University Casebook Series

October, 1986

ACCOUNTING AND THE LAW, Fourth Edition (1978), with Problems Pamphlet (Successor to Dohr, Phillips, Thompson & Warren)

George C. Thompson, Professor, Columbia University Graduate School of Business.
Robert Whitman, Professor of Law, University of Connecticut.
Ellis L. Phillips, Jr., Member of the New York Bar.
William C. Warren, Professor of Law Emeritus, Columbia University.

ACCOUNTING FOR LAWYERS, MATERIALS ON (1980)

David R. Herwitz, Professor of Law, Harvard University.

ADMINISTRATIVE LAW, Eighth Edition (1987), with 1983 Problems Supplement (Supplement edited in association with Paul R. Verkuil, Dean and Professor of Law, Tulane University)

Walter Gellhorn, University Professor Emeritus, Columbia University.
Clark Byse, Professor of Law, Harvard University.
Peter L. Strauss, Professor of Law, Columbia University.
Todd D. Rakoff, Professor of Law, Harvard University.

ADMIRALTY, Third Edition (1987), with Statute and Rule Supplement

Jo Desha Lucas, Professor of Law, University of Chicago.

ADVOCACY, see also Lawyering Process

AGENCY, see also Enterprise Organization

AGENCY—PARTNERSHIPS, Third Edition (1982)

Abridgement from Conard, Knauss & Siegel's Enterprise Organization, Third Edition.

ANTITRUST: FREE ENTERPRISE AND ECONOMIC ORGANIZATION, Sixth Edition (1983), with 1983 Problems in Antitrust Supplement and 1986 Case Supplement

Louis B. Schwartz, Professor of Law, University of Pennsylvania.
John J. Flynn, Professor of Law, University of Utah.
Harry First, Professor of Law, New York University.

BANKRUPTCY (1985)

Robert L. Jordan, Professor of Law, University of California, Los Angeles.
William D. Warren, Professor of Law, University of California, Los Angeles.

BUSINESS ORGANIZATION, see also Enterprise Organization

BUSINESS PLANNING, Temporary Second Edition (1984)

David R. Herwitz, Professor of Law, Harvard University.

BUSINESS TORTS (1972)

Milton Handler, Professor of Law Emeritus, Columbia University.

CHILDREN IN THE LEGAL SYSTEM (1983)

Walter Wadlington, Professor of Law, University of Virginia.
Charles H. Whitebread, Professor of Law, University of Southern California.
Samuel Davis, Professor of Law, University of Georgia.

CIVIL PROCEDURE, see Procedure

CLINIC, see also Lawyering Process

COMMERCIAL LAW (1983) with 1986 Bankruptcy Supplement

Robert L. Jordan, Professor of Law, University of California, Los Angeles.
William D. Warren, Professor of Law, University of California, Los Angeles.

COMMERCIAL LAW, CASES & MATERIALS ON, Fourth Edition (1985)

E. Allan Farnsworth, Professor of Law, Columbia University.
John Honnold, Professor of Law, University of Pennsylvania.

COMMERCIAL PAPER, Third Edition (1984)

E. Allan Farnsworth, Professor of Law, Columbia University.

COMMERCIAL PAPER (1983) (Reprinted from COMMERCIAL LAW)

Robert L. Jordan, Professor of Law, University of California, Los Angeles.
William D. Warren, Professor of Law, University of California, Los Angeles.

COMMERCIAL PAPER AND BANK DEPOSITS AND COLLECTIONS (1967), with Statutory Supplement

William D. Hawkland, Professor of Law, University of Illinois.

COMMERCIAL TRANSACTIONS—Principles and Policies (1982)

Alan Schwartz, Professor of Law, University of Southern California.
Robert E. Scott, Professor of Law, University of Virginia.

COMPARATIVE LAW, Fourth Edition (1980)

Rudolf B. Schlesinger, Professor of Law, Hastings College of the Law.

COMPETITIVE PROCESS, LEGAL REGULATION OF THE, Third Edition (1986), with 1986 Selected Statutes Supplement

Edmund W. Kitch, Professor of Law, University of Virginia.
Harvey S. Perlman, Dean of the Law School, University of Nebraska.

CONFLICT OF LAWS, Eighth Edition (1984), with 1986 Case Supplement

Willis L. M. Reese, Professor of Law, Columbia University.
Maurice Rosenberg, Professor of Law, Columbia University.

CONSTITUTIONAL LAW, Seventh Edition (1985), with 1986 Supplement

Edward L. Barrett, Jr., Professor of Law, University of California, Davis.
William Cohen, Professor of Law, Stanford University.

CONSTITUTIONAL LAW, CIVIL LIBERTY AND INDIVIDUAL RIGHTS, Second Edition (1982), with 1985 Supplement

William Cohen, Professor of Law, Stanford University.
John Kaplan, Professor of Law, Stanford University.

CONSTITUTIONAL LAW, Eleventh Edition (1985), with 1986 Supplement (Supplement edited in association with Frederick F. Schauer, Professor of Law, University of Michigan)

Gerald Gunther, Professor of Law, Stanford University.

CONSTITUTIONAL LAW, INDIVIDUAL RIGHTS IN, Fourth Edition (1986), (Reprinted from CONSTITUTIONAL LAW, Eleventh Edition), with 1986 Supplement (Supplement edited in association with Frederick F. Schauer, Professor of Law, University of Michigan)

Gerald Gunther, Professor of Law, Stanford University.

CONSUMER TRANSACTIONS (1983), with Selected Statutes and Regulations Supplement and 1987 Case Supplement

Michael M. Greenfield, Professor of Law, Washington University.

CONTRACT LAW AND ITS APPLICATION, Third Edition (1983)

The late Addison Mueller, Professor of Law, University of California, Los Angeles.
Arthur I. Rosett, Professor of Law, University of California, Los Angeles.
Gerald P. Lopez, Professor of Law, University of California, Los Angeles.

CONTRACT LAW, STUDIES IN, Third Edition (1984)

Edward J. Murphy, Professor of Law, University of Notre Dame.
Richard E. Speidel, Professor of Law, Northwestern University.

CONTRACTS, Fourth Edition (1982)

John P. Dawson, Professor of Law Emeritus, Harvard University.
William Burnett Harvey, Professor of Law and Political Science, Boston University.
Stanley D. Henderson, Professor of Law, University of Virginia.

CONTRACTS, Third Edition (1980), with Statutory Supplement

E. Allan Farnsworth, Professor of Law, Columbia University.
William F. Young, Professor of Law, Columbia University.

CONTRACTS, Second Edition (1978), with Statutory and Administrative Law Supplement (1978)

Ian R. Macneil, Professor of Law, Cornell University.

COPYRIGHT, PATENTS AND TRADEMARKS, see also Competitive Process; see also Selected Statutes and International Agreements

COPYRIGHT, PATENT, TRADEMARK AND RELATED STATE DOCTRINES, Second Edition (1981), with 1985 Case Supplement, 1986 Selected Statutes Supplement and 1981 Problem Supplement

Paul Goldstein, Professor of Law, Stanford University.

COPYRIGHT, Unfair Competition, and Other Topics Bearing on the Protection of Literary, Musical, and Artistic Works, Fourth Edition (1985), with 1985 Statutory Supplement

Ralph S. Brown, Jr., Professor of Law, Yale University.
Robert C. Denicola, Professor of Law, University of Nebraska.

CORPORATE ACQUISITIONS, The Law and Finance of (1986)

Ronald J. Gilson, Professor of Law, Stanford University.

CORPORATE FINANCE, Second Edition (1979), with 1984 Supplement

Victor Brudney, Professor of Law, Harvard University.
Marvin A. Chirelstein, Professor of Law, Columbia University.

CORPORATE READJUSTMENTS AND REORGANIZATIONS (1976)

Walter J. Blum, Professor of Law, University of Chicago.
Stanley A. Kaplan, Professor of Law, University of Chicago.

CORPORATION LAW, BASIC, Second Edition (1979), with 1983 Case and Documentary Supplement

Detlev F. Vagts, Professor of Law, Harvard University.

CORPORATIONS, see also Enterprise Organization

CORPORATIONS, Fifth Edition—Unabridged (1980), with 1986 Supplement

The late William L. Cary, Professor of Law, Columbia University.
Melvin Aron Eisenberg, Professor of Law, University of California, Berkeley.

CORPORATIONS, Fifth Edition—Abridged (1980), with 1986 Supplement

The late William L. Cary, Professor of Law, Columbia University.
Melvin Aron Eisenberg, Professor of Law, University of California, Berkeley.

CORPORATIONS, Second Edition (1982), with 1982 Corporation and Partnership Statutes, Rules and Forms

Alfred F. Conard, Professor of Law, University of Michigan.
Robert N. Knauss, Dean of the Law School, University of Houston.
Stanley Siegel, Professor of Law, University of California, Los Angeles.

CORPORATIONS COURSE GAME PLAN (1975)

David R. Herwitz, Professor of Law, Harvard University.

CORRECTIONS, SEE SENTENCING

CREDITORS' RIGHTS, see also Debtor-Creditor Law

CRIMINAL JUSTICE ADMINISTRATION, Third Edition (1986), with 1986 Case Supplement

Frank W. Miller, Professor of Law, Washington University.
Robert O. Dawson, Professor of Law, University of Texas.
George E. Dix, Professor of Law, University of Texas.
Raymond I. Parnas, Professor of Law, University of California, Davis.

CRIMINAL LAW, Third Edition (1983)

Fred E. Inbau, Professor of Law Emeritus, Northwestern University.
James R. Thompson, Professor of Law Emeritus, Northwestern University.
Andre A. Moenssens, Professor of Law, University of Richmond.

CRIMINAL LAW AND APPROACHES TO THE STUDY OF LAW (1986)

John M. Brumbaugh, Professor of Law, University of Maryland.

CRIMINAL LAW, Second Edition (1986)

Peter W. Low, Professor of Law, University of Virginia.
John C. Jeffries, Jr., Professor of Law, University of Virginia.
Richard C. Bonnie, Professor of Law, University of Virginia.

CRIMINAL LAW, Fourth Edition (1986)

Lloyd L. Weinreb, Professor of Law, Harvard University.

CRIMINAL LAW AND PROCEDURE, Sixth Edition (1984)

Rollin M. Perkins, Professor of Law Emeritus, University of California, Hastings College of the Law.
Ronald N. Boyce, Professor of Law, University of Utah.

CRIMINAL PROCEDURE, Second Edition (1980), with 1986 Supplement

Fred E. Inbau, Professor of Law Emeritus, Northwestern University.
James R. Thompson, Professor of Law Emeritus, Northwestern University.
James B. Haddad, Professor of Law, Northwestern University.
James B. Zagel, Chief, Criminal Justice Division, Office of Attorney General of Illinois.
Gary L. Starkman, Assistant U. S. Attorney, Northern District of Illinois.

CRIMINAL PROCESS, Third Edition (1978), with 1986 Supplement

Lloyd L. Weinreb, Professor of Law, Harvard University.

DAMAGES, Second Edition (1952)

Charles T. McCormick, late Professor of Law, University of Texas.
William F. Fritz, late Professor of Law, University of Texas.

DEBTOR-CREDITOR LAW (1984) with 1986 Supplement

Theodore Eisenberg, Professor of Law, Cornell University.

DEBTOR-CREDITOR LAW, Second Edition (1981), with Statutory Supplement

William D. Warren, Dean of the School of Law, University of California, Los Angeles.
William E. Hogan, Professor of Law, New York University.

DECEDENTS' ESTATES (1971)

Max Rheinstein, late Professor of Law Emeritus, University of Chicago.
Mary Ann Glendon, Professor of Law, Boston College.

DECEDENTS' ESTATES AND TRUSTS, Sixth Edition (1982)

John Ritchie, Emeritus Dean and Wigmore Professor of Law, Northwestern University.
Neill H. Alford, Jr., Professor of Law, University of Virginia.
Richard W. Effland, Professor of Law, Arizona State University.

DOMESTIC RELATIONS, see also Family Law

DOMESTIC RELATIONS, Successor Edition (1984) with 1987 Supplement

Walter Wadlington, Professor of Law, University of Virginia.

ELECTRONIC MASS MEDIA, Second Edition (1979)

William K. Jones, Professor of Law, Columbia University.

EMPLOYMENT DISCRIMINATION, Second Edition (1987)

Joel W. Friedman, Professor of Law, Tulane University.
George M. Strickler, Professor of Law, Tulane University.

ENERGY LAW (1983) with 1986 Case Supplement

Donald N. Zillman, Professor of Law, University of Utah.
Laurence Lattman, Dean of Mines and Engineering, University of Utah.

ENTERPRISE ORGANIZATION, Third Edition (1982), with 1982 Corporation and Partnership Statutes, Rules and Forms Supplement

Alfred F. Conard, Professor of Law, University of Michigan.
Robert L. Knauss, Dean of the Law School, University of Houston.
Stanley Siegel, Professor of Law, University of California, Los Angeles.

ENVIRONMENTAL POLICY LAW 1985 Edition, with 1985 Problems Supplement (Supplement in association with Ronald H. Rosenberg, Professor of Law, College of William and Mary)

Thomas J. Schoenbaum, Professor of Law, University of Georgia.

EQUITY, see also Remedies

EQUITY, RESTITUTION AND DAMAGES, Second Edition (1974)

Robert Childres, late Professor of Law, Northwestern University.
William F. Johnson, Jr., Professor of Law, New York University.

ESTATE PLANNING, Second Edition (1982), with 1985 Case, Text and Documentary Supplement

David Westfall, Professor of Law, Harvard University.

ETHICS, see Legal Profession, and Professional Responsibility

ETHICS AND PROFESSIONAL RESPONSIBILITY (1981) (Reprinted from THE LAWYERING PROCESS)

Gary Bellow, Professor of Law, Harvard University.
Bea Moulton, Legal Services Corporation.

EVIDENCE, Fifth Edition (1984)

John Kaplan, Professor of Law, Stanford University.
Jon R. Waltz, Professor of Law, Northwestern University.

EVIDENCE, Seventh Edition (1983) with Rules and Statute Supplement (1984)

Jack B. Weinstein, Chief Judge, United States District Court.
John H. Mansfield, Professor of Law, Harvard University.
Norman Abrams, Professor of Law, University of California, Los Angeles.
Margaret Berger, Professor of Law, Brooklyn Law School.

FAMILY LAW, see also Domestic Relations

FAMILY LAW Second Edition (1985)

Judith C. Areen, Professor of Law, Georgetown University.

FAMILY LAW AND CHILDREN IN THE LEGAL SYSTEM, STATUTORY MATERIALS (1981)

Walter Wadlington, Professor of Law, University of Virginia.

FEDERAL COURTS, Seventh Edition (1982), with 1986 Supplement

Charles T. McCormick, late Professor of Law, University of Texas.
James H. Chadbourn, late Professor of Law, Harvard University.
Charles Alan Wright, Professor of Law, University of Texas.

FEDERAL COURTS AND THE FEDERAL SYSTEM, Hart and Wechsler's Second Edition (1973), with 1981 Supplement

Paul M. Bator, Professor of Law, Harvard University.
Paul J. Mishkin, Professor of Law, University of California, Berkeley.
David L. Shapiro, Professor of Law, Harvard University.
Herbert Wechsler, Professor of Law, Columbia University.

FEDERAL PUBLIC LAND AND RESOURCES LAW, Second Edition (1987), with 1984 Statutory Supplement

George C. Coggins, Professor of Law, University of Kansas.
Charles F. Wilkinson, Professor of Law, University of Oregon.

FEDERAL RULES OF CIVIL PROCEDURE, 1986 Edition

FEDERAL TAXATION, see Taxation

FOOD AND DRUG LAW (1980), with Statutory Supplement

Richard A. Merrill, Dean of the School of Law, University of Virginia.
Peter Barton Hutt, Esq.

FUTURE INTERESTS (1958)

Philip Mechem, late Professor of Law Emeritus, University of Pennsylvania.

FUTURE INTERESTS (1970)

Howard R. Williams, Professor of Law, Stanford University.

FUTURE INTERESTS AND ESTATE PLANNING (1961), with 1962 Supplement

W. Barton Leach, late Professor of Law, Harvard University.
James K. Logan, formerly Dean of the Law School, University of Kansas.

GOVERNMENT CONTRACTS, FEDERAL, Successor Edition (1985)

John W. Whelan, Professor of Law, Hastings College of the Law.

GOVERNMENT REGULATION: FREE ENTERPRISE AND ECONOMIC ORGANIZATION, Sixth Edition (1985)

Louis B. Schwartz, Professor of Law, University of Pennsylvania.
John J. Flynn, Professor of Law, University of Utah.
Harry First, Professor of Law, New York University.

HINCKLEY JOHN W., TRIAL OF: A Case Study of the Insanity Defense

Peter W. Low, Professor of Law, University of Virginia.
John C. Jeffries, Jr., Professor of Law, University of Virginia.
Richard C. Bonnie, Professor of Law, University of Virginia.

INJUNCTIONS, Second Edition (1984)

Owen M. Fiss, Professor of Law, Yale University.
Doug Rendleman, Professor of Law, College of William and Mary.

INSTITUTIONAL INVESTORS, 1978

David L. Ratner, Professor of Law, Cornell University.

INSURANCE, Second Edition (1985)

William F. Young, Professor of Law, Columbia University.
Eric M. Holmes, Professor of Law, University of Georgia.

INTERNATIONAL LAW, see also Transnational Legal Problems, Transnational Business Problems, and United Nations Law

INTERNATIONAL LAW IN CONTEMPORARY PERSPECTIVE (1981), with Essay Supplement

Myres S. McDougal, Professor of Law, Yale University.
W. Michael Reisman, Professor of Law, Yale University.

INTERNATIONAL LEGAL SYSTEM, Second Edition (1981), with Documentary Supplement

Joseph Modeste Sweeney, Professor of Law, Tulane University.
Covey T. Oliver, Professor of Law, University of Pennsylvania.
Noyes E. Leech, Professor of Law, University of Pennsylvania.

INTRODUCTION TO LAW, see also Legal Method, On Law in Courts, and Dynamics of American Law

INTRODUCTION TO THE STUDY OF LAW (1970)

E. Wayne Thode, late Professor of Law, University of Utah.
Leon Lebowitz, Professor of Law, University of Texas.
Lester J. Mazor, Professor of Law, University of Utah.

JUDICIAL CODE and Rules of Procedure in the Federal Courts with Excerpts from the Criminal Code, 1984 Edition

Henry M. Hart, Jr., late Professor of Law, Harvard University.
Herbert Wechsler, Professor of Law, Columbia University.

JURISPRUDENCE (Temporary Edition Hardbound) (1949)

Lon L. Fuller, Professor of Law Emeritus, Harvard University.

JUVENILE, see also Children

JUVENILE JUSTICE PROCESS, Third Edition (1985)

Frank W. Miller, Professor of Law, Washington University.
Robert O. Dawson, Professor of Law, University of Texas.
George E. Dix, Professor of Law, University of Texas.
Raymond I. Parnas, Professor of Law, University of California, Davis.

LABOR LAW, Tenth Edition (1986), with 1986 Statutory Supplement

Archibald Cox, Professor of Law, Harvard University.
Derek C. Bok, President, Harvard University.
Robert A. Gorman, Professor of Law, University of Pennsylvania.

LABOR LAW, Second Edition (1982), with Statutory Supplement

Clyde W. Summers, Professor of Law, University of Pennsylvania.
Harry H. Wellington, Dean of the Law School, Yale University.
Alan Hyde, Professor of Law, Rutgers University.

LAND FINANCING, Third Edition (1985)

The late Norman Penney, Professor of Law, Cornell University.
Richard F. Broude, Member of the California Bar.
Roger Cunningham, Professor of Law, University of Michigan.

LAW AND MEDICINE (1980)

Walter Wadlington, Professor of Law and Professor of Legal Medicine, University of Virginia.
Jon R. Waltz, Professor of Law, Northwestern University.
Roger B. Dworkin, Professor of Law, Indiana University, and Professor of Biomedical History, University of Washington.

LAW, LANGUAGE AND ETHICS (1972)

William R. Bishin, Professor of Law, University of Southern California.
Christopher D. Stone, Professor of Law, University of Southern California.

LAW, SCIENCE AND MEDICINE (1984), with 1987 Supplement

Judith C. Areen, Professor of Law, Georgetown University.
Patricia A. King, Professor of Law, Georgetown University.
Steven P. Goldberg, Professor of Law, Georgetown University.
Alexander M. Capron, Professor of Law, Georgetown University.

LAWYERING PROCESS (1978), with Civil Problem Supplement and Criminal Problem Supplement

Gary Bellow, Professor of Law, Harvard University.
Bea Moulton, Professor of Law, Arizona State University.

LEGAL METHOD (1980)

Harry W. Jones, Professor of Law Emeritus, Columbia University.
John M. Kernochan, Professor of Law, Columbia University.
Arthur W. Murphy, Professor of Law, Columbia University.

LEGAL METHODS (1969)

Robert N. Covington, Professor of Law, Vanderbilt University.
E. Blythe Stason, late Professor of Law, Vanderbilt University.
John W. Wade, Professor of Law, Vanderbilt University.
Elliott E. Cheatham, late Professor of Law, Vanderbilt University.
Theodore A. Smedley, Professor of Law, Vanderbilt University.

LEGAL PROFESSION, THE, Responsibility and Regulation (1985)

Geoffrey C. Hazard, Jr., Professor of Law, Yale University.
Deborah L. Rhode, Professor of Law, Stanford University.

LEGISLATION, Fourth Edition (1982) (by Fordham)

Horace E. Read, late Vice President, Dalhousie University.
John W. MacDonald, Professor of Law Emeritus, Cornell Law School.
Jefferson B. Fordham, Professor of Law, University of Utah.
William J. Pierce, Professor of Law, University of Michigan.

LEGISLATIVE AND ADMINISTRATIVE PROCESSES, Second Edition (1981)

Hans A. Linde, Judge, Supreme Court of Oregon.
George Bunn, Professor of Law, University of Wisconsin.
Fredericka Paff, Professor of Law, University of Wisconsin.
W. Lawrence Church, Professor of Law, University of Wisconsin.

LOCAL GOVERNMENT LAW, Second Revised Edition (1986)

Jefferson B. Fordham, Professor of Law, University of Utah.

MASS MEDIA LAW, Third Edition (1987)

Marc A. Franklin, Professor of Law, Stanford University.

MENTAL HEALTH PROCESS, Second Edition (1976), with 1981 Supplement

Frank W. Miller, Professor of Law, Washington University.
Robert O. Dawson, Professor of Law, University of Texas.
George E. Dix, Professor of Law, University of Texas.
Raymond I. Parnas, Professor of Law, University of California, Davis.

MUNICIPAL CORPORATIONS, see Local Government Law

NEGOTIABLE INSTRUMENTS, see Commercial Paper

NEGOTIATION (1981) (Reprinted from THE LAWYERING PROCESS)

Gary Bellow, Professor of Law, Harvard Law School.
Bea Moulton, Legal Services Corporation.

NEW YORK PRACTICE, Fourth Edition (1978)

Herbert Peterfreund, Professor of Law, New York University.
Joseph M. McLaughlin, Dean of the Law School, Fordham University.

OIL AND GAS, Fifth Edition (1987)

Howard R. Williams, Professor of Law, Stanford University.
Richard C. Maxwell, Professor of Law, University of California, Los Angeles.
Charles J. Meyers, Dean of the Law School, Stanford University.
Stephen F. Williams, Professor of Law, University of Colorado.

ON LAW IN COURTS (1965)

Paul J. Mishkin, Professor of Law, University of California, Berkeley.
Clarence Morris, Professor of Law Emeritus, University of Pennsylvania.

UNIVERSITY CASEBOOK SERIES—Continued

PATENTS AND ANTITRUST (Pamphlet) (1983)

Milton Handler, Professor of Law Emeritus, Columbia University.
Harlan M. Blake, Professor of Law, Columbia University.
Robert Pitofsky, Professor of Law, Georgetown University.
Harvey J. Goldschmid, Professor of Law, Columbia University.

PERSPECTIVES ON THE LAWYER AS PLANNER (Reprint of Chapters One through Five of Planning by Lawyers) (1978)

Louis M. Brown, Professor of Law, University of Southern California.
Edward A. Dauer, Professor of Law, Yale University.

PLANNING BY LAWYERS, MATERIALS ON A NONADVERSARIAL LEGAL PROCESS (1978)

Louis M. Brown, Professor of Law, University of Southern California.
Edward A. Dauer, Professor of Law, Yale University.

PLEADING AND PROCEDURE, see Procedure, Civil

POLICE FUNCTION, Fourth Edition (1986), with 1986 Case Supplement

Reprint of Chapters 1–10 of Miller, Dawson, Dix and Parnas's CRIMINAL JUSTICE ADMINISTRATION, Third Edition.

PREPARING AND PRESENTING THE CASE (1981) (Reprinted from THE LAWYERING PROCESS)

Gary Bellow, Professor of Law, Harvard Law School.
Bea Moulton, Legal Services Corporation.

PREVENTIVE LAW, see also Planning by Lawyers

PROCEDURE—CIVIL PROCEDURE, Second Edition (1974), with 1979 Supplement

The late James H. Chadbourn, Professor of Law, Harvard University.
A. Leo Levin, Professor of Law, University of Pennsylvania.
Philip Shuchman, Professor of Law, Cornell University.

PROCEDURE—CIVIL PROCEDURE, Fifth Edition (1984), with 1986 Supplement

Richard H. Field, late Professor of Law, Harvard University.
Benjamin Kaplan, Professor of Law Emeritus, Harvard University.
Kevin M. Clermont, Professor of Law, Cornell University.

PROCEDURE—CIVIL PROCEDURE, Fourth Edition (1985)

Maurice Rosenberg, Professor of Law, Columbia University.
Hans Smit, Professor of Law, Columbia University.
Harold L. Korn, Professor of Law, Columbia University.

PROCEDURE—PLEADING AND PROCEDURE: State and Federal, Fifth Edition (1983), with 1986 Supplement

David W. Louisell, late Professor of Law, University of California, Berkeley.
Geoffrey C. Hazard, Jr., Professor of Law, Yale University.
Colin C. Tait, Professor of Law, University of Connecticut.

PROCEDURE—FEDERAL RULES OF CIVIL PROCEDURE, 1986 Edition

PRODUCTS LIABILITY (1980)

Marshall S. Shapo, Professor of Law, Northwestern University.

PRODUCTS LIABILITY AND SAFETY (1980), with 1985 Case and Documentary Supplement

W. Page Keeton, Professor of Law, University of Texas.
David G. Owen, Professor of Law, University of South Carolina.
John E. Montgomery, Professor of Law, University of South Carolina.

PROFESSIONAL RESPONSIBILITY, Third Edition (1984), with 1986 Selected National Standards Supplement

Thomas D. Morgan, Dean of the Law School, Emory University.
Ronald D. Rotunda, Professor of Law, University of Illinois.

PROPERTY, Fifth Edition (1984)

John E. Cribbet, Dean of the Law School, University of Illinois.
Corwin W. Johnson, Professor of Law, University of Texas.

PROPERTY—PERSONAL (1953)

S. Kenneth Skolfield, late Professor of Law Emeritus, Boston University.

PROPERTY—PERSONAL, Third Edition (1954)

Everett Fraser, late Dean of the Law School Emeritus, University of Minnesota.
Third Edition by Charles W. Taintor, late Professor of Law, University of Pittsburgh.

PROPERTY—INTRODUCTION, TO REAL PROPERTY, Third Edition (1954)

Everett Fraser, late Dean of the Law School Emeritus, University of Minnesota.

PROPERTY—REAL AND PERSONAL, Combined Edition (1954)

Everett Fraser, late Dean of the Law School Emeritus, University of Minnesota.
Third Edition of Personal Property by Charles W. Taintor, late Professor of Law, University of Pittsburgh.

PROPERTY—FUNDAMENTALS OF MODERN REAL PROPERTY, Second Edition (1982), with 1985 Supplement

Edward H. Rabin, Professor of Law, University of California, Davis.

PROPERTY—PROBLEMS IN REAL PROPERTY (Pamphlet) (1969)

Edward H. Rabin, Professor of Law, University of California, Davis.

PROPERTY, REAL (1984)

Paul Goldstein, Professor of Law, Stanford University.

PROSECUTION AND ADJUDICATION, Third Edition (1986), with 1986 Case Supplement

Reprint of Chapters 11–26 of Miller, Dawson, Dix and Parnas's CRIMINAL JUSTICE ADMINISTRATION, Third Edition.

PSYCHIATRY AND LAW, see Mental Health, see also Hinckley, Trial of

PUBLIC REGULATION OF DANGEROUS PRODUCTS (paperback) (1980)

Marshall S. Shapo, Professor of Law, Northwestern University.

PUBLIC UTILITY LAW, see Free Enterprise, also Regulated Industries

REAL ESTATE PLANNING (1980), with 1980 Problems, Statutes and New Materials Supplement

Norton L. Steuben, Professor of Law, University of Colorado.

REAL ESTATE TRANSACTIONS, Second Edition (1985), with 1985 Statute, Form and Problem Supplement

Paul Goldstein, Professor of Law, Stanford University.

RECEIVERSHIP AND CORPORATE REORGANIZATION, see Creditors' Rights

REGULATED INDUSTRIES, Second Edition, 1976

William K. Jones, Professor of Law, Columbia University.

REMEDIES (1982), with 1984 Case Supplement

Edward D. Re, Chief Judge, U. S. Court of International Trade.

RESTITUTION, Second Edition (1966)

John W. Wade, Professor of Law, Vanderbilt University.

SALES, Second Edition (1986)

Marion W. Benfield, Jr., Professor of Law, University of Illinois.
William D. Hawkland, Chancellor, Louisiana State Law Center.

SALES AND SALES FINANCING, Fifth Edition (1984)

John Honnold, Professor of Law, University of Pennsylvania.

SALES LAW AND THE CONTRACTING PROCESS (1982)

Reprint of Chapters 1–10 of Schwartz and Scott's Commercial Transactions.

SECURED TRANSACTIONS IN PERSONAL PROPERTY (1983) (Reprinted from COMMERCIAL LAW)

Robert L. Jordan, Professor of Law, University of California, Los Angeles.
William D. Warren, Professor of Law, University of California, Los Angeles.

SECURITIES REGULATION, Fifth Edition (1982), with 1986 Cases and Releases Supplement and 1986 Selected Statutes, Rules and Forms Supplement

Richard W. Jennings, Professor of Law, University of California, Berkeley.
Harold Marsh, Jr., Member of California Bar.

SECURITIES REGULATION (1982), with 1985 Supplement

Larry D. Soderquist, Professor of Law, Vanderbilt University.

SECURITY INTERESTS IN PERSONAL PROPERTY (1984)

Douglas G. Baird, Professor of Law, University of Chicago.
Thomas H. Jackson, Professor of Law, Stanford University.

SECURITY INTERESTS IN PERSONAL PROPERTY (1985) (Reprinted from Sales and Sales Financing, Fifth Edition)

John Honnold, Professor of Law, University of Pennsylvania.

SENTENCING AND THE CORRECTIONAL PROCESS, Second Edition (1976)

Frank W. Miller, Professor of Law, Washington University.
Robert O. Dawson, Professor of Law, University of Texas.
George E. Dix, Professor of Law, University of Texas.
Raymond I. Parnas, Professor of Law, University of California, Davis.

SOCIAL SCIENCE IN LAW, Cases and Materials (1985)

John Monahan, Professor of Law, University of Virginia.
Laurens Walker, Professor of Law, University of Virginia.

SOCIAL WELFARE AND THE INDIVIDUAL (1971)

Robert J. Levy, Professor of Law, University of Minnesota.
Thomas P. Lewis, Dean of the College of Law, University of Kentucky.
Peter W. Martin, Professor of Law, Cornell University.

TAX, POLICY ANALYSIS OF THE FEDERAL INCOME (1976)

William A. Klein, Professor of Law, University of California, Los Angeles.

TAXATION, FEDERAL INCOME, Successor Edition (1985)

Michael J. Graetz, Professor of Law, Yale University.

TAXATION, FEDERAL INCOME, Fifth Edition (1985)

James J. Freeland, Professor of Law, University of Florida.
Stephen A. Lind, Professor of Law, University of Florida.
Richard B. Stephens, Professor of Law Emeritus, University of Florida.

TAXATION, FEDERAL INCOME, Volume I, Personal Income Taxation, Successor Edition (1986), Volume II, Taxation of Partnerships and Corporations, Second Edition (1980), with 1985 Legislative Supplement

Stanley S. Surrey, late Professor of Law, Harvard University.
Paul R. McDaniel, Professor of Law, Boston College Law School.
Hugh J. Ault, Professor of Law, Boston College Law School.
Stanley A. Koppelman, Boston University

TAXATION, FEDERAL WEALTH TRANSFER, Second Edition (1982) with 1985 Legislative Supplement

Stanley S. Surrey, late Professor of Law, Harvard University.
William C. Warren, Professor of Law Emeritus, Columbia University.
Paul R. McDaniel, Professor of Law, Boston College Law School.
Harry L. Gutman, Instructor, Harvard Law School and Boston College Law School.

TAXATION, FUNDAMENTALS OF CORPORATE, Cases and Materials (1985)

Stephen A. Lind, Professor of Law, University of Florida.
Stephen Schwarz, Professor of Law, University of California, Hastings.
Daniel J. Lathrope, Professor of Law, University of California, Hastings.
Joshua Rosenberg, Professor of Law, University of San Francisco.

TAXATION, FUNDAMENTALS OF PARTNERSHIP, Cases and Materials (1985)

Stephen A. Lind, Professor of Law, University of California, Hastings.
Stephen Schwarz, Professor of Law, University of California, Hastings.
Daniel J. Lathrope, Professor of Law, University of California, Hastings.
Joshua Rosenberg, Professor of Law, University of San Francisco.

TAXATION, PROBLEMS IN THE FEDERAL INCOME TAXATION OF PARTNERSHIPS AND CORPORATIONS, Second Edition (1986)

Norton L. Steuben, Professor of Law, University of Colorado.
William J. Turnier, Professor of Law, University of North Carolina.

TAXATION, PROBLEMS IN THE FUNDAMENTALS OF FEDERAL INCOME, Second Edition (1985)

Norton L. Steuben, Professor of Law, University of Colorado.
William J. Turnier, Professor of Law, University of North Carolina.

TAXES AND FINANCE—STATE AND LOCAL (1974)

Oliver Oldman, Professor of Law, Harvard University.
Ferdinand P. Schoettle, Professor of Law, University of Minnesota.

TORT LAW AND ALTERNATIVES, Third Edition (1983)

Marc A. Franklin, Professor of Law, Stanford University.
Robert L. Rabin, Professor of Law, Stanford University.

TORTS, Seventh Edition (1982)

William L. Prosser, late Professor of Law, University of California, Hastings College.
John W. Wade, Professor of Law, Vanderbilt University.
Victor E. Schwartz, Professor of Law, American University.

TORTS, Third Edition (1976)

Harry Shulman, late Dean of the Law School, Yale University.
Fleming James, Jr., Professor of Law Emeritus, Yale University.
Oscar S. Gray, Professor of Law, University of Maryland.

TRADE REGULATION, Second Edition (1983), with 1985 Supplement

Milton Handler, Professor of Law Emeritus, Columbia University.
Harlan M. Blake, Professor of Law, Columbia University.
Robert Pitofsky, Professor of Law, Georgetown University.
Harvey J. Goldschmid, Professor of Law, Columbia University.

TRADE REGULATION, see Antitrust

TRANSNATIONAL BUSINESS PROBLEMS (1986)

Detlev F. Vagts, Professor of Law, Harvard University.

TRANSNATIONAL LEGAL PROBLEMS, Third Edition (1986) with Documentary Supplement

Henry J. Steiner, Professor of Law, Harvard University.
Detlev F. Vagts, Professor of Law, Harvard University.

TRIAL, see also Evidence, Making the Record, Lawyering Process and Preparing and Presenting the Case

TRIAL ADVOCACY (1968)

A. Leo Levin, Professor of Law, University of Pennsylvania.
Harold Cramer, of the Pennsylvania Bar.
Maurice Rosenberg, Professor of Law, Columbia University, Consultant.

TRUSTS, Fifth Edition (1978)

George G. Bogert, late Professor of Law Emeritus, University of Chicago.
Dallin H. Oaks, President, Brigham Young University.

TRUSTS AND SUCCESSION (Palmer's), Fourth Edition (1983)

Richard V. Wellman, Professor of Law, University of Georgia.
Lawrence W. Waggoner, Professor of Law, University of Michigan.
Olin L. Browder, Jr., Professor of Law, University of Michigan.

UNFAIR COMPETITION, see Competitive Process and Business Torts

UNITED NATIONS LAW, Second Edition (1967), with Documentary Supplement (1968)

Louis B. Sohn, Professor of Law, Harvard University.

WATER RESOURCE MANAGEMENT, Second Edition (1980), with 1983 Supplement

Charles J. Meyers, Dean of the Law School, Stanford University.
A. Dan Tarlock, Professor of Law, Indiana University.

WILLS AND ADMINISTRATION, Fifth Edition (1961)

Philip Mechem, late Professor of Law, University of Pennsylvania.
Thomas E. Atkinson, late Professor of Law, New York University.

WORLD LAW, see United Nations Law

University Casebook Series

CASES AND MATERIALS

ON

THE LAW OF EMPLOYMENT DISCRIMINATION

SECOND EDITION

By

JOEL WM. FRIEDMAN
Professor of Law
Tulane Law School

GEORGE M. STRICKLER, JR.
Associate Professor of Law
Tulane Law School

Mineola, New York
The Foundation Press, Inc.
1987

Printed in the United States of America

Library of Congress Cataloging in Publication Data

Friedman, Joel William, 1951–
Cases and materials on the law of employment discrimination.

iversity casebook series)
des index.
crimination in employment—Law and legislation—United States—Cases. I. Strickler, George
tle. III. Series.
74 1987 344.73'01133 86-27091
7-519-7 347.3041133

Discrim. 2nd Ed. UCB

TO

MY PARENTS

JWF

MY WIFE

GMS, Jr.

*

PREFACE

The nineteen years since the enactment of the omnibus 1964 Civil Rights Act has witnessed an explosion of administrative, legislative and judicial responses to the challenge of eradicating job discrimination and achieving equal employment opportunity for all workers in the United States. The materials herein seek to explore how the three branches of the federal and, to a lesser degree, state governments have attempted to make and enforce decisions that frequently involve controversial social policy as well as technical juridical judgments. In our experience, many students are attracted to a course in Employment Discrimination Law precisely because it offers them the opportunity to evaluate how different governmental institutions have addressed many inherently interesting and intellectually challenging issues steeped in social policy considerations. There are also, of course, a group of students who take an Employment Discrimination course with the intent of pursuing a career interest in this specialized field. Other students choose to study Employment Discrimination Law because the rich body of U.S. Supreme Court opinions in this area offers them more of a chance to analyze that Court's work than is available in many other courses. With this in mind, we have concluded that an effort to concentrate solely on providing a digest of the applicable legal rules serves the interests of neither the majority of our students nor their instructors. Accordingly, the book was developed with three goals in mind: First, to expose the students to the substantive law and, in so doing, improve their skills in statutory construction and case analysis. Second, to go beyond the decisions on the merits and examine the policy conflicts underlying the legal issues and evaluate the choices that were made. Third, because of the significant contribution to this body of caselaw by the U.S. Supreme Court, many of its opinions are used as a means of examining how the Court is functioning, on a substantive and methodological level, in one specialized field.

To accomplish these three goals, we have provided both hypothetical problems and specific interrogatories to raise issues discussed in and suggested by the statutes and cases and to generate discussion of other policy oriented and jurisprudential questions. Both were made available so that the instructor can choose the approach with which she or he is most comfortable. In addition, where certain portions of the course material demand it, background information is provided in narrative form.

Choosing the principal cases is always a difficult task. We have included, of course, all of the landmark opinions in this area. In addition, however, we have sought to include many very recent federal appellate court opinions that both raise important, novel and interesting issues and address them in a scholarly and pedagogically effective manner. To keep the size of this book within manageable limits, however, an effort has been made to avoid an encyclopedic approach. Accordingly, extensive string citations to cases and other authorities have been omitted in favor of providing a wider range of problems and questions. Finally, while this book is designed for a three hour course, there are several chapters which can be deleted to provide an integrated set of materials for a two hour course or seminar.

Cases and statute citations, as well as footnotes, of the court and commentators have been omitted without so specifying; numbered footnotes are from the original materials and retain the original numbering; lettered footnotes are those of the authors.

J. W. F.
G. M. S. Jr.

New Orleans, La.
January, 1983

PREFACE TO THE SECOND EDITION

The continuing accumulation of employment discrimination decisions and particularly the Supreme Court's willingness to return again and again to the area have led us to offer a second edition of this casebook which is now three years old.

Our experience with the first edition has convinced us that the basic organization of the book was sound and we have retained that organization in this edition. Our goals for the book have also remained essentially those we had in 1983. We designed the book to support a comprehensive survey course in an important species of labor law. We also wanted to provide materials that would allow the examination of the policy conflicts underlying both the passage of the modern civil rights statutes and their construction by the courts.

Because we were essentially satisfied with the structure of the original edition, updating the materials has created some difficulty. We realize that most teachers who will be using this book will do so in the context of a single two or three hour course. Simply adding the new decisions and developments to the existing material would have produced an overlong, unwieldy book. But because of developments in the law, we could not avoid expansion of some chapters, that on affirmative action being one example. Our response to the problem of keeping the book in manageable limits has been to compress more material into notes and textual discussion rather than to severely edit the principal cases. We have also shortened the chapter on class actions, which, as interesting as it was to one of us, is probably not covered in many courses.

Most of the principal cases from the first edition and the 1985 Supplement have been retained in this edition. Cases that have been overruled have, of course, been replaced. In several instances we have added cases that addressed previously unresolved issues and have substituted new decisions for those which we found did not "teach well." We also decided that, rather than rely on note material to cover some subjects, a principal case should be inserted.

We hope the new edition will prove to be an effective instructional tool.

G.M.S. Jr.
J.W.F.

New Orleans, Louisiana
November, 1986

*

ACKNOWLEDGMENTS

We wish to thank the following authors and copyright holders for permitting the inclusion of portions of their publications in this book.

Fisher, Franklin M., "Multiple Regression in Legal Proceedings," Columbia Law Review, Vol. 80, pp. 702, 705–06 (1980). Reprinted with permission of the Columbia Law Review.

Kanowitz, Leo, "Sex Based Discrimination in American Law III," Hastings Law Review, Vol. 20, pp. 305, 310–313 (1968); reprinted at L. KANOWITZ, WOMEN AND THE LAW: THE UNFINISHED REVOLUTION 103–105 (1969). Reprinted by permission of the publisher.

Reiss, Michael, "Requiem for an 'Independent Remedy': The Civil Rights Acts of 1866 and 1871 As Remedies for Employment Discrimination," Southern California Law Review, Vol. 50, pp. 961, 971–974 (1977). Reprinted with permission of the Southern California Law Review.

Preparation of this casebook was aided by the invaluable research assistance and proofreading of Roxanne L. Bland, Tulane '87.

*

SUMMARY OF CONTENTS

ANALYTICAL TABLE OF CONTENTS

PART I. INTRODUCTION: THE RESPONSE TO EMPLOYMENT DISCRIMINATION PRECEDING THE ENACTMENT OF TITLE VII OF THE 1964 CIVIL RIGHTS ACT

PART II. TITLE VII OF THE CIVIL RIGHTS ACT OF 1964

TABLE OF CASES

The principal cases are in italic type. Cases cited or discussed are in roman type. References are to pages.

CASES AND MATERIALS

ON

THE LAW OF EMPLOYMENT DISCRIMINATION

*

Part I

INTRODUCTION: THE RESPONSE TO EMPLOYMENT DISCRIMINATION PRECEDING THE ENACTMENT OF TITLE VII OF THE 1964 CIVIL RIGHTS ACT

Our legal system places numerous restraints on the terms and conditions employers and employee organizations may impose on employees and applicants for employment. The First Amendment to the United States Constitution and similar provisions in most state constitutions have been construed generally to prohibit the denial of public employment to persons because of their speech or beliefs. The federal government and some states have enacted legislation, such as the Occupational Safety and Health Act, directly affecting the conditions of the work place. In the Fair Labor Standards Act, Congress has created a statutory floor to the compensation that may be paid certain classes of wage earners and has prohibited altogether the employment of children in industry. The National Labor Relations Act and the Railway Labor Act were passed to prohibit employer interference with employee organization and to promote collective bargaining. Unions in turn are prohibited by the Landrum-Griffin Act from interfering with their members' right to speak out and seek internal political redress within the unions.

In addition to such statutory restraints, the employment relationship is often hedged by limitations of a contractual nature, ranging from collective bargaining agreements applying to thousands of employees and multiple employers, to the individual one-of-a-kind deals struck by first round picks in the National Football League draft and the teams which have obtained the rights to negotiate with them. Courts have at times imposed limits on the employer's freedom of action, even where no explicit contract exists, by finding implied contracts based on public policy or the course and history of the particular employment relationship.

The subject of this casebook is another type of legal restraint placed on employers and unions by legislatures and courts—the prohibition of certain employment actions based on characteristics of employees other than job performance or ability. The law of employment discrimination as so defined is in large part of very recent origin. Indeed, the bulk of the material contained in this book relates to legislative and judicial developments occurring after July, 1965, the effective date of Title VII of the 1964 Civil Rights Act. But in some circumstances, employment discrimination against racial minorities and women was prohibited even before 1964. The basis for such prohibitions will be explored in the remainder of this chapter.

SECTION A. THE CONSTITUTION

Read the Fourteenth Amendment to the U.S. Constitution.

KERR v. ENOCH PRATT FREE LIBRARY OF BALTIMORE

United States Court of Appeals, Fourth Circuit, 1945.
149 F.2d 212, cert. denied, 326 U.S. 721, 66 S.Ct. 26, 90 L.Ed. 427.

SOPER, CIRCUIT JUDGE.

This suit is brought by Louise Kerr, a young Negress, who complains that she has been refused admission to a library training class conducted by The Enoch Pratt Free Library of Baltimore City to prepare persons for staff positions in the Central Library and its branches. It is charged that the Library is performing a governmental function and that she was rejected in conformity with the uniform policy of the library corporation to exclude all persons of the colored race from the training school, and that by this action the State of Maryland deprives her of the equal protection of the laws in violation of § 1 of the Fourteenth Amendment of the Constitution of the United States and of the Civil Rights Act codified in 8 U.S.C.A. § 41. She asks for damages, as provided in that act, 8 U.S.C.A. § 43, for a permanent injunction prohibiting the refusal of her application, and for a declaratory judgment to establish her right to have her application considered without discrimination because of her race and color. Her father joins in the suit as a taxpayer, and asks that, if it be held that the library corporation is a private body not bound by the constitutional restraint upon state action, the Mayor and City Council of Baltimore be enjoined from making contributions to the support of the Library from the municipal funds on the ground that such contributions are ultra vires and in violation of the Fourteenth Amendment since they constitute a taking of his property without due process of law.

The defendants in the suit are the library corporation, nine citizens of Baltimore who constitute its board of trustees, the librarian and the Mayor and City Council of Baltimore. The defendants first named defend on two grounds: (1) That the plaintiff was not excluded from the Training School solely because of her race and color; and (2) that the Library is a private corporation, controlled and managed by the board of trustees, and does not perform any public function as a representative of the state. The municipality joins in the second defense and also denies that its appropriations to the Library are ultra vires or constitute a taking of property without due process of law. The District Judge sustained all of the defenses and dismissed the suit.

In our view it is necessary to consider only the first two defenses which raise the vital issues in the case. It is not denied that the applicant is well qualified to enter the training school. She is a native and resident of Baltimore City, twenty-seven years of age, of good character and reputation, and in good health. She is a graduate with high averages from the public high schools of Baltimore, from a public teachers' training school in Baltimore, has taken courses for three summers at the University of Pennsylvania, and has taught in the elementary public schools of the City. We must therefore consider whether in fact she was excluded from the training school because of her race, and if so, whether this action was contrary to the provisions of the federal constitution and laws.

There can be no doubt that the applicant was excluded from the school because of her race. The training course was established by the Library in 1928, primarily to prepare persons for the position of library assistant on the Library staff. There is no other training school for librarians in the state supported by public funds. Applicants are required to take a competitive entrance examination which, in view of the large number of applications for each class, is limited to fifteen or twenty persons who are selected by the director of the Library and his assistants as best qualified to function well in the work in view of their initiative, personality, enthusiasm and serious purpose. Members of the class are paid $50 monthly during training, since the practical work which they perform is equivalent to part time employment. In return for the training given, the applicant is expected to work on the staff one year after graduation, provided a position is offered. All competent graduates have been in fact appointed to the staff as library assistants, and during the past two or three years there have been more vacancies than graduates.

During the existence of the school, more than two hundred applications have been received from Negroes. All of them have been rejected. On June 14, 1933, the trustees of the Library formally resolved to make no change in the policy, then existing, not to employ Negro assistants on the Library service staff "in view of the public criticism which would arise and the effect upon the morale of the staff and the public." This practice was followed until 1942 when the trustees engaged two Negroes, who had not attended the Training School, as technical assistants for service in a branch of the Library which is patronized chiefly by Negroes. There are in all seventy senior and eighty junior library assistants employed at the Central Building and the twenty-six branches. There is no segregation of the races in any of them and white and colored patrons are served alike without discrimination. The population of Baltimore City is approximately eighty per cent white and twenty per cent colored.

Notwithstanding the appointment of two colored assistants in one branch of the Library, the board of trustees continued to exclude Negroes from the Training School for the reasons set forth in the following resolution passed by it on September 17, 1942:

> "Resolved that it is unnecessary and unpracticable to admit colored persons to the Training Class of The Enoch Pratt Free Library. The trustees being advised that there are colored persons

now available with adequate training for library employment have given the librarian authority to employ such personnel where vacancies occur in a branch or branches with an established record of preponderant colored use."

It was in accordance with this policy that the application made by the plaintiff on April 23, 1943, was denied.

The view that the action of the Board in excluding her was not based solely on her race or color rests on the contention that as the only positions as librarian assistants, which are open to Negroes, were filled at the time of her application, and as a number of adequately trained colored persons in the community were then available for appointment, should a vacancy occur, it would have been a waste of her time and a useless expense to the Library to admit her. The resolution of September 17, 1942, and the testimony given on the part of the defendants indicate that these were in fact the reasons which led to the plaintiff's rejection, and that the trustees were not moved by personal hostility or prejudice against the Negro race but by the belief that white library assistants can render more acceptable and more efficient service to the public where the majority of the patrons are white. The District Judge so found and we accept his finding. But it is nevertheless true that the applicant's race was the only ground for the action upon her application. She was refused consideration because the Training School is closed to Negroes, and it is closed to Negroes because, in the judgment of the Board, their race unfits them to serve in predominantly white neighborhoods. We must therefore determine whether, in view of the prohibition of the Fourteenth Amendment, the Board is occupying tenable ground in excluding Negroes from the Training School and from positions on the Library's staff.

The District Judge found that the Board of Trustees controls and manages the affairs of the Library as a private corporation and does not act in a public capacity as a representative of the state. Hence he held that the Board is not subject to the restraints of the Fourteenth Amendment which are imposed only upon state action that abridges the privileges or immunities of citizens of the United States or denies to any person the equal protection of the laws. His opinion reviews at length the corporate history of the institution and applies the rule, enunciated in state and federal courts, that to make a corporation a public one its managers must not only be appointed by public authority, but subject to its control.

The Court of Appeals of Maryland has used this test in somewhat similar cases and has held corporations to be private in character although public funds have been placed at their disposal to aid them in serving the public in the exercise of functions which could appropriately be performed by the state itself. For example, the rule was applied in Clark v. Maryland Institute, 87 Md. 643, 41 A. 126, where a colored youth was refused admission to an educational institution to which he had been appointed by a member of the City Council of Baltimore under a contract between the City and the Institute which authorized each member of the Council to make one appointment in consideration of an annual appropriation by the City of $9,000 per year for the education of the pupils. It was held that the Institute was within its rights in excluding colored persons because it was a private corporation and not an agency of the state, subject to the provisions of the Fourteenth Amendment.

These decisions are persuasive but in none of them was the corporation under examination completely owned and supported from its inception by the state as was the library corporation in the pending case. Moreover, a federal question is involved which the federal courts must decide for themselves so that a final and uniform interpretation may be given to the Constitution, the supreme law of the land; and in the performance of this duty in the pending case, we should not be governed merely by technical rules of law, but should appraise the facts in order to determine whether the board of trustees of the library corporation may be classified as "representatives of the state to such an extent and in such a sense that the great restraints of the Constitution set limits to their action." Nixon v. Condon, 286 U.S. 73, 88, 89, 52 S.Ct. 484, 487, 76 L.Ed. 984, 88 A.L.R. 458.

With this test in view, we must examine the legal background and the activities of the Library. It was established in 1882 through the philanthropy of Enoch Pratt, a citizen of Baltimore. His purpose was to create an institution which would belong to the City of Baltimore and serve all of its people; but he was fearful lest its management might fall into the hands of local politicians who would impair its efficiency by using it for selfish purposes. Accordingly, he erected and furnished a central library building at a cost of $225,000 and provided a fund of $833,000 and gave them to the city on condition that the city would create a perpetual annuity of $50,000 to be paid to the Board of Trustees for the maintenance of the Library and the erection and maintenance of four branches. But he also made it a condition of the gift that a Board of Trustees, to be selected by him from the citizens of Baltimore, be incorporated, with the power to manage the Library and fill all vacancies on the Board irrespective of religious or political grounds, and with the duty to make an annual report to the city showing the proceedings, the condition of the Library, and its receipts and disbursements for the year. These conditions were met; the corporation was formed, and the conveyances by gift were made to and accepted by the city which assumed the required obligations.

The steps by which these objects were given legal effect included an Act of the Legislature of Maryland of March 30, 1882, Acts 1882, Ch. 181; Ordinance No. 106 of the city of July 15, 1882, Ordinance No. 64 of May 14, 1883, and Ordinance No. 145 of October 10, 1884. The Act described the terms of the gift and the means which it offered to perpetually promote and diffuse knowledge among the people of the city, empowered the city to accept the gift and to agree by ordinance, to be approved by the voters of the city, to make the stipulated annual payment and directed the city to appoint a visitor to examine the books and accounts of the trustees annually and report to the city, and in case of abuse by the trustees to resort to the proper courts to enforce the performance of the trust. The Act also named nine citizens of Baltimore to constitute the Board of Trustees and to be a body corporate by the name of "The Enoch Pratt Free Library of Baltimore City," and empowered them to fill vacancies in the Board and to do all necessary things for the control and management of the Library and its branches, and to make all necessary by-laws and regulations for the administration of the trust and the appointment of necessary officers and agents. The trustees were directed to make an annual report to the city of their proceedings and of the condition of the Library, with a full account of receipts and disbursements. The real and personal property vested in the city by virtue of the act, as well as future acquisitions, were exempted from state and city taxes. The ordinances of the city contained appropriate provisions to give effect to the plan.

The Library was managed and conducted in accordance with these provisions until the year 1907 when Andrew Carnegie gave the city $500,000 for the erection of twenty additional branch buildings on the sole condition that the city should provide the sites and an annual sum of not less than ten per cent of the cost of the buildings for maintenance. The city accepted the gift upon these conditions by Ordinance No. 275 of May 11, 1907, and directed that the annual appropriation be expended by the trustees for the branch libraries in such manner as might be specified by the city from year to year in its ordinance of estimates. The legislature impliedly ratified the gift by the Act of 1908, Ch. 144, by enacting an amendment to the city charter empowering the city to appropriate and pay over such sums as it might deem proper for the equipment, maintenance or support of the library, provided that the title of ownership to the property should be vested in the Mayor and City Council of Baltimore.

By the year 1927 the central library had outgrown its quarters and the Legislature of the state, by the Act of 1927, Ch. 328, authorized the city, if the voters should approve, to issue bonds in the sum of $3,000,000 for the acquisition of additional real estate and the erection of a new building for a free public library in Baltimore City. The bond issue was authorized by Ordinance No. 1053 of April 13, 1927, which was submitted to and approved by the voters. Thereafter the city acquired the necessary land and erected thereon a modern library which constitutes the central building of the institution. Ordinance No. 1195, approved December 16, 1930, authorized the incorporation into the new site of the land previously occupied by the central building. The building has been completed and has been in use for some years past. The Library now includes this central building and twenty-six branches.

The existing fiscal arrangement between the city and the Library throws strong light on the question now under consideration. The work of the Library has been so expanded and its usefulness to the people of Baltimore has been so clearly demonstrated under the management of the Board of Trustees that the city has gradually increased its annual appropriations until they far exceed the obligations assumed by it under the gifts from Enoch Pratt and Andrew Carnegie. These obligations, as we have seen, amounted to the annual appropriation of $50,000 to meet the condition imposed by Mr. Pratt, offset by the income from the capital sum of $833,000 donated by him, and also the annual appropriation of $50,000 to meet the condition of Mr. Carnegie's gift. But in addition, the city has appropriated large additional sums. The total amounted to $511,575 in 1943 and $650,086.90 in 1944. In addition the city pays large sums for bond interest, bond retirement, and the retirement funds for library employees which in 1944 amounted to $82,160 for bond interest, $86,000 for bond retirement and $40,000 for the retirement fund, so that the city's total contribution to the Library for the year 1944 totaled the sum of $858,246.90.

Until ten years ago the appropriations made by the city were turned over to the trustees to be expended for library purposes; but for the past ten years all disbursements from city appropriations are made through the City Bureau of Control and Accounts on vouchers submitted by the trustees to the Bureau for payment. Salary checks are issued by the city's payroll officer and charged against the Library's appropriation. Library employees are not under the city's merit system, but their salaries conform to the city's salary scale and if an increase in salary or the creation of a new position is desired, the trustees are obliged to take up the matter with the Board of Estimates. The trustees submit an itemized budget to the city which is reviewed by the city's budget committee and the library budget is included in the regular city budget. All of the income of the Library is thus received from and disbursed by the city with the exception of an annual income of special gifts which has recently averaged from $6,000 to $8,000 annually, or about one per cent of the city's outlay.

By the Act of Legislature of 1939, Ch. 16, the city was authorized to include library employees within the municipal employees' retirement system, and this arrangement was accomplished upon the request of the trustees of the Library by Ordinance No. 961 of May 29, 1939. The annual contribution of the city to the retirement fund for library employees is about $40,000.

From this recital certain conclusions may be safely drawn. First. The purpose which inspired the founder to make the gift and led the state to accept it, was to establish an institution to promote and diffuse knowledge and education amongst all the people.

Second. The donor could have formed a private corporation under the general permissive statutes of Maryland with power both to own the property and to manage the business of the Library independent of the state. He chose instead to seek the aid of the state to found a public institution to be owned and supported by the city but to be operated by a self perpetuating board of trustees to safeguard it from political manipulation; and this was accomplished by special act of the legislature with the result that the powers and obligations of the city and the trustees were not conferred by Mr. Pratt but by the state at the very inception of the enterprise. They were in truth created by the state in accordance with a plan which was in quite general operation in the Southern and Eastern parts of the United States at the time.*

Third, during the sixty years that have passed since the Library was established, the city's interests have been greatly extended and increased, as the donor doubtless foresaw would be the case, until the existence and maintenance of the central library and its twenty-six branches as now conducted are completely dependent upon the city's voluntary appropriations. So great have become the demands upon the city that it now requires the budget of the Library to be submitted to the municipal budget authorities for approval and in this way the city exercises a control over the activities of the institution.

We are told that all of these weighty facts go for naught and that the Library is entirely bereft of governmental status because the executive control is vested in a self perpetuating board first named by Enoch Pratt. The District Court held that Pratt created in effect two separate trusts, one in the physical property, of which the city is the trustee, and the other a trust for management, committed to the board of trustees, and that the purpose and effect of the act of the legislature "was merely to ratify and approve the agreement between Mr. Pratt and the city, and to give the necessary authority of the state to the city to carry out the agreement"; and that the practical economic control of the Library by the city, by virtue of its large voluntary contributions, is immaterial, because "the problem must be resolved on the basis of the legal right to control and not possible practical control through withholding appropriations."

We do not agree with this analysis of the situation. It is generally recognized that the maintenance of a public library is a proper function of the state; and nowhere has the thought been better expressed than in Johnson v. Baltimore, 158 Md. 93, 103, 104, 148 A. 209, 213, 66 A.L.R. 1488, where the court said:

* We learn from Joeckel, The Government of the American Public Library, University of Chicago Press, 1935, that the oldest form of free public library existent today is that having a corporate existence. Accurate description of the libraries comprising this group is impossible because of the many variations of legal detail but the essential distinction between these and other public libraries lies in the fact that control and sometimes ownership is vested wholly or in part in a corporation, association or similar organization which is not part of the municipal or other government. Frequently there is some form of contractual relationship between the corporation and the city. But regardless of legal organization, these libraries all render service freely to all citizens on precisely the same terms as public libraries under direct municipal control. No less than 56 or 17% of all the public libraries in American cities having a population in excess of 30,000 fall into this category. Geographically these libraries are confined to the East and especially to the South where more than one-third of the cities in the 30,000 or over population group are served by libraries of this type. The Enoch Pratt Free Library belongs to this group.

"* * * At the present time it is generally recognized and conceded by all thoughtful people that such institutions form an integral part of a system of free public education and are among its most efficient and valuable adjuncts. An enlightened and educated public has come to be regarded as the surest safeguard for the maintenance and advancement of the progress of civilized nations. More particularly is this true in republican forms of government, wherein all citizens have a voice. It is also true that education of the people ought not to and does not stop upon their leaving school, but must be kept abreast of the time by almost constant reading and study. It would therefore seem that no more important duty or higher purpose is incumbent upon a state or municipality than to provide free public libraries for the benefit of its inhabitants."

It is equally true that the state may set up a board of trustees as an incorporated instrumentality to carry on its educational work, as it has done in the case of the University of Maryland. It is our view that although Pratt furnished the inspiration and the funds initially, the authority of the state was invoked to create the institution and to vest the power of ownership in one instrumentality and the power of management in another, with the injunction upon the former to see to it that the latter faithfully performed its trust. We know of no reason why the state cannot create separate agencies to carry on its work in this manner, and when it does so, they become subject to the constitutional restraints imposed upon the state itself.

We think that the special charter of the Library should not be interpreted as endowing it with the power to discriminate between the people of the state on account of race and that if the charter is susceptible of this construction, it violates the Fourteenth Amendment since the Board of Trustees must be deemed the representative of the state. The question of interpretation is not unlike that which was before the Supreme Court in Steele v. Louisville & N. R. Co., 323 U.S. 192, 65 S.Ct. 226, where it was held that a labor union which was empowered by the Federal Railway Labor Act to represent a whole craft of employees could not discriminate against Negro members thereof. The court said, 65 S.Ct. at pages 230, 232:

"If, as the state court has held, the Act confers this power on the bargaining representative of a craft or class of employees without any commensurate statutory duty towards its members, constitutional questions arise. For the representative is clothed with power not unlike that of a legislature which is subject to constitutional limitations on its power to deny, restrict, destroy or discriminate against the rights of those for whom it legislates and which is also under an affirmative constitutional duty equally to protect those rights. If the Railway Labor Act purports to impose on petitioner and the other Negro members of the craft the legal duty to comply with the terms of a contract whereby the representative has discriminatorily restricted their employment for the benefit and advantage of the Brotherhood's own members, we must decide the constitutional questions which petitioner raises in his pleading.

* * *

"We think that the Railway Labor Act imposes upon the statutory representative of a craft at least as exacting a duty to protect equally the interests of the members of the craft as the Constitution imposes upon a legislature to give equal protection to the interests of those for whom it legislates. Congress has seen fit to clothe the bargaining representative with powers comparable to those possessed by a legislative body both to create and restrict the rights of those whom it represents, but it has also imposed on the representative a corresponding duty. We hold that the language of the Act to which we have referred, read in the light of the purposes of the Act, expresses the aim of Congress to impose on the bargaining representative of a craft or class of employees the duty to exercise fairly the power conferred upon it in behalf of all those for whom it acts, without hostile discrimination against them."

For like reasons we think that the charter of the Library which empowers the Board of Trustees to manage the institution for a benevolent public purpose should not be construed to authorize them to pass a regulation in respect to the appointment of its agents which violates the spirit of the constitutional prohibition against race discrimination. Nor do we assume that the act would be so interpreted by the Court of Appeals of Maryland which in Mayor &c. v. Radecke, 49 Md. 217, 33 Am.Rep. 239, pointed out the duty of the courts to look beneath the language of an act to find the true purpose of a grant of legislative power. In that case the court said: "While we hold that this power of control by the Courts is one to be most cautiously exercised, we are yet of opinion there may be a case in which an Ordinance passed under grants of power like those we have cited, is so clearly unreasonable, so arbitrary, oppressive or partial, as to raise the presumption that the Legislature never intended to confer the power to pass it, and to justify the Courts in interfering and setting it aside as a plain abuse of authority."

In any event, it is our duty in this case in passing upon the nature of the library corporation and its relationship to the state not to be guided by the technical rules of the law of principal and agent, but to apply the test laid down in Nixon v. Condon, 286 U.S. 73, 52 S.Ct. 484, 76 L.Ed. 984, 88 A.L.R. 458, to which we have already referred. There the Supreme Court held that an executive committee of a political party, which had been authorized by a Texas statute to determine the qualification of the members of the party, was not acting merely for the political organization for which it spoke but was acting as a representative of the state when it excluded Negroes from participation in a primary election. In declaring that this action was subject to the condemnation of the

Fourteenth Amendment the court said (286 U.S. at pages 88, 89, 52 S.Ct. at page 487, 76 L.Ed. 984, 88 A.L.R. 458):

"* * * The pith of the matter is simply this, that, when those agencies are invested with an authority independent of the will of the association in whose name they undertake to speak, they become to that extent the organs of the state itself, the repositories of official power. They are then the governmental instruments whereby parties are organized and regulated to the end that government itself may be established or continued. What they do in that relation, they must do in submission to the mandates of equality and liberty that bind officials everywhere. They are not acting in matters of merely private concern like the directors or agents of business corporations. They are acting in matters of high public interest, matters intimately connected with the capacity of government to exercise its functions unbrokenly and smoothly. Whether in given circumstances parties or their committees are agencies of government within the Fourteenth or the Fifteenth Amendment is a question which this court will determine for itself. It is not concluded upon such an inquiry by decisions rendered elsewhere. The test is not whether the members of the executive committee are the representatives of the state in the strict sense in which an agent is the representative of his principal. The test is whether they are to be classified as representatives of the state to such an extent and in such a sense that the great restraints of the Constitution set limits to their action."

For further application of this principle, see Smith v. Allwright, 321 U.S. 649, 64 S.Ct. 757, 88 L.Ed. 987.

We have no difficulty in concluding that in the same sense the Library is an instrumentality of the State of Maryland. Even if we should lay aside the approval and authority given by the state to the library at its very beginning we should find in the present relationship between them so great a degree of control over the activities and existence of the Library on the part of the state that it would be unrealistic to speak of it as a corporation entirely devoid of governmental character. It would be conceded that if the state legislature should now set up and maintain a public library and should entrust its operation to a self perpetuating board of trustees and authorize it to exclude Negroes from its benefits, the act would be unconstitutional. How then can the well known policy of the Library, so long continued and now formally expressed in the resolution of the Board, be justified as solely the act of a private organization when the state, through the municipality, continues to supply it with the means of existence.

The plaintiff has been denied a right to which she was entitled and the judgment must be reversed and the case remanded for further proceedings.

Reversed and remanded.

NOTES FOR DISCUSSION

1. The Civil Rights Act, 8 U.S.C. § 41, referred to by the Fourth Circuit in *Kerr*, was the predecessor to the current 42 U.S.C. § 1983. That Act, passed in 1871, provides a federal cause of action for any person whose constitutional or federal statutory rights have been violated by any person acting "under color of any statute, ordinance, regulation, custom or usage, of any State or Territory * * *." Section 1983 is the most frequently used of the Reconstruction Era civil rights statutes. Its application in the employment discrimination context is discussed in Chapter 8, Section B, infra.

2. What is "the spirit of the constitutional prohibition against race discrimination" referred to by the Fourth Circuit? See Strauder v. West Virginia, 100 U.S. 303, 25 L.Ed. 664 (1880). If the library had a policy of admitting only men to the training program, would Kerr have had a cause of action under the Fourteenth Amendment? Compare Muller v. Oregon, 208 U.S. 412, 28 S.Ct. 324, 52 L.Ed. 551 (1908) and Goesaert v. Cleary, 335 U.S. 464, 69 S.Ct. 198, 93 L.Ed. 163 (1948) with Reed v. Reed, 404 U.S. 71, 92 S.Ct. 251, 30 L.Ed.2d 225 (1971).

3. The Fifth Amendment provides in part that "no person shall be * * * deprived of life, liberty, or property, without due process of law * * *." The due process clause has consistently been interpreted as forbidding the federal government from denying equal protection of the laws. Vance v. Bradley, 440 U.S. 93, 99 S.Ct. 939, 59 L.Ed.2d 171 (1979); Bolling v. Sharpe, 347 U.S. 497, 74 S.Ct. 693, 98 L.Ed. 884 (1954). In Davis v. Passman, 442 U.S. 228, 99 S.Ct. 2264, 60 L.Ed.2d 846 (1979), the Court held that a female employee of a U.S. Congressman who was discharged when the Congressman determined that "it was essential" her position be filled by a man, stated a cause of action for back pay and damages under the Fifth Amendment.

> "To withstand scrutiny under the equal protection component of the Fifth Amendment's Due Process Clause, 'classifications by gender must serve important governmental objectives and must be substantially related to achievement of those objectives.'" * * * The equal protection component of the Due Process Clause thus confers on petitioner a federal constitutional right to be free from gender discrimination which cannot meet these requirements.

442 U.S. at 234–235, (quoting Califano v. Webster, 430 U.S. 313, 97 S.Ct. 1192, 51 L.Ed.2d 360 (1977)) (footnotes omitted). Under what circumstances might discrimination against employees based on race or sex "serve important governmental objectives?" What about age? See, Vance v. Bradley, 440 U.S. 93, 99 S.Ct. 939, 59 L.Ed.2d 171 (1979).

4. The Fourteenth Amendment applies on its face only to states, but has been consistently interpreted as applying to any non-federal public body. Thus, the employment practices of cities, and other political subdivisions, as well as of agencies of the state itself, constitute state action for purposes of Fourteenth Amendment coverage. The "state action" requirement of the Fourteenth Amendment and the "under color of law" requirement of § 1983 are frequently treated as being one-and-the-same. See, United States v. Price, 383 U.S. 787, 794 n.7, 86 S.Ct. 1152, 1156 n.7, 16 L.Ed.2d 267, 272 n.7 (1966). The Supreme Court has stated, however, that the concepts "denote two separate areas of inquiry." Flagg Brothers, Inc. v. Brooks, 436 U.S. 149, 155–56, 98 S.Ct. 1729, ___, 56 L.Ed.2d 185 (1978). In Lugar v. Edmonson Oil Co., Inc., 457 U.S. 922,

102 S.Ct. 2744, 73 L.Ed.2d 482 (1982), the Court explained that "under color of state law" denotes only that the individual has acted with knowledge of and pursuant to law, but that such conduct by itself would not be state action. 457 U.S. at 935 n.18, 102 S.Ct. at 2752. Conduct which constitutes state action will, however, always satisfy the "color of law" requirement. Ibid. Because of the myriad ways in which the public and private sectors of society interact, a persistent problem has been in determining what constitutes sufficient state involvement to render an activity "state action." See, Graseck v. Mauceri, 582 F.2d 203 (2d Cir. 1978), cert. denied, 439 U.S. 1129, 99 S.Ct. 1048, 59 L.Ed.2d 91 (1979) ("one of the more slippery and troublesome areas of civil rights litigation").

In Burton v. Wilmington Parking Authority, 365 U.S. 715, 81 S.Ct. 856, 6 L.Ed.2d 45 (1961), the Court found state action in the racially discriminatory operation of a privately-owned restaurant that leased space from a publicly-owned parking garage, because the state had "so far insinuated itself into a position of interdependence with the restaurant that it must be recognized as a joint participant in the challenged activity." 365 U.S. at 725, 81 S.Ct. at 861. But in Moose Lodge No. 107 v. Irvis, 407 U.S. 163, 92 S.Ct. 1965, 32 L.Ed.2d 627 (1972), the Court held that state licensing of a private club did not constitute sufficient state action to make racial discrimination by the club violative of the Fourteenth Amendment. The Court noted that the state licensing did not "foster or encourage" discrimination and distinguished *Burton* on the ground that the Moose Lodge was not located on public property and did not have the sort of "symbiotic relationship" with the state enjoyed by the restaurant. 407 U.S. at 175, 92 S.Ct. at 1972.

In Blum v. Yaretsky, 457 U.S. 991, 102 S.Ct. 2777, 73 L.Ed.2d 534 (1982), a case challenging the discharge and transfer of patients from state regulated private nursing homes, the Court held that in order to establish state action the plaintiff must prove that the state "has exercised coercive power or has provided such significant encouragement, either overt or covert, that the choice must be in law deemed that of the State." 457 U.S. at 1004, 102 S.Ct. at 2785. Extensive state regulation of a private entity does not make it a state actor. Blum v. Yaretsky, supra; Jackson v. Metropolitan Edison Co., 419 U.S. 345, 95 S.Ct. 449, 42 L.Ed.2d 477 (1974). But see, Roberts v. Louisiana Downs, Inc., 742 F.2d 221 (5th Cir. 1984) (state action where state regulation is directly linked to challenged conduct). Nor will dependency on state funding make the state responsible for the actions of an otherwise private entity. See, Rendell-Baker v. Kohn, 457 U.S. 830, 102 S.Ct. 2764, 73 L.Ed.2d 418 (1982) (school's discharge of teacher was not state action although 90–99% of school's funding came from public sources); Blum v. Yaretsky, supra (nursing home's discharge of patients not state action even though state subsidized operating costs and paid medicaid for more than 90% of its patients).

In both *Rendell-Baker* and *Blum*, the Court emphasized that the challenged decisions had not been made by public officials or encouraged by state laws or policies. In light of the recent Supreme Court decisions, would *Kerr* be decided the same way today? With *Kerr* compare Gilliard v. New York Public Library System, 597 F.Supp. 1069, 1074–75 (S.D.N.Y.1984) (discharged employee's § 1983 suit against publicly funded library dismissed for lack of state action because of lack of control of city over personnel matters).

5. In *Kerr*, the defendant conceded a racially discriminatory employment policy while apparently denying that plaintiff was refused admission to the training program because of that policy. But if the library had no formalized

rule excluding blacks from the program, what kind of evidence would Kerr have had to present to prove that she was denied admission because of her race? Would the fact that, during the training school's existence, all 200 applications by blacks had been rejected be sufficient for a finder of fact to conclude that Kerr had been denied admission because of her race? Should such evidence even be admissible to prove discrimination against Kerr? See Chapter 3, infra.

6. Does the Fourth Circuit's reversal and remand for further proceedings mean that Kerr should be placed in the training program? What if all the positions in the program have been filled? If Kerr has an absolute constitutional right not to be discriminated against because of her race, what is the appropriate measure of relief?

SECTION B. FEDERAL CIVIL RIGHTS LEGISLATION AND EXECUTIVE ACTION

Following the Civil War, Congress passed a series of statutes intended to implement the commands of the Thirteenth, Fourteenth and Fifteenth Amendments by providing protection for black citizens from their former masters. The Reconstruction civil rights statutes were not, however, sympathetically received by the Supreme Court. In 1873 in The Slaughterhouse Cases, 83 U.S. (16 Wall.) 36, 21 L.Ed. 394 (1873), the Court upheld the validity of a Louisiana law which created a monopoly for a private slaughterhouse. A majority of the Court held that the law did not abridge the privileges and immunities of Louisiana citizens under the Fourteenth Amendment because such privileges and immunities encompassed only those rights which grew directly out of the relationship between the citizen and the national government, such as the right to sue in federal court, and did not include fundamental individual rights which arose only from state citizenship. The decision, though not directly involving the civil rights statutes, nonetheless affected them, because the Court construed the constitutional basis for much of the civil rights legislation in the narrowest possible way. The Slaughterhouse Cases was followed shortly by United States v. Cruikshank, 92 U.S. (2 Otto) 542, 23 L.Ed. 588 (1876), where the Court held that an indictment under a section of the post-war statutes, which charged that defendants conspired to prevent black citizens from assembling, was defective because of the failure to allege that the right to assemble grew out of the black citizens' relation to the federal government. Applying the *Slaughterhouse* doctrine to a statute, the Court held that the right to assemble peacefully was not an attribute of national citizenship unless the assemblage was for the purpose of petitioning the federal government. But even more significantly, the Court also announced that the first section of the Fourteenth Amendment consisted only of restrictions on the states and did not "add anything to the rights which one citizen has under the constitution against another." It followed that legislation founded on the Fourteenth Amendment could not reach private action. The combination of the narrow construction of the privileges and immunities clause in The

Slaughterhouse Cases and the elimination of private action from the reach of the Fourteenth Amendment in *Cruikshank* foreshadowed the effective negation of all the Reconstruction civil rights statutes.[a]

One of the series of legislative efforts which could have become a vehicle for protecting the employment rights of blacks was the Civil Rights Act of 1866, which provided that all citizens, without regard to color, were entitled in every state to the same right to contract, sue, give evidence, and to take, hold and convey property, and to the equal benefits of all laws for the security of persons and property as was enjoyed by white citizens. In 1903, a federal grand jury in Arkansas indicted a number of individuals for conspiring to violate the rights of black citizens protected by the 1866 Act. The indictment stated that a lumber mill in White Hall, Arkansas had employed eight black citizens as "laborers and workmen" such employment "being a right similar to that enjoyed in said state by the white citizens thereof." The indictment further alleged that:

> defendants being then and there armed with deadly weapons, threatening and intimidating the said workmen there employed, with the purpose of compelling them, by violence and threats and otherwise, to remove from said place of business, to stop said work, and to cease the enjoyment of said right and privilege, and by then and there wilfully, deliberately, and unlawfully compelling the employees to quit said work and abandon said place and cease the free enjoyment of all advantages under said contracts, the same being so done by said defendants and each of them for the purpose of driving the employees from said place of business and from their labor because they were colored men and citizens of African descent * * *.

A demurrer to the indictment on the ground that the offense created by the Civil Rights Act was not within the jurisdiction of the federal courts was overruled and the respondents were convicted. On appeal, the Supreme Court reversed. Hodges v. United States, 203 U.S. 1, 27 S.Ct. 6, 51 L.Ed. 65 (1906). The Court held that since the attempt to protect the employment rights of the black workers was directed against *private action*, the Fourteenth Amendment provided no basis for the prosecution. The Thirteenth Amendment, which outlawed slavery, was equally inapplicable because interference with an employee's right to contract was not the equivalent of forcing him into slavery or involuntary servitude. Concluding that neither the federal constitution, nor the laws passed pursuant thereto secured " 'to a citizen of the United States the right to work at a given occupation or particular calling free from injury, oppression, or interference by individual citizens,' " the court held that "the United States court had no jurisdiction of the wrongs charged in the indictment." The section of the 1866 Act at

[a] A good account of the post war civil rights legislation and of its judicial destruction is contained in Gressman, The Unhappy History of Civil Rights Legislation, 50 Mich.L.Rev. 1323 (1952).

issue in *Hodges* has survived as 42 U.S.C. § 1981.[b] Small wonder, however, that it and other of the post-war statutes remained deadletters during the first two thirds of this century. A modern resurrection of the 1866 Act, beginning with the decision in Jones v. Alfred H. Mayer Co., 392 U.S. 409, 88 S.Ct. 2186, 20 L.Ed.2d 1189 (1968), is described infra at 465.

After the practical nullification of the civil rights statutes by the Court, federal efforts to eliminate employment discrimination in the first half of this century were half-hearted at best. Religious discrimination in federal employment was prohibited by a civil service rule as early as 1883 (U.S. Civil Service Commission, Rule VIII, 1883), but not until 1940 was discrimination on the basis of race against federal employees and applicants for employment specifically barred. Ramspeck Act, 54 Stat. 1211, 1940, 5 U.S.C. § 631a, 1958.

In 1941 President Roosevelt issued Executive Order 8802, 6 Fed. Reg. 3,109 (1941) which "reaffirmed" the policy of the United States against "discrimination in the employment of workers in defense industries or government because of race, creed, color, or national origin."[c] The order established the Committee on Fair Employment Practice which could "receive and investigate complaints of discrimination" and "take appropriate steps to redress grievances which it finds to be valid." Those "appropriate steps" were not spelled out in subsequent Executive Orders, however, and the Committee was never given direct means of enforcing any directives it might issue. Twenty years later, President Kennedy issued Executive Order No. 10,925, 26 Fed. Reg. 1,977 (1961) which created the President's Committee on Equal Employment Opportunity, an agency charged with the responsibility of effectuating equal employment opportunity in government employment and in private employment on government contracts. Executive Order 10,925 was a dramatic break with the past. For while certain orders had imposed on government contractors an obligation not to discriminate on the basis of race, creed, color, or national origin, the Kennedy order required

[b] It is unclear why the Court in *Hodges* did not declare the 1866 Act unconstitutional as an unlawful assumption of state powers in violation of the 10th Amendment, as it did with other civil rights legislation in the Civil Rights Cases, 109 U.S. 3, 3 S.Ct. 18, 27 L.Ed. 835 (1883). Justice Harlan in his dissent in *Hodges* commented that "if the majority opinion's scope and effect are not wholly misapprehended by me, the court does adjudge that Congress cannot make it an offense against the United States for individuals to combine or conspire to prevent, even by force, citizens of African descent, solely because of their race, from earning a living." 203 U.S. at 8, 27 S.Ct. at 16.

[c] President Roosevelt was embarrassed into acting by the threat of a mass demonstration in Washington organized by A. Philip Randolph, President of the Brotherhood of Sleeping Car Porters, to protest racial discrimination by defense contractors. The march was scheduled for July 1, 1941. The administration, fearing international repercussions from such a demonstration, sought to dissuade Randolph, but he and other black leaders refused to cancel the march without a public commitment from the President to use his powers to obtain equal employment opportunity. Finally, on June 25th, the President promulgated Executive Order 8802. See Rochames, Race, Jobs & Politics 17–21 (1953); Comment, The Development of Modern Equal Employment Opportunity and Affirmative Action Law: A Brief Chronological Overview, 20 Howard L.J. 74, 75 (1977).

contractors to take affirmative action to make the policy effective and gave the Committee real enforcement powers. The Committee was authorized to: (a) publish the names of noncomplying contractors and unions; (b) recommend suits by the Department of Justice to compel compliance with contractual obligations not to discriminate; (c) recommend criminal actions against employers supplying false compliance reports; (d) terminate the contract of a noncomplying employer; and (e) forbid contracting agencies to enter into contracts with contractors guilty of discrimination. The work of the Committee and its successor agency, the Office of Federal Contract Compliance Programs, will be examined infra in Part V.

SECTION C. FEDERAL LABOR STATUTES

STEELE v. LOUISVILLE & NASHVILLE RAILROAD CO.

Supreme Court of the United States, 1944.
323 U.S. 192, 65 S.Ct. 226, 89 L.Ed. 173.

MR. CHIEF JUSTICE STONE delivered the opinion of the Court.

The question is whether the Railway Labor Act, 48 Stat. 1185, 45 U.S.C. § 151 et seq., 45 U.S.C.A. § 151 et seq., imposes on a labor organization, acting by authority of the statute as the exclusive bargaining representative of a craft or class of railway employees, the duty to represent all the employees in the craft without discrimination because of their race, and, if so, whether the courts have jurisdiction to protect the minority of the craft or class from the violation of such obligation.

The issue is raised by demurrer to the substituted amended bill of complaint filed by petitioner, a locomotive fireman, in a suit brought in the Alabama Circuit Court against his employer, the Louisville & Nashville Railroad Company, the Brotherhood of Locomotive Firemen and Enginemen, an unincorporated labor organization, and certain individuals representing the Brotherhood. The Circuit Court sustained the demurrer, and the Supreme Court of Alabama affirmed. We granted certiorari, the question presented being one of importance in the administration of the Railway Labor Act.

The allegations of the bill of complaint, so far as now material, are as follows: Petitioner, a Negro, is a locomotive fireman in the employ of respondent railroad, suing on his own behalf and that of his fellow employees who, like petitioner, are Negro firemen employed by the Railroad. Respondent Brotherhood, a labor organization, is, as provided under § 2, Fourth of the Railway Labor Act, the exclusive bargaining representative of the craft of firemen employed by the Railroad and is recognized as such by it and the members of the craft. The majority of the firemen employed by the Railroad are white and are members of the Brotherhood, but a substantial minority are Negroes who, by the constitution and ritual of the Brotherhood, are excluded from its membership. As the membership of the Brotherhood constitutes a majority of all firemen employed on respondent Railroad, and as under § 2, Fourth, the members because they are the majority have the right to choose and have chosen the Brotherhood to represent the craft, petitioner and other Negro firemen on the road have been required to accept the Brotherhood as their representative for the purposes of the Act.

On March 28, 1940, the Brotherhood, purporting to act as representative of the entire craft of firemen, without informing the Negro firemen or giving them opportunity to be heard, served a notice on respondent Railroad and on twenty other railroads operating principally in the southeastern part of the United States. The notice announced the Brotherhood's desire to amend the existing collective bargaining agreement in such manner as ultimately to exclude all Negro firemen from the service. By established practice on the several railroads so notified only white firemen can be promoted to serve as engineers, and the notice proposed that only "promotable", i.e., white, men should be employed as firemen or assigned to new runs or jobs or permanent vacancies in established runs or jobs.

On February 18, 1941, the railroads and the Brotherhood, as representative of the craft, entered into a new agreement which provided that not more than 50% of the firemen in each class of service in each seniority district of a carrier should be Negroes; that until such percentage should be reached all new runs and all vacancies should be filled by white men; and that the agreement did not sanction the employment of Negroes in any seniority district in which they were not working. The agreement reserved the right of the Brotherhood to negotiate for further restrictions on the employment of Negro firemen on the individual railroads. On May 12, 1941, the Brotherhood entered into a supplemental agreement with respondent Railroad further controlling the seniority rights of Negro firemen and restricting their employment. The Negro firemen were not given notice or opportunity to be heard with respect to either of these agreements, which were put into effect before their existence was disclosed to the Negro firemen.

Until April 8, 1941, petitioner was in a "passenger pool", to which one white and five Negro firemen were assigned. These jobs were highly desirable in point of wages, hours and other considerations. Petitioner had performed and was performing his work satisfactorily. Following a reduction in the mileage covered by the pool, all jobs in the pool were, about April 1, 1941, declared vacant. The Brotherhood and the Railroad, acting under the agreement, disqualified all the Negro firemen and replaced them with four white men, members of the Brotherhood, all junior in seniority to petitioner and no more competent or worthy. As a consequence petitioner was deprived of employment for sixteen days and then was assigned to more arduous, longer, and less remunerative work in local freight service. In conformity to the agreement, he was later replaced by a Brotherhood member junior to him, and assigned work on a switch engine, which was still harder and less remunerative, until January 3, 1942. On that date, after the bill of complaint in the present suit had been filed, he was reassigned to passenger service.

Protests and appeals of petitioner and his fellow Negro firemen, addressed to the Railroad and the Brotherhood, in an effort to secure relief and redress, have been ignored. Respondents have expressed their intention to enforce the agreement of February 18, 1941, and its subsequent modifications. The Brotherhood has acted and asserts the right to act as exclusive bargaining representative of the firemen's craft. It is alleged that in that capacity it is under an obligation and duty imposed by the Act to represent the Negro firemen impartially and in good faith; but instead, in its notice to and contracts with the railroads, it has been hostile and disloyal to the Negro firemen, has deliberately discriminated against them, and has sought to deprive them of their seniority rights and to drive them out of employment in their craft, all in order to create a monopoly of employment for Brotherhood members.

The bill of complaint asks for discovery of the manner in which the agreements have been applied and in other respects; for an injunction against enforcement of the agreements made between the Railroad and the Brotherhood; for an injunction against the Brotherhood and its agents from purporting to act as representative of petitioner and others similarly situated under the Railway Labor Act, so long as the discrimination continues, and so long as it refuses to give them notice and hearing with respect to proposals affecting their interests; for a declaratory judgment as to their rights; and for an award of damages against the Brotherhood for its wrongful conduct.

The Supreme Court of Alabama took jurisdiction of the cause but held on the merits that petitioner's complaint stated no cause of action.[1] It pointed out that the Act places a mandatory duty on the Railroad to treat with the Brotherhood as the exclusive representative of the employees in a craft, imposes heavy criminal penalties for willful failure to comply with its command, and provides that the majority of any craft shall have the right to determine who shall be the representative of the class for collective bargaining with the employer. It thought that the Brotherhood was empowered by the statute to enter into the agreement of February 18, 1941, and that by virtue of the statute the Brotherhood has power by agreement with the Railroad both to create the seniority rights of petitioner and his fellow Negro employees and to

1. The respondents urge that the Circuit Court sustained their demurrers on the ground that the suit could not be maintained against the Brotherhood, an unincorporated association, since by Alabama statute such an association cannot be sued unless the action lies against all its members individually, and on several other state-law grounds. They argue accordingly that the judgment of affirmance of the state Supreme Court may be rested on an adequate non-federal ground. As that court specifically rested its decision on the sole ground that the Railway Labor Act places no duty upon the Brotherhood to protect petitioner and other Negro firemen from the alleged discriminatory treatment, the judgment rests wholly on a federal ground, to which we confine our review.

destroy them. It construed the statute, not as creating the relationship of principal and agent between the members of the craft and the Brotherhood, but as conferring on the Brotherhood plenary authority to treat with the Railroad and enter into contracts fixing rates of pay and working conditions for the craft as a whole without any legal obligation or duty to protect the rights of minorities from discrimination or unfair treatment, however gross. Consequently it held that neither the Brotherhood nor the Railroad violated any rights of petitioner or his fellow Negro employees by negotiating the contracts discriminating against them.

If, as the state court has held, the Act confers this power on the bargaining representative of a craft or class of employees without any commensurate statutory duty toward its members, constitutional questions arise. For the representative is clothed with power not unlike that of a legislature which is subject to constitutional limitations on its power to deny, restrict, destroy or discriminate against the rights of those for whom it legislates and which is also under an affirmative constitutional duty equally to protect those rights. If the Railway Labor Act purports to impose on petitioner and the other Negro members of the craft the legal duty to comply with the terms of a contract whereby the representative has discriminatorily restricted their employment for the benefit and advantage of the Brotherhood's own members, we must decide the constitutional questions which petitioner raises in his pleading.

But we think that Congress, in enacting the Railway Labor Act and authorizing a labor union, chosen by a majority of a craft, to represent the craft, did not intend to confer plenary power upon the union to sacrifice, for the benefit of its members, rights of the minority of the craft, without imposing on it any duty to protect the minority. Since petitioner and the other Negro members of the craft are not members of the Brotherhood or eligible for membership, the authority to act for them is derived not from their action or consent but wholly from the command of the Act. Section 2, Fourth, provides: "Employees shall have the right to organize and bargain collectively through representatives of their own choosing. The majority of any craft or class of employees shall have the right to determine who shall be the representative of the craft or class for the purposes of this Act * * *." Under § 2, Sixth and Seventh, when the representative bargains for a change of working conditions, the latter section specifies that they are the working conditions of employees "as a class." Section 1, Sixth, of the Act defines "representative" as meaning "Any person or * * * labor union * * * designated either by a carrier or a group of carriers or by its or their employees, to act for it or them." The use of the word "representative," as thus defined and in all the contexts in which it is found, plainly implies that the representative is to act on behalf of all the employees which, by virtue of the statute, it undertakes to represent.

By the terms of the Act, § 2, Fourth, the employees are permitted to act "through" their representative, and it represents them "for the purposes of" the Act. Sections 2, Third, Fourth, Ninth. The purposes of the Act declared by § 2 are the avoidance of "any interruption to commerce or to the operation of any carrier engaged therein," and this aim is sought to be achieved by encouraging "the prompt and orderly settlement of all disputes concerning rates of pay, rules, or working conditions." Compare Texas & N. O. R. Co. v. Brotherhood of Railway & S. S. Clerks, 281 U.S. 548, 569, 50 S.Ct. 427, 433, 74 L.Ed. 1034. These purposes would hardly be attained if a substantial minority of the craft were denied the right to have their interests considered at the conference table and if the final result of the bargaining process were to be the sacrifice of the interests of the minority by the action of a representative chosen by the majority. The only recourse of the minority would be to strike, with the attendant interruption of commerce, which the Act seeks to avoid.

Section 2, Second, requiring carriers to bargain with the representative so chosen, operates to exclude any other from representing a craft. Virginian R. Co. v. System Federation, supra, 300 U.S. 545, 57 S.Ct. 598, 81 L.Ed. 789. The minority members of a craft are thus deprived by the statute of the right, which they would otherwise possess, to choose a representative of their own, and its members cannot bargain individually on behalf of themselves as to matters which are properly the subject of collective bargaining.

The labor organization chosen to be the representative of the craft or class of employees is thus chosen to represent all of its members, regardless of their union affiliations or want of them. As we have pointed out with respect to the like provision of the National Labor Relations Act, 29 U.S.C.A. § 151 et seq., in J. I. Case Co. v. National Labor Relations Board, supra, 321 U.S. 338, 64 S.Ct. 580, "The very purpose of providing by statute for the collective agreement is to supersede the terms of separate agreements of employees with terms which reflect the strength and bargaining power and serve the welfare of the group. Its benefits and advantages are open to every employee of the represented unit * * *." The purpose of providing for a representative is to secure those benefits for those who are represented and not to deprive them or any of them of the benefits of collective bargaining for the advantage of the representative or those members of the craft who selected it.

As the National Mediation Board said in In The Matter of Representation of Employees of the St. Paul Union Depot Company, Case No. R–635: "Once a craft or class has designated its representative, such representative is responsible under the law to act for all employees within the craft or class, those who are not members of the represented organization, as well as those who are members." [2]

2. The Mediation Board's decision in this case was set aside in Brotherhood of Railway & Steamship Clerks v. United Transport Service Employees, 78 U.S.App. D.C. 125, 137 F.2d 817, reversed on jurisdictional grounds 320 U.S. 715, 64 S.Ct.

Unless the labor union representing a craft owes some duty to represent non-union members of the craft, at least to the extent of not discriminating against them as such in the contracts which it makes as their representative, the minority would be left with no means of protecting their interests, or indeed, their right to earn a livelihood by pursuing the occupation in which they are employed. While the majority of the craft chooses the bargaining representative, when chosen it represents, as the Act by its terms makes plain, the craft or class, and not the majority. The fair interpretation of the statutory language is that the organization chosen to represent a craft is to represent all its members, the majority as well as the minority, and it is to act for and not against those whom it represents.[3] It is a principle of general application that the exercise of a granted power to act in behalf of others involves the assumption toward them of a duty to exercise the power in their interest and behalf, and that such a grant of power will not be deemed to dispense with all duty toward those for whom it is exercised unless so expressed.

We think that the Railway Labor Act imposes upon the statutory representative of a craft at least as exacting a duty to protect equally the interests of the members of the craft as the Constitution imposes upon a legislature to give equal protection to the interests of those for whom it legislates. Congress has seen fit to clothe the bargaining representative with powers comparable to those possessed by a legislative body both to create and restrict the rights of those whom it represents, cf. J. I. Case Co. v. National Labor Relations Board, supra, 321 U.S. 335, 64 S.Ct. 579, but it has also imposed on the representative a corresponding duty. We hold that the language of the Act to which we have referred, read in the light of the purposes of the Act, expresses the aim of Congress to impose on the bargaining representative of a craft or class of employees the duty to exercise fairly the power conferred upon it in behalf of all those for whom it acts, without hostile discrimination against them.

This does not mean that the statutory representative of a craft is barred from making contracts which may have unfavorable effects on

260. The Court of Appeals was of the opinion that a representative is not only required to act in behalf of all the employees in a bargaining unit, but that a labor organization which excludes a minority of a craft from its membership has no standing to act as such representative of the minority.

The Act has been similarly interpreted by the Emergency Board referred to in General Committee v. Southern Pacific Co., 320 U.S. 338, 340, 342, 343, 64 S.Ct. 142, 143, 144, 145, note. It declared in 1937: "When a craft or class, through representatives chosen by a majority, negotiates a contract with a carrier, all members of the craft or class share in the rights secured by the contract, regardless of their affiliation with any organization of employees. * * * the representatives of the majority represent the whole craft or class in the making of an agreement for the benefit of all * * *."

3. Compare the House Committee Report on the N.L.R.A. (H. Rep. No. 1147, 74th Cong., 1st Sess., pp. 20–22) indicating that although the principle of majority rule "written into the statute books by Congress in the Railway Labor Act of 1934" was to be applicable to the bargaining unit under the N.L.R.A., the employer was required to give "equally advantageous terms to nonmembers of the labor organization negotiating the agreement."

some of the members of the craft represented. Variations in the terms of the contract based on differences relevant to the authorized purposes of the contract in conditions to which they are to be applied, such as differences in seniority, the type of work performed, the competence and skill with which it is performed, are within the scope of the bargaining representation of a craft, all of whose members are not identical in their interest or merit. Cf. Carmichael v. Southern Coal & Coke Co., 301 U.S. 495, 509, 510, 512, 57 S.Ct. 868, 872, 873, 874, 81 L.Ed. 1245, 109 A.L.R. 1327, and cases cited; State of Washington v. Superior Court, 289 U.S. 361, 366, 53 S.Ct. 624, 627, 77 L.Ed. 1256, 89 A.L.R. 653; Metropolitan Casualty Ins. Co. v. Brownell, 294 U.S. 580, 583, 55 S.Ct. 538, 540, 79 L.Ed. 1070. Without attempting to mark the allowable limits of differences in the terms of contracts based on differences of conditions to which they apply, it is enough for present purposes to say that the statutory power to represent a craft and to make contracts as to wages, hours and working conditions does not include the authority to make among members of the craft discriminations not based on such relevant differences. Here the discriminations based on race alone are obviously irrelevant and invidious. Congress plainly did not undertake to authorize the bargaining representative to make such discriminations.

The representative which thus discriminates may be enjoined from so doing, and its members may be enjoined from taking the benefit of such discriminatory action. No more is the Railroad bound by or entitled to take the benefit of a contract which the bargaining representative is prohibited by the statute from making. In both cases the right asserted, which is derived from the duty imposed by the statute on the bargaining representative, is a federal right implied from the statute and the policy which it has adopted. It is the federal statute which condemns as unlawful the Brotherhood's conduct. "The extent and nature of the legal consequences of this condemnation, though left by the statute to judicial determination, are nevertheless to be derived from it and the federal policy which it has adopted." Deitrick v. Greaney, 309 U.S. 190, 200, 201, 60 S.Ct. 480, 485, 84 L.Ed. 694.

So long as a labor union assumes to act as the statutory representative of a craft, it cannot rightly refuse to perform the duty, which is inseparable from the power of representation conferred upon it, to represent the entire membership of the craft. While the statute does not deny to such a bargaining labor organization the right to determine eligibility to its membership, it does require the union, in collective bargaining and in making contracts with the carrier, to represent non-union or minority union members of the craft without hostile discrimination, fairly, impartially, and in good faith. Wherever necessary to that end, the union is required to consider requests of non-union members of the craft and expressions of their views with respect to collective bargaining with the employer and to give to them notice of and opportunity for hearing upon its proposed action.

Since the right asserted by petitioner "is * * * claimed * * * under the Constitution" and a "statute of the United States", the decision of the Alabama court adverse to that contention is reviewable here under § 237(b) of the Judicial Code, 28 U.S.C.A. § 344(b), unless the Railway Labor Act itself has excluded petitioner's claims from judicial consideration. The question here presented is not one of a jurisdictional dispute, determinable under the administrative scheme set up by the Act, or restricted by the Act to voluntary settlement by recourse to the traditional implements of mediation, conciliation and arbitration. There is no question here of who is entitled to represent the craft, or who are members of it, issues which have been relegated for settlement to the Mediation Board. Nor are there differences as to the interpretation of the contract which by the Act are committed to the jurisdiction of the Railroad Adjustment Board.

Section 3, First (i), which provides for reference to the Adjustment Board of "disputes between an employee or group of employees and a carrier or carriers growing out of grievances or out of the interpretation or application of agreements", makes no reference to disputes between employees and their representative. Even though the dispute between the railroad and the petitioner were to be heard by the Adjustment Board, that Board could not give the entire relief here sought. The Adjustment Board has consistently declined in more than 400 cases to entertain grievance complaints by individual members of a craft represented by a labor organization. "The only way that an individual may prevail is by taking his case to the union and causing the union to carry it through to the Board." Administrative Procedure in Government Agencies, S. Doc. No. 10, 77th Cong., 1st Sess., Pt. 4, p. 7. Whether or not judicial power might be exerted to require the Adjustment Board to consider individual grievances, as to which we express no opinion, we cannot say that there is an administrative remedy available to petitioner or that resort to such proceedings in order to secure a possible administrative remedy, which is withheld or denied, is prerequisite to relief in equity. Further, since § 3, First (c), permits the national labor organizations chosen by the majority of the crafts to "prescribe the rules under which the labor members of the Adjustment Board shall be selected" and to "select such members and designate the division on which each member shall serve", the Negro firemen would be required to appear before a group which is in large part chosen by the respondents against whom their real complaint is made. In addition § 3, Second, provides that a carrier and a class or craft of employees, "all acting through their representatives, selected in accordance with the provisions of this Act", may agree to the establishment of a regional board of adjustment for the purpose of adjusting disputes of the type which may be brought before the Adjustment Board. In this way the carrier and the representative against whom the Negro firemen have complained have power to supersede entirely the Adjustment Board's procedure and to create a tribunal of their own selection to interpret and apply the agreements now complained of to which they are the only parties. We cannot say that a hearing, if available, before either of these tribunals would constitute an adequate administrative remedy. There is no administrative means by which the Negro firemen can secure separate representation for the purposes of collective bargaining. For the Mediation Board "has definitely ruled that a craft or class of employees may not be divided into two or more on the basis of race or color for the purpose of choosing representatives." [4]

In the absence of any available administrative remedy, the right here asserted, to a remedy for breach of the statutory duty of the bargaining representative to represent and act for the members of a craft, is of judicial cognizance. That right would be sacrificed or obliterated if it were without the remedy which courts can give for breach of such a duty or obligation and which it is their duty to give in cases in which they have jurisdiction. * * * there can be no doubt of the justiciability of these claims. As we noted in General Committee v. Missouri-Kansas-Texas R. Co., supra, 320 U.S. 331, 64 S.Ct. 150, the statutory provisions which are in issue are stated in the form of commands. For the present command there is no mode of enforcement other than resort to the courts, whose jurisdiction and duty to afford a remedy for a breach of statutory duty are left unaffected. The right is analogous to the statutory right of employees to require the employer to bargain with the statutory representative of a craft, a right which this Court has enforced and protected by its injunction in Texas & N. O. R. Co. v. Brotherhood of Railway & S. S. Clerks, 281 U.S. 556, 557, 560, 50 S.Ct. 429, 430, 74 L.Ed. 1034, and in Virginian R. Co. v. System Federation, 300 U.S. 548, 57 S.Ct. 599, 81 L.Ed. 789, and like it is one for which there is no available administrative remedy.

We conclude that the duty which the statute imposes on a union representative of a craft to represent the interests of all its members stands on no different footing and that the statute contemplates resort to the usual judicial remedies of injunction and award of damages when appropriate for breach of that duty.

The judgment is accordingly reversed and remanded for further proceedings not inconsistent with this opinion.

Reversed.

MR. JUSTICE BLACK concurs in the result.

MR. JUSTICE MURPHY, concurring.

The economic discrimination against Negroes practiced by the Brotherhood and the railroad under color of Congressional authority raises a grave constitutional issue that should be squarely faced.

The utter disregard for the dignity and the well-being of colored citizens shown by this record is so pronounced as to demand the invocation of constitutional condemnation. To decide the case and to

4. National Mediation Board, The Railway Labor Act and the National Mediation Board, p. 17.

analyze the statute solely upon the basis of legal niceties, while remaining mute and placid as to the obvious and oppressive deprivation of constitutional guarantees, is to make the judicial function something less than it should be.

The constitutional problem inherent in this instance is clear. Congress, through the Railway Labor Act, has conferred upon the union selected by a majority of a craft or class of railway workers the power to represent the entire craft or class in all collective bargaining matters. While such a union is essentially a private organization, its power to represent and bind all members of a class or craft is derived solely from Congress. The Act contains no language which directs the manner in which the bargaining representative shall perform its duties. But it cannot be assumed that Congress meant to authorize the representative to act so as to ignore rights guaranteed by the Constitution. Otherwise the Act would bear the stigma of unconstitutionality under the Fifth Amendment in this respect. For that reason I am willing to read the statute as not permitting or allowing any action by the bargaining representative in the exercise of its delegated powers which would in effect violate the constitutional rights of individuals.

If the Court's construction of the statute rests upon this basis, I agree. But I am not sure that such is the basis. Suffice it to say, however, that this constitutional issue cannot be lightly dismissed. The cloak of racism surrounding the actions of the Brotherhood in refusing membership to Negroes and in entering into and enforcing agreements discriminating against them, all under the guise of Congressional authority, still remains. No statutory interpretation can erase this ugly example of economic cruelty against colored citizens of the United States. Nothing can destroy the fact that the accident of birth has been used as the basis to abuse individual rights by an organization purporting to act in conformity with its Congressional mandate. Any attempt to interpret the Act must take that fact into account and must realize that the constitutionality of the statute in this respect depends upon the answer given.

The Constitution voices its disapproval whenever economic discrimination is applied under authority of law against any race, creed or color. A sound democracy cannot allow such discrimination to go unchallenged. Racism is far too virulent today to permit the slightest refusal, in the light of a Constitution that abhors it, to expose and condemn it wherever it appears in the course of a statutory interpretation.

NOTES AND PROBLEMS FOR DISCUSSION

1. What was the "grave constitutional issue" which Justice Murphy in his concurring opinion wished to see "squarely faced?" Would the adoption by the Court of a constitutional basis for its decision have been of any practical benefit to the plaintiff class? The complaint in *Steele* prayed for an injunction prohibiting enforcement of the agreement between the Brotherhood and the Railroad and prohibiting the Brotherhood from acting as the plaintiffs' repre-

sentative so long as it refused to give them notice and a hearing with respect to actions affecting their interests. Why didn't the plaintiffs request an injunction requiring the Brotherhood to accept blacks as members? What relief does the Court actually afford the plaintiffs?

2. In BROTHERHOOD OF RAILROAD TRAINMEN v. HOWARD, 343 U.S. 768, 72 S.Ct. 1022, 96 L.Ed. 1283 (1952), black train porters complained that the segregated, all-white Brotherhood of Railroad Trainmen representing the craft of brakemen had entered into an agreement with the employer, the effect of which was to abolish the job of train porter and assign all porter functions to brakemen. The case differed from *Steele* in that the plaintiffs were not members of the bargaining unit represented by the defendant union, but were members of a different craft and were represented by a union of their own choosing. The question thus posed was whether the defendant union owed any duty under the Railway Labor Act not to discriminate against black employees which it did not represent as bargaining agent. In a brief opinion the majority, relying on *Steele*, concluded that "the Federal Act thus prohibits bargaining agents it authorizes from using their position and power to destroy colored workers' jobs in order to bestow them on white workers." 343 U.S. at 774. In dissent, Justice Minton, joined by Chief Justice Reed, argued that:

> The majority reaches out to invalidate the contract, not because the train porters are brakemen entitled to fair representation by the Brotherhood, but because they are Negroes who were discriminated against by the carrier at the behest of the Brotherhood. I do not understand that private parties such as the carrier and the Brotherhood may not discriminate on the ground of race. Neither a state government nor the Federal Government may do so, but I know of no applicable federal law which says that private parties may not. That is the whole problem underlying the proposed Federal Fair Employment Practices Code. Of course, this Court by sheer power can say this case is *Steele*, or even lay down a code of fair employment practices. But sheer power is not a substitute for legality.

343 U.S. at 777–778.

In light of *Steele*, what was the source of the union's duty not to discriminate against employees it did not represent? In CONLEY v. GIBSON, 355 U.S. 41, 78 S.Ct. 99, 2 L.Ed.2d 80 (1957), the *Steele* doctrine of fair representation was extended to apply to a union's failure to protect black employees in the bargaining unit from unilateral action by the employer. In that case the railroad eliminated forty-five jobs held by blacks in violation of a contract with the Brotherhood of Railway Clerks whose all-white local accepted the employer's excuses and refused to process grievances filed by the displaced employees. Because the district court dismissed the case on jurisdictional grounds, the Supreme Court could hold no more than that the complaint stated a cause of action under the Railway Labor Act. 355 U.S. at 45. Thus the question of exactly what relief black employees were entitled to against union or employer under the Act remained unanswered.[a] Could, for example, the employer be required to reinstate black employees discharged on racial grounds because of the union's failure to fairly represent? Also left open by *Steele* and its progeny

[a] On remand from the Supreme Court, seven years after the elimination of the black jobs, the district court is reported to have granted the defendants' motion to dismiss as to deceased plaintiffs and a motion for summary judgment as to the remaining plaintiffs' class action. See Herring, The "Fair Representation" Doctrine: An Effective Weapon Against Union Racial Discrimination?, 24 Md.L.Rev. 113, 127 (1964).

was the question of whether a union had an obligation to protest racially discriminatory employment practices preexisting the union's status as bargaining agent under the RLA. See Clark v. Norfolk & Western Railway, 37 L.R. R.M. 2685 (W.D. Va. 1956); Richardson v. Texas & New Orleans Railroad, 242 F.2d 230 (5th Cir. 1957).

3. The development of the fair representation doctrine occurred chiefly in litigation under the Railway Labor Act arising in the southern railroad industry. That development began with the filing of the *Steele* case and its federal court companion, Tunstall v. Brotherhood of Locomotive Firemen and Enginemen, 323 U.S. 210, 65 S.Ct. 235, 89 L.Ed. 187 (1944) in the early 1940s. It was not until 1955, however, that unions acting as bargaining agents under the National Labor Relations Act were held to have the same obligations toward minority employees that the railroad unions bore under the RLA. In Syres v. Oil Workers, 223 F.2d 739 (5th Cir. 1955), reversed, 350 U.S. 892, 76 S.Ct. 152, 100 L.Ed. 785, an all-black local filed suit against its white counterpart for injunctive relief and damages, alleging that the white union caused the employer to maintain segregated job classifications which relegated black workers to the lowest paying, least desirable positions. The Fifth Circuit affirmed the dismissal of the suit as one merely arising from a dispute between the locals, and involving no federal question. The Supreme Court reversed in a one sentence per curiam opinion citing *Steele* and Brotherhood of Railroad Trainmen v. Howard. In Humphrey v. Moore, 375 U.S. 335, 84 S.Ct. 363, 11 L.Ed.2d 370 (1964), the Court stated explicitly that a union operating under the NLRA has the same "responsibility and duty of fair representation" as that imposed on unions by the RLA. The National Labor Relations Board in Metal Worker's Union (Hughes Tool Co.), 56 L.R.R.M. 1289 (1964) held that a union's breach of its duty to fairly represent black workers constituted a violation of the NLRA, and warranted rescission of the union's certification as exclusive bargaining agent. See also Local Union 12, United Rubber, Cork, Linoleum and Plastic Workers v. National Labor Relations Board, 150 N.L.R.B. 312 (1964), enforced, 368 F.2d 12 (5th Cir. 1966) (union's refusal to process grievances based on belief that employee's discriminatory job conditions should continue found to be violation of duty of fair representation), and Houston Maritime Association, 168 N.L.R.B. 615 (1967) (duty of fair representation breached by union's policies which perpetuated effects of past discrimination). But in Handy Andy, Inc., 228 N.L.R.B. 447 (1977), the Board ruled that certification would not be withheld because of a union's history of discriminatory activities in *other* bargaining units.

4. *Steele* and the cases discussed above addressed the problem of racial discrimination by the employer initiated or tolerated by unions endowed with powers by the national labor laws. As a natural corollary to the fair representation cases, the practice of racial segregation of union membership itself came under attack. In James v. Marinship Corp., 25 Cal.2d 721, 155 P.2d 329 (1944) and Williams v. International Brotherhood of Boilermakers, Iron Shipbuilders & Helpers of America, 27 Cal.2d 586, 165 P.2d 903 (1946), all-white locals of the Boilermakers created segregated auxiliary locals for black employees and then sought to enforce closed shop agreements with employers by demanding discharge of black workers who refused to join such auxiliaries. The district court in *James* enjoined enforcement of the closed shop contracts against the black employees and also enjoined the white local from "refusing to admit into membership in said Local 6 on the same terms and conditions as white persons * * * plaintiffs and other Negro workers similarly situated." The Califor-

nia Supreme Court, basing its decision in part on the public policy of the state and in part on the special status of the unions as exclusive bargaining agents under the NLRA, affirmed and held that a union could not enforce a closed shop agreement while at the same time closing its membership. The court interpreted the district court's order, however, not as requiring the white local to admit black members, but only as prohibiting the union from maintaining *both* a closed shop and an arbitrarily closed or partially closed union. 155 P.2d at 342. The court's opinions in both *James* and *Williams* were expressly contingent on the findings that the black auxiliaries were inferior in status and authority to the white locals, thus leaving open the question whether a union with "separate but equal" segregated locals could enforce a closed shop contract against workers refusing to join a segregated local. In Betts v. Easley, 161 Kan. 459, 169 P.2d 831 (1946), the Kansas Supreme Court enjoined the Brotherhood of Railway Carmen, which had established racially segregated locals after becoming the certified bargaining agent for employees of the Santa Fe Railway, from acting as a bargaining agent for black employees as long as the latter "were not given equality in privileges and participation in union affairs." But in Oliphant v. Brotherhood of Locomotive Firemen and Enginemen, 262 F.2d 359 (6th Cir. 1958), cert. denied, 359 U.S. 935, 79 S.Ct. 648, 3 L.Ed.2d 636 (1959), where black employees sought an order requiring their admission to an all-white union on the ground that, as their recognized bargaining agent, it had negotiated a contract detrimental to their interests, the district court and court of appeals dismissed the complaint, finding the Brotherhood's certification under the RLA insufficient to make its discriminatory conduct the equivalent of government action. The Supreme Court denied review "in view of the abstract context in which the questions sought to be raised are presented in this record."

SECTION D. STATE LAW

Commencing in the 1940's, a number of states enacted fair employment practice statutes to combat discrimination in employment. These statutes took one of two forms: (1) those which expressed a public policy against discrimination in employment, but contained no remedial provisions, and (2) those which defined prohibited employment practices and provided an enforcement mechanism.[a] A series of statutes[b] enacted by the State of New York typified the second type of act: the New York laws, variously applicable to employers, employment agencies, and labor organizations, defined unlawful discrimination to include the refusal of an employer to hire or to discharge from employment because of an individual's race, color or creed. Discrimination with regard to "compensation or terms of employment" was also prohibited and labor unions were forbidden to discriminate against either their members or employers because of race, creed or color. Most importantly, the New York laws provided for enforcement by the State Commission for Human Rights. Upon the filing of a complaint of

[a] For a comprehensive survey of state legislation as of 1949, see Note, Fair Employment Practices—A Comparison of State Legislation and Proposed Bills, 24 N.Y.U.L.Q. 398 (1949).

[b] See, e.g., N.Y. Civil Rights Law, ch. 6, §§ 40–43; N.Y. Executive Law, ch. 18, §§ 290–301; N.Y. Labor Laws, ch. 31, § 220–e; N.Y. Penal Law, ch. 40, §§ 700–701, 514.

discrimination, the Commission was authorized to investigate, conduct hearings, issue judicially enforceable cease and desist orders and take other affirmative action.[c] Violators of the acts were subject to criminal prosecution as well as civil liability. An individual discriminated against by a labor union enjoyed a private right of action for damages, but when a labor organization was not implicated, the individual's exclusive remedy was before the Commission.

In RAILWAY MAIL ASSOCIATION v. CORSI, 326 U.S. 88, 65 S.Ct. 1483, 89 L.Ed. 2072 (1945), an association of postal workers which limited its membership to "Caucasians and native American Indians" charged that the New York statute prohibiting discriminatory exclusion from membership violated due process by denying to the group the right to select its own membership. Citing State v. Louisville & Nashville Railroad Co. and Tunstall v. Brotherhood of Locomotive Firemen and Engineers, a unanimous Supreme Court declared there was "no constitutional basis for the contention that a state cannot protect workers from exclusion solely on the basis of race, color or creed by an organization * * *." Significantly, the Court did not refer to United States v. Hodge, The Slaughterhouse Cases or any other judicial nullifications of federal civil rights legislation. But if a state was not constitutionally barred from prohibiting discrimination by private associations, could there be any constitutional barrier to such action by the federal government?

[c] Under N.Y. Executive Law, ch. 18, §§ 295–297, the Commission was authorized to issue cease and desist orders upon a finding that a violation was occurring; to order reinstatement, back pay, restoration of or admission to union membership; and to order payment of compensatory damages.

Part II

TITLE VII OF THE CIVIL RIGHTS ACT OF 1964

Chapter 1

AN OVERVIEW OF THE SUBSTANTIVE PROVISIONS

Of the several pieces of legislation enacted by Congress to promote the goal of equal employment opportunity, none has been the basis for more litigation, nor the subject of more intense and wideranging judicial and academic scrutiny, than Title VII of the Civil Rights Act of 1964,[a] as amended by the Equal Employment Opportunity Act of 1972.[b] The explosion of litigation that followed the enactment of Title VII can be traced, at least in part, to the expansive language Congress used to define the classes of persons and employment-related decisions subject to the Act's substantive proscriptions. Title VII prohibits employers, unions and employment agencies from discriminating with respect to a broadly defined class of employment-related decisions on the basis of five specifically enumerated classifications—race, color, religion, national origin and sex. It also created the Equal Employment Opportunity Commission (EEOC), a five member, presidentially-appointed agency, to administer and interpret its provisions. The following selection of cases and note materials addresses several issues relating to the coverage of this statute.

SECTION A. COVERED ENTITIES

Read Sections 701(a)–(i), 703(a)–(c), and 717(a) of Title VII.[c]

1. Employers

Title VII prohibits three types of employment-related institutions—employers, employment agencies, and unions—from engaging in discriminatory employment practices. Section 701(b) defines "employer" as [1] a "person", [2] "engaged in an industry affecting commerce", [3]

[a] The 1964 Civil Rights Act, Pub.L. 88–352; 78 Stat. 241; 42 U.S.C. §§ 1971, 1975a–d, 2000a et seq., is an omnibus civil rights statute designed to prohibit discrimination in, inter alia, public accommodations and facilities, participation in federally assisted programs, and education, as well as in employment.

[b] Pub.L. 92–261, 86 Stat. 103; 42 U.S.C. § 2000e et seq.

[c] All references to Title VII will be made to the Act's original section numbers rather than to the parallel U.S. Code citations.

who has at least fifteen employees for twenty weeks during the current or preceding calendar year. The broadly worded definitions in § 701 of "person" and "industry affecting commerce" clearly reflect Congress' desire to maximize the scope of Title VII's jurisdiction since they result in the inclusion of virtually all organizational structures used to further business purposes within the statutory definition of "employer". Consequently, the only significant limitation on the definition of this term is the requirement that an "employer" have fifteen "employees" within the prescribed time period. Moreover, while the Act originally required a covered employer to have twenty-five employees, the reduction of this requirement to fifteen employees effected by the 1972 Amendments is further evidence of the legislature's desire to expand the reach of Title VII. Several interpretative questions, nevertheless, have arisen in connection with this minimum employee requirement.

EQUAL EMPLOYMENT OPPORTUNITY COMMISSION v. RINELLA & RINELLA

United States District Court, Northern District of Illinois, 1975.
401 F.Supp. 175.

WILL, DISTRICT JUDGE.

* * * Arlene Nagy was employed by the defendants as a legal secretary from January 1971 to March 1973, when she resigned and from October 1973, when she was rehired, to July 10, 1974 when she was discharged. From March of 1974, she was also a member of Women Employed, an Illinois not-for-profit corporation whose purpose is to oppose discrimination based on sex and otherwise to work to improve the employment status and working conditions of women in Chicago, Illinois.

Between March 1973 and July 30, 1974, Ms. Nagy engaged in various activities in opposition to what she alleges to be unlawful employment practices by Rinella & Rinella, which discriminated against women. These activities included joining Women Employed, soliciting other women employees of Rinella & Rinella to join Women Employed, attending meetings and participating in the activities of Women Employed, and publicly alleging that Rinella & Rinella discriminated on the basis of sex in its health insurance benefits. On July 30, 1974, Samuel A. Rinella, the owner of the law firm, discharged Ms. Nagy because of her participation in these activities.

Women Employed, on August 26, 1974, filed a charge with the Commission stating that Rinella & Rinella, in violation of Section 704(a) of Title VII, 42 U.S.C. § 2000e–3(a), intentionally discriminated against Arlene Nagy by unlawfully discharging her, and that the firm, by and through its partner, Samuel Rinella, intentionally discriminated against other female employees by interrogating them concerning their membership in Women Employed and threatening to discharge them if they joined or participated in the activities of Women Employed. The Commission conducted a preliminary investigation and the District

Director of the Commission's Chicago District Office concluded, in accordance with Section 706(f)(2), that prompt judicial action in the form of preliminary relief was necessary to carry out the purposes of Title VII. Consequently, on October 7, 1974, the Commission filed a petition for preliminary relief against Rinella & Rinella pursuant to Section 706(f)(2) * * *.

During the pendency of this action, on February 24, 1975, the Commission under the signature of a deputy director of the Chicago District Office, issued a right-to-sue letter to Women Employed. Thereafter, on March 4, 1975, Women Employed, as agent for and on behalf of Arlene Nagy, and Arlene Nagy, filed the second lawsuit under Section 706(f)(1) of Title VII * * *.

The defendants have filed motions to dismiss both lawsuits raising numerous alleged jurisdictional and procedural deficiencies. Specifically, their totally non-frivolous claims include:

1. The court is without subject matter jurisdiction in that:

a. The defendant does not qualify as an employer engaged in an industry affecting interstate commerce.

b. The defendant has not continuously employed fifteen (15) or more persons.

* * *

For the reasons set forth hereinafter, we find none of defendants' arguments offered in support of their motions to be meritorious and, accordingly, their motions to dismiss will be denied.

The plaintiffs allege that the defendant law firm is an employer within the meaning of Section 701(b) of Title VII, and is, therefore, subject to the proscriptions of the Civil Rights Act of 1964. The term "employer" is defined by the Act as:

> * * * a person engaged in an industry affecting commerce who has fifteen or more employees for each working day in each of twenty or more calendar weeks in the current or preceding calendar year, and any agent of such person * * *.

Title VII goes on to define an "employee" in almost unrestricted terms:

> The term "employee" means an individual employed by an employer * * *.

The defendants admit that they employed at least eleven employees during the relevant period consisting of secretaries and other clerical personnel and law clerks. Ms. Nagy's status as an employee is contested by the defendants; however, it would appear that she constituted a twelfth employee. The firm also included a group of lawyers which ranged from six to eight during the period under investigation. It is the defendants' contention that, due to the nature of these attorneys' status, they were independent contractors and not employees of the firm. As such, defendants contend, their numbers may not be applied toward reaching the required fifteen employees, and, accordingly, the firm is beyond the purview of Title VII.

The defendants argue that a primary consideration in determining whether an individual is an employee is whether the employer had the power to direct, control and supervise the employee in the performance of his work. The defendants contend that the element of control is not present here. They stress that the lawyers associated with the firm divide fees on the basis of productivity pursuant to a pre-arranged agreement providing for periodic salary draws, that the attorneys have no fixed office hours, set their own vacation schedules, and fix the fees in those cases for which they have responsibility. They further claim that the lawyer to whom a case is assigned is solely responsible for working on that case and does not receive instructions or guidance.

While the defendants' representations would indicate that, as professionals, the attorneys associated with Rinella & Rinella are subject to minimal direct supervision, the conclusion that the defendants would have us accept—that professional employment situations are not covered by Title VII—clearly is not the case. That sections 701, 703 and 704(a) of Title VII were intended to reach "professionals" is borne out by the legislative history of the 1972 amendments to Title VII.

* * *

The courts also have found little distinction between professional and nonprofessional job situations, concluding that, since the primary objective of Title VII is the elimination of the major social ills of job discrimination, discriminatory practices in professional fields are not immune from attack.

Accordingly, we do not find that the greater independence and authority generally afforded attorneys associated with smaller law firms precludes their being employees of the firm. Rather, the court must examine the totality of the firm's arrangements to determine whether an employer-employee relationship in fact exists. In the instant case, the evidence overwhelmingly supports a finding that the attorneys associated with Samuel Rinella in Rinella & Rinella are employees.

Samuel Rinella admits to being the sole owner of the firm of Rinella & Rinella. All of the other attorneys are associated with him in the practice of law. Samuel Rinella hires each of his associates and he has the authority to fire them. Samuel Rinella maintains that the reason that he has associates is to accommodate the amount of business he attracts and so he can have control over the cases.

Samuel Rinella refers significant numbers of his cases to his associates. * * * Associates' cases which are not referred directly from Samuel Rinella are also apparently considered firm work as most of the associates deposit the fees from their own cases in the firm bank account * * *.

Samuel Rinella also exerts considerable control over the compensation paid to those associated with his firm. While the attorneys' compensation, regular or bi-weekly salary draws out of the firm account with quarterly adjustments, is the result of negotiation and mutual agreement between Samuel Rinella and the individual attorney, no one disputes that Samuel Rinella has the final say with respect to the sums involved. The lawyers' compensation strongly resembles a salary in that it is regular and in round numbers, and there is no indication that an attorney has ever returned money to the firm following a quarterly adjustment or paid any interest. These factors controvert the defendants' suggestion that the draws are merely loans to independent contractors based upon expected earnings. Samuel Rinella also determines and pays the salaries of all secretarial and clerical employees.

* * *

Finally, all outward appearances to the public indicate that the attorneys are employed by the firm. The list of names on the law office's outer door, as well as the letterhead on the firm's stationery and billhead, suggest that the attorneys are working for the firm. The firm's stationery and billhead are apparently used by the associates on their own cases as well as those referred to them by Samuel Rinella. The firm's listings in various legal directories also suggest that the associates are employees. Since the firm is not a partnership, and the associates are not listed as "of counsel," it is only reasonable to conclude that they are employed by the firm.

Based upon all of these considerations, it is inconceivable that the associates of Rinella & Rinella could be considered anything but employees of the firm. Added to the secretarial and other clerical employees whom defendants concede to be employees within the meaning of Title VII, the law firm does employ more than the requisite fifteen employees, and therefore comes within its coverage.

The defendants contend that they are not engaged in an industry affecting interstate commerce due to the local nature of their business which involves predominately divorce litigation. Few cases have dealt with whether the practice of law affects commerce. Of particular note is the National Labor Relations Board's decision in Evans and Kunz, Ltd., 194 NLRB 1216 (1972), involving unfair labor charges levied against a small Phoenix law firm which confines most, if not all, of its activities to the practice of law solely within the state of Arizona. In that case, the Board upheld the Trial Examiner's decision that the firm was engaged in operations affecting commerce within the meaning of the National Labor Relations Act, wherein "affecting commerce" is similarly defined. The Board, however, exercised its discretion and declined to assert its jurisdiction concluding that "the effect of a labor dispute on commerce is not sufficiently substantial to warrant the exercise of jurisdiction." While we do not find the Board's decision defining jurisdiction in the context of a different statute with different policies and purposes to be controlling here, we do find its determination that a predominantly local law firm affects commerce to be germane and instructive.

* * * [I]n keeping with the general principle that remedial legislation such as Title VII should be liberally construed for jurisdictional purposes, we find that the dynamics inherent in a general law practice necessarily affects interstate commerce. This is especially so in light of the cases interpeting the interstate commerce requirements of the Civil Rights Act of 1964, most notably, Katzenbach v. McClung, 379 U.S. 294, 85 S.Ct. 377, 13 L.Ed.2d 290 (1964), which held that Ollie's Barbeque, a family owned restaurant catering only to local trade, was within the definition of commerce contained in Title II of the Civil Rights Act of 1964.

The incidents of interstate commerce are far more apparent in the instant case than they were in Katzenbach v. McClung and many of its progeny. Notwithstanding the defendants' divorce orientation, they admit that their practice encompasses other types of business, i.e., corporate, probate and real estate. They further admit that various attorneys travel out of state on firm business. Samuel Rinella, for instance, travelled to London, England and to Arizona, and Richard Rinella travelled to Washington, D.C. The firm's long distance phone bill in calendar year 1974 was $1,277.01; its out-of-state travel expenses amounted to approximately $2,000 for the same year. The firm also purchased both office intercommunication equipment from an out-of-state company for $8,400, and law and reference books from out-of-state publishers billed at approximately $2,500. These various factors establish that Rinella & Rinella indeed affects interstate commerce and, accordingly, is subject to the proscriptions of Title VII.

* * *

In summary, defendants' motion to dismiss for lack of jurisdiction * * * [is] denied. Cause No. 74 C 2861 and Cause No. 75 C 702 will be consolidated for the purpose of further discovery and trial if necessary. An order consistent with the foregoing will enter.

NOTES AND PROBLEMS FOR DISCUSSION

1. Would the result in the principal case have been different if all the attorneys in the defendant law firm had been partners? See Burke v. Friedman, 556 F.2d 867 (7th Cir. 1977). Is a general rule the best approach or should decisions be made on an ad hoc basis? The EEOC has embraced the "economic realities" test, under which it looks to the economic realities of the plaintiff's employment situation, especially his or her ownership and management interest in the business. See EEOC Dec. No. 85–4, 53 L.W. 2492 (Apr. 9, 1985). For a suggestion that treating partners as "employees" is consistent with the purposes of Title VII, see Note, Applicability of Federal Antidiscrimination Legislation to the Selection of a Law Partner, 76 Mich.L.Rev. 282 (1977).

2. Jane Baker claims that she was refused a position as night manager by Pine Valley Motor Lodge on the basis of her sex. Pine Valley is a small, local business with only 10 employees. It is a wholly owned subsidiary, however, of Great American Hotel & Motel, Inc., a corporation with over one thousand

employees. After Baker filed a Title VII action against Pine Valley, the defendant moved to dismiss the case on the ground that it was not an employer within the meaning of the statute. How should the court rule on this motion? See Armbruster v. Quinn, 711 F.2d 1332 (6th Cir. 1983); Watson v. Gulf & Western Industries, 650 F.2d 990 (9th Cir. 1981); Baker v. Stuart Broadcasting Co., 560 F.2d 389 (8th Cir. 1977). Any different result if Pine Valley's payroll also included six part-time employees? See Pascutoi v. Washburn-McReavy Mortuary, 11 FEP Cases 1325 (D. Minn. 1975). What if each of these six also had another job? See Thurber v. Jack Reilly's Inc., 717 F.2d 633 (1st Cir. 1983), cert. denied, 466 U.S. 904, 104 S.Ct. 1678, 80 L.Ed.2d 153 (1984).

3. Bill Montes claims that on July 5, 1978, he was denied a promotion by his employer, Kondet Industries, Inc. because he is an Hispanic. He filed a timely charge of national origin and race discrimination with the EEOC on October 15, 1978. On December 1, 1978, Kondet was taken over by Amalgamated Production Company. Montes timely filed an amended charge against Amalgamated on January 1, 1979. Amalgamated subsequently moved to dismiss the complaint for failure to state a claim and for lack of subject matter jurisdiction. What result? Should this issue be left to private negotiation? Would the affected employees be a party to such negotiations? What effect would a rule imposing liability have the transferability of businesses? Could Montes have obtained an effective remedy from the prior owner? See In Re National Airlines, Inc., 700 F.2d 695 (11th Cir. 1983); Trujillo v. Longhorn Mfg. Co., 694 F.2d 221 (10th Cir. 1982); Dominguez v. Hotel Union, Local 64, 674 F.2d 732 (8th Cir. 1982); EEOC v. MacMillan Bloedel Containers, Inc., 503 F.2d 1086 (6th Cir. 1974); Brown v. Evening News Association, 473 F.Supp. 1242 (E.D. Mich. 1979). See generally, Barksdale, Successor Liability Under the National Labor Relations Act and Title VII, 54 Tex.L.Rev. 707 (1976).

4. Can the discharged employee of a McDonald's franchise bring a Title VII claim against McDonald's as well as against the owner/operator of the franchise? See Kennedy v. McDonald's Corp., 610 F.Supp. 203 (S.D.W.Va. 1985).

5. Section 701(b) includes "agents" of § 701(a) "persons" within the class of covered employers. Accordingly, an employer with less than fifteen employees can be covered by the Act if it is viewed as the agent of an organization with more than 15 employees. See e.g., Owens v. Rush, 636 F.2d 283 (10th Cir. 1980) (claim against County Sheriff, whose office employed fewer than 15 persons, is cognizable under Title VII as Sheriff is under contract of, and is therefore an agent of County, and County satisfied minimum employee requirement). Does this provision also mean that a company can be liable under Title VII for the discriminatory acts of its employees? Would it matter whether the discriminator was a supervisory or non-supervisory employee? What about the employer's prior knowledge of, or response to the discriminatory conduct? See Meritor Savings Bank, FSB v. Vinson, infra, at 99. Note, however, the absence in § 717 (the provision extending Title VII to federal government employees) of analogous "agent" language. Did Congress intend to apply a different rule to federal employers?

6. As originally enacted, Title VII did not apply to the employment practices of federal, state or local government employers. The 1972 amendments, however, broadened the definition of "person" in § 701(a) to include state and local governments, governmental agencies, and political subdivisions. In addition, the 1972 enactment added a new provision, § 717, bringing most federal government employees within the purview of Title VII. But see

Johnson v. Alexander, 572 F.2d 1219 (8th Cir. 1978) (uniformed armed forces personnel not covered by Title VII).

The Supreme Court upheld the constitutionality of the extension of Title VII to state and local government entities in Fitzpatrick v. Bitzer, 427 U.S. 445, 96 S.Ct. 2666, 49 L.Ed.2d 614 (1976). Rejecting the claim that awards of money judgments for back pay or attorneys' fees infringed upon state sovereignty guaranteed by the Eleventh Amendment, the Court held that enactment of the statutory amendment was a proper exercise of Congress' enforcement power under § 5 of the Fourteenth Amendment. For a thorough discussion of the constitutional challenges to Title VII's extension to public employment, see Note, Title VII and Public Employers: Did Congress Exceed Its Powers?, 78 Col. L.Rev. 372 (1978).

7. William Sheraton, a black attorney, is engaged in the private practice of criminal defense law. He claims that the trial judges in his jurisdiction do not appoint black attorneys to represent indigents in criminal cases. Attorneys receiving such appointments are paid under a local Criminal Justice Act. Mr. Sheraton files an action against the State under Title VII alleging that he is being discriminated against on the basis of his race. The State responds with a motion to dismiss. What result? See Thompson v. District of Columbia, 25 FEP Cases 943 (D.D.C.1980), affirmed, 672 F.2d 897 (D.C.Cir. 1981).

8. Note that while the court in *Rinella* indicated that Title VII defines "employee" in "almost unrestricted terms", § 701(f) does specifically exclude "any person elected to public office" and "any person chosen by such officer to be on such officer's personal staff" from the definition of employee. A plaintiff's status as an employee for Title VII purposes is a matter of federal, rather than state law. State law is relevant only insofar as it describes the plaintiff's position, duties and manner of supervision. In determining whether a complainant falls within the "personal staff" exception, the courts consider the following six factors: (1) whether the complainant is personally accountable to an elected official; (2) whether that elected official has plenary power to appoint and remove persons occupying the position in question; (3) whether the complainant represents the public official in the eyes of the public; (4) whether the elected official exercises a considerable amount of control over the position in question; (5) the level of the position within the organization's chain of command, and (6) the degree of intimacy of the working relationship between the elected official and the complainant. See Teneyuca v. Bexar County, 767 F.2d 148 (5th Cir. 1985); Goodwin v. Circuit Court of St. Louis County, 729 F.2d 541 (8th Cir. 1984), cert. denied, ___ U.S. ___, 105 S.Ct. 1194, 84 L.Ed.2d 339 (1985); Ramirez v. San Mateo County, 639 F.2d 509 (9th Cir. 1981); and Owens v. Rush, 654 F.2d 1370 (10th Cir. 1981).

9. Camella Judge is a secretary for Lois Ann, Inc., a producer of computer software products. Lois Ann has thirteen employees in its Los Angeles office and three sales representatives. The sales representatives do not work out of the corporate office. They sell other product lines besides those of Lois Ann and are paid no salary apart from commissions received for products sold. Ms. Judge brought a Title VII action against Lois Ann alleging that she was subjected to sexual harassment by Lois Ann's President, Alan Kopolow. Lois Ann files a motion to dismiss. What result? See Armbruster v. Quinn, 711 F.2d 1332 (6th Cir. 1983).

2. Employment Agencies

GREENFIELD v. FIELD ENTERPRISES, INC.

United States District Court, Northern District of Illinois, 1972.
4 FEP Cases 548.

McGARR, DISTRICT JUDGE.

The plaintiffs describe themselves as six " * * * female members of the employment market in the Chicago area * * * over twenty-one years of age." The defendants are corporations in the business of publishing newspapers and particularly newspapers containing classified advertisement sections in the Chicago area. The complaint alleges that these classified advertisement sections contain help-wanted listings under separate male and female headings without reference to whether sex is a bona fide occupational qualification reasonably necessary to the normal operation of the advertiser's business or enterprise. It is contended that this practice is a violation of Title VII of the Civil Rights Act of 1964 and particularly Section 703(b):

> It shall be an unlawful employment practice for an employment agency to fail or refuse to refer for employment, or otherwise to discriminate against, any individual because of his race, color, religion, sex, or national origin, or to classify or refer for employment any individual on the basis of his race, color, religion, sex, or national origin.

The definition of the phrase "employment agency" used in this section is found elsewhere in the same statute. Paragraph (c) reads in pertinent part as follows:

> The term 'employment agency' means any person regularly undertaking with or without compensation to procure employees for an employer or to procure for employees opportunities to work for an employer and includes an agent of such person. * * *

Plaintiffs allege that the publication of said listings causes them irreparable injury by depriving them of equal access to employment where sex is not a bona fide occupational qualification. * * * The complaint seeks a preliminary and permanent injunction against the defendants, prohibiting the listing of jobs under male and female headings where sex is not a bona fide occupational qualification.

Defendants have filed motions variously denominated motion to strike or dismiss, or motions for judgment on the pleadings, all seeking a final disposition of the case based on the contention that the complaint fails to state a cause of action cognizable before this court. * * *

* * *

The paramount issue in the adjudication of the motions now under consideration by this court involves the question whether the language of the statute controlling here, in its reference to employment agencies, was intended to apply, and does apply, to newspapers publishing classified ads. * * *

At the outset, we must examine Section 703(b), and consider it together with the definition of the term employment agency in Section 701(c). Those sections, together with such light as the legislative history may throw upon them, control this court's decision on these motions. To the extent that it is helpful, we must also consider the single case which seems closely in point, Brush v. San Francisco Newspaper Printing Co., 315 F.Supp. 577, and the equally relevant consideration that the Equal Employment Opportunity Commission, the agency charged with the administration of Title VII, has concluded that utilization by the employer of classified advertising such as is complained of here, is covered by Title VII, and has so stated as follows:

> "Job Opportunity Advertising. It is a violation of Title VII for a help-wanted advertisement to indicate a preference, limitation, specification, or discrimination based on sex unless sex is a bona fide occupational qualification for the particular job involved. The placement of an advertisement in columns classified by publishers on the basis of sex, such as columns headed 'Male' or 'Female', will be considered as expression of a preference, limitation, specification or discrimination based on sex."

The administrative interpretation of the Act by the enforcing agency is entitled to great deference. It is not, however, precisely in point in this case, nor is it, in the last analysis, binding upon the court.

The brief of the Equal Employment Opportunity Commission refers to an ancillary provision of the statute for the light it presumably throws on the issues here. It sets out the relevant portion of Section 704(b) of Title VII. The pleadings do not rely upon this section, and it has not otherwise been injected into the case except by this reference in the brief of the Equal Employment Opportunity Commission. Because it refers to printing and advertising, it seems apt at first glance. However, it throws no light on the principal issue, since it, too, is a section limited in its application to "an employment agency." We thus revert to the necessity of determining whether in the conduct of the activities complained of in the complaint, the newspaper defendants are employment agencies as contemplated by the statute.

In examining Section 701(c) of the Act, which defines employment agency, we note that it begins with the phrase "any person." Corporations are included in the meaning of the word person. The section goes on, "* * * regularly undertaking with or without compensation to procure employees for an employer or to procure for employees opportunities to work for an employer. * * *" This definition clearly describes the activities of an employment agency in the traditional and generally accepted sense of that term, that is, any agency in the business of finding jobs for its worker clientele and finding workers for its employer clientele. Nothing in the statute or legislative history suggests a broader or different meaning. Only the most forced and tortured construction of those words could bring within that definition a newspaper publishing corporation which, as part of its publishing activities, accepts and lists classified ads for compensation.

The final relevant phrase of the definition of the term employment agency, after defining this phrase in the words set forth above, concludes by saying, "* * * and includes an agent of such person. * * *" Plaintiffs' brief makes the point that if the newspapers in their classified ad activities are not employment agencies, that they certainly are the agents of employment agencies, and thus come within the statutory definition. The matter again is one of statutory construction. The definition of employment agency refers to a person regularly undertaking to procure employees for an employer or to procure opportunities to work for employees. Persons are defined by the statute as individuals, unions, partnerships, associations, corporations, legal representatives, mutual companies, joint stock companies, trusts, unincorporated associations, trustees, etc. This variety of legal entities having been included in the definition of persons, it made clear and obvious sense for the statutory draftsmen to inject into the description of activities by such persons constituting them as employment agencies in the traditional and recognized sense, the notion that entities in the business world act through and are responsible for the actions of their agents. Therefore, the meaning of the phrase, "* * * includes an agent of such person * * *" must necessarily mean an agent of such person engaged in the same activity as brings the person within the definition of the term employment agency. This, again, is the regular undertaking of procuring employees for an employer client or employers for employee clients. While the publishing of classified advertising may further the business of employment agencies, it does not constitute the business of employment agencies. The assistance that the newspapers may or may not furnish to their customers in the course of servicing their advertising requirements as set forth on page four of plaintiffs' memorandum may indeed constitute the newspaper defendants a link in the job procurement chain, may indeed make them indispensible to the successful operation of employment agencies. But these activities do not make them employment agencies themselves. Therefore, and for these reasons, this court agrees with the conclusions of District Judge Swygert in Brush v. San Francisco Newspaper Printing Co. In addition, as set forth in that opinion, the legislative history of the section under consideration is consistent with this interpretation, and while not controlling as a matter of statutory construction, lends support to the conclusions here reached. * * *

On the other side of this issue, and quite to the contrary, is the position of the Equal Employment Opportunity Commission. * * *

In view of the clear limitation of the applicable statute to employers and employment agencies, the Equal Employment Opportunity Commission Guideline must be similarly limited in its application. Thus read, it is appropriately promulgated, but not of probative value in this case.

If read in the broader sense that it was intended to extend Title VII to newspapers, it is obvious that this guideline promulgated by the Equal Employment Opportunity Commission is contrary to the interpretation of that section indicated in the earlier portions of this opinion. * * *

* * *

The plaintiffs' brief and the *amicus* brief contain much material suggesting the impropriety and undesirability of the separate classification by sex of help-wanted and employment opportunity ads. Much of this material is persuasive. It is the business and jurisdiction of this court to decide only the applicability of the statute upon which the cause of action here under consideration is predicated. That statute has been determined to be non-applicable and for this reason this court has no jurisdiction. It seems appropriate to suggest, however, to the defendant, however gratuitously, that the position of the plaintiffs is an idea whose time has come and that serious consideration be given to a revision of the classification practices in employment advertising without reference to and free from the compulsion of the jurisdiction of the court.

The several motions of the defendants to strike and dismiss and for judgment on the pleadings are hereby granted.

NOTES AND PROBLEMS FOR DISCUSSION

1. Would a contrary result in *Greenfield* have created a constitutional problem? In Pittsburgh Press Co. v. Pittsburgh Commission on Human Relations, 413 U.S. 376, 93 S.Ct. 2553, 37 L.Ed.2d 669 (1973), the Supreme Court upheld a state court order forbidding newspapers from publishing "help-wanted" advertisements in sex-designated columns except for jobs exempt from the provisions of a city antidiscrimination ordinance. The Court rejected the newspaper's claim that the court order infringed upon its constitutional right to free speech, on the ground that the First Amendment does not protect commercial advertising. Three years later, however, in Virginia State Pharmacy Board v. Virginia Consumer Council, 425 U.S. 748, 96 S.Ct. 1817, 48 L.Ed.2d 346 (1976), the Court indicated that its prior ruling in *Pittsburgh Press* was limited by the fact that the restriction on publication in that case applied only to otherwise illegal (sex discriminatory) commercial speech. The Court then struck down a Virginia statute which declared it unprofessional conduct for a licensed pharmacist to advertise prescription drug prices and specifically stated that commercial speech is entitled to some measure of First Amendment protection.

2. The court in *Greenfield* dealt with only one of the interpretative questions arising out of the statutory definition of employment agency. In addition to the "regularly undertaking" requirement discussed in *Greenfield*, 701(c) demands that an employment agency procure "employees" for an "employer". Accordingly, issues concerning the interpretation of these two words previously discussed in connection with suits against employers also must be examined in the employment agency context.

(a) Does Title VII apply, for example, to transactions between a statutory employment agency and a client with fewer than fifteen employees? See Schrock v. Altru Nurses Registry, 38 FEP Cases 1709 (N.D.Ill. 1985) (agency placed nurses with private patients).

(b) Section 701(c) imposes no size limitation on covered employment agencies. Note, however, that an employment agency also may qualify as an employer under § 701(b) vis-a-vis its own staff and thus be subject to the provisions of § 703(a) as well as § 703(b).

3. Is a law school placement office a statutory employment agency? If so, must it ensure that all prospective employers using its facilities or services employ non-discriminatory recruitment and hiring practices? See Kaplowitz v. University of Chicago, 387 F.Supp. 42 (N.D.Ill.1974). Cf. Dumas v. Town of Mt. Vernon, 436 F.Supp. 866 (S.D.Ala.1977), affirmed in relevant part, 612 F.2d 974 (5th Cir. 1980)) (County Personnel Board that tested, interviewed and certified job applicants for jobs with the defendant Town is an employment agency.) What about a State Board of Bar Examiners? See Tyler v. Vickery, 517 F.2d 1089 (5th Cir. 1975), cert. denied, 426 U.S. 940, 96 S.Ct. 2660, 49 L.Ed.2d 393 (1976).

3. Labor Organizations

Sections 701(d) and (e) define "labor organization" in such general terms that there are few reported cases dealing with the application of Title VII to unions. A statutory union must either (a) operate a hiring hall that procures employees for a statutory employer; or (b) have fifteen members *and* either (1) be a certified or otherwise recognized bargaining representative of employees of a statutory employer, or (2) be affiliated with a body that represents or is actively seeking to represent employees of a statutory employer. The statute, therefore, covers international, national, and state as well as local bodies. In addition, the statute applies to agents of covered unions.

HOWARD v. INTERNAL MOLDERS & ALLIED WORKERS UNION

United States Court of Appeals, Eleventh Circuit, 1986.
779 F.2d 1546.

TUTTLE, SENIOR CIRCUIT JUDGE:

This is an appeal from a judgment dismissing a complaint filed by a class of employees against the Clow Corporation and defendant Union on charges of racial discrimination in employment practices.

I. STATEMENT OF THE CASE

Early in the proceedings, a consent decree was entered between the Clow Corporation, the employer, and the class of plaintiffs. However, the suit continued as against the labor organization under the provisions of 42 U.S.C. § 2000e–2(c)(3).[1]

1. Section 42 U.S.C. 2000e–2(c)(3) provides:

It shall be an unlawful employment practice for a labor organization * * *

At the trial, plaintiffs laid great stress upon the discriminatory effect on blacks of the departmental system under which most blacks were employed in the lowest paying department and under which there was only departmental seniority for promotion. They also stressed the fact that as to certain jobs, an unvalidated test was required by the employer and that the labor organization failed adequately to oppose the unvalidated testing requirement.

The trial court held that the seniority policy of the employer was carried out in good faith and held that plaintiffs had failed to establish any discriminatory practice thereabouts. With respect to the unvalidated testing, however, the court adopted what it called the "*Terrell*" standard as measuring the duty of the Union under its obligation of fair representation. This standard was established in Terrell v. United States Pipe & Foundry Co., 644 F.2d 1112, 1120 (5th Cir., Unit B, 1981):

> We begin with established principles of law, Section 703(c)(3) of Title VII makes it unlawful for a union to "cause or attempt to cause an employer to discriminate." * * * 42 U.S.C. § 2000e–2(c)(3). We have recognized that under the Act: [l]abor organizations, as well as employers, have an affirmative duty to take corrective steps to prevent the perpetuation of past discrimination." [sic] Myers v. Gilman Paper Co., 544 F.2d 837, 850 (5th Cir.), modified in other respects on rehearing, 556 F.2d 758, cert. dismissed, 434 U.S. 801, 98 S.Ct. 28, 54 L.Ed.2d 59 (1977). (citation omitted).

Recognizing the effect of the *Terrell* decision, the trial court made the following findings of fact and conclusions of law:

> Plaintiffs allege that defendants violated 42 U.S.C. § 2000e–2(e)(3) by acquiescing in the administration by the employer of facially neutral tests that had an adverse impact on plaintiffs. To prevail on this claim, plaintiffs must establish first that the mechanical comprehension test used by the company violated Title VII, and second, that defendants failed to comply with the *Terrell* "every reasonable step" standard.[17]

* * *

Clow Corporation used the mechanical comprehension test as a condition to promotion from 1965 (the effective date of Title VII) until 1977 (when this suit was filed). During those years, 56% (103 of 184) of the white employees who took the test passed it; only 12.5% (10 of 80) of the black employees who took the test passed it. The court concludes that plaintiffs established their prima facie case of disparate impact discrimination. Defendants did not rebut this presumption with any proof that the test was job related. Accordingly, the court concludes that plaintiffs established that the company's mechanical

(3) To cause or attempt to cause an employer to discriminate against an individual in violation of this section.

17. Although the Fifth Circuit in *Terrell* and *Walker* applied this standard to situations involving seniority systems, this court assumes that the Fifth Circuit would always apply this standard to a labor organization's conduct that is challenged under 42 U.S.C. § 2000e–2(c)(3).

comprehension test, although neutral in form, had a discriminatory impact and violated Title VII.

Next the court must determine whether the union defendants satisfied the *Terrell* standard. Union representative Robert Hollman criticized the company's use of the test on January 19, 1970. White members of the union committee demanded that the company cease using the tests on August 11, 1975. The court has pointed out that the union members never demanded that the union attempt to persuade the company to stop using the tests through the grievance procedure in 1970. There was no evidence that the union committee ever demanded during the 1972, 1974, or 1977 negotiations that the company cease using the tests. Defendants did not establish that the company would have refused to stop using the tests.[18] The company's abandonment of the tests when this suit was filed illustrates that the company would have considered agreeing to halt the use of the tests. Accordingly, the court concludes that the local union violated 42 U.S.C. § 2000e–2(c)(3) because it did not satisfy the *Terrell* standard of taking every reasonable step to ensure that the employer complies with Title VII. * * *

An international union can be held liable for a discriminatory practice if it has a "sufficient connection" with the discriminatory practice. Myers v. Gilman Paper Corp., 544 F.2d 837, 851 (5th Cir.), cert. dismissed, 434 U.S. 801 [98 S.Ct. 28, 54 L.Ed.2d 59] (1977). The Fifth Circuit in *Myers* adopted the holding of the Fourth Circuit in Patterson v. American Tobacco Co., 535 F.2d 257, 270–71 (4th Cir.), cert. denied, 429 U.S. 920 [97 S.Ct. 314, 50 L.Ed.2d 286] (1976): "The Fourth Circuit recently held that a sufficient connection exists where, as here, the international union provided 'an advisor' to the local in its negotiations and the international approved the resultant collective bargaining agreement." Myers v. Gilman Paper Corp., 544 F.2d at 852. The court has found above that Hildridge Dockery, the International Molders representative for the Local Union, worked closely with the bargaining committee as an advisor from 1972 until 1980. The court concludes that Dockery's activities provide a sufficient connection of the International to the Local Union's violation of Title VII * * *. Accordingly, pursuant to Myers v. Gilman Paper Corp., the court concludes that the International also violated 42 U.S.C. § 2000e–2(c)(3) for its conduct regarding the company's mechanical comprehension test.

Thereafter, on the 21st day of June, 1983, the court entered the following order:

> In conformity with the findings of fact and conclusions of law entered herein on June 1, 1983, the court finds in favor of the plaintiffs and against the defendants for their violation of 42 U.S.C. § 2000e–2(c)(3) for its conduct regarding the use of the mechanical

18. This situation is to be compared to the seniority system situation: there this court found that "the company had no intention of making any further concessions regarding the seniority system."

comprehension test. The court denies all other claims made by the plaintiffs.

* * *

II. ISSUES

The issues before this Court are:

* * *

2. Did the district court correctly decide that the unions were liable to the plaintiff class on account of their failure adequately to insist on the elimination of the unvalidated testing?

* * *

III. DISCUSSION

* * *

* * * Once the trial court found that the mechanical aptitude test had, during its entire period of operation, a disparate impact on the minority class, it follows that it was the duty of the defendant unions under the *Terrell* standard to make every reasonable effort to see that these tests were brought to an end. This, the trial court found, they had failed to do. * * *

* * *

It is, therefore, clear that the unions in this case are liable, because they did not use all reasonable effort to cause the employer to put an end to the use of the non-validated tests for promotion.

NOTES AND PROBLEMS FOR DISCUSSION

1. Why did the court find the union in violation of the statute? What should the union have done to satisfy its statutory obligations?

2. Charles Embry claims that he was denied membership by the Independent Drugstore Workers Union #2 solely on the basis of his race. The Union has 50 members, consisting of all ten of the employees of each of the five independent drugstores with whom it engages in collective bargaining. How should the trial court rule on the defendant Union's motion to dismiss Embry's Title VII suit for lack of jurisdiction or failure to state a cause of action? See Renfro v. Office and Professional Employee's International Union, Local 277, 545 F.2d 509 (5th Cir. 1977).

3. Sally Jones is employed as an administrative assistant by a local union. The union is the exclusive bargaining representative for hundreds of hotel and motel employees and has a staff of ten full time employees. Sally claims that the union has refused to promote her because of her sex. Can she state a cause of action under any section of Title VII? What if the union's activities are governed by a board of directors made up of fifty members, all of whom are full time employees of the hotels and restaurants organized by this union and all of whom are paid on a per diem basis by the union for the days they conduct union business, such as the investigation of all grievances? See Chavero v. Local 241, 787 F.2d 1154 (7th Cir. 1986). See also §§ 703(a)(1), (c)(1).

4. Are public sector unions within the reach of Title VII? In EEOC v. CALIFORNIA TEACHERS ASSOCIATION, 534 F.Supp. 209 (N.D.Cal.1982), the defendant, a union representing public school teachers in California, claimed

that it was not engaged in an industry affecting commerce (as required by § 701(d)) and thus was not a statutory labor organization. Section 703(e) provides that a union can satisfy the § 701(d) standard if it represents employees of an employer that is engaged in an industry affecting commerce. In addition, § 701(h) includes "any governmental industry, business or activity" within its definition of industry affecting commerce. The combination of §§ 701(e) and (h), the plaintiff contended, demonstrated Congress' determination that public sector unions affect interstate commerce. The court rejected this argument. Governmental employers were added to § 701(h) as part of the 1972 amendments to Title VII, an enactment initiated pursuant to Congress' authority under § 5 of the fourteenth amendment, not the commerce clause. Since Congress did not consider the commerce clause in amending § 701(h), the court reasoned, the legislature cannot be deemed to have found that every governmental entity is an industry affecting commerce. Accordingly, the court concluded, the statute also cannot be read to include a presumption that all public sector unions satisfy the "industry affecting commerce" requirement. The court then allocated to the plaintiff the duty of proving the requisite nexus with interstate commerce by proving either that the union was itself an industry affecting commerce or that it represented employees of an employer engaged in an industry affecting commerce. Will it be difficult for the EEOC to carry that burden? But see Graves v. Methodist Youth Services, 624 F.Supp. 429 (N.D.Ill. 1985) (local social service agency providing free services is *not* engaged in an industry or activity affecting interstate commerce; $175 in annual long distance telephone charges and purchase of office supplies from out-of-state supplier are *de minimis* and do *not* affect interstate commerce).

SECTION B. COVERED EMPLOYMENT DECISIONS

Sections 703(a)–(c) set forth the substantive limitations placed by Title VII on employers, employment agencies, and labor organizations. Once again, Congress' use of broad language in these provisions reflects its desire to bring almost all employment-related decisions made by these three entities within the scope of the statute's proscriptions. The following case, however, is one of the few cases where the challenged employment decision was held to lie outside the jurisdiction of Title VII.

HISHON v. KING & SPALDING

Supreme Court of the United States, 1984.
457 U.S. 69, 104 S.Ct. 2229, 81 L.Ed.2d 59.

CHIEF JUSTICE BURGER delivered the opinion of the Court.

We granted certiorari to determine whether the District Court properly dismissed a Title VII complaint alleging that a law partnership discriminated against petitioner, a woman lawyer employed as an associate, when it failed to invite her to become a partner.

I

A

In 1972 petitioner Elizabeth Anderson Hishon accepted a position as an associate with respondent, a large Atlanta law firm established as a general partnership. When this suit was filed in 1980, the firm had more than 50 partners and employed approximately 50 attorneys as associates. Up to that time, no woman had ever served as a partner at the firm.

Petitioner alleges that the prospect of partnership was an important factor in her initial decision to accept employment with respondent. She alleges that respondent used the possibility of ultimate partnership as a recruiting device to induce petitioner and other young lawyers to become associates at the firm. According to the complaint, respondent represented that advancement to partnership after five or six years was "a matter of course" for associates "who receive[d] satisfactory evaluations" and that associates were promoted to partnership "on a fair and equal basis." Petitioner alleges that she relied on these representations when she accepted employment with respondent. The complaint further alleges that respondent's promise to consider her on a "fair and equal basis" created a binding employment contract.

In May 1978 the partnership considered and rejected Hishon for admission to the partnership; one year later, the partners again declined to invite her to become a partner.[1] Once an associate is passed over for partnership at respondent's firm, the associate is notified to begin seeking employment elsewhere. Petitioner's employment as an associate terminated on December 31, 1979.

B

Hishon filed a charge with the Equal Employment Opportunity Commission on November 19, 1979, claiming that respondent had discriminated against her on the basis of her sex in violation of Title VII of the Civil Rights Act of 1964. Ten days later the Commission issued a notice of right to sue, and on February 27, 1980, Hishon brought this action in the United States District Court for the Northern District of Georgia. She sought declaratory and injunctive relief, back pay, and compensatory damages "in lieu of reinstatement and promotion to partnership." This, of course, negates any claim for specific performance of the contract alleged.

The District Court dismissed the complaint on the ground that Title VII was inapplicable to the selection of partners by a partnership.[2] A

1. The parties dispute whether the partnership actually reconsidered the 1978 decision at the 1979 meeting. Respondent claims it voted not to reconsider the question and that Hishon therefore was required to file her claim with the Equal Employment Opportunity Commission within 180 days of the May 1978 meeting, not the meeting one year later, see 42 U.S.C. § 2000e–5(e). The District Court's disposition of the case made it unnecessary to decide that question, and we do not reach it.

2. The District Court dismissed under Fed.Rule Civ.Proc. 12(b)(1) on the ground that it lacked subject-matter jurisdiction over petitioner's claim. Although limited discovery previously had taken place concerning the manner in which respondent was organized, the court did not find any "jurisdictional facts" in dispute. See Thomson v. Gaskill, 315 U.S. 442, 446, 62 S.Ct. 673, 675, 86 L.Ed. 951 (1942). Its reasoning makes clear that it dismissed petitioner's complaint on the ground that her allegations did not state a claim cogni-

divided panel of the United States Court of Appeals for the Eleventh Circuit affirmed. We granted certiorari and we reverse.

II

At this stage of the litigation, we must accept petitioner's allegations as true. A court may dismiss a complaint only if it is clear that no relief could be granted under any set of facts that could be proved consistent with the allegations. The issue before us is whether petitioner's allegations state a claim under Title VII * * *.

A

Petitioner alleges that respondent is an "employer" to whom Title VII is addressed. She then asserts that consideration for partnership was one of the "terms, conditions, or privileges of employment" as an associate with respondent.[4] If this is correct, respondent could not base an adverse partnership decision on "race, color, religion, sex, or national origin."

Once a contractual relationship of employment is established, the provisions of Title VII attach and govern certain aspects of that relationship.[5] In the context of Title VII, the contract of employment may be written or oral, formal or informal; an informal contract of employment may arise by the simple act of handing a job applicant a shovel and providing a workplace. The contractual relationship of employment triggers the provision of Title VII governing "terms, conditions, or privileges of employment." Title VII in turn forbids discrimination on the basis of "race, color, religion, sex, or national origin."

Because the underlying employment relationship is contractual, it follows that the "terms, conditions, or privileges of employment" clearly include benefits that are part of an employment contract. Here, petitioner in essence alleges that respondent made a contract to consider her for partnership.[6] Indeed, this promise was allegedly a key contractual provision which induced her to accept employment. If the evidence at trial establishes that the parties contracted to have petitioner considered for partnership, that promise clearly was a term,

zable under Title VII. Our disposition makes it unnecessary to consider the wisdom of the District Court's invocation of Rule 12(b)(1), as opposed to Rule 12(b)(6).

4. Petitioner has raised other theories of Title VII liability which, in light of our disposition, need not be addressed.

5. Title VII also may be relevant in the absence of an existing employment relationship, as when an employer *refuses* to hire someone. See § 2000e–2(a)(1). However, discrimination in that circumstance does not concern the "terms, conditions, or privileges of employment," which is the focus of the present case.

6. Petitioner not only alleges that respondent promised to consider her for partnership, but also that it promised to consider her on a "fair and equal basis." This latter promise is not necessary to petitioner's Title VII claim. Even if the employment contract did not afford a basis for an implied condition that the ultimate decision would be fairly made on the merits, Title VII itself would impose such a requirement. If the promised consideration for partnership is a term, condition, or privilege of employment, then the partnership decision must be without regard to "race, color, religion, sex, or national origin."

condition, or privilege of her employment. Title VII would then bind respondents to consider petitioner for partnership as the statute provides, i.e., without regard to petitioner's sex. The contract she alleges would lead to the same result.

Petitioner's claim that a contract was made, however, is not the only allegation that would qualify respondent's consideration of petitioner for partnership as a term, condition, or privilege of employment. An employer may provide its employees with many benefits that it is under no obligation to furnish by any express or implied contract. Such a benefit, though not a contractual *right* of employment, may qualify as a "privileg[e]" of employment under Title VII. A benefit that is part and parcel of the employment relationship may not be doled out in a discriminatory fashion, even if the employer would be free under the employment contract simply not to provide the benefit at all. Those benefits that comprise the "incidents of employment," S.Rep. No. 867, 88th Cong., 2d Sess. 11 (1964),[7] or that form "an aspect of the relationship between the employer and employees," Allied Chemical & Alkali Workers v. Pittsburgh Plate Glass Co., 404 U.S. 157, 178, 92 S.Ct. 383, 397, 30 L.Ed.2d 341 (1971),[8] may not be afforded in a manner contrary to Title VII.

Several allegations in petitioner's complaint would support the conclusion that the opportunity to become a partner was part and parcel of an associate's status as an employee at respondent's firm, independent of any allegation that such an opportunity was included in associates' employment contracts. Petitioner alleges that respondent's associates could regularly expect to be considered for partnership at the end of their "apprenticeships," and it appears that lawyers outside the firm were not routinely so considered.[9] Thus, the benefit of partnership consideration was allegedly linked directly with an associate's status as an employee, and this linkage was far more than coincidental: petitioner alleges that respondent explicitly used the prospect of ultimate partnership to induce young lawyers to join the firm. Indeed, the importance of the partnership decision to a lawyer's status as an

7. Senate Report 867 concerned S. 1937, which the Senate postponed indefinitely after it amended a House version of what ultimately became the Civil Rights Act of 1964. See 110 Cong.Rec. 14,602 (1964). The report is relevant here because S. 1937 contained language similar to that ultimately found in the Civil Rights Act. It guaranteed "equal employment opportunity," which was defined to "include all the compensation, terms, conditions, and privileges of employment." S.Rep. No. 867, 88th Cong., 2d Sess. 24 (1964).

8. *Allied Chemical* pertains to Section 8(d) of the National Labor Relations Act (NLRA), which describes the obligation of employers and unions to meet and confer regarding "wages, hours, and other terms and conditions of employment." 49 Stat. 452, as added, 29 U.S.C. § 158(d). The meaning of this analogous language sheds light on the Title VII provision at issue here. We have drawn analogies to the NLRA in other Title VII contexts, see Franks v. Bowman Transportation Co., 424 U.S. 747, 768–770, 96 S.Ct. 1251, 1266–1267, 47 L.Ed.2d 444 (1976), and have noted that certain sections of Title VII were expressly patterned after the NLRA, *see* Albemarle Paper Co. v. Moody, 422 U.S. 405, 419, 95 S.Ct. 2362, 2372, 45 L.Ed.2d 280 (1975).

9. Respondent's own submissions indicate that most of respondent's partners in fact were selected from the ranks of associates who had spent their entire prepartnership legal careers (excluding judicial clerkships) with the firm.

associate is underscored by the allegation that associates' employment is terminated if they are not elected to become partners. These allegations, if proved at trial, would suffice to show that partnership consideration was a term, condition, or privilege of an associate's employment at respondent's firm, and accordingly that partnership consideration must be without regard to sex.

B

Respondent contends that advancement to partnership may never qualify as a term, condition, or privilege of employment for purposes of Title VII. First, respondent asserts that elevation to partnership entails a change in status from an "employee" to an "employer." However, even if respondent is correct that a partnership invitation is not itself an offer of employment, Title VII would nonetheless apply and preclude discrimination on the basis of sex. The benefit a plaintiff is denied need not *be* employment to fall within Title VII's protection; it need only be a term, condition, or privilege *of* employment. It is also of no consequence that employment as an associate necessarily ends when an associate becomes a partner. A benefit need not accrue before a person's employment is completed to be a term, condition, or privilege of that employment relationship. Pension benefits, for example, qualify as terms, conditions, or privileges of employment even though they are received only after employment terminates. Arizona Governing Committee for Tax Deferred Annuity & Deferred Compensation Plans v. Norris, 463 U.S. 1073, ___, 103 S.Ct. 3492, ___, 77 L.Ed.2d 1236 (1983). Accordingly, nothing in the change in status that advancement to partnership might entail means that partnership consideration falls outside the terms of the statute. See Lucido v. Cravath, Swaine & Moore, 425 F.Supp. 123, 128–129 (SDNY 1977).

Second, respondent argues that Title VII categorically exempts partnership decisions from scrutiny. However, respondent points to nothing in the statute or the legislative history that would support such a *per se* exemption.[10] When Congress wanted to grant an employer complete immunity, it expressly did so.[11]

10. The only legislative history respondent offers to support its position is Senator Cotton's defense of an unsuccessful amendment to limit Title VII to businesses with 100 or more employees. In this connection the Senator stated: "[W]hen a small businessman who employs 30 or 25 or 26 persons selects an employee, he comes very close to selecting a partner; and when a businessman selects a partner, he comes dangerously close to the situation he faces when he selects a wife." 110 Cong.Rec. 13,085 (1964); accord 118 Cong. Rec. 1524, 2391 (1972).

Because Senator Cotton's amendment failed, it is unclear to what extent Congress shared his concerns about selecting partners. In any event, his views hardly conflict with our narrow holding today: that in appropriate circumstances partnership consideration may qualify as a term, condition, or privilege of a person's employment with an employer large enough to be covered by Title VII.

11. For example, Congress expressly exempted Indian tribes and certain agencies of the District of Columbia, 42 U.S.C. § 2000e(b)(1), small businesses and bona fide private membership clubs, § 2000e(b)(2), and certain employees of religious organizations, § 2000e–1. Congress initially exempted certain employees of educational institutions, § 702, 78 Stat. 255 (1964), but later revoked that exemption, Equal Em-

Third, respondent argues that application of Title VII in this case would infringe constitutional rights of expression or association. Although we have recognized that the activities of lawyers may make a "distinctive contribution * * * to the ideas and beliefs of our society," NAACP v. Button, 371 U.S. 415, 431, 83 S.Ct. 328, 337, 9 L.Ed.2d 405 (1963), respondent has not shown how its ability to fulfill such a function would be inhibited by a requirement that it consider petitioner for partnership on her merits. Moreover, as we have held in another context, "[i]nvidious private discrimination may be characterized as a form of exercising freedom of association protected by the First Amendment, but it has never been accorded affirmative constitutional protections." Norwood v. Harrison, 413 U.S. 455, 470, 93 S.Ct. 2804, 2813, 37 L.Ed.2d 723 (1973). There is no constitutional right, for example, to discriminate in the selection of who may attend a private school or join a labor union. Runyon v. McCrary, 427 U.S. 160, 96 S.Ct. 2586, 49 L.Ed.2d 415 (1976); Railway Mail Association v. Corsi, 326 U.S. 88, 93–94, 65 S.Ct. 1483, 1487–1488, 89 L.Ed. 2072 (1945).

III

We conclude that petitioner's complaint states a claim cognizable under Title VII. Petitioner therefore is entitled to her day in court to prove her allegations. The judgment of the Court of Appeals is reversed, and the case is remanded for further proceedings consistent with this opinion.

It is so ordered.

JUSTICE POWELL, concurring.

I join the Court's opinion holding that petitioner's complaint alleges a violation of Title VII and that the motion to dismiss should not have been granted. Petitioner's complaint avers that the law firm violated its promise that she would be considered for partnership on a "fair and equal basis" within the time span that associates generally are so considered.[1] Petitioner is entitled to the opportunity to prove these averments.

I write to make clear my understanding that the Court's opinion should not be read as extending Title VII to the management of a law firm by its partners. The reasoning of the Court's opinion does not require that the relationship among partners be characterized as an "employment" relationship to which Title VII would apply. The relationship among law partners differs markedly from that between employer and employee—including that between the partnership and its

ployment Opportunity Act of 1972, § 3, 86 Stat. 103.

1. Law firms normally require a period of associateship as a prerequisite to being eligible to "make" partner. This need not be an inflexible period, as firms may vary from the norm and admit to partnership earlier than, or subsequent to, the customary period of service. Also, as the complaint recognizes, many firms make annual evaluations of the performances of associates, and usually are free to terminate employment on the basis of these evaluations.

associates.[2] The judgmental and sensitive decisions that must be made among the partners embrace a wide range of subjects.[3] The essence of the law partnership is the common conduct of a shared enterprise. The relationship among law partners contemplates that decisions important to the partnership normally will be made by common agreement, see, e.g., Memorandum of Agreement, King & Spalding, App. 153–164 (Respondent's partnership agreement), or consent among the partners.

Respondent contends that for these reasons application of Title VII to the decision whether to admit petitioner to the firm implicates the constitutional right to association. But here it is alleged that respondent as an employer is obligated by contract to consider petitioner for partnership on equal terms without regard to sex. I agree that enforcement of this obligation, voluntarily assumed, would impair no right of association.[4]

In admission decisions made by law firms, it is now widely recognized—as it should be—that in fact neither race nor sex is relevant. The qualities of mind, capacity to reason logically, ability to work under pressure, leadership and the like are unrelated to race or sex. This is demonstrated by the success of women and minorities in law schools, in the practice of law, on the bench, and in positions of community, state

2. Of course, an employer may not evade the strictures of Title VII simply by labeling its employees as "partners." Law partnerships usually have many of the characteristics that I describe generally here.

3. These decisions concern such matters as participation in profits and other types of compensation; work assignments; approval of commitments in bar association, civic or political activities; questions of billing; acceptance of new clients; questions of conflicts of interest; retirement programs; and expansion policies. Such decisions may affect each partner of the firm. Divisions of partnership profits, unlike shareholders' rights to dividends, involve judgments as to each partner's contribution to the reputation and success of the firm. This is true whether the partner's participation in profits is measured in terms of points or percentages, combinations of salaries and points, salaries and bonuses, and possibly in other ways.

4. The Court's opinion properly reminds us that "invidious private discrimination * * * has never been afforded affirmative constitutional protections." Op., at 2235. This is not to say, however, that enforcement of laws that ban discrimination will always be without cost to other values, including constitutional rights. Such laws may impede the exercise of personal judgment in choosing one's associates or colleagues. See generally, Fallon, To Each According to His Ability, From None According to His Race: The Concept of Merit in the Law of Antidiscrimination, 60 Boston Univ.L.Rev. 815, 844–860 (1980). Impediments to the exercise of one's right to choose one's associates can violate the right of association protected by the First and Fourteenth Amendments. Cf. NAACP v. Button, 371 U.S. 415, 83 S.Ct. 328, 9 L.Ed.2d 405 (1963); NAACP v. Alabama, 357 U.S. 449, 78 S.Ct. 1163, 2 L.Ed.2d 1488 (1958).

With respect to laws that prevent discrimination, much depends upon the standards by which the courts examine private decisions that are an exercise of the right of association. For example, the courts of appeals generally have acknowledged that respect for academic freedom requires some deference to the judgment of schools and universities as to the qualifications of professors, particularly those considered for tenured positions. Lieberman v. Gant, 630 F.2d 60, 67–68 (CA2 1980); Kunda v. Muhlenberg College, 621 F.2d 532, 547–548 (CA3 1980). Cf. Regents of the University of California v. Bakke, 438 U.S. 265, 311–315, 98 S.Ct. 2733, 2759–2761, 57 L.Ed.2d 750 (1978) (opinion of Justice Powell). The present case, before us on a motion to dismiss for lack of subject matter jurisdiction, does not present such an issue.

and national leadership. Law firms—and, of course, society—are the better for these changes.

NOTES AND PROBLEMS FOR DISCUSSION

1. In Lucido v. Cravath, Swaine & Moore, 425 F.Supp. 123 (S.D.N.Y.1977), discussed in the principal case, the trial judge refused to recognize "any First Amendment privacy or associational rights for a commercial, profit-making business organization" such as a law firm. Moreover, the court added, even if such a constitutional guarantee existed, the application of Title VII to the partnership selection process did not violate that right since it did not prevent the partners from associating for political, social, and economic goals. Does the right to freedom of association extend beyond a group's exercise of protected First Amendment rights of speech and petition? In Heart of Atlanta Motel v. United States, 379 U.S. 241, 85 S.Ct. 348, 13 L.Ed.2d 258 (1964), the Supreme Court declared that Title II of the 1964 Civil Rights Act, which prohibits discrimination or segregation on the basis of race, color, religion or national origin by certain places of public accommodation, did not infringe upon constitutional guarantees of personal liberty or due process. A town zoning ordinance restricting land use to one-family dwellings was challenged in Village of Belle Terre v. Boraas, 416 U.S. 1, 94 S.Ct. 1536, 39 L.Ed.2d 797 (1974). The ordinance's definition of "family" precluded occupancy of a single dwelling by more than two unrelated persons but permitted occupancy by an unlimited number of persons related by blood, marriage and adoption. Plaintiffs, six unrelated college students seeking to reside in a single home, claimed that the ordinance infringed upon their constitutional rights of privacy and association. The Supreme Court summarily rejected this contention. Subsequently, however, in Moore v. City of East Cleveland, 431 U.S. 494, 97 S.Ct. 1932, 52 L.Ed.2d 531 (1977) the Court ruled that a housing ordinance permitting only certain categories of related persons to live together constituted an intrusive regulation of family life and therefore infringed upon the freedom of personal choice in marriage and family matters protected by the Constitution. Nevertheless, the Court added, the statute could survive constitutional attack if it served an important governmental interest. Should the rights of associational privacy extend beyond marriage and family life matters to commercial relationships? If so, should this right overwhelm the government interest in eradicating employment discrimination embodied in Title VII? Are you persuaded by the Court's treatment of these issues in *Hishon*? For an interesting discussion of these questions, see Raggi, An Independent Right to Freedom of Association, 12 Harv.Civ.R.–Civ.L.L.Rev. 1 (1977).

2. In his concurring opinion, Justice Powell appears to wish to limit the Court's opinion by suggesting that Title VII would not apply to the business relationship among partners. His opinion implies that although the plaintiff Hishon was protected as a statutory "employee" while she was an associate (and therefore was entitled to nondiscriminatory treatment of the partnership decision—a privilege of employment), once she becomes a partner, Title VII would not apply to the manner in which the partnership treated her since her status would change from "employee" to "employer". Does this mean, for example, that the level of her participation in profits could be set lower than that awarded to a similarly situated male partner? If so, does she really enjoy an equal right to partnership consideration? Would it make a difference if the profit participation differential was instituted one minute or one month or one decade after the partnership decision? Should there be some limit to the

legislative involvement with the partnership relationship? Considering the realities of the modern, large law firm, is it appropriate to classify partners as owners rather than as employees? Moreover, would the result in *Hishon* have changed if the plaintiff had been an associate in a different law firm, seeking a lateral move to the partnership level?

There was no question in *Hishon* as to whether the defendant was a statutory employer. But what would the Court have done if the defendant law firm had been organized as a professional corporation rather than as a partnership and if all the workers were shareholders in that corporation? In EEOC v. Dowd & Dowd, Ltd., 736 F.2d 1177 (7th Cir. 1984), the court held that shareholders of a professional corporation engaged in the practice of law were not employees within the meaning of Title VII. The court interpreted Justice Powell's opinion in *Hishon* as implying that partners were owners and not employees and added that shareholders of a professional corporation should be similarly viewed.

3. David Ono was hired by Sokolow General Hospital as a surgical resident for a four year term. At the end of the term, Ono applied for staff privileges at the Hospital in order to have a place to perform surgery in connection with his upcoming private practice. The Hospital denies his request and Ono files a national origin discrimination claim against the Hospital under Title VII. Suppose Ono can prove that the Hospital always granted staff privileges to its residents upon completion of their residency and that he is the first to be denied such privileges and that all incoming residents are told of this benefit when they begin their residency, but that the contract of employment did not mention future staff privileges. Can Ono state a claim under Title VII? Is he an employee? Is *Hishon* relevant? See Doe v. St. Joseph's Hospital of Fort Wayne, 788 F.2d 411 (7th Cir. 1986); Amro v. St. Luke's Hospital, 39 FEP Cases 1574 (E.D.Pa.1986).

4. Perono Macaroni Co., Inc., restricts the sale of its corporate stock to persons of Italian ancestry and requires that all of its employees be stockholders. Does this violate Title VII? See Bonilla v. Oakland Scavenger Co., 697 F.2d 1297 (9th Cir. 1982), cert. denied, 467 U.S. 1251, 104 S.Ct. 3533, 82 L.Ed.2d 838 (1984).

5. Jose Alvarez, a U.S. citizen of Hispanic ancestry, is a physician and principal owner of a professional corporation that provides medical services to hospitals. On behalf of the corporation, Alvarez submitted a contract proposal to Veterans Hospital for the operation of the hospital's emergency room. Under this proposal, Alvarez would become director of the emergency room and the five other doctors in his corporation, all of whom are of Hispanic ancestry, would also work in the emergency room. The hospital rejected the proposal on the ground that it did not want its emergency room staffed with so many Hispanics. Can Alvarez bring a Title VII claim against the hospital on behalf of himself and/or the corporation? See Gomez v. Alexian Bros. Hospital, 698 F.2d 1019 (9th Cir. 1983).

SECTION C. PROSCRIBED BASES OF CLASSIFICATION

The protections of Title VII extend to all persons.[a] The statute prohibits discrimination by employers, unions and employment agen-

[a] Two relatively minor exceptions to this rule are found at §§ 702 and 703(f). See infra, at 53.

cies against "any individual". This does not mean, however, that all forms of discrimination are prohibited by this enactment. Title VII prohibits covered employment institutions from discriminating with respect to covered employment decisions on the basis of only five classifications—race, color, religion, sex and national origin. Thus, for example, while an alien, blind person or minor can assert a claim under Title VII alleging discrimination on the basis of national origin, race, or sex, the statute does not support a claim of discrimination on the basis of alienage, handicap, or age. Specific problems associated with each of the protected classifications are examined infra at 250.

SECTION D. EXEMPTIONS

Read Sections 701(b)(1), (2); 702; 703(e)(2), (f), (i).

The broad coverage of Title VII is subject to a few statutorily created exemptions. Indian tribes and bona fide private membership clubs are immune from Title VII liability. Businesses located on or near Indian reservations are permitted to give preferential treatment to Indians living on or near a reservation. Discrimination also is permitted against members of the Communist Party or Communist-front organizations and against alien employees of American businesses located abroad. State and federal statutes creating preferences for veterans enjoy a similar exemption from the provisions of Title VII. The most controversial of these exemptions is the immunity accorded religious institutions under § 702.

EQUAL EMPLOYMENT OPPORTUNITY COMMISSION v. MISSISSIPPI COLLEGE

United States Court of Appeals, Fifth Circuit, 1980.
626 F.2d 477, cert. denied, 453 U.S. 912, 101 S.Ct. 3143, 69 L.Ed.2d 994 (1981).

CHARLES CLARK, CIRCUIT JUDGE.

The Equal Employment Opportunity Commission [EEOC] appeals the district court's denial of its petition seeking enforcement of a subpoena issued in connection with its investigation of a charge of discrimination filed against Mississippi College [College]. At issue is a significant interplay between the effective enforcement of Title VII and the religious protections of the first amendment. We vacate the judgment appealed from and remand the action to the district court.

I. FACTS

A. The College

Mississippi College is a four-year coeducational liberal arts institution located in Clinton, Mississippi. The College is owned and operated by the Mississippi Baptist Convention [Convention], an organization composed of Southern Baptist churches in Mississippi.

The Convention conceives of education as an integral part of its Christian mission. It acquired the College in 1850 and has operated it to the present day to fulfill that mission by providing educational enrichment in a Christian atmosphere. As part of its policy, Mississippi College seeks to assure that faculty and administrative officers are committed to the principle that "the best preparation for life is a program of cultural and human studies permeated by the Christian ideal, as evidenced by the tenets, practices and customs of the Mississippi Baptist Convention and in keeping with the principles and scriptures of the Bible." In accordance with this purpose, the College has a written policy of preferring active members of Baptist churches in hiring. The evidence the College presented to the district court indicates that approximately ninety-five percent of the college's full-time faculty members are Baptists. The evidence also shows that eighty-eight percent of the College's students are Baptists. The undergraduate curriculum for all students, regardless of major, includes two courses in which the Bible is studied, and all students are required to attend chapel meetings held twice weekly. The College's facilities include prayer rooms available for use by the students and the College employs a full-time director of Christian activities. Because no woman has been ordained as a minister in a Southern Baptist church in Mississippi, the College hires only males to teach courses concerning the Bible.

B. The Charging Party

Dr. Patricia Summers, the charging party, obtained part-time employment with the College as an assistant professor in the psychology department for the 1975–76 school year. While employed by the College, Summers learned of a vacancy in the full-time faculty of the department of educational psychology created by the departure of Raymond Case, an experimental psychologist. She expressed her desire both orally and in writing to be considered for the position, but she was not interviewed by College officials. Instead, the College hired William Bailey to fill the vacant position. When Summers inquired why she had not been considered for the vacancy, the Vice President of Academic Affairs informed her that the College sought someone with a background in experimental psychology.

In May 1976, Summers filed a charge of discrimination with the EEOC, alleging that Mississippi College had discriminated against her on the basis of sex in hiring someone to fill the vacant full-time position in the psychology department. She later amended her charge to include the additional allegations that the College discriminated against women as a class with respect to job classifications, promotions, recruitment, and pay and that it discriminated on the basis of race in recruiting and hiring.

The evidence before the district court demonstrates that Summers had received a doctoral degree in education from the University of Virginia with a major in counseling and had engaged in post-doctoral studies at Harvard University and other nationally recognized schools. In an affidavit filed with the court, Summers averred that she previously had taught experimental psychology. The President of Mississippi

College, Dr. Lewis Nobles, stated both in an affidavit filed with the EEOC and in his testimony before the district court that the College sought to fill the vacancy with an experimental psychologist, that Bailey had been trained in this field, and that Summers' experience was in clinical psychology. Nobles also stated that an additional factor in the College's selection of Bailey was that he was a Baptist, while Summers was not. Although Summers had been baptized in the Baptist faith while a child, she joined the Presbyterian church, the faith of her husband, when she married in 1970.

Although the College did not hire Summers to fill the vacant full-time position, it did offer to renew her part-time contract for the 1976–77 school year at an increased salary. In offering to renew her contract the College did not indicate that it had any objections to her religious views.

C. The Subpoena Enforcement Proceedings

The College refused to comply voluntarily with the EEOC's request for information that the Commission considered necessary to investigate Summers' charge. * * * The College responded to the subpoena by filing a petition with the EEOC seeking revocation of the subpoena. The EEOC denied the College's petition. The College still declined to comply with the subpoena and the EEOC brought this action in the district court seeking enforcement of the subpoena under § 710 of Title VII.[4] After a hearing on the merits, the district court denied enforcement of the petition.

* * *

On this appeal the EEOC contends that the district court erred in denying its petition for enforcement. First, it asserts that Summers, although white, can assert a charge of race discrimination against the College because she has standing to assert discrimination that affects her "working environment." Second, it argues that § 702 does not exempt race or sex discrimination by a religious education institution from the scope of Title VII. Third, it maintains that its investigation of the College's hiring practices violates neither the establishment clause nor the free exercise clause of the first amendment.

II. SUMMERS' STANDING TO ASSERT A CHARGE OF RACIAL DISCRIMINATION

* * *

We conclude that § 706 of Title VII permits Summers to file a charge asserting that Mississippi College discriminates against blacks

4. Section 710 of Title VII grants to the EEOC, for the purposes of any hearing or investigation it conducts, the same investigatory powers exercised by the National Labor Relations Board under 29 U.S.C. § 161. Thus § 710 empowers the district court within whose jurisdiction either the EEOC is conducting its inquiry or the person resides against whom enforcement of the subpoena is sought to order any person who refuses to obey a subpoena issued by the EEOC to appear before the EEOC, to produce evidence if so ordered, or to give testimony concerning the matter under investigation. Any failure to obey is punishable as a contempt of court. *See* 29 U.S.C. § 161.

on the basis of race in recruitment and hiring.[8] Our decision today does not allow Summers to assert the rights of others. We hold no more than that, provided she meets the standing requirements imposed by Article III, Summers may charge a violation of her own personal right to work in an environment unaffected by racial discrimination.

* * *

III. SECTION 702 OF TITLE VII

Section 702 of Title VII exempts from the application of Title VII religious educational institutions "with respect to the employment of individuals of a particular religion to perform work connected with the carrying on by such * * * educational institution * * * of its activities." 42 U.S.C. § 2000e–1.

The EEOC contends that § 702 only exempts from the coverage of Title VII discrimination based upon religion, not discrimination predicated upon race, color, sex, or national origin. It argues that the College's mere assertion that it declined to hire Summers because of her religion should not prevent it from investigating to determine if the College used Summers' religion as a pretext for some other form of discrimination. The College asserts that its hiring decision falls squarely within the statutory exemption created by § 702.

This court previously rejected the argument that the exemption provided by § 702 applies to all of the actions of a religious organization taken with respect to an employee whose work was connected with its "religious activities." See McClure v. Salvation Army, 460 F.2d 553 (5th Cir.), cert. denied, 409 U.S. 896, 93 S.Ct. 132, 34 L.Ed.2d 153 (1972). In *McClure* we restricted the application of that exemption to a religious organization's discrimination in employment against an individual on the basis of religion, stating:

> The language and the legislative history of § 702 compel the conclusion that Congress did not intend that a religious organization be exempted from liability for discriminating against its employees on the basis of race, color, sex or national origin with respect to their compensation, terms, conditions or privileges of employment.

The College argues first that once it showed (1) an established policy of preferring Baptists in its hiring decisions, (2) that the individual hired for the position was Baptist, and (3) that the charging party was not a Baptist, § 702 prevented the EEOC from investigating further the charge of discrimination. *McClure* did not address the EEOC's authority to investigate an individual charge of race or sex discrimination asserted against a religious institution that presents evidence showing

8. We decide only the issue before us of whether a white employee can charge her employer with discriminating against blacks in violation of Title VII. We expressly pretermit the question of whether any form of discrimination other than racial discrimination can be charged by a person who is not a member of the group against whom the discrimination is directed. We likewise pretermit and intimate no opinion concerning Summers' adequacy as a class represenative for any blacks against whom the College may have discriminated.

that it made the challenged employment decision on the basis of an individual's religion. We conclude that if a religious institution of the kind described in § 702 presents convincing evidence that the challenged employment practice resulted from discrimination on the basis of religion, § 702 deprives the EEOC of jurisdiction to investigate further to determine whether the religious discrimination was a pretext for some other form of discrimination. This interpretation of § 702 is required to avoid the conflicts that would result between the rights guaranteed by the religion clauses of the first amendment and the EEOC's exercise of jurisdiction over religious educational institutions.

The College argues second, and more broadly, that the employment relationship between a religious educational institution and its faculty is exempt from Title VII. It relies on *McClure's* holding that the relationship between a church and its ministers was not intended by Congress to be covered by Title VII. The College's reliance on *McClure* as support for this argument is misplaced.

In *McClure* this court expressly restricted its decision to the context of the church-minister relationship. We concluded that matters touching the relationship between a church and its ministers, including the selection of a minister, determination of salary, and assignment of duties and location, are "matters of church administration and government and thus, purely of ecclesiastical cognizance." The facts distinguish this case from *McClure*. The College is not a church. The College's faculty and staff do not function as ministers. The faculty members are not intermediaries between a church and its congregation. They neither attend to the religious needs of the faithful nor instruct students in the whole of religious doctrine. That faculty members are expected to serve as exemplars of practicing Christians does not serve to make the terms and conditions of their employment matters of church administration and thus purely of ecclesiastical concern. The employment relationship between Mississippi College and its faculty and staff is one intended by Congress to be regulated by Title VII.

Because the College is not a church and its faculty members are not ministers, *McClure's* construction of Title VII does not bar the EEOC in the instant case from investigating Summers' allegations that the college engages in class discrimination against women and blacks.[10]

10. The College has asserted both before this court and before the district court that its desire to employ Southern Baptists whenever possible to facilitate the carrying out of its religious mission has resulted in its adoption of several recruiting and employment practices that tend to have a disparate impact upon women and blacks. The College contends, for example, that it recruits faculty members through the Association of Baptist Colleges, the member colleges of which have predominantly white student bodies. To the extent that this employment practice is based upon religious discrimination, § 702 exempts it from the application of Title VII. However, any choice by the College to recruit only among Baptist colleges that are predominantly white as opposed to all Baptist colleges is not protected by § 702 and could be investigated by the EEOC. Also, § 702 does not prevent the EEOC from investigating whether the College discriminates against any blacks who may apply from the schools at which it does recruit. The determination of which of the College's employment practices are based upon religious discrimination and therefore exempt under § 702 can best be made by the district court on remand. On remand

However, as pointed out above, § 702 may bar investigation of her individual claim. The district court did not make clear whether the individual employment decision complained of by Summers was based on the applicant's religion. Thus, we cannot determine whether the exemption of § 702 applies. If the district court determines on remand that the College applied its policy of preferring Baptists over non-Baptists in granting the faculty position to Bailey rather than Summers, then § 702 exempts that decision from the application of Title VII and would preclude any investigation by the EEOC to determine whether the College used the preference policy as a guise to hide some other form of discrimination. On the other hand, should the evidence disclose only that the College's preference policy could have been applied, but in fact it was not considered by the College in determining which applicant to hire, § 702 does not bar the EEOC's investigation of Summers' individual sex discrimination claim.

IV. FIRST AMENDMENT QUESTIONS

The EEOC contends that the district court erred in concluding that application of Title VII to a religious educational institution would foster the excessive government entanglement with religion prohibited by the establishment clause and would impermissibly burden the institution's practice of its religious beliefs in violation of the free exercise clause.

A. *Establishment Clause*

The establishment clause of the first amendment prohibits Congress from enacting any law "respecting an establishment of religion." In determining whether a congressional enactment violates the establishment clause, the Supreme Court has examined three principal criteria: (1) whether the statute has a secular legislative purpose, (2) whether the principal or primary effect of the statute is neither to advance nor to inhibit religion, and (3) whether the statute fosters "an excessive government entanglement with religion." Lemon v. Kurtzman, 403 U.S. 602, 612–13, 91 S.Ct. 2105, 2111, 29 L.Ed.2d 745, 752 (1971). The College does not contend that Title VII has no secular legislative purpose or that it inhibits or advances religion as its primary effect. We therefore focus our inquiry upon the third criteria: whether the statute fosters an excessive entanglement with religion.

In *Lemon* the Court evaluated three factors in determining whether government entanglement with religion is excessive:

> the character and purposes of the institutions that are benefited, the nature of the aid that the State provides, and the resulting relationship between the government and the religious authority.

the College should be granted a further opportunity to present evidence demonstrating which parts of the information sought concern practices based upon religious discrimination.

Although the Supreme Court generally has construed the establishment clause in the context of governmental action that benefited a religious activity, it is now clear that the establishment clause is implicated by a statute that potentially burdens religious activities. See N.L.R.B. v. Catholic Bishop of Chicago, 440 U.S. 490, 500–502, 99 S.Ct. 1313, 1319–20, 59 L.Ed.2d 533, 541–542 (1979). The three-prong test employed in *Lemon* to determine whether government entanglement is excessive applies with equal force to such cases.

The evidence presented to the district court makes it readily apparent that the character and purposes of the College are pervasively sectarian. The purpose of the College is to provide a college education in an atmosphere saturated with Christian ideals. The College is formally affiliated with the Mississippi Baptist Convention. Indeed, the College exists primarily to serve the evangelical mission of the Convention. The Convention selects the Board of Trustees that exercises effective control over the College.

The nature of the burden that might be imposed upon the College by the application of Title VII to it is largely hypothetical at this stage of the proceedings. The information requested by the EEOC's subpoena does not clearly implicate any religious practices of the College. The College's primary concern is that the EEOC's investigation will not cease should it comply with the subpoena, but instead will intrude further into its operations. The College worries that the EEOC will seek to require it to alter the employment practices by which it seeks to ensure that its faculty members are suitable examples of the Christian ideal advocated by the Southern Baptist faith. These hypothetical concerns are of limited validity. As noted previously, the exemption granted to religious institutions by § 702 of Title VII must be construed broadly to exclude from the scope of the act any employment decision made by a religious institution on the basis of religious discrimination. This construction of § 702 largely allays the College's primary concern that it will be unable to continue its policy of preferring Baptists in hiring. The only practice brought to the attention of the district court that is clearly predicated upon religious beliefs that might not be protected by the exemption of § 702 is the College's policy of hiring only men to teach courses in religion.[12] The bare potential that Title VII would affect this practice does not warrant precluding the application of Title VII to the College. Before the EEOC could require the College to alter that practice, the College would have an opportunity to litigate in a federal forum whether § 702 exempts or the first amendment protects that particular practice. We thus determine that, in the factual context before us, the application of Title VII to the College

12. In his testimony before the district court Dr. Nobles explained that the practice of not hiring women to teach religion courses was based upon Bible scriptures indicating that pastors and deacons should be men. He testified that to his knowledge no member church of the Mississippi Baptist Convention had an ordained woman preacher.

could have only a minimal impact upon the College's religion based practices.

The relationship between the federal government and the College that results from the application of Title VII does have limits both in scope and effect. It is true that the subpoena issued to the College by the EEOC presages a wide ranging investigation into many aspects of the College's hiring practices. Furthermore, should the EEOC conclude that cause exists to believe that the College discriminates on the basis of sex or race, the College in all likelihood would be subjected to a court action if it did not voluntarily agree to alter its actions. The College would, however, be entitled to a de novo determination of whether its practices violate Title VII. In that action the College could reassert the protection of the first amendment prior to being ordered to amend its practices. If the challenged employment practices survived the scrutiny of the district court, the EEOC could not attack again those particular practices absent some change in circumstances.

Although the College is a pervasively sectarian institution, the minimal burden imposed upon its religious practices by the application of Title VII and the limited nature of the resulting relationship between the federal government and the College cause us to find that application of the statute would not foster excessive government entanglement with religion. Employment practices based upon religious discrimination are exempt under § 702 from the coverage of Title VII and the College could not be required to alter any of its other employment practices until it exercised its opportunity to justify those practices on first amendment grounds before a federal district court. Because no religious tenets advocated by the College or the Mississippi Baptist Convention involve discrimination on the basis of race or sex, an investigation by the EEOC will only minimally intrude upon any of the College's or Convention's religious beliefs. No ongoing interference with the College's religious practices will result from an EEOC investigation of the charge filed by Summers. Therefore, we conclude that imposing the requirements of Title VII upon the College does not violate the establishment clause of the first amendment.

B. The Free Exercise Clause

The free exercise clause of the first amendment proscribes any congressional legislation "prohibiting the free exercise" of religion.

In determining whether a statutory enactment violates the free exercise of a sincerely held religious belief, the Supreme Court has examined (1) the magnitude of the statute's impact upon the exercise of the religious belief, (2) the existence of a compelling state interest justifying the burden imposed upon the exercise of the religious belief, and (3) the extent to which recognition of an exemption from the statute would impede the objectives sought to be advanced by the state.

As discussed previously, the impact of Title VII upon the exercise of the religious belief is limited in scope and degree. Section 702 excludes from the scope of Title VII those employment practices of the College that discriminate on the basis of religion. We acknowledge that, except for those practices that fall outside of Title VII, the impact of Title VII on the College could be profound. To the extent that the College's practices foster sexual or racial discrimination, the EEOC, if unable to persuade the College to alter them voluntarily, could seek a court order compelling their modification, imposing injunctive restraints upon the College's freedom to make employment decisions, and awarding monetary relief to those persons aggrieved by the prohibited acts. However, the relevant inquiry is not the impact of the statute upon the institution, but the impact of the statute upon the institution's exercise of its sincerely held religious beliefs. The fact that those of the College's employment practices subject to Title VII do not embody religious beliefs or practices protects the College from any real threat of undermining its religious purpose of fulfilling the evangelical role of the Mississippi Baptist Convention, and allows us to conclude that the impact of Title VII on the free exercise of religious beliefs is minimal.

Second, the government has a compelling interest in eradicating discrimination in all forms. Congress manifested that interest in the enactment of Title VII and the other sections of the Civil Rights Act of 1964. The proscription upon racial discrimination in particular is mandated not only by congressional enactments but also by the thirteenth amendment. We conclude that the government's compelling interest in eradicating discrimination is sufficient to justify the minimal burden imposed upon the College's free exercise of religious beliefs that results from the application of Title VII.

Moreover, we conclude that creating an exemption from the statutory enactment greater than that provided by § 702 would seriously undermine the means chosen by Congress to combat discrimination and is not constitutionally required. Although the number of religious educational institutions is minute in comparison to the number of employers subject to Title VII, their effect upon society at large is great because of the role they play in educating society's young. If the environment in which such institutions seek to achieve their religious and educational goals reflects unlawful discrimination, those discriminatory attitudes will be perpetuated with an influential segment of society, the detrimental effect of which cannot be estimated. Because the burden placed upon the free exercise of religion by the application of Title VII to religious educational institutions is slight, because society's interest in eradicating discrimination is compelling, and because the creation of an exemption greater than that provided by § 702 would seriously undermine Congress' attempts to eliminate discrimination, we conclude the application of Title VII to educational institutions such as Mississippi College does not violate the free exercise clause of the first amendment.

* * * We vacate the district court's findings of fact, its conclusions of law, and its initial opinion and remand for further proceedings

consistent with this opinion. We specifically note that on remand the district court * * * should allow the parties to present further evidence demonstrating which employment practices of Mississippi College are exempt from the coverage of Title VII under § 702 as construed by this opinion. We leave for resolution by the district court on remand the question of what portions of the EEOC's subpoena should be enforced.

Vacated and Remanded.

NOTES AND PROBLEMS FOR DISCUSSION

1. As originally enacted in 1964, § 702 permitted discrimination by religious institutions only with respect to the employment of individuals connected with the institution's religious activities. The 1972 amendments broadened this exemption to cover all secular as well as religious activities of religious organizations. Both enactments, however, permit discrimination only on religious grounds. Is the scope of the exemption as amended consistent with the interests § 702 was designed to serve? Does it reach a proper balance between the inevitably competing constitutional interests in permitting free exercise but prohibiting the establishment of religion?

(a) Should a religious organization be immune from Title VII liability with respect to its secular activities or does such a broad exclusion conflict with the establishment clause of the First Amendment? Why should a religious sect that owns and operates a restaurant or radio station be permitted to limit employment in those establishments to members of its sect? See King's Garden, Inc. v. Federal Communications Commission, 498 F.2d 51 (D.C.Cir. 1974), cert. denied, 419 U.S. 996, 95 S.Ct. 309, 42 L.Ed.2d 269; Amos v. Corporation of Presiding Bishop, 594 F.Supp. 791 (D.Utah 1984); Note, The Constitutionality of the 1972 Amendment to Title VII's Exemption for Religious Organizations, 73 Mich.L.Rev. 538 (1975). What about the Christian Science Monitor? See Feldstein v. The Christian Science Monitor, 555 F.Supp. 974 (D.Mass. 1983).

(b) On the other hand, does the exercise of government control over the relationship between a religious institution and employees associated exclusively with its religious functions infringe upon the institution's right of free exercise? The principal case examined two related aspects of this problem: (1) Whether there are circumstances under which Title VII was not intended to restrict the employment relationship between the parties; and (2) In those circumstances where Title VII does apply to religious institutions, the extent to which such regulation is consistent with the limitations on government conduct imposed by the free exercise clause of the First Amendment.

The former statutory issue was the focus of the court's attention in McClure v. Salvation Army, 460 F.2d 553 (5th Cir. 1972), cited in the principal case. There, the plaintiff, a commissioned officer with the status of ordained minister in the Salvation Army, alleged that she had suffered salary and assignment discrimination because of her sex. The court, after noting that the Salvation Army was a church, ruled that Congress did not intend for Title VII to regulate the employment relationship between a church and its ministers. The court acknowledged, however, that its interpretation of Congressional intent was prompted by its conclusion that a contrary interpretation of the statute would conflict with the principles embodied in the free exercise clause of the First

Amendment. *McClure* was distinguished in *Mississippi College*, however, on the ground that the defendant College was not a church and the plaintiff was not a minister. On the other hand, in Rayburn v. Seventh-Day Adventists, 772 F.2d 1164 (4th Cir. 1985), the court extended the *McClure* rationale to the claim of a female member of the church who had been denied a pastoral staff position of associate pastor by one of the Adventist churches on the basis of her sex. The position of associate pastor could be held by an ordained minister or a person (male or female) who has received seminary training but has not been ordained. The Adventist Church, however, did not permit women to stand for ordination. The court concluded that the *McClure* "ministerial exception" turned not on the presence of ordination but on the function of the position. It held that the exception should apply whenever the employee's "primary duties consist of teaching, spreading the faith, church governance, supervision of religious order, or supervision or participation in religious ritual and worship"; i.e., whenever "the position is important to the spiritual and pastoral mission of the church." Would *McClure* or *Rayburn* support a defense motion to dismiss a claim of sex discrimination brought by an editorial employee against a church-affiliated publishing house that publishes and sells religious materials for the sole purpose of carrying out the church's ministry? See EEOC v. Pacific Press Publishing Association, 676 F.2d 1272 (9th Cir. 1982). What about a theology teacher's claim against a religious seminary? Would it make a difference if the teacher also was a minister of that faith? In Maguire v. Marquette University, 627 F.Supp. 1499 (E.D.Wis. 1986), the defendant refused to hire a Catholic woman as an associate professor of theology because she was not a Jesuit (an order of the Catholic Church composed solely of men) and because of its perceptions of her views concerning the moral theology of abortion. The plaintiff filed a sex discrimination charge under Title VII and the defendant claimed that its policy was exempted from statutory scrutiny by the operation of § 703(e)(2). The court acknowledged that Marquette clearly constituted a religiously-supported and controlled educational institution within the meaning of § 703(e)(2). It then suggested that the position of theology professor at such an institution approached the relationship between a religion and its minister and held that judicial interference with the decision to hire a theology professor would deprive the defendant of its free exercise rights and constitute an establishment of religion by fostering excessive government entanglement with religion. The court also addressed the defendant's claim that the plaintiff's theological position on abortion indicated that she was not a Catholic and that, therefore, pursuant to § 703(e)(2) the University could refuse to hire a non-Catholic. The trial judge concluded that resolving this question would require him to determine whether the plaintiff was a Catholic and that such a determination was itself prohibited by the free exercise and establishment clauses. The court, however, did not examine the interesting question of whether a religious institution's religiously-premised policy of not hiring women (i.e., the policy of reserving positions for Jesuits, an all male order) was subject to Title VII attack. What if that minister taught history rather than theology? See EEOC v. Southwestern Baptist Theological Seminary, 651 F.2d 277 (5th Cir. 1981), cert. denied, 456 U.S. 905, 102 S.Ct. 1749, 72 L.Ed.2d 161 (1982). See generally, Note, Equal Employment or Excessive Entanglement? The Application of Employment Discrimination Statutes to Religiously Affiliated Organizations, 18 Conn.L.Rev. 581 (1986).

As to the second statutory issue, the court in *Mississippi College* concluded that where the defendant presents convincing evidence that its challenged employment decision was based on religious considerations, the free exercise clause precludes further investigation by the EEOC even if the plaintiff claims that religion is merely a pretext for another illegal form of discrimination. Does this represent an appropriate accommodation of the competing statutory and constitutional principles where the employee is not connected directly with the organization's religious activities? For example, should a church-owned and operated network of thrift stores be permitted to discharge one of its truckdrivers because he had been excommunicated? See Amos v. Corporation of Presiding Bishop of Church of Jesus Christ of Latter-Day Saints, 618 F.Supp. 1013 (D.Utah 1985).

2. Suppose a religious institution provided a fringe benefit to "head of household" employees and that this benefit was given only to single employees and married male employees because, according to its religious beliefs, the husband is the head of the household. Can a married female employee who is denied that benefit bring a Title VII sex discrimination claim? Is this a form of religious discrimination that, through the operation of § 702, exempts the institution from Title VII scrutiny? If not, would applying the statute in this situation nevertheless violate the First Amendment? The issue of whether sex discriminatory policies mandated by religious belief are immunized by § 702 was mentioned (in footnote 12), but not seriously considered by the court in *Mississippi College.* But in EEOC v. FREMONT CHRISTIAN SCHOOL, 781 F.2d 1362 (9th Cir. 1986), where the defendant school implemented the aforementioned type of sex-based head of household fringe benefit policy, the court rejected the church owned and operated school's § 702 and constitutional law defenses. On the statutory question, the court said simply that the statute only exempted religious classifications and that this was a policy that discriminated on the basis of sex. Then, noting that the Church had voluntarily dropped a similarly sex-based policy concerning wages, the court concluded that forcing the Church to abandon this discriminatory fringe benefit policy would only "minimally, if at all" interfere with the practice of its religious beliefs. Thus, in light of the government's substantial interest in ensuring equal employment opportunity, the application of the statute to the Church in this situation was held not to violate the First Amendment free exercise guarantee. Contrarily, in Dayton Christian Schools v. Ohio Civil Rights Commission, 766 F.2d 932 (6th Cir. 1985), rev'd on other grounds, ___ U.S. ___, 106 S.Ct. 2718, 91 L.Ed.2d 512 (1986), the Sixth Circuit ruled that application of an Ohio antidiscrimination statute (which did not contain a provision analogous to § 702) to a religious school's decision not to rehire a pregnant teacher would violate the First Amendment free exercise and establishment of religion clauses as made applicable to the States by the Fourteenth Amendment. Initially, the teacher had been informed that the decision not to rehire her was founded on the school's religiously-based desire to have a mother with pre-school age children at home. After learning of this decision, the teacher consulted an attorney, who communicated with the school and threatened legal action for violation of state and federal antidiscrimination statutes. Shortly thereafter, the teacher was discharged for consulting the attorney. A letter explaining the discharge stated that the teacher was terminated for failing to follow the Biblical Chain-of-Command, a biblical concept that was interpreted by the school as requiring the internal peaceful resolution of differences in order to maintain a united front. After the teacher had a filed a complaint under state law with the state Civil Rights Commission, the school brought a § 1983 action to enjoin that state agency from exercising jurisdiction over the school and for a declaratory

judgment that enforcement of the statute by the Commission in this circumstance violated the First and Fourteenth Amendments. The Sixth Circuit first noted the trial court findings that the school was a religious institution and that nonrenewal of the teaching contract for violating the Chain-of-Command was consistent with and compelled by the school board's sincerely held religious beliefs. On the basis of these facts and its evaluation of the importance of religion in the school's educational process and the unique role of the teacher in promoting the school's religious mission, the appellate court concluded that the exercise of jurisdiction by the state agency was unacceptably burdensome on the school board's exercise of religion. Moreover, it added, this burden was not overcome by the state's substantial interest in eradicating discrimination since accommodating the board's religious beliefs in this case resulted in only a limited interference with the state's ability to prohibit discrimination since the state still would be able to prohibit religious institutions from engaging in non-religious discrimination. The Supreme Court reversed, ruling that the trial court should have abstained from adjudicating the case under the federalism-premised abstention principles enunciated in Younger v. Harris. The Court stated that "however Dayton's constitutional claim should be decided on the merits, the Commission violates no constitutional rights by merely investigating the circumstances of Hoskinson's discharge in this case, if only to ascertain whether the ascribed religious-based reason was in fact the reason for the discharge". It was sufficient, the Court ruled, that the constitutional claims could be raised in state court judicial review of the anticipated administrative proceedings.

3. The Friendship, Commerce and Navigation Treaty between the U.S. and Japan provides that companies of either nation are permitted to hire certain classes of employees "of their choice". Two separate actions were brought against American-incorporated wholly-owned subsidiaries of Japanese companies claiming that the subsidiaries' policies of filling these positions solely with male Japanese citizens violated Title VII. The defendant subsidiaries contended that the Treaty immunized them from the application of local antidiscrimination law. In Spiess v. C. Itoh & Co., 643 F.2d 353 (5th Cir. 1981), vac'd and rem'd in light of Sumitomo Shoji America, Inc. v. Avagliano, 457 U.S. 1128, 102 S.Ct. 2951, 73 L.Ed.2d 1344 (1982), the Fifth Circuit found the Treaty applicable to an American subsidiary of a foreign corporation and held that the Treaty provision permitting Japanese companies to hire executives "of their choice" did exempt the company from American domestic employment discrimination laws. It reasoned that subsequently enacted federal legislation invalidates extant treaty obligations only when congressional intent to do so is clearly expressed and that no evidence of such an intent was manifested in Title VII. In Sumitomo Shoji America, Inc. v. Avagliano, 638 F.2d 552 (2d Cir. 1981), the Second Circuit also ruled that the Treaty applied to American-incorporated subsidiaries of Japanese companies, but concluded that the Treaty did not exempt such subsidiaries from the provisions of Title VII. The Supreme Court reversed the appellate court, 457 U.S. 176, 102 S.Ct. 2374, 72 L.Ed.2d 765 (1982), holding that the Treaty was not intended to cover locally-incorporated subsidiaries of foreign companies. Accordingly, it did not reach the question of whether the treaty superseded domestic law. For further discussion of this issue, see Recent Developments, 15 Tex.Int'l.L.J. 187 (1980).

4. Could a U.S. citizen working overseas for a U.S. corporation state a claim under Title VII? See Bryant v. International Schools Services, 502 F.Supp. 472 (D.N.J.1980), rev'd on other grounds, 675 F.2d 562 (3rd Cir. 1982).

If an American is working overseas for an American-owned corporation's foreign subsidiary, can she bring a Title VII action against her employer's American-owned parent corporation? See Marques v. Digital Equipment Corp., 637 F.2d 24 (1st Cir. 1980). For an interesting discussion of the impact of Title VII on multinational corporations see Note, Civil Rights in Employment and the Multinational Corporations, 10 Corn.Int'l L.J. 87 (1976).

5. Private membership clubs are exempted from the definition of employer in § 701(b)(2). Does this provision prevent an employee of a credit union from filing a claim under Title VII against his employer? See Quijano v. University Federal Credit Union, 617 F.2d 129 (5th Cir. 1980). What about the employee of a private retirement and nursing home sponsored by, and whose admittees must be members or the spouses of members of, a private membership club? See Fesel v. Masonic Home, 428 F.Supp. 573 (D.Del.1977).

Chapter 2

DEFINING DISCRIMINATION: THE CONCEPTUAL FRAMEWORK

SECTION A. INTRODUCTION

As the materials in the preceding chapter indicate, the intricate nature of Title VII's definitional and substantive provisions reflects Congress' desire to place a wide range of institutions and employment practices within the jurisdiction of the statute's antidiscrimination principle. While the statute sets forth an extensive list of unlawful employment practices, the word "discriminate" is contained within the definition of each group of proscribed practices. A reexamination of the definitional provisions, however, reveals that Congress did not provide a definition of this critical term. Is the meaning of discrimination so obvious that the concept does not need to be defined? Surely, no one would doubt that an employer's refusal to hire a qualified woman simply because of its determination that women belong at home and not in the work force would be prohibited by Title VII. But what if the employer rejected her because she failed to meet the company's policy that all employees be at least 59″ tall and weigh 150 pounds? Would your opinion change if the employer could prove that it would be happy to hire any woman who satisfied this height and weight requirement? Is a company, 95% of whose employees are women, discriminating on the basis of sex when it refuses to hire pregnant women or married women with pre-school aged children? What about an employer who refuses to hire any job applicant with an arrest record? with facial hair? Finally, assume the employer admittedly refused to hire Blacks before the effective date of Title VII but abolished that policy after Title VII was enacted. Is this company violating Title VII by granting promotions on the basis of total years of service with the firm?

The absence of any statutory definition of discrimination left the task of formulating a workable concept of discrimination to the courts. This has proven to be a more involved undertaking than one might expect. While discrimination at first blush may appear to be a relatively straightforward concept, it can manifest itself in subtle and indiscernible, as well as conspicuous ways. The following series of cases illustrates the difficulties encountered by the Supreme Court in its attempts at fashioning and articulating conceptual frameworks within which claims of employment discrimination are to be examined.

SECTION B. DISPARATE TREATMENT

The most easily recognized form of discrimination occurs when an employer, union or employment agency overtly accords different treatment to individuals based exclusively on their race, color, religion, sex or national origin. The manner in which such "disparate treatment" claims must be proved and defended against has been examined by the Supreme Court on four separate occasions within the space of eight years. In reading these opinions, examine whether they provide a coherent and consistent statement of the Court's position with respect to the nature of the burden of proof allocated to each party.

McDONNELL DOUGLAS CORP. v. GREEN

Supreme Court of the United States, 1973.
411 U.S. 792, 93 S.Ct. 1817, 36 L.Ed.2d 668.

MR. JUSTICE POWELL delivered the opinion of the Court.

The case before us raises significant questions as to the proper order and nature of proof in actions under Title VII of the Civil Rights Act of 1964.

Petitioner, McDonnell Douglas Corp., is an aerospace and aircraft manufacturer headquartered in St. Louis, Missouri, where it employs over 30,000 people. Respondent, a black citizen of St. Louis, worked for petitioner as a mechanic and laboratory technician from 1956 until August 28, 1964 when he was laid off in the course of a general reduction in petitioner's work force.

Respondent, a long-time activist in the civil rights movement, protested vigorously that his discharge and the general hiring practices of petitioner were racially motivated. As part of this protest, respondent and other members of the Congress on Racial Equality illegally stalled their cars on the main roads leading to petitioner's plant for the purpose of blocking access to it at the time of the morning shift change. * * *

On July 2, 1965, a "lock-in" took place wherein a chain and padlock were placed on the front door of a building to prevent the occupants, certain of petitioner's employees, from leaving. Though respondent apparently knew beforehand of the "lock-in" the full extent of his involvement remains uncertain.[3]

Some three weeks following the "lock-in," on July 25, 1965, petitioner publicly advertised for qualified mechanics, respondent's trade, and respondent promptly applied for re-employment. Petitioner turned down respondent, basing its rejection on respondent's participation in the "stall-in" and "lock-in." Shortly thereafter, respondent filed a formal complaint with the Equal Employment Opportunity Commission, claiming that petitioner had refused to rehire him because of his race and persistent involvement in the civil rights movement, in violation of §§ 703(a)(1) and 704(a) of the Civil Rights Act of 1964. The former section generally prohibits racial discrimination in any employment decision while the latter forbids discrimination against applicants

3. * * * In view of respondent's admitted participation in the unlawful "stall-in," we find it unnecessary to resolve the contradictory contentions surrounding this "lock-in."

or employees for attempting to protest or correct allegedly discriminatory conditions of employment.

The Commission made no finding on respondent's allegation of racial bias under § 703(a)(1), but it did find reasonable cause to believe petitioner had violated § 704(a) by refusing to rehire respondent because of his civil rights activity. After the Commission unsuccessfully attempted to conciliate the dispute, it advised respondent in March 1968, of his right to institute a civil action in federal court within 30 days.

On April 15, 1968, respondent brought the present action, claiming initially a violation of § 704(a) and, in an amended complaint, a violation of § 703(a)(1) as well.[5] The District Court dismissed the latter claim of racial discrimination in petitioner's hiring procedures on the ground that the Commission had failed to make a determination of reasonable cause to believe that a violation of that section had been committed. The District Court also found that petitioner's refusal to rehire respondent was based solely on his participation in the illegal demonstrations and not on his legitimate civil rights activities. The court concluded that nothing in Title VII or § 704 protected "such activity as employed by the plaintiff in the 'stall in' and 'lock in' demonstrations."

On appeal, the Eighth Circuit affirmed that unlawful protests were not protected activities under § 704(a),[6] but reversed the dismissal of respondent's § 703(a)(1) claim relating to racially discriminatory hiring practices, holding that a prior Commission determination of reasonable cause was not a jurisdictional prerequisite to raising a claim under that section in federal court. The court ordered the case remanded for trial of respondent's claim under § 703(a)(1).

In remanding, the Court of Appeals attempted to set forth standards to govern the consideration of respondent's claim. * * * In order to clarify the standards governing the disposition of an action challenging employment discrimination, we granted certiorari.

I

We agree with the Court of Appeals that absence of a Commission finding of reasonable cause cannot bar suit under an appropriate section of Title VII and that the District Judge erred in dismissing respondent's claim of racial discrimination under § 703(a)(1). * * * Accordingly, we remand the case for trial of respondent's claim of racial discrimination consistent with the views set forth below.

5. Respondent also contested the legality of his 1964 discharge by petitioner, but both courts held this claim barred by the statute of limitations. Respondent does not challenge those rulings here.

6. Respondent has not sought review of this issue.

II

The critical issue before us concerns the order and allocation of proof in a private, non-class action challenging employment discrimination. The language of Title VII makes plain the purpose of Congress to assure equality of employment opportunities and to eliminate those discriminatory practices and devices which have fostered racially stratified job environments to the disadvantage of minority citizens. * * *

* * * The broad, overriding interest, shared by employer, employee, and consumer, is efficient and trustworthy workmanship assured through fair and racially neutral employment and personnel decisions. In the implementation of such decisions, it is abundantly clear that Title VII tolerates no racial discrimination, subtle or otherwise.

In this case respondent, the complainant below, charges that he was denied employment "because of his involvement in civil rights activities" and "because of his race and color." Petitioner denied discrimination of any kind, asserting that its failure to re-employ respondent was based upon and justified by his participation in the unlawful conduct against it. Thus, the issue at the trial on remand is framed by those opposing factual contentions. The two opinions of the Court of Appeals and the several opinions of the three judges of that court attempted, with a notable lack of harmony, to state the applicable rules as to burden of proof and how this shifts upon the making of a prima facie case. We now address this problem.

The complainant in a Title VII trial must carry the initial burden under the statute of establishing a prima facie case of racial discrimination. This may be done by showing (i) that he belongs to a racial minority; (ii) that he applied and was qualified for a job for which the employer was seeking applicants; (iii) that, despite his qualifications, he was rejected; and (iv) that, after his rejection, the position remained open and the employer continued to seek applicants from persons of complainant's qualifications.[13] In the instant case, we agree with the Court of Appeals that respondent proved a prima facie case. Petitioner sought mechanics, respondent's trade, and continued to do so after respondent's rejection. Petitioner, moreover, does not dispute respondent's qualifications and acknowledges that his past work performance in petitioner's employ was "satisfactory."

The burden then must shift to the employer to articulate some legitimate, nondiscriminatory reason for the employee's rejection. We need not attempt in the instant case to detail every matter which fairly could be recognized as a reasonable basis for a refusal to hire. Here petitioner has assigned respondent's participation in unlawful conduct against it as the cause for his rejection. We think that this suffices to

13. The facts necessarily will vary in Title VII cases, and the specification above of the prima facie proof required from respondent is not necessarily applicable in every respect to differing factual situations.

discharge petitioner's burden of proof at this stage and to meet respondent's prima facie case of discrimination.

The Court of Appeals intimated, however, that petitioner's stated reason for refusing to rehire respondent was a "subjective" rather than objective criterion which "carr[ies] little weight in rebutting charges of discrimination." * * * [W]e think the court below seriously underestimated the rebuttal weight to which petitioner's reasons were entitled. Respondent admittedly had taken part in a carefully planned "stall-in," designed to tie up access to and egress from petitioner's plant at a peak traffic hour. Nothing in Title VII compels an employer to absolve and rehire one who has engaged in such deliberate, unlawful activity against it.[17] * * *

Petitioner's reason for rejection thus suffices to meet the prima facie case, but the inquiry must not end here. While Title VII does not, without more, compel rehiring of respondent, neither does it permit petitioner to use respondent's conduct as a pretext for the sort of discrimination prohibited by § 703(a)(1). On remand, respondent must * * * be afforded a fair opportunity to show that petitioner's stated reason for respondent's rejection was in fact pretext. Especially relevant to such a showing would be evidence that white employees involved in acts against petitioner of comparable seriousness to the "stall-in" were nevertheless retained or rehired. Petitioner may justifiably refuse to rehire one who was engaged in unlawful, disruptive acts against it, but only if this criterion is applied alike to members of all races.

Other evidence that may be relevant to any showing of pretext includes facts as to the petitioner's treatment of respondent during his prior term of employment; petitioner's reaction, if any, to respondent's legitimate civil rights activities; and petitioner's general policy and practice with respect to minority employment. On the latter point, statistics as to petitioner's employment policy and practice may be helpful to a determination of whether petitioner's refusal to rehire respondent in this case conformed to a general pattern of discrimination against blacks.[19] In short, on the retrial respondent must be given a full and fair opportunity to demonstrate by competent evidence that the presumptively valid reasons for his rejection were in fact a coverup for a racially discriminatory decision.

* * *

17. The unlawful activity in this case was directed specifically against petitioner. We need not consider or decide here whether, or under what circumstances, unlawful activity not directed against the particular employer may be a legitimate justification for refusing to hire.

19. The District Court may, for example, determine, after reasonable discovery that "the [racial] composition of defendant's labor force is itself reflective of restrictive or exclusionary practices." We caution that such general determinations, while helpful, may not be in and of themselves controlling as to an individualized hiring decision, particularly in the presence of an otherwise justifiable reason for refusing to rehire.

III

In sum, respondent should have been allowed to pursue his claim under § 703(a)(1). If the evidence on retrial is substantially in accord with that before us in this case, we think that respondent carried his burden of establishing a prima facie case of racial discrimination and that petitioner successfully rebutted that case. But this does not end the matter. On retrial, respondent must be afforded a fair opportunity to demonstrate that petitioner's assigned reason for refusing to re-employ was a pretext or discriminatory in its application. If the District Judge so finds, he must order a prompt and appropriate remedy. In the absence of such a finding, petitioner's refusal to rehire must stand.

The judgment is vacated and the cause is hereby remanded to the District Court for further proceedings consistent with this opinion.

So ordered.

NOTES AND PROBLEMS FOR DISCUSSION

1. Henry Wilson, a black man, was refused employment as a bricklayer by Supreme Contracting, Inc. After successfully completing the job interview and reference check portions of the application process, Wilson was sent to the company physician for a routine physical examination. The doctor reported to the personnel supervisor that Mr. Wilson was not physically qualified because of a previously undetected heart defect. Mr. Wilson's concern over such a finding led him to consult his own doctor, whose examination showed that Mr. Wilson was in perfect health. Mr. Wilson brought a letter to that effect from his physician to the plant personnel supervisor. The supervisor, however, refused to reconsider Wilson, stating that company policy precluded re-examination of applicants found unfit by the plant doctor. Two days later, the plant hired a white man for the bricklaying position sought by Wilson. Can Wilson establish a prima facie violation of Title VII? What arguments could the employer assert in response? Could plaintiff ultimately succeed on the merits? Would it make any difference if the plaintiff could persuade the factfinder that the company physician made a mistake? What if the plaintiff could show that only 5% of the bricklayers employed by Supreme Contracting are black, even though Blacks constitute 35% of the population of the surrounding community? See Weaden v. American Cyanamid Co., 14 FEP Cases 533 (N.D.Fla.1976).

2. Will it be difficult for most plaintiffs to establish a prima facie case under the standards set forth in *McDonnell Douglas*?

(a) Presumably, the most troublesome element in the Court's four-pronged test is the requirement that plaintiff prove that she was qualified for the job in question. Does this mean a plaintiff must prove that she was better qualified than the applicant who was chosen in order to establish a prima facie case? Equally qualified? Or, is it enough for a plaintiff to prove that she possessed the minimum qualifications prescribed for the job? See Burdine v. Texas Department of Community Affairs, 647 F.2d 513 (5th Cir. 1981); Aikens v. United States Postal Service Board, 665 F.2d 1057 (D.C.Cir. 1981); Hagans v. Andrus, 651 F.2d 622 (9th Cir. 1981), cert. denied, 454 U.S. 859, 102 S.Ct. 313, 70 L.Ed.2d 157; Davis v. Weidner, 596 F.2d 726 (7th Cir. 1979).

(b) Jane Reed applied for a position with Crystal Giant, Inc. on September 19, 1980. During her interview, Reed was told that there were no jobs open then and there was likely to be nothing available for the foreseeable future. Reed left her resume and application with the interviewer. One month later, Robert Green was hired for the same position sought by Ms. Reed. Assuming Ms. Reed can prove that she was qualified for that job, can she establish a prima facie case of disparate treatment? See Phillips v. Joint Legislative Committee, 637 F.2d 1014 (5th Cir. 1981), cert. denied, 456 U.S. 960, 102 S.Ct. 2035, 72 L.Ed.2d 483 (1982); McLean v. Phillips-Ramsey, Inc., 624 F.2d 70 (9th Cir. 1980). What if Ms. Reed had not applied for the job because notice of the vacancy was accomplished solely by word-of-mouth? See Lams v. General Waterworks Corp., 766 F.2d 386 (8th Cir. 1985).

3. How extensive is the burden of proof placed on a defendant after the plaintiff establishes a prima facie case? Examine carefully the language chosen by the Court to describe the burden defendant must sustain to rebut the plaintiff's prima facie case of discrimination: "The burden then must shift to the employer to articulate some legitimate, nondiscriminatory reason for the employee's rejection." 411 U.S. at 802. This terminology has generated a significant amount of controversy and additional litigation, all of which has focused on two issues.

(a) What significance, if any, should be accorded the Court's use of "articulate" rather than "prove" to describe the defendant's burden of proof? Does it mean that a defendant can meet its burden through an allegation in a pleading or by argument of counsel? If not, can the defendant satisfy this standard by coming forward with some credible evidence of a legitimate justification for its challenged action? Or, must the defendant sustain the more onerous burden of persuasion—i.e., prove the existence of a nondiscriminatory reason by a preponderance of the evidence?

(b) What factual issue is to be addressed by the defendant's offer of proof? Does a defendant satisfy its obligation to articulate *some* legitimate, nondiscriminatory reason by offering evidence of a single nondiscriminatory justification or must its evidence negate the presence of any discriminatory motive?

The ambiguity created by the Court's opinion in *McDonnell Douglas* resulted in inconsistent rulings on these issues by lower federal courts (compare, e.g., Barnes v. St. Catherine's Hospital, 563 F.2d 324 (7th Cir. 1977) with Turner v. Texas Instruments, Inc., 555 F.2d 1251 (5th Cir. 1977)) and, ultimately, led to three more attempts by the Court to explain its position. In reading the following three opinions, scrutinize the language employed by the Court. Do these decisions clarify the *McDonnell Douglas* formulation of the defendant's burden of proof? For an extensive discussion of the questions raised in this note see Friedman, The Burger Court and the Prima Facie Case in Employment Discrimination Litigation: A Critique, 65 Corn.L.Rev. 1 (1979).

4. What happens if the defendant does not discharge its burden of proof? Is the court compelled to grant a directed verdict in favor of the plaintiff? Does the prima facie case generate a presumption or an inference of discrimination? Does the Court address this issue in *McDonnell Douglas*? Is it discussed in the other three cases in this quartet?

FURNCO CONSTRUCTION CORP. v. WATERS

Supreme Court of the United States, 1978.
438 U.S. 567, 98 S.Ct. 2943, 57 L.Ed.2d 957.

MR. JUSTICE REHNQUIST delivered the opinion of the Court.

Respondents are three black bricklayers who sought employment with petitioner Furnco Construction Corp. Two of the three were never offered employment. The third was employed only long after he initially applied. * * * We granted certiorari to consider important questions raised by this case regarding the exact scope of the prima facie case under *McDonnell Douglas* and the nature of the evidence necessary to rebut such a case. Having concluded that the Court of Appeals erred in its treatment of the latter question, we reverse and remand to that court for further proceedings consistent with this opinion.

I

A few facts in this case are not in serious dispute. Petitioner Furnco, an employer within the meaning of §§ 701(b) and (h) of Title VII of the 1964 Civil Rights Act, specializes in refractory installation in steel mills and, more particularly, the rehabilitation or relining of blast furnaces with what is called in the trade "firebrick." Furnco does not, however, maintain a permanent force of bricklayers. Rather, it hires a superintendent for a specific job and then delegates to him the task of securing a competent work force. In August 1971, Furnco contracted with Interlake, Inc., to reline one of its blast furnaces. Joseph Dacies, who had been a job superintendent for Furnco since 1965, was placed in charge of the job and given the attendant hiring responsibilities. He did not accept applications at the jobsite, but instead hired only persons whom he knew to be experienced and competent in this type of work or persons who had been recommended to him as similarly skilled. He hired his first four bricklayers, all of whom were white, on two successive days in August, the 26th and 27th, and two in September, the 7th and 8th. On September 9 he hired the first black bricklayer. By September 13, he had hired 8 more bricklayers, 1 of whom was black; by September 17, 7 more had been employed, another of whom was black; and by September 23, 17 more were on the payroll, again with 1 black included in that number. From October 12 to 18, he hired 6 bricklayers, all of whom were black including respondent Smith, who had worked for Dacies previously and had applied at the jobsite somewhat earlier. Respondent Samuels and Nemhard were not hired, though they were fully qualified and had also attempted to secure employment by appearing at the jobsite gate. Out of the total of 1,819 man-days worked on the Interlake job, 242, or 13.3%, were worked by black bricklayers.

* * * The District Court elaborated at some length as to the "critical" necessity of insuring that only experienced and highly quali-

fied firebricklayers were employed. Improper or untimely work would result in substantial losses both to Interlake, which was forced to shut down its furnace and lay off employees during the relining job, and to Furnco, which was paid for this work at a fixed price and for a fixed time period. In addition, not only might shoddy work slow this work process down, but it also might necessitate costly future maintenance work with its attendant loss of production and employee layoffs; diminish Furnco's reputation and ability to secure similar work in the future; and perhaps even create serious safety hazards, leading to explosions and the like. These considerations justified Furnco's refusal to engage in on-the-job training or to hire at the gate, a hiring process which would not provide an adequate method of matching qualified applications to job requirements and assuring that the applicants are sufficiently skilled and capable. Furthermore, there was no evidence that these policies and practices were a pretext to exclude black bricklayers or were otherwise illegitimate or had a disproportionate impact or effect on black bricklayers. From late 1969 through late 1973, 5.7% of the bricklayers in the relevant labor force were minority group members, while, as mentioned before, 13.3% of the man-days on Furnco's Interlake job were worked by black bricklayers.

Because of the above considerations and following the established practice in the industry, most of the firebricklayers hired by Dacies were persons known by him to be experienced and competent in this type of work. The others were hired after being recommended as skilled in this type of work by his general foreman, an employee (a black), another Furnco superintendent in the area, and Furnco's General Manager John Wright. Wright had not only instructed Dacies to employ, as far as possible, at least 16% black bricklayers, a policy due to Furnco's self-imposed affirmative-action plan to insure that black bricklayers were employed by Furnco in Cook County in numbers substantially in excess of their percentage in the local union, but he had also recommended, in an effort to show good faith, that Dacies hire several specific bricklayers, who had previously filed a discrimination suit against Furnco, negotiations for the settlement of which had only recently broken down.

From these factual findings, the District Court concluded that respondents * * * had failed to prove a case of discrimination under McDonnell Douglas Corp. v. Green. It is not entirely clear whether the court thought respondents had failed to make out a prima facie case of discrimination under *McDonnell Douglas*, but the court left no doubt that it thought Furnco's hiring practices and policies were justified as a "business necessity" in that they were required for the safe and efficient operation of Furnco's business, and were "not used as a pretext to exclude Negroes." Thus, even if a prima facie case had been made out, it had been effectively rebutted. * * *

The Court of Appeals reversed, holding that respondents had made out a prima facie case under *McDonnell Douglas*, which Furnco had not effectively rebutted. Because of the "historical inequality of treatment of black workers" and the fact that the record failed to reveal that any white persons had applied at the gate, the Court of Appeals rejected Furnco's argument that discrimination had not been shown because a white appearing at the jobsite would have fared no better than respondents. That court also disagreed with Furnco's contention, which the District Court had adopted, that "the importance of selecting people whose capability had been demonstrated to defendant's brick superintendent is a 'legitimate, nondiscriminatory reason' for defendant's refusal to consider plaintiffs." Instead, the appellate court proceeded to devise what it thought would be an appropriate hiring procedure for Furnco, saying that "[i]t seems to us that there is a reasonable middle ground between immediate hiring decisions on the spot and seeking out employees from among those known to the superintendent." This middle course, according to the Court of Appeals, was to take written applications, with inquiry as to qualifications and experience, and then check, evaluate, and compare those claims against the qualifications and experience of other bricklayers with whom the superintendent was already acquainted. We granted certiorari to consider whether the Court of Appeals had gone too far in substituting its own judgment as to proper hiring practices in the case of an employer which claimed the practices it had chosen did not violate Title VII.

II

A

* * * [T]he Court of Appeals was justified in concluding that as a matter of law respondents made out a prima facie case of discrimination under *McDonnell Douglas*. * * * And here respondents carried that initial burden by proving they were members of a racial minority; they did everything within their power to apply for employment; Furnco has conceded that they were qualified in every respect for the jobs which were about to be opened, they were not offered employment * * * and the employer continued to seek persons of similar qualifications.

B

We think the Court of Appeals went awry, however, in apparently equating a prima facie showing under *McDonnell Douglas* with an ultimate finding of fact as to discriminatory refusal to hire under Title VII; the two are quite different and that difference has a direct bearing on the proper resolution of this case. The Court of Appeals, as we read its opinion, thought Furnco's hiring procedures not only must be reasonably related to the achievement of some legitimate purpose, but also must be the method which allows the employer to consider the qualifications of the largest number of minority applicants. We think the imposition of that second requirement simply finds no support either in the nature of the prima facie case or the purpose of Title VII.

* * * A prima facie case under *McDonnell Douglas* raises an inference of discrimination * * * because we presume these acts, if otherwise unexplained, are more likely than not based on the consideration of impermissible factors. And we are willing to presume this largely because we know from our experience that more often than not people do not act in a totally arbitrary manner, without any underlying reasons, especially in a business setting. Thus, when all legitimate reasons for rejecting an applicant have been eliminated as possible reasons for the employer's actions, it is more likely than not the employer, who we generally assume acts only with *some* reason, based his decision on an impermissible consideration such as race.

When the prima facie case is understood in the light of the opinion in *McDonnell Douglas*, it is apparent that the burden which shifts to the employer is merely that of proving that he based his employment decision on a legitimate consideration, and not an illegitimate one such as race. To prove that, he need not prove that he pursued the course which would both enable him to achieve his own business goal *and* allow him to consider the *most* employment applications. Title VII prohibits him from having as a goal a work force selected by any proscribed discriminatory practice, but it does not impose a duty to adopt a hiring procedure that maximizes hiring of minority employees. To dispel the adverse inference from a prima facie showing under *McDonnell Douglas*, the employer need only "articulate some legitimate, nondiscriminatory reason for the employee's rejection."

The dangers of embarking on a course such as that charted by the Court of Appeals here, where the court requires businesses to adopt what it perceives to be the "best" hiring procedures, are nowhere more evident than in the record of this very case. Not only does the record not reveal that the court's suggested hiring procedure would work satisfactorily, but also there is nothing in the record to indicate that it would be any less "haphazard, arbitrary, and subjective" than Furnco's method, which the Court of Appeals criticized as deficient for exactly those reasons. Courts are generally less competent than employers to restructure business practices, and unless mandated to do so by Congress they should not attempt it.

This is not to say, of course, that proof of a justification which is reasonably related to the achievement of some legitimate goal necessarily ends the inquiry. The plaintiff must be given the opportunity to introduce evidence that the proffered justification is merely a pretext for discrimination. And as we noted in *McDonnell Douglas*, this evidence might take a variety of forms. But the Court of Appeals, although stating its disagreement with the District Court's conclusion that the employer's hiring practices were a "legitimate, nondiscriminatory reason" for refusing to hire respondents, premised its disagreement on a view which we have discussed and rejected above. It did not conclude that the practices were a pretext for discrimination, but only that different practices would have enabled the employer to at least consider, and perhaps to hire, more minority employees. But courts may not impose such a remedy on an employer at least until a violation of Title VII has been proved, and here none had been under the reasoning of either the District Court or the Court of Appeals.

C

The Court of Appeals was also critical of petitioner's effort to employ statistics in this type of case. While the matter is not free from doubt, it appears that the court thought that once a *McDonnell Douglas* prima facie showing had been made out, statistics of a racially balanced work force were totally irrelevant to the question of motive. See 551 F.2d, at 1089. That would undoubtedly be a correct view of the matter if the *McDonnell Douglas* prima facie showing were the equivalent of an ultimate finding by the trier of fact that the original rejection of the applicant was racially motivated: A racially balanced work force cannot immunize an employer from liability for specific acts of discrimination. * * *

A *McDonnell Douglas* prima facie showing is not the equivalent of a factual finding of discrimination, however. Rather, it is simply proof of actions taken by the employer from which we infer discriminatory animus because experience has proved that in the absence of any other explanation it is more likely than not that those actions were bottomed on impermissible considerations. When the prima facie showing is understood in this manner, the employer must be allowed some latitude to introduce evidence which bears on his motive. Proof that his work force was racially balanced or that it contained a disproportionately high percentage of minority employees is not wholly irrelevant on the issue of intent when that issue is yet to be decided. We cannot say that such proof would have absolutely no probative value in determining whether the otherwise unexplained rejection of the minority applicants was discriminatorily motivated. Thus, although we agree with the Court of Appeals that in this case such proof neither was nor could have been sufficient to *conclusively* demonstrate that Furnco's actions were not discriminatorily motivated, the District Court was entitled to *consider* the racial mix of the work force when trying to make the determination as to motivation. The Court of Appeals should likewise give similar consideration to the proffered statistical proof in any further proceedings in this case.

III

* * * The judgment of the Court of Appeals is reversed, and the case is remanded for further proceedings consistent with this opinion.

MR. JUSTICE MARSHALL, with whom MR. JUSTICE BRENNAN joins, concurring in part and dissenting in part.

It is well established under Title VII that claims of employment discrimination because of race may arise in two different ways. Teamsters v. United States, 431 U.S. 324, 335–336, n. 15, 97 S.Ct. 1843, 1854, 52 L.Ed.2d 396 (1977). An individual may allege that he has been subjected to "disparate treatment" because of his race, or that he has been the victim of a facially neutral practice having a "disparate impact" on his racial group. The Court today concludes that the Court of Appeals was correct in treating this as a disparate-treatment case controlled by McDonnell Douglas Corp. v. Green, 411 U.S. 792, 93 S.Ct. 1817, 36 L.Ed.2d 668 (1973).

Under *McDonnell Douglas,* a plaintiff establishes a prima facie case of employment discrimination through disparate treatment by showing

> "(i) that he belongs to a racial minority; (ii) that he applied and was qualified for a job for which the employer was seeking applicants; (iii) that, despite his qualifications, he was rejected; and (iv) that, after his rejection, the position remained open and the employer continued to seek applicants from persons of complainant's qualifications."

Once a plaintiff has made out this prima facie case, the burden shifts to the employer who must prove that he had a "legitimate, nondiscriminatory reason for the [plaintiff's] rejection."

The Court of Appeals properly held that respondents had made out a prima facie case of employment discrimination under *McDonnell Douglas.* Once respondents had established their prima facie case, the question for the court was then whether petitioner had carried its burden of proving that respondents were rejected on the basis of legitimate nondiscriminatory considerations. The court, however, failed properly to address that question and instead focused on what other hiring practices petitioner might employ. I therefore agree with the Court that we must remand the case to the Court of Appeals so that it can address, under the appropriate standards, whether petitioner had rebutted respondents' prima facie showing of disparate treatment. I also agree that on remand the Court of Appeals is to address the other theories of liability which respondents have presented.

Where the Title VII claim is that a facially neutral employment practice actually falls more harshly on one racial group, thus having a disparate impact on that group, our cases establish a different way of proving the claim. As set out by the Court in Griggs v. Duke Power Co., to establish a prima facie case on a disparate-impact claim, a plaintiff need not show that the employer had a discriminatory intent but need only demonstrate that a particular practice in actuality "operates to exclude Negroes."

Once the plaintiff has established the disparate impact of the practice, the burden shifts to the employer to show that the practice has "a manifest relationship to the employment in question." The "touchstone is business necessity," and the practice "must be shown to be necessary to safe and efficient job performance to survive a Title VII challenge." Under this principle, a practice of limiting jobs to those with prior experience working in an industry or for a particular person, or to those who hear about jobs by word of mouth would be invalid if the practice in actuality impacts more harshly on a group protected under Title VII, unless the practice can be justified by business necessity.

There is nothing in today's opinion that is inconsistent with this approach or with our prior decisions. I must dissent, however, from the Court's apparent decision, to foreclose on remand further litigation on the *Griggs* question of whether petitioner's hiring practices had a disparate impact. Respondents claim that petitioner's practice of hiring from a list of those who had previously worked for the foreman foreclosed Negroes from consideration for the vast majority of jobs. Although the foreman also hired a considerable number of Negroes through other methods, respondents assert that the use of other methods to augment the representation of Negroes in the work force does not answer whether the primary hiring practice is discriminatory.

It is clear that an employer cannot be relieved of responsibility for past discriminatory practices merely by undertaking affirmative action to obtain proportional representation in his work force. As the Court said in *Teamsters,* and reaffirms today, a "company's later changes in its hiring and promotion policies could be of little comfort to the victims of the earlier * * * discrimination, and could not erase its previous illegal conduct or its obligation to afford relief to those who suffered because of it." Therefore, it is at least an open question whether the hiring of workers primarily from a list of past employees would, under *Griggs,* violate Title VII where the list contains no Negroes but the company uses additional methods of hiring to increase the numbers of Negroes hired.*

The Court today apparently assumes that the Court of Appeals affirmed the District Court's findings that petitioner's hiring practice had no disparate impact. I cannot agree with that assumption. Because the Court of Appeals disposed of this case under the *McDonnell Douglas* analysis, it had no occasion to address those findings of the District Court pertaining to disparate impact. Although the Court of Appeals did discuss *Griggs* in its opinion, as I read that discussion the court was merely rejecting petitioner's argument that it could defeat respondents' *McDonnell Douglas* claim by showing that the work force had a large percentage of Negro members. I express no view on the issue of whether respondents' claim should prevail on the facts presented here since that question is not presently before us, but I believe that respondents' opportunity to make their claim should not be foreclosed by this Court.

NOTES AND PROBLEMS FOR DISCUSSION

1. How does this opinion deal with the two defense burden of proof issues examined in connection with *McDonnell Douglas*? Does it provide a more

* Of course, the Court leaves open on remand the issue of whether Furnco's use of the list violated Title VII under a disparate-treatment theory.

precise delineation of either of these two aspects of the defendant's burden than *McDonnell Douglas*?

2. How does the Court describe the effect of a defendant's failure to sustain its burden of proof after the plaintiff has established a prima facie case? Is its position unambiguous?

3. Would the result in *Furnco* have been different if the Supreme Court had been convinced by evidence on the record that the Court of Appeals' suggested hiring procedure was less arbitrary and more effective than Furnco's system? If not, where was the error in the appellate court's analysis? On remand, the Seventh Circuit reversed its position and held that Furnco's interest in obtaining workers known from experience to be qualified did constitute a legitimate, nondiscriminatory reason for refusing to consider the plaintiffs and that, as to two of the three plaintiffs, this reason was not pretextual. It added, however, that since one of the plaintiffs had worked previously for a Furnco superintendent but was not on that superintendent's list of qualified workers, the refusal to consider his application at the gate was not supported by a legitimate, nondiscriminatory reason. Accordingly, the court reversed the judgment awarded against this plaintiff and remanded the case to the trial court for further consideration of his claim. Waters v. Furnco Construction Co., 688 F.2d 39 (7th Cir. 1982).

4. Why didn't the majority analyze this case under the disproportionate impact theory, as suggested by Justice Marshall?

5. David Fanning and Alan Marshall, employees at Anderson Manufacturing, Inc. applied for promotion to deputy plant supervisor. Fanning, a white employee, was chosen over Marshall, a black man, on the ground of his personal friendship with Mr. Anderson. Anderson admits that both applicants were qualified for the position and possessed equal seniority. Has the employer violated Title VII? Compare Thornton v. Coffey, 618 F.2d 686 (10th Cir. 1980), with Cooper v. University of Texas, 482 F.Supp. 187 (N.D.Tex.1979).

BOARD OF TRUSTEES OF KEENE STATE COLLEGE v. SWEENEY

Supreme Court of the United States, 1978.
439 U.S. 24, 99 S.Ct. 295, 58 L.Ed.2d 216.

PER CURIAM.

* * * In Furnco Construction Co. v. Waters, we stated that "[t]o dispel the adverse inference from a prima facie showing under *McDonnell Douglas*, the employer need only 'articulate some legitimate, nondiscriminatory reason for the employee's rejection.'" quoting McDonnell Douglas Corp. v. Green. We stated in *McDonnell Douglas* that the plaintiff "must * * * be afforded a fair opportunity to show that [the employer's] stated reason for [the plaintiff's] rejection was in fact pretext." The Court of Appeals in the present case, however, referring to *McDonnell Douglas*, stated that " in requiring the defendant to *prove absence of discriminatory motive*, the Supreme Court placed the burden squarely on the party with the greater access to such evidence." (emphasis added).[1]

1. While the Court of Appeals did make the statement that the dissent quotes, it also made the statement quoted in the text above. These statements simply contradict

While words such as "articulate," "show," and "prove," may have more or less similar meanings depending upon the context in which they are used, we think that there is a significant distinction between merely "articulat[ing] some legitimate, nondiscriminatory reason" and "prov[ing] absence of discriminatory motive." By reaffirming and emphasizing the *McDonnell Douglas* analysis in Furnco Construction Co. v. Waters, supra, we made it clear that the former will suffice to meet the employee's prima facie case of discrimination. Because the Court of Appeals appears to have imposed a heavier burden on the employer that *Furnco* warrants, its judgment is vacated and the case is remanded for reconsideration in the light of *Furnco.*[2]

MR. JUSTICE STEVENS, with whom MR. JUSTICE BRENNAN, MR. JUSTICE STEWART, and MR. JUSTICE MARSHALL join, dissenting.

Whenever this Court grants certiorari and vacates a court of appeals judgment in order to allow that court to reconsider its decision in the light of an intervening decision of this Court, the Court is acting on the merits. Such action always imposes an additional burden on circuit judges who—more than any other segment of the federal judiciary—are struggling desperately to keep afloat in the flood of federal litigation. For that reason, such action should not be taken unless the intervening decision has shed new light on the law which, if it had been available at the time of the court of appeals' decision, might have led to a different result.

In this case, the Court's action implies that the recent opinion in Furnco Construction Corp. v. Waters, made some change in the law as explained in McDonnell Douglas Corp. v. Green. When I joined the *Furnco* opinion, I detected no such change and I am still unable to discern one. In both cases, the Court clearly stated that when the complainant in a Title VII trial establishes a prima facie case of discrimination, "the burden which shifts to the employer is merely that

one another. The statement quoted in the text above would make entirely superfluous the third step in the *Furnco-McDonnell Douglas* analysis, since it would place on the employer at the second stage the burden of showing that the reason for rejection was not a pretext, rather than requiring such proof from the employee as a part of the third step. We think our remand is warranted both because we are unable to determine which of the two conflicting standards the Court of Appeals applied in reviewing the decision of the District Court in this case, and because of the implication in its opinion that there is no difference between the two standards. We, of course, intimate no view as to the correct result if the proper test is applied in this case.

2. We quite agree with the dissent that under *Furnco* and *McDonnell Douglas* the employer's burden is satisfied if he simply "explains what he has done" or "produc[es] evidence of legitimate nondiscriminatory reasons." But petitioners clearly did produce evidence to support their legitimate nondiscriminatory explanation for refusing to promote respondent during the years in question. Nonetheless, the Court of Appeals held that petitioners had not met their burden because the proffered legitimate explanation did not "rebut" or "disprove" respondent's prima facie case or "prove absence of nondiscriminatory motive." This holding by the Court of Appeals is further support for our belief that the court appears to have imposed a heavier burden on the employer than *Furnco*, and the dissent here, require.

of proving that he based his employment decision on a legitimate consideration, and not an illegitimate one such as race." [1]

The Court of Appeals' statement of the parties' respective burdens in this case is wholly faithful to this Court's teachings in *McDonnell Douglas.* The Court of Appeals here stated:

> "As we understand those cases, a plaintiff bears the initial burden of presenting evidence sufficient to establish a prima facie case of discrimination. *The burden then shifts to the defendant to rebut the prima facie case by showing that a legitimate, nondiscriminatory reason accounted for its actions.* If the rebuttal is successful, the plaintiff must show that the stated reason was a mere pretext for discrimination. *The ultimate burden of persuasion on the issue of discrimination remains with the plaintiff, who must convince the court by a preponderance of the evidence that he or she has been the victim of discrimination.*" (emphasis added).

This statement by the Court of Appeals virtually parrots this Court's statements in *McDonnell Douglas* and *Furnco.* Nonetheless, this Court vacates the judgment on the ground that "the Court of Appeals appears to have imposed a heavier burden on the employer than *Furnco* warrants." As its sole basis for this conclusion, this Court relies on a distinction drawn for the first time in this case "between merely 'articulat[ing] some legitimate, nondiscriminatory reason' and 'prov[ing] absence of discriminatory motive.' " [2] This novel distinction has two parts, both of which are illusory and were unequivocally rejected in *Furnco* itself.

First is a purported difference between "articulating" and "proving" a legitimate motivation. Second is the difference between affirming a nondiscriminatory motive and negating a discriminatory motive.

With respect to the first point, it must be noted that it was this Court in *Furnco,* not the Court of Appeals in this case, that stated that the employer's burden was to "*prov[e]* that he based his employment decision on a legitimate consideration." [3] Indeed, in the paragraph of this Court's opinion in *Furnco* cited earlier, the words "prove" and "articulate" were used interchangeably, and properly so. For they were descriptive of the defendant's burden in a trial context. In

1. This language is quoted from * * * *Furnco.*

2. The Court also suggests that "further support" for its decision is derived from the Court of Appeals' "holding" that "petitioners had not met their burden because the proffered legitimate explanation did not 'rebut' or 'disprove' respondent's prima facie case * * *." The actual "holding" of the Court of Appeals was that "the trial court's finding that sex discrimination impeded the plaintiff's second promotion was not clearly erroneous." The Court of Appeals reached this conclusion by considering all of the evidence presented by both parties to determine whether the evidence of discrimination offered by the plaintiff was "sufficient * * * to sustain the district court's findings" in light of the counter evidence offered by the employer. Such factual determinations by two federal courts are entitled to a strong presumption of validity.

3. It should also be noted that the Court of Appeals did not state that the petitioners' burden here was to "prove" anything; rather, the burden which shifted to them as defendants was to "show" a legitimate reason for their action.

litigation the only way a defendant can "articulate" the reason for his action is by adducing evidence that explains what he has done; when an executive takes the witness stand to "articulate" his reason, the litigant for whom he speaks is thereby proving those reasons. If the Court intends to authorize a method of articulating a factual defense without proof, surely the Court should explain what it is.

The second part of the Court's imaginative distinction is also rejected by *Furnco.* When an employer shows that a legitimate nondiscriminatory reason accounts for his action, he is simultaneously demonstrating that the action was not motivated by an illegitimate factor such as race. *Furnco* explicitly recognized this equivalence when it defined the burden on the employer as "that of proving that he based his employment decision on a legitimate consideration, and not an illegitimate one such as race." Whether the issue is phrased in the affirmative or in the negative, the ultimate question involves an identification of the real reason for the employment decision. On that question—as all of these cases make perfectly clear—it is only the burden of producing evidence of legitimate nondiscriminatory reasons which shifts to the employer; the burden of persuasion, as the Court of Appeals properly recognized, remains with the plaintiff.

In short, there is no legitimate basis for concluding that the Court of Appeals erred in this case—either with or without the benefit of *Furnco.* The Court's action today therefore needlessly imposes additional work on circuit judges who have already considered and correctly applied the rule the Court directs them to reconsider and reapply.

NOTES AND PROBLEMS FOR DISCUSSION

1. Why did the dissenters refuse to join the opinion of the Court? Did they disagree with the majority's ruling on the scope of the defendant's burden of proof? Or did the Justices simply disagree as to which proof standard had been applied by the appellate court?

2. Do you agree with the discussion in the dissenting opinion concerning the factual issue to be addressed by the defendant's evidence? Does proof of a legitimate motivation "simultaneously demonstrate" the absence of an illegitimate consideration? Is there always only one "real reason" for an employment decision? Can't an individual action be the product of both legitimate and illegitimate motives?

3. In this third stab at the problem, did the Court clearly and precisely declare which type of burden of proof defendants must sustain or the factual issue to which this offer of proof must be directed? Not specifically enough, apparently, to avoid a continued split among the federal circuit courts on these issues, especially with respect to the burden of proof question. Compare, e.g., Lieberman v. Gant, 630 F.2d 60 (2d Cir. 1980) (burden of production), and Jackson v. United States Steel Corp., 624 F.2d 436 (3d Cir. 1980) (burden of production) with Vaughn v. Westinghouse Electric Corp., 620 F.2d 655 (8th Cir. 1980) (burden of persuasion), and Burdine v. Texas Department of Community Affairs, 608 F.2d 563 (5th Cir. 1979) (burden of persuasion). This enduring state of judicial discord ultimately forced the Court to make a fourth attempt at resolving the ambiguities produced by its three prior opinions.

TEXAS DEPARTMENT OF COMMUNITY AFFAIRS v. BURDINE

Supreme Court of the United States, 1981.
450 U.S. 248, 101 S.Ct. 1089, 67 L.Ed.2d 207.

JUSTICE POWELL delivered the opinion of the Court.

This case requires us to address again the nature of the evidentiary burden placed upon the defendant in an employment discrimination suit brought under Title VII of the Civil Rights Act of 1964. The narrow question presented is whether, after the plaintiff has proved a prima facie case of discriminatory treatment, the burden shifts to the defendant to persuade the court by a preponderance of the evidence that legitimate, nondiscriminatory reasons for the challenged employment action existed.

I

[Respondent was employed as an accounting clerk in a division of the Petitioner Department that was funded completely by the federal government. To retain this funding, the Petitioner was forced to reduce its staff, which it accomplished by firing Respondent and two other employees, while retaining one male employee. Before her termination, Respondent had been denied a promotion to a supervisory position. She brought the instant action alleging that the failure to promote and subsequent decision to terminate her were the result of sex discrimination in violation of Title VII. The District Court, after a bench trial, ruled in favor of the defendant, finding no evidence to support plaintiff's claim that either decision had been based on gender discrimination.]

The Court of Appeals for the Fifth Circuit reversed in part. The court * * * affirmed the District Court's finding that respondent was not discriminated against when she was not promoted. The Court of Appeals, however, reversed the District Court's finding that Fuller's testimony sufficiently had rebutted respondent's prima facie case of gender discrimination in the decision to terminate her employment at PSC. The court reaffirmed its previously announced views that the defendant in a Title VII case bears the burden of proving by a preponderance of the evidence the existence of legitimate nondiscriminatory reasons for the employment action and that the defendant also must prove by objective evidence that those hired or promoted were better qualified than the plaintiff. The court found that Fuller's testimony did not carry either of these evidentiary burdens. It, therefore, reversed the judgment of the District Court and remanded the case for computation of backpay. Because the decision of the Court of Appeals as to the burden of proof borne by the defendant conflicts with interpretations of our precedents adopted by other courts of appeals, we granted certiorari. We now vacate the Fifth Circuit's decision and remand for application of the correct standard.

II

In McDonnell Douglas Corp. v. Green, we set forth the basic allocation of burdens and order of presentation of proof in a Title VII case alleging discriminatory treatment. First, the plaintiff has the burden of proving by the preponderance of the evidence a prima facie case of discrimination. Second, if the plaintiff succeeds in proving the prima facie case, the burden shifts to the defendant "to articulate some legitimate, nondiscriminatory reason for the employee's rejection." Third, should the defendant carry this burden, the plaintiff must then have an opportunity to prove by a preponderance of the evidence that the legitimate reasons offered by the defendant were not its true reasons, but were a pretext for discrimination.

The nature of the burden that shifts to the defendant should be understood in light of the plaintiff's ultimate and intermediate burdens. The ultimate burden of persuading the trier of fact that the defendant intentionally discriminated against the plaintiff remains at all time with the plaintiff. See Board of Trustees of Keene State College v. Sweeney. See generally 9 Wigmore, Evidence § 2489 (3d ed. 1940) (the burden of persuasion "never shifts"). The *McDonnell Douglas* division of intermediate evidentiary burdens serves to bring the litigants and the court expeditiously and fairly to this ultimate question.

The burden of establishing a prima facie case of disparate treatment is not onerous. The plaintiff must prove by a preponderance of the evidence that she applied for an available position, for which she was qualified, but was rejected under circumstances which give rise to an inference of unlawful discrimination.[6] The prima facie case serves an important function in the litigation: it eliminates the most common nondiscriminatory reasons for the plaintiff's rejection. * * * Establishment of the prima facie case in effect creates a presumption that the employer unlawfully discriminated against the employee. If the trier of fact believes the plaintiff's evidence, and if the employer is silent in the face of the presumption, the court must enter judgment for the plaintiff because no issue of fact remains in the case.[7]

The burden that shifts to the defendant, therefore, is to rebut the presumption of discrimination by producing evidence that the plaintiff was rejected, or someone else was preferred, for a legitimate, nondiscriminatory reason. The defendant need not persuade the court that it was actually motivated by the proffered reasons. It is sufficient if the

6. In the instant case, it is not seriously contested that respondent has proved a prima facie case. She showed that she was a qualified woman who sought an available position, but the position was left open for several months before she finally was rejected in favor of a male who had been under her supervision.

7. The phrase "prima facie case" may denote not only the establishment of a legally mandatory, rebuttable presumption, but also may be used by courts to describe the plaintiff's burden of producing enough evidence to permit the trier of fact to infer the fact at issue. 9 Wigmore, Evidence § 2494 (3d ed. 1940). *McDonnell Douglas* should have made it apparent that in the Title VII context we use "prima facie case" in the former sense.

defendant's evidence raises a genuine issue of fact as to whether it discriminated against the plaintiff.[8] To accomplish this, the defendant must clearly set forth, through the introduction of admissible evidence, the reasons for the plaintiff's rejection.[9] The explanation provided must be legally sufficient to justify a judgment for the defendant. If the defendant carries this burden of production, the presumption raised by the prima facie case is rebutted,[10] and the factual inquiry proceeds to a new level of specificity. Placing this burden of production on the defendant thus serves simultaneously to meet the plaintiff's prima facie case by presenting a legitimate reason for the action and to frame the factual issue with sufficient clarity so that the plaintiff will have a full and fair opportunity to demonstrate pretext. The sufficiency of the defendant's evidence should be evaluated by the extent to which it fulfills these functions.

The plaintiff retains the burden of persuasion. She now must have the opportunity to demonstrate that the proffered reason was not the true reason for the employment decision. This burden now merges with the ultimate burden of persuading the court that she has been the victim of intentional discrimination. She may succeed in this either directly by persuading the court that a discriminatory reason more likely motivated the employer or indirectly by showing that the employer's proffered explanation is unworthy of credence.

III

In reversing the judgment of the District Court that the discharge of respondent from PSC was unrelated to her sex, the Court of Appeals adhered to two rules it had developed to elaborate the defendant's burden of proof. First, the defendant must prove by a preponderance of the evidence that legitimate, nondiscriminatory reasons for the discharge existed. Second, to satisfy this burden, the defendant "must

8. This evidentiary relationship between the presumption created by a prima facie case and the consequential burden of production placed on the defendant is a traditional feature of the common law. "The word 'presumption' properly used refers only to a device for allocating the production burden." F. James & G. Hazard, Civil Procedure § 7.9, at 255 (2d ed. 1977) (footnote omitted). See Fed.Rule Evid. 301. Usually, assessing the burden of production helps the judge determine whether the litigants have created an issue of fact to be decided by the jury. In a Title VII case, the allocation of burdens and the creation of a presumption by the establishment of a prima facie case is intended progressively to sharpen the inquiry into the elusive factual question of intentional discrimination.

9. An articulation not admitted into evidence will not suffice. Thus, the defendant cannot meet its burden merely through an answer to the complaint or by argument of counsel.

10. In saying that the presumption drops from the case, we do not imply that the trier of fact no longer may consider evidence previously introduced by the plaintiff to establish a prima facie case. A satisfactory explanation by the defendant destroys the legally mandatory inference of discrimination arising from the plaintiff's initial evidence. Nonetheless, this evidence and inferences properly drawn therefrom may be considered by the trier of fact on the issue of whether the defendant's explanation is pretextual. Indeed, there may be some cases where the plaintiff's initial evidence, combined with effective cross-examination of the defendant, will suffice to discredit the defendant's explanation.

prove that those he hired * * * were somehow *better* qualified than was plaintiff; in other words, comparative evidence is needed."

A

The Court of Appeals has misconstrued the nature of the burden that *McDonnell Douglas* and its progeny place on the defendant. We stated in *Sweeney* that "the employer's burden is satisfied if he simply 'explains what he has done' or 'produc[es] evidence of legitimate nondiscriminatory reasons.'" It is plain that the Court of Appeals required much more: it placed on the defendant the burden of persuading the court that it had convincing, objective reasons for preferring the chosen applicant above the plaintiff.

The Court of Appeals distinguished *Sweeney* on the ground that the case held only that the defendant did not have the burden of proving the absence of discriminatory intent. But this distinction slights the rationale of *Sweeney* and of our other cases. We have stated consistently that the employee's prima facie case of discrimination will be rebutted if the employer articulates lawful reasons for the action; that is, to satisfy this intermediate burden, the employer need only produce admissible evidence which would allow the trier of fact rationally to conclude that the employment decision had not been motivated by discriminatory animus. The Court of Appeals would require the defendant to introduce evidence which, in the absence of any evidence of pretext, would *persuade* the trier of fact that the employment action was lawful. This exceeds what properly can be demanded to satisfy a burden of production.

The court placed the burden of persuasion on the defendant apparently because it feared that "[i]f an employer need only *articulate*—not prove—a legitimate, nondiscriminatory reason for his action, he may compose fictitious, but legitimate, reasons for his actions." We do not believe, however, that limiting the defendant's evidentiary obligation to a burden of production will unduly hinder the plaintiff. First, as noted above, the defendant's explanation of its legitimate reasons must be clear and reasonably specific. This obligation arises both from the necessity of rebutting the inference of discrimination arising from the prima facie case and from the requirement that the plaintiff be afforded "a full and fair opportunity" to demonstrate pretext. Second, although the defendant does not bear a formal burden of persuasion, the defendant nevertheless retains an incentive to persuade the trier of fact that the employment decision was lawful. Thus, the defendant normally will attempt to prove the factual basis for its explanation. Third, the liberal discovery rules applicable to any civil suit in federal court are supplemented in a Title VII suit by the plaintiff's access to the Equal Employment Opportunity Commission's investigatory files concerning her complaint. Given these factors, we are unpersuaded that the plaintiff will find it particularly difficult to prove that a proffered explanation lacking a factual basis is a pretext. We remain confident that the *McDonnell Douglas* framework permits the plaintiff meriting relief to demonstrate intentional discrimination.

B

The Court of Appeals also erred in requiring the defendant to prove by objective evidence that the person hired or promoted was more qualified than the plaintiff. *McDonnell Douglas* teaches that it is the plaintiff's task to demonstrate that similarly situated employees were not treated equally. The Court of Appeals' rule would require the employer to show that the plaintiff's objective qualifications were inferior to those of the person selected. If it cannot, a court would, in effect, conclude that it has discriminated.

* * *

The views of the Court of Appeals can be read, we think, as requiring the employer to hire the minority or female applicant whenever that person's objective qualifications were equal to those of a white male applicant. But Title VII does not obligate an employer to accord this preference. Rather, the employer has discretion to choose among equally qualified candidates, provided the decision is not based upon unlawful criteria. The fact that a court may think that the employer misjudged the qualifications of the applicants does not in itself expose him to Title VII liability, although this may be probative of whether the employer's reasons are pretexts for discrimination.

IV

In summary, the Court of Appeals erred by requiring the defendant to prove by a preponderance of the evidence the existence of nondiscriminatory reasons for terminating the respondent and that the person retained in her stead had superior objective qualifications for the position. When the plaintiff has proved a prima facie case of discrimination, the defendant bears only the burden of explaining clearly the nondiscriminatory reasons for its actions. The judgment of the Court of Appeals is vacated and the case is remanded for further proceedings consistent with this opinion.

It is so ordered.

NOTES AND PROBLEMS FOR DISCUSSION

1. How has the Court finally resolved the controversy over the scope and target of the defendant's burden of proof? Is this consistent with its three prior decisions?

2. What does the Court say about the effect of a prima facie case? Is this ruling consistent with the teachings of *Furnco* and *Sweeney*? How does the Court deal with the language employed in those cases? For a discussion of the use of presumptions and inferences in disparate treatment cases see Belton, Burdens of Pleading and Proof In Discrimination Cases: Toward a Theory of Procedural Justice, 34 Vand.L.Rev. 1205 (1981); Mendez, Presumptions of

Discriminatory Motive in Title VII Disparate Treatment Cases, 32 Stanf.L.Rev. 1129 (1980).

3. In International Brotherhood of Teamsters v. United States, 431 U.S. 324, 97 S.Ct. 1843, 52 L.Ed.2d 396 (1977), the Supreme Court noted that in a disparate treatment case, "[p]roof of discriminatory motive is critical * * *." Id., at 335 n. 15, 97 S.Ct. at 1854 n. 15. Does this comport with the *McDonnell Douglas* tripartite proof formula? If so, at which stage does evidence of intent become relevant? The *Teamster* Court's statement suggests that most disparate treatment cases will be disposed of at this stage. But can a plaintiff win without offering evidence of intent?

4. In each of the four preceding opinions, the Court required the defendant to articulate some "legitimate, nondiscriminatory reason". The *Burdine* Court added that this explanation must be "legally sufficient". Does this mean something other than nondiscriminatory? If so, under what standard must the reason be legitimate? Would it be sufficient for a court to conclude that the justification is silly? unethical? violative of some other statute or common law principle? See Curler v. City of Ft. Wayne, 591 F.Supp. 327 (N.D.Ind.1984). What if the employer's articulated defense consists of evidence of its subjective evaluation of the worker's performance in a case involving a refusal to reinstate after layoff or a promotion? Compare Miles v. M.N.C. Corp., 750 F.2d 867 (11th Cir. 1985) (where subjective evaluation was made by a white supervisor in absence of guidelines for evaluating performance and without either written work evaluations or regular checks on employee work habits, court finds situation a "ready mechanism for racial discrimination" and that this justification, without more, did not rebut the prima facie case) with Verniero v. Air Force Academy Sch. Dist. No. 20, 705 F.2d 388 (10th Cir. 1983) (subjective evaluation of applicant's ability to get along with co-workers did rebut the prima facie case).

UNITED STATES POSTAL SERVICE BOARD OF GOVERNORS v. AIKENS

Supreme Court of the United States, 1983.
460 U.S. 711, 103 S.Ct. 1478, 75 L.Ed.2d 403.

JUSTICE REHNQUIST delivered the opinion of the Court.

Respondent Louis Aikens filed suit under Title VII of the Civil Rights Act of 1964, claiming that petitioner, the United States Postal Service, discriminated against him on account of his race. Aikens, who is black, claimed that the Postal Service had discriminatorily refused to promote him to higher positions in the Washington, D.C. Post Office where he had been employed since 1937. After a bench trial, the District Court entered judgment in favor of the Postal Service, but the Court of Appeals reversed. We vacated the Court of Appeals' judgment and remanded for reconsideration in light of Texas Department of Community Affairs v. Burdine.

On remand, the Court of Appeals reaffirmed its earlier holding that the District Court had erred in requiring Aikens to offer direct proof of discriminatory intent. It also held that the District Court erred in requiring Aikens to show, as part of his *prima facie* case, that he was "as qualified or more qualified" than the people who were promoted.

665 F.2d 1057, 1058, 1059 (CADC 1981) (Per Curiam). We granted certiorari.[1]

The Postal Service argues that an employee who has shown only that he was black, that he applied for a promotion for which he possessed the minimum qualifications, and that the employer selected a nonminority applicant has not established a "*prima facie*" case of employment discrimination under Title VII. Aikens argues that he submitted sufficient evidence that the Postal Service discriminated against him to warrant a finding of a *prima facie* case.[2] Because this case was fully tried on the merits, it is surprising to find the parties and the Court of Appeals still addressing the question whether Aikens made out a *prima facie* case. We think that by framing the issue in these terms, they have unnecessarily evaded the ultimate question of discrimination *vel non.*[3]

By establishing a *prima facie* case, the plaintiff in a Title VII action creates a rebuttable "presumption that the employer unlawfully discriminated against" him. Texas Department of Community Affairs v. Burdine, 450 U.S. 248, 254, 101 S.Ct. 1089, 1094, 67 L.Ed.2d 207 (1981). See McDonnell Douglas Corp. v. Green, 411 U.S. 792, 93 S.Ct. 1817, 36 L.Ed.2d 668 (1973). To rebut this presumption, "the defendant must clearly set forth, through the introduction of admissible evidence, the reasons for the plaintiff's rejection." *Burdine,* supra, 450 U.S., at 255, 101 S.Ct., at 1094. In other words, the defendant must "produc[e] evidence that the plaintiff was rejected, or someone else was preferred, for a legitimate, nondiscriminatory reason." Id., at 254, 101 S.Ct., at 1094.

1. We have consistently distinguished disparate treatment cases from cases involving facially neutral employment standards that have disparate impact on minority applicants. See, e.g., Texas Department of Community Affairs v. Burdine, 450 U.S. 248, 252 n. 5, 101 S.Ct. 1089, 1093 n. 5, 67 L.Ed.2d 207 (1981); McDonnell Douglas Corp. v. Green, 411 U.S. 792, 802 n. 14, 93 S.Ct. 1817, 1824 n. 14, 36 L.Ed.2d 668 (1973).

2. Aikens showed that white persons were consistently promoted and detailed over him and all other black persons between 1966 and 1974. Aikens has been rated as "an outstanding supervisor whose management abilities are far above average." App. 8. There was no derogatory or negative information in his Personnel Folder. He had more supervisory seniority and training and development courses than all but one of the white persons who were promoted above him. He has a Masters Degree and has completed three years of residence towards a Ph.D. Aikens had substantially more education than the white employees who were advanced ahead of him; of the 12, only two had any education beyond high school and none had a college degree. He introduced testimony that the person responsible for the promotion decisions at issue had made numerous derogatory comments about blacks in general and Aikens in particular. If the District Court were to find, on the basis of this evidence, that the Postal Service did discriminate against Aikens, we do not believe that this would be reversible error.

3. As in any lawsuit, the plaintiff may prove his case by direct or circumstantial evidence. The trier of fact should consider all the evidence, giving it whatever weight and credence it deserves. Thus, we agree with the Court of Appeals that the District Court should not have required Aikens to submit direct evidence of discriminatory intent. See International Brotherhood of Teamsters v. United States, 431 U.S. 324, 358 n. 44, 97 S.Ct. 1843, 1866 n. 44, 52 L.Ed.2d 396 (1977) ("[T]he *McDonnell Douglas* formula does not require direct proof of discrimination").

But when the defendant fails to persuade the district court to dismiss the action for lack of a *prima facie* case,[4] and responds to the plaintiff's proof by offering evidence of the reason for the plaintiff's rejection, the fact finder must then decide whether the rejection was discriminatory within the meaning of Title VII. At this stage, the *McDonnell-Burdine* presumption "drops from the case," id., at 255, n. 10, 101 S.Ct., at 1095, n. 10, and "the factual inquiry proceeds to a new level of specificity." Id., at 255, 101 S.Ct., at 1095. After Aikens presented his evidence to the District Court in this case, the Postal Service's witnesses testified that he was not promoted because he had turned down several lateral transfers that would have broadened his Postal Service experience. The District Court was then in a position to decide the ultimate factual issue in the case.

The "factual inquiry" in a Title VII case is "whether the defendant intentionally discriminated against the plaintiff." *Burdine,* supra, at 253, 101 S.Ct., at 1093. In other words, is "the employer * * * treating 'some people less favorably than others because of their race, color, religion, sex, or national origin.'" Furnco Construction Corp. v. Waters, 438 U.S. 567, 577, 98 S.Ct. 2943, 2949, 57 L.Ed.2d 957 (1978), quoting Int'l Brotherhood of Teamsters v. United States, 431 U.S. 324, 335, n. 15, 97 S.Ct. 1843, 1854, n. 15, 52 L.Ed.2d 396 (1977). The *prima facie* case method established in *McDonnell Douglas* was "never intended to be rigid, mechanized, or ritualistic. Rather, it is merely a sensible, orderly way to evaluate the evidence in light of common experience as it bears on the critical question of discrimination." *Furnco,* supra, 438 U.S., at 577, 98 S.Ct., at 2949. Where the defendant has done everything that would be required of him if the plaintiff had properly made out a *prima facie* case, whether the plaintiff really did so is no longer relevant. The district court has before it all the evidence it needs to decide whether "the defendant intentionally discriminated against the plaintiff." *Burdine,* supra, 450 U.S., at 253, 101 S.Ct., at 1093.

On the state of the record at the close of the evidence, the District Court in this case should have proceeded to this specific question directly, just as district courts decide disputed questions of fact in other civil litigation.[5] As we stated in *Burdine:*

> "The plaintiff retains the burden of persuasion. [H]e may succeed in this either directly by persuading the court that a discriminatory reason more likely motivated the employer or indirectly by

4. It appears that at one point in the trial the District Court decided that Aikens had made out a *prima facie* case. When Aikens concluded his case in chief, the Postal Service moved to dismiss on the ground that there was no *prima facie* case. The District Court denied this motion.

5. Of course, the plaintiff must have an adequate "opportunity to demonstrate that the proffered reason was not the true reason for the employment decision," but rather a pretext. *Burdine,* supra, at 256, 101 S.Ct., at 1095. There is no suggestion in this case that Aikens did not have such an opportunity.

showing that the employer's proffered explanation is unworthy of credence." 450 U.S., at 256, 101 S.Ct., at 1095.

In short, the district court must decide which party's explanation of the employer's motivation it believes.

All courts have recognized that the question facing triers of fact in discrimination cases is both sensitive and difficult. The prohibitions against discrimination contained in the Civil Rights Act of 1964 reflect an important national policy. There will seldom be "eyewitness" testimony as to the employer's mental processes. But none of this means that trial courts or reviewing courts should treat discrimination differently from other ultimate questions of fact. Nor should they make their inquiry even more difficult by applying legal rules which were devised to govern "the allocation of burdens and order of presentation of proof," *Burdine,* supra, at 252, 101 S.Ct., at 1093, in deciding this ultimate question. The law often obliges finders of fact to inquire into a person's state of mind. As Lord Justice Bowen said in treating this problem in an action for misrepresentation nearly a century ago:

> "The state of a man's mind is as much a fact as the state of his digestion. It is true that it is very difficult to prove what the state of a man's mind at a particular time is, but if it can be ascertained it is as much a fact as anything else." Eddington v. Fitzmaurice, 29 Ch.Div. 459, 483 (1885).

The District Court erroneously thought that respondent was required to submit direct evidence of discriminatory intent, see n. 3, supra, and erroneously focused on the question of *prima facie* case rather than directly on the question of discrimination. Thus we cannot be certain that its findings of fact in favor of the Postal Service were not influenced by its mistaken view of the law. We accordingly vacate the judgment of the Court of Appeals, and remand the case to the District Court so that it may decide on the basis of the evidence before it whether the Postal Service discriminated against Aikens.

It is so ordered.

JUSTICE MARSHALL concurs in the judgment.

JUSTICE BLACKMUN, with whom JUSTICE BRENNAN joins, concurring.

I join the Court's opinion. I write to stress the fact, however, that, as I read its opinion, the Court today reaffirms the framework established by McDonnell Douglas Corp. v. Green, 411 U.S. 792, 93 S.Ct. 1817, 36 L.Ed.2d 668 (1973), for Title VII cases. Under that framework, once a Title VII plaintiff has made out a prima facie case and the defendant-employer has articulated a legitimate, nondiscriminatory reason for the employment decision, the plaintiff bears the burden of demonstrating that the reason is pretextual, that is, it is "not the true reason for the employment decision." Texas Dept. of Community Affairs v. Burdine, 450 U.S. 248, 256, 101 S.Ct. 1089, 1095, 67 L.Ed.2d 207 (1981). As the Court's opinion today implies, ante, at 1481, this burden "merges with the ultimate burden of persuading the court that [the plaintiff] has been the victim of intentional discrimination." 450 U.S., at 256, 101 S.Ct., at 1095.

This ultimate burden may be met in one of two ways. First, as the Court notes, a plaintiff may persuade the court that the employment decision more likely than not was motivated by a discriminatory reason. Ante, at 1481 and 1483. In addition, however, this burden is also carried if the plaintiff shows "that the employer's proffered explanation is unworthy of credence." *Burdine,* 450 U.S., at 256, 101 S.Ct., at 1095, citing *McDonnell Douglas,* 411 U.S., at 804–805, 93 S.Ct., at 1825–26. While the Court is correct that the ultimate determination of factual liability in discrimination cases should be no different from that in other types of civil suits, ante, at 1483, the *McDonnell Douglas* framework requires that a plaintiff prevail when at the third stage of a Title VII trial he demonstrates that the legitimate, nondiscriminatory reason given by the employer is in fact not the true reason for the employment decision.

NOTES AND PROBLEMS FOR DISCUSSION

1. On remand, the trial court found that the plaintiff had not sustained this burden, believing the defendant's nondiscriminatory explanation for the challenged decision. Aikens v. Bolger, 33 FEP Cases 1697 (D.D.C.1984).

2. In his separate concurring opinion, Justice Blackmun indicated that he understood the Court to reaffirm the *Burdine* formula, under which the plaintiff must prevail if it proves that the defendant's proffered reason is in fact not "the true reason" for its challenged decision. But what if the plaintiff convinces the fact finder that the defendant did not actually rely on its proffered reason yet does not offer sufficient evidence of a discriminatory motive beyond the establishment of a prima facie case? Consider CLARK v. HUNTSVILLE CITY BOARD OF EDUCATION, 717 F.2d 525 (11th Cir. 1983), wherein a Black employee challenged the defendant's decision to choose a white non-employee over the plaintiff for the job of director of vocational education for the Huntsville school system. At trial, the plaintiff established a prima facie case of discrimination and the defendant sought to rebut the resulting presumption through the introduction of evidence that it had selected the non-employee because of his superior qualifications. To demonstrate pretext, the plaintiff pointed to school board policies providing that vacancies would be filled by hiring qualified individuals from the outside only if the vacancies could not be filled by the promotion or transfer of incumbent employees and that qualified "insiders" would be given first consideration for promotions. The trial court construed these policies to prefer minimally qualified current employees over "outsiders" for promotion regardless of the relative qualifications of the insider and the outsider. It then held that the employer's reliance on the outsider's superior qualifications in the face of a policy to prefer minimally qualified insiders to all outsiders irrespective of the outsiders' superior qualifications rendered its articulated justification a pretext. The appellate court reversed, ruling that the trial court had misinterpreted the pretext component of the *Burdine* formula.

> "The lower court's misapprehension of the requirements for pretext melds with its confusion over the mental state that a Title VII disparate treatment defendant must have. Under *Burdine,* plaintiff must prove

'intentional discrimination' to prevail. * * * The issue of the proper intent standard and that of pretext overlap because plaintiff's burden of showing pretext 'merges' with the ultimate burden of demonstrating unlawful discrimination. Only when defendants' articulated reason is pretext 'for accomplishing a racially discriminatory purpose' will the plaintiff recover. The court thus may not circumvent the intent requirement of the plaintiff's ultimate burden of persuasion by couching its conclusion in terms of pretext; a simple finding that the defendant did not truly rely on its proffered reason, without a further finding that the defendant relied instead on race will not suffice to establish Title VII liability.[5]"

717 F.2d at 529. The Court of Appeals remanded for new findings on whether the defendants' articulated reason was their actual reason or whether the plaintiff was rejected because of his race. For the plaintiff to prevail, the court stated, he must convince the trial court that the defendants acted not in reliance on the successful applicant's greater qualifications but with a racially discriminatory motive. Is this consistent with *Burdine* and/or *Aikens?* Is the court requiring the plaintiff to offer additional evidence or simply asking the trial court to make more detailed findings of fact? If a plaintiff does nothing more than satisfy the requirements of the prima facie case and convince the fact finder that the defendant's sole articulated non-discriminatory reason is not credible, is it entitled to judgment? Is this where the *Aikens* Court's statement that the presumption "drops from the case" becomes significant? In King v. Palmer, 778 F.2d 878 (D.C.Cir. 1985), the D.C. Circuit held that the trial court had erroneously entered judgment in favor of the defendants where the plaintiff had established a prima facie case and had discredited the defendant's purported explanation. It ordered the lower court to enter judgment in favor of the plaintiff. See also Monroe v. Burlington Industries, 784 F.2d 568, 572 (4th Cir. 1986) (plaintiff established pretext by discrediting defendant's explanation).

3. In Bibbs v. Block, 749 F.2d 508 (8th Cir. 1984), the appellate court reversed the trial court's ruling that a plaintiff who had shown that race was a "discernible" factor in the challenged decision also was required to prove that the same decision would not have been reached if race had been disregarded. The court said that in mixed motivation cases, it was sufficient for the plaintiff to prove that race was a "discernible" factor and that it was irrelevant whether race was a major or minor factor. It rejected the adoption of the "same decision" standard articulated by the Supreme Court in Mt. Healthy City School District Board of Education v. Doyle, 429 U.S. 274, 97 S.Ct. 568, 50 L.Ed. 2d 471 (1977). In *Mt. Healthy,* the Court stated that a plaintiff asserting a constitutional cause of action was required to prove that the challenged decision would not have been made absent considerations of race. The court in *Bibbs* stated that this constitutional standard was inapplicable to cases involving statutory claims. It contended that the *Burdine* formula was satisfied by proof that race was a "but for" or "more likely than not" cause of the challenged decision and that this standard was satisfied by proving that race was a "discernible" factor without evidence that it was a "determining" or "substantial" factor. Do you agree that race can be a "but for" cause without also satisfying the rejected "same decision"/"determining factor" test?

5. * * * We state merely that the plaintiff must in fact persuade the court that the defendant acted with a discriminatory purpose.

On rehearing en banc, the circuit court modified its analysis. It stated that in mixed motivation cases it was appropriate to separate the issues of liability and remedy. Title VII, the court reasoned, precludes the use of race as a factor in the decisionmaking process. Accordingly, where the plaintiff establishes that race was such a "discernible" factor, the employer should be found liable under Title VII. It added, however, that where the plaintiff cannot establish but-for causation, i.e., where the court finds that the plaintiff would not have been selected even if race has been disregarded, awarding affirmative relief such as promotion or hiring would provide the plaintiff with a windfall. Accordingly, it ruled that in such a case, as here, the plaintiff was entitled only to declaratory and injunctive relief and should be considered a prevailing party for the purpose of an award of attorney's fees. 778 F.2d 1318 (8th Cir. 1985). See infra, at 184.

In *McDonnell Douglas,* the Supreme Court noted that the facts will vary in Title VII cases and that the four part test for establishing a prima facie case "is not necessarily applicable in every respect to differing factual situations." It reiterated this message in *Furnco,* where it stated that the four part standard was not intended to be "rigid, mechanized or ritualistic." This language reflects the Court's recognition that disparate treatment analysis can apply, in modified form, to other than the garden variety discharge or refusal to hire/promote case. For example, consider the following.

MERITOR SAVINGS BANK, FSB v. VINSON

Supreme Court of the United States, 1986.
___ U.S. ___, 106 S.Ct. 2399, 91 L.Ed.2d 49.

JUSTICE REHNQUIST delivered the opinion of the Court.

This case presents important questions concerning claims of workplace "sexual harassment" brought under Title VII of the Civil Rights Act of 1964.

I

In 1974, respondent Mechelle Vinson met Sidney Taylor, a vice president of what is now petitioner Meritor Savings Bank (the bank) and manager of one of its branch offices. When respondent asked whether she might obtain employment at the bank, Taylor gave her an application, which she completed and returned the next day; later that same day Taylor called her to say that she had been hired. With Taylor as her supervisor, respondent started as a teller-trainee, and thereafter was promoted to teller, head teller, and assistant branch manager. She worked at the same branch for four years, and it is undisputed that her advancement there was based on merit alone. In September 1978, respondent notified Taylor that she was taking sick leave for an indefinite period. On November 1, 1978, the bank discharged her for excessive use of that leave.

Respondent brought this action against Taylor and the bank, claiming that during her four years at the bank she had "constantly been subjected to sexual harassment" by Taylor in violation of Title VII.

She sought injunctive relief, compensatory and punitive damages against Taylor and the bank, and attorney's fees.

At the 11-day bench trial, the parties presented conflicting testimony about Taylor's behavior during respondent's employment.* Respondent testified that during her probationary period as a teller-trainee, Taylor treated her in a fatherly way and made no sexual advances. Shortly thereafter, however, he invited her out to dinner and, during the course of the meal, suggested that they go to a motel to have sexual relations. At first she refused, but out of what she described as fear of losing her job she eventually agreed. According to respondent, Taylor thereafter made repeated demands upon her for sexual favors, usually at the branch, both during and after business hours; she estimated that over the next several years she had intercourse with him some 40 or 50 times. In addition, respondent testified that Taylor fondled her in front of other employees, followed her into the women's restroom when she went there alone, exposed himself to her, and even forcibly raped her on several occasions. These activities ceased after 1977, respondent stated, when she started going with a steady boyfriend.

Respondent also testified that Taylor touched and fondled other women employees of the bank, and she attempted to call witnesses to support this charge. But while some supporting testimony apparently was admitted without objection, the District Court did not allow her "to present wholesale evidence of a pattern and practice relating to sexual advances to other female employees in her case in chief, but advised her that she might well be able to present such evidence in rebuttal to the defendants' cases." Vinson v. Taylor, 23 FEP Cases 37, 38–39, n. 1 (D DC 1980). Respondent did not offer such evidence in rebuttal. Finally, respondent testified that because she was afraid of Taylor she never reported his harassment to any of his supervisors and never attempted to use the bank's complaint procedure.

Taylor denied respondent's allegations of sexual activity, testifying that he never fondled her, never made suggestive remarks to her, never engaged in sexual intercourse with her and never asked her to do so. He contended instead that respondent made her accusations in response to a business-related dispute. The bank also denied respondent's allegations and asserted that any sexual harassment by Taylor was unknown to the bank and engaged in without its consent or approval.

The District Court denied relief, but did not resolve the conflicting testimony about the existence of a sexual relationship between respondent and Taylor. It found instead that

> "If [respondent] and Taylor did engage in an intimate or sexual relationship during the time of [respondent's] employment with [the bank], that relationship was a voluntary one having nothing to do

* Like the Court of Appeals, this Court was not provided a complete transcript of the trial. We therefore rely largely on the District Court's opinion for the summary of the relevant testimony.

with her continued employment at [the bank] or her advancement or promotions at that institution."

The court ultimately found that respondent "was not the victim of sexual harassment and was not the victim of sexual discrimination" while employed at the bank.

Although it concluded that respondent had not proved a violation of Title VII, the District Court nevertheless went on to address the bank's liability. After noting the bank's express policy against discrimination, and finding that neither respondent nor any other employee had ever lodged a complaint about sexual harassment by Taylor, the court ultimately concluded that "the bank was without notice and cannot be held liable for the alleged actions of Taylor."

The Court of Appeals for the District of Columbia Circuit reversed. 753 F.2d 141 (1985). Relying on its earlier holding in Bundy v. Jackson, 641 F.2d 934 (1981), decided after the trial in this case, the court stated that a violation of Title VII may be predicated on either of two types of sexual harassment: harassment that involves the conditioning of concrete employment benefits on sexual favors, and harassment that, while not affecting economic benefits, creates a hostile or offensive working environment. The court drew additional support for this position from the Equal Employment Opportunity Commission's Guidelines on Discrimination Because of Sex, 29 CFR § 1604.11(a) (1985), which set out these two types of sexual harassment claims. Believing that "Vinson's grievance was clearly of the [hostile environment] type," and that the District Court had not considered whether a violation of this type had occurred, the court concluded that a remand was necessary.

The court further concluded that the District Court's finding that any sexual relationship between respondent and Taylor "was a voluntary one" did not obviate the need for a remand. "[U]ncertain as to precisely what the [district] court meant" by this finding, the Court of Appeals held that if the evidence otherwise showed that "Taylor made Vinson's toleration of sexual harassment a condition of her employment," her voluntariness "had no materiality whatsoever." The court then surmised that the District Court's finding of voluntariness might have been based on "the voluminous testimony regarding respondent's dress and personal fantasies," testimony that the Court of Appeals believed "had no place in this litigation."

As to the bank's liability, the Court of Appeals held that an employer is absolutely liable for sexual harassment practiced by supervisory personnel, whether or not the employer knew or should have known about the misconduct. The court relied chiefly on Title VII's definition of "employer" to include "any agent of such a person," 42 U.S.C. § 2000e(b), as well as on the EEOC guidelines. The court held that a supervisor is an "agent" of his employer for Title VII purposes, even if he lacks authority to hire, fire, or promote, since "the mere existence—or even the appearance—of a significant degree of influence in vital job decisions gives any supervisor the opportunity to impose on employees."

In accordance with the foregoing, the Court of Appeals reversed the judgment of the District Court and remanded the case for further proceedings. A subsequent suggestion for rehearing en banc was denied, with three judges dissenting. We granted certiorari, and now affirm but for different reasons.

II

Title VII of the Civil Rights Act of 1964 makes it "an unlawful employment practice for an employer * * * to discriminate against any individual with respect to his compensation, terms, conditions, or privileges of employment, because of such individual's race, color, religion, sex, or national origin." 42 U.S.C. § 2000e–2(a)(1). The prohibition against discrimination based on sex was added to Title VII at the last minute on the floor of the House of Representatives. 110 Cong.Rec. 2577–2584 (1964). The principal argument in opposition to the amendment was that "sex discrimination" was sufficiently different from other types of discrimination that it ought to receive separate legislative treatment. See id., at 2577 (Statement of Rep. Celler quoting letter from United States Department of Labor); id., at 2584 (statement of Rep. Green). This argument was defeated, the bill quickly passed as amended, and we are left with little legislative history to guide us in interpreting the Act's prohibition against discrimination based on "sex."

Respondent argues, and the Court of Appeals held, that unwelcome sexual advances that create an offensive or hostile working environment violate Title VII. Without question, when a supervisor sexually harasses a subordinate because of the subordinate's sex, that supervisor "discriminate[s]" on the basis of sex. Petitioner apparently does not challenge this proposition. It contends instead that in prohibiting discrimination with respect to "compensation, terms, conditions, or privileges" of employment, Congress was concerned with what petitioner describes as "tangible loss" of "an economic character," not "purely psychological aspects of the workplace environment." Brief for Petitioner 30–31, 34. In support of this claim petitioner observes that in both the legislative history of Title VII and this Court's Title VII decisions, the focus has been on tangible, economic barriers erected by discrimination.

We reject petitioner's view. First, the language of Title VII is not limited to "economic" or "tangible" discrimination. The phrase "terms, conditions, or privileges of employment" evinces a congressional intent " 'to strike at the entire spectrum of disparate treatment of men and women' " in employment. Los Angeles Department of Water and Power v. Manhart, 435 U.S. 702, 707, n. 13, 98 S.Ct. 1370, 1375, n. 13, 55 L.Ed.2d 657 (1978), quoting Sprogis v. United Air Lines, Inc., 444 F.2d 1194, 1198 (CA7 1971). Petitioner has pointed to nothing in the Act to suggest that Congress contemplated the limitation urged here.

Second, in 1980 the EEOC issued guidelines specifying that "sexual harassment," as there defined, is a form of sex discrimination prohibited by Title VII. As an "administrative interpretation of the Act by the enforcing agency," Griggs v. Duke Power Co., 401 U.S. 424, 433–434, 91 S.Ct. 849, 855, 28 L.Ed.2d 158 (1971), these guidelines, " 'while not controlling upon the courts by reason of their authority, do constitute a body of experience and informed judgment to which courts and litigants may properly resort for guidance,' " General Electric Co. v. Gilbert, 429 U.S. 125, 141–142, 97 S.Ct. 401, 410–11, 50 L.Ed.2d 343 (1976), quoting Skidmore v. Swift & Co., 323 U.S. 134, 140, 65 S.Ct. 161, 164, 89 L.Ed. 124 (1944). The EEOC guidelines fully support the view that harassment leading to noneconomic injury can violate Title VII.

In defining "sexual harassment," the guidelines first decribe the kinds of workplace conduct that may be actionable under Title VII. These include "[u]nwelcome sexual advances, requests for sexual favors, and other verbal or physical conduct of a sexual nature." 29 CFR § 1604.11(a) (1985). Relevant to the charges at issue in this case, the guidelines provide that such sexual misconduct constitutes prohibited "sexual harassment," whether or not it is directly linked to the grant or denial of an economic *quid pro quo,* where "such conduct has the purpose or effect of unreasonably interfering with an individual's work performance or creating an intimidating, hostile, or offensive working environment." § 1604.11(a)(3).

In concluding that so-called "hostile environment" (i.e., non *quid pro quo*) harassment violates Title VII, the EEOC drew upon a substantial body of judicial decisions and EEOC precedent holding that Title VII affords employees the right to work in an environment free from discriminatory intimidation, ridicule, and insult. See generally 45 Fed.Reg. 74676 (1980). Rogers v. EEOC, 454 F.2d 234 (CA5 1971), cert. denied, 406 U.S. 957, 92 S.Ct. 2058, 32 L.Ed.2d 343 (1972), was apparently the first case to recognize a cause of action based upon a discriminatory work environment. In *Rogers,* the Court of Appeals for the Fifth Circuit held that a Hispanic complainant could establish a Title VII violation by demonstrating that her employer created an offensive work environment for employees by giving discriminatory service to its Hispanic clientele. The court explained that an employee's protections under Title VII extend beyond the economic aspects of employment:

> "[T]he phrase 'terms, conditions or privileges of employment' in [Title VII] is an expansive concept which sweeps within its protective ambit the practice of creating a working environment heavily charged with ethnic or racial discrimination * * *. One can readily envision working environments so heavily polluted with discrimination as to destroy completely the emotional and psychological stability of minority group workers * * *." 454 F.2d, at 238.

Courts applied this principle to harassment based on race, e.g., Firefighters Institute for Racial Equality v. St. Louis, 549 F.2d 506,

514–515 (CA8), cert. denied sub nom. Banta v. United States, 178 U.S.App.D.C. 91, 98, 434 U.S. 819, 98 S.Ct. 60, 54 L.Ed.2d 76 (1977); Gray v. Greyhound Lines, East, 178 U.S.App.D.C. 91, 98, 545 F.2d 169, 176 (1976), religion, e.g., Compston v. Borden, Inc., 424 F.Supp. 157 (SD Ohio 1976), and national origin, e.g., Cariddi v. Kansas City Chiefs Football Club, 568 F.2d 87, 88 (CA8 1977). Nothing in Title VII suggests that a hostile environment based on discriminatory *sexual* harassment should not be likewise prohibited. The guidelines thus appropriately drew from, and were fully consistent with, the existing caselaw.

Since the guidelines were issued, courts have uniformly held, and we agree, that a plaintiff may establish a violation of Title VII by proving that discrimination based on sex has created a hostile or abusive work environment. As the Court of Appeals for the Eleventh Circuit wrote in Henson v. Dundee, 682 F.2d 897, 902 (1982):

> "Sexual harassment which creates a hostile or offensive environment for members of one sex is every bit the arbitrary barrier to sexual equality at the workplace that racial harassment is to racial equality. Surely, a requirement that a man or woman run a gauntlet of sexual abuse in return for the privilege of being allowed to work and make a living can be as demeaning and disconcerting as the harshest of racial epithets."

Accord, Katz v. Dole, 709 F.2d 251, 254–255 (CA4 1983); Bundy v. Jackson, 205 U.S.App.D.C. 444, 641 F.2d, at 934–944 (1981); Zabkowicz v. West Bend Co., 589 F.Supp. 780 (ED Wisc.1984).

Of course, as the courts in both *Rogers* and *Henson* recognized, not all workplace conduct that may be described as "harassment" affects a "term, condition, or privilege" of employment within the meaning of Title VII. See Rogers v. EEOC, supra, at 238 ("mere utterance of an ethnic or racial epithet which engenders offensive feelings in an employee" would not affect the conditions of employment to sufficiently significant degree to violate Title VII); *Henson,* supra, at 904 (quoting same). For sexual harassment to be actionable, it must be sufficiently severe or pervasive "to alter the conditions of [the victim's] employment and create an abusive working environment." Ibid. Respondent's allegations in this case—which include not only pervasive harassment but also criminal conduct of the most serious nature—are plainly sufficient to state a claim for "hostile environment" sexual harassment.

The question remains, however, whether the District Court's ultimate finding that respondent "was not the victim of sexual harassment," effectively disposed of respondent's claim. The Court of Appeals recognized, we think correctly, that this ultimate finding was likely based on one or both of two erroneous views of the law. First, the District Court apparently believed that a claim for sexual harassment will not lie absent an *economic* effect on the complainant's employment. See ibid. ("It is without question that sexual harassment of female employees in which they are asked or required to submit to sexual demands as a *condition to obtain employment or to maintain employment or to obtain promotions* falls within protection of Title VII.") (emphasis added). Since it appears that the District Court made its findings without ever considering the "hostile environment" theory of sexual harassment, the Court of Appeals' decision to remand was correct.

Second, the District Court's conclusion that no actionable harassment occurred might have rested on its earlier "finding" that "[i]f [respondent] and Taylor did engage in an intimate or sexual relationship * * *, that relationship was a voluntary one." But the fact that sex-related conduct was "voluntary," in the sense that the complainant was not forced to participate against her will, is not a defense to a sexual harassment suit brought under Title VII. The gravamen of any sexual harassment claim is that the alleged sexual advances were "unwelcome." 29 CFR § 1604.11(a) (1985). While the question whether particular conduct was indeed unwelcome presents difficult problems of proof and turns largely on credibility determinations committed to the trier of fact, the District Court in this case erroneously focused on the "voluntariness" of respondent's participation in the claimed sexual episodes. The correct inquiry is whether respondent by her conduct indicated that the alleged sexual advances were unwelcome, not whether her actual participation in sexual intercourse was voluntary.

Petitioner contends that even if this case must be remanded to the District Court, the Court of Appeals erred in one of the terms of its remand. Specifically, the Court of Appeals stated that testimony about respondent's "dress and personal fantasies," which the District Court apparently admitted into evidence, "had no place in this litigation." Ibid. The apparent ground for this conclusion was that respondent's voluntariness *vel non* in submitting to Taylor's advances was immaterial to her sexual harassment claim. While "voluntariness" in the sense of consent is not a defense to such a claim, it does not follow that a complainant's sexually provocative speech or dress is irrelevant as a matter of law in determining whether he or she found particular sexual advances unwelcome. To the contrary, such evidence is obviously relevant. The EEOC guidelines emphasize that the trier of fact must determine the existence of sexual harassment in light of "the record as a whole" and "the totality of circumstances, such as the nature of the sexual advances and the context in which the alleged incidents occurred." 29 CFR § 1604.11(b) (1985). Respondent's claim that any marginal relevance of the evidence in question was outweighed by the potential for unfair prejudice is the sort of argument properly addressed to the District Court. In this case the District Court concluded that the evidence should be admitted, and the Court of Appeals' contrary conclusion was based upon the erroneous, categorical view that testimony about provocative dress and publicly expressed sexual fantasies "had no place in this litigation." While the District Court must carefully weigh the applicable considerations in deciding whether to admit evidence of this kind, there is no *per se* rule against its admissibility.

III

Although the District Court concluded that respondent had not proved a violation of Title VII, it nevertheless went on to consider the question of the bank's liability. Finding that "the bank was without notice" of Taylor's alleged conduct, and that notice to Taylor was not the equivalent of notice to the bank, the court concluded that the bank therefore could not be held liable for Taylor's alleged actions. The Court of Appeals took the opposite view, holding that an employer is strictly liable for a hostile environment created by a supervisor's sexual advances, even though the employer neither knew nor reasonably could have known of the alleged misconduct. The court held that a supervisor, whether or not he possesses the authority to hire, fire, or promote, is necessarily an "agent" of his employer for all Title VII purposes, since "even the appearance" of such authority may enable him to impose himself on his subordinates.

The parties and *amici* suggest several different standards for employer liability. Respondent, not surprisingly, defends the position of the Court of Appeals. Noting that Title VII's definition of "employer" includes any "agent" of the employer, she also argues that "so long as the circumstance is work-related, the supervisor is the employer and the employer is the supervisor." Brief for Respondent 27. Notice to Taylor that the advances were unwelcome, therefore, was notice to the bank.

Petitioner argues that respondent's failure to use its established grievance procedure, or to otherwise put it on notice of the alleged misconduct, insulates petitioner from liability for Taylor's wrongdoing. A contrary rule would be unfair, petitioner argues, since in a hostile environment harassment case the employer often will have no reason to know about, or opportunity to cure, the alleged wrongdoing.

The EEOC, in its brief as *amicus curiae,* contends that courts formulating employer liability rules should draw from traditional agency principles. Examination of those principles has led the EEOC to the view that where a supervisor exercises the authority actually delegated to him by his employer, by making or threatening to make decisions affecting the employment status of his subordinates, such actions are properly imputed to the employer whose delegation of authority empowered the supervisor to undertake them. Thus, the courts have consistently held employers liable for the discriminatory discharges of employees by supervisory personnel, whether or not the employer knew, should have known, or approved of the supervisor's actions. E.g., Anderson v. Methodist Evangelical Hospital, Inc., 464 F.2d 723, 725 (CA6 1972).

The EEOC suggests that when a sexual harassment claim rests exclusively on a "hostile environment" theory, however, the usual basis for a finding of agency will often disappear. In that case, the EEOC believes, agency principles lead to

> "a rule that asks whether a victim of sexual harassment had reasonably available an avenue of complaint regarding such harassment, and, if available and utilized, whether that procedure was reasonably responsive to the employee's complaint. If the employer has an expressed policy against sexual harassment and has implemented a procedure specifically designed to resolve sexual harassment claims, and if the victim does not take advantage of that procedure, the employer should be shielded from liability absent actual knowledge of the sexually hostile environment (obtained, e.g., by the filing of a charge with the EEOC or a comparable state agency). In all other cases, the employer will be liable if it has actual knowledge of the harassment or if, considering all the facts of the case, the victim in question had no reasonably available avenue for making his or her complaint known to appropriate management officials." Brief for United States and Equal Opportunity Employment Commission as *Amici Curiae,* 26.

As respondent points out, this suggested rule is in some tension with the EEOC guidelines, which hold an employer liable for the acts of its agents without regard to notice. 29 CFR § 1604.11(c) (1985). The guidelines do require, however, an "examin[ation of] the circumstances of the particular employment relationship and the job [f]unctions performed by the individual in determining whether an individual acts in either a supervisory or agency capacity." Ibid.

This debate over the appropriate standard for employer liability has a rather abstract quality about it given the state of the record in this case. We do not know at this stage whether Taylor made any sexual advances toward respondent at all, let alone whether those advances were unwelcome, whether they were sufficiently pervasive to constitute a condition of employment, or whether they were "so pervasive and so long continuing * * * that the employer must have become conscious of [them]," Taylor v. Jones, 653 F.2d 1193, 1197–1199 (CA8 1981) (holding employer liable for racially hostile working environment based on constructive knowledge).

We therefore decline the parties' invitation to issue a definitive rule on employer liability, but we do agree with the EEOC that Congress wanted courts to look to agency principles for guidance in this area. While such common-law principles may not be transferable in all their particulars to Title VII, Congress' decision to define "employer" to include any "agent" of an employer, 42 U.S.C. § 2000e(b), surely evinces an intent to place some limits on the acts of employees for which employers under Title VII are to be held responsible. For this reason, we hold that the Court of Appeals erred in concluding that employers are always automatically liable for sexual harassment by their supervisors. See generally Restatement (Second) of Agency §§ 219–237 (1958).

For the same reason, absence of notice to an employer does not necessarily insulate that employer from liability. Ibid.

Finally, we reject petitioner's view that the mere existence of a grievance procedure and a policy against discrimination, coupled with respondent's failure to invoke that procedure, must insulate petitioner from liability. While those facts are plainly relevant, the situation before us demonstrates why they are not necessarily dispositive. Petitioner's general nondiscrimination policy did not address sexual harassment in particular, and thus did not alert employees to their employer's interest in correcting that form of discrimination. App. 25. Moreover, the bank's grievance procedure apparently required an employee to complain first to her supervisor, in this case Taylor. Since Taylor was the alleged perpetrator, it is not altogether surprising that respondent failed to invoke the procedure and report her grievance to him. Petitioner's contention that respondent's failure should insulate it from liability might be substantially stronger if its procedures were better calculated to encourage victims of harassment to come forward.

IV

In sum, we hold that a claim of "hostile environment" sex discrimination is actionable under Title VII, that the District Court's findings were insufficient to dispose of respondent's hostile environment claim, and that the District Court did not err in admitting testimony about respondent's sexually provocative speech and dress. As to employer liability, we conclude that the Court of Appeals was wrong to entirely disregard agency principles and impose absolute liability on employers for the acts of their supervisors, regardless of the circumstances of a particular case.

Accordingly, the judgment of the Court of Appeals reversing the judgment of the District Court is affirmed, and the case is remanded for further proceedings consistent with this opinion.

It is so ordered.

JUSTICE MARSHALL, with whom JUSTICE BRENNAN, JUSTICE BLACKMUN, and JUSTICE STEVENS join, concurring in the judgment.

I fully agree with the Court's conclusion that workplace sexual harassment is illegal, and violates Title VII. Part III of the Court's opinion, however, leaves open the circumstances in which an employer is responsible under Title VII for such conduct. Because I believe that question to be properly before us, I write separately.

The issue the Court declines to resolve is addressed in the EEOC Guidelines on Discrimination Because of Sex, which are entitled to great deference. See Griggs v. Duke Power Co., 401 U.S. 424, 433–434, 91 S.Ct. 849, 854–55, 28 L.Ed.2d 158 (1971) (EEOC Guidelines on Employment Testing Procedures of 1966). The Guidelines explain:

> "Applying general Title VII principles, an employer * * * is responsible for its acts and those of its agents and supervisory

employees with respect to sexual harassment regardless of whether the specific acts complained of were authorized or even forbidden by the employer and regardless of whether the employer knew or should have known of their occurrence. The Commission will examine the circumstances of the particular employment relationship and the job functions performed by the individual in determining whether an individual acts in either a supervisory or agency capacity.

"With respect to conduct between fellow employees, an employer is responsible for acts of sexual harassment in the workplace where the employer (or its agents or supervisory employees) knows or should have known of the conduct, unless it can show that it took immediate and appropriate corrective action." 29 CFR §§ 1604.11(c), (d) (1985).

The Commission, in issuing the Guidelines, explained that its rule was "in keeping with the general standard of employer liability with respect to agents and supervisory employees * * * [T]he Commission and the courts have held for years that an employer is liable if a supervisor or an agent violates the Title VII, regardless of knowledge or any other mitigating factor." 45 Fed.Reg. 74676 (1980). I would adopt the standard set out by the Commission.

An employer can act only through individual supervisors and employees; discrimination is rarely carried out pursuant to a formal vote of a corporation's board of directors. Although an employer may sometimes adopt company-wide discriminatory policies violative of Title VII, acts that may constitute Title VII violations are generally effected through the actions of individuals, and often an individual may take such a step even in defiance of company policy. Nonetheless, Title VII remedies, such as reinstatement and backpay, generally run against the employer as an entity. The question thus arises as to the circumstances under which an employer will be held liable under Title VII for the acts of its employees.

The answer supplied by general Title VII law, like that supplied by federal labor law, is that the act of a supervisory employee or agent is imputed to the employer. Thus, for example, when a supervisor discriminatorily fires or refuses to promote a black employee, that act is, without more, considered the act of the employer. The courts do not stop to consider whether the employer otherwise had "notice" of the action, or even whether the supervisor had actual authority to act as he did. E.g., Flowers v. Crouch-Walker Corp., 552 F.2d 1277, 1282 (CA7 1977); Young v. Southwestern Savings and Loan Assn., 509 F.2d 140 (CA5 1975); Anderson v. Methodist Evangelical Hospital, Inc., 464 F.2d 723 (CA6 1972). Following that approach, every Court of Appeals that has considered the issue has held that sexual harassment by supervisory personnel is automatically imputed to the employer when the harassment results in tangible job detriment to the subordinate employee. See Horn v. Duke Homes, Inc., Div. of Windsor Mobile Homes, 755

F.2d 599, 604–606 (CA7 1985); Vinson v. Taylor, 243 U.S.App.D.C. 323, 329–334, 753 F.2d 141, 147–152 (1985); Craig v. Y & Y Snacks, Inc., 721 F.2d 77, 80–81 (CA3 1983); Katz v. Dole, 709 F.2d 251, 255, n. 6 (CA4 1983); Henson v. City of Dundee, 682 F.2d 897, 910 (CA11 1982); Miller v. Bank of America, 600 F.2d 211, 213 (CA9 1979).

The brief filed by the Solicitor General on behalf of the EEOC in this case suggests that a different rule should apply when a supervisor's harassment "merely" results in a discriminatory work environment. The Solicitor General concedes that sexual harassment that affects tangible job benefits is an exercise of authority delegated to the supervisor by the employer, and thus gives rise to employer liability. But, departing from the EEOC Guidelines, he argues that the case of a supervisor merely creating a discriminatory work environment is different because the supervisor "is not exercising, or threatening to exercise, actual or apparent authority to make personnel decisions affecting the victim." Brief for United States and EEOC as *Amicus Curiae* 24. In the latter situation, he concludes, some further notice requirement should therefore be necessary.

The Solicitor General's position is untenable. A supervisor's responsibilities do not begin and end with the power to hire, fire, and discipline employees, or with the power to recommend such actions. Rather, a supervisor is charged with the day-to-day supervision of the work environment and with ensuring a safe, productive, workplace. There is no reason why abuse of the latter authority should have different consequences than abuse of the former. In both cases it is the authority vested in the supervisor by the employer that enables him to commit the wrong: it is precisely because the supervisor is understood to be clothed with the employer's authority that he is able to impose unwelcome sexual conduct on subordinates. There is therefore no justification for a special rule, to be applied *only* in "hostile environment" cases, that sexual harassment does not create employer liability until the employee suffering the discrimination notifies other supervisors. No such requirement appears in the statute, and no such requirement can coherently be drawn from the law of agency.

Agency principles and the goals of Title VII law make appropriate some limitation on the liability of employers for the acts of supervisors. Where, for example, a supervisor has no authority over an employee, because the two work in wholly different parts of the employer's business, it may be improper to find strict employer liability. See 29 CFR § 1604.11(c) (1985). Those considerations, however, do not justify the creation of a special "notice" rule in hostile environment cases.

Further, nothing would be gained by crafting such a rule. In the "pure" hostile environment case, where an employee files an EEOC complaint alleging sexual harassment in the workplace, the employee seeks not money damages but injunctive relief. See Bundy v. Jackson, 205 U.S.App.D.C. 444, 446, 641 F.2d 934, 936, n. 12 (1981). Under Title VII, the EEOC must notify an employer of charges made against it within 10 days after receipt of the complaint. 42 U.S.C. § 2000e–5(b). If the charges appear to be based on "reasonable cause," the EEOC must attempt to eliminate the offending practice through "informal methods of conference, conciliation, and persuasion." Ibid. An employer whose internal procedures assertedly would have redressed the discrimination can avoid injunctive relief by employing these procedures after receiving notice of the complaint or during the conciliation period. Where a complainant, on the other hand, seeks backpay on the theory that a hostile work environment effected a constructive termination, the existence of an internal complaint procedure may be a factor in determining not the employer's liability but the remedies available against it. Where a complainant without good reason bypassed an internal complaint procedure she knew to be effective, a court may be reluctant to find constructive termination and thus to award reinstatement or backpay.

I therefore reject the Solicitor General's position. I would apply in this case the same rules we apply in all other Title VII cases, and hold that sexual harassment by a supervisor of an employee under his supervision, leading to a discriminatory work environment, should be imputed to the employer for Title VII purposes regardless of whether the employee gave "notice" of the offense.

NOTES AND PROBLEMS FOR DISCUSSION

1. As the Court noted in *Meritor*, the notion that Title VII affords employees protection against a threatening or coercive work environment originated in the context of racial and ethnic epithets. See Rogers v. EEOC, 454 F.2d 234 (5th Cir. 1971), cert. denied, 406 U.S. 957, 92 S.Ct. 2058, 32 L.Ed.2d 343 (1972); Cariddi v. Kansas City Chiefs Football Club, 568 F.2d 89 (8th Cir. 1977). The opinion in *Meritor* also reflects the recognition that sexual harassment, in both its *quid pro quo* and hostile work environment forms, constitutes an actionable form of sex discrimination. Consequently, most of the decisions now turn on the resolution of two subsidiary issues: (a) the level of severity and frequency of conduct needed to cross the line from acceptable banter to offensive harassment, and (b) respondeat superior.

(a) The *Meritor* Court, in adopting the position enunciated in the EEOC Guidelines, indicated that in a hostile environment case, as opposed to a *quid pro quo* case, the harassment must be sufficiently severe and persistent as to affect the average employee's work performance or create an "intimidating, hostile, or offensive working environment." This standard, however, may be easier to articulate than to apply. See e.g., Sand v. Johnson, 33 FEP Cases 716 (E.D.Mich.1982) (distinguishing between explicit sexual conduct and flirtatious conduct); Robinson v. du Pont Co., 33 FEP Cases 880 (D.Del.1979) (numerous sexual innuendos held to have been "irrationally misconstrued" by the plaintiff); Downes v. F.A.A., 775 F.2d 288 (Fed.Cir. 1985) (requiring a persistent pattern of offensive conduct but then ruling that evidence of five instances of such behavior during a three year period did not establish a pattern of harassment); Moffett v. Gene B. Blick Co., Inc., 621 F.Supp. 244, 269–270 (N.D.Ind.1985) ("Regular, almost daily exposure to terms such as 'stupid cunt', 'whore', 'bitch' and 'nigger lover' over the course of six to seven months, is, by any definition, a concerted pattern of continuous harassment which pollutes a working environment."). Yet, does sexual harassment have to take the form of a sexual advance or be undertaken for the purpose of obtaining sexual favors? See McKinney v. Dole, 765 F.2d 1129 (D.C.Cir. 1985) (any harassment, such as a pattern of threatened or actual use of physical force, regardless of whether it is taken with or without sexual overtones, constitutes prohibited sexual harassment if it would not occur but for the sex of the employee victim).

(b) Since Title VII only provides a cause of action against the "employer", it is essential to examine the issue of employer vicarious responsibility for the actions of its employees. As the Court indicated in *Meritor*, the extent of employer liability traditionally has turned on two factors: (1) whether the challenged conduct was undertaken by a supervisor or co-employee, and (2) whether the plaintiff is alleging *quid pro quo* or hostile environment harassment.

While it rejected the position taken by the EEOC and the D.C. Circuit that employers should be automatically liable for all forms of supervisory harassment, the Supreme Court did not adopt either of the two other standards that have been offered by the lower courts. Several circuits impose strict liability only when the supervisory conduct involves *quid pro quo* harassment. See e.g., Horn v. Duke Homes, 755 F.2d 599 (7th Cir. 1985), Henson v. City of Dundee, 682 F.2d 897 (11th Cir. 1982); Miller v. Bank of America, 600 F.2d 211 (9th Cir. 1979). Under this view, then, proof that the employer knew or should have known of the supervisor's conduct and failed to take quick remedial action is required where the plaintiff alleges hostile environment harassment by a supervisor. See e.g. Hamilton v. Rodgers, 783 F.2d 1308 (5th Cir. 1986); Katz v. Dole, 709 F.2d 251 (4th Cir. 1983); Ferguson v. E.I. Du Pont de Nemours & Co. Inc., 560 F.Supp. 1172 (D.Del.1983). Alternatively, other courts require actual or constructive knowledge and failure to take appropriate remedial action on the employer's part before they will impose liability for supervisory conduct in any type of harassment action. See Tomkins v. Public Service Electric & Gas Co., 568 F.2d 1044 (3d Cir. 1977). As to what constitutes sufficient corrective action, see Moffett v. Gene B. Glick Co., Inc., 621 F.Supp. 244, 270–71 (N.D.Ind.1985) ("This involves more than merely indicating the existence of an official policy against harassment or discrimination. The measures required are reasonable affirmative steps to eliminate the harassment which maintain an atmosphere free of racial intimidation and insults."). The strict liability standard is criticized in Conte & Gregory, Sexual Harassment in Employment—Some Proposals Toward More Realistic Standards of Liability, 32 Drake L.Rev. 407 (1982–83). For an interesting insight into the development of the EEOC Guidelines that adopted the strict liability standard, on the other hand, see Smith, Prologue to the EEOC Guidelines on Sexual Harassment, 10 Cap.U.L.Rev. 471 (1981).

Should an employer also be liable for harassment by a nonsupervisory co-employee? A federal government study indicated that co-worker harassment accounted for 65% of all reported incidents of sexual harassment in federal employment. U.S. Merit Systems Protection Board, Sexual Harassment In The Federal Workplace: Is It A Problem 59 (1981). Employers have been held liable for co-worker racial harassment where the employer was shown to have known of the harassment and failed to take corrective action. See Barrett v. Omaha National Bank, 726 F.2d 424 (8th Cir. 1984); DeGrace v. Rumsfeld, 614 F.2d 796 (1st Cir. 1980); Scott v. Sears, Roebuck & Co., 605 F.Supp. 1047 (N.D.Ill.1985); EEOC v. Murphy Motor Freight Lines, 488 F.Supp. 381

(D.Minn.1980). But see Smith v. Rust Engineering Co., 20 FEP Cases 1172 (N.D.Ala.1978) (co-worker sexual harassment claim dismissed for failure to show employment retaliation). A helpful discussion of this issue can be found in Allegretti, Sexual Harassment of Female Employees By Nonsupervisory Co-workers: A Theory of Liability, 15 Creighton L.Rev. 437 (1982); Significant Development, Employer Liability For Sexual Harassment Under Title VII, 61 B.U.L.Rev. 535 (1981); Note, Sexual Harassment Claims of Abusive Work Environment Under Title VII, 97 Harv.L.Rev. 1449 (1984). The EEOC Guidelines, which recognize the "discriminatory atmosphere" form of discrimination, 29 CFR 1604.11(a)(3) (1985), extend this analysis to sexual harassment cases by holding an employer liable for harassment between fellow employees where the employer or its supervisors "knows or should have known of the conduct, unless it can show that it took immediate and appropriate corrective action." 29 CFR 1604.11(d) (1985). This standard was adopted in Martin v. Norbar, Inc., 537 F.Supp. 1260 (S.D.Ohio 1982).

2. Can an employee state a claim under Title VII when she alleges that the harassment was committed by a non-employee? Would it matter whether the act occurred inside or outside of the workplace? See Whitaker v. Carney, 778 F.2d 216 (5th Cir. 1985). The EEOC Guidelines state that an employer "may also be responsible for the acts of non-employees, with respect to sexual harassment of employees in the workplace, where the employer (or its agents or supervisory employees) knows or should have known of the conduct and fails to take immediate and appropriate corrective action. 29 C.F.R. § 1604.11(e) (1985).

3. Can a supervisor state a claim of harassment by a subordinate? See Erebia v. Chrysler Plastic Products Corp., 772 F.2d 1250 (6th Cir. 1985) (supervisor can state claim under § 1981 for ethnic slurs by subordinates condoned by employer); Moffett v. Gene B. Glick Co., Inc., 621 F.Supp. 244, 272 (N.D.Ind.1985) (supervisor subjected to racially based harassment by subordinates can maintain action under Title VII).

4. Title VII has been held not to prohibit discrimination on the basis of sexual orientation. See infra, at 370. Does this mean that a gay male employee cannot state a claim under Title VII by alleging that a male supervisor conditioned his continued employment upon acceding to the supervisor's sexual demands? See Joyner v. AAA Cooper Transportation, 597 F.Supp. 537 (M.D.Ala.1983); Wright v. Methodist Youth Services, Inc., 511 F.Supp. 307 (N.D.Ill.1981). What about a bisexual supervisor? See Henson v. City of Dundee, 682 F.2d 897, 904 (11th Cir. 1982); Comment, Sexual Harassment and Title VII, 51 N.Y.U.L.Rev. 148 (1976).

5. Does Title VII provide an effective remedy, beyond injunctive relief, for proven acts of ethnic, racial or sexual harassment? As we will see, monetary damages are limited under Title VII to back pay. The courts uniformly have held that pain and suffering is not compensable under this statute. See infra, at 750. Presumably, this problem is most acute in cases of work environment harassment where, by definition, the plaintiff has not suffered a tangible job detriment. Is there any way around this problem? See Phillips v. Smalley Maintenance Services, Inc., 711 F.2d 1524 (11th Cir. 1983) (court can exercise pendent jurisdiction over state law invasion of privacy count in complaint

including Title VII sexual harassment claim); Rogers v. Lowes L'Enfant Plaza Hotel, 526 F.Supp. 523 (D.D.C.1981) (where male supervisor accused of making verbal and written sexually oriented advances to female employee and of making telephone calls to her home that included sexually offensive comments, plaintiff can state a claim for compensatory and punitive damages under common law theories of invasion of privacy, assault, battery and intentional infliction of emotional distress); Coley v. Consolidated Rail Corp., 561 F.Supp. 645 (E.D.Mich.1982) (plaintiff in sexual harassment case entitled to recover mental anguish and humiliation damages under state anti-discrimination law); Montgomery, Sexual Harassment in the Workplace: A Practitioner's Guide to Tort Actions, 10 Gold. Gate L.Rev. 879 (1980); Note, Sexual Harassment Claims of Abusive Work Environment Under Title VII, 97 Harv.L.Rev. 1449 (1984); Note, Legal Remedies for Employment-Related Sexual Harassment, 64 Minn.L. Rev. 151 (1979). One trial court has ruled that a plaintiff alleging a pattern and practice of sexual harassment can state a racketeering claim under the federal Racketeer Influenced and Corrupt Organizations Act (RICO). See Hunt v. Weatherbee, 626 F.Supp. 1097 (D.Mass.1986).

6. Betsy Garcelon and Dolly DuPonte applied for promotion to the same job with their employer. Ms. Garcelon received the promotion. Ms. DuPonte contends that Ms. Garcelon was chosen solely because Ms. Garcelon had a sexual relationship with the personnel officer who made the promotion decision. Can Ms. DuPonte state a claim of sexual harassment under Title VII? See King v. Palmer, 778 F.2d 878 (D.C.Cir. 1985); Priest v. Rotary, 634 F.Supp. 571 (N.D.Ca.1986). Would it make a difference if the unsuccessful applicant had been a man?

SECTION C. DISPROPORTIONATE IMPACT

The courts have recognized that the principles of Title VII can be violated by employment practices that do not result in overt differential treatment. Employment policies neutral on their face may deprive individuals of their statutory right to equal employment opportunity. Objective criteria can disqualify minority persons at a disproportionate rate because a history of societal discrimination has prevented many of them from achieving a competitive position in the labor force. The "disproportionate exclusionary impact" theory of discrimination, designed by the courts to address this problem, focuses primarily on the discriminatory impact of facially neutral policies rather than, as in disparate treatment cases, the intent underlying the defendant's action. Consequently, the nature of the proof required to establish the existence of this type of discrimination differs from that associated with claims of disparate treatment.

GRIGGS v. DUKE POWER CO.

Supreme Court of the United States, 1971.
401 U.S. 424, 91 S.Ct. 849, 28 L.Ed.2d 158.

MR. CHIEF JUSTICE BURGER delivered the opinion of the Court.

We granted the writ in this case to resolve the question whether an employer is prohibited by the Civil Rights Act of 1964, Title VII, from requiring a high school education or passing of a standardized general intelligence test as a condition of employment in or transfer to jobs when (a) neither standard is shown to be significantly related to successful job performance, (b) both requirements operate to disqualify Negroes at a substantially higher rate than white applicants, and (c) the jobs in question formerly had been filled only by white employees as part of a longstanding practice of giving preference to whites.

* * * [T]his proceeding was brought by a group of incumbent Negro employees against Duke Power Company. All the petitioners are employed at the Company's Dan River Steam Station, a power generating facility located at Draper, North Carolina. At the time this action was instituted, the Company had 95 employees at the Dan River Station, 14 of whom were Negroes; 13 of these are petitioners here.

The District Court found that prior to July 2, 1965, the effective date of the Civil Rights Act of 1964, the Company openly discriminated on the basis of race in the hiring and assigning of employees at its Dan River plant. The plant was organized into five operating departments: (1) Labor, (2) Coal Handling, (3) Operations, (4) Maintenance, and (5) Laboratory and Test. Negroes were employed only in the Labor Department where the highest paying jobs paid less than the lowest paying jobs in the other four "operating" departments in which only whites were employed. Promotions were normally made within each department on the basis of job seniority. Transferees into a department usually began in the lowest position.

In 1955 the Company instituted a policy of requiring a high school education for initial assignment to any department except Labor, and for transfer from the Coal Handling to any "inside" department (Operations, Maintenance, or Laboratory). When the Company abandoned its policy of restricting Negroes to the Labor Department in 1965, completion of high school also was made a prerequisite to transfer from Labor to any other department. From the time the high school requirement was instituted to the time of trial, however, white employees hired before the time of the high school education requirement continued to perform satisfactorily and achieve promotions in the "operating" departments. * * *

The Company added a further requirement for new employees on July 2, 1965, the date on which Title VII became effective. To qualify for placement in any but the Labor Department it became necessary to register satisfactory scores on two professionally prepared aptitude tests, as well as to have a high school education. Completion of high school alone continued to render employees eligible for transfer to the four desirable departments from which Negroes had been excluded if the incumbent had been employed prior to the time of the new requirement. In September 1965 the Company began to permit incumbent employees who lacked a high school education to qualify for transfer from Labor or Coal Handling to an "inside" job by passing two tests—the Wonderlic Personnel Test, which purports to measure general intelligence, and the Bennett Mechanical Comprehension Test.

Neither was directed or intended to measure the ability to learn to perform a particular job or category of jobs. The requisite scores used for both initial hiring and transfer approximated the national median for high school graduates.[3]

The District Court had found that while the Company previously followed a policy of overt racial discrimination in a period prior to the Act, such conduct had ceased. The District Court also concluded that Title VII was intended to be prospective only and, consequently, the impact of prior inequities was beyond the reach of corrective action authorized by the Act.

The Court of Appeals was confronted with a question of first impression, as are we, concerning the meaning of Title VII. After careful analysis a majority of that court concluded that a subjective test of the employer's intent should govern, particularly in a close case, and that in this case there was no showing of a discriminatory purpose in the adoption of the diploma and test requirements. On this basis, the Court of Appeals concluded there was no violation of the Act.

* * * In so doing, the Court of Appeals rejected the claim that because these two requirements operated to render ineligible a markedly disproportionate number of Negroes, they were unlawful under Title VII unless shown to be job related. We granted the writ on these claims.

The objective of Congress in the enactment of Title VII * * * was to achieve equality of employment opportunities and remove barriers that have operated in the past to favor an identifiable group of white employees over other employees. Under the Act, practices, procedures, or tests neutral on their face, and even neutral in terms of intent, cannot be maintained if they operate to "freeze" the status quo of prior discriminatory employment practices.

The Court of Appeals' opinion, and the partial dissent, agreed that, on the record in the present case, "whites register far better on the Company's alternative requirements" than Negroes.[6] This consequence would appear to be directly traceable to race. Basic intelligence must have the means of articulation to manifest itself fairly in a testing process. Because they are Negroes, petitioners have long received inferior education in segregated schools * * *. Congress did not intend by Title VII, however, to guarantee a job to every person regardless of qualifications. In short, the Act does not command that any person be hired simply because he was formerly the subject of discrimination, or because he is a member of a minority group. Dis-

3. The test standards are thus more stringent than the high school requirement, since they would screen out approximately half of all high school graduates.

6. In North Carolina, 1960 census statistics show that, while 34% of white males had completed high school, only 12% of Negro males had done so.

Similarly, with respect to standardized tests, the EEOC in one case found that use of a battery of tests, including the Wonderlic and Bennett tests used by the Company in the instant case, resulted in 58% of whites passing the tests, as compared with only 6% of the blacks.

criminatory preference for any group, minority or majority, is precisely and only what Congress has proscribed. What is required by Congress is the removal of artificial, arbitrary, and unnecessary barriers to employment when the barriers operate invidiously to discriminate on the basis of racial or other impermissible classification.

* * * The Act proscribes not only overt discrimination but also practices that are fair in form, but discriminatory in operation. The touchstone is business necessity. If an employment practice which operates to exclude Negroes cannot be shown to be related to job performance, the practice is prohibited.

On the record before us, neither the high school completion requirement nor the general intelligence test is shown to bear a demonstrable relationship to successful performance of the jobs for which it was used. Both were adopted, as the Court of Appeals noted, without meaningful study of their relationship to job-performance ability. Rather, a vice president of the Company testified, the requirements were instituted on the Company's judgment that they generally would improve the overall quality of the work force.

The evidence, however, shows that employees who have not completed high school or taken the tests have continued to perform satisfactorily and make progress in departments for which the high school and test criteria are now used.[7] The promotion record of present employees who would not be able to meet the new criteria thus suggests the possibility that the requirements may not be needed even for the limited purpose of preserving the avowed policy of advancement within the Company. * * *

The Court of Appeals held that the Company had adopted the diploma and test requirements without any "intention to discriminate against Negro employees." We do not suggest that either the District Court or the Court of Appeals erred in examining the employer's intent; but good intent or absence of discriminatory intent does not redeem employment procedures or testing mechanisms that operate as "built-in headwinds" for minority groups and are unrelated to measuring job capability.

The Company's lack of discriminatory intent is suggested by special efforts to help the undereducated employees through Company financing of two-thirds the cost of tuition for high school training. But Congress directed the thrust of the Act to the *consequences* of employment practices, not simply the motivation. More than that, Congress has placed on the employer the burden of showing that any given requirement must have a manifest relationship to the employment in question.

* * *

7. For example, between July 2, 1965, and November 14, 1966, the percentage of white employees who were promoted but who were not high school graduates was nearly identical to the percentage of nongraduates in the entire white work force.

The Company contends that its general intelligence tests are specifically permitted by § 703(h) of the Act.[8] That section authorizes the use of "any professionally developed ability test" that is not "designed, intended *or used* to discriminate because of race * * *." (Emphasis added.)

The Equal Employment Opportunity Commission, having enforcement responsibility, has issued guidelines interpreting § 703(h) to permit only the use of job-related tests.[9] The administrative interpretation of the Act by the enforcing agency is entitled to great deference. Since the Act and its legislative history support the Commission's construction, this affords good reason to treat the guidelines as expressing the will of Congress.

* * *

Nothing in the Act precludes the use of testing or measuring procedures; obviously they are useful. What Congress has forbidden is giving these devices and mechanisms controlling force unless they are demonstrably a reasonable measure of job performance. Congress has not commanded that the less qualified be preferred over the better qualified simply because of minority origins. Far from disparaging job qualifications as such, Congress has made such qualifications the controlling factor, so that race, religion, nationality, and sex become irrelevant. What Congress has commanded is that any tests used must measure the person for the job and not the person in the abstract.

The judgment of the Court of Appeals is, as to that portion of the judgment appealed from, reversed.

MR. JUSTICE BRENNAN took no part in the consideration or decision of this case.

NOTES AND PROBLEMS FOR DISCUSSION

1. How does the concept of discrimination recognized by the Court in *Griggs* differ from the one examined in *McDonnell Douglas*? To what extent are these theories premised on different interpretations of the concept of equality?

8. Section 703(h) applies only to tests. It has no applicability to the high school diploma requirement.

9. EEOC Guidelines on Employment Testing Procedures, issued August 24, 1966, provide:

"The Commission accordingly interprets 'professionally developed ability test' to mean a test which fairly measures the knowledge or skills required by the particular job or class of jobs which the applicant seeks, or which fairly affords the employer a chance to measure the applicant's ability to perform a particular job or class of jobs. The fact that a test was prepared by an individual or organization claiming expertise in test preparation does not, without more, justify its use within the meaning of Title VII."

The EEOC position has been elaborated in the new Guidelines on Employees Selection Procedures, 29 CFR § 1607, 35 Fed.Reg. 12333 (Aug. 1, 1970). These guidelines demand that employers using tests have available "data demonstrating that the test is predictive of or significantly correlated with important elements of work behavior which comprise or are relevant to the job or jobs for which candidates are being evaluated."

2. Is there any statutory authority for the Court's recognition of a disproportionate impact-based cause of action? For an interesting discussion of the development of disproportionate impact theory see Blumrosen, Strangers in Paradise: Griggs v. Duke Power Co. and the Concept of Employment Discrimination, 71 Mich.L.Rev. 59 (1972).

3. How much of a disproportionate impact must plaintiff show to establish a prima facie violation? The federal courts have not adopted a uniform quantitative standard for determining what constitutes a substantially disproportionate exclusionary impact. For a thorough and thoughtful discussion, see Shoben, Differential Pass-Fail Rates in Employment Testing: Statistical Proof Under Title VII, 91 Harv.L.Rev. 793 (1978).

On August 25, 1978, however, several federal agencies adopted a set of uniform testing guidelines to provide standards for ruling on the legality of selection procedures used by private and public employers subject to these agencies' rules. Section 4D, or the "four-fifths rule," provides that a selection rate for members of a protected group of less than 80% of the rate for the highest scoring group generally will create a prima facie case of disproportionate impact. This is only a rule of thumb; the agencies retain discretion to make adjustments in individual cases. See 4D, Fed.Reg. 38291, 297–98. The rule has been adopted by several courts. See Brown v. New Haven Civil Service Board, 474 F.Supp. 1256 (D.Conn.1979); Guardians Association v. Civil Service Commission, 630 F.2d 79 (2d Cir. 1980); United States v. City of Chicago, 21 FEP Cases 200 (N.D.Ill.1979).

4. Shortly after graduating from law school, James Stanton, a black man, failed the bar examination in the state in which he wanted to open up a private practice. He can prove that while 85% of the white applicants pass this examination, only 49% of all black applicants pass it. Can he successfully maintain a race discrimination claim under Title VII against the State Board of Bar Examiners? See Woodard v. Virginia Board of Bar Examiners, 598 F.2d 1345 (4th Cir. 1979).

5. Suppose a plaintiff can prove that one of the hiring standards used by the employer had a disproportionate exclusionary effect on blacks. The company, however, can show that its work force is racially balanced. Can the plaintiff establish a prima facie case of disproportionate impact discrimination? Must she offer evidence of a "bottom line" disproportionate impact to satisfy her initial burden of proof under *Griggs*?

CONNECTICUT v. TEAL

Supreme Court of the United States, 1982.
457 U.S. 440, 102 S.Ct. 2525, 73 L.Ed.2d 130.

JUSTICE BRENNAN delivered the opinion of the Court.

We consider here whether an employer sued for violation of Title VII of the Civil Rights Act of 1964 may assert a "bottom line" theory of defense. Under that theory, as asserted in this case, an employer's acts of racial discrimination in promotions—effected by an examination having disparate impact—would not render the employer liable for the racial discrimination suffered by employees barred from promotion if the "bottom line" result of the promotional process was an appropriate racial balance. We hold that the "bottom line" does not preclude respondent-employees from establishing a prima facie case, nor does it provide petitioner-employer with a defense to such a case.

I

Four of the respondents, Winnie Teal, Rose Walker, Edith Latney, and Grace Clark, are black employees of the Department of Income Maintenance of the State of Connecticut. Each was promoted provisionally to the position of Welfare Eligibility Supervisor and served in that capacity for almost two years. To attain permanent status as supervisors, however, respondents had to participate in a selection process that required, as the first step, a passing score on a written examination. This written test was administered on December 2, 1978, to 329 candidates. Of these candidates, 48 identified themselves as black and 259 identified themselves as white. The results of the examination were announced in March 1979. With the passing score set at 65,[3] 54.17 of the identified black candidates passed. This was approximately 68 percent of the passing rate for the identified white candidates.[4] The four respondents were among the blacks who failed the examination, and they were thus excluded from further consideration for permanent supervisory positions. In April 1979, respondents instituted this action in the United States District Court for the District of Connecticut against petitioners, the State of Connecticut, two state agencies, and two state officials. Respondents alleged, *inter alia,* that petitioners violated Title VII by imposing, as an absolute condition for consideration for promotion, that applicants pass a written test that excluded blacks in disproportionate numbers and that was not job related.

More than a year after this action was instituted, and approximately one month before trial, petitioners made promotions from the eligibility list generated by the written examination. In choosing persons from that list, petitioners considered past work performance, recommendations of the candidates' supervisors and, to a lesser extent, seniority. Petitioners then applied what the Court of Appeals characterized as an affirmative action program in order to ensure a significant number of minority supervisors. Forty-six persons were promoted to permanent supervisory positions, 11 of whom were black and 35 of whom were white. The overall result of the selection process was that, of the 48 identified black candidates who participated in the selection

3. The mean score on the examination was 70.4 percent. However, because the black candidates had a mean score 6.7 percentage points lower than the white candidates, the passing score was set at 65, apparently in an attempt to lessen the disparate impact of the examination.

4.

* * *

Petitioners do not contest the District Court's implicit finding that the examination itself resulted in disparate impact under the "eighty percent rule" of the Uniform Guidelines on Employee Selection Procedures adopted by the Equal Employment Opportunity Commission. Those guidelines provide that a selection rate that "is less than [80 percent] of the rate for the group with the highest rate will generally be regarded * * * as evidence of adverse impact."

process, 22.9 percent were promoted and of the 259 identified white candidates, 13.5 percent were promoted.[6] It is this "bottom-line" result, more favorable to blacks than to whites, that petitioners urge should be adjudged to be a complete defense to respondents' suit.

After trial, the District Court entered judgment for petitioners. The court treated respondents' claim as one of disparate impact under Griggs v. Duke Power Co., Albemarle Paper Co. v. Moody, and Dothard v. Rawlinson. However, the court found that, although the comparative passing rates for the examination indicated a prima facie case of adverse impact upon minorities, the result of the entire hiring process reflected no such adverse impact. Holding that these "bottom line" percentages precluded the finding of a Title VII violation, the court held that the employer was not required to demonstrate that the promotional examination was job related. The United States Court of Appeals for the Second Circuit reversed, holding that the District Court erred in ruling that the results of the written examination alone were insufficient to support a prima facie case of disparate impact in violation of Title VII. The Court of Appeals stated that where "an identifiable pass-fail barrier denies an employment opportunity to a disproportionately large number of minorities and prevents them from proceeding to the next step in the selection process," that barrier must be shown to be job related. We granted certiorari, and now affirm.

II

A

We must first decide whether an examination that bars a disparate number of black employees from consideration for promotion, and that has not been shown to be job related, presents a claim cognizable under Title VII. Section 703(a)(2) of Title VII provides in pertinent part:

> It shall be an unlawful employment practice for an employer—
>
> * * *
>
> (2) to limit, segregate, or classify his employees or applicants for employment in any way which would deprive or tend to deprive any individual of employment opportunities or otherwise adversely affect his status as an employee, because of such individual's race, color, religion, sex, or national origin.

Respondents base their claim on our construction of this provision in Griggs v. Duke Power Co., supra. * * *

Griggs and its progeny have established a three-part analysis of disparate impact claims. To establish a prima facie case of discrimination, a plaintiff must show that the facially neutral employment practice had a significantly discriminatory impact. If that showing is made, the employer must then demonstrate that "any given requirement [has]

6. The actual promotion rate of blacks was thus close to 170 percent that of the actual promotion rate of whites.

a manifest relationship to the employment in question," in order to avoid a finding of discrimination. *Griggs,* supra. Even in such a case, however, the plaintiff may prevail, if he shows that employer was using the practice as a mere pretext for discrimination. See Albemarle Paper Co.; Dothard, supra.[7]

* * *

Petitioners' examination, which barred promotion and had a discriminatory impact on black employees, clearly falls within the literal language of § 703(a)(2), as interpreted by *Griggs.*[8] The statute speaks, not in terms of jobs and promotions, but in terms of *limitations* and *classifications* that would deprive any individual of employment *opportunities.*[9] A disparate impact claim reflects the language of § 703(a)(2) and Congress' basic objectives in enacting that statute: "to achieve equality of employment *opportunities* and remove barriers that have operated in the past to favor an identifiable group of white employees over other employees." When an employer uses a nonjob-related barrier in order to deny a minority or woman applicant employment or promotion, and that barrier has a significant adverse effect on minorities or women, then the applicant has been deprived of an employment *opportunity* "because of * * * race, color, religion, sex, or national origin." In other words, § 703(a)(2) prohibits discriminatory "artificial, arbitrary, and unnecessary barriers to employment," that "limit * * * or classify * * * applicants for employment * * * in any way which would deprive or tend to deprive any individual of employment *opportunities.*"

Relying on § 703(a)(2), *Griggs* explicitly focused on employment "practices, procedures, or tests," that deny equal employment "opportunity." We concluded that Title VII prohibits "procedures or testing mechanisms that operate as 'built-in headwinds' for minority groups." We found that Congress' primary purpose was the prophylactic one of

7. Petitioners apparently argue both that the nondiscriminatory "bottom line" precluded respondents from establishing a prima facie case and, in the alternative, that it provided a defense.

8. The legislative history of the 1972 amendments to Title VII is relevant to this case because those amendments extended the protection of the Act to respondents here by deleting exemptions for state and municipal employers. That history demonstrates that Congress recognized and endorsed the disparate impact analysis employed by the Court in *Griggs.* Both the House and Senate reports cited *Griggs* with approval, the Senate Report noting that:

"Employment discrimination as viewed today is a * * * complex and pervasive phenomenon. Experts familiar with the subject now generally describe the problem in terms of 'systems' and 'effects' rather than simply intentional wrongs." In addition, the Section-by-Section Analyses of the 1972 amendments submitted to both houses explicitly stated that in any area not addressed by the amendments, present case law—which as Congress had already recognized included our then recent decision in *Griggs*—was intended to continue to govern.

9. In contrast, the language of § 703(a)(1), if it were the only protection given to employees and applicants under Title VII, might support petitioners' exclusive focus on the overall result. That subsection makes it an unlawful employment practice "to fail or refuse to hire or to discharge any individual, or otherwise to discriminate against any individual with respect to his compensation, terms, conditions or privileges of employment, because of such individual's race, color, religion, sex, or national origin."

achieving equality of employment "opportunities" and removing "barriers" to such equality. The examination given to respondents in this case surely constituted such a practice and created such a barrier.

Our conclusion that § 703(a)(2) encompasses respondents' claim is reinforced by the terms of Congress' 1972 extension of the protections of Title VII to state and municipal employees. See n. 8, supra. Although Congress did not explicitly consider the viability of the defense offered by the state employer in this case, the 1972 amendments to Title VII do reflect Congress' intent to provide state and municipal employees with the protection that Title VII, as interpreted by *Griggs,* had provided to employees in the private sector: equality of *opportunity* and the elimination of discriminatory *barriers* to professional development. The committee reports and the floor debates stressed the need for equality of opportunity for minority applicants seeking to obtain governmental positions. Congress voiced its concern about the wide-spread use by state and local governmental agencies of "invalid selection techniques" that had a discriminatory impact.

The decisions of this Court following *Griggs* also support respondents' claim. In considering claims of disparate impact under § 703(a)(2) this Court has consistently focused on employment and promotion requirements that create a discriminatory bar to *opportunities.* This Court has never read § 703(a)(2) as requiring the focus to be placed instead on the overall number of minority or female applicants actually hired or promoted. Thus Dothard v. Rawlinson, found that minimum statutory height and weight requirements for correctional counselors were the sort of arbitrary barrier to equal employment opportunity for women forbidden by Title VII. Although we noted in passing that women constituted 36.89 percent of the labor force and only 12.9 percent of correctional counselor positions, our focus was not on this "bottom line." We focused instead on the disparate effect that the minimum height and weight standards had on applicants: classifying far more women than men as ineligible for employment. Similarly, in Albemarle Paper Co. v. Moody, the action was remanded to allow the employer to attempt to show that the tests that he had given to his employees for promotion were job related. We did not suggest that by promoting a sufficient number of the black employees who passed the examination, the employer could avoid this burden. See also New York Transit Authority v. Beazer, 440 U.S. 568, 584, 99 S.Ct. 1355, 1365, 59 L.Ed.2d 587 (1979) ("A prima facie violation of the Act may be established by statistical evidence showing that an employment *practice* has the effect of denying members of one race equal access to employment *opportunities.*") (emphasis added).

In short, the District Court's dismissal of respondents' claim cannot be supported on the basis that respondents failed to establish a prima facie case of employment discrimination under the terms of § 703(a)(2). The suggestion that disparate impact should be measured only at the bottom line ignores the fact that Title VII guarantees these individual respondents the *opportunity* to compete equally with white workers on the basis of job-related criteria. Title VII strives to achieve equality of opportunity by rooting out "artificial, arbitrary and unnecessary" employer-created barriers to professional development that have a discriminatory impact upon individuals. Therefore, respondents' rights under § 703(a)(2) have been violated, unless petitioners can demonstrate that the examination given was not an artificial, arbitrary, or unnecessary barrier, because it measured skills related to effective performance in the role of Welfare Eligibility Supervisor.

B

The United States, in its brief as *amicus curiae,* apparently recognizes that respondents' claim in this case falls within the affirmative commands of Title VII. But it seeks to support the District Court's judgment in this case by relying on the defenses provided to the employer in § 703(h).[11] Section 703(h) provides in pertinent part:

> "Notwithstanding any other provision of this title, it shall not be an unlawful employment practice for an employer * * * to give and to act upon the results of any professionally developed ability test provided that such test, its administration or action upon the results is not designed, intended or used to discriminate because of race, color, religion, sex or national origin."

The Government argues that the test administered by the petitioners was not "used to discriminate" because it did not actually deprive disproportionate numbers of blacks of promotions. But the Government's reliance on § 703(h) as offering the employer some special haven for discriminatory tests is misplaced. We considered the relevance of this provision in *Griggs.* After examining the legislative history of § 703(h), we concluded that Congress, in adding § 703(h), intended only to make clear that tests that were *job related* would be permissible despite their disparate impact. As the Court recently confirmed, § 703(h), which was introduced as an amendment to Title VII on the Senate floor, "did not alter the meaning of Title VII, but 'merely clarifie[d] its present intent and effect.'" American Tobacco v. Patterson, 456 U.S. 63, 73, n. 11, 102 S.Ct. 1534, 1539, n. 11, 71 L.Ed.2d 748 (1982), quoting 110 Cong.Rec. 12723 (remarks of Sen. Humphrey). A nonjob-related test that has a disparate racial impact, and is used to "limit" or "classify" employees, is "used to discriminate" within the meaning of Title VII, whether or not it was "designed or intended" to have this effect and despite an employer's efforts to compensate for its discriminatory effect. See *Griggs.*

In sum, respondents' claim of disparate impact from the examination, a pass-fail barrier to employment opportunity, states a prima facie case of employment discrimination under § 703(a)(2), despite their

11. The Government's brief is submitted by the Department of Justice, which shares responsibility for federal enforcement of Title VII with the Equal Employment Opportunity Commission (EEOC). The EEOC declined to join this brief.

employer's nondiscriminatory "bottom line," and that "bottom line" is no defense to this prima facie case under § 703(h).

III

Having determined that respondents' claim comes within the terms of Title VII, we must address the suggestion of petitioners and some *amici curiae* that we recognize an exception, either in the nature of an additional burden on plaintiffs seeking to establish a prima facie case or in the nature of an affirmative defense, for cases in which an employer has compensated for a discriminatory pass-fail barrier by hiring or promoting a sufficient number of black employees to reach a nondiscriminatory "bottom line." We reject this suggestion, which is in essence nothing more than a request that we redefine the protections guaranteed by Title VII.[12]

Section 703(a)(2) prohibits practices that would deprive or tend to deprive "*any individual* of employment opportunities." The principal focus of the statute is the protection of the individual employee, rather than the protection of the minority group as a whole. Indeed, the entire statute and its legislative history are replete with references to protection for the individual employee. See, e.g., §§ 703(a)(1), (b), (c), 704(a). * * *

In suggesting that the "bottom line" may be a defense to a claim of discrimination against an individual employee, petitioners and *amici* appear to confuse unlawful discrimination with discriminatory intent. The Court has stated that a nondiscriminatory "bottom line" and an employer's good faith efforts to achieve a nondiscriminatory work force, might in some cases assist an employer in rebutting the inference that particular action had been intentionally discriminatory: "Proof that [a]

12. Petitioners suggest that we should defer to the EEOC Guidelines in this regard. But there is nothing in the Guidelines to which we might defer that would aid petitioners in this case. The most support petitioners could conceivably muster from the Uniform Guidelines on Employee Selection Procedures (now issued jointly by the EEOC, the Civil Service Commission, the Department of Labor, and the Department of Justice), is *neutrality* on the question whether a discriminatory barrier that does not result in a discriminatory overall result constitutes a violation of Title VII. Section 1607.4C of the Guidelines, relied upon by petitioners, states that as a matter of "*administrative and prosecutorial discretion, in the usual case,*" the agencies will not take enforcement action based upon the disparate impact of any component of a selection process if the total selection process results in no adverse impact. (Emphasis added.) The agencies made clear that the "guidelines do not address the underlying question of law," and that an individual "who is denied the job because of a particular component in a procedure which otherwise meets the 'bottom line' standard * * * retains the right to proceed through the appropriate agencies, and into Federal court." In addition, in a publication entitled, "Adoption of Questions and Answers to Clarify and Provide a Common Interpretation of the Uniform Guidelines on Employee Selection Procedures," the agencies stated:

> "Since the [bottom line] concept is not a rule of law, it does not affect the discharge by the EEOC of its statutory responsibilities to investigate charges of discrimination, render an administrative finding on its investigation, and engage in voluntary conciliation efforts. Similarly, with respect to the other issuing agencies, the bottom line concept applies not to the processing of individual charges, but to the initiation of enforcement action."

work force was racially balanced or that it contained a disproportionately high percentage of minority employees is not wholly irrelevant on the issue of intent when that issue is yet to be decided." Furnco Construction Corp. v. Waters, 438 U.S. 567, 580, 98 S.Ct. 2943, 2951, 57 L.Ed.2d 957 (1978). See also Teamsters v. United States, 431 U.S. 324, 340, n. 20, 97 S.Ct. 1843, 1856–1857, n. 20, 52 L.Ed.2d 396 (1977). But resolution of the factual question of intent is not what is at issue in this case. Rather, petitioners seek simply to justify discrimination against respondents, on the basis of their favorable treatment of other members of respondents' racial group. Under Title VII, "A racially balanced work force cannot immunize an employer from liability for specific acts of discrimination." Furnco Construction Corp.

> "It is clear beyond cavil that the obligation imposed by Title VII is to provide an equal opportunity for *each* applicant regardless of race, without regard to whether members of the applicant's race are already proportionately represented in the work force." Ibid. (emphasis in original).

It is clear that Congress never intended to give an employer license to discriminate against some employees on the basis of race or sex merely because he favorably treats other members of the employees' group. We recognized in Los Angeles Dept. of Water & Power v. Manhart, 435 U.S. 702, 98 S.Ct. 1370, 55 L.Ed.2d 657 (1978), that fairness to the class of women employees as a whole could not justify unfairness to the individual female employee because the "statute's focus on the individual is unambiguous." Similarly, in Phillips v. Martin Marietta Corp., 400 U.S. 542, 91 S.Ct. 496, 27 L.Ed.2d 613 (1971) (*per curiam*), we recognized that a rule barring employment of all married *women* with preschool children, if not a bona fide occupational qualification under § 703(e), violated Title VII, even though female applicants without preschool children were hired in sufficient numbers that they constituted 75 to 80 percent of the persons employed in the position plaintiff sought.

Petitioners point out that *Furnco, Manhart,* and *Phillips* involved facially discriminatory policies, while the claim in the instant case is one of discrimination from a facially neutral policy. The fact remains, however, that irrespective of the form taken by the discriminatory practice, an employer's treatment of other members of the plaintiffs' group can be "of little comfort to the victims of * * * discrimination." Teamsters v. United States, supra. Title VII does not permit the victim of a facially discriminatory policy to be told that he has not been wronged because other persons of his or her race or sex were hired. That answer is no more satisfactory when it is given to victims of a policy that is facially neutral but practically discriminatory. Every *individual* employee is protected against both discriminatory treatment and against "practices that are fair in form, but discriminatory in operation." Griggs v. Duke Power Co. Requirements and tests that have a discriminatory impact are merely some of the more subtle, but also the more pervasive, of the "practices and devices which have fostered racially stratified job environments to the disadvantage of minority citizens." McDonnell Douglas Corp. v. Green.

IV

In sum, petitioners' nondiscriminatory "bottom line" is no answer, under the terms of Title VII, to respondents' prima facie claim of employment discrimination. Accordingly, the judgment of the Court of Appeals for the Second Circuit is affirmed, and this case is remanded to the District Court for further proceedings consistent with this opinion.

It is so ordered.

JUSTICE POWELL, with whom THE CHIEF JUSTICE, JUSTICE REHNQUIST, and JUSTICE O'CONNOR join, dissenting.

In past decisions, this Court has been sensitive to the critical difference between cases proving discrimination under Title VII by a showing of disparate treatment or discriminatory intent and those proving such discrimination by a showing of disparate impact. Because today's decision blurs that distinction and results in a holding inconsistent with the very nature of disparate-impact claims, I dissent.

I

Section 703(a)(2), provides that it is an unlawful employment practice for an employer to

> "limit, segregate or classify his employees or applicants for employment in any way which would deprive or tend to deprive any individual of employment opportunities or otherwise adversely affect his status as an employee, because of such individual's race, color, religion, sex, or national origin."

Although this language suggests that discrimination occurs only on an individual basis, in *Griggs* the Court held that discriminatory intent on the part of the employer against an individual need not be shown when "employment procedures or testing mechanisms * * * operate as 'built-in headwinds' for minority groups and are unrelated to measuring job capability." Thus, the Court held that the "disparate impact" of an employer's practices on a racial group can violate § 703(a)(2) of Title VII. In *Griggs* and each subsequent disparate-impact case, however, the Court has considered, not whether the claimant as an individual had been classified in a manner impermissible under § 703(a)(2), but whether an employer's procedures have had an adverse impact on the protected *group* to which the individual belongs.

Thus, while disparate-*treatment* cases focus on the way in which an individual has been treated, disparate-*impact* cases are concerned with the protected group. This key distinction was explained in *Furnco Construction Corp.* (MARSHALL, J., concurring in part):

> "It is well established under Title VII that claims of employment discrimination because of race may arise in two different ways.

Teamsters v. United States, 431 U.S. 324, 335–336, n. 15, 97 S.Ct. 1843, 1854–1855, n. 15, 52 L.Ed.2d 396 (1977). An individual may allege that he has been subjected to 'disparate treatment' because of his race, or that he has been the victim of a facially neutral practice having a 'disparate impact' on his racial group."

In keeping with this distinction, our disparate impact cases consistently have considered whether the result of an employer's *total selection process* had an adverse impact upon the protected group.[2] If this case were decided by reference to the total process—as our cases suggest that it should be—the result would be clear. Here 22.9% of the blacks who entered the selection process were ultimately promoted, compared with only 13.5% of the whites. To say that this selection process had an unfavorable "disparate impact" on blacks is to ignore reality.

The Court, disregarding the distinction drawn by our cases, repeatedly asserts that Title VII was designed to protect individual, not group, rights. It emphasizes that some individual blacks were eliminated by the disparate impact of the preliminary test. But this argument confuses the *aim* of Title VII with the legal theories through which its aims were intended to be vindicated. It is true that the aim of Title VII is to protect individuals, not groups. But in advancing this commendable objective, Title VII jurisprudence has recognized two distinct methods of proof. In one set of cases—those involving direct proof of discriminatory intent—the plaintiff seeks to establish direct, intentional discrimination against him. In that type case, the individual is at the forefront throughout the entire presentation of evidence. In disparate impact cases, by contrast, the plaintiff seeks to carry his burden of proof by way of *inference*—by showing that an employer's selection process results in the rejection of a disproportionate number of members of a protected group to which he belongs. From such a showing a fair inference then may be drawn that the rejected applicant, as a member of that disproportionately excluded group, was himself a victim of that process's " 'built-in head winds.' " *Griggs*. But this method of proof—which actually *defines* disparate impact theory under Title VII—invites the plaintiff to prove discrimination by reference to the group rather than to the allegedly affected individual.[3] There can be

2. See Dothard v. Rawlinson, 433 U.S. 321, 329, 97 S.Ct. 2720, 2726–2727, 53 L.Ed. 2d 786 (1977) (statutory height and weight requirements operated as a bar to *employment* of disproportionate number of women); Albemarle Paper Co. v. Moody, 422 U.S. 405, 409–411, 95 S.Ct. 2362, 2367–2368, 45 L.Ed.2d 280 (1975) (seniority system allegedly locked blacks into lower paying jobs; applicants to skilled lines of progression were required to pass two tests); Griggs v. Duke Power Co., 401 U.S. 424, 431, 91 S.Ct. 849, 853, 28 L.Ed.2d 158 (1971) (tests were an absolute bar to transfers or hiring; the Court observed that all Congress requires is "the removal of artificial, arbitrary, and unnecessary barriers to *employment* * * *.") (emphasis added).

3. Initially, the plaintiff bears the burden of establishing a prima facie case that Title VII has been infringed. See Texas Dept. of Community Affairs v. Burdine. In a disparate-impact case, this burden is met by showing that an employer's selection process results in the rejection of a disproportionate number of members of a protected group. See Teamsters v. United States. Regardless of whether the plaintiff's prima facie case must itself focus on

no violation of Title VII on the basis of disparate impact in the absence of disparate impact on a *group*.

In this case the plaintiff seeks to benefit from a conflation of "discriminatory treatment" and "disparate impact" theories. But he cannot have it both ways. Having undertaken to prove discrimination by reference to one set of group figures (used at a preliminary point in the selection process), the plaintiff then claims that *non*discrimination cannot be proved by viewing the impact of the entire process on the group as a whole. The fallacy of this reasoning—accepted by the Court—is transparent. It is to confuse the individualistic *aim* of Title VII with the methods of proof by which Title VII rights may be vindicated. The respondent, as an individual, is entitled to the full personal protection of Title VII. But, having undertaken to prove a violation of his rights by reference to group figures, respondent cannot deny petitioner the opportunity to rebut his evidence by introducing figures of the same kind. Having pleaded a disparate impact case, the plaintiff cannot deny the defendant the opportunity to show that there was no disparate impact. As the Court of Appeals for the Third Circuit noted in EEOC v. Greyhound Lines, 635 F.2d 188, 192 (CA3 1980):

> "no violation of Title VII can be grounded on the disparate impact theory without proof that the questioned policy or practice has had a disproportionate impact on the employer's workforce. This conclusion should be as obvious as it is tautological: there can be no disparate impact unless there is [an ultimate] disparate impact."

Where, under a facially neutral employment process, there has been no adverse effect on the group—and certainly there has been none here—Title VII has not been infringed.

II

The Court's position is no stronger in case authority than it is in logic. None of the cases relied upon by the Court controls the outcome of this case.[5] Indeed, the disparate-impact cases do not even support the propositions for which they are cited. For example, the Court cites Dothard v. Rawlinson * * * and observes that "[a]lthough we noted

the defendant's overall selection process or whether it is sufficient that the plaintiff establish that at least one pass-fail barrier has resulted in disparate impact, the employer's presentation of evidence showing that its overall selection procedure does not operate in a discriminatory fashion certainly dispels any inference of discrimination. In such instances, at the close of the evidence, the plaintiff has failed to show disparate impact by a preponderance of the evidence.

5. The Court concentrates on cases of questionable relevance. Most of the lower courts that have squarely considered the question have concluded that there can be no violation of Title VII on a disparate-impact basis when there is no disparate impact at the *bottom line*. See, e.g., EEOC v. Greyhound Lines, 635 F.2d 188 (CA3 1980); EEOC v. Navajo Refining Co., 593 F.2d 988 (CA10 1979); Friend v. Leidinger, 588 F.2d 61, 66 (CA4 1978); Rule v. Ironworkers Local 396, 568 F.2d 558 (CA8 1977); Smith v. Troyan, 520 F.2d 492, 497–498 (CA6 1975), cert. denied, 426 U.S. 934, 96 S.Ct. 2646, 49 L.Ed.2d 385 (1976); Williams v. City & Cty. of San Francisco, 483 F.Supp. 335 (N.D.Cal.1979); Brown v. New Haven Civil Service Board, 474 F.Supp. 1256 (D.Conn.1979); Lee v. City of Richmond, 456 F.Supp. 756 (E.D.Va.1978).

in passing that women constituted 36.89 percent of the labor force and only 12.9 percent of correctional counselors, our focus was not on this bottom line. We focused instead on the disparate effect that the minimum height and weight standards had on applicants; classifying far more women than men as ineligible for employment." In *Dothard,* however, the Court was not considering a case in which there was any difference between the discriminatory effect of the employment standard and the number of minority members actually hired. The *Dothard* Court itself stated that

> "to establish a prima facie case of discrimination, a plaintiff need only show that the facially neutral standards in question *select* applicants *for hire* in a discriminatory pattern. Once it is shown that *the employment standards* are discriminatory in effect, the employer must meet 'the burden of showing that any given requirement [has] * * * a manifest relationship to the employment in question.'" (emphasis added).

The *Dothard* Court did not decide today's case. It addressed only a case in which the challenged standards had a discriminatory impact at the bottom line—the hiring decision. And the *Dothard* Court's "focus," referred to by the Court, is of no help in deciding the instant case.[6]

The Court concedes that the other major cases on which it relies, *Furnco,* and Phillips v. Martin Marietta Corp., "involved facially discriminatory policies, while the claim in the instant case is one of discrimination from a facially neutral policy." The Court nevertheless applies the principles derived from those cases to the case at bar. It does so by reiterating the view that Title VII protects *individuals,* not *groups,* and therefore that the manner in which an employer has treated other members of a group cannot defeat the claim of an individual who has suffered as a result of even a facially neutral policy. As appealing as this sounds, it confuses the distinction—uniformly recognized until today—between disparate *impact* and disparate *treatment.* Our cases, cited above, have made clear that discriminatory-impact claims cannot be based on how an individual is treated in isolation from the treatment of other members of the group. Such

6. The Court cites language from two other disparate-impact cases. The Court notes that in Albemarle Paper Co. v. Moody, the Court "remanded to allow the employer to attempt to show that the tests * * * given * * * for promotion were job related." But the fact that the Court did so without suggesting "that by promoting a sufficient number of black employees who passed the examination, the employer could avoid this hurdle," can hardly be precedent for the negative of that proposition when the issue was neither presented in the facts of the case nor addressed by the Court.

Similarly, New York Transit Authority v. Beazer, provides little support despite the language quoted by the Court. * * * In *Beazer,* the Court ruled that the statistical evidence actually presented was insufficient to establish a prima facie case of discrimination, and in doing so it indicated that it would have found statistical evidence of the number of applicants *and* employees in a methadone program quite probative. *Beazer* therefore does not justify the Court's speculation that the number of blacks and Hispanics actually employed were irrelevant to whether a case of disparate impact had been established under Title VII.

claims necessarily are based on whether the group fares less well than other groups under a policy, practice, or test. Indeed, if only one minority member has taken a test, a disparate-impact claim cannot be made, regardless of whether the test is an initial step in the selection process or one of several factors considered by the employer in making an employment decision.

III

Today's decision takes a long and unhappy step in the direction of confusion. Title VII does not require that employers adopt merit hiring or the procedures most likely to permit the greatest number of minority members to be considered for or to qualify for jobs and promotions. See Texas Dept. of Community Affairs v. Burdine; Furnco. Employers need not develop tests that accurately reflect the skills of every individual candidate; there are few if any tests that do so. Yet the Court seems unaware of this practical reality, and perhaps oblivious to the likely consequences of its decision. By its holding today, the Court may force employers either to eliminate tests or rely on expensive, job-related, testing procedures, the validity of which may or may not be sustained if challenged. For state and local governmental employers with limited funds, the practical effect of today's decision may well be the adoption of simple quota hiring.[8] This arbitrary method of employment is itself unfair to individual applicants, whether or not they are members of minority groups. And it is not likely to produce a competent workforce. Moreover, the Court's decision actually may result in employers employing *fewer* minority members. As Judge Newman noted in Brown v. New Haven Civil Service Comm'n, 474 F.Supp. 1256, 1263 (D.Conn.1979):

> "[A]s private parties are permitted under Title VII itself to adopt voluntary affirmative action plans, * * * Title VII should not be construed to prohibit a municipality's using a hiring process that results in a percentage of minority policemen approximating their percentage of the local population, instead of relying on the expectation that a validated job-related testing procedure will produce an equivalent result, yet with the risk that it might lead to substantially less hiring." (citations omitted).

Finding today's decision unfortunate in both its analytical approach and its likely consequences, I dissent.

8. Another possibility is that employers may integrate consideration of test results into one overall hiring decision based on that "factor" *and* additional factors. Such a process would not, even under the Court's reasoning, result in a finding of discrimination on the basis of disparate impact unless the actual hiring decisions had a disparate impact on the minority group. But if employers integrate test results into a single-step decision, they will be free to select *only* the number of minority candidates proportional to their representation in the workforce. If petitioner had used this approach, it would have been able to hire substantially fewer blacks without liability on the basis of disparate impact. The Court hardly could have intended to encourage this.

NOTES AND PROBLEMS FOR DISCUSSION

1. Does the Court's emphasis of individual interest terminology reflect a move away from the group interest-based theory of discrimination that it previously articulated in *Griggs?* Is the ruling in this case inconsistent with *Griggs* or does it simply shift the analysis of disproportionate impact to a different point in the selection process? If so, does this shift in emphasis reflect a changing conception of the notion of equality or nondiscrimination?

2. Do you agree with the dissent that there was no adverse effect on the group in this case? Is Justice Powell correct in assuming that a balanced bottom line dispels the inference of discrimination created by the plaintiff's prima facie showing? For a thorough discussion of *Teal* and its impact on the group interest concept that originated in *Griggs* see Blumrosen, The Group Interest Concept, Employment Discrimination, and Legislative Intent: The Fallacy of Connecticut v. Teal, 20 Harv.J.Leg. 99 (1983).

3. The New Bedford Police Department requires all applicants for police officer positions to meet a 5′6″ minimum height requirement. When one of its female police officers retired, the City decided that it needed to replace her with another woman because of some particular aspects of the job dealing with female prisoners. Plaintiff Mary Landry scored so high on the mandatory exam that she was ranked first on the eligibility list. After the interview, however, she was rejected for failure to satisfy the minimum height requirement, as were the women who ranked second and third on the eligibility list. The fourth ranked woman received the job. Mary can prove that 80% of the men and 20% of the women in the relevant population satisfied the minimum height requirement. Can Mary successfully bring suit under Title VII? See Costa v. Markey, 706 F.2d 1 (1st Cir. 1982), cert. denied 464 U.S. 1017, 104 S.Ct. 547, 78 L.Ed.2d 722 (1983).

4. While disproportionate impact theory most obviously relates to the use of aptitude and intelligence examinations, it has been utilized to invalidate other objective employment standards such as minimum height and weight requirements, Dothard v. Rawlinson, 433 U.S. 321, 97 S.Ct. 2720, 53 L.Ed.2d 786 (1977) (sex discrimination); prior experience requirement, Chrisner v. Complete Auto Transit, 645 F.2d 1251 (6th Cir. 1981) (sex discrimination); arrest record history, Gregory v. Litton Systems Inc., 316 F.Supp. 401 (C.D.Cal.1970), affirmed as modified 472 F.2d 631 (9th Cir. 1972) (racial discrimination); garnishment experience, Johnson v. Pike Corp. of America, 332 F.Supp. 490 (C.D.Cal.1971) (racial discrimination); parentage of illegitimate children, Davis v. America National Bank of Texas, 12 FEP Cases 1052 (N.D.Tex.1971) (sex and race discrimination); and record of criminal conviction other than minor traffic offenses, compare Green v. Missouri Pacific Railroad, 549 F.2d 1158 (8th Cir. 1977) with Richardson v. Hotel Corp. of America, 468 F.2d 951 (5th Cir. 1972).

Would an employer violate Title VII by refusing to hire persons with a history of drug use? See New York City Transit Authority v. Beazer, 440 U.S. 568, 99 S.Ct. 1355, 59 L.Ed.2d 587 (1979). What about a rule precluding spouses from working for the same employer? See Yuhas v. Libbey-Owens-Ford Co., 562 F.2d 496 (7th Cir. 1977), cert. denied 435 U.S. 934, 98 S.Ct. 1510, 55 L.Ed.2d 531 (1978). Can a gay employee state a *Griggs*-based Title VII claim based on an allegation that he was denied a promotion exclusively because of his sexual preference? Compare DeSantis v. Pacific Telephone & Telegraph Co., 608 F.2d 327 (9th Cir. 1979) and Gay Law Students Association v. Pacific Telephone &

Telegraph Co., 24 Cal.3d 458, 156 Cal.Rptr. 14, 595 P.2d 592 (1979), with Friedman, Constitutional and Statutory Challenges to Discrimination in Employment Based On Sexual Orientation, 64 Iowa L.Rev. 527, 566-68 (1979). Should the analysis of disproportionate impact claims be influenced by whether satisfaction of the challenged requirement is within or beyond the applicant's control?

5. Is the burden of proof placed upon defendants in disproportionate impact cases more onerous than that imposed when plaintiff establishes a prima facie case of disparate treatment? Compare NAACP v. Medical Center, Inc., 657 F.2d 1322 (3d Cir. 1981) with Johnson v. Uncle Ben's Inc., 657 F.2d 750 (5th Cir. 1981), cert. denied, 459 U.S. 967, 103 S.Ct. 293, 74 L.Ed.2d 277 (1983). See also Smith, Employer Defenses In Employment Discrimination Litigation: A Reassessment of Burdens of Proof and Substantive Standards Following Burdine, 55 Temple L.Rev. 372, 391–406 (1982). Does the opinion in *Griggs* offer defendants any guidance with respect to what they must prove to establish that a challenged employment practice is job-related?

ALBEMARLE PAPER CO. v. MOODY

Supreme Court of the United States, 1975.
422 U.S. 405, 95 S.Ct. 2362, 45 L.Ed.2d 280.

MR. JUSTICE STEWART delivered the opinion of the Court.

[A class of present and former black employees challenged the defendant's policy of requiring applicants for employment in skilled lines of progression to pass two general ability tests. Just before trial, the company hired an industrial psychologist to study the job relatedness of its two tests. The study compared the test scores of current employees working in some of the skilled job groupings with supervisorial judgments of these employees' competence. A statistically significant correlation between an individual's supervisorial rating and scores on both tests was found in two of the ten job groupings examined by the psychologist. Additionally, when studied separately, a statistically significant correlation with supervisorial ratings was found in three job groupings for one of the tests and in seven of the ten groupings for the other examination. On the basis of this study, the trial court concluded that the defendant had carried its burden of proving that its tests were job related. On appeal, the U.S. Fourth Circuit Court of Appeals reversed, finding that the validation study was not sufficiently comprehensive to warrant a determination of job-relatedness.]

* * *

In Griggs v. Duke Power Co. this Court unanimously held that Title VII forbids the use of employment tests that are discriminatory in effect unless the employer meets "the burden of showing that any given requirement [has] * * * a manifest relationship to the employment in question." This burden arises, of course, only after the complaining party or class has made out a prima facie case of discrimination, i.e., has shown that the tests in question select applicants for hire or promotion in a racial pattern significantly different from that of the pool of applicants. If an employer does then meet the burden of proving that its tests are "job related," it remains open to the complaining party to show that other tests or selection devices, without a similarly undesirable racial effect, would also serve the employer's legitimate interest in "efficient and trustworthy workmanship." Such a showing would be evidence that the employer was using its tests merely as a "pretext" for discrimination. In the present case, however, we are concerned only with the question whether Albemarle has shown its tests to be job related.

* * *

The EEOC has issued "Guidelines" for employers seeking to determine, through professional validation studies, whether their employment tests are job related. 29 CFR Part 1607. These Guidelines draw upon and make reference to professional standards of test validation established by the American Psychological Association. The EEOC Guidelines are not administrative "regulations" promulgated pursuant to formal procedures established by the Congress. But, as this Court has heretofore noted, they do constitute "[t]he administrative interpretation of the Act by the enforcing agency," and consequently they are "entitled to great deference." Griggs v. Duke Power Co.

The message of these Guidelines is the same as that of the Griggs case—that discriminatory tests are impermissible unless shown, by professionally acceptable methods, to be "predictive of or significantly correlated with important elements of work behavior which comprise or are relevant to the job or jobs for which candidates are being evaluated." 29 CFR § 1607.4(c).

Measured against the Guidelines, Albemarle's validation study is materially defective in several respects:

(1) Even if it had been otherwise adequate, the study would not have "validated" the Beta and Wonderlic test battery for all of the skilled lines of progression for which the two tests are, apparently, now required. The study showed significant correlations for the Beta Exam in only three of the eight lines. Though the Wonderlic Test's Form A and Form B are in theory identical and interchangeable measures of verbal facility, significant correlations for one form but not for the other were obtained in four job groupings. In two job groupings neither form showed a significant correlation. Within some of the lines of progression, one form was found acceptable for some job groupings but not for others. Even if the study were otherwise reliable, this odd patchwork of results would not entitle Albemarle to impose its testing program under the Guidelines. A test may be used in jobs other than those for which it has been professionally validated only if there are "no significant differences" between the studied and unstudied jobs. 29 CFR § 1607.4(c)(2). The study in this case involved no analysis of the attributes of, or the particular skills needed in, the studied job groups. There is accordingly no basis for concluding that "no significant differences" exist among the lines of progression, or among distinct job

groupings within the studied lines of progression. Indeed, the study's checkered results appear to compel the opposite conclusion.

(2) The study compared test scores with subjective supervisorial rankings. While they allow the use of supervisorial rankings in test validation, the Guidelines quite plainly contemplate that the rankings will be elicited with far more care than was demonstrated here. Albemarle's supervisors were asked to rank employees by a "standard" that was extremely vague and fatally open to divergent interpretations. * * * There is no way of knowing precisely what criteria of job performance the supervisors were considering, whether each of the supervisors was considering the same criteria or whether, indeed, any of the supervisors actually applied a focused and stable body of criteria of any kind.[32] There is, in short, simply no way to determine whether the criteria *actually* considered were sufficiently related to the Company's legitimate interest in job-specific ability to justify a testing system with a racially discriminatory impact.

(3) The Company's study focused, in most cases, on job groups near the top of the various lines of progression. In Griggs v. Duke Power Co., the Court left open "the question whether testing requirements that take into account capability for the next succeeding position or related future promotion might be utilized upon a showing that such long-range requirements fulfill a genuine business need." The Guidelines take a sensible approach to this issue, and we now endorse it:

> "If job progression structures and seniority provisions are so established that new employees will probably, within a reasonable period of time and in a great majority of cases, progress to a higher level, it may be considered that candidates are being evaluated for jobs at that higher level. However, where job progression is not so nearly automatic, or the time span is such that higher level jobs or employees' potential may be expected to change in significant ways, it shall be considered that candidates are being evaluated for a job at or near the entry level."

The fact that the best of those employees working near the top of a line of progression score well on a test does not necessarily mean that that test, or some particular cutoff score on the test, is a permissible measure of the minimal qualifications of new workers entering lower level jobs. In drawing any such conclusion, detailed consideration must be given to the normal speed of promotion, to the efficacy of on-the-job training in the scheme of promotion, and to the possible use of testing as a promotion device, rather than as a screen for entry into low-level jobs. The District Court made no findings on these issues. The issues take on special importance in a case, such as this one, where incumbent employees are permitted to work at even high-level jobs without passing the company's test battery.

32. It cannot escape notice that Albemarle's study was conducted by plant officials, without neutral, on-the-scene oversight, at a time when this litigation was about to come to trial. Studies so closely controlled by an interested party in litigation must be examined with great care.

(4) Albemarle's validation study dealt only with job-experienced, white workers; but the tests themselves are given to new job applicants, who are younger, largely inexperienced, and in many instances nonwhite. * * * The EEOC Guidelines * * * provide that "[d]ata must be generated and results separately reported for minority and nonminority groups wherever technically feasible." In the present case, such "differential validation" as to racial groups was very likely not "feasible," because years of discrimination at the plant have insured that nearly all of the upper level employees are white. But there has been no clear showing that differential validation was not feasible for lower level jobs. More importantly, the Guidelines provide:

> "If it is not technically feasible to include minority employees in validation studies conducted on the present work force, the conduct of a validation study without minority candidates does not relieve any person of his subsequent obligation for validation when inclusion of minority candidates becomes technically feasible." * * *

For all these reasons, we agree with the Court of Appeals that the District Court erred in concluding that Albemarle had proved the job relatedness of its testing program and that the respondents were consequently not entitled to equitable relief. The outright reversal by the Court of Appeals implied that an injunction should immediately issue against all use of testing at the plant. Because of the particular circumstances here, however, it appears that the more prudent course is to leave to the District Court the precise fashioning of the necessary relief in the first instance. During the appellate stages of this litigation, the plant has apparently been amending its departmental organization and the use made of its tests. The appropriate standard of proof for job relatedness has not been clarified until today. Similarly, the respondents have not until today been specifically apprised of their opportunity to present evidence that even validated tests might be a "pretext" for discrimination in light of alternative selection procedures available to the Company. We also note that the Guidelines authorize provisional use of tests, pending new validation efforts, in certain very limited circumstances. Whether such circumstances now obtain is a matter best decided, in the first instance, by the District Court. That court will be free to take such new evidence, and to exercise such control of the Company's use and validation of employee selection procedures, as are warranted by the circumstances and by the controlling law.

Accordingly, the judgment is vacated, and these cases are remanded to the District Court for proceedings consistent with this opinion.

It is so ordered.

MR. JUSTICE POWELL took no part in the consideration or decision of these cases.

[The concurring opinions of MR. JUSTICE MARSHALL and MR. JUSTICE REHNQUIST have been omitted.]

MR. JUSTICE BLACKMUN, concurring in the judgment.

I concur in the judgment of the Court, but I do not agree with all that is said in the Court's opinion.

* * * I * * * agree with the decision of the Court to vacate the judgment of the Court of Appeals insofar as it appeared to require an injunction against all testing by Albemarle. I cannot join, however, in the Court's apparent view that absolute compliance with the EEOC Guidelines is a sine qua non of pre-employment test validation. The Guidelines, of course, deserve that deference normally due agency statements based on agency experience and expertise. Nevertheless, the Guidelines in question have never been subjected to the test of adversary comment. Nor are the theories on which the Guidelines are based beyond dispute. The simple truth is that pre-employment tests, like most attempts to predict the future, will never be completely accurate. We should bear in mind that pre-employment testing, so long as it is fairly related to the job skills or work characteristics desired, possesses the potential of being an effective weapon in protecting equal employment opportunity because it has a unique capacity to measure all applicants objectively on a standardized basis. I fear that a too-rigid application of the EEOC Guidelines will leave the employer little choice, save an impossibly expensive and complex validation study, but to engage in a subjective quota system of employment selection. This, of course, is far from the intent of Title VII.

MR. CHIEF JUSTICE BURGER, concurring in part and dissenting in part.

* * *

The Court's treatment of the testing issue is * * * troubling. Its entire analysis is based upon a wooden application of EEOC Guidelines which, it says, are entitled to "great deference" as an administrative interpretation of Title VII under Griggs v. Duke Power Co. The Court's reliance upon Griggs is misplaced. There we were dealing with Guidelines which state that a test must be demonstrated to be job related before it can qualify for the exemption contained in § 703(h) of Title VII. * * * Because this interpretation of specific statutory language was supported by both the Act and its legislative history, we observed that there was "good reason to treat the guidelines as expressing the will of Congress."

In contrast, the Guidelines upon which the Court now relies relate to methods for *proving* job relatedness; they interpret no section of Title VII and are nowhere referred to in its legislative history. Moreover, they are not federal regulations which have been submitted to public comment and scrutiny as required by the Administrative Procedure Act.[3] Thus, slavish adherence to the EEOC Guidelines regarding test validation should not be required; those provisions are, as their

3. Such comment would not be a mere formality in light of the fact that many of the EEOC Guidelines are not universally accepted. For example, the Guideline relating to "differential validation," upon which the Court relies in this case, has been questioned by the American Psychological Association.

title suggests, guides entitled to the same weight as other well-founded testimony by experts in the field of employment testing.

The District Court so considered the Guidelines in this case and resolved any conflicts in favor of Albemarle's experts. Unless this Court is prepared to hold that this and similar factual findings are clearly erroneous, the District Court's conclusion that Albemarle had sustained its burden of showing that its tests were job related is entitled to affirmance, if we follow traditional standards of review. At the very least, the case should be remanded to the Court of Appeals with instructions that it reconsider the testing issue, giving the District Court's findings of fact the deference to which they are entitled.

NOTES AND PROBLEMS FOR DISCUSSION

1. Notice that in both *Griggs* and *Albemarle*, the defendants' failure to sustain their burden of proving the job-relatedness of their high school completion and intelligence examination requirements (after the plaintiff had established the disproportionate exclusionary impact of these criteria) resulted in the Court's finding them in violation of Title VII. By imposing this burden of validation upon defendants, has the Supreme Court created a presumption that all unvalidated selection devices generating a disproportionate exclusionary impact are invalid? If so, is such a presumption warranted? Do the opinions in these two cases suggest that the defendant can rebut this presumption and thus be relieved of the onerous burden of validating its employment criteria? If not, should all employers, regardless of size, be required to absorb the costs and effects on productivity associated with the validation process?

Of course, an employer can avoid these costs either by refusing to validate its criteria or by discontinuing its use of these selection devices. But are either of these alternatives consistent with the policies and goals of Title VII? For example, if an employer wants to continue to use a pre-employment test but does not want to incur the costs of validation, it might be encouraged to take steps to ensure that it will not be sued—i.e. by arbitrarily adjusting the minority and female composition of its work force. Is this consistent with Title VII? See § 703(j). In his dissenting opinion in Connecticut v. Teal, supra, Justice Powell suggested that it was and, moreover, that employers ought to be permitted to adjust the bottom line so that they are not forced either to eliminate tests or to incur the expense of a job validation study that may not survive court challenge. See 457 U.S. at 463, 102 S.Ct. at 2539. On the other hand, if the employer foregoes the use of objective selection devices, are alternative criteria less susceptible to manipulation and abuse? Moreover, is it clear that subjective standards, such as interviews or recommendations, are immune from the validation requirement? The Supreme Court has never specified what types of employment practices are subject to disparate impact analysis. In neither *Griggs* nor *Teal*, for example, did the Court differentiate between objective and subjective practices and procedures. Neither did it hold that impact theory was limited to a single employment criteria as opposed to a multi-factor system of practices that has an adverse impact. This issue has split the circuits.

In Pouncy v. Prudential Insurance Co., 668 F.2d 795 (5th Cir. 1982), the plaintiff proved that black employees were greatly over-represented in the lower levels of the defendant's work force and singled out three practices as responsible for the disparities. The suspect practices were the failure to post job vacancies, a system for promotions dependent in part on the employees' entry level jobs, and the use of largely subjective criteria for promotions. Despite the fact that the plaintiff had tried his case under the impact theory and the fact that the district judge had used impact analysis in deciding the case, the Court of Appeals held that "[n]one of the three Prudential 'employment practices' singled out by [the plaintiff] * * * are akin to the 'facially neutral employment practices' the disparate impact model was designed to test." 668 F.2d at 801. The Court then evaluated the evidence under the disparate treatment standard and concluded that plaintiff had failed to establish a prima facie case. See also, Lewis v. NLRB, 750 F.2d 1266 (5th Cir. 1985) (allegedly discriminatory promotion procedure subject only to disparate treatment analysis); Castaneda v. Pickard, 781 F.2d 456 (5th Cir. 1986) (allegations that school district's criteria for employment are vague, disorganized and undisclosed can be analyzed only under disparate treatment model).

The Eleventh Circuit has reached the opposite conclusion in a case in which a multi-component selection process for promotion was challenged as discriminatory.

> We have repeatedly held that subjective practices such as interviews and supervisory recommendations are capable of operating as barriers to minority advancement. * * * Exclusion of such subjective practices from the reach of the disparate impact model of analysis is likely to encourage employers to use subjective, rather than objective, selection criteria. Rather than validate education and other objective criteria, employers could simply take such criteria into account in subjective interviews or review panel decisions. It could not have been the intent of Congress to provide employers with an incentive to use such devices rather than validated objective criteria.

Griffin v. Carlin, 755 F.2d 1516, 1525 (11th Cir. 1985). See also, Hawkins v. Bounds, 752 F.2d 500 (10th Cir. 1985) (disparate impact analysis proper when it is claimed that the use of subjective employment practice has adverse impact on protected group); Segar v. Smith, 738 F.2d 1249 (D.C. Cir. 1984) (same employment practice may implicate both disparate treatment and impact analysis).

Is there any way a subjective system for making promotions could have a disparate impact on minority employees without those making the promotion decisions having engaged in intentional discrimination? If not, does it make any sense to allow proof of discrimination by a statistical showing less rigorous than that normally applied in disparate treatment cases? See Chapter 3, infra. In Atonio v. Wards Cove Packing Co., 768 F.2d 1120 (9th Cir. 1985), the court reasoned as follows.

> [T]he disparate impact model was created to challenge those specific, facially-neutral practices that result in a discriminatory impact and that by their nature make intentional discrimination difficult or impossible to prove. Were the facial neutrality threshold to disappear or be ignored, the distinction between disparate impact and disparate treatment would diminish and intent would become a largely discarded element. Rather than being an irrelevant factor as envisioned, race (or sex, etc.) could then become an overriding factor in employment decisions. Employers with work forces disproportionate to the minority representation in the labor force could then face the choice of either hiring by quota or defending their selection

procedures against Title VII attack. We do not find that such a result has been mandated by Congress or through Supreme Court interpretation of Title VII. Therefore, practices and policies such as lack of well-defined criteria, subjective decision making, hiring from different sources or channels, word-of-mouth recruitment, and segregated housing and messing, which are not facially neutral, lend themselves far better to scrutiny for intentional discrimination.

768 F.2d at 1133. Do you agree that these criteria are not facially neutral? Under the Ninth Circuit's standard, what kinds of employment practices would be considered "facially neutral"? For a further discussion of the application of Title VII to subjective criteria, see Bartholet, Application of Title VII to Jobs In High Places, 95 Harv.L.Rev. 945 (1982); 3 A. Larson, Employment Discrimination §§ 76.60–.64.

2. Did the Court in *Albemarle* add anything to the *Griggs* formula for proving claims of disproportionate impact? If so, does the inclusion of this new element suggest that intent can play an important role in such cases? According to the EEOC's Uniform Guidelines on Employee Selection Procedures, a validation study

> "should include * * * an investigation of suitable alternative selection procedures and suitable alternative methods of using the selection procedure which have as little adverse impact as possible, to determine the appropriateness of using or validating them in accord with these guidelines. Whenever the user is shown an alternative selection procedure with evidence of less adverse impact and substantial evidence of validity for the same job in similar circumstances, the user should investigate it to determine the appropriateness of using or validating it in accord with these guidelines."

29 CFR 1607.3B. Is this consistent with the burden of proof scheme outlined in *Albemarle*? Who should bear the burden of proof on this issue? The Supreme Court reaffirmed its position in Dothard v. Rawlinson, 433 U.S. 321, 329, 97 S.Ct. 2720, 2727, 53 L.Ed.2d 786, 797 (1977). But compare Wright v. Olin Corp., 697 F.2d 1172 (4th Cir. 1982) and Contreras v. City of Los Angeles, 656 F.2d 1267 (9th Cir. 1981) (placing burden of proof on the plaintiff to establish presence of less discriminatory alternative) with Kirby v. Colony Furniture Co., Inc., 613 F.2d 696 (8th Cir. 1980) (business necessity defense to policy producing discriminatory result requires the defendant to prove there is no alternative to the challenged practice).

3. (a) Is Chief Justice Burger's position concerning the deference to be accorded the EEOC Guidelines in *Albemarle* consistent with the Court's opinion in *Griggs*, which he authored? Are the issues presented in these two cases distinguishable?

(b) Should the Court defer to agency pronouncements promulgated without conforming to the notice and comment requirements of the Administrative Procedure Act? Why doesn't the EEOC have the rule-making and enforcement power granted by Congress to the National Labor Relations Board?

WASHINGTON v. DAVIS

Supreme Court of the United States, 1976.
426 U.S. 229, 96 S.Ct. 2040, 48 L.Ed.2d 597.

MR. JUSTICE WHITE delivered the opinion of the Court.

[Plaintiffs challenged the District of Columbia Metropolitan Police Department's administration of a written personnel test to all applicants for police officer positions. The test was used, along with certain other criteria, to select recruits for a seventeen week training program. The plaintiffs claimed that the use of a test which excluded a disproportionately high number of black applicants violated their rights under the due process clause of the Fifth Amendment, the 1866 Civil Rights Act and a local D.C. antidiscrimination ordinance. No claim was asserted under Title VII since it did not apply to federal government employees when the complaint was filed. Both sides filed motions for summary judgment with respect to the validity of the test. The Supreme Court ruled that the plaintiffs were not entitled to summary judgment on their constitutional claim. It then examined whether the defendants were entitled to summary judgment on the plaintiffs' statutory claims.]

The submission of the defendants in the District Court was that Test 21 complied with all applicable statutory as well as constitutional requirements; and they appear not to have disputed that under the statutes and regulations governing their conduct standards similar to those obtaining under Title VII had to be satisfied.[15] The District Court also assumed that Title VII standards were to control the case, identified the determinative issue as whether Test 21 was sufficiently job related and proceeded to uphold use of the test because it was "directly related to a determination of whether the applicant possesses sufficient skills requisite to the demands of the curriculum a recruit must master at the police academy." The Court of Appeals reversed because the relationship between Test 21 and training school success, if demonstrated at all, did not satisfy what it deemed to be the crucial requirement of a direct relationship between performance on Test 21 and performance on the policeman's job.

We agree with petitioners and the federal parties that this was error. The advisability of the police recruit training course informing the recruit about his upcoming job, acquainting him with its demands, and attempting to impart a modicum of required skills seems conceded. It is also apparent to us, as it was to the District Judge, that some minimum verbal and communicative skill would be very useful, if not essential, to satisfactory progress in the training regimen. Based on the evidence before him, the District Judge concluded that Test 21 was directly related to the requirements of the police training program and

15. In their memorandum supporting their motion for summary judgment, the federal parties argued:

> "In *Griggs*, supra, the Supreme Court set a job-relationship standard for the private sector employers which has been a standard for federal employment since the passage of the Civil Service Act in 1883. In that act Congress has mandated that the federal government must use '* * * examinations for testing applicants for appointment * * * which * * * as far as possible relate to matters that fairly test the relative capacity and fitness of the applicants for the appointments sought.' 5 U.S.C. § 3304(a)(1). Defendants contend that they have been following the job-related standards of *Griggs*, supra, for the past eighty-eight years by virtue of the enactment of the Civil Service Act which guaranteed open and fair competition for jobs."

They went on to argue that the *Griggs* standard had been satisfied. In granting the motions for summary judgment filed by petitioners and the federal parties, the District Court necessarily decided adversely to respondents the statutory issues expressly or tacitly tendered by the parties.

that a positive relationship between the test and training-course performance was sufficient to validate the former, wholly aside from its possible relationship to actual performance as a police officer. This conclusion of the District Judge that training-program validation may itself be sufficient is supported by regulations of the Civil Service Commission, by the opinion evidence placed before the District Judge, and by the current views of the Civil Service Commissioners who were parties to the case.[16] Nor is the conclusion foreclosed by either *Griggs* or Albemarle Paper Co. v. Moody, and it seems to us the much more sensible construction of the job-relatedness requirement.

The District Court's accompanying conclusion that Test 21 was in fact directly related to the requirements of the police training program was supported by a validation study, as well as by other evidence of record; [17] and we are not convinced that this conclusion was erroneous.

The federal parties, whose views have somewhat changed since the decision of the Court of Appeals and who still insist that training-program validation is sufficient, now urge a remand to the District Court for the purpose of further inquiry into whether the training-program test scores, which were found to correlate with Test 21 scores, are themselves an appropriate measure of the trainee's mastership of the material taught in the course and whether the training program itself is sufficiently related to actual performance of the police officer's task. We think a remand is inappropriate. The District Court's judgment was warranted by the record before it, and we perceive no good reason to reopen it, particularly since we were informed at oral argument that although Test 21 is still being administered, the training program itself has undergone substantial modification in the course of this litigation. If there are now deficiencies in the recruiting practices under prevailing Title VII standards, those deficiencies are to be

16. See n. 17, infra. Current instructions of the Civil Service Commission on "Examining, Testing, Standards, and Employment Practices" provide in pertinent part:

"S2-2—Use of applicant appraisal procedures

"a. *Policy.* The Commission's staff develops and uses applicant appraisal procedures to assess the knowledges, skills, and abilities of persons for jobs and not persons in the abstract.

"(1) Appraisal procedures are designed to reflect real, reasonable, and necessary qualifications for effective job behavior.

"(2) An appraisal procedure must, among other requirements, have a demonstrable and rational relationship to important job-related performance objectives identified by management, such as:

"(a) Effective job performance;

"(b) Capability;

"(c) Success in training;

"(d) Reduced turnover; or

"(e) Job satisfaction." 37 Fed.Reg. 21557 (1972).

17. The record includes a validation study of Test 21's relationship to performance in the recruit training program. * * * Findings of the study included data "support[ing] the conclusion that T[est] 21 is effective in selecting trainees who can learn the material that is taught at the Recruit School." * * *

The Court of Appeals was "willing to assume for purposes of this appeal that appellees have shown that Test 21 is predictive of further progress in Recruit School."

directly addressed in accordance with appropriate procedures mandated under that Title.

The judgment of the Court of Appeals accordingly is reversed.

So ordered.

MR. JUSTICE STEWART joins Parts I and II of the Court's opinion.

MR. JUSTICE STEVENS, concurring.

* * *

MR. JUSTICE BRENNAN, with whom MR. JUSTICE MARSHALL joins, dissenting.

* * *

The Court * * * says that its conclusion is not foreclosed by *Griggs* and *Albemarle*, but today's result plainly conflicts with those cases. *Griggs* held that "[i]f an employment practice which operates to exclude Negroes cannot be shown to be *related to job performance*, the practice is prohibited." Once a discriminatory impact is shown, the employer carries the burden of proving that the challenged practice "bear[s] a *demonstrable relationship to successful performance of the jobs* for which it was used." * * *

Albemarle read *Griggs* to require that a discriminatory test be validated through proof "by professionally acceptable methods" that it is " 'predictive of or significantly correlated with *important* elements of work behavior *which comprise or are relevant to the job or jobs* for which candidates are being evaluated.' " Further, we rejected the employer's attempt to validate a written test by proving that it was related to supervisors' job performance ratings, because there was no demonstration that the ratings accurately reflected job performance. We were unable "to determine whether the criteria *actually* considered were sufficiently related to the [employer's] legitimate interest in job-specific ability to justify a testing system with a racially discriminatory impact." To me, therefore, these cases read Title VII as requiring proof of a significant relationship to job performance to establish the validity of a discriminatory test. Petitioners do not maintain that there is a demonstrated correlation between Test 21 scores and job performance. Moreover, their validity study was unable to discern a significant positive relationship between training averages and job performance. Thus, there is no proof of a correlation—either direct or indirect—between Test 21 and performance of the job of being a police officer.

It may well be that in some circumstances, proof of a relationship between a discriminatory qualification test and training performance is an acceptable substitute for establishing a relationship to job performance. But this question is not settled, and it should not be resolved by the minimal analysis in the Court's opinion. Moreover, it is particularly inappropriate to decide the question on this record. "Professionally acceptable methods" apparently recognize validation by proof of a correlation with training performance, rather than job performance, if

(1) the training curriculum includes information proved to be important to job performance and (2) the standard used as a measure of training performance is shown to reflect the trainees' mastery of the material included in the training curriculum. But no authority, whether professional, administrative, or judicial, has accepted the sufficiency of a correlation with training performance in the absence of such proof. * * * [T]he record does not adequately establish either factor. As a result, the Court's conclusion cannot be squared with the focus on job performance in *Griggs* and *Albemarle*, even if this substitute showing is reconcilable with the holdings in those cases.

Today's reduced emphasis on a relationship to job performance is also inconsistent with clearly expressed congressional intent. A section-by-section analysis of the 1972 amendments to Title VII states as follows:

> "In any area where the new law does not address itself, or in any areas where a specific contrary intention is not indicated, it was assumed that the present case law as developed by the courts would continue to govern the applicability and construction of Title VII."

The pre-1972 judicial decisions dealing with standardized tests used as job qualification requirements * * * insist upon proof of a relationship to job performance to prove that a test is job related. * * *

Finally, it should be observed that every federal court, except the District Court in this case, presented with proof identical to that offered to validate Test 21 has reached a conclusion directly opposite to that of the Court today. Sound policy considerations support the view that, at a minimum, petitioners should have been required to prove that the police training examinations either measure job-related skills or predict job performance. Where employers try to validate written qualification tests by proving a correlation with written examinations in a training course, there is a substantial danger that people who have good verbal skills will achieve high scores on both tests due to verbal ability, rather than "job-specific ability." As a result, employers could validate any entrance examination that measures only verbal ability by giving another written test that measures verbal ability at the end of a training course. Any contention that the resulting correlation between examination scores would be evidence that the initial test is "job related" is plainly erroneous. It seems to me, however, that the Court's holding in this case can be read as endorsing this dubious proposition. Today's result will prove particularly unfortunate if it is extended to govern Title VII cases.

* * *

NOTES AND PROBLEMS FOR DISCUSSION

1. Are you persuaded by the Court's statement that its ruling on the job-relatedness of the defendants' test is not foreclosed by either *Griggs* or *Albemarle*? What about the points raised in Justice Brennan's dissenting opinion? Can the result perhaps be explained as an effort by the Court to moderate

the *Albemarle* standard which it now views as imposing too onerous a burden of validation upon employers?

2. Uniform Guidelines on Employee Selection Procedures, adopted by the EEOC, Civil Service Commission, and Departments of Labor and Justice two years after the decision in Washington v. Davis, and designed to establish a uniform federal position with respect to the requirement of equal employment legislation, provide:

> "Where performance in training is used as a criterion, success in training should be properly measured and the relevance of the training should be shown either through a comparison of the content of the training program with the critical or important work behavior(s) of the job(s), or through a demonstration of the relationship between measures of performance in training and measures of job performance. Measures of relative success in training include but are not limited to instructor evaluations, performance samples, or tests. Criterion measures consisting of paper and pencil tests will be closely reviewed for job relevance."

29 CFR 1607.14(B)(3)

> "Where a measure of success in a training program is used as a selection procedure and the content of a training program is justified on the basis of content validity, the use should be justified on the relationship between the content of the training program and the content of the job."

29 CFR 1607.14(C)(7).

Are these guidelines consistent with the validation standard set forth in Washington v. Davis?

3. Note the dissent's concerned reference to the possible extension of the majority's ruling to Title VII cases. Does the Court's opinion leave much doubt in your mind as to its likely resolution of that issue? The federal circuit courts, however, have not adopted a uniform position on this question. Compare Harless v. Duck, 619 F.2d 611 (6th Cir. 1980), cert. denied, 449 U.S. 872, 101 S.Ct. 212, 66 L.Ed.2d 92 (correlation between oral interview used to rank applicants and training academy performance does not satisfy Title VII validation requirement) and Blake v. City of Los Angeles, 595 F.2d 1367 (9th Cir. 1979), cert. denied, 446 U.S. 928, 100 S.Ct. 1865, 64 L.Ed.2d 281 (1980) (significant correlation between pre-employment test and training performance insufficient to establish Title VII validity in absence of showing training performance relationship to job performance), with United States v. Commonwealth of Virginia, 620 F.2d 1018 (4th Cir. 1980) (relationship between test and training course performance is sufficient basis for validation under Title VII).

4. Would the result have changed in Washington v. Davis if the challenged test had been used to determine not only admission into the training program but, also, selection as a permanent employee? In ENSLEY BRANCH OF NATIONAL ASSOCIATION FOR ADVANCEMENT OF COLORED PEOPLE v. SEIBELS, 616 F.2d 812 (5th Cir. 1980), Alabama law required the City of Birmingham to administer written examinations to applicants for all government jobs. Plaintiffs challenged the tests required of all applicants for police and firefighter positions. Applicants who passed the test for either position were ranked on an eligibility list in the order of their scores, with only those achieving the highest scores being certified to the appropriate department for final selection. The suit alleged that the use of tests that generated an adverse racial impact violated the Constitution, Title VII and other federal statutes.

The appellate court limited its inquiry to the claim asserted under Title VII. In their defense, the defendants attempted to validate the tests by offering evidence of a significant correlation between performance on these tests and grades received in the training academies. The trial court found that a significant correlation existed between these two criteria and that the training academies furnished skills or knowledge needed for performance on the job. It also found, however, that academy grades did not accurately predict job performance. These findings led the trial court to conclude that while completion of academy training was an accurate measure of job performance, academy grades were not and that neither of the challenged tests was a valid predictor of successful completion of the academy training program. Accordingly, the trial judge held that the defendants had failed to prove that the tests were job-related. The Fifth Circuit affirmed the lower court's holding:

> The Personnel Board's principal argument on appeal is based on the Supreme Court's opinion in Washington v. Davis. The Board focuses on the district court's finding that both the police test and the firefighter test bear a statistically significant correlation to training academy grades. With that focus the Board argues that the *Davis* case compels a decision in its favor. The Board contends that the *Davis* case stands for the general proposition that a test can be validated by showing that it predicts grades in a job-relevant training program, without regard to the test's ability to predict job performance. As discussed below, the *Davis* case held that the test there was properly validated because it was shown to predict whether those tested had the *minimum* reading and verbal skills necessary to *complete* a job-relevant training program. We do not believe the *Davis* [18] rationale can be extended, as the Board urges, to the general proposition that any test can be validated by showing a relationship to training. More specifically, we reject the Board's suggested extension of the *Davis* holding to this case, where the tests were not used to ascertain the minimum skills necessary to complete job-relevant training, but rather were used to rank job applicants according to their test scores and to select only the highest test scorers for job placement.
>
> * * *
>
> * * * Washington v. Davis holds that a selection device may be validated if it is shown to predict whether an applicant has the minimum amount of reading and verbal skills necessary to complete a job-relevant training program. We decline the Personnel Board's invitation to extend the *Davis* rationale by holding that any test can be validated against training, without respect to the test's ability to predict job performance. Such an extension would violate the requirement of job performance validation enunciated in *Griggs* and *Albemarle*, as well as the agency guidelines elaborating upon that requirement.
>
> Unlike the test upheld in Washington v. Davis, the tests used by the Personnel Board are not used to predict whether an applicant has the minimum amount of knowledge necessary to complete training [23]; rather, the tests are used to rank applicants according to their scores. Only those at the top of the eligibility list, those with the highest test scores, are

18. * * * Since we conclude that Washington v. Davis is factually distinguishable, we do not reach the question of its application to Title VII.

23. Indeed, the district court found * * * that neither test is a valid predictor of ability to pass the training curriculum.

certified for job placement. Even those who score a passing grade, and are deemed by the Personnel Board to possess the capacity to complete training, are not hired unless they are among the highest scorers. Use of a test for such ranking purposes, rather than as a *Davis*-like device to screen out candidates without minimum skills, is justified only if there is evidence showing that those with a higher test score do better on the job than those with a lower test score. Such evidence is utterly lacking here. The Board's validation studies show that higher test scores do *not* predict better job performance.[25]

Having accepted the district court's finding that the Personnel Board did not carry its burden of showing that the two tests are job-related, and having rejected the Board's suggestion that the *Davis* case can be extended to justify validation of these tests against training grades without regard to job performance, we affirm the district court's holding that the Personnel Board's use of the two tests violates Title VII.

616 F.2d at 819–822.

Did the Fifth Circuit accurately characterize and interpret the ruling in Washington v. Davis? Are the two cases distinguishable or did the appellate court merely emphasize insignificant factual disparities in order to limit the impact of a Supreme Court decision with which it disagreed?

SECTION D. RETALIATION

The preceding two sections in this chapter have examined judicial interpretations of the broad language of Title VII's general proscription against discrimination in employment. The statute, however, also prohibits another, more specifically described form of job bias. Section 704(a) states:

> "It shall be an unlawful employment practice for an employer to discriminate against any of his employees or applicants for employment, for an employment agency, or joint labor-management committee controlling apprenticeship or other training * * * to discriminate against any individual, or for a labor organization to discriminate against any member thereof or applicant for membership, because he has opposed any practice made an unlawful employment practice by this title, or because he has made a charge, testified, assisted, or participated in any manner in an investigation, proceeding or hearing under this title."

PAYNE v. McLEMORE'S WHOLESALE & RETAIL STORES

United States Court of Appeals, Fifth Circuit, 1981.
654 F.2d 1130, cert. denied, 455 U.S. 1000, 102 S.Ct. 1630,
71 L.Ed.2d 866 (1982).

SAM D. JOHNSON, CIRCUIT JUDGE:

This is a Title VII action alleging that in early 1971, defendant McLemore's Wholesale & Retail Stores, Inc. failed to rehire plaintiff

25. As previously noted, the Board's validation studies do show that the tests predict academy grades. However, academy grades cannot be used as the criterion with which the tests are compared, because the district court fcund that academy grades do not themselves predict job performance.

Charles Payne because of his participation in activities protected by section 704(a) of the Civil Rights Act of 1964. The district court concluded that plaintiff successfully carried his ultimate burden of proving discrimination. The district court found that plaintiff established a prima facie case of discrimination under section 704(a) by showing that the employer's failure to rehire plaintiff was caused by plaintiff's participation in boycott and picketing activities in opposition to an unlawful employment practice of the defendant. In addition, the district court found that plaintiff proved that the employer's proffered explanation for its failure to rehire the plaintiff—that plaintiff failed to reapply for a job with the employer—was merely pretextual. Because the finding of retaliatory discrimination is supported by requisite subsidiary facts, we affirm the district court judgment for the plaintiff.

During the period of time in which the actions challenged by plaintiff took place, McLemore's Wholesale & Retail Stores was a commercial partnership whose * * * operations included McLemore Wholesale Grocery, McLemore Jitney Jungle (a retail grocery operation), McLemore Farm Store (a light hardware, sporting goods, western wear, feed, seed, fertilizer, and chemical sales store), and Big M. Mobile Homes (a retail mobile home outlet). McLemore's Wholesale & Retail Stores, Inc., a Louisiana corporation, was incorporated August 26, 1975. In 1976, when this lawsuit was filed, the operation of McLemore's Wholesale & Retail Stores, Inc. had not changed significantly from the time it was a partnership; it continued to maintain the same operations that it had for the past several years. * * *

* * * Plaintiff originally worked in McLemore's fertilizer plant. The operation of the plant was seasonal in nature since the demand for fertilizer was dependent upon the farmers' planting seasons. During the first two years of plaintiff's employment with defendant, he was laid off for three months each year during the seasonal decline in work. In later years, during the off-season plaintiff was not laid off, but was instead shifted to positions in other parts of the defendant's operations. * * *

In November 1970, plaintiff was once again laid off due to the seasonal business decline. Two other black employees and two white employees were laid off at the same time. About a month later, plaintiff became involved in the formation and organization of the Franklin Parish Improvement Organization, a non-profit civil rights organization. * * * The organization was interested in improving social conditions of blacks in Franklin Parish, and it focused especially on the need to get blacks hired in retail stores in money-handling and supervisory positions in order to improve the treatment that blacks received while shopping in stores. Shortly after its formation, the members of the organization decided to boycott several retail businesses, including those of defendant * * *. Plaintiff organized and implemented the boycott and was actively involved in picketing McLemore's Jitney Jungle Food Stores. Defendant knew of plaintiff's involvement in the boycott and picketing. Moreover, the boycott and picketing were effective and defendant's business suffered as a result.

In previous years when he had been laid off, plaintiff had always gone back to work for defendant when the work picked back up. In the year of the boycott, however, he was not recalled or rehired.[3] * * *

On June 17, 1976, plaintiff filed this action in federal district court alleging that defendant's failure to rehire plaintiff was a result of plaintiff's race and his civil rights activity. In its answer, McLemore's denied that it had committed any discriminatory actions, and asserted that the reason the plaintiff was not rehired was because he failed to reapply for a position with McLemore's after he was laid off. The district court held that plaintiff did reapply for his job, but that he was not rehired because of his participation in boycotting and picketing activities. The court further found that participation in the boycott and picketing was protected activity under section 704(a) of Title VII; in other words, the district court concluded that the boycott and picketing were in opposition to an unlawful employment practice of the defendant. The court awarded plaintiff back pay, costs, and attorney's fees totalling $16,260.90.

The opposition clause of section 704(a) of Title VII provides protection against retaliation for employees who oppose unlawful employment practices committed by an employer. (Section 704(a) also contains a participation clause that protects employees against retaliation for their participation in the procedures established by Title VII to enforce its provisions. The participation clause is not involved in this lawsuit.) * * *

In this case, plaintiff contends that he was not rehired in retaliation for his boycott and picketing activities which were, according to plaintiff, in opposition to unlawful employment practices committed by McLemore's. Plaintiff asserted that the unlawful employment practices his boycott and picketing activities were intended to protest were McLemore's discrimination against blacks in hiring and promotion—specifically, McLemore's failure to employ blacks in money-handling, clerking, or supervisory positions. In demonstrating his contentions at trial, plaintiff had the initial burden of establishing a prima facie case of discrimination. McDonnell Douglas Corp. v. Green. The burden then shifted to the defendant to articulate a legitimate, nondiscriminatory reason for the failure to rehire the plaintiff. Finally, if the defendant carried his burden, the plaintiff was entitled to an opportunity to show that the defendant's stated reason for its failure to rehire plaintiff was in fact pretextual.

3. Of the four other employees who were laid off at the same time as plaintiff, only one was rehired—a black employee who was not involved in the boycott or picketing by the Franklin Parish Improvement Organization. Both plaintiff and Russell Brass (the other black employee who was laid off and not rehired) were involved in the boycott and picketing. According to defendant, the employee who was rehired was the only one of the five employees who were laid off that reapplied for a job.

"To establish a prima facie case under [section 704(a)] the plaintiff must establish (1) statutorily protected expression, (2) an adverse employment action, and (3) a causal link between the protected expression and the adverse action." Smalley v. City of Eatonville, 640 F.2d 765, 769 (5th Cir. 1981). The first element of the prima facie case—statutorily protected expression—requires conduct by the plaintiff that is in opposition to an unlawful employment practice of the defendant. Thus, for the plaintiff to prove that he engaged in statutorily protected expression, he must show that the boycott and picketing activity in which he participated was in opposition to conduct by McLemore's that was made unlawful by Title VII. According to the plaintiff, the purpose of the boycott and picketing was to oppose McLemore's discrimination against blacks in hiring and promotion. * * * [T]here is substantial evidence to support the district court finding that the purpose of the boycott and picketing was to oppose defendant's discrimination against blacks in certain employment opportunities [7]—an unlawful employment practice under section 703(a)(1).

Defendant argues, however, that plaintiff failed to establish his prima facie case because he failed to *prove* that defendant had committed any unlawful employment practices. Plaintiff responds that he was not required to *prove* the actual existence of those unlawful employment practices; instead, he asserts that it was sufficient to establish a prima facie case if he had a *reasonable belief* that defendant had engaged in the unlawful employment practices. We agree with plaintiff and conclude that it was not fatal to plaintiff's section 704(a) case that he failed to prove, under the *McDonnell Douglas* criteria for proving an unlawful employment practice under section 703(a)(1), that McLemore's discriminated against blacks in retail store employment opportunities.

The Ninth Circuit was apparently the first appellate court to decide whether the opposition clause of section 704(a) required proof of actual discrimination. Sias v. City Demonstration Agency, 588 F.2d 692 (9th Cir. 1978). In *Sias*, the plaintiff alleged that he was discharged by the City Demonstration Agency (an agency of the City of Los Angeles) in retaliation for his opposition to acts of racial discrimination by the City of Los Angeles. The City did not deny that plaintiff "was discharged for writing a letter of grievance to the Regional Administrator of the Department of Housing and Urban Development (HUD). Rather, it

7. Defendant claims that plaintiff did not engage in the boycott and picketing to oppose unlawful employment practices of McLemore's. Instead, it is McLemore's contention that the boycott and picketing were conducted to publicize the issues of integration of public facilities and common courtesy to blacks. To support this allegation, defendant points to the incident that initiated the formation of the Franklin Parish Improvement Organization—two black children being turned away from the town's segregated public swimming pool. * * * Although the Improvement Organization was, in part, occasioned by the position of blacks in Winnsboro in general, and although the boycott and picketing may have been to some extent a protest of this position, the district court's conclusion that the boycott and picketing activity was in opposition to unlawful employment practices of McLemore's is supported by substantial evidence.

contend[ed that, inasmuch as the trial court made no finding of actual discrimination, it [could not] be held to have violated" section 704(a). The Ninth Circuit concluded that "[s]uch a narrow interpretation * * * would not only chill the legitimate assertion of employee rights under Title VII but would tend to force employees to file formal charges rather than seek conciliation or informal adjustment of grievances." The *Sias* court quoted extensively from Hearth v. Metropolitan Transit Commission, 436 F.Supp. 685 (D.Minn.1977), which held that "as long as the employee had a reasonable belief that what was being opposed constituted discrimination under Title VII, the claim of retaliation does not hinge upon a showing that the employer was in fact in violation of Title VII." The *Hearth* court went on to state:

> But this Court believes that appropriate informal opposition to perceived discrimination must not be chilled by the fear of retaliatory action in the event the alleged wrongdoing does not exist. It should not be necessary for an employee to resort immediately to the EEOC or similar State agencies in order to bring complaints of discrimination to the attention of the employer with some measure of protection. The resolution of such charges without governmental prodding should be encouraged.
>
> The statutory language does not compel a contrary result. The elimination of discrimination in employment is the purpose behind Title VII and the statute is entitled to a liberal interpretation. When an employee reasonably believes that discrimination exists, opposition thereto is opposition to an employment practice made unlawful by Title VII even if the employee turns out to be mistaken as to the facts.

The Seventh Circuit has also adopted this position. Berg v. La Crosse Cooler Co., 612 F.2d 1041 (7th Cir. 1980). In *Berg*, the plaintiff was discharged when she challenged her employer's failure to provide pregnancy benefits as sex-based discrimination. After she was fired, the United States Supreme Court ruled that a disability benefits plan does not violate Title VII because of its failure to cover pregnancy related disabilities. The Seventh Circuit held that where the employee opposed a practice that she reasonably believed was an unlawful employment practice under Title VII, her opposition was protected from retaliatory discharge even where the practice was later determined not be an unlawful employment practice. The court concluded that to interpret the opposition clause to require proof of an actual unlawful employment practice

> undermines Title VII's central purpose, the elimination of employment discrimination by informal means; destroys one of the chief means of achieving that purpose, the frank and nondisruptive exchange of ideas between employers and employees; and serves no redeeming statutory or policy purposes of its own. Section 2000e–3(a) plays a central role in effectuating these objectives. By protecting employees from retaliation, it is designed to encourage employ-

ees to call to their employers' attention discriminatory practices of which the employer may be unaware or which might result in protracted litigation to determine their legality if they are not voluntarily changed.

The Fifth Circuit has not heretofore directly addressed the issue whether proof of an actual unlawful employment practice is necessary under the opposition clause, or whether an employee is protected from retaliation under the opposition clause if the employee reasonably believes that the employer is engaged in unlawful employment practices. To the extent that earlier Fifth Circuit cases provide guidance to this Court, however, they indicate that the reasonable belief test of the Seventh and Ninth Circuits comports with the decisions of this Circuit and the policies underlying Title VII. In Pettway v. American Cast Iron Pipe Co., 411 F.2d 998 (5th Cir. 1969), this Court held that an employee was protected by the participation clause of section 704(a) from discharge in retaliation for filing a charge with the EEOC, regardless of the truth or falsity of the contents of the charge. The Court stated that:

> There can be no doubt about the purpose of § 704(a). In unmistakable language it is to protect the employee who utilizes the tools provided by Congress to protect his rights. The Act will be frustrated if the employer may unilaterally determine the truth or falsity of charges and take independent action.

Thus, the Court held that where the communication with the EEOC satisfied the requirements of a "charge," the charging party could not be discharged for the writing and the court could not "either sustain any employer disciplinary action or deny relief because of the presence of * * * malicious material." Id. at 1007.[9]

9. Although this Court considers the reasoning of the *Pettway* decision to support the reasonable belief test in opposition clause cases, at least one district court has viewed the *Pettway* case quite differently. The district court in EEOC v. C & D Sportswear Corp., 398 F.Supp. 300 (M.D. Ga.1975), held that "baseless accusations" were protected "only as a means of protecting access to the Commission." Thus, that court concluded that the result in *Pettway* was limited to actions under the participation clause, and did not apply to actions under the opposition clause. The *C & D Sportswear* court held:

> Accordingly, the only reasonable interpretation to be placed on Section 704(a) is that where accusations are made in the context of charges before the EEOC, the truth or falsity of that accusation is a matter to be determined by the EEOC, and thereafter by the courts. However, where accusations are made outside the procedures set forth by Congress that accusation is made at the accuser's peril. In order to be protected, it must be established that the accusation is well-founded. If it is, there is, in fact, an unlawful employment practice and he has the right, protected by Section 704(a), to oppose it. However, where there is no underlying unlawful employment practice the employee has no right to make that accusation in derogation of the procedures provided by statute.

Id. at 306. We find the reasoning of the *C & D Sportswear* district court unpersuasive and the result unjustifiably restrictive. In *C & D Sportswear*, an employee called the president of the company a racist and was discharged for making that accusation. The district court reasoned that

> access to the EEOC must be protected. On the other hand, accusations of racism ought not to be made lightly. Unfounded accusations might well incite racism where none had previously existed. Were employees free to make unfounded accusations of racism against their em-

The Ninth Circuit recognized that the "considerations controlling the interpretation of the opposition clause are not entirely the same as those applying to the participation clause," and that the opposition clause "serves a more limited purpose" than does the participation clause. However, interpreting the opposition clause to require proof of an actual unlawful employment practice would "chill the legitimate assertion of employee rights under Title VII," just as surely as would interpreting the participation clause to require a truthful charge. On the other hand, interpreting the opposition clause to protect an employee who reasonably believes that discrimination exists "is consistent with a liberal construction of Title VII to implement the Congressional purpose of eliminating discrimination in employment."

* * *

To effectuate the policies of Title VII and to avoid the chilling effect that would otherwise arise, we are compelled to conclude that a plaintiff can establish a prima facie case of retaliatory discharge under the opposition clause of section 704(a) if he shows that he had a reasonable belief that the employer was engaged in unlawful employment practices.[11] While the district court made no explicit finding that plaintiff's opposition was based upon a reasonable belief that McLemore's hiring and promotional policies violated Title VII, such a finding is implicit and is sufficiently supported by evidence in the record. Thus, plaintiff established that he reasonably believed that defendant McLemore's discriminated against blacks in employment opportunities.

> ployers and fellow employees, racial discord, disruption, and disharmony would likely ensue. This would be wholly contrary to Congress' intention that race be removed, as far as possible, as an issue in employment.

While unfounded, inflammatory accusations of racism might, on balance, be found to provide the employer with a legitimate, nondiscriminatory reason for discharging an employee, this would neither require nor suggest that all unfounded accusations should be totally unprotected by the opposition clause of section 704(a). It is as important to protect an employee's right to oppose perceived discrimination by appropriate, informal means as it is to protect his right of access to the EEOC. An employee who engages in opposition activity should not be required to act at his own peril if it turns out that no unlawful employment practice actually exists, as long as the employee holds a reasonable belief that the unlawful employment practices do exist.

11. The First Circuit has adopted a somewhat different test than have the Seventh and Ninth Circuits. The First Circuit has not explicitly decided whether a section 704(a) plaintiff must "demonstrate that he harbored a 'reasonable belief' of discriminatory employer behavior" or whether the plaintiff must show that he harbored a " 'conscientiously held belief' of such misconduct." Monteiro v. Poole Silver Co., 615 F.2d 4, 8 (1st Cir. 1980) (footnote omitted). The *Monteiro* court found that "[u]nder either standard—the employer's conduct being non-discriminatory in fact—the plaintiff must show that his so-called opposition was in response to some *honestly held*, if mistaken, feeling that discriminatory practices existed." Id. (emphasis added) (footnote omitted). Thus, according to that court, if a reasonable person might have believed that the employer was engaged in unlawful employment practices, but the plaintiff actually did not in good faith hold such a belief, then the plaintiff's opposition conduct is unprotected. We need not decide here whether it is necessary to adopt a good faith requirement in addition to the reasonable belief requirement since, in the case before this Court, the plaintiff believed—reasonably and in good faith—that McLemore's was engaged in unlawful employment practices, and plaintiff's opposition conduct was in response to this belief.

Moreover, plaintiff showed that his boycott and picketing activities were in opposition to this unlawful employment practice. Defendant's failure to rehire the plaintiff was undoubtedly an adverse employment action. Finally, there was evidence to support an inference that defendant's failure to rehire plaintiff was causally related to plaintiff's boycott and picketing activities.[13] Thus, plaintiff successfully established a prima facie case, thereby raising an inference of unlawful discrimination under section 704(a). The burden then shifted to the defendant to "rebut the presumption of discrimination by producing evidence" of a legitimate, nondiscriminatory reason for its failure to rehire plaintiff.

Defendant McLemore's steadfastly maintained at trial that the *only* reason plaintiff was not rehired was because he failed to reapply for a position with defendant. This comprised the full and complete extent of the rebuttal evidence presented by the agents of the defendant in an effort to articulate a legitimate, nondiscriminatory reason for the failure to rehire the plaintiff. * * *

* * * This reason—the failure to reapply—would, if believed, be legally sufficient to justify a judgment for the defendant. Thus, the defendant carried its rebuttal burden at trial.

After the defendant has an opportunity to rebut plaintiff's prima facie case, the plaintiff has a corresponding opportunity to show that the defendant's proffered explanation was in fact pretextual. Here, plaintiff presented substantial evidence that he did reapply for a job with McLemore's. The trial court found "as a fact that Mr. Payne did reapply for his position with the defendant corporation." There is, therefore, substantial evidence in the record to support the district court's conclusion that the defendant's explanation for its failure to rehire the plaintiff was merely pretextual. The district court further found that members of McLemore's knew of plaintiff's participation in the boycott and picketing, and that there was a causal relationship between defendant's failure to rehire plaintiff and plaintiff's participation in the protest activity. There is also substantial evidence in the record to support the district court's conclusion in this regard. Thus, on the facts and arguments presented to the trial court, that court correctly held that the defendant's failure to rehire the plaintiff violated section 704(a); that is, that the defendant's stated reason for not rehiring the plaintiff (the plaintiff's failure to reapply for a job) was merely pretextual and that the defendant's actual reason for not rehiring the plaintiff was the plaintiff's participation in activities in opposition to unlawful employment practices of the defendant.

13. An inference that defendant's failure to rehire the plaintiff was caused by plaintiff's participation in the boycott and picketing activity was proper in view of the existence of evidence that the employer was aware of the plaintiff's activities and that, within a relatively short time after those activities took place, the adverse employment consequence occurred. The defendant was then entitled to an opportunity to introduce evidence to rebut this inference.

Now on appeal, for the first time, defendant contends that even if plaintiff's activity was in opposition to unlawful employment practices of defendant, plaintiff's actions were not protected by section 704(a) because the *form* of plaintiff's opposition was not covered by the statute. It is well-established that not all activity in opposition to unlawful employment practices is protected by section 704(a). Certain conduct—for example, illegal acts of opposition or unreasonably hostile or aggressive conduct—may provide a legitimate, independent, and nondiscriminatory basis for an employee's discharge. "There may arise instances where the employee's conduct in protest of an unlawful employment practice so interferes with the performance of his job that it renders him ineffective in the position for which he was employed. In such a case, his conduct, or form of opposition, is not covered by § 704(a)." Rosser v. Laborers' International Union, Local 438, 616 F.2d 221, 223 (5th Cir. 1980), cert. denied, 449 U.S. 886, 101 S.Ct. 241, 66 L.Ed.2d 112. In order to determine when such a situation exists, the court must engage in a balancing test: "[T]he courts have required that the employee conduct be reasonable in light of the circumstances, and have held that 'the employer's right to run his business must be balanced against the rights of the employee to express his grievances and promote his own welfare.'" Jefferies v. Harris County Community Action Association, 615 F.2d 1025, 1036 (5th Cir. 1980).

It appears that a number of cases have assumed that it is part of defendant's rebuttal burden to show that the form of plaintiff's opposition was unprotected by the statute. If the defendant took an adverse employment action against the plaintiff because of opposition conduct by the plaintiff that was outside the protection of the statute, then the defendant may have had a legitimate, nondiscriminatory reason to justify its actions. Thus, in the case before this Court, if the *form* of plaintiff's activities placed them outside the protection of section 704(a), then the defendant may have had a legitimate, nondiscriminatory reason for its failure to rehire the plaintiff. However, if the form of plaintiff's activities was the nondiscriminatory reason for the defendant's failure to rehire the plaintiff, it was the defendant's responsibility to introduce evidence to that effect at trial. * * *

In Gonzalez v. Bolger, 486 F.Supp. 595 (D.D.C.1980), the plaintiff, a former post office employee, brought an employment discrimination suit pursuant to section 704(a) alleging that he was discharged unlawfully in retaliation for his exercise of rights protected by Title VII. The district court made the following findings:

> At trial, plaintiff presented a *prima facie* case of retaliatory discrimination, by showing that he engaged in protected activities, that his employer was aware of the protected activities, and that he was subsequently discharged, within a relatively short time interval after his performance of the activities. This series of events is sufficient to enable a court to infer retaliatory motivation, absent further explanation from the employer. * * *

* * *

In rebuttal, however, defendant presented substantial proof, through testimony and documentary exhibits, that plaintiff's insubordination and disruptive outbursts were in fact the cause for his termination. These reasons, if accepted on the proof as a whole, would constitute a valid non-discriminatory explanation for defendant's action.

Since the court further found that plaintiff failed to establish that defendant's proffered justification was in fact pretextual, the court concluded that "[b]ecause plaintiff exceeded the limits of reasonable opposition activity on a continuing basis and his dismissal is attributable to these transgressions, the Court is forced to conclude that his termination was not pretextual, but rather was for valid non-discriminatory reasons." The *Gonzalez* court clearly placed the burden on defendant to show as part of its rebuttal burden, that the "plaintiff's excessive conduct was the cause for his termination."

* * *

It therefore becomes apparent that in the instant case, after plaintiff established his prima facie case, it was the responsibility of the defendant to show that the *form* of plaintiff's activities placed them outside the protection of section 704(a) and provided defendant with a legitimate reason for its failure to rehire the plaintiff. If the defendant intended to rely upon this contention, it was the defendant's responsibility to raise the issue at trial. Here, the defendant failed to offer *any* evidence at trial that its legitimate and nondiscriminatory reason for not rehiring the plaintiff was that plaintiff had engaged in hostile, unprotected activity that was detrimental to the employer's interests.[14] With respect to the defendant's burden of rebutting plaintiff's prima facie case, the *Burdine* Court stated that: "An articulation not admitted into evidence will not suffice. Thus, the defendant cannot meet its burden merely through an answer to the complaint or by argument of counsel." If the defendant cannot meet its rebuttal burden by answer to the complaint or by argument of counsel at trial, the defendant undoubtedly cannot meet its rebuttal burden solely by argument of counsel for the first time *on appeal.* It is not permissible for this Court to relate the defendant's arguments on appeal back to the time of trial in order to determine whether defendant met its rebuttal burden at trial. Since the defendant failed to present *any* evidence at trial that the egregious and disruptive form of plaintiff's opposition constituted the legitimate reason for defendant's failure to rehire plaintiff, the defendant surely did not carry its rebuttal burden on this issue at trial.

* * *

14. * * * The only contention made by the defendant that the conduct of the plaintiff was not protected by section 704(a) was that the boycott and picketing were not in opposition to an unlawful employment practice of the defendant and so did not satisfy the requirements of section 704(a). * * * While defendant did allege that plaintiff's activity was not in opposition to an unlawful employment practice of McLemore's, defendant did *not* assert that the form of plaintiff's activity was outside the scope of section 704(a).

[The court then refused to make its own determination as to whether the form of the plaintiff's activities provided the defendant with a legitimate, nondiscriminatory reason for not rehiring the plaintiff.]

* * * Since plaintiff made out his prima facie case of discrimination under section 704(a), and since the only explanation offered by the defendant for its failure to rehire plaintiff was correctly determined to be pretextual, the judgment of the district court for plaintiff is

Affirmed.

COLEMAN, CIRCUIT JUDGE, dissenting.

* * *

The gravamen of my concern is found in the concession of the majority opinion that "The Fifth Circuit has not heretofore directly addressed the issue whether proof of an actual unlawful employment practice is necessary under the opposition clause, or whether an employee is protected from retaliation under the opposition clause if the employee reasonably believes that the employer is engaged in unlawful employment practices".

The majority then proceeds to hold that reasonable belief is enough.

* * *

The statute speaks in terms of practices—not what someone "reasonably believes" to have been a practice when, in fact, the practice did not exist. I cannot believe that Congress intended (since it did not say so) to penalize employers for what an employee or applicant "believes" when, in fact, the employer is innocent. To hold otherwise is to deprive employers of their property rights in violation of the due process clause.

Finally, I dissent because, as the majority concedes, the District Court made no finding [the majority adds the word "explicit"] that the plaintiff's opposition was based upon "reasonable belief". In proceeding to make its own, inferential, findings of fact the majority cites not a single specific fact that would support a finding of reasonable belief. * * *

I respectfully dissent.

NOTES AND PROBLEMS FOR DISCUSSION

1. As *Payne* indicates, § 704(a) offers protection from retaliation directed at two types of conduct: "participation" in the formal Title VII enforcement process and informal "opposition" to a proscribed employment practice. Most of the cases arising under this section raise one or more of the following four interpretative questions: (a) whether the plaintiff's activities constitute participation or opposition; (b) the extent to which an employee should be immunized from retaliation when that participation or opposition is premised on a factually or legally erroneous belief that the employer is engaged in unlawful conduct; (c) whether the nature or form of the plaintiff's conduct removes it from the protection of the statute; and (d) whether the defendant's response constitutes retaliation. In many cases, (including *Payne*) of course, there also is an important factual dispute as to the causal connection between the plaintiff's

conduct and the defendant's response. Where causation is at issue, the plaintiff must prove that "but for" the protected activity, no action would have been taken. See De Anda v. St. Joseph Hospital, 671 F.2d 850 (5th Cir. 1982).

In light of the above issues, consider the following:

(a) Jane Leston, an electrical engineer with Chicago Industries, Inc., was denied a promotion to department supervisor in favor of her colleague, Bill Thomas. Shortly thereafter, Ms. Leston filed a sex discrimination charge under Illinois law with the appropriate Illinois administrative agency. When the company learned of Leston's charge, it asked Mr. Thomas to sign an affidavit prepared by the company to aid in its defense. Thomas refused and was demoted one week later. Can Thomas state a claim under § 704(a)? See Smith v. Columbus Metropolitan Housing Authority, 443 F.Supp. 61 (S.D.Ohio 1977). What if Leston's charge had alleged that she was denied the promotion because of her age? If the company terminated Leston after she filed that age discrimination claim, could she challenge the discharge under § 704(a)? See Hicks v. ABT Associates, Inc., 572 F.2d 960 (3d Cir. 1978).

(b) Karlen Construction, Inc. was awarded a contract by the federal government to help build a post office. The contract contained an affirmative action plan requiring Karlen to employ a specified percentage of minority workers. In the middle of construction, the company concluded that it could not afford to retain all four of the electricians it had hired for the post office project. To maintain compliance with the affirmative action plan, Karlen chose to lay off its three white electricians and retain its one black electrician. One of the laid off electricians, Fred Hill, circulated a letter around the site charging Karlen with racial discrimination in connection with the lay off of electricians. One month later, when its economic condition improved, Karlen rehired all of the laid off electricians, except for Hill. Hill subsequently filed a Title VII action alleging that Karlen's refusal to rehire him violated § 704(a). The trial court ruled in favor of the defendant, holding that the company's original decision to lay off the three white electricians and retain the black electrician did not violate Title VII and, therefore, that Hill's conduct after being laid off was not protected by § 704. How should the appellate court rule on Hill's appeal? See Sisco v. J. S. Alberici Construction Co., Inc., 655 F.2d 146 (8th Cir. 1981), cert. denied, 455 U.S. 976, 102 S.Ct. 1485, 71 L.Ed.2d 688 (1982).

Was the issue raised by this problem addressed by the court in *Payne*? Should the courts distinguish between mistakes of fact and law? Compare Parker v. Baltimore & Ohio Railroad Co., 652 F.2d 1012 (D.C.Cir. 1981) and Berg v. La Crosse Cooler Co., 612 F.2d 1041 (7th Cir. 1980) with Winsey v. Pace College, 394 F.Supp. 1324 (S.D.N.Y.1975).

In *Payne*, the court implied that persons engaged in participation enjoy a somewhat more expansive immunity than individuals engaged in opposition activities. Is such a distinction supported by any statutory language or policy consideration? See EEOC v. C & D Sportswear Corp., 398 F.Supp. 300 (M.D.Ga. 1975).

(c) Williams Steelworks, Inc. (W.S.I.), as a federal government contractor, was obliged to develop an affirmative action program and appoint one of its executives as director of the firm's equal opportunity programs. As equal opportunity director, Richard Kane was required to design the company's affirmative action programs and monitor their effectiveness. According to Kane, the company evidenced a lack of commitment to its equal opportunity obligation by continually ignoring his reports that detailed management's failure to accomplish the reforms outlined in the affirmative action programs. This ultimately led to Kane's filing a complaint against W.S.I. with the federal agency authorized to audit government contract compliance. When notified of the filing of this charge, the company asked Kane if he knew the identity of the charging party. He denied knowledge of this fact and continued to conceal his role as charging party while actively participating with the federal agency's investigation of his charge. During this period Kane also organized a clandestine meeting of minority employees to solicit complaints of discrimination. When W.S.I. learned of Kane's involvement with the federal investigation, Kane was fired. He subsequently brought suit against W.S.I. under § 704. What result? See Jennings v. Tinley Park School Dist., 796 F.2d 962 (7th Cir. 1986); Jones v. Flagship Int'l, 793 F.2d 714 (5th Cir. 1986); Holden v. Owens-Illinois, Inc., 793 F.2d 745 (6th Cir. 1986); E.E.O.C. v. Crown Zellerbach Corp., 720 F.2d 1008 (9th Cir. 1983); Smith v. Singer Co., 650 F.2d 214 (9th Cir. 1981); Novotny v. Great American Federal Savings & Loan Association, 539 F.Supp. 437 (W.D.Pa.1982). What if Kane also had filed a charge against W.S.I. with the EEOC before his discharge? See Gonzalez v. Bolger, 486 F.Supp. 595 (D.D.C.1980), affirmed, 656 F.2d 899 (D.C.Cir. 1981).

(d) Irish Pleshette filed a sex descrimination charge with the EEOC against her employer, Heavenly Foods, Inc., on March 16, 1976. She filed another charge on August 20, 1978. In both instances, the EEOC found no reasonable cause to believe discrimination had occurred and dismissed the charge. After EEOC dismissal of the second charge, Pleshette filed a Title VII action in federal court. The trial court granted the defendant's motion for summary judgment on March 16, 1980. Ms. Pleshette was discharged on April 30, 1980. Ms. Pleshette applied for a job with Consolidated Containers, Inc. on May 1, 1980. On May 5, 1980, John Newman, President of Heavenly Foods, refused Ms. Pleshette's request for a letter of recommendation. On May 8, 1980, Mr. Newman sent a letter to the Personnel Director of Consolidated, stating that Ms. Pleshette had filed charges of sex discrimination with the EEOC on two separate occasions, that both charges had been dismissed by the EEOC after lengthy investigations and that Ms. Pleshette had unsuccessfully pursued one of these claims in federal district court. Ms. Pleshette subsequently filed a second action against Heavenly Foods alleging that Newman's refusal to provide a letter of recommendation, and his sending of an unsolicited letter to Consolidated Containers violated § 704(a). What result? See § 701(f); Pantchenko v. C. B. Dolge Co., 581 F.2d 1052 (2d Cir. 1978); Rutherford v. American Bank of Commerce, 565 F.2d 1162 (10th Cir. 1977). What if the letter had been solicited by Consolidated? See Czarnowski v. Desoto, Inc., 518 F.Supp. 1252 (N.D.Ill.1981).

For a further discussion of these issues, see Kattan, Employee Opposition to Discriminatory Employment Practices: Protection From Reprisal Under Title VII, 19 Wm. & Mary L.Rev. 217 (1977).

2. Lou Bernstein and his daughter, Judy, worked for Martinez Paper Co. After the company denied Ms. Bernstein's application for a promotion, she filed a charge with the EEOC alleging that the denial of the promotion was based exclusively on her sex. Shortly after receiving notice of this charge, the company discharged Mr. Bernstein. Can he state a cause of action under § 704? See Kent v. R. J. Reynolds Tobacco Co., 27 FEP Cases 1628 (E.D.La. 1982).

3. Is an employer prohibited by § 704(a) from bringing a defamation suit against an employee who prosecutes a nonmeritorious Title VII claim? Would

the institution of such an action violate § 704(a)? What if the defamation suit was commenced in response to a letter sent by the employee to a local newspaper charging that the employer was a racist? While several courts have suggested, in dictum, that § 704 would not preclude a defamation action, see e.g., Noel v. McCain, 538 F.2d 633, 636 (4th Cir. 1976) (opposition case); Pettway v. American Cast Pipe Iron Co., 411 F.2d 998, 1008 n. 22 (5th Cir. 1969) (participation case); and Bartulica v. Paculdo, 411 F.Supp. 392, 397 n. 3 (W.D. Mo.1976) (opposition case), in the two cases in which this issue was directly addressed, the courts held that defamation suits instituted for retaliatory purposes would violate § 704. See EEOC v. Levi Strauss & Co., 515 F.Supp. 640 (N.D.Ill.1981); EEOC v. Virginia Carolina Veneer Corp., 495 F.Supp. 775 (W.D. Va.1980), appeal dismissed, 652 F.2d 380 (4th Cir. 1981). The court in *Levi Strauss*, however, noted that a good faith suit brought to attempt to rehabilitate the employer's reputation would not be proscribed by § 704.

4. When Title VII was amended in 1972, a new provision, § 717, was enacted to extend the statutory guarantee of equal employment opportunity to federal employees. Does the absence in § 717 of any language pertaining to retaliation suggest that federal employees are not protected against retaliation? See Canino v. E.E.O.C., 707 F.2d 468 (11th Cir. 1983); Smith v. Secretary of the Navy, 659 F.2d 1113 (D.C. Cir. 1981); Porter v. Adams, 639 F.2d 273 (5th Cir. 1981); Ayon v. Sampson, 547 F.2d 446 (9th Cir. 1976).

Chapter 3

PROVING DISCRIMINATION

SECTION A. THE PLAINTIFF'S BURDEN: PROOF OF THE PRIMA FACIE CASE AND OF PRETEXT

MILES v. M.N.C. CORPORATION

United States Court of Appeals, Eleventh Circuit, 1985.
750 F.2d 867.

CLARK, CIRCUIT JUDGE:

Mary Miles appeals from an adjudication that defendant-appellee M.N.C. Corporation (M.N.C.) did not discriminate against her on the basis of race in violation of Title VII of the Civil Rights Act. M.N.C. is a company engaged in the manufacture of cardboard boxes in Opelika, Alabama. Mary Miles claims that she was the victim of racial discrimination practiced by M.N.C. when the company did not rehire her after a temporary layoff. Miles started work for Rock-Tenn Company, M.N.C.'s predecessor in interest, on November 7, 1979 and was laid off on December 17, 1979. At the beginning of 1980, M.N.C. replaced Rock-Tenn as the owner of the business. Nick Constan, the major stockholder and president of M.N.C., served as plant manager for Rock-Tenn prior to M.N.C.'s purchase of the company. M.N.C. retained the same work force and managers and produced the same product under the same conditions as Rock-Tenn.[1]

At the time of Miles' layoff, two other full-time general production workers were also laid off. One of these workers, Lavelle Parmer, was white and the other worker, Sarah Wright, was black. Layoffs were according to seniority and these three women were the junior employees at the plant. Both Parmer and Wright had been employed a few days before Miles. One white male part-time worker, David Kinports, was also laid off. Miles claims that Dave Nichols, the plant supervisor, told her on two occasions that she would be recalled after the first of the year. Around January 23, 1980, Parmer, the white full-time worker, was reemployed and two white male part-time workers were employed. Part-time workers had the same duties as full-time general production workers. In June 1980, Parmer quit her job and was replaced by Karen Wilson, a white worker who had been employed by Rock-Tenn over two years, moved away and then returned to the Opelika area.

1. The district court was correct in finding that M.N.C. met the test under E.E.O.C. v. MacMillan Blodell Containers, 503 F.2d 1086, 1094 (6th Cir. 1974), of whether a successor corporation is liable for the acts of its predecessor.

After Parmer told Miles about her reemployment, Miles met with Nick Constan in January 1980. According to Miles, Constan told her at that time she would be recalled when work picked up before new employees were hired. Upon hearing about the employment of Wilson in June, Mary Miles spoke with Olin Henderson, plant manager, who told her she would be recalled when business picked up. Miles filed a charge of racial discrimination with the E.E.O.C. on November 1, 1980, received her right-to-sue letter in October 1981 and filed suit in federal court in December 1981.

After hearing testimony and receiving briefs, the district court found against Miles on her claim of racial discrimination. The district court applied a disparate treatment analysis to the facts and found that Miles had made out a prima facie case of discrimination.[2] Once the prima facie case is proved, the burden shifts to the employer to articulate a legitimate, nondiscriminatory reason for its acts with regard to the plaintiff. The burden on the defendant is one of production rather than persuasion.[3] If the employer carries this burden of production, the presumption raised by the prima facie case is rebutted and the employee must persuade the court that the reasons for not hiring plaintiff offered by the employer were pretextual. Texas Dept. of Community Affairs v. Burdine.

Miles contends that her direct evidence of discrimination, in the form of a racial slur made by Olin Henderson, changed the traditional burden of proof. Miles argues that a defendant cannot refute direct evidence of discrimination by mere articulation of other reasons for its actions. Instead, the defendant must rebut by proving by a preponderance of the evidence that it would have reached the same decision absent the presence of the illegal motive. The district court found that the racial slur evidence was struck from the record. The court held that both Parmer and Wilson were senior to the plaintiff, more experienced and more proficient. The court also noted that at the time the part-time employees were hired there was no need for full-time workers and that the plaintiff never applied for part-time work. The district court found that the statistical evidence lacked probity because it did not show the relative qualifications of black and white workers.

Mary Miles now appeals and claims that the district court made the following clearly erroneous findings of fact: 1) that seniority played a role in determining who was entitled to recall; 2) that Wilson's ability to operate a machine was the reason why she was hired; 3) that the

2. The court made that determination by applying the Eleventh Circuit modification of the *McDonnell Douglas* test for discharge cases. According to Lee v. Russell County Bd. of Education, 684 F.2d 769, 773 (11th Cir. 1982), the plaintiff must prove that he/she 1) is a member of a protected class; 2) was qualified for the position held; 3) was discharged; and 4) was replaced by a person outside the protected class. Mary Miles proved a prima facie case.

3. As the Court made clear in Texas Dept. of Community Affairs v. Burdine, the defendant does not have to persuade the court that it was actually motivated by the proffered reasons. It is sufficient if the defendant raises a genuine issue of fact as to whether it discriminated.

plaintiff did not apply for part-time employment; 4) that the statistical evidence was related to racial composition of the area; 5) that Olin Henderson's racial slur had been stricken from the record; 6) that the plaintiff offered no testimony as to the quality of her work; 7) that Parmer was an excellent block setter. The district court made several clearly erroneous findings of fact and erred with respect to the racial slur. The court then wrongfully concluded that M.N.C. would have reached the same decision regarding Miles even absent the illegal motivation. We reverse.

A court of appeals may not set aside district court findings of fact unless they are clearly erroneous. Fed.R.Civ.P. 52(a); Pullman-Standard v. Swint, 456 U.S. 273, 102 S.Ct. 1781, 72 L.Ed.2d 66 (1982). This standard imposes a heavy burden on the appellant in a case in which the evidence was largely testimonial and the district court had the advantage of observing the witnesses and making credibility determinations. A finding of fact is reversible under Rule 52(a) only when, after reviewing the entire record, the appellate court is convinced that an error has been made. The review this court conducts inquiries into whether a finding has substantial evidence to support it.

Because of the employee's easy burden of establishing a prima facie case and the employer's normal ability to articulate some legitimate nondiscriminatory reasons for its actions, most disparate treatment cases turn on the plaintiff's ability to demonstrate that the nondiscriminatory reason offered by the employer was a pretext for discrimination. B. Schlei & P. Grossman, Employment Discrimination Law 1316–1317 (1983). The same is true of the present case. Three types of evidence can be used by a plaintiff to prove pretext: 1) comparative evidence; 2) statistical evidence; and 3) direct evidence of discrimination, in the form of discriminatory statements and admissions. Miles proffered all three types of pretext evidence in this case. The district court made erroneous findings of fact with regard to each proffer: 1) in its determination that M.N.C. had legitimate reasons for hiring the two white workers in preference to Miles, 2) in its analysis of the statistical evidence offered at trial, and 3) in its decision as to the admissibility of the racial slur. The erroneous findings of fact in these three areas are crucial, and thereby affect the substantial rights of the plaintiff, because each determination made by the district court cut against the plaintiff's showing of pretext.[4]

I. Comparative Evidence

Miles attempted to prove that white workers in a comparable employment position to her own were treated more favorably than she

4. The plaintiff is always trying to show that the employer had a discriminatory motive for the actions it took. In trying to prove pretext, the plaintiff can demonstrate that the proffered reasons were not the true reasons for the employer's decision either by directly persuading the court a discriminatory reason more likely motivated the employer or indirectly by showing that the employer's proffered explanation is unworthy of credence. *Burdine,* supra.

was. The district court found that M.N.C. proved by a preponderance of the evidence that the workers in question could not be compared to Mary Miles. Since the district court offered distinct reasons why Parmer, Wilson and the part-time workers could not be compared to Miles, each rationale should be considered separately.

The district court found that Parmer, the first rehired full-time worker, was senior to Miles and more experienced and proficient. The president of M.N.C. indicated that Mary Miles was not considered a call-back employee because she had not served the ninety-day probationary period. Since Parmer had worked only a few days longer than Miles, it is clear that she, too, lacked vested seniority rights. Therefore, seniority could not have acted as a legitimate reason for recalling Parmer but not Miles. The district court's finding that seniority provided a basis for distinguishing between the two women is important. The only other reason for so distinguishing them, the work performance of each, was based upon subjective evaluation.

This circuit has frequently noted the problems associated with this type of worker assessment and noted that subjective evaluations involving white supervisors provide a ready mechanism for racial discrimination. Parson v. Kaiser Aluminum & Chemical Corp., 575 F.2d 1374, 1385 (5th Cir. 1978); Rowe v. General Motors Corp., 457 F.2d 348, 359 (5th Cir. 1972); Robbins v. White-Wilson Medical Clinic, 660 F.2d 1064, 1067 (5th Cir. Unit B 1981), vacated on other grounds, 456 U.S. 969, 102 S.Ct. 2229, 72 L.Ed.2d 842 (1982); Harris v. Birmingham Bd. of Educ., 712 F.2d 1377 (11th Cir. 1983).[5] This is because the supervisor is left free to indulge a preference, if he has one, for one race of workers over another. In addition, subjective and vague criteria may be insufficient reasons given by an employer for its failure to rehire because such criteria do not allow a reasonable opportunity for rebuttal.[6] The employee is left without any objective criteria to point to in order to show competence. Lee v. Russell County Bd. of Educ., 684 F.2d 769, 775–76 (11th Cir. 1982). All of the worker evaluations at M.N.C. were done by Olin Henderson. Evidence in the case established that there were no guidelines for evaluating performance, written worker evalua-

5. M.N.C. suggests that the principle in *Rowe* and its progeny applies only to cases where a class of plaintiffs is trying to show that the lack of formal evaluation processes can aid in establishing the existence of a pattern or practice that has a discriminatory impact. This circuit has not limited its concern about the dangers of subjective evaluations to cases involving disparate impact. Robbins v. White-Wilson Medical Clinic, Inc., supra (disparate treatment); Parson v. Kaiser Aluminum & Chemical Corp., supra (discriminatory impact and discriminatory treatment); Harris v. Birmingham Bd. of Educ., supra (appellate court analyzed the claim of one individual—disparate treatment). Furthermore, this court finds no reason to accept the idea that the problems which can stem from subjective evaluations would be any less serious in a disparate treatment case. Discriminatory motive can be expressed just as easily in actions against one individual as it can in an employment practice used against many. This case demonstrates this fact.

6. Plaintiff's witness, Louise Lyles, a co-worker with Miles at the plant, was not allowed to testify as to the quality of Miles' work. Lyles did testify that in early 1980 she asked both Henderson and Constan, separately, when Miles was going to be rehired. They both assured her that Miles would be recalled when there was an opening.

tions or regular checks done on the employee's work habits. This system appears to have resulted in management having more familiarity with the performance of some workers than others. Miles testified that in the period she worked at the company she never met her supervisor. M.N.C. president, Constan testified that he relied on Henderson for his evaluation of Miles' performance. Henderson's evaluation of Miles was that she was not a very good worker. At the same time, Henderson and Constan testified from personal knowledge Parmer was a superior worker who was quite efficient at all aspects of the work. What the court is left with as M.N.C.'s legitimate nondiscriminatory reason for failure to rehire Mary Miles is the subjective evaluation, without more, that she was not a good worker and Lavelle Parmer was. Considering the fact that Miles offered evidence which would tend to show that the evaluation process was tainted, see infra, M.N.C. has not met its burden with respect to Lavelle Parmer.

The district court held that at the time the part-time workers were hired there was no need for a full-time worker and that Miles had not applied for part-time employment. There was no evidence introduced into the record to show that Miles did not apply for part-time work or expressed an aversion for it. The only evidence is that from January until June of 1980 Mary Miles contacted M.N.C. several times about the possibility of working.

II. Statistical Evidence

As another part of her case of pretext, appellant offered statistical evidence to show that there was an overall discrimination in M.N.C. hiring in favor of whites. The district court found that the statistical evidence had methodological problems and, therefore, was not probative. In doing so, the court mischaracterized the evidence. The plaintiff's claim did not rest, as found by the district court, on the fact that M.N.C.'s general production positions were filled by white women in a community where the work force was predominantly black. Instead, Miles offered statistical proof which tended to show that the hiring rate for white applicants, referred to M.N.C. from the Alabama state employment service, far exceeded that of black applicants.[7] The statistical evidence introduced in the case compared the racial composition of the pool of qualified applicants with those actually hired. This is one of the appropriate statistical methods for demonstrating intentional discrimination.

The district court indicated that the statistical study lacked probative value because there was no data showing whether the white

7. The statistical evidence introduced by the plaintiff's expert showed: 1) among all applicants to M.N.C. the hiring rate was 38.7% for whites and 18.6% for blacks; 2) for general production positions the hiring rate for whites was 41.7% compared to 12.1% for blacks; and 3) for female applicants for general production positions (the same situation as the plaintiff) the hiring rate was 40.9% for white females and 12.2% for black females. The expert's conclusion was that the result showed a significant discrimination in favor of whites over blacks.

applicants were more experienced, more qualified or had better experience. At the same time, however, the court correctly noted that there were no specific qualification or criteria for employment at M.N.C. Various employees testified to widely differing past employment experiences. General production work was described as unskilled labor for which there were no particular qualifications. Several of the employees testified that the entire hiring process at M.N.C. consisted of filling out an application and having a very short conversation with the plant supervisor. Evidence introduced at trial showed that M.N.C. submitted job descriptions to the Alabama employment service and that office referred the applicants who were the basis for the statistical study. As a result, the statistics were not invalidated because they lacked variables to assess experience and qualifications.

It is true that the statistical study offered did not encompass all of the 1980–1981 hiring at M.N.C. Plaintiff's expert witnesses admitted that the study only compared the hiring rates between white and black workers referred from the state employment service and that out of the forty-nine persons reported hired during the relevant period only nineteen were referred from the Alabama state employment service.[8] The expert witness, however, did examine the racial composition of the pool hired from other sources and found that there was almost a three to one preference of whites over blacks. This information led the expert to conclude that the data available to him would underestimate any discrimination that would exist. Nevertheless, a study of the hiring rates did indicate what the expert characterized as significant discrimination in favor of whites over blacks. It is also true that the statistical study only measured hiring and therefore did not offer any information on rehiring.

However, the Supreme Court recognized in McDonnell Douglas v. Green, that statistics as to a defendant's employment policy and practice might be helpful to a determination of whether the refusal to rehire in a particular case conformed to a general pattern of discrimination against blacks. The Court also held that such general determinations, while helpful, may not control individualized hiring decisions, particularly in the presence of otherwise justifiable reasons for refusing to rehire. Miles never claimed that the statistical evidence proved her case of disparate treatment, but only that it showed a pattern of favoring whites over blacks at M.N.C. The statistical evidence supports such a claim. The district court was clearly erroneous in finding that the statistical evidence was compared to the general area population and that it was not useful because it did not reflect worker qualifica-

8. According to the appellant, the statistics were taken from the Alabama employment service referral lists because M.N.C. president Constan testified in deposition that employees at M.N.C. were hired by this method.

M.N.C. argues on appeal that size of the statistical pool makes it impossible to draw any reliable inference of discriminatory motivation. While it is true that Dr. Gundlach testified that the larger the statistical pool, the more accurate the conclusions, he also testified that the differences he found in the hiring rate were statistically significant for a sample of that size.

tions. The statistical evidence in this case provided a background against which to assess Miles' individual claim.

III. Direct Evidence of Discrimination

Appellant's final offer of evidence to prove pretext consisted of direct evidence of discrimination. Miles introduced a racial slur about the work abilities of blacks, made by Olin Henderson. Confusion has arisen over whether the racial slur was or should have been stricken from the record. Perhaps the best way to clarify the confusion is to quote from the record sequentially the court's rulings on the admissibility of the evidence. Plaintiff called Betty Rogers a white who had gone to work for the employer in 1979 and remained until 1982. She testified that there were no qualifications for the job. She stated that when she applied for the job two or three black women were simultaneously being interviewed for an opening but none of them were hired. The following from pages 82 to 111 are excerpts from the testimony of Betty Rogers and rulings of the court:

Q. Did you ever have occasion to discuss with Olin Henderson during normal business hours his reasons for not hiring black women as employees at the company?

[R. 86].

(Objection and colloquy between the court and counsel).

Q. Mrs. Rogers, do you of your own personal knowledge know who did the hiring of employees at this company in 1982?

* * *

A. Olin Henderson did the hiring.

[R. 89].

Q. Did you have occasion during the course of your employment during the normal company hours to discuss with Olin Henderson his reasons for not hiring black women as employees at the company?

A. Yes.

Q. What did he say?

[R. 90].

(Objection and colloquy between the court and counsel).

A. I asked Olin Henderson why they didn't have any blacks. He said, "Half of them weren't worth a shit."

[R. 92].

At page 105, the defendant moved to strike the testimony of Betty Rogers with respect to the racial slur on a ground that the evidence had failed to show that Henderson was responsible for hiring in 1980. At page 109, the trial court made the following ruling:

> And if Olin Henderson was not in charge of hiring and firing at the time he made the statement, it is not admissible against the company and I will sustain the motion to strike it.

Because of questions propounded to Nick Constan, president of M.N.C., the court reversed his rulings with respect to the admissibility of the racial slur. The following statements appear from the transcript:

> THE COURT: Well, it seems to me that you have, by examination—both of you—of this witness proved that Olin Henderson was competent to make the statement he made earlier about the hiring of blacks, and I will let that in.
>
> I will also let in the questions that you asked him, and you may state your questions and I will let him answer it.

[R. 166].

* * *

> THE COURT: All right. I think these * * * I think they opened the door for you by proving that Olin Henderson was very muchly in the picture as regards hiring and firing. By that, I think the statement he made about it is admissible.

[R. 167].

Without any further mention of the subject during the trial, the trial court in its final order finding in favor of the defendant ruled that racial slur was not admissible. The following appears from page 285 of the record:

> The Plaintiff's claim is largely resting upon the fact that the Defendant's general production positions are largely filled by white women in a community wherein the larger percentage of the work force is black, and the four positions—two full time and two part time—filled by re-employment after the Plaintiff's layoff were filled by white persons. Two white applicants who applied for full-time production work testified that they, along with black applicants, applied for work in full-time production and that they, but not the black applicants, were offered jobs. Neither of these are employed by Defendant. One of these, Ms. Rogers, testified without denial, as Plaintiff's brief points out, that Mr. Henderson was the hiring authority when he said they had no black employees because "they ain't worth a s___". Later, however, Ms. Rogers testified that Mr. Wiggins, not Mr. Henderson, did the hiring and firing at the time the remark was made and that Mr. Henderson had no authority to hire or fire. On motion, the Court struck from the evidence Mr. Henderson's racial slur which cannot be considered against the Defendant because Mr. Henderson had no authority to hire, fire or speak for the Defendant Company. This statement having been excluded, there was no occasion for Mr. Henderson to deny it. There is no evidence of the relative merits of the applicants, but

there were no written criteria to guide one entrusted with hiring for the Defendant.

[The Court held that the racial slur was admissible against the defendant as a statement made by an agent of a party about a matter within the scope of his employment under Rule 801(d)(2)(D) of the Federal Rules of Evidence.]

The district court's post-trial decision to strike the statement was critical to the plaintiff's case. Normally, the defendant in an employment discrimination case would only have to articulate legitimate, nondiscriminatory reasons for its failure to rehire an employee. The plaintiff who always retains the burden of persuasion would then have to show that the employer's reasons were pretextual. The *McDonnell Douglas* method of proving an employment discrimination case, however, pertains to situations where direct evidence of discrimination is lacking. Bell v. Birmingham Linen Service, 715 F.2d 1552, 1556 (11th Cir. 1983); Lee v. Russell County Bd. of Educ., 684 F.2d 769, 774 (11th Cir. 1982). Where a case of discrimination is proved by direct evidence, the defendant bears a heavier burden.[9] If the evidence consisted of direct testimony that the defendant acted with a discriminatory motive, and it is accepted by the trier of fact, the ultimate issue of discrimination has been proved. The employer can then rebut only by proving by a preponderance of the evidence that the same decision would have been reached even absent the presence of the discriminatory motive. The inquiry required is one which makes the employer show that it would be the same decision absent the discriminatory motive. Since the district court did not consider the statement admitted, the judge did not make any findings about whether Henderson put aside his bias in the rehiring recommendations and evaluations he gave to Constan. In a similar situation, the court in Bell v. Birmingham Linen Service found that absent a similar finding in that case it was impossible to conclude that Birmingham Linen Service met its burden of proving under a *Mt. Healthy*-type analysis, that it would have reached the same decision absent discrimination and remanded to the district court to evaluate the evidence under the *Mt. Healthy* standard. 715 F.2d at 1557. In the present case, however, it appears doubtful that M.N.C. could meet the heavier burden imposed under *Bell.* The person in charge of making employee evaluations and suggestions for rehiring and the person making the racial slur were the same individual.

9. As explained by the court in Lee v. Russell County Bd. of Education:

> Where the evidence for a prima facie case consists, as it does here, of direct testimony that defendants acted with a discriminatory motivation, if the trier of fact believes the prima facie evidence the ultimate issue of discrimination is proved; no inference is required. Defendant cannot rebut this type of showing of discrimination simply by articulating or producing evidence of legitimate, nondiscriminatory reasons. Once an unconstitutional motive is proved to have been a significant or substantial factor in an employment decision, defendant can rebut only by proving by a preponderance of the evidence that the same decision would have been reached even absent the presence of that factor.

684 F.2d 769, 774 (footnotes omitted).

Discrimination by M.N.C. in employment practices was proved by 1) Henderson's remark, 2) the statistical evidence, 3) the testimony of Betty Rogers that no blacks worked in production when she was employed in 1978 and Louise Lyles' testimony that she was the only black woman out of 20 production workers when employed in August 1979, and 4) Plaintiff's Exhibit 36 which showed that no blacks were employed in 1980. The district court found the plaintiff qualified. Consequently, we remand to give the defendant an opportunity to prove by a preponderance of evidence that the same employment decision would have been reached absent the presence of clearly discriminatory employment practices.

The judgment of the district court is reversed and remanded.

Reversed and Remanded.

CONNER v. FORT GORDON BUS CO.

United States Court of Appeals, Eleventh Circuit, 1985.
761 F.2d 1495.

JOHNSON, CIRCUIT JUDGE:

Marietta Lee Conner filed this employment discrimination suit against the Fort Gordon Bus Company under 42 U.S.C.A. § 1981 and Title VII of the Civil Rights Act of 1964. The district court ruled in favor of the employer, finding that it had articulated a legitimate non-discriminatory reason for terminating Conner and that Conner had failed to prove that the reason was a pretext for sex discrimination. We affirm the judgment of the district court.

On February 6, 1981, the Fort Gordon Bus Company hired Marietta Lee Conner as a bus driver. At that time two of the seventeen other bus drivers working for the company were women. On May 4, 1981, the president of the company, E.C. Walton, was driving in his car when he observed a company bus make a dangerous and illegal left turn. The incident angered him because a bus driver making a similar illegal turn had recently caused an accident which had resulted in a $35,000 liability for the company.[1] The next morning he determined that Conner had been driving the bus and he gave instructions to terminate her. Walton also fired a male bus driver, Sexton, that same day for reckless driving that endangered the safety of passengers.[2]

The company had no formal or written guidelines covering the termination of bus drivers for unsafe driving. Many of the male drivers had received traffic citations and were reprimanded rather than terminated. Walton testified that he terminated drivers whose performance, in his judgment, seriously endangered the safety of the passengers or buses. That policy was strictly enforced after the $35,000

1. The accident took place between 1979 and May of 1981. The record does not reveal a more specific date or the identity of the driver, other than the fact that he was a black male.

2. Sexton was terminated for operating a bus with the doors open. A representative of the company's insurer reported this safety violation to Walton.

accident but Sexton, Conner, and the driver who had caused the previous accident were the only drivers terminated for reckless driving. Approximately four other drivers had been involved in accidents but none of them had been at fault.

In order to prove discriminatory treatment in violation of Title VII or Section 1981, a plaintiff-employee must establish a prima facie case of discrimination.[3] A prima facie case of discrimination raises the inference that discriminatory intent motivated the discharge of the employee. So long as the prima facie case of discrimination does not include direct evidence of discrimination,[4] the employer may rebut the presumption by clearly articulating in a reasonably specific manner a legitimate non-discriminatory reason for the discharge. The plaintiff then must show that the proffered reason was a pretext for the true discriminatory reason. On this appeal, Conner challenges the district court's findings that the Company articulated legitimate reasons for the discharge and that she failed to prove the pretextual nature of those reasons.

ARTICULATION OF NON-DISCRIMINATORY REASON FOR DISCHARGE

According to the Supreme Court's opinion in *Burdine,* a prima facie case of discrimination does not place the burden of persuasion on the employer. The defendant rebuts the presumption of discrimination if it produces evidence that raises a genuine issue of fact as to whether it discriminated against the plaintiff; it must accomplish this by clearly setting forth, through the introduction of competent evidence, the reasons for the plaintiff's discharge. This Court has characterized this "exceedingly light" burden as being merely a burden of production and not a burden of proof. Perryman v. Johnson Products Co., Inc., 698 F.2d 1138, 1142 (11th Cir. 1983). Nevertheless, since the defendant's explanation must be clear and reasonably specific, *Burdine,* supra, some proffered reasons will be legally insufficient to rebut a prima facie case. For instance, a defendant relying on a purely subjective reason for discharge will face a heavier burden of production than it otherwise would. Robbins v. White-Wilson Medical Clinic, Inc., 660 F.2d 1064,

3. In discharge cases, a plaintiff must show that he or she (1) is a member of a protected class, (2) was qualified for the position held, (3) was discharged, and (4) was replaced by a person outside the protected class. Lee v. Russell County Bd. of Education, 684 F.2d 769, 773 (11th Cir. 1982). The employer in this case does not challenge the district court's finding that Conner presented a prima facie case.

4. Where a plaintiff proves discrimination through direct evidence of discrimination, such as discriminatory statements by the employer, the employer cannot rebut the prima facie case of discrimination simply by articulating a legitimate non-discriminatory reason for the discharge. Where the direct evidence proves the existence of a discriminatory intent, the employer may escape liability only by showing that the same decision would have been reached absent the illegal motive. Thompkins v. Morris Brown College, 752 F.2d 558 (11th Cir. 1985); Miles v. M.N.C. Corp., 750 F.2d 867 (11th Cir. 1985); Bell v. Birmingham Linen Service, 715 F.2d 1552 (11th Cir. 1983), cert. denied, 467 U.S. 1204, 104 S.Ct. 2385, 81 L.Ed.2d 344 (1984); Lee v. Russell Co. Bd. of Education, 684 F.2d 769 (11th Cir. 1982). Conner presented no direct evidence of discrimination in this case.

1067 (5th Cir. Unit B 1981), vacated on other grounds, 456 U.S. 969, 102 S.Ct. 2229, 72 L.Ed.2d 842 (1982). The plaintiff here contends that the company failed to articulate a clear and reasonably specific non-discriminatory ground for discharging her because the explanation offered by Walton was subjective.

Walton explained that Conner's discharge was based on his observation of an illegal left turn and his conclusion that the bus driver had endangered the safety of the passengers and the bus. This safety standard was interpreted by Walton alone; indeed, Walton never informed the drivers of the criterion he used for deciding when to terminate a driver. Yet neither of these circumstances renders this standard purely subjective. A standard known only to the employer and interpreted only by the employer could nevertheless be clear, specific and capable of objective evaluation, so long as the standard could be applied by a fact-finder after the discharge has taken place and the standard has been revealed.

The unpublicized nature of a decision-making standard does not affect its clarity or specificity at trial. If an employer articulates at trial a clear and specific reason for discharging an employee, the purposes of the employer's burden of production have been met. The employee is given a reasonable opportunity for rebuttal, for she is accorded the opportunity to show her competence according to the stated objective criteria. Title VII does not require employers to inform employees of the reasons behind their evaluations. Failure to explain decisions to employees may prove bad management but it does not necessarily prove discrimination. See Pace v. Southern Railway System, 701 F.2d 1383, 1392 n. 8 (11th Cir.), cert. denied, 464 U.S. 1018, 104 S.Ct. 549, 78 L.Ed.2d 724 (1983).

Neither is a proffered explanation insufficiently clear or specific simply because an employer has interpreted the standard without recourse to written guidelines. Previous decisions of this Court suggest that an employer's proffered reasons are too subjective to qualify as clear and specific reasons only where a factfinder cannot reasonably determine whether or not they apply to the plaintiff. For instance, the employer in *Robbins,* supra, cited the plaintiff's unpleasant personality as the reason she was not hired. While the court noted that such a reason would not be legally insufficient in every case, it held that the peculiar definition of "pleasant personality" used by the employer, equating pleasant personalities with "white" personalities, was legally insufficient to rebut a prima facie case. In Fowler v. Blue Bell, Inc., 737 F.2d 1007, 1010–11 (11th Cir. 1984), the employer refused to hire the plaintiff because of his prediction, based on the applicant's record, that he would not last long at the company. The Court found this reason sufficient to rebut the prima facie case and distinguished *Robbins,* stating that the proffered reason was "somewhat subjective, [but] not so incapable of objective evaluation as to render it inadequate to meet the defendant's burden of rebuttal." The employer's conclusion was based on a review of a written application, but he evaluated that material according to personal standards.

The standard used by the defendant in this case, unreasonable endangerment of passengers and property, is capable of objective evaluation. It resembles the objective duty of reasonable care employed by a court adjudicating tort claims. The plaintiff has not shown that Walton interpreted the standard in such an unusual manner, contrary to the normal meaning of the words, that a factfinder could not reasonably determine whether that standard was relied upon in any given case. The standard had a meaning accessible to Conner; she was able to question whether on a rational and objective basis her case fell within the described category. While it remains true that this Court disfavors subjective methods of evaluation because they provide a ready mechanism for racial discrimination, a legitimate ground for decision articulated by an employer, even a ground that requires interpretation on the part of the employer, is legally sufficient to satisfy the employer's burden of production so long as it is capable of objective evaluation.

Of course, the fact that an employer never formally announces a decisionmaking criterion and interprets it according to its own lights is relevant to a plaintiff's claim of discrimination. The use of unannounced policies, interpreted according to subjective criteria, will tend to support a plaintiff's claim of pretext. The articulated explanation in this case, however, was sufficiently clear and specific to force the plaintiff to prove, if she could, that it was a pretext.

PROOF OF PRETEXT

After the defendant articulates legitimate non-discriminatory reasons for a discharge, the plaintiff must prove by a preponderance of the evidence that the articulated reasons were not the sole causes of the discharge but rather that discrimination made a difference in the decision. O'Donnell v. Georgia Osteopathic Hospital, Inc., 748 F.2d 1543, 1550 (11th Cir. 1984). This Court may overturn a factual finding on the issue of pretext only if it is clearly erroneous.

In order to support her contention that the district court clearly erred in finding no pretext in this case, Conner points to three questionable aspects of Walton's decision. First, she emphasizes that Walton never stated before the time of trial that he terminated drivers for safety violations serious enough to place passengers and property in unreasonable danger, nor did he ever explain precisely what sort of safety violations would fall into this category.[5] As discussed earlier, the relative subjectivity of the employer's reason does support Conner's claim of pretext. Yet it cannot be said that a failure to find pretext is clearly erroneous whenever an employer's reason for discharge is an informal and unwritten policy subject to differing interpretations.

5. Walton stated during cross-examination that illegal turns were more reckless than most speeding violations. Counsel for Conner did not pursue the matter any further or ask Walton to explain his definition of recklessness.

Such criteria will not in and of themselves violate Title VII. See Allison v. Western Union Telegraph Co., 680 F.2d 1318, 1322 (11th Cir. 1982).

In this case Conner failed to present any evidence at all that the termination policy was unevenly applied. While Walton admitted that some male drivers had only been warned after receiving traffic citations from the police, he stated that those infractions had not been as serious as the ones committed by Conner and Sexton. Conner presented no evidence at all regarding the nature of the safety violations of drivers who were merely reprimanded, leaving Walton's testimony on the subject entirely uncontradicted. The only specific incidents of unsafe driving described at trial, those committed by Conner, Sexton, and the driver who had caused the $35,000 accident, had resulted in terminations.[6] Furthermore, Conner never argued that the criterion allegedly used by Walton was an unusual one in the industry or one that the bus company would be unlikely to use. In the absence of supporting evidence of this sort, the district court was not clearly erroneous to find in favor of the defendant even after Conner showed that Walton's basis for discharging her was an informal policy, subject to interpretation.

Second, Conner points out that Walton never attempted to confirm the accuracy of his belief that she had made an illegal left turn. An employer's lack of concern about the accuracy of its decision may support a claim of pretext, particularly where the possibility of error is great and confirmation could be easily obtained. Still, no court has held that lack of concern about the accuracy of a decision will, as a matter of law, establish a pretext. Further, Walton had no reason to doubt that a driver had made an illegal and dangerous left turn because he had seen it himself. The identity of the driver was duly ascertained by a search of business records. Under these circumstances, Walton's failure to seek further confirmation that Conner had committed a serious safety violation did not diminish the credibility of his proffered reason for discharge.

Finally, Conner argues on appeal that Walton did not decide to terminate the offending driver until after he had determined her identity. Proof of this fact would possibly establish pretext and the district court recognized as much by focusing on this matter in its findings of fact. The testimony of Walton on this topic contained an ambiguity, for he stated that "I determined who was driving the bus and I gave instructions that that person should no longer be a bus driver." The statement establishes when Walton gave the order to terminate but does not reveal when he made the decision to terminate. The court considered this testimony and the complete failure of the plaintiff to inquire into the issue before concluding that "I don't think

6. Conner testified that Sexton had a tendency to drive too quickly while turning and was not terminated for that reason. She did not produce any evidence, however, that any of these incidents came to the attention of Walton or any other official of the company.

that has been proven either way." Hence, the court found that Conner failed to meet her burden of proof. Given the lack of evidence on this point, we cannot conclude that the district court was clearly erroneous.

CONCLUSION

The reason given by Walton for his discharge of Conner was sufficiently clear and specific to meet the employer's burden of production. Even though there are reasons in this case to question whether Walton's explanation was a pretext for discrimination, none of them show that the district court clearly erred in its finding that Conner failed to prove discrimination by a preponderance of the evidence. Therefore, the judgment of the district court is affirmed.

HATCHETT, CIRCUIT JUDGE, Dissenting:

I agree with the law as announced by the majority: This court disfavors subjective methods of evaluation because they provide a ready mechanism for discrimination. We differ on the application of this rule of law to the facts in this case. I write to illuminate the facts because those who must apply this rule of law in the circuit may better do so when the facts, and all reasonable inferences to be drawn from them, are fully set forth and evaluated.

The facts in this case are more egregious than in any prior case involving subjective standards for hiring, promotion or termination. The majority fails to appreciate the fact that in this case, the claim is not merely that the employer used a subjective standard for termination; the claim is that the employer changed from one subjective standard to another subjective standard "in the twinkling of an eye." This is a "double dose" of the subjective policy problem.

Until Conner made the left turn (which she denies), the subjective policy was not to fire drivers for traffic violations. Even where the traffic violation resulted in the issuance of a traffic citation, it was the policy of the bus company not to terminate bus drivers. The policy, if sporadic day-by-day events may constitute a policy, was to reprimand the driver; yet even these reprimands were informal. The majority treats this case as a run of the mill subjective policy case without giving weight to the fact that this unwritten and unannounced policy applied to Conner was never applied to any other driver.[1] The policy which resulted in Conner's termination not only had never been applied to anyone else, but was formed by Walton after determining the identity of the bus driver. This case illustrates the reason for this circuit's strong disfavor for subjective standards when advanced to show a legitimate non-discriminatory reason for the action taken.

A comparison of our cases on the subject of subjective determinations shows how loosely the circuit rule is being applied in this case.

1. The fact that the bus company also fired Sexton, another driver, on the same day it fired Conner is of no moment; the facts of his case are not in this record, and that event without more is irrelevant. What happened in the months and years before the bus company fired Connor is what is relevant.

In Miles v. MNC, 750 F.2d 867 (11th Cir. 1985), Miles alleged racial discrimination when MNC, her employer, did not rehire her after a temporary layoff. The court found that MNC based its decision solely upon subjective evaluations of Miles's work performance. Further, "evidence in the case established that there were not guidelines for evaluating performance, written worker evaluations or regular work checks done on the employees' work habits." Additionally, the MNC plant manager, conducted all worker evaluations. We found MNC's subjective evaluations, without more, insufficient to sustain its burden of production, stating: "Subjective and vague criteria may be insufficient reasons given by an employer for its failure to rehire because such criteria do not allow a reasonable opportunity for rebuttal."

Miles is less egregious than this case. In this case, one management figure, the president, subjectively evaluated Conner's driving skills after learning her identity.[2] The bus company had not developed any guidelines or criteria upon which to assess worker performance. Because the bus company had no objective standards, Conner was unable to ascertain the consequences of her subsequent actions. Likewise, for the same reasons, she is denied a reasonable opportunity for rebuttal.

In Williams v. City of Montgomery, the City of Montgomery Fire Department discharged Williams, a black male, after he committed a felony. 742 F.2d 586 (11th Cir. 1984). The city maintained a mandatory policy requiring the discharge of any fire fighter convicted of a felony. Two years earlier, the city had terminated two white males because of their felony convictions; both fire fighters appealed to the Montgomery City-County Personnel Board, which reinstated them. The city did not reinstate Williams. We said: "The city and the Board submitted that the white fire fighters' offenses were less serious than Williams's offense and that the white fire fighters received more support from the fire department than did Williams. Besides being subjective, these reasons are irrelevant." We found the city's articulated reason insufficient to sustain its burden of production. In this case Conner's making of the left turn became more serious than any of the other many violations committed by other bus drivers. The company president's distinction between driver violations subject to termination and those rendered harmless remains undefined. As to dangerousness, the company's president "knows it when he sees it," and relies on the courts to unquestionably accept his determination. Absent from this record is anything to indicate the facts surrounding the alleged left turn. We are left to believe the company president that the "no firing for violations policy" changed and the turn was dangerous.

In Lee v. Conecuh County Board of Education, Gantt, a black male teacher, alleged racial discrimination because the Conecuh County Board of Education repeatedly failed to promote him to principal. 634 F.2d 959 (5th Cir. 1981). We found: "Despite the objective evidence of

2. Unfortunately, the record is not as clear as we would desire regarding the company president's knowledge of the identity of the offending bus driver or the president's method and timing in making that determination.

Gantt's superior qualifications, defendants contend that they refused to promote him because they consider him unfit for a principalship." The school board based its decision on subjective evaluations of Gantt's teaching ability, relying on the evaluations of a single supervisor. We stated: "Establishing qualifications is an employer's prerogative * * * but an employer may not utilize wholly subjective standards by which to judge its employees' qualifications and then plead lack of qualification when its promotion process, for example, is challenged as discriminatory." We found the school board's argument unpersuasive and insufficient to rebut Gantt's prima facie case.

Likewise, one Fort Gordon management figure terminated Conner based upon his subjective evaluations. Similar to *Lee,* an employer may not utilize wholly subjective standards by which to critique and discharge an employee and subsequently meet his burden of producing a legitimate non-discriminatory reason by arguing that the employee arguably violated safety standards about which she was totally unfamiliar.

In case after case, we have determined that subjective standard evidence is too unreliable to overcome a prima facie case of discrimination. Because the majority cites the rule, but fails to properly apply it in this case, I dissent.

NOTES AND PROBLEMS FOR DISCUSSION

1. What was the relevance of plaintiff's statistical evidence to the claim that she had not been rehired because of her race? Was there any explanation, other than racial discrimination, for the hiring patterns demonstrated by the plaintiff's evidence? If the plaintiff had been discharged or denied a promotion would the statistical showing made in this case have been probative on the issue of discrimination? Rule 401 of the Federal Rules of Evidence defines "relevant evidence" as "evidence having any tendency to make the existence of any fact that is of consequence to the determination of the action more probable or less probable than it would be without the evidence." Under Rule 406, evidence "of the routine practice of an organization * * * is relevant to prove that the conduct * * * of the organization on a particular occasion was in conformity with [it's] routine practice." Do these rules satisfactorily explain the use of the statistical evidence in *Miles?* Would the plaintiff's statistical showing have had any probative value absent the expert testimony of the plaintiff's expert? The role of statistics in proving discrimination will be discussed more extensively in Section B of this chapter.

2. Was Judge Hatchett correct in characterizing the facts of *Conner* as "more egregious" than those in *Miles?* Did the decision in *Miles* turn wholly on the fact that the employer's reasons for the challenged action were subjective in nature? The *McDonnell Douglas-Burdine* order of proof addresses two evidentiary problems common to Title VII cases: (1) direct proof of discriminatory intent either does not exist or is exceedingly hard to uncover; and (2) the employer enjoys greater access to (and control over) proof of its reasons for its own employment decisions. The formula was thus designed to apply where only circumstantial evidence of the employer's discriminatory intent exists. The Eleventh Circuit, as demonstrated by *Miles* and *Conner,* has developed the

"direct evidence" doctrine under which the ultimate issue of discrimination is established once plaintiff presents direct proof of discriminatory motivation which is "accepted" by the trier of fact. The burden of persuasion shifts to the employer to establish that the challenged action would have been taken absent discrimination. The direct evidence doctrine was first articulated in Lee v. Russell County Board of Education, 684 F.2d 769, 774 (11th Cir. 1982) and in Bell v. Birmingham Linen Service, 715 F.2d 1552, 1557 (11th Cir. 1983), cert. denied, 467 U.S. 1204, 104 S.Ct. 2385, 81 L.Ed.2d 344 (1984), where the court noted that McDonnell Douglas-Burdine was "not intended to be a Procrustean bed within which all disparate treatment cases must be forced to lie." Outside of the Eleventh Circuit, the formula has been explicitly adopted by the Sixth and Tenth Circuits. Blalock v. Metals Trades Inc., 775 F.2d 703, 707 (6th Cir. 1985); EEOC v. Wyoming Retirement System, 771 F.2d 1425, 1430 (10th Cir. 1985). Is it logical to impose the more stringent burden of proof on the employer when there is direct evidence of discriminatory motivation but not where the court is convinced that discrimination has been proved on the strength of plaintiff's circumstantial evidence? See, Milton v. Weinberger, 696 F.2d 94 (D.C.Cir. 1982). Is it fair to make credible evidence of bias tantamount to proof that the employer *acted* for a discriminatory reason? See Spanier v. Morrison's Management Services, 611 F.Supp. 642 (N.D.Ala.1985). What type of evidence should constitute "direct" proof of discrimination? See, Dybczak v. Tuskegee Institute, 737 F.2d 1524, 1528 (11th Cir. 1984), cert. denied, ___ U.S. ___, 105 S.Ct. 1180, 84 L.Ed.2d 328 (1985) (statistics are not direct evidence). How is the employer to know whether his burden is to merely "articulate" a non-discriminatory reason under *Burdine* or to meet the higher standard of the direct evidence rule? See, King v. Trans World Airlines, 738 F.2d 255 (8th Cir. 1984) (employer's reasons for failure to rehire female former employee not relevant in light of plaintiff's proof that her hiring interview was conducted differently from those of male applicants).

Even without the direct evidence doctrine, it is plain that the *McDonnell Douglas-Burdine* formula is not adaptable to all proof patterns which can arise in disparate treatment cases. See, e.g., Lams v. General Waterworks Corp., 766 F.2d 386 (8th Cir. 1985) (*McDonnell Douglas* formula of little use in deciding promotion claim by employees who were not considered for promotion because they did not know of vacancy until position was filled). In such cases what should be the employer's burden? Does the Supreme Court's decision in UNITED STATES POSTAL SERVICE v. AIKENS, supra, make the previous question of academic interest only?

3. Where the plaintiff has relied on the *McDonnell-Douglas-Burdine* formula and the employer has articulated non-discriminatory reasons for the challenged action, the plaintiff must be given a "fair opportunity" to show that the justification offered by the defendant "was in fact pretext." McDonnell Douglas Corp. v. Green, supra, 411 U.S. at 804, 93 S.Ct. at 1825. The Court's requirement in *Burdine* that "the defendant's explanation of its legitimate reasons * * * be clear and reasonably specific," 450 U.S. at 258, 101 S.Ct. at 1096, affords the plaintiff some protection against reasons so nebulous or vague as to make disproving them impossible. *Miles* and *Conner* state the accepted rule that the more subjective the standard by which employees or applicants are to be judged and the more subjective the manner in which the judging is done, the more likely that the court will find the employer's justifications pretextual when faced with evidence from which discrimination could be inferred. See, Robbins v. White-Wilson Medical Clinic, Inc., 660 F.2d 1064,

1067 (5th Cir. 1981), vacated and remanded on other grounds, 456 U.S. 969, 102 S.Ct. 2229, 72 L.Ed.2d 842 (1982) (employer's rejection of applicant because of her "yucky" attitude legally insufficient when viewed in context of evidence in plaintiff's prima facie case and testimony of defendant's chief witness on cross examination). Should use of a subjective evaluation system that allows judgments which may be tainted by unlawful prejudice to control employment decisions constitute a *per se* violation of Title VII? Compare, Abrams v. Johnson, 534 F.2d 1226, 1231 (6th Cir. 1976) (absolute discretion over employment decisions where subjective race prejudice may control inconsistent with Title VII) with Hopkins v. Price Waterhouse, 618 F.Supp. 1109 (D.D.C.1985) (Congress did not intend that courts police every instance where subjective judgments may be tainted by unarticulated, unconscious assumptions related to sex). A recurring problem in sex discrimination cases is whether employment decisions based on determinations of "inappropriate" behavior by female employees are influenced by sexual stereotyping. In *Hopkins,* the court noted that "[a]n employer who treats a woman with an assertive personality in a manner different than she would have been treated had she been male is guilty of sex discrimination." But, absent proof regarding identical conduct by male employees, the plaintiff in such a case will find it very difficult to show pretext. See, Bellissimo v. Westinghouse Electric Corp., 764 F.2d 175 (3d Cir. 1985), cert. denied, ___ U.S. ___ 106 S.Ct. 1244, 89 L.Ed.2d 353 (1986) (criticism of female attorney's dress and conduct, which included dancing with male client, resulting in her discharge did not constitute unlawful sex bias absent proof that plaintiff was treated differently from male employees—district court decision for plaintiff reversed as clearly erroneous); Macpherson v. Department of Water Resources, 734 F.2d 1103 (5th Cir. 1984) (finding that valuable female employee was discharged because of her "pertness" and not her gender not clearly erroneous); Brooks v. Ashtabula City Welfare Dept., 717 F.2d 263 (6th Cir. 1983), cert. denied, 466 U.S. 907, 104 S.Ct. 1687, 80 L.Ed.2d 160 (1984) (female employee refused promotion because of "abrasive" personality and "superior" attitude—district court decision for plaintiff reversed as clearly erroneous).

A plaintiff cannot prove that an employer's stated reasons are pretextual merely by showing that the employer was mistaken or relied on incorrect information. Only if the employer's articulated reason is shown to be a pretext for accomplishing a discriminatory purpose will the plaintiff prevail. Thus, a sincere, though mistaken, suspicion of dishonesty would satisfy the employer's *Burdine* burden. See, Williams v. Southwestern Bell Telephone Co., 718 F.2d 715, 717–718 (5th Cir. 1983) ("The trier of fact is to determine the defendant's intent, not adjudicate the merits of the facts or suspicions upon which it is predicated.")

Should any explanation of the employer's conduct which is not itself facially discriminatory be legally sufficient under *McDonnell Douglas-Burdine?* In Lombard v. School District of City of Erie, 463 F.Supp. 566, 570–571 (W.D.Pa. 1978), the court stated that:

> to avoid Title VII liability, the defendant need only articulate a reason for the apparently unequal treatment that is not sex related, and need not state that the selection was based upon merit. Stating that a man was selected over a woman for a job because the man had more friends in high places constitutes a 'non-discriminatory' reason for the unequal treatment sufficient to avoid liability under Title VII * * *.

Do you agree? Compare, Curler v. City of Fort Wayne, 591 F.Supp. 327, 336 (N.D.Ind.1984) (city's explanation that it chose black applicant over white applicant for vacancy because black applicant was union member was not a "legitimate non-discriminatory" reason under *McDonnell Douglas*). Should an employer's reliance on an affirmative action plan calling for preference for minority applicants constitute a "nondiscriminatory" reason for its decision? See, Johnson v. Transportation Agency, 770 F.2d 752 (9th Cir. 1984).

4. In *Burdine* the Supreme Court stated that one way the plaintiff can establish pretext is by "showing that the employer's proffered explanation is unworthy of credence." 450 U.S. at 256, 101 S.Ct. at 1095. This would suggest that, where the plaintiff has put on a prima facie case, a finding that the proffered justification is pretextual is equivalent to a finding that the employer intentionally discriminated. See, Duffy v. Wheeling Pittsburgh Steel Corp., 738 F.2d 1393 (3d Cir. 1984), cert. denied, ___ U.S. ___, 105 S.Ct. 592, 83 L.Ed.2d 702 (1984). A number of courts have held, however, that even a finding that the employer's articulated reasons were fabricated will not entitle plaintiff to judgment.

In Clark v. Huntsville City Board of Education, 717 F.2d 525 (11th Cir. 1983), the Court held that a simple finding that employer did not truly rely on its proffered reason, without a further finding that it relied instead on race, will not suffice to establish Title VII liability. See also, Baron v. Mary Elizabeth Day Nursery, 34 FEP Cases 1199 (N.D.Iowa 1984) (reasons for discharge "somewhat pretextual" but plaintiff failed to prove cause of termination was his sex); White v. Vathally, 732 F.2d 1037 (1st Cir. 1984), cert. denied, ___ U.S. ___, 105 S.Ct. 331, 83 L.Ed.2d 267 (1984) (mere showing that employer's explanation is not true reason for its employment decision, as distinguished from showing that reason is pretext for sex discrimination, does not satisfy burden of proving pretext); Johnson v. University of Wisconsin-Milwaukee, 783 F.2d 59 (7th Cir. 1986) (age discrimination act requires showing that proffered reason is not just pretext but pretext for discrimination). Do these decisions mean that the court may find that non-discriminatory reasons *not even proffered by the employer* were the "real" reasons for its actions? If so, how can the plaintiff be expected to prove that *unarticulated* reasons are pretextual? See, Miller v. WFLI Radio Inc., 687 F.2d 136 (6th Cir. 1982). What evidentiary role should the fact that the defendant concocted a false explanation play? See Williams v. City of Montgomery, 550 F.Supp. 662 (M.D.Ala.1982). Are all the above questions beside the point in light of the Supreme Court's decision in United States Postal Service Board of Governors v. Aikens, infra?

5. Once the employer has rebutted the plaintiff's prima facie case, must the plaintiff introduce additional evidence to show pretext, and, if so what kind of evidence? Relying on the statement in *Burdine* that, "there may be some cases where the plaintiff's initial evidence, combined with effective cross examination of the defendant, will suffice to discredit the defendant's explanation," 450 U.S. at 255 n. 10, 101 S.Ct. at 1094 n. 10, most courts have held that a finding of pretext can be based solely on the evidence constituting plaintiff's case in chief. See e.g., Monroe v. Burlington Industries, Inc., 784 F.2d 568 (4th Cir. 1986) (evidence that sufficed to establish prima facie case does not create a presumption of discrimination once the employer has rebutted with non-discriminatory explanation of its conduct but court may rely on same evidence in determining pretext); Dillon v. Coles, 746 F.2d 998 (3d Cir. 1984) (formula does not compartmentalize the evidence so as to limit its use to only one phase

of case: evidence might serve both to establish prima facie case and to discredit defendant's explanation).

See also, Easley v. Empire, Inc., 757 F.2d 923 (8th Cir. 1985) (evidence that only nine of employer's approximately 300 retail managers were women and that employer's policy manual said that men should be hired as managers supported finding that defendant's reasons for failing to promote female employee to retail manager were pretextual). Do such decisions impose on the employer, as a practical matter, a *greater* burden than that of merely "articulating" a non-discriminatory reason?

In Vaughn v. Westinghouse Electric Co., 702 F.2d 137 (8th Cir. 1983), the plaintiff alleged that she had been disqualified from a machine operator's job because of her race. The employer claimed that the disqualification resulted from the plaintiff's poor work performance. The district court, largely relying on plaintiff's statistics that showed a heavy preponderance of whites in the operator positions and in positions of supervision, found the employer's reasons to be pretextual and concluded that plaintiff's disqualification was motivated in substantial part by her race. The Court of Appeals affirmed and the Supreme Court granted certiorari, 464 U.S. 913, 104 S.Ct. 272, 78 L.Ed.2d 253 (1983). Two of the questions presented in Westinghouse's petition for certiorari were phrased as follows: (1) When the generalized prima facie case has been rebutted by defendant's proof of specific non-discriminatory reason for employment action, is plaintiff required to present evidence concerning particular conduct in issue in order to establish pretext? (2) Did district court's application of generalized evidence from prima facie case to meet plaintiff's pretext burden effectively foreclose defendant's opportunity to rebut inference drawn from prima facie case, and was it therefore clearly erroneous or inconsistent with previously enunciated legal standards? The Court subsequently vacated the grant of certiorari on the ground that review was "improvidently granted." 466 U.S. 521, 104 S.Ct. 2163, 80 L.Ed.2d 531 (1984).

RULE 52 AND FINDINGS OF FACT BY THE DISTRICT COURT

Rule 52(a) of the Federal Rules of Civil Procedure requires the district judge, in actions tried without a jury, to make separate findings of fact and conclusions of law in support of his judgment. The Rule further provides that "[f]indings of fact shall not be set aside unless clearly erroneous." The Supreme Court has held that "a finding is 'clearly erroneous' when although there is evidence to support it, the reviewing court on the entire evidence is left with the definite and firm conviction that a mistake has been committed." United States v. United States Gypsum Co., 333 U.S. 364, 395, 68 S.Ct. 525, 542, 92 L.Ed. 746, 766 (1948). Inherent in the clearly erroneous standard is the rule that a court of appeal does not try issues of fact *de novo* and does not set aside district court findings merely because, on the record before it, the appellate court would have reached a different conclusion. As the Eleventh Circuit noted in *Miles* and *Conner,* the appellant who challenges the lower court's factual findings has shouldered a heavy burden.

In an employment discrimination case in which the plaintiff alleges disparate treatment, it is thus highly important to the parties whether the trial court's findings concerning the employer's motivation or intent are treated as findings of "fact", conclusions of law, or mixed issues of fact and law. After the passage of Title VII several circuits, most notably the Fifth, characterized the issue of an employer's motivation as one of "ultimate fact" subject to plenary review, i.e., the same standard of review applied to conclusions of law. See for example, Joshi v. Florida State University, 646 F.2d 981, 986 (5th Cir. 1981), cert. denied, 456 U.S. 972, 102 S.Ct. 2233, 72 L.Ed.2d 845 (1982) (since trial court's finding of nondiscrimination resolved the ultimate issue in the case, court of appeals must make independent determination of appellant's allegations of discrimination while remaining bound by district court's credibility determinations and findings of subsidiary fact which are not clearly erroneous).

In PULLMAN–STANDARD v. SWINT, 456 U.S. 273, 102 S.Ct. 1781, 72 L.Ed.2d 66 (1982) the Court rejected the Fifth Circuit's "ultimate fact" standard of review as applied to findings of intent to discriminate and held the question of intent in a Title VII case to be a "pure question of fact, subject to rule 52's clearly erroneous standard [of review]." The Court declined to address the question of the applicability of Rule 52 to mixed questions of law and fact—"questions in which historical facts are admitted or established, the rule of law is undisputed, and the issue is whether the facts satisfy the statutory standard * * *," but noted that the circuits were divided on this question. 456 U.S. at 289 n. 19, 102 S.Ct. at 1790 n. 19.

Recently the Court returned to Rule 52's application to findings of fact in employment discrimination cases in ANDERSON v. CITY OF BESSEMER, 470 U.S. ___, 105 S.Ct. 1504, 84 L.Ed.2d 518 (1985). In *Anderson* the district court found that the plaintiff had been denied employment because of her sex and that the employer's explanation for preferring a male applicant were pretextual. Critical to the district court's determination were findings that the plaintiff was better qualified for the position than the male applicant who was given the job and that the plaintiff, but not the male applicants, was seriously questioned concerning her spouse's feelings about her working. The Fourth Circuit reversed on the ground that the district court's subsidiary factual findings were clearly erroneous. Stressing that "[i]f the district court's account of the evidence is plausible in light of the record viewed in its entirety, the court of appeals may not reverse it even though convinced that had it been sitting as the trier of fact, it would have weighed the evidence differently," the Supreme Court reversed.

With respect to the qualifications of the two candidates for the position, the Court noted that the district court's finding was based on essentially undisputed evidence regarding the respective backgrounds of the applicants and the duties of the position in question. The Court of Appeals, reading the same record differed with the district court as to the most important duty of the job and concluded that the male applicant was better qualified. The Supreme Court held that the court of appeals had overstepped its authority under Rule 52.

> Based on our own reading of the record, we cannot say that either interpretation of the facts is illogical or implausible. Each has support in inferences that may be drawn from the facts in the record; and if either interpretation had been drawn by a district court on the record before us, we would not be inclined to find it clearly erroneous. The question we must answer, however, is not whether the Fourth Circuit's interpretation of the facts was clearly erroneous, but whether the District Court's finding was clearly erroneous. The District Court determined that petitioner was better qualified, and, as we have stated above, such a finding is entitled to deference notwithstanding that it is not based on credibility determinations. When the record is examined in light of the appropriately deferential standard, it is apparent that it contains nothing that mandates a finding that the District Court's conclusion was clearly erroneous.

470 U.S. at ___, 105 S.Ct. at 1513.

As to the district court's finding that male candidates were not seriously questioned about the feelings of their wives toward the job in question, the Court held that the Court of Appeals had failed to give due regard to the ability of the district judge to interpret and discern the credibility of oral testimony.

> The trial judge was faced with the testimony of three witnesses, one of whom (Mrs. Boone) stated that none of the other candidates had been so questioned, one of whom (a male committee member) testified that [the successful male candidate] had been asked such a question "in a way," and one of whom (another committeeman) testified that all the candidates had been subjected to similar questioning. None of these accounts is implausible on its face, and none is contradicted by any reliable extrinsic evidence. Under these circumstances, the trial court's decision to credit Mrs. Boone was not clearly erroneous.

470 U.S. at ___, 105 S.Ct. at 1514.

Did the Eleventh Circuit in Miles v. M.N.C. Corp., comply with *Pullman-Standard* and *Anderson*? Was not the district judge entitled to believe that the supervisor's subjective evaluation of the plaintiff's work was the real reason she was not rehired?

In a case tried under the *McDonnell Douglas-Burdine* formula, the district judge will normally be called on at the end of the plaintiff's case to determine whether he has put on a prima facie case. Is that ruling a "pure question of fact," a question of law, or a mixture of the two? See, Gay v. Waiters' and Lunchmen's Union, Local 30, 694 F.2d 531, 539 (9th Cir. 1982). In light of the Supreme Court's ruling in UNITED STATES POSTAL SERVICE v. AIKENS, supra at 93, does it matter? See generally, Calleros, Title VII and Rule 52(c): Standards of Appellate Review in Disparate Treatment Cases—Limiting the Reach of Pullman Standard v. Swint, 58 Tul.L.Rev. 403 (1983).

BIBBS v. BLOCK

United States Court of Appeals, Eighth Circuit (en banc), 1985.
778 F.2d 1318.

ARNOLD, CIRCUIT JUDGE.

This is a Title VII case in which the plaintiff, an employee of the United States Department of Agriculture, claims that he was denied a promotion because of his race. The District Court found "that racial considerations probably did play a minor role in the selection process, * * * but that plaintiff would not have been selected for the position even if his race had been disregarded." It added that "race was not a determining factor in the decision to promote [another employee] rather than plaintiff." Judgment was entered in favor of defendant.

On appeal, a panel of this Court reversed. Bibbs v. Block, 749 F.2d 508 (8th Cir. 1984). Pointing to the District Court's finding that "race was a discernible factor at the time of the decision," the panel took the view that the additional finding that "the same decision would have been made absent racial considerations" was "inherently inconsistent." It vacated the judgment for defendant and remanded to the District Court "to enter a judgment in favor of plaintiff and to consider the necessary remedy to make plaintiff whole."

The defendant petitioned for rehearing. He asked that the panel modify its opinion to make clear that any relief ordered on remand could not include retroactive promotion and back pay at the higher level plaintiff had unsuccessfully sought. Such relief, defendant argued, could not be appropriate where the trier of fact had found that plaintiff would not have been promoted in any event. In the alternative, defendant asked for rehearing en banc. We granted the petition for rehearing en banc, thus automatically vacating the panel opinion. After oral argument, we now hold that plaintiff, having shown that race was a discernible factor at the time of the decision not to promote him, has established a violation of Title VII. The cause will be remanded for a determination of appropriate relief. As to retroactive promotion and back pay, the District Court should make a new finding, this time placing the burden of persuasion on defendant. If the court finds that defendant has shown by a preponderance of the evidence that plaintiff would not have been promoted in any event, retroactive promotion and back pay may not be ordered.

I.

Bibbs, who is black, is employed by the Agricultural Stabilization and Conservation Service (ASCS), a division of the Department of Agriculture. In September 1976, Bibbs applied for, but was denied, a promotion to a supervisory position in the ASCS print shop. Bibbs was one of seven individuals who applied for the position; he was the only black applicant. All seven applications were forwarded to a selection committee comprised of three individuals, all of whom were white. The committee was dominated by one member, Joseph Tresnak, who was most familiar with the print shop and the print-shop employees. The District Court found that Tresnak was the "key figure" in making the selection. Tresnak's central role in the selection process is significant in light of the direct evidence of Tresnak's use of racial slurs. One witness testified Tresnak had characterized Bibbs as a "black militant," while another testified Tresnak referred to another print-shop employee who was black as "boy" and "nigger." After interviewing each of the seven candidates, the committee selected Dennis Laube, who was white, for the position. The three members of the committee, after conclusion of all the interviews and without having agreed on any criteria for selection, selected the same top three candidates and each chose them in the same order. They did not discuss their views of the relative merits of the candidates before, during, or after the interviews.

In determining that the decision not to promote Bibbs was not racially motivated, the trial court noted that the work force in the print shop was racially integrated.[3] The trial court also found that Bibbs had a history of disciplinary and interpersonal problems and was not selected in part because he was difficult to work with and caused irritation among fellow workers. Given the diverse factors each of the members of the selection committee used, and the alleged absence of any discussion among them during the deliberation process, the trial court judged the selection committee members "not particularly credible, either in demeanor or in the substance of their testimony. * * * The committee members were extremely guarded in their responses to questions and were quite defensive in their positions on matters that might reflect negatively on their decision. The Court is skeptical that it has heard the complete story concerning the committee's deliberations." The trial court was particularly concerned about the committee members' lack of credibility given the subjective criteria considered by the committee. The trial court observed that a subjective procedure may provide a "convenient screen for discriminatory decision making, and must be carefully scrutinized."

After considering the evidence, the District Court made two factual findings. First, the court determined that race was a factor in the "selection process." The court initially stated race played a "minor role in the selection process," later, it stated race was a "discernible factor at the time of the decision." Second, the court found that Bibbs "would not have been selected for the position even if his race had been disregarded,". Thus, the court concluded race was not a "determining" factor or a "but for" factor, meaning a factor that ultimately made a

3. Such "bottom line" statistics do not insulate an employer from liability for intentional discrimination against an individual employee. See Connecticut v. Teal, 457 U.S. 440, 454, 102 S.Ct. 2525, 2534, 73 L.Ed.2d 130 (1982). But they are relevant evidence, to be considered along with all other factors.

difference in the decision, and that liability was therefore not established. It dismissed the complaint.

II.

In many Title VII cases, the proof proceeds on both sides on the premise that one motive only on the part of the employer—either an illegitimate one (e.g., race) or a legitimate one (e.g., ability to do the job)—has caused the adverse action of which the plaintiff complains. It is this type of case for which the familiar evidentiary framework of McDonnell Douglas Corp. v. Green, is designed. After the plaintiff establishes a prima facie case, and the defendant "articulates" (a verb that refers only to the burden of producing evidence) a legitimate, nondiscriminatory reason for the action complained of, the burden then shifts back to the plaintiff to persuade the trier of fact that the defendant's proffered reason was not the real one, but only a pretext hiding an impermissible racial motivation. Typically, the plaintiff will contend that one reason—race—was operative, the defendant will contend that another single reason—ability to do the job—motivated it, and the trier of fact will find one reason or the other (but not a combination) to be the true one. In such a case, the issues of motivation and causation are not distinctly separated, nor do they need to be. If the plaintiff shows the defendant's proffered reason to be a pretext for race, the case is over. Liability is established, and reinstatement is ordered (in a discharge case) absent extraordinary circumstances. The very showing that the defendant's asserted reason was a pretext for race is also a demonstration that but for his race plaintiff would have gotten the job. That is what pretext means: a reason *for the employment decision* that is not the true reason.

If the District Court in the case before us had found that defendant's reason or reasons for not promoting plaintiff were other than race, and that race played no part in the decisionmaking process, we should be required simply to affirm the dismissal of the complaint—assuming the finding was not clearly erroneous. But the court here conducted a more sensitive analysis of the various factors at work. It found that race was "a discernible factor," although not a but-for factor. It found, in other words, mixed motives.[4] In this situation, we believe analysis is aided best by separating the issues of liability and remedy. The District Court itself, citing Brodin, The Standard of Causation in the Mixed-Motive Title VII Action: A Social Policy Perspective, 82 Colum.

4. The District Court found that racial considerations were a discernible, though minor, factor in the selection process and in the decision of whom to promote, though not a determining factor in the "but for" sense. The court found that race was a motivating factor but that plaintiff had not shown that he would have received the job had race not been considered. In this situation, we think liability on the part of the defendant is established. The plaintiff, however, will actually be awarded the promotion (or comparable relief such as front pay or damages) only if defendant fails to show that it would have made the same decision absent consideration of the impermissible factor.

L.Rev. 292 (1982), suggested such an approach, but decided, in view of its "novelty," to leave to us whether to pursue it.

We accept the invitation. In doing so, we use as a factual predicate the District Court's findings of fact, which are not clearly erroneous. We look first to the statute.

As always, the words of the Congress are the best indications of its intention. It is not only failing to hire someone, or discharging him or her, because of race or sex, that is unlawful. The statute also forbids employers "otherwise to discriminate * * * with respect to compensation, terms, conditions, or privileges of employment, because of * * * race," § 703(a)(1), and makes it unlawful for employers "to limit * * * or classify * * * employees * * * in any way which would deprive *or tend to deprive* any individual of employment *opportunities or otherwise adversely affect*" him or her because of race. Section 703(a)(2). To put it in terms of the present case, it would be unlawful for defendant to put Bibbs at a disadvantage in the competition for promotion because of his race, as well as actually to deny him the promotion for this reason. (Indeed, if an employer requires black employees to meet a higher standard, the statute is violated even if they actually meet it and get the jobs in question.) Every kind of disadvantage resulting from racial prejudice in the employment setting is outlawed. Forcing Bibbs to be considered for promotion in a process in which race plays a discernible part is itself a violation of law, regardless of the outcome of the process. At the very least, such a process "tend[s] to deprive" him of an "employment opportunit[y]." Section 703(a)(2).

It does not follow, though, that retroactive promotion is an appropriate remedy. Unless the impermissible racial motivation was a but-for cause of Bibbs's losing the promotion, to place him in the job now would award him a windfall. He would be more than made whole. He would get a job that he would never have received whatever his race. At this point, we think, another provision of the statute, Section 706(g), 42 U.S.C. § 2000e–5(g) (1982), becomes important:

> (g) If the court finds that the respondent has intentionally engaged in or is intentionally engaging in an unlawful employment practice charged in the complaint, the court may enjoin the respondent from engaging in such unlawful employment practice, and order such affirmative action as may be appropriate, which may include, but is not limited to, reinstatement or hiring of employees with or without back pay * * *, or any other equitable relief as the court deems appropriate. * * * No order of the court shall require the admission or reinstatement of an individual as a member of a union, or the hiring, reinstatement, or promotion of an individual as an employee, or the payment to him of any back pay, if such individual was refused admission, suspended, or expelled, or was refused employment or advancement, or was suspended or discharged *for any reason other than discrimination on account of*

> *race,* color, religion, sex, or national origin or in violation of section 2000e–3(a) of this title.

(Emphasis added.)

Thus, the language of Title VII supports the separation of liability and remedy and allows an award of reinstatement or promotion and back pay only after a finding that discrimination was the but-for cause of the employment decision. After defining unlawful employment practices of an employer in Subsection 703(a) of the statute, Congress set forth the conditions on which courts may grant injunctive and affirmative relief. By the terms of the statute, injunctive relief may be awarded after a finding of intentional discrimination; and affirmative relief such as reinstatement and back pay may not be awarded if the employment decision was "for any reason other than discrimination." The "but-for" determination required for an award of affirmative relief is consistent with Title VII's intended purpose of making persons whole for injuries suffered on account of unlawful employment discrimination. Albemarle Paper Co. v. Moody. Focusing on Subsection 706(g) of the statute, the Supreme Court recently reaffirmed the principle of make-whole relief, stating that competitive seniority can be awarded only to actual victims of discrimination. Firefighters Local Union No. 1784 v. Stotts, 467 U.S. 561, 104 S.Ct. 2576, 2589, 81 L.Ed.2d 483 (1984).

The Supreme Court has not expressly addressed the mixed-motives problem in a Title VII case, but it has focused on it in other contexts. For example, in the context of legislative and administrative decision making, the Court has considered whether a decision motivated by both lawful and unlawful considerations violated the Equal Protection Clause. See Village of Arlington Heights v. Metropolitan Housing Development Corp., 429 U.S. 252, 265–66, 97 S.Ct. 555, 563–64, 50 L.Ed. 2d 450 (1977) ("When there is proof that a discriminatory purpose has been a *motivating* factor in the decision, * * * judicial deference [to the legislative/administrative decision] is no longer justified.") (emphasis added). The Court established the so-called same-decision test to review such decisions:

> Proof that the decision by the Village was motivated in part by a racially discriminatory purpose would not necessarily have required invalidation of the challenged decision. Such proof would, however, have shifted to the Village the burden of establishing that the same decision would have resulted even had the impermissible purpose not been considered. If this were established, the complaining party in a case of this kind no longer fairly could attribute the injury complained of to improper consideration of a discriminatory purpose. In such circumstances, there would be no justification for judicial interference with the challenged decision.

Id. at 270 n. 21, 97 S.Ct. at 566 n. 21. The Court also adopted the same-decision test for First Amendment retaliatory-discharge cases in Mt. Healthy City School District Board of Education v. Doyle, 429 U.S. 274, 97 S.Ct. 568, 50 L.Ed.2d 471 (1977), decided the same day as *Arlington*

Heights. See also Givhan v. Western Line Consolidated School District, 439 U.S. 410, 416–17, 99 S.Ct. 693, 697, 58 L.Ed.2d 619 (1979). The Court in *Mt. Healthy* articulated the proper standard of causation as follows:

> Initially, in this case, the burden was properly placed upon respondent to show that his conduct was constitutionally protected, and that this conduct was a "substantial factor"—or, to put it in other words, that it was a "motivating factor" in the Board's decision not to rehire him. Respondent having carried that burden, however, the District Court should have gone on to determine whether the Board had shown by a preponderance of the evidence that it would have reached the same decision as to respondent's reemployment even in the absence of the protected conduct.

429 U.S. at 287, 97 S.Ct. 568 at 576 (footnote omitted). See also NLRB v. Transportation Management Corp., 462 U.S. 393, 103 S.Ct. 2469, 76 L.Ed.2d 667 (1983) (similar mixed-motives analysis used in unfair-labor-practice cases).

In the *Mt. Healthy* group of cases, of course, the Supreme Court's mixed-motives analysis is used to establish the defendant's liability in the first place, not simply to determine the appropriate remedy. If the defendant establishes that it would have made the same decision in the absence of the illegitimate factor, it wins the case, and the complaint is dismissed. Our reading of Title VII is significantly different. In that statute, Congress has made unlawful any kind of racial discrimination, not just discrimination that actually deprives someone of a job. A defendant's showing that the plaintiff would not have gotten the job anyway does not extinguish liability. It simply excludes the remedy of retroactive promotion or reinstatement. In adopting this mode of analysis, we employ an approach similar to that used in King v. Trans-World Airlines, Inc., 738 F.2d 255, 259 (8th Cir. 1984) (discrimination in interview process not cured by defendant's legitimate reasons for not hiring plaintiff), approved in Easley v. Anheuser-Busch, Inc., 758 F.2d 251, 262 (8th Cir. 1985). Under this approach, once the plaintiff has established a violation of Title VII by proving that an unlawful motive played some part in the employment decision or decisional process, the plaintiff is entitled to some relief, including, as appropriate, a declaratory judgment, partial attorney's fees, and injunctive relief against future or continued discrimination. However, even after a finding of unlawful discrimination is made, the defendant is allowed a further defense in order to limit the relief. The defendant may avoid an award of reinstatement or promotion and back pay if it can prove by a preponderance of the evidence [5] that the plaintiff would not have been hired or promoted even in the absence of the proven discrimination.

5. Although several courts considering the weight of the employer's burden on the remedy question have imposed a "clear and convincing" proof requirement, see, e.g., *Toney,* 705 F.2d at 1373 (Tamm, J., concurring); Patterson v. Greenwood School District 50, 696 F.2d 293, 295; Ostroff v. Employment Exchange, Inc., 683 F.2d 302, 304 (9th Cir. 1982), we recently rejected that higher standard of proof in

This same-decision test will apply only to determine the appropriate remedy and only after plaintiff proves he or she was a victim of unlawful discrimination in some respect. For that reason, the burden of production *and* persuasion shifts from the plaintiff to the defendant. *King,* 738 F.2d at 259 ("The burden of showing that proven discrimination did not cause a plaintiff's rejection is properly placed on the defendant-employer because its unlawful acts have made it difficult to determine what would have transpired if all parties had acted properly.") (quoting League of United Latin American Citizens v. City of Salinas Fire Department, 654 F.2d 557, 559 (9th Cir. 1981)).

In the instant case, Bibbs has proved race was a discernible factor in the decision not to promote him. We hold such proof is sufficient in a mixed-motive context to establish intentional discrimination and liability under Title VII. We therefore vacate the judgment dismissing the complaint and remand for the entry of a declaratory judgment in favor of Bibbs and an injunction prohibiting the ASCS from future or continued discrimination against Bibbs on the basis of race. In addition, the District Court should consider Bibbs a prevailing party for the purpose of an award of attorney's fees. See 42 U.S.C. § 2000e–5(k); *King,* 738 F.2d at 259; Nanty v. Barrows Co., 660 F.2d 1327, 1334 n. 10 (9th Cir. 1981). Of course, in determining a reasonable fee, an adjustment based on the extent to which Bibbs has succeeded will be appropriate. See Hensley v. Eckerhart, 461 U.S. 424, 435–36, 103 S.Ct. 1933, 1940–41, 76 L.Ed.2d 40 (1983) (applying 42 U.S.C. § 1988). Nevertheless, we emphasize that "by proving unlawful discrimination, appellant prevailed on a significant issue in the litigation," *King,* 738 F.2d at 259, and thereby vindicated a major purpose of Title VII, the rooting out and deterrence of job discrimination.

III.

On this rehearing en banc the government did not challenge the panel's holding that defendant is liable. Instead, it challenged the scope of relief available when there has been no finding that discrimination was the "but-for" cause of the denial of promotion. Because we agree that a but-for or same-decision finding must be made before affirmative relief such as retroactive promotion and back pay may be awarded, we remand the case for further analysis of the remedy issue. As stated above, the District Court must consider whether Bibbs would have received the promotion but for the discrimination in the selection

Craik v. Minnesota State University Board, 731 F.2d 465, 470 n. 8 (8th Cir. 1984) (Title VII class action alleging a pattern or practice of sex discrimination). But cf. *King,* 738 F.2d 255, 257 (8th Cir. 1984). In *Craik* we stated: "The normal standard of proof in civil litigation is that of a preponderance of the evidence, and we do not believe that the public and private interests involved require altering that distribution of the risk of error between the litigants." 731 F.2d at 470 n. 8. We adhere to that view now. Cf. Herman & McLean v. Huddleston, 459 U.S. 375, 389–90, 103 S.Ct. 683, 685, 74 L.Ed.2d 548 (recovery under § 10(b) of the 1934 Securities Exchange Act, 15 U.S.C. § 78j(b), requires preponderance rather than clear and convincing evidence).

process. While the trial court's statement that "[i]t cannot be concluded that plaintiff would have been selected by a committee free of racial considerations" would satisfy the same-decision standard, the trial court apparently placed the burden on Bibbs to show why he was denied the promotion. We reiterate that to avoid an award of retroactive promotion and back pay, the defendant must prove by a preponderance of evidence that Bibbs would not have received the promotion even if race had not been considered.

Vacated and remanded with instructions.

LAY, CHIEF JUDGE, with whom HEANEY and MCMILLIAN, CIRCUIT JUDGES, join, concurring.

I concur in Judge Arnold's well-written opinion.

I write separately for two reasons: (1) to voice my disagreement with the dissent and (2) to state specially, although I fully join Judge Arnold's opinion, that I seriously question the propriety of applying the "same decision" test to "mixed motive" cases in a Title VII context.[1]

[That portion of Judge Lay's opinion which discusses his disagreement with the dissent is omitted]

The same decision test

I now address my view that the same decision test should not apply to mixed motive cases, even when the burden of proof is properly placed on the employer.

Title VII is designed to protect victims against invidious discrimination which *in any way* influences or motivates an employment decision. That the employer has other nondiscriminatory reasons which enter into the decision is irrelevant. It is clear under the relevant case law that racial discrimination need not be the "sole" cause motivating the employer. Race is either a factor in the employment decision or it is not.

There is precedent for use of the same decision test in employment discrimination cases where liability is based upon a class action or disparate impact context.[5] But to extend such a test to cases of disparate treatment will provide hollow victories to most victims of racial discrimination and little real relief. Many litigants who successfully prove racial discrimination in the employment decision will now find that the spoils do not go to the victim but only to the victim's

1. Notwithstanding my disagreement with the same decision test, in order to provide a majority opinion and a clear test to follow in this circuit I join Judge Arnold's application of the same decision test.

5. Cf. International Brotherhood of Teamsters v. United States, 431 U.S. 324, 359 n. 45, 97 S.Ct. 1843, 1867 n. 45, 52 L.Ed.2d 396 (1977). ("[T]he employer was in the best position to show why any individual employee was denied an employment opportunity. Insofar as the reasons related to available vacancies or the employer's evaluation of the applicant's qualifications, the company's records were the most relevant items of proof. If the refusal to hire was based on other factors, the employer and its agents knew best what those factors were and the extent to which they influenced the decision-making process.")

attorneys. Plaintiffs such as Bibbs will obtain attorneys' fees and perhaps injunctive or declaratory relief, but no award of back pay or reinstatement. After proving his or her case at the liability stage, to gain any other relief a plaintiff in an alleged mixed motive case will now face the additional uphill battle to rebut defendant's claim that the same decision would have been made absent race. Although Judge Arnold adopts the "but for" test for liability in McDonald v. Santa Fe Trail Transportation Co., 427 U.S. 273, 282 n. 10, 96 S.Ct. 2574, 2580 n. 10, 49 L.Ed.2d 493 (1976), the practical effect will be that before a plaintiff can recover damages in a Title VII case, he or she will have to convince the court that race was the sole cause. Surely Congress did not intend such a result.

Certain well-established principles should govern our review of the district court's decision. First, under the teaching of *Burdine,* "the ultimate burden of persuading the trier of fact that the defendant intentionally discriminated against the plaintiff remains at all times with the plaintiff." *Burdine,* 450 U.S. at 253, 101 S.Ct. at 1093. Second, as the district court acknowledged and as stated above, in a Title VII disparate treatment action a plaintiff need not prove that the sole reason for the employment decision was the discrimination, but is required to show no more than that race was a "but for" cause. *McDonald,* 427 U.S. at 282 n. 10, 96 S.Ct. at 2580 n. 10. The district court, reciting the confusion of our own cases and those of other circuits, resolved the apparent dilemma by finding that "racial considerations probably did play a minor role in the selection process, through the influence of Tresnak, but that plaintiff would not have been selected for the position even if his race had been disregarded." On the surface, the "same decision" reasoning is attractive and would simply relegate to appellate review the issue of whether the district court's factual findings are clearly erroneous. However, when race is shown to have been a discernible factor *in* the employment decision, as the district court found below, I conclude that the same-decision test is inappropriate under the principles of *Burdine.* Here, plaintiff has done far more than put forth a prima facie case of discrimination. He has successfully proven that race was a discriminatory factor *in* his employer's refusal to promote him. Rather than requiring proof that race was a "substantial" as opposed to a "minor" factor in the decision, Title VII simply requires that a plaintiff prove his or her claim of unlawful discrimination by persuading the court that "a discriminatory reason more likely [than not] motivated the employer." *Burdine,* 450 U.S. at 256, 101 S.Ct. at 1095. Nothing more is required of a plaintiff to establish liability under Title VII.

Once the trier of fact has found that race was a factor "in any way" influencing the decision, it is error to attempt to quantify race as a minor factor. See 42 U.S.C. § 2000e–2(a)(2) (1970 ed. Supp. V). Under the factual record presented here, once race was found to be a discernible factor in or influencing the decision, the additional conclusion that it was a minor factor is irrelevant to the Title VII analysis.

When race is shown at the liability stage to have been a factor in the employment decision, the employer should not be able to exculpate its proven invidious discriminatory practices by having a second chance to show that racial considerations did not affect the decision's outcome. This clearly contradicts Congress' purpose in enacting Title VII. I find that the record supports a finding that race clearly influenced the decision. Under these circumstances, I would reject as irrelevant and clearly erroneous the district court's unnecessary finding that "plaintiff would not have been selected for the position even if race had been disregarded."

The language of Title VII plainly recognizes the broad purpose of eliminating consideration of race from employment decisions. "Title VII prohibits *all* discrimination in employment based upon race, sex, and national origin. 'The broad, overriding interest, shared by employer, employee, and consumer, is efficient and trustworthy workmanship assured through fair and * * * neutral employment and personnel decisions.'" *Burdine,* 450 U.S. at 259, 101 S.Ct. at 1096 (emphasis added) (quoting McDonnell Douglas Corp. v. Green, 411 U.S. 792, 801, 93 S.Ct. 1817, 1823, 36 L.Ed.2d 668 (1973)). As Justice Marshall has stated:

> [I]t is important to bear in mind that Title VII is a remedial statute designed to eradicate certain invidious employment practices. The evils against which it is aimed are defined broadly: "to fail * * * to hire or to discharge * * * or otherwise to discriminate * * * with respect to * * * compensation, terms, conditions, or privileges of employment [because of such individual's race * * *]" and "to limit, segregate, or classify * * * in any way which would deprive or tend to deprive any individual of employment opportunities or otherwise adversely affect his status [* * * because of such individual's race * * *]." 42 U.S.C. § 2000e–2(a) (1970 ed., Supp. V) (emphasis deleted).

International Brotherhood of Teamsters, 431 U.S. at 381, 97 S.Ct. at 1878 (Marshall, J., concurring and dissenting).

Although proof of actual motivation would be within a defendant's knowledge, I find it highly inappropriate, under the *Burdine* principles governing Title VII cases, to adopt the *Mt. Healthy* rationale and shift the burden to the defendant to show that plaintiff would *not* have been promoted even if his race had not been considered. *Mt. Healthy* exacts a distinctly different standard relating to recovery and burden of proof in constitutionally-protected conduct cases than does *Burdine* which applied Title VII. A mixed motive case should be tried under the same tests set forth in *McDonald* and *Burdine.* To hold otherwise is to inject total confusion into the already difficult process faced by litigants who pursue relief under Title VII.[7]

7. This discussion finds analogous aid in causation principles developed in tort law. In order to establish liability, a plaintiff does not have to show that the defendant's negligence (or here, racial discrimination) was *the* sole proximate cause of the accident. The burden is on the plaintiff only to show that the defendant's negli-

BRIGHT, SENIOR CIRCUIT JUDGE, separately concurring.

I concur in Judge Arnold's opinion. I write separately to indicate that I do not join the separate concurrences of Chief Judge Lay and Judge McMillian, and to emphasize my view that liability in this case rests upon the district court's finding of a causal relationship between race discrimination and the employment decision; that is, that race discrimination played a role, albeit a minor one, in selecting the person to be promoted.

In my opinion, the existence of some racial prejudice in the workplace that does not affect the employment decision will not support a determination of liability against an employer, where the discrimination and the decision are not shown to be causally connected.

Finally, I express disagreement with the suggestion in Chief Judge Lay's opinion that the "same decision test" should be rejected in mixed motive cases—"same decision" meaning that the employer would have made the same employment decision regardless of racial factors which might have entered into the hiring or promotion decision.

A simple hypothetical will illustrate the logic of applying the same decision test. Assume a college seeks a new president. Five candidates, four Caucasians and one black constitute the finalists. All are qualified but one Caucasian possesses clearly superior talents. That person is selected, but during the selection process an individual on the committee states that he or she would not vote for a black person for president under any circumstances, and that bias is shown to have a minor impact on the decisionmaking process of the entire committee.[1] The mixed motive analysis offered by Chief Judge Lay seems to suggest that the college would be forced to hire and give backpay to the black applicant who would not have been selected as college president under a completely racially neutral selection process.

Under Judge Arnold's opinion, which I join, the college could limit the remedy, avoiding backpay and having to hire the rejected applicant, by showing by a preponderance of the evidence that the black applicant would not have received the appointment in any event.

In his dissent, Judge Ross construes the majority's use of the term "discernible factor" as containing no causal requirement. I disagree. I believe that term denotes the existence of a causal relationship in some degree in the present case, as shown by the district court's finding that "race played a minor role in the decision not to promote the plaintiff * * *." (Dist.Ct. Order at p. 8).

Thus, with the above explanation of my views, I agree with Judge Arnold's opinion for the court which imposes liability on the employer

gence was *a* proximate cause. In other words, the trier of fact must determine whether the defendant's negligence (discrimination) was *a* factor which served as *a* proximate cause of the accident (employment decision).

1. To make my position clear, I would add that the presence of racial bias by one member of the selection committee which does not on a causal basis enter into the employment decision of the committee will not impose liability on the employer.

but permits the defendant to restrict the remedy by proving by a preponderance of the evidence that Bibbs would not have been promoted even if his race had not been considered in the employment decision.

McMILLIAN, CIRCUIT JUDGE, concurring.

I concur in the decision to remand this case to the district court to determine whether appellant would have received the promotion but for the employer's discrimination in the selection process.

I agree with most of the analysis set forth in the majority opinion. I agree that proof of unlawful discrimination requires only proof that race was "a discernible factor" in the employment decision, a finding which would ordinarily entitle the plaintiff to declaratory relief, partial attorney's fees and prospective injunctive relief, and that, following proof of unlawful discrimination, the burden of persuasion and the burden of producing evidence on the issue of the scope of available retroactive relief are properly shifted to the employer. "The burden of showing that proven discrimination did not cause a plaintiff's rejection is properly placed on the defendant-employer because its unlawful acts have made it difficult to determine what would have transpired if all parties had acted properly." League of United Latin American Citizens v. City of Salinas Fire Department, 654 F.2d 557, 559 (9th Cir. 1981), citing Day v. Mathews, 530 F.2d 1083, 1086 (D.C.Cir. 1976) (per curiam).

However, I do not agree with the preponderance of the evidence standard of proof and would instead require the employer to prove by clear and convincing evidence that appellant would not have been promoted in the absence of discrimination. See, e.g., King v. Trans World Airlines, Inc., 738 F.2d 255, 259 (8th Cir. 1984).

> The requirement of clear and convincing proof * * * furthers Title VII's deterrent purpose. By making it more difficult for employers to defeat successful plaintiffs' claims to retroactive relief, the higher standard of proof may well discourage unlawful conduct by employers. In addition, the higher standard of proof is justified by the consideration that the employer is a wrongdoer whose unlawful conduct has made it difficult for the plaintiff to show what would have occurred in the absence of that conduct.

Toney v. Block, 705 F.2d 1364, 1373 (D.C.Cir. 1983) (Tamm, J., concurring) (citations omitted).

I would remand the case to the district court to determine whether the employer has shown by clear and convincing evidence that appellant would not have been promoted even in the absence of unlawful discrimination.

ROSS, CIRCUIT JUDGE, with whom FAGG and BOWMAN, CIRCUIT JUDGES, join, dissenting.

I dissent in part. I cannot agree with the majority's holding that proof that race was a "discernible factor" is sufficient in a mixed-motive context to establish intentional discrimination and liability under Title VII. I adhere to the position that when the evidence suggests mixed-motives the plaintiff must prove that race was a "motivating factor" before he or she can prevail at the liability stage. See Womack v. Munson, 619 F.2d 1292, 1297 n. 7 (8th Cir. 1980), cert. denied, 450 U.S. 979, 101 S.Ct. 1513, 67 L.Ed.2d 814 (1981). Retention of this standard is warranted by the language of the statute, the case law and by practical considerations.

Title VII prohibits employment practices that discriminate against any individual "because of" such individual's race, color, religion, sex or national origin. The "because of" language is crucial to employment discrimination suits brought under the statute and any adverse employment decision that is not arrived at "because of" one of the protected criteria is not unlawful under the statute. The majority, quite simply, ignores these operative words of the statute.

The "because of" requirement of the statute is not satisfied by the majority's "discernible factor" test.[2] While it is clear from the legislative history,[3] that the "because of" language does not require that a plaintiff, such as Bibbs, prove that race is the sole factor in the employment decision, at a minimum, it means that a plaintiff must prove some causal relationship between race and the employment decision. The "discernible factor" test is deficient because it contains no causal requirement. Title VII is not violated simply because an impermissible factor plays some minor part in the employer's decision. See Whiting v. Jackson State University, 616 F.2d 116, 121 (5th Cir. 1980). The Supreme Court has noted that to establish a violation of Title VII a plaintiff need only show that race was a "but for" cause. McDonald v. Sante Fe Trail Transportation Co., 427 U.S. 273, 282 n. 10, 96 S.Ct. 2574, 2580 n. 10, 49 L.Ed.2d 493 (1976).

I object to the majority's "discernible factor" test for the additional reason that it dilutes the requirement that every Title VII plaintiff must prove intentional discrimination. In every employment discrimination case brought pursuant to Title VII, the theory of disparate treatment requires the aggrieved employee to prove that the employer acted with a discriminatory intent based on an impermissible factor. The ultimate factual inquiry in a Title VII case is whether the defendant intentionally discriminated against the plaintiff. United States Postal Service Board of Governors v. Aikens, 460 U.S. 711, 103 S.Ct. 1478, 1482, 75 L.Ed.2d 403 (1983). The Title VII plaintiff bears the ultimate burden of persuading the trier of fact that the defendant intentionally discriminated against the plaintiff and that the plaintiff has been the victim of intentional discrimination. Texas Department of Community Affairs v. Burdine, 450 U.S. 248, 253–256, 101 S.Ct. 1089, 1093–95, 67 L.Ed.2d 207 (1981). The presence of an illegal factor in the

2. The majority clearly establishes a new test. Judge Arnold writes, "we now hold that plaintiff, having shown that race was a discernible factor at the time of the decision not to promote him, has established a violation of Title VII." Ante at 1319–1320.

3. The Senate and the House both rejected an amendment which would have added the word solely to subsection (a) of section 2000e–2. 110 Cong.Rec. 13,838 (1964); 110 Cong.Rec. 2728 (1964).

employment process, without more, does not in my opinion constitute intentional discrimination. The racial or discriminatory factor must be acted upon; it must be a basis for the employment decision, and not just perceived. As the Supreme Court has said, the plaintiff must demonstrate by competent evidence that whatever the stated reasons for his rejection, "the decision was in reality racially *premised.*" McDonnell Douglas Corp. v. Green, 411 U.S. 792, 805 n. 18, 93 S.Ct. 1817, 1825 n. 18, 36 L.Ed.2d 668 (1973) (emphasis added).

Because of the intentional discrimination requirement, the unlawful factor must be more than a "discernible factor"; it must be a "motivating factor". Proof of illegal motivation is critical to Title VII disparate treatment cases, International Brotherhood of Teamsters v. United States, 431 U.S. 324, 335 n. 15, 97 S.Ct. 1843, 1854 n. 15, 52 L.Ed.2d 396 (1977), and a plaintiff can meet his or her burden of proof "by persuading the court that a discriminatory reason more likely motivated the employer * * *." *Burdine,* supra, 450 U.S. at 256, 101 S.Ct. at 1095. Thus, a violation of Title VII is established when the plaintiff proves that the unlawful factor operated as a "motivating factor" in the employment process or decision [4]. By "motivating factor" is meant that the discriminatory purpose was acted upon and produced conduct or an employment decision affected by it.

This court applied a "motivating factor" approach prior to *Burdine,* supra. In Womack v. Munson, 619 F.2d 1292 (8th Cir. 1980), cert. denied, 450 U.S. 979, 101 S.Ct. 1513, 67 L.Ed.2d 814 (1981), this court noted:

> In cases challenging adverse employment actions as racially discriminatory under section 703(a), 42 U.S.C. § 2000e–2(a), we have held the court must look for the "motivating factor" when the evidence suggests mixed motives. See, e.g., Marshall v. Kirkland, 602 F.2d 1282 (8th Cir. 1979); Clark v. Mann, 562 F.2d 1104, 1116–17 (8th Cir. 1977) (42 U.S.C. § 1983 action. * * *

Id. at 1297 n. 7. Continued adherence to a "motivating factor" test is consistent with the language of the statute and current Supreme Court caselaw and I see no justification for reducing a Title VII plaintiff's burden to that of proving only that race was a "discernible factor." [5]

In addition to the legal considerations, I have concerns about the practical ramifications of the majority's holding that proof that race was a "discernible factor" is sufficient to establish liability in a Title VII mixed-motive case. First, the majority failed to define what it means by "discernible" and this omission will result in confusion for the district courts. Secondly, this holding is an open invitation to

4. The relevant inquiry is causation, not quantification.

5. Even the author relied upon by the majority, Brodin, The Standard of Causation in the Mixed-Motive Title VII Action: A Social Policy Perspective, 82 Colum.L. Rev. 292 (1982), takes the position that a plaintiff who establishes that a prohibited criterion was a *motivating factor* in the challenged decision thereby establishes a violation of the Act and thus the defendant's liability. Id. at 323 (emphasis added).

attorneys to file frivolous or extremely marginal cases so that they can get attorneys' fees for showing that an unlawful factor was "discernible."

It is for all of the above reasons that I cannot join the majority's adoption of a "discernible factor" test for Title VII mixed-motive cases. As for the disposition of the instant case, I would affirm the judgment of the district court [6] and dismiss Bibbs' complaint because he failed to establish that race was a "motivating factor" in his nonselection for promotion.

A true copy.

NOTES AND PROBLEMS FOR DISCUSSION

1. In addition to the majority's rule in *Bibbs,* courts have taken at least three other positions on the causation issue in "mixed motive" cases. Some courts have held that the plaintiff bears the burden of proving, not only discrimination, but that the illegal motivation was the "but for" cause of the challenged action, the position taken by the dissenters in *Bibbs.* See, Lewis v. University of Pittsburgh, 725 F.2d 910 (3rd Cir. 1983), cert. denied, ___ U.S. ___, 105 S.Ct. 266 (1984); La Montagne v. American Convenience Products, Inc., 750 F.2d 1405 (7th Cir. 1984); Cazalas v. U.S. Department of Justice, 569 F.Supp. 213 (E.D.La.1983), aff'd, 731 F.2d 280 (5th Cir. 1984), cert. denied, ___ U.S. ___, 105 S.Ct. 1169 (1985). Other courts have literally applied the *Mt. Healthy* doctrine to employment cases and held that, where discrimination is proved, the employer can avoid liability by proving that it would have made the "same decision" absent discrimination. See, Blalock v. Metals Trades, Inc., 775 F.2d 703 (6th Cir. 1985); Hill v. Seaboard Coast Line R. Co., 767 F.2d 771 (11th Cir. 1985). A number of circuits agree with Judge McMillian that, once plaintiff has proved that discrimination was a "discernible factor," the employer has the burden of proving by "clear and convincing evidence" that it would have made the same decision. See, King v. Trans World Airlines, Inc., 738 F.2d 255, 259 (8th Cir. 1984); Muntin v. State of California Parks and Recreation Dept., 738 F.2d 1054 (9th Cir. 1984); Day v. Matthews, 530 F.2d 1083 (D.C.Cir. 1976). Which of these rules is most consistent with the policies underlying Title VII? What is the difference, if any, between the "direct evidence" doctrine described in Miles v. M.N.C. Corp., supra, and the causation rule adopted by the majority in *Bibbs?*

2. Is the majority's rule in *Bibbs* applicable to cases involving discrimination in hiring or discharge? What relief would a discharged employee be entitled to if the employer proved that, absent discrimination, the employee would have been terminated?

3. It is logically possible that discrimination could exist in the employment unit at large and not have any bearing on the specific decision about which the plaintiff complains. For example, there could be racial discrimination in hiring but a black applicant might at the same time be objectively unqualified for the job. Is it however, inherently inconsistent to say that race was a "discernible factor" *in the particular employment decision for which relief is sought* (as the district court apparently found in *Bibbs*) but to also find that the same decision would have been reached on other grounds? If the plaintiff has established a

6. I agree with the majority's assessment that the district court's findings of fact are not clearly erroneous, ante at 1321.

prima facie case and the trier of fact has found the employer's explanation a pretext for discrimination, is it possible for the same trier of fact to apply the "same decision" rule? Is this Judge Lay's argument?

SECTION B: THE ROLE OF STATISTICS

HAZELWOOD SCHOOL DISTRICT v. UNITED STATES

Supreme Court of the United States, 1977.
433 U.S. 299, 97 S.Ct. 2736, 53 L.Ed.2d 768.

MR. JUSTICE STEWART delivered the opinion of the Court.

The petitioner Hazelwood School District covers 78 square miles in the northern part of St. Louis County, Mo. In 1973 the Attorney General brought this lawsuit against Hazelwood and various of its officials, alleging that they were engaged in a "pattern or practice" of employment discrimination in violation of Title VII of the Civil Rights Act of 1964, as amended.[1] The complaint asked for an injunction requiring Hazelwood to cease its discriminatory practices, to take affirmative steps to obtain qualified Negro faculty members, and to offer employment and give backpay to victims of past illegal discrimination.

Hazelwood was formed from 13 rural school districts between 1949 and 1951 by a process of annexation. By the 1967–1968 school year, 17,550 students were enrolled in the district, of whom only 59 were Negro; the number of Negro pupils increased to 576 of 25,166 in 1972–1973, a total of just over 2%.

From the beginning, Hazelwood followed relatively unstructured procedures in hiring its teachers. Every person requesting an application for a teaching position was sent one, and completed applications were submitted to a central personnel office, where they were kept on file.[2] During the early 1960's the personnel office notified all applicants whenever a teaching position became available, but as the number of applications on file increased in the late 1960's and early 1970's, this practice was no longer considered feasible. The personnel office thus began the practice of selecting anywhere from 3 to 10 applicants for interviews at the school where the vacancy existed. The personnel office did not substantively screen the applicants in determining which of them to send for interviews, other than to ascertain that each applicant, if selected, would be eligible for state certification by the

1. Under 42 U.S.C. § 2000e–6(a), the Attorney General was authorized to bring a civil action "[w]henever [he] has reasonable cause to believe that any person or group of persons is engaged in a pattern or practice of resistance to the full enjoyment of any of the rights secured by [Title VII], and that the pattern or practice is of such a nature and is intended to deny the full exercise of [those rights."] The 1972 amendments to Title VII directed that this function be transferred as of March 24, 1974, to the EEOC, at least with respect to private employers. § 2000e–6(c) (1970 ed. Supp. V); see also, § 2000e–5(f)(1) (1970 ed. Supp. V). The present lawsuit was instituted more than seven months before that transfer.

2. Before 1954 Hazelwood's application forms required designation of race, and those forms were in use as late as the 1962–1963 school year.

time he began the job. Generally, those who had most recently submitted applications were most likely to be chosen for interviews.[3]

Interviews were conducted by a department chairman, program coordinator, or the principal at the school where the teaching vacancy existed. Although those conducting the interviews did fill out forms rating the applicants in a number of respects, it is undisputed that each school principal possessed virtually unlimited discretion in hiring teachers for his school. The only general guidance given to the principals was to hire the "most competent" person available, and such intangibles as "personality, disposition, appearance, poise, voice, articulation, and ability to deal with people" counted heavily. The principal's choice was routinely honored by Hazelwood's Superintendent and the Board of Education.

In the early 1960's Hazelwood found it necessary to recruit new teachers, and for that purpose members of its staff visited a number of colleges and universities in Missouri and bordering States. All the institutions visited were predominantly white, and Hazelwood did not seriously recruit at either of the two predominantly Negro four-year colleges in Missouri.[4] As a buyer's market began to develop for public school teachers, Hazelwood curtailed its recruiting efforts. For the 1971–1972 school year, 3,127 persons applied for only 234 teaching vacancies; for the 1972–1973 school year, there were 2,373 applications for 282 vacancies. A number of the applicants who were not hired were Negroes.[5]

Hazelwood hired its first Negro teacher in 1969. The number of Negro faculty members gradually increased in successive years: six of 957 in the 1970 school year; 16 of 1,107 by the end of the 1972 school year; 22 of 1,231 in the 1973 school year. By comparison, according to 1970 census figures, of more than 19,000 teachers employed in that year in the St. Louis area, 15.4% were Negro. That percentage figure included the St. Louis City School District, which in recent years has followed a policy of attempting to maintain a 50% Negro teaching staff. Apart from that school district, 5.7% of the teachers in the county were Negro in 1970.

Drawing upon these historic facts, the Government mounted its "pattern or practice" attack in the District Court upon four different fronts. It adduced evidence of (1) a history of alleged racially discriminatory practices, (2) statistical disparities in hiring, (3) the standardless and largely subjective hiring procedures, and (4) specific instances of alleged discrimination against 55 unsuccessful Negro applicants for teaching jobs. Hazelwood offered virtually no additional evidence in

3. Applicants with student or substitute teaching experience at Hazelwood were given preference if their performance had been satisfactory.

4. One of those two schools was never visited even though it was located in nearby St. Louis. The second was briefly visited on one occasion, but no potential applicant was interviewed.

5. The parties disagree whether it is possible to determine from the present record exactly how many of the job applicants in each of the school years were Negroes.

response, relying instead on evidence introduced by the Government, perceived deficiencies in the Government's case, and its own officially promulgated policy "to hire all teachers on the basis of training, preparation and recommendations, regardless of race, color or creed."[6]

The District Court ruled that the Government had failed to establish a pattern or practice of discrimination. The court was unpersuaded by the alleged history of discrimination, noting that no dual school system had ever existed in Hazelwood. The statistics showing that relatively small numbers of Negroes were employed as teachers were found nonprobative, on the ground that the percentage of Negro pupils in Hazelwood was similarly small. The court found nothing illegal or suspect in the teacher-hiring procedures that Hazelwood had followed. Finally, the court reviewed the evidence in the 55 cases of alleged individual discrimination, and after stating that the burden of proving intentional discrimination was on the Government, it found that this burden had not been sustained in a single instance. Hence, the court entered judgment for the defendants. 392 F.Supp. 1276 (ED Mo.).

The Court of Appeals for the Eighth Circuit reversed. 534 F.2d 805. After suggesting that the District Court had assigned inadequate weight to evidence of discriminatory conduct on the part of Hazelwood before the effective date of Title VII,[7] the Court of Appeals rejected the trial court's analysis of the statistical data as resting on an irrelevant comparison of Negro teachers to Negro pupils in Hazelwood. The proper comparison, in the appellate court's view, was one between Negro teachers in Hazelwood and Negro teachers in the relevant labor market area. Selecting St. Louis County and St. Louis City as the relevant area,[8] the Court of Appeals compared the 1970 census figures, showing that 15.4% of teachers in that area were Negro, to the racial composition of Hazelwood's teaching staff. In the 1972–1973 and 1973–1974 school years, only 1.4% and 1.8%, respectively, of Hazelwood's teachers were Negroes. This statistical disparity, particularly when viewed against the background of the teacher hiring procedures that Hazelwood had followed, was held to constitute a prima facie case of a pattern or practice of racial discrimination.

6. The defendants offered only one witness, who testified to the total number of teachers who had applied and were hired for jobs in the 1971–1972 and 1972–1973 school years. They introduced several exhibits consisting of a policy manual, policy book, staff handbook, and historical summary of Hazelwood's formation and relatively brief existence.

7. As originally enacted, Title VII of the Civil Rights Act of 1964 applied only to private employers. The Act was expanded to include state and local governmental employers by the Equal Employment Opportunity Act of 1972, 86 Stat. 103, whose effective date was March 24, 1972. See 42 U.S.C. §§ 2000e(a), (b), (f), (h) (1970 ed. Supp. V).

The evidence of pre-Act discrimination relied upon by the Court of Appeals included the failure to hire any Negro teachers until 1969, the failure to recruit at predominantly Negro colleges in Missouri, and somewhat inconclusive evidence that Hazelwood was responsible for a 1962 Mississippi newspaper advertisement for teacher applicants that specified "white only."

8. The city of St. Louis is surrounded by, but not included in, St. Louis County. Mo.Ann.Stat. § 46.145 (1966).

In addition, the Court of Appeals reasoned that the trial court had erred in failing to measure the 55 instances in which Negro applicants were denied jobs against the four-part standard for establishing a prima facie case of individual discrimination set out in this Court's opinion in McDonnell Douglas Corp. v. Green. Applying that standard, the appellate court found 16 cases of individual discrimination,[10] which "buttressed" the statistical proof. Because Hazelwood had not rebutted the Government's prima facie case of a pattern or practice of racial discrimination, the Court of Appeals directed judgment for the Government and prescribed the remedial order to be entered.[11]

We granted certiorari * * * to consider a substantial question affecting the enforcement of a pervasive federal law.

The petitioners primarily attack the judgment of the Court of Appeals for its reliance on "undifferentiated work force statistics to find an unrebutted prima facie case of employment discrimination."[12] The question they raise, in short, is whether a basic component in the Court of Appeals' finding of a pattern or practice of discrimination—the comparatively small percentage of Negro employees on Hazelwood's teaching staff—was lacking in probative force.

This Court's recent consideration in International Brotherhood of Teamsters v. United States, of the role of statistics in pattern-or-practice suits under Title VII provides substantial guidance in evaluating the arguments advanced by the petitioners. In that case we stated that it is the Government's burden to "establish by a preponderance of the evidence that racial discrimination was the [employer's] standard operating procedure—the regular rather than the unusual practice."

10. The Court of Appeals held that none of the 16 prima facie cases of individual discrimination had been rebutted by the petitioners. See 534 F.2d, at 814.

11. The District Court was directed to order that the petitioners cease from discriminating on the basis of race or color in the hiring of teachers, promulgate accurate job descriptions and hiring criteria, recruit Negro and white applicants on an equal basis, give preference in filling vacancies to the 16 discriminatorily rejected applicants, make appropriate backpay awards, and submit periodic reports to the Government on its progress in hiring qualified Negro teachers. Id., at 819–820.

12. In their petition for certiorari and brief on the merits, the petitioners have phrased the question as follows:

> "Whether a court may disregard evidence that an employer has treated actual job applicants in a nondiscriminatory manner and rely on undifferentiated workforce statistics to find an unrebutted prima facie case of employment discrimination in violation of Title VII of the Civil Rights Act of 1964."

Their petition for certiorari and brief on the merits did raise a second question:

> "Whether Congress has authority under Section 5 of the Fourteenth Amendment to prohibit by Title VII of the Civil Rights Act of 1964 employment practices of an agency of a state government in the absence of proof that the agency purposefully discriminated against applicants on the basis of race."

That issue, however, is not presented by the facts in this case. The Government's opening statement in the trial court explained that its evidence was designed to show that the scarcity of Negro teachers at Hazelwood "is the result of purpose" and is attributable to "deliberately continued employment policies." Thus here, as in International Brotherhood of Teamsters v. United States, 431 U.S. 324, 97 S.Ct. 1843, 52 L.Ed.2d 396, "[t]he Government's theory of discrimination was simply that the [employer], in violation of § 703(a) of Title VII, regularly and purposefully treated Negroes * * * less favorably than white persons." Id., at 335, 97 S.Ct., at 1854 (footnote omitted).

We also noted that statistics can be an important source of proof in employment discrimination cases, since

> "absent explanation, it is ordinarily to be expected that nondiscriminatory hiring practices will in time result in a work force more or less representative of the racial and ethnic composition of the population in the community from which employees are hired. Evidence of long-lasting and gross disparity between the composition of a work force and that of the general population thus may be significant even though § 703(j) makes clear that Title VII imposes no requirement that a work force mirror the general population."

Where gross statistical disparities can be shown, they alone may in a proper case constitute prima facie proof of a pattern of practice of discrimination. Teamsters, supra.

There can be no doubt, in light of the Teamsters case, that the District Court's comparison of Hazelwood's teacher work force to its student population fundamentally misconceived the role of statistics in employment discrimination cases. The Court of Appeals was correct in the view that a proper comparison was between the racial composition of Hazelwood's teaching staff and the racial composition of the qualified public school teacher population in the relevant labor market.[13] The percentage of Negroes on Hazelwood's teaching staff in 1972–1973 was 1.4%, and in 1973–1974 it was 1.8%. By contrast, the percentage of qualified Negro teachers in the area was, according to the 1970 census, at least 5.7%.[14] Although these differences were on their face substan-

13. In Teamsters, the comparison between the percentage of Negroes on the employer's work force and the percentage in the general areawide population was highly probative, because the job skill there involved—the ability to drive a truck—is one that many persons possess or can fairly readily acquire. When special qualifications are required to fill particular jobs, comparisons to the general population (rather than to the smaller group of individuals who possess the necessary qualifications) may have little probative value. The comparative statistics introduced by the Government in the District Court, however, were properly limited to public school teachers, and therefore this is not a case like Mayor v. Educational Equality League, 415 U.S. 605, 94 S.Ct. 1323, 39 L.Ed.2d 630, in which the racial-composition comparisons failed to take into account special qualifications for the position in question. Id., at 620–621, 94 S.Ct., at 1333–1334.

Although the petitioners concede as a general matter the probative force of the comparative work-force statistics, they object to the Court of Appeals' heavy reliance on these data on the ground that applicant-flow data, showing the actual percentage of white and Negro applicants for teaching positions at Hazelwood, would be firmer proof. As we have noted, see n.5, supra, there was not clear evidence of such statistics. We leave it to the District Court on remand to determine whether competent proof of those data can be adduced. If so, it would, of course, be very relevant. Cf. Dothard v. Rawlinson, 433 U.S. 321, 330, 97 S.Ct. 2720, 2721, 53 L.Ed.2d 786.

14. As is discussed below, the Government contends that a comparative figure of 15.4%, rather than 5.7%, is the appropriate one. But even assuming arguendo that the 5.7% figure urged by the petitioners is correct, the disparity between that figure and the percentage of Negroes on Hazelwood's teaching staff would be more than fourfold for the 1972–1973 school year, and threefold for the 1973–1974 school year. A precise method of measuring the significance of such statistical disparities was explained in Castaneda v. Partida, 430 U.S. 482, 496–497, n.17, 97 S.Ct. 1272, 1281, n. 17, 51 L.Ed.2d 498, n.17. It involves calculation of the "standard deviation" as a measure of predicted fluctuations from the expected value of a sample. Using the 5.7% figure as the basis for calculating the expected value, the expected number of

tial, the Court of Appeals erred in substituting its judgment for that of the District Court and holding that the Government had conclusively proved its "pattern or practice" lawsuit.

The Court of Appeals totally disregarded the possibility that this prima facie statistical proof in the record might at the trial court level be rebutted by statistics dealing with Hazelwood's hiring after it became subject to Title VII. Racial discrimination by public employers was not made illegal under Title VII until March 24, 1972. A public employer who from that date forward made all its employment decisions in a wholly nondiscriminatory way would not violate Title VII even if it had formerly maintained an all-white work force by purposefully excluding Negroes.[15] For this reason, the Court cautioned in the Teamsters opinion that once a prima facie case has been established by statistical work-force disparities, the employer must be given an opportunity to show that "the claimed discriminatory pattern is a product of pre-Act hiring rather than unlawful post-Act discrimination."

The record in this case showed that for the 1972–1973 school year, Hazelwood hired 282 new teachers, 10 of whom (3.5%) were Negroes; for the following school year it hired 123 new teachers, 5 of whom (4.1%) were Negroes. Over the two-year period, Negroes constituted a total of 15 of the 405 new teachers hired (3.7%). Although the Court of Appeals briefly mentioned these data in reciting the facts, it wholly ignored them in discussing whether the Government had shown a pattern or practice of discrimination. And it gave no consideration at all to the possibility that post-Act data as to the number of Negroes hired compared to the total number of Negro applicants might tell a totally different story.[16]

What the hiring figures prove obviously depends upon the figures to which they are compared. The Court of Appeals accepted the Government's argument that the relevant comparison was to the labor market area of St. Louis County and the city of St. Louis, in which, according to the 1970 census, 15.4% of all teachers were Negro. The propriety of

Negroes on the Hazelwood teaching staff would be roughly 63 in 1972–1973 and 70 in 1973–1974. The observed number in those years was 16 and 22, respectively. The difference between the observed and expected values was more than six standard deviations in 1972–1973 and more than five standard deviations in 1973–1974. The Court in Castaneda noted that "[a]s a general rule for such large samples, if the difference between the expected value and the observed number is greater than two or three standard deviations," then the hypothesis that teachers were hired without regard to race would be suspect. 430 U.S. at 497 n.17, 97 S.Ct., at 1281 n.17.

15. This is not to say that evidence of pre-Act discrimination can never have any probative force. Proof that an employer engaged in racial discrimination prior to the effective date of Title VII might in some circumstances support the inference that such discrimination continued, particularly where relevant aspects of the decisionmaking process had undergone little change. Cf.Fed.Rule Evid. 406; Arlington Heights v. Metropolitan Housing Development Corp., 429 U.S. 252, 267, 97 S.Ct. 555, 564, 50 L.Ed.2d 450; 1 J. Wigmore, Evidence § 92, 2 id., §§ 302–305, 371, 375 (3d ed. 1940). And, of course, a public employer even before the extension of Title VII in 1972 was subject to the command of the Fourteenth Amendment not to engage in purposeful racial discrimination.

16. See n.13, supra, and n.21, infra. But cf. Teamsters, 431 U.S. at 364–367, 97 S.Ct., at 1868–1869.

that comparison was vigorously disputed by the petitioners, who urged that because the city of St. Louis has made special attempts to maintain a 50% Negro teaching staff, inclusion of that school district in the relevant market area distorts the comparison. Were that argument accepted, the percentage of Negro teachers in the relevant labor market area (St. Louis County alone) as shown in the 1970 census would be 5.7% rather than 15.4%.

The difference between these figures may well be important; the disparity between 3.7% (the percentage of Negro teachers hired by Hazelwood in 1972–1973 and 1973–1974) and 5.7% may be sufficiently small to weaken the Government's other proof, while the disparity between 3.7% and 15.4% may be sufficiently large to reinforce it.[17] In determining which of the two figures—or, very possibly, what intermediate figure—provides the most accurate basis for comparison to the hiring figures at Hazelwood, it will be necessary to evaluate such considerations as (i) whether the racially based hiring policies of the St. Louis City School District were in effect as far back as 1970, the year in which the census figures were taken;[18] (ii) to what extent those policies have changed the racial composition of that district's teaching staff from what it would otherwise have been; (iii) to what extent St. Louis' recruitment policies have diverted to the city, teachers who might otherwise have applied to Hazelwood;[19] (iv) to what extent Negro

17. Indeed, under the statistical methodology explained in Castaneda v. Partida, supra, 430 U.S., at 496–497, n.17, 97 S.Ct. 1272, at 1281, n.17, 51 L.Ed.2d 498, n.17, involving the calculation of the standard deviation as a measure of predicted fluctuations, the difference between using 15.4% and 5.7% as the areawide figure would be significant. If the 15.4% figure is taken as the basis for comparison, the expected number of Negro teachers hired by Hazelwood in 1972–1973 would be 43 (rather than the actual figure of 10) of a total of 282, a difference of more than five standard deviations; the expected number in 1973–1974 would be 19 (rather than the actual figure 5) of a total of 123, a difference of more than three standard deviations. For the two years combined, the difference between the observed number of 15 Negro teachers hired (of a total of 405) would vary from the expected number of 62 by more than six standard deviations. Because a fluctuation of more than two or three standard deviations would undercut the hypothesis that decisions were being made randomly with respect to race, 430 U.S. at 497 n.17, 97 S.Ct., at 1281 n.17, each of these statistical comparisons would reinforce rather than rebut the Government's other proof. If, however, the 5.7% areawide figure is used, the expected number of Negro teachers hired in 1972–1973 would be roughly 16, less than two standard deviations from the observed number of 10; for 1973–1974, the expected value would be roughly seven, less than one standard deviation from the observed value of 5; and for the two years combined, the expected value of 23 would be less than two standard deviations from the observed total of 15. A more precise method of analyzing these statistics confirms the results of the standard deviation analysis. See F. Mosteller, R. Rourke, & G. Thomas, Probability with Statistical Applications 494 (2d ed. 1970).

These observations are not intended to suggest that precise calculations of statistical significance are necessary in employing statistical proof, but merely to highlight the importance of the choice of the relevant labor market area.

18. In 1970 Negroes constituted only 42% of the faculty in St. Louis city schools, which could indicate either that the city's policy was not yet in effect or simply that its goal had not yet been achieved.

19. The petitioners observe, for example, that Harris Teachers College in St. Louis, whose 1973 graduating class was 60% Negro, is operated by the city. It is the petitioners' contention that the city's public elementary and secondary schools occupy an advantageous position in the recruitment of Harris graduates.

teachers employed by the city would prefer employment in other districts such as Hazelwood; and (v) what the experience in other school districts in St. Louis County indicates about the validity of excluding the City School District from the relevant labor market.

It is thus clear that a determination of the appropriate comparative figures in this case will depend upon further evaluation by the trial court. As this Court admonished in Teamsters: "[S]tatistics * * * come in infinite variety * * *. [T]heir usefulness depends on all of the surrounding facts and circumstances." Only the trial court is in a position to make the appropriate determination after further findings. And only after such a determination is made can a foundation be established for deciding whether or not Hazelwood engaged in a pattern or practice of racial discrimination in its employment practices in violation of the law.[20]

We hold, therefore, that the Court of Appeals erred in disregarding the post-Act hiring statistics in the record, and that it should have remanded the case to the District Court for further findings as to the relevant labor market area and for an ultimate determination whether Hazelwood engaged in a pattern or practice of employment discrimination after March 24, 1972.[21] Accordingly, the judgment is vacated, and the case is remanded to the District Court for further proceedings consistent with this opinion.

It is so ordered.

[The concurring opinion of JUSTICE BRENNAN and dissenting opinion of JUSTICE STEVENS are omitted].

DOTHARD v. RAWLINSON

Supreme Court of the United States, 1977.
433 U.S. 321, 97 S.Ct. 2720, 53 L.Ed.2d 786.

MR. JUSTICE STEWART delivered the opinion of the Court.

Appellee Dianne Rawlinson sought employment with the Alabama Board of Corrections as a prison guard, called in Alabama a "correctional counselor." After her application was rejected, she brought this class suit under Title VII of the Civil Rights Act of 1964 and under 42 U.S.C. § 1983, alleging that she had been denied employment because of her sex in violation of federal law. A three-judge Federal District Court for the Middle District of Alabama decided in her favor. Mieth v. Dothard, 418 F.Supp. 1169. We noted probable jurisdiction of this appeal from the District Court's judgment.

20. Because the District Court focused on a comparison between the percentage of Negro teachers and Negro pupils in Hazelwood, it did not undertake an evaluation of the relevant labor market, and its casual dictum that the inclusion of the city of St. Louis "distorted" the labor market statistics was not based upon valid criteria. 392 F.Supp. 1276, 1287 (ED Mo.).

21. It will also be open to the District Court on remand to determine whether sufficiently reliable applicant-flow data are available to permit consideration of the petitioners' argument that those data may undercut a statistical analysis dependent upon hirings alone.

I

At the time she applied for a position as correctional counselor trainee, Rawlinson was a 22-year-old college graduate whose major course of study had been correctional psychology. She was refused employment because she failed to meet the minimum 120-pound weight requirement established by an Alabama statute. The statute also establishes a height minimum of 5 feet 2 inches.[2]

After her application was rejected because of her weight, Rawlinson filed a charge with the Equal Employment Opportunity Commission, and ultimately received a right-to-sue letter. She then filed a complaint in the District Court on behalf of herself and other similarly situated women, challenging the statutory height and weight minima as violative of Title VII and the Equal Protection Clause of the Fourteenth Amendment.[4] A three-judge court was convened. While the suit was pending, the Alabama Board of Corrections adopted Administrative Regulation 204, establishing gender criteria for assigning correctional counselors to maximum-security institutions for "contact positions," that is, positions requiring continual close physical proximity to inmates of the institution. Rawlinson amended her class-action complaint by adding a challenge to regulation 204 as also violative of Title VII and the Fourteenth Amendment.

Like most correctional facilities in the United States, Alabama's prisons are segregated on the basis of sex. Currently the Alabama Board of Corrections operates four major all-male penitentiaries—Holman Prison, Kilby Corrections Facility, G.K. Fountain Correction Center, and Draper Correctional Center. The Board also operates the Julia Tutwiler Prison for Women, the Frank Lee Youth Center, the Number Four Honor Camp, the State Cattle Ranch, and nine Work Release Centers, one of which is for women. The Julia Tutwiler Prison for Women and the four male penitentiaries are maximum-security institutions. Their inmate living quarters are for the most part large dormitories, with communal showers and toilets that are open to the dormitories and hallways. The Draper and Fountain penitentiaries carry on extensive farming operations, making necessary a large num-

2. The statute establishes minimum physical standards for all law enforcement officers. In pertinent part, it provides:

"(d) *Physical qualifications.*—The applicant shall be not less than five feet two inches nor more than six feet ten inches in height, shall weigh not less than 120 pounds nor more than 300 pounds and shall be certified by a licensed physician designated as satisfactory by the appointing authority as in good health and physically fit for the performance of his duties as a law-enforcement officer. The commission may for good cause shown permit variances from the physical qualifications prescribed in this subdivision."

Ala.Code, Tit. 55, § 373(109) (Supp.1973).

4. A second plaintiff named in the complaint was Brenda Mieth, who, on behalf of herself and others similarly situated, challenged the 5′9″ height and 160-pound weight requirements for the position of Alabama state trooper as violative of the Equal Protection Clause. The District Court upheld her challenge, and the defendants did not appeal from that aspect of the District Court's judgment.

ber of strip searches for contraband when prisoners re-enter the prison buildings.

A correctional counselor's primary duty within these institutions is to maintain security and control of the inmates by continually supervising and observing their activities.[8] To be eligible for consideration as a correctional counselor, an applicant must possess a valid Alabama driver's license, have a high school education or its equivalent, be free from physical defects, be between the ages of 20½ years and 45 years at the time of appointment, and fall between the minimum height and weight requirements of 5 feet 2 inches, and 120 pounds, and the maximum of 6 feet 10 inches, and 300 pounds. Appointment is by merit, with a grade assigned each applicant based on experience and education. No written examination is given.

At the time this litigation was in the District Court, the Board of Corrections employed a total of 435 people in various correctional counselor positions, 56 of whom were women. Of those 56 women, 21 were employed at the Julia Tutwiler Prison for Women, 13 were employed in noncontact positions at the four male maximum-security institutions, and the remaining 22 were employed at the other institutions operated by the Alabama Board of Corrections. Because most of Alabama's prisoners are held at the four maximum-security male penitentiaries, 336 of the 435 correctional counselor jobs were in those institutions, a majority of them concededly in the "contact" classification.[9] Thus, even though meeting the statutory height and weight requirements, women applicants could under Regulation 204 compete equally with men for only about 25% of the correctional counselor jobs available in the Alabama prison system.

II

In enacting Title VII, Congress required "the removal of artificial, arbitrary, and unnecessary barriers to employment when the barriers operate invidiously to discriminate on the basis of racial or other impermissible classification." Griggs v. Duke Power Co., 401 U.S. 424, 431, 91 S.Ct. 849, 853, 28 L.Ed.2d 158. The District Court found that the minimum statutory height and weight requirements that applicants for employment as correctional counselors must meet constitute the sort of arbitrary barrier to equal employment opportunity that Title VII forbids. The appellants assert that the District Court erred both in finding that the height and weight standards discriminate against women, and in its refusal to find that, even if they do, these standards are justified as "job related."

8. The official job description for a correctional counselor position emphasizes counseling as well as security duties; the District Court found: "[C]orrectional counselors are persons who are commonly referred to as prison guards. Their duties primarily involve security rather than counseling." 418 F.Supp. 1169, 1175.

9. At the time of the trial the Board of Corrections had not yet classified all of its correctional counselor positions in the maximum-security institutions according to the criteria established in Regulation 204; consequently evidence of the exact number of "male only" jobs within the prison system was not available.

A

The gist of the claim that the statutory height and weight requirements discriminate against women does not involve an assertion of purposeful discriminatory motive. It is asserted, rather, that these facially neutral qualification standards work in fact disproportionately to exclude women from eligibility for employment by the Alabama Board of Corrections. We dealt in Griggs v. Duke Power Co., supra and Albemarle Paper Co. v. Moody, with similar allegations that facially neutral employment standards disproportionately excluded Negroes from employment, and those cases guide our approach here.

Those cases make clear that to establish a prima facie case of discrimination, a plaintiff need only show that the facially neutral standards in question select applicants for hire in a significantly discriminatory pattern. Once it is thus shown that the employment standards are discriminatory in effect, the employer must meet "the burden of showing that any given requirement [has] * * * a manifest relationship to the employment in question." Griggs v. Duke Power Co., supra. If the employer proves that the challenged requirements are job related, the plaintiff may then show that other selection devices without a similar discriminatory effect would also "serve the employer's legitimate interest in 'efficient and trustworthy workmanship.'" Albemarle Paper Co. v. Moody.

Although women 14 years of age or older compose 52.75% of the Alabama population and 36.89% of its total labor force, they hold only 12.9% of its correctional counselor positions. In considering the effect of the minimum height and weight standards on this disparity in rate of hiring between the sexes, the District Court found that the 5′2″-requirement would operate to exclude 33.29% of the women in the United States between the ages of 18–79, while excluding only 1.28% of men between the same ages. The 120-pound weight restriction would exclude 22.29% of the women and 2.35% of the men in this age group. When the height and weight restrictions are combined, Alabama's statutory standards would exclude 41.13% of the female population while excluding less than 1% of the male population.[12] Accordingly, the District Court found that Rawlinson had made out a prima facie case of unlawful sex discrimination.

12. Affirmatively stated, approximately 99.76% of the men and 58.87% of the women meet both these physical qualifications. From the separate statistics on height and weight of males it would appear that after adding the two together and allowing for some overlap the result would be to exclude between 2.35% and 3.63% of males from meeting Alabama's statutory height and weight minima. None of the parties has challenged the accuracy of the District Court's computations on this score, however, and the discrepancy is in any event insignificant in light of the gross disparity between the female and male exclusions. Even under revised computations the disparity would greatly exceed the 34% to 12% disparity that served to invalidate the high school diploma requirement in the *Griggs* case. 401 U.S., at 430, 91 S.Ct., at 853.

The appellants argue that a showing of disproportionate impact on women based on generalized national statistics should not suffice to establish a prima facie case. They point in particular to Rawlinson's failure to adduce comparative statistics concerning actual applicants for correctional counselor positions in Alabama. There is no requirement, however, that a statistical showing of disproportionate impact must always be based on analysis of the characteristics of actual applicants. See Griggs v. Duke Power Co. The application process might itself not adequately reflect the actual potential applicant pool, since otherwise qualified people might be discouraged from applying because of a self-recognized inability to meet the very standards challenged as being discriminatory. See International Brotherhood of Teamsters v. United States, 431 U.S. 324, 365–367, 97 S.Ct. 1843, 1869–1871, 52 L.Ed.2d 396. A potential applicant could easily determine her height and weight and conclude that to make an application would be futile. Moreover, reliance on general population demographic data was not misplaced where there was no reason to suppose that physical height and weight characteristics of Alabama men and women differ markedly from those of the national population.

For these reasons, we cannot say that the District Court was wrong in holding that the statutory height and weight standards had a discriminatory impact on women applicants. The plaintiffs in a case such as this are not required to exhaust every possible source of evidence, if the evidence actually presented on its face conspicuously demonstrates a job requirement's grossly discriminatory impact. If the employer discerns fallacies or deficiencies in the data offered by the plaintiff, he is free to adduce countervailing evidence of his own. In this case no such effort was made.

B

We turn, therefore, to the appellants' argument that they have rebutted the prima facie case of discrimination by showing that the height and weight requirements are job related. These requirements, they say, have a relationship to strength, a sufficient but unspecified amount of which is essential to effective job performance as a correctional counselor. In the District Court, however, the appellants produced no evidence correlating the height and weight requirements with the requisite amount of strength thought essential to good job performance. Indeed, they failed to offer evidence of any kind in specific justification of the statutory standards.[14]

14. In what is perhaps a variation on their constitutional challenge to the validity of Title VII itself, see n. 1, supra, the appellants contend that the establishment of the minimum height and weight standards by statute requires that they be given greater deference than is typically given private employer-established job qualifications. The relevant legislative history of the 1972 amendments extending Title VII to the States as employers does not, however, support such a result. Instead, Congress expressly indicated the intent that the same Title VII principles be applied to governmental and private employers alike. See H.R.Rep. No. 92–238, p. 17 (1971); S.Rep. No. 92–415, p. 10 (1971); U.S. Code Cong. & Admin.News 1972, p. 2137. See

If the job-related quality that the appellants identify is bona fide, their purpose could be achieved by adopting and validating a test for applicants that measures strength directly. Such a test, fairly administered, would fully satisfy the standards of Title VII because it would be one that "measure[s] the person for the job and not the person in the abstract." at 856. But nothing in the present record even approaches such a measurement.

For the reasons we have discussed, the District Court was not in error in holding that Title VII of the Civil Rights Act of 1964, as amended, prohibits application of the statutory height and weight requirements to Rawlinson and the class she represents.

* * *

[The Court held that the Board of Correction's regulation prohibiting the employment of women in "contact positions" in male, maximum security institutions did not violate Title VII because the defendants had shown sex to be a "bona fide occupational qualification" permitted by Section 703(e) of the Act.]

The judgment is accordingly affirmed in part and reversed in part, and the case is remanded to the District Court for further proceedings consistent with this opinion.

It is so ordered.

[The concurring opinion of JUSTICES REHNQUIST, BERGER and BLACKMUN and the concurring and dissenting opinion of JUSTICES MARSHALL and BRENNAN are omitted.]

MR. JUSTICE WHITE, concurring in No. 76–255 and dissenting in No. 76–422.

I join the Court's opinion in Hazelwood, School Dist. v. United States, but with reservations with respect to the relative neglect of applicant pool data in finding a prima facie case of employment discrimination and heavy reliance on the disparity between the areawide percentage of black public school teachers and the percentage of blacks on Hazelwood's teaching staff. Since the issue is whether Hazelwood discriminated against blacks in hiring after Title VII became applicable to it in 1972, perhaps the Government should have looked initially to Hazelwood's hiring practices in the 1972–1973 and 1973–1974 academic years with respect to the available applicant pool, rather than to history and to comparative work-force statistics from other school districts. Indeed, there is evidence in the record suggesting that Hazelwood, with a black enrollment of only 2%, hired a higher percentage of black applicants than of white applicants for these two years. The Court's opinion of course permits Hazelwood to introduce applicant pool data on remand in order to rebut the prima facie

also Schaeffer v. San Diego Yellow Cabs, 462 F.2d 1002 (CA9). Thus for both private and public employers, "[t]he touchstone is business necessity," *Griggs,* 401 U.S., at 431, 91 S.Ct., at 853; a discriminatory employment practice must be shown to be necessary to safe and efficient job performance to survive a Title VII challenge.

case of a discriminatory pattern or practice. This may be the only fair and realistic allocation of the evidence burden, but arguably the United States should have been required to adduce evidence as to the applicant pool before it was entitled to its prima facie presumption. At least it might have been required to present some defensible ground for believing that the racial composition of Hazelwood's applicant pool was roughly the same as that for the school districts in the general area, before relying on comparative work-force data to establish its prima facie case.

In Dothard v. Rawlinson, I have more trouble agreeing that a prima facie case of sex discrimination was made out by statistics showing that the Alabama height and weight requirements would exclude a larger percentage of women in the United States than of men. As in Hazelwood, the issue is whether there was discrimination in dealing with actual or potential applicants; but in Hazelwood there was at least a colorable argument that the racial composition of the area-wide teacher work force was a reasonable proxy for the composition of the relevant applicant pool and hence that a large divergence between the percentage of blacks on the teaching staff and the percentage in the teacher work force raised a fair inference of racial discrimination in dealing with the applicant pool. In Dothard, however, I am unwilling to believe that the percentage of women applying or interested in applying for jobs as prison guards in Alabama approximates the percentage of women either in the national or state population. A plaintiff could, of course, show that the composition of the applicant pool was distorted by the exclusion of nonapplicants who did not apply because of the allegedly discriminatory job requirement. But no such showing was made or even attempted here; and although I do not know what the actual fact is, I am not now convinced that a large percentage of the actual women applicants, or of those who are seriously interested in applying, for prison guard positions would fail to satisfy the height and weight requirements. Without a more satisfactory record on this issue, I cannot conclude that appellee Rawlinson has either made out a prima facie case for the invalidity of the restrictions or otherwise proved that she was improperly denied employment as a prison guard. There being no showing of discrimination, I do not reach the question of justification; nor, since she does not meet the threshold requirements for becoming a prison guard, need I deal with the gender-based requirements for contact positions. I dissent from the Court's judgment in Dothard insofar as it affirms the judgment of the District Court.

NOTES AND PROBLEMS FOR DISCUSSION

1. The Supreme Court has established two models of proof in disparate treatment cases. Individual treatment cases are governed by the *McDonnell Douglas-Burdine* formula. Class treatment cases, sometimes referred to as "pattern and practice" cases, follow the pattern established in *Teamsters* and *Hazelwood.* See Payne v. Travenol Laboratories, Inc., 673 F.2d 798 (5th Cir. 1982); Phillips v. Joint Legislative Committee, 637 F.2d 1014, 1024–27 (5th Cir.

1981), cert. denied, 456 U.S. 960, 102 S.Ct. 2035, 72 L.Ed.2d 483 (1982); Markey v. Tenneco Oil Co., 635 F.2d 497, 499 (5th Cir. 1981). Is the employer's burden of rebuttal greater in a class treatment case?

2. If applicant flow statistics were not necessary to establish a prima facie case in *Dothard,* why did Justice Stewart conclude in *Hazelwood* that the case should be remanded so that applicant flow statistics, which "might tell a totally different story," could be introduced? What relevant fact can be inferred from applicant flow data in *Hazelwood* that could not be inferred from such statistics in *Dothard*? Does the answer to this question turn on the fact that *Hazelwood* was a disparate treatment case and *Dothard* was tried under the disproportionate impact model? Focusing on the precise language of *Dothard* and *Teamsters*, one court has suggested that a significantly greater discrepancy (a "gross disparity") between the representation of the minority group in the employer's work force and its representation in the relevant labor market is required for a prima facie case of disparate treatment than is required to establish disproportionate impact where only a "marked disproportion" is necessary. Rivera v. City of Wichita Falls, 665 F.2d 531, 535 n. 5 (5th Cir. 1982). Do *Hazelwood* and *Dothard* also suggest that a higher "quality" of statistical evidence may be required in a treatment case than in one based on the disproportionate impact model? Will applicant flow statistics always provide a more accurate evidence of discrimination in hiring? See, EEOC v. Chicago Miniature Lamp Works, 622 F.Supp. 1281 (N.D.Ill.1985) (word of mouth recruiting made applicant flow statistics "not remotely representative" of the racial and ethnic composition of labor market).

3. *Hazelwood* and *Dothard* demonstrate a common use of statistical evidence in employment discrimination cases. To prove that a practice or policy is discriminatory in design or effect the composition of the employer's work force (or in a hiring case the pool of applicants) is compared to the composition of an outside "population." The difference between the work force composition and the composition of the population is used to prove the discriminatory effect in a disproportionate impact case and as circumstantial evidence of discriminatory intent in a disparate treatment case. The assumption underlying the evidentiary use of such comparisons is that, absent discrimination (effect or intent), the composition of the work force should reflect that of the outside population. The problem in both *Hazelwood* and *Dothard* is that the compositions of the relevant populations (the applicant pools) is unknown and the courts must assume that the compositions of larger populations (area work force statistics in *Hazelwood* and national population statistics in *Dothard*) are sufficiently similar to the relevant populations for the proper inferences to be drawn. The relevance and probative value of this type of statistical evidence thus turns on the validity of the assumption about the outside population. The critical question is whether the proper population has been used for comparison with the work force statistics. In *Dothard* for example, Justice White dissents because he does not believe that the plaintiffs proved that the female composition of the nation (the population) is an accurate reflection of the applicant pool for female prison guards in Alabama. Without such proof, or an assumption to that effect, there is no showing that the state's height and weight requirements would impact adversely on those women who wanted to be prison guards. Since he is unwilling to indulge in the assumption that women in the applicant pool share the same physical characteristics as women in the population as a whole, why is Justice White willing to assume in *Hazelwood* that the area-wide teacher work force (the population) was a "reasonable proxy" for the racial

composition of the applicant pool? What assumption about the applicant pool was made by the court in Miles v. M.N.C. Corp., supra?

In NEW YORK CITY TRANSIT AUTHORITY v. BEAZER, 440 U.S. 568, 99 S.Ct. 1355, 59 L.Ed.2d 587 (1979), the plaintiffs alleged that the Transit Authority's rule which denied employment of participants in methadone maintenance programs, including those who had successfully completed treatment, violated Title VII because it excluded a disproportionate number of blacks and Hispanics. Relying in part on evidence that 63% of the persons receiving methadone maintenance from public programs in New York City were black or Hispanic, the district court found that the plaintiffs had established a prima facie case which was not rebutted by defendant, and the Second Circuit affirmed. The Supreme Court reversed. The district court had inferred from the statistical proof that the Transit Authority's rule excluded a higher percentage of otherwise qualified minority applicants than it did whites. Beazer v. New York City Transit Authority, 414 F.Supp. 277, 279 (S.D.N.Y.1976), modified in part, 558 F.2d 97 (2d Cir. 1977). But the Supreme Court considered the statistical showing "virtually irrelevant" for that purpose because the figures told "nothing about the class of otherwise-qualified applicants and employees who have participated in methadone maintenance" and because the statistics included a substantial number of persons unqualified for other reasons or unavailable for work. 440 U.S. at 585–586, 99 S.Ct. at 1365–1366. In addition, the Court questioned whether the statistics accurately reflected the racial composition of all persons on methadone maintenance in New York because the figures omitted some 14,000 enrolled in private programs, "leaving open the possibility that the percentage of blacks and Hispanics in the class of methadone users is not significantly greater than the percentage of those minorities in the general population of New York City." 440 U.S. at 586, 99 S.Ct. at 1366. Without further proof, the Court was unwilling to indulge in two premises underlying the district court's inference of disproportionate impact: (1) that the plaintiffs' statistics reflected the racial composition of methadone users in the general population; and (2) that the percentage of minority methadone users in the general population reflected the percentage of such users in the class of otherwise qualified employees and applicants for employment. Is this consistent with the Court's discussion of the appropriate statistical pool in *Dothard* and *Teamsters*? See Friedman, The Burger Court and the Prima Facie Case In Employment Discrimination Litigation: A Critique, 65 Corn.L.Rev. 1, 48–52 (1979).

See also, Smith v. United Brotherhood of Carpenters and Joiners, 685 F.2d 164 (6th Cir. 1982) (in determining legality of high school diploma requirement for entry into carpentry apprentice program court should have compared blacks and whites who did not possess diploma rather than blacks and whites with only high school diploma which excluded persons possessing higher degrees); Kim v. Commandant, Defense Language Institute, 772 F.2d 521 (9th Cir. 1985) (applicant failed to show that test for job in language institute had disproportionate impact on Koreans because all those who took test were Korean).

Hazelwood and *Beazer* demonstrate the importance in a hiring case of "controlling" labor market statistics so as to create a "relevant" population for comparison purposes. Typically, gross labor market statistics must be controlled for both requisite skills and geographic scope.

Skill Requisites of the Job in Question. Where the job in question demands skills or abilities common to most people, the appropriate statistical pool will be either the general population or the adult work force. See *Hazelwood*, n.13.

Boykin v. Georgia-Pacific Corp., 706 F.2d 1384, 1392 (5th Cir. 1983), cert. denied, 465 U.S. 1006, 104 S.Ct. 999, 79 L.Ed.2d 231 (1984) (where unskilled persons are hired and then promoted on the basis of training received on the job unnecessary to standardize data for qualifications). Compare, Moore v. Hughes Helicopters, Inc., 708 F.2d 475 (9th Cir. 1983) (in absence of evidence that black females possessed requisite qualifications for higher paying positions, comparative statistics showing larger percentage of black females in low-pay jobs did not establish inference of discrimination). The difference between use of general population figures and adult work force figures will be small when the percentages of minority and majority persons working do not differ significantly. But the choice of general population as opposed to adult work force statistics will be critical where the percentage of the minority in the population differs greatly from its percentage in the available work force. In Dothard v. Rawlinson, for example, women over fourteen years of age comprised over 52% of the population of Alabama but only 37% of its total labor force. 433 U.S. at 329, 97 S.Ct. at 2726. Of course, where special skills or training are legitimate prerequisites to adequate performance of the job in question, the labor pool must be adjusted accordingly. In *Hazelwood* the Court of Appeals decided the proper comparison was between the racial composition of the school district's teaching staff and the racial composition of the teacher population of the St. Louis metropolitan area. What assumption was the Court of Appeals making when it used the percentage of blacks actually teaching in the market area as the comparison group? Did the Supreme Court accept this use of actual teachers as an appropriate measure of the percentage of available black teachers in the comparison group? Can you think of a better comparison group?

Geographic Area. The geographic area used to define the statistical pool may also significantly affect its composition. In *Hazelwood* the Court of Appeals ruled that the relevant labor market included the entire Metropolitan Statistical Area of St. Louis as calculated by the Census Bureau. The Supreme Court remanded for a determination by the district court of whether the appropriate labor market for the school district included the city of St. Louis or, as contended by the school board, should be limited to the rural area surrounding the city. What should the district court consider in making this determination? In his dissent, Justice Stevens noted that the record of the case showed that one third of the teachers hired by the school district in 1972–73 lived in the city of St. Louis at the time of initial employment. 433 U.S. at 315 n.2. Should not that fact alone demonstrate that the city was properly included in the relevant labor market? In Clark v. Chrysler Corp., 673 F.2d 921, 928–929 (7th Cir. 1982), the court determined the labor market for an employer which drew its labor force primarily from the county in which it was located, but also to some extent from peripheral areas, by weighing the minority availability statistics to reflect primarily the demographics of the employer's home county. See also, Markey v. Tenneco Oil Co., 707 F.2d 172 (5th Cir. 1983) (racial composition of labor market for employer that drew work force from four-county area calculated by weighing black population of each county according to percentage of actual applicants from that county).

The relevant labor pool will vary for employers in the same locality and even from job to job within a plant depending primarily on the salary of the job in question and the relative scarcity of such jobs. The higher the salary and the greater the scarcity, the greater the commuting distance the job will justify. The fact that applicants are willing to relocate for some jobs may also significantly affect the limits of the labor pool. See Johnson v. Goodyear Tire & Rubber Co., 491 F.2d 1364 (5th Cir. 1974).

It should also be obvious that, as with controls for skill, geographic limits may be chosen depending on what one seeks to prove by the statistical comparison. For example, in Dothard v. Rawlinson, the plaintiff demonstrated the sexually discriminatory nature of the height and weight requirements by showing the percentage of females nationwide who would be excluded by the minimum standards, and proved the discriminatory effect of the standards by comparing the actual percentage of women in correctional positions in Alabama with their percentage in the adult work force of the state. What should be relevant comparison population in a promotion case? See the following case.

LILLY v. HARRIS–TEETER SUPERMARKET

United States Court of Appeals, Fourth Circuit, 1983.
720 F.2d 326, cert. denied, 466 U.S. 951, 104 S.Ct. 2154, 80 L.Ed.2d 539 (1984).

HARRISON L. WINTER, CHIEF JUDGE:

In this class action charging racial discrimination in employment, Harris-Teeter Super Markets, Inc., (Harris-Teeter) appeals from a judgment of the district court entered upon findings that it had engaged in a pattern or practice of racial discrimination in terminations and promotions at its Mecklenburg County, North Carolina warehouse and retail stores, and that it had been guilty of specific instances of racial discrimination against thirteen of the named individual employees. We conclude that the suit was properly certified as a class action with respect to both promotions and terminations, and that various individual plaintiffs were properly permitted to intervene. We affirm the finding of a pattern or practice of racial discrimination in terminations, but reverse the finding of a pattern or practice of discrimination in promotions. We affirm the judgments of discrimination as to three named plaintiffs, but remand for further proceedings as to the individual plaintiffs alleging discrimination in promotions.

I.

Harris-Teeter is a retail grocery chain with offices, retail stores, and a warehouse located in Mecklenburg County. In January 1975, Harris-Teeter discharged Paul Lilly, a black warehouse employee. Lilly filed a charge with the Equal Employment Opportunity Commission (EEOC) alleging that he had been discharged for protesting racially discriminatory treatment on the job and that Harris-Teeter was engaged in systematic discrimination against blacks in its termination practices. Lilly later amended his EEOC charge to include allegations of systematic discrimination against blacks in hiring, promotions, personnel procedures, terminations, and supervisory practices. Lilly was subsequently issued a right-to-sue letter by EEOC and, in June 1976, he commenced the present action.

Lilly's complaint, brought under *both* 42 U.S.C. §§ 1981 and 2000e et seq., alleged that he had been terminated because of his race and in retaliation for protesting racial discrimination. He also claimed to represent a class of black Harris-Teeter employees who, from July 1974 on, had suffered racial discrimination in hiring, promotions, interviewing, terminations, supervision, and discipline. In support of his subsequent motion for class certification, Lilly presented statistical evidence purporting to show disparities in job classification and cited specific examples of alleged discrimination in promotions and terminations. The district court thereupon tentatively certified the class as requested.

In April 1979, twenty black Harris-Teeter employees filed a joint motion for permission to intervene as plaintiffs, in order to present their individual claims of racial discrimination. The claims of these individuals encompassed alleged discrimination in terminations, promotions, job placement, pay, and transfers. Although none of these individuals had exhausted their administrative (EEOC) remedies, the district court granted the motion for joint intervention. In addition, the district court consolidated the case with those of two other black Harris-Teeter employees, Gregory and Porter, who were alleging racial discrimination in demotions and hiring, respectively. Gregory and Porter had exhausted their EEOC remedies prior to filing their individual suits. Subsequently, the district court certified all twenty intervenors and Gregory as class representatives.

A bench trial was held from January through March, 1980. In August, 1980, the district court, 503 F.Supp. 29, filed a "Memorandum of Decision," in which the court found a generalized pattern of racial discrimination in hiring, promotions, and terminations. As practices that effectuated this discrimination, the court found that there were no written job descriptions, promotion criteria, job evaluations, or list of employees wanting to change jobs, that job openings were not posted, that the company rule that limited eligibility for promotions to employees in the same department and shift as the opening was strictly enforced as to blacks but not as to whites, that refusals by blacks to take on jobs were carefully remembered, although they were never asked if they had changed their minds, and that claimed previous job experience of blacks was either forgotten or disbelieved, while that of whites was credited and utilized. The district court also found that statistical evidence broadly supported the court's conclusion fr individualized testimony that blacks had less chance of g jobs and promotions than did whites. The district cou found that individual instances of discrimination ha ed as to fourteen of the named plaintiffs, but n Finally, the district court instructed plai proposed findings of fact and conclusio issues and as to the prevailing ir instructed to do likewise for tho to relief.[1]

[The court of appeals held that, adopted findings of fact submitted compliance with Rule 52(a) and that

1. Defendant's proposed opinion as to the ten unsuccessful plaintiffs was subse- quen not co

IV.

Harris-Teeter's next challenge is to the sufficiency of the evidence of a pattern or practice of racial discrimination with regard to both terminations and promotions. As to the former, plaintiffs' statistical evidence showed that blacks comprised, on average, 15.7 percent of the Harris-Teeter workforce from 1974 through 1978, but represented over 28 percent of the involuntary terminations during that period. Statistical analysis of the data underlying this disparity revealed that the number of involuntary "for cause" terminations of blacks was, over this period,[17] 9.71 standard deviations (by the binomial model [18]) greater than would be expected on the basis of chance.[19] Under the test discussed in EEOC v. American National Bank, 652 F.2d 1176, 1190–93 (4 Cir. 1981) (citing Hazelwood School District v. United States, 433 U.S. 299, 311 n. 17, 97 S.Ct. 2736, 2743 n. 17, 53 L.Ed.2d 768 (1977), and Castaneda v. Partida, 430 U.S. 482, 496 n. 17, 97 S.Ct. 1272, 1281 n. 17, 51 L.Ed.2d 498 (1977)), cert. denied, ___ U.S. ___, 103 S.Ct. 235, 74 L.Ed. 2d 186 (1982), because the number of standard deviations was more

17. If possible, it is highly preferable to examine the statistical data for the time period in combined form, rather than year by year. Combined data is more likely to demonstrate the "pattern or practice" of defendant's policies, whether discriminatory or not. Moreover, by increasing the absolute numbers in the data, chance will more readily be excluded as a cause of any disparities found. For example, if a coin were tossed ten times in the first day and came up heads four times, no one would think the coin was biased (0.632 standard deviations), but if this same ratio occurred for a total of 10,000 tosses, of which 4,000 were heads, the result could not be attributed to chance (20 standard deviations).

18. As we have touched upon previously, there are two common models of statistical analysis: the binomial model and the hypergeometric model. See EEOC v. Federal Reserve Bank of Richmond, 698 F.2d 633, 650 (4 Cir. 1983). The binomial model is appropriate where the "selection" (i.e., hiring, promotion, or termination) of the individuals does not significantly alter the racial composition of the pool from which [illegible]ture selections are to be made. This [illegible]uld be true, for instance, in selecting 50 [illegible]le to be hired for unskilled work from [illegible]e city, because making the selection [illegible]t, even if all those chosen as the [illegible]goes along are white, significantly [illegible] racial composition of the appli- [illegible] The hypergeometric model, on [illegible]and, is appropriate where the [illegible]ld significantly alter the ra- [illegible]on of the pool from which [illegible]s are to be made (that is, a finite pool). An example of this would be a situation in which 10 managers are to be promoted from a group of 30 foremen, of whom half are black and the other half white. The key distinction here is that the selection of a white for the first position will significantly alter the racial composition of the selection pool, from 15 of 30 (.500) to 15 of 29 (.517) black. Thus, if another white is chosen, the inference of discrimination will properly be heightened. See Peterson, Binomial v. Hypergeometric Employee Selection Models, 2 Personnel Research Report 1 (April 1983).

The binomial process is probably appropriate here because although the pool of persons who can be terminated is fixed at any given time, it is an open pool when examined over a five year period, as here, in that new employees will be hired and then themselves be subject to termination.

19. Under the binomial model,

n = total employees terminated

p = black percentage of the workforce

l–p = white percentage of the workforce

Q = actual number of black terminations

E = expected number of black terminations = np

s = standard deviation = $\sqrt{np(l-p)}$

number of standard deviations = (Q–E)/s

Here, n = 815, p = .1572, l–p = .8428, Q = 229, E = np = 128.12

s = 10.39, and the number of standard deviations = 9.71

than two or three, this statistical evidence conclusively ruled out chance as the cause of the disparity in the termination rates.[20]

In addition to this statistical evidence, the district court found that Harris-Teeter's terminations policy was highly discretionary [21] and had in specific instances been applied unevenly to blacks as against whites. The district court credited testimony that whites received disciplinary warnings, if at all, only after extensive absences or tardiness, while blacks, including Lilly, were terminated for insubstantial reasons. We think that the strong statistical evidence, when combined with the specific instances in which the discretion was unevenly exercised, is sufficient to support the district court's finding that Harris-Teeter engaged in a pattern or practice of racially discriminatory treatment of blacks in connection with its terminations policy.[22]

We turn next to the sufficiency of the proof of class-wide racial discrimination in promotions. The district court found that in 1976 the combined black promotion rate in the stores and warehouse was 69 percent of the white promotion rate, and that in the stores alone the black promotion rates for 1975 and 1976 were 70 percent and 67 percent, respectively, of the white promotion rates. The first problem with this data, however, is that its scope—covering the stores and warehouse for only 1976 and only the stores for 1975—is insufficient to prove discrimination from 1974 through 1978. Second, when additional, uncontested data from the record is added into the overall numbers, the black promotion rate rises to 86% of the white rate.[23] Moreover, a statistical disparity cannot, standing alone, make out a prima facie case of class-wide discrimination unless a standard deviation analysis has ruled out chance as the cause of the disparity. When such an analysis is performed on the promotions data, it appears that the number of blacks promoted is fewer than two standard deviations below what

20. By conclusively ruling out chance as the cause of the disparity in the termination rates, plaintiffs thereby made out a prima facie case of class-wide discrimination, thus shifting the burden to Harris-Teeter to come forward with a credible lawful explanation for the disparity.

21. The fact of this discretion is itself relevant. See Sledge v. J.P. Stevens & Co., 585 F.2d 625, 635 (4 Cir. 1978) ("where [strong statistical] proof is coupled with evidence that the defendant based hiring and other employment decisions upon the subjective opinions of white supervisors, the trial court is entitled to infer, as it did here, that the defendant illegally discriminated"), cert. denied, 440 U.S. 981, 99 S.Ct. 1789, 60 L.Ed.2d 241 (1979).

22. Harris-Teeter advanced no explanation for the disparity between the black and white termination rates, instead arguing that the plaintiffs' statistics "showed only that both blacks and whites had committed dischargeable offenses and had been discharged." That assertion is plainly incorrect, for the standard deviation analysis demonstrates that the significant disparity between the termination rates was not due to chance, but instead to some other cause. That cause is presumed to be unlawful discrimination until the defendant shows otherwise, see supra note 20, and Harris-Teeter failed to do so here.

23. The promotions data for the warehouse in 1975, available in the record, showed that more blacks were promoted than would be suggested by their proportion of the workforce. See infra note 24.

Of course, we do not suggest that a 14% disparity between black and white promotion rates is, if proved to be attributable to racial discrimination, any less illegal than a 30% disparity. However, it is less persuasive as proof that such discrimination did, in fact, exist.

would be expected from their proportion of the workforce; thus chance is not excluded as the cause of the disparity.[24]

In an attempt to demonstrate that discriminatory intent rather than chance was the cause of the disparity in the promotion rates, plaintiffs submitted statistical evidence demonstrating that fewer blacks were *hired* by Harris-Teeter than would have been expected from their proportion of the applicant pool. Standard deviation analysis of this data conclusively ruled out chance as the cause of the disparity in the hiring rates, thus raising a presumption that discriminatory intent was the explanation for the hiring disparity. The district court accepted this as being probative of a similar intent behind the disparity in the promotions data. On the present record, however, we cannot accept this analysis. We agree that evidence of discriminatory intent in one employment context (e.g., hiring) may be probative of discriminatory intent in a different context (e.g., promotions) where it has been demonstrated that the same company managerial personnel were responsible for decisionmaking in both contexts. In the present case, however, the district court made no finding that the store supervisors responsible for promotions were also responsible for hiring.[25] We therefore conclude that the inference of discriminatory intent with respect to hiring should not have been considered in determining whether discriminatory intent was the cause of the disparity in the promotions data.

The other factor relied upon by the district court to demonstrate an intentionally discriminatory pattern of racial discrimination was the testimony of the nine intervenors who prevailed on their promotion claims. But almost none of this testimony related to instances of direct

24. The promotions data, in the form found by the district court and with standard deviations by the binomial method provided, is:

		Employees		Promotions		# Standard
Unit	Year	White	Black	White	Black	Deviations
Ware.+ Stores	1976	1603	284	171	21	1.59
Stores	1975	1191	99	104	6	0.87
Stores	1976	1192	111	129	8	1.12

When adding the additional data mentioned in footnote 23, supra, the promotion figures are:

		Employees		Promotions		# Standard
Unit	Year	White	Black	White	Black	Deviations
Ware.	1975	223	192	18	21	−0.96
Ware.+ Stores	1975+ 1976	3017	575	293	48	0.97

25. Although ultimate formal responsibility for hiring, promotions, and terminations all rested in the district managers, the district court found that these managers adopted almost automatically the recommendations of the supervisors at the stores. There was no evidence that the district managers instructed or encouraged the store supervisors to make recommendations that were influenced by racial discrimination.

racial discrimination, and there certainly were too few instances of direct discrimination from which any pattern or practice of such discrimination could be inferred. Instead, most of the testimony dealt with the absence of written, objective criteria for promotion decisions. As we have noted, supra note 21, the possession by management of unbridled discretion will tend to confirm implications of racial discrimination drawn from statistical disparities. But here the promotions data did not reveal any statistically significant disparity between the black and white promotion rates. Thus, because Title VII and § 1981 prohibit racial discrimination, rather than simple arbitrariness or caprice, the mere existence of vague and subjective criteria is not alone proof of unlawful discrimination. The district court's finding of class-wide discrimination with respect to promotions therefore cannot stand.

V.

Harris-Teeter next challenges the district court's findings as to each of the thirteen named plaintiffs who prevailed. We turn first to the ten plaintiffs—Mobley, Reed, Gary,[26] McKinney, Torrence, Patterson, Jones, Sullivan, Bailey, and LeGrand—who alleged that they had been denied promotions because of racial discrimination. We conclude that, in light of our reversal of the district court's finding of class-wide discrimination in promotions, these cases must for two reasons be returned to the district court for further proceedings. First, in each instance, the district court appears to have grounded its conclusion, at least in part, on its earlier finding that the promotions system was, as a whole, discriminatorily applied as to blacks. Because the district court did not indicate explicitly whether this finding was a necessary, or merely a cumulative, piece of evidence, we must remand to the district court for a determination of whether any or all of the individual claims are made out in the absence of proof of class-wide discrimination. Second, the district court made no case-by-case findings as to the "subjective" criteria advanced by Harris-Teeter as the basis for its promotion decisions. As noted above, the district court may, where the statistical data reveals a disparity between the white and black promotion rates of sufficient magnitude to warrant an inference of discrimination, conclude that the subjective criteria do not overcome that inference. But the premise that the subjective criteria were mere pretexts for racial discrimination cannot stand as an across the board conclusion where, as here, the existence of class-wide discrimination is not demonstrated. Rather, the district court must, on a case-by-case basis, determine whether the subjective criteria advanced by Harris-Teeter were in fact utilized in making the individual decision, or whether the individual decision was based upon unlawful discrimination.

26. We also include here the "transfer" claimed by Gary, because the district court appears to have treated this claim along with Gary's promotion claim, and because Gary testified that this "transfer" would have included a pay raise, indicating that it too was actually a claimed promotion.

The district court next found that plaintiff Lilly had proven that his discharge from Harris-Teeter was based on racial discrimination. We agree. The evidence revealed that Lilly was discharged only two days after complaining about racial discrimination to Harris-Teeter's personnel director. Further, although Harris-Teeter claimed that Lilly's job performance in quantity checking had been deficient, it never introduced any written substantiation of these claims, and Lilly's supervisor admitted that he never checked as to whether the errors in counting might have been at the receiving end. Under these circumstances, the district court did not clearly err in rejecting Harris-Teeter's purported justification and in finding that Lilly had been the victim of racial discrimination.[27]

Next, the district court found that Richard Gregory's demotion and subsequent constructive discharge were based upon racial discrimination. The district court credited testimony that Gregory was assigned duties not given to whites at his level, that his termination of a white employee who had called him a "nigger" was reversed by his superiors, and that his job performance had been praised. Further, the district court noted that although Gregory had been discharged by a black, that was done on orders by, and in the presence of, a white territorial supervisor. We thus conclude that the district court's finding was not clearly erroneous.

The final individual claim decided by the district court was that of Edward Porter, who challenged Harris-Teeter's decision not to hire him as a tractor-trailer driver. The evidence showed that whites with less experience than Porter were hired by Harris-Teeter after he applied for the position. Harris-Teeter contended that they were hired instead of Porter because they came to the company when openings were available, but the district court found that, in at least one instance, Harris-Teeter had filled a subsequent position with a white who had applied before Porter, thus revealing that Harris-Teeter maintained, and utilized, its list of applicants on file. Moreover, the company's asserted statistics as to the percentage of black drivers are meaningless in the absence of data as to the pool of applicants for the positions. The district court's conclusion as to Porter is therefore also not clearly erroneous and will be sustained.

[An award of attorney's fees to plaintiffs was vacated for reconsideration in light of modifications to relief necessitated by the opinion.]

Affirmed in part; reversed in part; and remanded.

NOTES AND PROBLEMS FOR DISCUSSION

1. What is the difference, if any, between the statistical analysis used in *Lilly* and in *Hazelwood*? Are the statistics in one of the cases more probative of intentional discrimination than in the other? Does the fact that a number of

27. This conclusion is buttressed by the overwhelming statistical disparity between the black and white discharge rates, which proves class-wide racial discrimination in terminations.

individual store managers were responsible for terminations in their respective stores undermine the usefulness of the termination statistics? See, Mozee v. Jeffboat, Inc., 746 F.2d 365 (7th Cir. 1984). What assumption did the court make in determining that the appropriate labor market for the promotion claim was the existing work force? Compare, Regner v. City of Chicago, 601 F.Supp. 830 (N.D.Ill. 1985) with Maddox v. Claytor, 764 F.2d 1539 (11th Cir. 1985).

2. In some cases a simple comparison of data, for example the pay rates of men and women employed in the same job, may constitute a prima facie case of discrimination and will always be relevant as either confirming or rebutting an inference of discrimination raised by other evidence. But as *Lilly* demonstrates, not every statistical discrepancy, even when the proper comparative population is used, is probative of intentional discrimination.

> The plaintiffs vigorously contend that any discrepancy unfavorable to the class emerging from a simple comparison of the percentages is evidence of discrimination adequate to support a prima facie case. This argument flies in the face of rudimentary principles of sound statistical analysis. It is axiomatic that statistical significance may be attributed to an observed discrepancy only upon reduction to an acceptable level of the possibility that such a variation would, in the normal course of events, reasonably be expected to occur simply by random chance. * * *
>
> * * *
>
> The days—if they ever existed—of casual renditions of "broad conclusions from crude and incomplete statistics," * * * are indeed long since past.

Rivera v. City of Wichita Falls, 665 F.2d 531, 545, 547 (5th Cir. 1982); Fudge v. City of Providence Fire Dept., 766 F.2d 650 (1st Cir. 1985). Statisticians generally consider a discrepancy as statistically significant when it can be demonstrated that the probability of the discrepancy occurring by chance is no more than one in twenty. This is referred to as significant at the .05 level of significance. See White v. City of San Diego, 605 F.2d 455, 460 (9th Cir. 1979). Following *Hazelwood*, courts have routinely treated statistical discrepancies exceeding two standard deviations under the binomial theory as prima facie evidence of discrimination. See, Harrell v. Northern Electric Co., 679 F.2d 31 (5th Cir.), cert. denied, 459 U.S. 1037, 103 S.Ct. 449, 74 L.Ed.2d 603 (1982); EEOC v. Federal Reserve Bank of Richmond, 698 F.2d 633 (4th Cir. 1983). For a critical evaluation by statisticians of the use of the binomial significance test, see Meyer, Sacks and Zabell, What Happened in Hazelwood: Statistics, Employment Discrimination and the 80% Rule, 1984 Amer. Bar Found. Research J., 139 (1984).

It is important to remember that statistical proof plays different roles in treatment and impact cases. In the disproportionate impact case, the purpose of statistical evidence is to demonstrate the effect of the challenged procedure on different classes of persons. Where that effect can be demonstrated through relevant general population data, as was the case in Griggs v. Duke Power Co. and Dothard v. Rawlinson, no statistical analysis of the disparity is necessary, because the legally relevant impact is defined in terms of that population. But in some impact cases, particularly those arising from employment tests, no general population data is available. Thus, if an employer's aptitude test is failed by 40% of all white applicants and 50% of all black applicants, the pass rates are known only for those applicants who actually took the test. The applicants form only a sample of those persons in the relevant job market. Disparate impact in a sample drawn from the relevant population may not justify the conclusion that the test has a disparate impact on the population as a whole. In other words, there may be no difference in pass rates between blacks and whites in the population and the difference in the sample may be the result of chance—i.e. the peculiar abilities of the individuals in the sample. Courts have frequently assumed disparate impact on the population from the size of the disparity in the sample. See United States v. Chicago, 549 F.2d 415, 429 (7th Cir.), cert. denied, 434 U.S. 875 (1977); Bridgeport Guardians, Inc. v. Members of the Bridgeport Civil Service Commission, 482 F.2d 1333, 1335 (2d Cir. 1973), cert. denied, 421 U.S. 991, 95 S.Ct. 1997, 44 L.Ed.2d 481 (1975); Chance v. Board of Examiners, 458 F.2d 1167, 1171 (2d Cir. 1972). The Uniform Guidelines on Employment Selection Procedure, 29 CFR 1607.4D, 28 CFR 50.14(4)D (1981), adopted by the EEOC and other federal agencies, utilizes an arbitrary four-fifths rule of thumb to assess impact. Under this rule, a difference in pass rates between two racial, ethnic or sex groups is considered substantial if the pass rate for one group falls below four-fifths (80%) of the pass rate for the higher group. Depending on the size of the relevant population and that of the sample, the application of such a rule of thumb, or any intuitive guess work as to impact, may be statistically unwarranted. See Shoben, Differential Pass-Fail Rates in Employment Testing: Statistical Proof Under Title VII, 91 Harv.L.Rev. 793, 805–11 (1978). When only sample data is available, an inference of disparate impact on the population can only be based on a statistical analysis of the data to determine the likelihood that the observed pattern would occur by chance, if in fact there were no differences in the pass rates of the groups in the relevant population. Id. at 798.

In treatment cases statistical evidence is only probative if it can logically lead to an inference of discriminatory motivation or lack thereof. Thus, in *Hazelwood* and *Harris-Teeler Supermarket* the Courts used the binomial distribution analysis in evaluating statistical showings of discrepancies between actual work forces and relevant populations. The less the likelihood that such discrepancies could have occurred by chance, the more such evidence tends to prove that race was a factor in the hiring process. The use of the binomial analysis is appropriate when evaluating whether an observed pattern of events, each with only two possible outcomes, such as the hiring of either a black or white person from the relevant population, is likely to have occurred at random. But many treatment cases involve employment decisions, such as job assignment and wage setting, which have many possible outcomes. Typically, such decisions are influenced by multiple factors. For example, in a suit alleging that female employees are paid less than male employees because of their sex, a raw comparison of average wages of men and women shows that, on the average, females are paid less than males for the same kind of work. The employer claims that wages are set on the basis of education, experience, and productivity and that women on the average are not as well qualified as men. The employer's claim, if true, constitutes a valid defense. For the defense to be valid, however, it must not only be true that women are less qualified according to the various factors, but also that the difference in qualifications accounts for the difference in pay. If the employer does not pay experienced men more than less experienced men, then the factor of experience cannot account for the difference between male and female wages. In light of the defense claims, however, the comparison of average male and female wages may create a suspicion, but cannot prove discrimination, because there is no showing of a causative link between sex and the differential. Since one assumes an infinite variety of results from any given wage-setting decision, the binomial analysis cannot be used as an evaluative tool. A device is needed to filter out the various influencing factors and to identify, within bounds that are statistically significant, the suspect factor (in this case, sex) as playing a causative role in the setting of wages. For this kind of analysis, statisticians use a method called multiple regression. See generally Fisher, Multiple Regression in Legal Proceedings, 80 Colum.L.Rev. 702 (1980); Finkelstein, The Judicial Reception of Multiple Regression Studies in Race and Sex Discrimination Cases, 80 Colum.L. Rev. 737 (1980).

> [O]ne might describe multiple regression as a method used to extract a systematic signal from the noise prescribed by data. There are two primary problems involved in extracting such a signal. First, it is typically the case that the factor whose influence one wishes to test or measure is not the only major factor affecting the dependent variable. * * * Second, even if one can somehow account for the effects of the other important systematic factors, there typically remain chance components.
>
> * * *
>
> In multiple regression one first specifies the major variables that are believed to influence the dependent variable. * * * [In the above example this means specifying the factors that may affect wages.] There inevitably remain minor influences, each one perhaps small, but creating in combination a non negligible effect. These minor influences are treated by placing them in what is called a random disturbance term and assuming that their joint effect is not systematically related to the effects of the major variables being investigated—in other words by treating their effects as due to chance. Obviously, it is very desirable to have the random part of the relationships small, particularly relative to the systematic part. Indeed, the size of the random part provides an indication of how correctly one has judged what the systematic part is. Multiple regression thus provides a means not only for extracting the systematic effects from the data but also for assessing how well one has succeeded in doing so in the presence of the remaining random effects.
>
> The relationship between the dependent variable and the independent variable of interest is then estimated by extracting the effects of the other major variables (the systematic part). When this has been done, one has the best available substitute for controlled experimentation. The results of multiple regressions can be read as showing the effects of each variable on the dependent variable, holding the others constant. Moreover, those results allow one to make statements about the probability that the effect described has merely been observed as a result of chance fluctuation.

Fisher, supra, 80 Colum.L.Rev. at 705–06 (footnote omitted).

Increasingly, plaintiffs and defendants in Title VII class actions have resorted to multiple regression analysis to explain and explain away statistical discrepancies large and small. See Wilkins v. University of Houston, 654 F.2d 388 (5th Cir. 1981); Trout v. Lehman, 702 F.2d 1094 (D.C. Cir. 1983), vacated, 465 U.S. 1056, 104 S.Ct. 1404, 79 L.Ed.2d 732 (1984). Unlike binomial distribution analysis which, given relevant population statistics, can be applied by courts without expert assistance, the presentation of multiple regression evidence requires expert testimony from statisticians who have analyzed the relevant data, usually with the help of computers. One court has complained that Title VII class actions have become "contests between college professor statisticians who revel in discoursing about advanced statistical theory." Otero v. Mesa County Valley School District, 470 F.Supp. 326, 331 (D.Colo.1979), affirmed, 628 F.2d 1271 (10th Cir. 1980).

The most common problem with use of multiple regression analysis is the failure to take into account a factor, or independent variable, which may influence the dependent variable. In VALENTINO v. UNITED STATES POSTAL SERVICE, 674 F.2d 56 (D.C.Cir. 1982), the plaintiff introduced regression analyses attempting to measure the influence of sex on the salary of postal employees. The studies factored for sex, length of government service and years of education, but failed to control for type of education and job classification.

> In the setting we have here it would be irrational to assume "equal qualifications" to fill engineering or secretarial vacancies among persons educated the same number of years and employed by the government for the same length of time. Because Valentino's regression model ignores information central to understanding the causal relationships at issue, the district court could not accept her "centerpiece" proof as adequate to raise an inference that sex discrimination accounts for salary differences in the upper echelons at USPS Headquarters.

674 F.2d at 71. By contrast, in COMMONWEALTH v. LOCAL 542, INTERNATIONAL UNION OF OPERATING ENGINEERS, 469 F.Supp. 329 (E.D.Pa. 1978), affirmed, 648 F.2d 922 (3d Cir. 1981), the plaintiffs alleged that blacks were discriminated against in job referrals by union hiring halls and introduced a multiple regression to account for differences in age, geographic location, seniority, and occupational specialty, as well as race. The regression indicated that race was a highly significant factor influencing the number of hours worked by persons referred through the hiring halls, with whites working, on the average, some 109 hours per year more than blacks. The defendants argued that the analysis omitted the crucial factor of skill. The court rejected the argument because there was no evidence that skill varied by race (or was not accounted for by one of the other factors) and because there was no evidence that union hiring hall agents considered skill in making referrals. It should, of course, be the employer's burden to prove that a particular factor in fact influences the employment decision in question. In BAZEMORE v. FRIDAY, ___ U.S. ___, 106 S.Ct. 3000, 92 L.Ed.2d 315 (1986), a suit challenging class wide racial discrimination against black state agricultural agents, the plaintiffs relied in large part on regression analyses to demonstrate that black agents were paid less than similarly situated whites. Based on discovery from the defendant officials that four factors were determinative of salary: education, tenure, job title and job performance, the regressions used four independent variables—race, education, tenure, and job title. Both the district court and the Court of Appeals rejected the regression analyses as evidence of discrimination because they did not include "all measurable variables thought to have an effect on salary level." The Supreme Court reversed.

> The [Court of Appeals's] view of the evidentiary value of the regression analyses was plainly incorrect. While the omission of variables from a regression analysis may render the analysis less probative than it otherwise might be, it can hardly be said, absent some other infirmity, that an analysis which accounts for the major factors "must be considered unacceptable as evidence of discrimination." Normally, failure to in-

> clude variables will affect the analysis' probativeness, not its admissibility.
>
> Importantly, it is clear that a regression analysis that includes less than "all measurable variables" may serve to prove a plaintiff's case. A plaintiff in a Title VII suit need not prove discrimination with scientific certainty; rather, his or her burden is to prove discrimination by a preponderance of the evidence.

54 U.S.L.W. at 4975–76. The case was remanded with instructions to the Court of Appeals to consider the regression analyses along with all other evidence in the record.

Another frequently encountered problem is the use of inappropriate factors in the regression analysis. In JAMES v. STOCKHAM VALVES & FITTINGS CO., 559 F.2d 310 (5th Cir. 1977), cert. denied, 434 U.S. 1034, 98 S.Ct. 767, 54 L.Ed.2d 781 (1978), the defendant introduced a regression study to refute an inference of discrimination from the fact that black employees earned substantially less per hour than whites. Earnings were regressed for, among other factors, "merit rating" and "skill level." The court rejected the analysis because the factors were themselves tainted by discrimination. The "skill level" factor was derived from the employees' job class, but exclusion of blacks from higher level jobs was part of the discrimination alleged in the suit. As for merit ratings, the court found they were based on the totally subjective evaluation of the employer's all-white supervisory staff. A regression analysis incorporating a variable which is itself the product of racial bias cannot be used to test for the effect of racial discrimination in a series of employment decisions. Similarly, a factor may in fact influence employment decisions, but because it is not job-related, and has a disproportionate impact on the potential class, may be inappropriate for inclusion in a regression analysis. Finally, the data reflecting the factor may be sufficiently unavailable that a court would be unwarranted in basing any inference on a study which included it. Where the employer contends that a variable, not accounted for in the plaintiffs' analysis (for example, employees' disciplinary records), accounts for the discrepancy and plaintiffs contend that the variable itself is influenced by race, which party has the burden of proof on the issue of whether the variable factor is itself the result of bias? See, Coates v. Johnson & Johnson, 756 F.2d 524 (7th Cir. 1985).

The increasing complexity of statistical cases has led to expressions of judicial concern over the burden placed on the statistically unsophisticated judge, Garrett v. R. J. Reynolds Industries, Inc., 81 F.R.D. 25, 32–34 (M.D.N.C. 1978), and of fear that such evidence may actually be infringing on the judicial function.

> Excursions into the new and sometimes arcane corners of different disciplines is a familiar task of American trial lawyers and its generalist judges. But more is afoot here, and this court is uncomfortable with its implications. This concern has grown with the realization that the esoterics of econometrics and statistics which both parties have required this court to judge have a centripetal dynamic of their own. They push from the outside roles of tools for "judicial" decisions toward the core of decision making itself. Stated more concretely: the precision-like mesh of numbers tends to make fits of social problems when I intuitively doubt such fits. I remain wary of the siren call of the numerical display and hope that here the

> resistance was adequate; that the ultimate findings are the product of judgment, not calculation.
>
> * * *
>
> I write this unusual conclusion to this unusual opinion to make plain that this court did not select a numbers field for this contest but instead has been forced to judge a fight, there fought.
>
> To place the court's findings in perspective, an additional observation is required. Despite their recent recognition, the econometric techniques employed in this case are not discrimination CAT scanners—ready to detect alien discrimination in corporate bodies. It may reveal shadows but its resolution is seldom more precise.
>
> Ultimately the findings of fact here are not numerical products and sums but a human judgment that the facts found are more likely true than not true. With that standard, stripped to essentials, and within the decisional limits placed upon me by higher courts, this is what I think happened, approximately.

Vuyanich v. Republic National Bank of Dallas, supra, 505 F.Supp. at 224 (N.D.Tex.1981) vacated, 723 F.2d 1195 (5th Cir.) (*en banc*), cert. denied, ___ U.S. ___, 105 S.Ct. 567, 83 L.Ed.2d 507 (1984).

4. Despite the importance of statistical evidence, few, if any, disparate treatment cases are proved by such evidence alone. In individual cases following the *McDonnell Douglas* formula, no statistical pattern may exist or, because the work force is so small or the job qualifications so unique, statistically significant data may be unavailable. In individual cases where statistics are introduced the evidence is used to support rather than substitute for live testimony. See Miles v. M.N.C. Corp., *supra*, Diaz v. American Telephone & Telegraph, 752 F.2d 1356 (9th Cir. 1985) (statistics establishing general discriminatory pattern in employer's practices can create inference of discriminatory intent with respect to individual employment decision). Compare, Atkins v. City of Greensboro, 39 F.E.P. Cases 424 (M.D.N.C.1985) (statistical evidence that race has generally played role in employer's decisions "not very probative" on issue of whether race entered into discharge of four black employees accused of drug use). Virtually all class treatment cases are proved by a combination of statistical evidence and "anecdotal" testimony by the named plaintiffs or class members about specific instances of discrimination. Such testimony may "[bring] the cold numbers convincingly to life." *Teamsters*, supra, 431 U.S. at 339, 97 S.Ct. at 1856. The less persuasive the statistical evidence in such a case, the more important is live testimony in proving a pattern and practice of discrimination. See Wilkins v. University of Houston, supra, 654 F.2d at 410. Courts have demonstrated a marked reluctance to find intentional discrimination solely on the basis of statistical evidence. See, EEOC v. Sears, Roebuck & Co., 628 F.Supp. 1264 (N.D.Ill.1986); Sobel v. Yeshiva University, 566 F.Supp. 1166 (S.D.N.Y.1983).

In disproportionate impact cases non-statistical testimony will, of course, play a lesser role in the plaintiff's case-in-chief, but, as will be seen, may be critical in refuting the special defenses of business necessity and bona fide occupational qualifications.

5. In Harris-Teeter Supermarket's unsuccessful petition to the Supreme Court for certiorari it presented the issue as follows: "When corporate employer has discharged numerous employees, individually and for varied and sepa-

rate causes, and thereafter * * * it is shown numerically—but without trial of causes and circumstances of individual discharges—that proportion of white employees who were discharged was 21 percent and proportion of black employees who were discharged was 37.2 percent, do such statistics establish legal presumption that each and every discharged employee was discharged 'because' of being black?" 52 U.S.L.W. 3762. Was this a fair characterization of the Fourth Circuit's ruling? Compare, Mozee v. Jeffboat, Inc., supra. Does the decision mean that every discharged black is entitled to relief? See Chapter 14.

SECTION C. THE DEFENDANT'S CASE

1. General Rebuttal

If the plaintiff fails to put on sufficient proof to establish a prima facie case, the appropriate defense response is a motion for involuntary dismissal under Rule 41(b) of the Federal Rules of Civil Procedure (in cases tried without a jury), for a directed verdict under Rule 50(a) FRCP (jury case), or their state court equivalents. If the plaintiff has made out a prima facie case, the defendant's burden of going forward will vary with the type of claim made by the plaintiff. In an individual disparate treatment case following the Green v. McDonnell Douglas pattern, the defendant must only articulate a non-discriminatory explanation for the treatment accorded the plaintiff. In a class disparate treatment case, the plaintiff's establishment of a prima facie case shifts to the defendant the burden of demonstrating that plaintiff's proof is either inaccurate or insignificant. The defense may accomplish this by a direct attack on the validity of plaintiff's statistical evidence, apparently the tack taken by the school district in *Hazelwood*, or by a nondiscriminatory explanation for the disparity demonstrated by plaintiff—the route attempted by the defendants in Lilly v. Harris-Teeter Supermarket.

Disproportionate impact cases can be attacked by demonstrating the inaccuracy or irrelevancy of plaintiff's data, as was attempted in Dothard v. Rawlinson, but most impact cases are defended on the ground that the challenged practice has a legitimate business purpose. That defense and those available in disparate treatment cases are explored in the remainder of this chapter.

2. Special Defenses

a. Job Relatedness and Business Necessity

CONTRERAS v. CITY OF LOS ANGELES

United States Court of Appeals, Ninth Circuit, 1981.
656 F.2d 1267, cert. denied 455 U.S. 1021, 102 S.Ct. 1719, 72 L.Ed.2d 140 (1982).

WALLACE, CIRCUIT JUDGE.

Certain former and present city workers (appellants) appeal from the district court's judgment that they are entitled to no relief under Title VII of the Civil Rights Act of 1964, and 42 U.S.C. § 1981, for having lost their jobs by failing allegedly discriminatory civil service examinations. We affirm.

I

Contreras, E. Gonzalez, Mock, and Zavala (accountants) were employed by the City of Los Angeles (City) as Senior Accountants in the Training and Job Development Division of the Mayor's office. Maria Gonzalez (Gonzalez) was employed in the same division as an Auditor. Each had served efficiently in his or her position for more than one and one-half years, having been originally hired on the basis of oral interviews at a time when the Mayor's office was not subject to the stringent hiring requirements of the City's civil service rules and regulations.

In early 1976, when the City transferred the function of the Training and Job Development Division to the newly created Community Development Department, the senior accountant and auditor positions previously assigned to the Mayor's office became subject to the City's civil service commission. Consequently, appellants were required to pass written examinations before assuming senior accountant and auditor status in the new department. The City Council, in an effort to avoid possible inequities to appellants and others employed in the Mayor's office, proposed an amendment to the city charter exempting the employees from the examination requirement. Unfortunately for appellants, that amendment was defeated by the electorate in November 1976.

Prior to the rejection of the amendment, accountants took and failed the senior accountant examination. Gonzalez passed the auditor examination but scored too low to be employed as an auditor in the new office. Although accountants thus became ineligible for their former senior accountant positions, each of them scored high enough to be employed at his former salary [1] as regular civil service labor-market analysts. Gonzalez took a position with the State of California, but maintains her standing in this litigation by asserting a continuing interest in returning to her former auditor position.

Following voter rejection of the exempting amendment, appellants commenced this action in district court, claiming that the City's examinations unlawfully discriminated against Spanish-surnamed applicants. They requested that the district court enjoin the City from using the discriminatory examinations, order the City to develop examinations that accurately predict job performance, and order the City to retain appellants in their former positions until the new examinations are developed.

II

The three-step inquiry of Title VII actions is well-established, particularly in cases such as this where preemployment screening devices are

1. Mock would initially suffer a $1,000 per year decrease in salary from his former senior accountant position, but would be eligible for civil service advancement levels paying more than his former salary.

used.[2] At the outset, a plaintiff bears the burden of establishing a prima facie case that the employer's screening device selects employees in a significantly discriminatory pattern. Failure to meet this burden results in judgment for the employer. If the plaintiff succeeds in establishing a prima facie case of discrimination, the burden of proof then shifts to the employer to prove that the screening device is job related, i.e., that it actually measures skills, knowledge, or ability required for successful performance of the job sought by the applicant. Failure in this proof results in judgment for the plaintiff. If the employer succeeds in showing that the screening device does in fact measure job-related characteristics, the screening device does not violate Title VII unless the plaintiff then proves that the employer has available an alternative nondiscriminatory screening device that would effectively measure the capability of job applicants.

In this case the district judge accepted evidence probative of all three stages of the Title VII inquiry. After doing so, he ruled that appellants had failed to establish a prima facie case of discriminatory impact upon Spanish-surnamed applicants, that the City had proven the senior accountant and auditor examinations to be job related, and that appellants had failed to prove the existence of a non-discriminatory alternative that would select qualified employees with the same degree of accuracy as the written examination. We must first determine whether the district court's finding that appellants failed to present a prima facie case of discrimination is clearly erroneous. If it is not, we must affirm the district court's judgment for the defendants.

A. The Senior Accountant Examination

In attempting to prove that the senior accountant examination had a significantly discriminatory impact on Spanish-surnamed applicants, accountants introduced the following statistical evidence: 5 of 17 or 29.4 percent of the Spanish-surnamed applicants taking the examination passed, while 22 of 40 or 55 percent of the whites who took the examination passed; also, the mean score for Spanish-surnamed applicants was 60.7, 6½ points below the 67.2 mean score of white applicants. In addition to this statistical evidence, accountants introduced expert testimony that these statistics are reliable evidence of a discriminatory examination and that Spanish-surnamed individuals generally do worse than whites on written examinations.

The district judge, relying on evidence produced by the City, rejected the accountants' proof of a prima facie case for two reason [sic]. First, he placed little evidentiary weight on the examination results because the figures, although disparate, were not statistically significant when

2. This opinion is limited to consideration of appellants' claims under established Title VII principles. If plaintiffs have failed to meet their burden of proof under Title VII, they have also failed to establish their claim under 42 U.S.C. § 1981, whose standards are more stringent than those of Title VII. See Craig v. County of Los Angeles, 626 F.2d 659, 668 (9th Cir. 1980); Williams v. Dekalb County, 582 F.2d 2 (5th Cir. 1978) (per curiam); Chicano Police Officer's Ass'n v. Stover, 552 F.2d 918 (10th Cir. 1977) (per curiam).

tested at a .05 level of significance. Second, he concluded that the accountants scored low because they failed to study seriously in preparation for the examination. We will discuss his reasons separately.

In considering the district court's reliance on lack of statistical significance, we observe that the Supreme Court has stated: " '[s]tatistical analyses have served and will continue to serve an important role' in cases in which the existence of discrimination is a disputed issue." International Bhd. of Teamsters v. United States, 431 U.S. 324, 339, 97 S.Ct. 1843, 1856, 52 L.Ed.2d 396 (1977) ("*Teamsters*"), quoting Mayor of Philadelphia v. Educational Equality League, supra, 415 U.S. at 620, 94 S.Ct. at 1333. At the same time, however, the Court has cautioned that "[c]onsiderations such as small sample size may, of course, detract from the value of such evidence," *Teamsters,* supra, 431 U.S. at 340 n.20, 97 S.Ct. at 1857 n.20, and we have stated that the use of statistical evidence "is conditioned by the existence of proper supportive facts and the absence of variables which would undermine the reasonableness of the inference of discrimination which is drawn." United States v. Ironworkers Local 86, 443 F.2d 544, 551 (9th Cir.), cert. denied, 404 U.S. 984, 92 S.Ct. 447, 30 L.Ed.2d 367 (1971) (footnote omitted). See also Morita v. Southern California Permanente Medical Group, 541 F.2d 217, 220 (9th Cir. 1976), cert. denied, 429 U.S. 1050, 97 S.Ct. 761, 50 L.Ed.2d 765 (1977) ("statistical evidence derived from an extremely small universe * * * has little predictive value and must be disregarded"); Johnson v. Shreveport Garment Co., 422 F.Supp. 526, 539–40 (W.D.La.1976), aff'd, 577 F.2d 1132 (5th Cir. 1978).

A total of 17 Spanish-surnamed applicants took the senior accountant examination. The City's expert witness testified that the statistics calculable from such a small sample are not significant at a .05 level of statistical significance,[3] the level suggested by federal agency guidelines for the establishment of statistical proof. See e.g., 28 C.F.R. § 50.14, at § 12(b)(5) (1977). Thus, the expert testified, these statistics are not a reliable indicator of discriminatory effect. The unreliability of accountants' statistical base is illustrated by the fact that only three additional passing scores among Spanish-surnamed applicants would have produced a Spanish-surnamed passing rate sufficiently close to the white passing rate to preclude a finding of adverse impact under federal agency guidelines, even if one disregards the .05 level of significance requirement.[4] Although accountants produced expert testimony sug-

3. "[A] .05 level of statistical significance indicates that the demonstrated relationship between the variables would occur in a random sample five times out of one hundred and is generally recognized as the point at which statisticians draw conclusions from statistical data." White v. City of San Diego, 605 F.2d 455, 460 (9th Cir. 1979). In other words, the existence of a .05 level of statistical significance means that the disparate results of a pre-employment screening device would be the product of chance only one time in twenty. Nineteen times in twenty the disparate results would be the product of some discriminatory tendency of the screening device.

4. An additional three passing scores would have meant that eight of seventeen or 47.1 percent of the Spanish-surnamed applicants passed the examination. Such a percentage would not have been less than 4/5 or 80 percent of the white passing

gesting that the statistical disparity of the examination results is reliable, we recognize that the district judge may accept some statistical inferences and reject others based upon his perception of the oral and documentary evidence placed before him. "It is for the District Court, in the first instance, to determine whether these statistics appear sufficiently probative of the ultimate fact in issue—whether a given job qualification requirement has a disparate impact on some group protected by Title VII." Dothard v. Rawlinson, supra, 433 U.S. at 338, 97 S.Ct. at 2731 (Rehnquist, J., concurring).

As to the district judge's second reason, we begin with the premise that any statistical evidence produced by a plaintiff is subject to rebuttal by the employer. Id. at 331, 97 S.Ct. at 2727 (majority opinion); *Teamsters*, supra, 431 U.S. at 340, 97 S.Ct. at 1857. Employers "may endeavor to impeach the reliability of the statistical evidence, they may offer rebutting evidence, or they may disparage in arguments or in briefs the probative weight which the plaintiffs' evidence should be accorded." Dothard v. Rawlinson, supra, 433 U.S. at 338–39, 97 S.Ct. at 2731–32 (Rehnquist, J., concurring). In this case the City attacked accountants' statistical proof by introducing evidence that accountants failed to prepare seriously for the examination, and contended that such evidence further impeached the accuracy of the already dubious small sample size. Facts stipulated by the parties include the statement of a City official that accountants confessed to lack of preparation at a meeting held to air accountants' complaints about the examination. Although each accountant took the witness stand and expressly denied having made such an admission, the district judge did not believe their testimony and we must give "due regard * * * to the opportunity of the trial court to judge of the credibility of the witnesses." Fed.R.Civ.P. 52(a). See deLaurier v. San Diego Unified School District, supra, 588 F.2d at 679. The same City official who revealed accountants' admission to their lack of study filed a report describing the meeting at which the admission occurred. That report, prepared several months before accountants filed a complaint in the district court, related plausible reasons for their failure to study: they believed not only that the voters would pass the charter amendment exempting them from the examination requirements, but also that they would receive a second opportunity to take the examination if the amendment failed.

That accountants failed to prepare adequately for the examination is corroborated by their examination performance. Their average examination score, aside from being well below the established passing score, was 11.58 percent below the average score of the other 13 Spanish-surnamed applicants who took the test. Moreover, they scored

rate (55 percent) as required by 28 C.F.R. § 50.14, at § 4(b) (1977). An additional four passing scores among Spanish-surnamed applicants would have produced a 52.9 percent passing rate, nearly equal to the 55 percent rate achieved by whites. Statistics are not trustworthy when minor numerical variations produce significant percentage fluctuations.

well below the average Spanish-surnamed score in every examination category.

We conclude that the district court's finding that accountants failed to establish a prima facie case of discrimination was not clearly erroneous. In doing so we recognize the discriminatory implications of the disparate examination statistics and the expert testimony concerning their reliability. On the other hand, the City's expert testimony, the small statistical base, and the impeachment of the statistics by evidence of the accountants' failure to study, all convince us that the district court's conclusion was not an unreasonable interpretation of the evidence presented. "[W] here the evidence would support a conclusion either way but * * * the trial court has decided it to weigh more heavily for the defendant[,] [s]uch a choice between two permissible views of the weight of evidence is not 'clearly erroneous.'" United States v. Yellow Cab Co., 338 U.S. 338, 342, 70 S.Ct. 177, 179, 94 L.Ed. 150 (1949).

B. The Auditor Examination

Gonzalez also relied upon statistical evidence in attempting to prove the discriminatory impact of the auditor examination: 6 of 23 or 26.1 percent of the Spanish-surnamed applicants passed the examination, while 23 of 36 or 63.9 percent of the white applicants passed. The mean score of Spanish-surnamed applicants, 57.3, was more that 10 points below the 67.4 mean score of white applicants. The district judge expressly found that this evidence indicated a statistical adverse impact on Spanish-surnamed auditor applicants. Although Gonzalez passed the auditor examination, she failed to secure her desired position because she did not score highly enough. She relies upon the disproportionate pass rate to contend that she lost her job through an unlawfully discriminatory examination.

The district judge ruled that Gonzalez did not establish a prima facie case of discriminatory impact. He did so by combining the distribution of scores on the auditor examination with the results of a separate, senior auditor examination, on which Spanish-surnamed applicants performed better than any other ethnic group. Because 75 of the 125 questions on the senior auditor examination also appeared on the 100-question auditor examination, the district judge concluded that the auditor examination could not have discriminated against Spanish-surnamed applicants. The district judge also relied upon the fact that Gonzalez was denied employment not solely on the basis of her written examination score, but also on the basis of an oral interview score.

The district judge erred in concluding that Gonzalez failed to establish a prima facie case of discriminatory impact. The City did not rebut the statistical evidence produced by Gonzalez. Moreover, the district judge's reason for concluding that Gonzalez failed in her proof—the combined results of the senior auditor and auditor examinations—did not validly refute the clear import of Gonzalez' evidence. The senior auditor results were taken from an extremely small sample size, since only 9 Spanish-surnamed applicants took the test. It was clear error for the district court to conclude that these statistically insignificant results of the senior auditor examination permitted disregard of the statistical results of the auditor examination, particularly when there was no evidence that the Spanish-surnamed senior auditor applicants performed well on the same questions that the Spanish-surnamed auditor applicants failed. Indeed, the City's expert witness testified that it is not sound statistical procedure to combine the results of two separate examinations.

Nor does the fact that Gonzalez was denied employment on the basis of a combined oral interview and written examination score support the district court's ruling that Gonzalez failed in her proof. Gonzalez' written examination score, although high enough to pass, was lower than the average passing score. Her oral interview score, on the other hand, was well above average. Thus, it was her written examination score that most substantially impaired her chances of obtaining the auditor position.

Statistical disparities alone may constitute prima facie proof of discrimination. Although the prima facie case requirement is not automatically satisfied by statistical evidence of adverse impact, we hold that a prima facie case is established when such evidence of discriminatory impact is completely uncontroverted. Accordingly, we reverse the district court's ruling that Gonzalez failed to establish prima facie discrimination. We must therefore determine whether the City met its burden of proving that the auditor examination was job related.

III

A. *The Employer's Burden of Proof Under Title VII*

The allocation of proof in Title VII cases is well established. Once a plaintiff has met his or her burden of proving a prima facie case of discriminatory impact, the employer bears some burden of justifying the business practice in terms of business need. If this burden is met, the plaintiff then assumes the burden of proving the availability of an effective business alternative with less disparate racial impact.[5] De-

Test

5. The purpose of the procedure, as the Supreme Court recently spelled out is ultimately to focus the court's attention on the issue of discrimination. "In a Title VII case, the allocation of burdens * * * is intended progressively to sharpen the inquiry into the elusive factual question of intentional discrimination." Texas Department of Community Affairs v. Burdine, 450 U.S. 248, 255 n.8, 101 S.Ct. 1089, 1094 n.8, 67 L.Ed.2d 207 (1981).

This formulation was written in a disparate treatment case. In a disparate impact case the dialectic of the allocation of burdens sharpens the inquiry down to a factual question of discrimination, but not necessarily intentional discrimination in the sense of discrimination that is conscious and purposeful.

In the disparate impact case, the plaintiff will recover if the disparate impact stems from decisions or practices that cannot be given a genuine business justification. A practice that is unjustifiable in race and sex neutral business terms is not always the product of intentional discrimi-

spite this well-established procedure, courts differ on just what an employer must prove to discharge its burden. See Comment, The Business Necessity Defense to Disparate-Impact Liability Under Title VII, 46 U.Chi.L.Rev. 911, 912 (1979). Indeed, cases within this circuit might be read to differ on the weight of the employer's burden. Compare Craig v. County of Los Angeles, 626 F.2d 659 (9th Cir. 1980), and deLaurier v. San Diego Unified School District, 588 F.2d 674 (9th Cir. 1978), with Blake v. City of Los Angeles, 595 F.2d 1367 (9th Cir. 1979), and deLaurier v. San Diego Unified School District, supra, 588 F.2d at 685-92 (Hufstedler, J., dissenting). The question before us is: what must an employer show to meet its burden of proving that pre-employment test, having a disproportionate, adverse impact on a racial minority, are [sic] sufficiently justified by business need to survive a Title VII challenge?

In Craig v. County of Los Angeles, supra, we recently concluded that an employer must prove such tests to be "significantly job-related." 626 F.2d at 662. We stated that our standard for proof of job-relatedness was articulated by the Supreme Court:

> "[D]iscriminatory tests are impermissible unless shown, by professionally accepted methods, to be 'predictive of or significantly correlated with important elements of work behavior which comprise or are relevant to the job or jobs for which candidates are being evaluated.' 29 C.F.R. § 1607.4(c)."

626 F.2d at 662, quoting Albemarle Paper Co. v. Moody, supra, 422 U.S. at 431, 95 S.Ct. at 2378. We went on to state that an employer "must demonstrate a significant relation between the challenged selection device or criteria and the important elements of the job or training program, not merely some 'rational basis' for the challenged practice. However, the employer need not establish a perfect positive correlation between the selection criteria and the important elements of work." 626 F.2d at 664 (citation and footnote omitted).

The employer's burden in *Craig* comports with that applied in deLaurier v. San Diego Unified School District, supra, 588 F.2d 674, a case decided almost two years earlier. In *deLaurier* we applied a standard "commonly referred to as the 'business necessity' or 'job relatedness' defense * * *." Id. at 678. Although we stated that the employment practice in question must be shown to be " 'necessary to safe and efficient job performance,' " id. at 678, quoting Dothard v. Rawlinson, supra, 433 U.S. at 331 n.14, 97 S.Ct. at 2728 n.14, our application of this language to the facts demonstrated that the employer's burden is met with less than proof of absolute business necessity.

nation. The decision makers may simply have missed a less discriminatory option. In such an event we could speak of "negligent discrimination."

The chief point, however, and one that *Burdine* makes clear, is that Title VII does not ultimately focus on ideal social distributions of persons of various races and both sexes. Instead it is concerned with combating culpable discrimination. In disparate impact cases, culpable discrimination takes the form of business decisions that have a discriminatory impact and are not justified by their job-relatedness.

The school district in *deLaurier* attempted to justify its mandatory maternity leave policy with evidence that teaching ability declines as the date of delivery approaches, and that the school district needs advance notice to procure long-term teacher substitutes. 588 F.2d at 678 n.8. The school district did not thereby prove that its maternity leave policy, which required teachers to stop work at the start of their ninth month of pregnancy, was necessarily required for successful operation of the schools. See id. at 687–91 (Hufstedler, J., dissenting). Nonetheless, we upheld the maternity leave policy as a job-related employment practice. Id. at 678–79. We treated "job related" and "business necessity" as interchangeable terms, neither of which required proof that the challenged policy was absolutely necessary for operation of the business.

Gonzalez refers us to Blake v. City of Los Angeles, supra, 595 F.2d 1367, a case decided six months after *deLaurier.* *Blake* might be interpreted as adopting a much more demanding employer burden of proof than that required in *deLaurier*. In *Blake* we stated that an employer must prove not only that his screening device is job related; he must further prove it " 'necessary to safe and efficient job performance * * *.' " Id. at 1376, quoting, again, the phrase from Dothard v. Rawlinson, supra, 483 U.S. at 332 n.14, 97 S.Ct. 2728 n.14. Although both *deLaurier* and *Blake* quoted this language, it could be argued persuasively that *Blake* applied it more nearly literally than did *deLaurier*. *deLaurier* essentially applied a job-relatedness standard. *Blake* defined "job-related," quite properly, as "the capacity of selection devices to measure traits that are important to successful job performance." 595 F.2d at 1377. *Blake* also stated, however, that " 'job-relatedness' is relevant only for the purpose of trying to prove that the characteristics which the various tests select are directly related to the business necessity." Id. This formulation might seem to suggest that business necessity is something over and above job relatedness—that is, over and above what is "important to successful job performance." Id. On such a reading, *Blake's* use of the *Dothard* expression "necessary" would clearly mean something different from that expression's use in *Craig* and *deLaurier.* Thus, in order to determine the test to be applied to the auditor's examination given Gonzalez, we must first harmonize our cases.

Because it is the language from *Dothard* that is at the root of the issue before us, our effort to harmonize our cases must be guided by the Supreme Court's interpretation of that language. Before turning to the Supreme Court cases, we identify the issue in more detail.

The *Craig* test, by permitting job-related employment practices, views Title VII, as far as this case is concerned, as prohibiting only race-related employment criteria. The test maximizes employer freedom, restricting it only when employment decisions are made wholly or partially on the basis of race. It mandates employer color-blindness, but otherwise respects an employer's right to seek maximum employee productivity and efficiency. Thus, the *Craig/deLaurier* test tolerates a disparate impact on racial minorities so long as that impact is only an incidental product of criteria that genuinely predict or significantly correlate with successful job performance, and does not result from criteria that make race a factor in employment decisions.

The interpretation of *Blake* referred to above, on the other hand, views Title VII as much more restrictive of employer decision-making. That reading would not tolerate a disparate impact on racial minorities that results from job-related criteria. So understood, *Blake* would allow disparately impacting criteria only when forbidding them would seriously damage the business, that is, when they are "necessary" to operation of the business. Such a test would thus minimize an employer's freedom, permitting him to employ disproportionately-impacting criteria only if he can prove them necessary to the functioning of his enterprise. That such criteria are effective predictors of employee performance is insufficient under this view of Title VII. Thus, such a test would prohibit some pre-employment screening devices permitted by the *Craig/deLaurier* test: devices that actually predict employee performance, but that cannot be proven necessary to the operation of the business.

In determining whether Title VII requires application of the employer's burden of proof set forth in *Craig* and *deLaurier* or some other level of proof, we are not free to invoke our perception of ideal social policy. Rather, we must ascertain Congress' intent in enacting Title VII. Because the face of the statute does not clearly resolve the question before us, we look for guidance to the legislative history of Title VII, United States v. Culbert, 435 U.S. 371, 374 n.4, 98 S.Ct. 1112; 1114 n.4, 55 L.Ed.2d 349 (1978); Train v. Colorado Pub. Interest Research Group, Inc., 426 U.S. 1, 10, 96 S.Ct. 1938, 1942, 48 L.Ed.2d 434 (1976), and to interpretative pronouncements by the Supreme Court.

Congress' primary objective in passing Title VII was to eliminate race-related employment criteria. Senators Clark and Case, co-managers of Title VII on the Senate floor, issued an interpretative memorandum defining discrimination:

> To discriminate is to make a distinction, to make a difference in treatment or favor, and those distinctions or differences in treatment or favor which are prohibited by [Title VII] are those which are based on any of the five forbidden criteria: race, color, religion, sex, and national origin. Any other criterion or qualification for employment is not affected by this title.

110 Cong.Rec. 7213 (1964). Critics of the legislation were concerned that Title VII would intolerably burden employers and would force them to abandon employee selection practices based on productivity and efficiency. See Griggs v. Duke Power Co., 401 U.S. 424 at 434 & n. 10, 91 S.Ct. 849 at 855 & n.10, 28 L.Ed.2d 158. However, "[p]roponents of Title VII sought throughout the debate to assure the critics that the

Act would have no effect on job-related tests." Id. at 434, 91 S.Ct. at 855. Senator Case, in another interpretative memorandum, explained:

> Whatever its merits as a socially desirable objective, title VII would not require, and no court could read title VII as requiring, an employer to lower or change the occupational qualifications he sets for his employees simply because proportionately fewer Negroes than whites are able to meet them. * * *
>
> Title VII says merely that a covered employer cannot refuse to hire someone simply because of his color; * * * [I]t expressly protects the employer's right to insist that any prospective applicant, Negro or white, must meet the applicable job qualifications. Indeed, the very purpose of title VII is to promote hiring on the basis of job qualifications, rather than on the basis of race or color.

110 Cong.Rec. 7246–47 (1964). Senators Clark and Case assured the critics that "[a]n employer may set his qualifications as high as he likes * * *," id. at 7213, and Senator Humphrey stated that "[t]he employer will outline the qualifications to be met for the job. The employer, not the Government will establish the standards." Id. at 13088.

By enacting Title VII, "[d]iscriminatory preference for any group, minority or majority, is precisely and only what Congress has proscribed." Griggs v. Duke Power Co., supra, 401 U.S. at 431, 91 S.Ct. at 853. The legislative history, of Title VII clearly reveals that Congress was concerned about preserving employer freedom, and that it acted to mandate employer color-blindness with as little intrusion into the free enterprise system as possible. The question of preferential treatment has recently provided an occasion for the Supreme Court to state its understanding that Title VII "was not intended to 'diminish traditional management prerogatives.' " Texas Department of Community Affairs v. Burdine, 450 U.S. 248, 259, 101 S.Ct. 1089, 1096, 67 L.Ed.2d 207 (1981), quoting United Steelworkers of America v. Weber, 443 U.S. 193, 207, 99 S.Ct. 2721, 2729, 61 L.Ed.2d 480 (1979).

Therefore, we conclude that the employer's burden of proof required by *Craig* and *deLaurier* is more consistent with Congress' Title VII intent than the employer's burden of proof required by the interpretation of *Blake* suggested above. Our review of Supreme Court case law reinforces this conclusion.

The Supreme Court first considered an employer's duty under Title VII in Griggs v. Duke Power Co., supra, 401 U.S. 424, 91 S.Ct. at 850, and concluded that "Congress has placed on the employer the burden of showing that any given requirement must have a manifest relationship to the employment in question." Id. at 432, 91 S.Ct. at 854. *Griggs* suggests that the Court perceived "business necessity" to be the same standard as "job-related," and viewed both as requiring only that an employer prove that his employment practices are legitimately related to job performance:

> The Act proscribes not only overt discrimination but also practices that are fair in form but discriminatory in operation. The touch-

> stone is business necessity. If an employment practice which operates to exclude Negroes cannot be shown to be related to job performance, the practice is prohibited.

Id. at 431, 91 S.Ct. at 853.

Four years after the *Griggs* decision, the Supreme Court answered the very question considered by us today: "What must an employer show to establish that pre-employment tests racially discriminatory in effect, though not in intent, are sufficiently 'job related' to survive challenge under Title VII?" Albemarle Paper Co. v. Moody, supra, 422 U.S. at 408, 95 S.Ct. at 2367. The employer in *Albemarle* attempted to justify its use of aptitude tests that disproportionately excluded blacks by employing an expert to "validate" the tests in terms of job-relatedness. Various defects in the validation study convinced the Supreme Court that the employer had failed to satisfy its burden of proof. 422 U.S. at 431–36, 95 S.Ct. at 2378–80. Significantly, however, the Court did not interpret Title VII as requiring employer proof of a strong form of "business necessity." Indeed, the Court in *Albemarle* never used the term "business necessity." Rather, the Court "clarified" the "standard of proof for job relatedness," id. at 436, 95 S.Ct. at 2380, by articulating a standard that is "the same as that of the *Griggs* case—that discriminatory tests are impermissible unless shown, by professionally acceptable methods, to be 'predictive of or significantly correlated with important elements of work behavior which comprise or are relevant to the job or jobs for which the candidates are being evaluated.' " Id. at 431, 95 S.Ct. at 2378, quoting 29 C.F.R. § 1607.4(c). It was this articulation of an employer's Title VII burden that we relied upon in *Craig.* 626 F.2d at 662.

We now turn to the troublesome Supreme Court language that appears in Dothard v. Rawlinson, supra, 433 U.S. 321, 97 S.Ct. at 2723. *Dothard* invalidated a height and weight requirement for prison guards that disproportionately excluded women applicants and was not proven to be "job-related." 433 U.S. at 332, 97 S.Ct. at 2728. In doing so, the Court required employer proof identical to that required in its earlier cases: "the employer must meet 'the burden of showing that any given requirement [has] * * * a manifest relationship to the employment in question.' " Id. at 329, 97 S.Ct. at 2727, quoting Griggs v. Duke Power Co., supra, 401 U.S. at 432, 91 S.Ct. at 854. Although the holding tracks prior Supreme Court cases, an unnecessary footnote contains the few words that cause our present difficulty: "a discriminatory employment practice must be shown to be necessary to safe and efficient job performance to survive a Title VII challenge." 433 U.S. at 332 n.14, 97 S.Ct. at 2728 n.14. This footnote formulation is belied by the broader standard applied in the *Dothard* text. See id. at 329, 331–32, 97 S.Ct. at 2726, 2727–28.

Since *Dothard*, the Court has indicated that the *Griggs/Albemarle* standard, rather than the *Dothard* footnote, controls Title VII inquiries. In New York Transit Authority v. Beazer, 440 U.S. 568, 99 S.Ct. 1355,

59 L.Ed.2d 587 (1979), the plaintiffs challenged a Transit Authority (TA) refusal to hire narcotics users, specifically methadone users. The Court stated:

> Respondents recognize, and the findings of the District Court establish, that TA's legitimate employment goals of safety and efficiency require that exclusion of all users of illegal narcotics, barbiturates [sic], and amphetamines, and of a majority of all methadone users. The District Court also held that those goals require the exclusion of all methadone users from the 25% of its positions that are "safety sensitive." Finally, the District Court noted that those goals are significantly served by—*even if they do not require*—TA's rule as it applies to all methadone users including those who are seeking employment in nonsafety-sensitive positions. *The record thus demonstrates that TA's rule bears a "manifest relationship to the employment in question."* Griggs v. Duke Power Co., 401 U.S. 424, 432, 91 S.Ct. 849, 854, 28 L.Ed.2d 158. See Albemarle Paper Co. v. Moody, 422 U.S. 405, 425, 95 S.Ct. 2362, 2375, 45 L.Ed.2d 280.

Id. 440 U.S. at 587 n.31, 99 S.Ct. at 1366 n.31 (emphasis added) (citations omitted). Thus, the Court's most recent application of the employer's Title VII burden of proof not only follows the standards set forth in *Griggs* and *Albemarle*, but implicitly approves employment practices that significantly serve, but are neither required by nor necessary to, the employer's legitimate business interests.

We conclude that any employer burden of proof that could be suggested by the possible strong reading of *Blake's* "business necessity" language would be inconsistent with Supreme Court case law and the Congressional intent underlying Title VII. Accordingly, we reject that interpretation of *Blake.* We interpret *Blake* in line with our precedents decided before (*deLaurier*) and after (*Craig*) that case. We hold that discriminatory tests are impermissible unless shown, by professionally accepted methods, to be predictive of or significantly correlated with important elements of work behavior that comprise or are relevant to the job or jobs for which candidates are being evaluated.[6]

B. Validation of the Auditor Examination

The district court made two conclusions of law relevant to the validation issue:

> 4. The Defendants may demonstrate that a test is job related by any competent evidence. Washington v. Davis, 426 U.S. 229 [96

6. In Harriss v. Pan American World Airways, Inc., 649 F.2d 670 (9th Cir. 1980), our court again quoted the *Blake* standard. Id. at 675. It was, however, unnecessary to the disposition of that case to examine the possibility of conflict between *Blake* and *Craig.* Therefore our court did not reach the question we now consider, and *Harriss* does not compel any particular result here.

S.Ct. 2040, 48 L.Ed.2d 597] (1976); see also, Blake v. City of Los Angeles, [435 F.Supp. 55 (C.D.Cal.1977)].

* * *

6. There is no magic in any validating procedure, and the Defendants need only supply competent and relevant evidence upon the issue of the job-relatedness of their employment standards. Washington v. Davis, 426 U.S. 229 (1976) at 247 n.13 [96 S.Ct. 2040 at 2051 n.13, 48 L.Ed.2d 597].

These conclusions would be error if they implied that the evidence need not show that the screening device was validated "by professionally acceptable methods" to be "'predictive of or significantly correlated with important elements of work behavior which comprise or are relevant to the job or jobs for which candidates are being evaluated.'" Albemarle Paper Co. v. Moody, supra, 422 U.S. at 431, 95 S.Ct. at 2378, quoting 29 C.F.R. § 1607.4(c).

We doubt, however, that the district judge intended anything more than the appropriateness of accepting any competent and relevant evidence tending to establish the existence of a professionally acceptable validation. We so interpret the district judge's conclusion of law because footnote 13 of Washington v. Davis discusses three different standards adopted by the American Psychological Association, and itself cites *Albemarle* and 29 C.F.R. § 1607.[7] The language of the sixth conclusion of law, however, was borrowed from the district court opinion in Blake v. City of Los Angeles, supra, 435 F.Supp. at 65, and there is also a "*see*" cite to that opinion in the fourth finding. Although the district court opinion in *Blake* itself quoted from footnote 13 of Washington v. Davis, the district judge in *Blake* focused on only part of that footnote and took too broad a view of permissible validation procedures. We therefore believe it is necessary to confirm our view that the district judge in the present case was making no similar error. We will do this by reviewing the evidence before the district court in

7. Footnote 13 reads as follows:

It appears beyond doubt by now that there is no single method for appropriately validating employment tests for their relationship to job performance. Professional standards developed by the American Psychological Association in its Standards for Educational and Psychological Tests and Manuals (1966), accept three basic methods of validation: "empirical" or "criterion" validity (demonstrated by identifying criteria that indicate successful job performance and then correlating test scores and the criteria so identified); "construct" validity (demonstrated by examinations structured to measure the degree to which job applicants have identifiable characteristics that have been determined to be important in successful job performance); and "content" validity (demonstrated by tests whose content closely approximates tasks to be performed on the job by the applicant). These standards have been relied upon by the Equal Employment Opportunity Commission in fashioning its Guidelines on Employee Selection Procedures, 29 CFR pt. 1607 (1975), and have been judicially noted in cases where validation of employment tests has been in issue. See, e.g., Albemarle Paper Co. v. Moody, 422 U.S. 405, 431, 95 S.Ct. 2362, 2378, 45 L.Ed.2d 280 (1975); Douglas v. Hampton, 168 U.S.App.D.C., at 70, 512 F.2d, at 984; Vulcan Society v. Civil Service Comm'n, 490 F.2d 387, 394 (CA2 1973).

the light of the "professionally accepted methods" validation standard of *Albemarle*, and the arguments pressed by Gonzalez.

To satisfy this requirement, examinations such as the one used by the City to hire auditors must be " 'validated' in terms of job performance." Washington v. Davis, 426 U.S. 229, at 247, 96 S.Ct. 2040, 2051, 48 L.Ed.2d 597. Title VII requires no single method of examination validation, but only that the method chosen be professionally acceptable. See Albemarle Paper Co. v. Moody, supra, 422 U.S. at 431, 95 S.Ct. at 2378. To this end, the Equal Employment Opportunity Commission (EEOC) has issued guidelines defining minimum standards for professionally acceptable validation studies. See 29 C.F.R. § 1607.14 (1979). These standards are not mandatory, but they are "entitled to great deference," Griggs v. Duke Power Co., supra, 401 U.S. at 434, 91 S.Ct. at 855, and an employer who disregards them must articulate some cogent reason for doing so and generally bears a heavier than usual burden of proving job relatedness. United States v. City of Chicago, 549 F.2d 415, 430 (7th Cir. 1977); United States v. Georgia Power Co., 474 F.2d 906, 913 (5th Cir. 1973).

In *Craig*, we established a three-step procedure for validation of examinations used to select employees from among a group of applicants:

> The employer must first specify the particular trait or characteristic which the selection device is being used to identify or measure. The employer must then determine that that particular trait or characteristic is an important element of work behavior. Finally, the employer must demonstrate by "professionally acceptable methods" that the selection device is "predictive of or significantly correlated" with the element of work behavior identified in the second step.

Craig v. County of Los Angeles, 626 F.2d 659, 662 (9th Cir. 1980), quoting Albemarle Paper Co. v. Moody, supra, 422 U.S. at 431, 95 S.Ct. at 2378. Applying the *Craig* procedure to the facts of this case, we conclude that the City successfully validated the auditor examination in terms of job-relatedness.

The City's validation of the auditor examination consisted of two phases: a job-analysis phase and an examination-review phase. In the job-analysis phase, a number of auditors and auditor supervisors employed in various civil service positions throughout the city were organized as a group of job experts for the purpose of determining what skill, knowledge, and ability was essential to the position of auditor. These job experts held four meetings. At the first meeting, they compiled a list of the tasks performed by City-employed auditors. At the second meeting, they determined what skills, knowledge, and ability are required to perform those tasks. At the third meeting, these skills, knowledge, and ability, known as job "elements," were ranked by the job experts on the basis of their importance to the job of auditor. Each job expert ranked the elements himself or herself, without the help of other experts, and the results were averaged to produce a final ranking. From the results of this final ranking, a City personnel analyst compiled a list of elements "critical" to the position of auditor. By definition, these critical elements were the various skills, knowledge, or ability sufficiently essential to the job of auditor to be tested on the auditor examination. At the fourth meeting, the job experts weighted the critical elements according to their relative importance to the auditor position. Again, the weighting was done on an individual basis, the final weighting being an average of all of the job experts' results. Standard deviation analysis was performed on this average, and on the average produced at the third meeting, to protect against one expert skewing the results by extreme rankings or weightings. The final product of these meetings, a compilation of elements critical to the position of auditor, weighted according to their relative importance, was used by the City's examining division to create the 100-question auditor examination.

The examination review phase of the City's validation study occurred after the applicants had taken the examination. In this phase, a new group of job experts was selected from among civil service auditors and supervisors employed by the City. These experts individually reviewed each question and decided if it tested one of the critical elements identified in the first phase. Only if five of the seven job experts agreed that a question tested a critical element was the question considered job related. As a result of this procedure, all but five questions were determined to be job related.

This validation study satisfies our three-step procedure set forth in Craig v. County of Los Angeles, supra, 626 F.2d at 662. First, the initial meetings during the job-analysis phase specified the particular trait or characteristic which was to be measured by the examination. Second, the last two meetings during the job-analysis phase determined which characteristics or traits were important elements of the auditor position. Third, the examination-review phase demonstrated that the auditor examination was significantly correlated with those elements of work behavior identified in the job-analysis phase.

As mentioned earlier, a key requirement of this third step, a requirement essential to proof of job relatedness generally, is that the validation method be professionally acceptable. At trial, the City produced expert testimony that its validation procedures met professional standards. Gonzalez produced expert testimony that the procedures were professionally unacceptable. The district judge resolved this conflict of testimony in favor of the City's expert, not only by ruling that the examinations were job related, but also by resolving every testimonial dispute between these experts in favor of the City. We will not disturb such a credibility determination.[8] See United States v. City of Chicago, supra, 549 F.2d at 429–30, 434.

8. Even if the district judge had been under the misapprehension that validation might sometimes be possible under other than professionally acceptable methods, this error would not infect his credibility determinations as between two different expert views of professionally acceptable methods.

Gonzalez contends that various methodological defects in the City's validation study demonstrated that it was not conducted in a professionally acceptable manner.[9] These alleged defects were also the basis of her expert's opinion that the City's validation was unprofessional. Specifically, Gonzalez contends, and her expert testified, that the study did not protect against job-expert bias; did not ensure that the questions tested essential job attributes; did not attempt to eliminate questions that tested elements obtainable through a brief, on-the-job orientation; did not ensure that the level of question difficulty correlated with the level of job difficulty; and did not verify the level of the cutoff score. Methodological defects clearly may reduce the probative value of a validation study. Craig v. County of Los Angeles, supra, 626 F.2d at 664. Therefore, we must consider each of Gonzalez' alleged defects separately.

Gonzalez contends that the City did not protect against job-expert bias, and indeed risked such bias, by selecting experts from among its own employees and by informing the selected experts about the pending Title VII lawsuit. Although accountants attempted to introduce hearsay evidence of actual bias among job experts for the senior accountant examination, Gonzalez introduced no evidence of actual bias among job experts for the auditor examination. The existence of bias was left to inference from the fact that job experts were City employees who knew of the lawsuit. However, the Supreme Court has not found employee involvement in and knowledge of a lawsuit to be fatal defects in a validation study. See Albemarle Paper Co. v. Moody, supra, 422 U.S. at 433 n.32, 95 S.Ct. at 2379. Rather, the Court has cautioned that studies made by such employees "must be examined with great care." Id. The district judge saw no reason to suspect that City employees with knowledge of the lawsuit would be biased against Gonzalez or other Spanish-surnamed applicants. Their jobs were not threatened by the validation study, and there was no evidence that they were biased generally against Spanish-surnamed applicants. The entire validation process, which averaged the conclusions of many job experts and tested that average for unusual deviations, was carefully designed to neutralize the effect of any biases which may have existed. Thus, viewing the study with great care, we find that Gonzalez' first alleged defect does not undercut the study's validity.

Gonzalez next contends that the validation study's "most basic defect" occurred in the examination-review phase. Job experts were asked to determine whether each question tested a skill, knowledge, or ability *included in* one of the critical elements identified during the job

9. In attempting to show that the City's examinations were not job related, the major contention in appellants' brief is that successful employees would never fail a truly valid examination. Therefore, appellants contend that accountants' failure of the senior accountant examination proved that it was not job related. We do not reach this argument, because the accountants failed to establish prima facie discrimination, and thus the City was not required to prove the job relatedness of the senior accountant examination. Gonzalez passed the auditor examination; therefore, this argument does not apply to her.

analysis phase. Therefore, Gonzalez contends, the examination-review phase did not ensure that each question tested "*essential* knowledge, skills, or behaviors composing the job in question," 29 C.F.R. § 1607.5(a) (1977) (emphasis added), as required by EEOC guidelines. We disagree. The critical elements presented to the job experts in the examination-review phase had, in the job-analysis phase, been determined to be skills, knowledge or ability critical or essential to performance of the auditor function. Therefore, by determining that the trait tested by each question was included in a critical element, the experts in the examination-review phase determined that the question tested a trait essential to the position of auditor. Moreover, before a question would be validated as job-related, five of seven job experts in the examination-review phase had to agree that it tested a critical element.[10]

Gonzalez next alleges that the validation study was defective because it failed to identify questions that tested skills, knowledge, or ability obtainable through a brief, on-the-job orientation, as required by 29 C.F.R. § 1607.5(a) (1977). Again we disagree. When experts in the job-analysis phase identified critical elements of the auditor position, they selected only those traits that a "barely acceptable worker" at the "minimum level of proficiency" would need "on the first day on the job." Thus, the selected critical elements did not include skills, knowledge, or ability learned on the job. That the job experts of the examination-review phase were not expressly asked to determine whether the trait tested by each question was obtainable through a brief orientation, is irrelevant. By determining that each question tested traits included in a critical element, the job experts effectively determined that the skills, knowledge, or ability tested were those needed by minimally proficient employees at the commencement of their employment as auditors. Gonzalez does not refute this reasoning.

Gonzalez next contends that the examination-review phase failed to determine whether the difficulty level of the examination questions equaled the difficulty level of the auditor's position, as required by some cases. Even if we accepted this added requirement, Gonzalez would not be helped. As mentioned in the above discussion, those who identified the critical elements of the auditor position did so for the "barely acceptable worker" who functioned at a "minimum level of proficiency." Thus, the critical elements to which the questions were matched represented the requisite level of difficulty for success as an auditor. Moreover, the nature of the examination minimizes the importance of the level-of-difficulty equation. As the City's expert testified, the purpose of a civil service examination is not to identify all individuals who could function competently in the available job. Rather, the civil service examination, as required by the City charter, ranks the applicants so that only the best qualified are hired. The statistics of the auditor examination demonstrate the need for such ranking: 188

10. Evidence of specific questions that tested nonessential traits related only to the senior accountant examination, and therefore does not apply to the auditor examination.

applicants took the examination in hopes of obtaining positions for which only 16 individuals had been hired in the previous two years combined.

Finally, Gonzalez contends that the examination passing score of 65 was arbitrarily set by the City charter, with no analysis of whether that score actually excluded some qualified applicants. We have two responses. First, Gonzalez passed the examination. Thus, a lower cutoff score would have had no effect on whether she was hired. Second, as discussed above, the nature of a civil service examination minimizes the significance of the cutoff score. Where an examination is designed to rank applicants so that only the top few may be hired (Gonzalez ranked 12th overall and she was not hired), the cutoff score is more a formality than a matter of consequence. Those who failed the examination would not have been hired even if they had passed by virtue of a lower cutoff score.

In summary, we conclude that the City's validation study satisfied our previously established three-step criteria for validations of pre-employment examinations. That the validation was professionally acceptable is demonstrated by expert testimony in the record and the failure of each of Gonzalez' challenges. The City established, by professionally acceptable standards, that the auditor examination was predictive of or significantly correlated with important elements of the auditor position. Thus, we must finally consider whether Gonzalez established the existence of a less discriminatory alternative.

IV

"If an employer [meets] the burden of proving that its tests are 'job related,' it remains open to the complaining party to show that other tests or selection devices, without a similarly undesirable racial effect, would also serve the employer's legitimate interest in 'efficient and trustworthy workmanship.'" Albemarle Paper Co. v. Moody, supra, 422 U.S. at 425, 95 S.Ct. at 2375, quoting McDonnell-Douglas Corp. v. Green, 411 U.S. 792 at 801, 93 S.Ct. 1817, 1823, 36 L.Ed.2d 668. Gonzalez contends that the auditor examination, even if job related, violates Title VII because the City could have effectively screened auditor applicants by use of less discriminatory oral interviews. In making this contention, Gonzalez cites extensively from Crockett v. Green, 388 F.Supp. 912, 919–21 (E.D.Wis.1975), aff'd, 534 F.2d 715 (7th Cir. 1976), a case which places upon the employer the burden of proving that no alternative screening device was available. The district court opinion in *Crockett*, which was rendered before the Supreme Court's decision in Albemarle Paper Co. v. Moody, supra, 422 U.S. 405, 95 S.Ct. 2362, 45 L.Ed.2d 280, clearly misallocates the burden of proof. Once an employer has shown a selection device to be job related, it becomes the plaintiff's responsibility to prove that a less discriminatory alternative would satisfy the employer's hiring needs. With the burden of proof properly allocated in this case, we agree with the district court's conclusion that Gonzalez failed to prove the existence of less-discriminatory screening devices that would have satisfied the City's civil service hiring needs.

The only evidence produced by Gonzalez to establish the existence of alternative auditor selection methods was expert testimony that Spanish-surnamed individuals generally do better in oral interviews than on written examinations and that oral examinations could be used to screen applicants. However, even if the district court accepted this testimony as establishing that oral interviews have a less disparate impact on minorities, it does not satisfy Gonzalez' burden of proving that oral interviews, as an alternative to written examinations, would satisfy the City's civil service hiring needs.[11] That oral interviews were used in the past to hire auditors for the Mayor's office, a fact upon which Gonzalez relies, does not prove that such interviews would satisfy the merit hiring requirements of the new civil service division. Evidence in the record reveals that the oral interviews previously used were designed to meet the special needs of the Mayor's office, not those of a civil service classification. Moreover, that oral interviews were used to screen applicants in other job categories transferred out of the Mayor's office at the same time that the auditor position was transferred, another fact upon which Gonzalez relies, does not prove that such interviews would have satisfied the auditor-hiring needs of the new department. As the district court correctly concluded, Gonzalez did not prove that a less discriminatory alternative was available.

V

In summary, we conclude that accountants failed to establish a prima facie case of discriminatory impact by the senior accountant examination. Gonzalez, although successfully establishing a prima facie case of discriminatory impact by the auditor examination, failed to prove that a less discriminatory alternative was available to the City. Thus, the City's proof that its auditor examination was job related entitles it to judgment. Accordingly, we affirm the district court's decision that appellants are entitled to no relief under Title VII.

Affirmed.

TANG, CIRCUIT JUDGE, specially concurring in part and dissenting in part.

* * *

11. Civil service classifications and merit hiring are designed to eliminate the spoils system of political hiring, Kirkland v. New York State Department of Correctional Services, 520 F.2d 420, 428 (2d Cir. 1975), cert. denied 429 U.S. 823, 97 S.Ct. 73, 50 L.Ed.2d 84 (1976), and to require the government to hire individuals on the basis of superior qualifications. Id. It is unfortunate that appellants were not rehired in the positions at which they previously functioned effectively. However, that seemingly inequitable consequence is the result of a system that seeks to hire those who can best perform the jobs available.

III

The majority concedes that the district court committed legal error by requiring only that the City supply "competent and relevant evidence" on the issue of the job relatedness of their employment standards, ante, at 1279–1282, yet it concludes that despite this error the lower court's determination that the City met its burden of establishing a business necessity must be upheld on appeal. I cannot share this view. Accordingly, I respectfully dissent from this holding; rather than affirm the district court I would remand the case with instructions to reevaluate the evidence under the proper legal standard.

A district court's findings of subsidiary fact in Title VII disparate impact cases must normally be reviewed by an appellate court under the clearly erroneous standard. See Harriss v. Pan American World Airways, Inc., 637 F.2d 1297 (9th Cir. 1980). We would, therefore, usually accord great deference to the lower court's factual findings on the issue of business necessity defense and refrain from substituting our judgment for that of the district court.

When a district court's factual findings are induced by an erroneous conception of the law, however, we are not free to indulge in a deferential review. On the contrary, we must discard the clearly erroneous standard and independently review the record because it has long been acknowledged that a lower court's legal misconception can directly infect its findings. As a consequence, we must assume that the district court's findings in this case were infected by its erroneous understanding of the business necessity defense and independently review those findings.

The majority opinion not only fails to acknowledge this principle but blatantly states that we can deferentially review the lower court's findings:

> At trial, the City produced expert testimony that its validation procedures met professional standards. Gonzalez produced expert testimony that the procedures were professionally unacceptable. The district judge resolved this conflict of testimony in favor of the City's expert, not only by ruling that the examinations were job related, but also by resolving every testimonial dispute between these experts in favor of the City. We will not disturb such a credibility determination.

Ante at 1282.

This approach is an obvious application of the clearly erroneous standard and cannot be justified under the circumstances here presented. The district judge's conclusion that the examinations were job related is entirely without conclusive force because it rendered that determination under the incorrect assumption that job relatedness could be established and the defendant's burden met with the introduction of evidence that was merely "relevant" or "competent". Similarly, its determination that the City's expert was more credible cannot be insulated by a sympathetic appellate review because that conclusion was directly engendered by its erroneous assumption that the City could satisfy its burden of proof on the business necessity defense with the introduction [of] "relevant" or "competent" evidence.

Although the normal course in such a case would be an appellate *de novo* review of the district court's findings of fact, in view of the complexity of the evidence received and the possibility that the party's presentation of evidence was inhibited by the lower court's legal error, such an examination would more properly proceed at the district court level. I would, therefore, remand the case for an introduction and evaluation of evidence and a redetermination on the issue whether the City met its burden of proving job relatedness and validation.

NOTES AND PROBLEMS FOR DISCUSSION

1. What sort of purposes should justify an employer's practices under the business necessity defense? Can the desire to avoid union pressure or an attempt to satisfy customers' sexually stereotyped preconceptions constitute a legitimate business purpose? See Robinson v. Lorillard Corp., 444 F.2d 791, 799 (4th Cir.), cert. dismissed, 404 U.S. 1006, 92 S.Ct. 573, 30 L.Ed.2d 655 (1971); Diaz v. Pan American World Airways, Inc., 442 F.2d 385, 389 (5th Cir.), cert. denied, 404 U.S. 950, 92 S.Ct. 275, 30 L.Ed.2d 267 (1971). Should administrative convenience alone provide a satisfactory explanation for a practice with a discriminatory impact? In deLaurier v. San Diego Unified School District, 588 F.2d 674 (9th Cir. 1978), the Court of Appeals upheld a rule requiring school teachers to go on leave at the beginning of their ninth month of pregnancy as justified by the desire of the school district to predict with certainty the date of departure for the teachers in question. In the context of a private enterprise, should the desire to maximize profit justify any practice reasonably calculated to attain that goal? It is now generally accepted that the business necessity defense applies only in disproportionate impact cases to justify practices which "are fair in form but discriminatory in operation," Griggs v. Duke Power Co., supra, but not in disparate treatment cases. See Garcia v. Gloor, 609 F.2d 156 (5th Cir. 1980), cert. denied, 449 U.S. 1113, 101 S.Ct. 923, 66 L.Ed.2d 842 (1981); Pettway v. American Cast Iron Pipe Co., 494 F.2d 211, 244 (5th Cir. 1974), cert. denied, 439 U.S. 1115, 99 S.Ct. 1020, 59 L.Ed.2d 74 (1979).

2. In contrast to the Ninth Circuit's holdings in *Contreras* and *deLaurier*, a number of courts have held that the business necessity defense is not satisfied merely by proof that the employment practice serves a legitimate business purpose:

> [T]he applicable test is not merely whether there exists a business purpose for adhering to a challenged practice. The test is whether there exists an overriding legitimate business purpose such that the practice is necessary to the safe and efficient operation of the business. Thus, the business purpose must be sufficiently compelling to override any racial impact; the challenged practice must effectively carry out the business purpose it is alleged to serve; and there must be available no acceptable alternative policies or practices which would better accomplish the business purpose advanced, or accomplish it equally well with a lesser differential racial impact.

Robinson v. Lorillard Corp., supra, 444 F.2d at 798. In United States v. Bethlehem Steel Corp., 446 F.2d 652, 662 (2d Cir. 1971), the court emphasized that "[n]ecessity connotes an irresistible demand. * * * [A practice] must not only directly foster safety and efficiency of a plant, but also be essential to those goals." See also Green v. Missouri Pacific Railroad, 523 F.2d 1290 (8th Cir. 1975); United States v. Jacksonville Terminal Co., 451 F.2d 418 (5th Cir. 1971), cert. denied, 406 U.S. 906, 92 S.Ct. 1607, 31 L.Ed.2d 815 (1972). Under these cases, an employment practice not "sufficiently compelling to override [its] racial impact" will fail to establish the defense even though the practice serves a legitimate business purpose. As a corollary to the "stark necessity" version of the defense is the rule that the employer bears the burden of proving the *unavailability* of less discriminatory alternatives, because no less discriminatory alternatives could exist if the practice is absolutely necessary.

> It should go without saying that a practice is hardly "necessary" if an alternative practice better effectuates the intended purpose or is equally effective but less discriminatory.

Robinson v. Lorillard, supra, 444 F.2d at 798, n.7. See Local 189, Papermakers & Paperworkers v. United States, 416 F.2d 980 (5th Cir. 1969), cert. denied, 397 U.S. 919, 90 S.Ct. 926, 25 L.Ed.2d 100 (1970). Were the "stark necessity" cases in effect overruled by Dothard v. Rawlinson, *supra*? See, Clady v. County of Los Angeles, 770 F.2d 1421, 1432 n. 11 (9th Cir. 1985), cert. denied, ___ U.S. ___, 106 S.Ct. 1516, 89 L.Ed.2d 915 (1986) (where employer demonstrates job-relatedness of test, burden shifts to plaintiff to prove other selection methods with less discriminatory impact would serve employer's legitimate interest as well).

3. What exactly is the point of disagreement between the majority and the dissent in *Contreras*? To satisfy the business necessity defense, there must be a showing of a nexus between the practice and the business purpose, but what quantum of proof is required to establish that nexus? What standard was applied by the district court in *Contreras*? By the Court of Appeals?

In Spurlock v. United Airlines, Inc., 475 F.2d 216 (10th Cir.1972), the Court of Appeals addressed the question of whether certain requirements for the position of airline flight officer, including the requirement of a college degree, were job-related within the meaning of *Griggs*.

> When a job requires a small amount of skill and training and the consequences of hiring an unqualified applicant are insignificant, the courts should examine closely any pre-employment standard or criteria which discriminate against minorities. In such a case, the employer should have a heavy burden to demonstrate to the court's satisfaction that his employment criteria are job-related. On the other hand, when the job clearly requires a high degree of skill and the economic and human risks involved in hiring an unqualified applicant are great, the employer bears a corresponding lighter burden to show that his employment criteria are job-related. * * * The courts, therefore, should proceed with great caution before requiring an employer to lower his pre-employment standards for such a job.

475 F.2d at 219. Relying on *Spurlock*, a number of courts have significantly relaxed the evidentiary burden in disproportionate impact cases on employers of those entrusted with "the lives and well-being" of the public. See e.g., Hodgson v. Greyhound Lines, Inc., 499 F.2d 859, 863 (7th Cir.1974), cert. denied, 419 U.S. 1122, 95 S.Ct. 805, 42 L.Ed.2d 822 (1975); Chrisner v. Complete Auto Transit, Inc., 645 F.2d 1251, 1262–63 (6th Cir.1981). In Davis v. City of Dallas,

777 F.2d 205 (5th Cir.1985), a police department's requirement that applicants for the force have completed at least 45 semester hours of college credit with at least a "C" average was attacked under *Griggs.* The requirement had an adverse impact on black applicants. The defendant presented no empirical evidence that officers with college hours performed their duties better than those without such education although comparisons were possible because the department had formerly required only a high school diploma. Its validation evidence consisted of the opinions of several experts that, regardless of the area of study, college education "fill[ed] the gap of inexperience in the handling of a crisis situation for an inexperienced officer." The Court of Appeals concluded that the skills required for police work "were not definable with significant precision" and that "formal validation through the use of empirical evidence was a virtual impossibility." Citing *Spurlock,* the Court affirmed the district court's finding that the city had met its burden under *Griggs.* "Because of the professional nature of the job, coupled with the risks and public responsibility inherent in the position, * * * empirical evidence is not required to validate the job-relatedness of the educational requirement." 777 F.2d at 217. Does the *Spurlock* doctrine mean that certain employers may adopt practices with an adverse impact which, though not absolutely essential to the business, will provide a higher quality work force, while other employers, because of the nature of their business, will not be allowed such latitude? Compare, Rodriguez v. East Texas Motor Freight, 505 F.2d 40, 57 (5th Cir.1974), vacated on other grounds, 431 U.S. 395, 97 S.Ct. 1891, 52 L.Ed.2d 45 (1977) (policy prohibiting transfer of local drivers to over-the-road positions not justified by general concern for safety) with Hawkins v. Anheuser-Busch, Inc., 697 F.2d 810, (8th Cir.1983) (college degree requirement for supervisory position upheld on basis of opinion testimony by company personnel). See generally, Bartholet, Application of Title VII to Jobs in High Places, 95 Harv.L.Rev. 945 (1982).

Should an employer have a heavier burden of establishing business necessity when the challenged policy in fact perpetuates past intentional discrimination? In Walker v. Jefferson County Home, 726 F.2d 1554 (11th Cir.1984), the Court of Appeals noted that a nursing home's requirement of prior supervisory experience as a prerequisite for promotion to a supervisory position, though neutral on its face, impacted on black employees because of past discrimination in job assignments to supervisory positions and thus served to "freeze the status quo of prior discriminatory employment practices." In such a case the Court held that the employer should have a "heavy burden" of proving business necessity. The defendant failed to satisfy the burden because it did not prove that the job of supervisor was "highly skilled or that the economic and human risks involved as being an unqualified applicant [were] great." 726 F.2d at 1559. In United States v. Town of Cicero, 786 F.2d 331 (7th Cir.1986), the government challenged municipal ordinances which restricted city employment to persons who had been residents in the town for at least one year. The town was less than .05% black but adjoined two predominantly black communities. In its entire history the town had never employed a black. The district court denied a preliminary injunction on the ground that the ordinances were facially neutral. The Seventh Circuit reversed and remanded for reconsideration noting that under *Griggs,* even neutral practices cannot be maintained if they operate to freeze in the results of prior employment discrimination. But did the ordinances in fact "freeze" prior discrimination in employment or did they merely impact adversely on blacks because of discrimination in housing for which the city was arguably not responsible?

4. As noted previously at 99 and 174–175, employment tests which have a disproportionate impact violate the Act if they are unrelated to job capability. To pass muster under Title VII a test with disproportionate impact "must measure the person for the job and not the person in the abstract." Griggs v. Duke Power Co., supra, 401 U.S. at 436, 91 S.Ct. at 856. A test which accurately predicts job performance has "validity."

> Validity refers to the degree to which a test correlates with a relevant measure or criterion of job performance. Unless those people who score relatively high on a test are also likely to perform better on the job, a test lacks validity for that purpose and is useless for selecting personnel for the job in question.

J. Kirkpatrick, Testing and Fair Employment 6–7 (1968).

> Validation asks two fundamental questions. The first asks whether a relationship exists at all. If so, the second question is whether the relationship is strong enough to be useful.

R. M. Guion, Personnel Testing 131 (1965).

The Uniform Guidelines for Employee Selection Procedures, 29 CFR 1607 (1981), 28 CFR 50.14 (1981), promulgated by the EEOC and other federal agencies, describe three means of validating employment tests. (1) *Criterion-Related Validation.* Criterion validation was described by the Fifth Circuit in United States v. Georgia Power Co., 474 F.2d 906 (5th Cir. 1973).

> The most accurate way to validate an employment test is to administer the test to be validated to all applicants but proceed to select new employees without regard for their test achievement, and then, after an appropriate period of work experience, compare job performance with test scores. * * * An alternative is "concurrent validation", a process in which a representative sample of current employees is rated, then tested, and their scores are compared to their job ratings.

Of the three methods of validation, criterion-related validation is the only one which correlates test results with actual work performance and is thus considered preferable to methods based on less direct evidence. See United States v. Georgia Power, supra; Bridgeport Guardians, Inc. v. Members of the Bridgeport Civil Service Commission, 482 F.2d 1333, 1337 (2d Cir. 1973), cert. denied, 421 U.S. 991, 95 S.Ct. 1997, 44 L.Ed.2d 481 (1975). (2) *Content Validity.* A test which has content validity is one that tests for the actual skills or knowledge used in the job. Thus, if the job consists of transferring sacks of flour from a conveyor belt to a loading dock, a test of the applicant's physical ability to perform that task would have content validity. Evidence of the validity of a test by this method "should consist of data showing that the content of the selection procedure is representative of important aspects of performance on the job for which the candidates are to be evaluated." 29 CFR 1607.5B. Content validation must be based on a job analysis "of the important work behavior(s) required for successful performance and their relative importance and, if the behavior results in work product(s), an analysis of the work product(s)." 29 CFR 1607.14C(2). Courts have held that for a test to have content validity, it must measure "with proper relevant emphasis all or * * * most of the essential areas of knowledge and the traits needed for proper job performance." Bridgeport Guardians, Inc. v. Members of the Bridgeport Civil Service Commission, 354 F.Supp. 778, 792 (D.Conn.1973), affirmed in pertinent part, 482 F.2d 1333 (2d Cir. 1973), cert. denied, 421 U.S. 991, 95 S.Ct. 1997, 44 L.Ed.2d 481 (1975); Kirkland v. New York State

Department of Corrections, 374 F.Supp. 1361, 1378 (S.D.N.Y.1974), affirmed in pertinent part, 520 F.2d 420 (2d Cir. 1975), cert. denied, 429 U.S. 823, 97 S.Ct 73, 50 L.Ed.2d 84 (1976). Content validation can be used for tests which seek to measure specific skills or items of knowledge but is

> not appropriate for demonstrating the validity of selection procedures which purport to measure traits or constructs, such as intelligence, aptitude, personality, common sense, judgment, leadership, and spatial ability. Content validity is also not an appropriate strategy when the selection procedure involves knowledges, skills, or abilities which an employee will be expected to learn on the job.

29 CFR 1607.14C(1). (3) *Construct Validation.* Construct validation is the most complex and least understood of the validation methods. Very basically, it involves the identification of characteristics or traits which are important to successful performance of the job. A test which measures those traits has construct validity.

> The user should show by empirical evidence that the selection procedure is validly related to the construct and that the construct is validly related to the performance of critical or important work behavior(s). The relationship between the construct as measured by the selection procedure and the related work behavior(s) should be supported by empirical evidence from one or more criterion-related studies involving the job or jobs in question * * *.

29 CFR 1607.14D(3). In Washington v. Davis, the Supreme Court held that demonstration of a direct relationship between scores on an employment test and success in a police training program was sufficient to validate the test "wholly aside from its possible relationship to actual performance as a police officer." 426 U.S. at 250, 96 S.Ct. at 2052. Apparently there was no evidence in the record relating training program success to job performance. The Federal parties requested a remand to determine "whether the training program itself is sufficiently related to actual performance of the police officer's task." That request was rejected as inappropriate since the district court's judgment was "warranted by the record before it." 426 U.S. at 252, 96 S.Ct. at 2053. What method of test validation was used by the employer in *Contreras*?

5. The validation of physical tests for employment in police and fire departments has proved particularly troublesome as illustrated by Berkman v. City of New York, 536 F.Supp. 177 (E.D.N.Y.1982), aff'd, 705 F.2d 584 (2d Cir. 1983). There the court concluded that the job of firefighter required long-durational physical stamina and the ability to pace oneself so that a variety of tasks could be accomplished in emergency conditions. 536 F.Supp. at 212. The physical test adopted by the city of New York, which eliminated all female applicants, put a premium on the ability to perform certain tasks (running a mile, carrying a 100-plus pound "dummy" up a flight of stairs) in the shortest possible time. The court held that, in light of its adverse impact on women, the test violated Title VII because its various parts bore little, if any, resemblance to tasks actually performed by firefighters. The "dummy carry" portion of the exam, for example, "would be dangerous in the extreme to carrier and carried alike" if actually used in the course of a fire. 536 F.Supp. at 207. The Berkman court also rejected the city's use of test scores to rank order the candidates on the ground that the city was unable to demonstrate that a higher score was likely to result in better job performance. "Here, the lack of systematic study of the relationship between work behaviors observed (in the

validation study) and the abilities tested for in the test battery makes it apparent that the fine graduations of the rank order employed are hardly justified by the job analysis." 536 F.Supp. at 211. On remand from the Court of Appeals, the city did develop a test with content validity (a duplication of various tasks actually performed by firefighters), but the rank-ordered scoring system, based on time taken to complete the test, which eliminated from practical consideration for hiring virtually all women who passed the test, was again rejected as placing undue emphasis on aerobic capacities not required for the job. Berkman v. City of New York, 626 F.Supp. 591 (E.D.N.Y.1985). See also Burney v. City of Pawtucket, 559 F.Supp. 1089 (D.R.I.1983), vacated, 563 F.Supp. 1088 (D.R.I.1983)

b. Bona Fide Occupational Qualification

WILSON v. SOUTHWEST AIRLINES CO.

United States District Court, Northern District of Texas, 1981.
517 F.Supp. 292.

PATRICK E. HIGGINBOTHAM, DISTRICT JUDGE.

This case presents the important question whether femininity, or more accurately female sex appeal, is a bona fide occupational qualification ("BFOQ") for the jobs of flight attendant and ticket agent with Southwest Airlines. Plaintiff Gregory Wilson and the class of over 100 male job applicants he represents have challenged Southwest's open refusal to hire males as a violation of Title VII of the Civil Rights Act of 1964. The class further alleges that Southwest's published height-weight requirement for flight attendants operates to exclude from eligibility a greater proportion of male than female applicants.[1]

At the phase one trial on liability, Southwest conceded that its refusal to hire males was intentional. The airline also conceded that its height-weight restrictions would have an adverse impact upon male applicants, if actually applied. Southwest contends, however, that the BFOQ exception to Title VII's ban on sex discrimination, 42 U.S.C. § 703(e), justifies its hiring only females for the public contact positions of flight attendant and ticket agent. The BFOQ window through which Southwest attempts to fly permits sex discrimination in situations where the employer can prove that sex is a "bona fide occupational qualification reasonably necessary to the normal operation of that particular business or enterprise." Id. Southwest reasons it may discriminate against males because its attractive female flight attendants and ticket agents personify the airline's sexy image and fulfill its public promise to take passengers skyward with "love." Defendant claims maintenance of its females-only hiring policy is crucial to the airline's continued financial success.

1. The airline solicits applications from males for the flight attendant position and publishes a 5 foot, 9 inch eligibility requirement for males, though it has never hired and refuses to hire males. The evidence offered by Plaintiffs in support of their claim of adverse impact was not answered. See Plaintiff's Exhs. 22, 23.

Since it has been admitted that Southwest discriminates on the basis of sex, the only issue to decide is whether Southwest has proved [2] that being female is a BFOQ reasonably necessary to the normal operation of its particular business. As the application of § 703(e) depends, in large part, upon an analysis of the employer's "particular" business, it is necessary to set forth the factual background of this controversy as a predicate to consideration of Southwest's BFOQ defense. The facts are undisputed.

Factual Background

Defendant Southwest Airlines is a scheduled air carrier engaged in the transportation of passengers. Southwest's inaugural flight was June 18, 1971. It presently serves major cities in Texas, Oklahoma, Louisiana and New Mexico.

Southwest was incorporated in March of 1967 and filed its initial application with the Texas Aeronautics Commission ("TAC") in November of 1967 to serve the intrastate markets of Dallas, Houston and San Antonio. Southwest's proposed entry as an intrastate commuter carrier sparked a hostile reaction from the incumbent air carriers serving the Texas market. The airline's application to the TAC was bitterly contested and the original TAC decision to permit Defendant to begin serving Dallas, Houston and San Antonio was litigated for over four years through a succession of state and federal courts. The legal controversy was not resolved until December of 1970, when the U.S. Supreme Court denied the incumbent air carriers' petition for a *writ of certiorari*. According to Southwest's Chairman Herbert Kelleher, the airline in the interim had lost a commitment from a major insurance company to purchase $3 million of preferred stock; had lost a commitment for the sale of aircraft necessary to commence operations; had lost $2 million in subscriptions for stock by individual investors; and had spent over $530,000 in legal fees litigating the issue of its right to commence operations, all as a result of the defensive tactics of Southwest's competitors. In December of 1970, Southwest had $143 in the bank and was over $100,000 in debt, though no aircraft had ever left the ground.

Barely intact, Southwest, in early 1971, called upon a Dallas advertising agency, the Bloom Agency, to develop a winning marketing strategy. Planning to initiate service quickly, Southwest needed instant recognition and a "catchy" image to distinguish it from its competitors.

The Bloom Agency evaluated both the images of the incumbent competitor airlines as well as the characteristics of passengers to be

2. Once sex discrimination has been admitted or proved, the burden shifts to the defendant to prove that sex is a bona fide occupational qualification. Weeks v. Southern Bell Telephone & Telegraph, 408 F.2d 228, 232 (5th Cir. 1969). The placement of the burden of proof, however, is not outcome determinative in this case. That is, even if plaintiff's burden of persuasion required him to prove the inapplicability of the BFOQ, the result is the same.

served by a commuter airline. Bloom determined that the other carriers serving the Texas market tended to project an image of conservatism. The agency also determined that the relatively short haul commuter market which Southwest hoped to serve was comprised of predominantly male businessmen. Based on these factors, Bloom suggested that Southwest break away from the conservative image of other airlines and project to the traveling public an airline personification of feminine youth and vitality. A specific female personality description was recommended and adopted by Southwest for its corporate image:

> This lady is young and vital * * * she is charming and goes through life with great flair and exuberance * * * you notice first her exciting smile, friendly air, her wit * * * yet she is quite efficient and approaches all her tasks with care and attention. * * *

From the personality description suggested by The Bloom Agency, Southwest developed its now famous "Love" personality. Southwest projects an image of feminine spirit, fun and sex appeal. Its ads promise to provide "tender loving care" to its predominantly male, business passengers.[3] The first advertisements run by the airline featured the slogan, "AT LAST THERE IS SOMEBODY ELSE UP THERE WHO LOVES YOU." Variations on this theme have continued through newspaper, billboard, magazine and television advertisements during the past ten years.[4] Bloom's "Love" compaign was given a boost in 1974–1975 when the last of Southwest's competitors moved its operations to the new Dallas/Fort Worth Regional Airport, leaving Southwest as the only heavy carrier flying out of Dallas' convenient and fortuitously named, Love Field.

Over the years, Southwest gained national and international attention as the "love airline." Southwest Airlines' stock is traded on the New York Stock Exchange under the ticker symbol "LUV". During 1977 when Southwest opened five additional markets in Texas, the love theme was expanded to "WE'RE SPREADING LOVE ALL OVER TEXAS."

As an integral part of its youthful, feminine image, Southwest has employed only females in the high customer contact positions of ticket agent and flight attendant. From the start, Southwest's attractive personnel, dressed in high boots and hot-pants, generated public inter-

3. According to an October, 1979 onboard marketing survey commissioned before this lawsuit was filed, 69.01% of the respondents were male, while 58.41% of all respondents listed their occupation as either professional/technical, manager/administrator, or sales. Only 49.75% of the passengers surveyed, however, gave "business" as the reason for their trip.

4. Unabashed allusions to love and sex pervade all aspects of Southwest's public image. Its T.V. commercials feature attractive attendants in fitted outfits, catering to male passengers while an alluring feminine voice promises inflight love. On board, attendants in hot-pants (skirts are now optional) serve "love bites" (toasted almonds) and "love potions" (cocktails). Even Southwest's ticketing system features a "quickie machine" to provide "instant gratification."

est and "free ink." Their sex appeal has been used to attract male customers to the airline. Southwest's flight attendants, and to a lesser degree its ticket agents, have been featured in newspaper, magazine, billboard and television advertisements during the past ten years. Some attendants assist in promotional events for other businesses and civic organizations. Southwest flight attendants and ticket agents are featured in the company's in-flight magazine and have received notice in numerous other national and international publications.[5] The airline also encourages its attendants to entertain the passengers and maintain an atmosphere of informality and "fun" during flights. According to Southwest, its female flight attendants have come to "personify" Southwest's public image.

Southwest has enjoyed enormous success in recent years.[6] This is in no small part due to its marketing image. Though Southwest now enjoys a distinct advantage by operating its commuter flights out of "convenient" Love and Hobby Fields, the airline achieved a commanding position in the regional commuter market while flying "wing tip to wing tip" with national carriers who utilized the same airport, fares, schedules, and aircraft. The evidence was undisputed that Southwest's unique, feminized image played and continues to play an important role in the airline's success.[7]

Less certain, however, is Southwest's assertion that its females-only hiring policy is necessary for the continued success of its image and its business. Based on two onboard surveys, one conducted in October, 1979, before this suit was filed, and another in August, 1980, when the suit was pending,[8] Southwest contends its attractive flight attendants

5. For example, in 1974 a Southwest Airlines' flight attendant was featured on the cover of *Esquire* magazine as being "the best in America."

6. From 1979 to 1980, the company's earnings rose from $17 million to 28 million when most other airlines suffered heavy losses. As a percentage of revenues, Southwest's return is considered to be one of the highest in the industry.

7. Even Plaintiff Wilson in his original charge filed with the Equal Employment Opportunity Commission stated:

> The airline [Southwest] does not hire male flight attendants and has built its business by attracting businessmen and employing attractive female flight attendants.

8. The results of a briefer third survey conducted on March 10–11, 1981 at the request of Southwest's trial counsel cannot be considered. Conducted expressly to "determine" passenger preference for females in anticipation of trial, the survey showed bias and lacked statistical reliability for many reasons. Among other problems, the survey suffered from non-random sampling [passengers were sampled only at Love (Dallas) and Hobby (Houston) Fields, during the prime hours for business transportation (6:15–11:00 A.M.) and a disproportionately high (80%) number of males were included], and from a loaded setting [Southwest employed Kelly Temporary Services (59 of 60 interviewers were female) to conduct face-to-face interviews (the interviewers asked questions and recorded the responses) who identified themselves as agents of Southwest]. The survey also asked "loaded" and "double" questions, Question 10, for example, stated; "Southwest feels its 'Love Image' as featured by its attractive female flight attendants and ticket agents is one of the reasons people prefer to use Southwest over other airlines. If you could fly on another airline for the same price, out of the same airport, would you be as likely to use the services of Southwest, if Southwest changed this image—that is, would you be as likely to fly Southwest if they substituted males for some of the female flight attendants and ticket agents?" Given these deficiencies, and the failure to perform any test for statistical reliability, the

are the "largest single component" of its success. In the 1979 survey, however, of the attributes considered most important by passengers, the category "courteous and attentive hostesses" ranked fifth in importance behind (1) on time departures, (2) frequently scheduled departures, (3) friendly and helpful reservations and ground personnel, and (4) convenient departure times,[9] Defendant's Exh. 1 at 2 (¶ 17) and 39 (Question 14). Apparently, one of the remaining eight alternative categories, "attractive hostesses," was not selected with sufficient frequency to warrant being included in the reported survey results.

In another section of the 1979 survey labeled "likes/dislikes," where passengers were given an opportunity to select one or more attributes they liked about Southwest, the alternative "pleasant/friendly/courteous personnel/hostesses" was selected in "6.49% of the responses,"[10] while "attractive hostesses" got a 5.60% response. The categories "economical" (10.01%), "location" (Love and Hobby) (6.87%), and "convenience" (6.43%) were selected as, or more, often than the personnel/hostess attributes. Summing the two "hostess" percentages, the surveyors concluded that "their combined ratings make them the largest single component of your corporate image. *For many of your passengers, the hostesses are Southwest Airlines.*" (original emphasis) Defendant's Exh. 1, at 15. The Court, however, need not be versed in the techniques of opinion polling to question the soundness of this conclusion on the basis of summing the responses to the two hostess questions. Whatever the percentage figures represent, it is plain that in combining the figures, the survey corporation made no attempt to account for either passengers who selected both personnel/hostess responses, or for passengers who did not give any response at all. More objectionable is concluding that hostesses are the "largest single component" of the airline's image when no other attributes relating to image were presented. Even ignoring these and other deficiencies, the questions on their face say nothing about passenger preference, if any, for female flight attendants instead of males. At most, then, the responses indicate that pleasant, attractive personnel are attributes some passengers liked about Southwest.

The 1980 survey proves nothing more. *See* Defendant's Exh. 49 at 22, 23. Indeed, rather than Southwest's female personnel being the "sole factor" distinguishing the airline from its competitors, as Defendant contends, the 1980 survey lists Southwest's "personnel" as only one among five characteristics contributing to Southwest's public image. Id. at 25, Chart No. 27. Accordingly, there is no persuasive proof

survey conclusion that hiring males would have a negative impact on Southwest's business cannot be given weight.

9. Of the attributes reported, "delivering checked baggage promptly" ranked sixth in importance while "lower fares" ranked seventh.

10. Just what these percentage figures mean is impossible to determine from the survey report. The report does not indicate whether the percentage for each question represents the percentage of the sum of attributes selected, or the percentage of passengers who selected each attribute. Neither does the survey account for the passengers, if any, who did not respond at all to the "likes/dislikes" question.

that Southwest's passengers prefer female over male flight attendants and ticket agents, or, of greater importance, that they would be less likely to fly Southwest if males were hired.

In evaluating Southwest's BFOQ defense, therefore, the Court proceeds on the basis that "love," while important, is not everything in the relationship between Defendant and its passengers. Still, it is proper to infer from the airline's competitive successes that Southwest's overall "love image" has enhanced its ability to attract passengers. To the extent the airline has successfully feminized its image and made attractive females an integral part of its public face, it also follows that femininity and sex appeal are qualities related to successful job performance by Southwest's flight attendants and ticket agents. The strength of this relationship has not been proved. It is with this factual orientation that the Court turns to examine Southwest's BFOQ defense.

Interpretations of the Bona Fide Occupational Qualification

To begin, Section 703(a) of the 1964 Civil Rights Act, 42 U.S.C. § 2000e–2(a) (Title VII) provides:

> (a) It shall be an unlawful employment practice for an employer—
>
> (1) to fail or refuse to hire * * * or otherwise discriminate against any individual with respect to his compensation, terms, conditions, or privileges of employment, because of such individual's race, color, religion, sex, or national origin.

The broad scope of Title VII's coverage is qualified by Section 703(e), 42 U.S.C. § 2000e–2(e), the BFOQ exception. Section 703(e) states:

> (e) Notwithstanding any other provision of this subchapter,
>
> (1) It shall not be an unlawful employment practice for an employer to hire [an employee] * * * on the basis of his religion, sex, or national origin in those certain instances where religion, sex, or national origin is a bona fide occupational qualification reasonably necessary to the normal operation of that particular business or enterprise.

The BFOQ defense is available in cases involving intentional as well as unintentional discrimination.[11]

Congress provided sparse evidence of its intent when enacting the BFOQ exception to Title VII.[12] The only relevant remarks [13] from the

11. The BFOQ defense is not to be confused with the doctrine of "business necessity" which operates only in cases involving unintentional discrimination, when job criteria which are "fair in form, but discriminatory in operation" are shown to be "related to" job performance. See Swint v. Pullman-Standard, 624 F.2d 525, 534 (5th Cir. 1980), cert. granted in part 451 U.S. 906, 101 S.Ct. 1972, 68 L.Ed.2d 293 (1981); Miller v. Texas State Board of Barber Examiners, 615 F.2d 650, 653 (5th Cir.), cert. denied 449 U.S. 891, 101 S.Ct. 249, 66 L.Ed. 2d 117 (1980). Southwest has stipulated that it is flying only under the BFOQ defense.

12. Because sex was added as prohibited classification in a last minute attempt by opponents to block passage of the Civil Rights Bill, House consideration of the BFOQ exception for sex was limited to the final day for House debate on the Bill. See 110 Cong.Rec. 2577 (remarks of Rep.Smith) 2581–82 (remarks of Rep.Green) (1964). See also Barnes v. Costle, 561

13. See note 13 on page 261.

floor of the House were those of Representative Goodell of New York who proposed adding "sex" as a BFOQ category after sex was designated a prohibited classification under Title VII. She stated:

> There are so many instances where the matter of sex is a bona fide occupational qualification. For instance, I think of an elderly woman who wants a female nurse. There are many things of this nature which are bona fide occupational qualifications, and it seems to me they would be properly considered here as an exception.

110 Cong.Rec. 2718 (1964).

Most often relied upon [14] as a source of legislative intent is the Interpretative Memorandum of Title VII submitted by the Senate Floor Managers of the Civil Rights Bill. 110 Cong.Rec. 7212 (1964). The Memorandum referred to the BFOQ as a "limited exception" to the Act's prohibition against discrimination, conferring upon employers a "limited right to discriminate on the basis of religion, sex, or national origin where the reason for the discrimination is a bona fide occupational qualification." Id. at 7213. As examples of "legitimate discrimination," the memorandum cited "the preference of a French restaurant for a French cook, the preference of a professional baseball team for male players, and the preference of a business which seeks the patronage of members of particular religious groups for a salesman of that religion. * * * " Id. In Dothard v. Rawlinson, supra, 433 U.S. at 334, 97 S.Ct. at 2729, the Court cited the Memorandum in support of its conclusion that Congress intended the BFOQ as an "extremely narrow exception" to Title VII's prohibition against sex discrimination, ignoring Representative Goodell's broader construction. See Sirota, supra, note 12, at 1029 n.26. The Fifth Circuit in Swint v. Pullman-Standard, supra, 624 F.2d at 535, relied on this same Memorandum for the proposition that Congress intended that customer preference might be considered when applying the BFOQ exception.

The final indication of congressional intent is furnished by the Senate Debate on the Civil Rights Bill. By its actions, the Senate implied what it did not intend the BFOQ provision to mean. Pertinent to the inquiry in this case, the Senate defeated by a vote of 61 to 30 an amendment offered by Senator McClellan, which proposed that no unemployment practice would occur

> where *the employer involved believes*, on the basis of substantial evidence, that the hiring of such an individual of a particular race, color, sex, or national origin will be *more beneficial* to the normal

F.2d 983, 987 (D.C.Cir.1977); Sirota: "Sex Discrimination Title VII and the Bona Fide Occupational Qualification," 55 Tex.L.Rev. 1025, 1027 (1977).

13. Two other members inquired how the BFOQ would apply to specific situations, but their questions went unanswered. 110 Cong.Rec. 2720 (1964) (remarks of Reps. Mutler and Green).

14. See, e.g., Dothard v. Rawlinson, 433 U.S. 321, 334, 97 S.Ct. 2720, 2729, 53 L.Ed. 2d 786 (1977); Swint v. Pullman-Standard, supra, 624 F.2d at 535; Diaz v. Pan American World Airways, Inc., 311 F.Supp. 559, 569 (S.D.La.), rev'd 442 F.2d 385 (5th Cir.), cert. denied, 404 U.S. 950, 92 S.Ct. 275, 30 L.Ed.2d 267 (1971).

> operation of the particular business or enterprise involved, or to the *good will* thereof, than the hiring of an individual without consideration of his race, color, religion, sex or national origin, or * * * [where] an employer * * * fail[s] or refuse[s] to hire any individual in those certain instances where the employer involved believes, on the basis of substantial evidence, that the hiring of such individual would *not be in the best interests* of the particular business or enterprise involved, or for the *good will* thereof.

110 Cong.Rec. 13825–26 (1964) (emphasis added). See Barnes v. Costle, supra, 561 F.2d at 991 n.58. In debate, Senator McClellan had stated the amendment's purpose was to protect an employer's right to make hiring decisions based on its own business judgment. Senator Case, one of the Floor Managers, responded that passage of such a broad amendment would effectively nullify Title VII. As one commentator has noted, a plausible implication from defeat of the McClellan "best interests" Amendment, is that the Senate did not intend to weaken Title VII's prohibition against sex discrimination by allowing an employer to consider customer attitudes and preferences, a major component of good will, when making hiring decisions. See Sirota, supra, note 12, at 1030.

Early on, the Equal Employment Opportunity Commission ("EEOC"), created by Congress to administer Title VII, pronounced that "the bona fide occupational qualification as to sex should be interpreted narrowly." See EEOC Guidelines on Discrimination Because of Sex, 29 C.F.R. § 1604.2(a) (1965). The agency Guidelines further stated that the BFOQ exception did not justify "the refusal to hire an individual because of the preferences of * * * the employer, clients or customers," except where necessary for authenticity as provided in § 1604.2(a)(2). Id. at § 1604.2(a)(1)(iii); see also 1979 Guidebook to Fair Employment Practices (CCH).

To date, the Commission has steadfastly adhered to its position that customer preference gives rise to a bona fide occupational qualification for sex in one instance only, "[w]here it is necessary for the purpose of authenticity or genuineness * * * e.g. an actor or actress." Id. at § 1604.2(a)(2) as amended by 45 Fed.Reg. 74676 (Nov. 10, 1980). This exception is analogous to the example of a BFOQ for a French Cook in a French restaurant suggested by the Senate Floor Managers in their Interpretative Memorandum, supra, 110 Cong.Rec. at 7213 (1964).

An illustration of the EEOC's refusal to recognize a BFOQ for sex based on customer preference is EEOC Decision No. 71–2338, 1973 EEOC Dec. 4437 (1971). There, the Commission considered an employer's refusal to promote a female to the position of branch manager because the job involved accompanying male customers to football games, dinners and on hunting trips. The customer's preference for male hosts, the Commission held, did not warrant recognition of a BFOQ for sex. Id. at 4438. The EEOC also had occasion to consider an employer's refusal to hire a female as a courier guard-driver for an armored car. EEOC Decision No. 70–11, 1973 EEOC Dec. 4048 (1969). In rejecting the employer's defense that loss of customer confidence in the company's ability to provide security created a BFOQ for male sex, the Commission stated, "this argument is, in law, without merit, since it presumes that customers' desires may be accommodated even at the price of rendering nugatory the will of Congress." Id. at 4049. To this Court's knowledge, the EEOC has never recognized a BFOQ for sex except for positions in the entertainment industry where sex authenticity is an essential qualification.[15] See EEOC, "Toward Job Equality for Women" 5 (1969) (informal publication).

Those courts which have analyzed Title VII's BFOQ exception, however, have broadened its sweep. Consistent with the language of § 703(e), courts have held, or stated, that customer preference for one sex may be taken into account in those limited instances where satisfying customer preference is "reasonably necessary to the normal operation of the particular business or enterprise." See, e.g., Avigliano v. Sumitomo Shoji America, Inc., 638 F.2d 552 (2nd Cir. 1981).

This Circuit's decisions in Weeks v. Southern Bell Tel. & Tel. Co., 408 F.2d 228 (5th Cir. 1969) ("Weeks") and Diaz v. Pan American World Airways, Inc., 442 F.2d 385 (5th Cir.), cert. denied 404 U.S. 950, 92 S.Ct. 275, 30 L.Ed.2d 267 (1971) ("Diaz") have given rise to a two step BFOQ test: (1) does the particular *job* under consideration require that the worker be of one sex only; and if so, (2) is that requirement reasonably necessary to the "essence" of the employer's business. See, Usery v. Tamiami Trail Tours, Inc., 531 F.2d 224, 228 n.8, 234 nn.24–27 (5th Cir. 1976); [1977] Empl. Prac. Guide (CCH) ¶ 287. The first level of inquiry is designed to test whether sex is so essential to job performance that a member of the opposite sex simply could not do the same job. See Fernandez v. Wynn Oil Co., supra, 20 FEP Cases at 1164. As stated in *Weeks*, supra, 408 F.2d at 235:

> [T]o rely on the bona fide occupational qualification exception, an employer has the burden of proving that he had reasonable cause to believe, that is a factual basis for believing, that all or substantially all women would be unable to perform safely and efficiently the duties of the job involved.

The second level is designed to assure that the qualification being scrutinized is one so important to the operation of the business that the business would be undermined if employees of the "wrong" sex were hired. See, Usery v. Tamiami Trail Tours, Inc., supra, 531 F.2d at 235, n.27; Touhy v. Ford Motor Co., 22 FEP Cases 1492, 1494 (E.D.Mich. 1980). *Diaz's* "essence of the business" rule has now been adopted by

15. Deference is to be given the agency construction of the BFOQ exception because of its consistent adherence to and application of the "guidelines." Dothard v. Rawlinson, supra, 433 U.S. at 334, n.19, 97 S.Ct. at 2729, n.19; Diaz v. Pan American World Airways, Inc., supra, 442 F.2d at 389 (EEOC rejection of customer preference entitled to "great deference").

every Circuit that has considered the matter.[16] As the court there explained:

> * * * [T]he use of the word "necessary" in Section 703(e) requires that we apply a business *necessity* test, not a business *convenience* test. That is to say, discrimination based on sex is valid only when the *essence* of the business operation would be undermined by not hiring members of one sex exclusively.

Diaz, supra, 442 F.2d at 388 (original emphasis).[17]

Southwest concedes with respect to the *Weeks* test that males are able to perform safely and efficiently all the basic, mechanical functions required of flight attendants and ticket agents. Indeed, any argument to the contrary has been foreclosed by the decisions of this Circuit in *Diaz* and Hailes v. United Air Lines, 464 F.2d 1006, 1008 n.2 (5th Cir. 1972). ("It is settled law in this Circuit that female sex is not a bona fide occupational qualification for the position of airline cabin attendant"). See also, In re National Airlines, 14 FEP Cases 1806, 1816 (S.D.Fla.1977); EEOC Opinion, "Flight Cabin Attendant," 33 Fed.Reg. 3361 (1968).[18] Southwest's position, however, is that females are required to fulfill certain non-mechanical aspects of these jobs: to attract those male customers who prefer female attendants and ticket agents, and to preserve the authenticity and genuineness of Southwest's unique, female corporate personality.

A similar, though not identical, argument that females could better perform certain non-mechanical functions required of flight attendants was rejected in *Diaz.* There the airline argued and the trial court found that being female was a BFOQ because women were superior in "providing reassurance to anxious passengers, giving courteous personalized service and, in general, making flights as pleasurable as possible

16. Gunther v. Iowa State Men's Reformatory, 612 F.2d 1079, 1085 (8th Cir.) cert. denied 446 U.S. 966, 100 S.Ct. 2942, 64 L.Ed.2d 825 (1980); Arritt v. Grisell, 567 F.2d 1267, 1271 (4th Cir. 1977); Manhart v. Los Angeles Department of Water and Power, 553 F.2d 581, 587 (9th Cir. 1976), vacated on other grounds, 435 U.S. 702, 98 S.Ct. 1370, 55 L.Ed.2d 657 (1978); Hodgson v. Greyhound Lines, Inc., 499 F.2d 859, 862 (7th Cir. 1974) cert. denied sub nom., 419 U.S. 1122, 95 S.Ct. 805, 42 L.Ed.2d 822 (1975). See also, Dothard v. Rawlinson, supra, 433 U.S. at 333, 97 S.Ct. at 2728 (citing *Diaz* and *Weeks*).

17. Because *Diaz* adopted and added to the job based BFOQ test in *Weeks,* the decisional focus is not altogether clear. Although there is only one *Diaz* test, some courts have applied it in slightly different ways, at times focusing on the essence of the *employment position* in question, or the *particular business need* which the position fulfills, rather than focusing upon the relationship between the sex qualification and the essence of the *total business operation.* See, e.g., Swint v. Pullman-Standard, supra, 624 F.2d at 534 (dicta); Fernandez v. Wynn Oil Co., supra, 20 FEP Cases at 1165. See also Sirota, supra note 12, at 1043 n. 113. Practically, this difference in application will rarely be outcome determinative. A finding that one sex is essential to job performance will almost by necessity require the conclusion that the essence of the business operation would be undermined by not hiring members of that sex exclusively. The exception would be where the job or business need requiring employees of one sex only could be eliminated entirely without "undermining" the business itself. Such a situation is not presented here.

18. Citing numerous charges of airline discrimination against males, the EEOC in its 1968 "Flight Cabin Attendant" Opinion specifically concluded that "the basic duties of a flight cabin attendant * * * can be satisfactorily performed by members of both sexes."

within the limitations imposed by aircraft operations." Id. 442 F.2d at 387; 311 F.Supp. 559, 563 (S.D.Fla.1970). Although it accepted the trial court findings, the Court of Appeals reversed, holding that femininity was not a BFOQ, because catering to passengers psychological needs was only "tangential" to what was "reasonably *necessary*" for the business involved (original emphasis). Id. at 388. Characterizing the "essence" or "primary function" of Pan American's business as the safe transportation of passengers from one point to another, the court explained:

> While a pleasant environment, enhanced by the obvious cosmetic effect that female stewardesses provide as well as, according to the findings of the trial court, their apparent ability to perform the non-mechanical functions of the job in a more effective manner than most men, may all be important, they are tangential to the essence of the business involved. No one has suggested that having male stewards will so seriously affect the operation of the airline as to jeopardize or even minimize its ability to provide safe transportation from one place to another.

Id. at 388.

Similar reasoning underlay the appellate court's rejection of Pan American's claim that its customers' preference for female attendants justified its refusal to hire males.[19] Because the non-mechanical functions that passengers preferred females to perform were tangential to the airline's business, the court held, "the fact that customers prefer [females] cannot justify sex discrimination." Id. at 389. The Fifth Circuit in *Diaz* did not hold that customer preference could never give rise to a sex BFOQ. Rather, consistent with the EEOC's exception for authenticity and genuineness,[20] the Court allowed that customer preference could "be taken into account only when it is based on the company's inability to perform the primary function or service it offers," that is, where sex or sex appeal is itself the dominant service provided.[21]

Diaz and its progeny establish that to recognize a BFOQ for jobs requiring multiple abilities, some sex-linked and some sex-neutral, the sex-linked aspects of the job must predominate. Only then will an employer have satisfied *Weeks'* requirement that sex be so essential to successful job performance that a member of the opposite sex could not

19. Based upon a "scientific" opinion survey conducted by the Air Transport Association of America, as well as other evidence, the district court found that "Pan Am's passengers overwhelmingly prefer to be served by female stewardesses."

20. 29 C.F.R. 1604.2(a)(2) as amended by 45 Fed.Reg. 74676.

21. Except under limited circumstances, the *Diaz* court reasoned, the purpose of Title VII to overcome stereotyped thinking about the job abilities of the sexes would be undermined if customer expectations, preferences, and prejudices were allowed to determine the validity of sex discrimination in employment. Id. at 389; see also, Long v. Sapp, 502 F.2d 34, 40 (5th Cir. 1974) (subjective doubts about the ability of one sex to perform a particular job, which may themselves be based upon impermissible stereotypes, are no substitute for the objective evidence demanded by *Weeks*).

perform the job. An illustration of such dominance in sex cases is the exception recognized by the EEOC for authenticity and genuineness. Supra at note 20. In the example given in § 1604.2(a)(2), that of an actor or actress, the primary function of the position, its essence, is to fulfill the audience's expectation and desire for a particular role, characterized by particular physical or emotional traits. Generally, a male could not supply the authenticity required to perform a female role. Similarly, in jobs where sex or vicarious sexual recreation is the primary service provided, e.g. a social escort or topless dancer, the job automatically calls for one sex exclusively; the employee's sex and the service provided are inseparable. Thus, being female has been deemed a BFOQ for the position of a Playboy Bunny, female sexuality being reasonably necessary to perform the dominant purpose of the job which is forthrightly to titillate and entice male customers. See St. Cross v. Playboy Club, Appeal No. 773, Case No. CFS 22618–70 (New York Human Rights Appeal Board, 1971) (dicta); Weber v. Playboy Club, Appeal No. 774, Case No. CFS 22619–70 (New York Human Rights Appeal Board, 1971) (dicta). One court has also suggested, without holding, that the authenticity exception would give rise to a BFOQ for Chinese nationality where necessary to maintain the authentic atmosphere of an ethnic Chinese restaurant, Utility Workers v. Southern California Edison, 320 F.Supp. 1262, 1265 (C.D.Cal.1970).[22] Consistent with the language of *Diaz*, customer preference for one sex only in such a case would logically be so strong that the employer's ability to perform the primary function or service offered would be undermined by not hiring members of the authentic sex or group exclusively.[23]

The Court is aware of only one decision where sex was held to be a BFOQ for an occupation not providing primarily sex oriented services. In Fernandez v. Wynn Oil Co., 20 FEP Cases 1162 (C.D.Cal.1979), the court approved restricting to males the job of international marketing director for a company with extensive overseas operations. The position involved primarily attracting and transacting business with Latin American and Southeast Asian customers who would not feel comfortable doing business with a woman. The court found that the customers' attitudes, customs, and mores relating to the proper business roles of the sexes created formidable obstacles to successful job performance by a woman. South American distributors and customers, for example,

22. Similarly in Avigliano v. Sumitomo Shoji America, Inc., 638 F.2d 552 (2d Cir. 1981), the Second Circuit remanded for a determination whether being of Japanese nationality was a BFOQ for management positions in a Japanese firm's U.S. subsidiary.

23. Customer preference may also give rise to a BFOQ for one sex where the preference is based upon a desire for sexual privacy. The privacy right has been recognized in a variety of situations, including disrobing, sleeping, or performing bodily functions in the presence of the opposite sex. See, e.g., Fesel v. Masonic Home of Delaware, Inc., 428 F.Supp. 573 (D.Del. 1977); Mieth v. Dothard, 418 F.Supp. 1169, 1184–85 (M.D.Ala.1976) (three-judge District Court) aff'd in part, rev'd in part sub nom. Dothard v. Rawlinson, 433 U.S. 321, 97 S.Ct. 2720, 53 L.Ed.2d 786 (1977); Reynolds v. Wise, 375 F.Supp. 145, 151 (N.D.Tex.1973); EEOC, Toward Job Equality for Woman 5 (1969). See also, Sirota, supra, note 12, at 1060–65.

would have been offended by a woman conducting business meetings in her hotel room. Applying the *Diaz* test, the court concluded that hiring a female as international marketing director "would have totally subverted any business [defendant] hoped to accomplish in those areas of the world." Id. at 1165.[24] Because hiring a male was *necessary* to the Defendant's ability to continue its foreign operations, sex was deemed a BFOQ for the marketing position.

Application of the Bona Fide Occupational Qualification to Southwest Airlines

Applying the first level test for a BFOQ, with its legal gloss, to Southwest's particular operations results in the conclusion that being female is not a qualification required to perform successfully the jobs of flight attendant and ticket agent with Southwest. Like any other airline, Southwest's primary function is to transport passengers safely and quickly from one point to another.[25] See, e.g., *Diaz*, supra, 442 F.2d at 388. To do this, Southwest employs ticket agents whose primary job duties are to ticket passengers and check baggage, and flight attendants, whose primary duties are to assist passengers during boarding and deboarding, to instruct passengers in the location and use of aircraft safety equipment, and to serve passengers cocktails and snacks during the airline's short commuter flights. Mechanical, non-sex-linked duties dominate both these occupations. Indeed, on Southwest's short-haul commuter flights there is time for little else. That Southwest's female personnel may perform their mechanical duties "with love" does not change the result. "Love" is the manner of job performance, not the job performed.

While possession of female allure and sex appeal have been made qualifications for Southwest's contact personnel by virtue of the "love" campaign, the functions served by employee sexuality in Southwest's operations are not dominant ones. According to Southwest, female sex appeal serves two purposes: (1) attracting and entertaining male passengers and (2) fulfilling customer expectations for female service engendered by Southwest's advertising which features female personnel. As in *Diaz*, these non-mechanical, sex-linked job functions are only "tangential" to the essence of the occupations and business in-

24. In reaching its conclusion, the court followed *Diaz* in adopting a very narrow standard for weighing customer preference, stating:

> Customer preferences should not be bootstrapped to the level of business necessity. The only occasion where customer preference will rise to the dignity of a bona fide occupational qualification is where no customer will do business with a member of one sex either because it would destroy the essence of the business or would create serious safety and efficiency problems.

Id. at 1165.

25. Southwest's argument that its primary function is "to make a profit," not to transport passengers, must be rejected. Without doubt the goal of every business is to make a profit. For purposes of BFOQ analysis, however, the business "essence" inquiry focuses on the particular service provided and the job tasks and functions involved, not the business goal. If an employer could justify employment discrimination merely on the grounds that it is necessary to make a profit, Title VII would be nullified in short order.

volved. Southwest is not a business where vicarious sex entertainment is the primary service provided. Accordingly, the ability of the airline to perform its primary business function, the transportation of passengers, would not be jeopardized by hiring males.

Southwest does not face the situation anticipated in *Diaz* [26] and encountered in *Fernandez* where an established customer preference for one sex is so strong that the business would be undermined if employees of the opposite sex were hired. Southwest's claim that its customers prefer females rests primarily upon inferences drawn from the airline's success after adopting its female personality. But according to Southwest's own surveys, that success is attributable to many factors. There is no competent proof that Southwest's popularity derives directly from its females-only policy to the exclusion of other factors like dissatisfaction with rival airlines and Southwest's use of convenient Love and Hobby Fields. Nor is there competent proof that the customer preference for females is so strong that Defendant's male passengers would cease doing business with Southwest as was the case in *Fernandez*. In short, Southwest has failed in its proof to satisfy *Diaz's* business necessity requirement, without which customer preference may not give rise to a BFOQ for sex.

Southwest contends, nevertheless, that its females-only policy is reasonably necessary to the continued success of its "love" marketing campaign. Airline management testified that Southwest's customers will be disappointed if they find male employees after seeing only female personnel advertised. As a matter of law, this argument fails to support a BFOQ for sex. The court in *Diaz* emphasized that its test was one of business *necessity*, not business *convenience*. *Diaz,* supra, 442 F.2d at 388; Fernandez v. Wynn Oil Co., supra, 20 FEP at 1164. In Weeks v. Southern Bell Telephone and Telegraph Co., supra, 408 F.2d at 234–35, the Fifth Circuit expressly disapproved of the broad construction of the BFOQ exception in Bowe v. Colgate Palmolive Co., 272 F.Supp. 332, 362 (S.D.Ind.1967), aff'd in part and rev'd in part 416 F.2d 711 (7th Cir. 1969) which would have permitted sex discrimination where sex was "rationally related to an end which [the employer] has a right to achieve—production, profit, or business reputation."

It is also relevant that Southwest's female image was adopted at its discretion, to promote a business unrelated to sex. Contrary to the unyielding South American preference for males encountered by the Defendant company in *Fernandez*, Southwest exploited, indeed nurtured, the very customer preference for females it now cites to justify discriminating against males. See note 21, supra. Moreover, the fact that a vibrant marketing campaign was necessary to distinguish Southwest in its early years does not lead to the conclusion that sex discrimination was then, or is now, a business *necessity*. Southwest's

26. To reiterate, the Fifth Circuit in *Diaz*, supra, 442 F.2d at 389, announced that "* * * customer preference may be taken into account only when it is based on the company's inability to perform the primary function or service it offers."

claim that its female image will be tarnished by hiring males is, in any case, speculative at best.

The few cases on point support the conclusion that sex does not become a BFOQ merely because an employer chooses to exploit female sexuality as a marketing tool, or to better insure profitability. In Guardian Capital Corp. v. New York State Division of Human Rights, 46 App.Div.2d 832, 360 N.Y.S.2d 937 (1974), *app. dismissed* 48 A.D.2d 753, 368 N.Y.S.2d 594 (1975) for example, the court prohibited an employer from firing male waiters to hire sexually attractive waitresses in an attempt to change the appeal of the business and boost sales. Similarly, in University Parking, Inc. v. Hotel and Restaurant Employees & Bartenders' Int'l Un., 71–2 Lab.Arb.Awards 5360 (1971) (Peck, Arb.), the arbitrator denied an employer's right to replace three waitresses with waiters in order to "upgrade" his business and respond to customer desires for "classier" French service.[27] Merely because Southwest's female image was established in "good faith" [28] and has become its trademark does not distinguish Defendant's conduct from the discriminatory business decisions disapproved of in these cases.

Neither, in the final analysis, does Southwest's "battle-for-inches" with its competitors rise to the level of business *necessity.* *Diaz's* necessity test focuses on the company's ability "to perform the primary function or service it offers," not its ability to compete. *Diaz*, supra, 442 F.2d at 389. As one court has noted in the context of racial discrimination, "[t]he expense involved in changing from a discriminatory system * * * [fails to constitute] a business necessity that would justify the continuation of * * * discrimination." Bush v. Lone Star Steel Co., 373 F.Supp. 526, 533 (E.D.Tex.1974); see also Robinson v. Lorillard Corp., 444 F.2d 791, 799 n. 8 (4th Cir.), cert. dismissed 404 U.S. 1006, 92 S.Ct. 573, 30 L.Ed.2d 655 (1971) ("dollar cost alone is not determinative"). Similarly, a potential loss of profits or possible loss of competitive advantage following a shift to non-discriminatory hiring does not establish business necessity under *Diaz*. To hold otherwise would permit employers within the same industry to establish different hiring standards based on the financial condition of their respective businesses. A rule prohibiting only financially successful enterprises from discriminating under Title VII, while allowing their less successful competitors to ignore the law, has no merit.

Southwest, however, has failed to establish by competent proof that revenue loss would result directly from hiring males. Analogous to the holding in Guardian Capital Corp. v. New York State Division of Human Rights, supra, 360 N.Y.S.2d at 938–39, an employer's mere

27. The EEOC reached the same result in EEOC Decision No. YSF–9–058 1973 EEOC Dec. 4125 (1969).

28. Under Title VII, it is immaterial that Southwest's feminized marketing strategy was conceived and implemented in "good faith," not in a desire to discriminate against males. Even in cases of unintentional discrimination, the absence of bad motive or intent does not redeem employment practices with forbidden discriminatory consequences. See Griggs v. Duke Power Co., 401 U.S. 424, 432, 91 S.Ct. 849, 854, 28 L.Ed.2d 158 (1971); Vuyanich v. Republic National Bank, 78 F.R.D. 352, 358 (N.D.Tex.1978).

"beforehand belief" that sex discrimination is a financial imperative, alone, does not establish a BFOQ for sex.

Conclusion

In rejecting Southwest's BFOQ defense, this court follows Justice Marshall's admonition that the BFOQ exception should not be permitted to "swallow the rule." See Phillips v. Martin Marietta Corp., 400 U.S. 542, 545, 91 S.Ct. 496, 498, 27 L.Ed.2d 613 (1971) (Marshall, J. concurring). Southwest's position knows no principled limit. Recognition of a sex BFOQ for Southwest's public contact personnel based on the airline's "love" compaign opens the door for other employers freely to discriminate by tacking on sex or sex appeal as a qualification for any public contact position where customers preferred employees of a particular sex.[29] In order not to undermine Congress' purpose to prevent employers from "refusing to hire an individual based on stereotyped characterizations of the sexes," see Phillips v. Martin Marietta Corp., supra, 400 U.S. at 545, 91 S.Ct. at 498, a BFOQ for sex must be denied where sex is merely useful for attracting customers of the opposite sex, but where hiring both sexes will not alter or undermine the essential function of the employer's business. Rejecting a wider BFOQ for sex does not eliminate the commercial exploitation of sex appeal. It only requires, consistent with the purposes of Title VII, that employers exploit the attractiveness and allure of a sexually integrated workforce. Neither Southwest, nor the traveling public, will suffer from such a rule. More to the point, it is my judgment that this is what Congress intended.

One final observation is called for. This case has serious underpinnings, but it also has disquieting strains. These strains, and they were only that, warn that in our quest for non-racist, non-sexist goals, the demand for equal rights can be pushed to silly extremes. The rule of law in this country is so firmly embedded in our ethical regimen that little can stand up to its force—except literalistic insistence upon one's rights. And such inability to absorb the minor indignities suffered daily by us all without running to court may stop it dead in its tracks. We do not have such a case here—only warning signs rumbling from the facts.

NOTES AND PROBLEMS FOR DISCUSSION

1. If a loss of revenue or competitive advantage from the abandonment of a sexually discriminatory hiring practice will not, as a matter of law, establish sex as a BFOQ, why did the district court in *Wilson* allow the admission of such evidence? Given the fact that the airline's "primary business function" will continue to be the transportation of passengers, is there any way for Southwest to maintain its successful image without running afoul of Title VII? Compare, Chambers v. Omaha Girls Club, 629 F.Supp. 925 (D.Neb.1986).

29. See Note: "Developments in the Law—Employment Discrimination and Title VII of the Civil Rights Act of 1964," 84 Harv.L.Rev. 1109, 1185 (1971).

Except in the "authenticity" type case (as in a male preferred for role of *Hamlet*), the employer's perception of the physical inability of those of a particular sex to perform given job functions has never sustained a BFOQ defense. See Rosenfeld v. Southern Pacific Co., 444 F.2d 1219 (9th Cir. 1971); Bowe v. Colgate-Palmolive Co., 416 F.2d 711 (7th Cir. 1969); Weeks v. Southern Bell Telephone & Telegraph Co., 408 F.2d 228 (5th Cir. 1969). As noted in the *Wilson* opinion, efforts to justify discriminatory hiring practices on the basis of sexually stereotyped customer preferences have also met with little success. The BFOQ holding in Fernandez v. Wynn Oil Co., that hiring a male was necessary to the employer's continued foreign business, was reversed by the Ninth Circuit on the ground that foreign prejudice against women in business cannot justify non-enforcement of Title VII in this country. 653 F.2d 1273 (9th Cir. 1981). Cf. Avigliano v. Sumitomo Shoji America, Inc., 638 F.2d 552 (2d Cir. 1981), reversed on other grounds 456 U.S. 912, 102 S.Ct. 1764, 72 L.Ed.2d 171 (1982) ("acceptability to those persons with whom the company or branch does business" is one factor to be considered in determining whether executive position in American branch of Japanese company can be restricted to Japanese national).

If an airline cannot justify hiring only female flight attendants as necessary to its image, can it at least demand that its female attendants remain sexually attractive—i.e. slender? In Gerdom v. Continental Airlines, Inc., 692 F.2d 602 (9th Cir.1982) cert. dismissed, 460 U.S. 1074, 103 S.Ct. 1534, 75 L.Ed.2d 954 (1983), the Ninth Circuit rejected the defendants' argument that its weight restrictions for flight attendants (all of whom were female) was merely a sex-neutral "grooming" requirement outside of the purview of Title VII and held that the rule did not qualify as a BFOQ because, "Continental does not argue that only thin females can do the job." The airline's reliance on customer preference for slender female attendants was rejected for the same reasons as those expressed in *Wilson*. If the airline had employed male flight attendants who were subject to the same weight rules as the females, would the employer have to produce a business justification of any kind for its policy? Could an employer's desire that its employees be "real," ie. biological, men or women, qualify as a BFOQ? Would such a defense be necessary for the employer who discharged an otherwise qualified transsexual? See, Ulane v. Eastern Airlines, Inc., 581 F.Supp. 821 (N.D.Ill.1983), reversed, 742 F.2d 1081 (7th Cir.1984), cert. denied, ___ U.S. ___, 105 S.Ct. 2023, 85 L.Ed.2d 304 (1985).

Employers have met with more success in basing BFOQ on customer desires where those desires are related to personal privacy and modesty. In Fesel v. Masonic Home of Delaware, Inc., 447 F.Supp. 1346 (D.Del.1978), affirmed, 591 F.2d 1334 (3d Cir. 1979), numerous residents of a nursing home stated that they would leave if it abandoned its policy of hiring only female nurses. The court held that the home had sustained its burden of proving that the essence of its business would be undermined by employing members of the opposite sex:

> While these attitudes may be characterized as "customer preference," this is, nevertheless, not the kind of case governed by the regulatory provision that customer preference alone cannot justify a job qualification based upon sex. Here personal privacy interests are implicated which are protected by law and which have to be recognized by the employer in running its business.

447 F.Supp. at 1352. See also Backus v. Baptist Medical Center, 510 F.Supp. 1191 (E.D.Ark.1981) (hospital's exclusion of male nurses from obstetrics and gynecology department upheld as BFOQ); Philadelphia v. Pennsylvania

Human Relations Commission, 7 Pa.Commw. 500, 300 A.2d 97 (1973) (youth center whose personnel were required to monitor showers and conduct body searches allowed to restrict hiring to persons of same sex as inmates). As part of the employer's burden of proving BFOQ based on the privacy rights of others, however, it will be required to show that no selective system of job assignments could be made which would protect privacy and allow the employment of members of both sexes). See Backus v. Baptist Medical Center, supra, 510 F.Supp. at 1197; Fesel v. Masonic Homes of Delaware, supra, 447 F.Supp. at 1351. A minor, but certainly note-worthy, exception to the general rule that a BFOQ cannot be based in the discriminatory preference of customers, was established in Kern v. Dynalectron Corp., 577 F.Supp. 1196 (N.D.Tex.1983) aff'd, 746 F.2d 810 (5th Cir. 1984) which held that an employer's requirement that helicopter pilots hired to fly into Mecca be Moslem (adopted to comply with Arabian Law which prohibits entry of non-Moslems into Mecca) is a BFOQ, exempt from the religious discrimination provisions of Title VII. The district courts' opinion also deserves at least Honorable Mention in the category of judicial understatement.

> The Defendants' burden of producing a legitimate reason for the existing discrimination is properly sustained through the application of the B.F.O.Q. exception to Kern's case. * * * [T]his Court held that Dynalectron has proven a factual basis for believing that *all* non-Moslems would be unable to perform this job safely. Specifically, non-Moslems flying into Mecca are, if caught, beheaded.
>
> * * * [T]he essence of Dynalectron's business is to provide helicopter pilots * * * [t]hus, the essence of Dynalectron's business would be undermined by the beheading of all the non-Moslem pilots based in Jeddah.

577 F.Supp. at 1200. But in Abrams v. Baylor College of Medicine, 581 F.Supp. 1570 (S.D.Tex.1984), the court concluded that the "patronizing, paternalistic 'concerns'" of a medical school for the safety of Jewish staff members, did not justify, either under the BFOQ or business necessity rationales, its policy of excluding such employees from a program in Saudi Arabia. See, EEOC Decision No. 85–10 (1985), 38 FEP Cases 1873 (employer who refuses to hire woman for work in foreign country because it believes that country prohibits commingling of men and women in workplace will have its proffered reason for rejecting applicant viewed as pretextual unless it has "current, authoritative, and factual basis for its belief").

2. In Dothard v. Rawlinson, 433 U.S. 321, 97 S.Ct. 2720, 53 L.Ed.2d 786 (1977). Concerns for institutional or public safety have also underlaid successful BFOQ defenses. While the Court struck down Alabama's height and weight requirements for prison personnel as not justified by business necessity, it upheld a regulation explicitly barring employment of females in "contact positions" in all male penitentiaries as a BFOQ. Citing the "rampant violence" and "jungle atmosphere" in the state's prisons, the Court stated that:

> The essence of a correctional counselor's job is to maintain prison security. A woman's relative ability to maintain order in a male maximum-security unclassified penitentiary of the type Alabama now runs could be directly reduced by her womanhood.
>
> * * *
>
> The likelihood that inmates would assault a woman because she was a woman would pose a real threat not only to the victim of the assault but also to the basic control of the penitentiary and protection of its inmates and

> the other security personnel. The employee's very womanhood would then directly undermine her capacity to provide the security that is the essence of a correctional counselor's responsibility.

433 U.S. at 335, 336, 97 S.Ct. at 2729, 2730. Since *Dothard*, efforts to exclude females from institutional positions in prisons on "personal privacy" or safety grounds have met with little success. See e.g., Gunther v. Iowa State Men's Reformatory, 612 F.2d 1079, 1085–86 (8th Cir.), cert. denied, 446 U.S. 966, 100 S.Ct. 2942, 64 L.Ed.2d 825 (1980) (since Iowa prison was not the "stygian spectre" involved in *Dothard*, it was unlawful to exclude females from contact positions); Griffin v. Michigan Department of Corrections, 31 EPD ¶ 33,482 (E.D.Mich.1982) (neither prison security nor inmate privacy justified refusal to promote female to work as guard in men's prison); Hardin v. Stynchcomb, 691 F.2d 1364 (11th Cir. 1982) (inmate privacy no justification for refusal to hire female jail guards). Could hostile atmosphere in workplace undergoing desegregation justify requiring black applicants for supervisory position to be better qualified than white applicants? See, Parson v. Kaiser Aluminum & Chemical Corp., 727 F.2d 473 (5th Cir. 1984).

3. Section 703(e), which permits discrimination where sex, religion or national origin is a BFOQ, omits race from these exceptions to Title VII's requirements. It is permissible to take race into account in order to remedy past discrimination, Fullilove v. Klutznick, 448 U.S. 448, 100 S.Ct. 2758, 65 L.Ed.2d 902 (1980), United Steelworkers of America v. Weber, 443 U.S. 193, 99 S.Ct. 2721, 61 L.Ed.2d 480 (1979), but job assignments based on the racial stereotype that blacks work better with blacks constitutes a violation of Title VII. See Knight v. Nassau County Civil Service Commission, 649 F.2d 157 (2d Cir.), cert. denied, 454 U.S. 818, 102 S.Ct. 97, 70 L.Ed.2d 87 (1981); Miller v. Texas State Board of Barber Examiners, 615 F.2d 650 (5th Cir.), cert. denied, 449 U.S. 891, 101 S.Ct. 249, 66 L.Ed.2d 117 (1980). Unlike BFOQ, the business necessity defense can be raised in a racial discrimination case. Aside from that factor, is there any other significant difference between the business necessity and BFOQ defenses? See Harriss v. Pan American World Airways, Inc., 649 F.2d 670 (9th Cir. 1980).

4. What burden does the court in Wilson v. Southwest Airlines place on the defendant? Compare Backus v. Baptist Medical Center, supra, 510 F.Supp. at 1198 (employer has only to explain clearly the defense under *Burdine*) with Criswell v. Western Airlines, Inc., supra, 514 F.Supp. at 389 n.7 (defendant must establish BFOQ by a preponderance of the evidence). What, indeed, is the difference, if any, between raising a BFOQ defense and stating a non-discriminatory reason for the allegedly discriminatory act? See Saunders v. Hercules, Inc., 510 F.Supp. 1137, 1141–42 (W.D.Va.1981); Johnson v. Uncle Ben's, Inc., 657 F.2d 750, 752–53 (5th Cir. 1981). Is a finding that sex is or is not a BFOQ a finding of fact subject to Rule 52(a)'s "clearly erroneous" standard of review, or a mixed question of fact and law? See Smallwood v. United Airlines, 661 F.2d 303 (4th Cir. 1981); Dolter v. Wahlert High School, 483 F.Supp. 266 (N.D. Iowa 1980).

5. Should an employer's "fetal vulnerability" program, which excludes fertile women from jobs involving exposure to toxic chemicals, be analyzed as (1) a prima facie case of disparate treatment case which only obligates the employer to articulate a non-discriminatory reason for the policy; (2) a case where intentional sex discrimination has been established that can only be overcome by the statutory bona fide occupational qualification (b.f.o.q.) defense ; or (3) as a disproportionate impact case which casts on the employer the burden

of establishing the business necessity of the policy? On the one hand, such a policy can apply only to women, making it something like an explicit sexual classification. On the other hand, the policy is case in gender-neutral terms and does not affect all women simply because of their sex, making it somewhat like height and weight restrictions which impact predominantly on women. Recognizing that such a program does not fit precisely into any of the developed theories, the Fourth Circuit in Wright v. Olin Corp., 697 F.2d 1172 (4th Cir. 1982), concluded that the disparate impact-business necessity theory of claim and defense should be utilized and held that "under appropriate circumstances an employer may, as a matter of business necessity, impose otherwise impermissible restrictions on employment opportunity that are reasonably required to protect the health of unborn children of women workers against hazards of the workplace." 697 F.2d at 1189–1190. The Court also outlined how the defense may be established: (1) The burden is on the employer to prove the existence of significant risks of harm to the unborn children of female workers from their exposure during pregnancy to toxic chemicals in the workplace and that the hazard can be effectively eliminated by the policy; (2) The effectiveness of the actual program and the reality of the danger must be proved by the opinion evidence of qualified experts in relevant scientific fields; (3) To establish the requisite degree of risk of harm, it is not necessary to prove the existence of a general consensus on the issue within the qualified scientific community, but only to show that within that community there is so considerable a body of opinion that significant risk exists that an informed employer could not responsibly fail to act on the assumption that the opinion might be an accurate one. The prima facie defense may be rebutted by proof that there are acceptable alternative policies that would accomplish the business purpose. By showing an acceptable alternative that would accomplish the protective purpose equally well with less differential impact, the plaintiff may not only negate the employer's defense, but may prove that, behind the proven but prima facie-justified disparate impact of the program, there lay in fact discriminatory intent. 697 F.2d at 1190–92. Compare, Zuniga v. Kleberg County Hospital, 692 F.2d 986 (5th Cir.1982) and Hayes v. Shelby Memorial Hospital, 726 F.2d 1543 (11th Cir.1983) (discharge of pregnant X-ray technician, allegedly because of fear of harm to fetus, shown to be pretext for overt discrimination by proof of alternative, less discriminatory means of achieving business purpose). See also, Levin v. Delta Airlines, Inc., 730 F.2d 994 (5th Cir.1984) (airline's concern for passenger safety justified a blanket exclusion of pregnant stewardesses from flight duty).

c. Bona Fide Seniority Systems

INTERNATIONAL BROTHERHOOD OF TEAMSTERS v. UNITED STATES

Supreme Court of the United States, 1977.
431 U.S. 324, 97 S.Ct. 1843, 52 L.Ed.2d 396.

[The Court's discussion of the government's proof of post-Act discrimination is omitted].

MR. JUSTICE STEWART delivered the opinion of the Court.

This litigation brings here several important questions under Title VII of the Civil Rights Act of 1964. The issues grow out of alleged unlawful employment practices engaged in by an employer and a union. The employer is a common carrier of motor freight with nationwide operations, and the union represents a large group of its employees. The District Court and the Court of Appeals held that the employer had violated Title VII by engaging in a pattern and practice of employment discrimination against Negroes and Spanish-surnamed Americans, and that the union had violated the Act by agreeing with the employer to create and maintain a seniority system that perpetuated the effects of past racial and ethnic discrimination. In addition to the basic questions presented by these two rulings, other subsidiary issues must be resolved if violations of Title VII occurred—issues concerning the nature of the relief to which aggrieved individuals may be entitled.

I

The United States brought an action in a Tennessee federal court against the petitioner T.I.M.E.–D.C., Inc. (the company), pursuant to § 707(a) of the Civil Rights Act of 1964.[1] The complaint charged that the company had followed discriminatory hiring, assignment, and promotion policies against Negroes at its terminal in Nashville, Tenn.[2] The Government brought a second action against the company almost three years later in a Federal District Court in Texas, charging a pattern and practice of employment discrimination against Negroes and Spanish-surnamed persons throughout the company's transportation system. The petitioner International Brotherhood of Teamsters (union) was joined as a defendant in that suit. The two actions were consolidated for trial in the Northern District of Texas.

The central claim in both lawsuits was that the company had engaged in a pattern or practice of discriminating against minorities in

1. At the time of suit the statute provided as follows:

> "(a) Whenever the Attorney General has reasonable cause to believe that any person or group of persons is engaged in a pattern or practice of resistance to the full enjoyment of any of the rights secured by this subchapter, and that the pattern or practice is of such a nature and is intended to deny the full exercise of the rights herein described, the Attorney General may bring a civil action in the appropriate district court of the United States by filing with it a complaint (1) signed by him (or in his absence the Acting Attorney General), (2) setting forth facts pertaining to such pattern or practice, and (3) requesting such relief, including an application for a permanent or temporary injunction, restraining order or other order against the person or persons responsible for such pattern or practice, as he deems necessary to insure the full enjoyment of the rights herein described."

Section 707 was amended by § 5 of the Equal Employment Opportunity Act of 1972, 86 Stat. 107, 42 U.S.C. § 2000e–6(c) (1970 ed., Supp. V), to give the equal Employment Opportunity Commission, rather than the Attorney General, the authority to bring "pattern or practice" suits under that section against private-sector employers. In 1974, an order was entered in this action substituting the EEOC for the United States but retaining the United States as a party for purposes of jurisdiction, appealability, and related matters. See 42 U.S.C. § 2000e–6(d) (1970 ed., Supp. V).

2. The named defendant in this suit was T.I.M.E. Freight, Inc., a predecessor of T.I.M.E.–D.C., Inc. T.I.M.E.–D.C., Inc., is a nationwide system produced by 10 mergers over a 17-year period. See United States v. T.I.M.E.–D.C., Inc., 517 F.2d 299, 304, and n. 6 (CA5). It currently has 51 terminals and operates in 26 States and three Canadian Provinces.

hiring so-called line drivers. Those Negroes and Spanish-surnamed persons who had been hired, the Government alleged, were given lower paying, less desirable jobs as servicemen or local city drivers, and were thereafter discriminated against with respect to promotions and transfers.[3] In this connection the complaint also challenged the seniority system established by the collective-bargaining agreements between the employer and the union. The Government sought a general injunctive remedy and specific "make whole" relief for all individual discriminatees, which would allow them an opportunity to transfer to line-driver jobs with full company seniority for all purposes.

The cases went to trial[4] and the District Court found that the Government had shown "by a preponderance of the evidence that T.I.M.E.–D.C. and its predecessor companies were engaged in a plan and practice of discrimination in violation of Title VII * * *."[5] The court further found that the seniority system contained in the collective-bargaining contracts between the company and the union violated Title VII because it "operate[d] to impede the free transfer of minority groups into and within the company." Both the company and the union were enjoined from committing further violations of Title VII.

3. *Line drivers*, also known as over-the-road drivers, engage in long-distance hauling between company terminals. They compose a separate bargaining unit at the company. C. Other distinct bargaining units include *servicemen*, who service trucks, unhook tractors and trailers, and perform similar tasks; and *city operations*, composed of dockmen, hostlers, and city drivers who pick up and deliver freight within the immediate area of a particular terminal. All of these employees were represented by the petitioner union.

4. Following the receipt of evidence, but before decision, the Government and the company consented to the entry of a Decree in Partial Resolution of Suit. The consent decree did not constitute an adjudication on the merits. The company agreed, however, to undertake a minority recruiting program; to accept applications from all Negroes and Spanish-surnamed Americans who inquired about employment, whether or not vacancies existed, and to keep such applications on file and notify applicants of job openings; to keep specific employment and recruiting records open to inspection by the Government and to submit quarterly reports to the District Court; and to adhere to certain uniform employment qualifications respecting hiring and promotion to line driver and other jobs.

The decree further provided that future job vacancies at any company terminal would be filled first "[b]y those persons who may be found by the Court, if any, to be individual or class discriminatees suffering the present effects of past discrimination because of race or national origin prohibited by Title VII of the Civil Rights Act of 1964." Any remaining vacancies could be filled by "any other persons," but the company obligated itself to hire one Negro or Spanish-surnamed person for every white person hired at any terminal until the percentage of minority workers at that terminal equaled the percentage of minority group members in the population of the metropolitan area surrounding the terminal. Finally, the company agreed to pay $89,500 in full settlement of any backpay obligations. Of this sum, individual payments not exceeding $1,500 were to be paid to "alleged individual and class discriminatees" identified by the Government.

The Decree in Partial Resolution of Suit narrowed the scope of the litigation, but the District Court still had to determine whether unlawful discrimination had occurred. If so, the court had to identify the actual discriminatees entitled to fill future job vacancies under the decree. The validity of the collective-bargaining contract's seniority system also remained for decision, as did the question whether any discriminatees should be awarded additional equitable relief such as retroactive seniority.

5. The District Court's memorandum decision is reported at 6 FEP Cases 690 (1974) and 6 EPD ¶ 8979 (1973–1974).

With respect to individual relief the court accepted the Government's basic contention that the "affected class" of discriminatees included all Negro and Spanish-surnamed incumbent employees who had been hired to fill city operations or serviceman jobs at every terminal that had a line-driver operation.[6] All of these employees, whether hired before or after the effective date of Title VII, thereby became entitled to preference over all other applicants with respect to consideration for future vacancies in line-driver jobs.[7] Finding that members of the affected class had been injured in different degrees, the court created three subclasses. Thirty persons who had produced "the most convincing evidence of discrimination and harm" were found to have suffered "severe injury." The court ordered that they be offered the opportunity to fill line-driver jobs with competitive seniority dating back to July 2, 1965, the effective date of Title VII.[8] A second subclass included four persons who were "very possibly the objects of discrimination" and who "were likely harmed," but as to whom there had been no specific evidence of discrimination and injury. The court decreed that these persons were entitled to fill vacancies in line-driving jobs with competitive seniority as of January 14, 1971, the date on which the Government had filed its systemwide lawsuit. Finally, there were over 300 remaining members of the affected class as to whom there was "no evidence to show that these individuals were either harmed or not harmed individually." The court ordered that they be considered for line-driver jobs[9] ahead of any applicants from the general public but behind the two other subclasses. Those in the third subclass received no retroactive seniority; their competitive seniority as line drivers would begin with the date they were hired as line drivers. The court further decreed that the right of any class member to fill a line-driver vacancy was subject to the prior recall rights of laid-off line drivers, which under the collective-bargaining agreements then in effect extended for three years.[10]

6. The Government did not seek relief for Negroes and Spanish-surnamed Americans hired at a particular terminal after the date on which that terminal first employed a minority group member as a line driver.

7. See n. 4, supra.

8. If an employee in this class had joined the company after July 2, 1965, then the date of his initial employment rather than the effective date of Title VII was to determine his competitive seniority.

9. As with the other subclasses, there were a few individuals in the third group who were found to have been discriminated against with respect to jobs other than line driver. There is no need to discuss them separately in this opinion.

10. This provision of the decree was qualified in one significant respect. Under the Southern Conference Area Over-the-Road Supplemental Agreement between the employer and the union, line drivers employed at terminals in certain Southern States work under a "modified" seniority system. Under the modified system an employee's seniority is not confined strictly to his home terminal. If he is laid off at his home terminal he can move to another terminal covered by the Agreement and retain his seniority, either by filling a vacancy at the other terminal or by "bumping" a junior line driver out of his job if there is no vacancy. The modified system also requires that any new vacancy at a covered terminal be offered to laid-off line drivers at all other covered terminals before it is filled by any other person. The District Court's final decree, as amended slightly by the Court of Appeals, 517 F.2d 299, 323, altered this system by requiring that any vacancy be offered to all members of all three subclasses before it may be

The Court of Appeals for the Fifth Circuit agreed with the basic conclusions of the District Court: that the company had engaged in a pattern or practice of employment discrimination and that the seniority system in the collective-bargaining agreements violated Title VII as applied to victims of prior discrimination. 517 F.2d 299. The appellate court held, however, that the relief ordered by the District Court was inadequate. Rejecting the District Court's attempt to trisect the affected class, the Court of Appeals held that all Negro and Spanish-surnamed incumbent employees were entitled to bid for future line-driver jobs on the basis of their company seniority, and that once a class member had filled a job, he could use his full company seniority—even if it predated the effective date of Title VII—for all purposes, including bidding and layoff. This award of retroactive seniority was to be limited only by a "qualification date" formula, under which seniority could not be awarded for periods prior to the date when (1) a line-driving position was vacant,[11] *and* (2) the class member, met (or would have met, given the opportunity) the qualifications for employment as a line driver.[12] Finally, the Court of Appeals modified that part of the District Court's decree that had subjected the rights of class members to fill future vacancies to the recall rights of laid-off employees. Holding that the three-year priority in favor of laid-off workers "would unduly impede the eradication of past discrimination," id., at 322, the Court of Appeals ordered that class members be allowed to compete for vacancies with laid-off employees on the basis of the class members' retroactive seniority. Laid-off line drivers would retain their prior recall rights with respect only to "purely temporary" vacancies. Ibid.[13]

The Court of Appeals remanded the case to the District Court to hold the evidentiary hearings necessary to apply these remedial principles. We granted both the company's and the union's petitions for certiorari to consider the significant questions presented under the Civil Rights Act of 1964, 425 U.S. 990, 96 S.Ct. 2200, 48 L.Ed.2d 814.

* * *

B

The District Court and the Court of Appeals also found that the seniority system contained in the collective-bargaining agreements be-

filled by laid-off line drivers from other terminals.

11. Although the opinion of the Court of Appeals in this case did not specifically mention the requirement that a vacancy exist, it is clear from earlier and later opinions of that court that this requirement is a part of the Fifth Circuit's "qualification date" formula.

12. For example, if a class member began his tenure with the company on January 1, 1966, at which time he was qualified as a line driver and a line-driving vacancy existed, his competitive seniority upon becoming a line driver would date back to January 1, 1966. If he became qualified or if a vacancy opened opened up only at a later date, then that later date would be used.

13. The Court of Appeals also approved (with slight modification) the part of the District Court's order that allowed class members to fill vacancies at a particular terminal ahead of line drivers laid off at other terminals. See n.10, supra.

tween the company and the union operated to violate Title VII of the Act.

For purposes of calculating benefits, such as vacations, pensions, and other fringe benefits, an employee's seniority under this system runs from the date he joins the company, and takes into account his total service in all jobs and bargaining units. For competitive purposes, however, such as determining the order in which employees may bid for particular jobs, are laid off, or are recalled from layoff, it is bargaining-unit seniority that controls. Thus, a line driver's seniority, for purposes of bidding for particular runs [25] and protection against layoff, takes into account only the length of time he has been a line driver at a particular terminal.[26] The practical effect is that a city driver or serviceman who transfers to a line-driver job must forfeit all the competitive seniority he has accumulated in his previous bargaining unit and start at the bottom of the line drivers' "board."

The vice of this arrangement, as found by the District Court and the Court of Appeals, was that it "locked" minority workers into inferior jobs and perpetuated prior discrimination by discouraging transfers to jobs as line drivers. While the disincentive applied to all workers, including whites, it was Negroes and Spanish-surnamed persons who, those courts found, suffered the most because many of them had been denied the equal opportunity to become line drivers when they were initially hired, whereas whites either had not sought or were refused line-driver positions for reasons unrelated to their race or national origin.

The linchpin of the theory embraced by the District Court and the Court of Appeals was that a discriminatee who must forfeit his competitive seniority in order finally to obtain a line-driver job will never be able to "catch up" to the seniority level of his contemporary who was not subject to discrimination.[27] Accordingly, this continued, built-in disadvantage to the prior discriminatee who transfers to a line-driver job was held to constitute a continuing violation of Title VII, for which both the employer and the union who jointly created and maintain the seniority system were liable.

The union, while acknowledging that the seniority system may in some sense perpetuate the effects of prior discrimination, asserts that

25. Certain long-distance runs, for a variety of reasons, are more desirable than others. The best runs are chosen by the line drivers at the top of the "board"—a list of drivers arranged in order of their bargaining-unit seniority.

26. Both bargaining-unit seniority and company seniority rights are generally limited to service at one particular terminal, except as modified by the Southern Conference Area Over-the-Road Supplemental Agreement. See n. 10, supra.

27. An example would be a Negro who was qualified to be a line driver in 1958 but who, because of his race, was assigned instead a job as a city driver, and is allowed to become a line driver only in 1971. Because he loses his competitive seniority when he transfers jobs, he is forever junior to white line drivers hired between 1958 and 1970. The whites, rather than the Negro, will henceforth enjoy the preferable runs and the greater protection against layoff. Although the original discrimination occurred in 1958—before the effective date of Title VII—the seniority system operates to carry the effects of the earlier discrimination into the present.

the system is immunized from a finding of illegality by reason of § 703(h) of Title VII, 42 U.S.C. § 2000e–2(h), which provides in part:

> "Notwithstanding any other provision of this subchapter, it shall not be an unlawful employment practice for an employer to apply different standards of compensation, or different terms, conditions, or privileges of employment pursuant to a bona fide seniority * * * system, * * * provided that such differences are not the result of an intention to discriminate because of race * * * or national origin * * *."

It argues that the seniority system in this case is "bona fide" within the meaning of § 703(h) when judged in light of its history, intent, application, and all of the circumstances under which it was created and is maintained. More specifically, the union claims that the central purpose of § 703(h) is to ensure that mere perpetuation of *pre-Act* discrimination is not unlawful under Title VII. And, whether or not § 703(h) immunizes the perpetuation of *post-Act* discrimination, the union claims that the seniority system in this litigation has no such effect. Its position in this Court, as has been its position throughout this litigation, is that the seniority system presents no hurdle to *post-Act* discriminatees who seek retroactive seniority to the date they would have become line drivers but for the company's discrimination. Indeed, the union asserts that under its collective-bargaining agreements the union will itself take up the cause of the post-Act victim and attempt, through grievance procedures, to gain for him full "make whole" relief, including appropriate seniority.

The Government responds that a seniority system that perpetuates the effects of prior discrimination—pre-Act or post-Act—can never be "bona fide" under § 703(h); at a minimum Title VII prohibits those applications of a seniority system that perpetuate the effects on incumbent employees of prior discriminatory job assignments.

The issues thus joined are open ones in this Court.[28] We considered § 703(h) in Franks v. Bowman Transportation Co., 424 U.S. 747, 96 S.Ct. 1251, 47 L.Ed.2d 444, but there decided only that § 703(h) does not bar the award of retroactive seniority to job applicants who seek relief from an employer's post-Act hiring discrimination. We stated that "the thrust of [§ 703(h)] is directed toward defining what is and what is not an illegal discriminatory practice in instances in which the post-Act operation of a seniority system is challenged as perpetuating the effects

28. Concededly, the view that § 703(h) does not immunize seniority systems that perpetuate the effects of prior discrimination has much support. It was apparently first adopted in Quarles v. Philip Morris, Inc., 279 F.Supp. 505 (ED Va.). The court there held that "a departmental seniority system *that has it genesis in racial discrimination* is not a *bona fide* seniority system." Id., at 517 (first emphasis added). The Quarles view has since enjoyed wholesale adoption in the Courts of Appeals. Insofar as the result in Quarles and in the cases that followed it depended upon findings that the seniority systems were themselves "racially discriminatory" or had their "genesis in racial discrimination," 279 F.Supp., at 517, the decisions can be viewed as resting upon the proposition that a seniority system that perpetuates the effects of pre-Act discrimination cannot be bona fide if an intent to discriminate entered into its very adoption.

of discrimination occurring prior to the effective date of the Act." 424 U.S. at 761, 96 S.Ct., at 1263. Beyond noting the general purpose of the statute, however, we did not undertake the task of statutory construction required in this litigation.

(1)

Because the company discriminated both before and after the enactment of Title VII, the seniority system is said to have operated to perpetuate the effects of both pre- and post-Act discrimination. Post-Act discriminatees, however, may obtain full "make whole" relief, including retroactive seniority under Franks v. Bowman, supra, without attacking the legality of the seniority system as applied to them. *Franks* made clear and the union acknowledges that retroactive seniority may be awarded as relief from an employer's discriminatory hiring and assignment policies even if the seniority system agreement itself makes no provision for such relief.[29] 424 U.S., at 778–779, 96 S.Ct., at 1271. Here the Government has proved that the company engaged in a post-Act pattern of discriminatory hiring, assignment, transfer, and promotion policies. Any Negro or Spanish-surnamed American injured by those policies may receive all appropriate relief as a direct remedy for this discrimination.[30]

(2)

What remains for review is the judgment that the seniority system unlawfully perpetuated the effects of pre-Act discrimination. We must decide, in short, whether § 703(h) validates otherwise bona fide seniority systems that afford no constructive seniority to victims discriminated against prior to the effective date of Title VII, and it is to that issue that we now turn.

29. Article 38 of the National Master Freight Agreement between The Company and the union in effect as of the date of the systemwide lawsuit provided:

> "The Employer and the Union agree not to discriminate against any individual with respect to his hiring, compensation, terms or conditions of employment because of such individual's race, color, religion, sex, or national origin, nor will they limit, segregate or classify employees in any way to deprive any individual employee of employment opportunities because of his race, color, religion, sex, or national origin."

Any discrimination by the company would apparently be a "grievable" breach of this provision of the contract.

30. The legality of the seniority system insofar as it perpetuates post-Act discrimination nonetheless remains at issue in this case, in light of the injunction entered against the union. Our decision today in United Air Lines, Inc. v. Evans, 431 U.S. 553, 97 S.Ct. 1885, 52 L.Ed.2d 571, is largely dispositive of this issue. Evans holds that the operation of a seniority system is not unlawful under Title VII even though it perpetuates post-Act discrimination that has not been the subject of a timely charge by the discriminatee. Here, of course, the Government has sued to remedy the post-Act discrimination directly, and there is no claim that any relief would be time barred. But this is simply an additional reason not to hold the seniority system unlawful, since such a holding would in no way enlarge the relief to be awarded. See Franks v. Bowman Transportation Co., 424 U.S. 747, 778–779, 96 S.Ct. 1251, 1271, 47 L.Ed. 2d 444. Section 703(h) on its face immunizes all bona fide seniority systems, and does not distinguish between the perpetuation of pre- and post-Act discrimination.

The primary purpose of Title VII was "to assure equality of employment opportunities and to eliminate those discriminatory practices and devices which have fostered racially stratified job environments to the disadvantage of minority citizens." McDonnell Douglas Corp. v. Green, 411 U.S. at 800, 93 S.Ct., at 1823.[31] To achieve this purpose, Congress "proscribe[d] not only overt discrimination but also practices that are fair in form, but discriminatory in operation." Id., at 431, 91 S.Ct., at 853. Thus, the Court has repeatedly held that a prima facie Title VII violation may be established by policies or practices that are neutral on their face and in intent but that nonetheless discriminate in effect against a particular group.

One kind of practice "fair in form, but discriminatory in operation" is that which perpetuates the effects of prior discrimination.[32] As the Court held in Griggs: "Under the Act, practices, procedures, or tests neutral on their face, and even neutral in terms of intent, cannot be maintained if they operate to 'freeze' the status quo of prior discriminatory employment practices." 401 U.S. at 430, 91 S.Ct., at 853.

Were it not for § 703(h), the seniority system in this case would seem to fall under the Griggs rationale. The heart of the system is its allocation of the choicest jobs, the greatest protection against layoffs, and other advantages to those employees who have been line drivers for the longest time. Where, because of the employer's prior intentional discrimination, the line drivers with the longest tenure are without exception white, the advantages of the seniority system flow disproportionately to them and away from Negro and Spanish-surnamed employees who might by now have enjoyed those advantages had not the employer discriminated before the passage of the Act. This disproportionate distribution of advantages does in a very real sense "operate to 'freeze' the status quo of prior discriminatory employment practices." But both the literal terms of § 703(h) and the legislative history of Title VII demonstrate that Congress considered this very effect of many seniority systems and extended a measure of immunity to them.

Throughout the initial consideration of HR 7152, later enacted as the Civil Rights Act of 1964, critics of the bill charged that it would

31. We also noted in McDonnell Douglas:

> "There are societal as well as personal interests on both sides of this [employer-employee] equation. The broad, overriding interest, shared by employer, employee, and consumer, is efficient and trustworthy workmanship assured through fair and racially neutral employment and personnel decisions. In the implementation of such decisions, it is abundantly clear that Title VII tolerates no racial discrimination, subtle or otherwise." 411 U.S. at 801, 93 S.Ct., at 1823.

32. Local 53 Asbestos Workers v. Vogler, 407 F.2d 1047 (CA5), provides an apt illustration. There a union had a policy of excluding persons not related to present members by blood or marriage. When in 1966 suit was brought to challenge this policy, all of the union's members were white, largely as a result of pre-Act, intentional racial discrimination. The court observed: "While the nepotism requirement is applicable to black and white alike and is not on its face discriminatory, in a completely white union the present effect of its continued application is to forever deny to Negroes and Mexican-Americans any real opportunity for membership." Id., at 1054.

destroy existing seniority rights.[33] The consistent response of Title VII's congressional proponents and of the Justice Department was that seniority rights would not be affected, even where the employer had discriminated prior to the Act.[34] An interpretative memorandum placed in the Congressional Record by Senators Clark and Case stated:

> "Title VII would have no effect on established seniority rights. Its effect is prospective and not retrospective. Thus, for example, *if a business has been discriminating in the past and as a result has an all-white working force, when the title comes into effect the employer's obligation would be simply to fill future vacancies on a nondiscriminatory basis.* He would not be obliged—or indeed, permitted—to fire whites in order to hire Negroes, or to prefer Negroes for future vacancies, or, once Negroes are hired, to give them special seniority rights at the expense of the white workers hired earlier." 110 Cong.Rec. 7213 (1964) (emphasis added).[35]

A Justice Department statement concerning Title VII, placed in the Congressional Record by Senator Clark, voiced the same conclusion:

> "Title VII would have no effect on seniority rights existing at the time it takes effect. If, for example, a collective bargaining contract provides that in the event of layoffs, those who were hired last must be laid off first, such a provision would not be affected in the least by Title VII. *This would be true even in the case where owing to discrimination prior to the effective date of the title, white workers had more seniority than Negroes.*" Id., at 7207 (emphasis added).[36]

While these statements were made before § 703(h) was added to Title VII, they are authoritative indicators of that section's purpose.

33. E.g., H.R.Rep.No.914, 88th Cong., 1st Sess. 65–66, 71 (1963) (minority report); 110 Cong.Rec. 486–488 (1964) (remarks of Sen. Hill); id., at 2726 (remarks of Rep. Dowdy); id., at 7091 (remarks of Sen. Stennis).

34. In addition to the material cited in Franks v. Bowman Transportation Co., 424 U.S. at 759–762, 96 S.Ct., at 1261–1263, see 110 Cong.Rec. 1518 (1964) (remarks of Rep. Celler); id., at 6549 (remarks of Sen. Humphrey); id., at 6564 (remarks of Sen. Kuchel).

35. Senators Clark and Case were the "bipartisan captains" responsible for Title VII during the Senate debate. Bipartisan captains were selected for each title of the Civil Rights Act by the leading proponents of the Act in both parties. They were responsible for explaining their title in detail, defending it, and leading discussion on it. See id., at 6528 (remarks of Sen. Humphrey); Vaas, Title VII: Legislative History, 7 B.C.Ind. & Com.L.Rev. 431, 444–445 (1966).

36. The full text of the statement is set out in Franks v. Bowman Transportation Co., supra, at 760 n.16, 96 S.Ct., at 1262. Senator Clark also introduced a set of answers to questions propounded by Senator Dirksen, which included the following exchange:

> "Question. Would the same situation prevail in respect to promotions, when that management function is governed by a labor contract calling for promotions on the basis of seniority? What of dismissals? Normally, labor contracts call for 'last hired, first fired.' If the last hired are Negroes, is the employer discriminating if his contract requires they be first fired and the remaining employees are white?

> "Answer. Seniority rights are in no way affected by the bill. If under a 'last hired, first fired' agreement a Negro happens to be the 'last hired,' he can still be 'first fired' as long as it is done because of his status as 'last hired' and not because of his race." 110 Cong.Rec. 7217 (1964). See *Franks*, supra, at 760 n.16, 96 S.Ct., at 1262.

Section 703(h) was enacted as part of the Mansfield-Dirksen compromise substitute bill that cleared the way for the passage of Title VII.[37] The drafters of the compromise bill stated that one of its principal goals was to resolve the ambiguities in the House-passed version of HR 7152. See, e.g., 110 Cong.Rec. 11935–11937 (1964) (remarks of Sen. Dirksen); id., at 12707 (remarks of Sen. Humphrey). As the debates indicate, one of those ambiguities concerned Title VII's impact on existing collectively bargained seniority rights. It is apparent that § 703(h) was drafted with an eye toward meeting the earlier criticism on this issue with an explicit provision embodying the understanding and assurances of the Act's proponents: namely, that Title VII would not outlaw such differences in treatment among employees as flowed from a bona fide seniority system that allowed for full exercise of seniority accumulated before the effective date of the Act. It is inconceivable that § 703(h), as part of a compromise bill, was intended to vitiate the earlier representations of the Act's supporters by increasing Title VII's impact on seniority systems. The statement of Senator Humphrey, noted in *Franks*, 424 U.S. at 761, 96 S.Ct., at 1262, confirms that the addition of § 703(h) "merely clarifies [Title VII's] present intent and effect." 110 Cong.Rec. 12723 (1964).

In sum, the unmistakable purpose of § 703(h) was to make clear that the routine application of a bona fide seniority system would not be unlawful under Title VII. As the legislative history shows, this was the intended result even where the employer's pre-Act discrimination resulted in whites having greater existing seniority rights than Negroes. Although a seniority system inevitably tends to perpetuate the effects of pre-Act discrimination in such cases, the congressional judgment was that Title VII should not outlaw the use of existing seniority lists and thereby destroy or water down the vested seniority rights of employees simply because their employer had engaged in discrimination prior to the passage of the Act.

To be sure, § 703(h) does not immunize all seniority systems. It refers only to "bona fide" systems, and a proviso requires that any differences in treatment not be "the result of an intention to discriminate because of race * * * or national origin * * *." But our reading of the legislative history compels us to reject the Government's broad argument that no seniority system that tends to perpetuate pre-Act discrimination can be "bona fide." To accept the argument would require us to hold that a seniority system becomes illegal simply because it allows the full exercise of the pre-Act seniority rights of employees of a company that discriminated before Title VII was enacted. It would place an affirmative obligation on the parties to the seniority agreement to subordinate those rights in favor of the claims of pre-Act discriminatees without seniority. The consequence would be a perversion of the congressional purpose. We cannot accept the invita-

37. See Franks v. Bowman, Transportation Co., supra, at 761, 96 S.Ct., at 1251; Vaas, supra, n. 35, at 435.

tion to disembowel § 703(h) by reading the words "bona fide" as the Government would have us do.[38] Accordingly, we hold that an otherwise neutral, legitimate seniority system does not become unlawful under Title VII simply because it may perpetuate pre-Act discrimination. Congress did not intend to make it illegal for employees with vested seniority rights to continue to exercise those rights, even at the expenses of pre-Act discriminatees.[39]

That conclusion is inescapable even in a case, such as this one, where the pre-Act discriminatees are incumbent employees who accumulated seniority in other bargaining units. Although there seems to be no explicit reference in the legislative history to pre-Act discriminatees already employed in less desirable jobs, there can be no rational basis for distinguishing their claims from those of persons initially denied *any* job but hired later with less seniority than they might have had in the absence of pre-Act discrimination.[40] We rejected any such distinction in *Franks*, finding that it had "no support anywhere in Title VII or its legislative history," 424 U.S. at 768, 96 S.Ct., at 1266. As discussed above, Congress in 1964 made clear that a seniority system is not unlawful because it honors employees' existing rights,

38. For the same reason, we reject the contention that the proviso in § 703(h), which bars differences in treatment resulting from "an intention to discriminate," applies to any application of a seniority system that may perpetuate past discrimination. In this regard the language of the Justice Department memorandum introduced at the legislative hearings, is especially pertinent: "It is perfectly clear that when a worker is laid off or denied a chance for promotion because under established seniority rules he is 'low man on the totem pole' he is not being discriminated against because of his race. * * * Any differences in treatment based on established seniority rights would not be based on race and would not be forbidden by the title." 110 Cong.Rec. 7207 (1964).

39. The legislative history of the 1972 amendments to Title VII, summarized and discussed in Franks, 424 U.S. at 764–765, n.21, 96 S.Ct. at 1264; id., at 796–797, n.18, 96 S.Ct., at 1263 (Powell, J., concurring in part and dissenting in part), in no way points to a different result. As the discussion in Franks indicates, that history is itself susceptible of different readings. The few broad references to perpetuation of pre-Act discrimination or "de facto segregated job ladders," see, e.g., S.Rep.No.92–415, pp. 5, 9 (1971); H.R.Rep.No.92–238, pp. 8, 17 (1971), did not address the specific issue presented by this case. And the assumption of the authors of the Conference Report that "the present case law as developed by the courts would continue to govern the applicability and construction of Title VII," see *Franks*, supra, at 765 n.21, 96 S.Ct., at 1264, of course does not foreclose our consideration of that issue. More importantly, the section of Title VII that we construe here, § 703(h), was enacted in 1964, not 1972. The views of members of a later Congress, concerning different sections of Title VII, enacted after this litigation was commenced, are entitled to little if any weight. It is the intent of the Congress that enacted § 703(h) in 1964, unmistakable in this case, that controls.

40. That Title VII did not proscribe the denial of fictional seniority to *pre-Act* discriminatees who got no job was recognized even in Quarles v. Philip Morris, Inc., 279 F.Supp. 505 (ED Va.), and its progeny. Quarles stressed the fact that the references in the legislative history were to employment seniority rather than departmental seniority. Id., at 516. In Local 189, United Papermakers & Paperworkers v. United States, 416 F.2d 980 (CA5), another leading case in this area, the court observed: "No doubt, Congress, to prevent 'reverse discrimination' meant to protect certain seniority rights that could not have existed but for previous racial discrimination. For example a Negro who had been rejected by an employer on racial grounds before passage of the Act could not, after being hired, claim to outrank whites who had been hired before him but after his original rejection, even though the Negro might have had senior status but for the past discrimination." Id., at 994.

even where the employer has engaged in pre-Act discriminatory hiring or promotion practices. It would be as contrary to that mandate to forbid the exercise of seniority rights with respect to discriminatees who held inferior jobs as with respect to later hired minority employees who previously were denied any job. If anything, the latter group is the more disadvantaged. As in *Franks*, " 'it would indeed be surprising if Congress gave a remedy for the one [group] which it denied for the other.' " Ibid., quoting Phelps Dodge Corp. v. NLRB, 313 U.S. 177, 187, 61 S.Ct. 845, 849, 85 L.Ed. 1271.[41]

(3)

The seniority system in this litigation is entirely bona fide. It applies equally to all races and ethnic groups. To the extent that it "locks" employees into non-linedriver jobs, it does so for all. The city drivers and servicemen who are discouraged from transferring to linedriver jobs are not all Negroes or Spanish-surnamed Americans; to the contrary, the overwhelming majority are white. The placing of line drivers in a separate bargaining unit from other employees is rational, in accord with the industry practice, and consistent with National Labor Relations Board precedents.[42] It is conceded that the seniority system did not have its genesis in racial discrimination, and that it was negotiated and has been maintained free from any illegal purpose. In these circumstances, the single fact that the system extends no retroactive seniority to pre-Act discriminatees does not make it unlawful.

Because the seniority system was protected by § 703(h), the union's conduct in agreeing to and maintaining the system did not violate Title VII. On remand, the District Court's injunction against the union must be vacated.[43]

[The Court's discussion of the relief to be afforded victims of post-Act discrimination and the concurring and dissenting opinions of Justices Marshall and Brennan are omitted].

41. In addition, there is no reason to suppose that Congress intended in 1964 to extend less protection to legitimate departmental seniority systems than to plantwide seniority systems. Then, as now, seniority was measured in a number of ways, including length of time with the employer, in a particular plant, in a department, in a job, or in a line of progression. See Aaron, Reflections on the Legal Nature and Enforceability ofSeniority Rights, 75 Harv.L.Rev. 1532, 1534 (1962); Cooper & Sobol, Seniority and Testing under Fair Employment Laws: A General Approach to Objective Criteria of Hiring and Promotion, 82 Harv.L.Rev. 1598, 1602 (1969). The legislative history contains no suggestion that any one system was preferred.

42. See Georgia Highway Express, 150 N.L.R.B. 1649, 1651: "The Board has long held that local drivers and over-the-road drivers constitute separate appropriate units where they are shown to be clearly defined, homogeneous, and functionally distinct groups with separate interests which can effectively be represented separately for bargaining purposes. * * * In view of the different duties and functions, separate supervision, and different bases of payment, it is clear that the over-the-road drivers have divergent interests from those of the employees in the [city operations] unit * * * and should not be included in that unit."

43. The union will properly remain in this litigation as a defendant so that full relief may be awarded the victims of the employer's post-Act discrimination. Fed. Rule Civ.Proc. 19(a). See EEOC v. MacMillan Bloedel Containers, Inc., 503 F.2d 1086, 1095 (CA6).

CALIFORNIA BREWERS ASSOCIATION v. BRYANT

Supreme Court of the United States, 1980.
444 U.S. 598, 100 S.Ct. 814, 63 L.Ed.2d 55.

MR. JUSTICE STEWART delivered the opinion of the Court.

Title VII of the Civil Rights Act of 1964 makes unlawful, practices, procedures, or tests that "operate to 'freeze' the status quo of prior discriminatory employment practices." Griggs v. Duke Power Co., 401 U.S. 424, 430, 91 S.Ct. 849, 853, 28 L.Ed.2d 158. To this rule, § 703(h) of the Act, provides an exception:

> "[I]t shall not be an unlawful employment practice for an employer to apply different standards of compensation, or different terms, conditions, or privileges of employment pursuant to a bona fide seniority * * * system, * * * provided that such differences are not the result of an intention to discriminate because of race. * * * "

In Teamsters v. United States, 431 U.S. 324, 352, 97 S.Ct. 1843, 1863, 52 L.Ed.2d 396, the Court held that "the unmistakable purpose of § 703(h) was to make clear that the routine application of a bona fide seniority system would not be unlawful under Title VII * * * even where the employer's pre-Act discrimination resulted in whites having greater existing seniority rights than Negroes." [2]

The present case concerns the application of § 703(h) to a particular clause in a California brewery industry collective-bargaining agreement. That agreement accords greater benefits to "permanent" than to "temporary" employees, and the clause in question provides that a temporary employee must work at least 45 weeks in a single calendar year before he can become a permanent employee. The Court of Appeals for the Ninth Circuit held that the 45-week requirement was not a "seniority system" or part of a "seniority system" within the meaning of § 703(h). 585 F.2d 421. We granted certiorari to consider the important question presented under Title VII of the Civil Rights Act of 1964. 442 U.S. 916, 99 S.Ct. 2835, 61 L.Ed.2d 282.

I

In 1973, the respondent, a Negro, filed a complaint in the United States District Court for the Northern District of California, on behalf of himself and other similarly situated Negroes, against the California Brewers Association and seven brewing companies (petitioners here), as well as against several unions. The complaint alleged that the defendants had discriminated against the respondent and other Negroes in

2. United Air Lines, Inc. v. Evans, 431 U.S. 553, 97 S.Ct. 1885, 52 L.Ed.2d 571, extended this holding to preclude Title VII challenges to seniority systems that perpetuated the effects of discriminatory post-Act practices that had not been the subject of a timely complaint. See also International Brotherhood of Teamsters v. United States, 431 U.S. at 348, n.30, 97 S.Ct. at 1861.

violation of Title VII of the Civil Rights Act of 1964, 42 U.S.C. §§ 2000e et seq., and in violation of 42 U.S.C. § 1981.[3]

The complaint, as amended, alleged that the respondent had been intermittently employed since May 1968, as a temporary employee of one of the defendants, the Falstaff Brewing Corp. It charged that all the defendant employers had discriminated in the past against Negroes, that the unions had acted in concert with the employers in such discrimination, and that the unions had discriminated in referring applicants from hiring halls to the employers. The complaint further asserted that this historical discrimination was being perpetuated by the seniority and referral provisions of the collective-bargaining agreement (Agreement) that governed industrial relations at the plants of the seven defendant employers. In particular, the complaint alleged, the Agreement's requirement that a temporary employee work 45 weeks in the industry in a single calendar year to reach permanent status had, as a practical matter, operated to preclude the respondent and the members of his putative class from achieving, or from a reasonable opportunity of achieving, permanent employee status.[4] Finally, the complaint alleged that on at least one occasion one of the defendant unions had passed over the respondent in favor of more junior white workers in making referrals to job vacancies at a plant of one of the defendant employers.

The Agreement is a multiemployer collective-bargaining agreement negotiated more than 20 years ago, and thereafter updated, by the California Brewers Association (on behalf of the petitioner brewing companies) and the Teamsters Brewery and Soft Drink Workers Joint Board of California (on behalf of the defendant unions). The Agreement establishes several classes of employees and the respective rights of each with respect to hiring and layoffs. Three of these classes are pertinent here: "permanent," "temporary," and "new" employees.

A permanent employee is "any employee * * * who * * * has completed forty-five weeks of employment under this Agreement in one classification[5] in one calendar year as an employee of the brewing industry in [the State of California]." An employee who acquires permanent status retains that status unless he "is not employed under this Agreement for any consecutive period of two (2) years. * * *"[6]

3. The complaint also alleged, under 29 U.S.C. §§ 159 and 185, that the union defendants had breached their duty of fair representation by, among other things, negotiating "unreasonable privileges for some employees over others. * * *"

4. In this Court, the respondent emphasizes that he has not contended that there is anything illegal in classifying employees as permanent and temporary or in according greater rights to permanent than to temporary employees. His sole Title VII challenge in this respect has been to the 45-week rule on its face and as it has been applied by the defendant unions and employers.

5. The Agreement classifies employees into brewers, bottlers, drivers, shipping and receiving clerks, and checkers. Under the Agreement, separate seniority lists have to be maintained for each of these classifications of employees. The respondent is a brewer.

6. An employee may also lose permanent status if he "quits the industry" or is discharged for certain specified reasons.

A temporary employee under the Agreement is "any person other than a permanent employee * * * who worked under this agreement * * * in the preceding calendar year for at least sixty (60) working days. * * *" A new employee is any employee who is not a permanent or temporary employee.

The rights of employees with respect to hiring and layoffs depend in substantial part on their status as permanent, temporary, or new employees.[7] The Agreement requires that employees at a particular plant be laid off in the following order: new employees in reverse order of their seniority at the plant, temporary employees in reverse order of their plant seniority, and then permanent employees in reverse order of their plant seniority. Once laid off, employees are to be rehired in the reverse order from which they were laid off.

The Agreement also gives permanent employees special "bumping" rights. If a permanent employee is laid off at any plant subject to the Agreement, he may be dispatched by the union hiring hall to any other plant in the same local area with the right to replace the temporary or new employee with the lowest plant seniority at that plant.

Finally, the Agreement provides that each employer shall obtain employees through the local union hiring hall to fill needed vacancies. The hiring hall must dispatch laid-off workers to such an employer in the following order: first, employees of that employer in the order of their seniority with that employer; second, permanent employees registered in the area in order of their industry seniority; third, temporary employees in the order of their seniority in the industry; and fourth, new employees in the order of their industry seniority. The employer then "shall have full right of selection among" such employees.

The District Court granted the defendants' motions to dismiss the complaint for failure to state a claim on which relief could be granted. No opinion accompanied this order. A divided panel of the Court of Appeals reversed, 585 F.2d 421, concluding that the 45-week rule is not a "seniority system" or part of a "seniority system" within the meaning of § 703(h) of Title VII. In the appellate court's view the provision "lacks the fundamental component of such a system" which is "the concept that employment rights should increase as the length of an employee's service increases." 585 F.2d, at 426. The court pointed out that under the Agreement some employees in the industry could acquire permanent status after a total of only 45 weeks of work if those weeks were served in one calendar year, while others "could work for many years and never attain permanent status because they were always terminated a few days before completing 45 weeks of work in any one year." Id., at 426–427.

7. In addition, permanent employees are given preference over temporary employees with respect to various other employment matters, such as the right to collect supplemental unemployment benefits upon layoff, wages and vacation pay, and choice of vacation times.

The Court of Appeals concluded that "while the collective bargaining agreement does contain a seniority system, the 45-week provision is not a part of it." Id., at 427:

> "The 45-week rule is simply a classification device to determine who enters the permanent employee seniority line and this function does not make the rule part of a seniority system. Otherwise any hiring policy (e.g., an academic degree requirement) or classification device (e.g., merit promotion) would become part of a seniority system merely because it affects who enters the seniority line."

Id., at 427, n.11.[8] Accordingly, the Court of Appeals remanded the case to the District Court to enable the respondent to prove that the 45-week provision has had a discriminatory impact on Negroes under the standards enunciated in Griggs v. Duke Power Co., 401 U.S. 424, 91 S.Ct. 849, 28 L.Ed.2d 158. 585 F.2d at 427–428.[9]

II

Title VII does not define the term "seniority system," and no comprehensive definition of the phrase emerges from the legislative history of § 703(h).[10] Moreover, our cases have not purported to delineate the contours of its meaning.[11] It is appropriate, therefore, to begin with commonly accepted notions about "seniority" in industrial relations, and to consider those concepts in the context of Title VII and this country's labor policy.

In the area of labor relations, "seniority" is a term that connotes length of employment.[12] A "seniority system" is a scheme that, alone or in tandem with non-"seniority" criteria,[13] allots to employees ever

8. The Court of Appeals also observed that "the 45-week requirement makes the system particularly susceptible to discriminatory application since employers and unions can manipulate their manpower requirements and employment patterns to prevent individuals who are disfavored from ever achieving permanent status." 585 F.2d, at 427. This danger, according to the court, is almost never present in any "true" seniority system, in which rights "usually accumulate automatically over time. * * *" Ibid.

9. The Court of Appeals directed the trial court on remand to consider as well the respondent's claims under 42 U.S.C. § 1981 and 29 U.S.C. §§ 159 and 185.

10. See 100 Cong.Rec. 1518, 5423, 7207, 7213, 7217, 12723, 15893 (1964). The example of a "seniority system" most frequently cited in the congressional debates was one that provided that the "last hired" employee would be the "first fired." Nowhere in the debates, however, is there any suggestion that this model was intended to be anything other than an illustration.

11. See Trans World Airlines, Inc. v. Hardison, 432 U.S. 63, 97 S.Ct. 2264, 53 L.Ed.2d 113; United Air Lines, Inc. v. Evans, 431 U.S. 553, 97 S.Ct. 1885, 52 L.Ed.2d 571; Teamsters v. United States, 431 U.S. 324, 97 S.Ct. 1843, 52 L.Ed.2d 396; Franks v. Bowman Transportation Co., 424 U.S. 747, 96 S.Ct. 1251, 47 L.Ed.2d 444.

12. Webster's Third New International Dictionary 2066 (unabridged ed. 1961) defines "seniority," in pertinent part, as the "status attained by length of continuous service * * * to which are attached by custom or prior collective agreement various rights or privileges * * * on the basis of ranking relative to others. * * *"

13. A collective-bargaining agreement could, for instance, provide that transfers and promotions are to be determined by a mix of seniority and other factors, such as aptitude tests and height requirements. That the "seniority" aspects of such a scheme of transfer and promotion might be covered by § 703(h) does not mean that the

improving employment rights and benefits as their relative lengths of pertinent employment increase.[14] Unlike other methods of allocating employment benefits and opportunities, such as subjective evaluations or educational requirements, the principal feature of any and every "seniority system" is that preferential treatment is dispensed on the basis of some measure of time served in employment.

Viewed as a whole, most of the relevant provisions of the Agreement before us in this case conform to these core concepts of "seniority." Rights of temporary employees and rights of permanent employees are determined according to length of plant employment in some respects, and according to length of industry employment in other respects. Notwithstanding this fact, the Court of Appeals concluded that the 45-week rule should not be viewed, for purposes of § 703(h), as part of what might otherwise be considered a "seniority system." For the reasons that follow, we hold that this conclusion was incorrect.

First, by legislating with respect to "systems" [15] of seniority in § 703(h), Congress in 1964 quite evidently intended to exempt from the normal operation of Title VII more than simply those components of any particular seniority scheme that, viewed in isolation, embody or effectuate the principle that length of employment will be rewarded. In order for any seniority system to operate at all, it has to contain ancillary rules that accomplish certain necessary functions, but which may not themselves be directly related to length of employment.[16] For instance, every seniority system must include rules that delineate how and when the seniority timeclock begins ticking,[17] as well as rules that specify how and when a particular person's seniority may be forfeited.[18] Every seniority system must also have rules that define which passages of time will "count" towards the accrual of seniority and which will not.[19] Every seniority system must, moreover, contain rules that par-

aptitude tests or the height requirements would also be so covered.

14. See E. Beal, E. Wickersham, & P. Kienast, The Practice of Collective Bargaining 430–431 (1972); Cooper & Sobol, Seniority and Testing Under Fair Employment Laws: A General Approach to Objective Criteria of Hiring and Promotion, 82 Harv.L.Rev. 1598, 1602 (1969); Aaron, Reflections on the Legal Nature and Enforceability of Seniority Rights, 75 Harv.L.Rev. 1532, 1534 (1962).

15. Webster's Third New International Dictionary 2322 (unabridged ed. 1961) defines "system," in pertinent part, as a "complex unity formed of many often diverse parts subject to a common plan or serving a common purpose."

16. See generally S. Slichter, J. Healy, & E. Livernash, The Impact of Collective Bargaining on Management 115–135 (1960).

17. By way of example, a collective-bargaining agreement could specify that an employee begins to accumulate seniority rights at the time he commences employment with the company, at the time he commences employment within the industry, at the time he begins performing a particular job function, or only after a probationary period of employment.

18. For example, a collective-bargaining agreement could provide that accumulated seniority rights are permanently forfeited by voluntary resignation, by severance for cause, or by nonemployment at a particular plant or in the industry for a certain period.

19. For instance, the time an employee works in the industry or with his current employer might not be counted for the purpose of accumulating seniority rights, whereas the time the employee works in a particular job classification might determine his seniority.

ticularize the types of employment conditions that will be governed or influenced by seniority, and those that will not.[20] Rules that serve these necessary purposes do not fall outside § 703(h) simply because they do not, in and of themselves, operate on the basis of some factor involving the passage of time.[21]

Second, Congress passed the Civil Rights Act of 1964 against the backdrop of this Nation's longstanding labor policy of leaving to the chosen representatives of employers and employees the freedom through collective bargaining to establish conditions of employment applicable to a particular business or industrial environment. It does not behoove a court to second-guess either that process or its products. Seniority systems, reflecting as they do, not only the give and take of free collective bargaining, but also the specific characteristics of a particular business or industry, inevitably come in all sizes and shapes. As we made clear in the Teamsters case, seniority may be "measured in a number of ways" and the legislative history of § 703(h) does not suggest that it was enacted to prefer any particular variety of seniority system over any other. 431 U.S., at 355, n. 41, 97 S.Ct., at 1865.

What has been said does not mean that § 703(h) is to be given a scope that risks swallowing up Title VII's otherwise broad prohibition of "practices, procedures, or tests" that disproportionately affect members of those groups that the Act protects. Significant freedom must be afforded employers and unions to create differing seniority systems. But that freedom must not be allowed to sweep within the ambit of § 703(h) employment rules that depart fundamentally from commonly accepted notions concerning the acceptable contours of a seniority system, simply because those rules are dubbed "seniority" provisions or have some nexus to an arrangement that concededly operates on the basis of seniority. There can be no doubt, for instance, that a threshold requirement for entering a seniority track that took the form of an educational prerequisite would not be part of a "seniority system" within the intendment of § 703(h).

The application of these principles to the case at hand is straightforward. The Agreement sets out, in relevant part, two parallel seniority ladders. One allocates the benefits due temporary employees; the other identifies the benefits owed permanent employees. The propriety under § 703(h) of such parallel seniority tracks cannot be doubted after the Court's decision in the *Teamsters* case. The collective-bargaining agreement at issue there allotted one set of benefits according to each employee's total service with the company, and another set according to each employee's service in a particular job category. Just as in that case the separation of seniority tracks did not derogate from the

20. By way of example, a collective-bargaining agreement could provide that an employee's seniority will govern his entitlement to vacation time and his job security in the event of layoffs, but will have no influence on promotions or job assignments.

21. The examples in the text of the types of rules necessary to the operation of a seniority system are not intended to and do not comprise an exhaustive list.

identification of the provisions as a "seniority system" under § 703(h), so in the present case the fact that the system created by the Agreement establishes two or more seniority ladders does not prevent it from being a "seniority system" within the meaning of that section.

The 45-week rule, correspondingly, serves the needed function of establishing the threshold requirement for entry into the permanent-employee seniority track. As such, it performs the same function as did the employment rule in *Teamsters* that provided that a line driver began to accrue seniority for certain purposes only when he started to work as a line driver, even though he had previously spent years as a city driver for the same employer. In *Teamsters*, the Court expressed no reservation about the propriety of such a threshold rule for § 703(h) purposes. There is no reason why the 45-week threshold requirement at issue here should be considered any differently.

The 45-week rule does not depart significantly from commonly accepted concepts of "seniority." The rule is not an educational standard, an aptitude or physical test, or a standard that gives effect to subjectivity. Unlike such criteria, but like any "seniority" rule, the 45-week requirement focuses on length of employment.

Moreover, the rule does not distort the operation of the basic system established by the Agreement, which rewards employment longevity with heightened benefits. A temporary employee's chances of achieving permanent status increase inevitably as his industry employment and seniority accumulate. The temporary employees with the most industry seniority have the first choice of new jobs within the industry available for temporary employees. Similarly, the temporary employees with the most plant seniority have the first choice of temporary employee jobs within their plant and enjoy the greatest security against "bumping" by permanent employees from nearby plants. As a general rule, therefore, the more seniority a temporary employee accumulates, the more likely it is that he will be able to satisfy the 45-week requirement. That the correlation between accumulated industry employment and acquisition of permanent employee status is imperfect does not mean that the 45-week requirement is not a component of the Agreement's seniority system. Under any seniority system, contingencies such as illnesses and layoffs may interrupt the accrual of seniority and delay realization of the advantages dependent upon it.[22]

For these reasons, we conclude that the Court of Appeals was in error in holding that the 45-week rule is not a component of a "seniority system" within the meaning of § 703(h) of Title VII of the Civil Rights Act of 1964. In the District Court the respondent will remain free to show that, in respect to the 45-week rule or in other respects, the seniority system established by the Agreement is not

22. There are indications in the record of this case that a long-term decline in the California brewing industry's demand for labor is a reason why the accrual of seniority as a temporary employee has not led more automatically to the acquisition of permanent status. But surely, what would be part of a "seniority system" in an expanding labor market does not become something else in a declining labor market.

"bona fide," or that the differences in employment conditions that it has produced are "the result of an intention to discriminate because of race."

For the reasons stated, the judgment before us is vacated, and the case is remanded to the Court of Appeals for the Ninth Circuit for further proceedings consistent with this opinion.

It is so ordered.

MR. JUSTICE POWELL and MR. JUSTICE STEVENS took no part in the consideration or decision of this case.

MR. JUSTICE MARSHALL with whom MR. JUSTICE BRENNAN and MR. JUSTICE BLACKMUN join, dissenting.

In the California brewing industry, an employee's rights and benefits are largely dependent on whether he is a "permanent" employee within the meaning of the collective-bargaining agreement. Permanent employees are laid off after all other employees. If laid off at one facility, a permanent employee is permitted to replace the least senior nonpermanent employee at any other covered facility within the local area. Permanent employees are selected before temporary employees to fill vacancies. They have exclusive rights to supplemental unemployment benefits upon layoff and receive higher wages and vacation pay for the same work performed by other employees. Permanent employees have first choice of vacation times, less rigorous requirements for qualifying for holiday pay, exclusive access to veterans' reinstatement and seniority rights, and priority in assignment of overtime work among bottlers.

According to respondent's complaint, no Negro has ever attained permanent employee status in the California brewing industry.[1]

The provision of the collective-bargaining agreement at issue here defines a permanent employee as one "who * * * has completed forty-five weeks of employment * * * in one classification in one calendar year as an employee of the brewing industry in this State." An employee who works 44 weeks per year for his entire working life remains a temporary employee. By contrast, an employee who works 45 weeks in his first year in the industry attains permanent employee status. This simple fact belies the Court's conclusion that the 45-week requirement "does not depart significantly from commonly accepted concepts of 'seniority.'" Since I am unable to agree that the provision at issue is part of a "seniority system" under § 703(h) of Title VII, I dissent.

I

Neither Title VII nor its legislative history provides a comprehensive definition of the term "seniority system."[2] The Court is therefore

1. In the present procedural posture of the case, of course, the allegations of the complaint must be accepted as true.

2. The legislative history does, however, provide a bit more guidance than the Court admits. The fact that the sole example of

correct in concluding that the term must be defined by reference to "commonly accepted notions about 'seniority' in industrial relations" and "in the context of Title VII and this country's labor policy." Those "commonly accepted notions," however, do not lead to the Court's holding today. And I believe that the relevant policies do not support that holding, but instead require that it be rejected.

The concept of "seniority" is not a complicated one. The fundamental principle, as the Court recognizes, is that employee rights and benefits increase with length of service. This principle is reflected in the very definition of the term, as found in dictionaries [3] and treatises and articles in the field of industrial relations.[4] To quote from a few of the sources on which the Court purports to rely today: "Seniority is a system of employment preference based on length of service; employees with the longest service are given the greatest job security and the best opportunities for advancement." Aaron, Reflections on the Legal Nature and Enforceability of Seniority Rights, 75 Harv.L.Rev. 1532, 1534 (1962). "The variations and combinations of seniority principles are very great, but in all cases the basic measure is length of service, with preference accorded to the senior worker." Cooper & Sobol, Seniority

a seniority system given in the congressional debates is one in which rights increase with cumulative length of service is at least suggestive.

3. See, e.g., Webster's Third New International Dictionary 2066 (unabridged ed. 1961) ("a status attained by length of continuous service (as in a company * * *) to which are attached by custom or prior collective agreement various rights or privileges"); Random House Dictionary of the English Language 1299 (1966) ("priority, precedence, or status obtained as the result of a person's length of service"); Black's Law Dictionary 1222 (5th ed. 1979) ("As used with reference to job seniority, worker with most years of service is first promoted within range of jobs subject to seniority, and is the last laid off, proceeding so on down the line to the youngest in point of service"); Ballentine's Law Dictionary 1160 (1969) ("the principle in labor relations that length of employment determines the order of layoffs, rehirings, and advancements").

4. See, e.g. Roberts' Dictionary of Industrial Relations 390 (1966) ("The length of service an individual employee has in the plant. * * * The seniority principle rests on the assumption that the individuals with the greatest length of service within the company should be given preference in employment"); United States Department of Labor, Bureau of Labor Statistics, Bulletin No. 908–11, p. 1 (1949) ("A seniority program aims to provide maximum security in employment to those with the longest service"); E. Dangel & I. Shriber, The Law of Labor Unions § 15 (1941) ("Seniority * * * is an employment advantage in the matter of the choice of and the right to work in one's occupation on the basis of an employee's length of service"); BNA, Collective Bargaining Contracts, Techniques of Negotiation and Administration with Topical Classification of Clauses 488 (1941) ("The term [seniority] refers to length of service with the employer or in some division of an enterprise"); Meyers, The Analytic Meaning of Seniority, Industrial Relations Research Association, Proceedings of Eighteenth Annual Meeting 194 (1966) ("Seniority is the application of the criterion of length of service for the calculation of relative equities among employees"); McCaffrey, Development and Administration of Seniority Provisions, Proceedings of New York University Second Annual Conference on Labor 132 (1949) ("seniority may be defined as the length of company-recognized service as applied to certain employer-employee relationships"); Christenson, Seniority Rights Under Labor Union Working Agreements, 11 Temp.L.Q. 355 (1937) ("seniority is a rule providing that employers promote, lay-off and re-employ labor, according to length of previous service"). Cf. P. Selznick, Law, Society, and Industrial Justice 203 (1969) (referring to the " 'rather general feeling that a worker who has spent many years on his job has some stake in that job and in the business of which it is a part' ").

and Testing under Fair Employment Laws: A General Approach to Objective Criteria of Hiring and Promotion, 82 Harv.L.Rev. 1598, 1602 (1969). "Seniority grants certain preferential treatment to long-service employees almost at the expense of short-service employees. * * * [S]eniority is defined as length of service." E. Beal, E. Wickersham, & P. Kienast, The Practice of Collective Bargaining 430 (1972).

It is hardly surprising that seniority has uniformly been defined in terms of cumulative length of service. No other definition could accord with the policies underlying the recognition of seniority rights. A seniority system provides an objective standard by which to ascertain employee rights and protections, thus reducing the likelihood of arbitrariness or caprice in employer decisions. At the same time, it promotes stability and certainty among employees, furnishing a predictable method by which to measure future employment position. See, e.g., Sayles, Seniority: An Internal Union Problem, 30 Harv.Bus.Rev. 55 (1952); C. Golden & H. Ruttenberg, The Dynamics of Industrial Democracy 128–131 (1973); Cooper & Sobol, supra, at 1604–1605.

The Court concedes this general point, recognizing that a " 'seniority system' is a scheme that, alone or in tandem with non-'seniority' criteria, allots to employees ever improving employment rights and benefits as their relative lengths of pertinent employment increase." In my view, that concession is dispositive of this case. The principal effect of the 45-week requirement is to ensure that employee rights and benefits in the California brewing industry are not "ever improving" as length of service increases. Indeed, cumulative length of service is only incidentally relevant to the 45-week rule. The likelihood that a temporary employee will attain permanent employee status is largely unpredictable. The 45-week period, which is exclusive of vacation, leaves of absence, and time lost because of injury or sickness, represents almost 90% of the calendar year. Even if an employee is relatively senior among temporaries, his ability to work 45 weeks in a year will rest in large part on fortuities over which he has no control. The most obvious reason that employees have been prevented from attaining permanent employee status—a reason barely referred to by the Court—is that the brewing industry is a seasonal one. An employee may also be prevented from becoming permanent because of replacement by permanent employees or an employer's unexpected decision to lay off a particular number of employees during the course of a year.[5] It is no wonder that the accrual of seniority by temporary employees has not led with any regularity to the acquisition of permanent employee status.[6] In sum,

5. Indeed, the agreement expressly provides that a permanent employee laid off at one facility will replace (or "bump") the temporary employee with the lowest *plant* seniority, even if that employee has more industry seniority than others. As a result, temporaries who are relatively senior in terms of industry seniority may have less opportunity to work 45 weeks in a calendar year than temporaries with less industry seniority but more plant seniority. Thus, it is simply not true that temporary employees obtain permanent employee status in order of cumulative length of employment, for the requisite 45 weeks is computed on the basis of service in the industry rather than in particular plants.

6. The Court acknowledges this point, but responds that a system which would

the 45-week rule does not have the feature of providing employees with a reasonably certain route by which to measure future employment position. So understood, the 45-week rule has very little to do with seniority, for it makes permanent status turn on fortuities over which the employee has no control, not on length of service with the employer or in the relevant unit.

The Court avoids this conclusion by little more than assertion. It observes that the 45-week rule acts as a threshold requirement for entry onto the seniority track composed of permanent employees, but eliminates the force of that observation with the inevitable concession that such threshold requirements are not necessarily entitled to § 703(h) exemption.[7] It notes that the 45-week requirement "focuses on length of employment," and proceeds to the unexplained conclusion that it therefore "does not depart significantly from commonly accepted concepts of 'seniority.'" And it adds that more senior temporary employees tend to have a greater opportunity to obtain work and thus to attain permanent status through 45 weeks of employment in a calendar year.

The Court's analysis, of course, is largely dependent on its conclusion that since the 45-week requirement is one measured by time of service, it does not depart from common concepts of seniority. That conclusion, however, is foreclosed by the Court's own definition of a seniority system as one in which employee rights increase with cumulative length of service—not length of service within a calendar year. The mere fact that the 45-week rule is in some sense a measure of "time" does not demonstrate a valid relation to concepts of seniority. Such a conclusion would make the § 703(h) exemption applicable to a rule under which permanent employee status is dependent on number of days served within a week, or hours served within a day.[8]

Nor is there much force to the suggestion that the 45-week requirement somehow becomes part of a seniority system because permanent employee status is more easily achieved by the more senior temporary employees. I could agree with the Court's decision if petitioners

fall within § 703(h) in an expanding labor market does not lose that status by virtue of the fact that the labor market is contracting. In the Court's words, however, the question is whether the 45-week rule is a part of a seniority system because it "allots to employees ever improving employment rights and benefits as their relative lengths of pertinent employment increase." In that context it is surely relevant whether the 45-week provision does in fact operate to reward cumulative length of service, or serves instead as a virtually impassable barrier to advancement.

7. As the Court's own analysis suggests, the 45-week provision is entirely different from the seniority provisions involved in Teamsters v. United States, 431 U.S. 324, 97 S.Ct. 1843, 52 L.Ed.2d 396 (1977). At issue in that case was a seniority system granting some benefits on the basis of an employee's cumulative length of service with the company, and others on the basis of cumulative length of service in a particular job category. In both cases employee rights and benefits depended on total length of service in the relevant unit, not on the length of service within a calendar year.

8. For example, there can be no serious question that a provision making permanent status dependent on 7 days of work per week, or 12 hours per day, would not be part of a "seniority system" within the meaning of § 703(h).

demonstrated that the collective-bargaining agreement actually operates to reward employees in order of cumulative length of service. But at this stage of the litigation there is no evidence that temporary employees attain permanent status in a way correlating even roughly with total length of employment. The mere possibility that senior temporary employees are more likely to work for 45 weeks is, in my view, insufficient.[9] It might as well be said that a law conditioning permanent employee status on the attainment of a certain level of skill is a "seniority" provision since skills tend to increase with length of service. A temporary employee is always subject to a risk that for some reason beyond his control, he will be unable to work the full 45 weeks and be forced to start over again.

II

Since the 45-week rule operates as a threshold requirement with no relation to principles of seniority, I believe that the rule is for analytical purposes no different from an educational standard or physical test which, as the Court indicates, is plainly not entitled to § 703(h) exemption. Accordingly, I think it clear that the 45-week requirement is not part of a "seniority system" within the meaning of § 703(h). But if the question were perceived to be close, I would be guided by the familiar principle that exemptions to remedial statutes should be construed narrowly. "To extend an exemption to other than those plainly and unmistakably within its terms and spirit is to abuse the interpretative process and to frustrate the announced will of the people." Phillips Co. v. Walling, 324 U.S. 490, 493, 65 S.Ct. 807, 808, 89 L.Ed. 1095 (1945). The effect of § 703(h) is to exempt seniority systems from the general prohibition on practices which perpetuate the effects of racial discrimination. This exception is a limited one in derogation of the overarching purpose of Title VII, "the integration of blacks into the mainstream of American society," Steelworkers v. Weber, 443 U.S. 193, 202, 99 S.Ct. 2721, 2727, 61 L.Ed.2d 480 (1979). A statute designed to remedy the national disgrace of discrimination in employment should be interpreted generously to comport with its primary purpose; exemptions should be construed narrowly so as not to undermine the effect of the general prohibition. Today the Court not only refuses to apply this familiar principle of statutory construction, it does not even acknowledge it.

In my view, the Court's holding is fundamentally at odds with the purposes of Title VII and the basic function of the § 703(h) exemption. I dissent.[10]

9. I could understand, although I do not favor, a decision remanding this case for factual findings on the question whether temporary employees in fact acquire permanent status and, if so, whether they do so in order of cumulative length of service. In my view, it is extraordinary for the Court to conclude, in a factual vacuum and on the authority of nothing other than petitioners' word, that "the rule does not distort the operation of the basic system established by the Agreement, which rewards employment longevity with heightened benefits." See also n.5, supra.

10. To decide this case we are not required to offer a complete definition of the term "seniority system" within the mean-

NOTES AND PROBLEMS FOR DISCUSSION

1. Is a probationary period as a prerequisite to permanent status in a job a "seniority system" entitled to protection under § 703(h)? Assume the employer and the union negotiated prior to the effective date of Title VII, as part of a collective bargaining agreement, a 60 day probation period for each "skilled" position in the plant. During the probation period the new employee may be removed from the position on the subjective determination of the supervisor that the employee will have difficulty becoming proficient at the work. After becoming permanent in the position, an employee may only be removed for malfeasance. Assume also that alleged failure during the probation period is the chief reason that only a relative handful of black employees have advanced to the skilled positions. Will the black employees be entitled to elimination of the probation system if they can prove a pattern of disparate treatment? Is a rule under which employees hired on the same day are ranked in seniority according to their scores on preemployment tests a "seniority system" within the meaning of § 703(h)? See, United States v. City of Cincinnati, 771 F.2d 161 (6th Cir. 1985).

2. The Supreme Court has not directly addressed the question of what factors render a seniority system illegal. Obviously a system which itself contains a racial classification or one adopted after the effective date of Title VII with a discriminatory purpose is not protected by § 703(h). But what of a system which was adopted prior to passage of Title VII for discriminatory reasons, but which is facially neutral in its application? In an internal memorandum issued after the *Teamsters* decision, the EEOC took the position that a seniority system was protected under § 703(h) only if it was instituted prior to the effective date of the Act and only if evidence shows there was no discriminatory intent in the genesis or maintenance of the system. The memorandum also stated that when the employer or a union is made aware—by means of a grievance, EEOC charges or the like—that the seniority system is "locking in" minorities or females, discriminatory intent will be inferred if the system is maintained or renegotiated when an alternative is available.[a] But in American Tobacco Co. v. Patterson, 456 U.S. 63, 102 S.Ct. 1534, 71 L.Ed.2d 748 (1982), the Court held that § 703(h) is not limited to seniority systems predating passage of Title VII.

In James v. Stockham Valves & Fittings Co., 559 F.2d 310 (5th Cir. 1977), cert. denied, 434 U.S. 1034 (1978), the Court of Appeals interpreted *Teamsters* as follows:

> As we read the *Teamsters* opinion, the issue whether there has been purposeful discrimination in connection with the establishment or continuation of a seniority system is integral to a determination that the system is or is not bona-fide * * * The Court's analysis suggests that totality of the circumstances in the development and maintenance of the system is rele-

ing of § 703(h). Nor are we called upon to canvass and evaluate rules "ancillary" to seniority systems. The question whether all of the rules listed by the Court, are part of a seniority system is not at all easy, and the Court's own reasoning demonstrates that its discussion of those rules is gratuitous and does little to advance analysis of the 45-week requirement. That requirement serves none of the functions of an "ancillary" rule.

[a] The EEOC Interpretive Memorandum No. N–915 (July 14, 1977) was withdrawn from the Agency's Compliance Manual. The Memorandum is quoted in Note, The Seniority System Exemption in Title VII: International Brotherhood of Teamsters v. United States, 6 Hofstra L.Rev. 585, 607–08 (1978). See also 1 Federal Regulation of Employment Service, Job Discrimination, § 2.117.

vant to examining that issue * * * In *Teamsters* the Court focused on four factors:

> (1) whether the seniority system operates to discourage all employees equally from transferring between seniority units;
>
> (2) whether the seniority units are in the same or separate bargaining units (if the latter, whether that structure is rational and in conformance with industry practice);
>
> (3) whether the seniority system had its genesis in racial discrimination; and
>
> (4) whether the system was negotiated and has been maintained free from any illegal purpose.

559 F.2d at 351–352. Most post-*Teamsters* decisions have adopted the four-factor inquiry of *Stockham Valve.* See Sears v. Atchison, Topeka & Santa Fe R.R. Co., 645 F.2d 1365, 1372 at n.5 (10th Cir. 1981), cert. denied 456 U.S. 964, 102 S.Ct. 2045, 72 L.Ed.2d 490 (1982); Taylor v. Mueller Co., 26 FEP Cases 1695, 1699 (6th Cir. 1981); Younger v. Glamorgan Pipe & Foundry Co., 20 FEP Cases 776, 784 (W.D.Va.1979), affirmed per curiam, 621 F.2d 96 (4th Cir. 1980). In Miller v. Continental Can Co., 25 EPD ¶ 31,543 (S.D.Ga.1981), the district court defined a bona fide seniority system as one "that has not been an independent engine of racial discrimination, and, hence, one that has created 'legitimate expectations' in employees who have participated in the system without discriminatory motive." 25 EPD ¶ 31,543 at 19,299. The court relied on *Stockham Valve* as "the principle source of guidance in applying this 'legitimate expectations' test." Courts which have declared seniority systems illegal have generally found overt *post-Act* racial discrimination by employer, union, or both. See, Wattleton v. International Bro. of Boilermakers, 686 F.2d 586 (7th Cir. 1982), cert. denied, 459 U.S. 1208, 103 S.Ct. 1199, 75 L.Ed.2d 442 (1983); Veazie v. Southern Greyhound Lines, Inc., et al., 35 EPD ¶ 34,832 (E.D.La.1983); Terrell v. United States Pipe and Foundry Co., 39 FEP Cases 571 (N.D.Ala.1985). Should a court be able to infer discriminatory intent underlying a seniority system from evidence of the system's disproportionate impact on a protected class and its toleration by the employer and/or union?

In PULLMAN–STANDARD v. SWINT, 456 U.S. 273, 102 S.Ct. 1781, 72 L.Ed.2d 66 (1982), the Court held that:

> Differentials among employees that result from a seniority system are not unlawful employment practices unless the product of an intent to discriminate. It would make no sense, therefore to say that the intent to discriminate required by § 703(h) may be presumed from such an impact. As § 703(h) was construed in *Teamsters*, there must be a finding of actual intent to discriminate on racial grounds on the part of those who negotiated or maintained the system.

Id. at 4429. The Court also held that a finding of intent is a "pure question of fact subject to Rule 52's clearly erroneous standard" of review.

3. The Court in *California Brewers Ass'n* noted that on remand the plaintiff could still show that the 45-week rule was not a "bona fide" seniority system under § 703(h). Assume that the plaintiff is unable to prove that the rule was created or maintained for a discriminatory purpose, but does prove that it was used in a discriminatory fashion against him—i.e., that he was intentionally laid off because of his race to prevent him from obtaining permanent status. To what relief would he be entitled?

In FRANKS v. BOWMAN TRANSPORTATION CO., 424 U.S. 747, 96 S.Ct. 1251, 47 L.Ed.2d 444 (1976), the court held that § 703(h) does not preclude a court from awarding all appropriate relief, including retroactive seniority, to the victim of post-Act discrimination, notwithstanding the fact that the seniority system perpetuating that discrimination is not itself illegal. That decision was not affected by *Teamsters.* But a victim of post-Title VII discrimination in hiring or assignment must challenge the discrimination directly, and cannot let the statute of limitations run and then file a suit based upon the theory that the otherwise bona fide seniority system perpetuating the discrimination constitutes a "continuing violation." United Air Lines, Inc. v. Evans, 431 U.S. 553, 97 S.Ct. 1885, 52 L.Ed.2d 571 (1977).

Is a seniority system of a public employer which merely perpetuates the effect of past discrimination in hiring or job assignment, but was not designed or maintained for discriminatory purposes, protected by *Teamsters*? See Moore v. City of San Jose, 615 F.2d 1265, 1272 (9th Cir. 1980).

Chapter 4

THE PROHIBITED CLASSIFICATIONS: SPECIAL PROBLEMS

As noted in Chapter 1, Title VII was intended to proscribe a wide range of discriminatory employment practices. Congress intentionally drafted the provisions that define the covered employment institutions and decisions in broad and general terms. Nevertheless, Title VII, in one important respect, is a statute of limited application. It prohibits discrimination on the basis of five specifically enumerated classifications—race, color, sex, religion and national origin. Consequently, the courts have ruled, allegations of bias based on any other classification do not state a claim under this statute. On the other hand, however, keep in mind that the availability of disproportionate impact-based claims serves to expand the universe of practices perceived as discriminating on the basis of the enumerated categories. The materials in this chapter will examine several interpretative questions concerning the five statutory classifications.

SECTION A. RELIGION AND THE DUTY TO ACCOMMODATE

Title VII is the only federal statute that explicitly prohibits employment discrimination on the basis of religion. Section 701(j) defines religion as including "all aspects of religious observance and practice, as well as belief * * *." While the statute does not set out the limits of these general terms, the federal courts have uniformly adopted the interpretation given to the religious exemption provision of the selective service statutes by the Supreme Court in two conscientious objector cases, Welsh v. United States, 398 U.S. 333, 90 S.Ct. 1792, 26 L.Ed.2d 308 (1970); and United States v. Seeger, 380 U.S. 163, 85 S.Ct. 850, 13 L.Ed.2d 733 (1965). Accordingly, a plaintiff need only prove (1) that his belief is "religious" in his own scheme of things [a]; and (2) that it is sincerely held.

The statutory definition of religion was added to the Act by the 1972 amendments to Title VII. This new enactment, § 701(j), contains another provision which has been the subject of most of the controversy and litigation in the area of religious discrimination in employment.

[a] In *Welsh*, this was held to include moral or ethical beliefs which occupy the role of religion in an individual's life. Political or social ideologies, on the other hand, have been held to fall outside the limits of Title VII protected religious belief. See Bellamy v. Mason's Stores, Inc., 368 F.Supp. 1025 (E.D.Va.1973), affirmed on other grounds, 508 F.2d 504 (4th Cir. 1974) (racist and antisemitic philosophy espoused by Ku Klux Klan does not constitute religion). Atheism, however, does fit within the statutory definition of religion. Young v. Southwestern Savings & Loan Association, 509 F.2d 140 (5th Cir. 1975).

TRANS WORLD AIRLINES, INC. v. HARDISON

Supreme Court of the United States, 1977.
432 U.S. 63, 97 S.Ct. 2264, 53 L.Ed.2d 113.

MR. JUSTICE WHITE delivered the opinion of the Court.

Section 703(a)(1) of the Civil Rights Act of 1964, makes it an unlawful employment practice for an employer to discriminate against an employee or a prospective employee on the basis of his or her religion. At the time of the events involved here, a guideline of the Equal Employment Opportunity Commission (EEOC), required, as the Act itself now does, that an employer, short of "undue hardship," make "reasonable accommodations" to the religious needs of its employees. The issue in this case is the extent of the employer's obligation under Title VII to accommodate an employee whose religious beliefs prohibit him from working on Saturdays.

I

Petitioner Trans World Airlines (TWA) operates a large maintenance and overhaul base in Kansas City, Mo. On June 5, 1967, respondent Larry G. Hardison was hired by TWA to work as a clerk in the Stores Department at its Kansas City base. Because of its essential role in the Kansas City operation, the Stores Department must operate 24 hours per day, 365 days per year, and whenever an employee's job in that department is not filled, an employee must be shifted from another department, or a supervisor must cover the job, even if the work in other areas may suffer.

Hardison, like other employees at the Kansas City base, was subject to a seniority system contained in a collective-bargaining agreement that TWA maintains with petitioner International Association of Machinists and Aerospace Workers (IAM). The seniority system is implemented by the union steward through a system of bidding by employees for particular shift assignments as they become available. The most senior employees have first choice for job and shift assignments, and the most junior employees are required to work when the union steward is unable to find enough people willing to work at a particular time or in a particular job to fill TWA's needs.

In the spring of 1968 Hardison began to study the religion known as the Worldwide Church of God. One of the tenets of that religion is that one must observe the Sabbath by refraining from performing any work from sunset on Friday until sunset on Saturday. The religion also proscribes work on certain specified religious holidays.

When Hardison informed Everett Kussman, the manager of the Stores Department, of his religious conviction regarding observance of the Sabbath, Kussman agreed that the union steward should seek a job swap for Hardison or a change of days off; that Hardison would have his religious holidays off whenever possible if Hardison agreed to work the traditional holidays when asked; and that Kussman would try to find Hardison another job that would be more compatible with his religious beliefs. The problem was temporarily solved when Hardison transferred to the 11 p. m.–7 a. m. shift. Working this shift permitted Hardison to observe his Sabbath.

The problem soon reappeared when Hardison bid for and received a transfer from Building 1, where he had been employed, to Building 2, where he would work the day shift. The two buildings had entirely separate seniority lists; and while in Building 1 Hardison had sufficient seniority to observe the Sabbath regularly, he was second from the bottom on the Building 2 seniority list.

In Building 2 Hardison was asked to work Saturdays when a fellow employee went on vacation. TWA agreed to permit the union to seek a change of work assignments for Hardison, but the union was not willing to violate the seniority provisions set out in the collective-bargaining contract, and Hardison had insufficient seniority to bid for a shift having Saturdays off.

A proposal that Hardison work only four days a week was rejected by the company. Hardison's job was essential, and on weekends he was the only available person on his shift to perform it. To leave the position empty would have impaired supply shop functions, which were critical to airline operations; to fill Hardison's position with a supervisor or an employee from another area would simply have undermanned another operation; and to employ someone not regularly assigned to work Saturdays would have required TWA to pay premium wages.

When an accommodation was not reached, Hardison refused to report for work on Saturdays. A transfer to the twilight shift proved unavailing since that schedule still required Hardison to work past sundown on Fridays. After a hearing, Hardison was discharged on grounds of insubordination for refusing to work during his designated shift.

Hardison, having first invoked the administrative remedy provided by Title VII, brought this action for injunctive relief in the United States District Court * * *, claiming that his discharge by TWA constituted religious discrimination in violation of Title VII. * * * Hardison's claim of religious discrimination rested on 1967 EEOC guidelines requiring employers "to make reasonable accommodations to the religious needs of employees" whenever such accommodation would not work an "undue hardship," and on similar language adopted by Congress in the 1972 amendments to Title VII.

After a bench trial, the District Court ruled in favor of the defendants. * * * [T]he District Court rejected at the outset TWA's contention that requiring it in any way to accommodate the religious needs of its employees would constitute an unconstitutional establishment of religion. As the District Court construed the Act, however, TWA had satisfied its "reasonable accommodations" obligation, and any further accommodation would have worked an undue hardship on the company.

The Court of Appeals for the Eighth Circuit reversed the judgment for TWA. It agreed with the District Court's constitutional ruling, but held that TWA had not satisfied its duty to accommodate. * * *

In * * * [its] petition for certiorari TWA * * * contended that adequate steps had been taken to accommodate Hardison's religious observances and that to construe the statute to require further efforts at accommodation would create an establishment of religion contrary to the First Amendment of the Constitution. TWA also contended that the Court of Appeals improperly ignored the District Court's findings of fact.

* * * Because we agree with petitioner that * * * [its] conduct was not a violation of Title VII, we need not reach the other questions presented.

II

The Court of Appeals found that TWA had committed an unlawful employment practice under § 703(a)(1) of the Act * * *. The emphasis of both the language and the legislative history of the statute is on eliminating discrimination in employment; similarly situated employees are not to be treated differently solely because they differ with respect to race, color, religion, sex, or national origin. This is true regardless of whether the discrimination is directed against majorities or minorities.

The prohibition against religious discrimination soon raised the question of whether it was impermissible under § 703(a)(1) to discharge or refuse to hire a person who for religious reasons refused to work during the employer's normal workweek. In 1966 an EEOC guideline dealing with this problem declared that an employer had an obligation under the statute "to accommodate to the reasonable religious needs of employees * * * where such accommodation can be made without serious inconvenience to the conduct of the business."

In 1967 the EEOC amended its guidelines to require employers "to make reasonable accommodations to the religious needs of employees and prospective employees where such accommodations can be made without undue hardship on the conduct of the employer's business." The EEOC did not suggest what sort of accommodations are "reasonable" or when hardship to an employer becomes "undue."

This question—the extent of the required accommodation—remained unsettled when this Court, in Dewey v. Reynolds Metals Co., 402 U.S. 689, 91 S.Ct. 2186, 29 L.Ed.2d 267 (1971), affirmed by an equally divided Court the Sixth Circuit's decision. This discharge of an employee who for religious reasons had refused to work on Sundays was there held by the Court of Appeals not to be an unlawful employment practice because the manner in which the employer allocated Sunday work assignments was discriminatory in neither its purpose nor effect; and consistent with the 1967 EEOC guidelines, the employer had made a reasonable accommodation of the employee's beliefs by giving him the opportunity to secure a replacement for his Sunday work.

In part "to resolve by legislation" some of the issues raised in *Dewey*, Congress included the following definition of religion in its 1972 amendments to Title VII:

> "The term 'religion' includes all aspects of religious observance and practice, as well as belief, unless an employer demonstrates that he is unable to reasonably accommodate to an employee's or prospective employee's religious observance or practice without undue hardship on the conduct of the employer's business." § 701(j).

The intent and effect of this definition was to make it an unlawful employment practice under § 703(a)(1) for an employer not to make reasonable accommodations, short of undue hardship, for the religious practices of his employees and prospective employees. But like the EEOC guidelines, the statute provides no guidance for determining the degree of accommodation that is required of an employer. The brief legislative history of § 701(j) is likewise of little assistance in this regard.[9] * * *

* * * With this in mind, we turn to a consideration of whether TWA has met its obligation under Title VII to accommodate the religious observances of its employees.

III

The Court of Appeals held that TWA had not made reasonable efforts to accommodate Hardison's religious needs under the 1967 EEOC guidelines in effect at the time the relevant events occurred.[11] In its view, TWA had rejected three reasonable alternatives, any one of which would have satisfied its obligation without undue hardship. First, within the framework of the seniority system, TWA could have permitted Hardison to work a four-day week, utilizing in his place a supervisor or another worker on duty elsewhere. That this would have caused other shop functions to suffer was insufficient to amount to undue hardship in the opinion of the Court of Appeals. Second—according to the Court of Appeals, also within the bounds of the collective-bargaining contract—the company could have filled Hardi-

9. * * * The legislative history of the measure consists chiefly of a brief floor debate in the Senate, contained in less than two pages of the Congressional Record and consisting principally of the views of the proponent of the measure, Senator Jennings Randolph.

11. Ordinarily, an EEOC guideline is not entitled to great weight where, as here, it varies from prior EEOC policy and no new legislative history has been introduced in support of the change. But where "Congress has not just kept its silence by refusing to overturn the administrative construction, but has ratified it with positive legislation," Red Lion Broadcasting Co. v. FCC, 395 U.S. 367, 381–382, 89 S.Ct. 1794, 1802, 23 L.Ed.2d 371 (1969), the guideline is entitled to some deference, at least sufficient in this case to warrant our accepting the guideline as a defensible construction of the pre-1972 statute, *i.e.*, as imposing on TWA the duty of "reasonable accommodation" in the absence of "undue hardship." We thus need not consider whether § 701(j) must be applied retroactively to the facts of this litigation.

son's Saturday shift from other available personnel competent to do the job, of which the court said there were at least 200. That this would have involved premium overtime pay was not deemed an undue hardship. Third, TWA could have arranged a "swap between Hardison and another employee either for another shift or for the Sabbath days." In response to the assertion that this would have involved a breach of the seniority provisions of the contract, the court noted that it had not been settled in the courts whether the required statutory accommodation to religious needs stopped short of transgressing seniority rules, but found it unnecessary to decide the issue because, as the Court of Appeals saw the record, TWA had not sought, and the union had therefore not declined to entertain, a possible variance from the seniority provisions of the collective-bargaining agreement. The company had simply left the entire matter to the union steward who the Court of Appeals said "likewise did nothing."

We disagree with the Court of Appeals in all relevant respects. It is our view that TWA made reasonable efforts to accommodate and that each of the Court of Appeals' suggested alternatives would have been an undue hardship within the meaning of the statute as construed by the EEOC guidelines.

A

It might be inferred from the Court of Appeals' opinion and from the brief of the EEOC in this Court that TWA's efforts to accommodate were no more than negligible. The findings of the District Court, supported by the record, are to the contrary. In summarizing its more detailed findings, the District Court observed:

> "TWA established as a matter of fact that it did take appropriate action to accommodate as required by Title VII. It held several meetings with plaintiff at which it attempted to find a solution to plaintiff's problems. It did accommodate plaintiff's observance of his special religious holidays. It authorized the union steward to search for someone who would swap shifts, which apparently was normal procedure."

It is also true that TWA itself attempted without success to find Hardison another job. The District Court's view was that TWA had done all that could reasonably be expected within the bounds of the seniority system.

The Court of Appeals observed, however, that the possibility of a variance from the seniority system was never really posed to the union. This is contrary to the District Court's findings and to the record. The District Court found that when TWA first learned of Hardison's religious observances in April 1968, it agreed to permit the union's steward to seek a swap of shifts or days off but that "the steward reported that he was unable to work out scheduling changes and that he understood that no one was willing to swap days with plaintiff." Later, in March 1969, at a meeting held just two days before Hardison first failed to report for his Saturday shift, TWA again "offered to accommodate plaintiff's religious observance by agreeing to any trade of shifts or change of sections that plaintiff and the union could work out. * * * Any shift or change was impossible within the seniority framework and the union was not willing to violate the seniority provision set out in the contract to make a shift or change." * * *

* * *

B

We are also convinced, contrary to the Court of Appeals, that TWA itself cannot be faulted for having failed to work out a shift or job swap for Hardison. Both the union and TWA had agreed to the seniority system; the union was unwilling to entertain a variance over the objections of men senior to Hardison; and for TWA to have arranged unilaterally for a swap would have amounted to a breach of the collective-bargaining agreement.

(1)

Hardison and the EEOC insist that the statutory obligation to accommodate religious needs takes precedence over both the collective-bargaining contract and the seniority rights of TWA's other employees. We agree that neither a collective-bargaining contract nor a seniority system may be employed to violate the statute, but we do not believe that the duty to accommodate requires TWA to take steps inconsistent with the otherwise valid agreement. Collective bargaining, aimed at effecting workable and enforceable agreements between management and labor, lies at the core of our national labor policy, and seniority provisions are universally included in these contracts. Without a clear and express indication from Congress, we cannot agree with Hardison and the EEOC that an agreed-upon seniority system must give way when necessary to accommodate religious observances. * * *

* * *

Had TWA * * * circumvented the seniority system by relieving Hardison of Saturday work and ordering a senior employee to replace him, it would have denied the latter his shift preference so that Hardison could be given his. The senior employee would also have been deprived of his contractual rights under the collective-bargaining agreement.

It was essential to TWA's business to require Saturday and Sunday work from at least a few employees even though most employees preferred those days off. Allocating the burdens of weekend work was a matter for collective bargaining. In considering criteria to govern this allocation, TWA and the union had two alternatives: adopt a neutral system, such as seniority, a lottery, or rotating shifts; or allocate days off in accordance with the religious needs of its employees. TWA would have had to adopt the latter in order to assure Hardison and others like him of getting the days off necessary for strict observance of their religion, but it could have done so only at the expense of others who had strong, but perhaps nonreligious, reasons for not working on weekends. There were no volunteers to relieve Hardison on Saturdays, and to give Hardison Saturdays off, TWA would have had to deprive another employee of his shift preference at least in part because he did not adhere to a religion that observed the Saturday Sabbath.

Title VII does not contemplate such unequal treatment. The repeated, unequivocal emphasis of both the language and the legislative history of Title VII is on eliminating discrimination in employment, and such discrimination is proscribed when it is directed against majorities as well as minorities. * * * It would be anomalous to conclude that by "reasonable accommodation" Congress meant that an employer must deny the shift and job preference of some employees, as well as deprive them of their contractual rights, in order to accommodate or prefer the religious needs of others, and we conclude that Title VII does not require an employer to go that far.

(2)

Our conclusion is supported by the fact that seniority systems are afforded special treatment under Title VII itself. Section 703(h) provides in pertinent part:

> "Notwithstanding any other provision of this subchapter, it shall not be an unlawful employment practice for an employer to apply different standards of compensation, or different terms, conditions, or privileges of employment pursuant to a bona fide seniority or merit system * * * provided that such differences are not the result of an intention to discriminate because of race, color, religion, sex, or national origin * * *."

"[T]he unmistakable purpose of § 703(h) was to make clear that the routine application of a bona fide seniority system would not be unlawful under Title VII." International Brotherhood of Teamsters v. United States, 431 U.S. 324, 352, 97 S.Ct. 1843, 1863, 52 L.Ed.2d 396 (1977). * * * [A]bsent a discriminatory purpose, the operation of a seniority system cannot be an unlawful employment practice even if the system has some discriminatory consequences.

There has been no suggestion of discriminatory intent in this case. * * * The Court of Appeals' conclusion that TWA was not limited by the terms of its seniority system was in substance nothing more than a ruling that operation of the seniority system was itself an unlawful employment practice even though no discriminatory purpose had been shown. That ruling is plainly inconsistent with the dictates of § 703(h), both on its face and as interpreted in the recent decisions of this Court.[13]

13. Franks v. Bowman Transportation Co., is not to the contrary. In *Franks* we held that "once an illegal discriminatory practice occurring after the effective date

As we have said, TWA was not required by Title VII to carve out a special exception to its seniority system in order to help Hardison to meet his religious obligations.[14]

C

The Court of Appeals also suggested that TWA could have permitted Hardison to work a four-day week if necessary in order to avoid working on his Sabbath. Recognizing that this might have left TWA short-handed on the one shift each week that Hardison did not work, the court still concluded that TWA would suffer no undue hardship if it were required to replace Hardison either with supervisory personnel or with qualified personnel from other departments. Alternatively, the Court of Appeals suggested that TWA could have replaced Hardison on his Saturday shift with other available employees through the payment of premium wages. Both of these alternatives would involve costs to TWA, either in the form of lost efficiency in other jobs or higher wages.

To require TWA to bear more than a *de minimis* cost in order to give Hardison Saturdays off is an undue hardship.[15] Like abandon-

of the Act is proved," § 703(h) does not bar an award of retroactive seniority status to victims of that discriminatory practice. Here the suggested exception to the TWA–IAM seniority system would not be remedial; the operation of the seniority system itself is said to violate Title VII. In such circumstances, § 703(h) unequivocally mandates that there is no statutory violation in the absence of a showing of discriminatory purpose. See United Air Lines, Inc. v. Evans, 431 U.S. 553, 558–560, 97 S.Ct. 1885, 1889–1890, 52 L.Ed.2d 571 (1977).

14. Despite its hyperbole and rhetoric, the dissent appears to agree with—at last it stops short of challenging—the fundamental proposition that Title VII does not require an employer and a union who have agreed on a seniority system to deprive senior employees of their seniority rights in order to accommodate a junior employee's religous practices. This is the principal issue on which TWA and the union came to this Court. The dissent is thus reduced to (1) asserting that the statute requires TWA to accommodate Hardison even though substantial expenditures are required to do so; and (2) advancing its own view of the record to show that TWA could have done more than it did to accommodate Hardison without violating the seniority system or incurring substantial additional costs. We reject the former assertion as an erroneous construction of the statute. As for the latter, we prefer the findings of the District Judge who heard the evidence. Thus, the dissent suggests that through further efforts TWA or the union might have arranged a temporary or permanent job swap within the seniority system, despite the District Court's express finding, supported by the record, that "[t]he seniority provisions * * * precluded the possibility of plaintiff's changing his shift." Similarly, the dissent offers two alternatives—sending Hardison back to Building 1 or allowing him to work extra days without overtime pay—that it says could have been pursued by TWA or the union, even though neither of the courts below even hinted that these suggested alternatives would have been feasible under the circumstances. Furthermore, Buildings 1 and 2 had separate seniority lists, and insofar as the record shows, a return to Building 1 would not have solved Hardison's problems. Hardison himself testified that he "gave up" his Building 1 seniority when he came to Building 2, App. 104, and that the union would not accept his early return to Building 1 in part "because the problem of seniority came up again." We accept the District Court's findings that TWA had done all that it could do to accommodate Hardison's religious beliefs without either incurring substantial costs or violating the seniority rights of other employees.

15. The dissent argues that "the costs to TWA of either paying overtime or not replacing respondent would [not] have been more than *de minimis.*" This ignores, however, the express finding of the District Court that "[b]oth of these solutions would have created an undue burden

ment of the seniority system, to require TWA to bear additional costs when no such costs are incurred to give other employees the days off that they want would involve unequal treatment of employees on the basis of their religion. By suggesting that TWA should incur certain costs in order to give Hardison Saturdays off the Court of Appeals would in effect require TWA to finance an additional Saturday off and then to choose the employee who will enjoy it on the basis of his religious beliefs. While incurring extra costs to secure a replacement for Hardison might remove the necessity of compelling another employee to work involuntarily in Hardison's place, it would not change the fact that the privilege of having Saturdays off would be allocated according to religious beliefs.

As we have seen, the paramount concern of Congress in enacting Title VII was the elimination of discrimination in employment. In the absence of clear statutory language or legislative history to the contrary, we will not readily construe the statute to require an employer to discriminate against some employees in order to enable others to observe their Sabbath.

Reversed.

MR. JUSTICE MARSHALL, with whom MR. JUSTICE BRENNAN joins, dissenting.

* * *

Today's decision deals a fatal blow to all efforts under Title VII to accommodate work requirements to religious practices. The Court holds, in essence, that although the EEOC regulations and the Act state that an employer must make reasonable adjustments in his work demands to take account of religious observances, the regulation and Act do not really mean what they say. An employer, the Court concludes, need not grant even the most minor special privilege to religious observers to enable them to follow their faith. As a question of social policy, this result is deeply troubling, for a society that truly values religious pluralism cannot compel adherents of minority religions to make the cruel choice of surrendering their religion or their job. And as a matter of law today's result is intolerable, for the Court adopts the very position that Congress expressly rejected in 1972, as if we were free to disregard congressional choices that a majority of this Court thinks unwise. I therefore dissent.

I

With respect to each of the proposed accommodations to respondent Hardison's religious observances that the Court discusses, it ultimately notes that the accommodation would have required "unequal treatment," in favor of the religious observer. That is quite true. But if an

on the conduct of TWA's business," and it fails to take account of the likelihood that a company as large as TWA may have many employees whose religious observances, like Hardison's, prohibit them from working on Saturdays or Sundays.

accommodation can be rejected simply because it involves preferential treatment, then the regulation and the statute, while brimming with "sound and fury," ultimately "signif[y] nothing."

The accommodation issue by definition arises only when a neutral rule of general applicability conflicts with the religious practices of a particular employee. * * * What all * * * [the accommodation] cases have in common is an employee who could comply with the rule only by violating what the employee views as a religious commandment. In each instance, the question is whether the employee is to be exempt from the rule's demands. To do so will always result in a privilege being "allocated according to religious beliefs," unless the employer gratuitously decides to repeal the rule *in toto.* What the statute says, in plain words, is that such allocations are required unless "undue hardship" would result.

* * *

II

Once it is determined that the duty to accommodate sometimes requires that an employee be exempted from an otherwise valid work requirement, the only remaining question is whether this is such a case: Did TWA prove that it exhausted all reasonable accommodations, and that the only remaining alternatives would have caused undue hardship on TWA's business? To pose the question is to answer it, for all that the District Court found TWA had done to accommodate respondent's Sabbath observance was that it "held several meetings with [respondent] * * * [and] authorized the union steward to search for someone who would swap shifts." To conclude that TWA, one of the largest air carriers in the Nation, would have suffered undue hardship had it done anything more defies both reason and common sense.

The Court implicitly assumes that the only means of accommodation open to TWA were to compel an unwilling employee to replace Hardison; to pay premium wages to a voluntary substitute; or to employ one less person during respondent's Sabbath shift.[5] Based on this assumption, the Court seemingly finds that each alternative would have involved undue hardship not only because Hardison would have been given a special privilege, but also because either another employee would have been deprived of rights under the collective-bargaining agreement, or because "more than a *de minimis* cost," would have been imposed on TWA. But the Court's myopic view of the available options is not supported by either the District Court's findings or the evidence adduced at trial. Thus, the Court's conclusion cannot withstand analy-

5. It is true that these are the only options the Court of Appeals discussed. But that court found that TWA could have adopted these options without undue hardship; once that conclusion is rejected it is incumbent on this Court to decide whether any other alternatives were available that would not have involved such hardship.

sis, even assuming that its rejection of the alternatives it does discuss is justifiable.[6]

To begin with, the record simply does not support the Court's assertion, made without accompanying citations, that "[t]here were no volunteers to relieve Hardison on Saturdays." Everett Kussman, the manager of the department in which respondent worked, testified that he had made no effort to find volunteers, and the union stipulated that its steward had not done so either.[8] * * * Thus, respondent's religious observance might have been accommodated by a simple trade of days or shifts without necessarily depriving any employee of his or her contractual rights [10] and without imposing significant costs on

6. I entertain grave doubts on both factual and legal grounds about the validity of the Court's rejection of the options it considers. As a matter of fact, I do not believe the record supports the Court's suggestion that the costs to TWA of either paying overtime or not replacing respondent would have been more than *de minimis.* While the District Court did state, as the Court notes, that both alternatives "would have created an undue burden on the conduct of TWA's business," the court did not explain its understanding of the phrase "undue burden," and may have believed that such a burden exists whenever any cost is incurred by the employer, no matter how slight. Thus the District Court's assertion falls far short of a factual "finding" that the costs of these accommodations would be more than *de minimis.* Moreover, the record is devoid of any evidence documenting the extent of the "efficiency loss" TWA would have incurred had it used a supervisor or an already scheduled employee to do respondent's work, and while the stipulations make clear what overtime would have cost, the price is far from staggering: $150 for three months, at which time respondent would have been eligible to transfer back to his previous department. The Court's suggestion that the cost of accommodation must be evaluated in light of the "likelihood that * * * TWA may have many employees whose religious observances * * * prohibit them from working on Saturdays or Sundays," is not only contrary to the record, which indicates that only one other case involving a conflict between work schedules and Sabbath observance had arisen at TWA since 1945, but also irrelevant, since the real question is not whether such employees exist but whether they could be accommodated without significant expense. Indeed, to the extent that TWA employed Sunday as well as Saturday Sabbatarians, the likelihood of accommodation being costly would diminish, since trades would be more feasible.

As a matter of law, I seriously question whether simple English usage permits "undue hardship" to be interpreted to mean "more than *de minimis* cost," especially when the examples the guidelines give of possible undue hardship is the absence of a qualified substitute. I therefore believe that in the appropriate case we would be compelled to confront the constitutionality of requiring employers to bear more than *de minimis* costs. The issue need not be faced here, however, since an almost cost-free accommodation was possible.

8. The Court relies, on the District Court's conclusory assertion that "[a]ny shift or change was impossible within the seniority framework." But the District Court also found that "TWA did not take part in the search for employees willing to swap shifts * * * and it was admitted at trial that the Union made no real effort." Thus, the District Court's statement concerning the impact of "the seniority framework" lends no support to the Court's assertion that there were no volunteers. See also n. 10, infra.

10. If, as appears likely, no one senior to the substitute employee desired respondent's Sabbath assignment or his Thursday-Monday shift, then the substitute could have transferred to respondent's position without depriving anyone of his or her seniority expectations. Similarly, if, as also appears probable, no one senior to respondent desired the substitute's spot, respondent could have assumed it. Such a trade would not have deprived any employee of seniority expectations. The trade apparently still would have violated the collective-bargaining agreement, however, since the agreement authorized transfers only to vacant jobs. This is undoubtedly what the District Court meant when it found that "the seniority framework" precluded shift changes. Indeed, the first time in the District Court's opinion that such a finding appears, it is preceded by

TWA. Of course, it is also possible that no trade—or none consistent with the seniority system—could have been arranged. But the burden under the EEOC regulation is on TWA to establish that a reasonable accommodation was not possible. Because it failed either to explore the possibility of a voluntary trade or to assure that its delegate, the union steward, did so, TWA was unable to meet its burden.

Nor was a voluntary trade the only option open to TWA that the Court ignores; to the contrary, at least two other options are apparent from the record. First, TWA could have paid overtime to a voluntary replacement for respondent—assuming that someone would have been willing to work Saturdays for premium pay—and passed on the cost to respondent. In fact, one accommodation Hardison suggested would have done just that by requiring Hardison to work overtime when needed at regular pay. Under this plan, the total overtime cost to the employer—and the total number of overtime hours available for other employees—would not have reflected Hardison's Sabbath absences. Alternatively, TWA could have transferred respondent back to his previous department where he had accumulated substantial seniority, as respondent also suggested.[11] Admittedly, both options would have violated the collective-bargaining agreement; the former because the agreement required that employees working over 40 hours per week receive premium pay, and the latter because the agreement prohibited employees from transferring departments more than once every six months. But neither accommodation would have deprived any other employee of rights under the contract or violated the seniority system in any way.[12] Plainly an employer cannot avoid his duty to accommodate by signing a contract that precludes all reasonable accommodations; even the Court appears to concede as much. Thus I do not believe it can be even seriously argued that TWA would have suffered "undue hardship" to its business had it required respondent to pay the extra costs of his replacement, or had it transferred respondent to his former department.

What makes today's decision most tragic, however, is not that respondent Hardison has been needlessly deprived of his livelihood simply because he chose to follow the dictates of his conscience. Nor is

the finding that "there were no jobs open for bid."

Even if a trade could not have been arranged without disrupting seniority expectations TWA could have requested the Union Relief Committee to approve an exemption. The record reveals that the Committee's function was to ameliorate the rigidity of the system, and that on at least one occasion it had approved a permanent transfer apparently outside the seniority system.

11. The Court states, that because of TWA's departmental seniority system, such a transfer "would not have solved Hardison's problems." But respondent testified without contradiction that had he returned to his previous department he would have regained his seniority in that department, and thereby could have avoided work on his Sabbath. According to respondent, the only objection that was raised to this solution was that it violated the rule prohibiting transfers twice within six months.

12. The accommodations would have disadvantaged respondent to some extent, but since he suggested both options I do not consider whether an employer would satisfy his duty to accommodate by offering these choices to an unwilling employee.

the tragedy exhausted by the impact it will have on thousands of Americans like Hardison who could be forced to live on welfare as the price they must pay for worshiping their God.[14] The ultimate tragedy is that despite Congress' best efforts, one of this Nation's pillars of strength—our hospitality to religious diversity—has been seriously eroded. All Americans will be a little poorer until today's decision is erased.

I respectfully dissent.

NOTES AND PROBLEMS FOR DISCUSSION

1. Shirley Booker was hired by the Postal Service as a full time window clerk in 1971. Pursuant to an agreement between the Selective Service System and the Postal Service, the latter agency agreed to participate in the registration of young men for the draft. As of January 1, 1981, in addition to their other duties, all window clerks were required to provide, aid in the completion of and accept registration forms. They also were prohibited from refusing a tendered form for any reason. After receiving the standard training in handling such forms, Ms. Booker notified her supervisor of her conscientious objection to any involvement in the registration process, based on her moral opposition to war and conscription. She asked to be relieved of this duty in exchange for which she agreed to perform additional tasks not performed by window clerks. Her supervisor rejected this request, however, stating that such a compromise would violate the work assignment provisions of the collective bargaining agreement covering all postal employees. In addition, he told Booker that accepting her request could severely disrupt the efficient operation of the post office by setting a precedent that would encourage other employees to try to bargain their way out of undesired duties. Accordingly, he informed Booker that any failure to process registration forms would result in her dismissal. Nevertheless, Booker consistently avoided processing the forms by referring all potential registrants to other windows. Upon learning of Booker's conduct, and personally observing such a referral, the supervisor served Booker with a notice of dismissal for insubordination. After exhausting all available administrative remedies, Booker filed suit under Title VII in a federal district court claiming that the discharge constituted discrimination on the basis of her religion. How should the court rule? See McGinnis v. United States Postal Service, 512 F.Supp. 517 (N.D.Cal.1980).

2. Do you agree with Justice Marshall's contention that the majority in *Hardison* effectively nullified the statutory duty to accommodate through its interpretation of "undue hardship"? Can you conceive of an accommodation that would not impose an undue hardship under a literal reading of the Court's tripartite formulation of that term? Can the Court's restrictive interpretation of § 701(j) perhaps be explained as an attempt to avoid the constitutional issue that arises when a defendant is ordered to make some accommodation?

14. Ironically, the fiscal costs to society of today's decision may exceed the costs that would accrue if employers were required to make all accommodations without regard to hardship, since it is clear that persons on welfare cannot be denied benefits because they refuse to take jobs that would prevent them from observing religious holy days.

3. The courts have uniformly adopted the following allocation of the burden of proof in religious discrimination cases:

> "In order to establish a prima facie case of religious discrimination under [§§ 703(a) and 701(j)], a plaintiff must plead and prove that (1) he had a bona fide belief that compliance with an employment requirement is contrary to his religious faith; (2) he informed his employer about the conflict; and (3) he was discharged because of his refusal to comply with the employment requirement."

Brown v. General Motors Corp., 601 F.2d 956, 959 (8th Cir. 1979).

> "The burden [is] thereafter upon [the defendants] to prove that they made good faith efforts to accommodate [the plaintiff's] religious beliefs and, if these efforts were unsuccessful, to demonstrate that they were unable reasonably to accommodate his beliefs without undue hardship."

Anderson v. General Dynamics, 589 F.2d 397, 401 (9th Cir. 1978).

Does the employee's conduct have to be required by her religious beliefs? Is it enough to establish that the conduct is permitted or motivated by religious belief? See Dorr v. First Kentucky National Corp., 796 F.2d 179 (6th Cir. 1986).

4. Many collective bargaining agreements contain "union security" clauses which require all employees to pay union dues within a specific time after the effective date of the contract. These provisions also state that failure to make such payments shall result in the employee's discharge. Suppose an employee claims that her sincere religious beliefs forbid her from making contributions to labor organizations. She also states, however, that she is willing to contribute an amount equal to the union dues to a non-sectarian, non-union charity chosen by the union and her employer. If the union and employer reject this request and terminate her employment, can the employee successfully prosecute a Title VII claim of religious discrimination? Does a union have a § 701(j) duty to accommodate? If so, does the loss of the plaintiff's dues impose any undue hardship upon the union? Could this accommodation distress other employees, impair their job performance and thus result in an undue hardship upon the employer?

At least four federal circuit courts have concluded that the presence of the word "employer" in § 701(j) notwithstanding, unions are under a statutory duty to accommodate. See Nottelson v. Smith Steel Workers, 643 F.2d 445 (7th Cir. 1981), cert. denied, 454 U.S. 1046, 102 S.Ct. 587, 70 L.Ed.2d 488; Burns v. Southern Pacific Transportation Co., 589 F.2d 403 (9th Cir. 1978), cert. denied, 439 U.S. 1072, 99 S.Ct. 843, 59 L.Ed.2d 38 (1979), on remand, 22 FEP Cases 1229 (D.Ariz.1979); McDaniel v. Essex International Inc., 571 F.2d 338 (6th Cir. 1978), on remand, 509 F.Supp. 1055 (W.D.Mich.1981), affirmed, 696 F.2d 34 (6th Cir. 1982); and Cooper v. General Dynamics, 533 F.2d 163 (5th Cir. 1976). Moreover, in each of these cases except *Cooper*, the court held that neither the loss of an employee's union dues, nor the grumblings of other employees not offered such a choice, constituted undue hardship to the union or employer as a matter of law. While the courts recognized that the loss of dues generated by a large number of requests for substitute payments could result in undue hardship as a matter of fact, they stated that undue hardship could be established only by offering evidence of actual, as opposed to anticipated multiple requests for substitute payments. Accord, Haring v. Blumenthal, 471 F.Supp. 1172, 1182 (D.D.C.1979), affirmed, 24 EPD ¶ 31,412 (D.C.Cir. 1980). Accordingly, in *Nottelson, Burns* and *McDaniel*, the unions' and employers' blanket refusal to permit substitute payments and their failure to prove that this accommodation would result in undue hardship as a matter of fact, resulted in judgments for the plaintiffs.

Are these rulings consistent with the *Hardison* de minimis standard? Moreover, won't the accommodations required by the courts in these cases compel both the union and employer to violate the contractual union security clause? If so, is this permissible under *Hardison*? In *Nottelson*, the court distinguished *Hardison* on the ground that the defendant in that case would have been forced to ignore a seniority system protected by Title VII as well as the collective bargaining agreement. 643 F.2d at 452. Do you agree? See also McCormick v. Bd. of Educ., Belvidere, 32 FEP Cases 504 (N.D.Ill.1983); McDaniel v. Essex International Inc., 509 F.Supp. 1055, 1061 (W.D.Mich.1981). Finally, isn't it also true that the plaintiffs in *Nottelson, Burns* and *McDaniel* were accorded differential treatment because of their religion?

The National Labor Relations Act, 29 U.S.C. § 151 et seq., the federal statute governing the organizational and collective bargaining rights of employees, sanctions the type of union security clause discussed in this Note. Defendants frequently have relied on § 8(a)(3) of the N.L.R.A., the provision recognizing the legality of union security clauses, as the basis for their claim that a substituted charity accommodation would be inconsistent with the national labor policy of promoting union security agreements. The statute was amended in 1974, however, to provide that health care industry employees subject to a union security clause, but whose religious beliefs prevent them from paying union dues, could not be required to make such payments. 29 U.S.C. § 169. The amendment also states that a collective bargaining agreement can require these employees to make equivalent payments to a non-religious, non-labor organization charitable fund chosen by the employee from a list of at least three such funds designated in the contract, or, in the absence of such a contractual designation, to any such fund chosen by the employee. In 1980, these provisions were expanded to include all employees covered by the N.L.R.A. Does the 1980 amendment dispose of the defendants' argument? See Tooley v. Martin Marietta Corp., 648 F.2d 1239, 1242 (9th Cir. 1981). Has the employer satisfied its Title VII duty to accommodate an employee whose religious beliefs preclude him from paying union dues by requiring him to pay an equal amount to one of several nonreligious charities designated in the collective bargaining agreement? See Stern v. Teamsters Local 200, 626 F.Supp. 1043 (E.D.Wi.1986).

5. Section 702 exempts religious institutions from § 703's ban on religious discrimination. Does this mean that these institutions also are not subject to the § 701(j) duty to accommodate? See Larsen v. Kirkham, 499 F.Supp. 960 (D. Utah 1980).

6. If the employee and the company each propose a reasonable accommodation, does Title VII require the employer to accept the employee's proposal where it does not impose an undue hardship? See American Postal Workers Union v. Postmaster General, 781 F.2d 772 (9th Cir. 1986) (employer must accept employee's proposal where employer's attempted accommodation fails to eliminate the religious conflict); Philbrook v. Ansonia Bd. of Ed., 757 F.2d 476 (2d Cir. 1985), cert. granted, ___ U.S. ___, 106 S.Ct. 848, 88 L.Ed.2d 889 (1986).

7. Is a trial court's findings of undue hardship and reasonable accommodation to be upset on appeal only if they are clearly erroneous? Does the Supreme Court's opinion in *Anderson*, supra at 182 help resolve this problem? See Wisner v. Truck Central, A Sub. of Saunders Leasing, 784 F.2d 1571, 1573

(11th Cir. 1986) (holding finding on de minimis cost subject to Rule 52 standard).

8. Rabban County employs several social workers to provide counseling and therapy for the inmates in its prison facilities. One of these counselors, Lisa Germain, sincerely views herself as an evangelist with a mission to spread the Gospel. Accordingly, she offered religious counseling, including Bible reading and prayer, to amenable inmates as one method of combatting their psychological problems. Rabban County follows a policy of precluding all county-paid social workers from using religious counseling because it believes that it is constitutionally compelled to maintain an atmosphere of religious neutrality within its jails. The County also instructs all of its counselors to refer requests for religious counseling to the chaplains who make themselves available to the inmates. Ms. Germain maintains that praying and sharing scripture with the inmates is a religious practice and continues to offer religious counseling to inmates who desire it. After repeated warnings, she is discharged. Germain then brings a Title VII action against the County alleging religious discrimination. The County claims that, in light of the constitutional constraints upon its conduct, it has made a reasonable accommodation to her religious beliefs by allowing inmates access to voluntary chaplains of all faiths. How should the court rule? See Spratt v. County of Kent, 621 F.Supp. 594 (W.D.Mich.1985).

TOOLEY v. MARTIN–MARIETTA CORP.

United States Court of Appeals, Ninth Circuit, 1981.
648 F.2d 1239, cert. denied, 454 U.S. 1098, 102 S.Ct. 671, 70 L.Ed.2d 639.

Before HUG, TANG and FARRIS, CIRCUIT JUDGES.

FARRIS, CIRCUIT JUDGE.

* * *

In 1976, the Martin-Marietta Corporation and Steelworkers Local 8141 executed a collective bargaining agreement containing a "union shop" clause, under which the company was obligated to discharge all employees who failed to join the union. Plaintiffs Tooley, Bakke, and Helt are Seventh Day Adventists who, under the tenets of their faith, are prohibited from becoming members in or paying a service fee to a union. Plaintiffs informed the company and the union of this proscription, and offered to pay an amount equal to union dues to a mutually acceptable charity. The union refused.

After exhausting their administrative remedies, plaintiffs instituted this action, alleging that the union's and the company's refusal to honor the requested accommodation constituted religious discrimination under Title VII of the Civil Rights Act of 1964. In particular, the plaintiffs argued that both the union and the company were required under section 701(j) of the Act to make good faith efforts to institute their requested exemption unless it would result in undue hardship to either the Steelworkers or the company. The Steelworkers contended that the "substituted charity" accommodation was unreasonable, that its implementation would cause the union undue hardship, and that by authorizing such an accommodation, section 701(j) violated the Establishment Clause. The district court enjoined the union and the company from attempting to discharge the plaintiffs for failing to pay union dues so long as they make equivalent contributions to a mutually acceptible charity.

[The appellate court upheld as not clearly erroneous the trial judge's findings that the plaintiff's proposed accommodation was reasonable and did not impose an undue hardship upon the defendants. Consequently, the court was then obliged to consider the constitutional question left unanswered by the Supreme Court in *Hardison.*]

* * *

The Steelworkers argue that section 701(j) as applied here violates the Establishment Clause.[8] The district court held that section 701(j) withstood constitutional attack under the three-pronged test enunciated in Committee for Public Education & Religious Liberty v. Nyquist, 413 U.S. 756, 772–73, 93 S.Ct. 2955, 2965, 39 L.Ed.2d 948 (1973).

The Establishment Clause ensures government neutrality in matters of religion. But government neutrality "is not so narrow a channel that the slightest deviation from an absolutely straight course leads to condemnation." Sherbert v. Verner, 374 U.S. 398, 422, 83 S.Ct. 1790, 1803, 10 L.Ed.2d 965 (1963) (Harlan, J., dissenting). Courts have defined the government's obligation as one of "benevolent neutrality." Walz v. Tax Commission, 397 U.S. 664, 669, 90 S.Ct. 1409, 1411, 25 L.Ed.2d 697 (1970). While the government must avoid "partiality to any one group," Zorach v. Clauson, 343 U.S. 306, 313, 72 S.Ct. 679, 683, 96 L.Ed. 954 (1952), it may deviate from absolute rigidity to accommodate the religious practices of each group. *Walz*, 397 U.S. at 669, 90 S.Ct. at 1411.

Government can accommodate the beliefs and practices of members of minority religions without contravening the prohibitions of the Establishment Clause. Cf. Wisconsin v. Yoder, 406 U.S. 205, 234 n.22, 92 S.Ct. 1526, 1542 n.22, 32 L.Ed.2d 15 (1972) (exempting Amish children from state compulsory education laws); Sherbert v. Verner, 374 U.S. 398, 409, 83 S.Ct. 1790, 1796, 10 L.Ed.2d 965 (1963) (exempting Seventh-Day Adventists from state unemployment compensation requirements). Government may legitimately enforce accommodations of religious beliefs when the accommodation reflects the "obligation of

8. The plaintiffs contend that the constitutional validity of § 701(j) as applied here has been determined conclusively by the Supreme Court's dismissal of the appeal in Rankins v. Comm'n on Professional Competence, 24 Cal.3d 167, 593 P.2d 852, 154 Cal.Rptr. 907, appeal dismissed, 444 U.S. 986, 100 S.Ct. 515, 62 L.Ed.2d 416 (1979). There, the California state constitutional employment discrimination provision, construed to require the same accommodations as those required by Title VII's § 701(j), was held not to offend the Establishment Clause in requiring a school district to accommodate a teacher who refused to work on religious holidays. The dismissal of the appeal in *Rankins* binds this court only on "the precise issues presented and necessarily decided." Mandel v. Bradley, 432 U.S. 172, 176, 97 S.Ct. 2238, 2240, 53 L.Ed.2d 199 (1977). Because this case and *Rankins* involve entirely different kinds of religious accommodations, the constitutional dimension of each is necessarily different.

neutrality in the face of religious differences," and does not constitute "sponsorship, financial support, [or] active involvement of the sovereign in religious activities" with which the Establishment Clause is mainly concerned.

Like the accommodations allowed in Sherbert v. Verner and Wisconsin v. Yoder, the substituted charity accommodation satisfies these requirements. By exempting the plaintiffs from union membership or the payment of mandatory union dues, the accommodation places the plaintiffs on an equal footing with other employees whose religious convictions find no impediment in the workplace. To this extent, the accommodation reflects governmental neutrality in the face of religious differences. Further, the substituted charity accommodation does not involve government "sponsorship" or "financial support" of the Seventh-Day Adventist religion: the accommodation requires that the plaintiffs suffer the same economic loss as their co-workers who are not similarly restricted in paying union dues or in obtaining union membership. The accommodation demands neither direct nor indirect financial support of the plaintiffs' religion by the government, and cannot be reasonably construed as actively advancing or assisting their religion.

This same conclusion is compelled under the test enunciated in Committee for Public Education & Religious Liberty v. Nyquist. The *Nyquist* test, typically applied to state legislation, requires that for section 701(j) to be consistent with the demands of the Establishment Clause, it must (1) reflect a clearly secular purpose, (2) have a primary effect that neither inhibits nor advances religion, and (3) avoid excessive government entanglement with religion.

1. Legislative Purpose

The primary motivation for the enactment of section 701(j) was to resolve many of the issues left open by prior "Sabbatarian" cases, where employees refused to work on their Sabbath and requested that their employers accommodate them. *Hardison,* 432 U.S. at 73–74, 97 S.Ct. at 2271. The Steelworkers contend that because section 701(j) was intended to secure special treatment for Sabbatarians and other religious proponents, the legislation has an improper sectarian purpose.

Although section 701(j)'s enactment may have resolved certain problems confronting sectarians, this alone is insufficient to establish that the legislation lacks a clearly secular purpose. Section 701(j) was intended to promote Title VII's broader policy of prohibiting discrimination in employment. The bill's sponsor in the Senate, recognizing the problems confronting Sabbatarians in particular, stated that the legislation was intended to "assure that freedom from religious discrimination in the employment of workers is for all time guaranteed in law." Section 701(j) functions to "secure equal economic opportunity to members of minority religions." *Hardison,* 432 U.S. at 90 n.4 (Marshall, J., dissenting). Cf. Rankins v. Commission on Professional Competence, 24 Cal.3d 167, 177–78 (recognizing as secular the purpose of "promot[ing] equal employment opportunities for members of all religious faiths"), appeal dismissed, 444 U.S. 986 (1979). It therefore has a legitimate secular purpose.

2. Primary Effect

The Steelworkers contend that the substituted charity accommodation has the primary effect of advancing the plaintiffs' religion by conferring various alleged economic benefits. It is argued that as a consequence of the accommodation, the plaintiffs have a greater choice than their co-workers in determining how their money is spent, and are more easily able to make charitable contributions.

We reject this argument. It confuses ancillary or incidental benefits with primary benefits to those accommodated. It could be argued, for example, that the exemption allowed the Amish children in Wisconsin v. Yoder permitted the children to contribute additional economic benefit to their families, and that the exemption allowed in Sherbert v. Verner permitted the Seventh-Day Adventist to exercise a greater choice in determining which day of the week was to be free of employment responsibilities.

The substituted charity accommodation allows the plaintiffs to work without violating their religious beliefs, at a cost equivalent to that paid by their co-workers without similar beliefs. It neither increases nor decreases the advantages of membership in the Seventh-Day Adventist faith in a manner so substantial and direct that it "advances" or "inhibits" the plaintiffs' religion.

The Steelworkers also contend that the accommodation violates the Establishment Clause because it will ultimately result in either the union curtailing necessary services, or forcing the accommodation cost on other employees. In either case, the Steelworkers argue that the plaintiffs receive the benefit of their religious beliefs at the expense of their co-workers. As a result, it is urged that the accommodation impermissibly places the burdens of accommodation on unaccommodated private parties.

A religious accommodation does not violate the Establishment Clause merely because it can be construed in some abstract way as placing an inappreciable but inevitable burden on those not accommodated. Exemption of conscientious objectors from military conscription has been upheld despite the effect of requiring nonobjectors to serve in their stead. Sectarian institutions are exempt from the payment of property taxes, even though the effect may be to increase marginally the property taxes paid by unaccommodated private citizens. Walz v. Tax Commission, 397 U.S. 664, 90 S.Ct. 1409, 25 L.Ed.2d 697 (1970). Sunday closing laws have been upheld even though their effect may be to burden those who sincerely observe another Sabbath.

The substituted charity does not have a primary effect which either advances or inhibits the plaintiffs' religion.

3. Government Entanglement

Nor do we find that the accommodation here requires that the government become impermissibly entangled with the accommodation's administration. The Establishment Clause prohibits only *excessive* government entanglement. The implementation of the substituted charity accommodation requires a minimal amount of supervision and administrative cost. Once the sincerity of a religious objector's belief is established, the only administrative burden involves the employee and the union agreeing on a mutually acceptable charity. The Steelworkers have not demonstrated that the burden of administering this accommodation involves sufficiently significant amounts of time or money or that the goverment involvement is sufficiently "comprehensive, discriminating, and continuing" to draw into question the validity of the accommodation.

Affirmed.

NOTES AND PROBLEMS FOR DISCUSSION

1. The constitutionality of § 701(j) also was upheld by the Sixth and Seventh Circuits in Cummins v. Parker Seal Co., 516 F.2d 544 (6th Cir. 1975), vacated and remanded in light of *Hardison*, 433 U.S. 903, 97 S.Ct. 2965, 53 L.Ed.2d 1087 (1977); and Nottelson v. Smith Steel Workers, 643 F.2d 445 (7th Cir. 1981), cert. denied, 454 U.S. 1046, 102 S.Ct. 587, 70 L.Ed.2d 488 (1981), respectively. In *Cummins*, however, Judge Celebrezze authored a dissenting opinion in which he strongly disagreed with the majority's application of the *Nyquist* standard:

* * *

> There is no doubt that Congress acted with a valid secular purpose in banning employment discrimination based on religion through Title VII of the Civil Rights Act of 1964. The expressed purpose of that legislation was to end discrimination based on certain factors that had no relation to an individual's ability and initiative and, accordingly, to end the burden on interstate commerce imposed by various forms of invidious discrimination. The object was to make religion a meaningless factor in employment decisions.
>
> This secular purpose does not justify the 1972 religious accommodation amendment * * *. Section 2000e(j) defines religion so as to require that persons receive preferential treatment because of their religion. This contradicts the secular purpose behind the original Title VII. Rather than "putting teeth" into the Act, it mandates religious discrimination, thus departing from the Act's basic purpose.
>
> The second purportedly secular justification for the rule is that it recognizes that "certain persons will not compromise their religious convictions" and ensures "that they will not be punished for the supremacy of conscience."
>
> The absence of a religious accommodation rule, however, would not amount to punishment. It would simply be a "hands-off" attitude on government's part, allowing employers and employees to settle their own differences. The rule grants benefits to religious practitioners because of their religion. The second rationale the majority advances, therefore,

amounts to an assertion that it is a valid secular purpose to grant preferences to persons whose religious practices do not fit prevailing patterns. Indeed, the legislative history of the 1972 amendment reveals Congressional thinking that the Establishment Clause was not violated because "[i]n dealing with the free exercise [of religion], really, this promotes the constitutional demand in that respect."

It is, of course, fundamental that the First Amendment protects the free exercise of all religions, whatever the number of their practitioners. * * * Thus, Government may not penalize persons on the basis of their religion.

* * *

The fact that Government may not penalize particular religions does not mean that Congress may favor particular religions. On the contrary, it means that Congress may not. The argument that aid to religious institutions is justified under a broad reading of the Free Exercise Clause has been raised on behalf of aid to parochial schools and other benefits to religious groups. The argument has appeared in dissenting opinions, and Supreme Court majorities have consistently rejected it. * * * The Free Exercise Clause provides a shield against government interference with religion, but it does not offer a sword to cut through the strictures of the Establishment Clause. * * * There is no valid secular legislative purpose behind the rule. Its purpose is to protect and advance particular religions.

This purpose is clearly evident in the remarks of Senator Randolph, who authored the 1972 amendment. Although the majority cites his argument that the amendment would advance freedom from religious discrimination (despite its requiring discrimination on religious grounds), the majority fails to quote the real reason why Senator Randolph introduced the amendment:

> I say to the distinguished chairman of the Labor and Public Welfare Committee, who manages this bill, that there has been a partial refusal at times on the part of employees whose religious practices rigidly require them to abstain from work in the nature of hire on particular days. So there has been, because of understandable pressures, such as commitments of a family nature and otherwise, a dwindling of the membership of some of the religious organizations because of the situation to which I have just directed attention.

* * *

The purpose evident in these remarks is the promotion of certain religions whose followers' practices conflict with employers' schedules. The promotion of a particular religion is not a justifiable ground for legislation. Otherwise, the neutrality principle, which is the core of the First Amendment, would be violated.

Not only does the religious accommodation rule lack a secular purpose. It also fails the second test under *Nyquist*. It lacks "a primary effect that neither advances nor inhibits religion." It is, in other words, neither "even-handed in operation" nor "neutral in primary impact." The religious accommodation rule violates these principles in two respects.

First, the religious accommodation requirement discriminates between religion and non-religion. Only those with "religious practices" may benefit from the rule. Others are forced to submit to uniform work rules and to bear the burdens imposed by their employers' accommodation to religious practitioners. Thus, the rule discriminates against those with no religion, although the freedom not to believe is within the First Amendment's protection.

Second, it discriminates among religions. Only those which require their followers to manifest their belief in acts requiring modification of an employer's work rules benefit, while other employees are inconvenienced by the employer's accommodation. By singling out particular sects for government protection, the Federal Government has forfeited the pretense that the rule is merely part of the general ban on religious discrimination. * * *

* * *

Because the religious accommodation rule violates the First Amendment under the first two tests of *Nyquist*, it is unnecessary to consider whether it also fosters "excessive entanglement" of Church and State. It is fair to note, however, that the 1972 amendment is worded far more broadly than Regulation 1605.1. The 1972 amendment extends to "all aspects of religious observance and practice, as well as belief." * * * Disposition of complaints under the amendment will require inquiry into the sincerity with which beliefs are held and force consideration of the validity of the religious nature of claims, procedures which are not favored and may themselves be improper because they put courts in review of religious matters.

* * *

This is not to say that a wise employer could not decide that as a matter of sound business practice and good employee relations to accommodate to his employees' religious practices. Forbidding the government from *requiring* accommodation would not be a holding that accommodation may not be made by private or public employers.

Is Judge Celebrezze's discussion of the Free Exercise Clause on point? Does § 701(j) create a conflict between the Free Exercise and Establishment Clauses of the First Amendment? See Anderson v. General Dynamics, 489 F.Supp. 782, 790 (S.D.Cal.1980), reversed on other grounds, 648 F.2d 1247 (9th Cir. 1981). The Sixth Circuit's opinion in *Cummins*, decided before *Hardison*, originally was affirmed by an equally divided Supreme Court. On rehearing, however, the Supreme Court vacated the appellate court's opinion and remanded the case for reconsideration in light of *Hardison*. On remand, the Sixth Circuit concluded that a reasonable accommodation could not be achieved without undue hardship and, therefore, did not reach the constitutional issue.

2. In Rankins v. Commission on Professional Competence, cited at footnote eight of the principal case, the California Supreme Court, relying on § 701(j) cases, held that the California Constitution's prohibition of religious discrimination in employment implied a duty to accommodate equivalent to that found in § 701(j). The court also ruled that the imposition of this duty did not contravene the Establishment Clause of the federal Constitution. The U.S. Supreme Court dismissed the appeal taken in *Rankins* for want of a substantial federal question. The court in *Tooley* concluded that it was not bound on the constitutional issue by the U.S. Supreme Court's actions in *Rankins* since *Rankins* involved a plaintiff's religious objection to working on specified holy days, whereas plaintiff Tooley asserted a religious objection to paying union dues. Are you persuaded by this distinction? See Nottelson v. Smith Steel Workers, 643 F.2d 445, 453 (7th Cir. 1981).

3. U.S. Air Force regulations prohibit the wearing of headgear indoors except by armed security police in the performance of their duties. Dr. S. Simcha Goldman, an Orthodox Jew and ordained rabbi, while on active service as a clinical psychologist at an air force base mental health clinic, was permitted to wear his yarmulke in the health clinic and avoided controversy by wearing his service cap over the yarmulke when out of doors. He also wore the yarmulke while testifying as a witness at a court-martial. After a complaint was lodged with the Hospital Commander by the opposing counsel in that proceeding, the Commander declared that wearing the yarmulke was in violation of the regulations and ordered the psychologist not to wear it outside the hospital. Dr. Goldman refused and the Commander subsequently revised his order to prohibit Dr. Goldman from wearing the yarmulke even in the hospital. After receiving a formal letter of reprimand and a negative recommendation from the Hospital Commander in connection with his application to extend the term of his active service, Dr. Goldman brought suit alleging that the application of the regulation to prevent him from wearing his yarmulke infringed his First Amendment right to freely exercise his religious beliefs. In GOLDMAN v. WEINBERGER, ___ U.S. ___, 106 S.Ct. 1310, 89 L.Ed.2d 478 (1986), the Supreme Court rejected Dr. Goldman's claim. The Court noted that its review of military regulations challenged on First Amendment grounds was more deferential than that which would accompany analogous claims in the civilian sector. It added that deference was especially appropriate in connection with the professional judgment of military authorities concerning the importance of a particular military interest. Accordingly, the Court concluded, the regulation was supported by the military's perceived need for uniformity. While recognizing that this regulation might make military life more objectionable for individuals such as Dr. Goldman, the Court stated that the First Amendment did not require the military to accommodate such religious practices where such accommodation would detract from the uniformity sought by the regulations.

SECTION B. NATIONAL ORIGIN

ESPINOZA v. FARAH MANUFACTURING CO.

Supreme Court of the United States, 1973.
414 U.S. 86, 94 S.Ct. 334, 38 L.Ed.2d 287.

MR. JUSTICE MARSHALL delivered the opinion of the Court.

This case involves interpretation of the phrase "national origin" in Tit. VII of the Civil Rights Act of 1964. Petitioner Cecilia Espinoza is a lawfully admitted resident alien who was born in and remains a citizen of Mexico. She resides in San Antonio, Texas, with her husband, Rudolfo Espinoza, a United States citizen. In July 1969, Mrs. Espinoza sought employment as a seamstress at the San Antonio division of respondent Farah Manufacturing Co. Her employment application was rejected on the basis of a longstanding company policy against the employment of aliens. After exhausting their administrative remedies with the Equal Employment Opportunity Commission, petitioners commenced this suit in the District Court alleging that respondent had discriminated against Mrs. Espinoza because of her "national origin" in violation of § 703 of Tit. VII. The District Court granted petitioners' motion for summary judgment, holding that a refusal to hire because of lack of citizenship constitutes discrimination on the basis of "national origin." The Court of Appeals reversed, concluding that the statutory phrase "national origin" did not embrace citizenship. We granted the writ to resolve this question of statutory construction and now affirm.

* * * Certainly the plain language of the statute supports the result reached by the Court of Appeals. The term "national origin" on its face refers to the country where a person was born, or, more broadly, the country from which his or her ancestors came.

The statute's legislative history, though quite meager in this respect, fully supports this construction. The only direct definition given the phrase "national origin" is the following remark made on the floor of the House of Representatives by Congressman Roosevelt, Chairman of the House Subcommittee which reported the bill: "It means the country from which you or your forebears came. * * * You may come from Poland, Czechoslovakia, England, France, or any other country." 110 Cong. Rec. 2549 (1964). We also note that an earlier version of § 703 had referred to discrimination because of "race, color, religion, national origin, or *ancestry*." The deletion of the word "ancestry" from the final version was not intended as a material change, see H. R. Rep. No. 914, 88th Cong., 1st Sess., 87 (1963), suggesting that the terms "national origin" and "ancestry" were considered synonymous.

There are other compelling reasons to believe that Congress did not intend the term "national origin" to embrace citizenship requirements. Since 1914, the Federal Government itself, through Civil Service Commission regulations, has engaged in what amounts to discrimination against aliens by denying them the right to enter competitive examination for federal employment. But it has never been suggested that the citizenship requirement for federal employment constitutes discrimination because of national origin, even though since 1943, various Executive Orders have expressly prohibited discrimination on the basis of national origin in Federal Government employment.

Moreover, § 701(b) of Tit. VII, in language closely paralleling § 703, makes it "the policy of the United States to insure equal employment opportunities for Federal employees without discrimination because of * * * national origin * * *." The legislative history of that section reveals no mention of any intent on Congress' part to reverse the longstanding practice of requiring federal employees to be United States citizens. To the contrary, there is every indication that no such reversal was intended. Congress itself has on several occasions since 1964 enacted statutes barring aliens from federal employment. The Treasury, Postal Service, and General Government Appropriation Act, 1973, for example, provides that "no part of any appropriation contained in this or any other Act shall be used to pay the compensation of any officer or employee of the Government of the United States

* * * unless such person (1) is a citizen of the United States * * *."[3]

To interpret the term "national origin" to embrace citizenship requirements would require us to conclude that Congress itself has repeatedly flouted its own declaration of policy. This Court cannot lightly find such a breach of faith. So far as federal employment is concerned, we think it plain that Congress has assumed that the ban on national-origin discrimination in § 701(b) did not affect the historical practice of requiring citizenship as a condition of employment. And there is no reason to believe Congress intended the term "national origin" in § 703 to have any broader scope.

Petitioners have suggested that the statutes and regulations discriminating against noncitizens in federal employment are unconstitutional under the Due Process Clause of the Fifth Amendment. We need not address that question here, for the issue presented in this case is not whether Congress has the power to discriminate against aliens in federal employment, but rather, whether Congress intended to prohibit such discrimination in private employment. Suffice it to say that we cannot conclude Congress would at once continue the practice of requiring citizenship as a condition of federal employment and, at the same time, prevent private employers from doing likewise. Interpreting § 703 as petitioners suggest would achieve the rather bizarre result of preventing Farah from insisting on United States citizenship as a condition of employment while the very agency charged with enforcement of Tit. VII would itself be required by Congress to place such a condition on its own personnel.

The District Court drew primary support for its holding from an interpretative guideline issued by the Equal Employment Opportunity Commission which provides:

> "Because discrimination on the basis of citizenship has the effect of discriminating on the basis of national origin, a lawfully immigrated alien who is domiciled or residing in this country may not be discriminated against on the basis of his citizenship * * *." 29 CFR § 1606.1(d) (1972).

Like the Court of Appeals, we have no occasion here to question the general validity of this guideline insofar as it can be read as an expression of the Commission's belief that there may be many situations where discrimination on the basis of citizenship would have the effect of discriminating on the basis of national origin. In some instances, for example, a citizenship requirement might be but one part of a wider scheme of unlawful national-origin discrimination. In other cases, an employer might use a citizenship test as a pretext to disguise

3. Petitioners argue that it is unreasonable to attribute any great significance to these provisions in determining congressional intent because the barrier to employment of noncitizens has been tucked away in appropriations bills rather than expressed in a more affirmative fashion. We disagree. Indeed, the fact that Congress has occasionally enacted exceptions to the general barrier indicates to us that Congress was well aware of what it was doing.

what is in fact national-origin discrimination. Certainly Tit. VII prohibits discrimination on the basis of citizenship whenever it has the purpose or effect of discriminating on the basis of national origin. "The Act proscribes not only overt discrimination but also practices that are fair in form, but discriminatory in operation." Griggs v. Duke Power Co., 401 U.S. 424, 431, 91 S.Ct. 849, 853, 28 L.Ed.2d 158 (1971).

It is equally clear, however, that these principles lend no support to petitioners in this case. There is no indication in the record that Farah's policy against employment of aliens had the purpose or effect of discriminating against persons of Mexican national origin.[5] It is conceded that Farah accepts employees of Mexican origin, provided the individual concerned has become an American citizen. Indeed, the District Court found that persons of Mexican ancestry make up more than 96% of the employees at the company's San Antonio division, and 97% of those doing the work for which Mrs. Espinoza applied. While statistics such as these do not automatically shield an employer from a charge of unlawful discrimination, the plain fact of the matter is that Farah does not discriminate against persons of Mexican national origin with respect to employment in the job Mrs. Espinoza sought. She was denied employment, not because of the country of her origin, but because she had not yet achieved United States citizenship. In fact, the record shows that the worker hired in place of Mrs. Espinoza was a citizen with a Spanish surname.

The Commission's guideline may have significance for a wide range of situations, but not for a case such as this where its very premise—that discrimination on the basis of citizenship has the effect of discrimination on the basis of national origin—is not borne out.[6] It is also significant to note that the Commission itself once held a different view as to the meaning of the phrase "national origin." When first confronted with the question, the Commission, through its General Counsel, said: " 'National origin' refers to the country from which the individual or his forebears came * * *, not to whether or not he is a United States citizen * * *." EEOC General Counsel's Opinion Letter, 1 CCH Employment Prac. Guide ¶ 1220.20 (1967). The Commission's more recent interpretation of the statute in the guideline relied on by the District Court is no doubt entitled to great deference, but that deference must have limits where, as here, application of the guideline would be inconsistent with an obvious congressional intent not to reach

5. There is no suggestion, for example, that the company refused to hire aliens of Mexican or Spanish-speaking background while hiring those of other national origins. * * * While the company asks job applicants whether they are United States citizens, it makes no inquiry as to their national origin.

6. It is suggested that a refusal to hire an alien always disadvantages that person because of the country of his birth. A person born in the United States, the argument goes, automatically obtains citizenship at birth, while those born elsewhere can acquire citizenship only through a long and sometimes difficult process. The answer to this argument is that it is not the employer who places the burdens of naturalization on those born outside the country, but Congress itself, through laws enacted pursuant to its constitutional power "[t]o establish an uniform Rule of Naturalization." U.S.Const., Art. 1, § 8, cl. 4. * * *

the employment practice in question. Courts need not defer to an administrative construction of a statute where there are "compelling indications that it is wrong."

Finally, petitioners seek to draw support from the fact that Tit. VII protects all individuals from unlawful discrimination, whether or not they are citizens of the United States. We agree that aliens are protected from discrimination under the Act. That result may be derived not only from the use of the term "any individual" in § 703, but also as a negative inference from the exemption in § 702, which provides that Tit. VII "shall not apply to an employer with respect to the employment of aliens outside any State * * *." Title VII was clearly intended to apply with respect to the employment of aliens inside any State.

The question posed in the present case, however, is not whether aliens are protected from illegal discrimination under the Act, but what kinds of discrimination the Act makes illegal. Certainly it would be unlawful for an employer to discriminate against aliens because of race, color, religion, sex, or national origin—for example, by hiring aliens of Anglo-Saxon background but refusing to hire those of Mexican or Spanish ancestry. Aliens are protected from illegal discrimination under the Act, but nothing in the Act makes it illegal to discriminate on the basis of citizenship or alienage.

We agree with the Court of Appeals that neither the language of the Act, nor its history, nor the specific facts of this case indicate that respondent has engaged in unlawful discrimination because of national origin.

Affirmed.

MR. JUSTICE DOUGLAS, dissenting.

It is odd that the Court which holds that a State may not bar an alien from the practice of law or deny employment to aliens can read a federal statute that prohibits discrimination in employment on account of "national origin" so as to permit discrimination against aliens.

Alienage results from one condition only: being born outside the United States. Those born within the country are citizens from birth. It could not be more clear that Farah's policy of excluding aliens is *de facto* a policy of preferring those who were born in this country. Therefore the construction placed upon the "national origin" provision is inconsistent with the construction this Court has placed upon the same Act's protections for persons denied employment on account of race or sex.

In connection with racial discrimination we have said that the Act prohibits "practices, procedures, or tests neutral on their face, and even neutral in terms of intent," if they create "artificial, arbitrary, and unnecessary barriers to employment when the barriers operate invidiously to discriminate on the basis of racial *or other impermissible classification.*" Griggs v. Duke Power Co., 401 U.S. 424, 430–431, 91

S.Ct. 849, 28 L.Ed.2d 158 (1971) (emphasis added). There we found that the employer could not use test or diploma requirements which on their face were racially neutral, when in fact those requirements had a *de facto* discriminatory result and the employer was unable to justify them as related to job performance. The tests involved in *Griggs* did not eliminate all blacks seeking employment, just as the citizenship requirement here does not eliminate all applicants of foreign origin. Respondent here explicitly conceded that the citizenship requirement is imposed without regard to the alien's qualifications for the job.

These petitioners against whom discrimination is charged are Chicanos. But whether brown, yellow, black, or white, the thrust of the Act is clear: alienage is no barrier to employment here. *Griggs*, as I understood it until today, extends its protective principles to all, not to blacks alone. Our cases on sex discrimination under the Act yield the same result as *Griggs*.

The construction placed upon the statute in the majority opinion is an extraordinary departure from prior cases, and it is opposed by the Equal Employment Opportunity Commission, the agency provided by law with the responsibility of enforcing the Act's protections. The Commission takes the only permissible position: that discrimination on the basis of alienage *always* has the effect of discrimination on the basis of national origin. Refusing to hire an individual because he is an alien "is discrimination based on birth outside the United States and is thus discrimination based on national origin in violation of Title VII." The Commission's interpretation of the statute is entitled to great weight.

There is no legislative history to cast doubt on this construction.[3] Indeed, any other construction flies in the face of the underlying congressional policy of removing "artificial, arbitrary, and unnecessary barriers to employment." McDonnell Douglas Corp. v. Green, 411 U.S. 792, 806, 93 S.Ct. 1817, 1826, 36 L.Ed.2d 668 (1973).

Mrs. Espinoza is a permanent resident alien, married to an American citizen, and her children will be native-born American citizens. But that first generation has the greatest adjustments to make to their new country. Their unfamiliarity with America makes them the most vulnerable to exploitation and discriminatory treatment. They, of course, have the same obligation as American citizens to pay taxes, and they are subject to the draft on the same basis. But they have never received equal treatment in the job market. * * *

3. The only legislative history the majority points to is Congressman Roosevelt's definition of "national origin": "It means the country from which you or your forebears came. * * * You may come from Poland, Czechoslovakia, England, France, or any other country." But that only makes clear what petitioners here argue—that Mrs. Espinoza cannot be discriminated against because she comes from a foreign country. The majority's mention of the deletion of the word "ancestry," ibid., is certainly irrelevant. Obviously "national origin" comprehends "ancestry," but as Congressman Roosevelt pointed out it means more—not only where one's forebears were born, but where one himself was born.

The majority decides today that in passing sweeping legislation guaranteeing equal job opportunities, the Congress intended to help only the immigrant's children, excluding those "for whom there [is] no place at all." I cannot impute that niggardly an intent to Congress.

NOTES AND PROBLEMS FOR DISCUSSION

1. While foreign citizens are not protected by Title VII against private sector alienage bars, similarly restrictive employment practices used by a public employer can be challenged under the equal protection guarantees of the Fifth or Fourteenth Amendments to the U.S. Constitution. The Supreme Court has invalidated statutes that prevented aliens from entering a state's classified civil service, Sugarman v. Dougall, 413 U.S. 634, 93 S.Ct. 2842, 37 L.Ed.2d 853 (1973), practicing law, In re Griffiths, 413 U.S. 717, 93 S.Ct. 2851, 37 L.Ed.2d 910 (1973) and working as an engineer, Examining Board of Engineers v. Flores de Otero, 426 U.S. 572, 96 S.Ct. 2264, 49 L.Ed.2d 65 (1976). More recently, however, the Court upheld one state statute that excluded aliens from serving as "peace officers", Cabell v. Chavez-Salido, 454 U.S. 432, 102 S.Ct. 735, 70 L.Ed. 2d 677 (1982), another that prohibited aliens who did not manifest an intention to apply for U.S. citizenship from working as elementary and secondary school teachers, Ambach v. Norwick, 441 U.S. 68, 99 S.Ct. 1589, 60 L.Ed.2d 49 (1979), and a third that precluded aliens from working for a state police force, Foley v. Connelie, 435 U.S. 291, 98 S.Ct. 1067, 55 L.Ed.2d 287 (1978). These latter decisions indicate that, at least in certain situations, the Court is willing to apply a less demanding standard than the strict scrutiny traditionally accorded alienage classifications. See generally Griffith, The Alien Meets Some Constitutional Hurdles in Employment, Education and Aid Programs, 17 S.D.L.Rev. 201 (1980).

2. The EEOC Guidelines discussed in *Espinoza* were modified after that decision was rendered to provide that citizenship requirements violate Title VII only when they have the purpose or effect of discriminating on the basis of national origin. 29 CFR 1606.5 (1980).

3. Does an employer's rule prohibiting employees from speaking Spanish on the job unless they are communicating with Spanish-speaking customers constitute national origin discrimination? See Garcia v. Gloor, 618 F.2d 264 (5th Cir. 1980), cert. denied, 449 U.S. 1113, 101 S.Ct. 923, 66 L.Ed.2d 842 (1981). What about an employer that denies a promotion to an employee because of his foreign accent? See Carino v. University of Oklahoma, 750 F.2d 815 (10th Cir. 1984); Berke v. Ohio Dep't of Public Welfare, 628 F.2d 980 (6th Cir. 1980). Should the disposition of these cases be influenced by the degree to which the disqualifying characteristic is immutable? The principal case and the mutability/immutability question are examined in Note, Garcia v. Gloor: Mutable Characteristics Rationale Extended to National Origin Discrimination, 32 Merc. L.Rev. 1275 (1981).

4. Is an employer liable under Title VII if one of its supervisors makes derogatory references to a subordinate employee's heritage? See Cariddi v. Kansas City Chiefs Football Club, 568 F.2d 87 (8th Cir. 1977); Morales v. Dain, Kalman & Quail, Inc., 467 F.Supp. 1031 (D.Minn.1979). What if the speaker was a co-employee rather than a supervisor? In either situation, should it matter whether the company encouraged, acquiesced to, condemned, or was unaware of this conduct?

The EEOC Guidelines specifically address these issues:

"(a) The Commission has consistently held that harassment on the basis of national origin is a violation of Title VII. An employer has an affirmative duty to maintain a working environment free of harassment on the basis of national origin.

"(b) Ethnic slurs and other verbal or physical conduct relating to an individual's national origin constitute harassment when this conduct: (1) has the purpose or effect of creating an intimidating, hostile or offensive working environment; (2) has the purpose or effect of unreasonably interfering with an individual's work performance; or (3) otherwise adversely affects an individual's employment opportunities.

"(c) An employer is responsible for its acts and those of its agents and supervisory employees with respect to harassment on the basis of national origin regardless of whether the specific acts complained of were authorized or even forbidden by the employer and regardless of whether the employer knew or should have known of their occurrence. * * *

"(d) With respect to conduct between fellow employees, an employer is responsible for acts of harassment in the workplace on the basis of national origin, where the employer, its agents or supervisory employees, knows or should have known of the conduct, unless the employer can show that it took immediate and appropriate corrective action."

29 CFR 1606.8 (1980).

5. Can the owner of an Italian restaurant refuse to hire a non-Italian chef? Waiter?

6. Relying on *Griggs* disproportionate impact analysis, several courts have invalidated minimum height requirements on the ground that they disproportionately exclude members of certain national origin groups and are not related to job performance. See Craig v. County of Los Angeles, 626 F.2d 659 (9th Cir. 1980), cert. denied, 450 U.S. 919, 101 S.Ct. 1364, 67 L.Ed.2d 345 (1981); United States v. City of Buffalo, 457 F.Supp 612 (W.D.N.Y. 1978), affirmed as modified on remedies, 633 F.2d 643 (2d Cir. 1980).

SECTION C. RACE AND COLOR

McDONALD v. SANTA FE TRAIL TRANSPORTATION

Supreme Court of the United States, 1976.
427 U.S. 273, 96 S.Ct. 2574, 49 L.Ed.2d 493.

MR. JUSTICE MARSHALL delivered the opinion of the Court.

Petitioners, L. N. McDonald and Raymond L. Laird, brought this action in the United States District Court for the Southern District of Texas seeking relief against Santa Fe Trail Transportation Co. (Santa Fe) and International Brotherhood of Teamsters Local 988 (Local 988), which represented Santa Fe's Houston employees, for alleged violations of * * * Title VII of the Civil Rights Act of 1964, in connection with their discharge from Santa Fe's employment. The District Court dismissed the complaint on the pleadings. The Court of Appeals for the Fifth Circuit affirmed. In determining whether the decisions of these courts were correct, we must decide * * * whether a complaint alleging that white employees charged with misappropriating property from their employer were dismissed from employment, while a black employee similarly charged was not dismissed, states a claim under Title VII. * * *

Because the District Court dismissed this case on the pleadings, we take as true the material facts alleged in petitioners' complaint. On September 26, 1970, petitioners, both white, and Charles Jackson, a Negro employee of Santa Fe, were jointly and severally charged with misappropriating 60 one-gallon cans of antifreeze which was part of a shipment Santa Fe was carrying for one of its customers. Six days later, petitioners were fired by Santa Fe, while Jackson was retained. * * *

* * *

Title VII of the Civil Rights Act of 1964 prohibits the discharge of "any individual" because of "such individual's race," § 703(a)(1). Its terms are not limited to discrimination against members of any particular race. Thus, although we were not there confronted with racial discrimination against whites, we described the Act in Griggs v. Duke Power Co., as prohibiting "[d]iscriminatory preference for *any* [racial] group, *minority* or *majority*" (emphasis added). Similarly the EEOC, whose interpretations are entitled to great deference, has consistently interpreted Title VII to proscribe racial discrimination in private employment against whites on the same terms as racial discrimination against nonwhites, holding that to proceed otherwise would

> "constitute a derogation of the Commission's Congressional mandate to eliminate all practices which operate to disadvantage the employment opportunities of any group protected by Title VII, including Caucasians." EEOC Decision No. 74–31, 7 FEP 1326, 1328, CCH EEOC Decisions ¶ 6404, p. 4084 (1973).

This conclusion is in accord with uncontradicted legislative history to the effect that Title VII was intended to "cover white men and white women and all Americans," 110 Cong. Rec. 2578 (1964) (remarks of Rep. Celler), and create an "obligation not to discriminate against whites," id., at 7218 (memorandum of Sen. Clark). See also id., at 7213 (memorandum of Sens. Clark and Case); id., at 8912 (remarks of Sen. Williams). We therefore hold today that Title VII prohibits racial discrimination against the white petitioners in this case upon the same standards as would be applicable were they Negroes and Jackson white.

* * *

NOTES AND PROBLEMS FOR DISCUSSION

1. The absence of a statutory definition of "race" notwithstanding, few definitional problems have arisen in connection with this term. Since the statute also protects individuals from discrimination on the basis of color, national origin and religion, choosing the specific classification into which any particular claim fits usually is not a controversial issue. There are, however, two exceptions to this general rule. The bona fide occupational qualification defense provided in § 703(e) cannot be used to justify a classification based on

race. Thus, characterizing a claim as alleging national origin, as opposed to race discrimination, can be critical where the defendant wants to take advantage of this defense. Secondly, affirmative action policies often define the class included within their provisions by racial membership.

2. The very few reported cases dealing with "color", as divorced from race discrimination, have involved claims by a dark-skinned person that he was denied a position given to a light-skinned member of his race (or vice versa) with similar qualifications. See Ali v. National Bank of Pakistan, 508 F.Supp. 611 (S.D.N.Y.1981); EEOC Decision No. 72–0454 (Nov. 15, 1971). In light of this and the inapplicability of the BFOQ defense to race or color claims, would a movie producer violate Title VII by insisting on a dark-complexioned black actor to play the lead role in "The Idi Amin Story"?

3. Plaintiff, a white woman, was discharged from her job because she was involved in a social relationship with a black man. Can she state a claim under Title VII? Compare Parr v. Woodmen of the World Life Ins. Co., 791 F.2d 888 (11th Cir. 1986) and Whitney v. Greater New York Corp. of Seventh Day Adventists, 401 F.Supp. 1363 (S.D.N.Y.1975) with Ripp v. Dobbs Houses, Inc., 366 F.Supp. 205 (N.D.Ala.1973).

4. In Morton v. Mancari, 417 U.S. 535, 94 S.Ct. 2474, 41 L.Ed.2d 290 (1974), the Supreme Court rejected a claim that a 1934 federal statute granting qualified American Indians an employment preference in the Bureau of Indian Affairs was inconsistent with, and thus superseded by the anti-racial discrimination provisions of Title VII. In reaching this result, the Court noted that Title VII itself specifically exempts Indian tribes from its provisions and permits private businesses located on or near Indian reservations to give preferential treatment to Indians living on or near reservations.

SECTION D. SEX

KANOWITZ, SEX-BASED DISCRIMINATION IN AMERICAN LAW III: TITLE VII OF THE 1964 CIVIL RIGHTS ACT AND THE EQUAL PAY ACT OF 1963

20 Hastings L.Rev. 305, 310–12 (1968).

* * *

Any consideration of the sex provisions of Title VII of the 1964 Civil Rights Act requires a preliminary glance at what can only be described as their peculiar legislative history. In the light of its tremendous potential for profoundly affecting the daily lives of so many Americans—both men and women—Title VII's prohibition against sex-discrimination in employment had a rather inauspicious birth.

This is not to say that some species of federal legislation outlawing sex-based discrimination in employment might not have emerged eventually from a Congress in which male representatives out-numbered female representatives overwhelmingly. Agitation for such a law, after all, had been going on for many years. * * * But the prospects for the passage of legislation prohibiting sex discrimination in hiring and promotional practices in employment were exceedingly dim in 1964. Had the sex provisions of Title VII been presented then as a separate bill, rather than being coupled as they were in an effusion of Congressional gimmickry with legislation aimed at curbing racial and ethnic discrimination, their defeat in 1964 would have been virtually assured. We have no less an authority for this conclusion than Oregon's Representative Edith Green, whose strong advocacy of equal legal treatment for American women lends great force to her appraisal. In her view, stated in Congress, the legislation against sex discrimination in employment, "considered by itself, and * * * brought to the floor with no hearings and no testimony * * * would not [have] receive[d] one hundred votes."

In fact, it was not until the last day of the bill's consideration in Chairman Howard Smith's House Rules committee, where it had gone after a favorable report from the Judiciary Committee, that there first appeared a motion to add "sex" discrimination to the other types of employment discrimination that the original bill sought to curb. That motion was defeated in Committee by a vote of 8–7. But after almost two weeks of passionate floor debate in the House and just one day before the act was passed, Representative Smith, a principal opponent of the original bill, offered an amendment to include sex as a prohibited basis for employment discrimination. Under that amendment, the previously proposed sanctions against employers, unions, hiring agencies, or their agents, for discrimination in hiring or promotional practices against actual or prospective employees on the basis of race, creed, or national origin, were, with some exceptions, also to apply to discrimination based upon the "sex" of the job applicant or employee. Offering his amendment, Representative Smith remarked: "Now I am very serious * * * I do not think it can do any harm to this legislation; maybe it will do some good."

Despite Congressman Smith's protestations of seriousness, there was substantial cause to doubt his motives. For four months Congress had been locked in debate over the passage of the Civil Rights Act of 1964. Most southern Representatives and a few of their northern allies had been making every effort to block its passage. In the context of that debate and of the prevailing Congressional sentiment when the amendment was offered, it is abundantly clear that a principal motive in introducing it was to prevent passage of the basic legislation being considered by Congress, rather than solicitude for women's employment rights.

It is not surprising, therefore, that Representative Green, expressing her hope that "the day will come when discrimination will be ended against women," also registered her opposition to the proposed amendment, stating that it "will clutter up the bill and it may later—very well—be used to help destroy this section of the bill by some of the very people who today support it."

Despite these misgivings, and despite the apparent objectives of its sponsors to block passage of the entire Act, the legislation that finally emerged contained Representative Smith's amendment intact. As a result of this stroke of misfired political tactics, our federal positive law now includes a provision that had been desired for many years by those who were concerned with the economic, social and political status of American women, but which had been delayed because of the feeling that the time had not ripened for such legislation, and had been specifically opposed in this instance partly because of a belief that "discrimination based on sex involves problems sufficiently different from discrimination based on * * * other factors * * * to make separate treatment preferable."

What significance should be drawn from this peculiar legislative history of Title VII's prohibition against sex discrimination? It would be a most serious error to attribute to Congress as a corporate unit the apparently cynical motives of the amendment's sponsor. Though most members of Congress were intent on prohibiting employment discrimination based on race, religion and national origin, they did vote to do the same with respect to sex discrimination once the matter, regardless of its sponsor's apparent intentions, was brought to them for a vote. And when Congress adopts any legislation, especially a law with such important ramifications, one must infer a Congressional intention that such legislation be effective to carry out its underlying social policy—which in this case is to eradicate every instance of sex-based employment discrimination that is not founded upon a bona fide occupational qualification.

* * *

---

1. "Sex-Plus" Discrimination and Pregnancy

After the enactment of Title VII, the federal courts treated sex discrimination claims just like claims relating to the other classifications. The disparate treatment and disproportionate impact theories, which originated in race cases, were easily adapted to allegations of sex bias. In Dothard v. Rawlinson, 433 U.S. 321, 97 S.Ct. 2720, 53 L.Ed.2d 786 (1977), for example, the Supreme Court invalidated a minimum height and weight requirement for jobs with the Alabama Board of Corrections because of its disproportionate exclusionary impact on women. There was, however, one development in the treatment of Title VII claims that was peculiar to sex-based charges. Employers with a significant proportion of women employees began to implement policies that restricted employment opportunities to specific classes of women. For example, some companies refused to employ married or pregnant women, women over a certain age, or women with pre-school-age children. The employers contended that the presence of women on their payrolls negated claims that they discriminated on the basis of sex. Opponents of these policies, on the other hand, argued that the restrictions did violate Title VII since they applied only to female employees. Thus, the courts were faced with determining whether an employment policy that does not discriminate *solely* on the basis of sex, but on the basis of sex plus some other, facially neutral qualification, is violative of Title VII.

PHILLIPS v. MARTIN MARIETTA CORP.

Supreme Court of the United States, 1971.
400 U.S. 542, 91 S.Ct. 496, 27 L.Ed.2d 613.

PER CURIAM.

Petitioner Mrs. Ida Phillips commenced an action in the United States District Court for the Middle District of Florida under Title VII of the Civil Rights Act of 1964 alleging that she had been denied employment because of her sex. The District Court granted summary judgment for Martin Marietta Corp. (Martin) on the basis of the following showing: (1) in 1966 Martin informed Mrs. Phillips that it was not accepting job applications from women with pre-school-age children; (2) as of the time of the motion for summary judgment, Martin employed men with pre-school-age children; (3) at the time Mrs. Phillips applied, 70–75% of the applicants for the position she sought were women; 75–80% of those hired for the position, assembly trainee, were women, hence no question of bias against women as such was presented.

The Court of Appeals for the Fifth Circuit affirmed, and denied a rehearing *en banc*. We granted certiorari.

Section 703(a) of the Civil Rights Act of 1964 requires that persons of like qualifications be given employment opportunities irrespective of their sex. The Court of Appeals therefore erred in reading this section as permitting one hiring policy for women and another for men—each having pre-school-age children. The existence of such conflicting family obligations, if demonstrably more relevant to job performance for a woman than for a man, could arguably be a basis for distinction under § 703(e) of the Act. But that is a matter of evidence tending to show that the condition in question "is a bona fide occupational qualification reasonably necessary to the normal operation of that particular business or enterprise." The record before us, however, is not adequate for resolution of these important issues. Summary judgment was therefore improper and we remand for fuller development of the record and for further consideration.

Vacated and remanded.

MR. JUSTICE MARSHALL, concurring.

While I agree that this case must be remanded for a full development of the facts, I cannot agree with the Court's indication that a "bona fide occupational qualification reasonably necessary to the normal operation of" Martin Marietta's business could be established by a showing that some women, even the vast majority, with pre-school-age children have family responsibilities that interfere with job performance and that men do not usually have such responsibilities. Certainly, an employer can require that all of his employees, both men and women, meet minimum performance standards, and he can try to insure compliance by requiring parents, both mothers and fathers, to provide for the care of their children so that job performance is not interfered with.

But the Court suggests that it would not require such uniform standards. I fear that in this case, where the issue is not squarely before us, the Court has fallen into the trap of assuming that the Act permits ancient canards about the proper role of women to be a basis for discrimination. Congress, however, sought just the opposite result.

By adding the prohibition against job discrimination based on sex to the 1964 Civil Rights Act Congress intended to prevent employers from refusing "to hire an individual based on stereotyped characterizations of the sexes." Equal Employment Opportunity Commission, Guidelines on Discrimination Because of Sex, 29 CFR § 1604.1(a)(1)(ii). Even characterizations of the proper domestic roles of the sexes were not to serve as predicates for restricting employment opportunity. The exception for a "bona fide occupational qualification" was not intended to swallow the rule.

That exception has been construed by the Equal Employment Opportunity Commission, whose regulations are entitled to "great deference," Udall v. Tallman, 380 U.S. 1, 16, 85 S.Ct. 792, 801, 13 L.Ed.2d 616 (1965), to be applicable only to job situations that require specific physical characteristics necessarily possessed by only one sex. Thus the exception would apply where necessary "for the purpose of authenticity or genuineness" in the employment of actors or actresses, fashion models, and the like. If the exception is to be limited as Congress intended, the Commission has given it the only possible construction.

When performance characteristics of an individual are involved, even when parental roles are concerned, employment opportunity may be limited only by employment criteria that are neutral as to the sex of the applicant.

NOTES FOR DISCUSSION

1. While the Supreme Court did not employ "sex-plus" terminology in *Phillips*, this case, the first Title VII sex discrimination suit decided by the Court, clearly fits within that framework. Into which of the two previously discussed proof schemes—disparate treatment or disproportionate impact—does this type of claim fall?

2. What is your reaction to the majority's suggestion that sex might be a BFOQ? Justice Marshall contends that even if the premise upon which the application of that defense is predicated—that the responsibility for pre-school-age children more frequently falls on mothers than fathers—is statistically correct, Congress did not intend to sanction employment practices based on stereotyped characterizations of sex roles. Do you agree? The BFOQ defense is most frequently asserted in sex discrimination cases. For an extensive discussion of § 703(e) see Chapter 3, supra, at 255–274.

WILLINGHAM v. MACON TELEGRAPH PUBLISHING CO.

United States Court of Appeals, Fifth Circuit, 1975.
507 F.2d 1084.

SIMPSON, CIRCUIT JUDGE.

Alan Willingham, plaintiff-appellant, applied for employment with defendant-appellee Macon Telegraph Publishing Co., Macon, Georgia (Macon Telegraph) as a display or copy layout artist on July 28, 1970. Macon Telegraph refused to hire Willingham. The suit below alleged that the sole basis for refusal to hire was objection to the length of his hair. On July 30, 1970, he filed a complaint with the Equal Employment Opportunity Commission (E.E.O.C.), asserting discrimination by Macon in its hiring policy based on sex * * *.

The E.E.O.C. investigated the alleged discrimination and eventually advised Willingham that there was reasonable cause to believe that Macon Telegraph had violated the * * * Civil Rights Act of 1964, and that he was entitled to file suit. On December 17, 1971, Willingham filed suit, alleging *inter alia* that Macon Telegraph's hiring policy unlawfully discriminated on the basis of sex. On April 17, 1972, the district court granted summary judgment in favor of defendant Macon Telegraph, finding no unlawful discrimination. Upon Willingham's appeal from the district court decision a panel of this circuit reversed, finding the presence of a prima facie case of sexual discrimination and directing remand for an evidentiary hearing. Upon en banc consideration we vacate the remand order of the original panel and affirm the district court.

THE FACTS

* * *

* * * Macon Telegraph's management believed that the entire business community it served—and depended upon for business success—associated long hair on men with the counter-culture types who gained extensive unfavorable national and local exposure at the time of [a local music] * * * festival. Therefore the newspaper's employee grooming code, which required employees (male and female) who came into contact with the public to be neatly dressed and groomed in accordance with the standards customarily accepted in the business community, was interpreted to exclude the employing of men (but not women) with long hair. Willingham's longer than acceptable shoulder length hair was thus the grooming code violation upon which Macon Telegraph based its denial of employment.

* * * Willingham's argument is that Macon Telegraph discriminates amongst employees based upon their sex, in that female employees can wear their hair any length they choose, while males must limit theirs to the length deemed acceptable by Macon Telegraph. He asserts therefore that he was denied employment because of his sex: were he a girl with identical length hair and comparable job qualifica-

tions, he (she) would have been employed. A majority of the original panel which heard the case agreed, and remanded the cause to the district court for a finding of whether or not the discrimination might not be lawful under the "bona fide occupational qualification" (B.F.O.Q.) statutory exception to Sec. 703. Since we agree with the district court that Macon Telegraph's dress and grooming policy does not unlawfully discriminate on the basis of sex, the applicability of the B.F.O.Q. exception will not be considered in this opinion.

THE NATURE OF SEXUAL DISCRIMINATION

The unlawfulness vel non of employer practices with respect to the hiring and treatment of employees in the private sector, as contemplated by Sec. 703 and applied to the facts of this case, can be determined by way of a three step analysis: (1) has there been some form of discrimination, i.e., different treatment of similarly situated individuals; (2) was the discrimination based on sex; and (3) if there has been sexual discrimination, is it within the purview of the bona fide occupational qualification (BFOQ) exception and thus lawful? We conclude that the undisputed discrimination practiced by Macon Telegraph is based not upon sex, but rather upon grooming standards, and thus outside the proscription of Sec. 703. This determination pretermits any discussion of whether, if sexual discrimination were involved, it would be within the BFOQ exception.

Although our judicial inquiry necessarily focuses upon the proper statutory construction to be accorded Sec. 703, it is helpful first to define narrowly the precise issue to be considered. * * * [W]e are not concerned with discrimination based upon sex alone. That situation obtains when an employer refuses to hire, promote, or raise the wages of an individual solely because of sex, as, for instance, if Macon Telegraph had refused to hire any women for the job of copy layout artist because of their sex.

Willingham relies on a more subtle form of discrimination, one which courts and commentators have often characterized as "sex plus". In general, this involves the classification of employees on the basis of sex *plus* one other ostensibly neutral characteristic. The practical effect of interpreting Sec. 703 to include this type of discrimination is to impose an equal protection gloss upon the statute, i.e. similarly situated individuals of either sex cannot be discriminated against vis à vis members of their own sex unless the same distinction is made with respect to those of the opposite sex. Such an interpretation may be necessary in order to counter some rather imaginative efforts by employers to circumvent Sec. 703.

Inclusion of "sex plus" discrimination within the proscription of Sec. 703 has legitimate legislative and judicial underpinning. An amendment which would have added the word "solely" to the bill, modifying "sex", was defeated on the floor in the House of Representatives. Presumably, Congress foresaw the debilitating effect such a limitation might have upon the sex discrimination amendment. Further, the Supreme Court, in Phillips v. Martin Marietta Corp., 1971, 400 U.S. 542, 91 S.Ct. 496, 27 L.Ed.2d 613, found expressly that "sex plus" discrimination violates the Civil Rights Act. The employer in *Phillips* refused to accept job applications from women with pre-school age children, but had no such policy with respect to male applicants. The defendant argued that it was not discriminating between men and women, but only amongst women, and then only with respect to a neutral fact—pre-school age children. In a short per curiam decision, the Supreme Court held that if the legislative purpose of giving persons of like qualifications equal employment opportunity irrespective of sex were to be effected, employers could not have one hiring policy for men and another for women. Thus "sex plus" discrimination against being a woman *plus* having pre-school age children, was under the facts of that case just as unlawful as would have been discrimination based solely upon sex.

In this analytical context, then, the single issue in this case is precisely drawn: Does a particular grooming regulation applicable to men only constitute "sex plus" discrimination within the meaning of Sec. 703, as construed by the Supreme Court? Willingham and numerous amici curiae have advanced several arguments supporting an affirmative answer to the question. We proceed to consider these arguments.

The primary premise of Willingham's position is that "sex plus" must be read to intend to include "sex plus any sexual stereotype" and thus, since short hair is stereotypically male, requiring it of all male applicants violates Sec. 703. While the Supreme Court did not explicate the breadth of its rationale in *Phillips*, it seems likely that Mr. Justice Marshall at least might agree with Willingham. In his special concurrence he noted that any hiring distinction based upon stereotyped characterizations of the sexes violates the Act, and went on to say that such discrimination could never be a BFOQ exception, an issue expressly left open in the majority's per curiam opinion.

Willingham finds further comfort in Sprogis v. United Air Lines, Inc., 7 Cir. 1971, 444 F.2d 1194. Plaintiff there was a female stewardess who challenged an airline rule that stewardesses were not allowed to marry, but with no such provision for male stewards or other employees. The *Sprogis* court found the rule to be an unlawful form of "sex plus" discrimination, relying in part on *Phillips*. In reference to "sex plus" the court noted that "[i]n forbidding employers to discriminate against individuals because of their sex, Congress intended to strike at the entire spectrum of disparate treatment of men and women *resulting from sex stereotypes*." Treating the emphasized language in its broadest sense, it is possible that the court felt that all sexual stereotypes violate Sec. 703. Several district courts apparently agree with this construction, at least insofar as personal dress and appearance codes are concerned. See Aros v. McDonnell Douglas Corp., C.D.

Cal.1972, 348 F.Supp. 661 (dress and grooming code constitutes sexual discrimination when applied differently to males and females); Donohue v. Shoe Corp. of America, C.D.Cal.1972, 337 F.Supp. 1357 (rule requiring short hair on men, but not on women, is prima facie violation of Sec. 703); Roberts v. General Mills, Inc., N.D.Ohio 1971, 337 F.Supp. 1055 (rule allowing female employees to wear hairnets, but requiring men to wear hats—and therefore keep their hair short—violates Sec. 703).

Finally, the E.E.O.C. by administrative decision, regulation, and on amicus brief here, fully supports Willingham's position. In its administrative decisions, the Commission has uniformly held that dress and grooming codes that distinguish between sexes are within Sec. 703, and can only be justified if proven to be a BFOQ. * * *

SEXUAL STEREOTYPES AND LEGISLATIVE INTENT

The beginning (and often the ending) point of statutory interpretation is an exploration of the legislative history of the Act in question. We must decide, if we can there find any basis for decision, whether Congress intended to include *all* sexual distinctions in its prohibition of discrimination (based solely on sex or on "sex plus"), or whether a line can legitimately be drawn beyond which employer conduct is no longer within reach of the statute.

We discover, as have other courts earlier considering the problem before us, that the meager legislative history regarding the addition of "sex" in Sec. 703(a) provides slim guidance for divining Congressional intent. * * * And while it is argued that a lack of change in this section in the 1972 amendments to the Act evidences Congressional agreement with the position of the E.E.O.C., it may be argued with equal force that the law was insufficiently developed at the time the amendments were considered to support any change. We find the legislative history inconclusive at best and draw but one conclusion, and that by way of negative inference. Without more extensive consideration, Congress in all probability did not intend for its proscription of sexual discrimination to have significant and sweeping implications. We should not therefore extend the coverage of the Act to situations of questionable application without some stronger Congressional mandate.

We perceive the intent of Congress to have been the guarantee of equal job opportunity for males and females. Providing such opportunity is where the emphasis rightly lies. This is to say that the Act should reach any device or policy of an employer which serves to deny acquisition and retention of a job or promotion in a job to an individual *because* the individual is either male or female. * * *

Juxtaposing our view of the Congressional purpose with the statutory interpretations advanced by the parties to this action elucidates our reasons for adopting the more narrow construction. Equal employment *opportunity* may be secured only when employers are barred from discriminating against employees on the basis of immutable characteristics, such as race and national origin. Similarly, an employer cannot have one hiring policy for men and another for women *if* the distinction is based on some fundamental right. But a hiring policy that distinguishes on some other ground, such as grooming codes or length of hair, is related more closely to the employer's choice of how to run his business than to equality of employment opportunity. In *Phillips*, supra, the Supreme Court condemned a hiring distinction based on having pre-school age children, an existing condition not subject to change. In Sprogis v. United Air Lines, supra, the Seventh Circuit reached a similar result with respect to marital status. We have no difficulty with the result reached in those cases; but nevertheless perceive that a line must be drawn between distinctions grounded on such fundamental rights as the right to have children or to marry and those interfering with the manner in which an employer exercises his judgment as to the way to operate a business. Hair length is not immutable and in the situation of employer vis à vis employee enjoys no constitutional protection. If the employee objects to the grooming code he has the right to reject it by looking elsewhere for employment, or alternatively he may choose to subordinate his preference by accepting the code along with the job.

* * *

We adopt the view, therefore, that distinctions in employment practices between men and women on the basis of something other than immutable or protected characteristics do not inhibit employment *opportunity* in violation of Sec. 703(a). Congress sought only to give all persons equal access to the job market, not to limit an employer's right to exercise his informed judgment as to how best to run his shop.

* * *

CONCLUSION

Nothing that we say should be construed as disparagement of what many feel to be a highly laudable goal—maximizing individual freedom by eliminating sexual stereotypes. We hold simply that such an objective may not be read into the Civil Rights Act of 1964 without further Congressional action. Private employers are prohibited from using different hiring policies for men and women only when the distinctions used relate to immutable characteristics or legally protected rights. While of course not impervious to judicial scrutiny, even those distinctions do not violate Sec. 703(a) if they are applied to both sexes.

Affirmed.

NOTES AND PROBLEMS FOR DISCUSSION

1. As the court in *Willingham* noted, sex-plus theory has been used to strike down no-marriage rules applied only to female employees. Other courts have similarly invalidated policies that discriminate against unwed mothers, Dolter v. Wahlert High School, 483 F.Supp. 266 (N.D.Iowa 1980); female

homosexuals, Valdes v. Lumbermen's Mutual Casualty Co., 507 F.Supp. 10 (S.D. Fla.1980); black women, Jefferies v. Harris County Community Action Association, 615 F.2d 1025 (5th Cir. 1980); and women who did not use their husband's surname on personnel forms, Allen v. Lovejoy, 553 F.2d 522 (6th Cir. 1977). In each of the aforementioned cases, the "plus" factor was used only to disqualify women. Would the application of these factors to members of both sexes, however, necessarily insulate them from Title VII liability?

2. Several other courts have adopted the limitation imposed on sex plus theory by the Fifth Circuit in *Willingham*—i.e., that Title VII only prohibits policies which discriminate on the basis of "plus" characteristics that are either immutable or involve fundamental rights—and thereby upheld dress codes prohibiting women from wearing pants, La Von Lonigan v. Bartlett and Co. Grain, 466 F.Supp. 1388 (W.D.Mo.1979); the discharge of an "uppity woman" because of her aggressive personality, Oaks v. City of Fairhope, Alabama, 515 F.Supp. 1004 (S.D.Ala.1981); and a maximum weight policy for female flight attendants, EEOC v. Delta Airlines, Inc., 24 EPD ¶ 31,455 (S.D.Tex.1980). One court somewhat self-consciously attempted to justify its acceptance of sex-differentiated dress codes (a state trial judge's requirement that male attorneys wear a necktie before his court) as in keeping with contemporary fashion. See Devine v. Lonschein, 621 F.Supp. 894, 897 (S.D.N.Y.1985). Can an employer forbid its employees from wearing religious medallions on the job? What if the rule applies only to crucifixes? Is § 701(j) relevant here?

3. What happens if the "plus" factor can be possessed only by members of one gender? This issue most frequently arises in cases involving employment distinctions based on pregnancy. In GENERAL ELECTRIC CO. v. GILBERT, 429 U.S. 125, 97 S.Ct. 401, 50 L.Ed.2d 343 (1976), the plaintiffs claimed that the company's non-occupational disability plan was in violation of Title VII because it did not provide payment for any absence due to pregnancy. They contended that the employer's failure to include pregnancy disabilities on the same terms and conditions as other non-occupational disabilities discriminated against them on the basis of their sex. The Supreme Court rejected this claim, holding that the exclusion of pregnancy from an otherwise nearly comprehensive disability plan was not a gender-based discrimination nor a pretext for such discrimination, but simply an economically-motivated decision to remove one expensive risk from the list of compensable disabilities. In addition, the Court ruled, by failing to prove that the benefit package was worth more to men than to women, either financially or in terms of aggregate risk protection, the plaintiffs had not demonstrated that the pregnancy-related exclusion had a *Griggs*-like disproportionate discriminatory effect on women. This ruling, which contradicted both the unanimous position of the six federal appellate courts that had addressed the issue and the E.E.O.C. Guidelines, received a great deal of attention and criticism. See e.g., Comment, Differential Treatment of Pregnancy in Employment: The Impact of General Electric Co. v. Gilbert and Nashville Gas Co. v. Satty, 13 Harv.Civ.R.–Civ.Lib.L.Rev. 717 (1978); Comment, 27 Loy.L.Rev. 532 (1981); Comment, 1977 Utah L.Rev. 119 (1977). The Court soon thereafter had another opportunity to examine a pregnancy-based employment policy and used it to limit the impact of *Gilbert*.  In NASHVILLE GAS CO. v. SATTY, 434 U.S. 136, 98 S.Ct. 347, 54 L.Ed.2d 356 (1977), company policy required pregnant employees to take a formal leave of absence without pay and to forfeit their accumulated job seniority upon returning to work after childbirth. Employees disabled by non-occupational sickness or injury, however, were entitled to sick pay and retention of accumu-

lated seniority. The Court concluded that the sick leave policy was indistinguishable from General Electric's denial of disability benefits to pregnant employees. Accordingly, the Court ruled, *Gilbert* controlled and this portion of the case was remanded to allow the trial court to determine whether the sick leave plan was a pretext for sex discrimination. It was the Court's treatment of the seniority provision, however, that generated the most controversy. The Court held that while the company's practice of denying accumulated seniority to employees returning from pregnancy leave was neutral on its face, it nevertheless had a discriminatory effect upon women and thus violated Title VII. In reaching this conclusion, the *Satty* Court distinguished *Gilbert* in the following manner:

> "In *Gilbert*, there was no showing that General Electric's policy of compensating for all non-job-related disabilities except pregnancy favored men over women. No evidence was produced to suggest that men received more benefits from General Electric's disability insurance fund than did women; both men and women were subject generally to the disabilities covered and presumably drew similar amounts from the insurance fund. We therefore upheld the plan under Title VII. * * *
>
> "Here, by comparison, petitioner has not merely refused to extend to women a benefit that men cannot and do not receive, but has imposed on women a substantial burden that men need not suffer. The distinction between benefits and burdens is more than one of semantics. We held in *Gilbert* that sec. 703(a)(1) did not require that greater economic benefits be paid to one sex or the other "because of their differing roles in 'the scheme of human existence,'" 429 U.S., at 139 n. 17. But that holding does not allow us to read sec. 703(a)(2) to permit an employer to burden female employees in such a way as to deprive them of employment opportunities because of their different role."

In order to determine whether subsequent cases were governed by *Gilbert* or *Satty*, the courts sought to ascertain whether the challenged pregnancy-based classifications either denied women some additional economic benefit or deprived them of employment opportunities, or adversely affected their employee status by subjecting them to a burden not borne by male employees. Pursuant to this somewhat elusive benefit/burden analysis, the courts held that absent a business justification, Title VII prohibited a school board from vesting discretion in the Superintendent to determine when a teacher could return from maternity leave when the Superintendent was not provided with similar discretion with respect to teachers returning from sick leave, Clanton v. Orleans Parish School Board, 649 F.2d 1084 (5th Cir. 1981); or from requiring pregnant teachers to go on mandatory maternity leave at a fixed point in the pregnancy term, deLaurier v. San Diego Unified School District, 588 F.2d 674 (9th Cir. 1978); and precluded an employer from requiring women who had been on pregnancy leave to have sustained a normal menstrual cycle before they could return to work, Harper v. Thiokol Chemical Corp., 619 F.2d 489 (5th Cir. 1980). On the other hand, one court held that Title VII was not violated by a company rule granting employees on nonoccupational disability leave full seniority credit for the period of their absence but limiting female employees on maternity leave to a maximum of thirty days' service credit. In re Southwestern Bell Telephone Co. Maternity Benefits Litigation, 602 F.2d 845 (8th Cir. 1979).

Congress responded to the controversy and confusion surrounding *Gilbert* and *Satty* by passing the Pregnancy Discrimination Act of 1978. This amendment to Title VII added a new provision—§ 701(k)—designed specifically to reverse the rulings in *Gilbert* and *Satty* by declaring that all pregnancy-based distinctions constitute discrimination on the basis of sex and that pregnancy must be treated like other temporary disabilities for all employment-related purposes. As the Act did not become effective as to extant benefit and insurance programs until April 29, 1979, there are very few reported cases in which its substantive provisions have been addressed. Nevertheless, many interpretative questions concerning the meaning and scope of the amendment undoubtedly will be raised. The EEOC already has issued interpretative guidelines addressing many of these anticipated problems. 29 CFR 1604.10 (Appendix) (1979).

Read § 701(k) of Title VII

NEWPORT NEWS SHIPBUILIDNG AND DRY DOCK CO. v. EEOC

Supreme Court of the United States, 1983.
462 U.S. 669, 103 S.Ct. 2622, 77 L.Ed.2d 89.

JUSTICE STEVENS delivered the opinion of the Court.

In 1978 Congress decided to overrule our decision in General Electric Co. v. Gilbert, 429 U.S. 125, 97 S.Ct. 401, 50 L.Ed.2d 343 (1976), by amending Title VII of the Civil Rights Act of 1964 "to prohibit sex discrimination on the basis of pregnancy."[1] On the effective date of the act, petitioner amended its health insurance plan to provide its female employees with hospitalization benefits for pregnancy-related conditions to the same extent as for other medical conditions. The plan continued, however, to provide less favorable pregnancy benefits for spouses of male employees. The question presented is whether the amended plan complies with the amended statute.

Petitioner's plan provides hospitalization and medical-surgical coverage for a defined category of employees[3] and a defined category of dependents. Dependents covered by the plan include employees' spouses, unmarried children between 14 days and 19 years of age, and some older dependent children.[4] Prior to April 29, 1979, the scope of the plan's coverage for eligible dependents was identical to its coverage for employees. All covered males, whether employees or dependents, were treated alike for purposes of hospitalization coverage. All covered

1. The new statute (the Pregnancy Discrimination Act) amended the "Definitions" section of Title VII, 42 U.S.C. § 2000e (1976), to add a new subsection (k) reading in pertinent part as follows:

> "The terms 'because of sex' or 'on the basis of sex' include, but are not limited to, because of or on the basis of pregnancy, childbirth, or related medical conditions; and women affected by pregnancy, childbirth, or related medical conditions shall be treated the same for all employment-related purposes, including receipt of benefits under fringe benefit programs, as other persons not so affected but similar in their ability or inability to work, and nothing in section 2000e–2(h) of this title shall be interpreted to permit otherwise * * *."

3. On the first day following three months of continuous service, every active, full-time, production, maintenance, technical, and clerical area bargaining unit employee becomes a plan participant.

4. For example, unmarried children up to age 23 who are full-time college students solely dependent on an employee and certain mentally or physically handicapped children are also covered.

females, whether employees or dependents, also were treated alike. Moreover, with one relevant exception, the coverage for males and females was identical. The exception was a limitation on hospital coverage for pregnancy that did not apply to any other hospital confinement.[6]

After the plan was amended in 1979, it provided the same hospitalization coverage for male and female employees themselves for all medical conditions, but it differentiated between female employees and spouses of male employees in its provision of pregnancy-related benefits.[7] In a booklet describing the plan, petitioner explained the amendment that gave rise to this litigation in this way:

> "B. Effective April 29, 1979, maternity benefits for female employees will be paid the same as any other hospital confinement as described in question 16. This applies only to deliveries beginning on April 29, 1979 and thereafter.
>
> "C. Maternity benefits for the wife of a male employee will continue to be paid as described in part 'A' of this question."

In turn, Part A stated, "The Basic Plan pays up to $500 of the hospital charges and 100% of reasonable and customary for delivery and anesthesiologist charges." As the Court of Appeals observed, "To the extent that the hospital charges in connection with an uncomplicated delivery may exceed $500, therefore, a male employee receives less complete coverage of spousal disabilities than does a female employee."

After the passage of the Pregnancy Discrimination Act, and before the amendment to petitioner's plan became effective, the Equal Opportunity Employment Commission issued "interpretive guidelines" in the form of questions and answers. Two of those questions, numbers 21 and 22, made it clear that the EEOC would consider petitioner's amended plan unlawful. Number 21 read as follows:

> "21. Q. Must an employer provide health insurance coverage for the medical expenses of pregnancy-related conditions of the spouses of male employees? Of the dependents of all employees?
>
> "A. Where an employer provides no coverage for dependents, the employer is not required to institute such coverage. However, if an employer's insurance program covers the medical expenses of spouses of female employees, then it must equally cover the medical

6. For hospitalization caused by uncomplicated pregnancy, petitioner's plan paid 100% of the reasonable and customary physicians' charges for delivery and anesthesiology, and up to $500 of other hospital charges. For all other hospital confinement, the plan paid in full for a semiprivate room for up to 120 days and for surgical procedures; covered the first $750 of reasonable and customary charges for hospital services (including general nursing care, x-ray examinations, and drugs) and other necessary services during hospitalization; and paid 80 percent of the charges exceeding $750 for such services up to a maximum of 120 days.

7. Thus, as the EEOC found after its investigation, "the record reveals that the present disparate impact on male employees had its genesis in the gender-based distinction accorded to female employees in the past."

expenses of spouses of male employees, including those arising from pregnancy-related conditions.

But the insurance does not have to cover the pregnancy-related conditions of non-spouse dependents as long as it excludes the pregnancy-related conditions of such non-spouse dependents of male and female employees equally."[9]

On September 20, 1979, one of petitioner's male employees filed a charge with the EEOC alleging that petitioner had unlawfully refused to provide full insurance coverage for his wife's hospitalization caused by pregnancy; a month later the United Steelworkers filed a similar charge on behalf of other individuals. Petitioner then commenced an action in the United States District Court for the Eastern District of Virginia, challenging the Commission's guidelines and seeking both declaratory and injunctive relief. The complaint named the EEOC, the male employee, and the United Steelworkers of America as defendants. Later the EEOC filed a civil action against petitioner alleging discrimination on the basis of sex against male employees in the company's provision of hospitalization benefits. Concluding that the benefits of the new Act extended only to female employees, and not to spouses of male employees, the District Court held that petitioner's plan was lawful and enjoined enforcement of the EEOC guidelines relating to pregnancy benefits for employees' spouses. 510 F.Supp. 66 (1981). It also dismissed the EEOC's complaint. The two cases were consolidated on appeal.

A divided panel of the United States Court of Appeals for the Fourth Circuit reversed, reasoning that since "the company's health insurance plan contains a distinction based on pregnancy that results in less complete medical coverage for male employees with spouses than for female employees with spouses, it is impermissible under the statute." After rehearing the case en banc, the court reaffirmed the conclusion of the panel over the dissent of three judges who believed the statute was intended to protect female employees "in their ability or inability to work," and not to protect spouses of male employees. Because the important question presented by the case had been decided differently by the United States Court of Appeals for the Ninth Circuit, EEOC v.

9. Question 22 is equally clear. It reads:

"22. Q. Must an employer provide the same level of health insurance coverage for the pregnancy-related medical conditions of the spouses of male employees as it provides for its female employees?

"A. No. It is not necessary to provide the same level of coverage for the pregnancy-related medical conditions of spouses of male employees as for female employees. However, where the employer provides coverage for the medical conditions of the spouses of its employees, then the level of coverage for pregnancy-related medical conditions of the spouses of male employees must be the same as the level of coverage for all other medical conditions of the spouses of female employees. For example, if the employer covers employees for 100 percent of reasonable and customary expenses sustained for a medical condition, but only covers dependent spouses for 50 percent of reasonable and customary expenses for their medical conditions, the pregnancy-related expenses of the male employee's spouse must be covered at the 50 percent level."

Lockheed Missiles and Space Co., 680 F.2d 1243 (1982), we granted certiorari.[10]

Ultimately the question we must decide is whether petitioner has discriminated against its male employees with respect to their compensation, terms, conditions, or privileges of employment because of their sex within the meaning of § 703(a)(1) of Title VII. Although the Pregnancy Discrimination Act has clarified the meaning of certain terms in this section, neither that Act nor the underlying statute contains a definition of the word "discriminate." In order to decide whether petitioner's plan discriminates against male employees because of *their* sex, we must therefore go beyond the bare statutory language. Accordingly, we shall consider whether Congress, by enacting the Pregnancy Discrimination Act, not only overturned the specific holding in General Electric v. Gilbert, supra, but also rejected the test of discrimination employed by the Court in that case. We believe it did. Under the proper test petitioner's plan is unlawful, because the protection it affords to married male employees is less comprehensive than the protection it affords to married female employees.

I

At issue in General Electric v. Gilbert was the legality of a disability plan that provided the company's employees with weekly compensation during periods of disability resulting from nonoccupational causes. Because the plan excluded disabilities arising from pregnancy, the District Court and the Court of Appeals concluded that it discriminated against female employees because of their sex. This Court reversed.

After noting that Title VII does not define the term "discrimination," the Court applied an analysis derived from cases construing the Equal Protection Clause of the Fourteenth Amendment to the Constitution. The *Gilbert* opinion quoted at length from a footnote in Geduldig v. Aiello, 417 U.S. 484, 94 S.Ct. 2485, 41 L.Ed.2d 256 (1974), a case which had upheld the constitutionality of excluding pregnancy coverage under California's disability insurance plan. "Since it is a finding of sex-based discrimination that must trigger, in a case such as this, the finding of an unlawful employment practice under § 703(a)(1)," the Court added, "*Geduldig* is precisely in point in its holding that an exclusion of pregnancy from a disability-benefits plan providing general coverage is not a gender-based discrimination at all."

The dissenters in *Gilbert* took issue with the majority's assumption "that the Fourteenth Amendment standard of discrimination is coterminous with that applicable to Title VII."[13] As a matter of statutory interpretation, the dissenters rejected the Court's holding that the

10. Subsequently the Court of Appeals for the Seventh Circuit agreed with the Ninth Circuit. EEOC v. Joslyn Mfg. & Supply Co., 706 F.2d 1469 (1983).

13. As the text of the *Geduldig* opinion makes clear, in evaluating the constitutionality of California's insurance program, the Court focused on the "non-invidious" character of the State's legitimate fiscal interest in excluding pregnancy coverage. This justification was not relevant to the statutory issue presented in *Gilbert*. See n. 25, infra.

plan's exclusion of disabilities caused by pregnancy did not constitute discrimination based on sex. As JUSTICE BRENNAN explained, it was facially discriminatory for the company to devise "a policy that, but for pregnancy, offers protection for all risks, even those that are 'unique to' men or heavily male dominated." It was inaccurate to describe the program as dividing potential recipients into two groups, pregnant women and nonpregnant persons, because insurance programs "deal with future *risks* rather than historic facts." Rather, the appropriate classification was "between persons who face a risk of pregnancy and those who do not." The company's plan, which was intended to provide employees with protection against the risk of uncompensated unemployment caused by physical disability, discriminated on the basis of sex by giving men protection for all categories of risk but giving women only partial protection. Thus, the dissenters asserted that the statute had been violated because conditions of employment for females were less favorable than for similarly situated males.

When Congress amended Title VII in 1978, it unambiguously expressed its disapproval of both the holding and the reasoning of the Court in the *Gilbert* decision. It incorporated a new subsection in the "definitions" applicable "[f]or the purposes of this subchapter." The first clause of the Act states, quite simply: "The terms 'because of sex' or 'on the basis of sex' include, but are not limited to, because of or on the basis of pregnancy, childbirth, or related medical conditions."[14] The House Report stated, "It is the Committee's view that the dissenting Justices correctly interpreted the Act." Similarly, the Senate Report quoted passages from the two dissenting opinions, stating that they "correctly express both the principle and the meaning of title VII." Proponents of the bill repeatedly emphasized that the Supreme Court had erroneously interpreted Congressional intent and that amending legislation was necessary to reestablish the principles of Title VII law as they had been understood prior to the *Gilbert* decision. Many of them expressly agreed with the views of the dissenting Justices.

As petitioner argues, congressional discussion focused on the needs of female members of the work force rather than spouses of male employees. This does not create a "negative inference" limiting the scope of the act to the specific problem that motivated its enactment. Congress apparently assumed that existing plans that included benefits for dependents typically provided no less pregnancy-related coverage for the wives of male employees than they did for female employees. When the question of differential coverage for dependents was addressed in the Senate Report, the Committee indicated that it should be resolved "on the basis of existing title VII principles."[20] The legislative

14. The meaning of the first clause is not limited by the specific language in the second clause, which explains the application of the general principle to women employees.

20. "Questions were raised in the committee's deliberations regarding how this bill would affect medical coverage for dependents of employees, as opposed to employees themselves. In this context it

context makes it clear that Congress was not thereby referring to the view of Title VII reflected in this Court's *Gilbert* opinion. Proponents of the legislation stressed throughout the debates that Congress had always intended to protect *all* individuals from sex discrimination in employment—including but not limited to pregnant women workers.[21] Against this background we review the terms of the amended statute to decide whether petitioner has unlawfully discriminated against its male employees.

II

Section 703(a) makes it an unlawful employment practice for an employer to "discriminate against any individual with respect to his compensation, terms, conditions, or privileges of employment, because

must be remembered that the basic purpose of this bill is to protect women employees, it does not alter the basic principles of title VII law as regards sex discrimination. Rather, this legislation clarifies the definition of sex discrimination for title VII purposes. Therefore the question in regard to dependents' benefits would be determined on the basis of existing title VII principles." Leg.Hist. at 42–43.

This statement does not imply that the new statutory definition has no applicability; it merely acknowledges that the new definition does not itself resolve the question.

The dissent quotes extensive excerpts from an exchange on the Senate floor between Senators Hatch and Williams. Taken in context, this colloquy clearly deals only with the second clause of the bill, see n. 14, supra, and Senator Williams, the principal sponsor of the legislation, addressed only the bill's effect on income maintenance plans. Senator Williams first stated, in response to Senator Hatch, "With regard to more maintenance plans for pregnancy-related disabilities, I do not see how this language could be misunderstood." Upon further inquiry from Senator Hatch, he replied, "If there is any ambiguity, with regard to income maintenance plans, I cannot see it." At the end of the same response, he stated, "It is narrowly drawn and would not give any employee the right to obtain income maintenance as a result of the pregnancy of someone who is not an employee." These comments, which clearly limited the scope of Senator Williams' responses, are omitted from the dissent's lengthy quotation.

Other omitted portions of the colloquy make clear that it was logical to discuss the pregnancies of employees' spouses in connection with income maintenance plans. Senator Hatch asked, "what about the status of the woman coworker who is not pregnant but rides with a pregnant woman and cannot get to work once the pregnant female commences her maternity leave or the employed mother who stays home to nurse her pregnant daughter?" The reference to spouses of male employees must be understood in light of these hypothetical questions; it seems to address the situation in which a male employee wishes to take time off from work because his wife is pregnant.

21. See, e.g., 123 Cong.Rec. 7539 (1977) (remarks of Sen. Williams) ("the Court has ignored the congressional intent in enacting title VII of the Civil Rights Act—that intent was to protect all individuals from unjust employment discrimination, including pregnant workers"); id., at 29385, 29652. In light of statements such as these, it would be anomalous to hold that Congress provided that an employee's pregnancy is sex-based, while a spouse's pregnancy is gender-neutral.

During the course of the Senate debate on the Pregnancy Discrimination Act, Senator Bayh and Senator Cranston both expressed the belief that the new act would prohibit the exclusion of pregnancy coverage for spouses if spouses were otherwise fully covered by an insurance plan. Because our holding relies on the 1978 legislation only to the extent that it unequivocally rejected the *Gilbert* decision, and ultimately we rely on our understanding of general Title VII principles, we attach no more significance to these two statements than to the many other comments by both Senators and Congressmen disapproving the Court's reasoning and conclusion in *Gilbert*.

of such individual's race, color, religion, sex, or national origin * * *." Health insurance and other fringe benefits are "compensation, terms, conditions, or privileges of employment." Male as well as female employees are protected against discrimination. Thus, if a private employer were to provide complete health insurance coverage for the dependents of its female employees, and no coverage at all for the dependents of its male employees, it would violate Title VII.[22] Such a practice would not pass the simple test of Title VII discrimination that we enunciated in Los Angeles Department of Water & Power v. Manhart, 435 U.S. 702, 711, 98 S.Ct. 1370, 1377, 55 L.Ed.2d 657 (1978), for it would treat a male employee with dependents "in a manner which but for that person's sex would be different."[23] The same result would be reached even if the magnitude of the discrimination were smaller. For example, a plan that provided complete hospitalization coverage for the spouses of female employees but did not cover spouses of male employees when they had broken bones would violate Title VII by discriminating against male employees.

Petitioner's practice is just as unlawful. Its plan provides limited pregnancy-related benefits for employees' wives, and affords more extensive coverage for employees' spouses for all other medical conditions requiring hospitalization. Thus the husbands of female employees receive a specified level of hospitalization coverage for all conditions; the wives of male employees receive such coverage except for pregnancy-related conditions.[24] Although *Gilbert* concluded that an otherwise inclusive plan that singled out pregnancy-related benefits for exclusion was nondiscriminatory on its face, because only women can become pregnant, Congress has unequivocally rejected that reasoning. The 1978 Act makes clear that it is discriminatory to treat pregnancy-related conditions less favorably than other medical conditions. Thus petitioner's plan unlawfully gives married male employees a benefit

22. Consistently since 1970 the EEOC has considered it unlawful under Title VII for an employer to provide different insurance coverage for spouses of male and female employees.

Similarly, in our Equal Protection Clause cases we have repeatedly held that, if the spouses of female employees receive less favorable treatment in the provision of benefits, the practice discriminates not only against the spouses but also against the female employees on the basis of sex. Frontiero v. Richardson, 411 U.S. 677, 688, 93 S.Ct. 1764, 1771, 36 L.Ed.2d 583 (1973) (opinion of Brennan, J.) (increased quarters allowances and medical and dental benefits); Weinberger v. Wiesenfeld, 420 U.S. 636, 645, 95 S.Ct. 1225, 1231, 43 L.Ed.2d 514 (1975) (Social Security benefits for surviving spouses); Califano v. Goldfarb, 430 U.S. 199, 207–208, 97 S.Ct. 1021, 1027, 51 L.Ed.2d 270 (1977) (opinion of Brennan, J.) (Social Security benefits for surviving spouses); Wengler v. Druggists Mutual Ins. Co., 446 U.S. 142, 147, 100 S.Ct. 1540, 1543, 64 L.Ed.2d 107 (1980) (workers' compensation death benefits for surviving spouses).

23. The *Manhart* case was decided several months before the Pregnancy Discrimination Act was passed. Although it was not expressly discussed in the legislative history, it set forth some of the "existing title VII principles" on which Congress relied. * * *

24. This policy is analogous to the exclusion of broken bones for the wives of male employees, except that both employees' wives and employees' husbands may suffer broken bones, but only employees' wives can become pregnant.

package for their dependents that is less inclusive than the dependency coverage provided to married female employees.

There is no merit to petitioner's argument that the prohibitions of Title VII do not extend to discrimination against pregnant spouses because the statute applies only to discrimination in employment. A two-step analysis demonstrates the fallacy in this contention. The Pregnancy Discrimination Act has now made clear that, for all Title VII purposes, discrimination based on a woman's pregnancy is, on its face, discrimination because of her sex. And since the sex of the spouse is always the opposite of the sex of the employee, it follows inexorably that discrimination against female spouses in the provision of fringe benefits is also discrimination against male employees.[25] By making clear that an employer could not discriminate on the basis of an employee's pregnancy, Congress did not erase the original prohibition against discrimination on the basis of an employee's sex.

In short, Congress' rejection of the premises of General Electric v. Gilbert forecloses any claim that an insurance program excluding pregnancy coverage for female beneficiaries and providing complete coverage to similarly situated male beneficiaries does not discriminate on the basis of sex. Petitioner's plan is the mirror image of the plan at issue in *Gilbert.* The pregnancy limitation in this case violates Title VII by discriminating against male employees.[26]

The judgment of the Court of Appeals is affirmed.

JUSTICE REHNQUIST, with whom JUSTICE POWELL joins, dissenting.

In General Electric Co. v. Gilbert, we held that an exclusion of pregnancy from a disability-benefits plan is not discrimination "because of [an] individual's * * * sex" within the meaning of Title VII. In our view, therefore, Title VII was not violated by an employer's disability plan that provided all employees with non-occupational sickness and accident benefits, but excluded from the plan's coverage disabilities

25. See n. 22, supra. This reasoning does not require that a medical insurance plan treat the pregnancies of employees' wives the same as the pregnancies of female employees. For example, as the EEOC recognizes, see n. 9, supra (Question 22), an employer might provide full coverage for employees and no coverage at all for dependents. Similarly, a disability plan covering employees' children may exclude or limit maternity benefits. Although the distinction between pregnancy and other conditions is, according to the 1978 Act, discrimination "on the basis of sex," the exclusion affects male and female *employees* equally since both may have pregnant dependent daughters. The EEOC's guidelines permit differential treatment of the pregnancies of dependents who are not spouses.

26. Because the 1978 Act expressly states that exclusion of pregnancy coverage is gender-based discrimination on its face, it eliminates any need to consider the average monetary value of the plan's coverage to male and female employees.

The cost of providing complete health insurance coverage for the dependents of male employees, including pregnant wives, might exceed the cost of providing such coverage for the dependents of female employees. But although that type of cost differential may properly be analyzed in passing on the constitutionality of a State's health insurance plan, see Geduldig v. Aiello, supra, no such justification is recognized under Title II once discrimination has been shown. *Manhart,* supra ("It shall not be a defense under Title VII to a charge of sex discrimination in benefits that the cost of such benefits is greater with respect to one sex than the other.").

arising from pregnancy. Under our decision in *Gilbert,* petitioner's otherwise inclusive benefits plan that excludes pregnancy benefits for a male employee's spouse clearly would not violate Title VII. For a different result to obtain, *Gilbert* would have to be judicially overruled by this Court or Congress would have to legislatively overrule our decision in its entirety by amending Title VII.

Today, the Court purports to find the latter by relying on the Pregnancy Discrimination Act of 1978, a statute that plainly speaks only of female employees affected by pregnancy and says nothing about spouses of male employees. Congress, of course, was free to legislatively overrule *Gilbert* in whole or in part, and there is no question but what the Pregnancy Discrimination Act manifests congressional dissatisfaction with the result we reached in *Gilbert.* But I think the Court reads far more into the Pregnancy Discrimination Act than Congress put there, and that therefore it is the Court, and not Congress, which is now overruling *Gilbert.*

In a case presenting a relatively simple question of statutory construction, the Court pays virtually no attention to the language of the Pregnancy Discrimination Act or the legislative history pertaining to that language. * * *

The Court recognizes that this provision is merely definitional and that "[u]ltimately the question we must decide is whether petitioner has discriminated against its male employees * * * because of their sex within the meaning of § 703(a)(1)" of Title VII. Section 703(a)(1) provides in part:

> "It shall be an unlawful employment practice for an employer * * * to fail or refuse to hire or to discharge any individual, or otherwise to discriminate against any individual with respect to his compensation, terms, conditions, or privileges of employment, because of such individual's race, color, religion, sex, or national origin * * *."

It is undisputed that in § 703(a)(1) the word "individual" refers to an employee or applicant for employment. As modified by the first clause of the definitional provision of the Pregnancy Discrimination Act, the proscription in § 703(a)(1) is for discrimination "against any individual * * * *because of such individual's* * * * *pregnancy,* childbirth, or related medical conditions." This can only be read as referring to the pregnancy of an *employee.*

That this result was not inadvertent on the part of Congress is made very evident by the second clause of the Act, language that the Court essentially ignores in its opinion. When Congress in this clause further explained the proscription it was creating by saying that "women affected by pregnancy * * * shall be treated the same * * * as other persons not so affected but *similar in their ability or inability to* *work*" it could only have been referring to *female employees.* The Court of Appeals below stands alone in thinking otherwise.[3]

The Court concedes that this is a correct reading of the second clause. Ante, at n. 14. Then in an apparent effort to escape the impact of this provision, the Court asserts that "[t]he meaning of the first clause is not limited by the specific language in the second clause." Ante, at n. 14. I do not disagree. But this conclusion does not help the Court, for as explained above, when the definitional provision of the first clause is inserted in § 703(a)(1), it says the very same thing: the proscription added to Title VII applies only to female employees.

The plain language of the Pregnancy Discrimination Act leaves little room for the Court's conclusion that the Act was intended to extend beyond female employees. The Court concedes that "congressional discussion focused on the needs of female members of the work force rather than spouses of male employees." In fact, the singular focus of discussion on the problems of the *pregnant worker* is striking.

When introducing the Senate Report on the bill that later became the Pregnancy Discrimination Act, its principal sponsor, Senator Williams, explained:

> "Because of the Supreme Court's decision in the *Gilbert* case, this legislation is necessary to provide fundamental protection against sex discrimination for our Nation's 42 million *working women.* This protection will go a long way toward insuring that American women are permitted to assume their rightful place in our Nation's economy.
>
> "In addition to providing protection to *working women* with regard to fringe benefit programs, such as health and disability insurance programs, this legislation will prohibit other employment policies which adversely affect *pregnant workers.*"

* * * [T]he Congressional Record is overflowing with similar statements by individual members of Congress expressing their intention to insure with the Pregnancy Discrimination Act that working women are not treated differently because of pregnancy. Consistent with these views, all three committee reports on the bills that led to the Pregnancy Discrimination Act expressly state that the Act would require employers to treat pregnant employees the same as "other employees."

3. See EEOC v. Joslyn Manufacturing & Supply Co., 706 F.2d 1469, 1479 (CA7, 1983); EEOC v. Lockheed Missiles & Space Co., 680 F.2d 1243, 1245 (CA9 1982).

The Court of Appeals' majority, responding to the dissent's reliance on this language, excused the import of the language by saying: "The statutory reference to 'ability or inability to work' denotes disability and does not suggest that the spouse must be an employee of the employer providing the coverage. In fact, the statute says 'as other persons not so affected'; it does not say 'as other *employees* not so affected.'" This conclusion obviously does not comport with a common-sense understanding of the language. The logical explanation for Congress' reference to "persons" rather than "employees" is that Congress intended that the amendment should also apply to applicants for employment.

The Court tries to avoid the impact of this legislative history by saying that it "does not create a 'negative inference' limiting the scope of the act to the specific problem that motivated its enactment." This reasoning might have some force if the legislative history was silent on an arguably related issue. But the legislative history is not silent. The Senate Report provides:

> "Questions were raised in the committee's deliberations regarding how this bill would affect medical coverage for dependents of employees, as opposed to employees themselves. In this context it must be remembered that the basic purpose of this bill is to protect women employees, it does not alter the basic principles of Title VII law as regards sex discrimination. * * * [T]he question in regard to dependents' benefits would be determined on the basis of existing Title VII principles. * * * *[T]he question of whether an employer who does cover dependents, either with or without additional cost to the employee, may exclude conditions related to pregnancy from that coverage is a different matter.* Presumably because plans which provide comprehensive medical coverage for spouses of women employees but not spouses of male employees are rare, we are not aware of any Title VII litigation concerning such plans. It is certainly not this committee's desire to encourage the institution of such plans. If such plans should be instituted in the future, the question would remain whether, under Title VII, the affected employees were discriminated against on the basis of their sex as regards the extent of coverage for their dependents."

This plainly disclaims any intention to deal with the issue presented in this case. Where Congress says that it would not want "to encourage" plans such as petitioner's, it cannot plausibly be argued that Congress has intended "to prohibit" such plans. Senator Williams was questioned on this point by Senator Hatch during discussions on the floor and his answers are to the same effect.

> "MR. HATCH: * * * The phrase 'women affected by pregnancy, childbirth or related medical conditions,' * * * appears to be overly broad, and is not limited in terms of employment. It does not even require that the person so affected be pregnant.
>
> "*Indeed under the present language of the bill, it is arguable that spouses of male employees are covered by this civil rights amendment.* * * *
>
> "Could the sponsors clarify exactly whom that phrase intends to cover?
>
> * * *
>
> "MR. WILLIAMS: * * * I do not see how one can read into this any pregnancy other than that pregnancy that relates to the employee, and if there is any ambiguity, *let it be clear here and now that this is very precise. It deals with a woman, a woman who is an employee,* an employee in a work situation where all disabilities are covered under a company plan that provides income maintenance in

the event of medical disability; that her particular period of disability, when she cannot work because of childbirth or anything related to childbirth is excluded. * * *

* * *

"MR. HATCH: So the Senator is satisfied that, though the committee language I brought up, 'woman affected by pregnancy' seems to be ambiguous, what it means is that *this act only applies to the particular woman who is actually pregnant, who is an employee and has become pregnant after her employment?"*

* * *

"MR. WILLIAMS: "*Exactly.*" 123 Cong.Rec. S15,038–39 (daily ed. Sept. 16, 1977), Leg.Hist., at 80 (emphasis added).[7]

It seems to me that analysis of this case should end here. Under our decision in General Electric Co. v. Gilbert petitioner's exclusion of pregnancy benefits for male employee's spouses would not offend Title VII. Nothing in the Pregnancy Discrimination Act was intended to reach beyond female employees. Thus, *Gilbert* controls and requires that we reverse the Court of Appeals. But it is here, at what should be the stopping place, that the Court begins. * * *

The crux of the Court's reasoning is that even though the Pregnancy Discrimination Act redefines the phrases "because of sex" and "on the basis of sex" only to include discrimination against female employees affected by pregnancy, Congress also expressed its view that in *Gilbert* "the Supreme Court * * * erroneously interpreted Congressional intent." Somehow the Court then concludes that this renders all of *Gilbert* obsolete.

In support of its argument, the Court points to a few passages in congressional reports and several statements by various members of the 95th Congress to the effect that the Court in *Gilbert* had, when it construed Title VII, misperceived the intent of the 88th Congress. The Court also points out that "[m]any of [the members of 95th Congress] expressly agreed with the views of the dissenting Justices." Certainly

7. The Court suggests that in this exchange Senator Williams is explaining only that spouses of male employees will not be put on "income maintenance plans" while pregnant. This is utterly illogical. Spouses of employees have no income from the relevant employer to be maintained. Senator Williams clearly says that the Act is limited to female employees and as to such employees it will ensure income maintenance where male employees would receive similar disability benefits. Senator Hatch's final question and Senator Williams' response could not be clearer. The Act was intended to affect *only* pregnant workers. This is exactly what the Senate Report said and Senator Williams confirmed that this is exactly what Congress intended.

The only indications arguably contrary to the views reflected in the Senate Report and the exchange between Senators Hatch and Williams are found in two isolated remarks by Senators Bayh and Cranston. These statements, however, concern these two Senators' views concerning Title VII sex discrimination as it existed prior to the Pregnancy Discrimination Act. Their conclusions are completely at odds with our decision in General Electric Co. v. Gilbert, and are not entitled to deference here. We have consistently said that "[t]he views of members of a later Congress, concerning different [unamended] sections of Title VII * * * are entitled to little if any weight. It is the intent of the Congress that enacted [Title VII] in 1964 * * * that controls." Teamsters v. United States.

various members of Congress said as much. But the fact remains that *Congress as a body* has not expressed these sweeping views in the Pregnancy Discrimination Act.

Under our decision in General Electric Co. v. Gilbert, petitioner's exclusion of pregnancy benefits for male employee's spouses would not violate Title VII. Since nothing in the Pregnancy Discrimination Act even arguably reaches beyond female employees affected by pregnancy, *Gilbert* requires that we reverse the Court of Appeals. Because the Court concludes otherwise, I dissent.

NOTES AND PROBLEMS FOR DISCUSSION

1. It seems clear that absent the 1978 amendment, this case would have been controlled by the ruling in *Gilbert* that a distinction based on pregnancy does not constitute sex-based discrimination under Title VII. It also is clear that *Gilbert* would now be decided differently as a result of the 1978 amendment. The issue in *Newport News,* then, is the extent, if any, to which the second clause of section 701(k) limits the instances in which a pregnancy-based distinction constitutes discrimination on the basis of sex. More specifically, the question is whether a company's failure to provide pregnancy benefits to an employee's spouse constitutes sex-based discrimination in the terms and conditions of employment offered to the employee. Without clearly saying so, the Court appears to be stating that since *spousal* health care benefits, like other fringe benefits, are terms and conditions of employment, they are provided for "employment related purposes" and thus must cover pregnancy to the same extent as other medical conditions. Unfortunately, the somewhat confusing language employed in footnote 14 of its opinion, as the dissenters recognize, does not help the majority. On the other hand, is the dissent's evaluation of the legislative history convincing? Does the fact that the amendment was aimed predominantly at protecting women employees from discrimination mean that it should not be interpreted to prevent discrimination against male employees with respect to their receipt of fringe benefits? Finally, does it strike you that the language in the majority opinion sounds a bit too much like a gloating judicial "I told you so" on the part of those who had dissented in *Gilbert?*

2. Suppose an employer has no paid sick leave policy, but permits all employees to take up to two weeks unpaid sick leave before discharging them. Further assume that the employer uniformly discharged all persons who exceeded the two week limit. If the employer denies a female employee's request for additional unpaid time off for pregnancy and maternity leave, and discharges her upon the expiration of the two week period, can she successfully maintain a claim of sex discrimination? Is *Griggs* applicable? The EEOC has ruled that an employer's adherence to a facially neutral sick leave policy and its consequent refusal to provide pregnant employees with a reasonable leave of absence, in the absence of a showing of business necessity, discriminates on the basis of sex because of its disproportionate impact on women. See EEOC Dec. No. 74–112, 19 FEP Cases 1817 (April 15, 1974); EEOC Guidelines, 29 CFR § 1604.10(c). Is this consistent with the language in § 701(k) requiring pregnant employees to "be treated the same for all employee-related purposes" as non-pregnant employees? Does it amount to "reverse" sex discrimination? See Abraham v. Graphic Arts Int'l Union, 660 F.2d 811 (D.C. Cir. 1981); Kansas Ass'n v. EEOC, 33 FEP Cases 588 (D.Kans.1983); Note, 58 Wash. U.L.Q. 607

(1980). Does this analysis also suggest that an employee who provides infant care leave should make it available to workers of either gender? See Comment, The Pregnancy Discrimination Act: Protecting A Man's Right to Infant-Care Leave, 25 Santa Clara L.Rev. 435 (1985). What if a state antidiscrimination law prohibited employers from refusing to grant reasonable leaves of absence for pregnancy? See California Fed. S & L Ass'n v. Guerra, 758 F.2d 390 (9th Cir. 1985), cert. granted, ___ U.S. ___, 106 S.Ct. 783, 88 L.Ed.2d 762 (1986); Miller-Wohl Co. v. Commissioner of Labor, 515 F.Supp. 1264 (D.Mont.1981), vacated for lack of jurisdiction, 685 F.2d 1088 (9th Cir. 1982). For a thoughtful discussion of the issue, see Williams, Equality's Riddle: Pregnancy and the Equal Treatment/Special Treatment Debate, 13 NYU Rev. of L. & Soc. Ch. 325 (1984–85).

3. The federal Employee Retirement Income Security Act of 1974, 88 Stat. 829, 29 U.S.C. § 1001 et seq. (1976 ed. and Supp. V) (ERISA) subjects "employee benefit plans", such as pension and welfare plans, to federal regulation with respect to participation, funding and vesting. Section 514(a) of ERISA expressly preempts any and all state laws which relate to employee benefit plans covered by ERISA. The statute also, however, exempts from ERISA coverage (and thereby permits state regulation of) employee benefit plans maintained solely for the purpose of complying with applicable state workers' compensation, unemployment compensation or disability insurance laws. Finally, section 514(d) of ERISA provides that the statute cannot be construed to impair any other federal law. Prior to the enactment of the Pregnancy Discrimination Act, the New York State anti-discrimination statute had been interpreted to prohibit an employer from excluding pregnancy from its nonoccupational disability plan. This, of course, meant that the state law's provisions went beyond those of the federal statute as then interpreted by the Supreme Court in *Gilbert.* In SHAW v. DELTA AIR LINES, INC., 463 U.S. 85, 103 S.Ct. 2890, 77 L.Ed.2d 490 (1983), the Supreme Court held that the express preemption clause of ERISA prohibited state regulation of employee benefit plans insofar as the state statute prohibited practices that were lawful under Title VII. This ruling, the Court reasoned, gave effect to both the preemption of state law provision and the requirement that ERISA not be interpreted so as to impair or modify another federal statute. While the subsequent addition of subsection (k) to section 701 in 1978 limits the significance of this ruling with respect to the pregnancy provision of the New York State law, the Court noted that its decision might have further repercussions with respect to other provisions of state fair employment statutes that contain proscriptions broader than those in Title VII and that relate to employee benefit plans covered by ERISA.

4. Note also that the extent of protection afforded pregnancy classifications by section 701(k) may be limited by the availability of the business necessity and section 703(e) BFOQ defenses. Compare Harriss v. Pan American World Airways, Inc., 649 F.2d 670 (9th Cir. 1980) (policy requiring flight attendants to take maternity leave immediately upon discovery of pregnancy justified under BFOQ defense) with Burwell v. Eastern Air Lines, Inc., 633 F.2d 361 (4th Cir. 1980), cert. denied, 450 U.S. 965, 101 S.Ct. 1480, 67 L.Ed.2d 613 (1981) (business necessity defense justifies mandatory maternity leave only from the commencement of the 28th week of pregnancy.) Can a hospital justifiably discharge a pregnant radiation technologist on the ground that her exposure to X-rays created a risk of injury to the fetus and resultant liability to the hospital? See Zuniga v. Kleberg County Hospital, 692 F.2d 986 (5th Cir. 1982); Hayes v. Shelby Memorial Hospital, 726 F.2d 1543 (11th Cir. 1983). What if an employer

excludes all fertile women from jobs classified as requiring or possibly requiring contact with and exposure to known or suspected abortifacient or teratogenic agents? See Wright v. Olin Corp., 697 F.2d 1172 (4th Cir. 1982), on remand 585 F.Supp. 1447 (W.D.N.C.1984). See supra, at 273–274.

5. Some states have created income maintenance programs that pay benefits to persons who are unemployed because of a nonoccupational disability and finance such programs by employee contributions withheld from wages. Suppose that under such a statutory program the employer is required to withhold employee contributions from its employees' wages, transmit these funds to the state agency and perform record keeping functions, but does not make contributions of its own to the fund. If the program treats pregnancy differently than all other disabilities, is the employer liable under Title VII? See Barone v. Hackett, 602 F.Supp. 481 (D.R.I.1984).

6. Should the result in the principal case be given retroactive effect? Two federal appeals courts have concluded that retroactivity is justified in light of the presumption in favor of liability in Title VII cases announced by the Supreme Court in Albemarle Paper Co. v. Moody, see infra at p. 616, and the factors set forth in Chevron Oil Co. v. Huson, 404 U.S. 97, 92 S.Ct. 349, 30 L.Ed. 2d 296 (1971) for determining the appropriateness of retroactivity. Applying the *Chevron* standards, the court in EEOC v. Puget Sound Log S & G Bureau, 752 F.2d 1389 (9th Cir. 1985) stated that in light of extant EEOC guidelines on the Pregnancy Discrimination Act, analogous equal protection holdings by the Supreme Court, and several federal court decisions concerning the application of the PDA to nonemployees, the result in *Newport News* should not have come as a surprise to this defendant. In addition, the court noted, to deny retroactivity would frustrate the statutory make-whole purpose and would encourage employers to wait as long as possible to comply with the PDA. The court also reasoned that retroactivity would not impose an overly burdensome expense on the employer since it would only have to reimburse a relatively small, discrete number of male employees who had privately financed the cost of their nonemployee spouses' pregnancies. Accord, see EEOC v. Atlanta Gas Light Co., 751 F.2d 1188 (11th Cir. 1985).

7. Pregnancy and maternity policies used by public employers have been challenged under the Equal Protection and Due Process Clauses of the Constitution as well as under Title VII. In GEDULDIG v. AIELLO, 417 U.S. 484, 94 S.Ct. 2485, 41 L.Ed.2d 256 (1974), the Supreme Court rejected an equal protection attack upon an employee-funded California disability insurance system that specifically excluded pregnancy from its list of compensable disabilities. The Court held that the State's determination not to provide a totally comprehensive insurance program did not amount to invidious discrimination under the Equal Protection Clause. Since the plan provided equivalent aggregate risk protection to both sexes, the exclusion of pregnancy, though admittedly affecting only women, was not a sex-based classification for constitutional purposes. The decision to exclude pregnancy, the Court added, was not irrational but was supported by legitimate financial considerations. This reasoning later served as the foundation for the Court's ruling in *Gilbert*. The constitutionality of mandatory maternity leave for public school teachers was addressed in CLEVELAND BOARD OF EDUCATION v. LA FLEUR, 414 U.S. 632, 94 S.Ct. 791, 39 L.Ed.2d 52 (1974). The Court struck down the Board's policy requiring every pregnant teacher to take unpaid maternity leave at the end of the fourth month of pregnancy as violative of the Due Process Clause of the Fourteenth Amendment. This inflexible cutoff date, the Court reasoned, contained an

irrebuttable presumption—that all pregnant teachers become physically incapable of teaching at the same designated moment—and applied it even in the face of undisputed contrary medical evidence as to an individual teacher. Relying on several of its prior decisions, the Court concluded that the Due Process Clause could not tolerate an irrebuttable presumption that was not necessarily or universally true when the School Board had a reasonable alternative method of making individualized determinations as to physical competence. The Court applied this same analysis in also invalidating the Board's policy permitting teachers to return from maternity leave no sooner than the beginning of the regular semester following the date the teacher's child attained the age of three months. However, the Court's subsequent ruling in Weinberger v. Salfi, 422 U.S. 749, 95 S.Ct. 2457, 45 L.Ed.2d 522 (1975), in which it rejected a due process challenge to a Social Security Act provision that awarded benefits to a deceased wage earner's surviving widow and stepchildren only if they had been related to the deceased for at least nine months prior to his death, indicates that the Court has abandoned the irrebuttable presumption doctrine. See New York City Transit Authority v. Beazer, 440 U.S. 568, 592 n. 38, 99 S.Ct. 1355, 1369 n. 38, 59 L.Ed.2d 587, 606 n. 38 (1979) ("The District Court also concluded that TA's rule [refusing employment to methadone users] violates the Due Process Clause because it creates an 'irrebuttable presumption' of unemployability on the part of methadone users. Respondents do not rely on the due process argument in this Court, and we find no merit in it."). See generally Chase, the Premature Demise of Irrebuttable Presumptions, 47 U.Colo.L.Rev. 653 (1976). Consequently, most future challenges to public sector mandatory maternity leave programs are likely to rely principally upon Title VII rather than the Constitution.

8. Pregnancy, of course, is not the only "plus" characteristic restricted to members of one sex. Would an employer's refusal to hire all bearded applicants constitute a prima facie violation of Title VII? What if a restaurant owner imposed large breast size as a requirement for employment? Can either of these policies be justified under the BFOQ defense?

2. Sexual Harassment

Review the materials at pp. 99–114, supra.

3. Pension Funds

CITY OF LOS ANGELES, DEPARTMENT OF WATER AND POWER v. MANHART

Supreme Court of the United States, 1978.
435 U.S. 702, 98 S.Ct. 1370, 55 L.Ed.2d 657.

MR. JUSTICE STEVENS delivered the opinion of the Court.

As a class, women live longer than men. For this reason, the Los Angeles Department of Water and Power required its female employees to make larger contributions to its pension fund than its male employees. We granted certiorari to decide whether this practice discriminated against individual female employees because of their sex in violation of § 703(a)(1) of the Civil Rights Act of 1964, as amended.

For many years the Department has administered retirement, disability, and death-benefit programs for its employees. Upon retirement each employee is eligible for a monthly retirement benefit computed as a fraction of his or her salary multiplied by years of service.[3] The monthly benefits for men and women of the same age, seniority, and salary are equal. Benefits are funded entirely by contributions from the employees and the Department, augmented by the income earned on those contributions. No private insurance company is involved in the administration or payment of benefits.

Based on a study of mortality tables and its own experience, the Department determined that its 2,000 female employees, on the average, will live a few years longer than its 10,000 male employees. The cost of a pension for the average retired female is greater than for the average male retiree because more monthly payments must be made to the average woman. The Department therefore required female employees to make monthly contributions to the fund which were 14.84% higher than the contributions required of comparable male employees. Because employee contributions were withheld from paychecks, a female employee took home less pay than a male employee earning the same salary.

* * * In 1973, respondents brought this suit in the United States District Court for the Central District of California on behalf of a class of women employed or formerly employed by the Department. They prayed for an injunction and restitution of excess contributions.

While this action was pending, the California Legislature enacted a law prohibiting certain municipal agencies from requiring female employees to make higher pension fund contributions than males. The Department therefore amended its plan, effective January 1, 1975. The current plan draws no distinction, either in contributions or in benefits, on the basis of sex. On a motion for summary judgment, the District Court held that the contribution differential violated § 703(a)(1) and ordered a refund of all excess contributions made before the amendment of the plan. The United States Court of Appeals for the Ninth Circuit affirmed.

The Department and various *amici curiae* contend that: (1) the differential in take-home pay between men and women was not discrimination within the meaning of § 703(a)(1) because it was offset by a difference in the value of the pension benefits provided to the two classes of employees; (2) the differential was based on a factor "other than sex" within the meaning of the Equal Pay Act of 1963 and was therefore protected by the so-called Bennett Amendment; (3) the rationale of General Electric Co. v. Gilbert, 429 U.S. 125, 97 S.Ct. 401, 50 L.Ed.2d 343, requires reversal; and (4) in any event, the retroactive monetary recovery is unjustified. We consider these contentions in turn.

There are both real and fictional differences between women and men. It is true that the average man is taller than the average woman;

3. * * * The benefit is guaranteed for life.

it is not true that the average woman driver is more accident prone than the average man. Before the Civil Rights Act of 1964 was enacted, an employer could fashion his personnel policies on the basis of assumptions about the differences between men and women, whether or not the assumptions were valid.

It is now well recognized that employment decisions cannot be predicated on mere "stereotyped" impressions about the characteristics of males or females. Myths and purely habitual assumptions about a woman's inability to perform certain kinds of work are no longer acceptable reasons for refusing to employ qualified individuals, or for paying them less. This case does not, however, involve a fictional difference between men and women. It involves a generalization that the parties accept as unquestionably true: Women, as a class, do live longer than men. The Department treated its women employees differently from its men employees because the two classes are in fact different. It is equally true, however, that all individuals in the respective classes do not share the characteristic that differentiates the average class representatives. Many women do not live as long as the average man and many men outlive the average woman. The question, therefore, is whether the existence or nonexistence of "discrimination" is to be determined by comparison of class characteristics or individual characteristics. A "stereotyped" answer to that question may not be the same as the answer that the language and purpose of the statute command.

The statute makes it unlawful "to discriminate against any *individual* with respect to his compensation, terms, conditions, or privileges of employment, because of such *individual's* race, color, religion, sex, or national origin." The statute's focus on the individual is unambiguous. It precludes treatment of individuals as simply components of a racial, religious, sexual, or national class. If height is required for a job, a tall woman may not be refused employment merely because, on the average, women are too short. Even a true generalization about the class is an insufficient reason for disqualifying an individual to whom the generalization does not apply.

That proposition is of critical importance in this case because there is no assurance that any individual woman working for the Department will actually fit the generalization on which the Department's policy is based. Many of those individuals will not live as long as the average man. While they were working, those individuals received smaller paychecks because of their sex, but they will receive no compensating advantage when they retire.

It is true, of course, that while contributions are being collected from the employees, the Department cannot know which individuals will predecease the average woman. Therefore, unless women as a class are assessed an extra charge, they will be subsidized, to some extent, by the class of male employees.[14] It follows, according to the Department, that fairness to its class of male employees justifies the extra assessment against all of its female employees.

But the question of fairness to various classes affected by the statute is essentially a matter of policy for the legislature to address. Congress has decided that classifications based on sex, like those based on national origin or race, are unlawful. Actuarial studies could unquestionably identify differences in life expectancy based on race or national origin, as well as sex.[15] But a statute that was designed to make race irrelevant in the employment market, see Griggs v. Duke Power Co., 401 U.S. 424, 436, 91 S.Ct. 849, 856, 28 L.Ed.2d 158, could not reasonably be construed to permit a take-home-pay differential based on a racial classification.[16]

Even if the statutory language were less clear, the basic policy of the statute requires that we focus on fairness to individuals rather than fairness to classes. Practices that classify employees in terms of religion, race, or sex tend to preserve traditional assumptions about groups rather than thoughtful scrutiny of individuals. The generalization involved in this case illustrates the point. Separate mortality tables are easily interpreted as reflecting innate differences between the sexes; but a significant part of the longevity differential may be explained by the social fact that men are heavier smokers than women.

Finally, there is no reason to believe that Congress intended a special definition of discrimination in the context of employee group insurance coverage. It is true that insurance is concerned with events that are individually unpredictable, but that is characteristic of many employment decisions. Individual risks, like individual performance, may not be predicted by resort to classifications proscribed by Title VII. Indeed, the fact that this case involves a group insurance program highlights a basic flaw in the Department's fairness argument. For when insurance risks are grouped, the better risks always subsidize the poorer risks. Healthy persons subsidize medical benefits for the less healthy; unmarried workers subsidize the pensions of married workers; persons who eat, drink, or smoke to excess may subsidize pension benefits for persons whose habits are more temperate. Treating different classes of risks as though they were the same for purposes of group insurance is a common practice that has never been considered inherently unfair. To insure the flabby and the fit as though they were equivalent risks may be more common than treating men and women

14. The size of the subsidy involved in this case is open to doubt, because the Department's plan provides for survivors' benefits. Since female spouses of male employees are likely to have greater life expectancies than the male spouses of female employees, whatever benefits men lose in "primary" coverage for themselves, they may regain in "secondary" coverage for their wives.

15. For example, the life expectancy of a white baby in 1973 was 72.2 years; a nonwhite baby could expect to live 65.9 years, a difference of 6.3 years. See Public Health Service, IIA Vital Statistics of the United States, 1973, Table 5–3.

16. Fortifying this conclusion is the fact that some States have banned higher life insurance rates for blacks since the 19th century.

alike; [19] but nothing more than habit makes one "subsidy" seem less fair than the other.

An employment practice that requires 2,000 individuals to contribute more money into a fund than 10,000 other employees simply because each of them is a woman, rather than a man, is in direct conflict with both the language and the policy of the Act. Such a practice does not pass the simple test of whether the evidence shows "treatment of a person in a manner which but for that person's sex would be different." It constitutes discrimination and is unlawful unless exempted by the Equal Pay Act of 1963 or some other affirmative justification.

Shortly before the enactment of Title VII in 1964, Senator Bennett proposed an amendment providing that a compensation differential based on sex would not be unlawful if it was authorized by the Equal Pay Act, which had been passed a year earlier. The Equal Pay Act requires employers to pay members of both sexes the same wages for equivalent work, except when the differential is pursuant to one of four specified exceptions. The Department contends that the fourth exception applies here. That exception authorizes a "differential based on any other factor other than sex."

The Department argues that the different contributions exacted from men and women were based on the factor of longevity rather than sex. It is plain, however, that any individual's life expectancy is based on a number of factors, of which sex is only one. The record contains no evidence that any factor other than the employee's sex was taken into account in calculating the 14.84% differential between the respective contributions by men and women. * * *

* * *

The Department argues that reversal is required by General Electric Co. v. Gilbert, 429 U.S. 125, 97 S.Ct. 401, 50 L.Ed.2d 343. We are satisified, however, that neither the holding nor the reasoning of *Gilbert* is controlling.

In *Gilbert* the Court held that the exclusion of pregnancy from an employer's disability benefit plan did not constitute sex discrimination within the meaning of Title VII. Relying on the reasoning in Geduldig v. Aiello, 417 U.S. 484, 94 S.Ct. 2485, 41 L.Ed.2d 256, the Court first held that the General Electric plan did not involve "discrimination based upon gender as such." The two groups of potential recipients which that case concerned were pregnant women and nonpregnant persons. " 'While the first group is exclusively female, the second includes members of both sexes.' " In contrast, each of the two groups of employees involved in this case is composed entirely and exclusively

19. The record indicates, however, that the Department has funded its death-benefit plan by equal contributions from male and female employees. A death benefit—unlike a pension benefit—has less value for persons with longer life expectancies. Under the Department's concept of fairness, then, this neutral funding of death benefits is unfair to women as a class.

of members of the same sex. On its face, this plan discriminates on the basis of sex whereas the General Electric plan discriminated on the basis of a special physical disability.

In *Gilbert* the Court did note that the plan as actually administered had provided more favorable benefits to women as a class than to men as a class. This evidence supported the conclusion that not only had plaintiffs failed to establish a prima facie case by proving that the plan was discriminatory on its face, but they had also failed to prove any discriminatory effect.

In this case, however, the Department argues that the absence of a discriminatory effect on women as a class justifies an employment practice which, on its face, discriminated against individual employees because of their sex. But even if the Department's actuarial evidence is sufficient to prevent plaintiffs from establishing a prima facie case on the theory that the effect of the practice on women as a class was discriminatory, that evidence does not defeat the claim that the practice, on its face, discriminated against every individual woman employed by the Department.[30]

In essence, the Department is arguing that the prima facie showing of discrimination based on evidence of different contributions for the respective sexes is rebutted by its demonstration that there is a like difference in the cost of providing benefits for the respective classes. That argument might prevail if Title VII contained a cost-justification defense comparable to the affirmative defense available in a price discrimination suit. But neither Congress nor the courts have recognized such a defense under Title VII.

Although we conclude that the Department's practice violated Title VII, we do not suggest that the statute was intended to revolutionize the insurance and pension industries. All that is at issue today is a requirement that men and women make unequal contributions to an employer-operated pension fund. Nothing in our holding implies that it would be unlawful for an employer to set aside equal retirement contributions for each employee and let each retiree purchase the largest benefit which his or her accumulated contributions could command in the open market.[33] Nor does it call into question the insur-

30. Some *amici* suggest that the Department's discrimination is justified by business necessity. They argue that, if no gender distinction is drawn, many male employees will withdraw from the plan, or even the Department, because they can get a better pension plan in the private market. But the Department has long required equal contributions to its death-benefit plan, see n. 19, supra, and since 1975 it has required equal contributions to its pension plan. Yet the Department points to no "adverse selection" by the affected employees, presumably because an employee who wants to leave the plan must also leave his job, and few workers will quit because one of their fringe benefits could theoretically be obtained at a marginally lower price on the open market. In short, there has been no showing that sex distinctions are reasonably necessary to the normal operation of the Department's retirement plan.

33. Title VII and the Equal Pay Act primarily govern relations between employees and their employer, not between employees and third parties. We do not suggest, of course, that an employer can avoid his responsibilities by delegating discriminatory programs to corporate shells. Title VII applies to "any agent" of a cov-

ance industry practice of considering the composition of an employer's work force in determining the probable cost of a retirement or death benefit plan. Finally, we recognize that in a case of this kind it may be necessary to take special care in fashioning appropriate relief.

* * *

There can be no doubt that the prohibition against sex-differentiated employee contributions represents a marked departure from past practice. Although Title VII was enacted in 1964, this is apparently the first litigation challenging contribution differences based on valid actuarial tables. Retroactive liability could be devastating for a pension fund. The harm would fall in large part on innocent third parties. If, as the courts below apparently contemplated, the plaintiffs' contributions are recovered from the pension fund, the administrators of the fund will be forced to meet unchanged obligations with diminished assets. If the reserve proves inadequate, either the expectations of all retired employees will be disappointed or current employees will be forced to pay not only for their own future security but also for the unanticipated reduction in the contributions of past employees.

Without qualifying the force of the * * * presumption in favor of retroactive relief, we conclude that it was error to grant such relief in this case. Accordingly, although we agree with the Court of Appeals' analysis of the statute, we vacate its judgment and remand the case for further proceedings consistent with this opinion.

It is so ordered.

MR. JUSTICE BRENNAN took no part in the consideration or decision of this case.

MR. JUSTICE BLACKMUN, concurring in part and concurring in the judgment.

* * *

The Court's rationale, * * * is that Congress, by Title VII of the Civil Rights Act of 1964, as amended, intended to eliminate, with certain exceptions, "race, color, religion, sex, or national origin," as factors upon which employers may act. A program such as the one challenged here does exacerbate gender consciousness. But the program under consideration in *General Electric* did exactly the same thing and yet was upheld against challenge.

The Court's distinction between the present case and *General Electric*—that the permitted classes there were "pregnant women and nonpregnant persons," both female and male—seems to me to be just too easy. It is probably the only distinction that can be drawn. For me, it does not serve to distinguish the case on any principled basis. I therefore must conclude that today's decision cuts back on *General Electric*, and inferentially on *Geduldig*, the reasoning of which was

ered employer, and the Equal Pay Act applies to "any person acting directly or indirectly in the interest of an employer in relation to an employee." * * *

adopted there, and, indeed, makes the recognition of those cases as continuing precedent somewhat questionable. I do not say that this is necessarily bad. If that is what Congress has chosen to do by Title VII—as the Court today with such assurance asserts—so be it. I feel, however, that we should meet the posture of the earlier cases head on and not by thin rationalization that seeks to distinguish but fails in its quest.

* * *

MR. CHIEF JUSTICE BURGER, with whom MR. JUSTICE REHNQUIST joins, concurring in part and dissenting in part.

* * *

MR. JUSTICE MARSHALL, concurring in part and dissenting in part.

* * *

NOTES AND PROBLEMS FOR DISCUSSION

1. Do you agree with the majority or Justice Blackmun with respect to whether *Manhart* can be distinguished in any meaningful way from *Gilbert*? See generally, Rutherglen, Sexual Equality in Fringe-Benefit Plans, 65 Va.L. Rev. 199 (1979). To the extent that the two opinions are inconsistent, hasn't this problem been resolved by the enactment of the 1978 Pregnancy Discrimination Act and its subsequent interpretation by the Supreme Court in *Newport News*?

2. What impact should *Manhart* have on a pension plan under which women made contributions equal to those of men but receive smaller monthly benefits upon retirement? Would your response to this question change if the employee-funded retirement plan is administered by a private insurance company rather than by the employer? Each of these questions subsequently was addressed by the Court in ARIZONA GOVERNING COMMITTEE v. NORRIS, 463 U.S. 1073, 103 S.Ct. 3492, 77 L.Ed.2d 1236 (1983). The Court extended its ruling in *Manhart* to a deferred compensation plan that provided employees of the State of Arizona with the option of postponing the receipt of a portion of their wages until retirement by selecting among various plans offered by several companies chosen by the State to participate in its plan. The employees were not required to participate in the plan but participation was limited to a choice of one of the companies selected by the State; an employee could not invest its deferred compensation in any other way. The State was responsible for withholding the appropriate sum from a participating employee's wages but it did not contribute any money to supplement the employee's contribution. All of the companies selected by the State used sex-based mortality tables to calculate the monthly payments received by employees who chose to participate in a monthly annuity program. (The companies also offered a single lump-sum payment upon retirement option and an option making periodic payments of a fixed sum over a fixed time period.) Sex, however, was the only factor used to determine the longevity of individuals of the same age; other factors correlating with longevity such as smoking or alcohol consumption, weight, or medical history were not considered. The Court held that the use of sex-based actuarial tables was "no more permissible at the pay-out stage of a retirement plan than at the pay-in stage." In so holding, it rejected the State's contention that the plan did not violate Title VII because a man and woman who deferred the same

amount of wages would receive, upon retirement, annuity policies having approximately the same present actuarial value, since the lower value of each monthly payment received by a woman was offset by the likelihood that she would receive more payments. The defect in this argument, the Court declared, was that the plan calculated longevity solely on the basis of gender, a practice prohibited in *Manhart.* In addition, the Court noted that, as in *Manhart,* if a female employee wished to receive the same monthly benefits paid to a similarly situated man, she would have to make greater monthly contributions than that male employee.

The fact that participation in the plan was voluntary was irrelevant, the Court reasoned, since Title VII prohibits discrimination concerning all terms and conditions of employment and the option of participating in a deferred compensation plan constitutes a condition of employment. Similarly irrelevant was the fact that the plan provided other nondiscriminatory options such as the lump-sum and fixed-sum-over-fixed period alternatives. Offering nondiscriminatory benefits, the Court declared, did not excuse the provision of another benefit on a discriminatory basis. Finally, to avoid a potentially devastating financial impact on pension funds, a majority of the Court concluded that this case should fall outside the presumption in favor of awarding retroactive relief announced by the Court in Albemarle Paper Co. v. Moody, see infra at 700. Accordingly, it required employers to calculate benefits without regard to the sex of the employee only as to benefits derived from contributions collected after the effective date of the trial court's judgment. Benefits derived from contributions made prior to that date, a majority ruled, could be calculated as provided by the existing terms of the Arizona plan.

Justice O'Connor played the pivotal role in the resolution of this case. Four Justices—Marshall, Brennan, White and Stevens—concluded that the plan violated Title VII but also stated that this decision should apply retroactively to a limited extent. These four members of the Court declared that the Court's ruling in *Manhart* should have put the State of Arizona on notice that male and female employees who make the same contributions to a retirement plan must receive equal monthly benefits. Accordingly, they concluded, it was not unfair to require the State to eliminate any sex-based disparity in monthly benefits attributable to contributions made post-*Manhart.* Moreover, they said, the decision should apply to payments attributable to pre-*Manhart* contributions, if the trial court on remand would find that the employer, after *Manhart,* could have applied sex-neutral tables to pre-*Manhart* contributions without violating the contractual rights of male employees. While Justice O'Connor joined to form a majority on the issue of liability, she did not agree with this proposed remedy. The other four Justices—Powell, Burger, Blackmun and Rehnquist—in an opinion authored by Powell, concluded that the Arizona plan did not violate Title VII and that the trial court also erred in imposing liability on more than a purely prospective basis. Justice O'Connor joined with the Powell quartet on the remedies issue, thereby creating a majority on this question. In a separate concurring opinion, Justice O'Connor explained that the benefits should be calculated without regard to sex with respect only to those payments derived from contributions collected after the effective date of the judgment in this case. Does this mean that female benefits must be "topped up" to reach the level of men's benefits or can the men's benefits be reduced to achieve equality of benefit payments? Is it significant that the remedy is prospective only in its application? On remand, the Ninth Circuit ruled that the trial court had not abused its discretion in refusing to top up women's benefits since the *prospective* application of a gender-neutral benefit calculation would not, unlike a *retroactive* application, impair rights to expected benefits. Norris v. Arizona Governing Committee, 796 F.2d 1119 (9th Cir. 1986).

3. Will forbidding the use of sex-based mortality tables increase the cost of employing female workers? If so, can't it be argued that the decision in *Manhart* will have an adverse effect on the employment of women? For an interesting and insightful debate over the meaning and impact of *Manhart*, see Kimball, Reverse Sex Discrimination: Manhart, 1979 Am.B.Found.Res.J. 83; Benston, The Economics of Gender Discrimination in Employee Fringe Benefits: Manhart Revisited, 49 U.Chi.L.Rev. 489 (1982); Brilmayer, Hekeler, Laycock & Sullivan, Sex Discrimination in Employer-Sponsored Insurance Plans: A Legal and Demographic Analysis, 47 U.Chi.L.Rev. 505 (1980).

4. Sexual Preference Discrimination

DESANTIS v. PACIFIC TELEPHONE & TELEGRAPH CO., INC.

United States Court of Appeals, Ninth Circuit, 1979.
608 F.2d 327.

CHOY, CIRCUIT JUDGE.

Male and female homosexuals brought three separate federal district court actions claiming that their employers or former employers discriminated against them in employment decisions because of their homosexuality. They alleged that such discrimination violated Title VII of the Civil Rights Act of 1964 * * *.

I. *Statement of the Case*

A. *Strailey v. Happy Times Nursery School, Inc.*

Appellant Strailey, a male, was fired by the Happy Times Nursery School after two years' service as a teacher. He alleged that he was fired because he wore a small gold ear-loop to school prior to the commencement of the school year. He filed a charge with the Equal Employment Opportunity Commission (EEOC) which the EEOC rejected because of an alleged lack of jurisdiction over claims of discrimination based on sexual orientation. He then filed suit on behalf of himself and all others similarly situated, seeking declaratory, injunctive, and monetary relief. The district court dismissed the complaint as failing to state a claim * * *.

B. *DeSantis v. Pacific Telephone & Telegraph Co.*

DeSantis, Boyle, and Simard, all males, claimed that Pacific Telephone & Telegraph Co. (PT&T) impermissibly discriminated against them because of their homosexuality. DeSantis alleged that he was not hired when a PT&T supervisor concluded that he was a homosexual. According to appellants' brief, "BOYLE was continually harassed by his co-workers and had to quit to preserve his health after only three months because his supervisors did nothing to alleviate this condition." Finally, "SIMARD was forced to quit under similar conditions after almost four years of employment with PT&T, but he was harassed by his supervisors [as well] * * *. In addition, his personnel file has been marked as not eligible for rehire, and his applications for employment were rejected by PT&T in 1974 and 1976." Appellants DeSantis, Boyle, and Simard also alleged that PT&T officials have publicly stated that they would not hire homosexuals.

These plaintiffs also filed charges with the EEOC, also rejected by the EEOC for lack of jurisdiction. They then filed suit on behalf of themselves and all others similarly situated seeking declaratory, injunctive, and monetary relief under Title VII * * *. They also prayed that the district court issue mandamus commanding the EEOC to process charges based on sexual orientation. The district court dismissed their complaint. It held that the court lacked jurisdiction to compel the EEOC to alter its interpretation of Title VII. It also held that appellants had not stated viable claims under * * * Title VII * * *.

C. Lundin v. Pacific Telephone & Telegraph

Lundin and Buckley, both females, were operators with PT&T. They filed suit in federal court alleging that PT&T discriminated against them because of their known lesbian relationship and eventually fired them. They also alleged that they endured numerous insults by PT&T employees because of their relationship. * * * Appellants sought monetary and injunctive relief. The district court dismissed their suit as not stating a claim upon which relief could be granted. * * *

II. *Title VII Claim*

Appellants argue first that the district courts erred in holding that Title VII does not prohibit discrimination on the basis of sexual preference. They claim that in prohibiting certain employment discrimination on the basis of "sex," Congress meant to include discrimination on the basis of sexual orientation. They add that in a trial they could establish that discrimination against homosexuals disproportionately effects men and that this disproportionate impact and correlation between discrimination on the basis of sexual preference and discrimination on the basis of "sex" requires that sexual preference be considered a subcategory of the "sex" category of Title VII.

A. Congressional Intent in Prohibiting "Sex" Discrimination

In Holloway v. Arthur Andersen & Co., 566 F.2d 659 (9th Cir. 1977), plaintiff argued that her employer had discriminated against her because she was undergoing a sex transformation and that this discrimination violated Title VII's prohibition on sex discrimination. This court rejected that claim, writing:

> The cases interpreting Title VII sex discrimination provisions agree that they were intended to place women on an equal footing with men. [Citations omitted.]
>
> Giving the statute its plain meaning, this court concludes that Congress had only the traditional notions of "sex" in mind. Later legislative activity makes this narrow definition even more evident. Several bills have been introduced to *amend* the Civil Rights Act to prohibit discrimination against "sexual preference." None have [*sic*] been enacted into law.
>
> Congress has not shown any intent other than to restrict the term "sex" to its traditional meaning. Therefore, this court will not expand Title VII's application in the absence of Congressional mandate. The manifest purpose of Title VII's prohibition against sex discrimination in employment is to ensure that men and women are treated equally, absent a bona fide relationship between the qualifications for the job and the person's sex.

Following *Holloway*, we conclude that Title VII's prohibition of "sex" discrimination applies only to discrimination on the basis of gender and should not be judicially extended to include sexual preference such as homosexuality. See Smith v. Liberty Mutual Insurance Co., 569 F.2d 325, 326–27 (5th Cir. 1978).

B. Disproportionate Impact

Appellants argue that recent decisions dealing with disproportionate impact require that discrimination against homosexuals fall within the purview of Title VII. They contend that these recent decisions, like Griggs v. Duke Power Co., 401 U.S. 424, 91 S.Ct. 849, 28 L.Ed.2d 158 (1971), establish that any employment criterion that affects one sex more than the other violates Title VII. * * * They claim that in a trial they could prove that discrimination against homosexuals disproportionately affects men both because of the greater incidence of homosexuality in the male population and because of the greater likelihood of an employer's discovering male homosexuals compared to female homosexuals.

Assuming that appellants can otherwise satisfy the requirement of *Griggs*, we do not believe that *Griggs* can be applied to extend Title VII protection to homosexuals. In finding that the disproportionate impact of educational tests on blacks violated Title VII, the Supreme Court in *Griggs* sought to effectuate a major congressional purpose in enacting Title VII: protection of blacks from employment discrimination. * * *

The *Holloway* court noted that in passing Title VII Congress did not intend to protect sexual orientation and has repeatedly refused to extend such protection. Appellants now ask us to employ the disproportionate impact decisions as an artifice to "bootstrap" Title VII protection for homosexuals under the guise of protecting men generally.

This we are not free to do. Adoption of this bootstrap device would frustrate congressional objectives as explicated in *Holloway*, not effectuate congressional goals as in *Griggs*. It would achieve by judical "construction" what Congress did not do and has consistently refused to do on many occasions. It would violate the rule that our duty in construing a statute is to "ascertain * * * and give effect to the legislative will." We conclude that the *Griggs* disproportionate impact theory may not be applied to extend Title VII protection to homosexuals.

C. Differences in Employment Criteria

Appellants next contend that recent decisions have held that an employer generally may not use different employment criteria for men and women. They claim that if a male employee prefers males as sexual partners, he will be treated differently from a female who prefers male partners. They conclude that the employer thus uses different employment criteria for men and women and violates the Supreme Court's warning in Phillips v. Martin-Marietta Corp., 400 U.S. 542, 91 S.Ct. 496, 27 L.Ed.2d 613 (1971):

> The Court of Appeals therefore erred in reading this section as permitting one hiring policy for women and another for men * * *.

We must again reject appellants' efforts to "bootstrap" Title VII protection for homosexuals. While we do not express approval of an employment policy that differentiates according to sexual preference, we note that whether dealing with men or women the employer is using the same criterion: it will not hire or promote a person who prefers sexual partners of the same sex. Thus this policy does not involve different decisional criteria for the sexes.

D. Interference with Association

Appellants argue that the EEOC has held that discrimination against an employee because of the race of the employee's friends may constitute discrimination based on race in violation of Title VII. They contend that analogously discrimination because of the sex of the employees' sexual partner should constitute discrimination based on sex.

Appellants, however, have not alleged that appellees have policies of discriminating against employees because of the gender of their friends. That is, they do not claim that the appellees will terminate anyone with a male (or female) friend. They claim instead that the appellees discriminate against employees who have a certain type of relationship—i.e., homosexual relationship—with certain friends. As noted earlier, that relationship is not protected by Title VII. Thus, assuming that it would violate Title VII for an employer to discriminate against employees because of the gender of their friends, appellants' claims do not fall within this purported rule.

E. Effeminacy

Appellant Strailey contends that he was terminated by the Happy Times Nursery School because that school felt that it was inappropriate for a male teacher to wear an earring to school. He claims that the school's reliance on a stereotype—that a male should have a virile rather than an effeminate appearance—violates Title VII.

In *Holloway* this court noted that Congress intended Title VII's ban on sex discrimination in employment to prevent discrimination because of gender, not because of sexual orientation or preference. Recently the Fifth Circuit similarly read the legislative history of Title VII and concluded that Title VII thus does not protect against discrimination because of effeminacy. Smith v. Liberty Mutual Insurance Co., 569 F.2d at 326–27. We agree and hold that discrimination because of effeminacy, like discrimination because of homosexuality or transexualism (*Holloway*), does not fall within the purview of Title VII.

F. Conclusion as to Title VII Claim

Having determined that appellants' allegations do not implicate Title VII's prohibition on sex discrimination, we affirm the district court's dismissals of the Title VII claims.

SNEED, CIRCUIT JUDGE (concurring and dissenting).

* * *

I respectfully dissent from subpart B which holds that male homosexuals have not stated a Title VII claim under the disproportionate impact theories of Griggs v. Duke Power Co. My position is not foreclosed by our holding, with which I agree, that Title VII does not afford protection to homosexuals, male or female. The male appellants' complaint, as I understand it, is based on the contention that the use of homosexuality as a disqualification for employment, which for *Griggs'* purposes must be treated as a facially neutral criterion, impacts disproportionately on *males* because of the greater visibility of male homosexuals and a higher incidence of homosexuality among males than females.

To establish such a claim will be difficult because the male appellants must prove that as a result of the appellee's practices there exists discrimination against males *qua* males. That is, to establish a prima facie case under *Griggs* it will not be sufficient to show that appellees have employed a disproportionately large number of female *homosexuals* and a disproportionately small number of male *homosexuals*. Rather it will be necessary to establish that the use of homosexuality as a bar to employment disproportionately impacts on *males*, a class that enjoys Title VII protection. Such a showing perhaps could be made were male homosexuals a very large proportion of the total applicable male population.

My point of difference with the majority is merely that the male appellants in their *Griggs* claim are not using that case "as an artifice to 'bootstrap' Title VII protection for homosexuals under the guise of protecting men generally." Their claim, if established properly, would in fact protect males generally. I would permit them to try to make their case and not dismiss it on the pleadings.

NOTES AND PROBLEMS FOR DISCUSSION

1. Did the majority in *DeSantis* correctly analyze the plaintiff's disproportionate impact claim? Isn't Judge Sneed's dissenting opinion more on target?

2. Public sector employment policies that discriminate against gays are subject also to constitutional scrutiny. In BELLER v. MIDDENDORF, 632 F.2d 788 (9th Cir. 1980), cert. denied, 452 U.S. 905, 101 S.Ct. 3030, 69 L.Ed.2d 405 (1981), the court rejected the plaintiff's claim that the U. S. Navy's policy with respect to homosexuals violated the Due Process Clause of the Fifth Amendment. Navy regulations empowered the Secretary to discharge any person found to have engaged in homosexual acts, subject to the Secretary's exercise of discretion in rare situations for reasons unrelated to that individual's fitness to serve. The court declared that the Navy could rationally conclude that its policy was necessary to promote morale, discipline and efficiency in the service, "despite the evidence that attitudes toward homosexual conduct have changed among some groups in society * * *." 632 F.2d at 811. Moreover, the court noted, because of the important role played by the military, substantial deference traditionally has been accorded to its decisions. This limited level of review, the court concluded, coupled with the "relative impracticality at this time of achieving the Government's goals by regulations which turn more precisely on the fact of an individual case outweigh[ed] whatever solicitude is appropriate for consensual private homosexual conduct." 632 F.2d at 810. In those cases challenging anti-gay practices under the equal protection guarantees of the Fifth and Fourteenth Amendments, the courts have struck down policies that automatically exclude gays from all positions, but have noted that a defendant can defeat the plaintiff's claim by offering proof of a rational connection between sexual orientation and ability to perform the job. See e.g., Ashton v. Civiletti, 613 F.2d 923 (D.C.Cir. 1979); McKeand v. Laird, 490 F.2d 1262 (9th Cir. 1973); Comment, Employment Discrimination in the Armed Forces—An Analysis of Recent Decisions Affecting Sexual Preference Discrimination in the Military, 27 Vill.L.Rev. 351 (1981–82). Nevertheless, no reported case can be found in which a federal court has rejected the defendant's assertion of the existence of a rational nexus between homosexuality and job performance. Some of the justifications accepted by the courts include the susceptibility of gays to blackmail, the deleterious impact of homosexual employees on their co-employees or subordinates and the improper influence gay teachers have on their students. See also Childers v. Dallas Police Department, 513 F.Supp. 134 (N.D.Tex.1981), affirmed, 669 F.2d 732 (5th Cir. 1982) (police force's rejection of admittedly homosexual applicant did not violate his First Amendment rights of expression or association because hiring an acknowledged homosexual might subject the department to public ridicule and embarrassment and could create a security risk since this plaintiff sought a position that required the handling of evidence in offenses involving homosexual conduct.). In NATIONAL GAY TASK FORCE v. BOARD OF EDUC. OF OKLAHOMA CITY, 729 F.2d 1270 (10th Cir. 1984), however, the court struck down as

constitutionally invalid a state statute that permitted the dismissal or rejection for employment of teachers found to have engaged in public homosexual conduct or activity and to have been rendered unfit to hold a teaching position because of that conduct or activity. The statute defined "public homosexual conduct" as "advocating, soliciting, imposing, encouraging or promoting public or private homosexual activity in a manner that creates a substantial risk that such conduct will come to the attention of school children or school employees." "Public homosexual activity" was defined as the commission of a sex act with a person of the same sex in public. The court held that while the statute could permit a teacher to be fired for "public homosexual activity" without violating the constitutional right of privacy, the statutory definition of "public homosexual conduct" was facially overbroad. By prohibiting the "advocating", "encouraging", and "promoting" of homosexual activity, the statute prohibited protected First Amendment speech and therefore was unconstitutionally overbroad on its face. The court also held that the portion of the statute dealing with "public homosexual activity" was severable from the portion prohibiting "public homosexual conduct". Accordingly, it upheld the constitutionality of the former portion and struck down the statute only insofar as it punished "homosexual conduct" as that phrase was defined to include "advocating * * * encouraging or promoting" homosexual activity. This judgment was affirmed by an equally divided Supreme Court. ___ U.S. ___, 105 S.Ct. 1858, 84 L.Ed.2d 776 (1985).

The Navy policy attacked in *Beller* also was challenged in Dronenburg v. Zech, 741 F.2d 1388 (D.C.Cir. 1984) on the ground that it violated the plaintiff's constitutional right to privacy. The court rejected this claim, holding that the right to privacy did not extend to homosexual conduct. The D.C. Circuit's view subsequently was adopted by the Supreme Court. In BOWERS v. HARDWICK, ___ U.S. ___, 106 S.Ct. 2841, 92 L.Ed.2d 140 (1986), the Supreme Court denied relief in a suit for declaratory judgment challenging the constitutionality of a Georgia statute criminalizing sodomy as applied to consensual homosexual sodomy between adults in the respondent's home. A five member majority, in an opinion written by Justice White, reviewed its prior decisions concerning the constitutional right to privacy and concluded that those cases did not recognize a right to be free from state proscription of all kinds of private sexual conduct between consenting adults. More specifically, it concluded that there was no substantive fundamental right under the Due Process Clause to engage in consensual homosexual sodomy. Since homosexual consensual sodomy had been historically proscribed by state law, the Court reasoned, it could not be said to be either a fundamental liberty that was deeply rooted in the Nation's history and tradition or a right whose sacrifice would threaten the continued existence of liberty or justice. In addition, the fact that the statute proscribed activity undertaken in the privacy of the respondent's home was not of constitutional significance. The Court indicated that its prior ruling in Stanley v. Georgia, in which it overturned a statute that restricted the viewing of pornographic materials in the home, rested not on the right to privacy but on First Amendment concerns. The dissenters, led by Justice Blackmun, maintained that as the statute applied to heterosexual and homosexual sodomy, the case did not turn on the question of the right to engage in homosexual conduct. Rather, they declared, the issue was whether the right to privacy precluded state restriction of any sexual conduct in the home between consenting adults. The dissenters concluded that the right of an individual to conduct intimate relationships in the intimacy of his home is part of the fundamental right of privacy. Moreover, the state's purported interest in protecting a tradition of condemning homosexual activity as immoral did not justify an abridgment of this right.

Prior to 1981, Army regulations authorized separation for homosexuality. These regulations were modified in 1981 to mandate separation for homosexuality. In Watkins v. U.S. Army, 721 F.2d 687 (9th Cir. 1983), the plaintiff had admitted his homosexuality to the Army since his original induction in 1967. Pursuant to the changed regulations, the Army refused a subsequent request for reenlistment and discharged Watkins on the ground of homosexuality. The trial court held that the Army was estopped from using its regulations as a bar to his continued service and enjoined the Army from refusing to reenlist Watkins on that ground. The Ninth Circuit reversed, stating that the trial court's broad equitable powers could not be used to force the military to disobey its own regulations absent a determination that the regulations were repugnant to the Constitution or to statutory authority. As the trial court had declined to rule on the substantive legality of the regulations and in light of its own prior ruling upholding the Navy's similar regulations in *Beller*, the appellate court reversed the trial court's judgment. For a thorough discussion of the constitutional and statutory issues raised by anti-homosexual employment practices, see Friedman, Constitutional and Statutory Challenges to Discrimination in Employment Based on Sexual Orientation, 64 Iowa L.Rev. 527 (1979).

3. Employing the same analysis relied upon in the principal case, courts have held that Title VII does not prohibit discrimination against transsexuals, as long as the defendant does not distinguish between male and female transsexuals. See Ulane v. Eastern Airlines, 742 F.2d 1081 (7th Cir. 1984), cert. denied, ___ U.S. ___, 105 S.Ct. 2023, 85 L.Ed.2d 304 (1985); Holloway v. Arthur Andersen & Co., 566 F.2d 659 (9th Cir. 1977); Sommers v. Budget Marketing, Inc., 667 F.2d 748 (8th Cir. 1982); Powell v. Read's Inc., 436 F.Supp. 369 (D.Md. 1977).

4. While several cities and municipalities have local ordinances prohibiting private and/or public employment discrimination on the basis of sexual preference, no State fair employment statute has been interpreted to protect gays from job bias. See e.g. Gay Law Students Association v. Pacific Telephone & Telegraph Co., 24 Cal.3d 458, 156 Cal.Rptr. 14, 595 P.2d 592 (1979) (California law prohibiting sex discrimination does not extend to sexual orientation discrimination. However, discrimination by defendant public utility held to violate the equal protection guarantee of the California Constitution.).

5. "Protective" State Labor Legislation

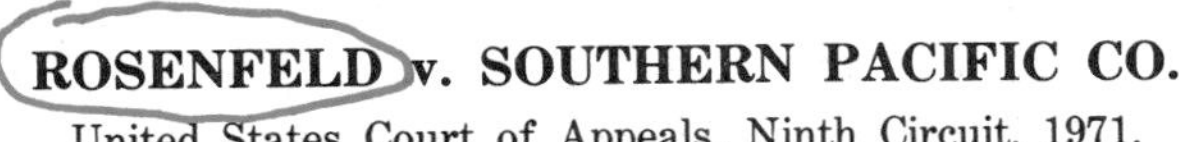

ROSENFELD v. SOUTHERN PACIFIC CO.

United States Court of Appeals, Ninth Circuit, 1971.
444 F.2d 1219.

HAMLEY, CIRCUIT JUDGE.

Leah Rosenfeld brought this action against Southern Pacific Company pursuant to section 706(f) of Title VII of the Civil Rights Act of 1964 (Act). Plaintiff, an employee of the company, alleged that in filling the position of agent-telegrapher at Thermal, California, in March, 1966,

Southern Pacific discriminated against her solely because of her sex, by assigning the position to a junior male employee.

* * *

On the merits, Southern Pacific argues that it is the company's policy to exclude women, generically, from certain positions. The company restricts these job opportunities to men for two basic reasons: (1) the arduous nature of the work-related activity renders women physically unsuited for the jobs; (2) appointing a woman to the position would result in a violation of California labor laws and regulations which limit hours of work for women and restrict the weight they are permitted to lift. Positions such as that of agent-telegrapher at Thermal fall within the ambit of this policy. The company concludes that effectuation of this policy is not proscribed by Title VII of the Civil Rights Act due to the exception created by the Act for those situations where sex is a "bona fide occupational qualification."

While the agent-telegrapher position at Thermal is no longer in existence, the work requirements which that position entailed are illustrative of the kind of positions which are denied to female employees under the company's labor policy described above. During the harvesting season, the position may require work in excess of ten hours a day and eighty hours a week.[6] The position requires the heavy physical effort involved in climbing over and around boxcars to adjust their vents, collapse their bunkers and close and seal their doors. In addition, the employee must lift various objects weighing more than twenty-five pounds and, in some instances, more than fifty pounds.

The critical question presented by this argument is whether, consistent with Title VII of the Civil Rights Act of 1964, the company may apply such a labor policy.* * *

* * *

* * * [T]he company points out that, apart from its intrinsic merit, its policy is compelled by California labor laws. One of the reasons Mrs. Rosenfeld was refused assignment to the Thermal position, and would presumably be refused assignment to like positions, is that she could not perform the tasks of such a position without placing the company in violation of California laws. Not only would the repeated lifting of weights in excess of twenty-five pounds violate the state's Industrial Welfare Order No. 9–63, but for her to lift more than fifty pounds as required by the job would violate section 1251 of the California Labor Code. Likewise, the peak-season days of over ten hours would violate section 1350 of the California Labor Code.

It would appear that these state law limitations upon female labor run contrary to the general objectives of Title VII of the Civil Rights Act of 1964 * * * and are therefore, by virtue of the Supremacy Clause, supplanted by Title VII. However, appellants * * * rely on

6. It was, indeed, this opportunity to earn overtime pay that made this position attractive to plaintiff.

section 703(e) and argue that since positions such as the Thermal agent-telegrapher required weight-lifting and maximum hours in excess of those permitted under the California statutes, being a man was indeed a bona fide occupational qualification. This argument assumes that Congress, having established by Title VII the policy that individuals must be judged as individuals, and not on the basis of characteristics generally attributed to racial, religious, or sex groups, was willing for this policy to be thwarted by state legislation to the contrary.

We find no basis in the statute or its legislative history for such an assumption. Section 1104 of the Act, provides that nothing contained in the Act should be construed as indicating an intent to occupy the field in which the Act operates, to the exclusion of State laws or the same subject matter, nor be construed as invalidating any provision of state law "* * * unless such provision is inconsistent with any of the purposes of this Act, or any provision thereof." This section was added to the Act to save state laws aimed at preventing or punishing discrimination, and as the quoted words indicate, not to save inconsistent state laws.

Still more to the point is section 708 of the Act, which provides that nothing in Title VII shall be deemed to exempt or relieve any person from any liability, duty, penalty, or punishment provided by any present or future state law "* * * other than any such law which purports to require or permit the doing of any act which would be an unlawful employment practice under this title." This section was designed to preserve the effectiveness of state antidiscrimination laws.[7]

The Commission, created by the provisions of Title VII of the Act, through its published Guidelines and Policy Statements has, albeit after considerable hesitation, taken the position that state "protective" legislation, of the type in issue here, conflicts with the policy of non-discrimination manifested by Title VII of the Act. * * * It is implicit in this Commission pronouncement that state labor laws inconsistent with the general objectives of the Act must be disregarded. The Supreme Court has recently observed that the administrative interpretation of the Act by the enforcing agency "is entitled to great deference." Griggs v. Duke Power Co., 401 U.S. 424, 91 S.Ct. 849, 28 L.Ed.2d 158 (1971).[10]

* * *

Under the principles set forth above, we conclude that Southern Pacific's employment policy is not excusable under * * * the state statutes. * * *

7. The legislative history is replete with statements making it clear that Congress was specifically aware that Title VII would undercut many state labor laws.

10. In the *Griggs* case, Chief Justice Burger, speaking for the Court, also pointed out that it is immaterial that the state laws in question, or the employer's labor policy, were not enacted or prescribed with an intent to discriminate. Said the Court:

> "Under the Act, practices, procedures, or tests neutral on their face, and even neutral in terms of intent, cannot be maintained if they operate to 'freeze' the status quo of prior discriminatory employment practices." * * *

In the district court one of the company's defenses was that of good faith reliance upon the Commission's Guidelines then in effect. This defense was relevant to plaintiff's prayer for damages. While the district court did not award damages, it did find that the company did not rely on any written interpretation or opinion of the Commission, and concluded that the company "discriminated" against plaintiff solely because of her sex by refusing to assign her to the Thermal position.

In our opinion the finding on the question of reliance is unnecessary to the disposition of the cause and, in any event, should not have been entered without according Southern Pacific an evidentiary hearing. Moreover, in view of the California statutes referred to above, the conclusion that the company engaged in "discrimination" in refusing to assign plaintiff to the Thermal position carries with it no invidious connotation. Prior to a judicial determination such as evidenced by this opinion, an employer can hardly be faulted for following the explicit provisions of applicable state law.

* * *

Affirmed.

CHAMBERS, CIRCUIT JUDGE (dissenting).

* * *

NOTES AND PROBLEMS FOR DISCUSSION

1. State "protective" labor statutes have been uniformly invalidated under the supremacy clause on the ground that their enforcement violates Title VII's ban on sex discrimination. Accordingly, the courts have struck down state laws imposing special requirements on women with respect to required rest periods, Ridinger v. General Motors Corp., 325 F.Supp. 1089 (S.D. Ohio 1971), reversed on other grounds, 474 F.2d 949 (6th Cir. 1972); seating arrangements, Manning v. General Motors Corp., 3 FEP Cases 968 (N.D. Ohio 1971), affirmed, 466 F.2d 812 (6th Cir. 1972), cert. denied, 410 U.S. 946, 93 S.Ct. 1366, 35 L.Ed.2d 613 (1973); and exclusion from certain occupations, Sail'er Inn, Inc. v. Kirby, 5 Cal.3d 1, 95 Cal.Rptr. 329, 485 P.2d 529 (1971). See generally, Kennedy, Sex Discrimination: State Protective Laws Since Title VII, 47 Not.D.Law. 514 (1972).

2. Do you agree with the ruling in the principal case that an employer should be insulated from back pay liability by its good faith reliance on extent state labor legislation? Is it appropriate to impose the cost of discrimination on innocent employees rather than on the innocent employer? Does this ruling create any disincentive on employees to challenge other potentially discriminatory state laws? The courts, as in *Rosenfeld*, refusing to compel employers to subject themselves to possible state prosecution in order to comply with Title VII, deny back pay upon a showing of employer good faith reliance on state protective legislation. See Williams v. General Foods Corp., 492 F.2d 399 (7th Cir. 1974); Manning v. General Motors Corp., 466 F.2d 812 (6th Cir. 1972), cert. denied, 410 U.S. 946, 93 S.Ct. 1366, 35 L.Ed.2d 613 (1973). What if a similar or identical statute of another state had been judicially invalidated before the employer's conduct occurred? See Alaniz v. California Processors, Inc., 785

F.2d 1412 (9th Cir. 1986) (employer liable for back pay from date it became aware of suspension of agency order restricting women from heavy lifting).

3. Once a court determines that a state protective labor statute conflicts with Title VII, what action should it take with respect to that enactment? Ordinarily, a court can achieve sexual parity in one of two alternative ways. It can invalidate the law entirely or it can take the benefit or restriction originally applicable only to women and extend it to all employees. The latter option, however, is not realistically available in the context of exclusionary statutes—i.e.—statutes that exclude women from certain occupations, from lifting objects over a specified weight, or from working more than a certain number of hours or days. In Hays v. Potlatch Forests, Inc., 465 F.2d 1081 (8th Cir. 1972), the court held that any conflict between Title VII and an Arkansas statute requiring employers to pay only women employees premium pay for time worked in excess of eight hours per day could be avoided by requiring employers to pay premium compensation to all employees after eight hours of daily work. The EEOC Guidelines go beyond *Hays* by requiring that the "benefits" of all sex-oriented State protective statutes be extended to both sexes. However, for all but minimum wage and premium pay statutes, the Guidelines recognize a business necessity defense to the extension requirement. See 29 CFR 1604.2(b)(3), (4) (1972). Do you agree with this result? Can it be argued that extension results in governmental imposition of terms and conditions of employment that should be left to private negotiation absent a clear declaration of legislative intent to intervene in this area? See Burns v. Rohr Corp., 346 F.Supp. 994 (S.D.Cal.1972) (refusing to order extension of California regulation requiring employers to give ten minute rest breaks every four hours to female employers). Doesn't extension of state laws by a federal court also raise a difficult issue of federal-state relations? See Homemakers, Inc. v. Division of Industrial Welfare, 509 F.2d 20 (9th Cir. 1974), cert. denied, 423 U.S. 1063, 96 S.Ct. 803, 46 L.Ed.2d 655 (1976) (refusing to extend California statute requiring payment of premium pay to covered women employees).

Chapter 5

PROCEDURAL REQUIREMENTS FOR PRIVATE SECTOR EMPLOYEES

SECTION A. EXHAUSTION OF ADMINISTRATIVE REMEDIES UNDER TITLE VII—SUITS BY PRIVATE PARTIES

1. The Timely E.E.O.C. Charge as a Prerequisite to Litigation

CHAPPELL v. EMCO MACHINE WORKS CO.

United States Court of Appeals, Fifth Circuit, 1979.
601 F.2d 1295.

Before WISDOM, CLARK and FAY, CIRCUIT JUDGES.

CHARLES CLARK, CIRCUIT JUDGE.

On August 31, 1973, the Emco Machine Works Company discharged Cleda Jean Chappell from her position as a shop clerk, giving her two weeks pay in lieu of notice. When, on September 18, 1973, Chappell visited the Texas Employment Commission to complain about Emco's treatment of her, one of the Commission's employees, Mr. Whitley, promised that he would promptly file a complaint on her behalf with the Equal Employment Opportunity Commission (EEOC). During the period between September 18 and February 24, 1974, Chappell repeatedly contacted Whitley regarding the status of her EEOC complaint, and was told that the complaint had been filed. On March 1, 1974, Chappell hired an attorney, who phoned the EEOC and discovered that the EEOC had not received Chappell's complaint. Despite Whitley's assurances, the EEOC did not receive the complaint until March 5, 1974, more than five months after Chappell's initial visit to the Texas Employment Commission. The reason for the delay in the EEOC's receipt of the complaint remains a mystery.

In processing Chappell's complaint, the EEOC found that Chappell had satisfied the jurisdictional requirements of Title VII of the Civil Rights Act of 1964 and that Emco had discharged her on the basis of her sex. On July 25, 1975, the EEOC issued Chappell a "right to sue" letter.

On September 2, 1975, Chappell brought suit in federal district court, alleging that her discharge violated Title VII. Emco moved for summary judgment, contending that Chappell had not met the requirements of 42 U.S.C. § 2000e–5(e),[1] which requires that a complaint of employment discrimination be filed with the EEOC within 180 days of the alleged incident of discrimination. Chappell appeals the district court's order granting that motion. We affirm.

Chappell urges that the 180-day period allowed for filing EEOC complaints under 42 U.S.C. § 2000e–5(e) should be treated as a statute of limitations and that the running of the period should be tolled during the time that she relied on Whitley's representations. She argues that she satisfied the filing requirements of § 2000e–5(e) when she spoke with Whitley and that, in any event, the 180-day period did not begin to run until September 15, the last day she received severance pay. She also contends that this court should defer to the EEOC's determination that she had satisfied the jurisdictional prerequisites of Title VII. Emco replies that the 180-day limitations period is jurisdictional and is therefore not subject to equitable tolling. Emco also asserts that the 180-day period commenced running when she was discharged on August 31, that the filing requirement is satisfied only when the EEOC receives the complaint, and that courts should not defer to EEOC's findings regarding jurisdictional matters.

I.

A.

Is the 180-day time period contained in § 2000e–5(e) subject to equitable delay or interruption? The answer is in the affirmative but requires close analysis of numerous precedents.

In McArthur v. Southern Airways, 569 F.2d 276 (5th Cir. 1978) (en banc), this court held that timely filing of a complaint with the EEOC was a jurisdictional prerequisite to bringing a Title VII action in federal court.[2] The *McArthur* plaintiffs were airline stewardesses who claimed that Southern Airways had discriminated against them on the basis of their sex. Even though the particular incidents of discrimina-

1. 42 U.S.C. § 2000e–5(e) provides:

A charge under this section shall be filed within one hundred and eighty days after the alleged unlawful employment practice occurred and notice of the charge (including the date, place and circumstances of the alleged unlawful employment practice) shall be served upon the person against whom such charge is made within ten days thereafter, except that in a case of an unlawful employment practice with respect to which the person aggrieved has initially instituted proceedings with a State or local agency with authority to grant or seek relief from such practice or to institute criminal proceedings with respect thereto upon receiving notice thereof, such charge shall be filed by or on behalf of the person aggrieved within three hundred days after the alleged unlawful employment practice occurred, or within thirty days after receiving notice that the State or local agency has terminated the proceedings under the State or local law, whichever is earlier, and a copy of such charge shall be filed by the Commission with the State or local agency.

2. But see Bethel v. Jefferson, 191 U.S. App.D.C. 108, 118 n. 64, 589 F.2d 631, 641 n. 64 (1978), and Laffey v. Northwest Airlines, Inc., 185 U.S.App.D.C. 322, 368, 567 F.2d 429, 475 (1976), cert. denied, 434 U.S. 1086, 98 S.Ct. 1281, 55 L.Ed.2d 792 (1978), in which the District of Columbia Circuit held that the timely filing was not a jurisdictional prerequisite and that equitable tolling principles applied.

tion had occurred more than 180 days prior to the filing of a complaint with the EEOC, plaintiffs contended that the requirement of timely filing had been met since they were victims of "continuing" discrimination. The en banc court rejected this argument, holding that " 'a discriminatory act which is not made the basis for a timely charge is the legal equivalent of a discriminatory act which occurred before the statute was passed.' " 569 F.2d at 277 (quoting United Air Lines v. Evans, 431 U.S. 553, 558, 97 S.Ct. 1885, 1887, 52 L.Ed.2d 571, 576 (1977)).

McArthur did not address the question whether equitable considerations could delay or interrupt the running of the 180-day period. But see *McArthur*, 569 F.2d at 279–80 (Rubin, J., dissenting). It could be argued, however, that *McArthur's* characterization of timely filing as a jurisdictional prerequisite to Title VII relief means that equity can play no part in determining whether timely filing has occurred. See Reich v. Dow Badische Co., 575 F.2d 363, 372–74 (2d Cir. 1978) (Danaher, Jr., concurring), cert. denied, 439 U.S. 1006, 99 S.Ct. 621, 58 L.Ed.2d 683 (1979). It is illogical to designate a particular fact as necessary to the court's jurisdiction, yet, in its absence, allow the court to adjudicate whether equities indicate that the jurisdictional defect should be ignored.

Supreme Court decisions regarding the consequences of the failure to comply with the provisions of Title VII, however, suggest that Title VII's § 2000e–5(e) is not a jurisdictional prerequisite in the same sense as other statutory requirements, such as the provision requiring the matter in controversy to exceed $10,000. See *Bethel*, supra, 191 U.S. App.D.C. at 118 n. 64, 589 F.2d at 641 n. 64; *McArthur*, supra, 569 F.2d at 280 (Rubin, J., dissenting). For example, the court has held that Title VII relief is, in certain circumstances, available to members of class actions who have not filed *any* complaint with the EEOC. These cases rely on the legislative history of Title VII, United Airlines v. McDonald, 432 U.S. 385, 389 n. 6, 92 S.Ct. 2464, 2467 n. 6, 53 L.Ed.2d 423, 429 n. 6 (1977); Franks v. Bowman Transportation Co., Inc., 424 U.S. 747, 771, 96 S.Ct. 1251, 1267, 47 L.Ed.2d 444, 465 (1976); Albermarle Paper Co. v. Moody, 422 U.S. 405, 414 n. 8, 95 S.Ct. 2362, 2370 n. 8, 45 L.Ed.2d 280, 294–95 n. 8 (1975). On the other hand, the court has strictly applied the amount in controversy requirement to bar participation in a class action suit by any potential class member not meeting the $10,000 limit. Zahn v. International Paper Co., 414 U.S. 291, 94 S.Ct. 505, 38 L.Ed.2d 511 (1973); Snyder v. Harris, 394 U.S. 332, 89 S.Ct. 1053, 22 L.Ed.2d 319 (1969).

In addition, both the Supreme Court and this court have, on various occasions, used equitable principles from the law concerning statutes of limitations to ameliorate the effects of Title VII provisions which are characterized as jurisdictional prerequisites.[3] In International Union

3. In Reeb v. Economic Opportunity Atlanta, Inc., 516 F.2d 924, 927 (5th Cir. 1975), Judge Wisdom noted the anomaly in using limitations law to analyze jurisdictional requirements:

of Electrical Workers v. Robbins & Myers, 429 U.S. 229, 97 S.Ct. 441, 50 L.Ed.2d 427 (1976), the Supreme Court addressed the question whether the statutory time period for filing complaints with the EEOC was amenable to equitable tolling. The *Robbins* plaintiffs contended that the statutory period should have been tolled during the pendency of arbitration procedures, asserting that "the policy of repose, designed to protect defendants is outweighed because the interests of justice require vindication of the plaintiffs' rights." 429 U.S. at 237, 97 S.Ct. at 447, 50 L.Ed.2d at 435–436. Noting that Title VII and union grievance procedures were independent remedies, the Court rejected plaintiffs' arguments. Although the *Robbins* Court found that timely filing was a jurisdictional prerequisite to a Title VII suit, 429 U.S. at 240, 97 S.Ct. at 441, 50 L.Ed.2d at 437, the Court distinguished Burnett v. New York Central R. Co., 380 U.S. 424, 85 S.Ct. 1050, 13 L.Ed.2d 941 (1965), a prior decision that found tolling appropriate. In *Burnett*, plaintiff had filed his Federal Employers' Liability Act suit in an Ohio state court which had jurisdiction over the matter, but which was an improper forum under Ohio venue law. After the Ohio court had dismissed his suit, plaintiff filed a complaint in federal district court against the same parties served in the state court suit, alleging the same cause of action. The Supreme Court held that the filing of the state court action was sufficient to toll the statutory limitations period contained in the Employers' Liability Act:

> Petitioner here did not sleep on his rights but brought an action within the statutory period in the state court of competent jurisdiction. Service of process was made upon the respondent notifying him that petitioner was asserting his cause of action.

380 U.S. at 429, 85 S.Ct. at 1055, 13 L.Ed.2d at 946; see Johnson v. Railway Express Agency, 421 U.S. 454, 95 S.Ct. 1716, 44 L.Ed.2d 295 (1975). The *Robbins* Court distinguished *Burnett* on its facts by finding

> [C]onceptual confusion springs from a court's describing the ninety day requirement as "jurisdictional" but proceeding on the basis of an analogy to how statutes of limitations have been construed. Statutes of limitations, designed as they are primarily to prevent stale claims, are traditionally thought to be subject to much more flexible construction than statutes which confer subject matter jurisdiction upon courts. For example, many courts hold that a party may waive the defense of statute of limitations, but virtually all courts insist that a lack of subject matter jurisdiction may never be waived and must be invoked by the court itself if the parties fail to raise it.

516 F.2d 927. Indicative of the inherent "conceptual confusion" recognized by Judge Wisdom, the terminology used by the Supreme Court in referring to Title VII's time periods has not been consistent. See Bethel v. Jefferson, 191 U.S.App.D.C. at 108, 118 n. 64, 589 F.2d 631, 641 n. 64 (D.C.Cir. 1978). In United Airlines v. Evans, 431 U.S. 553, 560, 97 S.Ct. 1885, 1890, 52 L.Ed.2d 571, 579 (1977); International Union of Electrical Workers v. Robbins & Myers, 429 U.S. 229, 240, 97 S.Ct. 441, 449, 50 L.Ed.2d 427, 437 (1976); and Alexander v. Gardner-Denver Co., 415 U.S. 36, 47, 94 S.Ct. 1011, 1019, 39 L.Ed.2d 147, 157 (1974), the Court referred to the time periods as "jurisdictional prerequisites." In United Airlines, Inc. v. McDonald, 432 U.S. 385, 392 & n. 11, 97 S.Ct. 2464, 2468 & n. 11, 53 L.Ed.2d 423, 430–31 & n. 11 (1977), and Occidental Life Insurance Co. v. EEOC, 432 U.S. 355, 371–72, 97 S.Ct. 2447, 2457, 53 L.Ed.2d 402, 414 (1977), the Court designated Title VII's time periods as "statutes of limitations."

that the *Robbins* petitioner, in filing the grievance proceedings, "was not asserting the same statutory claim in a different forum, nor giving notice to respondent of that statutory claim, but was asserting an independent claim based on a *contract* right." *Robbins*, supra, 429 U.S. at 238, 97 S.Ct. at 448, 50 L.Ed.2d at 436 (emphasis in the original). The *Robbins* Court also noted that the petitioner had not asserted that she was prevented from filing a claim with the EEOC within 90 days [4] of the discriminatory act, "indeed, it [was] conceded * * * that she could have filed it the following day, had she so wished." Id. at 237 n. 10, 97 S.Ct. at 447 n. 10, 50 L.Ed.2d at 436 n. 10. Thus, though *Robbins* rejected the union's claim, it recognized that equitable considerations can, in some circumstances, interrupt the running of Title VII's period for filing complaints.

Decisions of this court have also relied on equitable principles to forestall the strict, inflexible application of Title VII's jurisdictional prerequisites. In Reeb v. Economic Opportunity Atlanta, Inc., 516 F.2d 924 (5th Cir. 1975), plaintiff had not learned of the facts supporting her claim of illegal employment discrimination under Title VII until after the time period for filing a complaint with the EEOC had expired. This court held that even though the statute requires that the filing period commence to run from the date the discrimination has occurred, equitable considerations mandated that the period "not begin to run * * * until the facts that would support a charge of discrimination under Title VII were apparent or should have been apparent to a person with a reasonably prudent regard for his rights similarly situated to the plaintiff." 516 F.2d at 931. Although *McArthur's* designation of the time period as a jurisdictional prerequisite may have cast doubt on the validity of *Reeb*, see *McArthur*, 569 F.2d at 279–80 (Rubin, J., dissenting), we have recently indicated that the principle announced in *Reeb* is still valid. In Bickham v. Miller, 584 F.2d 736 (5th Cir. 1978), the question at issue was whether the running of one of Title VII's time periods should have been interrupted. The court noted that timely filing was a jurisdictional prerequisite, but reaffirmed the *Reeb* rule that commencement of the running of the period should be delayed until a "complainant learns or could be reasonably expected to learn of the discriminatory act." 584 F.2d at 738. The court then proceeded to determine that the facts did not warrant a delay in the commencement of the jurisdictional period.

One of our recent en banc decisions, White v. Dallas Independent School District, 581 F.2d 556 (5th Cir. 1978), also lends support to the proposition that Title VII's jurisdictional prerequisites are subject to equitable modification. The issue in *White* was whether Title VII requires the EEOC to defer to the procedures for remedying employment discrimination established by the laws of the State of Texas. Mrs. White had filed a complaint with the EEOC alleging that she was

4. Prior to its amendment in 1972, § 2000e–5(e) required that EEOC complaints be filed within ninety days of the incident of discrimination rather than the presently permitted 180 days.

discharged from her teaching post in the Dallas Independent School District solely because of a discriminatory policy on teacher pregnancy. Although, at the time White's complaint was filed, the EEOC was litigating the issue whether Title VII required deferral to the Texas statutory remedies, the EEOC sent Mrs. White two letters informing her that "timeliness and all other requirements have been met." Id. at 562. This court held that Title VII, 42 U.S.C. § 2000e–5(c), required the EEOC to defer to Texas procedures, even though in Mrs. White's case the state statute of limitations had run. The court also held that the EEOC's letters had substantially misled Mrs. White and therefore the EEOC's failure to defer "should not redound to her detriment." Id. at 562. The court expressly stated that it did not need to decide the issue whether deferral was a jurisdictional prerequisite to Title VII relief. Id. at 562 & n. 11. The only logical implication of the court's decision not to reach this issue is that even if the court had held deferral to be a jurisdictional prerequisite, White's failure to comply would not have barred her suit because of the equities flowing from the EEOC's misleading letters.

The legislative history of the recent amendments to the Age Discrimination in Employment Act (ADEA), 29 U.S.C. §§ 621–634, also provides support for the principle that Title VII's jurisdictional provisions are subject to equitable modification. The ADEA states that an individual may not file an action in district court unless, within 180 days of the alleged incident of discrimination, the person gives the Secretary of Labor notice of his or her intent to sue. 29 U.S.C. § 626(d). Since this provision is virtually identical to the 180-day time period established by § 2000e–5(e), and since the ADEA and Title VII share a common purpose, congressional statements concerning the correct construction of § 626(d) are highly relevant to interpreting § 2000e–5(e). Oscar Mayer & Co. v. Evans, 441 U.S. 750, 755, 99 S.Ct. 2066, 2071, 60 L.Ed.2d 609, 615 (1979); *Bethel*, supra, 191 U.S.App.D.C. at 118–19 n.64, 589 F.2d at 641–42 n.64; Smith v. American President Lines, Ltd., 571 F.2d 102, 109 n.13 (2d Cir. 1978). In the course of discussing the amendments to the ADEA, see Act of April 6, 1978, Pub.L.No. 95–256, 92 Stat. 190 (1978), the conference committee to which the amendments had been assigned concluded that "equitable modification for failing to file within the [180-day] time period will be available to plaintiffs under this act." [5] H.R.Rep.No. 95–950, 95th Cong., 2d Sess. 7, 12, reprinted in [1978] U.S.Code Cong. & Admin.News, pp. 504, 528, 534; also see S.Rep. No. 95–493, 95th Cong., 2 Sess. 1, 12–13, reprinted in [1978] U.S.Code Cong. & Admin.News, pp. 504, 515–16.

Since the decisions of the Supreme Court and of this court have recognized that equitable considerations can, in certain circumstances,

5. The committee report also states that timely filing is not a jurisdictional prerequisite to judicial relief under the ADEA. This circuit has held that timely filing is a jurisdiction matter, but has left open the question whether the time period is subject to equitable modification. Quina v. Owens-Corning Fiberglass Corp., 575 F.2d 1115 (5th Cir. 1978). But see Kephart v. Institute of Gas Technology, 581 F.2d 1287 (7th Cir. 1978).

mitigate the demands of § 2000e–5(e) of Title VII, holdings which characterize § 2000e–5(e) as jurisdictional do not preclude equitable modification of its requirements.

B.

Since some equitable modification of § 2000e–5(e)'s provisions is possible, are the circumstances presented by the instant case such as would justify suspending the statute's requirements? The answer is they are not.

In urging that equitable tolling is available to her, Chappell cites Franks v. Bowman Transportation Co., 495 F.2d 398 (5th Cir. 1974), rev'd in part on other grounds, 424 U.S. 747, 96 S.Ct. 1251, 47 L.Ed.2d 444 (1976).[6] After conciliation efforts with Franks' employer failed, the EEOC issued right-to-sue letters to Franks covering two discrimination complaints which Franks had filed with the EEOC. The letter was sent to Franks' mailing address, where his nine-year-old nephew received the letter and signed the postal receipt. The nephew subsequently lost the letter and never told Franks that the letter had arrived. About a year later, Franks contacted the EEOC about the processing of his complaint and was informed that the right-to-sue letter had been issued. After Franks filed another complaint with the EEOC presenting the same allegations contained in the original complaint, the EEOC issued another right-to-sue letter. Noting that, under then current § 2000e–5, a Title VII action must be filed within 30 days of the date the complainant receives notice that conciliation efforts have failed and that the EEOC does not intend to sue, the district court held that the 30-day period began to run on the date the first letter was delivered to Franks' mailing address and that the complaint was therefore time barred. This court reversed, holding that § 2000e–5 required that a person actually receive the notice before the running of the 30-day period commenced.

Chappell urges that *Franks* should govern here, quoting language from the opinion stating "that Congress did not intend to condition a claimant's right to sue under Title VII on fortuitous circumstances or events beyond his control which are not spelled out in the statute." 495 F.2d at 404. The issue in *Franks*, however, was, not tolling of a statutory period which had commenced, but rather whether the event which would start the running of the 30-day period had occurred; i.e., whether Franks had received notice of the EEOC's decision to administratively close his case. In the case at bar, however, Chappell asserts that even though the comparable 180-day period had properly started

6. Chappell also relies on Dartt v. Shell Oil Co., 539 F.2d 1256 (10th Cir. 1976), which held that equitable tolling was available to suspend the running of the 180-day filing requirement in the ADEA. On writ of certiorari to the Supreme Court, *Dartt* was affirmed by an equally divided court, 434 U.S. 99, 98 S.Ct. 600, 54 L.Ed.2d 270 (1977), the effect of which is to deprive *Dartt* of any precedential value in the Supreme Court or the lower courts. Hertz v. Woodmen, 218 U.S. 205, 213–14, 30 S.Ct. 621, 623, 54 L.Ed. 1001, 1005–1006 (1910); Smith v. American President Lines, Ltd., 571 F.2d 102, 109 (2d Cir. 1978). Thus, Chappell's reliance on *Dartt* is misplaced.

to run, equitable consideration should interrupt the period's progress. Thus, *Franks* does not control Chappell's case.

Other cases discussed in part I. A., supra, present situations in which equitable considerations have been applied to interrupt or delay the § 2000e–5(e) period. These cases have suspended the "jurisdictional" limitation in three distinct situations. First, the Supreme Court has upheld the tolling of the time period during the pendency of an action before a state court which had jurisdiction over the subject matter of the suit, but which was the wrong forum under state law, reasoning that the policy of repose inherent in the timely filing requirement was satisfied since the initial state court action was filed against the same parties served in the federal suit and alleged an identical cause of action. *Robbins*, supra, 429 U.S. at 238, 97 S.Ct. at 448, 50 L.Ed.2d at 436; see *Burnett*, supra, 380 U.S. at 429, 85 S.Ct. at 1055, 13 L.Ed.2d at 945. Second, this court has upheld deferring the commencement of the running of the 180-day period until the claimant knew or should have known the facts which would give rise to his Title VII claim. *Bickham*, supra, 584 F.2d at 738; *Reeb*, supra, 516 F.2d at 931. The rationale underlying this suspension of the statute's requirements is that it is unfair to allow a defendant to conceal facts that support the plaintiff's cause of action and then to rely on the statute of limitations to bar the suit when a duly diligent plaintiff was unable to discover those facts. *Reeb*, supra, 516 F.2d at 930. Third, this court has indicated that equitable modification is appropriate when the EEOC misleads a complainant about the nature of his rights under Title VII, *Page*, supra, 556 F.2d 346, 350–51; see *White*, supra, 581 F.2d at 562, concluding that a complainant "is entitled to rely on * * * seemingly authoritative statement[s] by the agency presumed to know the most about these matters." *Page*, supra, 556 F.2d at 351.

The facts of this case do not fit into any of the three categories discussed above. First, Chappell did not file a lawsuit on her Title VII cause of action in any court prior to the expiration of the 180-day period. Second, she has not alleged that she was unaware of the facts supporting her Title VII claim until after the 180-day period had expired. To the contrary, she attempted to file her complaint within a month of the alleged incident of discrimination. Third, she does not contend that the EEOC misled her about her rights under Title VII. Her only contention is that she was entitled to rely on Whitley's representations that her EEOC complaint had been filed.

While none of the cases discussed in part I.A. are on all-fours with the instant case, it is closest to the cases involving misleading statements made by the EEOC. Whitley, an employee of the Texas Employment Commission, was charged with aiding parties in obtaining remedies for employment discrimination and had actually filed EEOC complaints for various persons on prior occasions. He repeatedly informed Chappell that her EEOC complaint had been filed. We decline, however, to extend the tolling principle from the EEOC misrepresentation cases to embrace the situation presented here. Whitley was not an employee of the EEOC, and Chappell could easily have discovered whether her complaint was filed merely by writing or phoning the EEOC office. Yet, for five months, she relied on Whitley's representations, despite the fact that her own repeated inquiries obviously indicate that she knew something was awry. If we were to find that Chappell's reliance on Whitley tolled the time period, there would be no logical reason for denying tolling to a person who has relied on a lawyer or a relative or an acquaintance to file his or her complaint. A holding of this breadth would seriously undermine the policy of repose inherent in the timely filing period, a policy designed to protect employers from stale claims. See *Johnson*, supra, 421 U.S. at 467 n.14, 95 S.Ct. at 1724 n.14, 44 L.Ed.2d at 306 n.14; *Zambuto*, supra, 544 F.2d at 1335. Nor does the fact that Emco has alleged no prejudice as a result of Chappell's four-day delay in filing a complaint affect the result. The petitioner in *Robbins* raised a similar argument, which the Supreme Court rejected:

> Petitioners contend at some length that tolling would impose almost no costs * * *. But the principal answer to this contention is that Congress has already spoken with respect to what it considers acceptable when it established a 90-day limitations period, and gave no indications that it considered a "slight" delay followed by 90 days equally acceptable. In defining Title VII's jurisdictional prerequisites "with precision," * * * Congress did not leave to courts the decision as to which delays might or might not be "slight."

429 U.S. at 239–40, 97 S.Ct. at 449, 50 L.Ed.2d at 437. We therefore conclude that Chappell's reliance on Whitley's representations did not toll the running of the 180-day time period.

II.

Chappell asserts that her complaint was filed, within the meaning of § 2000e–5(e), when the employee of the Texas Employment Commission received it. This interpretation of the statute is erroneous. The statutory scheme clearly anticipates that the complaint must be filed with the EEOC. Only then is notice given to the employer and conciliation procedures commenced. See 42 U.S.C. § 2000e–5. Clearly, Chappell understood this. Indeed, it was the subject of her initial request to Whitley and all of her subsequent inquiries. Our decisions also have clearly held that timely filing *with the EEOC* is a jurisdictional prerequisite to Title VII relief. *McArthur*, supra, 569 F.2d at 276; Cutliff v. Greyhound Lines, Inc., 558 F.2d 803, 806 (5th Cir. 1977).

Chappell alternatively contends that the 180-day time period did not begin running until September 15, 1973, since she was paid through that date even though the termination occurred on August 31, 1973. The district court found that the statutory period began to run on August 31, 1973, since the incident of discrimination of which Chappell complained occurred on that date. This finding is not clearly erroneous.

Chappell also urges that this court should defer to the EEOC's determination that she had satisfied all of Title VII's jurisdictional prerequisites. It is clear, however, that a court must make an independent determination of whether jurisdiction exists rather than deferring to the EEOC. *Cutliff*, supra, 558 F.2d at 807; *Reeb*, supra, 516 F.2d at 926.

III.

Having found that Chappell failed to file a complaint with the EEOC within 180 days of the alleged incident of discrimination and that equitable delay or interruption of the 180-day period is unavailable under the circumstances of this case, we hold that Chappell's suit was time barred under 42 U.S.C. § 2000e–5(e) and that the district court properly dismissed her suit for want of jurisdiction.

Affirmed.

[A concurring opinion by JUDGE FAY is omitted.]

WISDOM, CIRCUIT JUDGE, dissenting.

With his usual thoroughness, Judge Clark has carefully analyzed the question whether the 180-day period contained in § 2000e–5(e) of Title VII is subject to equitable delay or interruption. I agree with his conclusion that equity must be considered in determining whether a timely filing occurred. I went at least that far in Reeb v. Economic Opportunity Atlanta, Inc., 5 Cir. 1975, 516 F.2d 924. Judge Clark has taken a long walk to the river, undressed, put on a bathing suit, tested the temperature of the water with his toe, and then decided that it was too cold for a swim. I would take the plunge.

Mrs. Chappell is the victim of a bureaucratic tangle. She filed her complaint with the Texas Employment Commission on September 18, 1973, eighteen days after she was fired. S. R. Whitley, a supervising interviewer for the Commission, stated in an affidavit that "in the regular course of business" he made "a memorandum or record * * * personally at the time of an interview with Mrs. Cleda J. Dykes [Chappell] on September 18, 1973". He continued: "These two pages of records represent an employment discrimination complaint. My records reflect that the complaint was forwarded to Equal Employment Opportunity Commission * * * on September 18, 1973 * * * [as] is customary in the usual course of business of Texas Employment Commission". The EEOC complaint, attached to Whitley's affidavit, is dated September 18, 1973. The Texas Employment Commission records reflect that her complaint was forwarded to the Albuquerque district office of the EEOC that day.

EEOC records, however, show that the complaint *bearing the notation of the Texas Employment Commission* was received on March 5, 1974. Although we do not know where the complaint was between

September 18, 1973 and March 5, 1974, we do know that Mrs. Chappell was in no way responsible for the delay in filing. The fault for the delay lies with the state agency, the EEOC district office, or the United States mails, in recent years not distinguished for efficiency.

The majority opinion acknowledges that equitable modification would be appropriate had Mrs. Chappell relied on an employee of the EEOC to file her complaint. A complainant "is entitled to rely on * * * seemingly authoritative statement[s] made by the agency presumed to know the most about these matters." Page v. U. S. Industries, Inc., 5 Cir. 1977, 556 F.2d 346, 351. The majority declines to apply this principle, however, in the case of seemingly authoritative statements made by the supervising interviewer of the Texas Employment Commission because, in its view, there is no logical stopping point between reliance on a state agency and reliance on a lawyer, relative, or an acquaintance to file the party's complaint. I consider that an officer or employee of a state agency may be presumed to do his duty in the regular course of business no less than an officer or employee of a federal agency.

State agencies occupy a special role in the statutory scheme of Title VII. Many of the procedural requirements of the Act reflect the judgment that *local*, more informal enforcement agencies are the preferred means of resolving employment discrimination grievances. Resort to state agencies reduces the EEOC caseload and conserves federal resources. The Seventh Circuit has noted that "as part of the compromise which made it possible to pass the Civil Rights Act of 1964, its sponsors agreed to the inclusion of provisions which * * * require a resort to state procedures, where available, as a condition precedent to a private action in the federal courts." Moore v. Sunbeam Corp., 7 Cir. 1972, 459 F.2d 811, 820–21. Indeed, the EEOC cannot act on a complaint unless it is first presented to the state agency if the agency is one empowered by the state's fair employment legislation to grant relief from the discriminatory act charged. 42 U.S.C. §§ 2000e–5(c) and 2000e–5(d). Although Mrs. Chappell was not *required* to file her complaint first with the Texas Employment Commission, since that agency is not a fair employment practice agency within the definition of § 2000e–5(c),[1] the Texas agency is charged with assisting claimants in obtaining remedies for employment discrimination and routinely handles EEOC complaints for litigants. Whitley's job was just exactly that.

In *Reeb*, we said that "the timing provisions [of the Act] will be subject to the same sort of equitable modifications that are applied to statutes of limitations, with the important additional requirement that these modifications will be applied in the interest of effectuating the

1. Section 2000e–5(c) defines that agency as one established in a state or political subdivision "which has a state or local law prohibiting the unlawful employment practice alleged and establishing or authorizing a state or local authority to grant or seek relief from such practice or to institute criminal proceedings with respect thereto. * * *" See also CFR Chptr. XIV, 1601.12. Cf. White v. Dallas Independent School District, 5 Cir. 1978, en banc, 581 F.2d 556.

broad remedial purposes of the statute." *Reeb,* supra, at 927. Modification should be applied if "doing so would further the purposes of the statute as a whole." Id.

It would be ironic for Mrs. Chappell to be penalized for resorting to a state forum when Title VII places great emphasis on resorting initially to state agencies to rectify unfair practices. Insistence on formalistic distinctions between the EEOC and its "agents" on the one hand and state agencies created to assist the individual in processing his grievance on the other hand is particularly indefensible in light of the avowed purpose of Title VII to provide a scheme whereby an unlettered layman can present his complaint without resort to a lawyer. Cf. Love v. Pullman Co., 1972, 404 U.S. 522, 92 S.Ct. 616, 30 L.Ed.2d 679. In this case Whitley specifically instructed Mrs. Chappell that she did not need a lawyer because the Texas agency would handle the matter for her.

Here, there is an absence of any prejudice to the defendant attributable to the delay in filing. The delay was minimal, only four days. It can even be said that in terms of the effect on the defendant of the statutory requirement of timeliness—there was no delay. March 1 was the 180th day. The law requires that the defendant be notified within ten days of the filing of a complaint; that is, 190 days from the date of the offense. Here, that would be March 11. The EEOC mailed the notice to the defendant on March 8. The defendant received the notice on March 11. Considering, therefore, notice to the defendant as integral to the ultimate purpose of the timely filing requirement, there was no delay, certainly no prejudicial delay.

The EEOC took the case on the merits, investigated, *and found discrimination.* Significantly, the EEOC itself, the agency Congress authorized to process employment discrimination complaints, considered the filing was timely. The EEOC "Determination" contains a finding of timeliness. And the district director of the EEOC stated that the "complaint was treated by my office as timely filed". The Commission found that the defendant's reasons for Mrs. Chappell's discharge were "so groundless as to warrant a conclusion that sex was the sole motivating factor for her discharge". In short, the facts cry out for justice.

Mrs. Chappell's reliance on Whitley's assurances was reasonable. To be sure, Mrs. Chappell's repeated inquiries regarding the status of her complaint "obviously indicate that she knew something was awry". But Whitley told Mrs. Chappell that the complaint had been forwarded and that the EEOC was in the process of taking action. It was reasonable for her to suppose that the delay was attributable to the slow turning of bureaucratic wheels. Her repeated inquiries demonstrate impatience; they do not show that she slept on her rights.

Mrs. Chappell actively pursued her remedies. She filed her complaint with an official state agency set up to carry out the broad purposes of Title VII by assisting laymen in initiating complaints with the EEOC. Bureaucratic ineptitude, whether of the Texas Employment

Commission or the EEOC district office, or perhaps the United States postal service, should not result in the forfeiture of her rights. I would, therefore, reverse the district court.

In ZIPES v. TRANS WORLD AIRLINES, INC., 455 U.S. 385, 102 S.Ct. 1127, 71 L.Ed.2d 234 (1982), the Supreme Court confirmed the position of most circuits by holding that "filing a timely charge of discrimination with the EEOC is not a jurisdictional prerequisite to suit in federal court, but a requirement that, like a statute of limitations is subject to waiver, estoppel, and equitable tolling". 455 U.S. at 393.

NOTES AND PROBLEMS FOR DISCUSSION

1. In Morgan v. Washington Manufacturing Co., 660 F.2d 710 (6th Cir. 1981), a discharged employee wrote a letter to President Carter within two months of her termination complaining of discrimination by her employer. The White House forwarded the letter to the Wage and Hour Office of the Department of Labor. The Labor Department sought more information from the potential plaintiff and finally referred the complaint to the EEOC shortly after the 180 day period had expired. The Sixth Circuit held that "in the absence of prejudice to the defendant or a showing of bad faith or lack of diligence by a claimant, equitable considerations should toll the 180 day period for filing a complaint under Title VII when the claimant makes a timely filing with a federal agency, like the Labor Department, which has jurisdiction in some fields of employment discrimination and when that complaint is forwarded to the EEOC shortly after the time period has expired." 660 F.2d at 712. The Sixth Circuit relied on the en banc decision of the Fifth Circuit in Coke v. General Adjustment Bureau, 640 F.2d 584 (5th Cir. 1981) (en banc), where that court held that the 180 day time period for the plaintiff to give the Secretary of Labor his notice of intent to sue under the ADEA would be equitably tolled by the employer's assurance, communicated to the plaintiff, that he would be reinstated to the position from which he had been removed. 640 F.2d at 595. The plaintiff in *Coke* submitted his notice within 180 days of the last such assurance, but more than 180 days after his demotion. Are these decisions consistent with the result in Chappell v. Emco Machine Works?

Courts have uniformly held that, in addition to the reasons stated in *Chappell,* misrepresentation, concealment, intimidation or other actions by the employer which it knew or reasonably should have known would cause a delay in filing the EEOC charge will toll the 180-day period. See, Felty v. Graves-Humphreys Co., 785 F.2d 516 (4th Cir. 1986) (offer of generous severence payment conditioned on not talking with other employees about termination); McClinton v. Alabama By-Products Corp., 743 F.2d 1483 (11th Cir. 1984) (failure to post notices of law in workplace as required by Act); Bilka v. Pepe's, Inc., 601 F.Supp 1254 (N.D.Ill.1985) (threats). Cf. Pruet Production Co. v. Ayles, 784 F.2d 1275 (5th Cir. 1986) (no misrepresentation or concealment that would have lulled employee into missing deadline); Dillman v. Combustion Engineering, Inc., 784 F.2d 57 (2d Cir. 1986) (offer of severance benefits not misleading when EEOC notices posted in workplace). Would failure to tell an employee why he was being demoted constitute the kind of misrepresentation that ought to toll the filing period? See, Klausing v. Whirlpool Corp., 623 F.Supp. 156 (S.D.Ohio 1985).

2. The period for filing the EEOC charge will not, however, be tolled by the pursuit of a remedy, separate and apart from Title VII, such as a grievance procedure contained in a collective bargaining agreement. In ALEXANDER v. GARDNER–DENVER CO., 415 U.S. 36, 94 S.Ct. 1011, 39 L.Ed.2d 147 (1974), the Court stressed that contractual rights and remedies are distinct from statutory rights and held that an employee does not waive his right to assert a Title VII claim by filing and pursuing a union grievance with respect to the practice alleged to be discriminatory. Since contractual rights are totally separate from and independent of the employee's rights under Title VII, the Court held in INTERNATIONAL UNION OF ELECTRICAL, RADIO AND MACHINE WORKERS, LOCAL 790 v. ROBBINS & MYERS, INC., 429 U.S. 229, 97 S.Ct. 441, 50 L.Ed.2d 427 (1976), that pursuit of relief through a grievance procedure does not interrupt the period for filing an EEOC charge. The *Robbins & Myers* Court rejected arguments that equitable tolling principles should be applied because the employee was not seeking to assert his statutory claim in the grievance proceeding. Presumably, the Court felt the employee could not be misled under these circumstances as to the legal effect of filing the grievance. Note that the filing of an EEOC charge does not toll the running of any other statute of limitations applicable to an independent claim. See Johnson v. Railway Express Agency, infra at p. 532.

Could the parties to a collective bargaining agreement provide that the internal grievance procedure is the *exclusive* remedy for charges of discrimination, thus precluding resort to the EEOC by an aggrieved employee? Should the employee's success at the grievance stage bar assertion of his Title VII claim? See Strozier v. General Motors Corp., 635 F.2d 424 (5th Cir. 1981).

3. Section 706(c) of Title VII provides that where a qualifying state or local agency[a] exists to remedy unlawful discrimination, "no charge may be filed * * * by the person aggrieved * * * [until] sixty days after state proceedings have been commenced * * * unless such proceedings have been earlier terminated." "Initial resort to state and local remedies is mandated, and recourse to the federal forums is appropriate only when the state law does not provide prompt or complete relief." New York Gaslight Club, Inc. v. Carey, 447 U.S. 54, 65, 100 S.Ct. 2024, 64 L.Ed.2d 723 (1980). Thus, if referral to state authorities is required and has not occurred when the EEOC receives a charge, it may not begin its inquiry into the merits of the claim. The Commission, however, does not completely reject such a premature charge. In LOVE v. PULLMAN, 404 U.S. 522, 92 S.Ct. 616, 30 L.Ed.2d 679 (1972), the Supreme Court approved the EEOC's "deferral" procedure, now incorporated in 29 CFR 1601.13, under which the Commission refers a charge to the appropriate state or local agency on behalf of the grievant and defers its own action until the period of reference to the agency expires. The charge is received by the EEOC but not "filed" within the meaning of the statute. In endorsing this procedure, the Court noted:

> Nothing in the Act suggests that the state proceedings may not be initiated by the EEOC acting on behalf of the complainant rather than by the complainant himself, nor is there any requirement that the complaint to the

[a] To qualify as a "706 Agency" three requirements of that section must be satisfied. The acts alleged must constitute an unlawful employment practice under Title VII; they must violate a state or local law; and the local agency must have authority to remedy the violation or to institute criminal proceedings. See 29 CFR 1601.70(a) and White v. Dallas Independent School District, 581 F.2d 556, 558–559 (5th Cir. 1978) (en banc).

> state agency be made in writing rather than by oral referral. Further, we cannot agree with the respondent's claim that the EEOC may not properly hold a complaint in "suspended animation," automatically filing it upon termination of the state proceedings.

404 U.S. at 525–526, 92 S.Ct. at 618.

Under § 706(e), the plaintiff, known at the administrative stage as the "charging party," has 180 days after the unlawful employment practice occurred to file his charge with the EEOC. In a state with a 706 agency, however, a person who has "initially instituted proceedings with a State or local agency" has 300 days to file such a charge or 30 days after receiving notice that the state or local agency has terminated its proceedings, whichever is earlier. In MOHASCO CORP. v. SILVER, 447 U.S. 807, 100 S.Ct. 2486, 65 L.Ed.2d 532 (1980), the charging party wrote the EEOC on June 15, 1976, 291 days after his discharge, complaining that his employer had discriminated against him because of his religion. The EEOC immediately referred the charge to the appropriate New York state agency which determined in due course that there was no merit to the charge. Approximately one year later the EEOC notified the complainant that he had a statutory right to file a private action and he thereafter filed suit. Granting summary judgment to the employer, the district court held that § 706(c) precluded any filing with the EEOC until a date 60 days after June 15th (the date of filing with the state agency), and because that date was 51 days beyond § 706(c)'s 300 day time limit for filing in deferral states, the charge was not timely filed. The Court of Appeals reversed, holding that the charge had been "filed" for purposes of § 706(e) when received by the EEOC and "filed" for purposes of § 706(c) at the end of the 60 day deferral period and that, therefore, the June 15th letter had been filed within the 300 days allowed by § 706(e). The Supreme Court reversed, holding that under § 706(k) the charge could not have been filed with the EEOC until 60 days after June 15th, by which time the applicable 300 day limitation of § 706(e) had already expired:

> Section [706(c)] was rather clearly intended to increase the role of States and localities in resolving charges of employment discrimination. And [§ 706(d)'s] longer time * * * for filing with the EEOC in deferral states was included to prevent forfeiture of a complainant's federal rights while participating in state proceedings.
>
> But neither this latter provision nor anything else in the legislative history contains any "suggestion that complainants in some States were to be allowed to proceed with less diligence than those in other states." Moore v. Sunbeam Corp., 459 F.2d 811, 825, n.35 (CA7 1972). The history identifies only one reason for treating workers in deferral States differently from workers in other States: to give state agencies an opportunity to redress the evil at which the federal legislation was aimed, and to avoid federal intervention unless its need was demonstrated. The statutory plan was not designed to give the worker in a deferral State the option of choosing between his state remedy and his federal remedy, nor indeed simply to allow him additional time in which to obtain state relief.

447 U.S. at 820–821, 100 S.Ct. at 2494.

Despite this language in *Mohasco,* there is substantial confusion over whether a charging party who has not filed with the appropriate state agency within the applicable *state* limitation period has the benefit of the 300-day deferral state period for filing with the EEOC. For example, in Jones v. Airco Carbide

Chemical Co., 691 F.2d 1200 (6th Cir. 1982), a former employee submitted his charge to the EEOC 231 days after his discharge. The EEOC sent the charge to the state agency which dismissed it because of the 180-day filing period in the state employment discrimination law. The district court, construing the 300-day period of § 706(c) as applicable only where a timely state charge had been filed, dismissed the complaint because the charge to the EEOC was outside of Title VII's 180-day filing period. The Sixth Circuit, relying on language in *Mohasco* that the claimant in a deferral state "need only file his charge within 240 days of the alleged discriminatory employment practice," 447 U.S. at 814 n. 16, 100 S.Ct. at 2491, reversed.

> [I]n commencing an action under * * * Section 706(c) of Title VII a timely filing under state law is not necessary in order to properly file with the EEOC. An untimely filed state proceeding is 'commenced' within the meaning of * * * Section 706(c) of Title VII so as to make available the 300-day filing period with the EEOC.

691 F.2d at 1204. A majority of the circuits have agreed with the Sixth that compliance with state time limitations is not a prerequisite for use of the 300-day filing period. See e.g., Thomas v. Florida Power and Light Co., 764 F.2d 768 (11th Cir. 1985); Smith v. Oral Roberts Evangelistic Assn., Inc., 731 F.2d 684 (10th Cir. 1984). The Seventh Circuit has avoided ruling on the issue by holding that timely filing with the state agency is not required to preserve one's Title VII rights if the state filing period is less than 180-days. Martinez v. UAW Local 1373, 772 F.2d 348 (7th Cir. 1985). Some district courts, stressing that Title VII was not intended to permit claimants in deferral states to be less diligent than in non-deferral states, continue to hold that timely filing with the state agency is a prerequisite to use of the expanded deferral state period for filing with the EEOC. See, Proffit v. Keycom Electronic Publishing, 625 F.Supp 400 (N.D.Ill.1985); Peters v. Wilson Plastics, 38 FEP Cases 937 (N.D.Ill. 1985). Since the 300-day period was intended to give the state agency time to investigate and conciliate before filing with the EEOC, does it make any sense to give the charging party, who has failed to comply with state law and thus cannot obtain a state investigation, an additional 120 days to file with the EEOC?

Under the liberal rule followed by most of the circuits, the state proceeding must be "commenced" at least 60 days prior to expiration of the 300-day period because of *Mohasco's* holding that the EEOC cannot consider the charge until 60 days after its filing with the state agency. Apparently this is the case even where, because of a late filing, the state agency will not consider the charge. See, Seredinski v. Clifton Precision Products Co., 776 F.2d 56 (3d Cir. 1985).

4. As noted by the majority in *Chappell*, Title VII relief is available to some persons joined as plaintiffs in a Title VII action even if they have not individually filed EEOC charges. See also, Snell v. Suffolk County, 782 F.2d 1094 (2d Cir. 1986). Thus, intervenors, who could have filed timely charges concerning the challenged practice, and members of a properly certified class are entitled to proceed in litigation without satisfying the requirements of § 706. See Oatis v. Crown Zellerbach Corp., infra at 420. However, before a non-filing class member or intervenor can benefit from a Title VII cause of action, at least one named plaintiff must have filed a timely EEOC charge and satisfied the other statutory prerequisites to a Title VII action. See Allen v. United States Steel Corp., 665 F.2d 689, 695–696 (5th Cir. 1982).

RES JUDICATA, COLLATERAL ESTOPPEL AND THE IMPACT OF STATE PROCEEDINGS ON TITLE VII LITIGATION

Section 706 of Title VII makes resort to state administrative remedies, in a state with a deferral agency, a prerequisite to litigation under the Act. It is important to understand, however, that, under certain circumstances, the *exhaustion* of state remedies may affect the claimant's right to a decision on the merits of his Title VII claim in federal court. In KREMER v. CHEMICAL CONSTRUCTION CORP., 456 U.S. 461, 102 S.Ct. 1883, 72 L.Ed.2d 262 (1982), the claimant, who alleged a discriminatory failure to rehire after a layoff, filed a charge with the EEOC which it, in turn, referred to the New York State Division of Human Rights (NYHRD), a qualifying agency under § 706. After an investigation, the NYHRD concluded there was no probable cause for the charge. Kremer sought a review of the agency's action in state court, as allowed New York's fair employment law. The state court affirmed the agency decision on the ground that it was not "arbitrary, capricious or an abuse of discretion." Subsequently, the EEOC issued a no-cause determination and a right-to-sue notice and Kremer filed a timely Title VII action in federal district court. The district court's dismissal of the complaint on grounds of res judicata was upheld by the Second Circuit. The Supreme Court, in a five-four decision, affirmed. While conceding that *initial resort* to state administrative remedies cannot deprive a charging party of a federal trial *de novo* on his Title VII claim, the majority found nothing in the legislative history of Title VII to suggest that Congress "considered it necessary or desirable to provide an absolute right to relitigate in federal court an issue resolved by a state court." 456 U.S. at 473, 102 S.Ct. at 1893. Since there was not a "clear and manifest" legislative purpose behind Title VII to deny res judicata or collateral estoppel to state court judgments on discrimination claims, the Court held that it would apply "the usual rule . . . that [the] merits of a claim once decided in a court of competent jurisdiction are not subject to redetermination in another forum." 456 U.S. at 485, 102 S.Ct. at 1899. Justice Blackmun, joined by Justices Brennan and Marshall in dissent, argued that state judicial review of an agency determination is merely part of the state "proceedings" under § 706(b) and (c) and that the Congressional intent was that a claimant could pursue his Title VII claim in federal court despite the conclusion of state "proceedings." Justice Blackmun warned:

> The lesson of the Court's ruling is: *An unsuccessful state discrimination complainant should not seek state judicial review.* If a discrimination complainant pursues state judicial review and loses—a likely result given the deferential standard of review in state court—he forfeits his right to seek redress in a federal court. If, however, he simply bypasses the state courts, he can proceed to the EEOC and ultimately to federal court. Instead of a deferential review of an agency record, he will receive in federal court a *de novo* hearing

> accompanied by procedural aids such as broad discovery rules and the ability to subpoena witnesses. Thus, paradoxically, the Court effectively has eliminated state reviewing courts from the fight against discrimination in an entire class of cases. Consequently, the state courts will not have chance to correct state agency errors when the agencies rule against discrimination victims, and the quality of decisionmaking can only deteriorate. It is a perverse sort of comity that eliminates the reviewing function of state courts in the name of giving their decisions due respect.

456 U.S. at 504–505, 102 S.Ct. at 1909. Justice Blackmun's assumption that charging parties can "simply bypass" state court review at the end of the state administrative process has not proved wholly correct. Courts have uniformly construed *Kremer* as applicable regardless of which party initiates the appeal to the state court. Thus, if the plaintiff prevails before the state agency and is *forced* into state court by the employer's appeal, the court's reversal of the agency's ruling will bar the federal Title VII action. See, Gonsalves v. Alpine Country Club, 727 F.2d 27 (1st Cir. 1984); Trujillo v. County of Santa Clara, 766 F.2d 1368 (9th Cir. 1985); Hickman v. Electronic Keyboarding, Inc., 741 F.2d 230 (8th Cir. 1984). The "lesson" of *Kremer* may be that, in a deferral state where judicial review of the agency process is possible, the claimant must abandon the agency proceedings *before* an appealable decision in order to guarantee his right to a federal forum.

According to the majority in *Kremer*, its decision was mandated by 28 USC § 1738 which requires federal courts to give the same preclusive effect to state court judgments that those judgments would be given in the courts of the state from which the judgments come. In McDonald v. City of West Branch, 466 U.S. 284, 104 S.Ct. 1799, 80 L.Ed. 2d 302 (1984), the Court held that an arbitration was not a "judicial proceeding" within the meaning of § 1738 and thus should have no preclusive effect on subsequent federal litigation involving the same issue which was arbitrated. There remained however the question of whether the doctrine of "administrative res judicata" should be applied in employment discrimination cases so that state agency decisions would be given preclusive effect where the agency had acted in a *judicial capacity*. The Seventh Circuit and several district courts had held that, where state administrative procedures provided the claimant with all the procedural safeguards normally associated with judicial proceedings, administrative decisions of such state agencies should be given the same preclusive effect as decisions of state courts. Buckhalter v. Pepsi Cola General Bottlers, 768 F.2d 842 (7th Cir. 1985); Zywicki v. Moxness Products, Inc., 610 F.Supp. 50 (E.D.Wis.1985); Parker v. National Corporation for Housing Partnerships, 619 F.Supp. 1061 (D.D.C.1985).

The Supreme Court dealt with the "administrative res judicata" issue in UNIVERSITY OF TENNESSEE v. ELLIOTT, ___ U.S. ___, 106 S.Ct. 3220, 92 L.Ed.2d 635 (1986). In *Elliott*, the plaintiff contested his proposed termination by the University of Tennessee before an administrative law judge under the state administrative procedures act. After hearing extensive evidence, the ALJ ruled that the university's charges against the plaintiff were not racially motivated as he had contended. The plaintiff did not seek review in the Tennessee courts, but instead proceeded with a suit filed in federal court under Title VII and Section 1983. The district court dismissed the suit on res judicata grounds, but the Sixth Circuit reversed, holding that the policies underlying Title VII and Section 1983 prevented the giving of preclusive effect to non judicial decisions. With respect to the Title VII claim, the Supreme Court affirmed the Court of Appeals and held that Congress did not intend unreviewed state administrative decisions to have preclusive effect on Title VII claims regardless of the nature of the state procedures. But as to the Section 1983 claim, the Court could "see no reason to suppose that Congress, in enacting the Reconstruction civil rights statutes, wished to foreclose the adaptation of traditional principles of preclusion to such subsequent developments as the burgeoning use of administrative adjudication in the 20th century." Accordingly, the Court held that when a state agency acting in a judicial capacity resolves disputed issues of fact which the parties had an adequate opportunity to litigate, federal courts in suits filed under the Reconstruction Era civil rights statutes must give the agency's factfinding the same preclusive effect to which it would be entitled in the courts of the state. Where the claimant prevails in the state court proceeding and obtains some relief, should he be barred from pursuing subsequent relief in a Title VII action by the doctrine of "bar and merger"? See, Patzer v. Board of Regents, 763 F.2d 851 (7th Cir. 1985). Should a claimant who obtains a decision from a state ALJ that the claimant was the victim of racial discrimination be able to preclude relitigation of the merits of his claim in a subsequent 1983 action for damages against his employer?

It is clear that the decision, whether by a state court or an agency operating in a "judicial capacity," can have no preclusive effect in subsequent litigation unless the state proceeding has afforded the plaintiff a "full and fair opportunity" to litigate the merits of the discrimination claim. See, Jones v. City of Alton, 757 F.2d 878 (7th Cir. 1985) (state court decision upholding plaintiff's discharge not entitled to res judicata effect where state court prevented plaintiff from presenting evidence of discrimination on mistaken theory that such evidence was irrelevant to grounds of discharge). Should a decision by a state court in an unemployment compensation proceeding that the plaintiff was terminated for "just cause" preclude a subsequent Title VII suit? See, Ross v. Communication Satellite Corp., 759 F.2d 355 (4th Cir. 1985); Harding v. Ramsay, Scarlett & Co., 599 F.Supp. 180 (D.Md.1984).

2. The Date of Discrimination: When Does the Period For Filing the Charge Begin to Run?

UNITED AIR LINES, INC. v. EVANS

Supreme Court of the United States, 1977.
431 U.S. 553, 97 S.Ct. 1885, 52 L.Ed.2d 571.

MR. JUSTICE STEVENS delivered the opinion of the Court.

Respondent was employed by United Air Lines as a flight attendant from November 1966 to February 1968. She was rehired in February 1972. Assuming, as she alleges, that her separation from employment in 1968 violated Title VII of the Civil Rights Act of 1964,[1] the question now presented is whether the employer is committing a second violation of Title VII by refusing to credit her with seniority for any period prior to February 1972.

Respondent filed charges with the Equal Employment Opportunity Commission in February 1973 alleging that United discriminated and continues to discriminate against her because she is a female. After receiving a letter granting her the right to sue, she commenced this action in the United States District Court for the Northern District of Illinois. Because the District Court dismissed her complaint, the facts which she has alleged are taken as true. They may be simply stated.

During respondent's initial period of employment, United maintained a policy of refusing to allow its female flight attendants to be married.[2] When she married in 1968, she was therefore forced to resign. Although it was subsequently decided that such a resignation violated Title VII, Sprogis v. United Air Lines, 444 F.2d 1194 (CA7 1971), cert. denied, 404 U.S. 991, 92 S.Ct. 536, 30 L.Ed.2d 543, respondent was not a party to that case and did not initiate any proceedings of her own in 1968 by filing a charge with the EEOC within 90 days of her separation.[3] A claim based on that discriminatory act is therefore barred.[4]

In November 1968, United entered into a new collective-bargaining agreement which ended the pre-existing "no marriage" rule and provid-

1. 78 Stat. 253. Title VII, as amended, is codified in 42 U.S.C. § 2000e et seq. (1970 ed. and Supp.V).

2. At that time United required that all flight attendants be female, except on flights between the mainland and Hawaii and on overseas military charter flights. See Sprogis v. United Air Lines, 444 F.2d 1194, 1203 (CA7 1971) (Stevens, J., dissenting); cert. denied, 404 U.S. 991, 92 S.Ct. 536, 30 L.Ed.2d 543.

3. Section 706(d), 78 Stat. 260, 42 U.S.C. § 2000e–5(e), then provided in part:

> "A charge under subsection (a) shall be filed within ninety days after the alleged unlawful employment practice occurred * * *."

The 1972 amendments to Title VII added a new subsection (a) to § 706. Consequently, subsection (d) was redesignated as subsection (e). At the same time it was amended to enlarge the limitations period to 180 days. See 86 Stat. 105, 42 U.S.C. § 2000e–5(e) (1970 ed., Supp.V).

4. Timely filing is a prerequisite to the maintenance of a Title VII action. Alexander v. Gardner-Denver Co., 415 U.S. 36, 47, 94 S.Ct. 1011, 1019, 39 L.Ed.2d 147. See Electrical Workers v. Robbins & Myers, Inc., 429 U.S. 229, 239–240, 97 S.Ct. 441, 448–449, 50 L.Ed.2d 427.

ed for the reinstatement of certain flight attendants who had been terminated pursuant to that rule. Respondent was not covered by that agreement. On several occasions she unsuccessfully sought reinstatement; on February 16, 1972, she was hired as a new employee. Although her personnel file carried the same number as it did in 1968, for seniority purposes she has been treated as though she had no prior service with United.[5] She has not alleged that any other rehired employees were given credit for prior service with United, or that United's administration of the seniority system has violated the collective-bargaining agreement covering her employment.[6]

Informal requests to credit her with pre-1972 seniority having been denied, respondent commenced this action.[7] The District Court dismissed the complaint, holding that the failure to file a charge within 90 days of her separation in 1968 caused respondent's claim to be time barred and foreclosed any relief under Title VII.[8]

A divided panel of the Court of Appeals initially affirmed; then, after our decision in Franks v. Bowman Transportation Co., 424 U.S. 747, 96 S.Ct. 1251, 47 L.Ed.2d 444, the panel granted respondent's petition for rehearing and unanimously reversed. 534 F.2d 1247 (CA7 1976). We granted certiorari, 429 U.S. 917, 97 S.Ct. 308, 50 L.Ed.2d 282, and now hold that the complaint was properly dismissed.

5. Respondent is carried on two seniority rolls. Her "company" or "system" seniority dates from the day she was rehired, February 16, 1972. Her "stewardess" or "pay" seniority dates from the day she completed her flight attendant training, March 16, 1972. One or both types of seniority determine a flight attendant's wages; the duration and timing of vacations; rights to retention in the event of layoffs and rights to re-employment thereafter; and rights to preferential selection of flight assignments.

6. Under the provisions of the collective-bargaining agreement between United and the Air Line Stewardesses and Flight Stewards as represented by the Air Line Pilots Association International for the period 1972–1974, seniority is irrevocably lost or broken after the separation from employment of a flight attendant "*who resigns or whose services with the Company are permanently severed for just cause.*" Brief for Respondent 6.

7. The relief requested in respondent's complaint included an award of seniority to the starting date of her initial employment with United and backpay "lost as a result of the discriminatory employment practices of [United]." In her brief in this Court, respondent states that she seeks backpay only since her date of rehiring, February 16, 1972, which would consist of the increment in pay and benefits attributable to her lower seniority since that time. Brief for Respondent 4.

8. The District Court recited that the motion was filed pursuant to Fed.Rule Civ. Proc. 12(b)(1) and dismissed the complaint on the ground that it had no jurisdiction of a time-barred claim. The District Court also held, however, that the complaint did not allege any continuing violation. For that reason, the complaint was ripe for dismissal under Rule 12(b)(6). The District Court stated:

> "Plaintiff asserts that by defendant's denial of her seniority back to the starting date of her original employment in 1966, United is currently perpetuating the effect of past discrimination.
>
> "Plaintiff, however, has not been suffering from any 'continuing' violation. She is seeking to have this court merely reinstate her November, 1966 seniority date which was lost solely by reason of her February, 1968 resignation. The fact that that resignation was the result of an unlawful employment practice is irrelevant for purposes of these proceedings because plaintiff lost her opportunity to redress that grievance when she failed to file a charge within ninety days of February, 1968. United's subsequent employment of plaintiff in 1972 cannot operate to resuscitate such a time-barred claim."

Respondent recognizes that it is now too late to obtain relief based on an unlawful employment practice which occurred in 1968. She contends, however, that United is guilty of a present, continuing violation of Title VII and therefore that her claim is timely.[9] She advances two reasons for holding that United's seniority system illegally discriminates against her: First, she is treated less favorably than males who were hired after her termination in 1968 and prior to her re-employment in 1972; second, the seniority system gives present effect to the past illegal act and therefore perpetuates the consequences of forbidden discrimination. Neither argument persuades us that United is presently violating the statute.

It is true that some male employees with less total service than respondent have more seniority than she. But this disparity is not a consequence of their sex, or of her sex. For females hired between 1968 and 1972 also acquired the same preference over respondent as males hired during that period. Moreover, both male and female employees who had service prior to February 1968, who resigned or were terminated for a nondiscriminatory reason (or for an unchallenged discriminatory reason), and who were later re-employed, also were treated as new employees receiving no seniority credit for their prior service. Nothing alleged in the complaint indicates that United's seniority system treats existing female employees differently from existing male employees, or that the failure to credit prior service differentiates in any way between prior service by males and prior service by females. Respondent has failed to allege that United's seniority system differentiates between similarly situated males and females on the basis of sex.

Respondent is correct in pointing out that the seniority system gives present effect to a past act of discrimination. But United was entitled to treat that past act as lawful after respondent failed to file a charge of discrimination within the 90 days then allowed by § 706(d). A discriminatory act which is not made the basis for a timely charge is the legal equivalent of a discriminatory act which occurred before the statute was passed. It may constitute relevant background evidence in a proceeding in which the status of a current practice is at issue, but separately considered, it is merely an unfortunate event in history which has no present legal consequences.

Respondent emphasizes the fact that she has alleged a *continuing* violation. United's seniority system does indeed have a continuing impact on her pay and fringe benefits. But the emphasis should not be placed on mere continuity; the critical question is whether any present *violation* exists. She has not alleged that the system discriminates against former female employees or that it treats former employees

9. Respondent cannot rely for jurisdiction on the single act of failing to assign her seniority credit for her prior service at the time she was rehired, for she filed her discrimination charge with the Equal Employment Opportunity Commission on February 21, 1973, more than one year after she was rehired on February 16, 1972. The applicable time limit in February 1972, was 90 days; effective March 24, 1972, this time was extended to 180 days, see n. 3, supra.

who were discharged for a discriminatory reason any differently from former employees who resigned or were discharged for a non-discriminatory reason. In short, the system is neutral in its operation.[10]

Our decision in Franks v. Bowman Transportation Co., supra, does not control this case. In *Franks* we held that retroactive seniority was an appropriate remedy to be awarded under § 706(g) of Title VII, 42 U.S.C. § 2000e–5(g) (1970 ed., Supp. V), after an illegal discriminatory act or practice had been proved, 424 U.S., at 762–768, 96 S.Ct., at 1263–1266. When that case reached this Court, the issues relating to the timeliness of the charge [11] and the violation of Title VII [12] had already been decided; we dealt only with a question of remedy. In contrast, in the case now before us we do not reach any remedy issue because respondent did not file a timely charge based on her 1968 separation and she has not alleged facts establishing a violation since she was rehired in 1972.[13]

The difference between a remedy issue and a violation issue is highlighted by the analysis of § 703(h) of Title VII in *Franks*.[14] As we held in that case, by its terms that section does not bar the award of retroactive seniority after a violation has been proved. Rather, § 703(h) "delineates which employment practices are illegal and thereby prohibited and which are not," 424 U.S., at 758, 96 S.Ct., at 1261.

That section expressly provides that it shall not be an unlawful employment practice to apply different terms of employment pursuant to a bona fide seniority system, provided that any disparity is not the result of intentional discrimination. Since respondent does not attack the bona fides of United's seniority system, and since she makes no charge that the system is intentionally designed to discriminate because of race, color, religion, sex, or national origin, § 703(h) provides an additional ground for rejecting her claim.

10. This case does not involve any claim by respondent that United's seniority system deterred her from asserting any right granted by Title VII. It does not present the question raised in the so-called departmental seniority cases. See, e.g., Quarles v. Philip Morris, Inc., 279 F.Supp. 505 (ED Va.1968).

11. The Court of Appeals had disposed of the timeliness issues in *Franks*, 495 F.2d 398, 405 (CA5 1974).

12. This finding of the District Court was unchallenged in the Court of Appeals, id., at 402, 403, and was assumed in this Court, 424 U.S., at 750, 96 S.Ct. at 1257.

In any event we noted in *Franks*: "The underlying legal wrong affecting [the class] is not the alleged operation of a racially discriminatory seniority system but of a racially discriminatory hiring system." Id., at 758, 96 S.Ct., at 1261.

13. At the time she was rehired in 1972, respondent had no greater right to a job than any other applicant for employment with United. Since she was in fact treated like any other applicant when she was rehired, the employer did not violate Title VII in 1972. And if the employer did not violate Title VII in 1972 by refusing to credit respondent with back seniority, its continued adherence to that policy cannot be illegal.

14. Section 703(h) 78 Stat. 257, 42 U.S.C. § 2000e–2(h), provides:

"Notwithstanding any other provision of this title, it shall not be an unlawful employment practice for an employer to apply different standards of compensation, or different terms, conditions, or privileges of employment pursuant to a bona fide seniority or merit system * * * provided that such differences are not the result of an intention to discriminate because of race, color, religion, sex, or national origin * * *."

The Court of Appeals read § 703(h) as intended to bar an attack on a seniority system based on the consequences of discriminatory acts which occurred prior to the effective date of Title VII in 1965,[15] but having no application to such attacks based on acts occurring after 1965. This reading of § 703(h) is too narrow. The statute does not foreclose attacks on the current operation of seniority systems which are subject to challenge as discriminatory. But such a challenge to a neutral system may not be predicated on the mere fact that a past event which has no present legal significance has affected the calculation of seniority credit, even if the past event might at one time have justified a valid claim against the employer. A contrary view would substitute a claim for seniority credit for almost every claim which is barred by limitations. Such a result would contravene the mandate of § 703(h).

The judgment of the Court of Appeals is reversed.

It is so ordered.

MR. JUSTICE MARSHALL, with whom MR. JUSTICE BRENNAN joins, dissenting.

But for her sex, respondent Carolyn Evans presently would enjoy all of the seniority rights that she seeks through this litigation. Petitioner United Air Lines has denied her those rights pursuant to a policy that perpetuates past discrimination by awarding the choicest jobs to those possessing a credential married women were unlawfully prevented from acquiring: continuous tenure with United. While the complaint respondent filed in the District Court was perhaps inartfully drawn,[1] it adequately draws into question this policy of United's.

For the reasons stated in the Court's opinion and in my separate opinion in Teamsters v. United States, 431 U.S. 324, 378, 97 S.Ct. 1843, 1875, 52 L.Ed.2d 396, I think it indisputable that, absent § 703(h), the seniority system at issue here would constitute an "unlawful employment practice" under Title VII, 42 U.S.C. § 2000e–2(a)(2) (1970 ed., Supp. V). And for the reasons developed at length in my separate opinion in *Teamsters*, I believe § 703(h) does not immunize seniority systems that perpetuate post-Act discrimination.

The only remaining question is whether Ms. Evans' complaint is barred by the applicable statute of limitations, 42 U.S.C. § 2000e–5(e) (1970 ed., Supp. V). Her cause of action accrued, if at all, at the time her seniority was recomputed after she was rehired. Although she apparently failed to file a charge with the EEOC within 180 days after her seniority was determined, Title VII recognizes that certain viola-

15. 534 F.2d, at 1251.

1. Although the District Court dismissed respondent's complaint for lack of jurisdiction pursuant to Fed.Rule Civ.Proc 12(b)(1), the basis for its ruling was that the complaint was time barred. Thus, the dismissal closely resembles a dismissal for failure to state a claim upon which relief can be granted, and the only issue before us is whether "it appears beyond doubt that the plaintiff can prove no set of facts in support of [her] claim which would entitle [her] to relief." Conley v. Gibson, 355 U.S. 41, 45–46, 78 S.Ct. 99, 101–102, 2 L.Ed. 2d 80 (1957).

tions, once commenced, are continuing in nature. In these instances, discriminatees can file charges at any time up to 180 days after the violation ceases. (They can, however, receive backpay only for the two years preceding the filing of charges with the Equal Employment Opportunity Commission. 42 U.S.C. § 2000e–5(g) (1970 ed., Supp. V).) In the instant case, the violation—treating respondent as a new employee even though she was wrongfully forced to resign—is continuing to this day. Respondent's charge therefore was not time barred, and the Court of Appeals judgment reinstating her complaint should be affirmed.[2]

DELAWARE STATE COLLEGE v. RICKS

Supreme Court of the United States, 1980.
449 U.S. 250, 101 S.Ct. 498, 66 L.Ed.2d 431.

JUSTICE POWELL delivered the opinion of the Court.

The question in this case is whether respondent, a college professor, timely complained under the civil rights laws that he had been denied academic tenure because of his national origin.

I

Columbus Ricks is a black Liberian. In 1970, Ricks joined the faculty at Delaware State College, a state institution attended predominantly by blacks. In February 1973, the Faculty Committee on Promotions and Tenure (the tenure committee) recommended that Ricks not receive a tenured position in the education department. The tenure committee, however, agreed to reconsider its decision the following year. Upon reconsideration, in February 1974, the committee adhered to its earlier recommendation. The following month, the Faculty Senate voted to support the tenure committee's negative recommendation. On March 13, 1974, the College Board of Trustees formally voted to deny tenure to Ricks.

Dissatisfied with the decision, Ricks immediately filed a grievance with the Board's Educational Policy Committee (the grievance committee), which in May 1974 held a hearing and took the matter under submission.[1] During the pendency of the grievance, the College admin-

2. It is, of course, true that to establish her entitlement to relief, respondent will have to prove that she was unlawfully forced to resign more than 180 days prior to filing her charge with the EEOC. But if that is sufficient to defeat her claim, then discriminatees will never be able to challenge "practices, procedures, or tests * * * [which] operate to 'freeze' the status quo of prior discriminatory employment practices," Griggs v. Duke Power Co., 401 U.S. 424, 430, 91 S.Ct. 849, 853, 28 L.Ed.2d 158 (1971), even though *Griggs* holds that such practices are impermissible, and the legislative history of the Equal Employment Opportunity Act of 1972, 86 Stat. 103, indicates that Congress agrees, see Teamsters v. United States, 431 U.S., at 391–393, 97 S.Ct., at 1883–1884 (MARSHALL, J., concurring in part and dissenting in part). The consequence of Ms. Evans' failure to file charges after she was discharged is that she has lost her right to backpay; not her right to challenge present wrongs.

1. According to the Court of Appeals, the grievance committee almost immediately recommended to the Board that Ricks' grievance be denied. Ricks v. Dela-

istration continued to plan for Ricks' eventual termination. Like many colleges and universities, Delaware State has a policy of not discharging immediately a junior faculty member who does not receive tenure. Rather, such a person is offered a "terminal" contract to teach one additional year. When that contract expires, the employment relationship ends. Adhering to this policy, the Trustees on June 26, 1974 told Ricks that he would be offered a one-year "terminal" contract that would expire June 30, 1975.[2] Ricks signed the contract without objection or reservation on September 4, 1974. Shortly thereafter, on September 12, 1974, the Board of Trustees notified Ricks that it had denied his grievance.

Ricks attempted to file an employment discrimination charge with the Equal Employment Opportunity Commission (EEOC) on April 4, 1975. Under Title VII, however, state fair employment practices agencies have primary jurisdiction over employment discrimination complaints. See 42 U.S.C. § 2000e–5(c). The EEOC therefore referred Ricks' charge to the appropriate Delaware agency. On April 28, 1975, the state agency waived its jurisdiction, and the EEOC accepted Ricks' complaint for filing. More than two years later, the EEOC issued a "right to sue" letter.

Ricks filed this lawsuit in the District Court on September 9, 1977.[3] The complaint alleged, *inter alia*, that the College had discriminated

ware State College, 605 F.2d 710, 711 (CA3 1979). Nothing in the record, however, reveals the date on which the grievance committee rendered its decision.

2. The June 26 letter stated:

"June 26, 1974

"Dr. Columbus Ricks
Delaware State College
Dover, Delaware

"Dear Dr. Ricks:

"On March 13, 1974, the Board of Trustees of Delaware State College officially endorsed the recommendations of the Faculty Senate at its March 11, 1974 meeting, at which time the Faculty Senate recommended that the Board not grant you tenure.

"As we are both aware, the Educational Policy Committee of the Board of Trustees has heard your grievance and it is now in the process of coming to a decision. The Chairman of the Educational Policy Committee has indicated to me that a decision may not be forthcoming until sometime in July. In order to comply with the 1971 Trustee Policy Manual and AAUP requirements with regard to the amount of time needed in proper notification of non-reappointment for non-tenured faculty members, the Board has no choice but to follow actions according to its official position prior to the grievance process, and thus, notify you of its intent not to renew your contract at the end of the 1974–75 school year.

"Please understand that we have no way of knowing what the outcome of the grievance process may be, and that this action is being taken at this time in order to be consistent with the present formal position of the Board and AAUP time requirements in matters of this kind. Should the Educational Policy Committee decide to recommend that you be granted tenure, and should the Board of Trustees concur with their recommendation, then of course, it will supersede any previous action taken by the Board.

"Sincerely yours,

"/s/Walton H. Simpson, President
Board of Trustees of Delaware State College"

3. In addition to the College itself, other defendants (petitioners in this Court) are Trustees Walton H. Simpson, William H. Davis, William G. Dix, Edward W. Hagemeyer, James C. Hardcastle, Delma Lafferty, James H. Williams, William S. Young, Burt C. Pratt, Luna I. Mishoe, and Pierre S. duPont IV (ex officio); the academic dean, M. Milford Caldwell (now de-

against him on the basis of his national origin in violation of Title VII and 42 U.S.C. § 1981.[4] The District Court sustained the College's motion to dismiss both claims as untimely. It concluded that the only unlawful employment practice alleged was the College's decision to deny Ricks' tenure, and that the limitations periods for both claims had commenced to run by June 26, 1974, when the President of the Board of Trustees officially notified Ricks that he would be offered a one-year "terminal" contract. See n.2, supra. The Title VII claim was not timely because Ricks had not filed his charge with the EEOC within 180 days after that date. Similarly, the § 1981 claim was not timely because the lawsuit had not been filed in the District Court within the applicable three-year statute of limitations.[5]

The Court of Appeals for the Third Circuit reversed. 605 F.2d 710 (1979). It agreed with the District Court that Ricks' essential allegation was that he had been denied tenure illegally. Id., at 711. According to the Court of Appeals, however, the Title VII filing requirement, and the statute of limitations for the § 1981 claim, did not commence to run until Ricks' "terminal" contract expired on June 30, 1975. The Court reasoned:

> "'[A] terminated employee who is still working should not be required to consult a lawyer or file charges of discrimination against his employer as long as he is still working, even though he has been told of the employer's present intention to terminate him in the future.'" Id., at 712, quoting Bonham v. Dresser Industries, Inc., 569 F.2d 187, 192 (CA3 1977), cert. denied, 439 U.S. 821, 99 S.Ct. 87, 58 L.Ed.2d 113 (1978).

The Court of Appeals believed that the initial decision to terminate an employee sometimes might be reversed. The aggrieved employee therefore should not be expected to resort to litigation until termination actually has occurred. Prior resort to judicial or administrative remedies would be

> "likely to have the negative side effect of reducing that employee's effectiveness during the balance of his or her term. Working relationships will be injured, if not sundered, and the litigation process will divert attention from the proper fulfillment of job responsibilities." 605 F.2d., at 712.

ceased); the education department chairman, George W. McLaughlin; and tenure committee members Romeo C. Henderson, Harriet R. Williams, Arthur E. Bragg, Ora Bunch, Ehsan Helmy, Vera Powell, John R. Price, Herbert Thompson, W. Richard Wynder, Ulysses Washington, and Jane Laskaris.

4. Section 1981 provides:

"All persons within the jurisdiction of the United States shall have the same right in every State and Territory to make and enforce contracts, to sue, be parties, give evidence, and to the full and equal benefit of all laws and proceedings for the security of persons and property as is enjoyed by white citizens, and shall be subject to like punishment, pains, penalties, taxes, licenses, and exactions of every kind, and to no other."

5. The statute of limitations in § 1981 cases is that applicable to similar claims under state law. Johnson v. Railway Express Agency, Inc., 421 U.S. 454, 462, 95 S.Ct. 1716, 1721, 44 L.Ed.2d 295 (1975). The parties in this case agree that the applicable limitations period under Delaware law is three years.

Finally, the Court of Appeals thought that a rule focusing on the last day of employment would provide a "bright line guide both for the courts and for the victims of discrimination." Id., at 712–713. It therefore reversed and remanded the case to the District Court for trial on the merits of Ricks' discrimination claims. We granted certiorari. 444 U.S. 1070, 100 S.Ct. 1012, 62 L.Ed.2d 751 (1980).

For the reasons that follow, we think that the Court of Appeals erred in holding that the filing limitations periods did not commence to run until June 30, 1975. We agree instead with the District Court that both the Title VII and § 1981 claims were untimely.[6] Accordingly, we reverse.

II

Title VII requires aggrieved persons to file a complaint with the EEOC "within one hundred and eighty days after the alleged unlawful employment practice occurred." 42 U.S.C. § 2000e–5(e).[7] Similarly, § 1981 plaintiffs in Delaware must file suit within three years of the unfavorable employment decision. See n.5, supra. The limitations periods, while guaranteeing the protection of the civil rights laws to those who promptly assert their rights, also protect employers from the burden of defending claims arising from employment decisions that are long past.

Determining the timeliness of Ricks' EEOC complaint, and this ensuing lawsuit, requires us to identify precisely the "unlawful employment practice" of which he complains. Ricks now insists that discrimination not only motivated the College in denying him tenure, but also in terminating his employment on June 30, 1975. Tr. of Oral Arg., at 25, 26, 31–32. In effect, he is claiming a "continuing violation" of the civil rights laws with the result that the limitations periods did not commence to run until his one-year "terminal" contract expired. This argument cannot be squared with the allegations of the complaint. Mere continuity of employment, without more, is insufficient to prolong the life of a cause of action for employment discrimination. United Air Lines v. Evans, supra, at 558, 97 S.Ct. at 1889. If Ricks intended to complain of a discriminatory discharge, he should have identified the alleged discriminatory acts that continued until, or occurred at the time of, the actual termination of his employment. But the complaint alleges no such facts.[8]

6. Because the claims were not timely filed, we do not decide whether a claim of national origin discrimination is cognizable under § 1981.

7. Under certain circumstances, the filing period is extended to 300 days. 42 U.S.C. § 2000e–5(e); see Mohasco Corp. v. Silver, 447 U.S. 807, 100 S.Ct. 2486, 65 L.Ed.2d 532 (1980).

8. Sixteen paragraphs in the complaint describe in detail the sequence of events surrounding the tenure denial. Only one paragraph even mentions Ricks' eventual departure from Delaware State, and nothing in that paragraph alleges any fact suggesting discrimination in the termination of Ricks' employment.

The complaint does allege that a variety of unusual incidents occurred during the 1974–1975 school year, including one in which the education department chairman, George W. McLaughlin, physically at-

Indeed, the contrary is true. It appears that termination of employment at Delaware State is a delayed, but inevitable, consequence of the denial of tenure. In order for the limitations periods to commence with the date of discharge, Ricks would have had to allege and prove that the manner in which his employment was terminated differed discriminatorily from the manner in which the College terminated other professors who also had been denied tenure. But no suggestion has been made that Ricks was treated differently from other unsuccessful tenure aspirants. Rather, in accord with the College's practice, Ricks was offered a one-year "terminal" contract, with explicit notice that his employment would end upon its expiration.

In sum, the only alleged discrimination occurred—and the filing limitations periods therefore commenced—at the time the tenure decision was made and communicated to Ricks.[9] That is so even though one of the *effects* of the denial of tenure—the eventual loss of a teaching position—did not occur until later. The Court of Appeals for the Ninth Circuit correctly held, in a similar tenure case, that "[t]he proper focus is upon the time of the *discriminatory acts*, not upon the time at which the *consequences* of the acts became most painful." Abramson v. University of Hawaii, 594 F.2d 202, 209 (1979) (emphasis added); see United Air Lines v. Evans, supra, at 558, 97 S.Ct. at 1889. It is simply insufficient for Ricks to allege that his termination "gives present effect to the past illegal act and therefore perpetuates the consequences of forbidden discrimination." Id. at 557, 97 S.Ct. at 1888. The emphasis is not upon the effects of earlier employment decisions; rather, it "is [upon] whether any present *violation* exists." Id. at 558, 97 S.Ct. at 1889 (emphasis in original).

III

We conclude for the foregoing reasons that the limitations periods commenced to run when the tenure decision was made and Ricks was notified. The remaining inquiry is the identification of this date.

A

Three dates have been advanced and argued by the parties. As indicated above, Ricks contended for June 30, 1975, the final date of his "terminal" contract, relying on a continuing violation theory. This contention fails, as we have shown, because of the absence of any allegations of facts to support it. The Court of Appeals agreed with

tacked Ricks. This incident allegedly resulted in McLaughlin's conviction for assault. Counsel for Ricks conceded at oral argument that incidents such as this were not independent acts of discrimination, Tr. of Oral Arg., at 29–30, but at most evidence that could be used at a trial.

9. Complaints that employment termination resulted from discrimination can present widely varying circumstances. In this case the only alleged discriminatory act is the denial of tenure sought by a college professor, with the termination of employment not occurring until a later date. The application of the general principles discussed herein necessarily must be made on a case-by-case basis.

Ricks that the relevant date was June 30, 1975, but it did so on a different theory. It found that the only alleged discriminatory act was the denial of tenure, 605 F.2d, at 711, but nevertheless adopted the "final date of employment" rule primarily for policy reasons. Ante, at 503. Although this view has the virtue of simplicity,[10] the discussion in Part II of this opinion demonstrates its fallacy as a rule of general application. Congress has decided that time limitations periods commence with the date of the "alleged unlawful employment practice." See 42 U.S.C. § 2000e-5(e). Where, as here, the only challenged employment practice occurs before the termination date, the limitations periods necessarily commence to run before that date.[11] It should not be forgotten that time-limitations provisions themselves promoted important interests; "the period allowed for instituting suit inevitably reflects a value judgment concerning the point at which the interests in favor of protecting valid claims are outweighed by the interests in prohibiting the prosecution of stale ones." Johnson v. Railway Express Agency, Inc., supra, at 463–464, 95 S.Ct. at 1721–1722.[12] See Mohasco Corp. v. Silver, 447 U.S. 807, at 820, 100 S.Ct. 2486, at 2494, 65 L.Ed.2d 532 (1980).

B

The EEOC, in its *amicus* brief, contends in the alternative for a different date. It was not until September 12, 1974, that the Board notified Ricks that his grievance had been denied. The EEOC therefore asserts that, for purposes of computing limitations periods, this was the date of the unfavorable tenure decision.[13] Two possible lines of reasoning underlie this argument. First, it could be contended that the Trustees' initial decision was only an expression of intent that did not become final until the grievance was denied. In support of this argu-

10. Brief for *amicus curiae* EEOC, at 19–22; Ricks v. Delaware State College, supra, at 712–713.

11. The Court of Appeals also thought it was significant that a final date of employment rule would permit the teacher to conclude his affairs at a school without the acrimony engendered by the filing of an administrative complaint or lawsuit. 605 F.2d at 712. It is true that "the filing of a lawsuit might tend to deter efforts at conciliation." Johnson v. Railway Express Agency, Inc., supra, at 461, 95 S.Ct. at 1720. But this is the "natural effect [ ] of the choice Congress has made," ibid., in explicitly requiring that the limitations period commence with the date of the "alleged unlawful employment practice," 42 U.S.C. § 2000e–5(c).

12. It is conceivable that the Court of Appeals' "final day of employment" rule might discourage colleges even from offering a "grace period," such as Delaware State's practice of one-year "terminal" contracts, during which the junior faculty member not offered tenure may seek a teaching position elsewhere.

13. If September 12 were the critical date, the § 1981 claim would be timely. Counting from September 12, the Title VII claim also would be timely if Ricks is entitled to 300 days, rather than 180 days, in which to file with the EEOC. In its brief before this Court, the EEOC as *amicus curiae* noted that Delaware is a state with its own fair employment practices agency. According to the EEOC, therefore, Ricks was entitled to 300 days to file his complaint. See n.7, supra. Because we hold that the time limitations periods commenced to run no later than June 26, 1974, we need not decide whether Ricks was entitled to 300 days to file under Title VII. Counting from the June 26 date, Ricks' filing with the EEOC was not timely even with the benefit of the 300-day period.

ment, the EEOC notes that the June 26 letter explicitly held out to Ricks the possibility that he would receive tenure if the Board sustained his grievance. See n.2, supra. Second, even if the Board's first decision expressed its official position, it could be argued that the pendency of the grievance should toll the running of the limitations periods.

We do not find either argument to be persuasive. As to the former, we think that the Board of Trustees had made clear well before September 12 that it had formally rejected Ricks' tenure bid. The June 26 letter itself characterized that as the Board's "official position." Ibid. It is apparent, of course, that the Board in the June 26 letter indicated a willingness to change its prior decision if Ricks' grievance were found to be meritorious. But entertaining a grievance complaining of the tenure decision does not suggest that the earlier decision was in any respect tentative. The grievance procedure, by its nature, is a *remedy* for a prior decision, not an opportunity to *influence* that decision before it is made.

As to the latter argument, we already have held that the pendency of a grievance, or some other method of collateral review of an employment decision, does not toll the running of the limitations periods. International Union of Electrical Workers v. Robbins & Myers, Inc., 429 U.S. 229, 97 S.Ct. 441, 50 L.Ed.2d 427 (1976).[14] The existence of careful procedures to assure fairness in the tenure decision should not obscure the principle that limitations periods normally commence when the employer's decision is made. Cf. id., at 234–235, 97 S.Ct. at 446.[15]

C

The District Court rejected both the June 30, 1975 date and the September 12, 1974 date, and concluded that the limitations periods had commenced to run by June 26, 1974, when the President of the Board notified Ricks that he would be offered a "terminal" contract for the 1974–1975 school year. We cannot say that this decision was erroneous. By June 26, the tenure committee had twice recommended that Ricks not receive tenure; the Faculty Senate had voted to support the tenure committee's recommendation; and the Board of Trustees formally had voted to deny Ricks tenure.[16] In light of this unbroken

14. See also B. Schlei & P. Grossman, Employment Discrimination Law, 235 (1979 Supp.), and cases cited therein.

15. We do not suggest that aspirants for academic tenure should ignore available opportunities to request reconsideration. Mere requests to reconsider, however, cannot extend the limitations periods applicable to the civil rights laws.

16. We recognize, of course, that the limitations periods should not commence to run so soon that it becomes difficult for a layman to invoke the protection of the civil rights statutes. See Oscar Mayer & Co. v. Evans, 441 U.S. 750, 761, 99 S.Ct. 2066, 2073 (1979); Love v. Pullman Co., 404 U.S. 522, 526–527, 92 S.Ct. 616, 618, 30 L.Ed.2d 679 (1972). But, for the reasons we have stated, there can be no claim here that Ricks was not abundantly forewarned. In NLRB v. Yeshiva University, 444 U.S. 672, 674, 100 S.Ct. 856, at 859, 63 L.Ed.2d 115 (1980), we noted that university boards of trustees customarily rely on the professional expertise of the tenured faculty, particularly with respect to decisions about hiring, tenure, termination, and promotion. Thus, the action of the Board of

array of negative decisions, the District Court was justified in concluding that the College had established its official position—and made that position apparent to Ricks—no later than June 26, 1974.[17]

We therefore reverse the decision of the Court of Appeals and remand to that Court so that it may reinstate the District Court's order dismissing the complaint.

Reversed.

JUSTICE STEWART, with whom JUSTICE BRENNAN and JUSTICE MARSHALL join, dissenting.

I agree with the Court that the unlawful employment practice alleged in the respondent's complaint was a discriminatory denial of tenure, not a discriminatory termination of employment. Nevertheless, I believe that a fair reading of the complaint reveals a plausible allegation that the College actually denied Ricks' tenure on September 12, 1974, the date on which the Board finally confirmed its decision to accept the faculty's recommendation that he not be given tenure.

Therefore, unlike the Court, I think Ricks should be allowed to prove to the District Court that the allegedly unlawful denial of tenure occurred on that date.[1] As noted by the Court, if Ricks succeeds in this proof, his § 1981 claim would certainly be timely, and the timeliness of his Title VII claim would then depend on whether his filing of a complaint with the Delaware Department of Labor entitled him to file his EEOC charge within 300 days of the discriminatory act, rather than within the 180 days limitation that the Court of Appeals and the District Court assumed to be applicable.[2]

A brief examination of the June 26, 1974 letter to Ricks from the Board of Trustees, quoted by the Court, provides a reasonable basis for

Trustees on March 13, 1974, affirming the faculty recommendation, was entirely predictable. The Board's letter of June 26, 1974 simply repeated to Ricks the Board's official position and acknowledged the pendency of the grievance through which Ricks hopes to persuade the Board to change that position.

17. We need not decide whether the District Court correctly focused on the June 26 date, rather than the date the Board communicated to Ricks its unfavorable tenure decision made at the March 13, 1974 meeting. As we have stated, see n.13, supra, both the Title VII and § 1981 complaints were not timely filed even counting from the June 26 date.

1. The Court treats the District Court's determination of June 26, 1974, as the date of tenure denial as a factual finding which is not clearly erroneous. But it must be stressed that the District Court dismissed Ricks' claims on the pleadings, and so never made factual determinations on this or any other issue.

2. Title VII would allow Ricks 300 days if he had "initially instituted" proceedings with a local or state agency with authority to grant him relief. 42 U.S.C. § 2000e–5(b); see Mohasco Corp. v. Silver, 447 U.S. 807, 808, 100 S.Ct. 2486, at 2488, 65 L.Ed. 2d 532. To benefit from this provision, however, Ricks would arguably have had to make a timely filing with the state agency. Delaware law requires that a charge of discrimination be filed with the Department of Labor within 90 days after the allegedly discriminatory practice occurred or within 120 days after the practice is discovered, whichever date is later. Del. Code Ann. tit. 19, § 712(d). Neither the District Court nor the Court of Appeals considered the timliness Ricks' filing with the state agency, nor the significance of the state agency's action in waiving jurisdiction over Ricks' charge, and so these questions would be appropriately addressed on remand.

the allegation that the College did not effectively deny Ricks' tenure until September 12. The letter informed Ricks of the Board's "intent not to renew" his contract at the end of the 1974–1975 academic year. And the letter suggested that the Board was so informing Ricks at that time only to ensure technical compliance with College and AAUP requirements in case it should *later* decide to abide by its earlier acceptance of the faculty's recommendation that Ricks be denied tenure. The Board expressly stated in the letter that it had "no way of knowing" what the outcome of the grievance process might be, but that a decision of the Board's Educational Policy Committee favorable to Ricks would "of course * * * supersede any previous action taken by the Board."

Thus, the Board itself may have regarded its earlier actions as tentative or preliminary, pending a thorough review triggered by the respondent's request to the Committee. The Court acknowledges that this letter expresses the Board's willingness to change its earlier view on Ricks' tenure, but considers the grievance procedure under which the decision might have been changed to be a remedy for an earlier tenure decision and not a part of the overall process of making the initial tenure decision. Ricks, however, may be able to prove to the District Court that at his College, the original Board response to the faculty's recommendation was not a virtually final action subject to reopening only in the most extreme cases, but a preliminary decision to shift the burden from the College to the tenure candidate, and to advance the tenure question to the Board's grievance committee as the next conventional stage in the process.[3]

Whether this is an accurate view of the tenure process at Delaware State College is, of course, a factual question we cannot resolve here. But Ricks lost his case in the trial court on a motion to dismiss. I think that motion was wrongly granted, and that Ricks was entitled to a hearing and a determination of this factual issue. See Abramson v. University of Hawaii, 594 F.2d 202 (CA9).

I would, therefore, vacate the judgment of the Court of Appeals and remand the case to the District Court so that it can make this determination and then, if necessary, resolve whether Title VII allowed Ricks 300 days from the denial of tenure to file his charge with the Commission.

JUSTICE STEVENS, dissenting.

The custom widely followed by colleges and universities of offering a one-year terminal contract immediately after making an adverse tenure decision is, in my judgment, analogous to the custom in many other personnel relationships of giving an employee two weeks advance notice

3. This view is consistent with the policies and model procedures of the American Association of University Professors, AAUP Policy Documents and Reports 15, 29 (1977); see Board of Regents v. Roth, 408 U.S. 564, 578–579, n.17, 92 S.Ct. 2701, 2710, n. 17, 33 L.Ed.2d 548; AAUP *Amicus* Brief, at 9–10, on whose requirements the Board of Trustees in this case expressly relied in explaining its action in the June 26 letter.

of discharge. My evaluation of this case can perhaps best be explained by that analogy.

Three different reference points could arguably determine when a cause of action for a discriminatory discharge accrues: (1) when the employer decides to terminate the relationship; (2) when notice of termination is given to the employee; and (3) when the discharge becomes effective. The most sensible rule would provide that the date of discharge establishes the time when a cause of action accrues and the statute of limitations begins to run. Prior to that date, the allegedly wrongful act is subject to change; more importantly, the effective discharge date is the date which can normally be identified with the least difficulty or dispute.[1]

I would apply the same reasoning here in identifying the date on which respondent's allegedly discriminatory discharge became actionable. See Egelston v. State University College at Geneseo, 535 F.2d 752, 755 (CA2 1976). Thus under my analysis the statute of limitations began to run on June 30, 1975, the termination date of respondent's one year contract. In reaching that conclusion, I do not characterize the college's discharge decision as a "continuing violation"; nor do I suggest that a teacher who is denied tenure and who remains in a school's employ for an indefinite period could file a timely complaint based on the tenure decision when he or she is ultimately discharged. Rather, I regard a case such as this one, in which a college denies tenure and offers a terminal one year contract as part of the adverse tenure decision, as a discharge case. The decision to deny tenure in this situation is in all respects comparable to another employer's decision to discharge an employee and, in due course, to give the employee notice of the effective date of that discharge. Both the interest in harmonious working relations during the terminal period of the employment relationship,[2] and the interest in certainty that is so important in litigation of this kind,[3] support this result.

1. Although few courts have had the occasion to consider the issue in the context of notice of discharge preceding actual termination, some courts have recognized that the date on which the employee actually ceases to perform services for the employer, and not a later date when the payment of benefits or accrued vacation time ceases, should determine the running of the statute of limitations. See Bonham v. Dresser Industries, Inc., 569 F.2d 187, 192 (CA3 1977), cert. denied, 439 U.S. 821, 99 S.Ct. 87, 58 L.Ed.2d 113 (1978); Krzyzewski v. Metropolitan Government of Nashville and Davidson County, 584 F.2d 802, 804–805 (CA6 1978).

2. This interest has special force in the college setting. Because the employee must file a charge with the EEOC within 180 days after the occurrence, the Court's analysis will necessitate the filing of a charge while the teacher is still employed. The filing of such a charge may prejudice any pending reconsideration of the tenure decision and also may impair the teacher's performance of his or her regular duties. Neither of these adverse consequences would be present in a discharge following a relatively short notice such as two weeks.

3. The interest in certainty lies not only in choosing the most easily identifiable date, but also in avoiding the involvement of the EEOC until the school's decision to deny tenure is final. The American Association of University Professors, as *amicus curiae* here, has indicated that under the "prevailing academic employment practices" of American higher education, which allow for maximum flexibility in tenure decisions, initial tenure determinations are often reconsidered, and the reconsideration process may take the better part of the

For these reasons, I would affirm the judgment of the Court of Appeals.

NOTES AND PROBLEMS FOR DISCUSSION

1. Is a denial of tenure fundamentally different from a notice of discharge? Should the period for filing in the latter case run from the date the employee learns of his discharge or from his last day of work? In CHARDON v. FERNANDEZ, 454 U.S. 6, 102 S.Ct. 28, 70 L.Ed.2d 6 (1981), a case filed under 42 U.S.C. § 1983, the Supreme Court concluded that that situation was indistinguishable from Delaware State College v. Ricks and held that the "unlawful employment practice" (from which date the limitation period runs) occurred when the allegedly unlawful decision to discharge occurred. Justice Brennan dissented:

> It is one thing to hold, as was held in Delaware State College v. Ricks, * * * that for the purpose of computing the limitations period, a cause of action for denial of a benefit such as tenure, and consequent damage, accrues when the plaintiff learns that he *has been* denied that benefit; it is quite another to hold, as the Court does here, that a cause of action for damages resulting from an unconstitutional termination of employment accrues when the plaintiff learns that he *will* be terminated. To my knowledge, such a rule has no analogue in customary principles of limitations law. See 4 A. Corbin, Contracts sec. 989 ("The plaintiff should not be penalized for leaving to the defendant an opportunity to retract his wrongful repudiation; and he will be so penalized if the statutory period of limitation is held to begin to run against him immediately.")
>
> The thrust of the Court's decision is to require a potential civil rights plaintiff to measure the time for filing his claim from the moment some form of injunctive relief first becomes available. The effect of this ruling will be to increase the number of unripe and anticipatory lawsuits in the federal courts—lawsuits that should not be filed until some concrete harm has been suffered, and until the parties, and the forces of time, have had maximum opportunity to resolve the controversy.

102 S.Ct. at 29.

The question of when the plaintiff knew or reasonably should have known of the alleged discriminatory action so as to trigger the filing period has continued to trouble the courts. In Janowiak v. City of South Bend, 750 F.2d 557 (7th Cir. 1984), a white applicant for a firefighter position was rejected because of an affirmative action plan that favored minority applicants. He filed his EEOC charge more than 180 days after the decision not to hire him, but less than 180 days after the last minority applicant was hired under the plan. The Court held that, although plaintiff was not informed in writing of the hiring decision, he should have learned of it within the filing period, because he had a copy of the minority and non-minority rankings under the plan and because of extensive publicity in the local news media. Compare, Shockley v. Vermont State Colleges, 38 FEP Cases 1523 (D.Vt.1984) (filing period for terminated faculty member tolled until last day of actual employment where plaintiff was led to believe he would be reappointed by fact that others in his position who received letters of non-reappointment were eventually reappointed and by statements

terminal contract year. American Association of University Professors *Amicus* Brief, at 6–11.

made by dean of institution that he expected plaintiff would return to work) with Mull v. Arco Durethene Plastics, Inc., 784 F.2d 284 (7th Cir. 1986) (neither employer's failure to send employee written notice of termination nor employee's optimistic hopes for continued employment based on his assignment to long-term projects tolled filing period where claimant knew that he would be terminated at year's end).

2. If a female employee is paid less than male employees who perform the same work, because she is a woman, when does the "unlawful employment practice" occur for purposes of beginning the Section 706 period for filing a charge? On the day her salary is set? On the day she learns of the discrimination? On her last day at work? See Hall v. Ledex, Inc., 669 F.2d 397, 398–399 (6th Cir. 1982); Roberts v. North American Rockwell Corp., 650 F.2d 823, 827–828 (6th Cir. 1981). But see Battle v. Clark Equipment, 524 F.Supp. 683 (N.D. Ind. 1981) (application of Delaware State College v. Ricks to alleged discriminatory distribution of supplemented unemployment pay). Should a refusal to hire constitute a continuing violation? Compare Acha v. Beame, 570 F.2d 57, 65 (2d Cir. 1978) with East v. Romine, Inc., 518 F.2d 332 (5th Cir. 1975) and Collins v. United Air Lines, Inc., 514 F.2d 594 (9th Cir. 1975). Does the failure to promote an employee constitute a continuing violation during his entire course of employment? Compare, Glass v. Petro-Tex Chemical Corp., 757 F.2d 1554 (5th Cir. 1985) (plaintiff could not be expected to know that first denial of promotion, five years before her EEOC charge, was itself actionable) with Woodard v. Lehman, 717 F.2d 909 (4th Cir. 1983) (no discriminatory action within filing period, *Evans* applied). Are there any circumstances under which a demotion could constitute part of a continuing violation? See, Taylor v. Homes Insurance Co., 777 F.2d 849 (4th Cir. 1985).

In Shehadeh v. Chesapeake & Potomac Telephone Co., 595 F.2d 711 (D.C.Cir. 1978), the Court of Appeals reversed the dismissal of an action filed by a woman who claimed she was discharged in violation of Title VII. The plaintiff alleged that she was fired because of her sex and because of her husband's national origin, and that the former employer had continued to discriminate against her by disseminating untrue information about her to prospective employers. The Court of Appeals upheld her right to bring suit despite her failure to file an EEOC charge until nearly five years after the original discharge. The court noted that "[w]hen * * * a continuing discriminatory employment practice is alleged, the administrative complaint may be timely filed notwithstanding that the conduct impugned is comprised in part of acts lying outside of the charge-filing period." 595 F.2d at 724. The court justified its ruling on the ground that the plaintiff had alleged that the employer harbored a continuing, unlawful bias against her. The charge "made plain that the specified event [which took place two years before the date of the charge] was illustrative of a long-lasting pattern of like events." 595 F.2d at 725. In Zipes v. Trans World Airlines, Inc., 455 U.S. 385, 102 S.Ct. 1127, 71 L.Ed.2d 234 (1982), the Court noted that the "particular purpose" of the filing requirement is "to give prompt notice to the employer." Is it fair to the employer to allow a former employee to challenge a five-year old discharge by alleging that a "continuing violation" has occurred? Does the *Shehadeh* decision mean that in a continuing violation case, the employee may obtain relief (for example, reinstatement) for the first of the discriminatory actions? See infra p. 782.

3. The Relation Between the Substance of the EEOC Charge and Suit

JENKINS v. BLUE CROSS MUTUAL HOSPITAL INSURANCE, INC.

United States Court of Appeals, Seventh Circuit, 1976.
538 F.2d 164, cert. denied, 429 U.S. 986, 97 S.Ct. 506, 50 L.Ed.2d 598.

SPRECHER, CIRCUIT JUDGE.

This appeal reheard in banc concentrates on whether the alleged victim of racial and sex discrimination made sufficiently like or reasonably related allegations in her charges to the Equal Employment Opportunity Commission to support, and out of which could grow or reasonably be expected to grow, the racial and sex allegations in her judicial complaint.

I.

The plaintiff brought this action on her own behalf and on behalf of other persons similarly situated as a class action, charging the defendants, her former employers, with denying her promotions and better assignments, and with ultimately terminating her employment because of her "race, sex, black styles of hair and dress," in violation of Title VII of the Civil Rights Act of 1964, 42 U.S.C. § 2000e et seq. and 42 U.S.C. § 1981. The plaintiff sought declaratory and injunctive relief, reinstatement with backpay and other money damages.

On July 17, 1974, the district court denied the plaintiff's motion seeking an order pursuant to F.R.Civ.P. 23(c)(1) determining that the action be maintainable as a class action.[1] The court stated that "a Title VII complaint must be viewed in relationship to the charges filed by the plaintiff against the defendant before the Equal Employment Opportunity Commission." The court's reasoning in denying certification of a class action was that: (1) "[i]t is clear that she did not raise sex before the EEOC * * *"; (2) "[w]hile there is an arguable connection to race by the allegation of hair style discrimination, such is not sufficient to raise the panorama of alleged [racial] evils plaintiff seeks to adjudicate in her complaint"; (3) "[h]er class could, therefore, only be composed of those persons denied promotion or not hired for wearing an Afro hair style"; and (4) "[n]o proof has been presented to the Court to show that this group of people would be so large that joinder of them in this action would be impracticable."

On January 21, 1975, the district court denied the plaintiff's motion for a preliminary injunction. The plaintiff's notice of appeal was from both the July 17, 1974 and January 21, 1975 orders.

1. Chronologically the defendants first filed a motion for a determination that the action *not* be maintainable as a class action and subsequently the plaintiff filed a cross motion for a determination that it be so maintainable. The district court order recites the existence of both motions and generally orders that "this action not be maintained as a class action" but in the accompanying "memorandum entry" only the plaintiff's motion is recited as denied.

Upon this appeal a panel of this court reversed the district court's judgment "[i]n light of the fact that the trial court dismissed the complaint because of the failure of the named plaintiff to qualify as representative of her class under Title VII, without giving consideration to the claim based on § 1981, and since we conclude that the relief claimed under § 1981 need not be based on any form of claim filed with the EEOC * * *." Jenkins v. Blue Cross Mutual Hospital Insurance, Inc., 522 F.2d 1235, 1241 (7th Cir. 1975). The case was remanded for the district court to give consideration to whether the plaintiff could qualify as a representative of the class upon her § 1981 claim, which alleged only racial discrimination, and thereafter to consider "what equitable relief the plaintiff may be entitled to." Id. at 1242.

* * *

* * * The district court had concluded that the plaintiff's EEOC charges limited her Title VII court complaint to charges of discrimination because of her wearing an Afro hair style. The original appeal panel consisting of Judges Tuttle,[3] Tone and Bauer was "unanimously of the view that the [EEOC] charge does not form the proper basis under Title VII for any complaint of discrimination on the basis of sex." 522 F.2d at 1241. Judges Tone and Bauer also agreed with the district court that the EEOC charge did not support allegations of racial discrimination beyond those due to wearing an Afro hair style. "Judge Tuttle would hold that the charge was sufficient under the announced standard to support the [racial] allegations of the complaint." Id.

Upon the rehearing in banc a majority of the entire court[4] concluded that the judgment should be reversed and remanded not only because of the § 1981 claim but also because the plaintiff's EEOC charges adequately support her judicial complaints of racial and sex discrimination.

The plaintiff's charge form, filed on June 8, 1971, with the EEOC, showed a check mark in the box on the form to indicate that the discrimination was because of "Race or Color" but no check mark appeared in the box preceded by the word "Sex." The explanation the plaintiff gave on the form for the discrimination was:

> I feel that I am being discriminated in the terms and conditions of my employment because of my race, Negro. I have worked for Blue Cross and Blue Shield approx. 3 years during which time I [had] no problem until May 1970 when I got my natural hair style. Later when I came up for promotion it was denied because my supervisor, Al Frymier, said I could never represent Blue Cross with my Afro. He also accused me of being the leader of the girls on the floor. The pressures I was working under kept me upset, therefore, I asked for

3. Honorable Elbert P. Tuttle, United States Circuit Judge, Fifth Circuit, had been sitting by designation, and wrote the panel's opinion.

4. The argument on rehearing and consideration of the case took place before the induction of Judge Harlington Wood, Jr., to fill the vacancy created by the elevation of Judge John Paul Stevens to the Supreme Court on December 19, 1975.

> a leave of absence. I was told I had to take a vacation before I could be granted leave of absence. I was granted a week vacation and on my return I was asked to take a 90 day leave, quit, or be fired, time they said to get myself together; and at the end of this time they would be able to place me on another job. A White employee who associated with me might have been denied her promotion because of her association with me.

The plaintiff received her statutory notice of her right to sue from the EEOC on August 4, 1972 and filed her complaint in the district court on August 28, 1972.

The entire court accepts the standard referred to in the panel decision as the guiding principle in its determination, namely that set forth in Danner v. Phillips Petroleum Co., 447 F.2d 159, 162 (5th Cir. 1971):

> The correct rule to follow in construing EEOC charges for purposes of delineating the proper scope of a subsequent judicial inquiry is that "the complaint in the civil action * * * may properly encompass any * * * discrimination like or reasonably related to the allegations of the charge and growing out of such allegations."

The majority parts with the panel in its application of the standard.

In Haines v. Kerner, 404 U.S. 519, 520, 92 S.Ct. 594, 596, 30 L.Ed.2d 652 (1972), the Supreme Court unanimously expressed its opinion that "we hold to less stringent standards [the allegations of a *pro se* complaint] than formal pleadings drafted by lawyers * * *." In a case also unanimously decided a few days later, Love v. Pullman Co., 404 U.S. 522, 527, 92 S.Ct. 616, 619, 30 L.Ed.2d 679 (1972), involving EEOC procedure, the Court said that "technicalities are particularly inappropriate in a statutory scheme in which laymen, unassisted by trained lawyers, initiated the process."

We have held that Title VII is to "be construed and applied broadly," Motorola, Inc. v. McLain, 484 F.2d 1339, 1344 (7th Cir. 1973), and in doing so, we have recognized that EEOC charges are in layman's language, Cox v. United States Gypsum Co., 409 F.2d 289, 290–291 (7th Cir. 1969). The context in which we must operate was well stated by Judge Bauer in Willis v. Chicago Extruded Metals Co., 375 F.Supp. 362, 365–366 (N.D.Ill.1974) (footnotes omitted):

> [T]he Civil Rights Act is designed to protect those who are least able to protect themselves. Complainants to the EEOC are seldom lawyers. To compel the charging party to specifically articulate in a charge filed with the Commission the full panoply of discrimination which he may have suffered may cause the very persons Title VII was designed to protect to lose that protection because they are ignorant of or unable to thoroughly describe the discriminatory practices to which they are subjected. * * *
>
> [T]he EEOC charges simply stated in laymen's language the "unfair thing that happened" to the plaintiff, that is, the discriminatory discharge * * *.

This policy of being "solicitous of the Title VII plaintiff" has been expressed by many courts. Gamble v. Birmingham Southern R.R., 514 F.2d 678, 687–689 (5th Cir. 1975); Danner v. Phillips Petroleum Co., supra, at 161–162; Sanchez v. Standard Brands, Inc., 431 F.2d 455, 463 (5th Cir. 1970).

In the present case the plaintiff checked the EEOC form box stating that the "discrimination [was] because of * * * Race or Color." She began describing the "unfair thing done" to her by saying that "I feel that I am being discriminated in the terms and conditions of my employment because of my race, Negro." She said that her supervisor denied her a promotion because she "could never represent Blue Cross with my Afro." A lay person's description of racial discrimination could hardly be more explicit. The reference to the Afro hairstyle was merely the method by which the plaintiff's supervisor allegedly expressed the employer's racial discrimination. The plaintiff stated that for three years prior to wearing her Afro hairstyle, she had no problem. As we have said, "[a] single charge may 'launch a full scale inquiry'" into racial discrimination. Motorola, Inc. v. McLain, supra, at 1346.

The majority agrees with Judge Tuttle's minority position in the panel decision that the EEOC charge was sufficient to support the racial discrimination allegations of the complaint. 522 F.2d at 1241. Judge Tuttle reached the same conclusion speaking for the Fifth Circuit in Smith v. Delta Air Lines, Inc., 486 F.2d 512 (5th Cir. 1973), where the court held that a charge alleging discrimination stemming from grooming requirements which applied particularly to black persons constituted a sufficient charge of racial discrimination when accompanied by substantially the same general allegation of racial discrimination as here.

In regard to sex discrimination, it is true that the plaintiff did not check the sex discrimination box on the EEOC form. In Sanchez v. Standard Brands, Inc., supra, at 462–464, the reverse situation had occurred. The plaintiff had checked only the box labeled "sex" and in her judicial complaint alleged discrimination because of her "national origin." The Fifth Circuit said:

> * * * [W]e decline to hold that the failure to place a check mark in the correct box is a fatal error. In the context of Title VII, no one—not even the unschooled—should be boxed out.

In Wetzel v. Liberty Mutual Insurance Co., 511 F.2d 199, 202–203 (3d Cir. 1975), vacated on other grounds, 424 U.S. 737, 96 S.Ct. 1202, 47 L.Ed.2d 435, 44 U.S.L.W. 4350 (1976), an alleged victim of sex discrimination checked the wrong box. The court held that lay persons were not to be denied access to the federal courts because of a technical error. Finally, in Vuyanich v. Republic National Bank, 409 F.Supp. 1083 (N.D.Tex.1976), the plaintiff's EEOC charge expressly stated only racial prejudice whereas her judicial complaint alleged both racial and sexual discrimination. The court held that she could proceed on both grounds inasmuch as her EEOC form stated that her superior told her that she [a black female] "probably did not need a job anyway, because her husband was a Caucasian." Id., at 1985. The court concluded that such a statement discriminated against both black persons and females since it could not be made to either a white person or a male. Id., at 1089.

In the present case, the plaintiff charged to the EEOC that her superior, in addition to referring to her Afro hairstyle, "also accused me of being a leader of the girls on the floor." The plaintiff then stated that "[a] White employee who associated with me might have been denied her promotion because of her association with me." These statements taken in conjunction with the charges of racial discrimination also charge sex discrimination.

In Danner v. Phillips Petroleum Co., supra, at 161–163, the case relied upon by the panel here in its original decision, the court held that the alleged victim of sex discrimination adequately charged it to the EEOC where all she charged was that "[t]herefore due to the fact that my position was not eliminated, just taken from me and given to a man, I feel that I have been mistreated and damaged."

The majority of this court conclude that the plaintiff sufficiently charged both racial and sex discrimination in her EEOC form in order to be eligible to represent a class composed of "all black and female persons who are employed, or might be employed, by Blue Cross-Blue Shield, Inc." * * *

The judgment is reversed and the case is remanded for further proceedings not inconsistent with this opinion.

TONE, CIRCUIT JUDGE, with whom PELL and BAUER, CIRCUIT JUDGES, (dissenting).

I agree with the majority's statement of the governing legal principles. My only disagreement is in the reading of plaintiff's charge filed with the EEOC, which is quoted in full in the majority opinion. The reader of these opinions can judge for himself whether the present challenges to defendant's recruitment and promotion practices, including testing, pay scale, and job-qualification standards (see 522 F.2d at 1240 n.9), are "like or reasonably related to the allegations of the [EEOC] charge and growing out of such allegations."* See Danner v. Phillips Petroleum Co., 447 F.2d 159, 162 (5th Cir. 1971). It appears to me that plaintiff made it clear she was not complaining about such practices when she said in her EEOC charge:

"I have worked for Blue Cross and Blue Shield approximately 3 years during which time I [had] no problem until May 1970 when I got my natural hair style."

* I do not include among the allegations which are not supported by the charge the one to the effect that black employees were required to observe white hair styles and dress styles (item b in footnote 9, 522 F.2d at 1240–1241), which I think does satisfy the *Danner* test.

I can find nothing elsewhere in the charge that contradicts or qualifies this statement and nothing that suggests a pattern and practice charge based on race or sex. (I attach no significance to the failure to check the box marked "Sex.") She seems to me to be saying that after three years of employment about which she has no complaints she had her hair styled in an Afro fashion, and was unfairly treated because of that. If the relatedness or growing-out-of requirement is to be abolished, I would have no objection. I cannot agree, however, that if there is to be such a requirement it has been satisfied with respect to the pattern and practice charges described above.

NOTES AND PROBLEMS FOR DISCUSSION

1. In Sanchez v. Standard Brands, Inc., the Fifth Circuit decision cited by the majority in *Jenkins*, the court clarified the "reasonably related" test as follows:

> [T]he civil action is much more intimately related to the EEOC investigation than to the words of the charge which originally triggered the investigation. Within this statutory scheme, it is only logical to limit the permissible scope of the civil action to the scope of the EEOC investigation which can reasonably be expected to grow out of the charge of discrimination.

431 F.2d at 466. See also Gamble v. Birmingham Southern Railroad Co., 514 F.2d 678, 688 (5th Cir. 1975) (*Sanchez* test hinges on whether broader EEOC investigation might be expected to grow from original charge). The Fifth Circuit's liberal standard for application of the "reasonably related" test has been adopted by most circuits. See, e.g., Smith v. American President Lines, 571 F.2d 102, 107 n.10 (2d Cir. 1978); EEOC v. Bailey Co., Inc., 563 F.2d 439, 446 (6th Cir. 1977), cert. denied, 435 U.S. 915, 98 S.Ct. 1468, 55 L.Ed.2d 506 (1978); Ostapowicz v. Johnson Bronze Co., 541 F.2d 394, 399 (3d Cir. 1976), cert. denied, 429 U.S. 1041, 97 S.Ct. 741, 50 L.Ed.2d 753 (1977). But see Nance v. Union Carbide Corp., 540 F.2d 718, 727 (4th Cir. 1976), vacated on other grounds, 431 U.S. 952, 97 S.Ct. 2671, 53 L.Ed.2d 268 (1977) (Title VII suit "may encompass only the 'discrimination stated in the charge itself or developed in the course of a reasonable investigation of that charge' "); King v. Seaboard Coast Line Railroad Co., 538 F.2d 581, 583 (4th Cir. 1976).

Some courts have interpreted *Sanchez* to mean that any practice which is an outgrowth of the kind of discrimination alleged in the charge can be challenged in the court suit. See Graniteville Co. v. EEOC, 438 F.2d 32, 41–42 (4th Cir. 1971) (discrimination in promotion related to discrimination in hiring); Falcon v. General Telephone Co., 626 F.2d 369, 377 (5th Cir. 1980), vacated on other grounds, 450 U.S. 1036 (1981), on remand, 647 F.2d 633 (5th Cir. 1981), cert. granted, 454 U.S. 1097, 102 S.Ct. 668, 70 L.Ed.2d 637; McBride v. Delta Air Lines, 551 F.2d 113, 115 (6th Cir. 1977), vacated on other grounds, 434 U.S. 916, 98 S.Ct. 387, 54 L.Ed.2d 273 (discharge claim justified review of all allegedly racially discriminatory practices). But could an EEOC investigation of religious discrimination "reasonably be expected" to grow out of a charge alleging only racial discrimination? See EEOC v. Bailey, supra. Is a charge of discrimination on the basis of national origin reasonably related to a claim of race discrimination? Compare Shah v. Mt. Zion Hospital & Medical Center, 642 F.2d 268 (9th Cir. 1981) with Kahn v. Pepsi Cola Bottling Group, 526 F.Supp. 1268 (E.D.N.Y. 1981).

What is the purpose of limiting the subject matter jurisdiction of the court to matters "reasonably related" to those in the EEOC charge? Is the purpose to give notice to the employer of the "ballpark" the charge is in or is it to insure that the EEOC has an opportunity to investigate all charges that may be litigated? See, Reiter v. Center Consolidated School District, 618 F.Supp. 1458 (D.Col.1985) (fact that plaintiff did not charge national origin discrimination in EEOC charge irrelevant since state FEP agency determined that plaintiff was discriminated against because of her perceived association with Hispanic community and employer was notified of finding before EEOC issued right to sue notice). Would it be consistent with the purposes of the Act to limit the court's jurisdiction to those matters *actually investigated* by either the EEOC or a state deferral agency? See, Babrocky v. Jewel Food Co., 773 F.2d 857, 863–64 (7th Cir. 1985); Henderson v. First National Bank, 344 F.Supp. 1373 (M.D.Ala.1972). Should amendments to an EEOC charge containing new allegations, made after expiration of the 180-period, "relate back" to the date the charge was originally filed? See, Hornsby v. Conoco, Inc., 777 F.2d 243 (5th Cir. 1985).

2. Must an employee whose employer has retaliated against him for filing an EEOC charge file a second charge to preserve his right to litigate the retaliation claim? In GUPTA v. EAST TEXAS STATE UNIVERSITY, 654 F.2d 411 (5th Cir. 1981), the plaintiff's EEOC charge alleged discrimination against him in terms of job assignments and salary. After the lawsuit was filed, the plaintiff was discharged. Although no EEOC charge was filed by the plaintiff regarding his termination, the retaliation issue was litigated at trial, and the Court of Appeals held that the district court had jurisdiction to hear the claim.

> [I]t is unnecessary for a plaintiff to exhaust administrative remedies prior to urging a retaliation claim growing out of an earlier charge; the district court has ancillary jurisdiction to hear such a claim when it grows out of an administrative charge that is properly before the court.

654 F.2d at 414. The court reasoned that requiring a plaintiff to file a second charge under the circumstances "would serve no purpose except to create additional procedural technicalities when a single filing would comply with the intent of Title VII." In addition, elimination of the procedural barrier would aid private enforcement of Title VII and would deter "employers from attempting to discourage employees from exercising their rights under Title VII." But if no EEOC charge on retaliation is filed, will the employer have an opportunity to resolve that claim before suit is filed? See EEOC v. St. Anne's Hospital, 664 F.2d 128, 131 (7th Cir. 1981) (separate retaliation charge unnecessary where employer informed during investigation that retaliation was an issue); Bickley v. University of Maryland, 527 F.Supp. 174 (D.Md. 1981) (timely filing of separate retaliation charge necessitated by language of statute and policy of encouraging conciliation).

3. Section 706(f)(1) of Title VII, 42 U.S.C. § 2000e–5(f)(1), provides in part that, "a civil action may be brought against the respondent named in the [EEOC] charge * * * by the person claiming to be aggrieved * * *" The degree of precision with which the employer must be identified in the charge is a matter of some uncertainty. In Dickey v. Greene, 710 F.2d 1003 (4th Cir. 1983), the plaintiff named only the institutional employer in the space on the EEOC charge form for listing the respondent, but in the narrative portion of the charge made allegations of discrimination against her supervisor whom she subsequently sued. The district court denied a motion for summary judgment by the individual defendant and held that by naming the individual in the narrative section of the charge, the EEOC was fairly appraised of his identity.

The Court of Appeals reversed. "The facts set forth by Dickey in her charge, including the reference to Greene in the narrative portion of the charge, can in no way be viewed as sufficient under the statute to charge Greene and thus to require the EEOC to enter into the obligatory conciliation proceedings with Greene * * * there is nothing in the record to suggest that Greene was ever involved in the conciliation efforts." 710 F.2d at 1006. By contrast, the Seventh Circuit held in Eggleston v. Chicago Journeymen Plumbers' Local Union No. 130, 657 F.2d 890, 905 (7th Cir. 1981), cert. denied, 455 U.S. 1017, 102 S.Ct. 1710, 72 L.Ed.2d 134 (1982) that, "where an unnamed party has been provided with adequate notice of the charge, under circumstances where the party has been given the opportunity to participate in conciliation proceedings aimed at voluntary compliance, the charge is sufficient to confer jurisdiction over that party." See also, Greenwood v. Ross, 778 F.2d 448 (8th Cir. 1985) (assistant coach who named university in EEOC charge should have been allowed to sue chancellor and athletic director who were not named in charge where those officials had acted on the university's behalf in controversy with the coach, had notice of the proceedings and had been represented by counsel throughout) and Dague v. Riverdale Athletic Ass'n., 99 F.R.D. 325 (N.D.Ga. 1983) (denying motion to dismiss filed by principle officers of the institutional defendant named in the charge). In *Dague* the court explained: "To dismiss the claims against these defendants solely on the fact that they were not named in the EEOC charge, without some showing of whether or not they had actual notice of the charge and an opportunity to participate in conciliation, would be to elevate form over substance and ignore the remedial purpose of the Act." 99 F.R.D. at 327. Do you agree? What purpose is served by correctly identifying the respondent in the original charge?

Courts are in general agreement that a charge which does not correctly identify an institutional respondent, is not fatal to a subsequent suit so long as the correct respondent was put on notice of the charge. See, Sedlacek v. Hach, 752 F.2d 333 (8th Cir. 1985) (charge named a "substantially identical related partnership"); Atonio v. Wards Cove Packing Co., Inc., 703 F.2d 329, 331 (9th Cir. 1982) (charge named business with same address as defendant and with common ownership and management).

4. In *Jenkins*, the plaintiff sought to represent a class apparently composed of all black and all female employees of the defendant company. The extent to which such a plaintiff may represent, through a class action, persons with factually dissimilar claims is discussed infra in Chapter 7 at p. 459.

4. Receipt of the "Right to Sue" Letter and Filing of the Timely Complaint

HARRIS v. FORD MOTOR CO.

United States District Court, Western District of Missouri, 1980.
487 F.Supp. 429.

MEMORANDUM AND ORDER

SCOTT O. WRIGHT, DISTRICT JUDGE.

Plaintiff sues for damages and injunctive and declaratory relief under Title VII of the Civil Rights Act of 1964, as amended 1972. Jurisdiction of this Court is invoked pursuant to 42 U.S.C. § 2000e–5(f), and 28 U.S.C. § 1343(4). Defendant has moved the Court for summary judgment on the grounds that plaintiff's claims are barred by the equitable doctrine of laches. Defendant's motion for summary judgment is denied.

Plaintiff was discharged from defendant's Claycomo, Missouri plant in September, 1973. Immediately after her discharge, plaintiff filed a charge of employment discrimination with the Equal Employment Opportunity Commission (EEOC). During June of 1976, the EEOC interviewed plaintiff and took her statement and the statement of her former supervisor at Ford, Donald Smith. The EEOC determined that there was no reasonable cause to believe that defendant was in violation of Title VII. Notice of the Right to Sue was sent to plaintiff on August 5, 1976. This Notice of the Right to Sue was returned to the EEOC as "unclaimed". Nearly two years later, plaintiff inquired about her claim, and the EEOC issued a second Right to Sue letter. Plaintiff filed this suit within ninety (90) days after receiving her second Notice of the Right to Sue.

Defendant argues that plaintiff's claims are barred by the equitable doctrine of laches because plaintiff's delay in filing suit was inexcusable and resulted in undue prejudice to the defendant. Defendant asserts that plaintiff's delay was inexcusable because she moved several times without notifying the EEOC of her change of address and she failed to take any action to find out the status of her claim. Defendant maintains that plaintiff's inexcusable delay caused them undue prejudice because memories of witnesses have dimmed and because plaintiff is attempting to recover back pay. If plaintiff is successful, the defendant will have to pay a substantial sum for work that they have already paid someone else to perform.

Plaintiff claims that the delay was excusable and resulted from a lack of diligence on the part of the EEOC. Even if plaintiff failed to inform the EEOC of each address change, she did provide them with an alternate address where she would be reached at all times. Plaintiff asserts that the delay was caused by EEOC's failure to send the letter to this alternate address and was, therefore, beyond the plaintiff's control.

The Court finds that the facts of this case and the law support the plaintiff's argument.

Section 2000e–5(f)(1) of 42 U.S.C. provides for a 90-day statute of limitations period from the time the aggrieved person receives a Notice of the Right to Sue from the EEOC. This provision has universally been interpreted to mean that actual notice of the Right to Sue triggers the running of the 90-day period.[1]

1. Section 2000e–5(f)(1), as amended in 1972 provides:

"If * * * the Commission has not entered into a conciliation agreement to which the person aggrieved is a party, the Commission * * * shall so notify the person aggrieved and *within ninety days after the giving of such notice a civil action may be brought* against the respondent named in the charge * * *." (Emphasis added.)

The purpose of the statutory notification is to inform the claimant that his administrative remedies with the Commission have been exhausted and that the ninety-day period has begun to run. This purpose has not been accomplished "unless the claimant is actually aware of the suit letter. In terms of the policy behind limitations periods generally, the claimant can hardly be said to have slept on his rights if he allows the [ninety-day] period to expire in ignorance of his right to sue." Franks v. Bowman Transportation Company, 495 F.2d at 404.

In Craig v. Department of Health, Education and Welfare, 581 F.2d 189 (8th Cir. 1978)[2], the Eighth Circuit Court of Appeals set out criteria for determining whether notice is sufficient in Title VII actions. The court stated that notice is sufficient if:

> "(1) A registered or certified letter, or other written notice requiring the recipient to acknowledge receipt therefor, is sent to the employee and the employee personally acknowledges such receipt; or
>
> "(2) A registered or certified letter, or other written notice requiring the recipient to acknowledge receipt therefor, is sent to the representative designated by the employee. Such notice must be addressed in accordance with the specific directions of the employee, and receipt must be acknowledged personally by the designated representative." 581 F.2d at 193.

Under this criteria, the first Notice of the Right to Sue in the pending case was insufficient because the employee, Carol Anne Harris, never personally acknowledged its receipt. The 90-day statute of limitation period did not begin to run until she received the second Right to Sue letter sometime in the spring of 1978. However, the defendant does not contend that plaintiff's suit is barred by the statute of limitations. Instead, defendant argues that plaintiff is barred by the equitable doctrine of laches. The Court must determine whether the plaintiff's conduct caused the delay which resulted from the EEOC's failure to contact the plaintiff.

Because laches is an equitable doctrine, it is within the discretion of the trial court to determine whether it applies. Laches has basically two elements: there must be an inexcusable delay in asserting any

Prior to the 1972 amendments, this section provided:

> "If * * * the Commission has been unable to obtain voluntary compliance with this title, *the Commission shall so notify the person aggrieved and a civil action may, within thirty days thereafter, be brought* against the respondent named in the charge * * *." 78 Stat. 259 (1964) (Emphasis added.)

Although the wording is different between the amended and the unamended statute, courts have consistently interpreted both to require actual notice. For the purposes of this opinion, no differentiation will be made between cases governed by the pre-1972 amendments and the current statute. See also, Plunkett v. Roadway Express, Inc., 504 F.2d 417 (10th Cir. 1974).

2. This action was brought under the Civil Rights Act of 1964, §§ 701 et seq., 717(c) as amended 42 U.S.C. §§ 2000e et seq., 2000e–16(c), which is applicable to federal employees. It differs in wording from § 2000e–5(f)(1) but courts interpret the two sections similarly. See Bell v. Brown, 557 F.2d 849 (D.C.Cir. 1977).

right or claim, and that delay must have caused undue prejudice to the party against whom the claim is asserted. See generally, 30A C.J.S. Equity §§ 115–6 (1965).

The defendant maintains, and the Court does not question, that the plaintiff's two-year delay in filing suit resulted in prejudice to the defendant. Memories of witnesses have dimmed, and steps to preserve testimony and evidence were not taken. However, as pointed out in her brief, plaintiff is also adversely affected by this lapse of time. Prejudice alone is not sufficient to bar the plaintiff's claims under the equitable doctrine of laches.

Defendant argues that it is additionally prejudiced by the plaintiff's claim for back pay. If successful, the plaintiff will be entitled to two more years of back pay than she would have been had the suit been filed within 90 days of the issuance of the first Notice of the Right to Sue. The Court understands that this may cause hardship on the defendant, but it is the policy of the courts to encourage back pay awards and to construe Title VII liberally in order to make the plaintiff "whole". See Albemarle Paper Co. v. Moody et al., 422 U.S. 405, 95 S.Ct. 2362, 45 L.Ed.2d 280 (1975). Unless the conduct of the plaintiff precludes an award of back pay, the Court may not arbitrarily deny it. For the reasons stated below, the Court finds that the plaintiff's conduct in this case does not preclude an award of back pay.

The defendant has demonstrated that it has been prejudiced by the two-year delay, but prejudice is not enough. The defendant must also show that the delay was inexcusable. On this point, the defendant falls short. There was no inexcusable delay on the part of this plaintiff. On the EEOC's own form, the plaintiff gave an address where she could be reached at all times. The defendant has offered no evidence that the EEOC attempted to notify plaintiff at this address. It would be difficult to say that plaintiff impermissibly slept on her rights when she was secure with the knowledge that the EEOC could reach her through this address even though she had moved several times.

Of course, plaintiff's omission to inform EEOC of her current address contributed to the delay. Had she timely notified them of her current address, the first Notice of the Right to Sue would have reached her. But, even though plaintiff's omission was a contributing factor to the delay, it is still not sufficient to bar her claim under the doctrine of laches. The question to ask is: Would the delay have been avoided except for the omission (or actions) of the plaintiff? The answer here is no. A reasonable amount of diligence on the part of the EEOC would have prevented the delay. They did not need to look further than their own Charge of Discrimination form to find an address where they could have reached plaintiff. The burden to notify the plaintiff of her Right to Sue is on the EEOC, and its lack of diligence in this case was the cause of the delay. To penalize the plaintiff here would be to ignore the legislative intent to construe Title VII cases liberally. See Albemarle Paper Co. v. Moody et al., supra.

For the reasons stated, it is hereby

Ordered that the defendant's motion for summary judgment is denied.

NOTES AND PROBLEMS FOR DISCUSSION

1. The language of Section 706(f)(1) of Title VII (quoted in footnote 1 in *Harris*) seems to require the EEOC to issue notice to the charging party within a 180-day period which begins the 90 day period for filing suit. In Zambuto v. American Telephone & Telegraph Co., 544 F.2d 1333, 1334 (5th Cir. 1977), the Court of Appeals recognized that, given the EEOC's workload, the 180 day period for completion of the administrative process could not be strictly enforced, and held that the Commission is not required to issue unsolicited 180 day "progress reports" which initiate the running of the 90 day period during which the charging party must decide whether to file suit. This construction of the statute was given apparent approval by the Supreme Court in Occidental Life Insurance Co. v. EEOC, 432 U.S. 355, 97 S.Ct. 2447, 53 L.Ed.2d 402 (1977). "An aggrieved person unwilling to await the conclusion of extended EEOC proceedings may institute a private lawsuit 180 days after a charge has been filed." 432 U.S. at 366, 97 S.Ct. at 2454. See also Turner v. Texas Instruments, 556 F.2d 1349 (5th Cir. 1977). The current EEOC Regulations only require the issuance of a notice of right to sue when the agency is requested to do so by the charging party after the expiration of the 180-day period. 29 CFR § 1601.28(a)(1).

The purpose of the 180 day mandatory delay between the charge and receipt of the right to sue letter is to allow time for the EEOC to investigate and attempt conciliation. Courts have uniformly held, however, that the "action or inaction of the EEOC cannot affect the grievant's substantive rights under the statute." Miller v. International Paper Co., 408 F.2d 283, 291 (5th Cir. 1969). See also Roberts v. Arizona Board of Regents, 661 F.2d 796, 800 (9th Cir. 1981). Thus, the failure or inability of the EEOC to investigate or attempt conciliation of a claim cannot bar the suit. See Miller v. International Paper Co., supra, 408 F.2d at 288–291; Allen v. Schwab Rehabilitation Hospital, 509 F.Supp. 151, 155 (N.D.Ill. 1981). Such failure will, however, bar a suit by the EEOC. See infra at 437.

There is substantial disagreement over the effect of a right to sue notice issued *before* the end of the 180 day period. EEOC Regulations permit issuance of such an early notice, on request of the charging party, "provided, that the District Director * * * has determined that it is probable that the Commission will be unable to complete its administrative processing of the charge within 180 days * * *." 29 C.F.R. § 1601.28(a)(2). A number of courts have held that early issuance of the notice does not preclude the filing of a suit. See Bryant v. California Brewers Association, 585 F.2d 421, 425 (9th Cir. 1978), vacated on other grounds, 444 U.S. 598, 100 S.Ct. 814, 63 L.Ed.2d 55 (1980); Weise v. Syracuse University, 522 F.2d 397, 412 (2d Cir. 1975). Other courts have held that since Section 706(c) does not provide for a notice of right to sue within the 180 day period, there is no jurisdiction to consider a claim filed prior to the expiration of that period. See True v. N.Y. Dept. of Correctional Services, 613 F.Supp. 27 (W.D.N.Y.1984); Grimes v. Pitney Bowes, Inc., 480 F.Supp. 1381, 1383-86 (N.D.Ga.1979); Hiduchenko v. Minneapolis Medical and

Diagnostic Center, 467 F.Supp. 103, 107 (D.Minn.1979). But if the EEOC is unable to process a charge within the 180 day period, is there any advantage to anyone in requiring the charging party to await the expiration of the period before bringing suit? See Hooks v. RCA Corp., 620 F.Supp. 1 (E.D.Pa.1984); Cattell v. Bob Frensley Ford Inc., 505 F.Supp. 617, 621–22 (M.D.Tenn.1980).

2. As indicated in Jenkins, procedural errors by the EEOC will not be allowed to rebound to the plaintiff's detriment. See White v. Dallas Independent School District, 581 F.2d 556, 562 (5th Cir. 1978) (en banc); Johnson v. Al Tech Specialties Steel Corp., 731 F.2d 143, (2nd Cir. 1984). Courts have been considerably less lenient, however, in allowing the mistakes of charging parties to equitably toll the 90 day period for filing suit. In Brown v. Mead Corp., 646 F.2d 1163 (6th Cir. 1981), the plaintiff received two right to sue notices. The first notice, accompanied by an EEOC determination that there was no cause to believe she had been discriminated against, was facially valid although it had been issued without proper authority. The plaintiff filed suit within 90 days of the second notice which included a determination that the charge was valid. The Court of Appeals affirmed the district court's dismissal of the suit, holding that the plaintiff could not invoke the equitable tolling principle, because she had not been misled by the first notice while the employer had "reason to conclude that the matter was resolved." 646 F.2d at 1168. And in McCloud v. National Railroad Passenger Corp., 25 FEP Cases 513 (D.D.C.1981), the plaintiff filed a timely suit in a court without jurisdiction. By the time the case was removed into a proper forum, the 90 day period had expired. The court dismissed, finding the case not an "appropriate [one] in which to apply a theory of equitable tolling." 25 FEP Cases at 515. Are these decisions consistent with the remedial purposes of Title VII?

3. What should constitute sufficient notice to the charging part of his right to sue so as to start the running of the 90-day period? In Espinoza v. Missouri Pacific R.R. Co., 754 F.2d 1247 (5th Cir. 1985), the plaintiff was out of town when the notice of right to sue was delivered to his home and he did not see it until he returned eight days later. He filed suit 92 days after the notice was delivered. The Court of Appeals held that the suit was not timely because the plaintiff had offered no explanation for his failure to file suit in the 82-day period that remained after he returned home. The Court noted that plaintiff had made no showing that he had been misled by the district court, the EEOC or the employer. EEOC regulations require that a charging party notify the agency of changes of address. 29 C.F.R. § 1601.7(b) (1981). The Seventh Circuit has held that the 90-day period begins running on the date the notice is delivered to the most recent address the claimant has provided the EEOC. St. Louis v. Alverno College, 744 F.2d 1314 (7th Cir. 1984). Compare, Franks v. Bowman Transportation Co., 495 F.2d 398 (5th Cir. 1974), reversed and remanded on other grounds, 424 U.S. 747, 96 S.Ct. 1251, 47 L.Ed.2d 444 (1976) (notice received by charging party's nine-year old nephew and lost; plaintiff allowed to proceed with suit one year later when he learned of notice) and Archie v. Chicago Truck Drivers Union, 585 F.2d 210 (7th Cir. 1978) (plaintiff's wife received notice 10 days before giving it to him; period did not begin to run until actual receipt by charging party). Are these various decisions consistent?

Should notice to the charging party's attorney start the period for filing suit? Most courts have held that notice to the attorney begins the running of the period where the attorney is representing the charging party and has been authorized to receive the notice. See, Josiah-Faeduwor v. Communications Satellite Corp., 785 F.2d 344 (D.C.Cir. 1986); Jones v. Madison Service Corp.,

744 F.2d 1309 (7th Cir. 1984); Gonzalez v. Stanford Applied Engineering, Inc., 597 F.2d 1298 (9th Cir. 1979). If the charging party has retained an attorney to represent her, when should the period begin if the client receives the notice before her attorney? See, Noe v. Ward, 754 F.2d 890 (10th Cir. 1985).

TOLLING THE 90–DAY PERIOD

Recognizing the difficulty often faced by claimants, particularly those who are indigent, in securing counsel to file civil rights actions and the remedial purposes of Title VII, a number of circuits have held that the filing of the EEOC right-to-sue letter with a federal court, within the 90-day period, either satisfied the filing requirement of 42 U.S.C. § 2000e–5(f)1) or tolled the running of the period for a reasonable time. See, Neal v. IAM Local Lodge 2386, 722 F.2d 247 (5th Cir. 1984); Judkins v. Beech Aircraft Corp., 723 F.2d 818 (11th Cir. 1984). In BALDWIN COUNTY WELCOME CENTER v. BROWN, 466 U.S. 147, 104 S.Ct. 1723, 80 L.Ed.2d 196 (per curiam 1984), however, the Supreme Court, held that the filing of a notice of right-to-sue and a request for appointment of counsel does not "commence" a Title VII action nor toll the running of the 90-day period. The plaintiff had sent her right-to-sue notice with a letter requesting appointment of counsel to the clerk of the district court within the 90-day period. A United States Magistrate entered an order requiring the plaintiff to make application for appointment of counsel using the court's motion form and supporting questionaire for indigents. The plaintiff did not return the questionaire until the 96th day after receipt of the notice and her request for appointment of counsel was denied for failure timely to comply with magistrate's order. The plaintiff retained counsel and, on the 130th day after receipt of the right-to-sue letter, filed an "amended complaint." The suit was dismissed by the district court as untimely. The Eleventh Circuit, in an unpublished opinion, reversed, holding that the filing of the right-to-sue letter had tolled the period for filing the complaint.

The Supreme Court, stressing that "[p]rocedural requirements by Congress for gaining access to the Federal courts are not to be disregarded by courts out of vague sympathy for particular litigants," reversed. The Court distinguished those lower court decisions that had relaxed the filing requirements where the notice was inadequate, where a formal motion for appointment of counsel was pending at the end of the 90-day period, and where the plaintiff was "lulled * * * into inaction" by the court or defendant. 466 U.S. at 151, 104 S.Ct. at 1726. Justice Stevens, joined by Justices Brennan and Marshall, dissented on two grounds: first, that the plaintiff's letter which accompanied the right-to-sue notice constituted a "short and plain statement of the claim" in compliance with Rule 8 of the Federal Rules of Civil Procedure and, second, that, in light of the remedial scheme of Title VII, "filing the right to sue letter and exercising reasonable diligence in the District Court in attempting to obtain counsel and file a formal complaint should toll the statute of limitations." 466 U.S. at 168, 104 S.Ct. at 1734.

Although the majority opinion in *Baldwin County* suggests that the equitable tolling doctrine is applicable only where responsibility for the late filing lies with the EEOC, the court, or the defendant, and not where the plaintiff has simply been unable to file a formal complaint, a number of courts have been inclined to limit the decision to its facts. In Brown v. J.I. Case Co., 756 F.2d 48 (7th Cir. 1985), the Court of Appeals held that a good faith request for appointment of counsel made within the 90-day period tolled the running of the time for filing suit until disposition of the motion. *Baldwin County* was distinguished on the ground that the plaintiff had "engaged in inequitable conduct" by not returning the magistrate's questionnaire until after the period had expired. Cf. Millard v. La Pointe's Fashion Store, 736 F.2d 501 (9th Cir. 1984). *Contra,* Firle v. Mississippi State Dept. of Education, 762 F.2d 487 (5th Cir. 1985). In Judkins v. Beech Aircraft Corp., 745 F.2d 1330 (11th Cir. 1984), the claimant filed his right-to-sue notice and a copy of his EEOC charge. The Eleventh Circuit held that the charge, which explained the factual basis for the discrimination claim in considerable detail, complied with the requirements of Rule 8(a)(2) of the Federal Rules of Civil Procedure so as to constitute a complaint.

If nothing else, *Baldwin County* highlights the importance to the claimant of obtaining legal assistance before the expiration of the filing period. Section 706(f)(1) of the Act authorizes the district court to appoint counsel "upon application by the complainant and in such circumstances as the court may deem just." Congress, however, has not created a fund (as it has for the Criminal Justice Act) from which appointed counsel can be compensated. Appointed counsel will be compensated only if the plaintiff wins the case and will probably have to bear the costs of the litigation pending its outcome. See Chapter 15, infra. Under these circumstances, courts have been reluctant to force private attorneys to take on employment discrimination cases and, in practice, "appointments" under Title VII are more like referrals to counsel who may accept or reject the cases. But locating a lawyer venturesome enough to take on a hard-to-prove case on a wholly contingent basis can prove difficult. In Bradshaw v. U.S. District Court for the Southern District of California, 742 F.2d 515 (9th Cir. 1984), the district court strove for over thirteen months to find an attorney who would agree to represent the plaintiff (twenty lawyers turned the case down) before directing the plaintiff to proceed *pro se.* On the plaintiff's petition for a writ of mandamus to compel the district court to appoint counsel, the Ninth Circuit held that district courts may resort to coercive appointments of counsel under Title VII but that the lower court had not abused its discretion in light of the litigious history of the plaintiff and the court's diligent search for counsel. In deciding whether to appoint counsel, the D.C. Circuit has held that the district court should take into account, in addition to the plaintiff's financial circumstances, the merits of the case, the efforts of plaintiff to secure counsel and the plaintiff's capacity to represent himself. Poindexter v. Federal Bureau of Investigation, 737 F.2d 1173 (D.C.Cir. 1984). The Sixth Circuit has held that the denial of a motion to appoint counsel in a Title VII case is not immediately appealable. Henry v. City of Detroit Manpower Dept., 763 F.2d 757 (6th Cir. 1985) (*en banc.*), cert. denied, ___ U.S. ___, 106 S.Ct. 604, 88 L.Ed.2d 582 (1985). A dissent in *Henry* argued that denial of appointment should be immediately appealable under the "death knell" doctrine and stressed the importance of representation by an attorney at the trial on the merits.

> Congress expressly recognized that a distinctive characteristic of civil rights plaintiffs is membership in a disadvantaged class. By contrast, civil rights defendants are typically institutions capable of wielding great resources and mustering extensive legal talent. * * * The civil rights action itself involves discovery and motions practice so complex that the plaintiff may drop the case before trial. * * * I am unwilling to assume "that civil rights plaintiffs are capable of prosecuting their own cases through trial * * * [and] that should they somehow succeed in doing so, they will have the determination and capability to perfect and conduct appeals properly and fully after they lose." [citing Bradshaw v. Zoological Society of San Diego, 662 F.2d 1301, 1310 (9th Cir. 1981).]

763 F.2d at 772 (Jones, J. dissenting).

SECTION B. SUITS BY THE EEOC

EQUAL EMPLOYMENT OPPORTUNITY COMMISSION v. SHERWOOD MEDICAL INDUSTRIES, INC.

United States District Court, Middle District of Florida, 1978.
452 F.Supp. 678.

MEMORANDUM OPINION

GEORGE C. YOUNG, CHIEF JUDGE.

This is a Title VII enforcement action brought by the Equal Employment Opportunity Commission against Sherwood Medical Industries, Inc. (Sherwood), alleging that Sherwood engaged in discriminatory employment practices with respect to race and male gender. Now before the Court is Sherwood's "Motion to Strike and/or for Dismissal for Failure to State a Claim and/or for Summary Judgment," which puts in issue the permissible scope of the Commission's judicial complaint in this cause. The decisive question raised is whether the EEOC is now foreclosed from prosecuting its claim of male sex discrimination because it neither included this claim in its reasonable cause determination nor afforded Sherwood an opportunity to conciliate the matter prior to filing suit.

I. BACKGROUND

This Title VII case was set in motion on July 16, 1973 when Larry C. Dilligard, a black male, filed a charge with the EEOC, complaining that he had been denied employment by defendant Sherwood solely because of his race. The details of his charge of discrimination, assumed to be true for the purpose of this motion, are as follows: Dilligard entered the personnel office of Sherwood's Deland facility on the morning of July 9, 1973 and requested an application for employment. He informed a caucasian female employee that he was seeking a clerical position and that he had a college degree in business. Dilligard was told that there were no vacancies in the clerical area and that there was no need to fill out an application because "we only accumulate a lot of applications and eventually throw them in the garbage can". Dilligard responded that he wished to complete an application in any event so that he could have one on file if a vacancy did occur. The employee refused to give him an application. Dilligard observed at the time a number of white job applicants waiting in a nearby reception center for interviews.

The EEOC responded to Dilligard's charge by sending Sherwood the statutory notice of charge and initiating a broad scale investigation into Sherwood's employment practices. In the course of its investigation the Commission compiled statistical data on the race and sex composition of Sherwood's clerical work force.

On February 18, 1975 the Commission issued a formal "reasonable cause determination" finding "reasonable cause to believe that respondent [Sherwood] failed to hire charging party because of his race." Despite the fact that the investigation clearly encompassed male gender discrimination, the determination made no finding on that issue and it invited conciliation only on Dilligard's narrow charge of race discrimination. Indeed, there were merely two references to male gender employment practices in the entire three page document:

> "The Commission also notes that all of respondent's clericals are female except one.
>
> The foregoing statistics coupled with the fact that there were clerical vacancies after July 9, 1973, is sufficient to establish that exclusion of blacks, and particularly black males, has occurred."

Apparently at no point during the conciliation negotiations that followed the Commission's determination did male gender employment discrimination emerge as a subject of concern. The conciliation agreement ultimately proposed by the Commission (and rejected by Sherwood) was completely silent on that issue; the agreement focused exclusively on Dilligard's charge of race discrimination. And from all that appears in the record it was not until the judicial complaint in this cause was filed that Sherwood first learned of the Commission's claim that it had discriminated against males.

Sherwood now argues that the Commission's failure to put it on notice of the sex discrimination claim and to afford it an opportunity to conciliate the matter bars the Commission from pressing that claim in this action. In substance, Sherwood's contention is that the Commission has filed to satisfy all of the statutory pre-requisites to its power to sue under Title VII, hence this Court lacks subject matter jurisdiction over the sex discrimination claim. The Commission's response is that it has satisfied the minimum conditions on its power to bring a Title VII enforcement action. It takes issue with the contention that the reasonable cause determination did not sufficiently apprise Sherwood of its claim of male gender discrimination. And it maintains that it can assert its sex discrimination claim even if that issue were never made an explicit subject of conciliation. Moreover, the Commission argues, the scope of matters sought to be conciliated is not a proper subject of judicial scrutiny and hence the Court should not even inquire into whether the sex claim was a subject of attempted conciliation.

II. THE SCOPE OF THE CHARGE AND THE INVESTIGATION

It is now well settled that the allowable scope of a civil enforcement action by the Commission is not fixed strictly by the allegations of the charging party's charge of discrimination. Rather, as the Fifth Circuit held in the often-cited decision of Sanchez v. Standard Brands, Inc., 431 F.2d 455 (1970), the scope of the civil action is to be determined by the "scope of the EEOC investigation which can reasonably be expected to grow out of the charge of discrimination." 431 F.2d at 466.[1] The charge should be viewed merely as the starting point for a reasonable investigation, not as a common-law pleading which narrowly circumscribes the Commission's freedom of action in carrying out its statutory duties. If the Commission uncovers during a reasonable investigation facts which support a charge of some form of discrimination other than that alleged in the original charge, it is free to develop these facts and, if necessary, to require the respondent to account for them. Judge Russell of the Fourth Circuit has astutely summarized this principle this way:

> "*So long as the new discrimination arises out of the reasonable investigation of the charge filed,* it can be the subject of a 'reasonable cause determination,' to be followed by an offer by the Commission of conciliation, and, if conciliation fails, by a civil suit, without

1. The post-*Sanchez* decisions have applied slightly different tests to determine whether the Commission's judicial complaint was unreasonably broad in light of the charge of discrimination. Compare e.g., Gamble v. Birmingham Southern R.R. Company, 514 F.2d 678, 687–89 (5th Cir. 1975); Oubichon v. North American Rockwell Corp., 482 F.2d 569, 571 (9th Cir. 1973); with MacBride v. Delta Airlines, Inc., 551 F.2d 113, 115 (6th Cir. 1977); EEOC v. General Electric Co., 532 F.2d 359, 365–66 (4th Cir. 1976). It is doubtful that there is any meaningful distinction between the tests employed. The inquiry in every case is essentially whether the additional charge of employment discrimination could reasonably have grown out of an investigation into the original charge.

the filing of a new charge on such claim of discrimination. In other words, the original charge is sufficient to support action by the EEOC as well as a civil suit under the Act for *any discrimination stated in the charge itself or developed in the course of the reasonable investigation of that charge,* provided such discrimination was included in the reasonable cause determination of the EEOC and was followed by compliance with the conciliation procedures fixed in the Act." (emphasis in original)

EEOC v. General Elec. Co., 532 F.2d 359, 366 (4th Cir. 1976).

In the present case the Commission's investigation clearly exceeded the scope of the charging party's charge of discrimination. For Dilligard's charge dealt solely with race and the Commission, in the course of its investigation of that charge, compiled statistical data on sex as well. But Sherwood does not say that the broader focus of the investigation was in any way improper or abusive in relation to the charge filed; indeed it appears to concede the reasonableness of the investigation. So there is no real question here about the scope of the judicial complaint per se. If the Commission complied with the statutory prerequisites to bringing suit, it was free to assert its sex claim against Sherwood because that claim arose out of a reasonable investigation of the original charge of discrimination. The scope of the complaint is in issue here only because it is contended that with respect to the sex discrimination claim the Commission has failed to comply with two statutory conditions on its power to sue: a reasonable cause determination and an effort to conciliate.

III. THE REASONABLE CAUSE DETERMINATION

Under 42 U.S.C. § 2000e–5(b), after the Commission investigates a charge of discrimination, it should "so far as practical not later than 120 days from the filing of the charge" make a determination on whether it believes the charge is true. This reasonable cause determination is a very crucial step in the administrative process. For it marks the conclusion of the Commission's investigation into a respondent's employment practices and it represents the Commission's formal opinion about what its investigation revealed. The determination may even bring the administrative process to an end with respect to many charges; if a "no cause" determination is made the charge of discrimination will be dismissed and the complaining party left to his private remedies in court. And where a "cause" determination is reached, the Commission, by law, must undertake an attempt to conciliate the dispute. See generally Occidental Life Ins. Co. v. EEOC, 432 U.S. 355 at 359, 97 S.Ct. 2447, 2451, 53 L.Ed.2d 402 at 407 (1977). In that event, the reasonable cause determination is intended to serve both as a formal means of placing the respondent on notice of the particular employment practice which the Commission views as violative of Title VII and as a framework for the conciliation efforts to follow.

Because of the importance of the reasonable cause determination, as a means of finally drawing the investigation to a close, as an embodiment of the Commission's legal conclusions from the evidence, as a means of notice to the respondent and as a device to frame the issues for conciliation, it seems evident that any and all of a respondents' employment practices viewed by the Commission as probably discriminatory, must be explicitly included in the determination. That is, the Commission must make an express finding in the determination concerning each employment practice which it concludes to be violative of Title VII. The Courts which have addressed themselves to this question have so concluded.

The reasonable cause determination at issue here falls far short of making any such finding on the sex discrimination claim now asserted against Sherwood. Indeed, the closest scrutiny of the determination could not have effectively placed Sherwood on notice that sex discrimination was a matter in issue. The only material reference to sex in the entire determination was the comment that statistical analysis indicated that there were clerical vacancies after July 9, 1973 sufficient to establish that "the exclusion of blacks, and particularly black males, has occurred." This comment was manifestly insufficient to afford Sherwood notice of the sex discrimination claim. If anything, the inference that should be drawn from the statement is that there was no discrimination against white males. Race discrimination was all that Sherwood could reasonably have viewed as being in dispute.

IV. THE FAILURE TO CONCILIATE

Conciliation is the final step in an EEOC administrative proceeding and a condition precedent to the Commission's power to sue. The language of the statute admits of no exception. If the Commission finds reasonable cause it "shall endeavor to eliminate any such unlawful employment practice by informal methods of conference, conciliation and persuasion", and only when conciliation "acceptable to the Commission" fails may it bring a civil action against the respondent. 42 U.S.C. § 2000e–5(b). The Courts have interpreted the statute to mean precisely what it says and it is thus now well established that failure to conciliate is fatal to a Title VII action brought by the Commission;[2] the suit or claim must be dismissed as premature.

The record in this case, as counsel for the Commission concedes, establishes that conciliation on the sex discrimination claim was never offered and never attempted. The only subject of conciliation efforts was Dilligard's race discrimination charge; when the negotiations on that charge failed, the Commission filed suit without ever attempting to settle the sex discrimination claim. It would thus seem to follow that the sex discrimination aspects of the Commission's claim against Sher-

2. By contrast, conciliation by the Commission is not a condition precedent to the institution of a private action for relief under Title VII by an individual plaintiff. See, Gamble v. Birmingham Southern R.R. Co., supra at 688–89; Danner v. Phillips Petroleum Co., 447 F.2d 159 (5th Cir. 1971).

wood would have to be stricken from this case. But the Commission argues that it would be error to do so because the Commission need conciliate only the original charge of discrimination, not the additional discrimination claims which come to life during an investigation of the original charge. That is, as the Commission views it, its duty is to conciliate the charging party's charge only and if it is unable to reach a conciliation agreement on that charge it is under no obligation to seek settlement with respect to additional discriminatory employment practices developed during the investigation of the original charge. Under this theory only Dilligard's charge was required to be conciliated.

This contention, if accepted, would run contrary to Congressional intent and could well have the affect of rendering the conciliation requirement an empty formality. The mandate that conciliation be attempted is unique to Title VII and it clearly reflects a strong Congressional desire for out-of-court settlement of Title VII violations. See Culpepper v. Reynolds Metal Co., 421 F.2d 888 (5th Cir. 1970); Oatis v. Crown Zellerbach, 398 F.2d 496 (5th Cir. 1968). The legislative history of the 1972 amendments confirms that Congress viewed judicial relief as a recourse of last resort, sought only after a settlement has been attempted and failed.[3] Conciliation is clearly the heart of the Title VII administrative process. In light of the clear Congressional preference for conciliation it would be anomalous to conclude that the Commission is under no obligation to conciliate a claim of discrimination simply because it originated during the course of its investigation rather than from an aggrieved person's charge.

Certainly one can find no support for the Commission's position in the decisions dealing with the scope of the judicial complaint. To the contrary, every decision recognizing a right in the Commission to expand its investigation—and ultimately its judicial complaint—beyond the scope of the charging party's charge, has presupposed that the additional employment practices complained of were included in the conciliation attempt along with the original charge. In EEOC v. Raymond Metal Prod. Co., 385 F.Supp. 907, 915 (D.Md.1974) for instance, the Court concluded:

> " * * * the judicial complaint in an EEOC civil action may properly embrace, in addition to those allegations contained in the

3. A reference to the legislative history of the Act appearing in EEOC v. Westvaco Corp., supra is particularly instructive:

"* * * Senator Dominick, the principle architect of the 1972 amendment that empowered the Commission to bring suit in its own name, stated that '[M]y amendment would take over at the level where conciliations fail' 118 Cong.Rec.S. 170 (Jan. 20, 1972). 'What the amendment does * * * is * * * provide for trial in the U.S. District Courts whenever the EEOC has investigated a charge, found reasonable cause to believe that an unlawful employment practice has occurred, and is *unable* to obtain voluntary compliance' 118 Cong.Rec.S. 221 (Jan. 21, 1972). Similarly, the Senior House Conferee on the 1972 amendment ventured the opinion that '*[O]nly if conciliation proves to be impossible* do we expect the Commission to bring action in federal district court to seek enforcement.' Cong.Rec.H. 1861 (Mar. 18, 1972). (remarks of Congressman Perkins, introduced in the Conference Report on House Resolution 1746)." (emphasis supplied) 372 F.Supp. at 988.

initial charge, any allegations of other discriminatory employment practices for which there has been *an investigation, a determination of reasonable cause and a genuine attempt at conciliation.*" (emphasis supplied)

The Fourth Circuit in EEOC v. General Electric Co., supra at 366, similarly stressed that the new discrimination developed from the Commission's investigation could be included in a civil suit provided that it was included in the reasonable cause determination and in the efforts to conciliate. Like language can be found in a long line of decisions concerning the scope of the Commission's judicial complaint. These decisions recognize a right in the Commission to pursue its investigation beyond the bounds of the original charge of discrimination. But in so doing they do not vest the Commission with the authority to pick and choose the matters to be conciliated.

The only construction of the statute which is at all in harmony with the Congressional desire for conciliation is that the Commission's authority to sue is conditioned upon full compliance with the administrative process—investigation, determination, and conciliation—with respect to each discriminatory practice alleged. "Congress, committed as it was to voluntary compliance, could not have intended that the Commission could attempt conciliation on one set of issues and, having failed, litigate a different set." EEOC v. E. I. duPont deNemours and Company, supra at 1336. Once having determined that a respondent has violated Title VII the Commission must make a genuine effort to conciliate with respect to each and every employment practice complained of. In this way, the respondent is afforded a fair opportunity to weigh all the factors which must be taken into account in deciding whether to settle a dispute out of court, even if the charge of discrimination in dispute arose from the Commission's own investigation rather than the charging party's charge. And if litigation then results, all parties are assured that they have had a fair opportunity to settle every matter in dispute. The Congressional mandate that litigation be a matter of last resort will have been observed.

It is contended, however, that this Court lacks jurisdiction to inquire into the degree of the Commission's compliance with the conciliation requirements of Title VII, hence Sherwood's complaint that it was afforded no opportunity to conciliate the sex discrimination claim may not be heard. Essentially, the Commission takes the position that the scope of the matters sought to be conciliated is not a proper subject of judicial scrutiny; the Courts inquiry into its jurisdiction must cease upon proof that conciliation was attempted on at least some matters in dispute. This contention is without merit. The Court recognizes that the conciliation requirement of the statute is phrased in terms of conciliation "acceptable to the Commission"; and thus district courts are not empowered to second guess the Commission with respect to particular settlement negotiations. But the question in this case is not whether the Commission properly exercised its discretion during settlement negotiations, but whether it afforded the respondent Sherwood the opportunity to conciliate at all with respect to one of the claims asserted in its judicial complaint. It is frivolous to contend that the court lacks jurisdiction to decide this question. If the Commission is to seek relief in federal court it must be prepared to show that it has satisfied the jurisdictional prerequisites—including submitting the matters in issue to conciliation. It has not done so here and it therefore follows that suit on the sex discrimination claim was premature. This is a matter of subject matter jurisdiction, not of Commission discretion.

V. CONCLUSION

As Judge Stapleton observed in EEOC v. E. I. duPont deNemours and Company, supra, the "Commission's power of suit and administrative process [are not] unrelated activities, [but] sequential steps in a unified scheme for securing compliance with Title VII". 373 F.Supp. at 1333. The Commission must substantially satisfy the requirements of each step in this process—investigation, determination and conciliation—before it can progress to the next. In the present case the Commission has bypassed two of the most essential—determination and conciliation. These defects may not be overlooked, and the sex discrimination claim must therefore be stricken. A separate order dismissing the Commission's sex discrimination claim will be entered. The race discrimination claim, of course, will remain pending and the issue for trial will be whether during the relevant period Sherwood discriminated against employees or prospective employees on the basis of race.

This Memorandum Opinion confirms the Court's ruling from the bench at the conclusion of the hearing on March 21, 1978.

JOHNSON v. NEKOOSA-EDWARDS PAPER CO.

United States Court of Appeals, Eighth Circuit, 1977.
558 F.2d 841, cert. denied 434 U.S. 920, 98 S.Ct. 394, 54 L.Ed.2d 276.

Before CLARK, ASSOCIATE JUSTICE, Retired,* GIBSON, CHIEF JUDGE, and HEANEY, CIRCUIT JUDGE.

HEANEY, CIRCUIT JUDGE.

This action was filed by Linda Johnson and the United Paperworkers International Union against Nekoosa Papers, Inc., alleging the existence of sex discrimination in its employment practices at Nekoosa's Ashdown, Arkansas, facilities. The named plaintiffs sought to represent a class including all past and present female employees and all female job applicants who were denied employment opportunities because of their sex. The Equal Employment Opportunity Commission (EEOC) was allowed to intervene. The District Court initially certified the class to include only present employees but later decertified the class entirely and ruled that "the EEOC may not expand the

* TOM C. CLARK, ASSOCIATE JUSTICE, Retired, Supreme Court of the United States, sitting by designation.

scope of this action beyond that which the Plaintiffs are permitted to pursue."[1] The District Court's decision to decertify the class and to limit the scope of the EEOC's intervention is challenged in this consolidated appeal.[2]

Prior to bringing this action, Johnson and the Union had filed a charge with the EEOC alleging that "[f]emale employees have been denied job opportunities, wages and fringe benefits because of their sex, including but not limited to the treatment of maternity conditions by the employer."[3] After an investigation, the EEOC found reasonable cause to believe that Nekoosa discriminated against women in violation of Title VII with respect to maternity benefits, job opportunities and wages. The EEOC issued its determination of probable cause on June 19, 1974, and indicated that an EEOC representative would be in contact with each party in the near future to begin conciliation. In early August, 1974, the attorney for Nekoosa contacted the EEOC by letter and telephone seeking to expedite the conciliation process. The EEOC did not respond to Nekoosa's overtures. The EEOC issued a right-to-sue letter to Johnson and the Union at their request on August 19, 1974. This action was filed on September 9, 1974.

* * *

[The Court held that the class decertification was not an appealable order. See infra at 463].

II.

We next consider whether the District Court properly held that the EEOC may not expand the scope of the action beyond that of the charge filed by the plaintiffs with the EEOC. The District Court certified the following questions to this Court pursuant to 28 U.S.C. § 1292(b).[6]

> 1. Whether the commission's suit in intervention properly enlarges the scope of the private plaintiffs' suit so as to include all forms of discrimination described in the Commission's Determination of Plaintiffs' underlying charges.
>
> 2. Whether the Court properly held that "the EEOC may not expand the scope of this action beyond that which the Plaintiffs are permitted to pursue" in view of the fact that the EEOC had not prior to the filing of its Motion to Intervene endeavored "to eliminate any such alleged, unlawful employment practice by informal

1. Linda Johnson and United Paperworkers International Union, AFL-CIO, and Equal Employment Opportunity Commission v. Nekoosa Papers Inc. (Ashdown, Arkansas), CA No. T–74–57–C (W.D.Ark., order filed June 8, 1976). Thus, the Equal Employment Opportunity Commission (EEOC) would not be able to raise the claims of those who were denied job opportunities because of their sex and to challenge the virtual exclusion of females from production jobs.

2. The above entitled cases were consolidated by this Court for the purpose of this opinion.

3. The charge was filed with the EEOC on November 29, 1973, by Johnson and the Union acting through their attorney.

6. The EEOC was granted permission to appeal by this Court in an order dated September 23, 1976.

methods of conference, conciliation, and persuasion" as required by § 706(b) of Title VII of the Civil Rights Act of 1964, 42 U.S.C. § 2000e–5(b) and that the EEOC had not as required by its rules, 29 CFR § 1601–23 (1974), notified the Defendant in writing "that such efforts have been unsuccessful and will not be resumed except on the Respondent's written request within the time specified in such notice."

3. Whether the Court abused its discretion in permitting the EEOC to intervene in this action in view of the fact that the EEOC had not, prior to the filing of its Motion for Intervention, endeavored to eliminate any alleged unlawful employment practice by informal methods of conference, conciliation and persuasion as required by § 706(b) of Title VII of the Civil Rights Act of 1964, 42 U.S.C. § 2000e–5(b) and that the EEOC had not, as required by its own rules, 29 CFR § 1601–23 (1974), notified the Defendant, in writing "that such efforts have been unsuccessful and will not be resumed except on the Respondent's written request with the time specified in such notice."

In order to resolve these questions relating to the permissible scope of the EEOC's suit in intervention, we are faced with the task of reconciling our holding in Equal Employment Op. Com'n v. Missouri Pacific R. Co., 493 F.2d 71 (8th Cir. 1974), with the EEOC's general obligation to conciliate.

In *Missouri Pacific*, this Circuit held "that, once the charging party has filed suit pursuant to a 'right to sue' notice the Commission is relegated to its right of permissive intervention." Id. at 75. The Court relied upon the express statutory scheme,[7] 42 U.S.C. § 2000e 5(f)(1), and the legislative history of the 1972 amendments to Title VII [8] in reaching its conclusion that duplicitous suits were barred by the statute. Accord, E.E.O.C. v. Continental Oil Co., 548 F.2d 884, 889–890 (10th Cir. 1977); Equal Employment Opportunity v. Occidental Life, 535 F.2d 533, 536 (9th Cir.) (dicta), cert. granted, 429 U.S. 1022, 97 S.Ct. 638, 50 L.Ed.2d 623 (1976).[9]

7. The scheme of the statute itself * * * negates the Commission's double-barreled approach. Once either the Commission or the charging party has filed suit, § 2000e–5(f)(1) speaks only in terms of intervention—the absolute right of the charging party to intervene if the Commission elects to file suit within 180 days; the permissive right of intervention on the part of the Commission in the private action. The statute cannot be read to warrant duplicitous lawsuits when both actions find their genesis in one unlawful employment practice charge. Equal Employment Op. Com'n v. Missouri Pacific R. Co., 493 F.2d 71, 74 (8th Cir. 1974).

8. H.R.Rep.No.92–238, 92d Cong., 2d Sess., 1972 U.S. Code Cong. & Admin.News p. 2148.

9. Other Circuits, have however, developed different approaches to the problem of duplicitous suits. The Fifth and Sixth Circuits, allow the EEOC to file suit if the EEOC suit would be broader in scope than the private action, even if a private suit based upon the same EEOC charge has already been filed. E.E.O.C. v. McLean Trucking Co. 525 F.2d 1007 (6th Cir. 1975); Equal Employment Op. Com'n v. Kimberly-Clark Corp., 511 F.2d 1352 (6th Cir. 1975), cert. denied, 423 U.S. 994, 96 S.Ct. 420, 46 L.Ed.2d 368 (1976); Equal Employment Op. Com'n v. Huttig Sash & Door Co., 511 F.2d 453 (5th Cir. 1975). This ap-

A problem arises, however, because different issues may be raised by the private suit and the suit filed by the EEOC even though the same charge originally filed with the EEOC serves as the basis for both suits. In this case, in its suit in intervention, the EEOC seeks to raise the claims of unsuccessful job applicants and to challenge the apparent exclusion of females from production jobs.[10] Thus, the scope of the EEOC suit is broader than that of the private suit which the District Court has limited to those issues raised by the charge filed with the EEOC which only alleged discrimination against present female employees.[11] The Court in *Missouri Pacific* recognized that the scope of the EEOC suit might be broader than that of the private suit when it stated that it was "fully confident that [the District Court] * * * will permit intervention and enlargement of the scope of the action by the Commission if necessary to the rendering of full and complete justice." Equal Employment Op. Com'n v. Missouri Pacific R. Co., supra at 75. My concurring opinion went one step further and would have required the District Court to broaden the scope of the suit to include those issues raised by the EEOC because the EEOC is charged with the responsibility of eliminating discriminatory employment practices and, thus, must be allowed to bring the broader issues before the court. Id. at 75 (J. Heaney concurring). Indeed, it would be anomalous if we did not allow the EEOC's suit in intervention to broaden the issues beyond those raised by the charge filed with the EEOC since the EEOC is not so restricted if it brings a direct suit. See E.E.O.C. v. General Elec. Co., 532 F.2d 359 (4th Cir. 1976); Equal Employment Op. Com'n v. Huttig Sash & Door Co., 511 F.2d 453 (5th Cir. 1975); cf. Equal Employment Op. Com'n v. Western Pub. Co., Inc., 502 F.2d 599 (8th Cir. 1974). We cannot, however, simply order that the EEOC be permitted

proach was rejected by the Tenth Circuit because it was unable to find any statutory basis for defining the EEOC's right to sue in terms of the scope of its suit. E.E.O.C. v. Continental Oil Co., 548 F.2d 884, 889 (10th Cir. 1977).

The Third Circuit reads the statute and the legislative history differently and places no limitation on the right of the EEOC to bring suit after a private action has been filed. Equal Emp. Opp. Com'n v. North Hills Passavant Hosp., 544 F.2d 664, 672 (3rd Cir. 1976). Any problem with duplicitous suits is to be resolved under Fed.R.Civ.P. 42(a) which provides for the consolidation of actions involving common questions of law and fact. Id. See generally Reiter, The Equal Employment Opportunity Commission and "Duplicitous Suits": An Examination of EEOC v. Missouri Pacific Railroad Co., 49 N.Y.U.L.Rev. 1130 (1974).

We adhere to our decision in Equal Employment Op. Com'n v. Missouri Pacific R. Co., 493 F.2d 71 (8th Cir. 1974), for the reasons stated in that opinion.

10. The EEOC investigation revealed that only 4.5% of Nekoosa's employees were female even though the community work force was 22.4% female. Moreover, 78.5% of the female Nekoosa employees occupied clerical positions.

11. We emphasize that we are without jurisdiction to review this aspect of the District Court's order. We note, however, that it has been held that a private suit is not necessarily restricted to the scope of the charge filed with the EEOC and may extend to those issues revealed by a reasonable investigation by the EEOC. See Jenkins v. Blue Cross Mutual Hospital Ins., Inc., 522 F.2d 1235, 1241 (7th Cir. 1975) (en banc); Danner v. Phillips Petroleum Co., 447 F.2d 159, 161–162 (5th Cir. 1971); Sanchez v. Standard Brands, Inc., 431 F.2d 455, 466 (5th Cir. 1970); cf. Parham v. Southwestern Bell Telephone Co., 433 F.2d 421, 425 (8th Cir. 1970).

to broaden the scope of its suit in intervention because we must also consider the obligation of the EEOC to attempt conciliation.

Because of the enormous backlog of cases pending before the EEOC, a private party will usually be able to bring an action before the EEOC has attempted conciliation and completed the administrative process.[12] When this occurs, as it did here, the EEOC is precluded from bringing a direct action and is relegated to its right of permissive intervention. If conciliation was required prior to intervention, the EEOC's motion to intervene might not be considered timely under Fed.R.Civ.P. 24 because the process of conciliation is often time-consuming. While conciliation is mandatory prior to direct suit by the EEOC, 42 U.S.C. § 2000e–5(f)(1); 29 C.F.R. § 1601.23; Patterson v. American Tobacco Company, 535 F.2d 257 (4th Cir.), cert. denied, 429 U.S. 920, 97 S.Ct. 314, 50 L.Ed.2d 286 (1976); Equal Employment Op. Com'n v. Hickey-Mitchell Co., 507 F.2d 944 (8th Cir. 1974); it is not mandatory under the statutory scheme prior to intervention by the EEOC.[13] 42 U.S.C. § 2000e–5(f)(1). Thus, the EEOC cannot be precluded from intervention because it failed to conciliate.

Conciliation is nonetheless an integral part of Title VII, Equal Employment Op. Com'n v. Hickey-Mitchell Co., supra, and is desirable for a variety of policy reasons including giving the defendant notice and

12. A charging party cannot bring a private action unless permission is received from the EEOC. However, the EEOC is required to issue a right-to-sue letter if it either dismisses a charge or does not bring suit within 180 days of the date the charge was filed. The charging party then has 90 days in which to initiate his own court action. 42 U.S.C. § 2000e–5(f)(1). It is, thus, possible for a charging party to bring suit within a short period of time after the charge has been filed.

While the EEOC can bring an action within 30 days after the charge has been filed, it can only do so if it finds reasonable cause to believe the charge to be true and if conciliation has failed. Since it has often taken the EEOC two to three years to attempt conciliation, Equal Employment Op. Com'n v. Kimberly-Clark Corp. supra at 1358; U.S. Comm'n on Civil Rights, The Federal Civil Rights Enforcement Effort—1974, 529 (1975), the EEOC will usually be unable to bring its own action before a private action has been filed. The EEOC's delay in processing cases is reflected by its backlog of cases. As of June 30, 1975, over 126,000 cases were pending before the EEOC. As the following table indicates, some of the pending charges date back to 1968.

Fiscal Year in Which Charge was Filed	Number of Open Charges
1968	2,213
1969	3,260
1970	4,245
1971	5,917
1972	8,114
1973	18,550
1974	30,812
1975	46,919
Unspecified	6,310
TOTAL	126,340

Report to the Congress by the Comptroller General of the United States, The Equal Employment Opportunity Commission Has Made Limited Progress in Eliminating Employment Discrimination 9 (September 28, 1976).

13. The EEOC has been permitted to intervene in three District Court cases even though it had not attempted to conciliate. Willis v. Allied Maintenance Corp., 13 FEP Cases 767 (S.D.N.Y.1976); NOW v. Minnesota Mining & Mfg., 11 FEP Cases 720 (D.Minn.1975); Jones v. Holy Cross Hospital Silver Springs, Inc., 64 F.R.D. 586 (D.Md.1974). In each case, the EEOC was not permitted to expand the scope of the action because it had not attempted to conciliate. Because we are ordering a stay to permit conciliation, the EEOC will be permitted to expand the scope of its action here.

an opportunity to respond to any additional claims revealed by the EEOC investigation and in order to avoid expensive and time-consuming court actions.[14] Because we believe strongly in the value of conciliation, we hold that while the EEOC is not barred from intervention by its failure to attempt to conciliate, it is under a continuing obligation to attempt to conciliate even after it has intervened in the action. To this end, we order the District Court to stay the action for sixty days and to require the EEOC to make a prompt offer to conciliate. If the offer is accepted by Nekoosa and if thereafter EEOC fulfills its obligation to conciliate in good faith and if no settlement is forthcoming by the end of the sixty-day period, the District Court is directed to then enter an order permitting the EEOC to expand its intervention in accordance with its petition. If Nekoosa refuses to conciliate, then the District Court's order permitting the EEOC to expand the scope of its intervention shall be issued forthwith.

We believe such a stay is not so long as to unduly prejudice the individual claimants. We realize that requiring the EEOC to expedite its conciliation process after intervention might be difficult for them because of their backlog of cases. We feel, however, it is the best balance between the right of the EEOC to intervene, the obligation of the EEOC to attempt conciliation and the right of the individual claimants to proceed with their action.

Accordingly, we reverse and remand this action to the District Court for action consistent with this opinion.

NOTES AND PROBLEMS FOR DISCUSSION

1. With *Johnson*, compare EEOC v. Kimberly-Clark Corp., 511 F.2d 1352, 1363 (6th Cir. 1975), cert. denied, 423 U.S. 994, 96 S.Ct. 420, 46 L.Ed.2d 368 (1975) ("The Congressional intent that duplicitous proceedings be avoided does not mean, however, that the EEOC should be limited to permissive intervention in a private suit when its investigation on the one charge has disclosed a number of violations which require judicial attention.") Although the EEOC's investigation of a charge, and thus the claims it may raise in a subsequent suit, may be considerably broader that the substance of the charge, claims which the EEOC has not attempted to conciliate with the defendant will be stricken from the suit. See EEOC v. Allegheny Airlines, 436 F.Supp. 1300, 1305–1307 (W.D. Pa.1977). But what kind of effort by the Commission to arrange conciliation is necessary? To what extent should the court delve into the conciliation process to determine whether an appropriate effort was made? See EEOC v. Klingler Electric Corp., 636 F.2d 104, 107 (5th Cir. 1981); EEOC v. Zia Co., 582 F.2d 527, 533 (10th Cir. 1978); EEOC v. Celotex Corp., 27 FEP Cases 324, 327 (W.D.Tenn. 1980). Would a court's review of the actual offers and counter offers of the parties during the conciliation process, to determine the EEOC's good faith, be fair to the parties?

14. We are aware that the conciliation process has to date been relatively unsuccessful. See Peck, The Equal Employment Opportunity Commission: Developments in the Administrative Process 1965, 1975, 51 Wash.L.Rev. 831, 852–853 (1976); Report to Congress by the Comptroller General of the United States, supra at 7–37. Action by the legislative and executive branches of the federal government is apparently necessary to make the process a more effective one.

2. May the EEOC bring an action based on a charge which has been settled by the employee? See EEOC v. North Hills Passavant Hospital, 544 F.2d 664 (3d Cir. 1976). What if the charging party's suit has been dismissed with prejudice? See EEOC v. Huttig Sash & Door Co., 511 F.2d 453 (5th Cir. 1975). Under § 706(i) of the Act, 42 U.S.C. § 2000e–5(i), the EEOC may seek enforcement of a decree entered in a case in which it was not a party. The courts are divided on the question of whether the Commission can seek modification of such decrees. Compare EEOC v. United Association of Journeymen, Local 189, 438 F.2d 408 (6th Cir. 1971), cert. denied, 404 U.S. 832, 92 S.Ct. 77, 30 L.Ed.2d 62, with EEOC v. First Alabama Bank, 595 F.2d 1050 (5th Cir. 1979).

3. Title VII imposes strict limits on the time within which private parties may file charges with the EEOC, but it does not contain an express limitation on the time within which the Commission may bring suit, nor are state statutes of limitation applicable to an EEOC action. But a Commission suit may be barred by the doctrine of laches when it has been inexcusably delayed and the defendant has been materially prejudiced by the delay. Occidental Life Insurance Co. v. EEOC, 432 U.S. 355, 373, 97 S.Ct. 2447, 2457, 53 L.Ed.2d 402 (1977). Laches is only available as a defense where *both* unreasonable delay and substantial or material prejudice to the defendant have occurred. The EEOC's workload has been rejected as an excuse for unreasonable delay. See EEOC v. Liberty Loan Corp., 584 F.2d 853, 857–858 (8th Cir. 1978). The burden of proving prejudice is on the defendant, EEOC v. Massey-Ferguson, Inc., 622 F.2d 271, 276 (7th Cir. 1980), and is normally established by demonstrating the unavailability of witnesses, changed personnel, or loss of pertinent records. See EEOC v. Alioto Fish Co., Limited, 623 F.2d 86, 88 (9th Cir. 1980) (virtually all witnesses dead or suffering from "dimmed memories"; charging party did not remember applying with defendant). EEOC v. Firestone Tire & Rubber Co., 626 F.Supp. 90 (N.D.Ga.1985) (individuals who could have been anticipated as favorable witnesses have become hostile because of intervening discharges and advancing age and poor health have made other witnesses' recall of past events impossible). But see, EEOC v. Great A & P Co., 735 F.2d 69 (3d Cir. 1984) (questioning whether, absent statutory authority, laches could ever be a defense against a federal agency).

4. Section 707 of Title VII originally granted to the Attorney General the authority to file suit under the Act when he had "reasonable cause to believe that any person * * * is engaged in a pattern or practice of resistance to the full enjoyment of any of the rights secured by this title * * *." Such a suit did not have to be based on a charge filed by an aggrieved employee or to have been preceded by investigation or attempted conciliation. The 1972 amendments to the Act transferred to the EEOC the authority to bring "pattern or practice" cases against private employers. The Justice Department retains jurisdiction over "pattern and practice" litigation against state and local governments. Does the transfer of the Attorney General's authority to bring private employer "pattern and practice" cases to the EEOC mean that the Commission can proceed in such cases without a § 706 charge?

5. Section 706(b) of Title VII provides for the initiation of proceedings by an aggrieved person or by "a member of the Commission". The statutory requirements for and procedures applicable to private charges and "Commissioner charges" are the same. Courts have tended, however, to require a good deal more specificity of Commissioner charges than of charges filed by private individuals. Disputes over the validity of Commissioner charges frequently arise during efforts by the Commission to enforce subpoenas issued in the

course of investigations. In EEOC v. Shell Oil Co., 466 U.S. 54, 104 S.Ct. 1621, 80 L.Ed.2d 41 (1984), the Commissioner's charge alleged that the company had engaged in a generic variety of unlawful practices from the effective date of Title VII to the present. The Court of Appeals held that the agency had failed to comply with § 706(b) because the notice had not included sufficient factual and statistical information about the charges nor informed the company of the approximate dates of the unlawful practices. Accordingly, it ordered that the agency subpoena not be enforced. The Supreme Court agreed that a charge and notice meeting the requirements of § 706 are jurisdictional prerequisites to judicial enforcement of an agency subpoena, but determined that in this case the requirements had been met and reversed. The Court concluded that the Eighth Circuit's holding would, in effect, have obliged the Commissioner to substantiate his allegations before the EEOC could investigate, thus impairing the agency's enforcement powers. The purpose of the notice requirement in § 706(b) is to give an employer fair notice of the existence and nature of the allegations against it, and not to impose a substantive constraint on the EEOC's investigative authority. The statute requires that a Commissioner charging a pattern or practice of discrimination should:

> Insofar as he is able * * * identify the groups of persons that he has reason to believe have been discriminated against, the categories of employment positions from which they have been excluded, the methods by which the discrimination may have been effected, and the periods of time in which he suspects the discrimination to have been practiced.

466 U.S. at 73, 104 S.Ct. at 1633. Should EEOC "harassment" of an employer constitute an affirmative defense to the Commission's suit? A basis for a counterclaim under the Federal Tort Claims Act? See EEOC v. First National Bank, 614 F.2d 1004 (5th Cir. 1980), cert. denied, 450 U.S. 917, 101 S.Ct. 1361, 67 L.Ed.2d 342 (1981).

EEOC ACTIONS AND THE RIGHTS OF INDIVIDUAL CLAIMANTS

ADAMS v. PROCTOR & GAMBLE MANUFACTURING CO.

United States Court of Appeals, Fourth Circuit, 1983.
697 F.2d 582, cert. denied, 465 U.S. 1041, 104 S.Ct. 1318, 79 L.Ed.2d 714 (1984).

Before WINTER, CHIEF JUDGE, RUSSELL, WIDENER, HALL, PHILLIPS, MURNAGHAN, SPROUSE, ERVIN, CHAPMAN, CIRCUIT JUDGES, and HAYNSWORTH, SENIOR CIRCUIT JUDGE, Sitting En Banc.

PER CURIAM:

This case, concerning the preclusive effect upon charging parties of a consent decree in an action brought against an employer by the EEOC, was first heard by a panel of this court. A majority of the panel held there was no preclusive effect, while Senior Judge Haynsworth dissented. Adams v. The Proctor & Gamble Mfg. Co., 678 F.2d 1190 (4th Cir. 1982). Thereafter, an order was entered granting rehearing *en banc.*

The question turns upon a proper interpretation of § 706(f)(1) of Title VII, 42 U.S.C.A. § 2000e–5(f)(1), which, insofar as pertinent, provides:

> (f)(1) If within thirty days after a charge is filed with the Commission * * *, the Commission has been unable to secure from the respondent a conciliation agreement acceptable to the Commission, the Commission may bring a civil action against any respondent not a government, governmental agency, or political subdivision named in the charge * * *. The person or persons aggrieved shall have the right to intervene in a civil action brought by the Commission * * *. If a charge filed with the Commission pursuant to subsection (b) of this section is dismissed by the Commission, or if within one hundred and eighty days from the filing of such charge * * *, the Commission has not filed a civil action under this section * * *, or the Commission has not entered into a conciliation agreement to which the person aggrieved is a party, the Commission * * * shall so notify the person aggrieved and within ninety days after the giving of such notice a civil action may be brought against the respondent named in the charge (A) by the person claiming to be aggrieved * * *.

In 1976 the EEOC brought an action against Proctor & Gamble alleging employment discrimination. Some two dozen Proctor & Gamble employees had filed charges with the EEOC, but none of them chose to intervene in the EEOC action, though each had an unqualified right to do so under § 706(f)(1). Negotiations between the employer and the EEOC resulted in a settlement of the action by consent decree. Thereafter, the EEOC issued right-to-sue letters to those charging parties who rejected awards under the decree. When sixteen of those Proctor & Gamble workers with right-to-sue letters sued individually, the district court granted the company's motion to dismiss on the ground that the letters were invalid.

Substantially for the reasons set forth in Judge Haynsworth's dissenting opinion when the case was before the panel, we hold the district court's dismissal was appropriate. We read § 706(f)(1) in these circumstances to preclude suits by individuals who are charging parties, but who have not intervened in the pending EEOC action in their behalf, once the EEOC action has been concluded by a consent decree.

Under § 706(f)(1) right-to-sue letters may be issued by the Commission to charging parties under several different circumstances, but there is no provision for the issuance of such a letter under any circumstance after the EEOC has filed an action on behalf of the charging parties. As noted by the panel dissenter, there must be an exception if the EEOC's action is concluded on technical grounds without a judgment on the merits. In every sense, however, this consent decree was a judgment on the merits, and it awarded benefits which were then available to the charging parties.

The statutory scheme is fair and reasonable. A charging party has an unqualified right to intervene in the EEOC's action. If he wishes to participate in settlement negotiations or to have the right to reject any settlement agreement negotiated by the EEOC, he may fully protect himself by intervening. If he does not intervene, it is not unfair to him to conclude that he placed the conduct of the litigation entirely upon the EEOC and expressed a conclusive willingness to be bound by the outcome, whether or not the outcome was negotiated.

General Telephone Co. of the Northwest, Inc., v. EEOC, 446 U.S. 318, 100 S.Ct. 1698, 64 L.Ed.2d 319 (1980), is not to the contrary. In that case the employer had sought a ruling that the EEOC could not obtain broad class relief without compliance with Federal Rule of Civil Procedure 23. There were only four charging parties in that case, but there were allegations of pervasive discrimination affecting a great many persons. In those circumstances, if the EEOC were required to comply with rule 23, the efficacy of the EEOC's § 706(f)(1) remedy would be substantially impaired. Thus, the Supreme Court observed that it was "unconvinced that it would be consistent with the remedial purpose of the statutes to bind all 'class' members * * * by the relief obtained under an EEOC judgment or settlement against the employer." Id. at 333, 100 S.Ct. at 1707–08.

The question before the Supreme Court in *General Telephone* was exclusively related to the effect of a possible judgment upon persons who were not charging parties and who had no right of intervention. The Court's dicta must be read as referable to them and entirely inapplicable to the question of the preclusive effect of a judgment upon charging parties who had not exercised their right of intervention.

Our interpretation of § 706(f)(1) is not unprecedented. See e.g., Jones v. Bell Helicopter Co., 614 F.2d 1389 (5th Cir. 1980); McClain v. Wagner Electric Corp., 550 F.2d 1115 (8th Cir. 1977); Crump v. Wagner Electric Corp., 369 F.Supp. 637 (E.D.Mo.1973). Cf. Truvillion v. King's Daughters Hospital, 614 F.2d 520 (5th Cir. 1980).

There has been some expression of concern among our dissenting brothers that a charging party may not recognize any reason to intervene in an EEOC action before an undesirable consent decree has been entered, by which time the right to intervene will have been lost. We appreciate their concern, but it cannot change the plain meaning of § 706(f)(1). Moreover, one who wishes to participate in tactical decisions which may substantially affect the outcome of the litigation or in settlement negotiations has reason for early intervention. In this, as in many other situations, one who invokes administrative and judicial machinery in his behalf should have a continuing interest or participation in it. If he does not intervene and leaves it to the EEOC to do whatever seems best to the EEOC for him, he should not be heard to complain of the consequences of his own indifference.

The judgment of the district court is affirmed.

Affirmed.

* * *

[The concurring opinion of JUDGE WIDENER is omitted]

PHILLIPS, CIRCUIT JUDGE, dissenting:

I respectfully dissent for the reasons expressed in the superseded panel opinion, 678 F.2d 1190, which held that plaintiffs' individual rights of action were not terminated by the institution of an EEOC action nor precluded by the entry in that action of a consent judgment to which they were not parties and whose terms they had affirmatively rejected. I continue to believe (as presumably does the EEOC, the federal agency charged with enforcing the statutory scheme in issue) that under the circumstances the EEOC was entitled under § 706(f)(1) to issue to these plaintiffs the right-to-sue letters upon which this action was brought and that the underlying rights of action are subsisting ones.

With all deference, nothing said in the per curiam opinion of the en banc court dissuades me from the interpretation given the controlling statutory provision by the original panel decision. As the majority opinion notes, those of us in dissent are particularly concerned that the contrary interpretation now reached imposes an utterly unrealistic burden upon Title VII charging parties. Under that interpretation, charging parties are required at their peril, and unaided by the principals, to follow the course of agency-employer conciliation or "settlement" efforts closely enough to protect their individual interests by formal intervention if, following institution of an agency action, those negotiations seem headed toward an unfavorable settlement.

There is nothing in the relevant statutory framework that lays upon the EEOC or the employer any obligation to keep charging parties advised of the details of those negotiations; of whether any "settlement" is imminent; of whether any settlement under consideration is to be expressed in a conciliation agreement or in a consent judgment; of the details or even the substance of a "settlement" that has been informally reached and remains only to be formalized by either means; of whether and when an agency action is to be commenced; of the fact that one has been commenced; or of anything else about the course of agency-employer dealings. The formal agency documents on file and a part of the record in this case contain no information along these lines of which charging parties might be held to have constructive notice. On oral argument we were given to understand by counsel for the EEOC, appearing as *amicus,* that the agency does not consider itself under any obligation and does not routinely keep all charging parties even generally apprised of the course of its conciliation-"settlement" negotiations. Certainly there is no suggestion that in this case—where presumably the normal course of proceedings was followed—these charging party-plaintiffs were ever sufficiently advised along these lines to make an informed decision that they must formally intervene—with the attendant expense—in order to protect their interests against an imminent consent judgment that did not satisfactorily protect them.

To the plain difficulty created for charging parties by its interpretation the en banc majority—which commendably concedes the difficulty—has only the meager response that the law after all affords these and comparably situated claimants the same means to protect their interests vis-a-vis agency action in their behalf that it does all persons in whose behalf federal agency action is undertaken. When the practicalities of the real-life situation involving these and comparably situated Title VII charging parties in their relation to EEOC-employer negotiations are frankly recognized, this assessment calls to mind—though with none of its implications of callousness—Anatole France's wry comment about actual as opposed to apparent impartiality of the law's general reach.[1]

If to all this it be rejoined that it is not our function to re-write statutes to cure perceived difficulties but simply to apply them according to their plain import, my response remains as it was in the panel majority opinion: that the dispositive statutory provision here is sufficiently ambiguous to require judicial interpretation drawing on the traditional aids. Among those traditional aids—in addition to the legislative history specifically alluded to in the panel opinion, see 678 F.2d at 1193–94—is that ancient and honorable canon of construction that when a literal interpretation ("conciliation" means only "conciliation") would lead to mischievous consequences, legislative intent is properly sought at deeper levels of purpose. See J. Sutherland, *Statutes and Statutory Construction* § 363 (2d ed. 1904). I continue to believe that in General Telephone Co. of the Northwest, Inc. v. EEOC, 446 U.S. 318, 100 S.Ct. 1698, 64 L.Ed.2d 319 (1980), the Supreme Court, by the clearest possible implication, and perhaps drawing *sub silentio* upon that canon, has already rejected the narrowly literal interpretation of § 706(f)(1) for which Proctor & Gamble has contended and which the en banc majority now adopts. See 678 F.2d at 1194–95 & n. 7. The *General Telephone* Court's careful discussion of the practical means by which employers entering into Title VII consent judgments with the EEOC may protect themselves against the private claims of employees—*including* charging parties—who may later reject the agency-employer settlement, see *General Telephone,* 446 U.S. at 333 & n. 15, 100 S.Ct. at 1708 & n. 15, is sensible only if it assumes that such judgments are not legally binding on those employees and that the employees' private rights of action are not terminated by mere institution of agency actions under § 706.

I am authorized to say that CHIEF JUDGE WINTER and JUDGE SPROUSE join in this opinion.

NOTES AND PROBLEMS FOR DISCUSSION

1. What steps might a district court take to protect the rights of employees who will be affected by the resolution of an EEOC suit? See, EEOC v. Pan American World Airways, 622 F.Supp. 633 (N.D.Cal.1985) and Chapter 7, infra.

1. "The law, in its majestic equality, forbids the rich as well as the poor to sleep under bridges, to beg in the streets, and to steal bread." A. France, *Le Lys Rouge* ch. 7 (1894), *quoted in* J. Cournos, *A Modern Plutarch* 27 (1928).

Chapter 6

PROCEDURAL REQUIREMENTS FOR PUBLIC SECTOR EMPLOYEES

SECTION A. FEDERAL GOVERNMENT EMPLOYEES

Read Section 717 of Title VII.

Title VII, as originally enacted, did not prohibit discrimination by public employers. As part of the Equal Employment Opportunity Act of 1972, however, Congress expanded the coverage of Title VII to include most federal, state and local government employees.[a] State and local governments were brought under the statute's jurisdiction through a broadened definition of "person" in § 701(a). A new provision—§ 717—was added to bring federal employees within the coverage of the Act. This latter section, in addition to its substantive provisions, designated the Civil Service Commission as the agency with jurisdiction over federal employee complaints of job discrimination. This function subsequently was transferred to the EEOC by § 3 of President Carter's Reorganization Plan No. 1 of 1978.

After this transfer of authority from the Civil Service Commission to the EEOC was effected, the EEOC adopted, with some minor changes, the procedural regulations previously used by the Civil Service Commission. These regulations, now codified at 29 CFR 1613 (1979), set forth the unique procedural rules that apply only to federal employees. Briefly, they require the aggrieved first to seek review of the challenged action within his or her own agency by consulting with that agency's Equal Employment Opportunity Counselor. If the employee is not satisfied with the Counselor's informal resolution of the matter, he or she can file a formal complaint with the official designated by the agency to receive such complaints. After an investigation and opportunity for a hearing, the agency EEO official renders a decision which is appealable to the agency head. If the aggrieved is not satisfied with the agency's final decision, he or she can either seek immediate judicial review of that decision or appeal to the EEOC.[b] The EEOC regulations

[a] The statute specifically exempts employees of the General Accounting Office, state or local elected officials, appointed members of the personal staff of such elected officials and appointed policy level state or local officials. See §§ 701(f), 717. While the statute has been interpreted to include civilian employees of the Army, Mares v. Marsh, 777 F.2d 1066 (5th Cir. 1985), it also has been construed to exclude uniformed members of the armed forces. See Gonzalez v. Department of Army, 718 F.2d 926 (9th Cir. 1983), and commissioned Public Health Service Officers, Salazar v. Heckler, 787 F.2d 527 (10th Cir. 1986).

[b] The 1978 reorganization plan also authorized the EEOC to delegate back to the Civil Service Commission (renamed the Merit Systems Protection Board by President Carter's Reorganization Plan #2 of 1978, § 201) the task of making prelimina-

also set forth time limits governing the various stages of this process. For example, if the aggrieved chooses to bypass the EEOC, both § 717 and the EEOC regulations authorize him or her to file a civil action in federal district court:

(a) Within thirty days of receipt of notice of final action taken by the employer agency on a complaint;[c] or

(b) After one-hundred eighty days from the filing of a complaint with the employer agency if there has been no decision.

ry rulings on any discrimination issue in so called "mixed cases"—i.e., those involving charges of discrimination prohibited by Title VII and employer conduct not covered by § 717. Additionally, the aggrieved individual retained the right to appeal the Merit Board's disposition of the § 717 issue to the EEOC. In cases involving only charges of discrimination cognizable under § 717, on the other hand, jurisdiction lies exclusively with the EEOC, which applies the same substantive standards used in connection with charges filed by private sector employees. This procedure was altered somewhat by the passage of the Civil Service Reform Act of 1978, 5 U.S.C. § 1101 et seq. This statute provides that where an employee or applicant seeks further administrative review of the employer agency's disposition of a Title VII challenge to certain specified kinds of employment decisions (removal, suspension for more than fourteen days, and reduction in grade or pay), the charge must be appealed from the agency to the MSPB, rather than the EEOC, regardless of whether it is a "mixed" or "pure" discrimination case. The charging party then can appeal the Board's decision to the EEOC which, if it disagrees with the Board's decision, must refer the case back to the Board for reconsideration. If the Board refuses to adopt the Commission's decision, and reaffirms its original ruling, it must certify the matter to a special three member panel consisting of a member of the Board, a member of the Commission and a Presidentially-appointed neutral. This panel then renders the final administrative decision in the case. See 5 U.S.C. §§ 7512, 7513, 7702 (1978). The Civil Service Reform Act also sets forth a separate series of limitations periods governing the filing of suit with respect to these limited types of personnel actions. Specifically, an aggrieved can file a civil action in federal district court after:

(a) the 120th day following the filing of a complaint with the employer agency where that complaint is appealable to the MSPB and there is no final decision by the agency and the aggrieved has not filed an appeal with the MSPB; or

(b) the 120th day after the filing of an appeal with the MSPB and there is no judicially reviewable action by the MSPB; or

(c) the 180th day after the filing of a petition with the EEOC and there is no final action by the EEOC.

The federal district court has jurisdiction over the entire case, including both the § 717 and non-§ 717 issues. See Christo v. MSPB, 667 F.2d 882 (10th Cir. 1981). Where, however, the Merit Systems Protection Board determines that the discrimination allegation in a "mixed" case is frivolous, review of the merits of the action lies exclusively with the Federal Circuit. The district court has appellate jurisdiction only where the discrimination claim in a "mixed" case is not frivolous. Hill v. Department of Air Force, 796 F.2d 1469 (Fed. Cir. 1986).

[c] The courts have split on the issue of whether a federal employee who petitions the EEOC to reconsider his claim must file suit within thirty days after the original decision or within thirty days from the disposition of the reconsideration petition. Compare Birch v. Lehman, 677 F.2d 1006 (4th Cir. 1982), cert. denied, 459 U.S. 1103, 103 S.Ct. 725, 74 L.Ed.2d 951 (1983) (reconsideration petition cannot extend filing period) with Donaldson v. T.V.A., 759 F.2d 535 (6th Cir. 1985) (reconsideration petition filed within 30 day period for bringing suit extends filing period to thirty days from receipt of notice of disposition of reconsideration petition) and Nordell v. Heckler, 749 F.2d 47 (D.C.Cir. 1984) (if reconsideration petition filed within time for bringing suit, such petition renders the initial decision no longer a "final action" and extends the deadline until thirty days from disposition of the reconsideration request) and with Martinez v. Orr, 738 F.2d 1107 (10th Cir. 1984) (reconsideration petition might be a basis in some circumstances for tolling the thirty day limit).

However, if the employee chooses to appeal the agency's action to the EEOC before bringing suit, the court action must be filed

(a) Within thirty days after receipt of notice of final action taken by the EEOC on the complaint; or

(b) After one-hundred eighty days from the date of filing an appeal with the EEOC if there has been no EEOC decision.

29 CFR 1613.281.

NOTES AND PROBLEMS FOR DISCUSSION

1. Federal employment discrimination, of course, can also violate the equal protection and due process guarantees of the Fifth Amendment as well as Executive Order 11478. A federal employee also might wish to challenge job discrimination under the 1866 or 1871 Civil Rights Acts and the Equal Pay Act. In BROWN v. G.S.A., 425 U.S. 820, 96 S.Ct. 1961, 48 L.Ed.2d 402 (1976), however, the Supreme Court held that Congress intended Title VII to be the exclusive and pre-emptive administrative and judicial remedy for federal employment discrimination claims. What about an employee of the government of the District of Columbia? See Cox v. University of District of Columbia, 24 FEP Cases 690 (D.D.C.1980). If, as noted supra, Title VII does not provide relief for the physical and emotional damages suffered by victims of sexual harassment, is a federal employee precluded by *Brown* from seeking relief under some other cause of action? See Langster v. Schweiker, 565 F.Supp. 407 (N.D.Ill.1983) (Title VII does not preempt other relief for conduct beyond the scope of Title VII); Epps v. Ripley, 30 FEP Cases 1632 (D.D.C.1982) (*Brown* interpreted as making Title VII the exclusive federal remedy and does not preempt state tort remedies); Stewart v. Thomas, 538 F.Supp. 891 (D.D.C.1982).

2. In light of the extensive administrative procedures available to a federal employee, to what extent should a federal judge be obliged to defer to the agency determinations in adjudicating a federal employee's Title VII claim? In CHANDLER v. ROUDEBUSH, 425 U.S. 840, 96 S.Ct. 1949, 48 L.Ed.2d 416 (1976), the Court concluded that federal employees enjoyed the same right to a judicial trial de novo of Title VII claims as private sector or state government employees. Central to this holding was the Court's determination that in enacting the 1972 amendment to extend Title VII to public employees, Congress intended to give federal employees the same measure of rights enjoyed by private employees. How, then, does this square with the ruling in *Brown*, decided the same day as *Chandler*, in light of the fact that private sector employees are not restricted to seeking relief for job discrimination under Title VII? It has been suggested that *Brown*'s divergence from the *Chandler* parity principle can be explained as a desire to compel federal employees to utilize the more elaborate administrative procedure provided to them in Title VII actions than is available to nonfederal workers. See C.A. Sullivan, M.J. Zimmer and R.F. Richards, Federal Statutory Law of Employment Discrimination, § 2.13 at 252–253 (1980). But doesn't the ruling in *Chandler* according federal courts the right to completely disregard agency findings of fact and law in suits brought by federal employees cut against that argument? Should the availability of de novo review depend upon whether the federal employee loses or wins before the EEOC? In Moore v. Devine, 780 F.2d 1559 (11th Cir. 1986), the court held that a final EEOC order favorable to a federal employee is binding on that employee's agency and is subject to an enforcement order by the district court without

de novo review if the agency fails to comply with the EEOC order. The court distinguished *Chandler*, stating that it was limited to cases where the federal employee had lost before the EEOC. Where the plaintiff wins, however, the court reasoned, the statute indicated that federal employees are to be treated differently than private or state employees, since it provides the EEOC with the authority to issue remedial orders upon a finding of discrimination by the federal government.

3. Who should bear the burden of establishing exhaustion of administrative remedies? Is it significant that since a federal employee must first seek redress within her or his own agency, the defendant would have custody of the relevant records? See Brown v. Marsh, 777 F.2d 8 (D.C. Cir. 1985).

SECTION B. STATE AND LOCAL GOVERNMENT EMPLOYEES

The Equal Employment Opportunity Act of 1972 extended the coverage of Title VII to state and local government employees. In Fitzpatrick v. Bitzer,[a] moreover, the Supreme Court ruled that the Eleventh Amendment did not preclude the granting of monetary damages against a state or local government defendant for back pay and attorney's fees in an action brought under that statute. While the Supreme Court has indicated that the proof standards applied to private Title VII claims also should govern claims against state and local governments,[b] there is one procedural difference between the enforcement of private and nonfederal public discrimination claims. Section 706(f)(1) authorizes the Attorney General, rather than the EEOC, to file a civil action against a nonfederal public employer.

NOTE FOR DISCUSSION

1. Should the exclusivity doctrine announced in Brown v. G.S.A. apply to state and local government employees? The courts are split on whether *Brown* should be read to preclude state employee claims under § 1983. Compare Alexander v. Chicago Park District, 773 F.2d 850 (7th Cir. 1985) (Title VII is exclusive remedy for state employee only when the right asserted by the plaintiff was created by Title VII; plaintiff can assert § 1983 claim based on violation of Fourteenth Amendment.); Trigg v. Fort Wayne Community Schools, 766 F.2d 299 (7th Cir. 1985) (Title VII does not preempt state employee's § 1983 claim alleging violation of equal protection clause of 14th Amendment); Nilsen v. City of Moss Point, Miss., 701 F.2d 556 (5th Cir. 1983) (Title VII and § 1983 claim based on Fourteenth Amendment violation must be joined in same suit to avoid invocation of res judicata principles); Poolaw v. City of Anadarko, 660 F.2d 459 (10th Cir. 1981), cert. denied, ___ U.S. ___, 105 S.Ct. 784, 83 L.Ed.2d 779 (1985) (permitting state employee to file claims under Title VII, §§ 1981 and 1983 without discussing the exclusivity issue) and Storey v. Bd. of Regents of Univ. of Wis., 600 F.Supp. 838 (W.D.Wi.1985) (Title VII does

[a] 427 U.S. 445, 96 S.Ct. 2666, 49 L.Ed.2d 614 (1976).

[b] See New York City Transit Authority v. Beazer, 440 U.S. 568, 99 S.Ct. 1355, 59 L.Ed.2d 587 (1979); Dothard v. Rawlinson, 433 U.S. 321, 331 n.14, 97 S.Ct. 2720, 2728 n.14, 53 L.Ed.2d 786, 799 n.14 (1977) ("* * * Congress expressly indicated that the same Title VII principles be applied to governmental and private employers alike.").

not preempt pre-existing remedy under § 1983 for violation of constitutional rights nor does it preempt Title IX remedy of state employee to the extent that Title IX provides a remedy—termination of federal funding—which is unavailable under Title VII) with Day v. Wayne County Board of Auditors, 749 F.2d 1199 (6th Cir. 1984) (Title VII precludes § 1983 claim based on violation of rights guaranteed by Title VII) and Tafoya v. Adams, 612 F.Supp. 1097 (D.Colo.1985) (Id.). See also Shapiro, Section 1983 Claims To Redress Discrimination In Public Employment: Are They Preempted By Title VII?, 35 Amer. U. L. Rev. 93 (1985); Comment, Trigg v. Fort Wayne Community Schools: State Employee Discrimination Claims—Is the Conflict Between Title VII and § 1983 Resolved?, 61 Notre Dame L. Rev. 88 (1986). Interestingly, however, the courts uniformly permit state employees to file § 1981 claims. See 512 infra. Is there any basis for this distinction? If the purpose of the exclusivity rule is to prevent federal employees from eschewing the extensive administrative scheme provided by the statute, why should state employees, who are not subject to this machinery, be subjected to the exclusivity principle? Do the rulings in these cases require any more than artful pleading? Is there any difference when the plaintiff asserts that a § 1983 claim is predicated on a Fourteenth Amendment rather than a Title VII violation? What about the requirement for establishing a prima facie case?

Chapter 7

CLASS ACTIONS

SECTION A. INTRODUCTION

Rule 23 of the Federal Rules of Civil Procedure provides in part:

(a) Prerequisites to a Class Action. One or more members of a class may sue or be sued as representative parties on behalf of all only if (1) the class is so numerous that joinder of all members is impracticable, (2) there are questions of law or fact common to the class, (3) the claims or defenses of the representative parties are typical of the claims or defenses of the class, and (4) the representative parties will fairly and adequately protect the interest of the class.

(b) Class Actions Maintainable. An action may be maintained as a class action if the prerequisites of subdivision (a) are satisfied, and in addition:

(1) The prosecution of separate actions by or against individual members of the class would create a risk of

(A) inconsistent or varying adjudications with respect to individual members of the class which would establish incompatible standards of conduct for the party opposing the class, or

(B) adjudications with respect to individual members of the class which would as a practical matter be dispositive of the interests of the other members not parties to the adjudications or substantially impair or impede their ability to protect their interests; or

(2) the party opposing the class has acted or refused to act on grounds generally applicable to the class, thereby making appropriate final injunctive relief or corresponding declaratory relief with respect to the class as a whole; or

(3) the court finds that the questions of law or fact common to the members of the class predominate over any questions affecting only individual members, and that a class action is superior to other available methods for the fair and efficient adjudication of the controversy. The matters pertinent to the findings include: (A) the interest of members of the class in individually controlling the prosecution or defense of separate actions; (B) the extent and nature of any litigation concerning the controversy already commenced by or against members of the class; (C) the desirability or undesirability of concentrating the litigation of the claims in the particular forum; (D) the difficulties likely to be encountered in the management of a class action.

(c) Determination by Order Whether Class Action to Be Maintained; Notice; Judgment; Actions Conducted Partially as Class Actions.

(1) As soon as practicable after the commencement of an action brought as a class action, the court shall determine by order whether it is to be so maintained. An order under this subdivision may be conditional, and may be altered or amended before the decision on the merits.

* * *

The class action did not originate with the adoption of the Federal Rules, but was "an invention of equity to enable it to proceed to a decree in suits where the number of those interested in the subject of the litigation is so great that their joinder as parties in conformity to the usual rules of procedure is impracticable." Hansberry v. Lee, 311 U.S. 32, 41, 61 S.Ct. 115, 85 L.Ed. 22 (1940). Following Brown v. Board of Education, 347 U.S. 483, 74 S.Ct. 686, 98 L.Ed. 873 (1954), the civil rights class action became a frequently used device for attacking racial discrimination in education, voting rights and housing. Typical of these cases were school desegregation suits where relief could not be granted to an individual plaintiff without, in effect, affording the same relief (i.e., desegregated schools) to a class composed of those sharing the same racial characteristic, whether the suit was denominated a "class" action or not. As the Fifth Circuit noted:

> There is at least considerable doubt that relief confined to individual specified Negro children either could be granted or, if granted, could be so limited in its operative effect. By the very nature of the controversy, the attack is on the unconstitutional practice of racial discrimination. Once that is found to exist, the court must order that it be discontinued. Such a decree, of course, might name the successful plaintiff as the party not to be discriminated against. But that decree may not—either expressly or impliedly—affirmatively authorize continued discrimination by reason of race against others. * * * Moreover, to require a school system to admit the specific successful plaintiff Negro child while others, having no such protection, were required to attend schools in a racially segregated system, would be for the court to contribute actively to the *class* discrimination * * *.

Potts v. Flax, 313 F.2d 284, 289 (5th Cir. 1963).

Rule 23 was revised in 1966 in part by the addition of section (b)(2) which was created specifically to facilitate civil rights actions "where a party is charged with discriminating unlawfully against a class, usually one whose members are incapable of specific enumeration." 1966 Advisory Committee's Note, 39 F.R.D. 98, 102. Not surprisingly, suits in which class-wide relief was automatic if the plaintiff prevailed did not result in close attention to the requirements of Rule 23.

Early employment discrimination class actions frequently attacked a whole range of employment practices (hiring, promotion, job assignment, pay scales, working conditions, etc.) and were referred to as "across the board" cases. Such cases, more often than not, fell into the mold set by the earlier civil rights litigation. "Whether in name or not, the suit is perforce a sort of class action for fellow employees similarly situated." Jenkins v. United Gas Corp., 400 F.2d 28, 33 (5th Cir. 1968). "[W]hether the Damoclean threat of racially discriminatory policy hangs over the racial class is a question of fact common to all the members of the class. The court is of the opinion, therefore, that a significant question of fact common to all members of the class exists in this case insofar as the complaint seeks the removal of the alleged discriminatory policies." Hall v. Werthan Bag Corp., 251 F.Supp. 184, 186 (M.D.Tenn.1966). With the increasing complexity of the employment practices challenged in class actions filed under Title VII, Section 1981 and other statutes, courts have increasingly demanded adherence to the requirements of Rule 23. Recent history demonstrates a progression away from the *pro forma* certification of broad classes of employees, former employees and applicants to evidentiary inquiries into the representative capacity of named plaintiffs and appropriate class composition.

SECTION B. THE SCOPE OF THE CLASS AND THE PROPER CLASS REPRESENTATIVE

JOHNSON v. GEORGIA HIGHWAY EXPRESS, INC.

United States Court of Appeal, Fifth Circuit, 1969.
417 F.2d 1122.

Before BROWN, CHIEF JUDGE, GODBOLD, CIRCUIT JUDGE, and CABOT, DISTRICT JUDGE.

CABOT, DISTRICT JUDGE.

This is an interlocutory appeal pursuant to 28 U.S.C. § 1292(b), from an order dated June 24, 1968, of the United States District Court for the Northern District of Georgia which denied appellant's motion to strike the appellee's demand for a jury trial and holding that appellant could not maintain this suit as a class action until he proved that he had been discharged because of race. Additionally, the order restricted the scope of the class to those persons who had been discharged because of their race. The issues to be decided, therefore, are whether or not the court erred with respect to these holdings.

Application of the rule pertaining to class actions is to be considered in the light of the particular circumstances of the case and generally, unless abuse is shown, the trial court's decision as to whether a proper class action has been brought is final. Cypress v. Newport News General and Non-Sectarian Hospital Assn., 4 Cir. 1967, 375 F.2d 648. We hold that such abuse does appear and the trial court must be reversed.

This suit is an employment discrimination action brought under Title VII of the Civil Rights Act of 1964, 42 U.S.C. § 2000e et seq. The appellant Johnson was employed by the appellee Georgia Highway Express, an interstate carrier of freight, in the capacity of a "stripper" and "stacker" in the appellee's Atlanta terminal for a number of years. It was alleged that in February of 1966 the company held a meeting with numerous Negro employees for the purpose of affording them an opportunity to present grievances to the company. The appellant, acting as spokesman for the group, inquired of the company how long it would be before Negro employees would be allowed to apply for jobs not then held by members of their race. Several weeks after the meeting appellant was discharged from his job. Appellant asserts that his discharge was racially motivated. The appellee denies that appellant was a spokesman for the group and contends that the appellant was discharged because of his failure to "regularly report to work" and to "regularly report to work on time."

On or about March 31, 1966, appellant filed a charge of racial discrimination with the Equal Employment Opportunities Commission (EEOC) complaining of certain policies and practices of the appellee all in violation of the Civil Rights Act of 1964, supra. The Commission notified appellant that while it had found reasonable cause to believe that the practices alleged by him had been committed by the company it had been unable to secure the company's voluntary compliance.

Upon the failure of EEOC to conciliate, the appellant on February 27, 1968, filed this complaint on behalf of himself and, pursuant to Rule 23 of the Federal Rules of Civil Procedure, on behalf of all other similarly situated Negroes seeking equal employment opportunities without discrimination on the grounds of race or color. The complaint set forth various acts of discrimination and coupled the same with an assertion of a company-wide policy of discrimination and segregation on the basis of race. The appellant sought to enjoin those practices and sought back pay. The appellee denied the material allegations of the complaint and moved to dismiss on the grounds that the suit was not a proper class action within the meaning of Rule 23 and requested a jury trial on "any issues of fact that may be lawfully tried by a jury." Appellant moved to strike the demand for jury trial. The district court denied the motion to strike and held that the class relief would be limited to persons discharged because of their race and that the suit could not be maintained as a class action until appellant proved that his discharge was for racial reasons and a determination made as to appellant's status in the event he should apply for re-employment.

I

The first point raised by appellant involves the district court's narrowing of the class, i.e., that the appellant, a discharged Negro employee, could only represent other discharged Negro employees. This was error as it is clear from the pleadings that the scope of appellant's suit is an "across the board" attack on unequal employment practices alleged to have been committed by the appellee pursuant to its policy of racial discrimination. Thus, the following language from a decision of this court, though appearing in a school desegregation case, seems applicable here:

> The peculiar rights of specific individuals were not in controversy. It [the suit] was directed at the system wide policy of racial discrimination. It sought obliteration of that policy of system-wide racial discrimination. In various ways this was sought through suitable declaratory orders and injunctions against any rule, regulation, custom or practice having any such consequence.

Potts v. Flax, 5 Cir. 1963, 313 F.2d 284, 289. While it is true, as the lower court points out, that there are different factual questions with regard to different employees, it is also true that the "Damoclean threat of a racially discriminatory policy hangs over the racial class [and] is a question of fact common to all members of the class." Hall v. Werthan Bag Corp., M.D.Tenn. 1966, 251 F.Supp. 184. Moreover, this court, in Jenkins v. United Gas Corp., 5 Cir. 1968, 400 F.2d 28, a Title VII Civil Rights action, refused to narrow a class based upon reasoning that there are different facts and circumstances involved in employment decisions, jobs, and qualifications. And assuming subsequent intervention after remand, if the lower court feels that it would be too burdensome due to the inapplicability of some issues to other members of the class, resort may be made to the use of sub-classes. See Oatis v. Crown Zellerbach Corp., 5 Cir. 1968, 398 F.2d 496. While the lower court was in doubt as to which class the appellant sought to represent, from the nature of the relief and subsequent briefs, it is obvious that he seeks to represent all Negro employees of the appellee, including discharged employees, as this is the class harmed by the alleged discrimination in hiring, firing, promotion, and maintenance of facilities.

In addition to impermissibly narrowing the class, the lower court refused to allow the appellant to represent the class until he proved his own right to relief. What the court held, therefore, was that the appellant was not a proper representative of the class. Two of the prerequisites to a class action are that the claims or defenses of the representative party are typical of the claims or defenses of the class, and that the representative party will fairly and adequately protect the interests of the class. Federal Rules of Civil Procedure, Rule 23(a)(3), (a)(4).

In this case it is clear that the appellant is a member of the class, i.e., a discharged Negro employee of the appellee, and his claim of racial discrimination is typical of the claims of the class. Whether he will adequately represent the class is a question of fact to be "raised and resolved in the trial court in the usual manner, * * *." Harris v. Palm Springs Alpine Estates, Inc., 9 Cir. 1964, 329 F.2d 909, 913. Therefore, the court below, if it doubted appellant's ability to protect the interests of the class, could have had, and on remand still can have, an evidentiary hearing on the issue. In this regard the standard to be applied is not whether appellant will prevail, but is as stated by Judge Medina:

> An essential concomitant of adequate representation is that the party's attorney be qualified, experienced, and generally able to conduct the proposed litigation. Additionally, it is necessary to eliminate so far as possible the likelihood that the litigants are involved in a collusive suit or that plaintiff has interests antagonistic to those of the remainder of the class.

Eisen v. Carlisle and Jacquelin, 2 Cir. 1968, 391 F.2d 555.

The plaintiff seeks relief against "limiting the use of company maintained facilities on the basis of race or color" but does not describe the facilities or the circumstances surrounding their use. If the defendant is not sufficiently advised of the charges made so as to be able to adequately meet its trial burdens, recourse may be had to a motion for more definite statement and to the various pretrial discovery devices.

The interstate character of defendant's business may well place a heavy management burden on the court, but surely not beyond the resourcefulness of the court to meet. For example, the court could well require appropriate notice to members of the class by letter, poster, etc., even though no notice is specifically required under Rule 23(b)(2), Fed. R.Civ.P., with which we are here concerned.

* * *

The order of the district court is reversed and the cause remanded for proceedings in accordance with this opinion.

GODBOLD, CIRCUIT JUDGE (specially concurring).

I concur in the reversal. As I understand it, we are telling the District Court that it defined the class too narrowly and that it must extend the limits outward. We are not, at the appellate level, attempting to stake out precise limits of an appropriate class. That can be done only when there are more precise pleadings, enabling the District Court to equate and balance what the appellant claims are the limits of the class against the tests of adequate representation, protection of the interests of the class, and manageability of the lawsuit.

The burden of telling the District Court enough that it can intelligibly proceed is on the complaining party in the first instance, not upon the court to do so by conducting hearings on adequacy of representation, or upon the defendant to flush out the claims by discovery. The status of the Title VII complainant as a private attorney general does not entitle him to proceed with all cards held to his chest or with no cards at all. The class action is a useful tool or device whose capacities are wide but not without limits.

The District Court was understandably in doubt as to just what class the appellant purported to represent. What is now obvious in this Court is that appellant hopes—and plans—to represent a class as broad as his ingenuity and syntax will allow, subject to whatever boundaries are court-established. The only specific allegations concern appellant's discharge from his position as "stripper," and the failure to promote Negro dock workers to city drivers, both occurring at appellee's Atlanta terminal. Georgia Highway is an interstate motor freight carrier operating in three states, with its principal office and largest terminal in Atlanta, where it allegedly employs over 600 persons. Its total employment is alleged to be more than 1,100 persons. According to the National Motor Carriers' Directory, it has 32 terminals.

Appellant alleges that appellee does not employ Negroes in administrative offices, but whether in Atlanta, elsewhere, or systemwide is not stated. There is an allegation, about as general as language can be made, that the appellee "pursues a policy and condones discrimination or segregation on the basis of race or color." Whether this refers to hiring, promotion, conditions of employment, or use of facilities, all concerned are left to guess. No defendant with a multiplant operation, and employees (some mobile and some fixed) scattered over several states and performing differing duties under presumably differing supervisors, can prepare a defense to this sort of charge. In the instant case over-the-road drivers, who, obviously do not work at the Atlanta terminal, are mentioned for the first time in the prayer for relief. Likewise the prayer asks for an end to unidentified discrimination in the "use of company maintained facilities."

The pleadings structure no class by defined acts, by time, by persons, by plant, by department, by supervisor, or by any other means. The appellant has done no more than name the preserve on which he intends to hunt. Over-technical limitation of classes by the district courts will drain the life out of Title VII, as will unduly narrow scope of relief once discriminatory acts are found. But without reasonable specificity the court cannot define the class, cannot determine whether the representation is adequate, and the employer does not know how to defend. And, what may be most significant, an over-broad framing of the class may be so unfair to the absent members as to approach, if not amount to, deprivation of due process. Envision the hypothetical attorney with a single client, filing a class action to halt all racial discrimination in all the numerous plants and facilities of one of America's mammoth corporations. One act, or a few acts, at one or a few places, can be charged to be part of a practice or policy quickening an injunction against all racial discrimination by the employer at all places. It is tidy, convenient for the courts fearing a flood of Title VII cases, and dandy for the employees if their champion wins. But what of the catastrophic consequences if the plaintiff loses and carries the class down with him, or proves only such limited facts that no practice or policy can be found, leaving him afloat but sinking the class?

In Oatis v. Crown Zellerbach, 398 F.2d 496 (1968), a single-plant case, plaintiff Hill claimed discrimination in several forms, one being the use of segregated locker rooms. This court allowed Oatis, Johnson and Young to appear as co-plaintiffs because each was employed in a separate and different department of the plant than Hill, but we held these co-plaintiffs "must proceed, however, within the periphery of the issues which Hill could assert," and that if necessary each co-plaintiff could represent a sub-class of persons in his department. *Oatis* represents a rational effort to structure classes and sub-classes based on the claims made as read against the factual context of the lawsuit. Jenkins v. United Gas Corporation, 400 F.2d 28 (1968) is not to the contrary. That case held that the plaintiff's acceptance of a promotion, after he filed a complaint charging specific racial discrimination in promotion and racial discrimination in general did not render the suit moot as to the class. The last paragraph of the opinion recognizes, as we do and as *Oatis* did, the power and duty to delineate rational classes and sub-classes.

One risk in the Title VII case is the normal reaction of the trial judge to shrink from holding that the single plaintiff, who has sufficient interest and motivation to sue, and his counsel, who has diligence to pursue, do not adequately represent the class, thereby implying possible lack of confidence in them. An additional risk is that of a collusive suit at the indirect and undisclosed behest of the employer, giving him the possibility of a whitewash of systemwide employment practices by a judicial inquiry of narrow scope in a forum far distant from numerous employees who may never have heard of the litigation, or, if they have heard, not in such manner as to impel them to grasp hold of the problem and make decisions about it.

Some of the difficulty may be sifted out by findings of the trial court at or during the trial that the plaintiff adequately represents the class. But this issue itself may be determined in the absence of 99.9% of those affected, who have had no notice or service of process or right to be heard and who may feel that the plaintiff in the particular case (or his counsel, or both) is the last person they want representing them.[1]

The broad brush approach of some of the Title VII cases is in sharp contrast to the diligence with which in other areas we carefully protect those whose rights may be affected by litigation. If this were an individual cross-action against an employee at one of appellee's remote terminals we would turn intellectual handsprings over questions of notice and process to him and opportunity to protect his interests—such issues as whether the marshal dropped the notice at the door or handed it to the child at the front gate. But when the problem is multiplied many-fold, counsel, and at times the courts, are moving blithely ahead tacitly assuming all will be well for surely the plaintiff will win and manna will fall on all members of the class. It is not quite that easy.

NOTES AND PROBLEMS FOR DISCUSSION

1. Would Judge Godbold's concern for the rights of class members be satisfied by notice after certification? What should such a notice say? Assuming adequate explanation in the notice of the nature of the suit and of the

1. Rule 23(b)(2) does not require notice.

potential significance of the litigation to the class member, what can the class member, as a practical matter, do to protect his rights? While notice is not required in Rule 23(b)(1) and (b)(2) actions, the court has discretion under Rule 23(d)(2) to order notice "to some or all members of any step in the action, or of the proposed extent of the judgment, or of the opportunity of members to signify whether they consider the representation fair and adequate, to intervene and present claims or defenses, or otherwise to come into the action." See Clark v. American Marine Corp., 297 F.Supp. 1305 (E.D.La.1969). What problem could such notice cause for the Title VII plaintiff? For the defendant?

2. Should the scope of the class be affected by the nature of the claim made on behalf of the class? For example, in a sex discrimination case against a nationwide company attacking the employer's company-wide maternity leave policy, a class composed of all of the company's female employees of child bearing age may be appropriate. See Wetzel v. Liberty Mutual Insurance Co., 511 F.2d 199 (3d Cir. 1975). But would a class of all female employees be appropriate where the claim was sex discrimination in promotions and company policy relegated promotional decisions to individual district managers?

3. Following Johnson v. Georgia Highway Express, "across the board" allegations of an employer's discriminatory policy said to infect a whole range of employment practices were generally held to satisfy the Rule 23(a)(2) requirement that the litigation raise questions of law and fact common to the class. See, Donaldson v. Pillsbury Co., 554 F.2d 825 (8th Cir. 1977), cert. denied, 434 U.S. 856, 98 S.Ct. 177, 54 L.Ed.2d 128; Lamphere v. Brown University, 71 F.R.D. 641 (D.R.I.1976), affirmed, 553 F.2d 714 (1st Cir. 1977); Kohn v. Royall, Koegel and Wells, 496 F.2d 1094 (2d Cir. 1974). But while an "across the board" allegation of class discrimination could satisfy the 23(a)(2) requirement, the plaintiff still had to demonstrate that the impact of the alleged discriminatory policies on him was not absent or wholly dissimilar from that experienced by other class members in order to comply with Rule 23(a)(3). See, e.g., Wells v. Ramsay, Scarlett & Co., Inc., 506 F.2d 436 (5th Cir. 1975) (the claims of a longshore foreman who was physically unable to perform longshore work and who had severed connections with the longshore union whose membership constituted the class the foreman sought to represent were not typical of the claims of the class of active longshoremen); Gibson v. Local 40 Supercargoes and Checkers of the International Longshoremen's and Warehousemen's Union, 543 F.2d 1259 (9th Cir. 1976) ("casual clerks" could not represent a class composed of full time clerks, a position none of named plaintiffs had sought). In an "across the board" case, however, the class member was not required to demonstrate a factual identity between his individual claim and the class claims in order to establish either typicality or commonality so long as his claim was "plainly rooted in the same bias asserted as the source of the [class] discrimination." Donaldson v. Pillsbury Co., supra, 554 F.2d at 831. For example, in Long v. Sapp, 502 F.2d 34 (5th Cir. 1974), a discharged black employee sought to represent a class composed not only of other discharged employees, but also of current black employees, applicants for employment and blacks "who would have applied for employment had the defendants not practiced racial discrimination in employment and recruiting." After trial, the district court dismissed the plaintiff's individual claims and denied class certification on the ground that since plaintiff had been employed by the defendant, her claims were not typical of those of putative class members who had never been employed. The Fifth Circuit reversed:

> * * * Mrs. Long directs her claims at racially discriminatory policies that she alleges pervade all aspects of the employment practices of Jackson County. Having shown herself to be a black and a former employee, albeit lawfully discharged, she occupies the position of one she says is suffering from the alleged discrimination. She has demonstrated the necessary nexus with the proposed class for membership therein. As a person aggrieved, she can represent other victims of the same policies, whether or not all have experienced discrimination in the same way.

502 F.2d at 43. The "common nexus" approach to determining typicality was widely adopted. See Donaldson v. Pillsbury Co., supra, 554 F.2d at 831; Gibson v. Local 40, Longshoremen's Union, 543 F.2d 1259, 1264 (9th Cir. 1976); Senter v. General Motors Corp., 532 F.2d 511, 523–524 (6th Cir. 1976). The development of the "across the board" case in employment discrimination litigation is described in Strickler, Protecting the Class: The Search For The Adequate Representative in Class Action Litigation, 34 DePaul L.Rev. 73, 110–124 (1984).

EAST TEXAS MOTOR FREIGHT SYSTEM, INC. v. RODRIGUEZ

Supreme Court of the United States, 1977.
431 U.S. 395, 97 S.Ct. 1891, 52 L.Ed.2d 453.

MR. JUSTICE STEWART delivered the opinion of the Court.

These cases, like International Brotherhood of Teamsters v. United States, involve alleged employment discrimination on the part of an employer and unions in the trucking industry. The employer, East Texas Motor Freight System, Inc., is a common carrier that employs city and over-the-road, or "line," truckdrivers. The company has a "no-transfer" policy, prohibiting drivers from transferring between terminals or from city-driver to line-driver jobs.[1] In addition, under the applicable collective-bargaining agreements between the company and the unions, competitive seniority runs only from the date an employee enters a particular bargaining unit, so that a line driver's competitive seniority does not take into account any time he may have spent in other jobs with the company.[2]

The respondents brought this suit against the company and the unions in a Federal District Court, challenging the above practices. Although their complaint denominated the cause as a class action, they did not move for class certification in the trial court. After a two-day hearing the court dismissed the class allegations of the complaint and decided against the individual respondents on the merits. The Court of Appeals for the Fifth Circuit reversed, after itself certifying what it considered an appropriate class and holding that the no-transfer rule and the seniority system violated the statutory rights of that class under 42 U.S.C. § 1981 and Title VII of the Civil Rights Act of 1964, 78

1. Under this policy a city driver must resign his job and forfeit all seniority in order to be eligible for a line-driver job. He gets no priority over other line-driver applicants by virtue of formerly having been with the company, and if he fails to become a line driver he is not automatically entitled to be restored to his city job.

2. For a fuller description of a similar seniority system, see International Brotherhood of Teamsters v. United States, 431 U.S. at 343–344, 97 S.Ct., at 1858–1859.

Stat. 253, as amended, 42 U.S.C. § 2000e et seq. (1970 ed. and Supp. V). 505 F.2d 40. This Court granted certiorari to review the judgment of the Court of Appeals.

I

The respondents are three Mexican-Americans who initiated this litigation as the named plaintiffs, Jesse Rodriguez, Sadrach Perez, and Modesto Herrera. They were employed as city drivers at the company's San Antonio terminal, and were members of Teamsters Local Union 657 and of the Southern Conference of Teamsters. There was no line-driver operation at the San Antonio terminal, and the respondents stipulated that they had not been discriminated against when they were first hired. In August 1970, some years after they were hired, each of them applied in writing for a line-driver job. In accord with its no-transfer policy, the company declined to consider these applications on their individual merits. The respondents then filed complaints with the Equal Employment Opportunity Commission, and after receiving "right to sue" letters from the Commission, see 42 U.S.C. § 2000e–5(e), they brought this lawsuit.

According to the complaint, the suit was brought on behalf of the named plaintiffs and all Negroes and Mexican-Americans who had been denied equal employment opportunities with the company because of their race or national origin. The complaint specifically alleged that the appropriate class should consist of all "East Texas Motor Freight's Mexican-American and Black in-city drivers included in the collective bargaining agreement entered into between East Texas Motor Freight and the Southern Conference of Teamsters covering the State of Texas. Additionally that such class should properly be composed of all Mexican-American and Black applicants for line driver positions with East Texas Motor Freight * * * from July 2, 1965 [the effective date of Title VII] to present."[3]

Despite the class allegations in their complaint, the plaintiffs did not move prior to trial to have the action certified as a class action pursuant to Fed.Rule Civ.Proc. 23, and no such certification was made by the District Judge. Indeed, the plaintiffs had stipulated before trial that " 'the only issue presently before the Court pertaining to the company is whether the failure of the Defendant East Texas Motor Freight to consider Plaintiffs' line driver applications constituted a

3. In addition to attacking the legality of the company's no-transfer and seniority policies, the complaint charged that the company excluded Negroes and Mexican-Americans from line-driver jobs, and that it had discharged plaintiff Perez and harassed plaintiff Rodriguez in retaliation for their having filed charges with the EEOC. The Southern Conference of Teamsters and Teamsters Local 657 were charged with participating in the exclusion of minority persons from line-driver jobs, acquiescing in the company's other discriminatory practices, and entering into collective-bargaining agreements that perpetuated the discrimination against Mexican-Americans and Negroes and erected "dual lines of seniority." In addition to other relief, the plaintiffs demanded that the company "merge its line-driver and city-driver seniority lists so as to provide for a singular seniority system based solely on an employee's anniversary date with the company."

violation of Title VII and 42 U.S.C. § 1981.'" App. 82. And the plaintiffs confined their evidence and arguments at trial to their individual claims. The defendants responded accordingly, with much of their proof devoted to showing that Rodriguez, Perez, and Herrera were not qualified to be line drivers.

Following trial, the District Court dismissed the class-action allegations. It stressed the plaintiffs' failure to move for a prompt determination of the propriety of class certification, their failure to offer evidence on that question, their concentration at the trial on their individual claims, their stipulation that the only issue to be determined concerned the company's failure to act on their applications, and the fact that, contrary to the relief the plaintiffs sought, see n. 3, supra, a large majority of the membership of Local 657 had recently rejected a proposal calling for the merger of city-driver and line-driver seniority lists with free transfer between jobs.[4]

The District Court also held against the named plaintiffs on their individual claims. It ruled that the no-transfer policy and the seniority system were proper business practices, neutrally applied, and that the company had not discriminated against the plaintiffs or retaliated against them for filing charges with the EEOC. The court further found: "None of the plaintiff employees could satisfy all of the qualifications for a road driver position according to the company manual due to age or weight or driving record. * * * The driving, work, and/or physical records of the plaintiffs are of such nature that only casual consideration need be given to determine that the plaintiffs cannot qualify to become road drivers." App. 64.

The Court of Appeals for the Fifth Circuit reversed. With respect to the propriety of the class action, the appellate court discounted entirely the plaintiffs' failure to move for certification. Determination of the class nature of a suit, the court ruled, is a "responsibility [that] falls to the court." 505 F.2d, at 50. Although the plaintiffs had acknowledged on appeal that only their individual claims had been tried, and had requested no more than that the case be remanded to the trial court for consideration of the class-action allegations, the Court of Appeals itself certified a class consisting of all of the company's Negro and Mexican-American city drivers covered by the applicable collective-bargaining agreements for the State of Texas. Stating that "the requirements of Rule 23(a) must be read liberally in the context of suits brought under Title VII and Section 1981," ibid., the court found that the named plaintiffs could "'fairly and adequately protect the interests of the class.'" Ibid. The court minimized the antagonism between the plaintiffs and other city drivers with respect to the complaint's demand that seniority lists be merged, since "[t]he disagreement * * * concerned only the proper remedy; there was no antagonism with regard to the

4. The large majority of the members of Local 657 at the meeting that rejected the proposal were Mexican-American or Negro city drivers, negating any possibility that the vote was controlled by white persons or by line drivers.

contention that the defendants practiced discrimination against the plaintiff class." Id., at 51.[5]

After certifying the class, the Court of Appeals went on to find classwide liability against the company and the union on the basis of the proof adduced at the trial of the individual claims. Contrary to the understanding of the judge who had tried the case, the appellate court determined that the trial had proceeded "as in a class action," with the acquiescence of the judge and the defendants. Id., at 52.[6] The parties' stipulation that the only issue before the trial court concerned the company's failure to consider the named plaintiffs' applications for line-driver jobs was discounted as no more than "an attempt to eliminate some confusion in the exposition of evidence at trial." Ibid.

Accordingly, the Court of Appeals concluded, upon the trial record, that the company had discriminated against Negroes and Mexican-Americans in hiring line drivers, that the company's no-transfer rule and seniority system perpetuated the past discrimination and were not justified by business necessity, that the company's requirement of three years of immediately prior line-haul experience was an illegal employment qualification, and that the unions had violated Title VII and 42 U.S.C. § 1981 by "their role in establishing separate seniority rosters that failed to make allowance for minority city drivers who had been discriminatorily relegated to city driver jobs." 505 F.2d, at 61. The Court of Appeals did not disturb the trial court's finding that none of the named plaintiffs was qualified to be a line driver; rather, it held only that that finding had been "premature," because each plaintiff, as a member of the class, would be entitled to have his application considered on the merits when future line-driver vacancies arose.[7]

II

It is our conclusion that on the record before it the Court of Appeals plainly erred in declaring a class action and in imposing upon the petitioners classwide liability. In arriving at this conclusion we do not reach the question whether a court of appeals should ever certify a class in the first instance. For it is inescapably clear that the Court of Appeals in any event erred in certifying a class in this case, for the

5. The court also stated that possible antagonism could be cured by tailoring the award of relief, but it did not suggest how such tailoring could be accomplished short of doing what it in fact did: awarding retroactive seniority to discriminatees and ignoring the named plaintiffs' separate demand that the seniority lines be merged.

6. The Court of Appeals apparently concluded on the basis of a colloquy appearing in the trial transcript that the parties and the trial judge understood the trial to concern the class claims as well as the individual claims. 505 F.2d, at 52, and n. 14. This was contrary to the understanding of the trial judge as reflected in his findings. Moreover, as the full colloquy reveals, the trial judge ruled that evidence concerning general company practice would be admitted, not because of the class allegations, but only because it was probative with respect to the plaintiffs' individual claims.

7. The Court of Appeals ordered that all class members be given an opportunity to transfer to line-driver jobs with retroactive seniority to be determined under the Fifth Circuit's "qualification date" principle. See International Brotherhood of Teamsters v. United States.

simple reason that it was evident by the time the case reached that court that the named plaintiffs were not proper class representatives under Fed.Rule Civ.Proc. 23(a).[8]

In short, the trial court proceedings made clear that Rodriguez, Perez and Herrera were not members of the class of discriminatees they purported to represent. As this Court has repeatedly held, a class representative must be part of the class and "possess the same interest and suffer the same injury" as the class members. The District Court found upon abundant evidence that these plaintiffs lacked the qualifications to be hired as line drivers.[9] Thus, they could have suffered no injury as a result of the alleged discriminatory practices, and they were, therefore, simply not eligible to represent a class of persons who did allegedly suffer injury. Furthermore, each named plaintiff stipulated that he had not been discriminated against with respect to his initial hire. In the light of that stipulation they were hardly in a position to mount a classwide attack on the no-transfer rule and seniority system on the ground that these practices perpetuated past discrimination and locked minorities into the less desirable jobs to which they had been discriminatorily assigned.

Apart from the named plaintiffs' evident lack of class membership, the record before the Court of Appeals disclosed at least two other strong indications that they would not "fairly and adequately protect the interests of the class."[10] One was their failure to move for class

8. Rule 23(a) provides:

"(a) Prerequisites to a Class Action. One or more members of a class may sue or be sued as representative parties on behalf of all only if (1) the class is so numerous that joinder of all members is impracticable, (2) there are questions of law or fact common to the class, (3) the claims or defenses of the representative parties are typical of the claims or defenses of the class, and (4) the representative parties will fairly and adequately protect the interests of the class."

9. Jesse Rodriguez did not have prior over-the-road experience with a truck line. His record as a city driver included at least three accidents and at least five personal injuries. Modesto Herrera had been involved in at least three accidents and seven injuries, resulting in much time lost from work. He had received four warning letters from the company, of which three concerned abnormally low productivity. Sadrach Perez had been fired from his city-driver job by the time of suit. The District Court found that on occasion Perez had claimed to be totally and permanently disabled and had then returned to work, and that customers had complained of his disrespect and discourteousness. The company had placed at least four warning letters in his file before discharging him, referring to his failure to make deliveries, poor production, absence from work, and violation of instructions and company policy. More than 10 customers had notified the company that they would refuse freight if Perez was sent to deliver it and would refuse to give up freight if Perez was sent to receive it. An arbitration committee convened in connection with Perez' discharge had decided in the company's favor.

In light of this evidence, the District Court's finding that none of the respondents was qualified to be a line driver was not clearly erroneous. Nor was this finding in any way "premature." The trial had concerned the company's failure to consider the respondents' individual line-driver applications, and the plaintiffs had requested backpay and transfer with carry-over seniority in addition to other relief. Even assuming, *arguendo*, that the company's failure even to consider the applications was discriminatory, the company was entitled to prove at trial that the respondents had not been injured because they were not qualified and would not have been hired in any event.

10. See Fed.Rule Civ.Proc. 23(a), quoted in n. 8, supra.

certification prior to trial. Even assuming, as a number of courts have held, that a district judge has an obligation on his own motion to determine whether an action shall proceed as a class action, the named plaintiffs' failure to protect the interests of class members by moving for certification surely bears strongly on the adequacy of the representation that those class members might expect to receive. Another factor, apparent on the record, suggesting that the named plaintiffs were not appropriate class representatives was the conflict between the vote by members of the class rejecting a merger of the city- and line-driver collective-bargaining units,[11] and the demand in the plaintiffs' complaint for just such a merger. See, e.g., Hansberry v. Lee, 311 U.S. 32, 44–45, 61 S.Ct. 115, 119, 85 L.Ed. 22.

We are not unaware that suits alleging racial or ethnic discrimination are often by their very nature class suits, involving classwide wrongs. Common questions of law or fact are typically present. But careful attention to the requirements of Fed.Rule Civ.Proc. 23 remains nonetheless indispensable. The mere fact that a complaint alleges racial or ethnic discrimination does not in itself ensure that the party who has brought the lawsuit will be an adequate representative of those who may have been the real victims of that discrimination.

For the reasons we have discussed, the District Court did not err in denying individual relief or in dismissing the class allegations of the respondents' complaint.[12] The judgment of the Court of Appeals is, accordingly, vacated, and the cases are remanded to that court for further proceedings consistent with this opinion.[13]

It is so ordered.

NOTES AND PROBLEMS FOR DISCUSSION

1. Were the named plaintiffs in *East Texas Motor Freight* ineligible to represent the class composed of minority drivers and minority applicants for

11. See supra, at 1895.

12. Obviously, a different case would be presented if the District Court had certified a class and only later had it appeared that the named plaintiffs were not class members or were otherwise inappropriate class representatives. In such a case, the class claims would have already been tried, and, provided the initial certification was proper and decertification not appropriate, the claims of the class members would not need to be mooted or destroyed because subsequent events or the proof at trial had undermined the named plaintiffs' individual claims. See, e.g., Franks v. Bowman Transportation Co., 424 U.S. 747, at 752–757, 96 S.Ct. 1251, 1258–1261, 47 L.Ed.2d 444; Moss v. Lane Co., 471 F.2d 853, 855–856 (CA4). Where no class has been certified, however, and the class claims remain to be tried, the decision whether the named plaintiffs should represent a class is appropriately made on the full record, including the facts developed at the trial of the plaintiffs' individual claims. At that point, as the Court of Appeals recognized in this case, "there [are] involved none of the imponderables that make the [class-action] decision so difficult early in litigation." 505 F.2d, at 51. See also Cox v. Babcock & Wilcox Co., 471 F.2d 13, 15–16 (CA4).

13. The union petitioners, in Nos. 75–651 and 75–715, also attack the judgments entered against them in Herrera v. Yellow Freight System, Inc., 505 F.2d 66 (CA5), and Resendis v. Lee Way Motor Freight, Inc., 505 F.2d 69 (CA5). The judgments against the unions in those related cases are also vacated, and the cases are remanded to the Court of Appeals for further consideration in light of this opinion and our opinion in International Brotherhood of Teamsters v. United States, 431 U.S. 324, 97 S.Ct. 1843, 52 L.Ed.2d 396.

line driver positions because they lacked the qualifications for the line driver position, because they failed to prove that they were the victims of discrimination, or for some other reason? The Court of Appeals found that the plaintiffs had proved class-wide discrimination, i.e., that the challenged employment practices excluded minority employees from the line driver position. Rodriguez v. East Texas Motor Freight System, Inc., 505 F.2d 40, 52–61 (5th Cir. 1974). Was this ruling on the merits of the class claim erroneous according to the Supreme Court? In footnote 12 of his opinion Justice Stewart stated that "[o]bviously, a different case would be presented if the District Court had certified a class and only later had it appeared that the named plaintiffs were not class members or were otherwise inappropriate class representatives." In light of the Court of Appeals' ruling that class wide discrimination had been proved, what exactly was the "obvious" difference between the case and one involving the same facts but with a pre-trial class certification? Should relief be denied class members who have been discriminated against because the named plaintiffs may not ultimately be entitled to relief? Does such a ruling further the policies underlying Rule 23?

If the plaintiffs were not adequate class representatives because their individual claims lacked merit, how can a class ever be certified without the named plaintiffs first trying and winning their individual cases? Note that Rule 23(c) requires that class certification be determined by the district court "as soon as practicable after commencement of an action * * *." Prior to *East Texas Motor Freight*, courts had uniformly rejected the argument that the likelihood of the plaintiffs' success on the merits was a factor to be considered in class certification. See Roberts v. Union Co., 487 F.2d 387, 389 (6th Cir. 1973); Huff v. N.D. Cass Co., 485 F.2d 710, 712 (5th Cir. 1973) (en banc); Parham v. Southwestern Bell Telephone Co., 433 F.2d 421, 428 (8th Cir. 1970); Johnson v. Georgia Highway Express, Inc., 417 F.2d 1122, 1124–25 (5th Cir. 1969). What would be the effect if *East Texas Motor Freight* was construed as overruling these cases? Would the court's class ruling have been the same if plaintiffs had won their individual cases?

2. Prior to 1970, East Texas Motor Freight had never employed a Mexican-American or a black as a line driver and by 1974 there was still not a single black on the force. Of the 575 city drivers, however, 111 were Spanish-surnamed and 95 were black. Rodriguez v. East Texas Motor Freight System, Inc., supra, 505 F.2d at 48. The plaintiffs alleged that a number of different employment practices locked minority drivers into the city driver jobs. 505 F.2d at 46–49. They also alleged that some class members were discriminated against in initial assignment to city jobs, but stipulated that they had not been themselves discriminated against in initial assignment. The Supreme Court cryptically noted that because of that stipulation, the plaintiffs were "hardly in a position to mount a classwide attack on the no-transfer rule and seniority system on the ground that these practices perpetuated past discrimination * * *." Does this mean that had plaintiffs proved discrimination against those employees who applied for city jobs initially but later sought to transfer to line positions, class relief would nevertheless be denied to those employees who were locked into city jobs to which they were discriminatorily assigned? If the root evil was the "lock in" effect of the no-transfer rule and seniority system, why shouldn't the class include all the minority employees affected by the practice regardless of how they came into the class?

3. Of what significance was the "conflict" between the relief requested by the named plaintiffs and the vote of union members rejecting merger of the city

and line driver bargaining units? Should a plaintiff be required to demonstrate the support of a majority of the putative class to obtain certification? In the opinion reversed by the Supreme Court, the Fifth Circuit noted that the memberships of the local union which voted on the merger and the class were not identical. The local included employees of firms other than East Texas Motor Freight, but was limited to residents of the San Antonio area, whereas the class was composed not only of drivers employed by East Texas but also encompassed all minority drivers working out of the company's twenty terminals in the state. 505 F.2d at 51. How might the interest of dissenting class members be protected? See Rule 23(e).

GENERAL TELEPHONE CO. OF THE SOUTHWEST v. FALCON

Supreme Court of the United States, 1982.
457 U.S. 147, 102 S.Ct. 2364, 72 L.Ed.2d 740.

JUSTICE STEVENS delivered the opinion of the Court.

The question presented is whether respondent Falcon, who complained that petitioner did not promote him because he is a Mexican-American, was properly permitted to maintain a class action on behalf of Mexican-American applicants for employment whom petitioner did not hire.

I

In 1969 petitioner initiated a special recruitment and training program for minorities. Through that program, respondent Falcon was hired in July 1969 as a groundman, and within a year he was twice promoted, first to lineman and then to lineman-in-charge. He subsequently refused a promotion to installer-repairman. In October 1972 he applied for the job of field inspector; his application was denied even though the promotion was granted several white employees with less seniority.

Falcon thereupon filed a charge with the Equal Employment Opportunity Commission stating his belief that he had been passed over for promotion because of his national origin and that petitioner's promotion policy operated against Mexican-Americans as a class. 626 F.2d 369, 372, n. 2 (CA5 1980). In due course he received a right to sue letter from the Commission and, in April 1975, he commenced this action under Title VII of the Civil Rights Act of 1964, 74 Stat. 253, as amended, 42 U.S.C. § 2000e et seq., in the United States District Court for the Northern District of Texas. His complaint alleged that petitioner maintained "a policy, practice, custom, or usage of: (a) discriminating against [Mexican-Americans] because of national origin and with respect to compensation, terms, conditions, and privileges of employment, and (b) * * * subjecting [Mexican-Americans] to continuous employment discrimination."[1] Respondent claimed that as a result of this policy whites with less qualification and experience and lower evaluation scores than respondent had been promoted more rapidly. The complaint contained no factual allegations concerning petitioner's hiring practices.

Respondent brought the action "on his own behalf and on behalf of other persons similarly situated, pursuant to Rule 23(b)(2) of the Federal Rules of Civil Procedure." The class identified in the complaint was "composed of Mexican-American persons who are employed, or who might be employed, by GENERAL TELEPHONE COMPANY at its place of business located in Irving, Texas, who have been and who continue to be or might be adversely affected by the practices complained of herein."[3]

After responding to petitioner's written interrogatories,[4] respondent filed a memorandum in favor of certification of "the class of all hourly Mexican American employees who have been employed, are employed, or may in the future be employed and all those Mexican Americans who have applied or would have applied for employment had the Defendant not practiced racial discrimination in its employment practices." His position was supported by the ruling of the United States Court of Appeals for the Fifth Circuit in Johnson v. Georgia Highway Express, Inc., 417 F.2d 1122 (1969), that any victim of racial discrimination in employment may maintain an "across the board" attack on all unequal employment practices alleged to have been committed by the

1. App. 14. In paragraph VI of the complaint, respondent alleged:

> "The Defendant has established an employment, transfer, promotional, and seniority system, the design, intent, and purpose of which is to continue and preserve, and which has the effect of continuing and preserving, the Defendant's policy, practice, custom and usage of limiting the employment, transfer, and promotional opportunities of Mexican-American employees of the company because of national origin."

Id., at 15.

3. App. 13–14. The paragraph of the complaint in which respondent alleged conformance with the requirements of Rule 23 continued:

> "There are common questions of law and fact affecting the rights of the members of this class who are, and who continue to be, limited, classified, and discriminated against in ways which deprive and/or tend to deprive them of equal employment opportunities and which otherwise adversely affect their status as employees because of national origin. These persons are so numerous that joinder of all members is impracticable. A common relief is sought. The interests of said class are adequately represented by Plaintiff. Defendant has acted or refused to act on grounds generally applicable to the Plaintiff."

Id., at 14.

4. Petitioner's Interrogatory No. 8 stated:

> "Identify the common questions of law and fact which affect the rights of the members of the purported class."

Id., at 26.

Respondent answered that interrogatory as follows:

> "The facts which affect the rights of the members of the class are the facts of their employment, the ways in which evaluations are made, the subjective rather than objective manner in which recommendations for raises and transfers and promotions are handled, and all of the facts surrounding the employment of Mexican-American persons by General Telephone Company. The questions of law specified in Interrogatory No. 8 call for a conclusion on the part of the Plaintiff."

Id., at 34.

employer pursuant to a policy of racial discrimination. Without conducting an evidentiary hearing, the District Court certified a class including Mexican-American employees and Mexican-American applicants for employment who had not been hired.[5]

Following trial of the liability issues, the District Court entered separate findings of fact and conclusions of law with respect first to respondent and then to the class. The District Court found that petitioner had not discriminated against respondent in hiring, but that it did discriminate against him in its promotion practices. The court reached converse conclusions about the class, finding no discrimination in promotion practices, but concluding that petitioner had discriminated against Mexican-Americans at its Irving facility in its hiring practices.[6]

After various post-trial proceedings, the District Court ordered petitioner to furnish respondent with a list of all Mexican-Americans who had applied for employment at the Irving facility during the period between January 1, 1973, and October 18, 1976. Respondent was then ordered to give notice to those persons advising them that they might be entitled to some form of recovery. Evidence was taken concerning the applicants who responded to the notice and backpay was ultimately awarded to 13 persons, in addition to respondent Falcon. The total recovery by respondent and the entire class amounted to $67,925.49, plus costs and interest.[7]

Both parties appealed. The Court of Appeals rejected respondent's contention that the class should have encompassed all of petitioner's operations in Texas, New Mexico, Oklahoma, and Arkansas.[8] On the other hand, the court also rejected petitioner's argument that the class had been defined too broadly. For, under the Fifth Circuit's across-the-board rule, it is permissible for "an employee complaining of one employment practice to represent another complaining of another

5. The District Court's pretrial order of February 2, 1976, provided, in part:

> "The case is to proceed as a class action and the Plaintiff is to represent the class. The class is to be made up of those employees who are employed and employees who have applied for employment in the Irving Division of the Defendant company, and no other division.
>
> * * *
>
> "Plaintiff and Defendant are to hold further negotiations to see if there is a possibility of granting individual relief to the Plaintiff, MARIANO S. FALCON." App. to Pet. for Cert. 48a–49a.

The District Court denied subsequent motions to decertify the class both before and after the trial.

6. The District Court ordered petitioner to accelerate its affirmative action plan by taking specified steps to more actively recruit and promote Mexican-Americans at its Irving facility. See id., at 41a–45a.

7. Respondent's individual recovery amounted to $1,040.33. A large share of the class award, $28,827.50, represented attorneys' fees. Most of the remainder resulted from petitioner's practice of keeping all applications active for only 90 days; the District Court found that most of the applications had been properly rejected at the time they were considered, but that petitioner could not justify the refusal to extend employment to disappointed applicants after an interval of 90 days. See 463 F.Supp. 315 (ND Tex.1978).

8. The Court of Appeals held that the District Court had not abused its discretion since each of petitioner's divisions conducted its own hiring and since management of the broader class would be much more difficult. 626 F.2d, at 376.

practice, if the plaintiff and the members of the class suffer from essentially the same injury. In this case, all of the claims are based on discrimination because of national origin." Id., at 375.[9] The court relied on Payne v. Travenol Laboratories, Inc., 565 F.2d 895 (1978), cert. denied, 439 U.S. 835, 99 S.Ct. 118, 58 L.Ed.2d 131, in which the Fifth Circuit stated:

> "Plaintiffs' action is an 'across the board' attack on unequal employment practices alleged to have been committed by Travenol pursuant to a policy of racial discrimination. As parties who have allegedly been aggrieved by some of these discriminatory practices, plaintiffs have demonstrated a sufficient nexus to enable them to represent other class members suffering from different practices motivated by the same policies." Id., at 900, quoted in 626 F.2d, at 375.

On the merits, the Court of Appeals upheld respondent's claim of disparate treatment in promotion,[10] but held that the District Court's findings relating to disparate impact in hiring were insufficient to support recovery on behalf of the class.[11] After this Court decided Texas Department of Community Affairs v. Burdine, 450 U.S. 248, 101 S.Ct. 1089, 67 L.Ed.2d 207, we vacated the judgment of the Court of Appeals and directed further consideration in the light of that opinion. 450 U.S. 1036, 101 S.Ct. 1752, 68 L.Ed.2d 234. The Fifth Circuit thereupon vacated the portion of its opinion addressing respondent's

9. The court continued:

> "While similarities of sex, race or national origin claims are not dispositive in favor of finding that the prerequisites of Rule 23 have been met, they are an extremely important factor in the determination, that can outweigh the fact that the members of the plaintiff class may be complaining about somewhat different specific discriminatory practices. In addition here, the plaintiff showed more than an alliance based simply on the same type of discriminatory claim. He also showed a similarity of interests based on job location, job function and other considerations."

626 F.2d, at 375–376 (citations omitted).

The court did not explain how job location, job function, and the unidentified other considerations were relevant to the Rule 23(a) determination.

10. The District Court found that petitioner's proffered reasons for promoting the whites, rather than respondent, were insufficient and subjective. The Court of Appeals held that respondent had made out a prima facie case under the test set forth in McDonnell Douglas Corp. v. Green, 411 U.S. 792, 802, 93 S.Ct. 1817, 1824, 36 L.Ed.2d 668, and that the District Court's conclusion that petitioner had not rebutted that prima facie case was not clearly erroneous. In so holding, the Court of Appeals relied on its earlier opinion in Burdine v. Texas Department of Community Affairs, 608 F.2d 563 (1979). Our opinion in *Burdine* had not yet been announced.

The Court of Appeals disposed of a number of other contentions raised by both parties, and reserved others pending the further proceedings before the District Court on remand. Among the latter issues was petitioner's objection to the District Court's theory for computing the class backpay awards. See n. 7, supra.

11. The District Court's finding was based on statistical evidence comparing the number of Mexican-Americans in the company's employ, and the number hired in 1972 and 1973, with the percentage of Mexican-Americans in the Dallas-Fort Worth labor force. See App. to Pet. for Cert. 39a. Since recovery had been allowed for the years 1973 through 1976 based on statistical evidence pertaining to only a portion of that period, and since petitioner's evidence concerning the entire period suggested that there was no disparate impact, the Court of Appeals ordered further proceedings on the class hiring claims. 626 F.2d, at 380–382.

promotion claim but reinstated the portions of its opinion approving the District Court's class certification. With the merits of both respondent's promotion claim and the class hiring claims remaining open for reconsideration in the District Court on remand, we granted certiorari to decide whether the class action was properly maintained on behalf of both employees who were denied promotion and applicants who were denied employment.

II

The class action device was designed as "an exception to the usual rule that litigation is conducted by and on behalf of the individual named parties only." Califano v. Yamasaki, 442 U.S. 682, 700–701, 99 S.Ct. 2545, 2557–2558, 61 L.Ed.2d 176. Class relief is "peculiarly appropriate" when the "issues involved are common to the class as a whole" and when they "turn on questions of law applicable in the same manner to each member of the class." Id., at 701, 99 S.Ct., at 2557. For in such cases, "the class-action device saves the resources of both the courts and the parties by permitting an issue potentially affecting every [class member] to be litigated in an economical fashion under Rule 23." Ibid.

Title VII of the Civil Rights Act of 1964, as amended, authorizes the Equal Employment Opportunity Commission to sue in its own name to secure relief for individuals aggrieved by discriminatory practices forbidden by the Act. See 42 U.S.C. § 2000e–5(f)(1). In exercising this enforcement power, the Commission may seek relief for groups of employees or applicants for employment without complying with the strictures of Rule 23. General Telephone Co. v. EEOC, 446 U.S. 318, 100 S.Ct. 1698, 64 L.Ed.2d 319. Title VII, however, contains no special authorization for class suits maintained by private parties. An individual litigant seeking to maintain a class action under Title VII must meet "the prerequisites of numerosity, commonality, typicality, and adequacy of representation" specified in Rule 23(a). Id., at 330, 100 S.Ct., at 1706. These requirements effectively "limit the class claims to those fairly encompassed by the named plaintiff's claims." Ibid.

We have repeatedly held that "a class representative must be part of the class and 'possess the same interest and suffer the same injury' as the class members." East Texas Motor Freight System, Inc. v. Rodriguez, 431 U.S. 395, 403, 97 S.Ct. 1891, 1896, 52 L.Ed.2d 453 (quoting Schlesinger v. Reservists Committee to Stop the War, 418 U.S. 208, 216, 94 S.Ct. 2925, 2929–2930, 41 L.Ed.2d 706). In *East Texas Motor Freight*, a Title VII action brought by three Mexican-American city drivers, the Fifth Circuit certified a class consisting of the trucking company's black and Mexican-American city drivers allegedly denied on racial or ethnic grounds transfers to more desirable line-driver jobs. We held that the Court of Appeals had "plainly erred in declaring a class action." 431 U.S., at 403, 97 S.Ct., at 1896. Because at the time the class was certified it was clear that the named plaintiffs were not qualified for line-driver positions, "they could have suffered no injury as a result of the allegedly discriminatory practices, and they were, therefore, simply not eligible to represent a class of persons who did allegedly suffer injury." Id., at 403–404, 97 S.Ct., at 1897.

Our holding in *East Texas Motor Freight* was limited; we noted that "a different case would be presented if the District Court had certified a class and only later had it appeared that the named plaintiffs were not class members or were otherwise inappropriate class representatives." Id., at 406, n. 12, 97 S.Ct., at 1898, n. 12. We also recognized the theory behind the Fifth Circuit's across-the-board rule, noting our awareness "that suits alleging racial or ethnic discrimination are often by their very nature class suits, involving classwide wrongs," and that "[c]ommon questions of law or fact are typically present." Id., at 405, 97 S.Ct., at 1898. In the same breath, however, we reiterated that "careful attention to the requirements of Fed. Rule Civ.Proc. 23 remains nonetheless indispensable" and that the "mere fact that a complaint alleges racial or ethnic discrimination does not in itself ensure that the party who has brought the lawsuit will be an adequate representative of those who may have been the real victims of that discrimination." Id., at 405–406, 97 S.Ct., at 1898.

We cannot disagree with the proposition underlying the across-the-board rule—that racial discrimination is by definition class discrimination.[12] But the allegation that such discrimination has occurred neither determines whether a class action may be maintained in accordance with Rule 23 nor defines the class that may be certified. Conceptually, there is a wide gap between (a) an individual's claim that he has been denied a promotion on discriminatory grounds, and his otherwise unsupported allegation that the company has a policy of discrimination, and (b) the existence of a class of persons who have suffered the same injury as that individual, such that the individual's claim and the class claims will share common questions of law or fact and that the individual's claim will be typical of the class claims.[13] For respondent to bridge that gap, he must prove much more than the

12. See Hall v. Werthan Bag Corp., 251 F.Supp. 184, 186 (MD Tenn.1966).

13. The commonality and typicality requirements of Rule 23(a) tend to merge. Both serve as guideposts for determining whether under the particular circumstances maintenance of a class action is economical and whether the named plaintiff's claim and the class claims are so interrelated that the interests of the class members will be fairly and adequately protected in their absence. Those requirements therefore also tend to merge with the adequacy-of-representation requirement, although the latter requirement also raises concerns about the competency of class counsel and conflicts of interest. In this case, we need not address petitioner's argument that there is a conflict of interest between respondent and the class of rejected applicants because an enlargement of the pool of Mexican-American employees will decrease respondent's chances for promotion. See General Telephone Co. v. EEOC, 446 U.S. 318, 331, 100 S.Ct. 1698, 1706–1707, 64 L.Ed.2d 319 ("In employment discrimination litigation, conflicts might arise, for example, between employees and applicants who were denied employment and who will, if granted relief, compete with employees for fringe benefits or seniority. Under Rule 23, the same plaintiff could not represent these classes."); see also East Texas Motor Freight System, Inc. v. Rodriguez, 431 U.S. 395, 404–405, 97 S.Ct. 1891, 1897–1898, 52 L.Ed. 2d 453.

validity of his own claim. Even though evidence that he was passed over for promotion when several less deserving whites were advanced may support the conclusion that respondent was denied the promotion because of his national origin, such evidence would not necessarily justify the additional inferences (1) that this discriminatory treatment is typical of petitioner's promotion practices, (2) that petitioner's promotion practices are motivated by a policy of ethnic discrimination that pervades petitioner's Irving division, or (3) that this policy of ethnic discrimination is reflected in petitioner's other employment practices, such as hiring, in the same way it is manifested in the promotion practices. These additional inferences demonstrate the tenuous character of any presumption that the class claims are "fairly encompassed" within respondent's claim.

Respondent's complaint provided an insufficient basis for concluding that the adjudication of his claim of discrimination in promotion would require the decision of any common question concerning the failure of petitioner to hire more Mexican-Americans. Without any specific presentation identifying the questions of law or fact that were common to the claims of respondent and of the members of the class he sought to represent,[14] it was error for the District Court to presume that respondent's claim was typical of other claims against petitioner by Mexican-American employees and applicants. If one allegation of specific discriminatory treatment were sufficient to support an across-the-board attack, every Title VII case would be a potential company-wide class action. We find nothing in the statute to indicate that Congress intended to authorize such a wholesale expansion of class-action litigation.[15]

The trial of this class action followed a predictable course. Instead of raising common questions of law or fact, respondent's evidentiary approaches to the individual and class claims were entirely different. He attempted to sustain his individual claim by proving intentional discrimination. He tried to prove the class claims through statistical evidence of disparate impact. Ironically, the District Court rejected the class claim of promotion discrimination, which conceptually might have borne a closer typicality and commonality relationship with respondent's individual claim, but sustained the class claim of hiring discrimination. As the District Court's bifurcated findings on liability demon-

14. See n. 4, supra.

15. If petitioner used a biased testing procedure to evaluate both applicants for employment and incumbent employees, a class action on behalf of every applicant or employee who might have been prejudiced by the test clearly would satisfy the commonality and typicality requirements of Rule 23(a). Significant proof that an employer operated under a general policy of discrimination conceivably could justify a class of both applicants and employees if the discrimination manifested itself in hiring and promotion practices in the same general fashion, such as through entirely subjective decisionmaking processes. In this regard it is noteworthy that Title VII prohibits discriminatory employment *practices*, not an abstract policy of discrimination. The mere fact that an aggrieved private plaintiff is a member of an identifiable class of persons of the same race or national origin is insufficient to establish his standing to litigate on their behalf all possible claims of discrimination against a common employer.

strate, the individual and class claims might as well have been tried separately. It is clear that the maintenance of respondent's action as a class action did not advance "the efficiency and economy of litigation which is a principal purpose of the procedure." American Pipe & Construction Co. v. Utah, 414 U.S. 538, 553, 94 S.Ct. 756, 766, 38 L.Ed. 2d 713.

We do not, of course, judge the propriety of a class certification by hindsight. The District Court's error in this case, and the error inherent in the across-the-board rule, is the failure to evaluate carefully the legitimacy of the named plaintiff's plea that he is a proper class representative under Rule 23(a). As we noted in Coopers & Lybrand v. Livesay, 437 U.S. 463, 98 S.Ct. 2454, 57 L.Ed.2d 351, "the class determination generally involves considerations that are 'enmeshed in the factual and legal issues comprising the plaintiff's cause of action.' " Id., at 469, 98 S.Ct., at 2458 (quoting Mercantile Nat. Bank v. Langdeau, 371 U.S. 555, 558, 83 S.Ct. 520, 522, 9 L.Ed.2d 523). Sometimes the issues are plain enough from the pleadings to determine whether the interests of the absent parties are fairly encompassed within the named plaintiff's claim, and sometimes it may be necessary for the court to probe behind the pleadings before coming to rest on the certification question. Even after a certification order is entered, the judge remains free to modify it in the light of subsequent developments in the litigation.[16] For such an order, particularly during the period before any notice is sent to members of the class, "is inherently tentative." 437 U.S., at 469, n. 11, 98 S.Ct., at 2458 n. 11. This flexibility enhances the usefulness of the class-action device; actual, not presumed, conformance with Rule 23(a) remains, however, indispensable.

III

The need to carefully apply the requirements of Rule 23(a) to Title VII class actions was noticed by a member of the Fifth Circuit panel that announced the across-the-board rule. In a specially concurring opinion in Johnson v. Georgia Highway Express, Inc., supra, at 1125–1127, Judge Godbold emphasized the need for "more precise pleadings," id., at 1125, for "without reasonable specificity the court cannot define the class, cannot determine whether the representation is adequate, and the employer does not know how to defend," id., at 1126. He termed as "most significant" the potential unfairness to the class members bound by the judgment if the framing of the class is overbroad. Ibid. And he pointed out the error of the "tacit assumption" underlying the across-the-board rule that "all will be well for surely the plaintiff will win and manna will fall on all members of the class." Id., at 1127. With the same concerns in mind, we reiterate today that a Title VII class action, like any other class action, may only be certified

16. "As soon as practicable after the commencement of an action brought as a class action, the court shall determine by order whether it is to be so maintained. An order under this subdivision may be conditional, and may be altered or amended before the decision on the merits." Fed. Rule Civ.Proc. 23(c)(1).

if the trial court is satisfied, after a rigorous analysis, that the prerequisites of Rule 23(a) have been satisfied.

The judgment of the Court of Appeals affirming the certification order is reversed and the case is remanded for further proceedings consistent with this opinion.

It is so ordered.

CHIEF JUSTICE BURGER, concurring in part and dissenting in part.

I agree with the Court's decision insofar as it states the general principles which apply in determining whether a class should be certified in this case under Rule 23. However, in my view it is not necessary to remand for further proceedings since it is entirely clear on this record that no class should have been certified in this case. I would simply reverse the Court of Appeals with instructions to dismiss the class claim.

As the Court notes, the purpose of Rule 23 is to promote judicial economy by allowing for litigation of common questions of law and fact at one time. Califano v. Yamasaki, 442 U.S. 682, 701, 99 S.Ct. 2545, 2557–2558, 61 L.Ed.2d 176 (1979). We have stressed that strict attention to the requirements of Rule 23 is indispensable in employment discrimination cases. East Texas Motor Freight System, Inc. v. Rodriguez, 431 U.S. 395, 405–406, 97 S.Ct. 1891, 1897–1898, 52 L.Ed.2d 453 (1977). This means that class claims are limited to those "fairly encompassed by the named plaintiff's claims." Ante at 2370; General Telephone Co. v. EEOC, 446 U.S. 318, 330, 100 S.Ct. 1698, 1706, 64 L.Ed.2d 319 (1980).

Respondent claims that he was not promoted to a job as field inspector because he is a Mexican-American. To be successful in his claim, which he advances under the "disparate treatment" theory, he must convince a court that those who were promoted were promoted not because they were better qualified than he was, but, instead, that he was not promoted for discriminatory reasons. The success of this claim depends on evaluation of the comparative qualifications of the applicants for promotion to field inspector and on analysis of the credibility of the reasons for the promotion decisions provided by those who made the decisions. Respondent's class claim on behalf of unsuccessful applicants for jobs with petitioner, in contrast, is advanced under the "adverse impact" theory. Its success depends on an analysis of statistics concerning petitioner's hiring patterns.*

The record in this case clearly shows that there are no common questions of law or fact between respondent's claim and the class claim; the only commonality is that respondent is a Mexican-American and he seeks to represent a class of Mexican-Americans. See ante, 2368–2369

* There is no allegation that those who made the hiring decisions are the same persons who determined who was promoted to field inspector. Thus there is no claim that the same person or persons who made the challenged decisions were motivated by prejudice against Mexican-Americans, and that this prejudice manifested itself in both the hiring decisions and the decisions not to promote respondent.

& n. 9. We have repeatedly held that the bare fact that a plaintiff alleges racial or ethnic discrimination is not enough to justify class certification. Ante at 2370; *East Texas Motor Freight*, supra, 431 U.S., at 405–406, 97 S.Ct., at 1897–1898. Accordingly, the class should not have been certified.

Moreover, while a judge's decision to certify a class is not normally to be evaluated by hindsight, ante, at 2372, since the judge cannot know what the evidence will show, there is no reason for us at this stage of these lengthy judicial proceedings not to proceed in light of the evidence actually presented. The Court properly concludes that the Court of Appeals and the District Court failed to consider the requirements of Rule 23. In determining whether to reverse and remand or to simply reverse, we can and should look at the evidence. The record shows that there is no support for the class claim. Respondent's own statistics show that 7.7% of those hired by petitioner between 1972 and 1976 were Mexican-American while the relevant labor force was 5.2% Mexican-American. Falcon v. General Telephone Company of the Southwest, 626 F.2d 369, 372, 381 n. 16. Petitioner's unchallenged evidence shows that it hired Mexican-Americans in numbers greater than their percentage of the labor force even though Mexican-Americans applied for jobs with petitioner in numbers smaller than their percentage of the labor force. Id., at 373 n. 4. This negates any claim of Falcon as a class representative.

Like so many Title VII cases, this case has already gone on for years, draining judicial resources as well as resources of the litigants. Rather than promoting judicial economy, the "across-the-board" class action has promoted multiplication of claims and endless litigation. Since it is clear that the class claim brought on behalf of unsuccessful applicants for jobs with petitioner cannot succeed, I would simply reverse and remand with instructions to dismiss the class claim.

NOTES AND PROBLEMS FOR DISCUSSION

1. What precisely is the holding of General Telephone Co. v. Falcon? Is it that a named plaintiff may represent a class composed only of those persons who have been affected by a discriminatory policy in exactly the same manner as the plaintiff? Or does the decision merely stand for the proposition that the district court may not assume a sufficient nexus between the individual and class claims absent a factual showing of a link between the two?

The Court in *General Telephone* states that proof sufficient to establish Falcon's individual claim would not necessarily support a finding of class discrimination. Presumably, in a case where proof of the individual claim would support an inference of class discrimination, the commonality and typicality requirements of Rule 23(a) would be satisfied. Thus, if a company's policy was to refuse employment to pregnant women, presumably a female employee discharged because of pregnancy would be allowed under *General Telephone* to represent a class composed of discharged employees and persons refused employment because of that policy. But is the converse true? If proof of class-wide discrimination is sufficiently relevant to plaintiff's individual claim to be admissible in support of that claim, would the commonality and typicality requirements be satisfied? In McDonnell Douglas Corp. v. Green, the Court noted that "statistics as to petitioner's employment policy and practice may be helpful to a determination of whether petitioner's refusal to rehire respondent * * * conformed to a general pattern of discrimination against blacks." After *General Telephone,* could Green represent a class composed of disappointed black applicants as well as discharged employees, assuming that he alleged such a general pattern of discrimination?

2. Does the Court's decision in *General Telephone* suggest that the remedial purposes of Title VII are irrelevant to class certification under Rule 23? Does the language or legislative history of Rule 23 require such a result? See, Advisory Committee's Note to 1966 Amendments to Rule 23, 39 F.R.D. 98, 102. In *General Telephone,* the plaintiff actively sought to represent a class even larger than that certified by the district court and at trial put on substantial proof to support the class claims. Assuming that Falcon was an "adequate" representative of the class in the sense that he had both the desire and the means to vigorously pursue the class claims, does the decision in *General Telephone* further the goals of Title VII? Was Falcon's "across the board" suit unfair to the defendant in the manner suggested by Judge Godbold in his separate opinion in Johnson v. Georgia Highway Express? Does the decision serve to protect the interests of Mexican-American applicants for employment with General Telephone? For a discussion of the different meanings of "adequacy" see Strickler, Protecting the Class: The Search For The Adequate Representative in Class Action Litigation, 34 DePaul L.Rev. 73 (1984).

Falcon has not resulted in the complete demise of the broad-based class action. Focusing on footnote 15 of the Supreme Court's opinion, a number of courts have certified or refused to decertify classes composed of persons whose relation to defendant differ distinctly from that of the named plaintiff on the ground that the various discriminatory practices were infected by the same "subjective decision making processes." See e.g., Carpenter v. Stephen F. Austin State University, 706 F.2d 608 (5th Cir. 1983) (former custodial workers were proper representatives of class composed of past, present and future black and female employees in all job classifications); Richardson v. Byrd, 709 F.2d 1016 (5th Cir.), cert. denied, 464 U.S. 1009, 104 S.Ct. 527, 78 L.Ed.2d 710 (1983) (employee may represent class composed in part of unsuccessful applicants); Kraszewski v. State Farm Insurance Co., 36 FEP Cases 1352 (N.D.Cal.1982) (plaintiff alleged general policy of discrimination manifested in subjective decision-making processes in hiring and promotion). Other courts have mechanically applied *Falcon* to deny certification of classes composed of applicants and employees, Walker v. Jim Dandy Co., 747 F.2d 1360 (11th Cir. 1984); Hawkins v. Fulton County, 95 F.R.D. 88 (N.D.Ga.1982), employees in different positions, Roby v. St. Louis Southwestern Railway Co., 775 F.2d 959 (8th Cir. 1985), and employees and those terminated, Briggs v. Anderson, 787 F.2d 1262 (8th Cir. 1986).

Can representational adequacy problems under *Falcon* be cured by allowing intervention of additional named plaintiffs as subclass representatives? See, Hill v. Western Electric Co., 672 F.2d 381 (4th Cir. 1982), cert. denied, 459 U.S. 981, 103 S.Ct. 318, 74 L.Ed.2d 294 (1982) and Note, Reinstating Vacated Findings in Employment Discrimination Class Actions: Reconciling General Telephone Co. v. Falcon with Hill v. Western Electric Co., 1983 Duke L.J. 821 (1983).

SECTION C. THE SIZE OF THE CLASS

GARCIA v. GLOOR

United States Court of Appeals, Fifth Circuit, 1980.
618 F.2d 264, cert. denied, 449 U.S. 1113, 101 S.Ct. 923, 66 L.Ed.2d 842.

ALVIN B. RUBIN, CIRCUIT JUDGE.

It is ordered that this court's opinion reported at 609 F.2d 156 (5th Cir. 1980) be withdrawn and the following is substituted:

Invoking Title VII, the Equal Employment Opportunity Act, 42 U.S.C. § 2000e–2 [EEO Act], Hector Garcia, a native-born American of Mexican descent, challenges as discriminatory his employer's rule that prohibits employees engaged in sales work from speaking Spanish on the job. Because the group of employees Mr. Garcia sought to represent was not numerous enough to constitute a class, we affirm the trial court's denial of class action certification. We conclude that the "speak-only-English" rule, as it was applied to Mr. Garcia by his employer, does not discriminate on the basis of national origin. We therefore affirm the district court's judgment that Mr. Garcia's discharge for violating the rule was not unlawful.

[The court affirmed the district court's denial of relief on the ground that the employee's rule, which prohibited all bilingual employees from speaking Spanish on the job except to Spanish-speaking customers, did not discriminate on the basis of national origin.]

II.

Mr. Garcia properly complains that the court arrived at its denial of class certification by deciding that he had no case on the merits. The question of class certification is a procedural one, distinct from the merits of the action. Huff v. N. D. Cass Co., 5 Cir. 1973 (en banc), 485 F.2d 710; Miller v. Mackey International, Inc., 5 Cir. 1971, 452 F.2d 424, 427–28. Whether a class should be certified depends entirely on whether the proposal satisfies the requirements of Fed.R.Civ.P. 23. See generally 7 C. Wright & A. Miller, Federal Practice and Procedure: Civil §§ 1759–1770 (1972).

However, the result reached by the trial judge was correct. A prerequisite for a class action is that the class be "so numerous that joinder of all members is impracticable." Fed.R.Civ.P. 23(a)(1). "The raison d'etre of the class suit doctrine is necessity, which in turn depends upon the question of number." 3B Moore's Federal Practice ¶ 23.05, at 23–149 (2d ed. 1979). This depends on the facts of each case and no arbitrary rules have been established, Wright & Miller, Federal Practice and Procedure: Civil § 1762 (1972), nor indeed should be. The basic question is practicability of joinder, not number of interested persons per se. Practicability of joinder depends on size of the class, ease of identifying its members and determining their addresses, facility of making service on them if joined and their geographic dispersion. See id.; 3B Moore's Federal Practice ¶ 23.05 (2d ed. 1979).

Only thirty-one persons, those Gloor employees who were Hispanic, were affected by the English-only rule. Their identity and addresses were readily ascertainable, and they all lived in a compact geographical area. The suggested class therefore failed to meet the elementary requirements that supports the whole theory of class actions—representation by one person of a group so numerous that joinder in one suit would be impracticable.

NOTES AND PROBLEMS FOR DISCUSSION

1. If impracticability of joinder is not solely a question of numbers, what factors are involved? In Gay v. Waiters' and Lunchmen's Union, Local 30, 549 F.2d 1330 (9th Cir. 1977), the Court of Appeals reversed a district court's denial of class certification on numerosity grounds and held that the trial court "must consider the broad remedial purposes of Title VII and must liberally interpret and apply Rule 23 so as not to undermine the purpose and effectiveness of Title VII in eradicating class-based discrimination." 549 F.2d at 1334. Compare Cypress v. Newport News General and Nonsectarian Hospital Association, 375 F.2d 648, 653 (4th Cir. 1967) (class consisting of seventeen physicians considered sufficiently numerous to permit certification); Sabala v. Western Gillette Inc., 362 F.Supp. 1142 (S.D.Tex.1973), affirmed in part and reversed in part on other grounds, 516 F.2d 1251 (5th Cir. 1975), vacated and remanded on other grounds, 431 U.S. 951, 97 S.Ct. 2670, 53 L.Ed.2d 268 (1977) (class of twenty-six employees allowed). A number of courts have recognized that the fear by putative class members of filing individual actions is a relevant consideration in determining practicability of joinder and justifies the certification of relatively small classes. See, Arkansas Education Ass'n. v. Board of Education, 446 F.2d 763, 765 (8th Cir. 1971) (approximately 17 in class); Slanina v. William Penn Parking Corp., 106 F.R.D. 419 (W.D.Pa.1984) (class of 25 employees sufficiently large because of fear of reprisals if forced to sue individually); Rosario v. Cook County, 101 F.R.D. 659 (N.D.Ill.1983) (class of 20 Hispanic correctional officers sufficiently numerous because of reluctance of individuals to bring employer into court). Most courts which have denied class certification on numerosity grounds, like the Fifth Circuit in Garcia v. Gloor, have focused on ease of identification, lack of geographic dispersion and facility of effectuating service. See Carey v. Greyhound Bus Co., 500 F.2d 1372, 1381 (5th Cir. 1974); Wilburn v. Steamship Trade Association, 376 F.Supp. 1228, 1233 (D.Md.1974).

2. In International Brotherhood of Teamsters v. United States, 431 U.S. 324, 364, 97 S.Ct. 1843, 1869, 52 L.Ed.2d 396 (1977), the Supreme Court stated that persons deterred from seeking employment because of the known discriminatory policies of an employer are entitled to relief in a Title VII action on the same basis as actual applicants, where they can demonstrate that they had an interest in the job in question and that application would have been futile. Such persons are, as a practical matter, unidentifiable at the class certification stage. May a class composed of a potentially large, but unidentifiable group of persons be certified? Does the inability to identify class members automatically make joinder impracticable? See Jones v. Diamond, supra, 519 F.2d at 1100 (smaller classes are less objectionable when plaintiff seeks relief for future class members). See also Barnett v. W. T. Grant Co., 518 F.2d 543 (4th Cir. 1975); Jack v. American Linen Supply, 498 F.2d 122 (5th Cir. 1974); Morrow v.

Crisler, 3 F.E.P. Cases 1162 (S.D.Miss.1971), affirmed in part, 479 F.2d 960 (5th Cir. 1973), affirmed on rehearing, 491 F.2d 1053 (5th Cir.) (en banc), cert. denied, 419 U.S. 895, 95 S.Ct. 173, 42 L.Ed.2d 139 (1974).

3. Assuming that joinder of class members is not impracticable and class certification is denied, how may joinder be effected? See Rules 19 and 20, Federal Rules of Civil Procedure. Can class-type relief be afforded to members of an uncertified "class"? See Carey v. Greyhound, supra, 500 F.2d 1372 (5th Cir. 1974), and Comment, To What Extent Can A Court Remedy Classwide Discrimination In An Individual Suit Under Title VII?, 20 St. Louis U.L.J. 388 (1976). If the class cannot be certified, may the plaintiff, or his attorney, contact putative class members and urge their intervention? See, In re Primus, 436 U.S. 412, 98 S.Ct. 1893, 56 L.Ed.2d 417 (1978).

4. The numerosity requirement has a converse prohibition—the class cannot be too large. Certification may be denied if the court determines the plaintiff lacks the resources to adequately represent the class. Eisen v. Carlisle & Jacquelin, 417 U.S. 156, 94 S.Ct. 2140, 40 L.Ed.2d 732 (1974); Ralston v. Volkswagonwerk, A.G., 61 F.R.D. 427 (W.D.Mo. 1973); Sayre v. Abraham Lincoln Federal Savings & Loan Association, 65 F.R.D. 379 (E.D.Pa. 1974). In assessing manageability, the financial resources of the plaintiff, his attorney's ability to pursue extensive and costly discovery, the geographic dispersion of class members, problems of communication and the reconciling of adverse interests will be considered. When an extremely large class is proposed, courts may permit discovery, prior to certification, of plaintiff and his counsel as to their ability to manage the class. See Guse v. J.C. Penney Co., 409 F.Supp. 28 (E.D.Wis. 1976), reversed on other grounds, 562 F.2d 6 (7th Cir. 1977).

SECTION D. THE CLASS ACTION AND THE PREREQUISITES TO TITLE VII LITIGATION

OATIS v. CROWN ZELLERBACH CORP.

United States Court of Appeals, Fifth Circuit, 1968.
398 F.2d 496.

Before BELL, AINSWORTH, and GODBOLD, CIRCUIT JUDGES.

GRIFFIN B. BELL, CIRCUIT JUDGE.

This appeal presents the issue whether membership in a class action brought under § 706(e) of the Civil Rights Act of 1964, 42 U.S.C.A. § 2000e–5(e), is restricted to individuals who have filed charges with the Equal Employment Opportunity Commission. The District Court answered in the affirmative. Mondy v. Crown Zellerbach Corporation, E.D.La., 1967, 271 F.Supp. 258, 264–266. Being of the view that the class was unduly restricted, we reverse.

The suit giving rise to this issue was instituted on March 1, 1967 by four Negro employees (Hill, Oatis, Johnson and Young) of Crown Zellerbach Corporation. The suit was filed against the company and the two local unions representing employees at the Bogalusa, Louisiana plant of the company. Each plaintiff sued on behalf of himself and all present and prospective Negro employees of the plant, as a class, seeking injunctive relief against unfair employment practices as defined by Title VII of the Civil Rights Act of 1964, 42 U.S.C.A. §§ 2000e–2 and 3.

Prior to this action Hill filed a formal charge against the defendants with the Equal Employment Opportunity Commission (EEOC) in the manner provided for under § 706(a) of the Act, 42 U.S.C.A. § 2000e–5(a). The Commission informed Hill by letter that it had been unable to obtain voluntary compliance from appellees within the 60 days required by the Act. The suit was commenced two weeks later.

Crown and the unions filed motions to dismiss. They contended that an action under Title VII of the Act, 42 U.S.C.A. § 2000e et seq., cannot be brought on behalf of a class, and that in any event plaintiffs Oatis, Johnson and Young could not join in the action as co-plaintiffs inasmuch as they had not filed a charge with the EEOC. The Attorney General, representing the EEOC, was permitted to intervene. See § 706(e) of the Act, supra.

The District Court ruled that the action could be maintained as a class action, but that the class was limited to those Negro employees who had filed charges with EEOC pursuant to § 706(a) of the Act, 271 F.Supp., supra, at pp. 264–266. Oatis, Johnson and Young had not filed such a charge and the motions to dismiss were granted as to them. It is from this dismissal that they appeal.[1]

Under the enforcement provisions of Title VII an aggrieved person is required to file a written charge with the EEOC. § 706(a), supra. Assuming the EEOC finds reasonable cause to believe the charge is true, informal efforts to settle with the employer or union are to be made through conference, conciliation, and persuasion.[2] The filing of such a charge is a condition precedent to seeking judicial relief. See § 706(e).[3] It is thus clear that there is great emphasis in Title VII on

1. The express determination and direction required by Rule 54(b) F.R.Civ.P., in connection with the entry of judgment has been made and appeal is proper although the case is still pending as to Hill's complaint. See Dore v. Link Belt Company, 5 Cir., 1968, 391 F.2d 671.

2. § 706(a):

> Whenever it is charged in writing under oath by a person claiming to be aggrieved, or a written charge has been filed by a member of the Commission where he has reasonable cause to believe a violation of this subchapter has occurred * * * that an employer, employment agency, or labor organization has engaged in an unlawful employment practice, the Commission shall furnish such employer, employment agency, or labor organization * * * with a copy of such charge and shall make an investigation of such charge, provided that such charge shall not be made public by the Commission. If the Commission shall determine, after such investigation, that there is reasonable cause to believe that the charge is true, the Commission shall endeavor to eliminate any such alleged unlawful employment practice by informal methods of conference, conciliation, and persuasion. * * *

3. § 706(e):

> If within thirty days after a charge is filed with the Commission * * * the Commission has been unable to obtain voluntary compliance with this subchapter, the Commission shall so notify the person aggrieved and a civil action may, within thirty days thereafter, be brought against the respondent named in the charge (1) by the person claiming to be aggrieved, or (2) if such charge was filed by a member of the Commission, by any person whom the charge alleges was aggrieved by the alleged unlawful employment practice * * *.

private settlement and the elimination of unfair practices without litigation.

The plaintiffs-appellants maintain that a class action will lie if at least one aggrieved person has filed a charge with the EEOC. Defendants, on the other hand, assert that the administrative, private remedy intent and purposes of the statute will be circumvented and avoided if only one person may follow the administrative route dictate of the Act and then sue on behalf of the other employees. This, they urge, would result in the courts displacing the EEOC role in fostering the purposes of the Act. Defendants also argue that the Act provides for protection of the rights of a class in that § 707(a), 42 U.S.C.A. § 2000e–6, envisions a suit by the Attorney General when he finds that a pattern or practice of discrimination exists. This provision, they say, militates against the position of plaintiffs.

The arguments of defendants are not persuasive for several reasons. A similar argument regarding a suit by the Attorney General was rejected by this court in a case brought under Title II of the Civil Rights Act of 1964. Lance v. Plummer, 5 Cir., 1965, 353 F.2d 585. We again reject it. The Act permits private suits and in nowise precludes the class action device.

Moreover, it does not appear that to allow a class action, within proper confines, would in any way frustrate the purpose of the Act that the settlement of grievances be first attempted through the office of the EEOC. It would be wasteful, if not vain, for numerous employees, all with the same grievance, to have to process many identical complaints with the EEOC. If it is impossible to reach a settlement with one discriminatee, what reason would there be to assume the next one would be successful. The better approach would appear to be that once an aggrieved person raises a particular issue with the EEOC which he has standing to raise, he may bring an action for himself and the class of persons similarly situated and we proceed to an examination of this view.

Plaintiff Hill raised several claims in the charge which he filed with the EEOC. One of these was that he was being discriminated against by the use of segregated locker rooms. Under the District Court's ruling Hill might bring suit and be placed in the white locker room. Other Negroes would have to wait until they could process their charges through EEOC before they could obtain the same relief from the same employer. We do not believe that Congress intended such a result from the application of Title VII. The class should not be so narrowly restricted. This conclusion is in line with several District Court decisions.

The Supreme Court recently made an apt comment on the nature of suits brought under the Civil Rights Act of 1964. See Newman v. Piggie Park Enterprises, 1968, 390 U.S. 400, 88 S.Ct. 964, 19 L.Ed.2d 1263, where the court stated:

"A Title II suit is thus private in form only. When a plaintiff brings an action under that Title, he cannot recover damages. If he obtains an injunction, he does so not for himself alone, but also as a 'private attorney general', vindicating a policy that Congress considered of the highest priority."

Clearly the same logic applies to Title VII of the Act. Racial discrimination is by definition class discrimination, and to require a multiplicity of separate, identical charges before the EEOC, filed against the same employer, as a prerequisite to relief through resort to the court would tend to frustrate our system of justice and order.

We thus hold that a class action is permissible under Title VII of the Civil Rights Act of 1964 within the following limits. First, the class action must, as it does here, meet the requirements of Rule 23(a) and (b)(2). Next, the issues that may be raised by plaintiff in such a class action are those issues that he has standing to raise (i.e., the issues as to which he is aggrieved, see § 706(a), supra), and that he has raised in the charge filed with the EEOC pursuant to § 706(a). Here then the issues that may be considered in the suit are those properly asserted by Hill in the EEOC charge and as are reasserted in the complaint.

Additionally, it is not necessary that members of the class bring a charge with the EEOC as a prerequisite to joining as co-plaintiffs in the litigation. It is sufficient that they are in a class and assert the same or some of the issues. This emphasizes the reason for Oatis, Johnson and Young to appear as co-plaintiffs. They were each employed in a separate department of the plant. They were representative of their respective departments, as Hill was of his, in the class action. They, as co-plaintiffs, must proceed however, within the periphery of the issues which Hill could assert. Under Rule 23(a) they would be representatives of the class consisting of the Negro employees in their departments so as to fairly and adequately protect their interests. This follows from the fact that due to the inapplicability of some of the issues to all members of the class, the proceeding might be facilitated by the use of subclasses. In such event one or more of the co-plaintiffs might represent a subclass. It was error, therefore, to dismiss appellants. They should have been permitted to remain in the case as plaintiffs but with their participation limited to the issues asserted by Hill.

Reversed and remanded for further proceedings not inconsistent herewith.

NOTES AND PROBLEMS FOR DISCUSSION

1. Does the court in *Oatis* mean that plaintiff Hill could not have represented a class composed of all black employees of the Bogalusa plant without the intervention of the employees working in other departments? If the claim is segregated facilities on a plant-wide basis, are sub-classes necessary or even beneficial?

2. The court held that the intervenors, "must proceed * * * within the periphery of the issues which Hill could assert." As discussed supra at 418, 423, the claims in a Title VII cause of action are limited to some degree by the allegations in the EEOC charge filed pursuant to § 706(a). The complaint may raise issues which can "reasonably be expected to grow out of the [EEOC] charge of discrimination." Sanchez v. Standard Brands, Inc., 431 F.2d 455, 466 (5th Cir. 1970).

Although all the circuits adhere to the "like or related" test of *Sanchez* for determining the proper scope of class allegations in a Title VII action, there is substantial divergence among the courts as to the application of that standard. In Fellows v. Universal Restaurants, Inc., 701 F.2d 447 (5th Cir. 1983), the court held that neither a class allegation in the EEOC charge nor a class investigation by the EEOC was a prerequisite to a class suit. All that was required was that the substance of the charge afford "a reasonable expectation that the EEOC's investigation could encompass not only Universal's alleged discrimination against Ms. Fellows but also that against all female applicants and employees." 701 F.2d at 451. But in Evans v. U.S. Pipe & Foundry Co., 696 F.2d 925 (11th Cir. 1983), the district court dismissed class allegations of discrimination in initial job assignments, promotions, layoffs, discipline and termination on behalf of all black employees of the defendant, because the plaintiff's EEOC charge had only alleged racial discrimination in the areas of promotion and job assignment and because the EEOC investigation had been limited to those matters. The Eleventh Circuit, while recognizing contrary authority, affirmed.

> The record reveals that the substantive inquiry by the Commission was limited to defendants' [sic] claims of discrimination in promotion and harassment. Appellants' concept of widespread discrimination rooted in the subjective decision-making of the white supervisory staff was not a part of the investigation by the Commission. Among the principles underlying the 'like or related' rule is the belief that the Commission should have the first opportunity to investigate the alleged discriminatory practices to permit it to perform its role in obtaining voluntary compliance and promoting conciliation efforts. In light of these principles, we cannot say that the district court erred in finding that plaintiff's broad class included members whose claims were beyond the scope of Evans' EEOC charge.

696 F.2d at 929. Does the *Evans* rationale make sense in light of the EEOC's own policy of limiting its investigation only to those charges that directly affect a charging party in order to reduce its backlog? See EEOC Compliance Manual [BNA] § 2.1(e) (May, 1979).

In one type of case, actions against the federal government, class actions must be preceded by an administrative class complaint clearly denominated as such. Federal regulations governing EEOC charges distinguish between individual and class-type claims in both charge form and handling. 29 C.F.R. §§ 1601.6–1601.21 (1981). These rules have been uniformly interpreted as making the filing of an administrative class charge and the exhaustion of administrative remedies on the class allegations prerequisites to class actions against federal agencies. See e.g. Patton v. Brown, 95 F.R.D. 205 (E.D.Pa.1982); Downes v. Adams, 35 F.R.Serv.2d 1309 (E.D.N.Y.1982); Johnson v. Bond, 94 F.R.D. 125 (N.D.Ill.1982); Moore v. Orr, 33 FEP Cases 523 (D.Col.1982).

CROWN, CORK & SEAL CO., INC. v. PARKER

Supreme Court of the United States, 1983.
462 U.S. 345, 103 S.Ct. 2392, 76 L.Ed.2d 628.

JUSTICE BLACKMUN delivered the opinion of the Court.

The question that confronts us in this case is whether the filing of a class action tolls the applicable statute of limitations, and thus permits all members of the putative class to file individual actions in the event that class certification is denied, provided, of course, that those actions are instituted within the time that remains on the limitations period.

I

Respondent Theodore Parker, a Negro male, was discharged from his employment with petitioner Crown, Cork & Seal Company, Inc., in July 1977. In October of that year, he filed a charge with the Equal Employment Opportunity Commission (EEOC) alleging that he had been harassed and then discharged on account of his race. On November 9, 1978, the EEOC issued a Determination Letter finding no reasonable cause to believe respondent's discrimination charge was true, and, pursuant to § 706(f) of the Civil Rights Act of 1964 (Act), sent respondent a Notice of Right to Sue.

Two months earlier, while respondent's charge was pending before the EEOC, two other Negro males formerly employed by petitioner filed a class action in the United States District Court for the District of Maryland. Pendleton v. Crown, Cork & Seal Co., Civ. No. M–78–1734. The complaint in that action alleged that petitioner had discriminated against its Negro employees with respect to hiring, discharges, job assignments, promotions, disciplinary actions, and other terms and conditions of employment, in violation of Title VII of the Act. The named plaintiffs purported to represent a class of "black persons who have been, continue to be and who in the future will be denied equal employment opportunities by defendant on the grounds of race or color." App. to Brief for Petitioner 2a. It is undisputed that respondent was a member of the asserted class.

In May 1979, the named plaintiffs in Pendleton moved for class certification. Nearly a year and a half later, on September 4, 1980, the District Court denied the motion. App. to Brief for Petitioner 7a. The court ruled that the named plaintiffs' claims were not typical of those of the class, that the named plaintiffs would not be adequate representatives, and that the class was not so numerous as to make joinder impracticable. Thereafter, Pendleton proceeded as an individual action on behalf of its named plaintiffs.[1]

1. The named plaintiffs in Pendleton later settled their claims, and their action was dismissed with prejudice. Respondent Parker, as permitted by United Airlines, Inc. v. McDonald, 432 U.S. 385, 392–395, 97 S.Ct. 2464, 2468–2470, 53 L.Ed.2d 423

On October 27, 1980, within 90 days after the denial of class certification but almost two years after receiving his Notice of Right to Sue, respondent filed the present Title VII action in the United States District Court for the District of Maryland, alleging that his discharge was racially motivated. Respondent moved to consolidate his action with the pending Pendleton case, but petitioner opposed the motion on the ground that the two cases were at substantially different stages of preparation. The motion to consolidate was denied. The District Court then granted summary judgment for petitioner, ruling that respondent had failed to file his action within 90 days of receiving his Notice of Right to Sue, as required by the Act's § 706(f)(1).

The United States Court of Appeals for the Fourth Circuit reversed. 677 F.2d 391 (1982). Relying on American Pipe & Constr. Co. v. Utah, 414 U.S. 538, 94 S.Ct. 756, 38 L.Ed.2d 713 (1974), the Court of Appeals held that the filing of the Pendleton class action had tolled Title VII's statute of limitations for all members of the putative class. Because the Pendleton suit was instituted before respondent received his Notice, and because respondent had filed his action within 90 days after the denial of class certification, the Court of Appeals concluded that it was timely.

Two other Courts of Appeals have held that the tolling rule of American Pipe applies only to putative class members who seek to intervene after denial of class certification, and not to those who, like respondent, file individual actions.[2] We granted certiorari to resolve the conflict.

II

A

American Pipe was a federal antitrust suit brought by the State of Utah on behalf of itself and a class of other public bodies and agencies. The suit was filed with only 11 days left to run on the applicable statute of limitations. The District Court eventually ruled that the suit could not proceed as a class action, and eight days after this ruling a number of putative class members moved to intervene. This Court ruled that the motions to intervene were not time-barred. The Court reasoned that unless the filing of a class action tolled the statute of limitations, potential class members would be induced to file motions to intervene or to join in order to protect themselves against the possibility that certification would be denied. The principal purposes of the

(1977), then intervened in that lawsuit for the limited purpose of appealing the denial of class certification. He failed, however, to take a timely appeal.

2. See Pavlak v. Church, 681 F.2d 617 (CA9 1982), cert. pending, No. 82–650; Stull v. Bayard, 561 F.2d 429, 433 (CA2 1977), cert. denied, 434 U.S. 1035, 98 S.Ct. 769, 54 L.Ed.2d 783 (1978); Arneil v. Ramsey, 550 F.2d 774, 783 (CA2 1977).

class action procedure—promotion of efficiency and economy of litigation—would thereby be frustrated. Ibid. To protect the policies behind the class action procedure, the Court held that "the commencement of a class action suspends the applicable statute of limitations as to all asserted members of the class who would have been parties had the suit been permitted to continue as a class action."

Petitioner asserts that the rule of American Pipe was limited to intervenors, and does not toll the statute of limitations for class members who file actions of their own.[3] Petitioner relies on the Court's statement in American Pipe that "the commencement of the original class suit tolls the running of the statute for all purported members of the class *who make timely motions to intervene* after the court has found the suit inappropriate for class action status." While American Pipe concerned only intervenors, we conclude that the holding of that case is not to be read so narrowly. The filing of a class action tolls the statute of limitations "as to all asserted members of the class," not just as to intervenors.

The American Pipe Court recognized that unless the statute of limitations was tolled by the filing of the class action, class members would not be able to rely on the existence of the suit to protect their rights. Only by intervening or taking other action prior to the running of the statute of limitations would they be able to ensure that their rights would not be lost in the event that class certification was denied. Much the same inefficiencies would ensue if American Pipe's tolling rule were limited to permitting putative class members to intervene after the denial of class certification. There are may reasons why a class member, after the denial of class certification, might prefer to bring an individual suit rather than intervene. The forum in which the class action is pending might be an inconvenient one, for example, or the class member might not wish to share control over the litigation with other plaintiffs once the economies of a class action were no longer available. Moreover, permission to intervene might be refused for reasons wholly unrelated to the merits of the claims.[4] A putative class

3. Petitioner also argues that American Pipe does not apply in Title VII actions, because the time limit contained in § 706(f)(1), 42 U.S.C. § 2000e–5(f)(1) [42 U.S.C.S. § 2000e–5(f)(1)], is jurisdictional and may not be tolled. This argument is foreclosed by the Court's decisions in Zipes v. Trans World Airlines, Inc., 455 U.S. 385, 398, 102 S.Ct. 1127, 1135, 71 L.Ed.2d 234 (1982), and Mohasco Corp. v. Silver, 447 U.S. 807, 811, 100 S.Ct. 2486, 2489 and n. 9, 65 L.Ed.2d 532 (1980).

4. Putative class members frequently are not entitled to intervene as of right under Fed.Rule Civ.Proc. 24(a), and permissive intervention under Fed.Rule Civ.Proc. 24(b) may be denied in the discretion of the District Court. American Pipe, 414 U.S. at 559–560, 94 S.Ct. at 769; id., at 562, 94 S.Ct. at 770 (concurring opinion); see Railroad Trainmen v. Baltimore & Ohio R.Co., 331 U.S. 519, 524–525, 67 S.Ct. 1387, 1389–1390, 91 L.Ed. 1646 (1947). In exercising its discretion the District Court considers "whether the intervention will unduly delay or prejudice the adjudication of the rights of the original parties," Fed.Rule Civ.Proc. 24(b), and a court could conclude that undue delay or prejudice would result if many class members were brought in as plaintiffs upon the denial of class certification. Thus, permissive intervention well

member who fears that class certification may be denied would have every incentive to file a separate action prior to the expiration of his own period of limitations. The result would be a needless multiplicity of actions—precisely the situation that Federal Rule of Civil Procedure 23 and the tolling rule of American Pipe were designed to avoid.

B

Failure to apply American Pipe to class members filing separate actions also would be inconsistent with the Court's reliance on American Pipe in Eisen v. Carlisle & Jacquelin, 417 U.S. 156, 94 S.Ct. 2140, 40 L.Ed.2d 732 (1974). In Eisen, the Court held that Rule 23(c)(2) required individual notice to absent class members, so that each class member could decide whether to "opt out" of the class and thereby preserve his right to pursue his own lawsuit. The named plaintiff in Eisen argued that such notice would be fruitless because the statute of limitations had long since run on the claims of absent class members. This argument, said the Court, was "disposed of by our recent decision in American Pipe * * * which established that commencement of a class action tolls the applicable statute of limitations as to all members of the class."

If American Pipe's tolling rule applies only to intervenors, this reference to American Pipe is misplaced and makes no sense. Eisen's notice requirement was intended to inform the class member that he could "preserve his opportunity to press his claim *separately*" by opting out of the class. But a class member would be unable to "press his claim separately" if the limitations period had expired while the class action was pending. The Eisen Court recognized this difficulty, but concluded that the right to opt out and press a separate claim remained meaningful because the filing of the class action tolled the statute of limitations under the rule of American Pipe. If American Pipe were limited to intervenors, it would not serve the purpose assigned to it by Eisen; no class member would opt out simply to intervene. Thus, the Eisen Court necessarily read American Pipe as we read it today, to apply to class members who choose to file separate suits.[5]

may be an uncertain prospect for members of a proposed class.

5. Several members of the Court have indicated that American Pipe's tolling rule can apply to class members who file individual suits, as well as to those who seek to intervene. See Johnson v. Railway Express Agency, Inc., 421 U.S. 454, 474–475, 95 S.Ct. 1716, 1727, 44 L.Ed.2d 295 (1975) (Marshall, J., joined by Douglas and Brennan, JJ., concurring in part and dissenting in part) ("In American Pipe we held that initiation of a timely class action tolled the running of the limitation period as to individual members of the class, enabling them to institute separate actions after the District Court found class action an inappropriate mechanism for the litigation"); United Airlines, Inc. v. McDonald, 432 U.S. 385, 402, 97 S.Ct. 2464, 2474, 53 L.Ed.2d 423 (1977) (Powell, J., joined by The Chief Justice and White, J., dissenting) ("Under American Pipe, the filing of a class action complaint tolls the statute of limitations until the District Court makes a decision regarding class status. If class status is denied, * * * the statute of limitations begins to run again as to class members

C

The Court noted in American Pipe that a tolling rule for class actions is not inconsistent with the purposes served by statutes of limitations. Limitations periods are intended to put defendants on notice of adverse claims and to prevent plaintiffs from sleeping on their rights, but these ends are met when a class action is commenced. Class members who do not file suit while the class action is pending cannot be accused of sleeping on their rights; Rule 23 both permits and encourages class members to rely on the named plaintiffs to press their claims. And a class complaint "notifies the defendants not only of the substantive claims being brought against them, but also of the number and generic identities of the potential plaintiffs who may participate in the judgment." The defendant will be aware of the need to preserve evidence and witnesses respecting the claims of all the members of the class. Tolling the statute of limitations thus creates no potential for unfair surprise, regardless of the method class members choose to enforce their rights upon denial of class certification.

Restricting the rule of American Pipe to intervenors might reduce the number of individual lawsuits filed against a particular defendant but, as discussed above, this decrease in litigation would be counterbalanced by an increase in protective filings in all class actions. Moreover, although a defendant may prefer not to defend against multiple actions in multiple forums once a class has been decertified, this is not an interest that statutes of limitations are designed to protect. Other avenues exist by which the burdens of multiple lawsuits may be avoided; the defendant may seek consolidation in appropriate cases, see Fed.Rule Civ.Proc. 42(a); 28 U.S.C. § 1404 [28 U.S.C.S. § 1404] (change of venue), and multidistrict proceedings may be available if suits have been brought in different jurisdictions, see 28 U.S.C. § 1407 [28 U.S.C.S. § 1407].[6]

III

We conclude, as did the Court in American Pipe, that "the commencement of a class action suspends the applicable statute of limitations as to all asserted members of the class who would have been parties had the suit been permitted to continue as a class action." Once the statute of limitations has been tolled, it remains tolled for all members of the putative class until class certification is denied. At that point, class members may choose to file their own suits or to intervene as plaintiffs in the pending action.

excluded from the class. In order to protect their rights, such individuals must seek to intervene in the individual action (or possibly file an action of their own) before the time remaining in the limitations period expires").

6. Petitioner's complaints about the burden of defending multiple suits ring particularly hollow in this case, since petitioner opposed respondent's efforts to consolidate his action with Pendleton.

In this case, respondent clearly would have been a party in Pendleton if that suit had been permitted to continue as a class action. The filing of the Pendleton action thus tolled the statute of limitations for respondent and other members of the Pendleton class. Since respondent did not receive his Notice of Right to Sue until after the Pendleton action was filed, he retained a full 90 days in which to bring suit after class certification was denied. Respondent's suit was thus timely filed.

The judgment of the Court of Appeals is affirmed.

SEPARATE OPINION

JUSTICE POWELL, with whom JUSTICE REHNQUIST and JUSTICE O'CONNOR join, concurring.

I join the Court's opinion. It seems important to reiterate the view expressed by Justice Blackmun in American Pipe & Constr. Co. v. Utah, 414 U.S. 538, 94 S.Ct. 756, 38 L.Ed.2d 713 (1974). He wrote that our decision "must not be regarded as encouragement to lawyers in a case of this kind to frame their pleadings as a class action, intentionally, to attract and save members of the purported class who have slept on their rights." The tolling rule of American Pipe is a generous one, inviting abuse. It preserves for class members a range of options pending a decision on class certification. The rule should not be read, however, as leaving a plaintiff free to raise different or peripheral claims following denial of class status.

In American Pipe we noted that a class suit "notifies the defendants not only of the substantive claims being brought against them, but also of the number and generic identities of the potential plaintiffs who participate in the judgment. Within the period set by the statute of limitations, the defendants have the essential information necessary to determine both the subject matter and size of the prospective litigation." When thus notified, the defendant normally is not prejudiced by tolling of the statute of limitations. It is important to make certain, however, that American Pipe is not abused by the assertion of claims that differ from those raised in the original class suit. As Justice Blackmun noted, a district court should deny intervention under Rule 24(b) to "preserve a defendant whole against prejudice arising from claims for which he has received no prior notice." Similarly, when a plaintiff invokes American Pipe in support of a separate lawsuit, the district court should take care to ensure that the suit raises claims that "concern the same evidence, memories, and witnesses as the subject matter of the original class suit," so that "the defendant will not be prejudiced." Ibid. Claims as to which the defendant was not fairly placed on notice by the class suit are not protected under American Pipe and are barred by the statute of limitations.

In this case, it is undisputed that the Pendleton class suit notified petitioner of respondent's claims. The statute of limitations therefore was tolled under American Pipe as to those claims.

NOTES AND PROBLEMS FOR DISCUSSION

1. What if Parker had received his right-to-sue letter *before* the class action was filed? Would the 90-day period have been merely suspended during the pendency of the action or would the period have begun to run anew when class certification was denied? In American Pipe & Construction Co. v. Utah, the anti-trust action discussed in Crown, Cork & Seal, the Court held that the filing of class action suspended the running of the limitation period. In that case the controlling statute of limitations was established by the Clayton Act which also provided for suspension when the period was tolled. *American Pipe* did not establish a general rule on tolling applicable to all federal actions. In CHARDON v. SOTO, 462 U.S. 650, 103 S.Ct. 2611, 77 L.Ed.2d 74 (1983), a suit filed under 42 U.S.C. § 1983, the Court held that where federal law is silent, state law must be looked to for both the applicable statute of limitations and to determine the tolling effect of a class action unless they are "inconsistent with the Constitution and laws of the United States." Under Puerto Rican law applicable in *Chardon,* the statute of limitations began to run anew when tolling ceases. Unlike § 1983, Title VII provides the applicable limitations period, but does not provide for the "tolling effect" of a class action. What rule should apply?

How similar must the claims raised in the original class action be to those in the subsequent suit for the tolling doctrine to apply? In Davis v. Bethlehem Steel Corp., et al., 769 F.2d 210 (4th Cir.), cert. denied, ___ U.S. ___, 106 S.Ct. 573, 88 L.Ed.2d 557 (1985), the Court of Appeals held that a class action filed in 1971 containing a "laundry list" of pattern and practice allegations was not specific enough to put the defendants on notice of the discriminatory acts alleged in a 1982 complaint thus precluding the application of *Crown, Cork & Seal.* Should the rule that the statute of limitations is tolled for all class members until class certification is denied or until they opt out of the class be limited to those members who can prove reliance on the pendency of the class action? See, Tosti v. City of Los Angeles, 754 F.2d 1485 (9th Cir. 1985). Does the rule in *Crown, Cork & Seal* apply to subsequently filed *class* actions as well as individual cases? See, Smith v. Flagship International, 609 F.Supp. 58 (N.D. Tex.1985).

2. As Oatis holds, employees who have not filed EEOC charges, may be represented in a Title VII class action by one who has and may even intervene as named plaintiffs under the "umbrella" of the first plaintiff's EEOC charge. But it is also clear that the class may include only those persons who had viable claims at the time the class representative on whom they depend filed a charge with the EEOC. See e.g., Laffey v. Northwest Airlines, Inc., 567 F.2d 429, 472–73 (D.C.Cir. 1976), cert. denied, 434 U.S. 1086, 98 S.Ct. 1281, 55 L.Ed.2d 792 (1977); Moses v. Avco Corp., 97 F.R.D. 20 (D.Conn.1982); Gill v. Monroe County Dept. of Social Services, 79 F.R.D. 316, 331 (W.D.N.Y.1978). For example, in a Title VII class action on behalf of persons unlawfully denied employment, the named plaintiff would have necessarily filed an EEOC charge within 180 days (in a non-deferral state) of the defendant's rejection of his application. Thus, only those persons who were denied employment within 180 days prior to the date on which the named plaintiff filed his EEOC charge (i.e., those persons who *could* have filed an EEOC charge at the same time the plaintiff did) may be included in the class. McDonald v. United Airlines, Inc., 587 F.2d 357, 361 n. 10 (7th Cir. 1978), cert. denied, 442 U.S. 934, 99 S.Ct. 2869, 61 L.Ed.2d 303 (1979); Wetzel v. Liberty Mutual Insurance Co., 508 F.2d 239, 246 (3d Cir.), cert.

denied, 421 U.S. 1011, 95 S.Ct. 2415, 44 L.Ed.2d 679 (1975); Zahorik v. Cornell University, 579 F.Supp. 349 (N.D.N.Y.1982). For those persons rejected by the employer more than 180 days prior to the date on which the named plaintiff filed his charge, their rights to either file their own suit or participate in a class action under Title VII ended 180 days after they were turned down for employment. As the Supreme Court noted in United Air Lines, Inc. v. Evans, the discrimination against such persons "is merely an unfortunate event in history which has no present legal consequences.", supra at 403. It follows that a person without a valid claim at the time the class representative's charge was filed may not intervene as a named plaintiff. Hill v. AT & T Technologies, Inc., 731 F.2d 175 (4th Cir. 1984).

In United Airlines, Inc. v. McDonald, 432 U.S. 385, 97 S.Ct. 2464, 53 L.Ed.2d 423 (1977), the Supreme Court held that where the class representative refuses to appeal the denial of certification, a putative class member, even one who has not filed an EEOC charge, should be allowed to intervene for purposes of carrying forward the appeal. But should the same rule apply where the named plaintiff's individual claim is dismissed before any class determination is made? In other words, should a person who could not file a Title VII action on his own, for failure to file an EEOC charge, be allowed to intervene to represent a class where the named plaintiff, who did file a charge, is otherwise precluded, as a matter of law, from litigating his claim? See Wakeen v. Hoffman House, Inc., 724 F.2d 1238 (7th Cir. 1983).

SECTION E. CERTIFICATION UNDER RULE 23(b)(2) AND 23(b)(3): NOTICE TO THE CLASS AND THE RIGHT TO OPT OUT

Once class certification is requested and the court finds that the mandatory requirements of Rule 23(a) are satisfied, it must determine whether the proposed class can be maintained under subsection (b)(1), (b)(2) or (b)(3) of the rule. Because of its language, subsection (b)(1) is seldom utilized [1] and, as a practical matter, the choice in almost all class litigation is between certification under (b)(2) or (b)(3).

A (b)(2) class is permitted when the defendant has "acted or refused to act on grounds generally applicable to the class, thereby making appropriate final injunctive relief or corresponding declaratory relief with respect to the class as a whole." The drafters of the rule intended (b)(2) to be applicable to actions involving very cohesive classes when injunctive relief applicable to all class members was sought. The civil rights class action challenging racial discrimination which affected all

1. Rule 23(b)(1) emphasizes the effect individual adjudications of the claims of putative class members might have on defendants and other class members and was apparently designed to encompass cases where separate actions by individual members of the class would be dismissed for failure to join indispensable parties. See, Homburger, State Class Actions and the Federal Rules, 71 Col.L.Rev. 609, 633 (1971). Thus, if the court determines that individual lawsuits by or against class members do not pose a threat of inconsistent adjudications that might cause hardship on the opposing party or that separate proceedings would not prejudice the other class members, the action cannot be maintained as a class action unless it qualifies under another subsection of 23(b). Because few actions fall within the requirements of (b)(1) or, if they do, overlap with one of the other subsections, there is little litigation concerning the (b)(1) classes. See, 7A Wright & Milier, Federal Practice and Procedure, § 1772, p. 5.

class members in the same way typified the kind of case to which (b)(2) was to be applicable. See, Advisory Committee's Note to Proposed Amendments to Rule 23, 39 F.R.D. 69, 102 (1966). Rule 23(b)(3) was intended to apply to a more heterogeneous class when questions of law or fact common to the class predominate over questions affecting only individual members. It was contemplated that (b)(3) certification would be appropriate when monetary relief was requested on behalf of class members who had suffered similar injuries. Advisory Committee Note, supra, at 103.

Under Rule 23, a final judgment in a class action, regardless of subsection utilized for certification, is binding on all members of the class. The major difference between certification under (b)(2) and (b)(3) lies in the notice and opt out provisions of section (c) of the rule. Because a (b)(2) action does not require notice to the class, a final judgment can be entered binding class members without any notice or opportunity to participate in or to be excluded from the proceeding. In a (b)(3) action, however, Rule 23(c)(2) requires that "the best notice practicable under the circumstances" be directed to class members at the time of certification, and that such members be allowed to exclude themselves from the action (and thus not be bound by any decision) with a timely notice to the court. The rule's authors believed that, because of differences that might exist between class members in the (b)(3) class, particularly where personal monetary relief was sought for class members, individual members might wish to pursue their personal claims in their own suits. Such class members were thus entitled to notice and the opportunity to opt out of the class action at the certification stage. Advisory Committee Note, supra, at 104–05. By contrast, the (b)(2) class was viewed as so unified in interest as to make notice and the opt-out provision unnecessary because any injunctive relief granted would necessarily affect all class members identically whether they remained members of the class or not. See, Katz v. Carte Blanche Corp., 496 F.2d 747, 759 (3d Cir. 1973), cert. denied, 419 U.S. 885, 95 S.Ct. 152, 42 L.Ed.2d 125 (1974); Advisory Committee Note, supra, at 104–05.

The Title VII class action has posed problems under Rule 23(b) because typically both broad injunctive relief and individual monetary awards in the form of back pay are requested for the class. Back pay, which will normally be in different amounts for individual class members depending on their length of employment, job classification and personal employment history, resembles the kind of relief thought by the drafters to be peculiarly appropriate for (b)(3) treatment. On the other hand, injunctive relief, either to prohibit class-wide discrimination in the future or as a remedy for past wrongs, is the kind of relief the (b)(2) class was designed to facilitate. The question of which subsection to utilize for certification is far from academic because of the Supreme Court's ruling in Eisen v. Carlisle & Jacquelin, 417 U.S. 156, 94 S.Ct. 2140, 40 L.Ed.2d 732 (1974) that in (b)(3) actions the plaintiff must bear all the costs of notice. The defendant in a class action thus has a strong incentive to see the action certified under (b)(3): where the class is large and geographically spread out, the cost of the notice required by (c)(2) may as a practical matter kill the action because of the plaintiff's inability to bear the expense. The employer-defendant will also benefit from class members opting out. Experience has shown that few if any employees will opt out because they want to bring individual cases and, if a sufficient number opt out, the class itself can fail for lack of numerosity.

The problem of designating which subsection is applicable in an employment case is illustrated by Wetzel v. Liberty Mutual Insurance Co., 508 F.2d 239 (3d Cir.), cert. denied, 421 U.S. 1011, 95 S.Ct. 2415, 44 L.Ed.2d 679 (1975) where plaintiffs sought certification of a nation-wide class of female employees in several job classifications. During the course of the litigation, the employer made changes in its hiring and promotional practices obviating the need for injunctive relief. On appeal, the employer argued that the case should have been certified as a (b)(3) action and notice required because, by the time the case reached judgment, the class no longer satisfied the requirements of 23(b)(2). The Third Circuit affirmed the district court's (b)(2) certification.

> [A] Title VII suit against discriminatory hiring and promotion is necessarily a suit to end discrimination because of a common class characteristic, in this case sex. * * * The conduct of the employer is actionable 'on grounds generally applicable to the class,' and the relief sought is 'relief with respect to the class as a whole.' Thus a Title VII action is particularly fit for (b)(2) treatment, and the drafters of Rule 23 specifically contemplated that suits against discriminatory hiring and promotion policies would be appropriately maintained under (b)(2). * * * Since a Title VII suit is essentially equitable in nature, it cannot be characterized as one seeking exclusively or predominantly money damages.

508 F.2d at 250–51. The Court also noted that the language of (b)(2) did not limit use of the subsection only to those cases where final injunctive relief was necessary, but merely required that the type of conduct by the party opposing the class be the kind that is subject to equitable relief.

> Liberty Mutual's policies at the time these charges were made were such that final injunctive relief was appropriate. This satisfies the language of the rule.

Ibid. It is far from clear that the drafters of Rule 23 contemplated anything like the modern Title VII class action when they devised (b)(2),[2] but most courts have agreed with the Third Circuit that Title VII class actions should be certified under (b)(2) where both monetary and

2. The civil rights cases cited in the Advisory Committee Note to the proposed revisions of Rule 23 involved challenges to overt, state-imposed policies of racial segregation in which all members of the class were necessarily affected by the discriminatory practices in the same way. Advisory Committee Note, supra, at 102. See, Strickler, Protecting the Class: The Search For the Adequate Representative in Class Action Litigation, 34 DePaul L.Rev. 73, 114 (1984);

injunctive relief is sought. See generally, Rutherglen, Notice, Scope and Preclusion in Title VII Class Actions, 69 Va.L.Rev. 11, 23 (1983). The Fifth Circuit has held that such "hybrid" class actions fall within the ambit of (b)(2) because the "demand for back pay is not in the nature of a claim for damages, but rather is an integral part of the statutory equitable remedy, to be determined through the exercise of the courts discretion." Johnson v. Georgia Highway Express, 417 F.2d 1122, 1125 (5th Cir. 1969). See also, Pettway v. American Cast Iron Pipe Co., 494 F.2d 211, 256–57 (5th Cir. 1974) (*Pettway III*).

Though not mandatory in a (b)(2) action, notice to the class at the time of certification may be ordered at the district court's discretion under Rule 23(d)(2).[3] See, Clark v. American Marine Corp., 297 F.Supp. 1305 (E.D.La.1969); Walthall v. Blue Shield of California, 16 FEP Cases 625 (N.D.Cal.1977). The notice may be issued for purely informational purposes, Avagliano v. Sumitomo Shoji America, Inc., 614 F.Supp. 1397 (S.D.N.Y.1985), or to encourage intervention, Woods v. New York Life Insurance Co., 686 F.2d 578 (7th Cir. 1982). The courts are divided over whether it is within the district court's discretion, at least at the certification stage, to allow class members to opt out of a (b)(2) action. Compare, Dosier v. Miami Valley Broadcasting Corp., 656 F.2d 1295, 1299 (9th Cir. 1981); Laskey v. International Union, United Automotive, Aerospace & Agricultural Implement Workers, 638 F.2d 954, 956 (6th Cir. 1981); Fowler v. Birmingham News Co., 608 F.2d 1055, 1058 (5th Cir. 1979); Kincade v. General Tire & Rubber Co., 635 F.2d 501, 507 (5th Cir. 1981).

Title VII class actions are usually tried in two stages. Liability is litigated first. If the court finds class-wide liability, the relief to which class members are entitled, including back pay, is determined in the second stage. See infra, Chapter 14. Because stage two, with its individualized relief determinations, is functionally similar to the type of litigation for which (b)(3) classes (common issues of fact and law) were designed, some courts have held that (b)(2) class members are entitled to notice and the right to opt out (or to pursue their individual monetary claims in stage two with their own attorneys) after liability is established in stage one. Holmes v. Continental Can Co., 706 F.2d 1144, 1155 (11th Cir. 1983); Officers for Justice v. Civil Service Commission, 688 F.2d 615, 634–35 (9th Cir. 1982), cert. denied, 459 U.S. 1217, 103 S.Ct. 1219, 75 L.Ed.2d 456 (1983). The Eleventh Circuit has held that, until the monetary relief stage in a (b)(2) class action brought under Title VII is reached, an opt out is always inappropriate. Cox v.

3. Rule 23(d) provides in part:

ORDERS IN CONDUCT OF CLASS ACTIONS. In the conduct of actions to which this rule applies, the court may make appropriate orders: . . . (2) requiring, for the protection of the members of the class or otherwise for the fair conduct of the action, that notice be given in such manner as the court may direct to some or all of the members of any step in the action, or of the proposed extent of the judgment, or of the opportunity of members to signify whether they consider the representation fair and adequate, to intervene and present claims or defenses, or otherwise to come into the action; * * *

American Cast Iron Pipe Co., 784 F.2d 1546, 1554 (11th Cir. 1986). In *Cox* the district court allowed the employer to send out notices and opt out questionaires to the previously certified class of employees. On the basis of the returns (roughly half of the potential class opted out), the court decertified the class for lack of numerosity. The Court of Appeals reversed.

> Such a procedure would only tend to promote what was actually accomplished here—the improper use of a court-approved opt-out procedure designed to force class members to take a stand against their employers in order to stay in a controversial lawsuit. To authorize such a procedure was abuse of discretion.

784 F.2d at 1554–55. The problem of determining class-wide relief at stage two is discussed infra in Chapter 14.

When a class action is settled, regardless of what type of class it is, Rule 23(e) requires notice to the class members of the terms of the settlement and judicial approval of the agreement before it is implemented. Rule 23(e) notice does not serve the same function as notice of an opt out right at the time of certification. Most courts have held that in a (b)(2) action, class members have no automatic right to opt out of the settlement because they disagree with its terms. Kincaide v. General Tire and Rubber Co., supra, 635 F.2d at 507; Pettway v. American Cast Iron Pipe Co., 576 F.2d 1157 (5th Cir. 1978) (*Pettway IV*), cert. denied, 439 U.S. 1115, 99 S.Ct. 1020, 59 L.Ed.2d 74 (1979). The notice of the proposed settlement is intended to alert class members whose rights will be determined by the agreement to its terms and allow them to oppose judicial approval. See, Parker v. Anderson, 667 F.2d 1204 (5th Cir.), cert. denied, 459 U.S. 828, 103 S.Ct. 63, 74 L.Ed.2d 65 (1982). In Holmes v. Continental Can Co., supra, however, the court held that it was an abuse of discretion for the trial judge not to allow class members to opt out of a settlement they opposed where their individual monetary claims were not typical of those made by other class members and the settlement provided the objectors with relatively little relief.[4] Where a class action is settled, can there be any reason for *not* allowing class members who are not satisfied with the settlement terms from opting out and pursuing their claims in individual suits?

SECTION F. THE PRECLUSIVE EFFECT OF THE CLASS ACTION JUDGMENT ON THE CLAIMS OF INDIVIDUAL CLASS MEMBERS

The concern expressed by Judge Godbold in Johnson v. Georgia Highway Express, Inc., supra, over the "catastrophic consequences if the plaintiff loses and carries the class down with him," refers to the preclusive effect of a judgment against the class on the claims of

4. The Court of Appeals was influenced by the fact that approximately one half of a relatively small lump-sum back pay award was to be divided among the eight named plaintiffs with the remainder to be distributed to 118 members of the class.

individual class members. As a general rule, a judgment entered in a properly certified class action binds, by way of res judicata or collateral estoppel, all class members on the issues decided in the case. But does this mean that a class member loses the right to prove that he was individually a victim of discrimination because a court decides that there was no class-wide discrimination? In COOPER v. FEDERAL RESERVE BANK OF RICHMOND, 467 U.S. 867, 104 S.Ct. 2794, 81 L.Ed.2d 718 (1984), a properly certified (b)(2) action on behalf of former and current employees of the bank, the plaintiffs tried but failed to prove a pattern and practice of racial discrimination in promotions. Thereafter, several class members filed separate actions, each alleging that he had been denied promotions because of race. The Bank moved to dismiss the complaints on the ground that each of the plaintiffs was a member of the class certified in the prior action and that they were bound by the determination that no class-wide discrimination had occurred. The district court denied the motions to dismiss but certified its order for an interlocutory appeal under 28 U.S.C. § 1292(b). The Fourth Circuit reversed, holding that under the doctrine of res judicata the judgment in the class action precluded the individual class members from maintaining their claims. The Supreme Court in turn reversed the Court of Appeals holding that it had erred in the preclusive effect accorded the class action judgment.

> That judgment (1) bars the class members from bringing another class action against the Bank alleging a pattern or practice of discrimination for the relevant time period and (2) precludes the class members in any other litigation with the Bank from relitigating the question whether the Bank engaged in a pattern and practice of discrimination against black employees during the relevant time period. The judgment is not, however, dispositive of the individual claims the * * * petitioners have alleged in their separate action. Assuming they establish a prima facie case of discrimination under *McDonnell Douglas,* the Bank will be required to articulate a legitimate reason for each of the challenged decisions, and if it meets that burden, the ultimate questions regarding motivation in their individual cases will be resolved by the District Court.

467 U.S. at 880, 104 S.Ct. at 2802. To rule otherwise the Court stated "would be tantamount to requiring that every member of the class be permitted to intervene [in the class action] to litigate the merits of his individual claim" and would defeat the purpose of the class device as a procedure for the efficient adjudication of common questions of law or fact. Ibid.

Left somewhat unsettled by *Cooper* is the effect of the class ruling on the evidence in the individual cases. The Court rather cryptically stated that the determination in the class action that the Bank had not engaged in a general pattern of discrimination "would be relevant on the issue of pretext." 467 U.S. at 880, 104 S.Ct. at 2802. Will *Cooper* preclude the plaintiff from introducing evidence of discrimination against other employees, who were also members of the class, as circumstantial evidence of discrimination against him? At what point would the use of such evidence constitute relitigation of the pattern and practice issue?

If a class member is allowed to opt out of the class and the court subsequently finds class-wide discrimination, of what use is that determination to the claimant in his individual case? See, Smith v. Western Electric Co., 770 F.2d 520 (5th Cir. 1985). Can *Cooper* be read to entitle a class member who is disatisfied with the settlement of the class claim to litigate his individual claim in a separate proceeding? See, Ivy v. Dole, 610 F.Supp. 165 (E.D.Va.1985). The effect of a judgment in favor of the class on the claims of class members is discussed infra Chapter 14.

SECTION G. APPEALABILITY OF CLASS CERTIFICATION DETERMINATIONS

In Gardner v. Westinghouse Broadcasting Co., 437 U.S. 478, 98 S.Ct. 2451, 57 L.Ed.2d 364 (1978), the Supreme Court held that the denial of class certification does not constitute a refusal to grant injunctive relief within the meaning of 28 U.S.C. § 1292(a) and thus cannot be reviewed by an interlocutory appeal. The Court expressly limited its opinion to cases in which the request for class certification was not accompanied by a motion for preliminary injunction. 437 U.S. at 479, n. 3, 98 S.Ct. at 2453, n. 3. See Jenkins v. Blue Cross Mutual Hospital Insurance, Inc., supra. *Gardner* means that, in most employment discrimination class actions, review of a denial of class certification may be obtained only after a determination on the merits of the plaintiffs' individual case—i.e., a "final" decision. But if, as suggested in East Texas Motor Freight v. Rodriguez, supra, the scope of review of a class denial after trial is in part determined by the decision on the merits of the plaintiff's claim, may full review of the class issue always be obtained? The Court in *Gardner* implied that full review of a class denial could be obtained through post-judgment intervention by putative class members. United Airlines, Inc. v. McDonald, 432 U.S. 385, 97 S.Ct. 2464, 53 L.Ed.2d 423 (1977). But in light of the practical difficulty of such would-be class members learning of the action, retaining counsel and taking the necessary steps to intervene and appeal within the time allowed by the Federal Rules, is that mechanism for review likely to be used?

SECTION H. CLASS ACTIONS AND THE E.E.O.C.

Section 706(c) of Title VII authorizes the EEOC, after unlawful employment practice charges against a private employer are filed with it and it is unable to secure conciliation, to bring a civil action against the employer seeking all relief authorized by the Act. See supra at 433. In General Telephone Co. v. EEOC, 446 U.S. 318, 100 S.Ct. 1698, 64

L.Ed.2d 319 (1980), the Supreme Court resolved a conflict among the circuits by holding that the EEOC may seek class-wide relief without being certified as a class representative and without complying with the requirements of Rule 23(a) and (b). The Court concluded that to force compliance by the EEOC with Rule 23 requirements would be contrary to the purpose of Section 706, under which the Commission was to act not merely as a representative of private interests, but to vindicate public policy. Moreover, some actions authorized by Section 706 would be foreclosed by requiring EEOC compliance with Rule 23 requirements such as numerosity or typicality. The Court also noted that it would not be consistent with the remedial purpose of Title VII to bind all "class" members with discrimination grievances against an employer by the relief obtained by an EEOC judgment or settlement against the employer, especially in view of the possible differences between the public and private interests involved.

Part III

OTHER FEDERAL ANTI-DISCRIMINATION LEGISLATION

Chapter 8

THE RECONSTRUCTION CIVIL RIGHTS ACTS—42 U.S.C.A. §§ 1981, 1983, 1985(c)

SECTION A. THE CIVIL RIGHTS ACT OF 1866—42 U.S.C.A. § 1981

REISS, REQUIEM FOR AN "INDEPENDENT REMEDY": THE CIVIL RIGHTS ACTS OF 1866 AND 1871 AS REMEDIES FOR EMPLOYMENT DISCRIMINATION

50 So.Cal.L.Rev. 961, 971–974 (1977).

* * *

In 1865, with the ratification of the thirteenth amendment, Congress obtained authority to pass laws designed to eradicate slavery and its incidents. The Civil Rights Act of 1866 [46] was enacted pursuant to that authority. Section 1 furthered two goals: first, it granted citizenship to all persons born in the United States; and second, it granted those persons the same rights as white citizens. There was some question at the time whether the thirteenth amendment authorized legislation this broad. These doubts, coupled with fears that the Act could easily be repealed in the future, constituted part of the impetus

46. Act of Apr. 9, 1866, ch. 31, § 1, 14 Stat. 27. Section 1 of the Civil Rights Act of 1866 provided:

> *That all persons born in the United States* and not subject to any foreign power, excluding Indians not taxed, *are* hereby declared to be *citizens* of the United States; *and such citizens,* of every race and color, without regard to any previous condition of slavery or involuntary servitude, except as a punishment for crime whereof the party shall have been duly convicted, *shall have the same right,* in every State and Territory in the United States, *to make and enforce contracts, to sue, be parties, and give evidence,* to inherit, purchase, lease, sell, hold, and convey real and personal property, *and to full and equal benefit of all laws and proceedings for the security of person and property, as is enjoyed by white citizens, and shall be subject to like punishment, pains, and penalties, and to none other,* any law, statute, ordinance, regulation, or custom, to the contrary notwithstanding.

14 Stat. 27 (1866) (emphasis added). The italicized portion is similar to, though not identical with, § 1981. The portion dealing with property rights is similar to what is now 42 U.S.C. § 1982.

for the subsequent adoption of the fourteenth amendment in 1868. Two years later, Congress reenacted the 1866 Act with only a minor change in wording, removing any doubts concerning its constitutionality. Years later, as part of a general recodification of federal law, the original section 1 was split into two separate statutes—sections 1981 and 1982. Section 1982 grants all persons the same *property* rights as white citizens, while section 1981 involves *other* rights, including the right to make and enforce contracts. Courts have held that the right "to make and enforce contracts" on an equal basis, referred to in section 1981, includes the right to enter into and enforce *employment* contracts. Thus, section 1981 prohibits discriminatory employment practices in recruitment, hiring, compensation, assignment, promotion, layoff, and discharge of employees.

* * *

* * * Although section 1981, by its terms, would seem to prohibit a broad range of *private* as well as public acts of discrimination, courts have narrowly construed the statute throughout most of its history. In 1883, in the *Civil Rights Cases,* the Supreme Court struck down other civil rights legislation which prohibited discrimination in public accommodations. The Court reasoned that Congress lacked the constitutional authority to reach wholly *private* conduct. Although the Civil Rights Act of 1866 was not directly involved in that case, the Court indicated that the statute should also be limited to situations involving state action. In 1948 the Court expressly declared that "governmental action" was required in a suit based on the Civil Rights Act of 1866.[54]

More than one hundred years after passage of the statute, the Supreme Court, in Jones v. Alfred H. Mayer Co.,[55] finally dispensed with the state action requirement and held that the Civil Rights Act of 1866 reached purely private acts of discrimination. While Jones v. Mayer involved the application of section 1982, it was immediately apparent that the rationale of the decision applied equally to section 1981. Following Jones v. Mayer, section 1981 was increasingly used by plaintiffs, in addition to Title VII, to attack discriminatory employment practices in the private sector. In each instance where a court of appeals had the opportunity to rule on the question, the court held that section 1981 did provide the basis for an independent federal cause of action against racial discrimination in employment. Finally, in Johnson v. Railway Express Agency, Inc.,[57] the Supreme Court affirmed that view. Courts have held section 1981 applicable not only to discrimination by private employers, but also to discrimination by labor unions. In other contexts, not directly involving employment, courts have held section 1981 applicable to contracts involving the purchase of tickets to an amusement park, the admission of patients to a private hospital, membership in private clubs, and, most recently, attendance in private

54. Hurd v. Hodge, 334 U.S. 24, 31 (1948).

55. 392 U.S. 409 (1968).

57. 421 U.S. 454 (1975).

schools. Thus, in the private sector, the coverage of section 1981 is at least as broad as the coverage of Title VII. In fact, it is certainly broader.

Title VII has always applied to employers and unions whose "operations affect commerce," if of a minimum size. The original minimum of one hundred members or employees has been reduced to fifteen. Section 1981 contains no statutory minimum, simply providing that "all persons * * * shall have the same right * * * to make and enforce contracts * * * as * * * white citizens." While it is not likely that all enterprises employing fewer than fifteen employees will be covered by section 1981,[66] the statute clearly does extend its protection to millions of workers in millions of small business establishments not covered by Title VII.

* * *

Read 42 USC § 1981 at p. 1042.

BOBO v. ITT, CONTINENTAL BAKING CO.

United States Court of Appeals, Fifth Circuit, 1981.
662 F.2d 340.

AINSWORTH, CIRCUIT JUDGE.

The principal issue raised by this appeal is whether 42 U.S.C. § 1981, derived primarily from the Civil Rights Act of 1866, 14 Stat. 27, encompasses claims of sex discrimination. The clear answer is that it does not.

Alice Bobo, a black woman, brought this action against her former employer, ITT, Continental Baking Company (ITT). She alleged that ITT discharged her because she had refused to wear a hat that co-employees allegedly were not required to wear. She also averred that prior to her firing, she had been the victim of other discriminatory employment conditions because of her race and sex. Bobo sought relief under Title VII of the Civil Rights Act of 1964 and 42 U.S.C. § 1981. Upon motion by ITT, partial summary judgment was entered against Bobo by the district court. The court ruled that Bobo's Title VII claim was barred because of her failure to sue within 90 days of receipt of her

66. At the far end of the size spectrum, small employment relationships can include not only family businesses, small partnerships, and sole proprietorships, but also the hiring of babysitters, live-in caretakers, and the like. It is simply not likely that all such employment relationships will be covered by § 1981. Two techniques are available for judicially establishing such limits: statutory construction and constitutional analysis. Courts may conclude either that § 1981 was not intended to reach certain of these very small, associational relationships or that the Constitution prohibits such regulation, regardless of Congress' intent. The Supreme Court has, to date, avoided reaching a decision on this question. In Sullivan v. Little Hunting Park, Inc., 396 U.S. 229 (1969), and Tillman v. Wheaton-Haven Recreation Ass'n, 410 U.S. 431 (1973), the district courts had refused to apply § 1981 to "bona fide private clubs." The Supreme Court avoided deciding whether such an exemption existed, and if it did, whence it derived, by holding instead that the two organizations did not qualify as private clubs under Title II of the Civil Rights Act of 1964. More recently, in Runyon v. McCrary, 427 U.S. 160 (1976), the Court again skirted the issue of whether § 1981 covered small, "truly private" schools.

right to sue letter from the Equal Employment Opportunity Commission. The court also held that since § 1981 did not reach claims of sex discrimination, Bobo was entitled to a trial only on the issue of whether she had been subjected to racial discrimination.

* * *

On appeal, Bobo attacks the district court's * * * determination that sex discrimination is not cognizable under § 1981.

Sex Discrimination Under § 1981

Section 1981 generally forbids racial discrimination in the making and enforcement of private contracts, including private employment contracts, whether the aggrieved party is black or white. Runyon v. McCrary, 427 U.S. 160, 168, 96 S.Ct. 2586, 2593, 49 L.Ed.2d 415 (1976); McDonald v. Santa Fe Trial Transportation Co., 427 U.S. 273, 295, 96 S.Ct. 2574, 2586, 49 L.Ed.2d 493 (1976); Johnson v. Railway Express Agency, 421 U.S. 454, 459–60, 95 S.Ct. 1716, 1719–20, 44 L.Ed.2d 295 (1975). * * *

Although § 1981 strikes at many forms of racial discrimination, no court has held that allegations of gender based discrimination fall within its purview. Courts at every level of the federal judiciary have considered the question and reached the opposite result. The Supreme Court, in framing the question for decision in *Runyon*, explained that the case did not involve "the right of a private school to limit its student body to boys, to girls, or to adherents of a particular religious faith, since 42 U.S.C. § 1981 is in no way addressed to such categories of selectivity." Even if we were to heed Bobo's invitation to regard this statement as dictum and therefore not dispositive of the issue, we could not ignore the Supreme Court's consistent emphasis on the racial character of § 1981, as indicated by the law's language and legislative history. The Court has interpreted the phrase "as is enjoyed by white citizens * * *" in § 1981 as reflecting its drafters' intention that the statute ban racial discrimination.

The Court's view of the 1866 Act's purpose was expressed in Georgia v. Rachel, 384 U.S. 780, 86 S.Ct. 1783, 16 L.Ed.2d 925 (1966), which construed its removal provisions. In examining the legislative history, the Court noted that the "white citizens" language was not a part of the original Senate bill, but was added later "apparently to emphasize the racial character of the rights being protected." The Court considered the legislative history of the 1866 Act and concluded that it "clearly indicates that Congress intended to protect a limited category of rights, specifically defined in terms of racial equality." Two terms later, while determining the breadth of 42 U.S.C. § 1982 [4] in Jones v. Alfred H. Mayer Co., the Court repeatedly referred to the 1866 Act's aim of eliminating racial discrimination. The Court observed that unlike the

4. Section 1982 proscribes discrimination with respect to real or personal property interests. Like § 1981, § 1982 is principally derived from § 1 of the Civil Rights Act of 1866.

Fair Housing Title (Title VIII) of the Civil Rights Act of 1968, § 1982 was addressed only to racial discrimination. Finally, in perhaps its most extensive discussion of the legislative history of the 1866 Act, the Court reaffirmed the limits on § 1981 in *McDonald*. Though extending the statute's protection to claims of racial discrimination by whites, the Court ruled that the 1866 Act's goal was to promote equality among the races by precluding discrimination in the making and enforcement of contracts either for or against any particular race.

Bobo nevertheless argues that the term "white citizens" should be deemed synonymous with "most favored group," thereby permitting those who find themselves somehow less favored to advance discrimination charges under § 1981. A sweeping interpretation of this sort, however, would thwart the statute's evident meaning and purpose. As the Supreme Court has explained, Congress enacted § 1 of the 1866 Act with the ambitious goal of ensuring equal citizenship for the newly freed slaves. Statements in the legislative history, carefully reviewed in *McDonald*, reflect this objective and confirm that the "white citizens" language was added specifically to preclude a construction that might expand the statute's coverage to other groups. Representative Wilson, who proposed amending the original bill to add the "white citizens" language, stated that "the reason for offering [the amendment] was this: it was thought by some persons that unless these qualifying words were incorporated in the bill, those rights might be extended to all citizens, whether male or female, majors or minors." * * *

Bobo further contends that since women obviously lacked equal legal rights during the Reconstruction era, "white citizens" should be read as "white men." But as the legislative history quoted above indicates, Congress meant precisely what it said. The drafters of § 1981 had no intention to disturb public or private authority to discriminate against women. Outlawing such discrimination in the United States in 1866 would have signaled an extraordinary social transformation, a result clearly not desired by Congress. Public sensitivity to the ills of gender discrimination is of more recent origin. We cannot ascribe contemporary attitudes to a Congress acting over a century ago when its views to the contrary are so plainly stated.

* * * [T]here is no direct holding by this court that gender based discrimination is not within the acts forbidden by § 1981. At least two other circuits, however, have so held. Movement for Opportunity and Equality v. General Motors Corp., 622 F.2d 1235, 1278 (7th Cir. 1980) (adopting district court opinion); DeGraffenreid v. General Motors Assembly Div., St. Louis, 558 F.2d 480, 486 n. 2 (8th Cir. 1977). A procession of district court opinions is in agreement with this view. * * *

Bobo cites Guerra v. Manchester Terminal Corp., 498 F.2d 641 (5th Cir. 1974) in support of a broader reading of § 1981. In *Guerra* a Mexican citizen lawfully residing in the United States complained that he was the victim of discrimination as a result of a collective bargaining agreement which targeted American citizens for more desirable jobs. The court held that § 1981 reached charges of discrimination based on alienage by private employers. In light of *Runyon* and *McDonald*, discussed above, we have previously characterized *Guerra* as a broad construction of § 1981 in a case with "strong racial overtones." Whatever vitality it may retain, *Guerra* did not propose extending § 1981 to sex discrimination, and thus lends no support to Bobo's contentions.

In the face of seemingly unambiguous statutory language, emphatic contemporaneous statements by legislators and an unbroken tide of case law rejecting Bobo's arguments, we conclude that the district court properly held that sex discrimination is not cognizable under § 1981.

* * *

For the foregoing reasons, the judgment of the district court is affirmed.

Affirmed.

NOTES AND PROBLEMS FOR DISCUSSION

1. The court in *Bobo* noted that § 1981 was held to apply to charges of discrimination based on alienage by the Fifth Circuit in Guerra v. Manchester Terminal Corp. Suppose the plaintiff in *Guerra* had been a U.S. citizen of Mexican ancestry and claimed that he had been discriminated against on the basis of his national origin. Could he state a claim under § 1981? While the courts agree that § 1981 was intended to prohibit discrimination on the basis of race and not national origin, most nevertheless allow national origin claims to proceed under § 1981 where they can be characterized as racial in nature. See e.g. Al-Khazraji v. St. Francis College, 784 F.2d 505 (3d Cir. 1986) (§ 1981 applies to race claim of ethnic Arab as race defined as "a group that is ethnically and physiognomically distinctive."); Bullard v. OMI Georgia, Inc., 640 F.2d 632 (5th Cir. 1981) (Black and white employees discharged and replaced by persons of Korean ancestry can state claim under § 1981 because complaint included allegation of race as well as national origin discrimination); Gonzalez v. Stanford Applied Engineering, Inc., 597 F.2d 1298 (9th Cir. 1979) (Mexican-American alleging discrimination because of his having brown skin can state a claim under § 1981); Manzanares v. Safeway Stores, Inc., 593 F.2d 968, 970 (10th Cir. 1979) (Mexican-American stated a claim of racial discrimination under § 1981 since the group to which he belonged is "of such an identifiable nature that the treatment afforded its members may be measured against that afforded Anglos.") One judge offered the following assessment of the treatment of national origin claims under § 1981:

> "The terms 'race' and 'racial discrimination' may be of such doubtful sociological validity as to be scientifically meaningless, but these terms nonetheless are subject to a commonly-accepted, albeit sometimes vague, understanding. Those courts which have extended the coverage of § 1981 have done so on a realistic basis, within the framework of this common meaning and understanding. On this admittedly unscientific basis, whites are plainly a 'race' susceptible to 'racial discrimination'; Hispanic persons and Indians, like blacks, have been traditional victims of group discrimination, and, however inaccurately or stupidly, are frequently and even com-

monly subject to a 'racial' identification as 'non-whites.' There is accordingly both a practical need and a logical reason to extend § 1981's proscription against exclusively 'racial' employment discrimination to these groups of potential discriminatees."

Budinsky v. Corning Glass Works, 425 F.Supp. 786, 787–788 (W.D.Pa.1977). See also Ortiz v. Bank of America, 547 F.Supp. 550 (E.D.Cal.1982) (§ 1981 protects members of any distinctive group that has been treated differently than and is perceived as distinguishable from white citizens.). But see Anooya v. Hilton Hotels Corp., 733 F.2d 48 (7th Cir. 1984) (§ 1981 complaint dismissal upheld where the plaintiff did not explicitly or implicitly allege facts from which court could equate the evil of race discrimination to the alleged national origin animus experienced on account of his Iraqi descent).

The courts also have ruled that § 1981 does not cover claims of discrimination on the basis of age, Barkley v. Carraux, 533 F.Supp. 242 (S.D.Tex.1982); religion, Khawaja v. Wyatt, 494 F.Supp. 302 (W.D.N.Y.1980); or sexual preference, Grossman v. Bernards Township Board of Education, 11 FEP Cases 1196 (D.N.J.1975), affirmed, 538 F.2d 319 (3d Cir. 1976), cert. denied, 429 U.S. 897, 97 S.Ct. 261, 50 L.Ed.2d 181 (1976). Could a Jewish plaintiff assert a claim of racial discrimination under § 1981? See Shaare Tefila Congregation v. Cobb, 785 F.2d 523 (4th Cir. 1986).

2. Can § 1981 be used to fill in some of the gaps in Title VII's coverage? For example, § 701(b) exempts Indian tribes from the antidiscrimination provisions of Title VII. Can a non-Indian denied employment by an Indian tribe bring a race discrimination action under § 1981? See Wardle v. Ute Indian Tribe, 623 F.2d 670 (10th Cir. 1980). Is a race discrimination claim brought by a uniformed member of the armed services cognizable under § 1981? See Taylor v. Jones, 653 F.2d 1193 (8th Cir. 1981). What about an employee of a private, tax-exempt membership club? Compare Guesby v. Kennedy, 580 F.Supp. 1280 (D.Kans.1984) with Kemerer v. Davis, 520 F.Supp. 256 (E.D.Mich. 1981). Can you think of other situations where § 1981 might apply to a case which is not covered by Title VII? In Valenzuela v. Kraft, Inc., 739 F.2d 434 (9th Cir. 1984), the Ninth Circuit held that Title VII falls within the federal courts' exclusive subject matter jurisdiction. Should this ruling also apply to § 1981 actions? See DeHorney v. Bank of America National Trust & Savings Association, 777 F.2d 440 (9th Cir. 1985).

3. In BROWN v. GENERAL SERVICES ADMINISTRATION, 425 U.S. 820, 96 S.Ct. 1961, 48 L.Ed.2d 402 (1976), the Supreme Court ruled that Title VII is the exclusive judicial remedy available to federal employees complaining of job discrimination. State and local government employees, however, are not limited to the remedies available under Title VII and thus can bring claims of racial or alienage discrimination under § 1981. See e.g., Bridgeport Guardians, Inc. v. Bridgeport Civil Service Commission, 482 F.2d 1333 (2d Cir. 1973), cert. denied 421 U.S. 991, 95 S.Ct. 1997, 44 L.Ed.2d 481 (1975) (municipal police force); Carter v. Gallagher, 452 F.2d 315 (8th Cir. 1972), cert. denied 406 U.S. 950, 92 S.Ct. 2045, 32 L.Ed.2d 338 (municipal civil service commission). The Eleventh Amendment, however, has been held to bar suits for damages in federal courts against states, or state officials where the damage award would be paid out of the state treasury, absent a waiver of sovereign immunity. Does this limit state employees to claims for equitable relief or personal damage claims against state officials in § 1981 cases? Has Congress implicitly overridden the states' constitutional immunity to damage suits by enacting § 1981? In FITZPATRICK v. BITZER, 427 U.S. 445, 96 S.Ct. 2666, 49 L.Ed.2d 614 (1976),

the Supreme Court ruled that Congress could and did abrogate the states' Eleventh Amendment immunity to damage actions through the 1972 amendment to Title VII authorizing private damage actions against states since that statute was enacted for the purpose of enforcing the provisions of the Fourteenth Amendment. On the other hand, in QUERN v. JORDAN, 440 U.S. 332, 99 S.Ct. 1139, 59 L.Ed.2d 358 (1979), the Court reaffirmed its prior ruling in Edelman v. Jordan, 415 U.S. 651, 94 S.Ct. 1347, 39 L.Ed.2d 662 (1974) that the Eleventh Amendment precluded the assertion of a federal court action for damages against a state under 42 U.S.C. § 1983 even where the complaint alleged a violation of the Fourteenth Amendment. Is it significant that Title VII, unlike §§ 1981 and 1983, specifically authorizes the awarding of money damages against a state? But does § 1981 specifically provide a damage remedy for private sector employees? See Rucker v. Higher Educational Aids Board, 669 F.2d 1179 (7th Cir. 1982); Gibson v. State of Wisconsin Department of Health, 489 F.Supp. 1048 (E.D.Wis.1980).

While local and municipal governments do not enjoy Eleventh Amendment immunity from damage actions, a common law immunity from such suits is generally recognized. In enacting § 1981, did Congress intend to override municipal immunity? The Supreme Court has ruled that municipalities do not enjoy a common law immunity from compensatory damage claims in actions brought under § 1983 where the challenged conduct is attributable directly to the municipality. Monell v. Department of Social Services of City of New York, 436 U.S. 658, 98 S.Ct. 2018, 56 L.Ed.2d 611 (1978). The Court, however, has also held that municipalities retain their immunity from punitive damages in § 1983 suits. City of Newport v. Fact Concerts, Inc., 453 U.S. 247, 101 S.Ct. 2748, 69 L.Ed.2d 616 (1981). With respect to § 1981, the courts are split. Compare Sethy v. Alameda County Water District, 545 F.2d 1157 (9th Cir. 1976) (§ 1981 abolishes immunity) and Boyd v. Shawnee Mission Public Schools, 522 F.Supp. 1115 (D.Kan.1981) (§ 1981 abolishes immunity from punitive damages) with Poolaw v. City of Anadarko, 738 F.2d 364 (10th Cir. 1984), cert. denied, ___ U.S. ___, 105 S.Ct. 784, 83 L.Ed.2d 779 (1985) (municipality immune from punitive damages under § 1981) and Heritage Homes of Attleboro, Inc. v. Seekonk Water District, 670 F.2d 1 (1st Cir. 1982) (municipality immune from punitive damages in § 1981 action).

4. Do claims of retaliation fall within the scope of § 1981? Would it matter whether the plaintiff was retaliated against for initially challenging the employer's personnel practices under Title VII or § 1981? See Choudhury v. Polytechnic Institute, 735 F.2d 38 (2d Cir. 1984); Goff v. Continental Oil Co., 678 F.2d 593 (5th Cir. 1982). What if the retaliation was motivated by sex or religious discrimination? While a few courts have held that retaliation is not cognizable under § 1981, most have ruled that retaliation can be challenged under § 1981 if it was motivated by racial discrimination. See e.g., Sisco v. J.S. Alberici Construction Co., Inc., 655 F.2d 146 (8th Cir. 1981), cert. denied, 455 U.S. 976, 102 S.Ct. 1485, 71 L.Ed.2d 688 (1982); London v. Coopers & Lybrand, 644 F.2d 811 (9th Cir. 1981).

5. Can an employee bring a § 1981 action against its union? If so, is a federal employee limited by Brown v. G.S.A. to a Title VII action against its union? See Jennings v. American Postal Workers Union, 672 F.2d 712 (8th Cir. 1982).

Prior to the Supreme Court's ruling in Washington v. Davis, 426 U.S. 229, 96 S.Ct. 2040, 48 L.Ed.2d 597 (requiring plaintiffs alleging violations of the Fourteenth Amendment to prove discriminatory intent in their prima facie case), most federal circuit courts applied Title VII proof standards to cases brought under § 1981 and therefore did not require proof of discriminatory purpose for such claims. The decision in *Washington* caused many circuit courts to reexamine the proof standard for § 1981 claims and led almost all of them to require a showing of intent in the prima facie case. The issue was finally addressed by the Supreme Court in the following case:

GENERAL BUILDING CONTRACTORS ASSOCIATION, INC. v. PENNSYLVANIA

Supreme Court of the United States, 1982.
458 U.S. 375, 102 S.Ct. 3141, 73 L.Ed.2d 835.

JUSTICE REHNQUIST delivered the opinion of the Court.

Respondents, the Commonwealth of Pennsylvania and a class of racial minorities who are skilled or seek work as operating engineers in the construction industry in Eastern Pennsylvania and Delaware, commenced this action under a variety of federal statutes protecting civil rights, including 42 U.S.C. § 1981. The complaint sought to redress racial discrimination in the operation of an exclusive hiring hall established in contracts between Local 542 of the International Union of Operating Engineers and construction industry employers doing business within the Union's jurisdiction. Respondents also alleged discrimination in the operation of an apprenticeship program established by Local 542 and several construction trade associations. Named as defendants were Local 542, the trade associations, the organization charged with administering the trade's apprenticeship program, and a class of approximately 1,400 construction industry employers. Petitioners, the defendant contractors and trade associations, seek review of a judgment granting an injunction against them. The questions we resolve are whether liability under 42 U.S.C. § 1981 requires proof of discriminatory intent and whether, absent such proof, liability can nevertheless be imposed vicariously on the employers and trade associations for the discriminatory conduct of the Union.

I

The hiring hall system that is the focus of this litigation originated in a collective bargaining agreement negotiated in 1961 by Local 542 and four construction trade associations in the Philadelphia area, three of whom are petitioners in this Court. The agreement was concluded only after a ten-week strike prompted by the resistance of the trade associations to the Union's demand for an exclusive hiring hall. Under the terms of the agreement, the Union was to maintain lists of operating engineers, or would-be engineers, classified according to the extent of their recent construction experience. Signatory employers were contractually obligated to hire operating engineers only from among those referred by the Union from its current lists. Workers affiliated with the Union were barred from seeking work with those employers except through Union referrals. Thus, the collective bargaining agreement effectively channeled all employment opportunities through the hiring hall. Since 1961 this requirement has been a constant feature of contracts negotiated with Local 542 by the trade associations, as well as of contracts signed with the Union by employers who were not represented by one of those associations in collective bargaining.

Among the means of gaining access to the Union's referral lists is an apprenticeship program established in 1965 by Local 542 and the trade associations. The program, which involves classroom and field training, is administered by the Joint Apprenticeship and Training Committee (JATC), a body of trustees half of whom are appointed by the Union and half by the trade associations. While enrolled in the program, apprentices are referred by the Union for unskilled construction work. Graduates of the program become journeymen operating engineers and are referred for heavy equipment jobs.

This action was filed in 1971 by the Commonwealth of Pennsylvania and 12 black plaintiffs representing a proposed class of minority group members residing within the jurisdiction of Local 542. The complaint charged that the Union and the JATC had violated numerous state and federal laws prohibiting employment discrimination, including Title VII of the Civil Rights Act of 1964 and 42 U.S.C. § 1981. The complaint alleged that these defendants had engaged in a pattern and practice of racial discrimination, by systematically denying access to the Union's referral lists, and by arbitrarily skewing referrals in favor of white workers, limiting most minority workers who did gain access to the hiring hall to jobs of short hours and low pay. The contractor employers and trade associations were also named as defendants, although the complaint did not allege a Title VII cause of action against them.[4]

The District Court divided the trial into two stages. The first stage, from which petitioners appeal, addressed issues of liability; assessment of damages was deferred to a second stage. For purposes of the first phase of the proceedings, the court certified a plaintiff class of minority operating engineers and would-be engineers, as well as a defendant class consisting of all trade associations and employers who had been parties to labor contracts with Local 542. A single employer, petitioner Glasgow, Inc., was certified to represent the defendant subclass of approximately 1,400 contractor employers.

The District Court's opinion in the liability phase of the trial is lengthy. For our purposes, however, the relevant findings and conclusions can be summarized briefly. First, the court found that the hiring hall system established by collective bargaining was neutral on its face.

4. The complaint did not assert a Title VII cause of action against petitioners because they were not named in the complaint filed by the plaintiffs with the EEOC, a precondition to suit in federal court.

Indeed, after May 1, 1971, the contracts contained a provision expressly prohibiting employment discrimination on the basis of race, religion, color, or national origin. But the court found that Local 542, in administering the system, "practiced a pattern of intentional discrimination and that union practices in the overall operation of a hiring hall for operating engineers created substantial racial disparities." The court made similar findings regarding the JATC's administration of the job training program. On the basis of these findings, the District Court held that Local 542 and the JATC had violated Title VII, both because they intentionally discriminated and because they enforced practices that resulted in a disparate racial impact. The court also interpreted 42 U.S.C. § 1981 to permit imposition of liability "on roughly the same basis as a Title VII claim," and therefore concluded that the Union and the JATC had also violated § 1981.

Turning to petitioners' liability under § 1981, the court found that the plaintiffs had failed to prove "that the associations or contractors viewed simply as a class were actually aware of the union discrimination," and had failed to show "intent to discriminate by the employers as a class." Nevertheless, the court held the employers and the associations liable under § 1981 for the purpose of imposing an injunctive remedy "as a result of their contractual relationship to and use of a hiring hall system which in practice effectuated intentional discrimination, whether or not the employers and associations knew or should have known [of the Union's conduct] ." The court reasoned that liability under § 1981 "requires no proof of purposeful conduct on the part of any of the defendants." Instead, it was sufficient that "(1) the employers delegated an important aspect of their hiring procedure to the union; [and that] (2) the union, in effectuating the delegation, intentionally discriminated or, alternatively, produced a discriminatory impact." "[P]laintiffs have shown that the requisite relationship exists among employers, associations, and union to render applicable the theory of *respondeat superior*, thus making employers and associations liable injunctively for the discriminatory acts of the union."

Following an appeal authorized by 28 U.S.C. § 1292(b), the Court of Appeals for the Third Circuit, sitting en banc, affirmed the judgment of liability against petitioners by an equally divided vote. We granted certiorari and we now reverse.

II

The District Court held that petitioners had violated 42 U.S.C. § 1981 notwithstanding its finding that, as a class, petitioners did not intentionally discriminate against minority workers and neither knew nor had reason to know of the Union's discriminatory practices. The first question we address, therefore, is whether liability may be imposed under § 1981 without proof of intentional discrimination.[8]

8. The District Court concluded, by analogy to Title VII, that a violation of § 1981 could be made out by "proof of disparate impact alone." The court re-

Title 42 U.S.C. § 1981 provides:

> "All persons within the jurisdiction of the United States shall have the same right in every State and Territory to make and enforce contracts, to sue, be parties, give evidence, and to the full and equal benefit of all laws and proceedings for the security of persons and property as is enjoyed by white citizens, and shall be subject to like punishment, pains, penalties, taxes, licenses, and exactions of every kind, and to no other."

We have traced the evolution of this statute and its companion, 42 U.S.C. § 1982, on more than one occasion, and we will not repeat the narrative again except in broad outline.

The operative language of both laws apparently originated in § 1 of the Civil Rights Act of 1866, 14 Stat. 27, enacted by Congress shortly after ratification of the Thirteenth Amendment.[10] "The legislative history of the 1866 Act clearly indicates that Congress intended to protect a limited category of rights, specifically defined in terms of racial equality." Georgia v. Rachel, 384 U.S. 780, 791 (1966). The same Congress also passed the joint resolution that was later adopted as the Fourteenth Amendment. As we explained in Hurd v. Hodge, 334 U.S. 24, 32–33 (1948) (footnotes omitted):

> "Frequent references to the Civil Rights Act are to be found in the record of the legislative debates on the adoption of the Amendment. It is clear that in many significant respects the statute and the Amendment were expressions of the same general congressional

ferred to Griggs v. Duke Power Co., 401 U.S. 424 (1971), in which we held that Title VII forbids the use of employment tests that produce a disproportionate racial impact unless the employer shows "a manifest relationship to the employment in question."

The District Court's holding on this issue is contrary to the holding of every Court of Appeals that has addressed the matter, including that of the Third Circuit in a subsequent case. See Guardians Assn. v. Civil Service Comm'n, 633 F.2d 232, 263–268 (CA2 1980), cert. granted, No. 81–431 (Jan. 11, 1982); Croker v. Boeing Co., 662 F.2d 975, 984–989 (CA3 1981) (en banc); Williams v. DeKalb Cty., 582 F.2d 2 (CA5 1978); Mescall v. Burrus, 603 F.2d 1266, 1269–1271 (CA7 1979); Craig v. County of Los Angeles, 626 F.2d 659, 668 (CA9 1980), cert. denied, 450 U.S. 919 (1981); Chicano Police Officer's Assn. v. Stover, 552 F.2d 918, 920–921 (CA10 1977). Two other circuits have approved a requirement of discriminatory intent in dicta. See Des Vergnes v. Seekonk Water Dist., 601 F.2d 9, 14 (CA1 1979); Detroit Police Officers' Assn. v. Young, 608 F.2d 671, 692 (CA6 1979), cert. denied, 452 U.S. 938 (1981). See also Johnson v. Alexander, 572 F.2d 1219, 1223–1224 (CA8), cert. denied, 439 U.S. 986 (1978); Donnell v. General Motors Corp., 576 F.2d 1292, 1300 (CA8 1978). But see Kinsey v. First Regional Securities, Inc., 557 F.2d 830, 838, n. 22 (CADC 1977).

10. Section 1 of the Act of Apr. 9, 1866, read in part:

> "That all persons born in the United States and not subject to any foreign power, * * * are hereby declared to be citizens of the United States; and such citizens, of every race and color, without regard to any previous condition of slavery or involuntary servitude, * * * shall have the same right, in every State and Territory in the United States, to make and enforce contracts, to sue, be parties, and give evidence, to inherit, purchase, lease, sell, hold, and convey real and personal property, and to full and equal benefit of all laws and proceedings for the security of person and property, as is enjoyed by white citizens, and shall be subject to like punishment, pains, and penalties, and to none other, any law, statute, ordinance, regulation, or custom, to the contrary notwithstanding."

policy. Indeed, as the legislative debates reveal, one of the primary purposes of many members of Congress in supporting the adoption of the Fourteenth Amendment was to incorporate the guaranties of the Civil Rights Act of 1866 in the organic law of the land. Others supported the adoption of the Amendment in order to eliminate doubt as to the constitutional validity of the Civil Rights Act as applied to the States."

Following ratification of the Fourteenth Amendment, Congress passed what has come to be known as the Enforcement Act of 1870, 16 Stat. 140, pursuant to the power conferred by § 5 of the Amendment. Section 16 of that Act contains essentially the language that now appears in § 1981.[11] Indeed, the present codification is derived from § 1977 of the Revised Statutes of 1874, which in turn codified verbatim § 16 of the 1870 Act. Section 16 differed from § 1 of the 1866 Act in at least two respects. First, where § 1 of the 1866 Act extended its guarantees to "citizens, of every race and color," § 16 of the 1870 Act—and § 1981—protects "all persons." Second, the 1870 Act omitted language contained in the 1866 Act, and eventually codified as § 1982, guaranteeing property rights equivalent to those enjoyed by white citizens. Thus, "[a] lthough the 1866 Act rested only on the Thirteenth Amendment * * * and, indeed, was enacted before the Fourteenth Amendment was formally proposed, * * * the 1870 Act was passed pursuant to the Fourteenth, and changes in wording may have reflected the language of the Fourteenth Amendment." Tillman v. Wheaton-Haven Recreation Assn., 410 U.S. 431, 439–440, n. 11 (1973).

In determining whether § 1981 reaches practices that merely result in a disproportionate impact on a particular class, or instead is limited to conduct motivated by a discriminatory purpose, we must be mindful of the "events and passions of the time" in which the law was forged. The Civil War had ended in April 1865. The First Session of the Thirty-ninth Congress met on December 4, 1865, some six months after the preceding Congress had sent to the States the Thirteenth Amendment and just two weeks before the Secretary of State certified the Amendment's ratification. On January 5, 1866, Senator Trumbull introduced the bill that would become the 1866 Act.

The principal object of the legislation was to eradicate the Black Codes, laws enacted by Southern legislatures imposing a range of civil

11. "That all persons within the jurisdiction of the United States shall have the same right in every State and Territory in the United States to make and enforce contracts, to sue, be parties, give evidence, and to the full and equal benefit of all laws and proceedings for the security of person and property as is enjoyed by white citizens, and shall be subject to like punishment, pains, penalties, taxes, licenses, and exactions of every kind, and none other, any law, statute, ordinance, regulation, or custom to the contrary notwithstanding. No tax or charge shall be imposed or enforced by any State upon any person immigrating thereto from a foreign country which is not imposed and enforced upon every person immigrating to such State from any other foreign country; and any law of any State in conflict with this provision is hereby declared null and void." 16 Stat. 144.

Section 18 of the 1870 Act also re-enacted the 1866 Act and declared that § 16 "shall be enforced according to the provisions of said act." 16 Stat. 144.

disabilities on freedmen. Most of these laws embodied express racial classifications and although others, such as those penalizing vagrancy, were facially neutral, Congress plainly perceived all of them as consciously conceived methods of resurrecting the incidents of slavery. Senator Trumbull summarized the paramount aims of his bill:

> "Since the abolition of slavery, the Legislatures which have assembled in the insurrectionary States have passed laws relating to the freedmen, and in nearly all the States they have discriminated against them. They deny them certain rights, subject them to severe penalties, and still impose upon them the very restrictions which were imposed upon them in consequence of the existence of slavery, and before it was abolished. The purpose of the bill under consideration is to destroy all these discriminations, and to carry into effect the [Thirteenth] amendment." Cong. Globe, 39th Cong., 1st Sess. 474 (1866).

Senator Trumbull emphasized: "This bill has nothing to do with the political rights or *status* of parties. It is confined exclusively to their civil rights, such rights as should appertain to every free man."

Of course, this Court has found in the legislative history of the 1866 Act evidence that Congress sought to accomplish more than the destruction of state-imposed civil disabilities and discriminatory punishments. We have held that both § 1981 and § 1982 "prohibit all racial discrimination, whether or not under color of law, with respect to the rights enumerated therein." Jones v. Alfred H. Mayer Co., 392 U.S., at 436. See Johnson v. Railway Express Agency, 421 U.S. 454, 459–460 (1975); Runyon v. McCrary, 427 U.S., at 168. Nevertheless, the fact that the prohibitions of § 1981 encompass private as well as governmental action does not suggest that the statute reaches more than purposeful discrimination, whether public or private. Indeed, the relevant opinions are hostile to such an implication. Thus, although we held in *Jones*, supra, that § 1982 reaches private action, we explained that § 1 of the 1866 Act "was meant to prohibit all *racially motivated* deprivations of the rights enumerated in the statute." Similarly, in Runyon v. McCrary, supra, we stated that § 1981 would be violated "if a private offeror refuses to extend to a Negro, *solely because he is a Negro*, the same opportunity to enter into contracts as he extends to white offerees."

The immediate evils with which the Thirty-ninth Congress was concerned simply did not include practices that were "neutral on their face, and even neutral in terms of intent," Griggs v. Duke Power Co., 401 U.S. 424, 430 (1971), but that had the incidental effect of disadvantaging blacks to a greater degree than whites. Congress instead acted to protect the freedmen from intentional discrimination by those whose object was "to make their former slaves dependent serfs, victims of unjust laws, and debarred from all progress and elevation by organized social prejudices." Cong. Globe, 39th Cong., 1st Sess. 1839 (1866) (Rep. Clarke). The supporters of the bill repeatedly emphasized that the legislation was designed to eradicate blatant deprivations of civil rights, clearly fashioned with the purpose of oppressing the former slaves. To infer that Congress sought to accomplish more than this would require stronger evidence in the legislative record than we have been able to discern.[15]

Our conclusion that § 1981 reaches only purposeful discrimination is supported by one final observation about its legislative history. As noted earlier, the origins of the law can be traced to both the Civil Rights Act of 1866 and the Enforcement Act of 1870. Both of these laws, in turn, were legislative cousins of the Fourteenth Amendment. The 1866 Act represented Congress' first attempt to ensure equal rights for the freedmen following the formal abolition of slavery effected by the Thirteenth Amendment. As such, it constituted an initial blueprint of the Fourteenth Amendment, which Congress proposed in part as a means of "incorporat[ing] the guaranties of the Civil Rights Act of 1866 in the organic law of the land." The 1870 Act, which contained the language that now appears in § 1981, was enacted as a means of enforcing the recently ratified Fourteenth Amendment. In light of the close connection between these Acts and the Amendment, it would be incongruous to construe the principal object of their successor, § 1981, in a manner markedly different from that of the Amendment itself.[17]

15. We attach significance to the fact that throughout much of the congressional debates, S.B. 61, which became the 1866 Act, contained an opening declaration that "there shall be no discrimination in civil rights or immunities among citizens of the United States in any State or Territory of the United States *on account of race, color, or previous condition of slavery.*" This passage had occasioned controversy in both the Senate and the House because of the breadth of the phrase "civil rights and immunities." After the Senate had passed the bill and as debates in the House were drawing to a close, the bill's floor manager, Rep. Wilson, introduced an amendment proposed by the House Judiciary Committee, of which he was also the chairman. That amendment deleted the language quoted above and left the bill as it would read when ultimately enacted. Rep. Wilson explained that the broad language of the original bill could have been interpreted to encompass the right of suffrage and other political rights. "To obviate that difficulty and the difficulty growing out of any other construction beyond the specific rights named in the section, our amendment strikes out all of those general terms and leaves the bill with the rights specified in the section." Cong. Globe 39th Cong. 1st Sess., 1367. The deleted language, emphasized above, strongly suggests that Congress was primarily concerned with intentional discrimination. That the passage was removed in an effort to *narrow* the scope of the legislation sharply undercuts the view that the 1866 Act reflects broader concerns.

17. It is true that § 1981, because it is derived in part from the 1866 Act, has roots in the Thirteenth as well as the Fourteenth Amendment. Indeed, we relied on that heritage in holding that Congress could constitutionally enact § 1982, which is also traceable to the 1866 Act, without limiting its reach to "state action." See Jones v. Alfred H. Mayer Co., 392 U.S., at 438. As we have already intimated, however, the fact that Congress acted in the shadow of the Thirteenth Amendment does not demonstrate that Congress sought to eradicate more than purposeful discrimination when it passed the 1866 Act. For example, Congress also enacted 42 U.S.C. § 1985(3) in part to implement the commands of the Thirteenth Amendment. See Griffin v. Breckenridge, 403 U.S. 88, 104–105 (1971). While holding that § 1985(3) does not require state action but also reaches private conspiracies, we have emphasized that a violation of the statute requires "some racial, or perhaps otherwise class-based, invidiously discriminatory animus behind the conspirators' action." We need not decide whether the Thirteenth Amendment itself reaches practices

With respect to the latter, "official action will not be held unconstitutional solely because it results in a racially disproportionate impact," Arlington Heights v. Metropolitan Housing Dev. Corp., 429 U.S. 252, 264–265 (1977). "[E]ven if a neutral law has a disproportionately adverse impact upon a racial minority, it is unconstitutional under the Equal Protection Clause only if that impact can be traced to a discriminatory purpose." Personnel Administrator of Mass. v. Feeney, 442 U.S. 256, 272 (1979). See Washington v. Davis, 426 U.S. 229 (1976). The same Congress that proposed the Fourteenth Amendment also passed the Civil Rights Act of 1866, and the ratification of that amendment paved the way for the Enforcement Act of 1870. These measures were all products of the same milieu and were directed against the same evils. Although Congress might have charted a different course in enacting the predecessors to § 1981 than it did in proposing the Fourteenth Amendment, we have found no convincing evidence that it did so.

We conclude, therefore, that § 1981, like the Equal Protection Clause, can be violated only by purposeful discrimination.

III

The District Court held petitioners liable under § 1981 notwithstanding its finding that the plaintiffs had failed to prove intent to discriminate on the part of the employers and associations as a class. In light of our holding that § 1981 can be violated only by intentional discrimination, the District Court's judgment can stand only if liability under § 1981 can properly rest on some ground other than the discriminatory motivation of the petitioners themselves. Both the District Court and respondents have relied on such grounds, but we find them unconvincing.

A

The District Court reasoned that liability could be vicariously imposed upon the employers and associations, based upon the intentional discrimination practiced by Local 542 in its operation of the hiring hall. The court's theory was that petitioners had delegated to the "union hiring hall" the authority to select workers as "the agent for two principals—the union and the contractors, with their respective associations." Since the hiring hall came into existence only through the agreement of petitioners, and since the exclusive hiring hall was the means by which "the intentional discrimination of the union was able to work its way broadly into the common workforce of operating engineers," the court concluded that "[t]he acts of the union therefore

with a disproportionate effect as well as those motivated by discriminatory purpose, or indeed whether it accomplished anything more than the abolition of slavery. We conclude only that the existence of that Amendment, and the fact that it authorized Congress to enact legislation abolishing the "badges and incidents of slavery," *Civil Rights Cases*, 109 U.S. 3, 20 (1883), do not evidence congressional intent to reach disparate effects in enacting § 1981.

justify imposition of responsibility upon those employers participating in the original delegation." The effect of this holding, as the court recognized, was to impose a "duty to see that discrimination does not take place in the selection of one's workforce," regardless of where the discrimination originates.

As applied to the petitioner associations, the District Court's theory is flawed on its own terms. The doctrine of *respondeat superior*, as traditionally conceived and as understood by the District Court, enables the imposition of liability on a principal for the tortious acts of his agent and, in the more common case, on the master for the wrongful acts of his servant. "Agency is the fiduciary relation which results from the manifestation of consent by one person to another that the other shall act on his behalf and subject to his control, and consent by the other so to act." Restatement (Second) of Agency § 1 (1958). A master-servant relationship is a form of agency in which the master employs the servant as "an agent to perform service in his affairs" and "controls or has the right to control the physical conduct of the other in the performance of the service." Id., § 2. See 2 F. Harper & F. James, The Law of Torts § 26.6 (1956). Local 542, in its operation of the hiring hall, simply performed no function as the agent or servant of the associations. The record demonstrates that the associations themselves do not hire operating engineers, and never have. Their primary purpose is to represent certain employers in contract negotiations with the Union. Even if the doctrine of *respondeat superior* were broadly applicable to suits based on § 1981, therefore, it would not support the imposition of liability on a defendant based on the acts of a party with whom it had no agency or employment relationship.[18]

We have similar difficulty in accepting the application of traditional *respondeat superior* doctrine to the class of contract or employers. In the run of cases, the relationship between an employer and the union that represents its employees simply cannot be accurately characterized as one between principal and agent or master and servant. Indeed, such a conception is alien to the fundamental assumptions upon which the federal labor laws are structured.

At the core of agency is a "fiduciary relation" arising from the "consent by one person to another that the other shall act on his behalf and subject to his control." Restatement (Second) of Agency § 1. Equally central to the master-servant relation is the master's control over or right to control the physical activities of the servant. The District Court found that the requirement of control was satisfied

18. In this case, the associations were held liable because they negotiated an agreement, fair on its face, which was later implemented by another party in a manner that was not only discriminatory but in violation of the agreement itself *and* in a manner of which the associations were neither aware nor had reason to be aware. Since the associations' only role was as agent for employers whose hiring would actually be governed by the agreement, the District Court's theory presumably would also permit the imposition of liability on the attorneys who actually conducted the contract negotiations. We are unaware of any authority supporting such an extended application of *respondeat superior*.

because "the employers retained power to oppose the union discrimination." However, the "power to oppose" the Union, even when the opposition is grounded in the terms of the collective bargaining agreement, is not tantamount to a "right to control" the Union.[19] Indeed, a rule equating the two would convert every contractual relationship into an agency relationship, a result clearly unsupported by the common-law doctrines on which the District Court relied.

The District Court's assumptions about the relation between the Union and the class of employers with whom it has contracted also runs counter to the premises on which the federal labor laws have been constructed. While authorizing collective bargaining and providing means of enforcing the resultant contracts, the National Labor Relations Act expressly prohibits employers from compromising the independence of labor unions. The entire process of collective bargaining is structured and regulated on the assumption that "[t]he parties—even granting the modification of views that may come from a realization of economic interdependence—still proceed from contrary and to an extent antagonistic viewpoints and concepts of self-interest." NLRB v. Insurance Agents, 361 U.S. 477, 488 (1960). We have no reason to doubt the validity of that assumption in the instant case.

Respondents also suggest that petitioners can be held vicariously liable for the discriminatory conduct of the JATC. They argue that the JATC is properly viewed as an agent of both Local 542 and the associations, emphasizing that half of the trustees charged with administering the JATC are appointed by the associations and that the JATC is wholly funded by mandatory contributions from the employers. We note initially that the District Court premised petitioners' liability not on the actions of the JATC, but on the discriminatory conduct of the Union. The record, therefore, contains no findings regarding the relationship between the JATC and petitioners, beyond those noted above, that might support application of *respondeat superior*.

The facts emphasized by respondents, standing alone, are inadequate. That the employers fund the activities of the JATC does not render the JATC the employers' servant or agent any more than an independent contractor is rendered an agent simply because he is compensated by the principal for his services. The employers must also enjoy a right to control the activities of the JATC, and there is no record basis for believing that to be the case. Neither is a right of control inferable merely from the power of the associations to appoint half of the JATC's trustees. It is entirely possible that the trustees, once appointed, owe a fiduciary duty to the JATC and the apprentices enrolled in its programs, rather than to the entities that appointed

19. According to respondents, the District Court's conclusion that petitioners retained the power to control the hiring hall was a finding of fact that cannot be set aside unless clearly erroneous. We disagree. The District Court found that petitioners had the "power to oppose" the Union, a conclusion we do not question. Whether the power to oppose the Union is equivalent to a right of control sufficient to invoke the doctrine of *respondeat superior* is, however, a legal question to which we must devote our independent judgment.

them. On the assumption that *respondeat superior* applies to suits based on § 1981, there is no basis for holding either the employers or the associations liable under that doctrine without evidence that an agency relationship existed at the time the JATC committed the acts on which its own liability was premised.

B

The District Court also justified its result by concluding that § 1981 imposes a "nondelegable duty" on petitioners "to see that discrimination does not take place in the selection of [their] workforce." The concept of a nondelegable duty imposes upon the principal not merely an obligation to exercise care in his own activities, but to answer for the well being of those persons to whom the duty runs. See Restatement (Second) of Agency § 214. The duty is not discharged by using care in delegating it to an independent contractor. Consequently, the doctrine creates an exception to the common-law rule that a principal normally will not be liable for the tortious conduct of an independent contractor. So understood, a nondelegable duty is an affirmative obligation to ensure the protection of the person to whom the duty runs.

In a sense, to characterize such a duty as "nondelegable" is merely to restate the duty. Thus, in this litigation the question is not whether the employers and associations are free to delegate their duty to abide by § 1981, for whatever duty the statute imposes, they are bound to adhere to it. The question is *what* duty does § 1981 impose. More precisely, does § 1981 impose a duty to refrain from intentionally denying blacks the right to contract on the same basis as whites or does it impose an affirmative obligation to ensure that blacks enjoy such a right? The language of the statute does not speak in terms of duties. It merely declares specific rights held by "[a]ll persons within the jurisdiction of the United States." We are confident that the Thirty-ninth Congress meant to do no more than prohibit the employers and associations in these cases from intentionally depriving black workers of the rights enumerated in the statute, including the equal right to contract. It did not intend to make them the guarantors of the workers' rights as against third parties who would infringe them.

Our earlier holding that § 1981 reaches only intentional discrimination virtually compels this conclusion. It would be anomalous to hold that § 1981 could be violated only by intentional discrimination and then to find this requirement satisfied by proof that the individual plaintiffs did not enjoy "the same right * * * to make and enforce contracts * * * as is enjoyed by white citizens" and that the defendants merely failed to ensure that the plaintiffs enjoyed employment opportunities equivalent to that of whites. Such a result would be particularly inappropriate in the case of the associations, who are not engaged in the construction business, do not employ operating engineers, and consequently did not delegate to the Union any hiring functions which they otherwise would have performed themselves.

Neither the District Court nor respondents identify anything in the language or legislative history of the statute to support a contrary conclusion.[21]

* * *

The judgment of the Court of Appeals is reversed and the case is remanded for proceedings consistent with this opinion.

It is so ordered.

JUSTICE O'CONNOR, with whom JUSTICE BLACKMUN joins, concurring.

* * *

I would briefly note the limits of the Court's holding. Once this case has been remanded to the District Court, nothing in the Court's opinion prevents the respondents from litigating the question of the employers' liability under § 1981 by attempting to prove the traditional elements of *respondeat superior.*

* * *

JUSTICE STEVENS, concurring in part and concurring in the judgment.

As I noted in my separate opinion in Runyon v. McCrary, 427 U.S. 160, 189, the Congress that enacted § 1 of the Civil Rights Act of 1866 "intended only to guarantee all citizens the same legal capacity to make and enforce contracts, to obtain, own, and convey property, and to litigate and give evidence." Any violation of that guarantee—whether deliberate, negligent, or purely accidental—would, in my opinion, violate 42 U.S.C. § 1981. The statute itself contains no requirement that an intent to discriminate must be proved.

The Court has broadened the coverage of § 1981 far beyond the scope actually intended by its authors; in essence, the Court has converted a statutory guarantee of equal rights into a grant of equal opportunities. Whether or not those decisions faithfully reflect the intent of Congress, the enlarged coverage of the statute "is now an important part of the fabric of our law." *Runyon,* supra, at 190 (STEVENS, J., concurring).

Since I do not believe Congress intended § 1981 to have any application at all in the area of employment discrimination generally covered by Title VII of the Civil Rights Act of 1964, an analysis of the motives and intent of the Reconstruction Congress cannot be expected to tell us

21. Respondents also contend that petitioners can be held liable on the theory that the hiring hall was a "joint enterprise" involving petitioners as well as the Union. They point to language in the District Court's opinion holding that "the union hiring hall was the agent for two principals—the union and the contractors with their respective associations." Even this theory, however, requires, among other things, the existence of a mutual right of control as between the members of the enterprise. See Restatement (Second) of Torts § 491. For reasons we have already stated, there is no record basis for finding that petitioners had a right to control Local 542 in its administration of the hiring hall. We also doubt the validity of the assumption that the hiring hall is a separate entity, except perhaps as a physical structure. The District Court did not find, and respondents do not assert, that the hiring hall has a separate juridical existence.

whether proof of intentional discrimination should be required in the judicially-created portion of the statute's coverage. Since Congress required no such proof in the statute it actually enacted, a logician would be comfortable in concluding that no such proof should ever be required. Nevertheless, since that requirement tends to define the entire coverage of § 1981 in a way that better reflects the basic intent of Congress than would a contrary holding, I concur in the conclusion reached by the Court in Part II of its opinion insofar as it relates to the statutory protection of equal opportunity but, perhaps illogically, would reach a different conclusion in a case challenging a denial of a citizen's civil rights.

Accordingly, I join the Court's judgment and Parts III and IV of its opinion.

JUSTICE MARSHALL, with whom JUSTICE BRENNAN joins, dissenting.

Today the Court reaches out and decides that 42 U.S.C. § 1981 requires proof of an intent to discriminate—an issue that is not at all necessary to the disposition of this case. Because I find no support for the majority's resolution of this issue, and because I disagree with its disposition of this case even if proof of intent should ordinarily be required, I respectfully dissent.

I

The question whether intent generally should be required in § 1981 actions is at most tangentially related to this case. There was unquestionably intentional discrimination on the part of both the union (Local 542) and the Joint Apprenticeship and Training Committee (JATC), a body, composed of officials from the union and the petitioner contracting associations, which jointly administered the apprenticeship and training program. As a result, the only question that the Court need address today is whether limited injunctive liability may be vicariously imposed upon an employer when the person or entity to whom it delegates a large portion of its hiring decisions intentionally discriminates on the basis of race. However, because the majority has chosen to reach first the more general question whether proof of intent is a prerequisite to recovery in a § 1981 action, I likewise will address this issue first.

* * * The plain language does not contain or suggest an intent requirement. A violation of § 1981 is not expressly conditioned on the motivation or intent of any person. The language focuses on the effects of discrimination on the protected class, and not on the intent of the person engaging in discriminatory conduct. Nothing in the statutory language implies that a right denied because of sheer insensitivity, or a pattern of conduct that disproportionately burdens the protected class of persons, is entitled to any less protection than one denied because of racial animus.

The Court attaches no significance to the broad and unqualified language of § 1981. Furthermore, the majority finds no support for its conclusion that intent should be required in the legislative history to § 1 of the 1866 Act, the precursor to § 1981. Instead, in the face of this unqualified language and the broad remedial purpose § 1981 was intended to serve, the majority assumes that Congress intended to restrict the scope of the statute to those situations in which racial animus can be proved on the ground that the legislative history contains no "convincing evidence" to the contrary. In my view, this approach to statutory construction is not only unsound, it is also contrary to our prior decisions, which have consistently given § 1981 as broad an interpretation as its language permits.

The fallacy in the Court's approach is that, in construing § 1981 and its legislative history, the Court virtually ignores Congress' broad remedial purposes and our paramount national policy of eradicating racial discrimination and its pernicious effects. When viewed in this light, it is clear that proof of intentional discrimination should not be required in order to find a violation of § 1981.

Although the Thirty-ninth Congress that passed the Civil Rights Act of 1866 did not specifically address the question whether intent should be required, the conclusion is inescapable that the congressional leadership intended to effectuate "the *result* of a change from a centuries old social system based on involuntary labor, with all the notions of racial unsuitability for the performance of anything but menial labor under close supervision, to the free labor system." Croker v. Boeing Co., 662 F.2d 975, 1006 (CA3 1981) (Gibbons, J., with whom Higginbotham and Sloviter, JJ., joined, dissenting in part) (emphasis in original). When this Congress convened, the Thirteenth Amendment had been ratified, abolishing slavery as a legal status. However, it was clear that in reality, Negroes were hardly accorded the employment and other opportunities accorded white persons generally. Thus, this Congress undertook to provide *in fact* the rights and privileges that were available to Negroes in theory. Four separate but related measures were proposed in an effort to accomplish this purpose.[1]

In this general climate, the 1866 Civil Rights Act was not an isolated technical statute dealing with only a narrow subject. Instead, it was an integral part of a broad congressional scheme intended to work a major revolution in the prevailing social order.[2] It is inconceivable that the

1. These measures included the Civil Rights Act of 1866 passed over President Johnson's veto; the Freedman's Bureau bill, which would have created a federal agency to ensure that a free labor system in which Negroes had equal participation would *in fact* be accomplished, and which commanded a clear majority in Congress, but failed to pass over a presidential veto; a constitutional amendment sponsored by Representative Bingham but not recommended; and the Fourteenth Amendment.

2. As the majority recognizes, one of the principal changes Congress hoped to achieve was the elimination of the infamous Black Codes. These included state laws regulating the terms and conditions of employment. In many States, these oppressive laws were facially neutral, literally applying to all laborers without regard to race. The laws prohibited such conduct as refusing to perform work and disobeying an employer, or inducing an employee away from his employer, and many provid-

Congress which enacted this statute would permit this purpose to be thwarted by excluding from the statute private action that concededly creates serious obstacles to the pursuit of job opportunities by Negroes solely because the aggrieved persons could not prove that the actors deliberately intended such a result. Even less conceivable is the notion, embraced by the Court's opinion today, that this Congress intended to absolve employers from even injunctive liability imposed as a result of intentional discrimination practiced by the persons to whom they had delegated their authority to hire employees.

The legislative history demonstrates that the Thirty-ninth Congress intended not merely to provide a remedy for preexisting rights, but to eradicate the "badges of slavery" that remained after the Civil War and the enactment of the Thirteenth Amendment. Congress was acutely aware of the difficulties that federal officials had encountered in effectuating the change from the system of slavery to a system of free labor even though the legal and constitutional groundwork for this change had already been laid. * * *

* * * [T]he leaders of Congress set about to enact legislation that would ensure to Negroes the opportunity to participate equally in the free labor system by providing an instrument by which they could strike down barriers to their participation, whether those barriers were erected with the conscious intent to exclude or with callous indifference to exclusionary effects. Congress knew that this attitude could manifest itself in a number of different ways and intended to protect Negro workers against not only flagrant, intentional discrimination, but also against more subtle forms of discrimination which might successfully camouflage the intent to oppress through facially neutral policies. * * *

Unfortunately, this awareness seems utterly lacking in the Court's opinion today. In order to hold that § 1981 requires a showing of intent, the majority must assume that the rights guaranteed under § 1981—to make and enforce contracts on the same basis as white persons—can be adequately protected by limiting the statute to cases where the aggrieved person can prove intentional discrimination. In taking this extraordinarily naive view, the Court shuts its eyes to reality, ignoring the manner in which racial discrimination most often infects our society. Today, although flagrant examples of intentional discrimination still exist, discrimination more often occurs "on a more sophisticated and subtle level," the effects of which are often as cruel and "devastating as the most crude form of discrimination." Pennsylvania v. Local 542, Int'l Union of Operating Engineers, 469 F.Supp. 329, 337 (ED Pa.1978) (Higginbotham, Circuit J., sitting by designation).

ed for forfeiture of wages if the employee did not fulfill the terms of his employment contract. Other Codes included vagrancy laws, which were vague and broad enough to encompass virtually all Negro adults, and many were facially neutral, applying to white persons as well as to Negroes. The Black Codes were constantly discussed during the debates over the Civil Rights Act of 1866, and Congress clearly intended that the Act would eliminate even those Codes which were facially neutral.

I think that Judge Higginbotham most accurately recognized this problem when he noted that "[t]he facts of the instant case * * * demonstrate the complexity and subtlety of the interrelationship of race, collective bargaining, craft unions, the employment process and that ultimate goal—real jobs." He further noted that "[a]t the critical level of viable jobs and equal opportunities, there were intentional and persistent efforts to exclude and discourage most of the minorities who, but for their race, would have been considered for entry into the union and for the more lucrative jobs."

* * * The purposes behind § 1981, and the profound national policy of blotting out all vestiges of racial discrimination, are no less frustrated when equal opportunities are denied through cleverly masked or merely insensitive practices, where proof of actual intent is nearly impossible to obtain, than when instances of intentional discrimination escape unremedied. For this reason, I cannot accept the Court's glib and unrealistic view that requiring proof of intent in § 1981 actions does not frustrate that statute's purpose of protecting against the devastating effects of racial discrimination in employment.

II

Even if I agreed with the Court that intent must be proved in a § 1981 action, I could not agree with its conclusion that the petitioner contracting associations should be immunized, even from injunctive liability, for the intentional discrimination practiced by the union hall to which they delegated a major portion of their hiring decisions. Under § 1981, minorities have an unqualified right to enter into employment contracts on the same basis as white persons. It is undisputed that in this case, the respondent class was denied this right through intentional discrimination. The fact that the associations chose to delegate a large part of the hiring process to the local union hiring hall, which then engaged in intentional discrimination, does not alter the fact that respondents were denied the right to enter into employment contracts with the associations on the same basis as white persons.

At the very least, § 1981 imposes on employers the obligation to make employment decisions free from racial considerations. The hiring decisions made by the contracting associations in this case were fraught with racial discrimination. Solely because of their race, hundreds of minority operating engineers were totally excluded from the industry and could not enter into employment contracts with any employer. Those minorities allowed into the industry suffered discrimination in referrals, and thus they too were denied the same right as white persons to contract with the contracting associations. Not one of the petitioner contracting associations has ever claimed, nor could they, that minorities had the same right as white operating engineers to contract for employment.

Instead, the contracting associations attempt to hide behind the veil of ignorance, shifting their responsibility under § 1981 to the very entity which they chose to assist them in making hiring decisions. The suggestion that an employer's responsibility under § 1981 depends upon its own choice of a hiring agent finds no support in the statute, nor does any other source of law authorize the circumvention of § 1981 that the contracting associations seek here. Their obligation to make employment contracts free from racial discrimination is a nondelegable one—it does not disappear when, as is often the case, the actual employer designates a particular agent to assist in the hiring process. In my view, the fact that the discriminating entity here is a union hiring hall, and not a person or corporation which has a traditional agent-principal relationship with the employer, does not alter this analysis.

The majority does not really analyze the question whether petitioners should be held injunctively liable because § 1981 imposes upon them a nondelegable duty. Instead the majority argues that, because it has held that § 1981 is intended only to reach intentional discrimination, the statute cannot make employers "guarantors of the workers' rights as against third parties who would infringe them." This argument does not withstand analysis. The majority does not assert that employers may escape liability under § 1981 by delegating their hiring decisions to a third party agent. Indeed, in light of the importance attached to the rights § 1981 is intended to safeguard, the duty to abide by this statute must be nondelegable, as the majority apparently recognizes. Instead, the majority argues that because § 1981 imposes only the duty to refrain from intentional discrimination in hiring, it somehow automatically follows that this duty could not have been violated in this case. However, it was precisely this duty that was violated here. The District Court found, and this Court does not disagree, that the entity to whom the petitioner associations effectively delegated their hiring decisions *intentionally discriminated* against the respondent class on the basis of race in making these decisions. Even under the Court's own narrow view of the scope of the duty imposed by § 1981, then, the duty was unquestionably violated in this case.

The majority obfuscates the issue by suggesting that the District Court imposed upon the contracting associations an obligation to seek out and eliminate discrimination by unrelated third parties wherever it may occur. In reality, the District Court did nothing more than impose limited injunctive liability upon the associations for violating their nondelegable duty under § 1981 when the union hiring hall, which effectively made hiring decisions for the associations, engaged in intentional discrimination on the basis of race in making these decisions.

By immunizing the employer from the injunctive relief necessary to remedy the intentional discrimination practiced by those through whom the employer makes its hiring decisions, the Court removes the person most necessary to accord full relief—the entity with whom the aggrieved persons will ultimately make a contract. I believe that the District Court appropriately rejected the petitioners' argument when it explained: "With intensity some employers urge that they agreed to the exclusive hiring hall system solely as a matter of economic survival at the end of a destructive ten week strike when the union would not compromise for any other hiring alternative. Yet economic pressures, however strong and harmful they might be, do not create immunity for employers, at least not in [the injunctive] liability phase."

Section 1981 provides Negroes "the same right" to make contracts as white persons enjoy. In the present case, this unqualified right was violated, and the violation is made no more palatable because the persons who actually made the hiring decisions and referrals, and not the employer itself, engaged in intentional discrimination.[5] The devastating violation of their rights under § 1981 remains the same and will go at least partially unremedied when the person with whom the ultimate employment contract must be made is immunized from even injunctive relief. I cannot impute to the Congress which enacted § 1981 the intention to reach such an inequitable and nonsensical result. Accordingly, I must dissent.

NOTES AND PROBLEMS FOR DISCUSSION

1. What impact is the decision in *General Building Contractors Association* likely to have on the future viability of § 1981 as a remedy for employment discrimination? For a contrary interpretation of § 1981, see Friedman, The Burger Court and the Prima Facie Case in Employment Discrimination Litigation: A Critique, 65 Corn.L.Rev. 1, 31–43 (1979).

2. In JOHNSON v. RYDER TRUCK LINES, INC., 575 F.2d 471 (4th Cir. 1978), cert. denied, 440 U.S. 979, 99 S.Ct. 1785, 60 L.Ed.2d 239 (1979), the Fourth Circuit ruled that the bona fide seniority system exemption provided by § 703(h) of Title VII should be read into § 1981 to promote uniformity of result under the two statutes. This interpretation of § 1981 subsequently was adopted by several other circuit courts. See Freeman v. Motor Convoy, Inc., 700 F.2d 1339 (11th Cir. 1983); Boilermakers, Wattleton v. International Broth. of Boiler Makers, 686 F.2d 586 (7th Cir. 1982), cert. denied, 459 U.S. 1208, 103 S.Ct. 1199, 75 L.Ed.2d 442 (1983); Terrell v. United States Pipe and Foundry Co., 644 F.2d 1112 (5th Cir. 1981). But see Bolden v. Pennsylvania State Police, 578 F.2d 912 (3d Cir. 1978) (§ 703(h) does not apply to § 1981 claims). What effect should the decision in *General Building Contractors Association* have on this issue?

3. One continuing advantage of § 1981 suits is the absence of any exhaustion of administrative remedies requirement. Plaintiffs in § 1981 actions can seek immediate judicial relief, unlike Title VII plaintiffs who must first pass through the complex administrative mechanism detailed in that statute. The procedural requirements attendant to bringing suit under § 1981, however, had to be outlined by the courts since the statute is silent on this subject. In

5. I agree with the JUSTICE O'CONNOR'S observation that nothing in the Court's opinion prevents the District Court on remand from holding the petitioner associations liable for discrimination practiced by the JATC. Specifically, they may be held liable because the trustees administering the JATC are appointed by the petitioner associations, the JATC is funded by employer contributions, and the associations exercise control over the JATC's actions. * * *

JOHNSON v. RAILWAY EXPRESS AGENCY, INC., 421 U.S. 454, 95 S.Ct. 1716, 44 L.Ed.2d 295 (1975) the Supreme Court, noting that Congress intended for Title VII and § 1981 to be separate and independent, rather than mutually exclusive remedies for employment discrimination, ruled that the prosecution of a Title VII suit did not toll the limitations period applicable to an action based on the same facts brought under § 1981. The Court recognized that its ruling on the tolling issue would likely encourage a plaintiff interested in retaining its § 1981 claim to file a separate action under that statute pending EEOC action on the related Title VII claim, a result inconsistent with Congress' expressed desire to encourage administrative resolution of discrimination claims. It suggested, however, with some misgivings, that this undesirable consequence could be moderated if the plaintiff requested the court in the § 1981 action to stay that proceeding until the Title VII administrative efforts had been completed. Moreover, the court concluded, the potential for discouraging reliance on the Title VII administrative machinery was overwhelmed by Congress' clear intent to retain § 1981 as an independent remedy for civil rights claimants.

The independent nature of these two remedies has been underscored by rulings that state administrative proceedings undertaken in connection with a Title VII claim do not operate as res judicata on the related § 1981 federal court action. See Kern v. Research Libraries, 27 FEP Cases 1007 (S.D.N.Y. 1979). However, where a state administrative agency's decision has been reviewed by a state court, the principles of res judicata and collateral estoppel have been applied to preclude relitigation of the same issues in a § 1981 suit. See Mitchell v. National Broadcasting Co., 553 F.2d 265 (2d Cir. 1977) (§ 1981 case dismissed as result of state court's action upholding state agency dismissal of complaint brought under state antidiscrimination law since issue of race discrimination identical in both actions). Is this analysis consistent with the Supreme Court's resolution of the same question in the Title VII context in *Kremer*? A ruling on the merits of a § 1981 claim has been held to preclude the assertion of an identical Title VII cause of action under the doctrine of collateral estoppel. See Lartius v. Iowa Dep't of Trans., 705 F.2d 1018 (8th Cir. 1983).

The Court in Johnson v. Railway Express also declared that in the absence of a limitations period built into § 1981 or any other relevant federal statute, the controlling period would ordinarily be the most appropriate one provided by state law. How does a trial judge decide whether a state limitations statute applicable to tort, contract, federal statutory or civil rights claims is the most analogous one in any particular situation? Moreover, since different states often prescribe different limitations periods for the same type of claim, won't reliance on state limitations law create the opportunity for forum-shopping? Could forum-shopping be reduced by requiring that all § 1981 actions be governed by the limitations statute of the state where the alleged discrimination occurred? In BURNETT v. GRATTAN, 468 U.S. 42, 104 S.Ct. 2924, 82 L.Ed.2d 36 (1984), the Supreme Court addressed the factors to be considered in choosing the "most appropriate" state limitations statute. The plaintiffs, student recruiters at a predominantly black college, were notified that their contracts would not be renewed. In response, they filed charges of racial discrimination with the EEOC. While these charges were pending, the plaintiffs, who were white, filed suit in state court asserting claims of sex and race discrimination under, inter alia, §§ 1981, 1983 and 1985. The defendants removed the case to federal court and then filed a motion to dismiss on the ground that the claims were barred by the applicable statute of limitations. The trial court borrowed the limitations period of a state employment discrimination statute which had been modeled after Title VII and which required claimants to file complaints with a state administrative body within six months of the alleged occurrence of discrimination. Since the state suit had not been filed within this six month period, the federal trial court granted the motion and dismissed the complaint. The Fourth Circuit reversed, finding that a state law governing the limitation of purely informal and conciliatory administrative proceedings was inappropriate for suits brought under the Federal Civil Rights Acts. Instead, it applied a three year general limitations statute applicable to all civil actions for which an express limitations period had not been furnished. Since the state suit was brought about eight months after the cause of action arose, the court held that the suit was timely filed and remanded to the trial court. The question before the Supreme Court, then, was whether a state limitations statute applicable to state administrative proceedings was applicable to claims brought under federal civil rights laws. (The Court noted that it had not been asked to decide whether the statute of limitations inquiry would vary depending upon the particular federal civil rights statute under which a claim was asserted.) It affirmed the ruling of the circuit court, agreeing with that court that the trial judge had erred in applying the administrative limitations statute. The Court set forth a two part standard for determining the "most appropriate" state limitations period. First, it declared, the state law must take into account and be responsive to the particular characteristics of litigation under the federal civil rights claims. In this regard, the Court noted, the dominant characteristic of the federal statutes was that they are judicially enforced without prior resort to administrative relief. And, it added, a claimant must prepare for this litigation in a much more thorough manner than someone who seeks to invoke an administrative remedy. Thus, while the limitations period provided by the state administrative statute reflected the relative lack of preparation needed for an administrative complainant, it was not sufficient for the federal claimant who bears a more substantial burden of preparation. The second factor, the Court continued, was whether the concerns reflected in the state limitations statute were consistent with the policies and goals of the federal civil rights acts. Here, according to the Court, the policies of the federal and state enactments diverged. The federal Act's goal, the Court maintained, was compensation, whereas the state law, which did not provide for a private right of action and which created an administrative agency with limited remedial authority, was concerned with encouraging private resolution of disputes through conciliation. In addition, the state's short limitations period reflected in part a judgment that factors such as minimizing the diversion of state government officials' attention from their duties outweighed the interest in providing employees ready access to a forum to resolve their claims of job discrimination. Such a judgment, the Court concluded, was inconsistent with the central objective of the federal statutes to provide relief to individuals whose statutory rights had been abridged. Accordingly, it held, borrowing this statute of limitations was inappropriate. In a concurring opinion, Justice Rehnquist, joined by the Chief Justice and Justice O'Connor, agreed that the trial judge had applied the wrong limitations period, but disagreed with the standard by which the majority reached this result. He contended that the courts should determine whether the state legislature intended for the statute under question to apply to the federal claim and, if it answers this question in the affirmative, should apply that statute unless it concludes that the statute discriminates against federal claimants or does not provide a reasonable amount of time in which to file a claim. He then viewed the differences in policy between the federal and state statutes as evidence that the legislature never intended for this limitations period to apply to federal civil rights claims. Does the Court's opinion dispose of either of the concerns raised in this paragraph? For a comprehensive examination of these issues see Section D, infra at 571. See also Comment, Developments In the Law—Section 1981, 15 Harv.Civ.R.-Civ.L.L.Rev. 29, 219–239 (1980).

4. In light of the intent requirement announced in *General Building Contractors Ass'n,* should the test for successor employer liability under Title VII be extended to § 1981 cases? See Musikawamba v. Essi, Inc., 760 F.2d 740 (7th Cir. 1985).

SECTION B. THE CIVIL RIGHTS ACT OF 1871, SECTION ONE—42 U.S.C.A. § 1983

Read 42 USC § 1983 at p. 12.

PERSONNEL ADMINISTRATOR OF MASSACHUSETTS v. FEENEY

Supreme Court of the United States, 1979.
442 U.S. 256, 99 S.Ct. 2282, 60 L.Ed.2d 870.

MR. JUSTICE STEWART delivered the opinion of the Court.

This case presents a challenge to the constitutionality of the Massachusetts Veterans Preference Statute, Mass.Gen.Laws, ch. 31, § 23, on the ground that it discriminates against women in violation of the Equal Protection Clause of the Fourteenth Amendment. Under ch. 31, § 23,[1] all veterans who qualify for state civil service positions must be considered for appointment ahead of any qualifying nonveterans. The preference operates overwhelmingly to the advantage of males.

The appellee Helen B. Feeney is not a veteran. She brought this action pursuant to 42 U.S.C. § 1983 alleging that the absolute preference formula established in ch. 31, § 23 inevitably operates to exclude women from consideration for the best Massachusetts civil service jobs and thus unconstitutionally denies them the equal protection of the laws.[2] The three-judge District Court agreed, one judge dissenting. Anthony v. Commonwealth of Massachusetts, 415 F.Supp. 485 (1976).[3]

1. For the text of ch. 31, § 23, see n. 10, infra. The general Massachusetts Civil Service law, Mass.Gen.Laws, ch. 31, was recodified on Jan. 1, 1979, 1978 Mass. Acts, ch. 383, and the veterans' preference is now found at Mass.Gen.Laws Ann., ch. 31, § 26 (West 1979). Citations in this opinion, unless otherwise indicated, are to the ch. 31 codification in effect when this litigation was commenced.

2. No statutory claim was brought under Title VII of the Civil Rights Act of 1964, 42 U.S.C. § 2000e et seq. Section 712 of the Act, 42 U.S.C. § 2000e–11, provides that "nothing contained in this subchapter shall be construed to repeal or modify any Federal, State, territorial or local law creating special rights or preference for veterans." The parties have evidently assumed that this provision precludes a Title VII challenge.

3. The appellee's case had been consolidated with a similar action brought by Carol B. Anthony, a lawyer whose efforts to obtain a civil service Counsel I position had been frustrated by ch. 31, § 23. In 1975, Massachusetts exempted all attorney positions from the preference, 1975 Mass. Acts, ch. 134, and Anthony's claims were accordingly found moot by the District Court. Anthony v. Commonwealth of Massachusetts, 415 F.Supp. 485, 495.

The District Court found that the absolute preference afforded by Massachusetts to veterans has a devastating impact upon the employment opportunities of women. Although it found that the goals of the preference were worthy and legitimate and that the legislation had not been enacted for the purpose of discriminating against women, the court reasoned that its exclusionary impact upon women was nonetheless so severe as to require the State to further its goals through a more limited form of preference. Finding that a more modest preference formula would readily accommodate the State's interest in aiding veterans, the court declared ch. 31, § 23 unconstitutional and enjoined its operation.[4]

Upon an appeal taken by the Attorney General of Massachusetts,[5] this Court vacated the judgment and remanded the case for further consideration in light of our intervening decision in Washington v. Davis, 426 U.S. 229, 96 S.Ct. 2040, 48 L.Ed.2d 597. Commonwealth of Massachusetts v. Feeney, 434 U.S. 884, 98 S.Ct. 252, 54 L.Ed.2d 169 (1977). The *Davis* case held that a neutral law does not violate the Equal Protection Clause solely because it results in a racially disproportionate impact; instead the disproportionate impact must be traced to a purpose to discriminate on the basis of race. 426 U.S., at 238–244, 96 S.Ct., at 2046–2050.

Upon remand, the District Court, one judge concurring and one judge again dissenting, concluded that a veterans' hiring preference is inherently nonneutral because it favors a class from which women have traditionally been excluded, and that the consequences of the Massachusetts absolute preference formula for the employment opportunities of women were too inevitable to have been "unintended." Accordingly, the court reaffirmed its original judgment. Feeney v. Commonwealth of Massachusetts, 451 F.Supp. 143. The Attorney General again appealed to this Court pursuant to 28 U.S.C. § 1253, and probable jurisdiction of the appeal was noted. 434 U.S. 884, 98 S.Ct. 252, 54 L.Ed.2d 169.

I

A

The Federal Government and virtually all of the States grant some sort of hiring preference to veterans.[6] The Massachusetts preference,

4. The District Court entered a stay pending appeal, but the stay was rendered moot by the passage of an interim statute suspending ch. 31, § 23 pending final judgment and replacing it with an interim provision granting a modified point preference to veterans. 1976 Mass.Acts, ch. 200, now codified at Mass.Gen.Law Ann., ch. 31, § 26 (West 1979).

5. The Attorney General appealed the judgment over the objection of other state officers named as defendants. In response to our certification of the question whether Massachusetts law permits this, see Commonwealth of Massachusetts v. Feeney, 429 U.S. 66, 97 S.Ct. 345, 50 L.Ed.2d 224, the Supreme Judicial Court answered in the affirmative. Feeney v. Commonwealth, 366 N.E.2d 1262 (Mass.1977).

6. The first comprehensive federal veterans' statute was enacted in 1944. Veterans' Preference Act of 1944, ch. 287, 58 Stat. 387. The Federal Government has, however, engaged in preferential hiring of

which is loosely termed an "absolute lifetime" preference, is among the most generous.[7] It applies to all positions in the State's classified civil service, which constitute approximately 60% of the public jobs in the State. It is available to "any person, male or female, including a nurse," who was honorably discharged from the United States Armed Forces after at least 90 days of active service, at least one day of which was during "wartime." [8] Persons who are deemed veterans and who are otherwise qualified for a particular civil service job may exercise the preference at any time and as many times as they wish.[9]

Civil service positions in Massachusetts fall into two general categories, labor and official. For jobs in the official service, with which the proofs in this action were concerned, the preference mechanics are uncomplicated. All applicants for employment must take competitive

veterans, through official policies and various special laws, since the Civil War. See, e.g., Res. of March 3, 1865. No. 27, 13 Stat. 571 (hiring preference for disabled veterans). See generally The Provision of Federal Benefits for Veterans, An Historical Analysis of Major Veterans' Legislation, 1862–1954, Committee Print No. 171, 84th Cong., 1st Sess. (House Comm. on Vets. Affairs, Dec. 28, 1955) 258–265. For surveys of state veterans' preference laws, many of which also date back to the late 19th century, see State Veterans' Laws, Digest of State Laws Regarding Rights, Benefits and Privileges of Veterans and Their Dependents, House Committee on Veterans' Affairs, 91st Cong., 1st Sess. (1969); Fleming & Shanor, Veterans Preferences in Public Employment: Unconstitutional Gender Discrimination? 26 Emory L.J. 13 (1977).

7. The forms of veterans' hiring preferences vary widely. The Federal Government and approximately 41 States grant veterans a point advantage on civil service examinations, usually 10 points for a disabled veteran and 5 for one who is not disabled. See Fleming & Shanor, supra n. 6, 26 Emory L.J., at 17, and n. 12 (citing statutes). A few offer only tie-breaking preferences. Id. n. 14 (citing statutes). A very few States, like Massachusetts, extend absolute hiring or positional preferences to qualified veterans. Id. n. 13. See, e.g., N.J.Stat.Ann. 11:27–4 (West 1977); S.D. Comp.Laws Ann. § 33–3–1 (1968); Utah Code Ann. § 34–30–11; Wash.Rev.Code §§ 41.04.010, 73.16.010 (1976).

8. Mass.Gen.Laws Ann., ch. 4, § 7, cl. 43 (West 1976), which supplies the general definition of the term "veteran," reads in pertinent part: "Veteran" shall mean any person, male or female, including a nurse, (a) whose last discharge or release from his wartime service, as defined herein, was under honorable conditions and who (b) served in the army, navy, marine corps, coast guard, or air force of the United States for not less than ninety days active service, at least one day of which was for wartime service * * *. Persons awarded the Purple Heart, ch. 4, § 7, cl. 43, or one of a number of specified campaign badges or the Congressional Medal of Honor are also deemed veterans. Mass. Gen.Laws Ann., ch. 31, § 21.

"Wartime service" is defined as service performed by a "Spanish War veteran," a "World War I veteran," a "World War II veteran," a "Korean veteran," a "Vietnam veteran," or a member of the "WAAC." Mass.Gen.Laws Ann., ch. 4, § 7, cl. 43 (West 1976). Each of these terms is further defined to specify a period of service. The statutory definitions, taken together, cover the entire period from September 16, 1940 to May 7, 1975. See ibid.

"WAAC" is defined as follows: "any woman who was discharged and so served in any corps or unit of the United States established for the purpose of enabling women to serve with, or as auxiliary to, the armed forces of the United States and such woman shall be deemed to be a veteran. Ibid.

9. The Massachusetts preference law formerly imposed a residency requirement, see 1954 Mass.Acts, ch. 627, § 3 (eligibility conditioned upon Massachusetts domicile prior to induction or five years residency in State). The distinction was invalidated as violative of the Equal Protection Clause in Stevens v. Campbell, 332 F.Supp. 102, 105 (D.C.Mass.1971). Cf. August v. Bronstein, 369 F.Supp. 190 (S.D.N.Y.1974) (upholding, inter alia, nondurational residency requirement in N.Y. veterans' preference statute), summarily aff'd, 417 U.S. 901, 94 S.Ct. 2596, 41 L.Ed.2d 208.

examinations. Grades are based on a formula that gives weight both to objective test results and to training and experience. Candidates who pass are then ranked in the order of their respective scores on an "eligible list." Ch. 31, § 23 requires, however, that disabled veterans, veterans, and surviving spouses and surviving parents of veterans be ranked—in the order of their respective scores—above all other candidates.[10]

Rank on the eligible list and availability for employment are the sole factors that * * * determine which candidates are considered for appointment to an official civil service position. When a public agency has a vacancy, it requisitions a list of "certified eligibles" from the state personnel division. Under formulas prescribed by civil service rules, a small number of candidates from the top of an appropriate list, three if there is only one vacancy, are certified. The appointing agency is then required to choose from among these candidates.[11] Although the veterans' preference thus does not guarantee that a veteran will be appointed, it is obvious that the preference gives to veterans who achieve passing scores a well-nigh absolute advantage.

B

The appellee has lived in Dracut, Mass., most of her life. She entered the work force in 1948, and for the next 14 years worked at a variety of jobs in the private sector. She first entered the state civil service system in 1963, having competed successfully for a position as Senior Clerk Stenographer in the Massachusetts Civil Defense Agency. There she worked for four years. In 1967, she was promoted to the position of Federal Funds and Personnel Coordinator in the same agency. The agency, and with it her job, was eliminated in 1975.

During her 12-year tenure as a public employee, Ms. Feeney took and passed a number of open competitive civil service examinations. On several she did quite well, receiving in 1971 the second highest score on an examination for a job with the Board of Dental Examiners, and in 1973 the third highest on a test for an Administrative Assistant

10. Chapter 31, § 23, provides in full:

"The names of persons who pass examinations for appointment to any position classified under the civil service shall be placed upon the eligible lists in the following order:—

"(1) Disabled veterans * * * in the order of their respective standing; (2) veterans in the order of their respective standing; (3) person described in section twenty-three B [the widow or widowed mother of a veteran killed in action or who died from a service-connected disability incurred in wartime service and who has not remarried] in the order of their respective standing; (4) other applicants in the order of their respective standing. Upon receipt of a requisition, names shall be certified from such lists according to the method of certification prescribed by the civil service rules. A disabled veteran shall be retained in employment in preference to all other persons, including veterans."

A 1977 amendment extended the dependents' preference to "surviving spouses," and "surviving parents." 1977 Mass.Acts, ch. 815.

11. A 1978 amendment requires the appointing authority to file a written statement of reasons if the person whose name was not highest is selected. 1978 Mass. Acts, ch. 393, § 11, currently codified at Mass.Gen.Laws Ann., ch. 31, § 27 (West 1979).

position with a mental health center. Her high scores, however, did not win her a place on the certified eligible list. Because of the veterans' preference, she was ranked sixth behind five male veterans on the Dental Examiner list. She was not certified, and a lower scoring veteran was eventually appointed. On the 1973 examination, she was placed in a position on the list behind 12 male veterans, 11 of whom had lower scores. Following the other examinations that she took, her name was similarly ranked below those of veterans who had achieved passing grades.

Ms. Feeney's interest in securing a better job in state government did not wane. Having been consistently eclipsed by veterans, however, she eventually concluded that further competition for civil service positions of interest to veterans would be futile. In 1975, shortly after her civil defense job was abolished, she commenced this litigation.

C

The veterans' hiring preference in Massachusetts, as in other jurisdictions, has traditionally been justified as a measure designed to reward veterans for the sacrifice of military service, to ease the transition from military to civilian life, to encourage patriotic service, and to attract loyal and well-disciplined people to civil service ocupations.[12] * * *

* * *

* * * The Massachusetts law dates back to 1884, when the State, as part of its first civil service legislation, gave a statutory preference to civil service applicants who were Civil War veterans if their qualifications were equal to those of nonveterans. 1884 Mass. Acts, ch. 320, § 16. This tie-breaking provision blossomed into a truly absolute preference in 1895, when the State enacted its first general veterans preference law and exempted veterans from all merit selection requirements. 1895 Mass. Acts, ch. 501, § 2. In response to a challenge brought by a male non-veteran, this statute was declared violative of state constitutional provisions guaranteeing that government should be for the "common good" and prohibiting hereditary titles. Brown v. Russell, 166 Mass. 14, 43 N.E. 1005 (1896).

The current veterans' preference law has its origins in an 1896 statute, enacted to meet the state constitutional standards enunciated in Brown v. Russell. That statute limited the absolute preference to

12. Veterans' preference laws have been challenged so often that the rationale in their support has become essentially standardized. See, e.g., Koelfgen v. Jackson, 355 F.Supp. 243 (D.C.Minn.1972), summarily aff'd, 410 U.S. 976, 93 S.Ct. 1502, 36 L.Ed.2d 173; August v. Bronstein, 369 F.Supp. 190 (S.D.N.Y.1974), summarily aff'd, 417 U.S. 901, 94 S.Ct. 2596, 41 L.Ed. 2d 208; Rios v. Dillman, 499 F.2d 329 (CA5 1974); cf. Mitchell v. Cohen, 333 U.S. 411, 419 n. 12, 68 S.Ct. 518, 522 n. 12, 92 L.Ed. 774. See generally Blumberg, De Facto and De Jure Sex Discrimination Under the Equal Protection Clause: A Reconsideration of the Veterans' Preference in Public Employment, 26 Buffalo L.Rev. 3 (1977). For a collection of early cases, see Annot., Veterans' Preference Laws, 161 A.L.R. 494 (1946).

veterans who were otherwise qualified.[13] 1896 Mass. Acts, ch. 517, § 2. A closely divided Supreme Judicial Court, in an advisory opinion issued the same year, concluded that the preference embodied in such a statute would be valid. Opinion of the Justices, 166 Mass. 589, 44 N.E. 625 (1896). In 1919, when the preference was extended to cover the veterans of World War I, the formula was further limited to provide for a priority in eligibility, in contrast to an absolute preference in hiring. 1919 Mass. Acts, ch. 150, § 2.[14] See Corliss v. Civil Service Comm'rs, 242 Mass. 61, 136 N.E. 356. In Mayor of Lynn v. Comm'r of Civil Service, 269 Mass. 410, 414, 169 N.E. 502, the Supreme Judicial Court, adhering to the views expressed in its 1896 advisory opinion, sustained this statute against a state constitutional challenge.

Since 1919, the preference has been repeatedly amended to cover persons who served in subsequent wars, declared or undeclared. See 1943 Mass. Acts, ch. 194; 1949 Mass. Acts, ch. 642, § 2 (World War II); 1954 Mass. Acts, ch. 627 (Korea); 1968 Mass. Acts, ch. 531, § 1 (Vietnam).[15] The current preference formula in ch. 31, § 23 is substantially the same as that settled upon in 1919. This absolute preference—even as modified in 1919—has never been universally popular. Over the years it has been subjected to repeated legal challenges, see Hutcheson v. Director of Civil Service, supra (collecting cases), criticism by civil service reform groups, see, e.g., Report of the Massachusetts Committee on Public Service on Initiative Bill Relative to Veterans' Preference, S. No. 279 (Feb. 1926); Report of Massachusetts Special Commission on Civil Service and Public Personnel Administration 37–43 (June 15, 1967) (hereinafter 1967 Report), and in 1926 to a referendum in which it was reaffirmed by a majority of 51.9%. See 1967 Report, supra, at 38. The present case is apparently the first to challenge the Massachusetts veterans' preference on the simple ground that it discriminates on the basis of sex.[16]

13. 1896 Mass. Acts, ch. 517, § 2. The statute provided that veterans who passed examinations should "be preferred in appointment to all persons not veterans * * *." Ibid. A proviso stated: "But nothing herein contained shall be construed to prevent the certification and employment of women."

14. 1919 Mass. Act, ch. 150, § 2. The amended statute provided that "The names of veterans who pass examinations * * * shall be placed upon the * * * eligible lists in the order of their respective standing, above the names of all other applicants," and further provided that "upon receipt of a requisition not especially calling for women, names shall be certified from such lists * * *." The exemption for "women's requisitions" was retained in substantially this form in subsequent revisions, see, e.g., 1954 Mass. Act, ch. 627, § 4. It was eliminated in 1971, 1971 Mass. Acts, ch. 219, when the State made all-single sex examinations subject to the prior approval of the Massachusetts Commission Against Discrimination, 1971 Mass. Acts, ch. 221.

15. A provision requiring public agencies to hire disabled veterans certified as eligible was added in 1922. 1922 Mass. Acts, ch. 463. It was invalidated as applied in Hutcheson v. Civil Service Comm'n, 361 Mass. 480, 281 N.E.2d 53 (1973) (suit by veteran arguing that absolute preference for disabled veterans arbitrary on facts). It has since been eliminated and replaced with a provision giving disabled veterans an absolute preference in retention. See Mass.Gen.Laws Ann., ch. 31, § 26 (West 1979). See n. 10, supra.

16. For cases presenting similar challenges to the veterans' preference laws of other States, see Ballou v. State Department of Civil Service, 75 N.J. 365, 382 A.2d 1118 (1978) (sustaining New Jersey absolute preference); Feinerman v. Jones, 356

D

The first Massachusetts veterans' preference statute defined the term "veterans" in gender-neutral language. See 1896 Mass. Acts, ch. 517, § 2 ("any person" who served in the United States army or navy), and subsequent amendments have followed this pattern, see, e.g., 1919 Mass. Acts, ch. 150, § 1 ("any person" who served * * *); 1954 Mass. Acts, ch. 531, § 1 ("any person, male or female, including a nurse"). Women who have served in official United States military units during wartime, then, have always been entitled to the benefit of the preference. In addition, Massachusetts, through a 1943 amendment to the definition of "wartime service," extended the preference to women who served in unofficial auxiliary women's units. 1943 Mass. Acts, ch. 194.[17]

When the first general veterans' preference statute was adopted in 1896, there were no women veterans.[18] The statute, however, covered only Civil War veterans. Most of them were beyond middle age, and relatively few were actively competing for public employment.[19] Thus, the impact of the preference upon the employment opportunities of nonveterans as a group and women in particular was slight.[20]

Notwithstanding the apparent attempts by Massachusetts to include as many military women as possible within the scope of the preference, the statute today benefits an overwhelmingly male class. This is attributable in some measure to the variety of federal statutes, regula-

F.Supp. 252 (M.D.Pa.1973) (sustaining Pennsylvania point preference); Branch v. DuBois, 418 F.Supp. 1128 (N.D.Ill.1976) (sustaining Illinois modified point preference); Wisconsin Nat'l Organization for Women v. Wisconsin, 417 F.Supp. 978 (W.D.Wis.1976) (sustaining Wisconsin point preference).

17. The provision, passed shortly after the creation of the Women's Auxiliary Army Corps (WAAC), see n. 21, infra, is currently found at Mass.Gen.Laws Ann., ch. 4, § 7, cl. 43 (West 1976), see n. 8, supra. "Wartime service" is defined as service performed by a * * * member of the "WAAC." A "WAAC" is "any woman who was discharged and so served in any corps or unit of the United States established for the purpose of enabling women to serve with, or as auxiliary to, the armed forces of the United States and such woman shall be deemed to be a veteran." Ibid.

18. Small numbers of women served in combat roles in every war before the 20th century in which the United States was involved, but usually unofficially or disguised as men. See Binkin and Bach, Women and the Military 5 (1977). Among the better-known are Molly Pitcher (Revolutionary War); Deborah Sampson (Revolutionary War), and Lucy Brewer (War of 1812). Passing as one "George Baker," Brewer served for three years as a gunner on the U.S.S. Constitution ("Old Ironsides") and distinguished herself in several major naval battles in the War of 1812. See Laffin, Women in Battle 116–122 (1967).

19. By 1887, the average age of Civil War veterans in Massachusetts was already over 50. Third Annual Report, Mass. Civil Service Comm'n 22 (Jan. 10, 1887). The tie-breaking preference which had been established under the 1884 statute had apparently been difficult to enforce, since many appointing officers "prefer younger men." Ibid. The 1896 statute which established the first valid absolute preference, see text, at p. 2289, supra, again covered only Civil War veterans. 1896 Mass. Acts, ch. 517, § 1.

20. In 1896, for example, 2,804 persons applied for civil service positions: 2,031 were men, of whom only 32 were veterans; 773 were women. Of the 647 persons appointed, 525 were men, of whom only 9 were veterans; 122 were women. Thirteenth Annual Report, Mass. Civil Service Comm'n 5, 6 (Dec. 4, 1896). The average age of the applicants was 38. Ibid.

tions, and policies that have restricted the numbers of women who could enlist in the United States Armed Forces,[21] and largely to the simple fact that women have never been subjected to a military draft. See generally M. Binkin and S. Bach, Women and the Military 4–21 (1977).

When this litigation was commenced, then, over 98% of the veterans in Massachusetts were male; only 1.8% were female. And over one-quarter of the Massachusetts population were veterans. During the decade between 1963 and 1973 when the appellee was actively participating in the State's merit selection system, 47,005 new permanent appointments were made in the classified official service. Forty-three percent of those hired were women, and 57% were men. Of the women appointed, 1.8% were veterans, while 54% of the men had veteran status. A large unspecified percentage of the female appointees were serving in lower paying positions for which males traditionally had not applied.[22] On each of 50 sample eligible lists that are part of the record

21. The Army Nurse Corps, created by Congress in 1901, was the first official military unit for women, but its members were not granted full military rank until 1944. See M. Binkin and S. Bach, Women and the Military 4–21 (1977) (hereinafter Binkin and Bach); M. E. Treadwell, The Women's Army Corps 6 (Dept. of Army, Office of Chief of Military History, 1954) (hereinafter Treadwell). During World War I, a variety of proposals were made to enlist women for work as doctors, telephone operators and clerks, but all were rejected by the War Department. See ibid. The Navy, however, interpreted its own authority broadly to include a power to enlist women as Yeoman F's and Marine F's. About 13,000 women served in this rank, working primarily at clerical jobs. These women were the first in the United States to be admitted to full military rank and status. See Treadwell 10.

Official military corps for women were established in response to the massive personnel needs of the Second World War. See generally Binkin and Bach; Treadwell. The Women's Army Auxiliary Corps (WAAC)—the unofficial predecessor of the Women's Army Corps (WAC)—was created on May 14, 1942, followed two months later by the WAVES (Women Accepted for Voluntary Emergency Service). See Binkin and Bach 7. Not long after, the U.S. Marine Corps Women's Reserve and the Coast Guard Women's Reserve (SPAR) were established. See ibid. Some 350,000 women served in the four services; some 800 women also served as Women's Airforce Service Pilots (WASPS). Ibid. Most worked in health care, administration, and communications; they were also employed as airplane mechanics, parachute riggers, gunnery instructors, air traffic controllers, and the like.

The authorizations for the women's units during World War II were temporary. The Women's Armed Services Integration Act of 1948, 62 Stat. 356–375, established the women's services on a permanent basis. Under the Act, women were given regular military status. However, quotas were placed on the numbers who could enlist; 62 Stat. 357, 360–361 (no more than 2% of total enlisted strength); eligibility requirements were more stringent than those for men, and career opportunities were limited. Binkin and Bach 11–12. During the 1950's and 1960's, enlisted women constituted little more than 1% of the total force. In 1967, the 2% quota was lifted, Act of Nov. 8, 1967, Pub.L. 90–130, § 1(b), 81 Stat. 376, and in the 1970's many restrictive policies concerning women's participation in the military have been eliminated or modified. See generally Binkin and Bach, supra. In 1972, women still constituted less than 2% of the enlisted strength. Id., at 14. By 1975, when this litigation was commenced, the percentage had risen to 4.0%. Ibid.

22. The former exemption for "women's requisitions," see nn. 13, 14, supra, may have operated in the 20th century to protect these types of jobs from the impact of the preference. However, the statutory history indicates that this was not its purpose. The provision dates back to the 1896 veterans' preference law and was retained in the law substantially unchanged until it was eliminated in 1971. See n. 14, supra. Since veterans in 1896 were a small but an exclusively male class, such a provision was apparently included to ensure that the

in this case, one or more women who would have been certified as eligible for appointment on the basis of test results were displaced by veterans whose test scores were lower.

At the outset of this litigation the State conceded that for "many of the permanent positions for which males and females have competed" the veterans' preference has "resulted in a substantially greater proportion of female eligibles than male eligibles" not being certified for consideration. The impact of the veterans' preference law upon the public employment opportunities of women has thus been severe. This impact lies at the heart of the appellee's federal constitutional claim.

II

The sole question for decision on this appeal is whether Massachusetts, in granting an absolute lifetime preference to veterans, has discriminated against women in violation of the Equal Protection Clause of the Fourteenth Amendment.

A

The Equal Protection guarantee of the Fourteenth Amendment does not take from the States all power of classification. Massachusetts Bd. of Retirement v. Murgia, 427 U.S. 307, 314, 96 S.Ct. 2562, 2567, 49 L.Ed. 2d 520. Most laws classify, and many affect certain groups unevenly, even though the law itself treats them no differently from all other members of the class described by the law. When the basic classification is rationally based, uneven effects upon particular groups within a class are ordinarily of no constitutional concern. New York City Transit Authority v. Beazer, 440 U.S. 568, 99 S.Ct. 1355, 59 L.Ed.2d 587; Jefferson v. Hackney, 406 U.S. 535, 548, 92 S.Ct. 1724, 1732, 32 L.Ed.2d 285. Cf. James v. Valtierra, 402 U.S. 137, 91 S.Ct. 1331, 28 L.Ed.2d 678. The calculus of effects, the manner in which a particular law reverberates in a society, is a legislative and not a judicial responsibility. Dandridge v. Williams, 397 U.S. 471, 90 S.Ct. 1153, 25 L.Ed.2d 491; San Antonio Bd. of Education v. Rodriguez, 411 U.S. 1, 93 S.Ct. 1278, 36 L.Ed.2d 16. In assessing an equal protection challenge, a court is called upon only to measure the basic validity of the legislative classification. Barrett v. Indiana, 229 U.S. 26, 29–30, 33 S.Ct. 692, 693, 57 L.Ed. 1050; Railway Express Co. v. New York, 336 U.S. 106, 69 S.Ct. 463, 93 L.Ed. 533. When some other independent right is not at stake, see, e.g., Shapiro v. Thompson, 394 U.S. 618, 89 S.Ct. 1322, 22 L.Ed.2d 600 and

statute would not be construed to outlaw a pre-existing practice of single-sex hiring explicitly authorized under the 1884 Civil Service Statute. See Rule XIX.3, Mass. Civil Service Law, Rules and Regs. of Comm'rs (1884) ("In case the request for any * * * certification, or any law or regulation shall call for persons of one sex, those of that sex shall be certified; otherwise sex shall be disregarded in certification.") The veterans' preference statute at no point endorsed this practice. Historical materials indicate, however, that the early preference law may have operated to encourage the employment of women in positions from which they previously had been excluded. See Thirteenth Annual Report, Mass. Civil Service Comm'n 5, 6 (Dec. 4, 1896); Third Annual Report, Mass. Civil Service Comm'n 23 (Jan. 10, 1887).

when there is no "reason to infer antipathy," Vance v. Bradley, 440 U.S. 93, 99 S.Ct. 939, 59 L.Ed.2d 171, it is presumed that "even improvident decisions will eventually be rectified by the democratic process * * *." Ibid.

Certain classifications, however, in themselves supply a reason to infer antipathy. Race is the paradigm. A racial classification, regardless of purported motivation, is presumptively invalid and can be upheld only upon an extraordinary justification. Brown v. Board of Education, 347 U.S. 483, 74 S.Ct. 686, 98 L.Ed. 873; MacLaughlin v. Florida, 379 U.S. 184, 85 S.Ct. 283, 13 L.Ed.2d 222. This rule applies as well to a classification that is ostensibly neutral but is an obvious pretext for racial discrimination. Yick Wo v. Hopkins, 118 U.S. 356, 6 S.Ct. 1064, 30 L.Ed. 220; Guinn v. United States, 238 U.S. 347, 35 S.Ct. 926, 59 L.Ed. 1340; cf. Lane v. Wilson, 307 U.S. 268, 59 S.Ct. 872, 83 L.Ed. 1281; Gomillion v. Lightfoot, 364 U.S. 339, 81 S.Ct. 125, 5 L.Ed.2d 110. But, as was made clear in Washington v. Davis, 426 U.S. 229, 96 S.Ct. 2040, 48 L.Ed.2d 597 and Village of Arlington Heights v. Metropolitan Housing Development Corp., 429 U.S. 252, 97 S.Ct. 555, 50 L.Ed.2d 450, even if a neutral law has a disproportionately adverse effect upon a racial minority, it is unconstitutional under the Equal Protection Clause only if that impact can be traced to a discriminatory purpose.

Classifications based upon gender, not unlike those based upon race, have traditionally been the touchstone for pervasive and often subtle discrimination. Caban v. Mohammed, 441 U.S. 380, 398, 99 S.Ct. 1760, 1771, 60 L.Ed.2d 297 (STEWART, J., dissenting). This Court's recent cases teach that such classifications must bear a "close and substantial relationship to important governmental objectives." Craig v. Boren, 429 U.S. 190, 197, 97 S.Ct. 451, 50 L.Ed.2d 397 and are in many settings unconstitutional. Although public employment is not a constitutional right, Massachusetts Bd. of Retirement v. Murgia, supra, and the States have wide discretion in framing employee qualifications, see, e.g., New York City Transit Authority v. Beazer, 440 U.S. 568, 99 S.Ct. 1355, 59 L.Ed.2d 587, these precedents dictate that any state law overtly or covertly designed to prefer males over females in public employment would require an exceedingly persuasive justification to withstand a constitutional challenge under the Equal Protection Clause of the Fourteenth Amendment.

B

The cases of Washington v. Davis, supra, and Village of Arlington Heights v. Metropolitan Housing Development Corp., supra, recognize that when a neutral law has a disparate impact upon a group that has historically been the victim of discrimination, an unconstitutional purpose may still be at work. But those cases signalled no departure from the settled rule that the Fourteenth Amendment guarantees equal laws, not equal results. *Davis* upheld a job-related employment test that white people passed in proportionately greater numbers than

Negroes, for there had been no showing that racial discrimination entered into the establishment or formulation of the test. *Arlington Heights* upheld a zoning board decision that tended to perpetuate racially segregated housing patterns, since apart from its effect, the board's decision was shown to be nothing more than an application of constitutionally neutral zoning policy. Those principles apply with equal force to a case involving alleged gender discrimination.

When a statute gender-neutral on its face is challenged on the ground that its effects upon women are disproportionably adverse, a two-fold inquiry is thus appropriate. The first question is whether the statutory classification is indeed neutral in the sense that it is not gender-based. If the classification itself, covert or overt, is not based upon gender, the second question is whether the adverse effect reflects invidious gender-based discrimination. See Village of Arlington Heights v. Metropolitan Housing Development Corp., supra, 429 U.S., at 266, 97 S.Ct., at 564. In this second inquiry, impact provides an "important starting point," 429 U.S., at 266, 97 S.Ct. 564 but purposeful discrimination is "the condition that offends the Constitution." Swann v. Board of Education, 402 U.S. 1, 16, 91 S.Ct. 1267, 1276, 28 L.Ed.2d 554.

It is against this background of precedent that we consider the merits of the case before us.

III

A

The question whether ch. 31, § 23 establishes a classification that is overtly or covertly based upon gender must first be considered. The appellee has conceded that ch. 31, § 23 is neutral on its face. She has also acknowledged that state hiring preferences for veterans are not *per se* invalid, for she has limited her challenge to the absolute lifetime preference that Massachusetts provides to veterans. The District Court made two central findings that are relevant here: first, that ch. 31, § 23 serves legitimate and worthy purposes; second, that the absolute preference was not established for the purpose of discriminating against women. The appellee has thus acknowledged and the District Court has thus found that the distinction between veterans and nonveterans drawn by ch. 31, § 23 is not a pretext for gender discrimination. The appellee's concession and the District Court's finding are clearly correct.

If the impact of this statute could not be plausibly explained on a neutral ground, impact itself would signal that the real classification made by the law was in fact not neutral. See Washington v. Davis, supra, 426 U.S., at 242, 96 S.Ct., at 2049; Village of Arlington Heights v. Metropolitan Housing Development Corp., supra, 429 U.S., at 266, 97 S.Ct., at 564. But there can be but one answer to the question whether this veteran preference excludes significant numbers of women from preferred state jobs because they are women or because they are nonveterans. Apart from the fact that the definition of "veterans" in the statute has always been neutral as to gender and that Massachusetts has consistently defined veteran status in a way that has been inclusive of women who have served in the military, this is not a law that can plausibly be explained only as a gender-based classification. Indeed, it is not a law that can rationally be explained on that ground. Veteran status is not uniquely male. Although few women benefit from the preference the nonveteran class is not substantially all-female. To the contrary, significant numbers of nonveterans are men, and all nonveterans—male as well as female—are placed at a disadvantage. Too many men are affected by ch. 31, § 23 to permit the inference that the statute is but a pretext for preferring men over women.

Moreover, as the District Court implictly found, the purposes of the statute provide the surest explanation for its impact. Just as there are cases in which impact alone can unmask an invidious classification, cf. Yick Wo v. Hopkins, supra, there are others, in which—notwithstanding impact—the legitimate noninvidious purposes of a law cannot be missed. This is one. The distinction made by ch. 31, § 23, is, as it seems to be, quite simply between veterans and nonveterans, not between men and women.

B

The dispositive question, then, is whether the appellee has shown that a gender-based discriminatory purpose has, at least in some measure, shaped the Massachusetts veterans' preference legislation. As did the District Court, she points to two basic factors which in her view distinguish ch. 31, § 23 from the neutral rules at issue in the Washington v. Davis and *Arlington Heights* cases. The first is the nature of the preference, which is said to be demonstrably gender-biased in the sense that it favors a status reserved under federal military policy primarily to men. The second concerns the impact of the absolute lifetime preference upon the employment opportunities of women, an impact claimed to be too inevitable to have been unintended. The appellee contends that these factors, coupled with the fact that the preference itself has little if any relevance to actual job performance, more than suffice to prove the discriminatory intent required to establish a constitutional violation.

1

The contention that this veterans' preference is "inherently non-neutral" or "gender-biased" presumes that the State, by favoring veterans, intentionally incorporated into its public employment policies the panoply of sex-based and assertedly discriminatory federal laws that have prevented all but a handful of women from becoming veterans. There are two serious difficulties with this argument. First, it is wholly at odds with the District Court's central finding that Massachusetts has not offered a preference to veterans for the purpose of discriminating against women. Second, it cannot be reconciled with the assumption made by both the appellee and the District Court that a more limiting hiring preference for veterans could be sustained. Taken together, these difficulties are fatal.

To the extent that the status of veteran is one that few women have been enabled to achieve, every hiring preference for veterans, however modest or extreme, is inherently gender-biased. If Massachusetts by offering such a preference can be said intentionally to have incorporated into its state employment policies the historical gender-based federal military personnel practices, the degree of the preference would or should make no constitutional difference. Invidious discrimination does not become less so because the discrimination accomplished is of a lesser magnitude.[23] Discriminatory intent is simply not amenable to calibration. It either is a factor that has influenced the legislative choice or it is not. The District Court's conclusion that the absolute veterans' preference was not originally enacted or subsequently reaffirmed for the purpose of giving an advantage to males as such necessarily compels the conclusion that the State intended nothing more than to prefer "veterans." Given this finding, simple logic suggests that an intent to exclude women from significant public jobs was not at work in this law. To reason that it was, by describing the preference as "inherently non-neutral" or "gender-biased," is merely to restate the fact of impact, not to answer the question of intent.

To be sure, this case is unusual in that it involves a law that by design is not neutral. The law overtly prefers veterans as such. As opposed to the written test at issue in *Davis*, it does not purport to define a job related characteristic. To the contrary, it confers upon a specifically described group—perceived to be particularly deserving—a competitive head start. But the District Court found, and the appellee has not disputed, that this legislative choice was legitimate. The basic distinction between veterans and nonveterans, having been found not gender-based, and the goals of the preference having been found worthy, ch. 31 must be analyzed as is any other neutral law that casts a greater burden upon women as a group than upon men as a group. The enlistment policies of the armed services may well have discriminated on the basis of sex. See Frontiero v. Richardson, 411 U.S. 677, 93 S.Ct. 1764, 36 L.Ed.2d 583; cf. Schlesinger v. Ballard, 419 U.S. 498, 95 S.Ct. 572, 42 L.Ed2d 610. But the history of discrimination against women in the military is not on trial in this case.

2

The appellee's ultimate argument rests upon the presumption, common to the criminal and civil law, that a person intends the natural

23. This is not to say that the degree of impact is irrelevant to the question of intent. But it is to say that a more modest preference, while it might well lessen impact and, as the State argues, might lessen the effectiveness of the statute in helping veterans, would not be any more or less "neutral" in the constitutional sense.

and foreseeable consequences of his voluntary actions. Her position was well stated in the concurring opinion in the District Court:

> "Conceding * * * that the goal here was to benefit the veteran, there is no reason to absolve the legislature from awareness that the means chosen to achieve this goal would freeze women out of all those state jobs actively sought by men. To be sure, the legislature did not wish to harm women. But the cutting-off of women's opportunities was an inevitable concomitant of the chosen scheme—as inevitable as the proposition that if tails is up, heads must be down. Where a law's consequences are *that* inevitable, can they meaningfully be described as unintended?" 451 F.Supp. 143, 151.

This rhetorical question implies that a negative answer is obvious, but it is not. The decision to grant a preference to veterans was of course "intentional." So, necessarily, did an adverse impact upon nonveterans follow from that decision. And it cannot seriously be argued that the legislature of Massachusetts could have been unaware that most veterans are men. It would thus be disingenuous to say that the adverse consequences of this legislation for women were unintended, in the sense that they were not volitional or in the sense that they were not foreseeable.

"Discriminatory purpose," however, implies more than intent as volition or intent as awareness of consequences. See United Jewish Organizations v. Carey, 430 U.S. 144, 179, 97 S.Ct. 996, 1016, 51 L.Ed.2d 229 (concurring opinion).[24] It implies that the decisionmaker, in this case a state legislature, selected or reaffirmed a particular course of action at least in part "because of," not merely "in spite of," its adverse effects upon an identifiable group.[25] Yet, nothing in the record demonstrates that this preference for veterans was originally devised or subsequently re-enacted because it would accomplish the collateral goal of keeping women in a stereotypic and predefined place in the Massachusetts Civil Service.

To the contrary, the statutory history shows that the benefit of the preference was consistently offered to "any person" who was a veteran.

24. Proof of discriminatory intent must necessarily usually rely on objective factors, several of which were outlined in Village of Arlington Heights v. Metropolitan Housing Development Corp., 429 U.S. 252, 266, 97 S.Ct. 555, 564, 50 L.Ed.2d 397. The inquiry is practical. What a legislature or any official entity is "up to" may be plain from the results its actions achieve, or the results they avoid. Often it is made clear from what has been called, in a different context, "the give and take of the situation." Cramer v. United States, 325 U.S. 1, 32–33, 65 S.Ct. 918, 934, 89 L.Ed. 1441. (Jackson, J.)

25. This is not to say that the inevitability or foreseeability of consequences of a neutral rule has no bearing upon the existence of discriminatory intent. Certainly, when the adverse consequences of a law upon an identifiable group are as inevitable as the gender-based consequences of ch. 31, § 23, a strong inference that the adverse effects were desired can reasonably be drawn. But in this inquiry—made as it is under the Constitution—an inference is a working tool, not a synonym for proof. When as here, the impact is essentially an unavoidable consequence of a legislative policy that has in itself always been deemed to be legitimate, and when, as here, the statutory history and all of the available evidence affirmatively demonstrate the opposite, the inference simply fails to ripen into proof.

That benefit has been extended to women under a very broad statutory definition of the term veteran.[26] The preference formula itself, which is the focal point of this challenge, was first adopted—so it appears from this record—out of a perceived need to help a small group of older Civil War veterans. It has since been reaffirmed and extended only to cover new veterans.[27] When the totality of legislative actions establishing and extending the Massachusetts veterans' preference are considered, see Washington v. Davis, supra, 426 U.S., at 242, 96 S.Ct., at 2049, the law remains what it purports to be: a preference for veterans of either sex over nonveterans of either sex, not for men over women.

IV

Veterans' hiring preferences represent an awkward—and, many argue, unfair—exception to the widely shared view that merit and merit alone should prevail in the employment policies of government. After a war, such laws have been enacted virtually without opposition. During peacetime they inevitably have come to be viewed in many quarters as undemocratic and unwise.[28] Absolute and permanent preferences, as the troubled history of this law demonstrates, have always been subject to the objection that they give the veteran more than a square deal. But the Fourteenth Amendment "cannot be made a refuge from ill-advised * * * laws." District of Columbia v. Brooke, 214 U.S. 138, 150, 29 S.Ct. 560, 563, 53 L.Ed. 941. The substantial edge granted to veterans by ch. 31, § 23 may reflect unwise policy. The appellee, however, has simply failed to demonstrate that the law in any way reflects a purpose to discriminate on the basis of sex.

The judgment is reversed, and the case is remanded for further proceedings consistent with this opinion.

MR. JUSTICE STEVENS, with whom MR. JUSTICE WHITE joins, concurring.

While I concur in the Court's opinion, I confess that I am not at all sure that there is any difference between the two questions posed at p. 2293, ante. If a classification is not overtly based on gender, I am inclined to believe the question whether it is covertly gender-based is

26. See nn. 8, 17, supra.

27. The appellee has suggested that the former statutory exception for "women's requisitions," see nn. 13, 14, supra, supplies evidence that Massachusetts, when it established and subsequently reaffirmed the absolute preference legislation, assumed that women would not or should not compete with men. She has further suggested that the former provision extending the preference to certain female dependents of veterans, see n. 10, supra, demonstrates that ch. 31, § 23 is laced with "old notions" about the proper roles and needs of the sexes. See Califano v. Goldfarb, 430 U.S. 199, 97 S.Ct. 1021, 51 L.Ed.2d 270; Weinberger v. Wiesenfeld, 420 U.S. 636, 95 S.Ct. 1225, 43 L.Ed.2d 514. But the first suggestion is totally belied by the statutory history, see pp. 2290–2292 and nn. 19, 20, supra, and the second fails to account for the consistent statutory recognition of the contribution of women to this Nation's military efforts.

28. See generally Veterans' Preference Oversight Hearings before Subcomm. on Civil Service, 95th Cong., 1st Sess. (1977); Report of Comptroller General, Conflicting Congressional Policies: Veterans' Preference and Apportionment vs. Equal Employment Opportunity (Sept. 29, 1977).

the same as the question whether its adverse effects reflect invidious gender-based discrimination. However the question is phrased, for me the answer is largely provided by the fact that the number of males disadvantaged by Massachusetts' Veterans Preference (1,867,000) is sufficiently large—and sufficiently close to the number of disadvantaged females (2,954,000)—to refute the claim that the rule was intended to benefit males as a class over females as a class.

MR. JUSTICE MARSHALL, with whom MR. JUSTICE BRENNAN joins, dissenting.

Although acknowledging that in some circumstances, discriminatory intent may be inferred from the inevitable or foreseeable impact of a statute, ante, at 2296 n. 25, the Court concludes that no such intent has been established here. I cannot agree. In my judgment, Massachusetts' choice of an absolute veterans' preference system evinces purposeful gender-based discrimination. And because the statutory scheme bears no substantial relationship to a legitimate governmental objective, it cannot withstand scrutiny under the Equal Protection Clause.

I

The District Court found that the "prime objective" of the Massachusetts Veterans Preference Statute, Mass.Gen.Laws, ch. 31, § 23, was to benefit individuals with prior military service. 415 F.Supp. 485, 497 (Mass.1976). See 451 F.Supp. 143, 145 (Mass.1978). Under the Court's analysis, this factual determination "necessarily compels the conclusion that the State intended nothing more than to prefer 'veterans.' Given this finding, simple logic suggests than an intent to exclude women from significant public jobs was not at work in this law." Ante, at 2295. I find the Court's logic neither simple nor compelling.

That a legislature seeks to advantage one group does not, as a matter of logic or of common sense, exclude the possibility that it also intends to disadvantage another. Individuals in general and lawmakers in particular frequently act for a variety of reasons. As this Court recognized in Arlington Heights v. Metropolitan Housing Development Corp., 429 U.S. 252, 265, 97 S.Ct. 555, 563, 50 L.Ed.2d 450 (1977), "[r]arely can it be said that a legislature or administrative body operating under a broad mandate made a decision motivated by a single concern." Absent an omniscience not commonly attributed to the judiciary, it will often be impossible to ascertain the sole or even dominant purpose of a given statute. See McGinnis v. Royster, 410 U.S. 263, 276–277, 93 S.Ct. 1055, 1062–1063, 35 L.Ed.2d 282 (1973); Ely, Legislative and Administrative Motivation in Constitutional Law, 79 Yale L.J. 1205, 1214 (1970). Thus, the critical constitutional inquiry is not whether an illicit consideration was the primary or but-for cause of a decision, but rather whether it had an appreciable role in shaping a given legislative enactment. Where there is "proof that a discriminatory purpose has been *a* motivating factor in the decision, * * * judicial deference is no longer justified." Arlington Heights v. Metropolitan Housing Corp., supra, 429 U.S., at 265–266, 97 S.Ct., at 563 (emphasis added).

Moreover, since reliable evidence of subjective intentions is seldom obtainable, resort to inference based on objective factors is generally unavoidable. See Beer v. United States, 425 U.S. 130, 148–149, n. 4, 96 S.Ct. 1357, 1367, n. 4, 47 L.Ed.2d 629 (1976) (MARSHALL, J., dissenting); cf. Palmer v. Thompson, 403 U.S. 217, 224–225, 91 S.Ct. 1940, 1944–1945, 29 L.Ed.2d 438 (1971); United States v. O'Brien, 391 U.S. 367, 383–384, 88 S.Ct. 1673, 1682–1683, 20 L.Ed.2d 672 (1968). To discern the purposes underlying facially neutral policies, this Court has therefore considered the degree, inevitability, and foreseeability of any disproportionate impact as well as the alternatives reasonably available. See Monroe v. Board of Commissioners, 391 U.S. 450, 459, 88 S.Ct. 1700, 1705, 20 L.Ed.2d 733 (1968); Goss v. Board of Education, 373 U.S. 683, 688–689, 83 S.Ct. 1405, 1408–1409, 10 L.Ed.2d 632 (1963); Gomillion v. Lightfoot, 364 U.S. 339, 81 S.Ct. 125, 5 L.Ed.2d 110 (1960); Griffin v. Illinois, 351 U.S. 12, 17 n. 11, 76 S.Ct. 585, 590 n. 11, 100 L.Ed. 891 (1956). Cf. Albemarle Paper Co. v. Moody, 422 U.S. 405, 425, 95 S.Ct. 2362, 2375, 45 L.Ed.2d 280 (1975).

In the instant case, the impact of the Massachusetts statute on women is undisputed. Any veteran with a passing grade on the civil service exam must be placed ahead of a nonveteran, regardless of their respective scores. The District Court found that, as a practical matter, this preference supplants test results as the determinant of upper-level civil service appointments. 415 F.Supp., at 488–489. Because less than 2% of the women in Massachusetts are veterans, the absolute preference formula has rendered desirable state civil service employment an almost exclusively male prerogative. 451 F.Supp., at 151 (Campbell, J., concurring).

As the District Court recognized, this consequence followed foreseeably, indeed inexorably, from the long history of policies severely limiting women's participation in the military.[1] Although neutral in

1. See 415 F.Supp. 485, 490, 495–499 (Mass.1976); 451 F.Supp. 143, 145, 148 (Mass.1978). In addition to the 2% quota on women's participation in the armed forces, see ante, at 2291 n. 21, enlistment and appointment requirements have been more stringent for females than males with respect to age, mental and physical aptitude, parental consent, and educational attainment. M. Binkin and S. Bach, Women and the Military (1977) (hereinafter Binkin and Bach); Note, The Equal Rights Amendment and the Military, 82 Yale L.J. 1533, 1539 (1973). Until the 1970's, the armed forces precluded enlistment and appointment of women, but not men, who were married or had dependent children. See 415 F.Supp. at 490; App. 85; Exs. 98, 99, 103, 104. Sex-based restrictions on advancement and training opportunities also diminished the incentives for qualified women to enlist. See Binkin and Bach 10–17; Beans, Sex Discrimination in the Military, 67 Milit.L.Rev. 19, 59–83 (1979). Cf. Schlesinger v. Ballard, 419 U.S. 498, 508, 95 S.Ct. 572, 577, 42 L.Ed.2d 610 (1975).

Thus, unlike the employment examination in Washington v. Davis, 426 U.S. 229, 96 S.Ct. 2040, 48 L.Ed.2d 597 (1976), which the Court found to be demonstrably job-related, the Massachusetts preference statute incorporates the results of sex-based military policies irrelevant to women's current fitness for civilian public employment. See 415 F.Supp., at 498–499.

form, the statute is anything but neutral in application. It inescapably reserves a major sector of public employment to "an already established class which, as a matter of historical fact, is 98% male." Ibid. Where the foreseeable impact of a facially neutral policy is so disproportionate, the burden should rest on the State to establish that sex-based considerations played no part in the choice of the particular legislative scheme. Cf. Castaneda v. Partida, 430 U.S. 482, 97 S.Ct. 1272, 51 L.Ed.2d 498 (1977); Washington v. Davis, 426 U.S. 229, 241, 96 S.Ct. 2040, 2048, 48 L.Ed.2d 597 (1976); Alexander v. Louisiana, 405 U.S. 625, 632, 92 S.Ct. 1221, 1226, 31 L.Ed.2d 536 (1972); see generally Brest, Palmer v. Thompson: An Approach to the Problem of Unconstitutional Legislative Motive, 1971 Sup.Ct.L.Rev. 95, 123.

Clearly, that burden was not sustained here. The legislative history of the statute reflects the Commonwealth's patent appreciation of the impact the preference system would have on women, and an equally evident desire to mitigate that impact only with respect to certain traditionally female occupations. Until 1971, the statute and implementing civil service regulations exempted from operation of the preference any job requisitions "especially calling for women." 1954 Mass. Acts, ch. 627, § 5. See also 1896 Mass. Acts, ch. 517, § 6; 1919 Mass. Acts, ch. 150, § 2; 1945 Mass. Acts, ch. 725, § 2(e); 1965 Mass. Acts, ch. 53, § 2; ante, at 2289, nn. 13, 14. In practice, this exemption, coupled with the absolute preference for veterans, has created a gender-based civil service hierarchy, with women occupying low grade clerical and secretarial jobs and men holding more responsible and remunerative positions. See 415 F.Supp., at 488; 451 F.Supp., at 148 n. 9.

Thus, for over 70 years, the Commonwealth has maintained, as an integral part of its veteran's preference system, an exemption relegating female civil service applicants to occupations traditionally filled by women. Such a statutory scheme both reflects and perpetuates precisely the kind of archaic assumptions about women's roles which we have previously held invalid. See Orr v. Orr, 440 U.S. 268, 99 S.Ct. 1102, 59 L.Ed.2d 306 (1979); Califano v. Goldfarb, 430 U.S. 199, 210–211, 97 S.Ct. 1021, 1028–1029, 51 L.Ed.2d 270 (1977); Stanton v. Stanton, 421 U.S. 7, 14, 95 S.Ct. 1373, 1377, 43 L.Ed.2d 688 (1975); Weinberger v. Wiesenfeld, 420 U.S. 636, 645, 95 S.Ct. 1225, 1231, 43 L.Ed.2d 514 (1975). Particularly when viewed against the range of less discriminatory alternatives available to assist veterans,[2] Massachusetts' choice of a formula that so severely restricts public employment opportunities for women cannot reasonably be thought gender-neutral. Cf. Albemarle Paper Co. v. Moody, supra, 422 U.S., at 425, 95 S.Ct., at 2375. The

2. Only four States afford a preference comparable in scope to that of Massachusetts. See Fleming and Shanor, Veterans' Preferences and Public Employment: Unconstitutional Gender Discrimination?, 26 Emory L.J. 13, 17 n. 13 (1977) (citing statutes). Other States and the Federal Government grant point or tie-breaking preferences that do not foreclose opportunities for women. See id., at 13, and nn. 13, 14; ante, at 2287 n. 7; Hearings before the Subcommittee on Civil Service of the House Committee on Post Office and Civil Service, 95th Cong., 1st Sess., 4 (1977) (statement of Alan Campbell, Chairman, U.S.Civil Service Commission).

Court's conclusion to the contrary—that "nothing in the record" evinces a "collateral goal of keeping women in a stereotypic and predefined place in the Massachusetts Civil Service," ante, at 2296—displays a singularly myopic view of the facts established below.[3]

II

To survive challenge under the Equal Protection Clause, statutes reflecting gender-based discrimination must be substantially related to the achievement of important governmental objectives. See Califano v. Webster, 430 U.S. 313, 316–317, 97 S.Ct. 1192, 1194–1195, 51 L.Ed.2d 360 (1977); Craig v. Boren, 429 U.S. 190, 197, 97 S.Ct. 451, 456, 50 L.Ed.2d 397 (1976); Reed v. Reed, 404 U.S. 71, 76, 92 S.Ct. 251, 254, 30 L.Ed.2d 225 (1971). Appellants here advance three interests in support of the absolute preference system: (1) assisting veterans in their readjustment to civilian life; (2) encouraging military enlistment; and (3) rewarding those who have served their country. Brief for Appellants 24. Although each of those goals is unquestionably legitimate, the "mere recitation of a benign compensatory purpose" cannot of itself insulate legislative classifications from constitutional scrutiny. Weinberger v. Wiesenfeld, supra, 420 U.S., at 648, 95 S.Ct., at 1233. And in this case, the Commonwealth has failed to establish a sufficient relationship between its objectives and the means chosen to effectuate them.

With respect to the first interest, facilitating veterans' transition to civilian status, the statute is plainly overinclusive. Cf. Trimble v. Gordon, 430 U.S. 762, 770–772, 97 S.Ct. 1459, 1465–1466, 52 L.Ed.2d 31 (1971); Jimenez v. Weinberger, 417 U.S. 628, 637, 94 S.Ct. 2496, 2502, 41 L.Ed.2d 363 (1974). By conferring a permanent preference, the legislation allows veterans to invoke their advantage repeatedly, without regard to their date of discharge. As the record demonstrates, a substantial majority of those currently enjoying the benefits of the system are not recently discharged veterans in need of readjustment assistance.[4]

Nor is the Commonwealth's second asserted interest, encouraging military service, a plausible justification for this legislative scheme. In its original and subsequent re-enactments, the statute extended benefits retroactively to veterans who had served during a prior specified period. See ante, at 2289. If the Commonwealth's "actual purpose" is to induce enlistment, this legislative design is hardly well-suited to that

3. Although it is relevant that the preference statute also disadvantages a substantial group of men, see ante, at 2285 (STEVENS, J., concurring), it is equally pertinent that 47% of Massachusetts men over 18 are veterans, as compared to 0.8% of Massachusetts women. App. 83. Given this disparity, and the indicia of intent noted at p. 2287, supra, the absolute number of men denied preference cannot be dispositive, especially since they have not faced the barriers to achieving veteran status confronted by women. See n. 1, supra.

4. The eligibility lists for the positions Ms. Feeney sought included 95 veterans for whom discharge information was available. Of those 95 males, 64 (67%) were discharged prior to 1960. App. 106, 150–151, 169–170.

end. See Califano v. Webster, supra, 430 U.S., at 317, 97 S.Ct., at 1195; Weinberger v. Wiesenfeld, supra, 420 U.S., at 648, 95 S.Ct., at 1233. For I am unwilling to assume what appellants made no effort to prove, that the possibility of obtaining an *ex post facto* civil service preference significantly influenced the enlistment decisions of Massachusetts residents. Moreover, even if such influence could be presumed, the statute is still grossly overinclusive in that it bestows benefits on men drafted as well as those who volunteered.

Finally, the Commonwealth's third interest, rewarding veterans, does not "adequately justify the salient features" of this preference system. Craig v. Boren, 429 U.S., at 202, 97 S.Ct., at 459. See Orr v. Orr, 440 U.S., at 281, 99 S.Ct., at 1113. Where a particular statutory scheme visits substantial hardship on a class long subject to discrimination, the legislation cannot be sustained unless "carefully tuned to alternative considerations." Trimble v. Gordon, supra, 430 U.S., at 772, 97 S.Ct., at 1466. See Caban v. Mohammed, 441 U.S. 380, 392 n. 13, 99 S.Ct. 1760, 1768, n. 13, 60 L.Ed.2d 297 (1979); Mathews v. Lucas, 427 U.S. 495, 96 S.Ct. 2755, 49 L.Ed.2d 651 (1976). Here, there are a wide variety of less discriminatory means by which Massachusetts could effect its compensatory purposes. For example, a point preference system, such as that maintained by many States and the Federal Government, see n. 2, supra, or an absolute preference for a limited duration, would reward veterans without excluding all qualified women from upper level civil service positions. Apart from public employment, the Commonwealth, can, and does, afford assistance to veterans in various ways, including tax abatements, educational subsidies, and special programs for needy veterans. See Mass.Gen.Laws Ann., ch. 59, § 5 (West Supp.1979); Mass.Gen.Laws Ann., ch. 69, §§ 7, 7B (West Supp.1979); and Mass.Gen.Laws Ann., chs. 115, 115A (West Supp.1978). Unlike these and similar benefits, the costs of which are distributed across the taxpaying public generally, the Massachusetts statute exacts a substantial price from a discrete group of individuals who have long been subject to employment discrimination,[5] and who, "because of circumstances totally beyond their control, have [had] little if any chance of becoming members of the preferred class." 415 F.Supp., at 499. See n. 1, supra.

In its present unqualified form, the Veterans Preference Statute precludes all but a small fraction of Massachusetts women from obtaining any civil service position also of interest to men. See 451 F.Supp., at 151 (Campbell, J., concurring). Given the range of alternatives available, this degree of preference is not constitutionally permissible.

I would affirm the judgment of the court below.

5. See Frontiero v. Richardson, 411 U.S. 677, 689 n. 23, 93 S.Ct. 1764, 1772 n. 23, 36 L.Ed.2d 583 (1973); Kahn v. Shevin, 416 U.S. 351, 353–354, 94 S.Ct. 1734, 1736–1737, 40 L.Ed.2d 189 (1974); United States Bureau of the Census, Current Population Reports, No. 107, Money Income and Poverty Status of Families and Persons in the United States: 1976 (Advance Report) (Table 7) (Sept. 1977).

NOTES AND PROBLEMS FOR DISCUSSION

1. If a private business enacted its own veterans' preference rule, would a suit similar to *Feeney*, but with a cause of action based on Title VII, be likely to produce a different result? Could the plaintiff establish a prima facie case by the introduction of evidence similar to that introduced in *Feeney*? Would the employer's desire to reward veterans for their military service constitute a defense under Title VII? See infra, at Chapter 2, Section C.

2. Had the majority of the Court in *Feeney* found that a bias against women, at least in part, underlay the veteran's preference law, would the plaintiff necessarily have prevailed? As indicated in the majority opinion, in equal protection cases under the Fifth and Fourteenth amendments, "strict scrutiny" is applied to classifications drawn along lines of race, i.e., "suspect" classifications. Such classifications are allowed to stand only if the state can demonstrate that they serve a "compelling" governmental interest that cannot be achieved by other means. See McLaughlin v. Florida, 379 U.S. 184, 85 S.Ct. 283, 13 L.Ed.2d 222 (1964). Despite the similarities between classifications based on sex and those based on race, the Supreme Court has declined to treat sex as a "suspect" classification so as to call for "strict-scrutiny", although, at one time, four members of the Court expressed this view. See Frontiero v. Richardson, 411 U.S. 677, 93 S.Ct. 1764, 36 L.Ed.2d 583 (1973). The Court instead has applied an intermediate standard of review under which sex based classifications which serve "important" governmental interests and are "substantially related" to the achievement of those objectives, are upheld as not violative of equal protection. See Craig v. Boren, 429 U.S. 190, 97 S.Ct. 451, 50 L.Ed.2d 397 (1976); Orr v. Orr, 440 U.S. 268, 99 S.Ct. 1102, 59 L.Ed.2d 306 (1979); Mississippi University for Women v. Hogan, 458 U.S. 718, 102 S.Ct. 3331, 73 L.Ed.2d 1090 (1982). See also Tribe, American Constitutional Law, p. 1063–1066 (1978). What level of scrutiny do Justices Marshall and Brennan feel the veterans' preference should be subjected to?

3. In WASHINGTON v. DAVIS, 426 U.S. 229, 96 S.Ct. 2040, 48 L.Ed.2d 597 (1976), unsuccessful black applicants for the Washington, D.C. police force alleged that employment policies of the department violated the due process clause of the Fifth Amendment, 42 U.S.C. § 1981, and certain provisions of the D.C. Code. Although it was uncontradicted that black applicants failed a pre-employment screening test at a rate four times greater than white applicants, the district court granted summary judgment to defendants in part on the ground that there was no evidence of intentional discrimination. Relying on Griggs v. Duke Power Co., the Court of Appeals reversed, holding that the disproportionate impact of the test on black applicants was sufficient to establish a constitutional violation, absent evidence that the test was job related, and that the plaintiffs were not required to show that racial considerations prompted defendants to use the test. The Supreme Court reversed. To make out a prima facie case of discrimination under the Due Process Clause of the Fifth Amendment or the Equal Protection Clause of the Fourteenth Amendment, plaintiffs must produce evidence that the defendants' actions resulted from discriminatory purposes. If the plaintiff makes such a showing, the burden shifts to the defendant "to rebut the presumption of unconstitutional action." 426 U.S. at 241, 96 S.Ct., at 2048. But, standing alone, disproportionate impact, though relevant, "does not trigger the rule * * * that racial classifications are to be subjected to the strictest scrutiny and are justifiable only by the weightiest of considerations." 426 U.S. at 242, 96 S.Ct. at 2049. In

VILLAGE OF ARLINGTON HEIGHTS v. METROPOLITAN HOUSING DEVELOPMENT CORP., 429 U.S. 252, 97 S.Ct. 555, 50 L.Ed.2d 450 (1977), a suit alleging that the refusal of a municipality to allow the construction of low income multi-family dwellings was racially discriminatory, the Court reaffirmed that evidence of disproportionate impact alone was insufficient to establish a prima facie case of discrimination under the Fourteenth Amendment. The Court noted, however, that the plaintiff is not required to show that a discriminatory purpose was the *sole* basis for the challenged action. "When there is proof that a discriminatory purpose has been a motivating factor in the decision" the rules regarding strict scrutiny are applicable. 429 U.S. at 265–266, 97 S.Ct., at 563–564.

As noted in both the majority and dissenting opinion in *Feeney*, courts have frequently inferred intent and motivation from an individual's ability to foresee the natural consequences of his acts. What more does the majority in *Feeney* require that the plaintiff show to establish intent? Does the decision mean that intent may not be proved by circumstantial evidence alone? As a practical matter, direct proof of illegal intent, the proverbial "smoking gun," is rare.

> "[I]t is difficult and often futile—to obtain direct evidence of the official's intentions. Rather than announce his intention of violating antidiscrimination laws, it is far more likely that the state official 'will pursue his discriminatory practices in ways that are devious, by methods subtle and illusive—for we deal with an area in which subtleties of conduct * * * play no small part.' "

United States v. Texas Education Agency, 532 F.2d 380, 388 (5th Cir. 1976), vacated for reconsideration in light of Washington v. Davis, 429 U.S. 990, 97 S.Ct. 517, 50 L.Ed.2d 603 (1976). The Fifth Circuit has also stated that:

> Neither the Supreme Court nor this Court, however, has denied relief when the weight of the evidence proved a plan to intentionally discriminate, even when its true purpose was cleverly cloaked in the guise of propriety. The existence of a right to redress does not turn on the degree of subtlety with which a discriminatory plan is effectuated. Circumstantial evidence, of necessity, must suffice, so long as the inference of discriminatory intent is clear.

Lodge v. Buxton, 639 F.2d 1358, 1363 (5th Cir. 1981), affirmed, 458 U.S. 613, 102 S.Ct. 3272, 73 L.Ed.2d 1012 (1982). If the district court in *Feeney* had found a discriminatory purpose underlying the veterans' preference act, would that finding have been "clearly erroneous" under Rule 52(a) of the Federal Rules of Civil Procedure? See Arlington Heights v. Metropolitan Housing Development Corp., supra, 429 U.S. at 266, 97 S.Ct., at 563.

Should impact-type evidence be more probative of improper intent in a non-legislative context? For example, assume a public employer has hired an unbroken string of white applicants to fill job openings for each of which there were equally qualified black applicants. The employer denies any racial motivation and explains that in each case his decision was based on his subjective determination of who would do the best job. Would such evidence establish a prima facie case of an equal protection violation under the *Feeney* rationale? Is there any reason to impose on plaintiffs with constitutional causes of action a higher burden than is placed on plaintiffs alleging disparate treatment under Title VII?

4. As noted in *Feeney,* Section 1983 is a remedial statute that does not create substantive rights but provides a remedy for the violation of rights

created elsewhere. Most 1983 actions, like *Feeney,* are based on constitutional violations. In Maine v. Thiboutot, 448 U.S. 1, 100 S.Ct. 2502, 65 L.Ed.2d 555 (1980), the Court held that Section 1983 also provides a remedy for actions taken under color of state law which contravene federal substantive statutes. The right to base a Section 1983 action on a Title VII violation would significantly expand the relief available to plaintiffs with employment discrimination claims against public agencies. In Day v. Wayne County Board of Auditors, 749 F.2d 1199 (6th Cir. 1984), the plaintiff filed an action against his employer under Title VII and Section 1983. The district court found that the employer had retaliated against the plaintiff for filing EEOC charges in violation of § 704 and granted back pay and injunctive relief. The court also found that the plaintiff had failed to establish discrimination on the basis of race or age and denied damages relief under § 1983. The plaintiff appealed, arguing that under Maine v. Thiboutot the Title VII violation constituted as a matter of law a violation of § 1983. The Court of Appeals affirmed.

> Though the issue is not without doubt, we believe Title VII provides the exclusive remedy when the only § 1983 cause of action is based on a violation of Title VII. * * * It would be anomalous to hold that when the only unlawful employment practice consists of the violation of a right created by Title VII, the plaintiff can by-pass all of the administrative processes of Title VII and go directly into court under § 1983.

749 F.2d at 1204. See also, Morgan v. Humboldt County School District, 623 F.Supp 440 (D.Nev.1985) (statutory scheme of age discrimination act would be thwarted if employee could pursue § 1983 suit based on ADEA violation).

The Sixth Circuit in *Day* was careful to distinguish that case from one in which the § 1983 claim was based on a constitutional violation.

> Where an employee establishes employer conduct which violates both Title VII and rights derived from another source—the Constitution or a federal statute—which existed at the time of the enactment of Title VII, the claim based on the other source is independent of the Title VII claim, and the plaintiff may seek the remedies provided by § 1983 in addition to those created by Title VII.

749 F.2d at 1205. See also, Tafoya v. Adams, 612 F.Supp. 1097 (D.Colo.1985); Meyett v. Coleman, 613 F.Supp. 39 (W.D.Wis.1985). Other courts have concluded, however, that the 1972 Amendments to Title VII, which extended the Act to public employers, made Title VII the *exclusive* remedy for employment discrimination by public agencies thus precluding § 1983 suits regardless of the substantive cause of action. See, Keller v. Prince George's County Dept. of Social Services, 616 F.Supp. 540 (D.Md.1985); Torres v. Wisconsin Dept. of Health & Social Services, 592 F.Supp. 922 (E.D.Wis.1984) and supra, Chapter 6, Section B.

If a Title VII suit is dismissed for failure to comply with the administrative prerequisites should a subsequent Section 1983 suit, based on the same facts alleged in the Title VII action, be barred by the doctrine of *res judicata?* See, Nilsen v. Moss Point, 701 F.2d 556 (5th Cir. 1983) (*en banc*).

5. A continuing problem for plaintiffs in Section 1983 litigation is in determining the appropriate party defendant. In MONROE v. PAPE, 365 U.S. 167, 81 S.Ct. 473, 5 L.Ed.2d 492 (1961), the Supreme Court held that because of the explicit language of the Act ("Every person who * * * subjects or causes to be subjects or causes to be subjected any citizen * * *"), only human beings and not institutions or corporate political bodies were proper

party defendants in a § 1983 case. See also City of Kenosha v. Bruno, 412 U.S. 507, 93 S.Ct. 2222, 37 L.Ed.2d 109 (1973). Thus, for a number of years § 1983 actions were normally filed against the public officials whose actions were challenged rather than the agency or political body which they represented. See Aldinger v. Howard, 427 U.S. 1, 96 S.Ct. 2413, 49 L.Ed.2d 276 (1976). (Note that *Feeney*, filed in 1975, was a suit against the administrator, not his agency.) But in 1977, the Supreme Court, following the lead of a number of circuits, recognized that a direct action under the Fourteenth Amendment could be instituted against a public body if jurisdiction was proper under 28 U.S.C. § 1331 (general federal question jurisdiction), Mt. Healthy City School District Board of Education v. Doyle, 429 U.S. 274, 277–278, 97 S.Ct. 568, 571, 50 L.Ed. 2d 471 (1977), and in MONELL v. DEPARTMENT OF SOCIAL SERVICES, 436 U.S. 658, 98 S.Ct. 2018, 56 L.Ed.2d 611 (1978), the Court finally overruled Monroe v. Pape and held that local governing bodies could be sued as "persons" under 42 U.S.C. § 1983 for monetary, declaratory, and injunctive relief where the unlawful action implemented or executed "a policy or custom" of the governing unit. The Court made clear, however, that public agencies would not be liable for all illegal acts of their employees on the theory of *respondeat superior*. "Instead, it is when execution of a government's policy or custom, whether made by its lawmakers or by those whose edicts or acts may fairly be said to represent official policy, inflicts the injury that the government as an entity is responsible under § 1983." 436 U.S. at 691–95, 98 S.Ct. 2036–2038. Since individual officials will often be unable to pay damage awards, a critical question in post-*Monell* litigation is whether the actions of the officials in question reflect or establish the "policy" of the public body. See e.g., Oklahoma City v. Tuttle, 471 U.S. ___, 105 S.Ct. 2427, 85 L.Ed.2d 791 (1985) (fact that official has discretion in exercise of particular functions does not without more give rise to municipal liability based on exercise of that discretion); Pembaur v. Cincinnati, et al., ___ U.S. ___, 106 S.Ct. 1292, 89 L.Ed.2d 452 (1986) (if decision to adopt particular course of action is directed by those who establish government policy, the municipality is responsible whether that action is taken only once or repeatedly); Schnapper, Civil Rights Litigation After Monell, 79 Colum.L.Rev. 213, 217–19 (1979). In the employment context, the personnel decisions of officials with the final authority over hiring and firing will probably be treated as the official policy of the agency. See, Williams v. Butler, 746 F.2d 431, 438 (8th Cir. 1984) (city that gave municipal judge carte blanche authority to make personnel decisions and provided no internal procedure for redress of grievances is liable for illegal discharge of judge's clerk); Gross v. San Jacinto Junior College, 588 F.2d 96, 98, vacated and modified in part on other grounds, 595 F.2d 1119 (5th Cir. 1979) (president of college who discharged teacher was one whose acts represent official policy).

6. It is not necessary to exhaust available state administrative remedies as a prerequisite to filing a Section 1983 action. This is the case even if the relief available at the administrative level would fully compensate the claimant. PATSY v. BOARD OF REGENTS OF THE STATE OF FLORIDA, 457 U.S. 496, 102 S.Ct. 2557, 73 L.Ed.2d 172 (1982). The claimant may find it useful to take advantage of the internal grievance procedure of the agency before filing his federal suit, but if the final stage of such procedure is a *judicial* review, he may be precluded by the doctrine of res judicata from litigating the federal claim. See, supra, Chapter 5, at 398.

SECTION C. THE CIVIL RIGHTS ACT OF 1871, SECTION TWO—42 U.S.C.A. § 1985(c)

Section 2 of the Civil Rights Act of 1871,[a] now codified at 42 U.S.C. § 1985(c), was enacted primarily to provide protection to southern blacks and Union sympathizers from the violent activities of the Ku Klux Klan, by outlawing conspiracies to deprive persons of "the equal protection of the laws, or of equal privileges and immunities under the law." Since § 1985(c)—like its statutory counterpart, § 1983 (originally § 1 of the 1871 Act)—was enacted pursuant to the Fourteenth Amendment, it was interpreted initially to prohibit only those conspiracies involving state action. In Griffin v. Breckenridge,[b] however, the Supreme Court ruled that black plaintiffs claiming that they were beaten by a group of private white citizens could state a cause of action under § 1985(c) without alleging either state action or that the defendants acted under color of state law, since their complaint alleged a "class-based invidiously discriminatory" conspiracy to deprive them of their thirteenth amendment right to be free from slavery and constitutional right of interstate travel. Since the decision in *Griffin*, several questions have arisen in connection with the application of § 1985(c) to employment discrimination claims.[c] For example, did the Court intend to preclude the extension of § 1985(c) to private conspiracies aimed at depriving persons of other constitutionally or statutorily guaranteed rights? In addition, is the requirement of a "class-based" discriminatory intent restricted to conspiracies motivated by racial animus? Finally, can a plaintiff satisfy the statutory "two or more persons" requirement where the complaint alleges a conspiracy between a corporation and its agents?

Read 42 USCA § 1985 at p. 1043.

GREAT AMERICAN FEDERAL SAVINGS & LOAN ASSOCIATION v. NOVOTNY

Supreme Court of the United States, 1979.
442 U.S. 366, 99 S.Ct. 2345, 60 L.Ed.2d 957.

MR. JUSTICE STEWART delivered the opinion of the Court.

More than a century after their passage, the Civil Rights Acts of the Reconstruction era continue to present difficult problems of statutory construction. Cf. Chapman v. Houston Welfare Rights Org., 441 U.S. 600, 99 S.Ct. 1905, 60 L.Ed.2d 508. In the case now before us, we consider the scope of 42 U.S.C. § 1985(c), the surviving version of § 2 of the Civil Rights Act of 1871.

[a] Act of April 20, 1871, ch. 22, § 2, 17 Stat. 13 (1871).

[b] 403 U.S. 88, 91 S.Ct. 1790, 29 L.Ed.2d 338 (1971).

[c] For a provocative critique of the application of § 1985(c) to employment discrimination claims, see Comment, A Construction of § 1985(c) In light of Its Original Purpose, 46 U.Chi.L.Rev. 402 (1979).

I

The respondent, John R. Novotny, began his career with the Great American Federal Savings and Loan Association (hereinafter the Association) in Allegheny County, Pa., in 1950. By 1975, he was secretary of the Association, a member of its board of directors, and a loan officer. According to the allegations of the complaint in this case the Association "intentionally and deliberately embarked upon and pursued a course of conduct the effect of which was to deny to female employees equal employment opportunity * * *." When Novotny expressed support for the female employees at a meeting of the board of directors, his connection with the Association abruptly ended. He was not re-elected as secretary; he was not re-elected to the board; and he was fired. His support for the Association's female employees, he alleges, was the cause of the termination of his employment.

Novotny filed a complaint with the Equal Employment Opportunity Commission under Title VII of the Civil Rights Act of 1964. After receiving a right-to-sue letter, he brought this lawsuit against the Association and its directors in the District Court for the Western District of Pennsylvania. He claimed damages under 42 U.S.C. § 1985(c), contending that he had been injured as the result of a conspiracy to deprive him of equal protection of and equal privileges and immunities under the laws.[4] The District Court granted the defendants' motion to dismiss. It held that § 1985(c) could not be invoked because the directors of a single corporation could not, as a matter of law and fact, engage in a conspiracy.[5]

Novotny appealed. After oral argument before a three-judge panel, the case was reargued before the en banc Court of Appeals for the Third Circuit, which unanimously reversed the District Court's judgment. The Court of Appeals ruled that Novotny had stated a cause of action under § 1985(c). It held that conspiracies motivated by an invidious animus against women fall within § 1985(c), and that Novotny, a male allegedly injured as a result of such a conspiracy, had standing to bring suit under that statutory provision. It ruled that Title VII could be the source of a right asserted in an action under § 1985(c), and that intracorporate conspiracies come within the intendment of the section. Finally, the court concluded that its construction of § 1985(c) did not present any serious constitutional problem.[6]

4. His complaint also alleged, as a second cause of action, that his discharge was in retaliation for his efforts on behalf of equal employment opportunity, and thus violated § 704(a) of Title VII. * * *

5. As to the Title VII claim, the District Court held that Novotny was not a proper plaintiff under § 704(a).

6. The Court of Appeals ruled that Novotny had also stated a valid cause of action under Title VII. It held that § 704(a) applies to retaliation for both formal and informal actions taken to advance the purposes of the Act. That holding is not now before this Court.

We note the relative narrowness of the specific issue before the Court. It is unnecessary for us to consider whether a plaintiff would have a cause of action under § 1985(c) where the defendant was not subject to suit under Title VII or a comparable statute. Nor do we think it necessary to

We granted certiorari, 439 U.S. 1066, 99 S.Ct. 830, 59 L.Ed.2d 30, to consider the applicability of § 1985(c) to the facts alleged in Novotny's complaint.

II

The legislative history of § 2 of the Civil Rights Act of 1871, of which § 1985(c) was originally a part, has been reviewed many times in this Court. The section as first enacted authorized both criminal and civil actions against those who have conspired to deprive others of federally guaranteed rights. Before the 19th century ended, however, the Court found the criminal provisions of the statute unconstitutional because they exceeded the scope of congressional power, and the provisions thus invalidated were later formally repealed by Congress. The civil action provided by the Act remained, but for many years was rarely, if ever, invoked.

The provisions of what is now § 1985(c) were not fully considered by this Court until 1951, in the case of Collins v. Hardyman, 341 U.S. 651, 71 S.Ct. 937, 95 L.Ed.2d 1253. There the Court concluded that the section protected citizens only from injuries caused by conspiracies "under color of state law." Twenty years later, in Griffin v. Breckenridge, 403 U.S. 88, 91 S.Ct. 1790, 29 L.Ed.2d 338, the Court unanimously concluded that the *Collins* Court had accorded to the provisions of § 1985(c) too narrow a scope. The fears concerning congressional power that had motivated the Court in the *Collins* case had been dissolved by intervening cases. Therefore, the Court found that § 1985(c) did provide a cause of action for damages caused by purely private conspiracies.

The Court's opinion in *Griffin* discerned the following criteria for measuring whether a complaint states a cause of action under § 1985(c):

> "To come within the legislation a complaint must allege that the defendants did (1) 'conspire or go in disguise on the highway or on the premises of another' (2) 'for the purpose of depriving, either directly or indirectly, any person or class of persons of the equal protection of the laws, or of equal privileges and immunities under the laws.' It must then assert that one or more of the conspirators (3) did, or caused to be done, 'any act in furtherance of the object of [the] conspiracy,' whereby another was (4a) 'injured in his person of property' or (4b) 'deprived of having and exercising any right or privilege of a citizen of the United States.' "

Section 1985(c) provides no substantive rights itself; it merely provides a remedy for violation of the rights it designates. The primary question in the present case, therefore, is whether a person injured by a conspiracy to violate § 704(a) of Title VII of the Civil Rights Act of 1964

consider whether § 1985(c) creates a remedy for statutory rights other than those fundamental rights derived from the Constitution.

is deprived of "the equal protection of the laws, or of equal privileges and immunities under the laws" within the meaning of § 1985(c).[11]

Under Title VII, cases of alleged employment discrimination are subject to a detailed administrative and judicial process designed to provide an opportunity for nonjudicial and nonadversary resolution of claims. * * *

* * * The majority of the federal courts have held that the Act does not allow a court to award general or punitive damages. The Act expressly allows the prevailing party to recover his attorney's fees, and, in some cases, provides that a district court may appoint counsel for a plaintiff. Because the Act expressly authorizes only equitable remedies, the courts have consistently held that neither party has a right to a jury trial.

If a violation of Title VII could be asserted through § 1985(c), a complainant could avoid most if not all of these detailed and specific provisions of the law. Section 1985(c) expressly authorizes compensatory damages; punitive damages might well follow. The plaintiff or defendant might demand a jury trial. The short and precise time limitations of Title VII would be grossly altered. Perhaps most importantly, the complainant could completely bypass the administrative process, which plays such a crucial role in the scheme established by Congress in Title VII.

The problem in this case is closely akin to that in Brown v. GSA, 425 U.S. 820, 96 S.Ct. 1961, 48 L.Ed.2d 402. There, we held that § 717 of Title VII provides the exclusive remedy for employment discrimination claims of those federal employees that it covers. Our conclusion was based on the proposition that

> "[t]he balance, completeness, and structural integrity of § 717 are inconsistent with the petitioner's contention that the judicial remedy afforded by § 717(c) was designed merely to supplement other putative judicial relief."

Here the case is even more compelling. In *Brown*, the Court concluded that § 717 displaced other causes of action arguably available to assert substantive rights similar to those granted by § 717. Section 1985(c), by contrast, *creates* no rights. It is a purely remedial statute, providing a civil cause of action when some otherwise defined federal right—to equal protection of the laws or equal privileges and immunities under the laws—is breached by a conspiracy in the manner defined by the section. Thus, we are not faced in this case with a question of implied repeal. The right Novotny claims under § 704(a) did not even arguably exist before the passage of Title VII. The only question here, therefore, is whether the rights created by Title VII may be asserted within the *remedial* framework of § 1985(3).

11. For the purposes of this question, we assume but certainly do not decide that the directors of a single corporation can form a conspiracy within the meaning of § 1985(c).

This case thus differs markedly from the cases recently decided by this Court that have related the substantive provisions of last century's Civil Rights Acts to contemporary legislation conferring similar substantive rights. In those cases we have held that substantive rights conferred in the 19th century were not withdrawn, *sub silentio*, by the subsequent passage of the modern statutes. * * *

* * *

This case, by contrast, does not involve two "independent" rights, and for the same basic reasons that underlay the Court's decision in Brown v. GSA, supra, reinforced by the other considerations discussed in this opinion, we conclude that § 1985(c) may not be invoked to redress violations of Title VII. It is true that a § 1985(c) remedy would not be coextensive with Title VII, since a plaintiff in an action under § 1985(c) must prove both a conspiracy and a group animus that Title VII does not require. While this incomplete congruity would limit the damage that would be done to Title VII, it would not eliminate it. Unimpaired effectiveness can be given to the plan put together by Congress in Title VII only by holding that deprivation of a right created by Title VII cannot be the basis for a cause of action under § 1985(c).

Accordingly, the judgment of the Court of Appeals is vacated, and the case is remanded to that Court for further proceedings consistent with this opinion.

It is so ordered.

MR. JUSTICE POWELL, concurring.

* * *

The Court's specific holding is that 42 U.S.C. § 1985(c) may not be invoked to redress violations of Title VII. The broader issue argued to us in this case was whether this Civil War era remedial statute, providing no substantive rights itself, was intended to provide a remedy generally for the violation of subsequently created statutory rights. For essentially the reasons suggested by MR. JUSTICE STEVENS, I would hold that § 1985(c) should not be so construed, and that its reach is limited to conspiracies to violate those fundamental rights derived from the Constitution.

The Court's unanimous decision in Griffin v. Breckenridge, 403 U.S. 88, 91 S.Ct. 1790, 29 L.Ed.2d 338 (1971), is to this effect. The alleged conspiracy there was an attempt by white citizens, resorting to force and violence, to deprive Negro citizens of the right to use interstate highways. In sustaining a cause of action under § 1985(c), the Court found that the alleged conspiracy—if implemented—would violate the constitutional "right of interstate travel" as well as the right of Negro citizens to be free from "invidiously discriminatory" action. The Court declared:

> "That the statute was meant to reach private action does not, however, mean that it was intended to apply to all tortious, conspiratorial interferences with the rights of others. For, though the

supporters of the legislation insisted on coverage of private conspiracies, they were equally emphatic that they did not believe, in the words of Representative Cook, 'that Congress has a right to punish an assault and battery when committed by two or more persons within a State.' The constitutional shoals that would lie in the path of interpreting § 1985[(c)] as a general federal tort law can be avoided by giving full effect to the congressional purpose—by requiring, as an element of the cause of action, the kind of invidiously discriminatory motivation stressed by the sponsors of the limiting amendment. The language requiring intent to deprive of *equal* protection, or *equal* privileges and immunities, means that there must be some racial, or perhaps otherwise class-based, invidiously discriminatory animus behind the conspirators' action. The conspiracy, in other words, must aim at a deprivation of the equal enjoyment of rights secured by the law to all."

* * *

By contrast, this Court has never held that the right to any particular private employment is a "right of national citizenship," or derives from any other right created by the Constitution. Indeed, even Congress, in the exercise of its powers under the Commerce Clause of the Constitution, has accorded less than full protection to private employees. It excluded several classes of employers from the coverage of Title VII, for example, employers of fewer than 15 employees. Nor does the Constitution create any right to be free of gender-based discrimination perpetuated solely through private action.

The rationale of *Griffin* accords with the purpose, history, and common understanding of this Civil War era statute. Rather than leave federal courts in any doubt as to the scope of actions under § 1985(c), I would explicitly reaffirm the constitutional basis of *Griffin.**

MR. JUSTICE STEVENS, concurring.

* * *

Sections 1983 and 1985(c) of Title 42 of the United States Code are the surviving direct descendants of §§ 1 and 2 of the Civil Rights Act of 1871. Neither of these sections created any substantive rights. Earlier this Term we squarely held that § 1983 merely provides a remedy for certain violations of certain federal rights, and today the Court unequivocally holds that § 1985(c) "provides no substantive rights itself; it merely provides a remedy for violation of the rights it designates."

* * * The import of the language [of §§ 1983 and 1985(c)] as well as the relevant legislative history, suggests that the Congress which

* The doubts which will remain after the Court's decision are far from insubstantial. At least one federal court, for example, has held that although Title VII rights may not be asserted through § 1985(c), claims based on § 3 of the Equal Pay Act of 1963, may be raised in a § 1985(c) suit. I would take advantage of the present opportunity to make clear that this Civil War era statute was intended to provide a remedy *only* for conspiracies to violate fundamental rights derived from the Constitution.

enacted both provisions was concerned with providing federal remedies for deprivations of rights protected by the Constitution and, in particular, the newly ratified Fourteenth Amendment. If a violation was effected "under color of any law, statute, ordinance, regulation, custom, or usage of any State," § 1983 afforded redress; if a violation was caused by private persons who "conspire or go in disguise on the highway," § 1985(c) afforded redress. Thus, the former authorized a remedy for state action depriving an individual of his constitutional rights, the latter for private action.

Some privileges and immunities of citizenship, such as the right to engage in interstate travel and the right to be free of the badges of slavery, are protected by the Constitution against interference by private action, as well as impairment by state action. Private conspiracies to deprive individuals of these rights are, as this Court held in Griffin v. Breckenridge, 403 U.S. 88, 91 S.Ct. 1790, 29 L.Ed.2d 338, actionable under § 1985(c) without regard to any state involvement.

Other privileges and immunities of citizenship such as the right to due process of law and the right to the equal protection of the laws are protected by the Constitution only against state action. Shelley v. Kraemer, 334 U.S. 1, 13, 68 S.Ct. 836, 842, 92 L.Ed. 1161. If a state agency arbitrarily refuses to serve a class of persons—Chinese Americans, for example, see Yick Wo v. Hopkins, 118 U.S. 356, 6 S.Ct. 1064, 30 L.Ed. 220—it violates the Fourteenth Amendment. Or if private persons take conspiratorial action that prevents or hinders the constituted authorities of any State from giving or securing equal treatment, the private persons would cause those authorities to violate the Fourteenth Amendment; the private persons would then have violated § 1985(c).

If, however, private persons engage in purely private acts of discrimination—for example, if they discriminate against women or against lawyers with a criminal practice, they do not violate the Equal Protection Clause of the Fourteenth Amendment. The rights secured by the Equal Protection and Due Process Clauses of the Fourteenth Amendment are rights to protection against unequal or unfair treatment by the State, not by private parties. Thus, while § 1985(c) does not require that a defendant act under color of state law, there still can be no claim for relief based on a violation of the Fourteenth Amendment if there has been no involvement by the State. The requirement of state action, in this context, is no more than a requirement that there be a constitutional violation.

Here, there is no claim of such a violation. Private discrimination on the basis of sex is not prohibited by the Constitution. The right to be free of sex discrimination by other private parties is a statutory right that was created almost a century after § 1985(c) was enacted. Because I do not believe that statute was intended to provide a remedy for the violation of statutory rights—let alone rights created by statutes that had not yet been enacted—I agree with the Court's conclusion that it does not provide respondent with redress for injuries caused by private conspiracies to discriminate on the basis of sex.

With this additional explanation of my views, I join the Court's opinion.

MR. JUSTICE WHITE, with whom MR. JUSTICE BRENNAN and MR. JUSTICE MARSHALL join, dissenting.

The Court today releases employers acting with invidious discriminatory animus in concert with others from liability under 42 U.S.C. § 1985(c) for the injuries they inflict. Because for both respondent in this case and as a general matter § 1985(c) is an entirely consistent supplement to Title VII, I dissent.

* * * [T]he majority holds that the claim under § 1985(c) must be dismissed because "deprivation of a right created by Title VII cannot be the basis for a cause of action under § 1985(c)."

Unfortunately, the majority does not explain whether the "right created by Title VII" to which it refers is the right guaranteed to women employees under § 703(a) or the right guaranteed to respondent under § 704(a). Although in stating its view of the issue before the Court, the majority intimates that it is relying on the fact that respondent has a claim directly under § 704(a), the reasoning of the majority opinion in no way indicates why the existence of a § 704(a) claim should prevent respondent from seeking to vindicate under § 1985(c) the entirely separate right provided by § 703(a).

Clearly, respondent's right under § 704(a)—to be free from retaliation for efforts to aid others asserting Title VII rights—is distinct from the Title VII right implicated in his claim under § 1985(c), which is the right of women employees not to be discriminated against on the basis of their sex. Moreover, that respondent in this case is in a position to assert claims under both § 1985(c) and § 704(a) is due solely to the peculiar facts of this case, rather than to any necessary relationship between the two provisions. First, it is of course possible that a person could be injured in the course of a conspiracy to deny § 703(a) rights—as respondent claims under his § 1985(c) cause of action—by some means other than retaliatory discrimination prohibited under § 704(a). Second, § 704(a) itself protects only employees and applicants for employment; others, such as customers or suppliers, retaliated against in the course of a conspiracy to violate § 703(a) are not expressly protected under any provision of Title VII. Indeed, if respondent in this case had been only a director, rather than both a director and an employee, of the Great American Federal Savings and Loan Association, he apparently would not be able to assert a claim under § 704(a).

Because the existence of a § 704(a) claim is due entirely to the peculiar facts of this case, I interpret the majority's broad holding that "deprivation of a right created by Title VII cannot be the basis for a cause of action under § 1985(c)" to preclude respondent from suing under § 1985(c) not because he coincidentally has a § 704(a) claim, but because the purpose of conspiracy alleging resulting in injury to him was to deny § 703(a) rights.

The pervasive and essential flaw in the majority's approach to reconciliation of § 1985(c) and Title VII proceeds from its characterization of the former statute as solely a "remedial" provision. It is true that the words "equal privileges and immunities under the laws" in § 1985(c) refer to substantive rights created or guaranteed by other federal law, be it the Constitution or federal statutes other than § 1985(c);[5] and in this case it is a conspiracy to deny a substantive right created in § 703(a) of Title VII[6] that is part of the basis for respondent's suit under § 1985(c).[7] However, § 1985(c), unlike a remedial statute such as 42 U.S.C. § 1983, does not merely provide a cause of action for persons deprived of rights elsewhere guaranteed. Because § 1985(c) provides a remedy for *any person* injured as a result of deprivation of a substantive federal right, it must be seen as itself creating rights in persons other than those to whom the underlying federal right extends.

In this case, for instance, respondent is seeking to redress an injury inflicted upon *him*, which injury is distinct and separate from the injury inflicted upon the female employees whose § 703(a) rights were allegedly denied. The damages available to a person such as respondent suing under § 1985(c) are not dependent upon the amount of injury caused persons deprived of "equal privileges and immunities under the laws," but upon the gravity of the separate injury inflicted upon the person suing.

5. The majority opinion does not reach the issue whether § 1985(c) encompasses federal statutory rights other than those proceeding in "fundamental" fashion from the Constitution itself. I am not certain in what manner the Court conceives of sex discrimination by private parties to proceed from explicit constitutional guarantees. In any event, I need not pursue this issue because I think it clear that § 1985(c) encompasses all rights guaranteed in federal statutes as well as rights guaranteed directly by the Constitution. As originally introduced, § 2 of the Civil Rights Act of 1871, encompassed "rights, privileges, or immunities * * * under the Constitution and laws of the United States." The substitution of the terms "the equal protection of the laws" and "equal privileges and immunities under the laws," did not limit the scope of the rights protected but added a requirement of certain "class-based, invidiously discriminatory animus behind the conspirators' action." We have repeatedly held that 18 U.S.C. § 241 (derived from § 6 of the Civil Rights Act of 1870, 16 Stat. 141), which is the "closest remaining criminal analogue to § 1985[c] ," Griffin v. Breckenridge, supra, at 98, 91 S.Ct., at 1796, encompasses all federal statutory rights. Similarly, we have stated that 42 U.S.C. § 1983, derived from § 1 of the 1871 Civil Rights Act, encompasses federal statutory as well as constitutional rights.

6. Although Griffin v. Breckenridge, supra, at 102 n. 9, 91 S.Ct., at 1798, did not reach the issue whether discrimination on a basis other than race may be vindicated under § 1985(c), the Court correctly assumes that the answer to this question is yes. The statute broadly refers to all privileges and immunities, without any limitation as to the class of persons to whom these rights may be granted. It is clear that sex discrimination may be sufficiently invidious to come within the prohibition of § 1985(c).

7. This is analogous to United States v. Johnson, supra, where the basis for a prosecution under 18 U.S.C. § 241 was a conspiracy to deny the substantive right to equality in public accommodations guaranteed under Title II of the Civil Rights Act of 1964.

In this circumstance—where the § 1985(c) plaintiff is seeking redress for injury caused as a result of the denial of other persons' Title VII rights—it makes no sense to hold that the remedies provided in Title VII are exclusive, for such a § 1985(c) plaintiff has no Title VII remedy. It thus can hardly be asserted that allowing this § 1985(c) plaintiff to seek redress of his injury would allow such individual to "completely bypass" the administrative and other "detailed and specific" enforcement mechanisms provided in Title VII.

In enacting § 1985(c), Congress specifically contemplated that persons injured by private conspiracies to deny the federal rights of others could redress their injuries, quite apart from any redress by those who are the object of the conspiracy. Nothing in the Court's opinion suggests any warrant for refusal to recognize this cause of action simply because Title VII rights are involved.

I am also convinced that persons whose own Title VII rights have allegedly been violated retain the separate right to seek redress under § 1985(c). In seeking to accommodate the civil rights statutes enacted in the decade after the Civil War and the civil rights statutes of the recent era, the Court has recognized that the later statutes cannot be said to have impliedly repealed the earlier unless there is an irreconcilable conflict between them. Of course, the mere fact of overlap in modes of redressing discrimination does not constitute such irreconcilable conflict. * * *

It is clear that such overlap as may exist between Title VII and § 1985(c) occurs only because the latter is directed at a discrete and particularly disfavored form of discrimination, and examination of § 1985(c) shows that it constitutes a compatible and important supplement to the more general prohibition and remedy provided in Title VII. Thus, while it may be that in many cases persons seeking redress under § 1985(c) also have a claim directly under Title VII,[10] this is not sufficient reason to deprive those persons of the right to sue for the compensatory and punitive damages to which they are entitled under the post-Civil War statute.

As previously indicated, the majority's willingness to infer a silent repeal of § 1985(c) is based on its view that the provision only gives a remedy to redress deprivations prohibited by other federal law. But this narrow view of § 1985(c) is incorrect even as to § 1985(c) plaintiffs themselves denied Title VII rights. Because only conspiracies to deprive persons of federal rights are subject to redress under § 1985(c), that statute, like 18 U.S.C. § 241, is itself a prohibition, separate and apart from the prohibitions stated in the underlying provisions of federal law. Moreover, only those deprivations imbued with "invidiously discriminatory motivation" amounting to "class-based * * * animus," are encompassed by § 1985(c). Viewed in this manner, the right

10. It is, of course, theoretically possible that an individual could be injured by a conspiracy to violate his Title VII rights even though that conspiracy was never brought to fruition and thus there was no violation of Title VII itself.

guaranteed by § 1985(c) is the right not to be subjected to an invidious conspiracy to deny other federal rights. This discrete category of deprivations to which § 1985(c) is directed stands in sharp contrast to the broad prohibition on discrimination provided in § 703(a) of Title VII, see Griggs v. Duke Power Co., 401 U.S. 424, 91 S.Ct. 849, 28 L.Ed. 2d 158 (1971). If, as the majority suggests, it would not recognize an implied repeal of an earlier statute granting a separate but overlapping right, then it should not do so in this case; for respondent has alleged a violation of § 703(a) in a manner independently prohibited by § 1985(c), and under the majority's approach should be allowed to redress *both* deprivations.

* * *

Because respondent exhausted his administrative remedies under Title VII, there is no need in this case to reach the question whether persons whose Title VII rights have been violated may bring suit directly in federal court alleging an invidious conspiracy to deny those Title VII rights. I note, however, that the majority's desire not to undercut the administrative enforcement scheme, including the encouragement of voluntary conciliation, provided by Title VII would be completely fulfilled by insisting that § 1985(c) plaintiffs exhaust whatever Title VII remedies they may have. The concerns expressed in the majority opinion do not provide a basis for precluding redress altogether under § 1985(c).

NOTES AND PROBLEMS FOR DISCUSSION

1. Should the holding in *Novotny* be extended to cases where the plaintiff alleges a conspiracy to deprive him or someone else of a right guaranteed by some federal statute other than Title VII? While Justices Powell and Stevens would restrict § 1985(c) to claimed deprivations of constitutional rights, and Justices White, Brennan and Marshall would not, the four other members of the majority did not address this issue. One year after its decision in *Novotny*, however, in MAINE v. THIBOUTOT, 448 U.S. 1, 100 S.Ct. 2502, 65 L.Ed.2d 555 (1980) the Court interpreted the language in § 1983 requiring plaintiffs to allege a deprivation of rights secured by the Constitution "and laws" to embrace claims of statutory as well as constitutional violations. Nevertheless, relying on the Court's ruling in *Novotny*, several lower federal courts have held that a § 1985(c) action cannot be based on a conspiracy to deprive persons of their rights under the Age Discrimination in Employment Act, Wippel v. Prudential Ins. Co., 33 FEP Cases 412 (D.Md.1982) and the Equal Pay Act, Whitten v. Petroleum Club of Lafayette, 508 F.Supp. 765 (W.D.La.1981). In both of these situations, however, the court was dealing with a statute that was enacted substantially after § 1985(c) and which provided for administrative review of discrimination claims prior to the institution of suit. What if a § 1985(c) complaint alleged a private conspiracy to deprive persons of their rights under a statute—such as § 1981—that was enacted before § 1985(c) and that did not require pre-suit exhaustion of administrative remedies? See Witten v. A.H. Smith & Co., 567 F.Supp. 1063 (D.Md.1983) (§ 1981 is proper substantive basis for § 1985(c) claim since Congress' purpose in enacting the 1871 Act was to enforce the provisions of the 1866 Act); Hudson v. Teamsters

Local 957, 536 F.Supp. 1138 (S.D.Ohio 1982) (plaintiff can bring § 1985(c) action for conspiracy to violate § 1981). Cf. Brett v. Sohio Construction Co., 518 F.Supp. 698 (D. Alaska 1981) (§ 1985(c) covers claim based on Labor Management Reporting & Disclosure Act). What about an alleged deprivation of a state statutory right? See Life Insurance Co. of North America v. Reichardt, 591 F.2d 499 (9th Cir. 1979). The principal case is noted at 61 B.U.L.Rev. 1007 (1981); 65 Corn.L.Rev. 114 (1979).

2. Paul Jones, a black man, received a notice from his foreman that because of excessive lateness he was recommending to the plant manager that Jones be discharged. After unsuccessfully requesting his union representative to intervene on his behalf, Jones spoke personally with the plant manager and convinced the manager to reject the foreman's recommendation in light of the company's lenient policy with respect to lateness. Jones subsequently brought a § 1985(c) action in federal court against the foreman and union representative charging that they conspired to deprive him of his rights under Title VII by strictly applying the tardiness rule to him because of his race. Jones' complaint alleged that no white employee had ever been fired because of excessive lateness. How should the court rule on the defendant's motion to dismiss for failure to state a cause of action? Note that in footnote six of *Novotny,* the Court explained that it was not ruling on whether a claim would lie under § 1985(c) where the defendant was not subject to suit under Title VII. Should the result be different under those circumstances?

The other manner in which this issue arises was addressed in Justice White's dissenting opinion—i.e., the availability of a § 1985(c) cause of action to a third party injured by a conspiracy directed at others. Do you agree with Justice White's conclusion that Congress intended to protect advocates of the victimized class? Does this interpretation promote the policy behind the act? What about Justice White's claim that without such a cause of action, the plaintiff is left remediless?

3. In his concurring opinion in *Novotny,* Justice Powell cited the passage in Griffin v. Breckenridge where a unanimous Court declared that a claim brought under § 1985(c) must allege "some racial, or perhaps otherwise class-based, invidiously discriminatory animus behind the conspirators' action." The majority in *Novotny* did not have to decide whether that language could be interpreted to permit a § 1985(c) claim challenging discrimination on the basis of a non-racial classification.

In UNITED BROTHERHOOD OF CARPENTERS AND JOINERS OF AMERICA, LOCAL 610 v. SCOTT, 463 U.S. 825, 103 S.Ct. 3352, 77 L.Ed.2d 1049 (1983), two non-union employees were beaten by local residents during a citizen protest against an employer's policy of hiring workers without regard to union membership. The company and these two employees brought suit under § 1985(c) against several local unions, a local trades council and various individuals, alleging that these defendants conspired to deprive the plaintiffs of their First Amendment right to associate with their fellow non-union employees and that this curtailment was a deprivation of the equal protection of the laws within the meaning of § 1985(c). This caused the Court to examine whether § 1985(c) reaches conspiracies other than those motivated by racial animus. In a 5–4 decision, the majority opined that "it is a close question whether Section 1985(c) was intended to reach any class-based animus other than animus against Negroes and those who championed their cause, most notably Republicans." The Court examined the legislative history and concluded that as the predominant purpose of the statute was to combat the then prevalent animus against Blacks and their supporters, it could not be construed to protect every political group from any injury perpetrated by a rival organization. While the majority did not hold that all political groups were excluded from the coverage of § 1985(c), it ruled that this provision did not reach conspiracies motivated by economic or commercial, as opposed to racial animus. Group actions resting on economic motivations were deemed outside the reach of the statute. Of course, this decision continued to leave unresolved the issue of whether § 1985(c) prohibits conspiracies aimed at non-racial groups that are motivated by other than economic animus. The four dissenters, on the other hand, would interpret § 1985(c) to include conspiracies to hinder any group or class of persons in the exercise of their legal rights because of an invidious animus towards members of that class.

Relying on *Scott,* the Tenth Circuit subsequently held that the class of handicapped persons was not a protected class under § 1985(c). Wilhelm v. Continental Title Co., 720 F.2d 1173 (10th Cir. 1983). Other pre-*Scott* lower federal courts, however, have extended § 1985(c) to discrimination on the basis of sex, Padway v. Palches, 665 F.2d 965 (9th Cir. 1982); religion and national origin, Marlowe v. Fisher Body, 489 F.2d 1057 (6th Cir. 1973), Schneider v. Bahler, 564 F.Supp. 1449 (N.D.Ind.1983); and age, Pavlo v. Stiefel Laboratories, Inc., 22 FEP Cases 489 (S.D.N.Y.1979). Still other courts have refused to apply the protection of § 1985(c) to homosexuals, DeSantis v. Pacific Tel. & Tel. Co., Inc., 608 F.2d 327 (9th Cir. 1979), or to public drunks, Wagar v. Hasenkrug, 486 F.Supp. 47 (D.Mont.1980). Can a rational distinction be drawn between the protected and unprotected classes? See Note, Protected Rights and Classes under 42 U.S.C. § 1985(3); United Brotherhood of Carpenters v. Scott, 17 Conn. L.Rev. 165 (1984); Gormley, Private Conspiracies and the Constitution: A Modern Vision of 42 U.S.C. § 1985(c), 64 Tex.L.Rev. 527 (1985).

4. While the federal appellate court in *Novotny* ruled that agents of a single corporation could form a conspiracy within the meaning of § 1985(c), the Supreme Court reserved decision on whether a conspiracy could occur between a single corporation and its agents or among several of the agents of one corporation. Where the employees are found to have acted in the scope of their employment, rather than in pursuit of their personal interests, most courts have refused to recognize intracorporate conspiracies. The majority of courts reason that because a corporation acts through its officers, directors and employees, action taken by a corporation and its agents within the scope of their employ constitutes conduct by only a single entity. Thus, these courts conclude, the statutory requirement of a conspiracy between "two or more persons" is not satisfied—i.e., an entity cannot conspire with itself. Similarly, where the corporation's agents alone are sued and charged with acting in concert, they usually are viewed as acting on behalf of, or as, a single entity—the corporation—rather than as independent individuals. See e.g., Herrmann v. Moore, 576 F.2d 453 (2d Cir. 1978), cert. denied 439 U.S. 1003, 99 S.Ct. 613, 58 L.Ed.2d 679; Dombrowski v. Dowling, 459 F.2d 190, 196 (7th Cir. 1972) ("[I]f the challenged conduct is essentially a single act of discrimination by a single business entity, the fact that two or more agents participated in the decision or in the act itself will normally not constitute the conspiracy contemplated by this statute."). But see An-Ti Chai v. Michigan Technological University, 493 F.Supp. 1137 (W.D.Mich.1980) (can state § 1985(c) conspiracy claim where plaintiff alleges multiple acts of discrimination by corporate agents). For further discussion of intracorporate conspiracies see Note, Intracorporate Con-

spiracies Under 42 U.S.C. § 1985(c), 13 Ga.L.Rev. 591 (1979); Note, Intracorporate Conspiracies Under 42 U.S.C. § 1985(c), 92 Harv.L.Rev. 470 (1978).

5. Must a § 1985(c) plaintiff prove discriminatory intent as part of its prima facie case? See Taylor v. St. Louis, 702 F.2d 695 (8th Cir. 1983).

SECTION D. THE APPLICABLE STATUTES OF LIMITATION

The Reconstruction Era civil rights acts discussed above do not contain their own statutes of limitation and there is no "catch all" federal limitation period. 42 U.S.C. § 1988 provides, however, that if in a civil rights case federal law is "deficient," the court should apply the law "of the State wherein the court having jurisdiction of such [claim] is held, so far as the same is not inconsistent with the Constitution and laws of the United States * * * " It is settled that federal courts will look to state law to determine the statutes of limitations for suits filed pursuant to Sections 1981, 1983 and 1985. See, Board of Regents v. Tomanio, 446 U.S. 478, 100 S.Ct. 1790, 64 L.Ed.2d 440 (1980) (courts should borrow "the state law of limitations governing an analogous cause of action"); Johnson v. Railway Express Agency, Inc., 421 U.S. 454, 95 S.Ct. 1716, 44 L.Ed.2d 295 (1975) (federal court should use "that [limitation period] which the State would apply if the action had been brought in a state court"). The problem of deciding which state limitation period is applicable to a civil rights action has continued to trouble the courts.

In BURNETT v. GRATTAN, 468 U.S. 42, 104 S.Ct. 2924, 82 L.Ed.2d 36 (1984), the plaintiffs, alleging that they were discharged by a state college because of their race and sex, filed suit under §§ 1981, 1983 and 1985. The district court applied a limitations period from a state fair employment law (modeled after Title VII) which allowed a 180-day period for filing an administrative complaint with a state agency, and dismissed the suit. The Court of Appeals reversed, holding that the state's three-year residual statute of limitations applicable to all civil actions for which the law did not specifically furnish a limitation period should be applied. The Supreme Court affirmed. "A state law is not 'appropriate' if it fails to take into account practicalities that are involved in litigating federal civil rights claims and policies that are analogous to the goals of the Civil Rights Acts." 104 S.Ct. at 2930. The Court observed that a person who files a civil rights suit in court has a significantly greater burden in terms of preparation than one who merely initiates a charge with an agency which will then bear the burden of investigation and development of the case. The Court concluded that the practical differences between state administrative proceedings and the civil rights claims in federal court as well as the "divergence in the objective" of the state and federal laws made adoption of the administrative limitation period inappropriate. The *Burnett* opinion did not, however, specify how a claim under the civil rights statutes should be characterized for purposes of finding the "appropriate" state statute of limitations and thus gave little guidance to the lower courts in determining which state limitation period should be adopted among those that were arguably applicable.

In WILSON v. GARCIA, 471 U.S. 261, 105 S.Ct. 1938, 85 L.Ed.2d 254 (1985), the Court resolved matters, at least for Section 1983 cases, by adopting a bright-line approach to the problem. The Court held that all Section 1983 actions should be treated as claims for violation of personal rights and that the state statute governing tort actions for the recovery of damages for personal injuries provides the appropriate limitation period. "[T]his choice is supported by the nature of the [Section] 1983 remedy, and by the federal interest in insuring that the borrowed period of limitations not discriminate against the federal civil rights remedy." 471 U.S. at ___, 105 S.Ct. at 1947. *Wilson* was a police brutality damage action, but the court made clear that its ruling applied to all Section 1983 actions, including employment discrimination claims, since allowing courts to choose the applicable limitation period based on the facts of each case has led to "uncertainty and time-consuming litigation that is foreign to the central purpose of [Section] 1983." 471 U.S. at ___, 105 S.Ct. at 1945. The Court expressly rejected the possibility that states' residuary statutes of limitations be applied in Section 1983 actions. "The relative scarcity of statutory claims when § 1983 was enacted makes it unlikely that Congress would have intended to apply the catchall periods of limitations for statutory claims that were later enacted by many States." 471 U.S. at ___, 105 S.Ct. at 1948. *Wilson* has not ended all confusion in the area, because some states have more than one limitation period applicable to personal injury actions. Compare, Gates v. Spinks, 771 F.2d 916 (5th Cir. 1985), cert. denied, ___ U.S. ___, 106 S.Ct. 1378, 89 L.Ed.2d 603 (1986) and Shorters v. Chicago, 617 F.Supp. 661 (N.D.Ill. 1985).

Unlike Section 1983, Section 1981 creates a substantive cause of action for racial discrimination in making and enforcing contracts and is applicable to private concerns. Because of these fundamental differences in the statutes, it is unclear what impact *Wilson* will have on Section 1981 litigation. The Third Circuit, relying on *Wilson*, held in Goodman v. Lukens Steel Co., 777 F.2d 113 (3d Cir. 1985), that the state personal injury statute of limitation should be applied to Section 1981 actions. "[B]ecause employment discrimination cases under § 1983, regardless of their affinity to contractual actions, are now governed by the personal injury statute of limitations, and because the same considerations which led to [*Wilson*] are also present in § 1981 cases, we conclude that the same limitations period applies." 777 F.2d at 120. Other courts have continued to follow pre-*Wilson* doctrine and look for the limitation period applicable to the state cause of action most analogous to the claim made under Section 1981. See, Hess v. United Tel. Co. of Ohio, 40 FEP Cases 1487 (N.D.Ohio 1986); Keller v. Association of American Medical Colleges, 38 EPD 35,761 (D.D.C. 1985).

As stated in Delaware State College v. Ricks, Chapter 5, supra, the question of when the applicable statute of limitations accrues or begins to run in a suit under the federal civil rights statutes is a matter of federal law. The question of what "tolls" or stops the running of the limitation period is, however, controlled by state law. In Board of Regents v. Tomanio, supra, the Court held that when a federal court borrows a state statute of limitations it must also use the state's tolling rules as well, unless to do so would conflict with the federal policies of compensation and deterrence underlying the civil rights acts. 446 U.S. at 484, 100 S.Ct. at 1795. State law also controls the effect of tolling, i.e. the amount of time remaining in the period to file suit after tolling has ended. In Chardon v. Soto, 462 U.S. 650, 103 S.Ct. 2611, 77 L.Ed.2d 74 (1983), the Court held that Puerto Rican law under which the limitation period starts running anew once tolling has occurred was not inconsistent with the policies behind Section 1983.

Chapter 9

THE EQUAL PAY ACT

In 1963, Congress passed the first modern statute directed at eliminating discrimination in the job market—the Equal Pay Act (EPA).[a] Enacted as an amendment to the Fair Labor Standards Act,[b] the EPA proscribes a limited range of discriminatory employment practices—sex-based wage differentials between employees performing "equal work". Subject to four statutorily created exceptions, an employer is prohibited from paying an employee of one sex less than an employee of the opposite sex for "equal work on jobs the performance of which requires equal skill, effort, and responsibility, and which are performed under similar working conditions * * * ". The Act also provides that compliance with its equal pay mandate cannot be achieved by reducing the wages of the higher paid employee.

As it is part of the Fair Labor Standards Act (FLSA), coverage under and enforcement of the Equal Pay Act is tied to the provisions of the FLSA.

Employers can fall within the general jurisdiction of the FLSA under either of two theories. The first ("employee") test focuses on the individual employee and asks whether he or she is "engaged in commerce" or engaged "in the production of goods for commerce." All employees who satisfy this requirement are protected by the FLSA. The use of this criterion, however, can result in one employer having both protected and unprotected employees, depending upon the nature of their particular job duties. To eliminate this problem, the FLSA was amended in 1966 to add a new basis for coverage that focuses on the general nature of the employer's business. Under this "enterprise" standard, all the employees of a particular enterprise are covered, regardless of their individual job responsibilities, if the enterprise is (a) engaged in interstate commerce or in the production of goods for interstate commerce, (b) has 2 or more employees so engaged, and (c) except for a few specified industries, makes at least $325,000 in annual gross.

Coverage under the EPA, however, may not be limited to the "employee" and "enterprise" standards that govern inclusion within the minimum wage provisions of the FLSA. The EPA states that an employer cannot discriminate against "employees subject to any provision of this section" within any "establishment" in which such employees are employed. The absence of any reference in this section to "engaged in commerce", as well as the use of "establishment" instead of "enterprise", has led Professor Larson, among others, to conclude

[a] Pub.L. 88–38, 77 Stat. 56, 29 USC § 206(d).

[b] Pub.L. 75–718, 52 Stat. 1060, 29 U.S.C. §§ 201–209.

that an employer is covered so long as it has at least one male and one female worker engaged in commerce or in the production of goods for commerce.[c]

In 1974, the FLSA was amended to apply to federal, state and local government employees. The Supreme Court, in National League of Cities v. Usery,[d] struck down the extension of the statute's wage and hour provisions to state and local government workers on the ground that the Tenth Amendment precluded Congress' exercise of its Commerce Clause authority to regulate the relationship between a state and its employees. This ruling was overruled, however, in GARCIA v. SAN ANTONIO METROPOLITAN TRANSIT AUTHORITY,[e] where the Court held that the extension of the FLSA wage and hour provisions to state and local governments did not constitute an unconstitutional exercise of Congress' authority under the Commerce Clause. Prior to the ruling in *Garcia*, the majority of lower federal courts distinguished the Equal Pay Act portions of the FLSA from the wage and hour provisions addressed in *National League of Cities*. Consistent with their treatment of similar amendments to Title VII and the Age Discrimination In Employment Act, these courts upheld the constitutionality of the application of the EPA to state and local agencies on either of two grounds. Some distinguished *Usery* by reasoning that Congress extended the coverage of the EPA pursuant to its authority under § 5 of the Fourteenth Amendment, rather than the Commerce Clause.[f] Others maintained that the EPA does not constitute an impermissible federal intrusion into state sovereignty because paying sex-differentiated wages is not a function essential to the separate and independent existence of the states.[g]

The Equal Pay Act, unlike the other portions of the FLSA, specifically mentions labor organizations, forbidding them from causing or attempting to cause an employer to violate the Act.[h]

In Northwest Airlines, Inc. v. Transport Workers Union of America,[i] the Supreme Court stated that the EPA does not expressly create a private right of action for monetary relief against unions but reserved decision on whether the EPA provided employees with an implied right of action for monetary relief. It noted, however, that the lower federal courts generally had refused to find that the Act created such an implied right of action.[j]

[c] See 1 A. Larson, Employment Discrimination, § 6.41 (1981).

[d] 426 U.S. 833, 96 S.Ct. 2465, 49 L.Ed.2d 245 (1976).

[e] 469 U.S. 528, 105 S.Ct. 1005, 83 L.Ed.2d 1016 (1985).

[f] See e.g. Marshall v. Owensboro-Daviess County Hospital, 581 F.2d 116 (6th Cir. 1978); Marshall v. City of Sheboygan, 577 F.2d 1 (7th Cir. 1978).

[g] See Marshall v. A & M Consolidated Independent School District, 605 F.2d 186 (5th Cir. 1979).

[h] The EPA does not contain a minimum member requirement for labor organizations.

[i] 451 U.S. 77, 101 S.Ct. 1571, 67 L.Ed.2d 750 (1981).

[j] The Court also ruled that where an employer was held liable under the EPA for sex-based wage differentials that were collectively bargained with a union, the

The Department of Labor was designated by the FLSA as the agency responsible for interpreting and enforcing its provisions. This task was transferred, however, to the EEOC by President Carter's Reorganization Plan No. 1 of 1978. While an aggrieved employee is entitled to file a complaint of an EPA violation with the EEOC, these proceedings need not be invoked prior to filing suit. An employee can bring a private action under the EPA in either federal or state court for amounts withheld in violation of the Act. The EEOC can bring such an action on that employee's behalf, but its exercise of this authority terminates the employee's right to file suit and the EPA, unlike Title VII, does not grant the individual a right to intervene in the EEOC action.[k] In addition, the EEOC can seek injunctive relief and liquidated damages as well as backpay. Finally, a two year statute of limitations applies to EPA suits for backpay, except that a case arising out of a willful violation is subject to a three year limitations period.[l]

The remaining materials in this Chapter will address the three most frequently litigated issues in cases brought under the EPA: (1) the meaning of the statutory equal work standard, (2) the scope of the statutory exceptions, and (3) the relationship between the EPA and Title VII.

Read 29 U.S.C. §§ 206(d) and 216 at pp. 1043–1045.

BRENNAN v. PRINCE WILLIAM HOSPITAL CORP.

United States Court of Appeals, Fourth Circuit, 1974.
503 F.2d 282, cert. denied, 420 U.S. 972.

BUTZNER, CIRCUIT JUDGE.

The Secretary of Labor appeals from the dismissal of an action against Prince William Hospital to equalize pay of male hospital

employer did not possess either a federal statutory or federal common law right to contribution from that union.

[k] Intervention may be sought, however, under F.R.Civ.P. 24. In the absence of any express conciliation requirement, one court has held that the EPA does not require the EEOC to attempt conciliation before instituting suit. EEOC v. Home of Economy, Inc., 712 F.2d 356 (8th Cir. 1983).

In Immigration and Naturalization Service v. Chadha, 462 U.S. 919, 103 S.Ct. 2764, 77 L.Ed.2d 317 (1983), the Supreme Court held that a legislative provision that gave one house of the Congress the power to veto the act of the Attorney General suspending deportation proceedings violated the constitutional separation of powers doctrine and the constitutional requirement that legislation be accomplished by action of both houses of Congress and by presentment to the President. Reorganization Plan No. 1 was promulgated by President Carter pursuant to the Reorganization Act of 1977, which statute authorized the President to reorganize federal agencies subject to veto by only one house of Congress. The courts are split as to whether the EEOC's authority to file lawsuits under the EPA survives the ruling in *Chadha.* Compare EEOC v. Allstate Ins. Co., 570 F.Supp. 1224 (S.D.Miss.1983) (entire Act is unconstitutional as one-house veto provision was not severable from remainder of statute), appeal dismissed for want of jurisdiction, 467 U.S. 1232, 104 S.Ct. 3499, 82 L.Ed.2d 810 (1984) with EEOC v. Hernando Bank, 724 F.2d 1188 (5th Cir. 1984) (one-house veto provision is severable from rest of Reorganization Act).

[l] To establish a willful violation, the plaintiff must prove that the defendant knew or should have known that its conduct was governed by the Act. See EEOC v. McCarthy, 768 F.2d 1 (1st Cir. 1985); EEOC v. Central Kansas Medical Center, 705 F.2d 1270 (10th Cir. 1983); Hill v. J.C. Penney Co., 688 F.2d 370 (5th Cir. 1982).

orderlies and female nurses' aides in conformity with the Equal Pay Act of 1963. The district court noted that the facts were not in dispute and that the controversy centered on the inferences to be drawn from them. It found that although aides and orderlies do the same type of patient care work, the following differences exist between the jobs: the proportions of routine care tasks are not the same; aides do work which orderlies are neither required nor permitted to do; and, most important, orderlies do work, including extra tasks, which aides are neither required nor permitted to do. It concluded, therefore, that the Secretary had failed to establish that the aides and orderlies perform substantially equal work.

We believe that the district court gave undue significance to these differences because it misapprehended the statutory definition of equal work, which embraces the concepts of "skill, effort, and responsibility." Since it applied an improper legal standard to the relevant facts, we reverse and remand for the entry of judgment for the Secretary.

In applying the Congressional mandate of equal pay for equal work on jobs which require equal skill, effort, and responsibility, there are two extremes of interpretation that must be avoided. Congress realized that the majority of job differentiations are made for genuine economic reasons unrelated to sex. It did not authorize the Secretary or the courts to engage in wholesale reevaluation of any employer's pay structure in order to enforce their own conceptions of economic worth. But if courts defer to overly nice distinctions in job content, employers may evade the Act at will. The response to this dilemma has been to require the Secretary to prove substantial equality of skill, effort, and responsibility as the jobs are actually performed.

One of the most common grounds for justifying different wages is the assertion that male employees perform extra tasks. These may support a wage differential if they create significant variations in skill, effort, and responsibility between otherwise equal jobs. But the semblance of the valid job classification system may not be allowed to mask the existence of wage discrimination based on sex. The Secretary may therefore show that the greater pay received by the male employees is not related to any extra tasks and thus is not justified by them. Higher pay is not related to extra duties when one or more of the following circumstances exists:

> Some male employees receive higher pay without doing the extra work.
>
> Female employees also perform extra duties of equal skill, effort, and responsibility.
>
> Qualified female employees are not given the opportunity to do the extra work.
>
> The supposed extra duties do not in fact exist.
>
> The extra task consumes a minimal amount of time and is of peripheral importance.

Third persons who do the extra task as their primary job are paid less than the male employees in question.

In all of these * * * [circumstances] the basic jobs were substantially equal. Despite claims to the contrary, the extra tasks were * * * makeweights. This left sex—which in this context refers to the availability of women at lower wages than men—as the one discernible reason for the wage differential. That, however, is precisely the criterion for setting wages that the Act prohibits.

Although a number of courts have applied the Equal Pay Act to hospital and nursing home aides and orderlies, varied employment practices among institutions have prevented the development of an industry-wide standard. The Act must be applied on a case by case basis to factual situations that are, for practical purposes, unique. It is therefore necessary to examine in some detail the employment practices of Prince William Hospital, even though the material facts are not in dispute.

Prince William is a 154 bed general hospital in Manassas, Virginia. It contains four medical and surgical units, intensive care and cardiac facilities, an obstetric floor with a nursery, four operating rooms, and an emergency room. Average occupancy is 120 patients, 60% female.

Floor orderlies and nurses' aides provide routine patient care under the supervision of nurses. The hospital hires only men as orderlies and only women as aides. Their numbers varied during the time covered by this case, ranging between 30–40 aides and 5–10 orderlies. When the case was tried, there were four full-time floor orderlies and thirty-four full-time aides, plus three part-time orderlies and three part-time aides. Full-time employees work five eight-hour shifts per week.

The hospital has maintained a pay differential between the two jobs since 1969. It uses a pay system with thirteen pay grades and five steps within each grade. Grades are assigned to positions and steps within grade show merit or longevity. All nurses' aides are in grade I, in which the hourly pay ranges from $1.98 to $2.31, and all orderlies are in grade II, in which the hourly pay ranges from $2.08 to $2.43, depending on the step in which the employee has been placed.

Before 1969 aides and orderlies had been paid the same wages, but the hospital had difficulty in hiring orderlies. The hospital's administrator believed that a higher wage was needed to attract orderlies because of the limited number of men willing to do housekeeping and personal care work. When the orderlies' wage was raised, they were given the additional duty of catheterizing male patients.

Hiring criteria for aides and orderlies are identical: a tenth grade education, personal cleanliness, and a desire to work with people. Experience, though desirable, is unnecessary. Although the educational level of the aides was somewhat lower, both groups included individuals who had not finished high school. The pay differential follows neither experience nor education. An aide with prior hospital experience starts in grade I step 2 ($2.06), while a completely inexperienced orderly starts in grade II step 1 ($2.08).

Aides and orderlies are the least skilled persons who care for patients. They participate in a common orientation program, but much of their training is acquired on the job. Each is assigned six to eight patients who require routine care. Whenever possible orderlies are assigned to male patients and aides to female, but the shortage of orderlies requires aides to care for males. Most of the time, aides and orderlies are occupied with tasks related to routine patient care that do not require the skills of a trained nurse.

The principal duties of both, which the hospital's director of nursing stated were identical, can be divided into four groups: patient care, which includes oral hygiene, back rubs, baths, bed-making, answering calls, giving bed pans, feeding, transporting the patient, and assistance with ambulation; minor treatment, which includes weighing, taking pulse, temperature, or blood pressure, draping and positioning the patient, administering heat pads and ice packs, assistance with dressing changes, and giving enemas; housekeeping, which includes room cleaning, equipment care and cleaning, work area cleaning, and obtaining supplies; and miscellaneous tasks, including answering the phone, running errands, and transportation to the morgue.

The hospital emphasized statistical evidence which shows that aides and orderlies do not perform all of their routine tasks with equal frequency. One of its exhibits, for example, shows that aides write charts, make beds, give baths, rub backs, and fetch bed pans more often than orderlies. Orderlies, on the other hand, bring supplies, run errands, and assist the nurses with their duties more often than aides. These distinctions, however, do not show any difference in skill, effort, or responsibility. All of the routine tasks are relatively simple. None performed more frequently by the orderlies requires the exertion of significantly more skill, effort, or responsibility than those performed more frequently by the aides. As hired, trained, and employed, the orderlies and aides are practical substitutes for one another in the performance of their basic duties. Disproportionate frequency in the performance of the same routine tasks does not make the job unequal.

The district court also found that aides perform certain duties which orderlies do not. Specifically, it found that some of the aides work in the obstetric department and care for infants in the nursery. Orderlies were not assigned to obstetrics, according to the director of nursing, for two reasons: there were no male patients and their lifting ability was unneeded there. Aides assigned to obstetrics performed the same duties as those on the medical and surgical wards.

These facts do not show any differences in skill, effort, or responsibility. Unless there is a difference of working conditions involved, which is not contended here, there is no reason why the performance of the same duties in a different location should be a significant difference in the jobs.

The final—and in some respects the most difficult—aspect of this case pertains to extra duties throughout the hospital that are assigned to the orderlies but not to the aides. These duties are specified in the job description of the orderlies. The district court found that the following extra duties were the most significant: heavy lifting, assisting in the emergency room, performing surgical preps on male patients, providing physical security by dealing with combative or hysterical persons, and catheterization of male patients.

Job descriptions and titles, however, are not decisive. Actual job requirements and performance are controlling. This aspect of the case, therefore, turns primarily on the extent to which the aides and orderlies actually perform the extra duties nominally assigned to the orderlies and on the skill, effort, and responsibility involved in those tasks which the orderlies alone perform.

In addition to caring for assigned patients, orderlies are required to answer calls to different parts of the hospital. On these excursions, called floating, they perform either their basic duties or the extra tasks. Floating itself adds nothing to the level of skill or responsibility, for that depends on the work done in the other locations. It might add to the degree of effort involved if the orderlies, in addition, had to perform their full basic workload. This, however, is not the case. According to the director of nursing, an orderly's routine duties at his assigned station are reassigned to other staff personnel, including the aides, when he is in another part of the hospital.

The job description states that orderlies are expected to perform total lifting of heavy or helpless patients and to set up traction equipment. The district court, however, found that the same tasks are performed by aides when no orderly is available and that aides assist orderlies in these tasks. Due to the small number of orderlies, there are rarely more than two on duty each shift, and from time to time no orderly is available on some of the shifts. It sometimes takes more than one aide, or mechanical assistance, to replace an orderly, but there is no evidence that any heavy lifting cannot be done without male assistance. The performance of tasks involving physical strength, therefore, though necessary to the operation of the hospital, is not a peculiar aspect of the orderlies' job. Strength is not a factor in the hiring of orderlies, except in the very general sense that the hospital assumes that a man is usually stronger than a woman. A large, burly woman would not be hired as an orderly, nor would a small, delicate man be hired as an aide. But the converse is not true. One of the orderlies is 52″ tall and weighs 125 lbs., while one aide is 61″ and weighs 225 lbs. The wage differential therefore can not be justified on the grounds that the hospital is maintaining a reserve of strong men for essential tasks.

Heavy lifting does not add significantly to the effort involved in the orderlies' job. In the ten working days covered by the hospital's survey of activities, the orderlies set up traction only once and lifted or assisted patients of unknown weight 54 times. Aides set up traction and lifted or ambulated patients a proportionate number of times. The extra effort, if any, is not substantial.

The emergency room is staffed by an orderly whose status is not questioned in this action. The hospital's claim that floor orderlies "assisted" there is supported only by the job description, but a mere job description without evidence of actual performance does not establish the existence of extra duties. Aides were also called to work in the emergency room. The record proves no more than that both aides and orderlies performed their normal duties with minor variations in a different location.

All surgical preps during the day shifts are done by the operating room staff. On the evening and night shifts, surgical preps on men are done by orderlies, and on women by aides or nurses. Aides also do surgical preps in the obstetric ward. A person performing a prep explains to the patient what is about to be done, shaves the area where the incision will be made, and washes it with antiseptic soap. The skill, effort, and responsibility involved are identical regardless of the patient's sex.

Physical security, as an extra duty, has two components. Because of his size and sex, the presence of a male orderly is claimed to reassure the other staff and exert a calming and deterrent effect on potentially violent patients or intruders. Because of his superior strength, he is given the primary responsibility for restraining actually violent persons. According to the hospital, he therefore possesses a special skill and is required to exert extra effort.

The hospital's contention, however, is contradicted by the record. Although in theory the orderly deals with disturbances, in practice the nearest staff member is expected to do so until assistance comes. Aides are expected to restrain violent or disoriented patients themselves when possible. They also deal with intruders. The hospital's tabulation of orderly and aide activity shows aides spending a larger proportion of their time than orderlies in applying restraining devices to patients. There is no evidence that orderlies do more actual physical restraint than aides.

No doubt the physical presence of a man in the house does have a comforting effect on the staff. It is doubtful, though, that this is a significant component of the orderly job. Unlike hospitals in which providing physical security has been found significant, Prince William Hospital does not handle psychiatric, alcoholic, criminal, or other potentially dangerous patients. There is no evidence that episodes caused by violent or confused patients are so frequent or dangerous that orderlies are necessary for the safety of the staff. Security guards are called to deal with violent episodes even when orderlies are available. Moreover, the ability to deal with confused or violent patients, according to the director of nursing, is as much a function of attitude and experience as of size and strength. If the orderly's superior strength is an extra skill, it is a peripheral part of his employment.

The hospital places great emphasis on the fact that orderlies insert Foley catheters in male patients. It contends that the task is a highly skilled and responsible procedure, requiring 30 to 45 minutes of an orderly's time.

A Foley catheter is a sterile tube which is inserted in the patient's urethra to drain the bladder. Orderlies catheterize male patients with unobstructed urinary tracts. If any difficulty is foreseen or experienced a physician catheterizes the patient. Nurses catheterize female patients. They are competent to catheterize males, but prefer not to do so for reasons of modesty. Since the hospital has enough nurses to catheterize women, aides are not assigned this duty. The orderly's job therefore does call for the exercise of skill and responsibility which is not required of the aides.

However, no more than one or two routine catheterizations are usually performed each week. When no floor orderly is present, other qualified male personnel are available to do them. The hospital looks for no special skill in this regard from its prospective orderlies but concedes that "any reasonably dextrous person can learn male catheterization on the job." Orderlies were assigned this duty only when the hospital decided that a higher wage rate was needed to attract men for routine care work, and new orderlies who have not yet learned to catheterize are nevertheless paid at the higher rate.

Like any other extra duty, catheterization must be evaluated as part of the entire job. In Hodgson v. Fairmont Supply Co., 454 F.2d 490, 496 (4th Cir. 1972), we pointed out that when jobs were substantially equal, a minimal amount of extra skill, effort, or responsibility cannot justify wage differentials. Infrequent performance of catheterizations, unaccompanied by other extra skills and responsibilities, has never been held to support a pay differential between aides and orderlies. The orderlies in Hodgson v. William and Mary Nursing Hotel, 20 W.H. Cases 10 (M.D.Fla.1971), for example, a case in which the district court found catheterization to be a significant extra duty, also moved heavy equipment, administered suction therapy, and did other demanding work not done by aides. Catheterizations, moreover, were frequent and difficult in that geriatric nursing home. Similarly, catheterization was only one element of the orderlies' duties, which differed fundamentally from the aides', in Hodgson v. Good Shepherd Hospital, 327 F.Supp. 143 (E.D.Tex.1971). In contrast, catheterization which only consumed a minimal amount of time was considered to be an insubstantial difference in Shultz v. Brookhaven General Hospital, 305 F.Supp. 424 (E.D. Tex.1969), aff'd in part and remanded in part sub nom. Hodgson v. Brookhaven General Hospital, 436 F.2d 719 (5th Cir. 1970), on remand 20 W.H. Cases 54 (E.D.Tex.1971), aff'd, 470 F.2d 729 (5th Cir. 1972). We conclude, therefore, that the orderlies' pay differential cannot be justified on the basis of the occasional extra work involved in catheterizing male patients.

In sum, the work performed by aides and orderlies is not identical. But, as we have previously held, application of the Equal Pay Act is not restricted to identical work. The basic routine tasks of the aides and orderlies are equal. The variations that the district court found, when tested by the Act's standard of "equal skill, effort, and responsibility," do not affect the substantial equality of their overall work.

The judgment of the district court is reversed, and this case is remanded for entry of judgment for the Secretary.

NOTES AND PROBLEMS FOR DISCUSSION

1. State University operates campuses in three different cities in the State—North, South and West. Undergraduate instruction is offered at the North and South campuses, while the graduate and professional schools are located on the West campus. Robert Force, a Professor of English at North with 10 years seniority, receives an annual salary of $25,000. Ruth Morris, a Professor of English at South with comparable credentials and identical seniority is paid $20,000 per year. Prof. Morris brings an action under the EPA. What result? See Brennan v. Goose Creek Consolidated Independent School District, 519 F.2d 53 (5th Cir. 1975). But see Grumbine v. United States, 586 F.Supp. 1144 (D.D.C.1984). Could Force successfully bring an action under Title VII? See Bartelt v. Berlitz School of Languages of America, Inc., 698 F.2d 1003 (9th Cir. 1983), cert. denied, 464 U.S. 915, 104 S.Ct. 277, 78 L.Ed.2d 257 (1983). What if Force was a Professor of Chemistry at South? See Melanson v. Rantoul, 536 F.Supp. 271 (D.R.I.1982). Does the statute suggest that a lesser degree of similarity is required with respect to working conditions than skill, effort and responsibility? See Lanegan—Grimm v. Library Ass'n of Portland, 560 F.Supp. 486, 493 (D.Or.1983).

2. Federal Airlines pays identical salaries to its male and female flight attendants. During layovers, female flight attendants are required to share double rooms while male attendants are provided with single rooms. In addition, male attendants are given a monthly uniform cleaning allowance. No such allowance is provided to female attendants. Can a female attendant state a claim under the EPA? See Laffey v. Northwest Airlines, Inc., 642 F.2d 578 (D.C.Cir. 1980); Donovan v. KFC Services, Inc., 547 F.Supp. 503 (E.D.N.Y.1982).

3. Does the application of the EPA to a religious organization violate the establishment or free exercise clauses of the First Amendment? See Russell v. Belmont College, 554 F.Supp. 667 (M.D.Tenn.1982).

KOUBA v. ALLSTATE INSURANCE CO.

United States Court of Appeals, Ninth Circuit, 1982.
691 F.2d 873.

CHOY, CIRCUIT JUDGE:

This appeal calls into question the scope of the "factor other than sex" exception to the Equal Pay Act of 1963 as incorporated into Title

VII of the Civil Rights Act of 1964 by the Bennett Amendment.[2] Because the district court misconstrued the exception, we reverse and remand.

I

Allstate Insurance Co. computes the minimum salary guaranteed to a new sales agent on the basis of ability, education, experience, and prior salary. During an 8-to-13 week training period, the agent receives only the minimum. Afterwards, Allstate pays the greater of the minimum and the commissions earned from sales. A result of this practice is that, on the average, female agents make less than their male counterparts.

Lola Kouba, representing a class of all female agents, argued below that the use of prior salary caused the wage differential and thus constitutes unlawful sex discrimination. Allstate responded that prior salary is a "factor other than sex" within the meaning of the statutory exception. The district court entered summary judgment against Allstate, reasoning that (1) because so many employers paid discriminatory salaries in the past, the court would presume that a female agent's prior salary was based on her gender unless Allstate presented evidence to rebut that presumption, and (2) absent such a showing (which Allstate did not attempt to make), prior salary is not a factor other than sex.

II

The Equal Pay Act prohibits differential payments between male and female employees doing equal work except when made pursuant to any of three specific compensation systems or "any other factor other than sex." These exceptions are affirmative defenses which the employer must plead and prove. Corning Glass Works v. Brennan, 417 U.S. 188, 196–97, 94 S.Ct. 2223, 2229, 41 L.Ed.2d 1 (1974) (claim brought under the Equal Pay Act).

Because Kouba brought her claim under Title VII rather than directly under the Equal Pay Act,[3] Allstate contends that the standard Title VII rules govern the allocation of evidentiary burdens. It cites Texas Department of Community Affairs v. Burdine, 450 U.S. 248, 253, 101 S.Ct. 1089, 1091, 67 L.Ed.2d 207 (1981), for the proposition that under Title VII an employee alleging sex discrimination bears the

2. The Bennett Amendment, which incorporates into Title VII the affirmative defenses fixed in the Equal Pay Act, states:

> It shall not be an unlawful employment practice under this subchapter [Title VII] for any employer to differentiate upon the basis of sex in determining the amount of the wages or compensation paid or to be paid to employees of such employer if such differentiation is authorized by the provisions of section 206(d) of title 29 [Equal Pay Act].

3. Her apparent reasons for bringing a Title VII action were the uncertainty at that time how the Equal Pay Act affected Title VII and the apparently less-demanding class-consent requirements under Title VII. Kuhn v. Philadelphia Electric Co., 475 F.Supp. 324, 326 (E.D.Pa.1979).

burden of persuasion at all times as to all issues and concludes that Kouba failed to carry the burden of showing that the wage differential did not result from a factor other than sex.[4]

Allstate misallocates the burden. In County of Washington v. Gunther, 452 U.S. 161, 170–71, 101 S.Ct. 2242, 2248–49, 68 L.Ed.2d 751 (1981), the Supreme Court recognized that very different principles govern the standard structure of Title VII litigation, including burdens of proof, and the structure of Title VII litigation implicating the "factor other than sex" exception to an equal-pay claim (though the Court reserved judgment on specifically how to structure an equal-pay claim under Title VII). Accordingly, we have held that even under Title VII, the employer bears the burden of showing that the wage differential resulted from a factor other than sex. Piva v. Xerox Corp., 654 F.2d 591, 598–601 (9th Cir. 1981); Gunther v. County of Washington, 623 F.2d 1303, 1319 (9th Cir. 1979) (supplemental opinion denying rehearing), aff'd, 452 U.S. 161, 101 S.Ct. 2242, 68 L.Ed.2d 751 (1981). Nothing in *Burdine* converts this affirmative defense, which the employer must plead and prove under *Corning Glass,* into an element of the cause of action, which the employee must show does not exist.

III

In an effort to carry its burden, Allstate asserts that if its use of prior salary caused the wage differential,[5] prior salary constitutes a factor other than sex. An obstacle to evaluating Allstate's contention is the ambiguous statutory language. The parties proffer a variety of possible interpretations of the term "factor other than sex."

A

We can discard at the outset three interpretations manifestly incompatible with the Equal Pay Act. At one extreme are two that would tolerate all but the most blatant discrimination. Kouba asserts that Allstate wrongly reads "factor other than sex" to mean any factor that either does not refer on its face to an employee's gender or does not result in all women having lower salaries than all men. Since an employer could easily manipulate factors having a close correlation to gender as a guise to pay female employees discriminatorily low salaries, it would contravene the Act to allow their use simply because they also are facially neutral or do not produce complete segregation. Not surpisingly, Allstate denies relying on either reading of the exception.

At the other extreme is an interpretation that would deny employers the opportunity to use clearly acceptable factors. Kouba insists that in order to give the Act its full remedial force, employers cannot use any factor that perpetuates historic sex discrimination. The court

4. Allstate does not dispute that otherwise Kouba established a prima facie case. Thus, for purposes of this appeal, we assume that she has.

5. Allstate questions whether its use of prior salary caused the wage differential. We leave that issue for the district court on remand.

below adopted a variation of this interpretation: the employer must demonstrate that it made a reasonable attempt to satisfy itself that the factor causing the wage differential was not the product of sex discrimination. Kouba v. Allstate Insurance Co., 523 F.Supp. 148, 162 (E.D.Cal. 1981). But while Congress fashioned the Equal Pay Act to help cure longstanding societal ills, it also intended to exempt factors such as training and experience that may reflect opportunities denied to women in the past. H.R.Rep. No. 309, 88th Cong., 1st Sess. 3, reprinted in 1963 U.S. Code Cong. & Ad. News 687, 689. Neither Kouba's interpretation nor the district court's variation can accommodate practices that Congress and the courts have approved.

B

All three interpretations miss the mark in large part because they do not focus on the reason for the employer's use of the factor. The Equal Pay Act concerns business practices. It would be nonsensical to sanction the use of a factor that rests on some consideration unrelated to business. An employer thus cannot use a factor which causes a wage differential between male and female employees absent an acceptable business reason.[6] Conversely, a factor used to effectuate some business policy is not prohibited simply because a wage differential results.

Even with a business-related requirement, an employer might assert some business reason as a pretext for a discriminatory objective. This possibility is especially great with a factor like prior salary which can easily be used to capitalize on the unfairly low salaries historically paid to women. See Futran v. RING Radio Co., 501 F.Supp. 734, 739 n. 2 (N.D.Ga.1980) (expressing concern that the use of prior salary would perpetuate the traditionally lower salaries paid women). The ability of courts to protect against such abuse is somewhat limited, however. The Equal Pay Act entrusts employers, not judges, with making the often uncertain decision of how to accomplish business objectives. We have found no authority giving guidance on the proper judicial inquiry absent direct evidence of discriminatory intent. A pragmatic standard, which protects against abuse yet accommodates employer discretion, is that the employer must use the factor reasonably in light of the employer's stated purpose as well as its other practices. The specific relevant considerations will of course vary with the situation. In Part IV of this opinion, we outline how the court below should apply this test to the business reasons given by Allstate for its use of prior salary.

C

Relying on recent Supreme Court precedent, Kouba would limit the category of business reasons acceptable under the exception to those

6. Not every reason making economic sense is acceptable. See Corning Glass Works v. Brennan, 417 U.S. at 205, 94 S.Ct. at 2233. This appeal does not, however, require us to compile a complete list of unacceptable factors or even formulate a standard to distinguish them from acceptable ones. We leave those tasks for another day.

that measure the value of an employee's job performance to his or her employer. In County of Washington v. Gunther, 452 U.S. at 170–71 n. 11, 101 S.Ct. at 2248–49 n. 11, the Court reported that Congress added the exception "because of a concern that bona fide job evaluation systems used by American businesses would otherwise be disrupted." In Corning Glass Works v. Brennan, 417 U.S. at 199, 94 S.Ct. at 2230, the Court explained that these systems "took into consideration four separate factors in determining job value—skill, effort, responsibility and working conditions—and each of these four components was further systematically divided into various subcomponents." Our study of the legislative history of the Equal Pay Act confirms that Congress discussed only factors that reflect job value.

In drafting the Act, however, Congress did not limit the exception to job-evaluation systems. Instead, it excepted "any other factor other than sex" and thus created a "broad general exception." H.R.Rep. No. 309, 88th Cong., 1st Sess. 3, reprinted in 1963 U.S. Code Cong. & Ad. News 687, 689. While a concern about job-evaluation systems served as the impetus for creating the exception, Congress did not limit the exception to that concern.

Other language in the Act supports this conclusion. The statutory definition of equal work incorporates the four factors listed in *Corning Glass* as the standard components in job-evaluation systems. (The Act refers to "equal work on jobs the performance of which requires equal skill, effort, and responsibility, and which are performed under similar working conditions.") It would render the "factor other than sex" exception surplusage to limit the exception to the same four factors. And while we might be able to distinguish other factors that also reflect job value, the scope of the exception would be exceedingly narrow if limited to other apparently uncommon factors. The broad language of the exception belies such limitation.

Accordingly, no court or other authority has inferred a job-evaluation requirement. We, too, reject that limitation on the "factor other than sex" exception.

IV

Allstate provides two business reasons for its use of prior salary that the district court must evaluate on remand.[7] We will discuss each explanation in turn without attempting to establish a comprehensive framework for its evaluation. The district court should mold its inquiry to the particular facts that unfold at trial.

7. A third reason given by Allstate is that an individual with a higher prior salary can demand more in the marketplace. Courts disagree whether market demand can ever justify a wage differential. Compare, e.g., Horner v. Mary Institute, 613 F.2d 706, 714 (8th Cir. 1980) (allowing it in limited situations), with Futran v. RING Radio Co., 501 F.Supp. 734, 739 (N.D.Ga. 1980) (disallowing it always). We need not rule whether Congress intended to prohibit the use of market demand. Because Allstate did not present any evidence to support its use of prior salary in response to market demand, the district court properly disposed of that reason on summary judgment.

A

Allstate asserts that it ties the guaranteed monthly minimum to prior salary as part of a sales-incentive program. If the monthly minimum far exceeds the amount that the agent earned previously, the agent might become complacent and not fulfill his or her selling potential. By limiting the monthly minimum according to prior salary, Allstate hopes to motivate the agent to make sales, earn commissions, and thus improve his or her financial position. Presumably, Allstate cannot set a uniform monthly minimum so low that it motivates all sales agents, because then prospective agents with substantially higher prior salaries might not risk taking a job with Allstate.

This reasoning does not explain Allstate's use of prior salary during the initial training period. Because the agents cannot earn commissions at that time, there is no potential reward to motivate them to make sales.

When commissions become available, we wonder whether Allstate adjusts the guaranteed minimum regularly and whether most agents earn commission-based salaries. On remand, the district court should inquire into these and other issues that relate to the reasonableness of the use of prior salary in the incentive program.

B

Reasoning that salary corresponds roughly to an employee's ability, Allstate also claims that it uses prior salary to predict a new employee's performance as a sales agent. Relevant considerations in evaluating the reasonableness of this practice include (1) whether the employer also uses other available predictors of the new employee's performance, (2) whether the employer attributes less significance to prior salary once the employee has proven himself or herself on the job, and (3) whether the employer relies more heavily on salary when the prior job resembles the job of sales agent.

V

In conclusion, the Equal Pay Act does not impose a strict prohibition against the use of prior salary. Thus while we share the district court's fear that an employer might manipulate its use of prior salary to underpay female employees the court must find that the business reasons given by Allstate do not reasonably explain its use of that factor before finding a violation of the Act.

Reversed and Remanded.

* * *

NOTES AND PROBLEMS FOR DISCUSSION

1. Mel's Clothing Store has separate departments for men's and women's clothing. The merchandise in the men's department is of better quality and

higher price than the women's merchandise, and yields a higher profit margin than the women's clothing. Only women were hired for the women's department and only men were permitted to work in the men's department. It is conceded that the sales personnel in both departments perform equal work. Mel's, however, pays all its salesmen a higher base salary than is paid to its saleswomen. The store maintains that this differential is justified by the greater profitability and dollar volume of gross sales produced by the salespersons in the men's department. Is Mel's violating the EPA? Is the plaintiff in this problem really asserting a claim of unequal pay? Or is she alleging that she was a victim of a discriminatory job assignment? If the latter, shouldn't the action be brought under Title VII rather than the EPA? See Hodgson v. Robert Hall Clothes, Inc., 473 F.2d 589 (3d Cir. 1973), cert. denied, 414 U.S. 866, 94 S.Ct. 50, 38 L.Ed.2d 85. Does the principal case address any of these issues? See Sullivan, The Equal Pay Act of 1963: Making and Breaking A Prima Facie Case, 31 Ark.L.Rev. 545 (1978).

2. Buff Spas Inc. operates a chain of health spas, each of which is divided into a men's and women's division. Men operate the men's division and women operate the women's division. The manager of each division is paid by commissions based on gross sales of memberships. Male managers are paid 6% of their spa's gross sales of memberships to men; female managers are paid 4% of gross sales of memberships to women. Over the course of the company's existence, the gross volume of membership sales to women was 50% higher than the gross volume of membership sales to men. There is no difference in the job duties of male and female managers and they perform their jobs under similar working conditions. The total remuneration received by males and females was substantially equal, however, because while females received a commission based on a lower percentage of gross sales, they sold more memberships than the males. The company says that it pays different commission rates so that men and women will be paid substantially equal compensation for equal work performed. Is the company in violation of the Equal Pay Act? See Bence v. Detroit Health Corp., 712 F.2d 1024 (6th Cir. 1983), cert. denied, 465 U.S. 1025, 104 S.Ct. 1282, 79 L.Ed.2d 685 (1984).

3. In connection with the opening of a family planning center, Good Samaritan Hospital sought to hire two additional gynecologists. From a pool of twenty male and two female applicants for the posts, the hospital made offers to Dr. Arlene DeRoy and Dr. Paul Barron. After both joined the Hospital's staff, Dr. Barron discovered that Dr. DeRoy's salary was $10,000 higher than his. Both Drs. Barron and DeRoy were 1975 graduates of the same medical school with comparable prior experience and medical school records. The Hospital contends that because of the great demand and extremely limited supply of female gynecologists, it was compelled to offer Dr. DeRoy a higher salary to lure her away from other offers of employment. Has the Hospital violated the Equal Pay Act? Compare Horner v. Mary Institute, 613 F.2d 706 (8th Cir. 1980) with Hodgson v. Brookhaven General Hospital, 436 F.2d 719 (5th Cir. 1970).

4. In CORNING GLASS WORKS v. BRENNAN, 417 U.S. 188, 94 S.Ct. 2223, 41 L.Ed.2d 1 (1974), discussed in the principal case, the employer paid a higher base wage to male night shift inspectors than it paid to female inspectors who performed the same job duties during the day shift. It also paid a separate premium to all workers on the night shift. The defendant argued that since day shift work was not "performed under similar working conditions" as night shift work, the plaintiff Secretary of Labor had failed to prove that

Corning was paying unequal pay for equal work. The Secretary contended that day and night shift work were performed under similar working conditions and that while night shift work could constitute a "factor other than sex" defense, Corning had failed to prove that the higher base wage paid to male night shift inspectors was based on a non-sex factor. The Court agreed with the Secretary:

> While a layman might well assume that time of day worked reflects one aspect of a job's "working conditions," the term has a different and much more specific meaning in the language of industrial relations. As Corning's own representative testified at the hearings, the element of working conditions encompasses two subfactors: "surroundings" and "hazards." "Surroundings" measures the elements, such as toxic chemicals or fumes, regularly encountered by a worker, their intensity, and their frequency. "Hazards" takes into account the physical hazards regularly encountered, their frequency, and the severity of injury they can cause. This definition of "working conditions" is not only manifested in Corning's own job evaluation plans but is also well accepted across a wide range of American industry.
>
> Nowhere in any of these definitions is time of day worked mentioned as a relevant criterion. The fact of the matter is that the concept of "working conditions," as used in the specialized language of job evaluation systems, simply does not encompass shift differentials. Indeed, while Corning now argues that night inspection work is not equal to day inspection work, all of its own job evaluation plans, including the one now in effect, have consistently treated them as equal in all respects, including working conditions. * * * We agree with the Second Circuit that the inspection work at issue in this case, whether performed during the day or night, is "equal work" as that term is defined in the Act.
>
> This does not mean, of course, that there is no room in the Equal Pay Act for nondiscriminatory shift differentials. Work on a steady night shift no doubt has psychological and physiological impacts making it less attractive than work on a day shift. The Act contemplates that a male night worker may receive a higher wage than a female day worker, just as it contemplates that a male employee with 20 years' seniority can receive a higher wage than a woman with two years' seniority. Factors such as these play a role under the Act's four exceptions—the seniority differential under the specific seniority exception, the shift differential under the catch-all exception for differentials "based on any other factor other than sex."

417 U.S. at 202–204, 94 S.Ct. at 2231–2233, 41 L.Ed.2d at 14–15.

What is the significance of this ruling?

The Court concluded that Corning had not sustained its burden of proving that the higher base rate paid for night work was based on a factor other than sex, since prior to 1966, Corning allowed only men to work the night shift and the men would not work at the low wage paid to women inspectors. Would the Court have reached a different conclusion if state law had precluded women from working at night? Can an employer justify a sex-based wage differential on the ground that the state minimum wage law establishes a higher minimum wage for women? See Wirtz v. Rainbo Baking Co. of Lexington, 303 F.Supp. 1049 (E.D.Ky.1967). Should the response to these questions differ from the treatment of the conflict between state "protective" labor legislation and Title VII? Does the language of the EPA offer any guidance as to how such state laws are to be interpreted in order to comply with the federal Act's equal pay standard?

5. The Robin Morris Institute determined that the salaries of its female researchers were significantly lower than those of its similarly qualified male researchers. Accordingly, it designed a formula for increasing the salaries of its female researchers to remedy that discrimination. Raises resulting from the application of that formula were given to the female researchers. A group of male researchers claims that the Morris Institute violated the EPA by giving raises solely to its female researchers. What result? See Ende v. Board of Regents, 757 F.2d 176 (7th Cir. 1985).

COUNTY OF WASHINGTON v. GUNTHER

Supreme Court of the United States, 1981.
452 U.S. 161, 101 S.Ct. 2242, 68 L.Ed.2d 751.

JUSTICE BRENNAN delivered the opinion of the Court.

The question presented is whether § 703(h) of Title VII of the Civil Rights Act of 1964 restricts Title VII's prohibition of sex-based wage discrimination to claims of equal pay for equal work.

I

This case arises over the payment by petitioner, the County of Washington, Or., of substantially lower wages to female guards in the female section of the county jail than it paid to male guards in the male section of the jail. Respondents are four women who were employed to guard female prisoners and to carry out certain other functions in the jail.[2] In January 1974, the county eliminated the female section of the jail, transferred the female prisoners to the jail of a nearby county, and discharged respondents.

Respondents filed suit against petitioner in Federal District Court under Title VII, seeking backpay and other relief.[3] They alleged that they were paid unequal wages for work substantially equal to that performed by male guards, and in the alternative, that part of the pay differential was attributable to intentional sex discrimination. The latter allegation was based on a claim that, because of intentional discrimination, the county set the pay scale for female guards, but not for male guards, at a level lower than that warranted by its own survey of outside markets and the worth of the jobs.

After trial, the District Court found that the male guards supervised more than 10 times as many prisoners per guard as did the female guards, and that the females devoted much of their time to less-valuable clerical duties. It therefore held that respondents' jobs were not substantially equal to those of the male guards, and that respon-

2. Oregon requires that female inmates be guarded solely by women, Or.Rev.Stat. §§ 137.350, 137.360, and the District Court opinion indicates that women had not been employed to guard male prisoners. For purposes of this litigation, respondents concede that gender is a bona fide occupational qualification for some of the female guard positions.

3. Respondents could not sue under the Equal Pay Act because the Equal Pay Act did not apply to municipal employees until passage of the Fair Labor Standards Amendments of 1974. Title VII has applied to such employees since passage of the Equal Employment Opportunity Act of 1972.

dents were thus not entitled to equal pay. The Court of Appeals affirmed on that issue, and respondents do not seek review of the ruling.

The District Court also dismissed respondents' claim that the discrepancy in pay between the male and female guards was attributable in part to intentional sex discrimination. It held as a matter of law that a sex-based wage discrimination claim cannot be brought under Title VII unless it would satisfy the equal work standard of the Equal Pay Act. The Court therefore permitted no additional evidence on this claim, and made no findings on whether petitioner's pay scales for female guards resulted from intentional sex discrimination.

The Court of Appeals reversed, holding that persons alleging sex discrimination "are not precluded from suing under Title VII to protest * * * discriminatory compensation practices" merely because their jobs were not equal to higher-paying jobs held by members of the opposite sex. The Court remanded to the District Court with instructions to take evidence on respondents' claim that part of the difference between their rate of pay and that of the male guards is attributable to sex discrimination. We granted certiorari, and now affirm.

We emphasize at the outset the narrowness of the question before us in this case. Respondents' claim is not based on the controversial concept of "comparable worth," under which plaintiffs might claim increased compensation on the basis of a comparison of the intrinsic worth or difficulty of their job with that of other jobs in the same organization or community. Rather, respondents seek to prove, by direct evidence, that their wages were depressed because of intentional sex discrimination, consisting of setting the wage scale for female guards, but not for male guards, at a level lower than its own survey of outside markets and the worth of the jobs warranted. The narrow question in this case is whether such a claim is precluded by the last sentence of § 703(h) of Title VII, called the "Bennett Amendment." [8]

Title VII makes it an unlawful employment practice for an employer "to discriminate against any individual with respect to his compensation, terms, conditions, or privileges of employment, because of such individual's * * * sex * * *." The Bennett Amendment to Title VII, however provides:

> "It shall not be an unlawful employment practice under this subchapter for any employer to differentiate upon the basis of sex in determining the amount of the wages or compensation paid or to be paid to employees of such employer if such differentiation is authorized by the provisions of section 206(d) of title 29."

8. We are not called upon in this case to decide whether respondents have stated a prima facie case of sex discrimination under Title VII, or to lay down standards for the further conduct of this litigation. The sole issue we decide is whether respondents' failure to satisfy the equal work standard of the Equal Pay Act in itself precludes their proceeding under Title VII.

To discover what practices are exempted from Title VII's prohibitions by the Bennett Amendment, we must turn to * * * the Equal Pay Act * * *. On its face, the Equal Pay Act contains three restrictions pertinent to this case. First, its coverage is limited to those employers subject to the Fair Labor Standards Act. Thus, the Act does not apply, for example, to certain businesses engaged in retail sales, fishing, agriculture, and newspaper publishing. Second, the Act is restricted to cases involving "equal work on jobs the performance of which requires equal skill, effort, and responsibility, and which are performed under similar working conditions." Third, the Act's four affirmative defenses exempt any wage differentials attributable to seniority, merit, quantity or quality of production, or "any other factor other than sex."

Petitioner argues that the purpose of the Bennett Amendment was to restrict Title VII sex-based wage discrimination claims to those that could also be brought under the Equal Pay Act, and thus that claims not arising from "equal work" are precluded. Respondents, in contrast, argue that the Bennett Amendment was designed merely to incorporate the four affirmative defenses of the Equal Pay Act into Title VII for sex-based wage discrimination claims. Respondents thus contend that claims for sex-based wage discrimination can be brought under Title VII even though no member of the opposite sex holds an equal but higher-paying job, provided that the challenged wage rate is not based on seniority, merit, quantity or quality of production, or "any other factor other than sex." The Court of Appeals found respondents' interpretation the "more persuasive." While recognizing that the language and legislative history of the provision are not unambiguous, we conclude that the Court of Appeals was correct.

The language of the Bennett Amendment suggests an intention to incorporate only the affirmative defenses of the Equal Pay Act into Title VII. The Amendment bars sex-based wage discrimination claims under Title VII where the pay differential is "authorized" by the Equal Pay Act. Although the word "authorize" sometimes means simply "to permit," it ordinarily denotes affirmative enabling action. * * * The question, then, is what wage practices have been affirmatively authorized by the Equal Pay Act.

The Equal Pay Act is divided into two parts: a definition of the violation, followed by four affirmative defenses. The first part can hardly be said to "authorize" anything at all: it is purely prohibitory. The second part, however, in essence "authorizes" employers to differentiate in pay on the basis of seniority, merit, quantity or quality of production, or any other factor other than sex, even though such differentiation might otherwise violate the Act. It is to these provisions, therefore, that the Bennett Amendment must refer.

Petitioner argues that this construction of the Bennett Amendment would render it superfluous. Petitioner claims that the first three affirmative defenses are simply redundant of the provisions elsewhere in § 703(h) of Title VII that already exempt bona fide seniority and merit systems and systems measuring earnings by quantity or quality of production, and that the fourth defense—"any other factor other than sex"—is implicit in Title VII's general prohibition of sex-based discrimination.

We cannot agree. The Bennett Amendment was offered as a "technical amendment" designed to resolve any potential conflicts between Title VII and the Equal Pay Act. Thus, with respect to the first three defenses, the Bennett Amendment has the effect of guaranteeing that courts and administrative agencies adopt a consistent interpretation of like provisions in both statutes. Otherwise, they might develop inconsistent bodies of case law interpreting two sets of nearly identical language.

More importantly, incorporation of the fourth affirmative defense could have significant consequences for Title VII litigation. Title VII's prohibition of discriminatory employment practices was intended to be broadly inclusive, proscribing "not only overt discrimination but also practices that are fair in form, but discriminatory in operation." Griggs v. Duke Power Co. The structure of Title VII litigation, including presumptions, burdens of proof, and defenses, has been designed to reflect this approach. The fourth affirmative defense of the Equal Pay Act, however, was designed differently, to confine the application of the Act to wage differentials attributable to sex discrimination. Equal Pay Act litigation, therefore, has been structured to permit employers to defend against charges of discrimination where their pay differentials are based on a bona fide use of "other factors other than sex." Under the Equal Pay Act, the courts and administrative agencies are not permitted "to substitute their judgment for the judgment of the employer * * * who [has] established and employed a bona fide job rating system," so long as it does not discriminate on the basis of sex. 109 Cong.Rec. 9209 (statement of Rep. Goodell, principal exponent of the Act). Although we do not decide in this case how sex-based wage discrimination litigation under Title VII should be structured to accommodate the fourth affirmative defense of the Equal Pay Act, we consider it clear that the Bennett Amendment, under this interpretation, is not rendered superfluous.

We therefore conclude that only differentials attributable to the four affirmative defenses of the Equal Pay Act are "authorized" by that Act within the meaning of § 703(h) of Title VII.[14]

* * *

14. The argument in the dissent that under our interpretation, the Equal Pay Act would be impliedly repealed and rendered a nullity is mistaken. Not only might the substantive provisions of the Equal Pay Act's affirmative defenses affect the outcome of some Title VII sex-based wage discrimination cases, but the procedural characteristics of the Equal Pay Act also remain significant. For example, the statute of limitations for backpay relief is more generous under the Equal Pay Act than under Title VII, and the Equal Pay Act, unlike Title VII, has no requirement of filing administrative complaints and awaiting administrative conciliation efforts. Given these advantages, many

Our interpretation of the Bennett Amendment draws additional support from the remedial purposes of Title VII and the Equal Pay Act. Section 703(a) of Title VII makes it unlawful for an employer "to fail or refuse to hire or to discharge any individual, or *otherwise to discriminate* against any individual with respect to his compensation, terms, conditions, or privileges of employment" because of such individual's sex. (emphasis added). As Congress itself has indicated, a "broad approach" to the definition of equal employment opportunity is essential to overcoming and undoing the effect of discrimination. S.Rep.No. 867, 88th Cong., 2d Sess., 12 (1964). We must therefore avoid interpretations of Title VII that deprive victims of discrimination of a remedy, without clear congressional mandate.

Under petitioner's reading of the Bennett Amendment, only those sex-based wage discrimination claims that satisfy the "equal work" standard of the Equal Pay Act could be brought under Title VII. In practical terms, this means that a woman who is discriminatorily underpaid could obtain no relief—no matter how egregious the discrimination might be—unless her employer also employed a man in an equal job in the same establishment, at a higher rate of pay. Thus, if an employer hired a woman for a unique position in the company and then admitted that her salary would have been higher had she been male, the woman would be unable to obtain legal redress under petitioner's interpretation. Similarly, if an employer used a transparently sex-biased system for wage determination, women holding jobs not equal to those held by men would be denied the right to prove that the system is a pretext for discrimination. Moreover, to cite an example arising from a recent case, Los Angeles Department of Water & Power v. Manhart, 435 U.S. 702, 98 S.Ct. 1370, 55 L.Ed.2d 657 (1978), if the employer required its female workers to pay more into its pension program than male workers were required to pay, the only women who could bring a Title VII action under petitioner's interpretation would be those who could establish that a man performed equal work: a female auditor thus might have a cause of action while a female secretary might not. Congress surely did not intend the Bennett Amendment to insulate such blatantly discriminatory practices from judicial redress under Title VII.[19]

Moreover, petitioner's interpretation would have other far-reaching consequences. Since it rests on the proposition that any wage differentials not prohibited by the Equal Pay Act are "authorized" by it, petitioner's interpretation would lead to the conclusion that discriminatory compensation by employers not covered by the Fair Labor Standards Act is "authorized"—since not prohibited—by the Equal Pay Act.

plaintiffs will prefer to sue under the Equal Pay Act rather than Title VII.

19. The dissent attempts to minimize the significance of the Title VII remedy in these cases on the ground that the Equal Pay Act already provides an action for sex-biased wage discrimination by women who hold jobs not *currently* held by men. But the dissent's position would still leave remediless all victims of discrimination who hold jobs *never* held by men.

Thus it would deny Title VII protection against sex-based wage discrimination by those employers not subject to the Fair Labor Standards Act but covered by Title VII. There is no persuasive evidence that Congress intended such a result, and the EEOC has rejected it since at least 1965. Indeed, petitioner itself apparently acknowledges that Congress intended Title VII's broader coverage to apply to equal pay claims under Title VII, thus impliedly admitting the fallacy in its own argument.

* * *

Petitioner argues strenuously that the approach of the Court of Appeals places "the pay structure of virtually every employer and the entire economy * * * at risk and subject to scrutiny by the federal courts." It raises the spectre that "Title VII plaintiffs could draw any type of comparison imaginable concerning job duties and pay between any job predominantly performed by women and any job predominantly performed by men." But whatever the merit of petitioner's arguments in other contexts, they are inapplicable here, for claims based on the type of job comparisons petitioner describes are manifestly different from respondents' claim. Respondents contend that the County of Washington evaluated the worth of their jobs; that the county determined that they should be paid approximately 95% as much as the male correctional officers; that it paid them only about 70% as much, while paying the male officers the full evaluated worth of their jobs; and that the failure of the county to pay respondents the full evaluated worth of their jobs can be proven to be attributable to intentional sex discrimination. Thus, respondents' suit does not require a court to make its own subjective assessment of the value of the male and female guard jobs, or to attempt by statistical technique or other method to quantify the effect of sex discrimination on the wage rates.

We do not decide in this case the precise contours of lawsuits challenging sex discrimination in compensation under Title VII. It is sufficient to note that respondents' claims of discriminatory undercompensation are not barred by § 703(h) of Title VII merely because respondents do not perform work equal to that of male jail guards. The judgment of the Court of Appeals is therefore

Affirmed.

JUSTICE REHNQUIST, with whom THE CHIEF JUSTICE, JUSTICE STEWART, and JUSTICE POWELL join, dissenting.

The Court today holds a plaintiff may state a claim of sex-based wage discrimination under Title VII without even establishing that she has performed "equal or substantially equal work" to that of males as defined in the Equal Pay Act. Because I believe that the legislative history of both the Equal Pay Act and Title VII clearly establishes that there can be no Title VII claim of sex-based wage discrimination without proof of "equal work," I dissent.

Because the Court never comes to grips with petitioners' argument, it is necessary to restate it here. Petitioners argue that Congress in adopting the Equal Pay Act of 1963 specifically addressed the problem of sex-based wage discrimination and determined that there should be a remedy for claims of unequal pay for equal work, but not for "comparable" work. Petitioners further observe that nothing in the legislative history of Title VII, enacted just one year later in 1964, reveals an intent to overrule that determination. Quite the contrary, petitioner notes that the legislative history of Title VII, including the adoption of the so-called Bennett Amendment, demonstrates Congress' intent to require all sex-based wage discrimination claims, whether brought under the Equal Pay Act or under Title VII, to satisfy the "equal work" standard. Because respondents have not satisfied the "equal work" standard, petitioners conclude that they have not stated a claim under Title VII.

In rejecting that argument, the Court ignores traditional canons of statutory construction and relevant legislative history. * * * It insists that there simply *must* be a remedy for wage discrimination *beyond* that provided in the Equal Pay Act. The Court does not explain *why* that must be so, nor does it explain *what* that remedy might be. And, of course, the Court cannot explain why it and not Congress is charged with determining what is and what is not sound public policy.

The closest the Court can come in giving a reason for its decision is its belief that interpretations of Title VII which "deprive victims of discrimination of a remedy, without clear congressional mandate" must be avoided. But that analysis turns traditional canons of statutory construction on their head. It has long been the rule that when a legislature enacts a statute to protect a class of persons, the burden is on the plaintiff to show statutory coverage, not on the defendant to show that there is a "clear congressional mandate" for *excluding* the plaintiff from coverage. Such a departure from traditional rules is particularly unwarranted in this case, where the doctrine of *in pari materia* suggests that all claims of sex-based wage discrimination are governed by the substantive standards of the previously enacted and more specific legislation, the Equal Pay Act.

Because the decision does not rest on any reasoned statement of logic or principle, it provides little guidance to employers or lower courts as to what types of compensation practices might now violate Title VII. The Court correctly emphasizes that its decision is narrow, and indeed one searches the Court's opinion in vain for a hint as to what pleadings or proof other than that adduced in this particular case, would be sufficient to state a claim of sex-based wage discrimination under Title VII. * * * All we know is that Title VII provides a remedy when, as here, plaintiffs seek to show by *direct* evidence that their employer *intentionally* depressed their wages. And, for reasons that go largely unexplained, we also know that a Title VII remedy may not be available to plaintiffs who allege theories different than that alleged here, such as the so-called "comparable worth" theory. One has the sense that the decision today will be treated like a restricted railroad ticket, "good for this day and train only."

In the end, however, the flaw with today's decision is not so much that it is so narrowly written as to be virtually meaningless, but rather that its legal analysis is wrong. The Court is obviously more interested in the consequences of its decision than in discerning the intention of Congress. In reaching its desired result, the Court conveniently and persistently ignores relevant legislative history and instead relies wholly on what it believes Congress *should* have enacted.

The starting point for any discussion of sex-based wage discrimination claims must be the Equal Pay Act of 1963, enacted as an amendment to the Fair Labor Standards Act of 1938. It was there that Congress, after 18 months of careful and exhaustive study, specifically addressed the problem of sex-based wage discrimination. The Equal Pay Act states that employers shall not discriminate on the basis of sex by paying different wages for jobs that require equal skill, effort, and responsibility. In adopting the "equal pay for equal work" formula, Congress carefully considered and ultimately rejected the "equal pay for comparable worth" standard advanced by respondents and several *amici.* As the legislative history of the Equal Pay Act amply demonstrates, Congress realized that the adoption of the comparable worth doctrine would ignore the economic realities of supply and demand and would involve both governmental agencies and courts in the impossible task of ascertaining the worth of comparable work, an area in which they have little expertise.

* * *

* * * Instead, Congress concluded that governmental intervention to equalize wage differentials was to be undertaken only within one circumstance: when men's and women's jobs were identical or nearly so, hence unarguably of equal worth. It defies common sense to believe that the same Congress—which, after 18 months of hearings and debates, had decided in 1963 upon the extent of federal involvement it desired in the area of wage rate claims—intended *sub silentio* to reject all of this work and to abandon the limitations of the equal work approach just one year later, when it enacted Title VII.

* * * The question is whether Congress intended to completely turn its back on the "equal work" standard enacted in the Equal Pay Act of 1963 when it adopted Title VII only one year later.

The Court answers that question in the affirmative, concluding that Title VII must be read more broadly than the Equal Pay Act. In so holding, the majority wholly ignores this Court's repeated adherence to the doctrine of *in pari materia,* namely, that "where there is no clear intention otherwise, a specific statute will not be controlled or nullified by a general one, regardless of the priority of enactment." * * *

Applying those principles to this case, there can be no doubt that the Equal Pay Act and Title VII should be construed *in pari materia.* The Equal Pay Act is the more specific piece of legislation, dealing solely with sex-based wage discrimination, and was the product of exhaustive congressional study. Title VII, by contrast, is a general antidiscrimination provision, passed with virtually no consideration of the specific problem of sex-based wage discrimination. See *General Electric Co. v. Gilbert,* 429 U.S. 125, 143, 97 S.Ct. 401, 411, 50 L.Ed.2d 343 (1976) (the legislative history of the sex discrimination amendment is "notable primarily for its brevity").[4] Most significantly, there is absolutely nothing in the legislative history of Title VII which reveals an intent by Congress to repeal by implication the provisions of the Equal Pay Act. Quite the contrary, what little legislative history there is on the subject * * * indicates that Congress intended to incorporate the substantive standards of the Equal Pay Act into Title VII so that sex-based wage discrimination claims would be governed by the equal work standard of the Equal Pay Act and by that standard alone. * * *

* * *

In response to questions by Senator Dirksen, Senator Clark, the floor manager for the bill, prepared a memorandum in which he attempted to put to rest certain objections which he believed to be unfounded. Senator Clark's answer to Senator Dirksen reveals that Senator Clark believed that all cases of wage discrimination under Title VII would be treated under the standards of the Equal Pay Act:

> "*Objection.* The sex anti-discrimination provisions of the bill duplicate the coverage of the Equal Pay Act of 1963. But more than this, they extend far beyond the scope and coverage of the Equal Pay Act. *They do not include the limitation in that Act with respect to equal work on jobs requiring equal skills in the same establishments, and thus, cut across different jobs.*
>
> "*Answer.* The Equal Pay Act is a part of the Wage Hour Law, with different coverage and with numerous exemptions unlike Title VII. Furthermore, under Title VII, jobs can no longer be classified as to sex, except where there is a rational basis for discrimination on the ground of bona fide occupational qualification. *The standards in the Equal Pay Act for determining discrimination as to wages, of course, are applicable to the comparable situation under Title VII.*" 110 Cong. Rec. 7217 (1964) (emphasis added).

4. Indeed, Title VII was originally intended to protect the rights of Negroes. On the final day of consideration by the entire House, Representative Smith added an amendment to prohibit sex discrimination. It has been speculated that the amendment was added as an attempt to thwart passage of Title VII. The amendment was passed by the House that same day, and the entire bill was approved two days later and sent to the Senate without any consideration of the effect of the amendment on the Equal Pay Act. The attenuated history of the sex amendment to Title VII makes it difficult to believe that Congress thereby intended to wholly abandon the carefully crafted equal work standard of the Equal Pay Act.

In this passage, Senator Clark asserted that the sex discrimination provisions of Title VII were necessary, notwithstanding the Equal Pay Act, because (a) the Equal Pay Act had numerous exemptions for various types of businesses, and (b) Title VII covered discrimination in access (e.g., assignment and promotion) to jobs, not just compensation. In addition, Senator Clark made clear that in the compensation area the equal work standard would continue to be the applicable standard. He explained, in answer to Senator Dirksen's concern, that when *different jobs* were at issue, the Equal Pay Act's legal standards—the "equal work" standard—would apply to limit the reach of Title VII. Thus Senator Clark rejected as unfounded the objections that the sex provisions of Title VII were unnecessary on the one hand, or extended beyond the equal work standard on the other.

Notwithstanding Senator Clark's explanation, Senator Bennett remained concerned that, absent an explicit cross reference to the Equal Pay Act, the "wholesale assertion" of the word "sex" in Title VII could nullify the carefully conceived Equal Pay Act standard. 110 Cong.Rec. 13647 (1964). Accordingly, he offered, and the Senate accepted, the * * * amendment to Title VII * * *.

Although the language of the Bennett Amendment is ambiguous, the most plausible interpretation of the Amendment is that it incorporates the substantive standard of the Equal Pay Act—the equal pay for equal work standard—into Title VII. A number of considerations support that view. In the first place, that interpretation is wholly consistent with, and in fact confirms, Senator Clark's earlier explanation of Title VII. Second, in the limited time available to Senator Bennett when he offered his amendment—the time for debate having been limited by cloture—he explained the Amendment's purpose.

> "Mr. President, after many years of yearning by members of the fair sex in this country, and after careful study by the appropriate committees of Congress, last year Congress passed the so-called Equal Pay Act, which became effective only yesterday.
>
> "By this time, programs have been established for the effective administration of this Act. Now when the Civil Rights Bill is under consideration in which the word sex has been inserted in many places, I do not believe sufficient attention may have been paid to possible conflicts between the wholesale insertion of the word sex in the bill and the Equal Pay Act. *The purpose of my amendment is to provide that in the event of conflicts, the provisions of the Equal Pay Act shall not be nullified.*" 110 Cong.Rec. 13647 (1964) (emphasis supplied).

It is obvious that the principal way in which the Equal Pay Act could be "nullified" would be to allow plaintiffs unable to meet the "equal pay for equal work" standard to proceed under Title VII asserting some other theory of wage discrimination, such as "comparable worth." If plaintiffs can proceed under Title VII without showing that they satisfy the "equal work" criterion of the Equal Pay Act, one would expect all plaintiffs to file suit under the "broader" Title VII standard. Such a result would, for all practical purposes, constitute an implied repeal of the equal work standard of the Equal Pay Act and render that Act a nullity. This was precisely the result Congress sought to avert when it adopted the Bennett Amendment, and the result the Court today embraces.

Senator Bennett confirmed this interpretation just one year later. The Senator expressed concern as to the proper interpretation of his Amendment and offered his written understanding of the Amendment.

> "The Amendment therefore means that it is not an unlawful employment practice: * * * (b) to have different standards of compensation for nonexempt employees, where such differentiation is not prohibited by the Equal Pay Amendment to the Fair Labor Standards Act.
>
> "Simply stated, *the [Bennett] Amendment means that discrimination and compensation on account of sex does not violate Title VII unless it also violates that Equal Pay Act.*" 111 Cong.Rec. 13359 (1965) (emphasis supplied).

Senator Dirksen agreed that this interpretation was "precisely" the one that he, Senator Humphrey, and their staffs had in mind when the Senate adopted the Bennett Amendment. He added, "I trust that that will suffice to clear up in the minds of anyone, whether in the Department of Justice or elsewhere, what the Senate intended when that Amendment was accepted." [6]

* * *

The Court blithely ignores all of his legislative history and chooses to interpret the Bennett Amendment as incorporating only the Equal Pay Act's four affirmative defenses, and not the equal work requirement.[10] That argument does not survive scrutiny. In the first place,

6. There is undoubtedly some danger in relying on subsequent legislative history. But that does not mean that such subsequent legislative history is wholly irrelevant, particularly where, as here, the *sponsor* of the legislation makes a clarifying statement which is not inconsistent with the prior ambiguous legislative history.

The Court suggests Senator Bennett's 1965 comments should be discounted because Senator Clark criticized them. Senator Clark did indeed criticize Senator Bennett, but only because Senator Clark read Senator Bennett's explanation as suggesting that Title VII protection would not be available to those employees not within the Equal Pay Act's coverage. Senator Clark's view was that employees not covered by the Equal Pay Act could still bring Title VII claims. He did not dispute, however, the proposition that the "equal work" standard of the Equal Pay Act was incorporated into Title VII claims. Quite the contrary, Senator Clark placed into the record a letter from the Chairman of the National Committee for Equal Pay which stated that:

> "Our best understanding of the implications of the [Bennett Amendment] at the time it was adopted was that its intent and effect was to make sure that equal pay would be applied and interpreted under the Civil Rights Act in the same way as under the earlier statute, the Equal Pay Act. *That is, the Equal Pay Act standards, requiring equal work * * * would also be applied under the Civil Rights Act.*"

10. In reaching this conclusion, the Court relies far too heavily on a definition of the word "authorize." Rather than "make a fortress out of the dictionary," the Court should instead attempt to implement the legislative intent of Congress. Even if dictionary definitions were to be our guide, the language of the amendment draws no distinction between the Equal Pay Act's standard for liability—equal pay for equal work—and the Act's defenses. Nor does any Senator or Congressman even come close to suggesting that the Amendment incorporates the Equal Pay Act's affirmative defenses into Title VII, but not the equal work standard itself. Quite the contrary, the concern was that Title VII would render the Equal Pay Act a nullity. It is only too obvious that reading just the four affirmative defenses of the Equal Pay Act into Title VII does not protect the careful draftsmanship of the Equal Pay Act. * * * In this case, it stands Congress' concern on its head to suppose that Congress sought to incorporate the affirmative defenses, but not the equal work standard. It would be surprising if Congress in 1964 sought to reverse its decision in 1963 to require a showing of "equal work" as a predicate to an equal pay claim and at the same time carefully preserve the four affirmative defenses.

Moreover, even on its own terms the Court's argument is unpersuasive. The Equal Pay Act contains four statutory defenses: different compensation is permissible if the differential is made by way of (1) a seniority system, (2) a merit system, (3) a system which measures earnings by quantity or quality of production, or (4) is based on any other factor other than sex. The flaw in interpreting the Bennett Amendment as incorporating only the four defenses of the Equal Pay Act into Title VII is that Title VII, even without the Bennett Amendment, contains those very same defenses. The opening sentence of § 703(h) protects differentials and compensation based on seniority, merit, or quantity or quality of production. These are three of the four EPA defenses. The fourth EPA defense, "a factor other than sex," is already implicit in Title VII because the statute's prohibition of sex discrimination applies only if there is discrimination on the basis of sex. Under the Court's interpretation, the Bennett Amendment, the second sentence of § 703(h), is mere surplusage. The Court's answer to this argument is curious. It suggests that repetition ensures that the provisions would be consistently interpreted by the courts. But that answer only speaks to the purpose for incorporating the defenses in each statute, not for stating the defenses twice in the same statute. Courts are not quite as dense as the majority assumes.

In sum, Title VII and the Equal Pay Act, read together, provide a balanced approach to resolving sex-based wage discrimination claims. Title VII guarantees that qualified female employees will have access to all jobs, and the Equal Pay Act assures that men and women performing the same work will be paid equally. Congress intended to remedy wage discrimination through the Equal Pay Act standards, whether suit is brought under that statute or under Title VII. What emerges is

the word "authorized" has been defined to mean exactly what petitioners contend. Black's Law Dictionary defines "authorized" to mean "to permit a thing to be done in the future." (4th ed. 1968). Accordingly, the language of the Bennett Amendment suggests that those differentiations which are authorized under the Equal Pay Act—and thus Title VII—are those based on "skill, effort, responsibility and working conditions" and those related to the four affirmative defenses. * * *

that Title VII would have been construed *in pari materia* even without the Bennett Amendment, and that the Amendment serves simply to insure that the equal work standard would be the standard by which all wage compensation claims would be judged.

Perhaps recognizing that there is virtually no support for its position in the legislative history, the Court rests its holding on its belief that any other holding would be unacceptable public policy. It argues that there must be remedy for wage discrimination beyond that provided for in the Equal Pay Act. Quite apart from the fact that that is an issue properly left to Congress and not the Court, the Court is wrong even as a policy matter. The Court's parade of horribles that would occur absent a distinct Title VII remedy simply do not support the result it reaches.

First, the Court contends that a separate Title VII remedy is necessary to remedy the situation where an employer admits to a female worker, hired for a unique position, that her compensation would have been higher had she been male. Stated differently, the Court insists that an employer could isolate a predominantly female job category and arbitrarily cut its wages because no men currently perform equal or substantially equal work. But a Title VII remedy is unnecessary in these cases because an Equal Pay Act remedy is available. Under the Equal Pay Act, it is not necessary that every Equal Pay Act violation be established through proof that members of the opposite sex are *currently* performing equal work for greater pay. However, unlikely such an admission might be in the bullpen of litigation, an employer's statement that "if my female employees performing a particular job were males, I would pay them more simply because they are males" would be admissible in a suit under that Act. Overt discrimination does not go unremedied by the Equal Pay Act. In addition, insofar as hiring or placement discrimination caused the isolated job category, Title VII already provides numerous remedies (such as backpay, transfer and constructive seniority) without resort to job comparisons. In short, if women are limited to low paying jobs against their will, they have adequate remedies under Title VII for denial of job opportunities even under what I believe is the correct construction of the Bennett Amendment.

The Court next contends that absent a Title VII remedy, women who work for employers exempted from coverage of the Equal Pay Act would be wholly without a remedy for wage discrimination. The Court misapprehends petitioners' argument. As Senator Clark explained in his memorandum, Congress sought to incorporate into Title VII the substantive standard of the Equal Pay Act—the "equal work" standard—not the employee coverage provisions. Thus, to say that the "equal pay for equal work" standard is incorporated into Title VII does not mean that employees are precluded from bringing compensation discrimination claims under Title VII. It means only that if employees choose to proceed under Title VII, they must show that they have been deprived of "equal pay for equal work."

There is of course a situation in which petitioners' position *would* deny women a remedy for claims of sex-based wage discrimination. A remedy would not be available where a lower paying job held primarily by women is "comparable," but not substantially equal to, a higher paying job performed by men. That is, plaintiffs would be foreclosed from showing that they received unequal pay for work of "comparable worth" or that dissimilar jobs are of "equal worth." The short, and best, answer to that contention is that Congress in 1963 explicitly chose not to provide a remedy in such cases. And contrary to the suggestion of the Court, it is by no means clear that Title VII was enacted to remedy *all* forms of alleged discrimination. * * * Congress balanced the need for a remedy for wage discrimination against its desire to avoid the burdens associated with governmental intervention into wage structures. The Equal Pay Act's "equal pay for equal work" formula reflects the outcome of this legislative balancing. In construing Title VII, therefore, the courts cannot be indifferent to this sort of political compromise.

Even though today's opinion reaches what I believe to be the wrong result, its narrow holding is perhaps its saving feature. The opinion does not endorse the so-called "comparable worth" theory: though the Court does not indicate how a plaintiff might establish a prima facie case under Title VII, the Court does suggest that allegations of unequal pay for unequal, but comparable, work will not state a claim on which relief may be granted. The Court, for example, repeatedly emphasizes that this is not a case where plaintiffs ask the court to compare the value of dissimilar jobs or to quantify the effect of sex discrimination on wage rates. * * *

Given that implied repeals of legislation are disfavored, we should not be surprised that the Court disassociates itself from the entire notion of "comparable worth." In enacting the Equal Pay Act in 1963, Congress specifically prohibited the courts from comparing the wage rates of dissimilar jobs: there can only be a comparison of wage rates where jobs are "equal or substantially equal." Because the legislative history of Title VII does not reveal an intent to overrule that determination, the courts should strive to harmonize the intent of Congress in enacting the Equal Pay Act with its intent in enacting Title VII. Where, as here, the policy of prior legislation is clearly expressed, the Court should not "transfuse the successor statute with a gloss of its own choosing."

Because there are no logical underpinnings to the Court's opinion, all we may conclude is that even absent a showing of equal work there is a cause of action under Title VII where there is direct evidence that an employer has *intentionally* depressed a woman's salary because she is a woman. The decision today does not approve a cause of action based on a *comparison* of the wage rates of dissimilar jobs.

For the foregoing reasons, however, I believe that even that narrow holding cannot be supported by the legislative history of the Equal Pay Act and Title VII. This is simply a case where the Court has superimposed upon Title VII a "gloss of its own choosing."

NOTES AND PROBLEMS FOR DISCUSSION

1. The Court in *Gunther* only went so far as to permit a litigant to bring an action for intentional sex-based wage discrimination under Title VII without satisfying the EPA's equal work standard. It left to the lower courts, however, the difficult task of formulating the proof standards to be applied to plaintiffs in such cases. In WILKINS v. UNIVERSITY OF HOUSTON, 654 F.2d 388 (5th Cir. 1981), vacated and remanded, 459 U.S. 809, 103 S.Ct. 34, 74 L.Ed.2d 47 (1982), affirmed on remand, 695 F.2d 134 (5th Cir. 1983), a post-*Gunther* case, the plaintiffs' Title VII claim was similar in theory to the one that had been asserted in *Gunther*. Their complaint alleged that the University evaluated all of the jobs held by its professional and administrative staff employees and classified each of them into one of nine levels. Although they did not offer evidence that women were paid less than men for equal work, the plaintiffs did show that in the University's academic division, a disproportionate number of those employees paid less than the minimum salary established for the level of their jobs were women and that all of the employees who received a salary in excess of the maximum assigned to their job levels were men. This statistical evidence of disparate wage treatment effected through the discriminatory application of a job classification system, the court held, established a prima facie Title VII violation. Similarly, in Bartelt v. Berlitz School of Languages of America, Inc., 698 F.2d 1003 (9th Cir. 1983), cert. denied, 464 U.S. 915, 104 S.Ct. 277, 78 L.Ed.2d 257 (1983), an allegation that an employer paid female employees in one establishment less than male employees in its other establishments was held to state a claim under Title VII even though it would not support an EPA claim due to the failure to satisfy the EPA's single establishment requirement.

A more difficult question is posed by plaintiffs seeking recovery under a "comparable worth" theory. The *Gunther* court emphasized that the complaint before it did not rely on that concept and thus it specifically reserved decision on whether such a claim was cognizable under Title VII. The availability of a comparable worth cause of action has generated a measure of support among the commentators. See e.g., Gasaway, Comparable Worth: A Post-Gunther Overview, 69 Geo.L.J. 1123 (1981); Note, Equal Pay, Comparable Work, and Job Evaluation, 90 Yale L.J. 657 (1981). Under this theory, employees would be entitled to equal pay for jobs that are not substantially equal but are comparable in their value to the employer. This, its proponents contend, would respond to the general undervaluation of jobs traditionally dominated by women, which goes unremedied under traditional Equal Pay doctrine because of the absence of male workers in those positions. See Blumrosen, Wage Discrimination, Job Segregation and Title VII of the Civil Rights Act of 1964, 12 U.Mich.J.L.Ref. 397 (1979). Its opponents argue that such a theory would result in an unacceptable intrusion into the labor market and require courts to engage in a comparative appraisal of the value of unrelated jobs, an area in which they have little institutional expertise. In BRIGGS v. CITY OF MADISON, 536 F.Supp. 435 (W.D.Wis.1982), the first reported post-*Gunther* case addressing the comparable worth issue, the court rejected the contention that plaintiffs could establish a prima facie case of wage discrimination under Title VII simply by showing that women occupied a sex-segregated job classification in which they were paid less than men occupying a sex-segregated job classification. It added, however, that a prima facie violation could be established if the plaintiffs also proved that the female and male sex-segregated jobs were "similar" in their requirements of skill, effort, responsibility and working conditions and were of comparable value to the employer. In POWER v. BARRY COUNTY, 539 F.Supp. 721 (W.D.Mich.1982), on the other hand, the court refused to recognize the plaintiff's Title VII comparable worth-based claim. Referring to *Gunther*, the court stated:

> A review of the legislative history leads me to conclude that the Supreme Court's recognition of intentional discrimination may well signal the outer limit of the legal theories cognizable under Title VII. There is no indication in Title VII's legislative history that the boundaries of the Act can be expanded to encompass the theory of comparable worth. Nor is there convincing evidence that Congress intended to make such a theory available to those seeking redress for real or imaginary wage inequalities. Nothing in the legislative history indicates support for an independent claim of recovery where the outcome of the case is dependent upon a court's evaluation of the relative worth of two distinct jobs. * * * [I]f Plaintiffs are able to demonstrate their wages are lower solely because they are women, then a claim under Title VII will exist. That is a quantum leap from the theory of comparable worth advanced by plaintiffs, wherein the Court is required to evaluate the worth of different jobs and rank them according to their relative values. Similarly, the legislative history provided by Plaintiffs fails to buttress their intention that comparable worth is a cognizable and independent cause of action.

539 F.Supp. at 726. This same analysis was employed in Connecticut Employees Ass'n v. State of Conn., 530 F.Supp. 618 (D.Ct.1982) (plaintiffs stated a Title VII claim of intentional discrimination where complaint alleged that lower rates of compensation were paid for work which the employer had determined to be of comparable or equal value to dissimilar, higher-paying jobs.). See also Cox v. American Cast Iron Pipe Co., 784 F.2d 1546 (11th Cir. 1986) (plaintiff can state Title VII claim when alleging that traditionally male jobs are compensated "objectively" based on system of detailed job descriptions, standardized evaluations, job classifications, pay scales and review provisions. while compensation for women's jobs is subjectively determined); Spaulding v. University of Washington, 740 F.2d 686 (9th Cir. 1984), cert. denied, ___ U.S. ___, 105 S.Ct. 511, 83 L.Ed.2d 401 (1984).

In Plemer v. Parsons-Gilbane, 713 F.2d 1127 (5th Cir. 1983), a female plaintiff based her Title VII action on the claim that the dissimilarities between her and a male employee's jobs did not justify the differential in salary paid to these two employees. The court rejected this claim, stating that unless the plaintiff could show that the employer had assessed the value of the two jobs, it was not prepared to make a subjective assessment of the value of differing duties and responsibilities. Does this ruling imply that an employer is under no duty to make such assessments? Moreover, doesn't it discourage employers from undertaking job valuation studies for fear of facing statutory liability for their failure to adjust salary structures in light of the report? The latter scenario befell the State of Washington in AFSCME v. State of Washington, 578 F.Supp, 846 (W.D.Wa.1983). The State commissioned an independent study of civil service positions which concluded that clear indications of pay differences existed between job groups predominantly held by men and those predominantly held by women and that the jobs were of comparable worth. The report also computed the cost of eliminating discrimination. The outgoing Governor then included a budget appropriation to implement the report's recommendations in his proposed budget, but the incoming Governor took the appropriation out of her budget despite a state budget surplus large enough to finance the remedial measures. In addition, the state legislature took no action to implement the report until after the filing of the instant lawsuit. The court held that the State's failure to eliminate an admittedly discriminatory compensation system constituted an intentional violation of Title VII since it did not present convincing evidence of a good faith reason for its failure to pay women their evaluated worth. This judgment was reversed on appeal. 770 F.2d 1401 (9th Cir. 1985) The Ninth Circuit reasoned that employers should be commended rather than penalized for undertaking job evaluation studies and held, therefore, that the State's failure to adopt the recommendations of a study that it had commissioned did not establish the discriminatory motive required in a disparate treatment claim. It also rejected the plaintiff's attempt to challenge the State's compensation scheme under disproportionate impact analysis. The plaintiff had claimed that the State's policy of requiring that state employee salaries reflect prevailing market rates generated an adverse impact on women by perpetuating the historical pattern of paying lower wages to women. The court reasoned that disproportionate impact analysis was only applicable to cases challenging a "specific, clearly delineated" employment standard and not to situations, as here, where the employer's policy was based on a multitude of such complex factors as market surveys, administrative hearings and recommendations, budget proposals, executive actions and legislative enactments. Moreover, the court added, in terms of disparate treatment analysis, reliance on market rates did not raise an inference of discriminatory motive since the employer did not create the extant market disparity and had not been shown to have been motivated by sex-based considerations in its decision to rely on the market. To the contrary, the court declared, nothing in the legislative history of Title VII indicated that Congress intended to prevent employers from competing in the labor market and relying on market forces in establishing their compensation schemes. Shortly after the ruling by the Ninth Circuit, the parties reached an out-of-court settlement in which the State agreed to spend over $46 million to correct the sex-based inequities in its wage scales. The settlement provided for review and approval of its terms by the state legislature and the trial court. For more on this case see Gender Discrimination: "Comparable Worth"—AFSCME v. Washington, 9 Harv.J.L. & Pub. Pol. 253 (1986). See generally, Market Value As A Factor "Other Than Sex" In Sex-Based Wage Discrimination Claims, 1985 U.Ill.L.Rev. 1027 (1985).

The Ninth Circuit's reasoning in *AFSCME* had been adumbrated by an Illinois federal trial court's decision in American Nurses Ass'n v. State of Illinois, 606 F.Supp. 1313 (N.D.Ill.1985). There, the defendant had not implemented the findings of an evaluative study that it had funded and conducted. The court reasoned that the mere funding and performance of a study did not compel the employer to adopt its results and implement a wage scale that the study found to be more equitable than the existing schedule. To do otherwise, the court declared, would create a disincentive to employers to conduct job evaluation studies. Title VII, the court ruled, only required that any action taken as the result of such a study be undertaken on a nondiscriminatory basis. Thus, since the defendant here did not implement any of the findings of its report, it was found not to have violated the Act. This decision, however, was reversed by the Seventh Circuit. 783 F.2d 716 (7th Cir. 1986). The appellate court agreed that "if all that the plaintiffs in this case are complaining about is the State of Illinois' failure to implement a comparable worth study, they have no case and it was properly dismissed." Similarly, it stated, no claim for intentional discrimination would lie if the refusal to implement the study had been intended as a reaffirmation of the State's commitment to pay market wages. But, the court concluded, the imprecise wording of the compaint permitted the interpretation that the plaintiffs were alleging intentionally discriminatory conduct actionable under Title VII, i.e., either that the State had refused to implement the study's recommendations because it believed that women should be paid less than men for equal work or that the State had refused to hire women for jobs traditionally reserved for men. Accordingly, it reversed the trial court's dismissal of the complaint and provided the plaintiffs with the opportunity to make additional efforts to prove a case of intentional discrimination.

Is the Equal Pact Act ever relevant to a comparable worth claim? See Comparable Worth in the Equal Pay Act, 51 U.Chi.L.Rev. 1078 (1984). For more on the potential viability of comparable worth claims, see Loudon & Loudon, Applying Disparate Impact to Title VII Comparable Worth Claims: An Incomparable Task, 61 Ind.L.J. 165 (1986); Newman & Vonhof, "Separate But Equal—Job Segregation and Pay Equity in the Wake of *Gunther*, 1981 U.Ill.L. Rev. 269 (1981); Note, Women, Wages and Title VII: The Significance of County of Washington v. Gunther, 43 U.Pitt.L.Rev. 467 (1982).

2. Assuming a plaintiff established a prima facie case of wage discrimination under Title VII, does the Court's treatment of the Bennett Amendment issue in *Gunther* suggest that the defendant in such a case must shoulder a heavier burden of proof than it would confront in a non-wage Title VII claim? Does *Gunther* suggest that *Burdine* will not apply to wage claims under Title VII? Moreover, did the Court imply that defendants in Title VII wage discrimination cases are limited to the four EPA defenses? Compare Crockwell v. Blackmon-Mooring Steamatic, Inc., 627 F.Supp. 800, 806 (W.D.Tenn.1985); *Briggs*, 536 F.Supp. 435, 447–48, (W.D.Wis.1982) and Boyd v. Madison County Mutual Insurance Co., 653 F.2d 1173, 1177–78 (7th Cir. 1981), cert. denied, 454 U.S. 1146, 102 S.Ct. 1008, 71 L.Ed.2d 299 (1982), with Kouba v. Allstate Insurance Co., 691 F.2d 873, 875 (9th Cir. 1982); Schulte v. Wilson Industries, Inc., 547 F.Supp. 324 (S.D.Tex.1982). If so, does this mean that the BFOQ defense is inapplicable to Title VII-based claims of compensation discrimination? Does the language of § 703(e) support such a conclusion? See Hodgson v. Robert Hall Clothes, Inc., 326 F.Supp. 1264 (D.Del.1971), modified on other grounds, 473 F.2d 589 (3d Cir.), cert. denied, 414 U.S. 866, 94 S.Ct. 50, 38 L.Ed. 2d 85 (1973). See also Barnett, Comparable Worth and the Equal Pay Act—Proving Sex-Based Wage Discrimination Claims After Gunther, 28 Wayne L.Rev. 1669, 1692–1700 (1982).

3. Several states, including California (public employment only), North Dakota, Oklahoma, Oregon and South Dakota have passed statutes requiring employers to provide equal pay for comparable work.

4. To the extent that a federal employee's wage discrimination claim falls within the jurisdiction of Title VII as well as the Equal Pay Act, does the exclusivity rule announced by the Supreme Court in Brown v. G.S.A., supra at 454, preclude that individual from bringing an action under the EPA? See Epstein v. Secretary, U.S. Dep't of Treasury, 552 F.Supp. 436 (N.D.Ill.1982).

Chapter 10

THE AGE DISCRIMINATION IN EMPLOYMENT ACT

SECTION A. OVERVIEW OF STATUTORY PROVISIONS

The Age Discrimination in Employment Act of 1967 (ADEA),[a] as amended in 1974 [b] and 1978,[c] is the exclusive federal statutory remedy for age discrimination in employment. Before the enactment of the ADEA, federal protection against age discrimination was limited to government workers (through the equal protection and due process clauses of the Constitution) and employees of federal contractors and subcontractors (through Executive Order 11141 [d]).[e] The ADEA, like Title VII, applies to employers, labor organizations and employment agencies. It defines employers as private business organizations that are engaged in commerce and have at least twenty employees,[f] their agents, and state and local government entities.[g] A separate provision,

[a] P.L. 90–202, 81 Stat. 602, 29 U.S.C. §§ 621–634 (1976).

[b] P.L. 93–259, 88 Stat. 74, 29 U.S.C. §§ 630(b), (c), (f), 633a, 634 (1976).

[c] P.L. 95–256, 92 Stat. 189, 29 U.S.C. §§ 623, (f)(2), 624, 626(c), (d), (e), 631, 633a(a), (f), (g), 634 (1981).

[d] 3 CFR 179 (1964), 29 Fed.Reg. 2477 (1964).

This Order, promulgated by President Johnson, provides that federal contractors and subcontractors shall not discriminate on the basis of age except upon the basis of a bona fide occupational qualification, retirement plan or statutory requirement. For further discussion of this and other Executive Orders, see infra at 802.

[e] A few states, such as Arizona, Hawaii, Idaho, Kentucky, Texas and Utah, had enacted state laws prohibiting age discrimination in employment before the passage of the ADEA.

[f] At least four federal courts have ruled that an American working outside of the U.S. for an American company is not covered by the ADEA because the ADEA incorporates the FLSA provisions that prohibit application of that statute outside the boundaries of the U.S. See Zahourek v. Arthur Young & Co., 750 F.2d 827 (10th Cir. 1984); Pfeiffer v. Wm. Wrigley Co., 755 F.2d 554 (7th Cir. 1985); Thomas v. Brown & Root, Inc., 745 F.2d 279 (4th Cir. 1984); Cleary v. U.S. Lines, Inc., 728 F.2d 607 (3d Cir. 1984). Congress filled this gap when it enacted the Older American Act Amendments of 1984, Pub.L. 98–459, 98 Stat. 1767. Section 802 of this statute explicitly extends the coverage of the ADEA to U.S. citizens employed abroad by American corporations or their subsidiaries except in cases where application of the ADEA would violate the law of the nation in which the U.S. citizen is employed. In Pfeiffer v. Wm. Wrigley Co., 755 F.2d 554 (7th Cir. 1985), the court held that the amendment should not be applied retroactively, on the ground that the legislative history was silent as to whether the amendment was intended either to change the scope of the original ADEA, to state the intended meaning of the original statute more clearly, or to limit the ADEA's intended extraterritorial effect to countries that did not possess inconsistent domestic law. For a helpful discussion of the standard used to determine employee status see EEOC v. Zippo Mfg. Co., 713 F.2d 32 (3d Cir. 1983) (adopting hybrid common law "right to control"/"economic realities" standard). See also Gazder v. Air India, 574 F.Supp. 134 (S.D.N.Y.1983) (airline owned by foreign government is an "employer" under ADEA).

[g] The constitutionality of the extension of the ADEA to state and local government employees was upheld by the Supreme

patterned exactly after sec. 717 of Title VII, extends the coverage of the Act to federal employees. Similarly, the ADEA's definition of labor organizations and employment agencies, with one minor exception, duplicates the language of the corresponding Title VII provisions.[h]

The substantive portions of the ADEA, including the prohibitions against retaliation and discriminatory advertising, are also virtually identical to the antidiscrimination provisions of Title VII. The major difference, of course, is that the ADEA only prohibits discrimination on the basis of age and, as to non-federal employees, applies solely to persons between the ages of forty and seventy. Finally, an aggrieved can bring a private cause of action under the ADEA, but only, as with Title VII claims, after he or she has pursued certain administrative remedies. The materials in this chapter are designed to offer a more detailed examination of the substantive and procedural components of the ADEA.

Court in EEOC v. Wyoming, 460 U.S. 226, 103 S.Ct. 1054, 75 L.Ed.2d 18 (1983). The Court rejected the contention that the statutory amendment violated the Tenth Amendment on the ground that the Tenth Amendment prohibits federal interference in certain core state functions and that requiring state and local governments to comply with the ADEA did not directly impair a state's ability to structure integral operations in areas of traditional governmental functions. In this case, a Wyoming statute required employer approval of the employment of game wardens who reach age 55. The Court ruled that the degree of federal intrusion occasioned by the application of the ADEA to this state law was not significant enough to override Congress' choice to extend its anti-age bias policy to the states. The ADEA would only require the state to make individualized tests of fitness and did not prohibit the state from pursuing its goal of maintaining worker fitness. Moreover, the court noted, the state could retain its policy if it could prove that age was a BFOQ for that position.

In Fitzpatrick v. Bitzer, 427 U.S. 445, 96 S.Ct. 2666, 49 L.Ed.2d 614 (1976), the Court upheld the constitutionality of the extension of Title VII to state government employment practices by ruling that the extension was effected through Congress' exercise of its authority under Section 5 of the Fourteenth Amendment rather than its power under the Commerce Clause. The *Wyoming* Court did not rule on whether the Fourteenth Amendment or the Commerce Clause was the constitutional basis for Congress' ADEA action. Accordingly, it did not use the *Fitzpatrick* rationale to reject the defendant's Tenth Amendment defense. This refusal to rule on whether the statute was an exercise of Congress' Fourteenth Amendment authority leaves open the question of whether a state can be held liable for money damages under the ADEA, since the Court in *Fitzpatrick* held only that the states enjoyed no Eleventh Amendment sovereign immunity from an award of money damages issued pursuant to a federal statute enacted under Congress' Fourteenth Amendment authority. In Ramirez v. Puerto Rico Fire Service, 715 F.2d 694 (1st Cir. 1983), the First Circuit addressed this question, ruling that the amendment extending the ADEA to public employees was enacted pursuant to Congress' authority under § 5 of the Fourteenth Amendment. Moreover, the court held, the legislative history evidenced sufficient Congressional intent to abrogate the states' Eleventh Amendment immunity to enforce the Fourteenth Amendment and, thus, that a state could be held liable for money damages under the ADEA.

[h] The ADEA requires statutory labor organizations that do not operate a hiring hall to have twenty-five members, whereas only fifteen members are required by Title VII. The ADEA, like the Equal Pay Act, incorporates the remedial scheme of the FLSA. The FLSA authorizes an employee to bring an action for damages against an "employer" and expressly excludes labor organizations from the definition of "employer". Accordingly, it has been held that an employee cannot recover damages against a union under the ADEA. See Neuman v. Northwest Airlines, 28 FEP Cases 1488 (N.D.Ill.1982).

SECTION B. SUBSTANTIVE PROVISIONS

Read § 4 of the ADEA at pp. ___.

TRANS WORLD AIRLINES, INC. v. THURSTON

Supreme Court of the United States, 1985.
469 U.S. 111, 105 S.Ct. 613, 83 L.Ed.2d 523.

JUSTICE POWELL delivered the opinion of the Court.

Trans World Airlines, Inc. (TWA), a commercial airline, permits captains disqualified from serving in that capacity for reasons other than age to transfer automatically to the position of flight engineer. In this case, we must decide whether the Age Discrimination in Employment Act of 1967 (ADEA) requires the airline to afford this same "privilege of employment" to those captains disqualified by their age. We also must decide what constitutes a "willful" violation of the ADEA, entitling a plaintiff to "liquidated" or double damages.

I

A

TWA has approximately 3,000 employees who fill the three cockpit positions on most of its flights.[1] The "captain" is the pilot and controls the aircraft. He is responsible for all phases of its operation. The "first officer" is the copilot and assists the captain. The "flight engineer" usually monitors a side-facing instrument panel. He does not operate the flight controls unless the captain and the first officer become incapacitated.

In 1977, TWA and the Air Line Pilots Association (ALPA) entered into a collective-bargaining agreement, under which every employee in a cockpit position was required to retire when he reached the age of 60. This provision for mandatory retirement was lawful under the ADEA, as part of a "bona fide seniority system." See United Air Lines, Inc. v. McMann, 434 U.S. 192, 98 S.Ct. 444, 54 L.Ed.2d 402 (1977). On April 6, 1978, however, the Act was amended to prohibit the mandatory retirement of a protected individual because of his age. TWA officials became concerned that the company's retirement policy, at least as it applied to flight engineers, violated the amended ADEA.[3]

On July 19, 1978, TWA announced that the amended ADEA prohibited the forced retirement of flight engineers at age 60. The company

1. On certain long-distance flights, a fourth crew member, the "international relief officer," is in the cockpit. On some types of aircraft, there are only two cockpit positions.

3. A regulation promulgated by the Federal Aviation Administration prohibits anyone from serving after age 60 as a pilot on a commercial carrier. 14 CFR § 121.383(c) (1984). Captains and first officers are considered "pilots" subject to this regulation; flight engineers are not. Therefore, TWA officials were concerned primarily with the effect that the 1978 amendments had on the company's policy of mandatory retirement of flight engineers.

thus proposed a new policy, under which employees in all three cockpit positions, upon reaching age 60, would be allowed to continue working as flight engineers. TWA stated that it would not implement its new policy until it "had the benefit of [ALPA's] views." ALPA's views were not long in coming. The Union contended that the collective-bargaining agreement prohibited the employment of a flight engineer after his 60th birthday and that the proposed change was not required by the recently amended ADEA.

Despite opposition from the Union, TWA adopted a modified version of its proposal. Under this plan, any employee in "flight engineer status" at age 60 is entitled to continue working in that capacity. The new plan, unlike the initial proposal, does not give 60-year-old captains [6] the right automatically to begin training as flight engineers. Instead, a captain may remain with the airline only if he has been able to obtain "flight engineer status" through the bidding procedures outlined in the collective-bargaining agreement. These procedures require a captain, prior to his 60th birthday, to submit a "standing bid" for the position of flight engineer. When a vacancy occurs, it is assigned to the most senior captain with a standing bid. If no vacancy occurs prior to his 60th birthday, or if he lacks sufficient seniority to bid successfully for those vacancies that do occur, the captain is retired.[7]

Under the collective-bargaining agreement, a captain displaced for any reason besides age need not resort to the bidding procedures. For example, a captain unable to maintain the requisite first-class medical certificate, see 14 CFR § 67.13 (1984), may displace automatically, or "bump," a less senior flight engineer.[8] The medically disabled captain's ability to bump does not depend upon the availability of a vacancy.[9] Similarly, a captain whose position is eliminated due to reduced manpower needs can "bump" a less senior flight engineer.[10] Even if a captain is found to be incompetent to serve in that capacity,

6. The term "captain" will hereinafter be used to refer to both the positions of captain and first officer.

7. In 1980, TWA imposed an additional restriction on captains bidding for flight engineer positions. Successful bidders were required to "fulfill their bids in a timely manner." Under this amended practice, captains who bid successfully for positions as flight engineers were required to "activate" their bids immediately. As a result, many captains under age 60 were trained for and assumed flight engineer positions, with resulting lower pay and responsibility.

8. The pilot must be able to obtain the second-class medical certificate that is required for the position of flight engineer. See 14 CFR § 67.15 (1984).

9. If the disabled captain lacks sufficient seniority to displace, he is not discharged. Rather, he is entitled to go on unpaid medical leave for up to five years, during which time he retains and continues to accrue seniority.

10. Only those flight engineers in the current and last former domiciles of the displaced captain may be "bumped." If a captain has insufficient seniority to displace a flight engineer at either of these domiciles, he is not discharged. Instead, he is placed in furlough status for a period of up to 10 years, during which time he continues to accrue seniority for purposes of a recall.

he is not discharged,[11] but is allowed to transfer to a position as flight engineer without resort to the bidding procedures.[12]

Respondents Harold Thurston, Christopher J. Clark, and Clifton A. Parkhill, former captains for TWA, were retired upon reaching the age of 60. Each was denied an opportunity to "bump" a less senior flight engineer. Thurston was forced to retire on May 26, 1978, before the company adopted its new policy. Clark did not attempt to bid because TWA had advised him that bidding would not affect his chances of obtaining a transfer. These two captains thus effectively were denied an opportunity to become flight engineers through the bidding procedures. The third captain, Parkhill, did file a standing bid for the position of flight engineer. No vacancies occurred prior to Parkhill's 60th birthday, however, and he too was forced to retire.

B

Thurston, Clark, and Parkhill filed this action against TWA and ALPA in the United States District Court for the Southern District of New York. They argued that the company's transfer policy violated ADEA § 4(a)(1). The airline allowed captains displaced for reasons other than age to "bump" less senior flight engineers. Captains compelled to vacate their positions upon reaching age 60, they claimed, should be afforded this same "privilege of employment." * * *

The District Court entered a summary judgment in favor of defendants TWA and ALPA. Air Line Pilots Assn. v. Trans World Air Lines, 547 F.Supp. 1221 (SDNY 1982). The court held that the plaintiffs had failed to establish a prima facie case of age discrimination under the test set forth in McDonnell Douglas Corp. v. Green. None could show that at the time of his transfer request a vacancy existed for the position of flight engineer. Furthermore, the court found that two affirmative defenses justified the company's transfer policy. 29 U.S.C. § 623(f)(1) and (f)(2). The United States Court of Appeals for the Second Circuit reversed the District Court's judgment. 713 F.2d 940 (1983). It found the *McDonnell Douglas* formula inapposite because the plaintiffs had adduced *direct* proof of age discrimination. Captains disqualified for reasons other than age were allowed to "bump" less senior flight engineers. Therefore, the company was required by ADEA § 4(a)(1) to afford 60-year-old captains this same "privilege of employment." The Court of Appeals also held that the affirmative defenses of the ADEA did not justify the company's discriminatory transfer policy.[14] TWA was held liable for "liquidated" or double

11. Although the collective-bargaining agreement does not address disciplinary downgrades, TWA's Vice President of Flight Operations, J.E. Frankum, stated that such downgrades had occurred "many times over many years."

12. Captains disqualified for other reasons also are allowed to "bump" less senior flight engineers. For example, the collective-bargaining agreement provides that a captain who fails to "requalify" in that position will not be discharged.

14. The Court of Appeals also found that ALPA had violated ADEA § 4(c), 29 U.S.C. § 623(c), which prohibits unions from causing or attempting to cause an employer to engage in unlawful discrimination. The court found, however, that

damages because its violation of the ADEA was found to be "willful." According to the court, an employer's conduct is "willful" if it "knows or shows reckless disregard for the matter of whether its conduct is prohibited by the ADEA." Because "TWA was clearly aware of the 1978 ADEA amendments," the Court of Appeals found the respondents entitled to double damages.

TWA filed a petition for a writ of certiorari in which it challenged the Court of Appeals' holding that the transfer policy violated the ADEA and that TWA's violation was "willful." The Union filed a cross-petition raising only the liability issue. We granted certiorari in both cases, and consolidated them for argument. We now affirm as to the violation of the ADEA, and reverse as to the claim for double damages.

II

A

The ADEA "broadly prohibits arbitrary discrimination in the workplace based on age." Lorillard v. Pons, 434 U.S. 575, 577, 98 S.Ct. 866, 868, 55 L.Ed.2d 40 (1978). Section 4(a)(1) of the Act proscribes differential treatment of older workers "with respect to * * * [a] privileg[e] of employment." Under TWA's transfer policy, 60-year-old captains are denied a "privilege of employment" on the basis of age. Captains who become disqualified from serving in that position for reasons other than age automatically are able to displace less senior flight engineers. Captains disqualified because of age are not afforded this same "bumping" privilege. Instead, they are forced to resort to the bidding procedures set forth in the collective-bargaining agreement. If there is no vacancy prior to a bidding captain's 60th birthday, he must retire.[15]

ALPA was not liable for damages. It held that the ADEA does not permit the recovery of monetary damages, including back pay, against a labor organization. It noted that the ADEA incorporates the remedial scheme of the FLSA, which does not allow actions against unions to recover damages.

In its petition for a writ of certiorari, TWA raised the issue of a union's liability for damages under the ADEA. Although we granted the petition in full, we now conclude that the Court is without jurisdiction to consider this question. TWA was not the proper party to present this question. The airline cannot assert the right of others to recover damages against the Union.

Both the individual respondents and the EEOC argue that the issue of union liability is properly before the Court. But the respondents failed to file a cross-petition raising this question. A prevailing party may advance any ground in support of a judgment in his favor. Dandridge v. Williams, 397 U.S. 471, 475 n. 6, 90 S.Ct. 1153, 1156 n. 6, 25 L.Ed.2d 491 (1970). An argument that would modify the judgment, however, cannot be presented unless a cross-petition has been filed. Federal Energy Admin. v. Algonquin SNG, Inc., 426 U.S. 548, 560 n. 11, 96 S.Ct. 2295, 2302 n. 11, 49 L.Ed.2d 49 (1976). In this case, the judgment of the Court of Appeals would be modified by the arguments advanced by the EEOC and the individual plaintiffs, as they are contending that the Union should be liable to them for monetary damages.

15. The discriminatory transfer policy may violate the Act even though 83% of the 60-year-old captains were able to obtain positions as flight engineers through the bidding procedures. See Phillips v. Martin Marietta Corp., 400 U.S. 542, 91 S.Ct. 496, 27 L.Ed.2d 613 (1971) (*per curiam*).

It also should be noted that many of the captains who obtained positions as flight engineers were forced to assume that posi-

The Act does not require TWA to grant transfer privileges to disqualified captains. Nevertheless, if TWA does grant some disqualified captains the "privilege" of "bumping" less senior flight engineers, it may not deny this opportunity to others because of their age. In Hishon v. King & Spalding, 457 U.S. ——, 104 S.Ct. 2229, 81 L.Ed.2d 59 (1984), we held that "[a] benefit that is part and parcel of the employment relationship may not be doled out in a discriminatory fashion, even if the employer would be free * * * not to provide the benefit at all." This interpretation of Title VII of the Civil Rights Act of 1964 applies with equal force in the context of age discrimination, for the substantive provisions of the ADEA "were derived *in haec verba* from Title VII." Lorillard v. Pons, supra.

TWA contends that the respondents failed to make out a prima facie case of age discrimination under McDonnell Douglas v. Green, because at the time they were retired, no flight engineer vacancies existed. This argument fails, for the *McDonnell Douglas* test is inapplicable where the plaintiff presents direct evidence of discrimination. See Teamsters v. United States, 431 U.S. 324, 358 n. 44, 97 S.Ct. 1843, 1866 n. 44, 52 L.Ed.2d 396 (1977). The shifting burdens of proof set forth in *McDonnell Douglas* are designed to assure that the "plaintiff [has] his day in court despite the unavailability of direct evidence." Loeb v. Textron, Inc., 600 F.2d 1003, 1014 (CA1 1979). In this case there is direct evidence that the method of transfer available to a disqualified captain depends upon his age. Since it allows captains who become disqualified for any reason other than age to "bump" less senior flight engineers, TWA's transfer policy is discriminatory on its face.

B

Although we find that TWA's transfer policy discriminates against disqualified captains on the basis of age, our inquiry cannot end here. Petitioners contend that the age-based transfer policy is justified by two of the ADEA's five affirmative defenses. Petitioners first argue that the discharge of respondents was lawful because age is a "bona fide occupational qualification" (BFOQ) for the position of captain. Furthermore, TWA claims that its retirement policy is part of a "bona fide seniority system," and thus exempt from the Act's coverage.

Section 4(f)(1) of the ADEA provides that an employer may take "any action otherwise prohibited" where age is a "bona fide occupational qualification." In order to be permissible under § 4(f)(1), however, the age-based discrimination must relate to a "particular business." Every court to consider the issue has assumed that the "particular business" to which the statute refers is the job from which the protected individual is excluded. In Weeks v. Southern Bell Tel. & Tel. Co., 408 F.2d 228 (CA5 1969), for example, the court considered the Title VII

tion prior to reaching age 60. See n. 7, supra. They were adversely affected by the discriminatory transfer policy despite the fact that they obtained positions as flight engineers.

claim of a female employee who, because of her sex, had not been allowed to transfer to the position of switchman. In deciding that the BFOQ defense was not available to the defendant, the court considered only the job of switchman.

TWA's discriminatory transfer policy is not permissible under § 4(f)(1) because age is not a BFOQ for the "particular" position of flight engineer. It is necessary to recognize that the airline has two age-based policies: (i) captains are not allowed to serve in that capacity after reaching the age of 60; and (ii) age-disqualified captains are not given the transfer privileges afforded captains disqualified for other reasons. The first policy, which precludes individuals from serving as captains, is not challenged by respondents.[17] The second practice does not operate to exclude protected individuals from the position of captain; rather it prevents qualified 60-year-olds from working as flight engineers. Thus, it is the "particular" job of flight engineer from which the respondents were excluded by the discriminatory transfer policy. Because age under 60 is not a BFOQ for the position of flight engineer,[18] the age-based discrimination at issue in this case cannot be justified by § 4(f)(1).

TWA nevertheless contends that its BFOQ argument is supported by the legislative history of the amendments to the ADEA. In 1978, Congress amended ADEA § 4(f)(2) to prohibit the involuntary retirement of protected individuals on the basis of age. Some Members of Congress were concerned that this amendment might be construed as limiting the employer's ability to terminate workers subject to a valid BFOQ. The Senate proposed an amendment to § 4(f)(1) providing that an employer could establish a mandatory retirement age where age is a BFOQ. S.Rep. No. 95–493, pp. 11, 24 (1977), U.S.Code Cong. & Admin. News 1978, p. 504. In the Conference Committee, however, the proposed amendment was withdrawn because "the [Senate] conferees agreed that * * * [it] neither added to nor worked any change upon present law." H.R.Conf.Rep. No. 95–950, p. 7 (1978), U.S.Code Cong. & Admin.News 1978, p. 529. The House Committee Report also indicated that an individual could be compelled to retire from a position for which age was a BFOQ. H.R.Rep. No. 95–527 pt. 1, p. 12 (1977).

The legislative history of the 1978 Amendments does not support petitioners' position. The history shows only that the ADEA does not prohibit TWA from retiring all disqualified captains, including those who are incapacitated because of age. This does not mean, however, that TWA can make dependent upon the age of the individual the availability of a transfer to a position for which age is not a BFOQ.

17. In this litigation, the respondents have not challenged TWA's claim that the FAA regulation establishes a BFOQ for the position of captain. The EEOC guidelines, however, do not list the FAA's age-60 rule as an example of a BFOQ because the EEOC wishes to avoid any appearance that it endorses the rule. 46 Fed.Reg. 47724, 47725 (1981).

18. The petitioners do not contend that age is a BFOQ for the position of flight engineer. Indeed, the airline has employed at least 148 flight engineers who are over 60 years old.

Nothing in the legislative history cited by petitioners indicates a congressional intention to allow an employer to discriminate against an older worker seeking to transfer to another position, on the ground that age was a BFOQ for his *former* job.

TWA also contends that its discriminatory transfer policy is lawful under the Act because it is part of a "bona fide seniority system." The Court of Appeals held that the airline's retirement policy is not mandated by the negotiated seniority plan. We need not address this finding; any seniority system that includes the challenged practice is not "bona fide" under the statute. The Act provides that a seniority system may not "require or permit" the involuntary retirement of a protected individual because of his age. Although the FAA "age 60 rule" may have caused respondents' retirement, TWA's seniority plan certainly "permitted" it within the meaning of the ADEA. Moreover, because captains disqualified for reasons other than age are allowed to "bump" less senior flight engineers, the mandatory retirement was age-based. Therefore, the "bona fide seniority system" defense is unavailable to the petitioners.

In summary, TWA's transfer policy discriminates against protected individuals on the basis of age, and thereby violates the Act. The two statutory defenses raised by petitioners do not support the argument that this discrimination is justified. The BFOQ defense is meritless because age is not a bona fide occupational qualification for the position of flight engineer, the job from which the respondents were excluded. Nor can TWA's policy be viewed as part of a bona fide seniority system. A system that includes this discriminatory transfer policy permits the forced retirement of captains on the basis of age.

III

A

Section 7(b) of the ADEA provides that the rights created by the Act are to be "enforced in accordance with the powers, remedies, and procedures" of the Fair Labor Standards Act. See Lorillard v. Pons, 434 U.S., at 579, 98 S.Ct., at 869 (1978). But the remedial provisions of the two statutes are not identical. Congress declined to incorporate into the ADEA several FLSA sections. Moreover, § 16(b) of the FLSA, which makes the award of liquidated damages mandatory, is significantly qualified in ADEA § 7(b) by a proviso that a prevailing plaintiff is entitled to double damages "only in cases of willful violations." In this case, the Court of Appeals held that TWA's violation of the ADEA was "willful," and that the respondents therefore were entitled to double damages. We granted certiorari to review this holding.

The legislative history of the ADEA indicates that Congress intended for liquidated damages to be punitive in nature. The original bill proposed by the administration incorporated § 16(a) of the FLSA, which imposes criminal liability for a willful violation. See 113 Cong.Rec. 2199 (1967). Senator Javits found "certain serious defects" in the administration bill. He stated that "difficult problems of proof * * * would arise under a criminal provision," and that the employer's invocation of the Fifth Amendment might impede investigation, conciliation, and enforcement. 113 Cong.Rec. 7076 (1967). Therefore, he proposed that "the [FLSA's] criminal penalty in cases of willful violation * * * [be] eliminated and a double damage liability substituted." Ibid. Senator Javits argued that his proposed amendment would "furnish an effective deterrent to willful violations [of the ADEA]," ibid., and it was incorporated into the ADEA with only minor modification, S. 788, 90th Cong., 1st Sess. (1967).

This Court has recognized that in enacting the ADEA, "Congress exhibited * * * a detailed knowledge of the FLSA provisions and their judicial interpretation * * *." Lorillard v. Pons, 434 U.S. 575, 581, 98 S.Ct. 866, 870, 55 L.Ed.2d 40 (1978). The manner in which FLSA § 16(a) has been interpreted therefore is relevant. In general, courts have found that an employer is subject to criminal penalties under the FLSA when he "wholly disregards the law * * * without making any reasonable effort to determine whether the plan he is following would constitute a violation of the law." Nabob Oil Co. v. United States, 190 F.2d 478, 479 (CA10), cert. denied, 342 U.S. 876, 72 S.Ct. 167, 96 L.Ed. 659 (1951); see also Darby v. United States, 132 F.2d 928 (CA5 1943).[19] This standard is substantially in accord with the interpretation of "willful" adopted by the Court of Appeals in interpreting the liquidated damages provision of the ADEA. The court below stated that a violation of the Act was "willful" if "the employer * * * knew or showed reckless disregard for the matter of whether its conduct was prohibited by the ADEA." Given the legislative history of the liquidated damages provision, we think the "reckless disregard" standard is reasonable.

The definition of "willful" adopted by the above cited courts is consistent with the manner in which this Court has interpreted the term in other criminal and civil statutes. In United States v. Murdock, 290 U.S. 389, 54 S.Ct. 223, 78 L.Ed. 381 (1933), the defendant was prosecuted under the Revenue Acts of 1926 and 1928, which made it a misdemeanor for a person "willfully" to fail to pay the required tax. The *Murdock* Court stated that conduct was "willful" within the meaning of this criminal statute if it was "marked by careless disregard [for] whether or not one has the right so to act." In United States v. Illinois Central R., 303 U.S. 239, 58 S.Ct. 533, 82 L.Ed. 773 (1938), the Court applied the *Murdock* definition of "willful" in a civil case. There, the defendant's failure to unload a cattle car was "willful," because it

19. Courts below have held that an employer's action may be "willful," within the meaning of § 16(a) of the FLSA, even though he did not have an evil motive or bad purpose. See Nabob Oil Co. v. United States, 190 F.2d 478 (CA10), cert. denied, 342 U.S. 876, 72 S.Ct. 167, 96 L.Ed. 659 (1951). We do not agree with TWA's argument that unless it intended to violate the Act, double damages are inappropriate under § 7(b) of the ADEA. Only one court of appeals has expressed approval of this position. See Loeb v. Textron, Inc., 600 F.2d 1003, 1020 n. 27 (CA1 1979).

showed a disregard for the governing statute and an indifference to its requirements.

The respondents argue that an employer's conduct is willful if he is "cognizant of an appreciable possibility that the employees involved were covered by the [ADEA]." In support of their position, the respondents cite § 6 of the Portal-to-Portal Act of 1947 (PPA), 29 U.S.C. § 255(a), which is incorporated in both the ADEA and the FLSA. Section 6 of the PPA provides for a 2-year statute of limitations period unless the violation is willful, in which case the limitations period is extended to three years. Several courts have held that a violation is willful within the meaning of § 6 if the employer knew that the ADEA was "in the picture." See, e.g., Coleman v. Jiffy June Farms, Inc., 458 F.2d 1139, 1142 (CA5 1971), cert. denied, 409 U.S. 948, 93 S.Ct. 292, 34 L.Ed.2d 219 (1972); EEOC v. Central Kansas Medical Center, 705 F.2d 1270, 1274 (CA10 1983). Respondents contend that the term "willful" should be interpreted in a similar manner in applying the liquidated damages provision of the ADEA.

We are unpersuaded by respondents' argument that a violation of the Act is "willful" if the employer simply knew of the potential applicability of the ADEA. Even if the "in the picture" standard were appropriate for the statute of limitations, the same standard should not govern a provision dealing with liquidated damages.[21] More importantly, the broad standard proposed by the respondents would result in an award of double damages in almost every case. As employers are required to post ADEA notices, it would be virtually impossible for an employer to show that he was unaware of the Act and its potential applicability. Both the legislative history and the structure of the statute show that Congress intended a two-tiered liability scheme. We decline to interpret the liquidated damages provision of ADEA § 7(b) in a manner that frustrates this intent.[22]

21. The Courts of Appeals are divided over whether Congress intended the "willfulness" standard to be identical for determining liquidated damages and for purposes of the limitations period. Compare Spagnuolo v. Whirlpool Corp., 641 F.2d 1109, 1113 (CA4), cert. denied, 454 U.S. 860, 102 S.Ct. 316, 70 L.Ed.2d 158 (1981) (standards are identical), with Kelly v. American Standard, Inc., 640 F.2d 974, 979 (CA9 1981) (standards are different).

22. The "in the picture" standard proposed by the respondents would allow the recovery of liquidated damages even if the employer acted reasonably and in complete "good faith." Congress hardly intended such a result.

The Court interpreted the FLSA, as originally enacted, as allowing the recovery of liquidated damages any time that there was a violation of the Act. See Overnight Motor Transportation Co. v. Missel, 316 U.S. 572, 62 S.Ct. 1216, 86 L.Ed. 1682 (1942). In response to its dissatisfaction with that harsh interpretation of the provision, Congress enacted the Portal-to-Portal Act of 1947. See Lorillard v. Pons, 434 U.S. 575, 581–582 n. 8, 98 S.Ct. 866, 870 n. 8, 55 L.Ed.2d 40 (1978). Section 11 of the PPA, 29 U.S.C. § 260, provides the employer with a defense to a mandatory award of liquidated damages when it can show good faith and reasonable grounds for believing it was not in violation of the FLSA. Section 7(b) of the ADEA does not incorporate § 11 of the PPA, contra Hays v. Republic Steel Corp., 531 F.2d 1307 (CA5 1976). Nevertheless, we think that the same concerns are reflected in the proviso to § 7(b) of the ADEA.

B

As noted above, the Court of Appeals stated that a violation is "willful" if "the employer either knew or showed reckless disregard for the matter of whether its conduct was prohibited by the ADEA." Although we hold that this is an acceptable way to articulate a definition of "willful," the court below misapplied this standard. TWA certainly did not "know" that its conduct violated the Act. Nor can it fairly be said that TWA adopted its transfer policy in "reckless disregard" of the Act's requirements. The record makes clear that TWA officials acted reasonably and in good faith in attempting to determine whether their plan would violate the ADEA.

Shortly after the ADEA was amended, TWA officials met with their lawyers to determine whether the mandatory retirement policy violated the Act. Concluding that the company's existing plan was inconsistent with the ADEA, David Crombie, the airline's Vice President for Administration, proposed a new policy. Despite opposition from the Union, the company adopted a modified version of this initial proposal. Under the plan adopted on August 10, 1978, any pilot in "flight engineer status" on his 60th birthday could continue to work for the airline. On the day the plan was adopted, the Union filed suit against the airline claiming that the new retirement policy constituted a "major" change in the collective-bargaining agreement, and thus was barred by the § 6 of the Railway Labor Act, 45 U.S.C. § 156. Nevertheless, TWA adhered to its new policy.

As evidence of "willfulness," respondents point to comments made by J.E. Frankum, the Vice President of Flight Operations. After Crombie was hospitalized in August 1978, Frankum assumed responsibility for bringing TWA's retirement policy into conformance with the ADEA. Despite legal advice to the contrary, Frankum initially believed that the company was not required to allow any pilot over 60 to work. Frankum later abandoned this position in favor of the plan approved on August 10, 1978. Frankum apparently had been concerned only about whether flight engineers could work after reaching the age of 60. There is no indication that TWA was ever advised by counsel that its new transfer policy discriminated against captains on the basis of age.

There simply is no evidence that TWA acted in "reckless disregard" of the requirements of the ADEA. The airline had obligations under the collective-bargaining agreement with the Air Line Pilots Association. In an attempt to bring its retirement policy into compliance with the ADEA, while at the same time observing the terms of the collective-bargaining agreement, TWA sought legal advice and consulted with the Union. Despite opposition from the Union, a plan was adopted that permitted cockpit employees to work as "flight engineers" after reaching age 60. Apparently TWA officials and the airline's attorneys failed to focus specifically on the effect of each aspect of the new retirement policy for cockpit personnel. It is reasonable to believe that the parties involved, in focusing on the larger overall problem, simply overlooked the challenged aspect of the new plan.[23] We conclude that TWA's violation of the Act was not willful within the meaning of § 7(b), and that respondents therefore are not entitled to liquidated damages.

IV

The ADEA requires TWA to afford 60-year-old captains the same transfer privileges that it gives to captains disqualified for reasons other than age. Therefore, we affirm the Court of Appeals on this issue. We do not agree with its holding that TWA's violation of the Act was willful. We accordingly reverse its judgment that respondents are entitled to liquidated or double damages.

It is so ordered.

NOTES AND PROBLEMS FOR DISCUSSION

1. With respect to the prima facie case, the lower courts have agreed that a plaintiff must prove that age was a "determining" or "but for" cause of the employer's conduct. See La Montagne v. American Convenience Products, 750 F.2d 1405 (7th Cir. 1984); Blackwell v. Sun Elec. Corp., 696 F.2d 1176 (6th Cir. 1983); Cuddy v. Carmen, 694 F.2d 853 (D.C.Cir. 1982); Staniewicz v. Beecham, Inc., 687 F.2d 526 (1st Cir. 1982).

2. The company asserted two arguments in *Thurston.* First, it contended that the plaintiff had failed to establish a prima facie case. Second, it alternatively argued that even if a prima facie case had been established, its policy was justified by two of the ADEA's five affirmative defenses. Suppose, that instead of relying on the statutory defenses, the company had sought to rebut the plaintiffs' disparate treatment-based prima facie case with evidence of "some legitimate nondiscriminatory reason" for its decision. Would it have been subjected to the same burden of proof?

In Douglas v. Anderson, 656 F.2d 528 (9th Cir. 1981), the manager of a law school bookstore alleged that he had been discharged because of his age. The defendants claimed that Douglas had been terminated after an audit of the financial records of the bookstore revealed several substantial management problems which led the auditors to conclude that the plaintiff had performed unsatisfactorily as business manager of the store. The court, applying the *McDonnell Douglas* formula, found that the plaintiff had established a prima facie case and that this shifted the burden to the employer "to produce evidence of a legitimate nondiscriminatory reason for terminating Douglas's employment." (Note, however, that this same circuit court, in Kouba v. Allstate Ins., supra at 583, stated that the employer bears the burden of "showing" that its challenged policy falls within the analogous "factor other than sex" defense of the Equal Pay Act.)

23. In his dissent, Judge Van Graafeiland also focused on the larger problem, rather than on the discriminatory transfer policy. Judge Van Graafeiland stated: "TWA is the only trunk airline that voluntarily has permitted [persons] * * * over 60 to continue working as flight engineers. Instead of receiving commendation for what it has done, TWA is held liable as a matter of law for age discrimination," 713 F.2d 940, 957 (1983).

Section 4(f) of the ADEA sets forth four defenses to claims of age bias. Under this provision, a defendant will be found not to have violated the statute:

(1) where age is a bona fide occupational qualification reasonably necessary to the normal operations of the particular business;

(2) where the differentiation is based on reasonable factors other than age;

(3) where the defendant has observed the terms of a bona fide seniority system or bona fide employee benefit plan that is not a subterfuge to evade the purposes of the Act and is not used to involuntarily retire an employee because of his or her age; or

(4) where the discharge or discipline was based on good cause.

Wasn't the defendant in *Douglas* asserting the second of these four defenses? If so, then why did it bear only the burden of production when the *Thurston* Court implied that the defendant would bear the burden of persuasion as to its assertion of the first and third listed defenses? Is there a justifiable distinction between these three types of defenses? Consider this analysis offered by the Fifth Circuit:

> "The reason for that distinction is clear. A defendant who seeks to establish a BFOQ is essentially asserting an 'affirmative defense'—one in the nature of confession and avoidance. An age-related BFOQ permits an employer to admit that he had discriminated on the basis of age, but to avoid any penalty. Establishment of a BFOQ relating to age justifies an employer's violation of the heart of the ADEA, allowing him to apply a general exclusionary rule to otherwise statutorily protected individuals solely on the basis of class membership. The good cause and differentiating factor exceptions, on the other hand, are denials of the plaintiff's prima facie case. Plaintiff says that the employer fired him because of his age; employer replies, in effect, not so, plaintiff was fired for excessive absences, general inability, or some other non-discriminatory reason. The natural tendency of the court to place the burden of proof upon the party desiring change and the special policy considerations disfavoring the statutory exceptions both justify the distinction between these defenses."

Marshall v. Westinghouse Electric Corp., 576 F.2d 588, 591 (5th Cir. 1978).

3. Were you satisfied with the Court's treatment of the BFOQ issue in *Thurston?* Did the Court rest its decision on the company's failure to contend that age was a BFOQ for the flight engineer position? Or did it take into account that the company had employed over 148 flight engineers over the age of sixty? Should it have made such a factual determination or should it have remanded for further consideration?

The questions of the nature and quantity of evidence necessary to establish a BFOQ were not addressed in *Thurston.* The lower federal courts have tended to agree that in certain situations, such as those where the employer asserts safety as a consideration for its challenged decision, a lesser showing is required. In Spurlock v. United Airlines, Inc., 475 F.2d 216, 219 (10th Cir. 1973), a disproportionate impact Title VII case in which the defendant raised the defense of business necessity, the court stated that where the job in question "requires a small amount of skill and training and the consequences of hiring an unqualified applicant are insignificant, the * * * employer should have a heavy burden to demonstrate * * * that his employment criteria are job-related. On the other hand, when the job clearly requires a high degree of skill and the economic and human risks involved in hiring an unqualified applicant are great, the employer bears a correspondingly lighter burden * * *." See also Tuohy v. Ford Motor Co., 675 F.2d 842, 845 (6th Cir. 1982) ("The presence of an overriding safety factor might well lead a court to conclude as a matter of policy that the level of proof required to establish the reasonable necessity of a BFOQ is relatively low."). But see Usery v. Tamiami Trail Tours, Inc., 531 F.2d 224 (5th Cir. 1976) (distinguishing Spurlock as a non-BFOQ case).

A precise comparison of the interpretations accorded the BFOQ defense under these two statutes had been impeded by the federal appellate courts' failure to agree upon a uniform application of this defense in ADEA cases as well as the absence of a Supreme Court ruling on the age/BFOQ issue. Most of these courts agreed that two elements must be proven by the defendant to establish a BFOQ: (1) that the job qualifications used to justify discrimination are reasonably necessary to the essence of the business; and (2) that there is a substantial factual basis for believing that all or substantially all members of the excluded class are unable to safely and efficiently perform the job, or that there is no practical basis other than the challenged classification for determining an individual applicant's ability to safely and efficiently perform the job. Nevertheless, they disagreed with respect to the nature and amount of evidence needed to satisfy the second element of the defense. Compare Hodgson v. Greyhound Lines, Inc., 499 F.2d 859, 865 (7th Cir. 1974), cert. denied, 419 U.S. 1122, 95 S.Ct. 805, 42 L.Ed.2d 822 (1975) (bus company that refuses to hire new drivers over age 35 need only show that its policy was based on a good faith judgment that passenger safety could be assured by its age limitation and was not merely the result of "an arbitrary belief lacking in objective reason or rationale.") with Smallwood v. United Air Lines, Inc., 661 F.2d 303 (4th Cir. 1981) (airline policy denying employment to pilot applicants over age 35 violates ADEA as employer did not offer significant evidence tending to prove that substantially all applicants over age 35 would be unable to satisfy job requirements and company's extant physical examination program could be used to screen out unsafe applicants on an individual basis) and Usery v. Tamiami Trail Tours, Inc., 531 F.2d 224 (5th Cir. 1976) (bus company's refusal to hire new drivers over age 40 upheld because employer demonstrated that age was the only practical basis for determining which applicants would be unsafe drivers even though court found employer did not demonstrate a factual basis for assuming that all applicants over 40 would be unsafe drivers). For further discussion of these cases see Note, The Scope of the Bona Fide Occupational Qualification Exemption Under the ADEA, 57 Chi.Kent L.Rev. 1145 (1981); Note, The Age Discrimination in Employment Act of 1967, 90 Harv.L.Rev. 380, 400–410 (1976).

The Supreme Court addressed this controversy in WESTERN AIR LINES, INC. v. CRISWELL, ___ U.S. ___, 105 S.Ct. 2743, 86 L.Ed.2d 321 (1985). It upheld the two pronged BFOQ inquiry developed in *Tamiani* and described herein. More significantly, perhaps, it rejected the employer's contention that the ADEA required only that an employer establish a "rational basis in fact" for believing that identification of those individuals lacking suitable qualifications could not occur on an individualized basis. The limited BFOQ defense, the Court reasoned, required the defendant to establish a substantial basis for believing that all or nearly all employees above the designated retirement age lacked the qualifications required for the job in question.

Moreover, in JOHNSON v. MAYOR AND CITY COUNCIL OF BALTIMORE, ___ U.S. ___, 105 S.Ct. 2717, 86 L.Ed.2d 286 (1985), decided the same day as *Western Air Lines*, the Court stated that a federal mandatory retirement rule applicable to a class of federal employees did not establish an absolute BFOQ defense to a state or local government rule imposing an identical pre-age 70 mandatory retirement age on analogous state and local government workers. It concluded that the federal statute relied on by the defendants in this case was not intended by Congress to apply to nonfederal employees. The Court also concluded that the decision to impose an age 55 mandatory retirement provision was not based on a Congressional determination that age was a bona fide occupational qualification for the subject class (federal firefighters), but, rather, on the idiosyncratic problems of federal civil servants and Congress' desire to create an image of a "young man's service." Accordingly, the Court stated that the presence of a federal statute authorizing pre-age 70 mandatory retirement for federal firefighters was not relevant to the question of whether age is a BFOQ for firefighters. The Court did add, however, that if, in another case, there was evidence that Congress had based its early retirement statute on the same considerations that would support the finding of a BFOQ, then such evidence "might" be admissible as evidence to determine the existence of a BFOQ for nonfederal employees and that the extent of the probativity of such a Congressional determination would depend upon the level of congruity between the federal and nonfederal occupations under question. Finally, it declared that if Congress had expressly extended the BFOQ to nonfederal occupations, that determination would be dispositive.

4. Luther Clark, a 45 year old former Air Force pilot, applied for a pilot position with Ace Airlines, Inc. The company rejected his application in a letter stating that while Clark was otherwise qualified for the job, airline policy precluded hiring pilots over the age of 35. Ace maintains a pilot training and progression system under which all pilot applicants are hired as Second Officers, are promoted to First Officers after 8 to 10 years of service with Ace and are advanced to Captain after an additional 6 to 8 years. The company contends that substantial costs are involved in operating its pilot training and progression system and, when coupled with an F.A.A. requirement that all pilots retire at 60, a maximum age of 35 at initial hire is necessary to achieve peak pilot productivity. Has Ace violated the ADEA? Compare Smallwood v. United Air Lines, Inc., 661 F.2d 303 (4th Cir. 1981), cert. denied, 456 U.S. 1007, 102 S.Ct. 2299, 73 L.Ed.2d 1302 (1982), with Murname v. American Airlines, Inc., 667 F.2d 98 (D.C.Cir. 1981), cert. denied, 456 U.S. 915, 102 S.Ct. 1770, 72 L.Ed.2d 174.

5. Kevin Conroy was discharged as Manager of the men's clothing department of Watson's Department Store one month after his 55th birthday. At the time of his discharge, Conroy had worked at Watson's for 25 years and was earning $47,000. Conroy's position eventually was filled by Mark Dix, a 25 year old who had worked as an assistant buyer at Watson's for 3 years. The store contends that a sharp decrease in revenues has forced it to employ several cost-cutting techniques, including reducing its payroll, and that Conroy's discharge was one of several personnel actions taken pursuant to that policy. Has Watson's violated the ADEA? See Leftwich v. Harris-Stowe State College, 702 F.2d 686 (8th Cir. 1983); Geller v. Markham, 635 F.2d 1027 (2d Cir. 1980). What if Watson's had offered to retain Conroy at the $21,000 salary it subsequently offered to Dix? Would that violate § 4(a)(3) of the ADEA, which makes it unlawful for an employer "to reduce the wage rate of any employee in order to comply with the Act"? See generally, Note, The Cost Defense Under the ADEA, 1982 Duke L.J. 580 (1982).

6. Johanson Insurance Co. decides to reduce the number of its insurance salesmen in response to a decline in sales. It offers an early retirement option to any of its sales personnel whose age plus total years of service is equal to or greater than 75. The plan pays $750 per month to all qualifying employees. David Filvaroff, a 60 year old employee, brings an ADEA claim against the company, alleging that by providing equal monthly early retirement benefits, younger qualifying employees will receive greater total benefits since they will be receiving monthly payments over a longer period of time. What result? See Dorsch v. L.B. Foster Co., 782 F.2d 1421 (7th Cir. 1986).

7. The 1978 amendments to the ADEA contained two major substantive changes. The upper level of the protected age group was extended for non-federal employees from 65 to 70 and involuntary retirement of non-federal employees before age 70 was outlawed. As originally enacted, § 4(f)(2) of the ADEA permitted an employer to make age-based decisions in order "to observe the terms of a bona fide seniority system or any employee benefit plan such as a retirement, pension or insurance plan which is not a subterfuge to evade the purposes of the Act." This provision meant, for example, that an employer could involuntarily retire an employee before age 65 so long as: (1) it was "observing" (2) the terms of a "bona fide" retirement or pension plan (3) that was not a "subterfuge to evade the purposes of the Act." The courts, moreover, held that an employer was "observing" such a plan as long as the plan placed the option of retirement in the hands of the employer—i.e., the statute protected plans whether the employer was required to involuntarily retire all employees at a certain age or simply had the option of so doing. See e.g. Benzel v. Valley National Bank, 633 F.2d 1325 (9th Cir. 1980). Retirement plans were held to be "bona fide" as long as they paid benefits and gave the employees notice of the age at which the employer could force them to retire. See Sexton v. Beatrice Foods Co., 630 F.2d 478 (7th Cir. 1980). Finally, in United Air Lines, Inc. v. McMann, 434 U.S. 192, 98 S.Ct. 444, 54 L.Ed.2d 402 (1977), the Supreme Court ruled that as long as a pension plan was established before the passage of the ADEA, it could not be a "subterfuge to evade the purposes of the Act."

The 1978 amendments to the ADEA, however, contained a provision designed to curtail these relatively broad interpretations of this statutory defense. Section 4(f)(2) was amended to prohibit the involuntary retirement of non-federal employees under 70 years of age. The 1978 legislation, however, also created two exceptions to this rule. Executive or high policy-making employees entitled to immediate non-forfeitable annual payments from a benefit plan of at least $44,000 and tenured college and university employees could be involuntarily retired at age 65. (The exemption for tenured university employees expired on July 1, 1982.) In Whittlesey v. Union Carbide Corp., 567 F.Supp. 1320 (S.D.N.Y.1983), one of the first cases examining the scope of the "high policy making" exemption, the court held that the employer's chief labor counsel did not fall within this exemption when it determined that he did not exercise important executive and policymaking responsibilities. The predominant part of the attorney's time was devoted to legal matters and giving legal advice, rather than to formulating company policy. In addition, while he was the senior labor attorney, his supervisory duties were minimal and occupied a very small portion of his time. Secondly, the amendment to § 4(f)(2) did not become applicable to employees covered by labor agreements in effect on September 1, 1977, until either the expiration of those agreements, or January 1, 1980, whichever came first. In addition, the prohibition against mandatory retirement remains subject to the statutory BFOQ defense. Suppose an employer imposes a mandatory retirement age for all employees in its business on the ground that age is a BFOQ. Must that employer prove that age is a BFOQ for every position or for the business in general? Compare EEOC v. City of St. Paul, 671 F.2d 1162 (8th Cir. 1982) (statutory challenge to application to district fire chief of ordinance establishing mandatory retirement age for all uniformed fire employees required separate consideration as to whether age was BFOQ for that particular position) with EEOC v. City of Janesville, 630 F.2d 1254 (7th Cir. 1980) (inquiry should be limited to whether age is a BFOQ for generic class of law enforcement personnel rather than position of police chief) and with Mahoney v. Trabucco, 738 F.2d 35 (1st Cir.), cert. denied, ___ U.S. ___. 105 S.Ct. 513, 83 L.Ed.2d 403 (1984) (apply BFOQ test to a recognized vocation rather than to a particularized set of job duties or to a generic classification). In *Thurston*, the Supreme Court addressed this conflict, concluding that the "particular business" referred to in the BFOQ provision meant the particular job from which the aggrieved was excluded and that age was not a BFOQ for the position of flight engineer.

A 1986 amendment to the ADEA, however, now prohibits mandatory retirement at any age (with a seven year exemption for professors, law enforcement personnel and firefighters) by nonfederal employers and requires such employers to continue group health care insurance for workers over 70.

8. While the 1978 amendment to § 4(f)(2) terminated the right previously afforded employers by the Act to involuntarily retire an employee within the protected age group on the basis of age, the original version of § 4(f)(2) still applies to all other age-based actions taken pursuant to the terms of bona fide employee benefit or seniority plans. For example:

(a) All employees of York Enterprises, Inc., are covered by an employer-funded disability, life and health insurance benefits plan. Because of the significantly higher cost of premiums for employees over age 60, York's employee benefits plan terminates disability, life and health insurance benefits to all employees at age 60. Does the ADEA prohibit this practice? Must York absorb the extra cost or, at least, make equal premium contributions for over-60 employees and simply provide reduced coverage? See Germann v. Levy, 553 F.Supp. 700 (N.D.Ill.1982). Alternatively, could York require employees over age 60 to contribute the difference to maintain their coverage under the plan? See EEOC Interpretations of the ADEA, 29 CFR 1625.10(a)(1), (d)(4), 46 Fed.Reg. 47724 (Sept. 29, 1981) (adopting Department of Labor's Interpretative Bulletin on Employee Benefit Plans, 29 CFR 860.120 (1979): "The legislative history of [§ 4(f)(2)] * * * indicates that its purpose is to permit age-based reductions in employee benefit plans where such reductions are justified by significant cost considerations."); Gitt, The 1978 Amendments to the ADEA—A Legal Overview, 64 Marq.L.Rev. 607, 647–655 (1981).

(b) Walker Tool & Die Co. has a generous retirement plan that provides substantial benefits to all employees who have at least ten years seniority and who remain with Walker until retirement at age 70. Joe Mason, a 62 year old master mechanic, unsuccessfully applied for a job with Walker. The company admitted that while Mason was qualified for an available job, since he could not satisfy the ten year seniority requirement in its retirement plan before facing mandatory retirement at age 70, he was not eligible for employment. Has Walker violated the ADEA? If so, must it hire Mason and include him within its retirement plan?

9. In EEOC v. County of Allegheny, 705 F.2d 679 (3d Cir. 1983), the court rejected the defendant's claim that its reliance upon a state statute that conflicted with the provisions of the ADEA constituted a "differentiation based on factors other than age".

10. The 1978 amendments also eliminated the upper limit of the protected age group for federal employees, so that virtually all federal employees above age 40 are protected against all forms of age discrimination. (The Act does create exceptions for air traffic controllers, Panama Canal and Alaska Railroad employees, law enforcement officers and firefighters.) Accordingly, absent the showing of a bona fide occupational qualification, the federal government is precluded from involuntarily retiring any covered federal employee solely on the basis of age.

Public sector age classifications, however, also have been scrutinized under the equal protection and due process requirements of the Fourteenth and Fifth Amendments of the U. S. Constitution. In MASSACHUSETTS BOARD OF RETIREMENT v. MURGIA, 427 U.S. 307, 96 S.Ct. 2562, 49 L.Ed.2d 520 (1976), noted in the principal case, a Massachusetts statute requiring uniformed state police officers to retire at age fifty was held not to violate the equal protection clause. (No claim was made under the ADEA.) The Supreme Court stated that an age classification need only pass the rationality, rather than strict scrutiny standard; and that mandatory retirement at age 50 rationally furthered Massachusetts' interest in protecting the public by assuring the physical preparedness of the uniformed police. Similarly, in VANCE v. BRADLEY, 440 U.S. 93, 99 S.Ct. 939, 59 L.Ed.2d 171 (1979), a federal statute mandating retirement at age 60 of Foreign Service personnel was upheld in the face of an equal protection challenge. The Supreme Court held that the retirement provision rationally furthered Congress' legitimate objective of maintaining a competent Foreign Service. However, in light of the virtual identity in language between § 15 of the ADEA and § 717 of Title VII, should the ruling in Brown v. General Services Administration, 425 U.S. 820, 96 S.Ct. 1961, 48 L.Ed. 2d 402 (1976), be extended to make the ADEA the exclusive remedy for federal employee claims of age discrimination, or should age claimants enjoy a parallel constitutional remedy? See Purtill v. Harris, 658 F.2d 134 (3d Cir. 1981); Paterson v. Weinberger, 644 F.2d 521 (5th Cir. 1981). Similarly, should the ADEA apply to an age discrimination claim of a uniformed member of the armed forces? See Lear v. Schlesinger, 17 FEP Cases 337 (W.D.Mo.1978).

SECTION C. PROCEDURAL REQUIREMENTS

Read §§ 7, 14 and 15 of the ADEA.

As the result of two events in 1978—the passage of the ADEA amendments and the promulgation of a governmental reorganization plan by President Carter [a]—litigants proceeding under the ADEA are subject to most of the same procedural requirements placed before Title VII claimants. Prior to 1978, the ADEA required complainants to file a notice of intent to sue with the Secretary of Labor before instituting suit and instructed the Secretary to seek voluntary compliance through conciliation. The Secretary also was given the authority to sue on behalf of the aggrieved and the exercise of that authority terminated

[a] Reorganization Plan No. 1 of 1978, § 2, 43 Fed.Reg. 19,807, 3 CFR 321 (1978).

the individual's private right of action. The 1978 amendments and reorganization plan effected a few important changes in this procedure. The reorganization plan transferred all ADEA administration and enforcement functions from the Secretary of Labor to the EEOC.[b] The amendments required an aggrieved person to file a "charge" of discrimination, rather than a notice of intent to sue, with the EEOC.[c] These changes, however, did not resolve all of the procedural questions surrounding litigation under the ADEA.

OSCAR MAYER & CO. v. EVANS

Supreme Court of the United States, 1978.
441 U.S. 750, 99 S.Ct. 2066, 60 L.Ed.2d 609.

MR. JUSTICE BRENNAN delivered the opinion of the Court.

* * *

This case presents three questions * * *. First, whether § 14(b) requires an aggrieved person to resort to appropriate state remedies before bringing suit under § 7(c) of the ADEA. Second, if so, whether the state proceedings must be commenced within time limits specified by state law in order to preserve the federal right of action. Third, if so, whether any circumstances may excuse the failure to commence timely state proceedings.

We hold that § 14(b) mandates that a grievant not bring suit in federal court under § 7(c) of the ADEA until he has first resorted to appropriate state administrative proceedings. We also hold, however, that the grievant is not required by § 14(b) to commence the state proceedings within time limits specified by state law. In light of these holdings, it is not necessary to address the question of the circumstances, if any, in which failure to comply with § 14(b) may be excused.

[b] The Reorganization Plan also authorized the EEOC to file lawsuits under the ADEA. This Plan was promulgated pursuant to the Reorganization Act of 1977, which authorized the President to reorganize federal agencies subject to veto by only one house of Congress. In light of the Supreme Court's ruling in *Chadha* as to the unconstitutionality of the one-house veto, see supra at 576 n. j, does the EEOC retain this right to sue? Compare EEOC v. CBS, Inc., 743 F.2d 969 (2d Cir. 1984) with Muller Optical Co. v. EEOC, 743 F.2d 380 (6th Cir. 1984).

[c] The EEOC promulgated regulations, effective January 3, 1983, setting forth the procedures it will follow in processing age discrimination charges. Under these regulations a "charge" may be filed with the EEOC by or on behalf of the aggrieved alleging a violation has occurred or is about to occur. The regulations retained the time limits for filing age bias charges that were prescribed by the ADEA as originally enacted; i.e., (a) within 180 days of the alleged discriminatory act, or (b) where the alleged act of discrimination occurred in a state having a law prohibiting age discrimination and an agency authorized to grant or seek relief from such practices, within 300 days of the alleged discrimination or 30 days after receipt of notice of the termination of proceedings under state law, whichever comes first. The provision in the original Act prohibiting the filing of suit until 60 days after the commencement of federal administrative action also was adopted by the Commission.

The Regulations also adopt the Commission's rules governing Title VII claims with respect to referral to and from state agencies, investigations and conciliation efforts. 29 C.F.R. § 1626, 48 F.Reg. 138 (1983).

Respondent Joseph Evans was employed by petitioner Oscar Mayer & Co. for 23 years until his involuntary retirement in January 1976. On March 10, 1976, respondent filed with the United States Department of Labor a notice of intent to sue the company under the ADEA. Respondent charged that he had been forced to retire because of his age in violation of the Act. At approximately this time respondent inquired of the Department whether he was obliged to file a state complaint in order to preserve his federal rights. The Department informed respondent that the ADEA contained no such requirement. Relying on this official advice, respondent refrained from resorting to state proceedings. On March 7, 1977, after federal conciliation efforts had failed, respondent brought suit against petitioner company and company officials in the United States District Court for the Southern District of Iowa.

Petitioners moved to dismiss the complaint on the grounds that the Iowa State Civil Rights Commission was empowered to remedy age discrimination in employment and that § 14(b) required resort to this state remedy prior to the commencement of the federal suit. The District Court denied the motion, and the Court of Appeals for the Eighth Circuit affirmed. * * * We reverse.

Petitioners argue that § 14(b) mandates that in States with agencies empowered to remedy age discrimination in employment (deferral States) a grievant may not bring suit under the ADEA unless he has first commenced a proceeding with the appropriate state agency. Respondent, on the other hand, argues that the grievant has the option of whether to resort to state proceedings, and that § 14(b) requires only that grievants choosing to resort to state remedies wait 60 days before bringing suit in federal court. The question of construction is close, but we conclude that petitioners are correct.

Section 14(b) of the ADEA was patterned after and is virtually *in haec verba* with § 706(c) of Title VII of the Civil Rights Act of 1964 * * *.

* * *

* * * Because state agencies cannot even attempt to resolve discrimination complaints not brought to their attention, the section has been interpreted to require individuals in deferral States to resort to appropriate state proceedings before bringing suit under Title VII.

Since the ADEA and Title VII share a common purpose, the elimination of discrimination in the workplace, since the language of § 14(b) is almost *in haec verba* with § 706(c), and since the legislative history of § 14(b) indicates that its source was § 706(c), we may properly conclude that Congress intended that the construction of § 14(b) should follow that of § 706(c). We therefore conclude that § 14(b), like § 706(c), is intended to screen from the federal courts those discrimination complaints that might be settled to the satisfaction of the grievant in state proceedings. We further conclude that prior resort to appropriate state proceedings is required under § 14(b), just as under § 706(c).

The contrary arguments advanced by respondent in support of construing § 14(b) as merely optional are not persuasive. Respondent notes first that under Title VII persons aggrieved must file with a state antidiscrimination agency before filing with the Equal Employment Opportunity Commission (EEOC). Under the ADEA, by contrast, grievants may file with state and federal agencies simultaneously.[4] From this respondent concludes that the ADEA pays less deference to state agencies and that, as a consequence, ADEA claimants have the option to ignore state remedies.

We disagree. The ADEA permits concurrent rather than sequential state and federal administrative jurisdiction in order to expedite the processing of age-discrimination claims. The premise for this difference is that the delay inherent in sequential jurisdiction is particularly prejudicial to the rights of "older citizens to whom, by definition, relatively few productive years are left."

The purpose of expeditious disposition would not be frustrated were ADEA claimants required to pursue state and federal administrative remedies simultaneously. Indeed, simultaneous state and federal conciliation efforts may well facilitate rapid settlements. There is no reason to conclude, therefore, that the possibility of concurrent state and federal cognizance supports the construction of § 14(b) that ADEA grievants may ignore state remedies altogether.

Respondent notes a second difference between the ADEA and Title VII. Section 14(a) of the ADEA, for which Title VII has no counterpart, provides that upon commencement of an action under ADEA, all state proceedings are superseded. From this, respondent concludes that it would be an exercise in futility to require aggrieved persons to file state complaints since those persons may, after only 60 days, abort their involuntary state proceeding by filing a federal suit.

We find no merit in the argument. Unless § 14(b) is to be stripped of all meaning, state agencies must be given at least some opportunity to solve problems of discrimination. While 60 days provides a limited time for the state agency to act, that was a decision for Congress to make and Congress apparently thought it sufficient. * * *

* * *

We consider now the consequences of respondent's failure to file a complaint with the Iowa State Civil Rights Commission. Petitioners argue that since Iowa's 120-day age-discrimination statute of limitations has run, it is now too late for respondent to remedy his procedural omission and that respondent's federal action is therefore jurisdictionally barred. Respondent pleads that since his failure to file was due to incorrect advice by the Department of Labor, his tardiness should be excused.

4. ADEA grievants may file with the State before or after they file with the Secretary of Labor.

Both arguments miss the mark. Neither questions of jurisdiction nor questions of excuse arise unless Congress mandated that resort to state proceedings must be within time limits specified by the State. We do not construe § 14(b) to make that requirement. Section 14(b) requires only that the grievant *commence* state proceedings. Nothing whatever in the section requires the respondent here to commence those proceedings within the 120 days allotted by Iowa law in order to preserve a right of action under § 7(c).

* * * By its terms, * * * the section requires only that state proceedings be commenced 60 days before federal litigation is instituted; besides commencement no other obligation is placed upon the ADEA grievant. In particular, there is no requirement that, in order to commence state proceedings and thereby preserve federal rights, the grievant must file with the State within whatever time limits are specified by state law. * * *

This implication is made express by the last sentence of § 14(b), which specifically provides:

> "If any requirement for the commencement of such proceedings is imposed by a State authority other than a requirement of the filing of a written and signed statement of the facts upon which the proceeding is based, the proceeding shall be deemed to have been commenced for the purposes of this subsection at the time such statement is sent by registered mail to the appropriate State authority."

State limitations periods are, of course, requirements "other than a requirement of the filing of a written and signed statement of the facts upon which the proceeding is based." Therefore, even if a State were to make timeliness a precondition for commencement, rather than follow the more typical pattern of making untimeliness an affirmative defense, a state proceeding will be deemed commenced for purposes of § 14(b) as soon as the complaint is filed.

* * *

This construction of the statute is fully consistent with the ADEA's remedial purposes and is particularly appropriate "in a statutory scheme in which laymen, unassisted by trained lawyers, initiate the process."

It is also consistent with the purposes of § 14(b). Section 14(b) does not stipulate an exhaustion requirement. The section is intended only to give state agencies a limited opportunity to settle the grievances of ADEA claimants in a voluntary and localized manner so that the grievants thereafter have no need or desire for independent federal relief. Individuals should not be penalized if States decline, for whatever reason, to take advantage of these opportunities. Congress did not intend to foreclose federal relief simply because state relief was also foreclosed.

The structure of the ADEA reinforces the conclusion that state procedural defaults cannot foreclose federal relief and that state limitations periods cannot govern the efficacy of the federal remedy. * * * Congress could not have intended to consign federal lawsuits to the "vagaries of diverse state limitations statutes," ibid, particularly since, in many States, including Iowa, the limitations periods are considerably shorter than the 180-day period allowed grievants in nondeferral States by 29 U.S.C. § 626(d)(1).

That Congress regarded incorporation as inconsistent with the federal scheme is made clear by the legislative history of § 706(c)'s definition of commencement—the same definition later used in § 14(b). Proponents of Title VII were concerned that localities hostile to civil rights might enact sham discrimination ordinances for the purpose of frustrating the vindication of federal rights. The statutory definition of commencement as requiring the filing of a state complaint and nothing more was intended to meet this concern while at the same time avoiding burdensome case-by-case inquiry into the reasonableness of various state procedural requirements.[11]

* * *

We therefore hold that respondent may yet comply with the requirements of § 14(b) by simply filing a signed complaint with the Iowa State Civil Rights Commission. That Commission must be given an opportunity to entertain respondent's grievance before his federal litigation can continue. Meanwhile, the federal suit should be held in abeyance. If, as respondent fears, his state complaint is subsequently dismissed as untimely, respondent may then return to federal court. But until that happens, or until 60 days have passed without a settlement, respondent must pursue his state remedy.

Accordingly, the judgment of the Court of Appeals is reversed, and the case is remanded to that court with instructions to enter an order directing the District Court to hold respondent's suit in abeyance until respondent has complied with the mandate of § 14(b).

It is so ordered.

MR. JUSTICE BLACKMUN, concurring.

* * *

MR. JUSTICE STEVENS, with whom THE CHIEF JUSTICE, MR. JUSTICE POWELL, and MR. JUSTICE REHNQUIST join, concurring in part and dissenting in part.

11. Moreover, even the danger that state remedies will be *inadvertently* by passed by otherwise proper ADEA plaintiffs will soon become nonexistent. After July 1, 1979, the EEOC will administer the ADEA. Discrimination charges will have to be filed with the EEOC within time limits specified by federal law, and the EEOC already has a regular procedure whereby discrimination complaints are automatically referred to appropriate agencies as soon as they are received. See Love v. Pullman Co., 404 U.S. 522, 92 S.Ct. 616, 30 L.Ed.2d 679 (1972); 29 CFR 1601.13 (1978). Thus, the deference to state agencies required by § 14(b) will soon become automatic. * * *

Section 14(b) of the Age Discrimination in Employment Act of 1967, 81 Stat. 607, 29 U.S.C. § 633(b), explicitly states that "no suit may be brought" under the Act until the individual has first resorted to appropriate state remedies. Respondent has concededly never resorted to state remedies. In my judgment, this means that his suit should not have been brought and should now be dismissed.

* * *

* * * If respondent should decide at this point to resort to state remedies, and if his complaint there is found to be time barred, and if he should then seek relief in federal court, the question addressed in * * * the Court's opinion—whether § 14(b) requires resort to state remedies "within time limits specified by the State"—would then be presented. But that question is not presented now, and I decline to join or to render any advisory opinion on its merits. I would simply order that this suit be dismissed in accordance with "the mandate of § 14(b)."

NOTES FOR DISCUSSION

1. Does the Court's ruling that the plaintiff need not file a state administrative charge within the state limitations period mean that there is no time limit for filing that state administrative charge? What about the combined effect of the requirement that the plaintiff must wait for sixty days after the state filing before filing its federal action and the two/three year statute of limitation set forth in § 55 of the FLSA made applicable to ADEA actions by § 7(e) of the ADEA? Moreover, do the answers to these questions affect the availability of the 300 day period for filing with the EEOC? Must a plaintiff file a timely state law charge with the state agency to qualify for the 300 day limit for filing with the EEOC? In fact, must a plaintiff file the state agency before filing its EEOC charge in order to take advantage of the 300 day filing limit? See Reinhard v. Fairfield Maxwell, Ltd., 707 F.2d 697 (2d Cir. 1983) (must file state administrative charge at least sixty days before expiration of three year period for filing claim of willful violation in federal court); Aronsen v. Crown Zellerbach, 662 F.2d 584 (9th Cir. 1981), cert. denied, 459 U.S. 1200, 103 S.Ct. 1183, 75 L.Ed.2d 431 (1983) (plaintiff can utilize 300 day period regardless of when state charge is filed); Fugate v. Allied Corp., 582 F.Supp. 780 (N.D.Ill.1984) (ADEA contains no time requirement for commencement of state proceedings as long as state charge filed at least sixty days before filing federal suit)

In *Thurston,* the Court stated that for purposes of determining the availability of punitive damages, a violation of the ADEA would be characterized as "willful" if the defendant knew or showed reckless disregard for the issue of whether its conduct was prohibited by the statute. It, however, declined to rule on whether the same standard of willfulness would apply for purposes of the statutory limitations period, while noting that the lower courts were divided on this issue. In Donovan v. Bel-Loc Diner, Inc., 780 F.2d 1113 (4th Cir. 1985), a minimum wage and overtime case brought under the FLSA, the court stated that the definition of "willful" announced in *Thurston* for punitive damage purposes should not be extended to the statute of limitations context. It reasoned that the willfulness standard under the limitations provision should be less stringent than that applied under its quasi-criminal liquidated damages counterpart since the purpose served by the limitations period (to extend the period of recovery of wrongfully withheld back wages) differed from the punitive purpose of the liquidated damages provision of the FLSA. Accordingly, it held that a violation of the FLSA is "willful" for limitations period purposes if the employer knew the Act was "in the picture"; i.e., knew of the potential applicability of the statute. This approach also has been adopted by the First Circuit. Secretary of Labor v. Daylight Dairy, 779 F.2d 784 (1st Cir. 1985). But see Walton v. United Consumers Club, Inc., 786 F.2d 303 (7th Cir. 1986) (rejecting "in the picture" standard and indicating that limitations standard should be *more* stringent than double damages standard in a FLSA case) and Michaels v. Jones & Laughlin Steel Corp., 628 F.Supp. 48, 50 (W.D.Pa. 1985) (applying, without discussion, *Thurston* standard to statute of limitations issue).

2. Should the invocation of state remedies requirement announced in *Oscar Mayer* be extended to ADEA actions brought by the EEOC? See Marshall v. Chamberlain Manufacturing Corp., 601 F.2d 100 (3d Cir. 1979). What is the extent of the EEOC's statutory duty to attempt to achieve conciliation prior to instituting suit? Should the trial court dismiss or stay an EEOC age suit where it finds the EEOC has not fulfilled this statutory obligation? See Marshall v. Sun Oil Co., 592 F.2d 563 (10th Cir. 1979), cert. denied 444 U.S. 826, 100 S.Ct. 49, 62 L.Ed.2d 33 (1979); Brennan v. Ace Hardware Corp., 495 F.2d 368 (8th Cir. 1974).

It is conceivable that the EEOC's conciliation efforts could extend beyond the two/three year period within which suit must be brought. Congress addressed this potential problem in its 1978 amendments to the ADEA by providing that the limitations period shall be tolled for up to one year when the EEOC seeks to effect voluntary compliance. Section 7(d) requires an individual to wait at least sixty days after filing an EEOC charge before commencing suit in order to give the EEOC a chance to resolve the dispute at the administrative level. Is this sixty day waiting period a jurisdiction requirement? Does your response to this question depend upon your answer to the immediately preceding question? See Vance v. Whirlpool Corp., 707 F.2d 483 (4th Cir. 1983), cert. denied, 465 U.S. 1102, 104 S.Ct. 1600, 80 L.Ed.2d 130 (1984).

3. Is a grievant's failure to file a timely charge with the EEOC fatal to a court's exercise of ADEA jurisdiction or is the filing requirement subject to equitable tolling? In ZIPES v. TRANS WORLD AIRLINES, INC., 455 U.S. 385, 102 S.Ct. 1127, 71 L.Ed.2d 234 (1982), the Supreme Court held that the timely filing of an EEOC charge is not a jurisdictional prerequisite to a Title VII suit in federal court but, rather, a precondition subject to waiver, estoppel and equitable tolling. In light of the comments made by the Supreme Court in the principle case concerning the relationship between Title VII and the ADEA, should the *Zipes* ruling be extended to ADEA actions? See Vance v. Whirlpool Corp., 716 F.2d 1010 (4th Cir. 1983). If so, under what circumstances would tolling be appropriate? See Dillman v. Combustion Engineering, Inc., 784 F.2d 57 (2d Cir. 1986); Price v. Litton Business Systems, Inc., 694 F.2d 963 (4th Cir. 1982) (filing period can be tolled if untimeliness is result of employer's deliberate design or conduct employer unmistakeably should have understood would cause delay); Franci v. Avco Corp., Avco Lycoming Division, 538 F.Supp. 250 (D.Conn.1982); Barber v. Commercial Union Insurance Co., 27 FEP Cases 703 (E.D.Pa.1981).

4. Does § 15 of the ADEA suggest that federal employees are under a different procedural scheme than the one governing non-federal employees? For example, must the federal employee invoke administrative remedies prior

to suit? If so, what limitations periods govern the commencement of agency or court proceedings? See Ray v. Nimmo, 704 F.2d 1480 (11th Cir. 1983) (notice of intent to sue requirement is not an absolute jurisdictional requirement but is subject to modification or excuse for equitable reasons).

5. Section 7(c) provides that suit by the EEOC terminates the individual's right to bring a separate action under the ADEA. Does an EEOC suit similarly preclude the aggrieved from pursuing his or her state law remedies? See Dunlop v. Pan American World Airways, Inc., 672 F.2d 1044 (2d Cir. 1982). Must a trial court dismiss a pending private ADEA action when the EEOC subsequently decides to file suit? See EEOC v. Eastern Airlines, Inc., 736 F.2d 635 (11th Cir. 1984); Burns v. Equitable Life Assurance Society, 696 F.2d 21 (2d Cir. 1982), cert. denied, 464 U.S. 933, 104 S.Ct. 336, 78 L.Ed.2d 306 (1983).

6. In light of the many procedural prerequisites to filing an action under the ADEA, should a state employee be permitted to file an age discrimination charge under § 1983? See Frye v. Grandy, 625 F.Supp. 1573, 1576 (D.Md.1986).

Chapter 11

THE REHABILITATION ACT OF 1973

Read §§ 7(7), 501 and 503–505 of the Rehabilitation Act.

PREWITT v. UNITED STATES POSTAL SERVICE

United States Court of Appeals, Fifth Circuit, 1981.
662 F.2d 292.

TATE, CIRCUIT JUDGE.

Claiming that the United States Postal Service unlawfully denied him employment due to his physical handicap, the plaintiff, George Dunbar Prewitt, Jr., brought this action against the postal service. Prewitt contended that he was physically able to perform the job for which he applied despite his handicap, even though the postal service's physical requirements indicate that only persons in "good physical condition" can perform the job because it involves "arduous" work. Prewitt alleged, inter alia, that the postal service thus violated his rights under the Rehabilitation Act of 1973, Prewitt filed this suit as a class action, after he was denied employment as a clerk/carrier at the Greenville, Mississippi post office. The district court granted the postal service's motion for summary judgment. On Prewitt's appeal, we find that the plaintiff has raised genuine issues of material fact as to 1) whether the postal service's physical requirements for postal employment are sufficiently "job related" to provide lawful grounds for the refusal to hire Prewitt, and 2) whether the postal service has breached its duty to make "reasonable accommodation" for handicapped persons such as Prewitt. Accordingly, we reverse the summary judgment of the district court, and remand the case for further proceedings in accordance with this opinion.

The Factual Background

The plaintiff Prewitt is a disabled Vietnam war veteran. Due to gunshot wounds, he must endure limited mobility of his left arm and shoulder. Nevertheless, in May *1970* (prior to his rejection for re-employment in 1978 that gave rise to this lawsuit), Prewitt applied for a position as a distribution clerk in the Jackson, Mississippi post office, a position which, according to the job description, "require[s] arduous physical exertion involving prolonged standing, throwing, reaching, and may involve lifting sacks of mail up to 80 pounds." [1] Prewitt was hired after passing the requisite written and medical examinations, and it is undisputed that, despite his handicap, he performed his duties in a competent, entirely satisfactory manner.

1. These physical requirements of Prewitt's 1970 position as distribution clerk are similar to those for the position of clerk/carrier for which he applied in 1978.

Prewitt resigned his position at the Jackson post office in September 1970 to return to school. He testified in his affidavit, which we must regard as true for summary judgment purposes, that his physical condition did not diminish in any significant way between May 1970 and September 1978, when he applied for the position at the Greenville post office that gave rise to this lawsuit. Prewitt questions the failure of the postal service to re-employ him in 1978, due to a physical handicap, for a position as clerk/carrier, a position with similar physical requirements to those of the job that he had satisfactorily performed in 1970.

* * *

According to the postal services qualification standards, the duties of a carrier "are arduous and require that the incumbent be in good physical condition." Thus, a medical form which was given to Prewitt indicates that applicants for this position must meet a wide range of physical criteria, including, inter alia, the ability to see, hear, lift heavy weights, carry moderate weights, reach above shoulder, and use fingers and both hands. According to the affidavit of Postmaster Charles Hughes, the duties of a clerk/carrier require stooping, bending, squatting, lifting up to seventy pounds, standing for long periods, stretching arms in all directions, reaching above and below the shoulder, and some twisting of the back.

To determine whether Prewitt could meet these physical standards, the Greenville postal authorities asked Prewitt to authorize the Veteran's Administration (VA) to release his medical records to the postal service for examination, and Prewitt complied with this request. The VA records, which apparently were made in 1970 before Prewitt was awarded disability benefits, indicated that Prewitt had a 30% service-related disability that caused "limitation of motion of left shoulder and atrophy of trapezius," as well as that he had a kidney disease, hypertension, and an eye condition not related to his armed forces service. The VA report was analyzed by Dr. Cenon Baltazar, a postal medical officer, who reported: "Limited records pertaining to [Prewitt] showed limitation of left shoulder and atrophy of trapezius muscle. This is not suitable for full performance as required of postal service positions unless it is a desk job." Prewitt subsequently received from Hughes a terse, two sentence letter informing him that Dr. Baltazar had determined that he was "medically unsuitable for postal employment." The letter did not state any reasons for this finding of unsuitability.

After receiving word of this adverse determination, Prewitt contacted Hughes to dispute the conclusion of the medical officer. Hughes told Prewitt that there was no appeal from the decision, but that the decision would be reconsidered at the local level if Prewitt would undergo an examination, at his own expense, by a private physician. In fact, Prewitt did have the right to appeal to the postal service's regional medical director. After belatedly learning of this right, Prewitt exercised his right to appeal, but he chose not to undergo a new physical examination. The regional medical officer, Dr. Gedney, examined the VA report and concluded that Prewitt was medically unsuitable. Unlike Dr. Baltazar, who relied solely on Prewitt's shoulder injury as the basis for his adverse determination, Dr. Gedney also mentioned the kidney disease (which Dr. Gedney stated is an unpredictably progressive disease that could possibly be aggravated by arduous duty) and hypertension. Based on Dr. Gedney's report, the regional office sustained the adverse determination and told Prewitt that there were no further medical appeal rights. Again, the letter did not inform Prewitt of the medical reasons upon which this conclusion was based.

Although the regional office correctly stated that there were no further *medical* appeal rights, in fact Prewitt had available to him an entirely independent chain of administrative review of the adverse determination through the postal service's equal employment opportunity (EEO) office. Prewitt filed an EEO complaint, alleging that the postal service had discriminated against him on the basis of his handicap by finding him unsuitable for postal employment. The EEO office conducted an investigation and found that the same medical officer who had disqualified Prewitt had ruled three other disabled or physically handicapped applicants suitable for postal employment. The investigation also revealed that the Greenville post office had hired fourteen persons classified as disabled and/or physically handicapped. Relying on these findings, the EEO office found no discrimination and advised Prewitt that he could appeal its decision to the Office of Appeals and Review of the Equal Employment Opportunity Commission (EEOC).

As permitted by statute, 42 U.S.C. § 2000e–16(c), made applicable to the handicapped by 29 U.S.C. § 794a(a)(1), instead of appealing to the EEOC, Prewitt filed this suit in the district court. No contention is made by the postal service that Prewitt did not exhaust administrative remedies. The postal service responded to Prewitt's complaint with a motion for summary judgment, contending that it had rejected Prewitt for valid medical reasons, and that Prewitt's refusal to take a physical examination had precluded it from making a re-evaluation. The plaintiff responded that postal service regulations required that applicants be given a current physical examination before a medical determination is made, and therefore, even though Prewitt was afforded an opportunity to take a physical after his determination was made, the determination of medical unfitness was invalid. Prewitt further argued that the regulations entitled him to a free physical examination, so that he was not required to bear the expense of an examination by a private physician. Finally, Prewitt noted that in view of the undisputed fact that he had been able to perform competently a similar job in 1970, the postal service had failed to articulate any legitimate reason for its finding of medical unsuitability.

* * *

Only since 1978 have handicapped individuals been entitled to bring private actions against federal agencies for violations of the Rehabilitation Act. This is apparently the first case in which a federal appellate court has been called upon to determine the nature and extent of this newly-created private right. We shall therefore examine the history of this legislation in some detail.

Congress passed the Rehabilitation Act of 1973 for the express purpose, inter alia, of "promot[ing] and expand[ing] employment opportunities in the public and private sectors for handicapped individuals." In addition to creating a number of wide-ranging federally-funded programs designed to aid handicapped persons in assuming a full role in society, the Act, in its Title V, established the principle that (a) the federal government, (b) federal contractors, and (c) recipients of federal funds cannot discriminate against the handicapped.

The duties of each of these three classes of entities were set forth in separate sections. Section 503 of the Act, required federal contractors to include in their contracts with the United States a provision mandating that, in employing persons to carry out the contract, "the party contracting with the United States shall take affirmative action to employ and advance in employment qualified handicapped individuals. * * * " Section 504, which imposed duties on recipients of federal funds, provided: "No otherwise qualified handicapped individual * * * shall, solely by reason of his handicap, be excluded from participation in, be denied the benefits of, or be subjected to discrimination under any program or activity receiving federal financial assistance."

The duties of the federal government itself were set forth in section 501(b), which stated:

> Each department, agency, and instrumentality (including the United States Postal Service and the Postal Rate Commission) in the executive branch shall * * * submit to the Civil Service Commission and to the [Interagency Committee on Handicapped Employees] an affirmative action program plan for the hiring, placement, and advancement of handicapped individuals in such department, agency, or instrumentality. Such plan shall include a description of the extent to which and methods whereby the special needs of handicapped employees are being met. * * *

* * *

Under the original 1973 Rehabilitation Act, a private cause of action founded on handicap discrimination was not recognized upon section 501 as against a federal government employer; the literal statutory wording merely required federal agencies to *submit* affirmative actions plans. However, due to differences in statutory wording, all courts that considered the issue found that section 504 established a private cause of action for handicapped persons subjected to discrimination by recipients of federal funds, while the federal courts split on the question whether the same was true under section 503 for individuals subjected to handicap discrimination by federal contractors.

In 1978, the Rehabilitation Act was amended to provide a private cause of action in favor of persons subjected to handicap discrimination by the federal government employing agencies. In the House, an amendment was adopted and ultimately enacted by the Congress that extended section 504's proscription against handicap discrimination to "any program or activity conducted by an Executive agency or by the United States Postal Service;" the legislative history, as well as the judicial interpretations, fully recognized that a private right of action had been created by section 504.

The Senate, at the same time, added a new section 505(a)(1) to the Rehabilitation Act, which created a private right of action under section 501. The provision states:

> The remedies, procedures, and rights set forth in section 717 of the Civil Rights Act of 1964, including the application of sections 706(f) through 706(k), shall be available, with respect to any complaint under section 501 of this Act, to any employee or applicant for employment aggrieved by the final disposition of such complaint, or by the failure to take final action on such complaint.

Section 717 of Title VII of the Civil Rights Act, to which section 501 is explicitly tied by the new section 505, mandates that all federal personnel actions be made "free from any discrimination based on race, color, religion, sex, or national origin." The provision further provides for a private right of action in favor of those whose claims of discrimination have not been satisfactorily resolved by administrative procedures. However, before an individual can bring a section 717 action in court, strict procedural requirements with respect to exhaustion of administrative remedies must be fulfilled. Once administrative remedies have been exhausted, however, an individual is entitled to de novo consideration of his discrimination claims in the district court; however, prior administrative findings made with respect to an employment discrimination claim may be admitted into evidence at the trial de novo.

* * *

The scope of the federal government's obligations under section 501 received Senate attention during debate on a proposed amendment to the proposed new section 505(a)(1). An amendment offered by Senator McClure would have added the following clause at the end of section 505(a)(1): "provided, however, that no equitable relief or affirmative action remedy disproportionately exceeding actual damages in the case shall be available under this section." Senator McClure explained that his amendment "would provide that the federally financed affirmative action remedy * * * could not be used to initiate massive construction projects for relatively minor temporal damages."

Senators Cranston and Stafford spoke in opposition to the McClure amendment. Senator Cranston remarked:

> I believe that the requirement with respect to Federal Contractors and grantees should be no less stringent than the requirements

attached to the Federal Government. The amendment offered by the Senator from Idaho would create an unwise and unrealistic distinction with respect of [sic] employment between the obligations of the Federal Government and the obligations of Federal contractors and grantees. Ironically, the Senator's amendment would limit— with a financial test—the Federal Government's obligation of being an equal opportunity employer. Federal contractors and grantees would—appropriately—continue to be required to be equal opportunity employers. Rather than a leader in this field, the Federal Government would become a distant also-ran requiring more of its grantees and contractors than it would be willing to require of itself.

The dispute was resolved when Senator McClure and the managers of the bill agreed upon the following compromise language: "In fashioning an equitable or affirmative action remedy under such section [section 501], a court may take into account the reasonableness of the cost of any necessary workplace accommodation, and the availability of alternative therefor or other appropriate relief." Id. at S15667. As thus amended, the new section 505(a)(1) was enacted into law * * *.

In summary, the 1978 amendments to the Rehabilitation Act 1) established a private right of action, subject to the same procedural constraints (administrative exhaustion, etc.) set forth in Title VII of the Civil Rights Act, in favor of section 501 claimants, and 2) extended section 504's proscription against handicap employment discrimination to cover the activities of the federal government itself.

Thus, by its 1978 amendments to the Rehabilitation Act, Congress clearly recognized both in section 501 and in section 504 that individuals now have a private cause of action to obtain relief for handicap discrimination on the part of the federal government and its agencies. The amendments to section 504 were simply the House's answer to the same problem that the Senate saw fit to resolve by strengthening section 501. The joint House-Senate conference committee could have chosen to eliminate the partial overlap between the two provisions, but instead the conference committee, and subsequently Congress as a whole, chose to pass both provisions, despite the overlap. "When there are two acts upon the same subject, the rule is to give effect to both if possible." United States v. Borden Co., 308 U.S. 188, 198, 60 S.Ct. 182, 188, 84 L.Ed. 181 (1939). By this same principle, in order to give effect to *both* the House and the Senate 1978 amendments finally enacted, we must read the exhaustion of administrative remedies requirement of section 501 into the private remedy recognized by both section 501 and section 504 for federal government handicap discrimination.

In the present suit, Prewitt claims that, despite his handicap, he is physically able to perform the job for which he applied, but that the postal service's physical requirements, neutral on their face, had *disparate impact* upon a person with his particular handicap and that they excluded him from employment that in fact he was physically able to perform. The present case was dismissed on summary judgment, through a failure to take into account the principles applicable to the federal government by the Rehabilitation Act of 1973, as amended in 1978; due to disputed issues of material fact, as will be stated, summary judgment was improvidently granted.

* * *

One of the chief physical factors upon which the postal service bases its refusal to hire Prewitt is that, due to Prewitt's inability to lift his left arm above shoulder level, the employing authority feels that he cannot "case" (sort) the mail that he would be required to deliver on his route. Because a carrier is required to lift above shoulder level with both hands to remove stacks of mail from a six-foot-high top ledge, the postal service contends that Prewitt would not be able to do this part of the job without some workplace modification—however, the postal service witness admitted, for instance, that Prewitt could be accommodated simply by lowering the legs to which the shelves are attached.[18] Only if Prewitt, despite his handicap, can perform the essential duties of the position in question, without the need for any workplace accommodation, can it be said that he was a victim of "disparate impact" discrimination. However, even if Prewitt cannot so perform, he might still be entitled to relief if he was a victim of "surmountable barrier" discrimination, i.e., if he was rejected even though he could have performed the essentials of the job if afforded reasonable accommodation.[19]

Since both issues will arise on the remand, we will therefore note the principles applicable to judicial determination of both cases involving claims of "disparate impact" and also of "surmountable barrier" ("the duty to make reasonable accommodation") discrimination against a handicapped person.

Preliminarily, however, we should observe that section 501 requires affirmative action on the part of federal agencies; unlike section 504 of the Rehabilitation Act and Title VII of the Civil Rights Act which

18. The second principal factor upon which the postal service relies is the severe pain that a VA report indicates that Prewitt suffers after lifting. Prewitt denies the pain or at least its severity. This type of handicap may be either a surmountable or insurmountable employment barrier.

19. Commentators have identified four distinct types of discriminatory barriers that handicapped persons must confront when seeking employment: 1. Intentional discrimination for reasons of social bias (racial, sexual, religion, handicap, etc.); 2. neutral standards with disparate impact; 3. surmountable impairment barriers; and 4. insurmountable impairment barriers.

The present complaints by Prewitt involve alleged "disparate impact" and a "surmountable barrier" handicap-discrimination.

The Title VII jurisprudence is, we believe, for the most part applicable to intentional social-bias discrimination against handicapped persons. *See* Texas Department of Corrections v. Burdine, 450 U.S. 248, 101 S.Ct. 1089, 67 L.Ed.2d 207 (1981) and McDonnell Douglas Corp. v. Green, 411 U.S. 792, 93 S.Ct. 1817, 36 L.Ed.2d 668 (1973). Likewise, as will be noted in the text, the Title VII disparate impact decisions are relevant in the determination of disparate impact handicap discrimination. Surmountable and insurmountable barriers raise issues that for the most part are peculiar to handicap discrimination.

usually require only nondiscrimination. In Ryan v. Federal Deposit Insurance Corp., 565 F.2d 762, 763 (D.C.Cir. 1977), the court held, and we agree, especially in light of the 1978 amendments, that section 501 requires that federal agencies do more than just *submit* affirmative plans—section 501 "impose[s] a duty upon federal agencies to structure their procedures and programs so as to ensure that handicapped individuals are afforded equal opportunity in both job assignment and promotion." Although *Ryan*, which was decided prior to the 1978 amendments, did not recognize a private right of action under section 501, the court held that the defendant federal agency should amend its procedures to provide an administrative forum through which handicapped individuals could enforce their section 501 rights. Subsequent to *Ryan*, the Civil Service Commission, and its successor enforcement agency, the EEOC, promulgated administrative regulations that define the section 501 duties of federal agencies, which for instance (see below) include the duty to make reasonable accommodation to employ a handicapped person. These regulations are the administrative interpretation of the Act by the enforcing agency and are therefore entitled to some deference in our attempt to determine the applications of this statute.

* * *

The EEOC regulations adopt a *Griggs*-type approach in the disparate impact handicap discrimination context. They require federal agencies not to use any selection criterion that "screens out or tends to screen out qualified handicapped persons or any class of handicapped persons" unless the criterion, as used by the agency, is shown to be "job-related for the position in question." The test is whether a handicapped individual who meets all employment criteria except for the challenged discriminatory criterion "can perform the essential functions of the position in question without endangering the health and safety of the individuals or others." If the individual can so perform, he must not be subjected to discrimination.

In our opinion, in the disparate impact context, there should be only minor differences in the application of the *Griggs* principles to handicap discrimination claims. One difference, however, is that, when assessing the disparate impact of a facially-neutral criterion, courts must be careful not to group all handicapped persons into one class, or even into broad subclasses. This is because "the fact that an employer employs fifteen epileptics is not necessarily probative of whether he or she has discriminated against a blind person."

In a section 504 handicap discrimination case, the Supreme Court held that the Rehabilitation Act does not require redress of "insurmountable barrier" handicap discrimination—that the statutory language prohibiting discrimination against an "otherwise qualified handicapped individual" means qualified *"in spite" of* his handicap, not qualified in all respects except for being handicapped. Southeastern

Community College v. Davis, 442 U.S. 397, 406, 99 S.Ct. 2361, 2367, 60 L.Ed.2d 980 (1979) (emphasis added).

The *Davis* rationale is equally controlling in the employment discrimination context. Accordingly, employers subject to the Rehabilitation Act need not hire handicapped individuals who cannot fully perform the required work, even with accommodation. However, while *Davis* demonstrates that only individuals who are qualified "in spite of" their handicaps need be hired, *Griggs* and its progeny dictate that the employer must bear the burden of proving that the physical criteria are job related. If the employer does this, then the burden of persuasion to show that he can satisfy these criteria rests on the handicapped applicant.

Federal employers, including the postal service, are obliged by section 501(b) to provide reasonable accommodation for the handicapped.[21] As the *Davis* Court pointed out, section 501(b), unlike section 504, explicitly requires federal government employers to undertake "affirmative action" on behalf of the handicapped. And the new section 505, added by Congress in 1978, explicitly permits courts to fashion "an equitable or affirmative action remedy" for violations of section 501, with the caveat that "the reasonableness of the cost of any necessary workplace accommodation" should be taken into account. The legislative intent reflected in the creation of a handicap discrimination private action clearly shows that federal government employers must make reasonable accommodation for handicapped job applicants.

There is a dearth of decisional law on this issue.[22] However, the EEOC administrative regulations, which, as noted above, are entitled to deference, provide some basis for outlining the contours of the surmountable barrier accommodation duty.

The relevant EEOC regulation, 29 C.F.R. § 1613.704, provides:

> (a) An agency shall make reasonable accommodation to the known physical or mental limitations of a qualified handicapped applicant or employee unless the agency can demonstrate that the

21. This court has consistently held that section 504 also mandates reasonable accommodation, thus prohibiting surmountable barrier discrimination by federal grantees against the handicapped.

22. Outside the handicap discrimination context, the "reasonable accommodation" issue has arisen in cases involving persons who claim a right to accommodation of their religious duty to refrain from working on certain days. In Trans World Airlines v. Hardison, 432 U.S. 63, 84, 97 S.Ct. 2264, 2277, 53 L.Ed.2d 113 (1977), the Supreme Court interpreted § 701(j) of the Civil Rights Act of 1964, 42 U.S.C. § 2000e(j), which requires employers to accommodate such religious practices, unless to do so would impose "undue hardship." The Court held that an employer need not accommodate such persons if the accommodation would require "more than a *de minimis* cost."

The *Hardison* principles are not applicable in the federal-employer handicap discrimination context. Congress clearly intended the federal government to take measures that would involve more than a *de minimis* cost. As the debate over the McClure amendment shows, Congress was even unwilling to approve language that would have limited the government's duty to make reasonable accommodation to instances in which the cost of accommodation does not "disproportionately exceed[ ] actual damages."

accommodation would impose an undue hardship on the operation of its program.

(b) Reasonable accommodation may include, but shall not be limited to: (1) Making facilities readily accessible to and usable by handicapped persons, and (2) job restructuring, part-time or modified work schedules, acquisition or modification of equipment or devices, appropriate adjustment or modification of examinations, the provision of readers and interpreters, and other similar actions.

(c) In determining pursuant to paragraph (a) of this section whether an accommodation would impose an undue hardship on the operation of the agency in question, factors to be considered include: (1) The overall size of the agency's program will respect to the number of employees, number and type of facilities and size of budget; (2) the type of agency operation, including the composition and structure of the agency's work force; and (3) the nature and the cost of the accommodation.

Thus, under subsection (a) of this provision, the burden of proving inability to accommodate is upon the employer. The administrative reasons for so placing the burden likewise justify a similar burden of proof in a private action based upon the Rehabilitation Act. The employer has greater knowledge of the essentials of the job than does the handicapped applicant. The employer can look to its own experience, or, if that is not helpful, to that of other employers who have provided jobs to individuals with handicaps similar to those of the applicant in question. Furthermore, the employer may be able to obtain advice concerning possible accommodations from private and government sources.

Although the burden of persuasion in proving inability to accommodate always remains on the employer, we must add one caveat. Once the employer presents credible evidence that indicates accommodation of the plaintiff would not reasonably be possible, the plaintiff may not remain silent. Once the employer presents such evidence, the plaintiff has the burden of coming forward with evidence concerning his individual capabilities and suggestions for possible accommodations to rebut the employer's evidence.

In addition, subsections (a) and (c) of 29 C.F.R. § 1613.704, which limit the employer's duty to accommodate to instances where accommodation would not impose "undue hardship" and define the factors to be used in determining whether a particular accommodation would impose "undue hardship," accurately express congressional intent. The second sentence of section 505, which admonishes the courts to "take into account the reasonableness of the cost of any necessary workplace accommodation," was added as compromise language in response to Senator McClure's concern that federal employers might be obliged "to initiate massive construction projects." The EEOC regulations adequately respond to this concern.

The factual showing before the district court was that the postal service rejected Prewitt's application for employment because it felt, on the basis of the medical records supplied to it, that Prewitt could not perform the "arduous" duties of the position. In view of the undisputed fact that Prewitt had satisfactorily performed a similar postal job in 1970 despite his physical handicap, as well as of his *uncontradicted* affidavit that his physical condition was substantially unchanged since then, Prewitt raised a genuine dispute issue of material fact as to whether the postal service's physical standards for employment are sufficiently "job related" to justify the employer's refusal to hire him. Under the applicable legal principles earlier set forth, therefore, the postal service is not shown under the facts thus far educed to have been justified as a matter of law in denying Prewitt's application. The summary judgment must therefore be reversed.

We should note that the postal service contends that the postal service rejected him because he refused its request that he take a current physical examination to establish his medical suitability for employment. This contention is based upon the showing that, *after* Prewitt was found medically unsuitable for employment, he was informally advised by the local postmaster that he would be reconsidered if he secured a new medical examination.

However, the record reveals that Prewitt's application was rejected because he was found to be medically unsuitable (without notifying Prewitt of the specific medical reasons), not because he refused to furnish any further or more current medical information. Indeed, Prewitt's essential position was that his physical condition and the effect of his disability was unchanged since 1970 and that, even accepting the disability reflected by the VA medical reports upon which the postal service relied, he was physically qualified to perform the duties of the position for which he applied, as instanced by his earlier satisfactory performance of the duties of a similar postal position.

On the basis of the factual showing thus far made, we reverse the summary judgment dismissing Prewitt's handicap-discrimination claim. We remand for further proceedings in accordance with the views set forth in this opinion. To summarize:

(1) Prewitt, the disabled claimant, may establish a prima facie of unlawful discrimination by proving that: (a) except for his physical handicap, he is qualified to fill the position; (b) he has a handicap that prevents him from meeting the physical criteria for employment; and (c) the challenged physical standards have a disproportionate impact on persons having the same handicap from which he suffers. To sustain this prima facie case, there should also be a facial showing or at least plausible reasons to believe that the handicap can be accommodated or that the physical criteria are not "job related."

(2) Once the prima facie case of handicap discrimination is established, the burden of persuasion shifts to the federal employer to show that the physical criteria offered as justification for refusal to hire the

plaintiff are "job related," *i.e.,* that persons who suffer from the handicap plaintiff suffers and who are, therefore, unable to meet the challenged standards, cannot safely and efficiently perform the essentials of the position in question. If the issue of reasonable accommodation is raised, the agency must then be prepared to make a further showing that accommodation cannot reasonably be made that would enable the handicapped applicant to perform the essentials of the job adequately and safely; in this regard, the postal service must "demonstrate that the accommodation would impose an undue hardship on the operation of its program," 29 C.F.R. § 1613.704(a), taking into consideration the factors set forth by 704(c) of the cited regulation.

(3) If the employer proves that the challenged requirements are job related, the plaintiff may then show that other selection criteria without a similar discriminatory effect would also serve the employer's legitimate interest in efficient and trustworthy workmanship. When the issue of reasonable accommodation is raised, the burden of persuasion in proving inability to accommodate always remains on the employer; however, once the employer presents credible evidence that reasonable accommodation is not possible or practicable, the plaintiff must bear the burden of coming forward with evidence that suggests that accommodation may in fact be reasonably made.

We of course express no opinion as to the merits of Prewitt's claim. If he is unable to perform the essentials of the position for which he has applied, with or without reasonable accommodation, the postal service need not hire him. The ultimate test is whether, with or without reasonable accommodation, a handicapped individual who meets all employment criteria except for the challenged discriminatory criterion "can perform the essential functions of the position in question without endangering the health and safety of the individuals or others." 28 CFR 1613.702(f). Since a disputed issue of material fact is shown as to this issue, the summary judgment granted by the district court must be reversed.

* * *

NOTES AND PROBLEMS FOR DISCUSSION

1. As the court in *Prewitt* noted, few cases have addressed the scope of a § 501 or § 504 defendant's duty to make a reasonable accommodation for handicapped employees or job applicants. In SOUTHEASTERN COMMUNITY COLLEGE v. DAVIS, 442 U.S. 397, 99 S.Ct. 2361, 60 L.Ed.2d 980 (1979), the Supreme Court discussed the accommodation issue in the context of a § 504 action brought by a hearing-impaired applicant who had been denied admission by the defendant college to its associate degree nursing program. The college maintained that the plaintiff was not "otherwise qualified" for its program because her inability to understand speech directed to her without the aid of lipreading prevented her from participating safely in both the clinical training program and her proposed profession. The Court agreed, thereby finding that the decision to exclude her was not discrimination within the meaning of § 504. Moreover, the Court rejected the plaintiff's claim that § 504 compelled the

college to make whatever adjustments would be necessary to permit her safe participation in its nursing program. While personal supervision by a nursing instructor or a waiver of the clinical requirement might have enabled the plaintiff to participate in the training program, this accommodation would have resulted in a substantial modification of an essential feature of the training program. In other words, the Court implicitly concluded that the plaintiff was a victim of "insurmountable barrier" discrimination since the proposed accommodation would not have rendered her capable of successfully performing all the normal and necessary duties of a registered nurse. Accordingly, the failure to redress this discrimination did not violate § 504. Nevertheless, while the Court ruled that the defendant was not obliged to make an accommodation under those circumstances, it noted that "situations may arise where a refusal to modify an existing program might become unreasonable and discriminatory." It did not elaborate, however, on the duty to accommodate in the face of surmountable barrier discrimination. This issue, however, as the *Prewitt* court noted, has been addressed by the EEOC in its Equal Federal Employment Opportunity Guidelines. 29 CFR 1613.704(c) (1981). The tripartite standard proposed by the Guidelines has been adopted by at least one federal trial court in a surmountable barrier case. See Bey v. Bolger, 540 F.Supp. 910 (E.D.Pa.1982). Does the reasonable accommodation obligation compel an employer to consider the handicapped plaintiff for positions other than those for which she applied? See Dexler v. Carlin, 40 FEP Cases 633 (D.Conn.1986).

The *Prewitt* court implied that the more specific guidelines articulated in *Hardison* with respect to accommodation to religious beliefs would not apply in the handicap context. Is this a proper implication? Is it likely that Congress intended to demand less of employers in an area where it clearly and explicitly created a duty to accommodate? Does the absence of a First Amendment limitation support a more extensive accommodation duty as to handicapped persons? See Note, Protecting the Handicapped From Employment Discrimination in Private Sector Employment: A Critical Analyses of § 503 of the Rehabilitation Act of 1973, 54 Tul.L.Rev. 717, 734–37 (1980); Note, Accommodating the Handicapped: The Meaning of Discrimination under § 504 of the Rehabilitation Act, 55 N.Y.U.L.Rev. 881 (1980).

The Third Circuit, in Strathie v. Department of Transp., 716 F.2d 227, 231 (3d Cir. 1983), offered this standard:

> A handicapped individual who cannot meet all of a program's requirements is not otherwise qualified if there is a factual basis in the record reasonably demonstrating that accommodating that individual would require either a modification of the essential nature of the program, or impose an undue burden on the recipient of federal funds.

For a comprehensive discussion of the application of § 504 see Wegner, The Antidiscrimination Model Reconsidered: Ensuring Equal Opportunity Without Respect To Handicap Under Section 504 of the Rehabilitation Act of 1973, 69 Corn.L.Rev. 403 (1984).

2. In *Prewitt*, the court discussed the defenses available to an employer in a disproportionate impact-based claim of handicap discrimination. What defenses are available when the plaintiff asserts a claim of disparate treatment? For example, can an employer justify its refusal to employ handicapped persons by pointing to an anticipated increase in workmen's compensation insurance premiums? See Panettieri v. C. V. Hill Refrigeration, 159 N.J. 472, 388 A.2d 630 (1978). What if the employer refuses to hire a handicapped person on this

ground, but also can point to that individual's history of unsafe job performance?

3. Does an employee of a federal grantee have to exhaust the available administrative remedies prior to filing an action under § 504? Did *Prewitt* address this question? The ruling by the Fifth Circuit in *Prewitt* that § 504 federal employee complainants are subject to an exhaustion requirement has been adopted by the Ninth and Sixth Circuits. See Boyd v. United States Postal Service, 752 F.2d 410 (9th Cir. 1985); Smith v. United States Postal Service, 742 F.2d 257 (6th Cir. 1984). Each federal agency is responsible for formulating and imposing remedies for § 504 violations by its recipient institutions. Accordingly, the agencies have established procedures for investigating and adjudicating claims of discrimination. Most of these agencies have adopted the same compliance procedures used to enforce Title VI of the 1964 Civil Rights Act and Title IX of the Education Amendments of 1972. The Supreme Court, in CANNON v. UNIVERSITY OF CHICAGO, 441 U.S. 677, 99 S.Ct. 1946, 60 L.Ed.2d 560 (1979), held that a Title IX plaintiff was not required to pursue administrative remedies prior to filing suit. Several courts have seized on these two facts, plus the notion that the available administrative remedy—termination of funding—does not compensate the individual discriminatee, to conclude that a § 504 plaintiff should not be subject to an exhaustion requirement. See Camenisch v. University of Texas, 616 F.2d 127 (5th Cir. 1980), vacated and remanded for mootness, 451 U.S. 390, 101 S.Ct. 1830, 68 L.Ed.2d 175 (1981); Cain v. Archdiocese of Kansas City, Kansas, 508 F.Supp. 1021 (D.Kan.1981); Whitaker v. Board of Education of the City of New York, 461 F.Supp. 99 (E.D.N.Y.1978). But see Peterson v. Gentry, 28 FEP Cases 273 (S.D. Iowa 1981) (§ 504 action dismissed for failure to exhaust state law administrative remedies that can provide remedy plaintiff seeks). Does a handicapped beneficiary of a program receiving federal funding have a private right of action under § 504 against the Secretary of the funding federal department for allegedly failing to investigate the beneficiary's complaint? See Salvador v. Bell, 622 F.Supp. 438 (N.D.Ill.1985) (availability of § 504 action against recipient of funding renders such a suit incompatible with the integrity of the § 504 enforcement scheme and is therefore nor permitted).

4. Since actions brought under § 501 are governed by the provisions of § 717 of Title VII, such suits presumably are subject to the limitations periods applied to federal employee Title VII claims. Similarly, a § 501 plaintiff will be required to invoke administrative remedies prior to filing suit. See Connolly v. United States Postal Service, 579 F.Supp. 305 (D.Mass.1984). Can *Prewitt* be read to imply that the Title VII limitations rules also control federal employee suits under § 504? See Brown v. United States Postal Service, 28 FEP Cases 825 (N.D.Ga.1980). What about the § 504 claims of employees of federal grantees? See Hutchings v. Erie City and County Library Board of Directors, 516 F.Supp. 1265 (W.D.Pa.1981).

5. The Postal Service refused to hire an applicant for one of its truck driver positions on the ground that he was an epileptic who admittedly had suffered an average of one grand mal seizure a year. During the trial of the unsuccessful applicant's § 501 action against the Service, the defendant introduced evidence of the plaintiff's medical condition which it had not possessed at the time it refused to hire him. Should the court permit the introduction of this evidence? Would it matter whether the evidence was offered to rebut the plaintiff's claim that he was "otherwise qualified" or to prove the existence of a

nondiscriminatory reason for the Service's decision? See Mantolete v. Bolger, 767 F.2d 1416 (9th Cir. 1985).

6. After his unsuccessful application for employment as a clerk/carrier with the Greenville, Mississippi post office, the plaintiff in the principal case applied for a substitute rural carrier job. Once again, he was found medically unsuitable for employment. He filed a second action alleging discrimination because of his handicap, which was dismissed with prejudice by the federal trial judge. The appellate court reversed this dismissal and noted that if the plaintiff prevailed on the merits, he would receive an award of back pay. Prewitt v. United States Postal Service, 662 F.2d 311 (5th Cir. 1981) (Prewitt II). Was the court correct in assuming, without discussion, that a private right of action for damages, as opposed to injunctive and declaratory relief, can be asserted under § 504? Compare Miener v. State of Missouri, 673 F.2d 969 (8th Cir. 1982) (damages are awardable under § 504) with Ruth Anne M. v. Alvin Independent School District, 532 F.Supp. 460 (S.D.Tex.1982) (private § 504 action limited to equitable relief).

CONSOLIDATED RAIL CORP. v. DARRONE

Supreme Court of the United States, 1984.
465 U.S. 624, 104 S.Ct. 1248, 79 L.Ed.2d 568.

JUSTICE POWELL delivered the opinion of the Court.

This case requires us to clarify the scope of the private right of action to enforce § 504 of the Rehabilitation Act of 1973, that prohibits discrimination against the handicapped by federal grant recipients. There is a conflict among the circuits.

I

The Rehabilitation Act of 1973 establishes a comprehensive federal program aimed at improving the lot of the handicapped. Among its purposes are to "promote and expand employment opportunities in the public and private sectors for handicapped individuals and place such individuals in employment." To further these purposes, Congress enacted § 504 of the Act. That section provides that:

> No otherwise qualified handicapped individual * * * shall, solely by reason of his handicap, be excluded from the participation in, be denied the benefits of, or be subjected to discrimination under any program or activity receiving Federal financial assistance.

The language of the section is virtually identical to that of § 601 of Title VI of the Civil Rights Act of 1964, that similarly bars discrimination (on the ground of race, color, or national origin) in federally-assisted programs.

In 1978, Congress amended the Rehabilitation Act to specify the means of enforcing its ban on discrimination. In particular, § 505(a)(2), made available the "remedies, procedure, and rights set forth in Title VI of the Civil Rights Acts of 1964" to victims of discrimination in violation of § 504 of the Act.[1]

1. Section 505(a)(2) provides in full: "The remedies, procedures, and rights set forth in title VI of the Civil Rights Act of 1964 shall be available to any person ag-

Petitioner, Consolidated Rail Corporation ("Conrail"), was formed pursuant to subchapter III of the Regional Rail Reorganization Act, 45 U.S.C. §§ 701 et seq. The Act, passed in response to the insolvency of a number of railroads in the Northeast and Midwest, established Conrail to acquire and operate the rail properties of the insolvent railroads and to integrate these properties into an efficient national rail transportation system. Under § 216 of the Act, 45 U.S.C. § 726, the United States, acting through the United States Railway Association, purchases debentures and series A preferred stock of the corporation "at such times and in such amounts as may be required and requested by the corporation," but "in accordance with the terms and conditions * * * prescribed by the Association * * *." Id. § 726(b)(1). The statute permits the proceeds from these sales to be devoted to maintenance of rail properties, capital needs, refinancing of indebtedness, or working capital. Ibid. Under this statutory authorization, Conrail has sold the United States $3.28 billion in securities.

Conrail also received federal funds under subchapter V of the Act, now repealed, to provide for reassignment and retraining of railroad workers whose jobs were affected by the reorganization. And Conrail now receives federal funds under § 1143(a) of the Northeast Rail Service Act, 45 U.S.C. § 797a, that provides termination allowances of up to $25,000 to workers who lose their jobs as a result of reorganization.

II

In 1979, Thomas LeStrange filed suit against petitioner for violation of rights conferred by § 504 of the Rehabilitation Act.[2] The complaint alleged that the Erie Lackawanna Railroad, to which Conrail is the successor in interest, had employed the plaintiff as a locomotive engineer; that an accident had required amputation of plaintiff's left hand and forearm in 1971; and that, after LeStrange was disabled, the Erie Lackawanna Railroad, and then Conrail, had refused to employ him although it had no justification for finding him unfit to work.

The District Court, following the decision of Trageser v. Libbie Rehabilitation Center, Inc., 590 F.2d 87 (CA4 1978), cert. denied, 442 U.S. 947, 99 S.Ct. 2895, 61 L.Ed.2d 318 (1979), granted petitioner's motion for summary judgment on the ground that the plaintiff did not have "standing" to bring a private action under § 504.[3] In *Trageser,* the Fourth Circuit had held that § 505(a)(2) of the Rehabilitation Act

grieved by any act or failure to act by any recipient of Federal assistance or Federal provider of such assistance under § 794 of this title."

Section 505(a)(1) generally makes available the remedies of Title VII of the Civil Rights Act to persons aggrieved by violation of § 791 of the Rehabilitation Act, which governs the federal government's employment of the handicapped.

2. Respondent, the administratrix of LeStrange's estate, was substituted as a party before this Court upon the death of LeStrange.

3. The District Court previously had dismissed constitutional claims raised by LeStrange, 501 F.Supp. 964 (MD Pa.1980).

incorporated into that act the limitation found in § 604 of Title VI, which provides that employment discrimination is actionable only when the employer receives federal financial assistance the "primary objective" of which is "to provide employment." The District Court concluded that the aid provided to petitioner did not satisfy the "primary objective" test.[4]

The Court of Appeals reversed and remanded to the District Court. 687 F.2d 767 (CA3 1982). There was no opinion for the court, but all three judges of the panel agreed that the cause of action for employment discrimination under § 504 was not properly limited to situations "where a primary objective of the federal financial assistance is to provide employment." Judge Bloch, noting that North Haven Board of Education v. Bell, 456 U.S. 512, 102 S.Ct. 1912, 72 L.Ed.2d 299 (1982), had construed Title IX to create a private cause of action for employment discrimination in all federally funded education programs, concluded that the language and legislative history of § 504 required the same broad construction of that section. Judge Adams, concurring in the judgment, found the result compelled by *North Haven Board of Education* and by the Third Circuit's decision in Grove City College v. Bell, aff'd, ante, p. 555.[5] Judge Weis, concurring, argued that Congress had not intended the Rehabilitation Act to incorporate Title VI's "primary objective" limitation: that limitation was designed to temper the government's decision to terminate federal funds, a decision that has more drastic consequences for the funded programs than do private suits for individual relief.

We granted certiorari to resolve the conflict among the circuits and to consider other questions under the Rehabilitation Act.[6] We affirm.

III

We are met initially by petitioner's contention that the death of the plaintiff LeStrange has mooted the case and deprives the Court of jurisdiction for that reason.[7] Petitioner concedes, however, that there

4. Under the analysis of *Trageser*, a private plaintiff also may have "standing" to sue for employment discrimination if he can show "that discrimination in employment necessarily causes discrimination against" the intended beneficiaries of the federal aid, even where that aid itself was not intended to further employment. App. to Pet. for Cert. 33. The District Court found as well that this prong of the *Trageser* test was not satisfied here.

5. The Third Circuit Court of Appeals had held in *Grove City College* that an entire educational institution is subject to the anti-discrimination provisions of Title IX if any department of the institution receives federal aid.

6. Three other Courts of Appeals have agreed substantially with the Fourth Circuit decision in *Trageser*. See Scanlon v. Atascadero State Hospital, 677 F.2d 1271 (CA9 1982); United States v. Cabrini Medical Center, 639 F.2d 908 (CA2 1981); Carmi v. Metropolitan St. Louis Sewer District, 620 F.2d 672 (CA8), cert. denied, 449 U.S. 892, 101 S.Ct. 249, 66 L.Ed.2d 117 (1980).

7. In addition, Conrail argued below, and again in its opening brief, that § 504 does not create a private right of action for employment discrimination. This argument was abandoned at page 3 of Conrail's reply brief. See also Tr. of Oral Arg. 13. In view of this concession it is unnecessary to address the question here beyond noting that the courts below relied on Cannon v. University of Chicago, 441 U.S. 677, 99 S.Ct. 1946, 60 L.Ed.2d 560 (1979), in hold-

remains a case or controversy if LeStrange's estate may recover money that would have been owed to LeStrange.[8] Without determining the extent to which money damages are available under § 504, we think it clear that § 504 authorizes a plaintiff who alleges intentional discrimination to bring an equitable action for backpay. The case therefore is not moot.

In Guardians Ass'n v. Civil Service Comm'n, 463 U.S. 582, 103 S.Ct. 3221, 77 L.Ed.2d 866 (1983), a majority of the Court expressed the view that a private plaintiff under Title VI could recover backpay; and no member of the Court contended that backpay was unavailable, at least as a remedy for intentional discrimination.[9] It is unnecessary to review here the grounds for this interpretation of Title VI. It suffices to state that we now apply this interpretation to § 505(a)(2), that, as we have noted, provides to plaintiffs under § 504 the remedies set forth in Title VI. Therefore, respondent, having alleged intentional discrimination, may recover backpay in the present § 504 suit.[10]

IV

A

The Court of Appeals rejected the argument that petitioner may be sued under § 504 only if the primary objective of the federal aid that it receives is to promote employment. Conrail relies particularly on § 604 of Title VI. This section limits the applicability of Title VI to "employment practice[s] * * * where a *primary objective* of the federal financial assistance is to provide employment" (emphasis added).[11]

ing that such a private right exists under § 504.

8. Petitioner also concedes that respondent, as representative of LaStrange's estate, may assert any right to monetary relief under § 504 that was possessed by LeStrange.

9. A majority of the Court agreed that retroactive relief is available to private plaintiffs for all discrimination, whether intentional or unintentional, that is actionable under Title VI. Justice Marshall, and Justice Stevens, joined by Justices Brennan and Blackmun, argued that both prospective and retroactive relief were fully available to Title VI plaintiffs. 463 U.S., at 624–634, 635–639, 103 S.Ct., at 3245–3249. Justice O'Connor agreed that both prospective and retroactive equitable relief were available, while reserving judgment on the question whether there is a private cause of action for damages relief under Title VI. Id., at 621, n. 1, 103 S.Ct., at 3237, n. 1. Justice White, joined by Justice Rehnquist, while contending that only relief ordering future compliance with legal obligations was available in other private actions under Title VI, put aside the situation of the private plaintiff who alleged intentional discrimination. Id., at 597, 103 S.Ct., at 3237. The Chief Justice and Justice Powell did not reach the question, as they would have held that petitioners in that case had no private right of action and had not made the showing of intentional discrimination required to establish a violation of Title VI. Id., at 596, 103 S.Ct., at 3236.

10. Although the legislative history of the 1978 amendments does not explicitly indicate that Congress intended to preserve the full measure of courts' equitable power to award backpay, the few references to the question are consistent with our holding. Congress clearly intended to make backpay available to victims of discrimination by the federal government, see S.Rep. No. 95–890, p. 19 (1978); and statements made in relation to subsequent legislation by the Senate Committee on Labor and Human Resources, the committee responsible for the 1978 amendments, endorse the availability of backpay. S.Rep. No. 96–316, pp. 12–13 (1979).

11. Section 604 provides in full: "Nothing contained in this subchapter shall be

As noted above, § 505(a)(2) of the Rehabilitation Act, as amended in 1978, adopted the remedies and rights provided in Title VI. Accordingly, Conrail's basic position in this case is that § 604's limitation was incorporated expressly into the Rehabilitation Act. The decision of the Court of Appeals therefore should be reversed, Conrail contends, as the primary objective of the federal assistance received by Conrail was not to promote employment.

It is clear that § 504 itself contains no such limitation. Section 504 neither refers explicitly to § 604 nor contains analogous limiting language; rather, that section prohibits discrimination against the handicapped under "*any* program or activity receiving Federal financial assistance." And it is unquestionable that the section was intended to reach employment discrimination.[12] Indeed, enhancing employment of the handicapped was so much the focus of the 1973 legislation that Congress the next year felt it necessary to amend the statute to clarify whether § 504 was intended to prohibit other types of discrimination as well. See § 111(a), Pub.L. 93–516, 88 Stat. 1617, 1619 (1974), *amending* 29 U.S.C. § 706(6).[13] Thus, the language of § 504 suggests that its bar

construed to authorize action under this subchapter by any department or agency with respect to any employment practice of any employer, employment agency, or labor organization except where a primary objective of the Federal financial assistance is to provide employment." 42 U.S.C. § 2000d–3.

12. Congress recognized that vocational rehabilitation of the handicapped would be futile if those who were rehabilitated could not obtain jobs because of discrimination. Employment discrimination thus would have "a profound effect on the provision of relevant and effective [rehabilitation] services." 119 Cong.Rec. 5862 (1973) (remarks of Sen. Williams). See, e.g., S.Rep. No. 93–318, p. 4 (1973); 119 Cong.Rec. 24587 (1973) (remarks of Sen. Taft), 24588 (remarks of Sen. Williams). Several other sections of Title V of the Rehabilitation Act also were aimed at discrimination in employment: § 501 and § 503 require all federal employers and federal contractors to adopt affirmative action programs for the handicapped.

13. We note further that the Court in an analogous statutory context rejected the contention that the terms used in § 504 implicitly contain a "primary objective" limitation. § 901 of Title IX, like § 504, borrowed the language of § 601 of Title VI. North Haven Board of Education v. Bell, 456 U.S. 512, 102 S.Ct. 1912, 72 L.Ed.2d 299 (1982), found, however, that Title IX's prohibition of employment discrimination did not incorporate § 604's "primary objective" requirement. The Court stated that, had Congress wished so to limit Title IX, it would have enacted in that Title counterparts to both § 601 and § 604. Id., at 530, 102 S.Ct., at 1922–1923.

Petitioner suggests that *North Haven* is inapplicable to the construction of § 504 because the Congress considered but rejected a provision explicitly incorporating the language of § 604 of Title VI into Title IX. And other aspects of the legislative history also supported the Court's interpretation of § 901, see id., at 523–529, 102 S.Ct., at 1919–1922. In contrast, Congress did not advert to a "primary objective" limitation when drafting § 504.

Clearly, petitioner's observations do not touch on that aspect of *North Haven* —its analysis of the language of § 601—that is relevant to the present case. But even without the analysis of *North Haven*, petitioner's interpretation of § 504's language is unfounded. For language is broad as that of § 504 cannot be read in isolation from its history and purposes. In these respects, § 504 differs from Title VI in ways that suggest that § 504 cannot sensibly be interpreted to ban employment discrimination only in programs that receive federal aid the "primary objective" of which is to promote employment. The "primary objective" limitation of Title VI gave the antidiscrimination provision of that Title a scope that well fits its underlying purposes—to ensure "that funds of the United States are not used to support racial discrimination" but "are spent in accordance with the Constitution and the moral sense of the Nation." 110 Cong.Rec. 6544 (1964) (remarks of Sen. Humphrey). As the Court of Appeals observed, it was

on employment discrimination should not be limited to programs that receive federal aid the primary purpose of which is to promote employment.

The legislative history, executive interpretation, and purpose of the 1973 enactment all are consistent with this construction. The legislative history contains no mention of a "primary objective" limitation, although the legislators on numerous occasions adverted to § 504's prohibition against discrimination in employment by programs assisted with federal funds. See, e.g., S.Rep. No. 93–318, at 4, 18, 50, 70 (1973), U.S.Code Cong. & Admin.News 1973, 2076; 119 Cong.Rec. 5862 (remarks of Sen. Cranston), 24587–24588 (1973) (remarks of Sen. Williams, chairman of the Committee on Labor and Public Welfare). Moreover, the Department of Health, Education and Welfare, the agency designated by the President to be responsible for coordinating enforcement of § 504, see Exec. Order No. 11914, from the outset has interpreted that section to prohibit employment discrimination by all recipients of federal financial aid, regardless of the primary objective of that aid.[14] This Court generally has deferred to contemporaneous regulations issued by the agency responsible for implementing a congressional enactment. See, e.g., NLRB v. Bell Aerospace Co., 416 U.S. 267, 274–275, 94 S.Ct. 1757, 1761–1762, 40 L.Ed.2d 134 (1974). The regulations particularly merit deference in the present case: the responsible congressional committees participated in their formulation, and both these committees and Congress itself endorsed the regulations in their final form.[15] Finally, application of § 504 to all programs receiving federal financial assistance fits the remedial purpose of the Rehabilitation Act "to promote and expand employment opportunities" for the handicapped. 29 U.S.C. § 701(8).

unnecessary to extend Title VI more generally to ban employment discrimination, as Title VII comprehensively regulates such discrimination.

In contrast, the primary goal of the Act is to increase employment of the handicapped, see supra, at 1253 and n. 13. However, Congress chose to ban employment discrimination against the handicapped, not by all employers, but only by the federal government and recipients of federal contracts and grants. As to the latter, Congress apparently determined that it would require contractors and grantees to bear the costs of providing employment for the handicapped as a *quid pro quo* for the receipt of federal funds. Cf. 118 Cong.Rec. 32305 (1972) (remarks of Sen. Javits). But this decision to limit § 504 to the recipients of federal aid does not require us to limit that section still further, as petitioner urges.

14. See 39 Fed.Reg. 18562, 18582 (1974) (revising pre-existing provisions to implement § 504); 41 Fed.Reg. 29548, 29552, 29563 (1976) (proposed department regulations), *promulgated,* 42 Fed.Reg. 22678 (§ 84.2), 22680 (§ 84.11), 22688 ("Employment Practices") (1977); 43 Fed.Reg. 2132, 2138 (1978) (final coordinating regulations).

The Department of Justice, now responsible for coordinating agency implementation of § 504, see Executive Order No. 12250, 45 Fed.Reg. 72995 (1980), adopted the HEW guidelines, 46 Fed.Reg. 440686 (1981). The Department of Transportation, from which Conrail receives federal aid, also has construed § 504 to prohibit employment discrimination in all programs receiving federal financial assistance. 44 Fed.Reg. 31442, 31468 (1979), codified at 49 CFR Pt. 27. See id. § 27.31.

15. See S.Rep. No. 93–1297, p. 25 (1974). In adopting § 505(a)(2) in the amendments of 1978, Congress incorporated the substance of the Department's regulations into the statute. See infra, at n. 17.

B

Nor did Congress intend to enact the "primary objective" requirement of § 604 into the Rehabilitation Act when it amended that Act in 1978. The amendments, as we have noted, make "available" the remedies, procedures and rights of Title VI for suits under § 504 against "*any* recipient of federal assistance." § 505(a)(2). These terms do not incorporate § 604's "primary objective" limitation. Rather, the legislative history reveals that this section was intended to codify the regulations of the Department of Health, Education and Welfare governing enforcement of § 504, see S.Rep. No. 95–890, at 19, that prohibited employment discrimination regardless of the purpose of federal financial assistance.[16] And it would be anomalous to conclude that the section, "designed to enhance the ability of handicapped individuals to assure compliance with [§ 504]," id., at 18, silently adopted a drastic limitation on the handicapped individual's right to sue federal grant recipients for employment discrimination.

V

Section 504, by its terms, prohibits discrimination only by a "program or activity receiving Federal financial assistance." This Court on two occasions has considered the meaning of the terms "program or activity" as used in Title IX. Grove City College v. Bell, 465 U.S. 553, 104 S.Ct. 1211, 78 L.Ed.2d 516 (1984); North Haven Board of Education v. Bell, 456 U.S., at 535–540, 102 S.Ct., at 1925–1928. Clearly, this language limits the ban on discrimination to the specific program that receives federal funds. Neither opinion, however, provides particular guidance as to the appropriate treatment of the programs before us. *Grove City College* considered grants of financial aid to students. The Court specifically declined to analogize these grants to nonearmarked direct grants and, indeed, characterized them as "*sui generis.*" 465 U.S., at 573, 104 S.Ct., at 1221. North Haven Board of Education did not undertake to define the term "program" at all, finding that, in the procedural posture of that case, that task should be left to the District Court in the first instance.[17]

16. The Committee noted that "the regulations promulgated by the Department of Health, Education and Welfare with respect to procedures, remedies, and rights under § 504 conform with those promulgated under Title VI. Thus, this amendment codifies existing practice as a specific statutory requirement." S.Rep. No. 95–890, at 19. Although these Department regulations incorporated Title VI regulations governing "complaint and enforcement procedures," see 42 Fed.Reg., at 22685, 22694–22701, the regulations implementing § 504 did not incorporate § 80.3 of the Title VI regulations, which limit Title VI's application to employment discrimination in federal programs to increase employment. The § 504 regulations banned employment discrimination in programs receiving any form of federal financial assistance. See n. 15, supra.

17. The Court held that the Court of Appeals in that case had erroneously suggested that HEW regulations issued under Title XI to govern employment discrimination need not be program specific.

The procedural posture of the case before us is the same as that of *North Haven Board of Education.* The District Court granted a motion for summary judgment on grounds unrelated to the issue of "program specificity." That judgment was reversed by the Court of Appeals and the case remanded for further proceedings. Thus, neither the District Court nor the Court of Appeals below considered the question whether respondent's decedent had sought and been denied employment in a "program * * * receiving federal financial assistance." [18] Nor did the District Court develop the record or make the factual findings that would be required to define the relevant "program." We therefore do not consider whether federal financial assistance was received by the "program or activity" that discriminated against LeStrange.[19]

VI

We conclude that respondent may recover backpay due to her decedent under § 504 and that this suit for employment discrimination may be maintained even if petitioner receives no federal aid the primary purpose of which is to promote employment. The judgment of the Court of Appeals is therefore affirmed.

It is so ordered.

NOTES AND PROBLEMS FOR DISCUSSION

1. The issue raised at Note 2 following *Prewitt* was discussed, but not resolved by the Court in *Darrone.* While it extended its prior holding in *Guardian's Association* to Section 504 actions, declaring that a Section 504 plaintiff could *not* recover backpay where it did not allege intentional discrimination, it reserved judgment on the extent to which money damages *are* available under Section 504. *Guardian's Ass'n.* involved an action brought under Title VI of the 1964 Civil Rights Act. This statute, in language almost identical to that later used in § 504, prohibits discrimination on the basis of race, color and national origin in federally funded programs. The Court held that grantees should be permitted to terminate their receipt of federal assistance rather than be compelled to assume the obligations necessary for compliance as well as any liability for noncompliance. The Court recognized that in cases of intentional discrimination the grantee could not deny its awareness of the antidiscrimination obligation or its failure to meet that obligation and thus the victim of such intentional discrimination might be entitled to compensation. Nevertheless, it also concluded that in a case of unintentional discrimination, it was not obvious that a grantee was aware that it was administering its program in violation of the statute or accompanying regulations and, therefore, the grantee should not be subject to financial sanction. See also Martin v. Cardinal Glennon Memorial Hospital, 599 F.Supp. 284 (E.D.Mo.1984) (neither punitive

18. Although Judge Adams cited the Third Circuit opinion in *Grove City College,* he did so merely to support his rejection of the *Trageser* "standing" analysis. See supra, at 1252.

19. Conrail does not contest that it receives Federal financial assistance within the meaning of § 504. Apparently, the government's payments to Conrail exceed the fair market value of the securities issued by Conrail to the government.

damages nor recovery for humiliation and embarrassment available under § 504).

The Court took another shot at a limited aspect of this question in ATASCADERO STATE HOSPITAL v. SCANLON, ___ U.S. ___, 105 S.Ct. 3142, 87 L.Ed.2d 171 (1985). In this case, the plaintiff, a diabetic, allegedly was denied employment as a graduate student assistant recreational therapist by a state hospital because of his physical handicaps. His complaint sought injunctive and compensatory relief from the hospital and the California Department of Mental Health. The defendants moved to dismiss the complaint on the ground, *inter alia,* that the Eleventh Amendment barred such an action for damages in federal court. The trial court granted the motion and the Ninth Circuit reversed, ruling that the State's participation in programs funded by the Rehabilitation Act constituted an implicit consent to be sued in federal court in actions brought under that statute. The Supreme Court reversed the Court of Appeals. In a 5–4 decision, the Court, speaking through Justice Powell, stated that while Congress can abrogate a State's Eleventh Amendment immunity from suit in federal court by acting pursuant to Section 5 of the Fourteenth Amendment, it can do so only "by making its intention unmistakably clear in the language of the statute." Such an explicit intention was required, the Court declared, because the Eleventh Amendment "implicates the fundamental constitutional balance between the Federal Government and the States. Undertaking this inquiry, the Court rejected the plaintiff's claim that the language in Section 505 providing remedies for Section 504 violations by "*any* recipient of Federal assistance" constituted such a clear expression of Congressional intent to subject States to federal suit. The Court reasoned that States cannot be treated like any other class of recipients and that such a general authorization for federal suit did not constitute "the kind of unequivocal statutory language sufficient to abrogate the Eleventh Amendment. When Congress chooses to subject the States to federal jurisdiction, it must do so specifically." The Court went further and stated that if the Rehabilitation Act were viewed as an enactment pursuant to the Spending Clause of Article I, rather than to Section 5 of the Fourteenth Amendment, the fact that various provisions of the Act were addressed to the States did not render participation by a State in programs funded under the Act an express or implied consent to be sued under that statute. Again, the Court reasoned that the Act did not contain any express language clearly manifesting an intent to condition participation in funded programs on a State's consent to waive its constitutional immunity. Thus, the State could not be said to have consented to federal jurisdiction by participating in funded programs. Finally, the majority declared that a California State Constitution provision authorizing suits against the State in such manner as "directed by law" did not constitute a waiver of the State's constitutional immunity from federal court jurisdiction. They ruled that to constitute such a waiver, the state statute or constitutional provision must specify the State's intention to subject itself to suit in federal court. This state constitutional provision was interpreted as merely authorizing the state legislature to waive the State's sovereign immunity and did not constitute an unequivocal waiver specifically applicable to federal court jurisdiction. In an exhaustive review of the history of the Eleventh Amendment, Justice Brennan, in a dissenting opinion joined in by the three other dissenting members, objected to what he saw as the Court's continually expanding view of the States' sovereign immunity from federal court jurisdiction. In short, he stated that the majority's notion that the sovereign immunity doctrine was essential to basic notions of federalism resulted only in a scheme capable of protecting States that violate federal law from the legal consequences of their conduct. He also concluded that Congress clearly intended to impose on States the same obligations and remedial liabilities under the Act that it imposed on all participants in federally funded programs.

2. The Supreme Court's opinion in *Guardians Ass'n.* also included a discussion of the standard of proof required to establish a violation of Title VI. The Justices wrote six separate opinions, none of which was adopted in full by a majority of the Court. Nevertheless, seven Justices agreed that proof of discriminatory intent was necessary to establish a statutory violation. A majority of five, however, also concluded that a *Griggs* -type showing of disproportionate impact would suffice in a suit brought to enforce administrative regulations issued pursuant to the statute. Should this ruling apply also to claims brought under § 504? This question was not addressed by the Supreme Court in *Consolidated Rail* since the plaintiff therein had alleged intentional discrimination.

The issue was raised, however, by the parties in ALEXANDER v. CHOATE, 469 U.S. 287, 105 S.Ct. 712, 83 L.Ed.2d 661 (1985). There, the director of the Tennessee Medicaid program decided to institute a variety of cost-cutting measures to respond to projected Medicaid costs in excess of the State's Medicaid budget. One of the proposed changes was to reduce from twenty to fourteen the number of inpatient hospital days per fiscal year that Tennessee Medicaid would pay to hospitals on behalf of Medicaid patients. A class of Tennessee Medicaid recipients brought an action under Section 504 to enjoin this proposed change on the ground that the reduced limitation on inpatient coverage would have a disproportionately disadvantageous impact on the handicapped. It was undisputed that 27.4% of all handicapped users of hospital services who received Medicaid in the 1979–1980 fiscal year required more than 14 days of care, whereas only 7.8% of the nonhandicapped users of hospital services required more than 14 days of inpatient care. The defendant State of Tennessee, relying on the Court's ruling in *Guardians Ass'n,* claimed that § 504 prohibited only purposeful discrimination against the handicapped. The trial court dismissed the complaint for failure to state a claim under Section 504. The Sixth Circuit reversed, holding that the plaintiffs had established a prima facie case by claiming that the State's proposed action would have a disproportionately discriminatory effect on the handicapped. It remanded the case to give the State an opportunity to rebut the prima facie case either by demonstrating the unavailability of an alternative cost-saving proposal with a less disproportionate impact on the handicapped or offering a substantial justification for its adoption of the proposed plan. The Supreme Court reversed, but refused to rule explicitly on whether an impact-based claim was cognizable under either § 504 or its implementing regulations. The Court stated that its opinion in *Guardians Ass'n.* was not dispositive of this issue since the decision in *Guardians Ass'n.* that a Title VI violation required proof of discriminatory purpose was controlled by the stare decisis effect of the Court's prior decision in *Bakke,* a restriction which did not apply to the interpretation of § 504. It also mentioned that the legislative history of § 504 reflected both Congress' recognition that most discrimination against the handicapped was the product of indifference rather than animus and its intention to proscribe this manifestation of bias. Moreover, it noted that all the federal circuit courts that had addressed the issue had agreed that § 504 reaches some form of impact discrimination. Nevertheless, the Court expressed its concern that a broad ruling that § 504 reached all action with a disproportionate impact on the handicapped would create a potentially unwieldy administrative and adjudicative burden. Consequently, the Court was unwilling to adopt such a broad interpretation of the statute. In addition, it chose not to decide whether 504 would ever extend to an impact-based discrimination claim. Instead, it assumed arguendo that Section 504 or its implementing regulations reached some conduct that creates a disproportionate impact and ruled that the disproportionate effect of Tennessee's challenged action did not fall within the class of impact that the federal statute or regulations might reach. The reduction in inpatient coverage, the Court reasoned, did not adversely affect the handicapped since all users of hospital services were subject to the same limitation. To do otherwise, the Court declared, would require singling out the handicapped for more than fourteen days of coverage and improperly read into § 504 an obligation to guarantee equal results from the provision of state Medicaid payments to the handicapped. Because the handicapped, like all other hospital service users, retained meaningful and equal access to fourteen days of Medicaid coverage for inpatient care, the Court concluded, Tennessee's proposed action did not create the type of disproportionate impact on the handicapped which might be prohibited by Section 504 or its implementing regulations. Is this analysis reminiscent of the Court's approach in General Electric v. Gilbert, supra at 344? For a detailed discussion of the methods of proving discrimination in § 504 cases, see Wegner, the Antidiscrimination Model Reconsidered: Ensuring Equal Opportunity Without Respect to Handicap Under § 504 of the Rehabilitation Act of 1973, 69 Corn.L.Rev. 401 (1984).

3. Louise Ross, an associate professor of physics, was dismissed shortly after she was involved in an automobile accident that left her blind and paralyzed from the waist down. The University contended that her disability made it impossible for Professor Ross to engage in the type of research activity expected of a teacher in her chosen field. In addition, the University indicated that while it received a substantial amount of federal funding, all of those monies were used to finance scholarships for minority students in the foreign language, mathematics and history departments. Is there any basis upon which the University could move to dismiss Ross' Sec. 504 claim for failure to state a cause of action? Title IX of the Education Amendments of 1972, 20 U.S.C. §§ 1001–1686 (1976), in language similar to that subsequently used in § 504, provides that "no person in the United States shall, on the basis of sex, be excluded from participation in, be denied the benefits of, or be subjected to discrimination under any education program or activity receiving Federal financial assistance * * *." The Department of Education, pursuant to what it viewed as its statutory authority to enforce the provisions of Title IX, issued regulations that prohibit sex-based discrimination in employment by any school receiving federal funds. Has the agency acted within the scope of its authority or did Congress intend for this statute to protect only students from sex-based discrimination? In NORTH HAVEN BOARD OF EDUCATION v. BELL, 456 U.S. 512, 102 S.Ct. 1912, 72 L.Ed.2d 299 (1982), cited in *Consolidated Rail,* the Supreme Court held that Title IX did apply to the employment practices of covered educational institutions.

Because of the program-specific language in Title IX, the problems examined in the preceding paragraph with respect to the Rehabilitation Act also arise under Title IX. While the Supreme Court in *North Haven* noted that the Act's remedial provisions apply only to those particular programs that are found to have violated Title IX, it did not define "program or activity". Should

Title IX apply to a sex discrimination claim filed by a university custodial employee? Is this worker involved in an "education program or activity"? See Walters v. President and Fellows of Harvard College, 601 F.Supp. 867 (D.Mass. 1985); Friedman, Congress, The Courts and Sex-Based Employment Discrimination in Higher Education: A Tale of Two Titles, 34 Vand.L.Rev. 37, 54–68 (1981). The Supreme Court finally addressed this issue in the following Title IX case.

GROVE CITY COLLEGE v. BELL

Supreme Court of the United States, 1984.
465 U.S. 555, 104 S.Ct. 1211, 79 L.Ed.2d 516.

JUSTICE WHITE delivered the opinion of the Court.

Section 901(a) of Title IX of the Education Amendments of 1972 prohibits sex discrimination in "any education program or activity receiving Federal financial assistance," [1] and § 902 directs agencies awarding most types of assistance to promulgate regulations to ensure that recipients adhere to that prohibition. Compliance with departmental regulations may be secured by termination of assistance "to the particular program, or part thereof, in which * * * noncompliance has been * * * found" or by "any other means authorized by law." § 902.[2]

1. Section 901(a), 20 U.S.C. § 1681(a), provides, in pertinent part:

> "No person in the United States shall, on the basis of sex, be excluded from participation in, be denied the benefits of, or be subjected to discrimination under any education program or activity receiving Federal financial assistance * * *."

Nine statutory exemptions, none of which is relevant to the disposition of this case, follow. See §§ 901(a)(1)–(9), 20 U.S.C. §§ 1681(a)(1)–(9).

2. Section 902, 20 U.S.C. § 1682, provides:

> "Each Federal department and agency which is empowered to extend Federal financial assistance to any education program or activity, by way of grant, loan, or contract other than a contract of insurance or guaranty, is authorized and directed to effectuate the provisions of section [901] with respect to such program or activity by issuing rules, regulations, or orders of general applicability which shall be consistent with achievement of the objectives of the statute authorizing the financial assistance in connection with which the action is taken. No such rule, regulation, or order shall become effective unless and until approved by the President. Compliance with any requirement adopted pursuant to this section may be effected (1) by the termination of or refusal to grant or to continue assistance under such program or activity to any recipient as to whom there has been an express finding on the record, after opportunity for hearing, of a failure to comply with such requirement, but such termination or refusal shall be limited to the particular political entity, or part thereof, or other recipient, as to whom such a finding has been made, and shall be limited in its effect to the particular program, or part thereof, in which such noncompliance has been so found, or (2) by any other means authorized by law: *Provided, however,* That no such action shall be taken until the department or agency concerned has advised the appropriate person or persons of the failure to comply with the requirement and has determined that compliance cannot be secured by voluntary means. In the case of any action terminating, or refusing to grant or continue, assistance because of failure to comply with a requirement imposed pursuant to this section, the head of the Federal department or agency shall file with the committees of the House and Senate having legislative jurisdiction over the program or activity involved a full written report of the circumstances and the grounds for such action. No such action shall become effective until thirty days have elapsed after the filing of such report." (emphasis in original).

This case presents several questions concerning the scope and operation of these provisions and the regulations established by the Department of Education. We must decide, first, whether Title IX applies at all to Grove City College, which accepts no direct assistance but enrolls students who receive federal grants that must be used for educational purposes. If so, we must identify the "education program or activity" at Grove City that is "receiving Federal financial assistance" and determine whether federal assistance to that program may be terminated solely because the College violates the Department's regulations by refusing to execute an Assurance of Compliance with Title IX. Finally, we must consider whether the application of Title IX to Grove City infringes the First Amendment rights of the College or its students.

I

Petitioner Grove City College is a private, coeducational, liberal arts college that has sought to preserve its institutional autonomy by consistently refusing state and federal financial assistance. Grove City's desire to avoid federal oversight has led it to decline to participate, not only in direct institutional aid programs, but also in federal student assistance programs under which the College would be required to assess students' eligibility and to determine the amounts of loans, work-study funds, or grants they should receive. Grove City has, however, enrolled a large number of students who receive Basic Educational Opportunity Grants (BEOGs), 20 U.S.C. § 1070a, under the Department of Education's [4] Alternate Disbursement System (ADS).[5]

The Department concluded that Grove City was a "recipient" of "Federal financial assistance" as those terms are defined in the regulations implementing Title IX, 34 CFR §§ 106.2(g)(1), (h) (1982),[6] and, in

4. The Department of Health, Education, and Welfare's functions with respect to BEOGs were transferred to the Department of Education by § 301(a)(3) of the Department of Education Organization Act, Pub.L. 96–88, 93 Stat. 678, 20 U.S.C. § 3441(a)(3). We will refer to both HEW and DOE as "the Department."

5. The Secretary, in his discretion, has established two procedures for computing and disbursing BEOGs. Under the Regular Disbursement System (RDS), the Secretary estimates the amount that an institution will need for grants and advances that sum to the institution, which itself selects eligible students, calculates awards, and distributes the grants by either crediting students' accounts or issuing checks. 34 CFR §§ 690.71–.85 (1982). Most institutions whose students receive BEOGs participate in the RDS, but the ADS is an option made available by the Secretary to schools that wish to minimize their involvement in the administration of the BEOG program. Institutions participating in the program through the ADS must make appropriate certifications to the Secretary, but the Secretary calculates awards and makes disbursements directly to eligible students. 34 CFR §§ 690.91–.96 (1982).

6. The Title IX regulations were recodified in 1980, without substantive change, at 34 CFR pt. 106 in connection with the establishment of the Department of Education. 45 Fed.Reg. 30802, 30962–30963 (1980). All references herein are to the currently effective regulations.

"Federal financial assistance" is defined in 34 CFR § 106.2(g)(1) (1982) to include:

"A grant or loan of Federal financial assistance, including funds made available for:

* * *

(ii) Scholarships, loans, grants, wages or other funds extended to any entity for payment to or on behalf of students admitted to that entity, or extended directly to such students for payment to that entity."

July 1977, it requested that the College execute the Assurance of Compliance required by 34 CFR § 106.4 (1982). If Grove City had signed the Assurance, it would have agreed to

> "[c]omply, to the extent applicable to it, with Title IX * * * and all applicable requirements imposed by or pursuant to the Department's regulation * * * to the end that * * * no person shall, on the basis of sex, be * * * subjected to discrimination under any education program or activity for which [it] receives or benefits from Federal financial assistance from the Department." App. to Pet. for Cert. 126–127.

When Grove City persisted in refusing to execute an Assurance, the Department initiated proceedings to declare the College and its students ineligible to receive BEOGs.[8] The Administrative Law Judge held that the federal financial assistance received by Grove City obligated it to execute an Assurance of Compliance and entered an order terminating assistance until Grove City "corrects its noncompliance with Title IX and satisfies the Department that it is in compliance" with the applicable regulations.

Grove City and four of its students then commenced this action in the District Court for the Western District of Pennsylvania, which concluded that the students' BEOGs constituted "Federal financial assistance" to Grove City but held, on several grounds, that the Department could not terminate the students' aid because of the College's refusal to execute an Assurance of Compliance. Grove City College v. Harris, 500 F.Supp. 253 (1980).[9] The Court of Appeals reversed. 687 F.2d 684 (CA3 1982). It first examined the language and legislative history of Title IX and held that indirect, as well as direct, aid triggered coverage under § 901(a) and that institutions whose students financed their educations with BEOGs were recipients of federal financial assistance within the meaning of Title IX. Although it recognized that Title IX's provisions are program-specific, the court likened the assistance

A "recipient" is defined in 34 CFR § 106.2(h) (1982) to include:

> "[A]ny public or private agency, institution, or organization, or other entity, or any person, to whom Federal financial assistance is extended directly or indirectly or through another recipient, and which operates an education program or activity which receives or benefits from such assistance * * *."

See also 34 CFR §§ 106.11, 106.31(a) (1982).

8. The Department also sought to terminate Guaranteed Student Loans (GSLs), 20 U.S.C. § 1071, received by Grove City's students.

9. The District Court held, first, that GSLs were "contract[s] of insurance or guaranty" that could not be terminated under § 902 of Title IX. The Department did not challenge this conclusion on appeal, and we express no view on this aspect of the District Court's reasoning. The court also concluded that Grove City could not be required to execute an Assurance of Compliance because Subpart E of the Title IX regulations, which prohibits discrimination in employment, was invalid. As the Court of Appeals recognized, we have since upheld the validity of Subpart E. North Haven Board of Education v. Bell, 456 U.S. 512, 102 S.Ct. 1912, 72 L.Ed.2d 299 (1982). The District Court held, in the alternative, that § 902 permitted termination only upon an actual finding of sex discrimination and that Grove City's refusal to execute an Assurance could not justify a termination of assistance. Finally, the court reasoned that affected students were entitled to hearings before their aid could be discontinued.

flowing to Grove City through its students to nonearmarked aid, and, with one judge dissenting, declared that "[w]here the federal government furnishes indirect or non-earmarked aid to an institution, it is apparent to us that the institution itself must be the 'program.'" 687 F.2d, at 700.[10] Finally, the Court of Appeals concluded that the Department could condition financial aid upon the execution of an Assurance of Compliance and that the Department had acted properly in terminating federal financial assistance to the students and Grove City despite the lack of evidence of actual discrimination.

We granted certiorari and we now affirm the Court of Appeals' judgment that the Department could terminate BEOGs received by Grove City's students to force the College to execute an Assurance of Compliance.

II

In defending its refusal to execute the Assurance of Compliance required by the Department's regulations, Grove City first contends that neither it nor any "education program or activity" of the College receives any federal financial assistance within the meaning of Title IX by virtue of the fact that some of its students receive BEOGs and use them to pay for their education. We disagree.

Grove City provides a well-rounded liberal arts education and a variety of educational programs and student services. The question is whether any of those programs or activities "receiv[es] Federal financial assistance" within the meaning of Title IX when students finance their education with BEOGs. The structure of the Education Amendments of 1972, in which Congress both created the BEOG program and imposed Title IX's nondiscrimination requirement, strongly suggests an affirmative conclusion. BEOGs were aptly characterized as a "centerpiece of the bill," 118 Cong.Rec. 20297 (1972) (Rep. Pucinski), and Title IX "relate[d] directly to [its] central purpose." 117 Cong.Rec. 30412 (1971) (Sen. Bayh). In view of this connection and Congress' express recognition of discrimination in the administration of student financial aid programs, it would indeed be anomalous to discover that one of the primary components of Congress' comprehensive "package of federal

10. In reaching this conclusion, the Court of Appeals accepted the position argued by respondents. As respondents acknowledged in the oral argument before this Court, the Department's position has not been a model of clarity. The Department initially took the position that the receipt of student financial aid would trigger institution-wide coverage under Title IX and construed its regulations to that effect. It pressed that position in the lower courts. In their brief in opposition to the petition for certiorari, respondents did not defend this aspect of the Court of Appeals' opinion, but argued instead that the question need not be resolved to decide this case. In their brief on the merits and in the oral argument, however, respondents conceded that the Court of Appeals erred in holding that Grove City itself constituted the "program or activity" subject to regulation under Title IX. The Department's regulations, it was represented, may be construed in a program-specific manner and hence are not inconsistent with the statute. This concession, of course, is not binding on us and does not foreclose our review of the judgment below.

aid," id., at 2007 (Sen. Pell), was not intended to trigger coverage under Title IX.

It is not surprising to find, therefore, that the language of § 901(a) contains no hint that Congress perceived a substantive difference between direct institutional assistance and aid received by a school through its students. The linchpin of Grove City's argument that none of its programs receives any federal assistance is a perceived distinction between direct and indirect aid, a distinction that finds no support in the text of § 901(a).[12] Nothing in § 901(a) suggests that Congress elevated form over substance by making the application of the nondiscrimination principle dependent on the manner in which a program or activity receives federal assistance. There is no basis in the statute for the view that only institutions that themselves apply for federal aid or receive checks directly from the federal government are subject to regulation. As the Court of Appeals observed, "by its all inclusive terminology [§ 901(a)] appears to encompass *all* forms of federal aid to education, direct or indirect." We have recognized the need to " 'accord [Title IX] a sweep as broad as its language,' ". North Haven Board of Education v. Bell, 456 U.S. 512, 521, 102 S.Ct. 1912, 1918, 72 L.Ed.2d 299 (1982) (quoting United States v. Price, 383 U.S. 787, 801, 86 S.Ct. 1152, 1160, 16 L.Ed.2d 267 (1966)), and we are reluctant to read into § 901(a) a limitation not apparent on its face.

Our reluctance grows when we pause to consider the available evidence of Congress' intent. The economic effect of direct and indirect assistance often is indistinguishable, and the BEOG program was structured to ensure that it effectively supplements the College's own financial aid program.[13] Congress undoubtedly comprehended this re-

12. Grove City itself recognizes the problematic nature of the distinction it advances. Although its interpretation of § 901(a) logically would exclude from coverage under Title IX local school districts that receive federal funds through state educational agencies, see, e.g., 20 U.S.C. §§ 3801 et seq., Grove City wisely does not attempt to defend this result. In fact, the College concedes that "[b]ecause federal assistance is often passed through state agencies, this type of indirect assistance leads to Title IX jurisdiction *over the education program or activity* which ultimately receives the assistance." Grove City has proposed no principled basis for treating differently federal assistance received through students and federal aid that is disbursed by a state agency.

13. Grove City's students receive BEOGs to pay for the education they receive at the College. Their eligibility for assistance is conditioned upon continued enrollment at Grove City and on satisfactory progress in their studies. 20 U.S.C. §§ 1091(a)(1), (3). Their grants are based on the "cost of attendance" at Grove City, 20 U.S.C. § 1070a(a)(2)(B)(i), which includes the College's tuition and fees, room and board, and a limited amount for books, supplies, and miscellaneous expenses. 34 CFR § 690.51 (1982). The amount that students and their families can reasonably be expected to contribute is subtracted from the maximum BEOG to ensure that the assistance is used solely for educational expenses, 20 U.S.C. § 1070a(a)(2)(A)(i), and students are required to file affidavits stating that their awards will be "used solely for expenses related to attendance" at Grove City. 20 U.S.C. § 1091(a)(5); see 34 CFR §§ 690.79, 690.94(a)(2) (1982).

Grove City's attempt to analogize BEOGs to food stamps, Social Security benefits, welfare payments, and other forms of general-purpose governmental assistance to low-income families is unavailing. First, there is no evidence that Congress intended the receipt of federal money in this manner to trigger coverage under Title IX. Second, these general assistance programs, unlike student aid programs, were not designed to assist colleges and universities. Third, educational institutions have no

ality in enacting the Education Amendments of 1972. The legislative history of the amendments is replete with statements evincing Congress' awareness that the student assistance programs established by the amendments would significantly aid colleges and universities. In fact, one of the stated purposes of the student aid provisions was to "provid[e] assistance to institutions of higher education." 20 U.S.C. § 1070(a)(5).

Congress' awareness of the purpose and effect of its student aid programs also is reflected in the sparse legislative history of Title IX itself. Title IX was patterned after Title VI of the Civil Rights Act of 1964. The drafters of Title VI envisioned that the receipt of student aid funds would trigger coverage,[15] and, since, they approved identical language, we discern no reason to believe that the Congressmen who voted for Title IX intended a different result.

The few contemporaneous statements that attempted to give content to the phrase "receiving Federal financial assistance," while admittedly somewhat ambiguous, are consistent with Senator Bayh's declaration that Title IX authorizes the termination of "all aid that comes through the Department of Health, Education, and Welfare."[16] Such statements by individual legislators should not be given controlling effect, but, at least in instances where they are consistent with the plain language of Title IX, Senator Bayh's remarks are "an authoritative guide to the statute's construction." North Haven Board of Education v. Bell, 456 U.S., at 527, 102 S.Ct., at 1921. The contemporaneous legislative history, in short, provides no basis for believing that Title

control over, and indeed perhaps no knowledge of, whether they ultimately receive federal funds made available to individuals under general assistance programs, but they remain free to opt out of federal student assistance programs. Fourth, individuals' eligibility for general assistance is not tied to attendance at an educational institution.

15. Appendix A to the initial Title VI regulations identified several programs making assistance available through payments to students among those to which the regulations applied, 29 Fed.Reg. 16298, 16304 (1964), as did the version in force when Title IX was enacted. 45 CFR pt. 80, app. A. (1972). The current list of programs covered by Title VI includes BEOGs and GSLs, 34 CFR pt. 100, app. A (1982), and Grove City's assumption that Congress would have excluded BEOGs from coverage under Title VI if the program had been operational in 1964 is baseless.

16. Grove City relies heavily on a colloquy between Senators Bayh and Dominick:

"Mr. Dominick: The Senator is talking about every program under HEW?

"Mr. Bayh: Let me suggest that I would imagine that any person who was sitting at the head of [HEW], administering the program, would be reasonable and would use only such leverage as was necessary against the institution.

"It is unquestionable, in my judgment, that this would not directed at specific assistance that was being received by individual students, but would be directed at the institution, and the Secretary would be expected to use good judgment as to how much leverage to apply, and where it could best be applied." 117 Cong.Rec. 30408 (1971).

Grove City contends that Senator Bayh's statement demonstrates an intent to exclude student aid from coverage under Title IX. We believe that his answer is more plausibly interpreted as suggesting that, although the Secretary is empowered to terminate student aid, he probably would not need to do so where leverage could be exerted by terminating other assistance. The students, of course, always remain free to take their assistance elsewhere.

IX's broad language is somehow inconsistent with Congress' underlying intent.

Persuasive evidence of Congress' intent concerning student financial aid may also be gleaned from its subsequent treatment of Title IX. We have twice recognized the probative value of Title IX's unique postenactment history, North Haven Board of Education v. Bell, supra, at 535, 102 S.Ct., at 1925; Cannon v. University of Chicago, supra, at 687, n. 7, 702–703, 99 S.Ct., at 1952, n. 7, 1960–1961, and we do so once again. The Department's sex discrimination regulations made clear that "[s]cholarships, loans, [and] grants * * * extended directly to * * * students for payment to" an institution constitute federal financial assistance to that entity. Under the statutory "laying before" procedure of the General Education Provisions Act, 20 U.S.C. § 1232(d)(1), Congress was afforded an opportunity to invalidate aspects of the regulations it deemed inconsistent with Title IX. The regulations were clear, and Secretary Weinberger left no doubt concerning the Department's position that "the furnishing of student assistance to a student who uses it at a particular institution * * * [is] Federal aid which is covered by the statute." Yet, neither House passed a disapproval resolution. Congress' failure to disapprove the regulations is not dispositive, but, as we recognized in North Haven Board of Education v. Bell, it strongly implies that the regulations accurately reflect congressional intent. Congress has never disavowed this implication and in fact has acted consistently with it on a number of occasions.[19]

With the benefit of clear statutory language, powerful evidence of Congress' intent, and a longstanding and coherent administrative construction of the phrase "receiving Federal financial assistance," we have little trouble concluding that Title IX coverage is not foreclosed because federal funds are granted to Grove City's students rather than directly to one of the College's educational programs. There remains the question, however, of identifying the "education program or activi-

19. Although "Congress has proceeded to amend § 901 when it has disagreed with HEW's interpretation of the statute," North Haven Board of Education v. Bell, supra, at 534, 102 S.Ct., at 1924, it has acquiesced in the Department's longstanding assessment of the types of federal aid that trigger coverage under Title IX. In considering the 1976 Education Amendments, for example, Congress rejected an amendment proposed by Senator McClure that would have defined federal financial assistance as "assistance received by the institution directly from the federal government." Senator Pell objected that the amendment would remove from the scope of Title IX funds provided under the BEOG program and pointed out that, "[w]hile these dollars are paid to students they flow through and ultimately go to institutions of higher education * * *." Senator Bayh raised a similar objection and the amendment was rejected. Id., at 28147.

* * *

The statutory authorization for BEOGs, moreover, has been renewed three times. Each time, Congress was well aware of the administrative interpretation under which such grants were believed to trigger coverage under Title IX. The history of these re-enactments makes clear that Congress regards BEOGs and other forms of student aid as a critical source of support for educational institutions. In view of Congress' consistent failure to amend either Title IX or the BEOG statute in a way that would support Grove City's argument, we feel fully justified in concluding that "the legislative intent has been correctly discerned." North Haven Board of Education v. Bell, supra, at 535, 102 S.Ct., at 1925.

ty" of the College that can properly be characterized as "receiving" federal assistance through grants to some of the students attending the College.[20]

III

An analysis of Title IX's language and legislative history led us to conclude in North Haven Board of Education v. Bell that "an agency's authority under Title IX both to promulgate regulations and to terminate funds is subject to the program-specific limitations of §§ 901 and 902." Although the legislative history contains isolated suggestions that entire institutions are subject to the nondiscrimination provision whenever one of their programs receives federal assistance, we cannot accept the Court of Appeals' conclusion that in the circumstances present here Grove City itself is a "program or activity" that may be regulated in its entirety. Nevertheless, we find no merit in Grove City's contention that a decision treating BEOGs as "Federal financial assistance" cannot be reconciled with Title IX's program-specific language since BEOGs are not tied to any specific "education program or activity."

If Grove City participated in the BEOG program through the RDS, we would have no doubt that the "education program or activity receiving Federal financial assistance" would not be the entire College; rather, it would be its student financial aid program.[21] RDS institutions receive federal funds directly, but can use them only to subsidize or expand their financial aid programs and to recruit students who might otherwise be unable to enroll. In short, the assistance is

20. Justice Stevens' assertion that we need not and have no jurisdiction to decide this question is puzzling. Title IX coverage is triggered only when an "education program or activity" is receiving federal aid. Unless such a program can be and is identified, there is no basis for ordering the College to execute an Assurance of Compliance. The Court of Appeals understood as much and ruled that the entire College is the covered educational program. Until and unless that view of the statute is overturned, there will be outstanding an authoritative Court of Appeals' judgment that the certificate Grove City must execute relates to the entire College and that without such a certificate, the Department would be entitled to terminate grants to Grove City students.

Grove City asks to be relieved of that judgment on the grounds that none of its educational programs is receiving any federal aid and that if any of its programs is receiving aid, it is only its administration of the BEOG program. Grove City is entitled to have these issues addressed, for otherwise it must deal with the undisturbed judgment of the Court of Appeals that the entire College is subject to Federal oversight under Title IX. Even though the Secretary has changed his position and no longer agrees with the expansive construction accorded the statute by the Court of Appeals, it is still at odds with Grove City as to the extent of the covered program; and in any event, its modified stance can hardly overturn or modify the judgment below or eliminate Grove City's legitimate and substantial interest in having its submissions adjudicated.

21. There is no merit to Grove City's argument that the Department may regulate only the administration of the BEOG program. Just as employees who "work in an education program that receive[s] federal assistance," North Haven Board of Education v. Bell, supra, at 540, 102 S.Ct., at 1927, are protected under Title IX even if their salaries are "not funded by federal money," ibid., so also are students who participate in the College's federally assisted financial aid program but who do not themselves receive federal funds protected against discrimination on the basis of sex.

earmarked for the recipient's financial aid program. Only by ignoring Title IX's program-specific language could we conclude that funds received under the RDS, awarded to eligible students, and paid back to the school when tuition comes due represent federal aid to the entire institution.

We see no reason to reach a different conclusion merely because Grove City has elected to participate in the ADS. Although Grove City does not itself disburse students' awards, BEOGs clearly augment the resources that the College itself devotes to financial aid. As is true of the RDS, however, the fact that federal funds eventually reach the College's general operating budget cannot subject Grove City to institution-wide coverage. Grove City's choice of administrative mechanisms, we hold, neither expands nor contracts the breadth of the "program or activity"—the financial aid program—that receives federal assistance and that may be regulated under Title IX.

To the extent that the Court of Appeals' holding that BEOGs received by Grove City's students constitute aid to the entire institution rests on the possibility that federal funds received by one program or activity free up the College's own resources for use elsewhere, the Court of Appeals' reasoning is doubly flawed. First, there is no evidence that the federal aid received by Grove City's students results in the diversion of funds from the College's own financial aid program to other areas within the institution.[22] Second, and more important, the Court of Appeals' assumption that Title IX applies to programs receiving a larger share of a school's own limited resources as a result of federal assistance earmarked for use elsewhere within the institution is inconsistent with the program-specific nature of the statute. Most federal educational assistance has economic ripple effects throughout the aided institution, and it would be difficult, if not impossible, to determine which programs or activities derive such indirect benefits. Under the Court of Appeals' theory, an entire school would be subject to Title IX merely because one of its students received a small BEOG or because one of its departments received an earmarked federal grant. This result cannot be squared with Congress' intent.

The Court of Appeals' analogy between student financial aid received by an educational institution and nonearmarked direct grants provides a more plausible justification for its holding, but it too is faulty. Student financial aid programs, we believe, are *sui generis*. In neither purpose nor effect can BEOGs be fairly characterized as unrestricted grants that institutions may use for whatever purpose they desire. The BEOG program was designed; not merely to increase the total resources available to educational institutions, but to enable them

22. Until 1980, institutions whose students received BEOGs and other forms of assistance were required to provide assurance that they would "continue to spend on [their] own scholarship and student-aid program[s], from sources other than funds received under [the federal programs], not less than the average expenditure per year made for that purpose during the most recent period of three fiscal years." This requirement was altered in the Education Amendments of 1980, and no longer applies to schools whose students receive only BEOGs.

to offer their services to students who had previously been unable to afford higher education. It is true, of course, that substantial portions of the BEOGs received by Grove City's students ultimately find their way into the College's general operating budget and are used to provide a variety of services to the students through whom the funds pass. However, we have found no persuasive evidence suggesting that Congress intended that the Department's regulatory authority follow federally aided students from classroom to classroom, building to building, or activity to activity. In addition, * * * the economic effect of student aid is far different from the effect of nonearmarked grants to institutions themselves since the former, unlike the latter, increases both an institution's resources and its obligations. In that sense, student financial aid more closely resembles many earmarked grants.

We conclude that the receipt of BEOGs by some of Grove City's students does not trigger institution-wide coverage under Title IX. In purpose and effect, BEOGs represent federal financial assistance to the College's own financial aid program, and it is that program that may properly be regulated under Title IX.

IV

Since Grove City operates an "education program or activity receiving Federal financial assistance," the Department may properly demand that the college execute an Assurance of Compliance with Title IX. Grove City contends, however, that the Assurance it was requested to sign was invalid, both on its face and as interpreted by the Department, in that it failed to comport with Title IX's program-specific character. Whatever merit that objection might have had at the time, it is not now a valid basis for refusing to execute an Assurance of Compliance.

The Assurance of Compliance regulation itself does not, on its face, impose institution-wide obligations. Recipients must provide assurance only that "each education program or activity operated by * * * [them] *and to which this part applies* will be operated in compliance with this part." The regulations apply, by their terms, "to every recipient and to *each education program or activity* operated by such recipient *which receives or benefits from Federal financial assistance.*" These regulations, like those at issue in North Haven Board of Education v. Bell, "conform with the limitations Congress enacted in §§ 901 and 902." Nor does the Department now claim that its regulations reach beyond the College's student aid program. Furthermore, the Assurance of Compliance currently in use, like the one Grove City refused to execute, does not on its face purport to reach the entire College; it certifies compliance with respect to those "education programs and activities receiving Federal financial assistance." Under this opinion, consistent with the program-specific requirements of Title IX, the covered education program is the College's financial aid program.

A refusal to execute a proper program-specific Assurance of Compliance warrants termination of federal assistance to the student financial aid program. The College's contention that termination must be preceded by a finding of actual discrimination finds no support in the language of § 902, which plainly authorizes that sanction to effect "[c]ompliance with any requirement adopted pursuant to this section." Regulations authorizing termination of assistance for refusal to execute an Assurance of Compliance with Title VI had been promulgated, 45 CFR § 80.4 (1964), and upheld, Gardner v. Alabama, 385 F.2d 804 (CA5 1967), cert. denied, 389 U.S. 1046, 88 S.Ct. 773, 19 L.Ed.2d 839 (1968), long before Title IX was enacted, and Congress no doubt anticipated that similar regulations would be developed to implement Title IX. We conclude, therefore, that the Department may properly condition federal financial assistance on the recipient's assurance that it will conduct the aided program or activity in accordance with Title IX and the applicable regulations.

V

Grove City's final challenge to the Court of Appeals' decision—that conditioning federal assistance on compliance with Title IX infringes First Amendment rights of the College and its students—warrants only brief consideration. Congress is free to attach reasonable and unambiguous conditions to federal financial assistance that educational institutions are not obligated to accept. Grove City may terminate its participation in the BEOG program and thus avoid the requirements of § 901(a). Students affected by the Department's action may either take their BEOGs elsewhere or attend Grove City without federal financial assistance. Requiring Grove City to comply with Title IX's prohibition of discrimination as a condition for its continued eligibility to participate in the BEOG program infringes no First Amendment rights of the College or its students.

Accordingly, the judgment of the Court of Appeals is affirmed.

JUSTICE POWELL, with whom CHIEF JUSTICE BURGER and JUSTICE O'CONNOR join, concurring.

As I agree that the holding in this case is dictated by the language and legislative history of Title IX, and the Regulations of the Department of Education, I join the Court's decision. I do so reluctantly and write briefly to record my view that the case is an unedifying example of overzealousness on the part of the Federal Government.

Grove City College (Grove City) may be unique among colleges in our country; certainly there are few others like it. Founded more than a century ago in 1876, Grove City is an independent, coeducational liberal arts college. * * * At the time of this suit, it had about 2,200 students and tuition was surprisingly low for a private college. Some 140 of the College's students were receiving Basic Educational Opportunity Grants (BEOGs), and 342 had obtained Guaranteed Student Loans (GSLs). The grants were made directly to the students through the

Department of Education, and the student loans were guaranteed by the federal government. Apart from this indirect assistance, Grove City has followed an unbending policy of refusing all forms of government assistance, whether federal, state or local. It was and is the policy of this small college to remain wholly independent of government assistance, recognizing—as this case well illustrates—that with acceptance of such assistance one surrenders a certain measure of the freedom that Americans always have cherished.

This case involves a Regulation adopted by the Department to implement § 901(a) of Title IX. * * * The sole purpose of the statute is to make unlawful *"discrimination"* by recipients of federal financial assistance on the "basis of sex." The undisputed fact is that Grove City does not discriminate—and so far as the record in this case shows—never has discriminated against anyone on account of sex, race, or national origin. This case has nothing whatever to do with discrimination past or present. The College therefore has complied to the letter with the sole purpose of § 901(a).

As the Court describes, the case arises pursuant to a Regulation adopted under Title IX that authorizes the Secretary to obtain from recipients of federal aid an "Assurance of Compliance" with Title IX and regulations issued thereunder. At the outset of this litigation, the Department insisted that by accepting students who received BEOG awards, Grove City's entire institution was subject to regulation under Title IX. The College, in view of its policies and principles of independence and its record of non-discrimination, objected to executing this Assurance. One would have thought that the Department confronted as it is with cases of national importance that involve actual discrimination, would have respected the independence and admirable record of this college. But common sense and good judgment failed to prevail. The Department chose to litigate, and instituted an administrative proceeding to compel Grove City to execute an agreement to operate all of its programs and activities in full compliance with all of the regulations promulgated under Title IX—despite the College's record as an institution that had operated to date in full accordance with the letter and spirit of Title IX. * * *

* * *

The effect of the Department's termination of the student grants and loans would not have been limited to the College itself. Indeed, the most direct effect would have been upon the students themselves. Absent the availability of other scholarship funds, many of them would have had to abandon their college education or choose another school. It was to avoid these serious consequences that this suit was instituted. The College prevailed in the District Court but lost in the Court of Appeals. Only after Grove City had brought its case before this Court, did the Department retreat to its present position that Title IX applies only to Grove City's financial aid office. On this narrow theory, the Department has prevailed, having taken this small independent college, which it acknowledges has engaged in no discrimination whatever, through six years of litigation with the full weight of the federal government opposing it. I cannot believe that the Department will rejoice in its "victory."

JUSTICE STEVENS, concurring in part and concurring in the result.

For two reasons, I am unable to join part III of the Court's opinion. First, it is an advisory opinion unnecessary to today's decision, and second, the advice is predicated on speculation rather than evidence.

The controverted issue in this litigation is whether Grove City College may be required to execute the "Assurance of Compliance with Title IX" tendered to it by the Secretary in order to continue receiving the benefits of the federal financial assistance provided by the BEOG program. The Court of Appeals affirmed the District Court's decision that Grove City is a "recipient" of federal financial assistance, and reversed its decision that the Secretary could not terminate federal financial assistance because Grove City refused to execute the Assurance. The Court today holds (in part II of its opinion) that Grove City is a recipient of federal financial assistance within the meaning of Title IX, and (in part IV) that Grove City must execute the Assurance of Compliance in order to continue receiving that assistance. These holdings are fully sufficient to sustain the judgment the Court reviews, as the Court acknowledges by affirming that judgment.

In part III of its opinion, the Court holds that Grove City is not required to refrain from discrimination on the basis of sex except in its financial aid program. In so stating, the Court decides an issue that is not in dispute. The Assurance of Compliance merely requires that it comply with Title IX "to the extent applicable to it." See ante, at 1215. The Secretary, who is responsible for administering Title IX, construes the statute as applicable only to Grove City's financial aid program. All the Secretary seeks is a judgment that Title IX requires Grove City to promise not to discriminate in its financial aid program. The Court correctly holds that this program is subject to the requirements of Title IX, and that Grove City must promise not to discriminate in its operation of the program. But, there is no reason for the Court to hold that Grove City need not make a promise that the Secretary does not ask it to make, and that it in fact would not be making by signing the Assurance, in order to continue to receive federal financial assistance. It will be soon enough to decide the question discussed in part III when and if the day comes that the Secretary asks Grove City to make some further promise in order to continue to receive federal financial assistance.

Moreover, the record in this case is far from adequate to decide the question raised in part III. Assuming for the moment that participation in the BEOG program could not in itself make Title IX applicable to the entire institution, a factual inquiry is nevertheless necessary as to which of Grove City's programs and activities can be said to receive or benefit from federal financial assistance. This is the import of the applicable regulation, upheld by the Court today, which states that

Title IX applies "to every recipient and to each education program or activity operated by such recipient which receives or benefits from Federal financial assistance." The Court overlooks the fact that the regulation is in the disjunctive; Title IX coverage does not always depend on the actual receipt of federal financial assistance by a given program or activity. The record does not tell us how important the BEOG program is to Grove City, in either absolute or relative terms; nor does it tell us anything about how the benefits of the program are allocated within the institution. The Court decides that a small scholarship for just one student should not subject the entire school to coverage. But why should this case be judged on the basis of that hypothetical example instead of a different one? What if the record showed—and I do not suggest that it does—that all of the BEOG money was reserved for, or merely happened to be used by, talented athletes and that their tuition payments were sufficient to support an entire athletic program that would otherwise be abandoned? Would such a hypothetical program be covered by Title IX? [1] And if this athletic program discriminated on the basis of sex, could it plausibly be contended that Congress intended that BEOG money could be used to enable such a program to survive? Until we know something about the character of the particular program, it is inappropriate to give advice about an issue that is not before us.

Accordingly, while I subscribe to the reasoning in parts I, II, and IV of the Court's opinion, I am unable to join part III.

JUSTICE BRENNAN, with whom JUSTICE MARSHALL joins, concurring in part and dissenting in part.

The Court today concludes that Grove City College is "receiving Federal financial assistance" within the meaning of Title IX of the Education Amendments of 1972 because a number of its students receive federal education grants. As the Court persuasively demonstrates in Part II of its opinion, that conclusion is dictated by "the need to accord [Title IX] a sweep as broad as its language," by reference to the analogous statutory language and legislative history of Title VI of the Civil Rights Act of 1964, by reliance on the unique postenactment history of Title IX and by recognition of the strong congressional intent that there is no "substantive difference between direct institutional assistance and aid received by a school through its students". For these same reasons, however, I cannot join Part III of the Court's opinion, in which the Court interprets the language in Title IX that limits application of the statute to "any education program or activity"

1. Indeed, if we are to speculate about hypothetical cases, why not consider a school comparable to the private institutions discussed in Blum v. Yaretsky, 457 U.S. 991, 102 S.Ct. 2777, 73 L.Ed.2d 534 (1982), in which over 90% of the patients received funds from public sources? It is at least theoretically possible that an educational institution might be financed entirely by tuition, and that virtually all of the students at an institution could receive a federal subsidy. Again, I do not suggest that Grove City College is such an institution, but I do suggest that it is improper for the Court to decide a legal issue on the basis of hypothetical examples that are selected to support a particular result.

receiving federal monies. By conveniently ignoring these controlling indicia of congressional intent, the Court also ignores the primary purposes for which Congress enacted Title IX. The result—allowing Title IX coverage for the College's financial aid program, but rejecting institution-wide coverage even though federal monies benefit the entire College—may be superficially pleasing to those who are uncomfortable with federal intrusion into private educational institutions, but it has no relationship to the statutory scheme enacted by Congress.

I

The Court has twice before had occasion to ascertain the precise scope of Title IX. See North Haven Board of Education v. Bell; Cannon v. University of Chicago. In both cases, the Court emphasized the broad congressional purposes underlying enactment of the statute. In *Cannon,* while holding that Title IX confers a private cause of action on individual plaintiffs, we noted that the primary congressional purpose behind the statute was "to avoid the use of federal resources to support discriminatory practices," and that this purpose "is generally served by the statutory procedure for the termination of federal financial support for institutions engaged in discriminatory practices." In *North Haven,* while holding that employment discrimination is within the reach of Title IX, we expressed "no doubt that 'if we are to give [Title IX] the scope that its origins dictate, we must accord it a sweep as broad as its language.'" And although we acknowledged that an agency's authority "both to promulgate regulations and to terminate funds is subject to the program-specific limitation of §§ 901 and 902," we explicitly refused to define "program" at that time.

When reaching that question today,[1] the Court completely disregards the broad remedial purposes of Title IX that consistently have controlled our prior interpretations of this civil rights statute. Moreover, a careful examination of the statute's legislative history, the accepted meaning of similar statutory language in Title VI, and the postenactment history of Title IX will demonstrate that the Court's narrow definition of "program or activity" is directly contrary to congressional intent.

A

The statute that was eventually enacted as Title IX had its genesis in separate proposals considered by the House and the Senate, in 1970 and 1971, respectively. In the House, the Special Subcommittee on Education, under the leadership of Representative Edith Green, held extensive hearings during the summer of 1970 on "Discrimination Against Women." At that time, the subcommittee was considering a

1. There is much to commend the suggestion, made by JUSTICE STEVENS, that Part III of the Court's opinion is no more than an advisory opinion, unnecessary to the resolution of this case and unsupported by any factual findings made below. Because the Court has not heeded that suggestion, however, I feel compelled to express my view on the merits of the issue decided by the Court.

package of legislation that included a simple amendment adding the word "sex" to the list of discriminations prohibited by Title VI of the Civil Rights Act of 1964. Testimony offered during those hearings, however, focused on the evidence of pervasive sex discrimination in educational institutions.[3] It therefore was not surprising that the version of the subcommittee's proposal that was eventually passed by the full House was limited in its application to federally assisted *education* programs or activities. More important for present purposes, however, the House-passed bill retained the overall format of the subcommittee proposal, and therefore continued to incorporate the "program or activity" language and its enforcement provisions from Title VI.

In the Senate, action began on Title IX in 1971, when Senator Bayh first introduced a floor amendment to the comprehensive education legislation then being considered. As then written, Senator Bayh's proposal was clearly intended to cover an entire institution whenever any education program or activity conducted by that institution was receiving federal monies. In particular, the amendment expressly prohibited discrimination on the basis of sex "under any program or activity conducted by a public institution of higher education, or any school or department of graduate education, which is a recipient of Federal financial assistance for any education program or activity." As explained by its sponsor, the amendment would have prohibited sex discrimination "by any public institution of higher education or any institution of graduate education receiving Federal educational financial assistance."

The 1971 amendment was eventually ruled nongermane, so Senator Bayh was forced to renew his efforts during the next session. When reintroduced, the amendment had been modified to conform in substantial part with the version of Title IX that had been passed by the House. This change was apparently made to ensure adoption of the antidiscrimination provisions by the Conference Committee that would soon convene. * * * There is thus nothing to suggest that the Senate had retreated from the underlying premise of the original amendment proposed by Senator Bayh in 1971—that sex discrimination would be prohibited in any educational institution receiving Federal financial

3. Also during those hearings, representatives of the executive branch first raised objections about the expansive reach of the proposal being considered by the subcommittee. Specifically, it was noted by witnesses testifying on behalf of the Department of Health, Education, and Welfare that the proposed legislation would apply to institutions that were traditionally noncoeducational and to facilities and services within an institution, such as dormitories or physical recreation areas, that might properly be limited to one sex. To eliminate this alleged overreaching, the Department of Justice offered its own legislation that was recognized at the time as far *narrower* in its reach than the subcommittee's proposal. Nonetheless, even with this more limited scope, the alternative offered by the administration would have prohibited sex-based discrimination by a "recipient of Federal financial assistance for any education program or activity," and would have covered facilities or services at educational institutions that did not themselves receive direct educational grants. The administration proposal was eventually rejected by the full House in favor of the bill reported by Representative Green and her subcommittee.

assistance. Indeed, Senator Bayh's willingness to conform the language of his amendment to the bill already enacted by the House proved successful, as Title IX was approved by the Conference Committee and enacted into law.

In sum, although the contemporaneous legislative history does not definitively explain the intended meaning of the program-specific language included in Title IX, it lends no support to the interpretation adopted by the Court. What is clear, moreover, is that Congress intended enforcement of Title IX to mirror the policies and procedures utilized for enforcement under Title VI.

B

"Title IX was patterned after Title VI of the Civil Rights Act of 1964." *Cannon,* supra, at 694, 99 S.Ct., at 1956. Except for the substitution of the word "sex" in Title IX to replace the words "race, color, or national origin" in Title VI, and for the limitation of Title IX to "Education" programs or activities, the two statutes use identical language to describe their scope. The interpretation of this critical language as it already existed under Title VI is therefore crucial to an understanding of congressional intent in 1972 when Title IX was enacted using the same language.

The voluminous legislative history of Title VI is not easy to comprehend, especially when one considers the emotionally and politically charged atmosphere operating at the time of its enactment. And there are no authoritative committee reports explaining the many compromises that were eventually enacted, including the program-specific limitations that found their way into Title VI. Moreover, as might be expected, statements were made by various Members of Congress that can be cited to support a whole range of definitions for the "program or activity" language. For every instance in which a legislator equated the word "program" with a particular grant statute, there is an example of a legislator defining "program or activity" more broadly.

Without completely canvassing several volumes of the *Congressional Record,* I believe it is safe to say that, by including the programmatic language in Title VI, Congress sought to allay fears on the part of many legislators that one isolated violation of the statute's antidiscrimination provisions would result in the wholesale termination of federal funds. * * *

But even accepting that there is some uncertainty concerning the 1964 understanding of "program or activity," we need not be overly concerned with whatever doubt surrounds the precise intent, if any, of the 88th Congress. For what is crucial in ascertaining the meaning of the program-specific language included in Title IX is the understanding that the 92d Congress had at the time it enacted the identical language. And there were two principal indicators of the accepted interpretation of the program-specific language in Title VI that were available to Members of Congress in 1972 when Title IX was enacted—the existing administrative regulations promulgated under Title VI, and the available judicial decisions that had already interpreted those provisions.

The Title VI regulations first issued by the Department of Health, Education, and Welfare during the 1960's, and remaining in effect during 1972, could not have been clearer in the way they applied to educational institutions. See generally 45 CFR Part 80 (1972). * * *

It must have been clear to the Congress enacting Title IX, therefore, that the administrative interpretation of that statute would follow a similarly expansive approach. * * *

Nor were there any outstanding court decisions in 1972 that would have led Congress to believe that Title VI was much narrower in scope. The principal judicial interpretations of Title VI prior to 1972 were announced by the United States Court of Appeals for the Fifth Circuit. In a school desegregation case, for example, the court expressly approved the Department's desegregation guidelines, while noting the broad purposes underlying the prohibitory section of Title VI. United States v. Jefferson County Board of Education, 372 F.2d 836, 881–882 (CA5 1966), adopted en banc, 380 F.2d 385 (CA5 1967) (per curiam) ("'The legality is based on the general power of Congress to apply reasonable conditions * * *. In general, it seems rather anomalous that the Federal Government should aid and abet discrimination on the basis of race, color or national origin by granting money and other kinds of financial aid.'") In another desegregation case, the court noted that Title VI "states a reasonable condition that the United States may attach to any grant of financial assistance and may enforce by refusal or withdrawal of federal assistance." Bossier Parish School Board v. Lemon, 370 F.2d 847, 852 (CA5 1967). More significantly, the court went on to equate a local school system with a "program or activity" receiving federal aid, noting that the "School Board accepted federal financial assistance in November 1964, and thereby brought its school system within the class of programs subject to the section 601 prohibition against discrimination."

Finally, in Board of Public Instruction v. Finch, 414 F.2d 1068 (CA5 1969), the court spoke more directly to the program-specific limitation in Title VI. Although the court refused "to assume * * * that defects in one part of a school system automatically infect the whole," and rejected the definition of the term program offered by the Department, the court also noted that "the purpose of the Title VI cutoff is best effectuated by separate consideration of the use or intended use of federal funds under each grant statute." In particular, although "there will * * * be cases from time to time where a particular program, within a state, within a county, within a district, even within a school * * *, is effectively insulated from otherwise unlawful activities," termination of federal funds is proper "if they are administered in a discriminatory manner, or if they support a program which is infected by a discriminatory environment." To this end, the court remanded the case to the Department for specific findings on the relationship, if any, between the three types of federal grants received by the school system (federal aid for the education of children from low-income families, for supplementary education centers, and for adult education) and the system's discriminatory practices.

In short, the judicial interpretations of Title VI existing in 1972 were either in agreement with the expansive reach of the Department's regulations, *Bossier Parish,* supra; *Jefferson County,* supra, or sanctioned a broad-based termination of federal aid if the funded programs were affected by discriminatory practices, *Finch,* supra. * * * Like the existing administrative regulations, therefore, they provide strong support for the view that Congress intended an expansive interpretation of the program-specific language included in Title IX. Because Members of Congress "repeated[ly] refer[red] to Title VI and its modes of enforcement, we are especially justified in presuming both that those representatives were aware of the prior interpretation of Title VI and that that interpretation reflects their intent with respect to Title IX." *Cannon,* supra.

C

If any doubt remains about the congressional intent underlying the program-specific language included in Title IX, it is removed by the unique, postenactment history of the statute. * * *

Regulations promulgated by the Department to implement Title IX, both as proposed and as finally adopted included an interpretation of program specificity consistent with the view of Title VI and with the congressional intent behind Title IX outlined above. In particular, the regulations prohibited sex discrimination "under any academic, extracurricular, research, occupational training, or other education program or activity operated by a recipient which receives or benefits from Federal financial assistance." Introductory remarks explained the basis for the agency's decision:

> "[T]itle IX will be consistent with the interpretation of similar language contained in title VI of the Civil Rights Act of 1964 * * *. Therefore, an education program or activity or part thereof operated by a recipient of Federal financial assistance administered by the Department will be subject to the requirements of this regulation if it receives or benefits from such assistance.[8] This interpretation is consistent with the only case specifically ruling on the language contained in title VI, which holds that Federal funds may be terminated under title VI upon a finding that they 'are infected by a discriminatory environment.' "

Thus, the agency charged with the statute's implementation initially interpreted the program-specific language of Title IX in a manner

8. In *North Haven,* we concluded that the word "it" in this sentence refers to "education program or activity" rather than "recipient." Even with this limiting construction, however, the regulations still apply to any education program or activity which "receives *or benefits*" from federal assistance. In any event, given the Department's own interpretation of the words quoted in the text, our limiting construction may have been unjustified. * * *

consistent with the view of Congress' intent outlined above—to allow for application of the statute to an entire institution if the institution is comprised of education programs or activities that receive or benefit from federal monies.

Moreover, pursuant to § 431(d)(1) of the General Education Provisions Act, these regulations were submitted to Congress for review. As we explained in *North Haven,* supra, this "laying before" procedure afforded Congress an opportunity to disapprove any regulation that it found to be "inconsistent with the Act from which it derives its authority." And although the regulations interpreting the program-specific limitations of Title IX were explicitly considered by both Houses of Congress, no resolutions of disapproval were passed by the Legislature.

In particular, two resolutions to invalidate the Department's regulations were proposed in the Senate, each specifically challenging the regulations because of the program-specificity requirements of Title IX. One resolution would have provided a blanket disapproval of the regulations, premised in part on the view that "[t]he regulations are inconsistent with the enactment in that they apply to programs or activities not receiving Federal funds such as athletics and extracurricular activities." The other resolution was aimed more particularly at the regulation of athletic programs and activities not receiving direct federal monies, but also was premised on the program-specific limitations in the statute.[9] Neither resolution, however, was acted upon after referral to the appropriate committee.

* * *

Although the failure of Congress to disapprove the Department's regulations is not itself determinative, it does "len[d] weight to the argument" that the regulations were consistent with congressional intent. *North Haven,* supra. Moreover, "the relatively insubstantial interest given the resolutions of disapproval that were introduced seems particularly significant since Congress has proceeded to amend [Title IX] when it has disagreed with [the Department's] interpretation of the statute." *North Haven.* Indeed, those amendments, by exempting from the reach of Title IX various facilities or services at educational institutions that themselves do not receive direct federal aid, strongly suggest that Congress understands the statute otherwise to encompass such programs or activities.[12]

9. * * * The opinion for the Court, limited as it is to a college that receives only "[s]tudent financial aid . . . [that] is *sui generis,*" obviously does not decide whether athletic programs operated by colleges receiving other forms of federal financial assistance are within the reach of Title IX.

12. In 1974, after the Department had published its proposed regulations for Title IX, the Congress excepted social fraternities and sororities and voluntary youth service organizations from the statute's reach. Later, in 1976, Congress provided statutory exemptions for activities related to Boys/Girls State/Nation conferences, father-son or mother-daughter activities (if reasonable opportunities exist for the opposite sex), and collegiate scholarships awarded to "beauty" pageant winners. Obviously, since none of these activities receive direct federal support, these amendments would have been superfluous unless Title IX was otherwise to be applied to such activities

In conclusion, each of the factors relevant to the interpretation of the program-specificity requirements of Title IX, taken individually or collectively, demonstrates that the Court today limits the reach of Title IX in a way that was wholly unintended by Congress. The contemporaneous legislative history of Title IX, the relevant interpretation of similar language in Title VI, and the administrative and legislative interpretations of Title IX since the statute's original enactment all lead to the same conclusion: that Title IX coverage for an institution of higher education is appropriate if federal monies are received by or benefit the entire institution.

II

A proper application of Title IX to the circumstances of this case demonstrates beyond peradventure that the Court has unjustifiably limited the statute's reach. Grove City College enrolls approximately 140 students who utilize Basic Educational Opportunity Grants (BEOGs) to pay for their education at the College. Although the grant monies are paid directly to the students, the Court properly concludes that the use of these federal monies at the College means that the College "receives Federal financial assistance" within the meaning of Title IX. The Court also correctly notes that a principal purpose underlying congressional enactment of the BEOG program is to provide funds that will benefit colleges and universities as a whole. It necessarily follows, in my view, that the entire undergraduate institution operated by Grove City College is subject to the antidiscrimination provisions included in Title IX.

A

In determining the scope of Title IX coverage, the primary focus should be on the purposes meant to be served by the particular federal funds received by the institution.[13] In this case, Congress has clearly

when conducted by educational institutions receiving federal funds.

Other congressional developments since the issuance of the Department's regulations, which have not resulted in amendments to the statute, lend even more support to the broader view of Title IX. After the Department's final regulations went into effect in 1975, for example, Senator Helms introduced amendments to Title IX which would have defined "education programs and activities" to mean "only programs or activities which are an integral part of the required curriculum of an educational institution." No action was taken on the bill. Similarly, in 1976, Senator McClure sponsored an amendment to define "education program or activity" as "such programs or activities as are curriculum or graduation requirements of the institutions." This amendment was rejected in a recorded vote. Finally, the 98th Congress has recently reaffirmed its commitment to Title IX and to the regulations originally issued thereunder. In particular, the House passed (414–8) a resolution expressing its belief that Title IX and its regulations "should not be amended or altered in any manner which will lessen the comprehensive coverage of such statute in eliminating gender discrimination throughout the American educational system." After today's Court decision, it will take another reaffirmation of congressional intent, in the form of a clarifying amendment to Title IX, to ensure that the original legislative will is no longer frustrated.

13. Because I believe that BEOG monies are intended by Congress to benefit institutions of higher education in their entirety, I find it unnecessary in this case

indicated that BEOG monies are intended to benefit any college or university that enrolls students receiving such grants. * * *

In many respects, therefore, Congress views financial aid to students, and in particular BEOGs, as the functional equivalent of general aid to institutions. Given this undeniable and clearly stated congressional purpose, it would seem to be self-evident that Congress intended colleges or universities enrolling students who receive BEOGs to be covered, in their entirety, by the anti-discrimination provisions of Title IX. That statute's primary purpose, after all, is to ensure that federal monies are not used to support discriminatory practices.

Under the Court's holding, in contrast, Grove City College is prohibited from discriminating on the basis of sex in its own "financial aid program," but is free to discriminate in other "programs or activities" operated by the institution. Underlying this result is the unstated and unsupportable assumption that monies received through BEOGs are meant only to be utilized by the College's financial aid program. But it is undisputed that BEOG monies, paid to the institution as tuition and fees and used in the general operating budget, are utilized to support most, and perhaps all, of the facilities and services that together comprise Grove City College.[14]

The absurdity of the Court's decision is further demonstrated by examining its practical effect. According to the Court, the "financial aid program" at Grove City College may not discriminate on the basis of sex because it is covered by Title IX, but the College is not prohibited from discriminating in its admissions, its athletic programs, or even its various academic departments. The Court thus sanctions practices that Congress clearly could not have intended: for example, after today's decision, Grove City College would be free to segregate male and female students in classes run by its mathematics department. This would be so even though the affected students are attending the College with the financial assistance provided by federal funds. If anything about Title IX were ever certain, it is that discriminatory practices like the one just described were meant to be prohibited by the statute.

B

The Court, moreover, does not offer any defensible justification for its holding. First, the Court states that it has "no doubt" that BEOGs

to decide whether Title IX's-reach would be the same when more targeted federal aid is being received by an institution. For such cases, it may be appropriate to examine carefully not only the purposes but also the actual effects of the federal monies received.

14. Although Justice Stevens properly notes that there have been no findings of fact on this particular point, even the Court is forced to concede the obvious ("It is true, of course, that substantial portions of the BEOGs received by Grove City's students ultimately find their way into the College's general operating budget and are used to provide a variety of services to the students through whom the funds pass."). The Court nonetheless ignores its own concession by claiming that there is "no persuasive evidence" that Congress intended to cover an entire institution of higher education in this situation. As I explain in Part II, however, the evidence of congressional intent is quite persuasive, if not convincing.

administered through the Regular Disbursement System (RDS) are received, not by the entire College, but by its financial aid program. Thus, the Court reasons, BEOGs administered through the Alternate Disbursement Systems (ADS) must also be received only by the financial aid program. The premise of this syllogism, however, simply begs the question presented; until today's decision, there was considerable doubt concerning the reach of Title IX in a college or university administering BEOGs through the RDS. Indeed, the extent to which Title IX covers an educational institution receiving BEOGs is the same regardless of the procedural mechanism chosen by the College to disburse the student aid. With this argument, therefore, the Court is simply restating the question presented by the case.

Second, the Court rejects the notion that the federal funds disbursed under the BEOG program are received by the entire institution because they effectively "free up" the College's own resources for use by all programs or activities that are operated by Grove City College. But coverage of an entire institution that receives BEOGs through its students is not dependent upon such a theory. Instead, Title IX coverage for the whole undergraduate institution at Grove City College is premised on the congressional intent that BEOG monies would provide aid for the college or university as a whole. Therefore, whatever merit the Court's argument may have for federal monies that are intended solely to benefit a particular aspect of an educational institution, such as a research grant designed to assist a specific laboratory or professor, see n. 13, supra, the freeing-up theory is simply irrelevant when the federal financial assistance is meant to benefit the entire institution.

Third, the Court contradicts its earlier recognition that BEOGs are no different from general aid to a college or university by claiming that "student financial aid programs * * * are *sui generis.*" Ante, at 1221. Although this assertion serves to limit severely the effect of the Court's holding, it is wholly unexplained, especially in light of the forceful evidence of congressional intent to the contrary. Indeed, it would be more accurate to say that financial aid for students is the prototypical method for funneling federal aid to institutions of higher education.

Finally, although not explicitly offered as a rationale, the Court's holding might be explained by its willingness to defer to the Government's position as it has been represented to this Court. But until the Government filed its briefs in this case, it had consistently argued that Title IX coverage for the entire undergraduate institution operated by Grove City College was authorized by the statute. The latest position adopted by the Government, irrespective of the motivations that might underlie this recent change, is therefore entitled to little, if any, deference. * * * The interpretation of statutes as important as Title IX should not be subjected so easily to shifts in policy by the executive branch.

III

In sum, the program-specific language in Title IX was designed to ensure that the reach of the statute is dependent upon the scope of federal financial assistance provided to an institution. When that financial assistance is clearly intended to serve as federal aid for the entire institution, the institution as a whole should be covered by the statute's prohibition on sex discrimination. Any other interpretation clearly disregards the intent of Congress and severely weakens the antidiscrimination provisions included in Title IX. I therefore cannot join in Part III of the Court's opinion.

NOTES AND PROBLEMS FOR DISCUSSION

1. Do you agree with the majority's conclusion that student grants cannot be characterized as unrestricted grants, particularly when the Court itself emphasized that the BEOG funds must be used exclusively for educational expenses and admitted the difficulty of tracking the ultimate destination of such funds?

2. Does Title IX imply a private right of action for damages in a case alleging employment discrimination? Should the ruling in *Guardians Ass'n.* extend to Title IX in light of the fact that Title IX, like § 504, was patterned directly after Title VI? Is the existence of a Title VII remedy a relevant consideration? See Minor v. Northville Public Schools, 605 F.Supp. 1185 (E.D. Mich.1985) (Title IX provides private right of action in case also cognizable under Title VII but Title IX claim barred here by application of most analogous state limitations statute); Storey v. Board of Regents, 604 F.Supp. 1200 (W.D. Wis.1985).

3. The Supreme Court did not address the issue of program-specificity in the § 504 context in *Consolidated Rail* since that question had not been considered by the courts below. Instead, it remanded the case and directed the trial court to define the relevant "program". In O'CONNOR v. PERU STATE COLLEGE, 781 F.2d 632 (8th Cir. 1986), a woman hired as a physical education teacher and women's basketball coach filed a claim under, *inter alia,* Title IX, alleging that the defendant refused to rehire her either for discriminatory purposes or in retaliation for her criticism of the school's treatment of women athletes. The school received no federal funding other than a Title III grant designed to help establish a central research facility to aid student and faculty research. The trial court dismissed the claim on the ground that the plaintiff had failed to show that the federal funding was given to the physical education department and, therefore, that the physical education department did not constitute a "program or activity" within the meaning of Title IX. The appellate court stated that the trial court had employed the wrong standard for determing whether the physical education department satisfied this statutory requirement. It reasoned that *Grove City* required it to examine the purposes for which grants under the enabling statute *could* be used to determine the relevant "program or activity". Title III funds, it continued, were to be used "to improve academic quality". Therefore, the court declared, the appropriate "program or activity" was the entire academic component of the college. Furthermore, rather than looking to where the funding was spent, the appellate court concluded, it was appropriate to see where it could have been used in

conformity with the purpose of the funding statute. The court ruled that while any academic program would constitute a "program or activity", intercollegiate sports did not constitute "academics" and, therefore, Title IX coverage could not extend to the college's athletic programs. Does this opinion exceed the reasoning of *Grove City?* In UNITED STATES DEPARTMENT OF TRANSPORTATION v. PARALYZED VETERANS OF AMERICA, ___ U.S. ___, 106 S.Ct. 2705, 91 L.Ed.2d 494 (1986), the Supreme Court concluded that the financial assistance provided to airport operators from a Trust Fund created by the Airport and Airway Development Act of 1970 did not render § 504 applicable to commercial airlines. The Court reasoned that as these funds were given directly and exclusively to entities that own or manage airports for construction and other projects strictly limited to airports, the recipients of federal financial assistance were the airport operators and not the commercial airlines. While the airlines may have benefitted from these federal disbursements, the majority announced, § 504 applied only to recipients, and not beneficiaries, of federal funding. The Court also rejected the claim that because airports and airlines were "inextricably intertwined", they should be viewed as a single "program or activity" within the meaning of § 504. Finally, the Court held that the provision of an air traffic control system by the federal government was not a form of federal financial assistance to the airlines. Since this federally conducted program was owned and operated by the federal government, the Court stated, it did not constitute federal financial assistance.

4. Is a charitable organization that receives an exemption from federal income taxation covered by § 504? Is it "receiving federal financial assistance"? See Martin v. Delaware Law School, 625 F.Supp. 1288, 1302 (D.Del. 1985). What about a private social service agency that receives funding from a state agency? What if the state agency is reimbursed by the federal government? See Graves v. Methodist Youth Services, 624 F.Supp. 429 (N.D.Ill.1985). Must the defendant have received federal funding at the time of the challenged employment decision in order for the plaintiff to state a claim under § 504? See Niehaus v. Kansas Bar Ass'n, 793 F.2d 1159 (10th Cir. 1986).

DAVIS v. UNITED AIR LINES, INC.

United States Court of Appeals, Second Circuit, 1981.

662 F.2d 120, cert. denied, 456 U.S. 965, 102 S.Ct. 2045, 72 L.Ed.2d 490 (1982).

OAKES, CIRCUIT JUDGE.

This case involves the issue whether section 503 of the Vocational Rehabilitation Act of 1973, as amended, gives an employee a private right of action against an employer contracting with the federal government for alleged discrimination in employment on the basis of physical handicap. The question has been answered contrarily by a number of district courts, with differing views among the district judges in the Second Circuit, but the only courts of appeal passing on the question, the Fifth, Sixth, and Seventh, Circuits, have held that there is no such private judicial remedy. We agree with the extended analysis of this question by Judge Alvin Rubin for the panel majority in the Fifth Circuit in Rogers v. Frito-Lay, Inc., 611 F.2d 1074 (5th Cir. 1980), and our examination of the cases decided in the Supreme Court and in our own court since *Rogers* was handed down reenforces the conclusion in *Rogers* that no private right of action may be inferred from section 503.

Accordingly, we reverse the judgment of the United States District Court for the Eastern District of New York, Jack B. Weinstein, Chief Judge, which found the reasoning of courts upholding a private right of action "persuasive" in light of the factors identified by the Supreme Court in Cort v. Ash, 422 U.S. 66, 95 S.Ct. 2080, 45 L.Ed.2d 26 (1975). * * *

* * * Thomas Davis had worked for United Air Lines, Inc. ("United") since 1966 as a ramp serviceman, servicing aircraft and loading and unloading cargo. In 1969 he was diagnosed as having epilepsy and from time to time until mid-September 1974, he experienced seizures that did not interfere with his satisfactory performance of duties as a ramp serviceman. After he experienced a seizure in mid-September 1974, he was placed on restricted duties, and he was ultimately confined to working in the bag room. In June 1977, he was placed on "extended illness status" because of his epilepsy; he was officially discharged on February 15, 1980.

In December 1978 Davis filed a complaint with the Department of Labor as provided by section 503(b), charging that United had discriminated against him on the basis of his physical handicap. The Department of Labor has not acted on his complaint. In October 1979, he filed a private suit against United in the Eastern District of New York claiming that United had violated his rights under section 503. Judge Weinstein denied United's motion for judgment on the pleadings, and certified his order for appeal in accordance with 28 U.S.C. § 1292(b). It is assumed for purposes of this appeal that Davis is physically "handicapped" within the meaning of the Act, that United holds government contract subject to the requirements of section 503, and that Davis was discharged because of his handicap.

The law may be briefly stated as follows. Under section 503(a), any contract in excess of $2,500 entered into by the federal government must "contain a provision requiring that * * * [the contractor] shall take affirmative action to employ and advance in employment qualified handicapped individuals. * * * " Section 503(b) provides that if any handicapped individual "believes any contractor has failed or refuse[d] to comply with the provisions of his [federal] contract," that "such individual may file a complaint with the Department of Labor" which shall "promptly investigate" and "take such action * * * as the facts and circumstances warrant * * *."

Because section 503 creates no explicit private judicial remedy against federal contractors charged with employment discrimination against the handicapped, the federal courts have had to determine whether a private right of action may be inferred. The starting points for our analysis must be the four factors set out in Cort v. Ash * * *.

Under *Cort* the initial consideration is whether the plaintiff is a member of a class for "whose *especial* benefit the statute was enacted." Although section 503 was generally intended to benefit handicapped persons, that alone does not establish that Congress intended to "create a federal right in favor of the plaintiff."

The Supreme Court has suggested that a private right of action may be more readily implied when the language of a statute is "right-creating" rather than merely "duty-creating." See Cannon v. University of Chicago. Statutory language has been found right-creating when it focuses explicitly on the benefited class. See, e.g., id. at 682 n. 3, 99 S.Ct. at 2487 ("no person * * * shall, on the basis of sex, be excluded * * *," 20 U.S.C. § 1681).

Section 504 of the Vocational Rehabilitation Act of 1973, which is not at issue in this case, invokes just such right-creating language: "No otherwise qualified handicapped individual * * * shall, solely by reason of his handicap, be excluded from the participation in, be denied the benefits of, or be subjected to discrimination under any program or activity receiving Federal financial assistance." Accordingly, a number of courts have held that section 504 creates a private cause of action for handicapped persons.

By contrast, section 503 contains only duty-creating language, directing federal departments and agencies to provide in all federal contracts that contractors are obligated to take affirmative steps to employ and advance handicapped persons. Nowhere does section 503 confer an express right upon the handicapped, nor impose a direct duty on federal contractors. As Judge Rubin noted in *Rogers*, the use of duty-creating rather than right-creating phrases, though "not conclusive," makes "inference of a private cause of action more difficult." Indeed, the Supreme Court has stated that langauge such as that contained in section 503 militates against inferring a private right of action:

> There would be far less reason to infer a private remedy in favor of individual persons if Congress, instead of drafting Title IX with an unmistakable focus on the benefited class, had written it simply as a ban on discriminatory conduct by recipients of federal funds or as a prohibition against the disbursement of public funds to educational institutions engaged in discriminatory practices.

Cannon v. University of Chicago.

The second inquiry under *Cort* is whether there is any legislative history evidencing congressional intent to create or deny a private remedy. We read *Cort* * * * as requiring a very close, even microscopic, examination of the legislative history of the particular statute involved. This reading of the legislative history must be done with an enlightened judicial eye, giving full attention to the underlying congressional purpose, the very heart of statutory analysis, but also with a healthy skepticism of "casual statements from floor debates," as Justice Jackson warned us so pointedly in Schwegmann Bros. v. Calvert Distillers Co., 341 U.S. 384, 396, 71 S.Ct. 745, 751, 95 L.Ed. 1035 (1951).

Taking such a view of section 503, we find nothing in the history of the original Rehabilitation Act of 1973 that casts any light on whether Congress intended to create a private right of action. Given Congress's initial silence, we may seek some guidance from the 1974 and 1978 amendments to the Act. In giving weight to these amendments, we would choose a middle road between the panel majority in Rogers v. Frito-Lay, Inc. ("[W]hat happened after a statute was enacted may be history and it may come from members of the Congress, but it is not part of the legislative history of the original enactment"), and Judge Goldberg's dissent in *Rogers* ("it is a well-established principle that the post-enactment treatment of a statute by Congress is cogent evidence of the intent of Congress at the time of its passage"). We believe our view is called for by Cannon v. University of Chicago, in which the Court, while partially relying on subsequent legislative history, noted that "we cannot accord these remarks the weight of contemporary legislative history * * *."

The subsequent legislative history of the Rehabilitation Act is internally conflicting. The 1974 amendments deal expressly with section 504, equating it with Title VI (race discrimination) and Title IX (sex discrimination). Senate Report No. 93–1297, which urged overriding the President's veto of the 1974 amendments, expressly noted that section 504 permits a private right of action.

In contrast, the Senate Conference Committee never explicitly stated that section 503 confers a private right of action. Although the report did state that "[i]t is intended that sections 503 and 504 be administered in such a manner that a consistent uniform and effective Federal approach to discrimination against handicapped persons would result," this appears to refer simply to the desirability of cooperation between the Department of Health, Education, and Welfare, which was assigned to enforce section 504, and the Department of Labor, which was assigned to enforce section 503. This separate assignment may even indicate that section 503, unlike 504, was not intended to be privately enforced; the Department of Labor, unlike the Department of Health, Education, and Welfare, lacked experience in dealing with private lawsuits.

The only indication that a "uniform" approach to combatting employment discrimination against the handicapped might entail a private right of action under section 503 as well as section 504 is the remarks of a senator who was not a member of the conference committee, although he was one of the principal sponsors of the original Act and its subsequent amendments. Senator Robert Stafford of Vermont stated on the floor in 1974 that enforcement under both sections 503 and 504 should be similar to enforcement under Title VI and Title IX. These remarks were not, however, included in the conference committee report. Furthermore, although an exchange of correspondence between the Senate Committee on Labor and Public Welfare and the Secretary of Labor regarding the enforcement of section 503 is appended to the report, nowhere in that correspondence is there any hint that the statute was to be enforced through private lawsuits. * * *

With the exception of Senator Stafford's statement on the floor, then, the legislative intent demonstrated by the history of the 1974 amendments simply does not support implication of a private right of action under section 503. In 1978, however, when Congress again amended the Act by adding section 505 to provide for attorney's fees "[i]n any action or proceeding to enforce or charge a violation of [the Act]," the accompanying Senate Report clearly assumed that a private judicial remedy was available under section 503: "[T]he availability of attorney's fees should assist in vindicating private rights of action in the case of section 502 and 503 cases, as well as those arising under section 501 and 504." H.R. Rep.No. 95–1149 (Education and Labor Committee), spoke in exactly the same terms.[8]

Neither the Senate nor the House Reports, however, contained any reference to the existing case law from the district courts. Although two district court cases had found that there was a private right of action under section 503, three cases had held that no implied right of action existed.

This failure to note the conflicting case law of the time indicates that the reference to private rights of action being available in section 502 and 503 cases as well as those arising under sections 501 and 504 was inadvertent. This seems especially true in light of the Senate Report's extensive reference to the testimony of Deborah Kaplan of the Disability Rights Center before the Subcommittee on the Handicapped. Her testimony quoted in the Senate Report related only to sections 501 and 504:

> Unfortunately, the disabled citizens who are protected by section 501 as well as section 504 stand alone among minority groups in this country, since they remain largely unaffected by the recently enacted Civil Rights Attorney's Fees Awards Act of 1976, Public Law 94–559, and because the legislation which protects their civil rights contains no attorney's fees provision. Thus many disabled people, who desperately need to vindicate their rights through the courts, have been utterly frustrated and disillusioned because they could neither afford an attorney, locate one able to represent them without a fee, nor seek an attorney's fee award from the courts.

We note also the Seventh Circuit's point in Simpson v. Reynolds Metals Co., 629 F.2d 1226, 1242 (7th Cir. 1980), that allowing attorney's fees in actions or proceedings brought under section 503 may have been intended to provide for attorney's fees either in a section 503(b) proceeding before the Department of Labor or in a judicial proceeding brought pursuant to the Department of Labor's regulations permitting the

8. The House Report stated: "The new section permits courts, at their discretion, to award to the prevailing party, other than the United States, in any action to enforce sections 501, 503 or 504 of the act, a reasonable allowance to cover the costs of attorneys' fees."

director of the Office of Federal Contract Compliance Programs (OFCCP) to seek appropriate judicial action to enforce the affirmative action contractual provisions required under the Act. In short, even giving appropriate weight to the subsequent legislative history reflected in the 1978 amendment, we find nothing that compels us to the conclusion that a private right of action exists under section 503. The assumption in the 1978 congressional reports simply "cannot be relied upon as a faithful indicator of prior congressional intent." Simpson v. Reynolds Metals Co.

Given the somewhat ambiguous legislative history, however, we must proceed to the third question under Cort v. Ash: whether it is consistent with the underlying purposes of the legislative scheme to infer a private right of action for the handicapped person discriminated against by his employor. Here we note, as did the *Rogers* majority, that Congress provided a rather complete administrative scheme to remedy section 503 violations and that the implementing regulations, emphasize resolving complaints to the Department of Labor "by informal means, including conciliation, and persuasion, whenever possible." The regulations provide as remedies withholding of progess payments, termination of existing contracts, or debarment from receiving future contracts, rather than remedies running to the discriminated-against employee. In this regard, the administrative procedures established by the Act and implementing regulations are remarkably consistent with those under the Comprehensive Employment and Training Act (CETA) discussed in CETA Workers' Organizing Committee v. New York, 617 F.2d 926 (2d Cir. 1980). * * * [A]s in *CETA Workers*, we believe that the underlying congressional purpose was to provide an administrative procedure for the determination of complaints under which the administering agency was to use its powers to enforce the section in question. And though the Rehabilitation Act failed directly to provide for judicial review of such an administrative procedure, the Department of Labor evidently thought that such review might be possible * * *. The implementing regulations do incorporate the elaborate and sophisticated hearing practice and procedure used to enforce equal opportunity under Executive Order No. 11,246; these elaborate hearing provisions culminate, or may culminate, in a final administrative order, which is in our view reviewable like other administrative orders under the Administrative Procedure Act and particularly 5 U.S.C. §§ 701–706.

To be sure, the regulations' failure to specify time limits has presented a problem that is particularly evident in the case at bar. The Department of Labor has, contrary to the will of Congress, been unable to comply speedily with the provisions of the Rehabilitation Act. This has resulted in the Department's taking the position in the past, although it takes no position here, that a private cause of action should be permitted in order to remedy section 503 violations more effectively and indeed an acknowledgment that "[t]he net effect of [OFCCP] discretion is that there is no assurance that compliance decisions are not tempered by political, procurement, personal or other potentially competing or conflicting requirements," OFCCP Task Force, Preliminary Report on the Revitalization of the Federal Contract Compliance Program (1977). The agency backlog and its position in favor of recognition of a private remedy are set forth in an affidavit by the director of the OFCCP * * *. While lack of executive resources to enforce an act of Congress is regrettable, it is hardly the judiciary's role to redress that lack by inferring a judicial remedy.

Moreover, although a department's position on whether an implied private cause of action exists is entitled to judicial consideration, an agency's expertise, "[e]ven if the agency spoke with a consistent voice, * * * is of limited value when the narrow legal issue is one peculiarly reserved for judicial resolution, namely whether a cause of action should be implied by judicial interpretation in favor of a particular class of litigants." Piper v. Chris-Craft Industries, 430 U.S. at 41 n. 27, 97 S.Ct. at 949. * * *

In any case, an after-the-fact acknowledgment of inadequacy because of limited departmental resources is not the equivalent of a long-held, firmly established, well-reasoned position that the agency has made known to Congress and to the courts over the years, such as in *Cannon* * * *.

We need not deal with the fourth Cort v. Ash factor; it is plain enough that discrimination against the disabled has not been a matter traditionally relegated to state law. But we conclude, as have the other three courts of appeals that have passed upon the question, that no implied private right of action exists under section 503, recognizing that the glass through which we see is by no means crystal clear but is so cloudy as to be barely translucent.

Judgment reversed.

IRVING R. KAUFMAN, CIRCUIT JUDGE (dissenting).

* * *

The threshold question under *Cort* is whether the plaintiff was one of the class for whose "especial benefit" § 503 was enacted. This inquiry focuses on whether Congress intended to benefit a clearly defined class rather than to protect the general public. Looking to the language of the statute may provide evidence of this intent. Here, the language of § 503(a) and (b) specifically identifies the class, "handicapped individuals," and provides equal employment opportunities for all who fall within it. Indeed, relying on this approach to the first *Cort* factor, virtually all of the district courts analyzing § 503, including those that ultimately found no private right of action, have concluded that the statute was enacted for the "especial benefit" of the handicapped.

The majority, however, contends that when § 503 is examined for "right- or duty-creating language," Cannon v. University of Chicago, no indication of an intention to establish a federal right in favor of the plaintiff can be found. While the absence of such a "talismanic incantation," is less relevant than the substance of the obligations created, the affirmative action language of § 503 may appear to create, when scrutinized closely, a duty for federal agencies, it is argued, not for employers.

Although the duty-creating phrases are not conclusive in either direction, an analysis of the second and more important *Cort* factor, contrary to the majority's position, offers exceedingly strong evidence for giving a right of action to the handicapped individual. In considering whether the legislative history of § 503 sheds light on the private right of action question, three statutes carry weight and are directly relevant to our determination: the 1973 Rehabilitation Act, the Rehabilitation Act Amendments of 1974, and the attorney's fees provisions of the Rehabilitation, Comprehensive Services, and Developmental Disabilities Amendments of 1978.

I do not quarrel with the assertion that the legislative history of the 1973 Act provides little assistance. Debate primarily focused on the establishment of federally-funded programs for the handicapped, not on the relatively non-controversial antidiscrimination provisions of §§ 503 and 504. Nor is an examination of the history surrounding the 1974 Amendments to the Act particularly enlightening, because discussion centered on redefining "handicapped individual," not on explicating the full meaning of §§ 503 and 504. The conference report, however, lends guidance. It states that § 504 permits a "judicial remedy through private action," and notes, as the majority recognizes, that both sections will be administered to effect a uniform appropach to discrimination against handicapped persons. Such langauge, I believe, should fairly be read to suggest that, since Congress recognized a private right of action under § 504, such a remedy would not be inconsistent with Congress's purpose in § 503. In addition, during the Senate debate, Senator Robert Stafford, one of the principal sponsors of the original Act and its later amendments, stated that enforcement of both sections would be similar to that of § 601 of the Civil Rights Act and § 901 of the Education Amendments of 1972. Although a private right of action was found to exist for the Education Amendments in *Cannon*, supra, the majority denigrates the value of Senator Stafford's remarks.

More conclusive evidence of a congressional intent to authorize a private action is found in the 1978 attorney's fees amendments. This provision explicitly presumes private judicial actions because attorney's fees are made available to parties "other than the United States" and because the language looks to actions before "courts," not administrative agencies. The Senate Report and Senate debates also indicate that private actions were envisioned. The majority concedes that the accompanying Senate Report explicitly stated that the availability of attorney's fees was intended to aid handicapped individuals in "vindicating private rights of action in the case of section * * * 503 cases." The majority further acknowledges that H.R.Rep.No.1149, took precisely the same position.

My brothers have decided that this legislative material is "unpersuasive" and virtually dismiss it. They adopt the rationale that failure to discuss the then-existing case law indicates that references to the availability of a § 503 private right of action were "inadvertent." I realize that "even Homer nods," but such a bald refusal to acknowledge a clear, express statement of congressional intent is inexcusable. Granted, the evidence surrounding the passage of the 1978 attorney's fees amendments carries less weight than contemporary legislative history, but this evidence is strongly relevant in determining what members of Congress assumed they had done several years previously. It is clear from the legislative history that Congress premised the attorney's fees provision on the existence of an implied remedy. Furthermore, interpreting an attorney's fees amendment to reveal Congress's intent is surely not a novel method of construction, as the majority's position would appear to suggest. In *Cannon*, interpretation of the legislative background of the attorney's fees amendment to § 901 of Title IX served as the basis for the Court's recognition of a private right of action. Indeed, Congress is generally considered to be a creditable interpreter of its actions, and judicial deference to these interpretations is appropriate.

Here, the notion that the view of a subsequent Congress forms a weak foundation for inferring the intent of an earlier one, is not a persuasive argument. Many members of the relevant committees in 1978 were also members of those committees in 1973. I doubt that these distinguished members of Congress who labored over trail-blazing legislation would have forgotten what they had intended a mere five years before the 1978 amendments. Contrary to the majority's poorly-supported and tenuous conclusion that the legislative history is ambiguous, the legislative history clearly indicates that Congress, in passing the attorney's fees amendments of 1978, assumed that a private right of action was created with the passage of § 503 in 1973. This assumption does not reflect a subsequent desire to amend the original enactment; rather, it illuminates the initial intent of the draftsmen.

The third factor of the *Cort* analysis considers whether a private right of action would support Congress's purpose in enacting the statutory scheme. Implication of a private right of action is not inconsistent with the underlying purpose of § 503—effective administrative enforcement. The Department of Labor and its office of Federal Contract Compliance Programs, it is interesting to note, have stated that the existence of an implied remedy would enhance informal conciliation and administrative enforcement in general. Although the majority lightly dismisses these agency opinions, courts generally believe they are deserving of substantial weight.

My brothers, in concluding that the mandates of the third *Cort* factor are not fulfilled, rely on an analysis contained in CETA Workers' Org. Comm. v. City of New York. Such reliance is misplaced because *CETA* is readily distinguishable. The statutory presumption in favor of administrative enforcement is much more potent under the Comprehensive Employment and Training Act ("CETA") than it is under the Rehabilitation Act. Section 106 provides, in great detail, a sophisticated scheme for enforcement of CETA. In particular, the Secretary of Labor is required to reach a final determination on a complaint within 120 days. This complex enforcement mechanism suggests the "primacy" and "exclusivity" of the administrative grievance procedures.

No such detailed machinery exists under the Rehabilitation Act, and even the accompanying Regulations contain no deadlines for the processing of complaints. Surely, it does not require straining the legislative interpretation to envision a private right of action complementing the statutory enforcement mechanism for § 503. Indeed, the Department of Labor endorses this view. I submit that analysis of the third *Cort* factor differs for the two statutes. More importantly, it indicates that Congress would be more inclined to create a private right of action for a statute where provisions for administrative enforcement are not detailed and precise. But the majority, admitting that the CETA scheme is more fully developed, still finds the distinctions between the two of little significance even in light of the Department of Labor's statement that an implied right of action for § 503 violations should be permitted. The majority, it appears, attaches greater weight to tangential *exempla* than to direct, explicit evidence.

* * *

* * * I believe the only reasonable conclusion to be reached from applying the *Cort* analysis is that Congress intended handicapped individuals to have a private remedy under § 503. * * *

NOTES AND PROBLEMS FOR DISCUSSION

1. Does the opinion in the principal case evidence the operation of a presumption against the recognition of an implied private right of action? In his dissenting opinion in CANNON v. UNIVERSITY OF CHICAGO, 441 U.S. 677, 749, 99 S.Ct. 1946, 1985, 60 L.Ed.2d 560, 608 (1979), Justice Powell recommended that the Court "not condone the implication of any private action from a federal statute absent the most compelling evidence that Congress in fact intended such an action to exist." Should such a presumption operate in the context of a civil rights statute whose administrative remedy not only does not redress, but may compound, the injury suffered by the individual discriminatee? For a proposal urging the adoption of a presumption in favor of recognizing private rights of action under these circumstances, see Note, Implied Rights of Action Under the Rehabilitation Act of 1973, 68 Geo.L.J. 1229, 1254–1260 (1980). See also, Note, Implied Rights of Action to Enforce Civil Rights: The Case For a Sympathetic View, 87 Yale L.J. 1378 (1978).

2. Could a plaintiff avoid the ruling in *Davis* by asserting a claim as a third party beneficiary of the affirmative action provision in the employer's contract with the government? See D'Amato v. Wisconsin Gas Co., 760 F.2d 1474 (7th Cir. 1985) (rejecting third party beneficiary claim on the grounds that the parties to the contract did not intend to make the handicapped direct beneficiaries of their contracts and that Congress intended that the administrative scheme be the sole avenue of redress for the handicapped); Hodges v. Atchison,

T. & S.F. Ry., 728 F.2d 414 (10th Cir. 1984), cert. denied, 469 U.S. 822, 105 S.Ct. 97, 83 L.Ed.2d 43 (1985) (rejecting third party beneficiary claim as "but another aspect of the implied right of action argument").

3. Assume a state university entered into a contract to provide scientific research for the federal government and discriminated against a handicapped applicant for a job in that federally financed program. Can the applicant bring a private action against the university under 42 U.S.C. § 1983 alleging that the university deprived him of rights secured by § 503 of the Rehabilitation Act? Is the holding in *Davis* relevant to this issue? See Meyerson v. State of Arizona, 709 F.2d 1235 (9th Cir. 1983), vacated and remanded on other grounds in light of Consolidated Rail v. Darrone, 465 U.S. 1095, 104 S.Ct. 1584, 80 L.Ed. 2d 118 (1984).

4. The 1974 amendments to the Rehabilitation Act broadened the definition of "handicapped individual" to include any person who:

> "(i) has a physical or mental impairment which substantially limits one or more of such person's major life activities,
>
> "(ii) has a record of such impairment, or
>
> "(iii) is regarded as having such an impairment."

29 U.S.C. § 706(7) (1976).

In determining what constitutes a handicap for the purposes of the Act, the courts and federal agencies have concentrated on interpreting two key statutory terms—"impairment" and "substantially limits". The first of these two definitional problems has arisen most frequently in connection with so-called voluntary disabilities. Alcoholics, for example, have been held to be handicapped within the meaning of the Act. Whitaker v. Board of Higher Education, 461 F.Supp. 99 (E.D.N.Y.1978). So have drug addicts. Davis v. Bucher, 451 F.Supp. 791 (E.D.Pa.1978). These rulings, of course, only meant that present, former or perceived alcoholics and drug addicts could not be discriminated against if they were "otherwise qualified"—i.e., if the disability did not impair their job performance. In 1978, Congress amended the statutory definition of handicapped persons to exclude from protection under §§ 503 and 504 any current alcohol or drug abuser whose current use prevents the user from performing his or her job duties or whose use constitutes a threat to property or the safety of others. 29 U.S.C. § 706(7)B (Supp.1980); see infra at 1055. Does this mean that a federal employee who is a current drug or alcohol abuser can state a claim under § 501 and require the government to make a reasonable accommodation to his or her condition? See Whitlock v. Donovan, 598 F.Supp. 126 (D.D.C.1984) (federal government required to make reasonable accommodation to alcoholic employee under § 501).

A question also has been raised as to whether the handicap must result in a present impairment. Consider the following:

A city police department refused to hire an applicant when a pre-employment physical examination revealed that he suffered from a degenerative knee condition. According to the examining physician's report, while the applicant's knees were fully functional at present, there was a significant likelihood of degenerative changes in his knees in the future. These changes, the report concluded, would prevent the applicant from performing several job duties that put pressure on a patrol officer's knees. Assuming the police department receives federal funding, has it violated § 504? Compare Chicago, Milwaukee, St. Paul & Pacific Railroad Co. v. Washington State Human Rights Commission, 11 FEP Cases 854 (Wash.Super.Ct.1975), reversed in part and vacated in part on other grounds, 87 Wn.2d 802, 557 P.2d 307 (1976); with Chrysler Outboard Corp. v. Department of Industry, Labor & Human Relations, 14 FEP Cases 344 (Wis.Cir.Ct. 1976). See also Miller, Hiring the Handicapped: An Analysis of Laws Prohibiting Discrimination Against the Handicapped in Employment, 16 Gonz.L.Rev. 23 (1980).

The U.S. Postal Service refused to hire an epileptic applicant who had a history of one grand mal seizure per year for a position that would involve driving a vehicle or using dangerous machinery with moving parts. It contended that this person was not an "otherwise qualified" handicapped person on the ground that she would create an "elevated risk" of injury to herself or others. The court stated that in some cases it is necessary to screen out job applicants on the basis of possible future injury. To do so, however, the court added, the defendant must show a "reasonable probability of substantial harm" based on an ad hoc analysis of the plaintiff's work and medical history and the requirements of the job in question. Mantolete v. Bolger, 767 F.2d 1416 (9th Cir. 1985).

While the courts have tended to define "impairment" on an ad hoc basis, the federal agencies have chosen to include in their regulations a list of specific disabilities they view as falling within the ambit of the statute. For example, the Department of Health and Human Services' regulations include cosmetic disfigurement, sight, speech, hearing, reproductive and learning impairment, and mental retardation as covered disabilities. They also specifically exclude economic, cultural and environmental disadvantages, prison records, homosexuality and age. See 45 CFR 84.3(i) (1979). In addition, one federal trial court denied a motion to dismiss for failure to state a claim in a § 501 case brought against the Postal Service by a transsexual who alleged that she was handicapped by reason of her medically and psychologically established need for gender reassignment surgery and that this impairment substantially limited her major life activity of working. Doe v. United States Postal Service, 37 FEP Cases 1867 (D.D.C.1985). Should the statute apply to contagious diseases such as, for example, tuberculosis? See Arline v. School Board of Nassau County, 772 F.2d 759 (11th Cir. 1985), cert. granted, 475 U.S. ___, 106 S.Ct. 1633, 90 L.Ed.2d 179 (1986). Can being left-handed constitute an "impairment"? See de La Torres v. Bolger, 781 F.2d 1134 (5th Cir. 1986). What about AIDS? Would it make a difference whether an employer receiving federal financial assistance refused an applicant because that individual was suffering from the disabling effects of AIDS or whether the employer's decision was based on its fear or belief that the applicant was capable of transmitting the disease? On June 23, 1986, the Justice Department released a memorandum which it had sent to the U.S. Department of Health and Human Services (HHS). In this memo, the Justice Department concluded that § 504 prohibited covered employers from discriminating on the basis of the disabling effects of AIDS but that the statute did not prevent employers from taking measures to prevent the spread of the disease. Thus, according to this opinion, while a covered employer would violate the statute by discriminating against an otherwise qualified applicant because that individual is suffering from the effects of AIDS, the statute would not prohibit discrimination against an individual, regardless of whether that person was or was not suffering from the effects of AIDS, as long as the decision was based exclusively on the employer's belief that the applicant was capable of transmitting AIDS. This distinction was predicated on the conclusion that while the disabling effects of AIDS on its victims qualify as handicaps, the ability to transmit a disease is not a "handicap" within the meaning of the statute because it does not constitute an "impairment that substantially limits a major life activity". Accordingly, the perception that an individual is able to spread the disease does not satisfy the statutory standard of being "regarded as having . . . an impairment". The memorandum also stated that a uniform rule could not be applied to individuals who have AIDS-related complex (described as "signs and symptoms that are suggestive of the syndrome but do not manifest the secondary complications of the disease") because the determination of whether the disabling effects of ARC constitute a handicap must be made on an *ad hoc* basis. Finally, the Department opinion declared that individuals who test positive for antibodies to the HTLV–III virus cannot be classified as handicapped solely on the basis of such seropositivity since such individuals have not yet suffered any substantial adverse health consequences.

Under this memorandum's interpretation of § 504, would it matter whether the employer's fear of communicability was unreasonable? See e.g., Mann et. al., Prevalence of HTLV–III/LAV In Household Contacts of Patients With Confirmed AIDS and Controls in Kinshasa, Zaire, 256 J.A.M.A. 721 (1986) (finding no evidence of AIDS transmission within households of persons with AIDS). In the educational context, at least one court has interpreted § 504 to protect a child's right to attend school even if the child has AIDS. See Application of District 27 Community School Board v. Board of Education, 130 Misc.2d 398, 502 N.Y.S.2d 325 (Sup.Ct.1986). This opinion is consistent with prior caselaw concerning children with Hepatitis B. See e.g., New York State Ass'n for Retarded Children, Inc. v. Carey, 466 F.Supp. 479 (E.D.N.Y.1978), affirmed, 612 F.2d 644 (2d Cir. 1979).

Does the Justice Department's memorandum require an employer to respond to fear of communicability consistently among different ailments? For example, a state government employee was discharged from a clerical job after the employer learned that he had AIDS. The employee filed a complaint under § 504; the government agency responded that it was concerned about communicability. The employee countered that several of his co-workers were permitted to smoke in the office even though doctors could not assure that exposure to smoke would not cause lung cancer. The employee has prevailed in two rounds of administrative proceedings and this case is pending before a federal district court. Shuttleworth v. Broward County, 639 F.Supp. 654 (S.D.Fla.1986); 1 Aids Policy & Law #7 (BNA) (April 23, 1986), at 1–2. See generally, Leonard, Employment Discrimination Against Persons With AIDS, 10 U. of Dayton L.Rev. 681 (1985); Note, AIDS: Does It Qualify As A "Handicap" Under The Rehabilitation Act of 1973?, 61 Not.D.L.Rev. 572 (1986).

With respect to the second interpretative question, the Department of Labor's Office of Federal Contract Compliance Programs regulations state that a handicapped person is "substantially limited" if she or he is "likely to experience difficulty in securing, retaining or advancing in employment" because of the handicap. Does this mean that a worker who is denied a particular position because of her handicap, but who can successfully perform several other similar or related jobs, is covered by the Act? In E.E. Black, Limited v. Marshall, 497 F.Supp. 1088 (D.Ha.1980), the trial court reversed the Assistant Secretary of Labor's determination that an individual was substantially limited if the impairment operated to bar him from the particular job of his choice. At the same time, the court refused to limit statutory protection to persons whose disability precluded almost any type of employment. The court concluded that Congress' use of "substantially" to modify "limits" reflected its intent to cover individuals whose disability impaired employment in their chosen field. See also Jasany v. United States Postal Service, 755 F.2d 1244 (6th Cir. 1985) (adopting *E.E. Black* interpretation of "substantially limited"). In Forrisi v. Bowen, 794 F.2d 931 (4th Cir. 1986), for example, the court concluded that an individual with acrophobia—fear of heights—was not "substantially limited" simply because he could not perform his chosen occupation in a setting that also required him to climb stairways and ladders.

5. The Rehabilitation Act is not the only source of employment rights enjoyed by handicapped persons. State and local government employees can look to the Fourteenth Amendment for redress from handicap discrimination. Absolute rules precluding all employment on the basis of specified disabilities, it has been held, use irrebutable presumptions in violation of the Due Process Clause. See e.g., Gurmankin v. Costanzo, 556 F.2d 184 (3d Cir. 1977) (local school board's refusal to allow blind applicants to take qualifying exam violates Due Process Clause of Fourteenth Amendment). The irrebutable presumption doctrine, however, is no longer favored by the Supreme Court. Accordingly, constitutional challenges to handicap discrimination by state and local government workers are likely to focus on the Equal Protection Clause. Such was the case, for example, in NEW YORK CITY TRANSIT AUTHORITY v. BEAZER, 440 U.S. 568, 99 S.Ct. 1355, 59 L.Ed.2d 587 (1979). The trial court had ruled that the defendant's blanket exclusion of methadone users from all positions violated the Due Process Clause because it created an irrebutable presumption of unemployability as to all methadone users. The Supreme Court noted that the respondent employees no longer asserted that argument and, moreover, that it was without merit. The Court then turned to the respondent's equal protection claim and found that it survived scrutiny under the rationality standard.

Can a federal employee state a constitutional cause of action for handicap discrimination? Does § 505 of the Rehabilitation Act suggest that the Court's ruling in Brown v. G.S.A. should be extended to make the Rehabilitation Act the exclusive remedy for such federal employee claims? See Shirey v. Campbell, 27 FEP Cases 1142 (D.D.C. 1980), reversed and remanded on other grounds, 670 F.2d 1188 (D.C.Cir. 1982); Connolly v. United States Postal Service, 579 F.Supp. 305 (D.Mass.1984); Ruth Anne M. v. Alvin Independent School District, 532 F.Supp. 460 (S.D.Tex.1982).

Employees of private businesses that neither receive federal funding nor perform under federal contracts or subcontracts exceeding $2500, of course, are not covered by the Rehabilitation Act at all. They also have no remedy against handicap bias under the other federal antidiscrimination statutes. Congress has repeatedly rejected attempts to amend Title VII to include handicap as a prohibited basis of discrimination. Handicapped persons have been held to not fall within the class of traditional victims of invidious discrimination covered by § 1985(c). See Cain v. Archdiocese of Kansas City, Kansas, 508 F.Supp. 1021 (D.Kan.1981). While no reported case can be found in which a plaintiff asserted a claim of handicap discrimination under § 1981, it is unlikely that the statute would be interpreted to extend to such an action. Of course, if a private employer's handicap bar operates to disproportionately exclude members of a Title VII-protected class, relief may be available under Title VII. See New York City Transit Authority v. Beazer, supra.

As a result of the unavailability of a federal statutory remedy, state law occupies the preeminent position with respect to private sector employee claims of handicap bias. Over forty states have enacted legislation that prohibits discrimination against handicapped persons. Interestingly, though, while the federal statute encompasses mental and physical disability unrelated to job performance, the laws in seventeen states define handicap solely in terms of physical disablity.

6. In addition to its obligations under § 503, any federal contractor or subcontractor involved with a federal contract in the amount of $10,000 or more for the procurement of personal property and non-personal services (including construction), is required by the Vietnam Era Veterans Assistance Act of 1974, as amended, 38 U.S.C. § 2012 (Supp.1981), to take affirmative action to employ and advance in employment disabled veterans of the Vietnam era. If a covered veteran believes that a contractor has not complied with this requirement, the statute athorizes him to file a complaint with the Secretary of Labor. The Act also requires all federal executive departments and agencies to include in the affirmative action hiring and advancement plans required by § 501 of the Rehabilitation Act, a separate specification of their plans to employ and advance disabled Vietnam era veterans. 38 U.S.C. § 2014.

7. Can an aggrieved employee file suit to compel the Secretary of Labor to institute § 503(b) enforcement proceedings against a government contractor? See Moon v. Donovan, 29 FEP Cases 1780 (N.D.Ga.1982) (plaintiff can bring such a cause of action under Administrative Procedure Act). See also Salvador v. Bell, 622 F.Supp. 438 (N.D.Ill.1985) (handicapped individual participating in program that received funding from U.S. Department of Education does not have private right of action under § 504 against Secretary of Education for allegedly failing to investigate his handicap discrimination complaint).

Part IV

REMEDIES

Chapter 12

MONETARY RELIEF

ALBEMARLE PAPER CO. v. MOODY

Supreme Court of the United States, 1975.
422 U.S. 405, 95 S.Ct. 2362, 45 L.Ed.2d 280.

[The facts of the case are set out at p. 133, supra. The district court found that black employees had been locked into lower paying job descriptions by a discriminatory seniority system and ordered defendants to implement a system of plant-wide seniority. The court refused, however, to award back pay to the plaintiff's class on the grounds that (1) the employer's breach of Title VII was not in "bad faith," and (2) the plaintiffs had delayed making their back pay claim until five years after the complaint was filed, thereby prejudicing the defendants. The Court of Appeals reversed, holding that back pay could properly be requested by amending the pleadings and that an award could not be denied merely because the employer had not acted in "bad faith."]

* * *

II

Whether a particular member of the plaintiff class should have been awarded any backpay and, if so, how much, are questions not involved in this review. The equities of individual cases were never reached. Though at least some of the members of the plaintiff class obviously suffered a loss of wage opportunities on account of Albemarle's unlawfully discriminatory system of job seniority, the District Court decided that *no* backpay should be awarded to *anyone* in the class. The court declined to make such an award on two stated grounds: the lack of "evidence of bad faith non-compliance with the Act," and the fact that "the defendants would be substantially prejudiced" by an award of backpay that was demanded contrary to an earlier representation and late in the progress of the litigation. Relying directly on Newman v. Piggie Park Enterprises, 390 U.S. 400, 88 S.Ct. 964, 19 L.Ed.2d 1263 (1968), the Court of Appeals reversed, holding that backpay could be denied only in "special circumstances." The petitioners argue that the Court of Appeals was in error—that a district court has virtually unfettered discretion to award or deny backpay, and that there was no abuse of that discretion here.[8]

Piggie Park Enterprises, supra, is not directly in point. The Court held there that attorneys' fees should "ordinarily" be awarded—i.e., in all but "special circumstances"—to plaintiffs successful in obtaining injunctions against discrimination in public accommodations, under Title II of the Civil Rights Act of 1964. While the Act appears to leave Title II fee awards to the district court's discretion, 42 U.S.C. § 2000a–3(b), the court determined that the great public interest in having injunctive actions brought could be vindicated only if successful plaintiffs, acting as "private attorneys general," were awarded attorneys' fees in all but very unusual circumstances. There is, of course, an equally strong public interest in having injunctive actions brought under Title VII, to eradicate discriminatory employment practices. But this interest can be vindicated by applying the *Piggie Park* standard to the *attorneys' fees* provision of Title VII, 42 U.S.C. § 2000e–5(k), see Northcross v. Memphis Board of Education, 412 U.S. 427, 428, 93 S.Ct. 2201, 2202, 37 L.Ed.2d 48 (1973). For guidance as to the granting and denial of *backpay,* one must, therefore, look elsewhere.

The petitioners contend that the statutory scheme provides no guidance, beyond indicating that backpay awards are within the district court's discretion. We disagree. It is true that backpay is not an automatic or mandatory remedy; like all other remedies under the Act, it is one which the courts "may" invoke.[9] The scheme implicitly

8. The petitioners also contend that no backpay can be awarded to those unnamed parties in the plaintiff class who have not themselves filed charges with the EEOC. We reject this contention. The Courts of Appeals that have confronted the issue are unanimous in recognizing that backpay may be awarded on a class basis under Title VII without exhaustion of administrative procedures by the unnamed class members. See, e.g., Rosen v. Public Service Electric & Gas Co., 409 F.2d 775, 780 (CA3 1969), and 477 F.2d 90, 95–96 (CA3 1973); Robinson v. Lorillard Corp., 444 F.2d 791, 802 (CA4 1971); United States v. Georgia Power Co., 474 F.2d 906, 919–921 (CA5 1973); Head v. Timken Roller Bearing Co., supra, at 876; Bowe v. Colgate-Palmolive Co., 416 F.2d 711, 719–721 (CA7 1969); United States v. N. L. Industries, Inc., 479 F.2d 354, 378–379 (CA8 1973). The Congress plainly ratified this construction of the Act in the course of enacting the Equal Employment Opportunity Act of 1972, Pub.L. 92–261, 86 Stat. 103. The House of Representatives passed a bill, H.R. 1746, 92d Cong., 1st Sess., that would have barred, in § 3(e), an award of backpay to any individual who "neither filed a charge [with the EEOC] nor was named in a charge or amendment thereto." But the Senate Committee on Labor and Public Welfare recommended, instead, the re-enactment of the backpay provision without such a limitation, and cited with approval several cases holding that backpay was awardable to class members who had not personally filed, nor been named in, charges to the EEOC, S.Rep. No. 92–415, p. 27 (1971). See also 118 Cong.Rec. 4942 (1972). The Senate passed a bill without the House's limitation, id., at 4944, and the Conference Committee adopted the Senate position. A Section-by-Section Analysis of the Conference Committee's resolution notes that "[a] provision limiting class actions was contained in the House bill and specifically rejected by the Conference Committee," id., at 7168, 7565. The Conference Committee bill was accepted by both Chambers. Id., at 7170, 7573.

9. Title 42 U.S.C. § 2000e-5(g) (1970 ed., Supp. III) provides:

"If the court finds that the respondent has intentionally engaged in or is intentionally engaging in an unlawful employment practice charged in the complaint, the court may enjoin the respondent from engaging in such unlawful employment practice, and order such affirmative action as may be appropriate, which

recognizes that there may be cases calling for one remedy but not another, and—owing to the structure of the federal judiciary—these choices are, of course, left in the first instance to the district courts. However, such discretionary choices are not left to a court's "inclination, but to its judgment; and its judgment is to be guided by sound legal principles." United States v. Burr, 25 F.Cas.No.14,692d, pp. 30, 35 (CC Va.1807) (Marshall, C. J.). The power to award backpay was bestowed by Congress, as part of a complex legislative design directed at a historic evil of national proportions. A court must exercise this power "in light of the large objectives of the Act," Hecht Co. v. Bowles, 321 U.S. 321, 331, 64 S.Ct. 587, 592, 88 L.Ed. 754 (1944). That the court's discretion is equitable in nature, see Curtis v. Loether, 415 U.S. 189, 197, 94 S.Ct. 1005, 1010, 39 L.Ed.2d 260 (1974), hardly means that it is unfettered by meaningful standards or shielded from thorough appellate review. In Mitchell v. Robert DeMario Jewelry, 361 U.S. 288, 292, 80 S.Ct. 332, 335, 4 L.Ed.2d 323 (1960), this Court held, in the face of a silent statute, that district courts enjoyed the "historic power of equity" to award lost wages to workmen unlawfully discriminated against under § 17 of the Fair Labor Standards Act of 1938, 52 Stat. 1069, as amended, 29 U.S.C. § 217 (1958 ed). The Court simultaneously noted that "the statutory purposes [leave] little room for the exercise of discretion not to order reimbursement." 361 U.S., at 296, 80 S.Ct. at 337.

It is true that "[e]quity eschews mechanical rules * * * [and] depends on flexibility." Holmberg v. Armbrecht, 327 U.S. 392, 396, 66 S.Ct. 582, 584, 90 L.Ed. 743 (1946). But when Congress invokes the Chancellor's conscience to further transcendent legislative purposes, what is required is the principled application of standards consistent with those purposes and not "equity [which] varies like the Chancellor's foot."[10] Important national goals would be frustrated by a regime of discretion that "produce[d] different results for breaches of duty in situations that cannot be differentiated in policy." Moragne v. States Marine Lines, 398 U.S. 375, 405, 90 S.Ct. 1772, 1790, 26 L.Ed.2d 339 (1970).

may include, but is not limited to, reinstatement or hiring of employees, with or without back pay (payable by the employer, employment agency, or labor organization, as the case may be, responsible for the unlawful employment practice), or any other equitable relief as the court deems appropriate. Back pay liability shall not accrue from a date more than two years prior to the filing of a charge with the Commission. Interim earnings or amounts earnable with reasonable diligence by the person or persons discriminated against shall operate to reduce the back pay otherwise allowable. No order of the court shall require the admission or reinstatement of an individual as a member of a union, or the hiring, reinstatement, or promotion of an individual as an employee, or the payment to him of any back pay, if such individual was refused admission, suspended, or expelled, or was refused employment or advancement or was suspended or discharged for any reason other than discrimination on account of race, color, religion, sex, or national origin or in violation of section 2000e–3(a) of this title."

10. Eldon, L. C., in Gee v. Pritchard, 2 Swans. *403, *414, 36 Eng.Rep. 670, 674 (1818).

The District Court's decision must therefore be measured against the purposes which inform Title VII. As the Court observed in Griggs v. Duke Power Co., 401 U.S., at 429–430, 91 S.Ct., at 853, the primary objective was a prophylactic one:

> "It was to achieve equality of employment opportunities and remove barriers that have operated in the past to favor an identifiable group of white employees over other employees."

Backpay has an obvious connection with this purpose. If employers faced only the prospect of an injunctive order, they would have little incentive to shun practices of dubious legality. It is the reasonably certain prospect of a backpay award that "provide[s] the spur or catalyst which causes employers and unions to self-examine and to self-evaluate their employment practices and to endeavor to eliminate, so far as possible, the last vestiges of an unfortunate and ignominious page in this country's history." United States v. N. L. Industries, Inc., 8 Cir., 479 F.2d at 354, 379 (CA8 1973).

It is also the purpose of Title VII to make persons whole for injuries suffered on account of unlawful employment discrimination. This is shown by the very fact that Congress took care to arm the courts with full equitable powers. For it is the historic purpose of equity to "secur[e] complete justice," Brown v. Swann, 10 Pet. 497, 503, 9 L.Ed. 508 (1836); see also Porter v. Warner Holding Co., 328 U.S. 395, 397–398, 66 S.Ct. 1086, 1088–1089, 90 L.Ed. 1332 (1946). "[W]here federally protected rights have been invaded, it has been the rule from the beginning that courts will be alert to adjust their remedies so as to grant the necessary relief." Bell v. Hood, 327 U.S. 678, 684, 66 S.Ct. 773, 777, 90 L.Ed. 939 (1946). Title VII deals with legal injuries of an economic character occasioned by racial or other antiminority discrimination. The terms "complete justice" and "necessary relief" have acquired a clear meaning in such circumstances. Where racial discrimination is concerned, "the [district] court has not merely the power but the duty to render a decree which will so far as possible eliminate the discriminatory effects of the past as well as bar like discrimination in the future." Louisiana v. United States, 380 U.S. 145, 154, 85 S.Ct. 817, 822, 13 L.Ed.2d 709 (1965). And where a legal injury is of an economic character,

> "[t]he general rule is, that when a wrong has been done, and the law gives a remedy, the compensation shall be equal to the injury. The latter is the standard by which the former is to be measured. The injured party is to be placed, as near as may be, in the situation he would have occupied if the wrong had not been committed." Wicker v. Hoppock, 6 Wall. 94, 99, 18 L.Ed. 752 (1867).

The "make whole" purpose of Title VII is made evident by the legislative history. The backpay provision was expressly modeled on the backpay provision of the National Labor Relations Act.[11] Under

11. Section 10(c) of the NLRA, 49 Stat. 454, as amended, 29 U.S.C. § 160(c), provides that when the Labor Board has found that a person has committed an "unfair

that Act, "[m]aking the workers whole for losses suffered on account of an unfair labor practice is part of the vindication of the public policy which the Board enforces." Phelps Dodge Corp. v. NLRB, 313 U.S. 177, 197, 61 S.Ct. 845, 854, 85 L.Ed. 1271 (1941). See also Nathanson v. NLRB, 344 U.S. 25, 27, 73 S.Ct. 80, 82, 97 L.Ed. 23; NLRB v. J. H. Rutter-Rex Mfg. Co., 396 U.S. 258, 263, 90 S.Ct. 417, 420, 24 L.Ed.2d 405 (1969). We may assume that Congress was aware that the Board, since its inception, has awarded backpay as a matter of course—not randomly or in the exercise of a standardless discretion, and not merely where employer violations are peculiarly deliberate, egregious, or inexcusable.[12] Furthermore, in passing the Equal Employment Opportunity Act of 1972, Congress considered several bills to limit the judicial power to award backpay. These limiting efforts were rejected, and the backpay provision was re-enacted substantially in its original form.[13] A Section-by-Section Analysis introduced by Senator Williams to accompany the Conference Committee Report on the 1972 Act strongly reaffirmed the "make whole" purpose of Title VII:

labor practice," the Board "shall issue" an order "requiring such person to cease and desist from such unfair labor practice, and to take such affirmative action including reinstatement of employees with or without back pay, as will effectuate the policies of this subchapter." The backpay provision of Title VII provides that when the court has found "an unlawful employment practice," it "may enjoin" the practice "and order such affirmative action as may be appropriate, which may include, but is not limited to, reinstatement or hiring of employees, with or without back pay * * *." 42 U.S.C. § 2000e–5(g) (1970 ed., Supp. III). The framers of Title VII stated that they were using the NLRA provision as a model. 110 Cong.Rec. 6549 (1964) (remarks of Sen. Humphrey); id., at 7214 (interpretative memorandum by Sens. Clark and Case). In early versions of the Title VII provision on remedies, it was stated that a court "may" issue injunctions, but "shall" order appropriate affirmative action. This anomaly was removed by Substitute Amendment No. 656, 110 Cong.Rec. 12814, 12819 (1964). The framers regarded this as merely a "minor language change," id., at 12723–12724 (remarks of Sen. Humphrey). We can find here no intent to back away from the NLRA model or to denigrate in any way the status of backpay relief.

12. "The finding of an unfair labor practice and discriminatory discharge is presumptive proof that some back pay is owed by the employer," NLRB v. Mastro Plastics Corp., 354 F.2d 170, 178 (CA2 1965). While the backpay decision rests in the NLRB's discretion, and not with the courts, NLRB v. J. H. Rutter-Rex Mfg. Co., 396 U.S. 258, 263, 90 S.Ct. 417, 420, 24 L.Ed.2d 405 (1969), the Board has from its inception pursued "a practically uniform policy with respect to these orders requiring affirmative action." NLRB, First Annual Report 124 (1936).

"[I] all but a few cases involving discriminatory discharges, discriminatory refusals to employ or reinstate, or discriminatory demotions in violation of section 8(3), the Board has ordered the employer to offer reinstatement to the employee discriminated against and to make whole such employee for any loss of pay that he has suffered by reason of the discrimination." NLRB Annual Report, Second p. 148 (1937).

13. As to the unsuccessful effort to restrict class actions for backpay, see n. 8, *supra*. In addition, the Senate rejected an amendment which would have required a jury trial in Title VII cases involving backpay, 118 Cong.Rec. 4917, 4919–4920 (1972) (remarks of Sens. Ervin and Javits), and rejected a provision that would have limited backpay liability to a date two years prior to filing a complaint in court. Compare H.R. 1746, which passed the House, with the successful Conference Committee bill, analyzed at 118 Cong.Rec. 7168 (1972), which adopted a substantially more liberal limitation, i.e., a date two years prior to filing a charge with the EEOC. See 42 U.S.C. § 2000e–5(g) (1970 ed., Supp. III).

> "The provisions of this subsection are intended to give the courts wide discretion exercising their equitable powers to fashion the most complete relief possible. In dealing with the present section 706(g) the courts have stressed that the scope of relief under that section of the Act is intended to make the victims of unlawful discrimination whole, and that the attainment of this objective rests not only upon the elimination of the particular unlawful employment practice complained of, but also requires that persons aggrieved by the consequences and effects of the unlawful employment practice be, so far as possible, restored to a position where they would have been were it not for the unlawful discrimination." 118 Cong.Rec. 7168 (1972).

As this makes clear, Congress' purpose in vesting a variety of "discretionary" powers in the courts was not to limit appellate review of trial courts, or to invite inconsistency and caprice, but rather to make possible the "fashion[ing] [of] the most complete relief possible."

It follows that, given a finding of unlawful discrimination, backpay should be denied only for reasons which, if applied generally, would not frustrate the central statutory purposes of eradicating discrimination throughout the economy and making persons whole for injuries suffered through past discrimination.[14] The courts of appeals must maintain a consistent and principled application of the backpay provision, consonant with the twin statutory objectives, while at the same time recognizing that the trial court will often have the keener appreciation of those facts and circumstances peculiar to particular cases.

The District Court's stated grounds for denying backpay in this case must be tested against these standards. The first ground was that Albemarle's breach of Title VII had not been in "bad faith." [15] This is not a sufficient reason for denying backpay. Where an employer *has* shown bad faith—by maintaining a practice which he knew to be illegal or of highly questionable legality—he can make no claims whatsoever on the Chancellor's conscience. But, under Title VII, the mere absence of bad faith simply opens the door to equity; it does not depress the scales in the employer's favor. If backpay were awardable only upon a showing of bad faith, the remedy would become a punishment for moral turpitude, rather than a compensation for workers' injuries. This would read the "make whole" purpose right out of Title VII, for a worker's injury is no less real simply because his employer did not inflict it in "bad faith." [16] Title VII is not concerned with the employ-

14. It is necessary, therefore, that if a district court does decline to award backpay, it carefully articulate its reasons.

15. The District Court thought that the breach of Title VII had not been in "bad faith" because judicial decisions had only recently focused directly on the discriminatory impact of seniority systems. The court also noted that Albemarle had taken some steps to recruit black workers into one of its departments and to eliminate strict segregation through the 1968 departmental merger.

16. The backpay remedy of the NLRA on which the Title VII remedy was modeled, see n. 11, supra, is fully available even where the "unfair labor practice" was committed in good faith. See, e.g., NLRB v. J. H. Rutter-Rex Mfg. Co., 396 U.S., at 265, 90 S.Ct. 417, 421, 24 L.Ed.2d 405;

er's "good intent or absence of discriminatory intent" for "Congress directed the thrust of the Act to the *consequences* of employment practices, not simply the motivation." Griggs v. Duke Power Co., 401 U.S., at 432, 91 S.Ct., at 854. See also Watson v. City of Memphis, 373 U.S. 526, 535, 83 S.Ct. 1314, 1319–1320, 10 L.Ed.2d 529 (1963); Wright v. Council of City of Emporia, 407 U.S. 451, 461–462, 92 S.Ct. 2196, 2202–2203, 33 L.Ed.2d 51 (1972).[17] To condition the awarding of backpay on a showing of "bad faith" would be to open an enormous chasm between injunctive and backpay relief under Title VII. There is nothing on the face of the statute or in its legislative history that justifies the creation of drastic and categorical distinctions between those two remedies.[18]

The District Court also grounded its denial of backpay on the fact that the respondents initially disclaimed any interest in backpay, first asserting their claim five years after the complaint was filed. The court concluded that the petitioners had been "prejudiced" by this conduct. The Court of Appeals reversed on the ground "that the broad aims of Title VII require that the issue of back pay be fully developed and determined even though it was not raised until the post-trial stage of litigation," 474 F.2d, at 141.

It is true that Title VII contains no legal bar to raising backpay claims after the complaint for injunctive relief has been filed, or indeed after a trial on that complaint has been had.[19] Furthermore, Fed.Rule Civ.Proc. 54(c) directs that

> "every final judgment shall grant the relief to which the party in whose favor it is rendered is entitled, even if the party has not demanded such relief in his pleadings."

But a party may not be "entitled" to relief if its conduct of the cause has improperly and substantially prejudiced the other party. The respondents here were not merely tardy, but also inconsistent, in demanding backpay. To deny backpay because a *particular* cause has been prosecuted in an eccentric fashion, prejudicial to the other party,

American Machinery Corp. v. NLRB, 5 Cir., 424 F.2d 1321, 1328–1330 (CA5 1970); Laidlaw Corp. v. NLRB, 7 Cir., 414 F.2d 99, 107 (CA7 1969).

17. Title VII itself recognizes a complete, but very narrow, immunity for employer conduct shown to have been undertaken "in good faith, in conformity with, and in reliance on any written interpretation or opinion of the [Equal Employment Opportunity] Commission." 42 U.S.C. § 2000e–12(b). It is not for the courts to upset this legislative choice to recognize only a narrowly defined "good faith" defense.

18. We note that some courts have denied backpay, and limited their judgments to declaratory relief, in cases where the employer discriminated on sexual grounds in reliance on state "female protective" statutes that were inconsistent with Title VII. See, e.g., Kober v. Westinghouse Electric Corp., 3 Cir., 480 F.2d 240 (CA3 1973); LeBlanc v. Southern Bell Telephone & Telegraph Co., 5 Cir., 460 F.2d 1228 (CA5 1972); Manning v. General Motors Corp., 466 F.2d 812 (CA6 1972); Rosenfeld v. Southern Pacific Co., 9 Cir., 444 F.2d 1219 (CA9 1971). There is no occasion in this case to decide whether these decisions were correct. As to the effect of Title VII on state statutes inconsistent with it, see 42 U.S.C. § 2000e–7.

19. See Rosen v. Public Service Electric & Gas Co., 409 F.2d, at 780 n. 20; Robinson v. Lorillard Corp., 444 F.2d, at 802–803; United States v. Hayes International Corp., 5 Cir., 456 F.2d 112, 116, 121 (CA5 1972).

does not offend the broad purposes of Title VII. This is not to say, however, that the District Court's ruling was necessarily correct. Whether the petitioners were in fact prejudiced, and whether the respondents' trial conduct was excusable, are questions that will be open to review by the Court of Appeals, if the District Court, on remand, decides again to decline to make any award of backpay.[20] But the standard of review will be the familiar one of whether the District Court was "clearly erroneous" in its factual findings and whether it "abused" its traditional discretion to locate "a just result" in light of the circumstances peculiar to the case, Langnes v. Green, 282 U.S. 531, 541, 51 S.Ct. 243, 247, 75 L.Ed. 520 (1931). On these issues of procedural regularity and prejudice, the "broad aims of Title VII" provide no ready solution.

Judgment vacated and case remanded.

[The concurring opinion of JUSTICES MARSHALL and REHNQUIST and the concurring and dissenting opinion of CHIEF JUSTICE BURGER are omitted.]

NOTES AND PROBLEMS FOR DISCUSSION

1. The only special circumstance that courts have generally recognized as relieving an employer, which has violated Title VII, of back pay liability is where good faith compliance with a state law has caused the violation. In Alaniz v. California Processors, Inc., 785 F.2d 1412 (9th Cir. 1986), for example, back pay was denied where the employer had refused to assign female employees to certain jobs because of the state's prohibition of employment of women in any position requiring lifting of more than 25 pounds. The defendant's good faith was demonstrated by the fact that it abandoned its practice as soon as it was advised that the state had ended enforcement of the regulation. See also, LeBeau v. Libbey-Owens-Ford Co., 727 F.2d 141 (7th Cir. 1984) (within district court's discretion to deny back pay where employer complied with state law restricting overtime work of women); Schaeffer v. San Diego Yellow Cabs, Inc., 462 F.2d 1002 (9th Cir. 1972) (continued reliance on state law after notice of contrary EEOC regulations concerning state protective laws demonstrated lack of good faith). Are these decisions consistent with *Albemarle's* holding that the employer's "good faith" or lack of intent to violate the Act is not a special circumstance justifying a denial of back pay? See *Albemarle,* supra, n. 18.

2. Under the *Albemarle* standard, does the district court in fact have any discretion over whether or not to award back pay in a case where the plaintiff has proved a violation of Title VII? In ARIZONA GOVERNING COMMITTEE v. NORRIS, 463 U.S. 1073, 103 S.Ct. 3492, 77 L.Ed.2d 1236 (1983), the Court followed its decision in Los Angeles Dept. of Water & Power v. Manhart, supra, p. 361, by holding that a state retirement plan that paid lower benefits to women than to men solely because of their longer life expectancy, violated Title VII. The Court limited retroactive relief to the plaintiff class so that benefits derived from employer contributions made prior to the decision in *Manhart* would be calculated under the terms of the existing plan because, prior to that

20. The District Court's stated grounds for denying backpay were, apparently, cumulative rather than independent. The District Court may, of course, reconsider its backpay determination in light of our ruling on the "good faith" question.

decision, the employer could have reasonably assumed that the plan was lawful, and full retroactive application would have a devastating effect on the employer and the pension plan.

EQUAL EMPLOYMENT OPPORTUNITY COMMISSION v. FORD MOTOR CO.

United States Court of Appeals, Fourth Circuit, 1981.
645 F.2d 183.

Before WINTER and BUTZNER, CIRCUIT JUDGES, and HOFFMAN, SENIOR DISTRICT JUDGE.

WINTER, CIRCUIT JUDGE.

The Equal Employment Opportunity Commission (EEOC) brought suit against Ford Motor Company for violating Title VII. EEOC alleged that Ford had discriminated against several women in its hiring practices at a parts warehouse in Charlotte, North Carolina. The district court found that Ford had discriminated against ten individual women and awarded them back pay. We affirm, but remand the case to the district court for consideration of additional relief.

I.

Ford operates a parts warehouse in Charlotte. A number of the workers at the warehouse are "picker-packers." These employees fill order for automotive parts by "picking" out ordered parts from storage and "packing" them for delivery. Until 1972 when two women were hired as temporary workers, no woman had ever worked as a picker-packer at the warehouse. Ford did not hire a woman to work as a picker-packer on a permanent basis until 1975.

In 1971, Judy Gaddis applied for employment as a picker-packer at the warehouse. When she did not receive a job, she filed a sex discrimination charge with the EEOC. The EEOC, after unsuccessfully trying to secure an acceptable conciliation agreement, sued Ford under Title VII on behalf of two groups of women. The first group consisted of Gaddis and two others who applied for picker-packer jobs which Ford filled with men in the summer of 1971. The second group consisted of eleven women who applied for a single picker-packer opening in 1973. Again in 1973 Ford had chosen a man, not a woman, to work at the warehouse.

The 1971 woman applicants were Gaddis, Rebecca Starr and Zettie Smith. In response to proof that as of 1971 it had never hired women as picker-packers and proof of a discriminatory hiring policy, Ford attempted to demonstrate that it had not in fact discriminated against women in its hiring practices at the Charlotte warehouse. Further, Ford tried to show that these particular women had not applied before the 1971 openings were filled. The district court rejected Ford's arguments, finding that Ford had followed a discriminatory hiring policy and that the three women had applied prior to the time in 1971 when Ford hired three men.

With the aid of a special master, the district court calculated the back pay due Gaddis, Starr, and Smith. Based upon the employment history of the three men who were hired in 1971,[1] the district court decided that, if the women had been hired in 1971, they would have worked at Ford until the time of trial. The special master thus began the back pay period with the date of the 1971 hirings and ended it at the date of trial in 1977.

With respect to Gaddis and Starr only, Ford attempted to terminate its back pay liability at three different junctures: in 1973 when they were recalled for one year by their former employer General Motors, later in 1973 when they rejected job offers from Ford, and in 1975 when they entered a CETA nurses training program. The district court refused to truncate the back pay periods at any of these points. Further, the district court rejected Ford's request to subtract unemployment compensation from the back pay awards.

In 1973, Ford filled a vacancy by hiring a man, Robert Simpson, even though eleven women had applied for the position. The district court ruled that EEOC proved a prima facie case of sex discrimination, in this instance based upon Ford's hiring procedures. After referral, the special master found that Simpson was hired in part because a warehouse employee took an interest in his application and that Ford did not seriously consider the applications of the eleven women. The special master determined that Ford did not intentionally discriminate against the women when it hired Simpson. But the special master concluded that Ford's practice of hiring new employees on the recommendation of present workers, who were all male, without giving other applications full consideration, had a discriminatory effect upon the women applicants. The district court accepted the conclusion of the special master.

Pursuant to the district court's instructions, the special master determined the back pay due each of the women who had applied for the 1973 opening. Smith was among the eleven who had applied, but she was not included in the 1973 group because her injury was remedied by the award she received as a member of the 1971 group. Of the remaining ten applicants, seven appeared before the special master and demonstrated their financial injury.[2] Under the district court's directions, the special master divided each woman's award by seven, since the seven women had applied for a single vacancy.

1. Ford filled four positions with men in August, 1971. One of those positions was created especially for a man, Parks, who transferred from a Ford warehouse in another city. The district court instructed the special master to base the back pay pay periods of the three women on the employment histories of Blanchard, Coe, and Rogers, the three men hired to fill the other three positions in which vacancies had occurred in the regular course of operations.

2. The seven women were Gloria Gaither, Betty Erwin, Mary Luckey, Frances McGinnis Gantz, Mary Cox, Arlene Brown, and Frankie Benson Grier. Because Mary Luckey had died in the interim, a representative of her estate appeared before the special master.

Ford attempted to reduce its back pay liability by arguing that the back pay periods of the seven women should terminate with the end of Simpson's employment at Ford. Simpson was laid off by Ford in 1974. He was not recalled; instead, Ford hired a woman, its first permanent female picker-packer, to fill his job. The special master found, however, that it was Ford's usual practice to recall employees who had been laid off. Therefore, the special master refused to end the back pay period with Simpson's termination, and the district court approved that decision.

The district court granted the two groups of women no additional relief beyond back pay. No mention of additional relief was made in the report of the special master, nor did the district court discuss other remedies in its findings of fact and conclusions of law, its referral order, or its final order.

Finally, the district court ordered Ford to report in the future about the company's efforts to hire women. The court declined however, to grant general prospective relief against sex discrimination at the warehouse, due to the vigorous affirmative action program Ford had pursued since 1975.

* * *

[The court affirmed the district court's findings that Gaddis, Starr and Smith had applied for warehouse positions in 1971 and had been denied employment because they were women as not "clearly erroneous."]

(2) *Back Pay*

In order to remedy the effects of discrimination against Gaddis, Starr, and Smith, the district court awarded them back pay. With the help of a special master, following the direction of this court in UTU v. Norfolk & Western Railway, 532 F.2d 336, 341 (4 Cir. 1975), cert. denied, 425 U.S. 934, 96 S.Ct. 1664, 48 L.Ed.2d 175 (1976), the court constructed the hypothetical work histories which the three women would have had at Ford if they had not been victims of discrimination. The court then used these hypothetical work histories to calculate back pay. The district court determined that if the women had been hired in 1971, they would have been working at Ford at the time of trial in 1977, as were two of the men who were hired in 1971. Accordingly, the court granted the women back pay from the time the men were hired in 1971 through 1977.

Ford urges that the back pay periods of Gaddis and Starr should have been terminated at three different points short of the date of trial. In addition, Ford insists that the awards of all three women should be reduced by the amount of unemployment compensation they received during the period.

(a) *Subsequent Recall*

Before Gaddis and Starr applied for the Ford warehouse jobs, they had worked in similar positions for General Motors. In 1971 Gaddis and Starr applied for work at the Ford warehouse because they had been laid off from their General Motors jobs. In January, 1973, Gaddis and Starr were recalled to General Motors. They worked at General Motors for approximately one year and were then laid off for a final time.

The district court subtracted their earnings at General Motors from their back pay awards. Ford insists that the district court should have gone further. Ford contends that the back pay period of Gaddis and Starr should have been terminated when they rejoined General Motors.

Ford's argument misses the point of a Title VII back pay award. Under Title VII, a district court awards back pay in order to put the discrimination victim in the position she would have occupied if the defendant had not discriminated against her. Albemarle Paper Co. v. Moody. Pursuant to this purpose, the district court constructed the claimants' hypothetical employment histories, calculated what they would have earned if they had not been victims of discrimination, subtracted what they actually earned during the period, and awarded the difference in back pay. We prescribed this formula in *UTU*, 532 F.2d at 341, because it makes the discrimination victim whole while denying her a double recovery. If the back pay period ended when a discrimination victim obtained substantially equivalent temporary employment, as Ford suggests, the discrimination victim would not be made whole, because her back pay period would be shorter than her hypothetical work history. Ford's proposed rule is thus contrary to the intent of Title VII, since it does not fully compensate the discrimination victim.

Moreover, the procedure followed by the district court is completely in accord with the statute. In 42 U.S.C. § 2000e–5(g), Congress provided: "Interim earnings or amounts earnable with reasonable diligence by the person or persons discriminated against shall operate to reduce the back pay otherwise allowable." Thus, the statute requires only that interim earnings be deducted from the back pay award, the very procedure implemented by the district court; but it does not require, as Ford urges, that the back pay period end when a discrimination victim accepts other temporary employment. The back pay period may continue past the acceptance of another job by a discrimination victim, as long as the victim's earnings are subtracted from the back pay award.

In this case, the district court properly found that the hypothetical employment histories of the women would extend beyond their employment at General Motors. The two men who were hired instead of Gaddis and Starr worked until the time of trial. Unlike the women, who were unable to continue at General Motors, the two male Ford workers were steadily employed from 1971 until 1977. Thus, if Ford had hired Gaddis and Starr in 1971, in all probability they would have worked until 1977.[6]

Ford also argues that the result reached by the district court is contrary to the method followed by the National Labor Relations Board under the National Labor Relations Act, 29 U.S.C. § 160. Ford contends that the NLRB has implemented a rule of ending back pay periods when a discrimination victim obtains substantially equivalent employment, even if the discrimination victim is subsequently laid off.

In fact, the approach under the NLRA is identical to the approach adopted by the district court. In NLRB v. Mastro Plastics Corp., 354 F.2d 170 (2 Cir. 1965), cert. denied, 384 U.S. 972, 86 S.Ct. 1862, 16 L.Ed. 2d 682 (1966),[7] the guilty employer made the same argument advanced by Ford. Both the Board and the court rejected the employer's position. The court explained:

> Several discriminatees secured substantially equivalent employment or became self-employed during the back pay period and yet suffered additional losses thereafter. Mastro argues that the taking of such employment terminates completely its back pay obligation. We do not agree. The only issue here is whether the discriminatee willfully incurred a loss of earnings. It would be unjust to require him to mitigate his damages to the greatest extent possible but then to penalize him for substantial but short-lived success. Unless in taking substantially equivalent or self-employment the discriminatee willfully forwent greater earnings, his back pay should not be reduced beyond the interim earnings he in fact received.

Id. at 179.

This passage highlights the central weakness of Ford's argument. If the back pay period ended completely when a discrimination victim accepted substantially equivalent employment, then a discrimination

6. Ford submits that this focus on the work histories of the men who were actually hired is punitive. But the best evidence of the female applicants' probable work histories at Ford was the work histories of the men who held the 1971 positions. By constructing the hypothetical work histories of the women through reliance on the work histories of the men, the district court acted only to compensate the discrimination victims, not to punish Ford.

7. See note 11, *infra*.

Furthermore, the back pay formula employed by the district court in this case is the back pay formula used under the NLRA. The Board estimates the back pay the discrimination victim would have earned but for the discrimination and subtracts actual earnings to determine the back pay award. NLRB v. Gullett Gin Co., 340 U.S. 361, 71 S.Ct. 337, 95 L.Ed. 337 (1951); Phelps Dodge Corp. v. NLRB, 313 U.S. 177, 61 S.Ct. 845, 85 L.Ed. 1271 (1941); F. W. Woolworth Co., 90 NLRB 289 (1950).

We also note that the NLRB decisions cited by Ford are inapposite to this case. In Circle Bindery, Inc., 232 NLRB 1185, 1187–88 (1977), the Board terminated the back pay period when the discrimination victim accepted permanent employment, but because the discrimination victim would have left the temporary job from which he had been discriminatorily discharged when he accepted the permanent job. Thus, the acceptance of the permanent job marked the end of his hypothetical work history for the temporary employer. In Star Baby Co., 140 NLRB 678, 683–84 (1963), the Board ended the back pay periods when the discrimination victims found permanent employment, but did not address the problem faced in the instant case. *Star Baby* was complicated by the fact that the employer had gone out of business.

victim would be discouraged from mitigating damages. She could accept equivalent employment only by forfeiting continued back pay rights, with the risk that her new job might end and leave her without income from any source. Many discrimination victims might choose unemployment and continuing back pay over employment which might be short-lived. Title VII, like the NLRA, should be interpreted so as to encourage mitigation of damages by discrimination victims in order to reduce the back pay liability of Title VII defendants. [That policy] would be ill-served by a rule which encouraged discrimination victims to remain idle.[8]

Therefore, by refusing to terminate the back pay period when Gaddis and Starr returned to General Motors, the district court furthered two policies underlying Title VII. It made Gaddis and Starr whole, by awarding them back pay during their entire hypothetical work histories at Ford. At the same time, the district court followed a rule which induces Title VII discrimination victims to mitigate damages. Without reservation, we affirm the district court's decision.

(b) *Job Offers*

Later in 1973, while Gaddis and Starr were working at General Motors, Ford offered a permanent warehouse job to Gaddis. She declined the offer. Then Ford offered the job to Starr, who likewise declined. Ford asserts that its back pay liability cannot extend past the time when Gaddis and Starr turned down the offers.

The district court found that one principal reason why Gaddis and Starr rejected Ford's offer was because they would have been forced to abandon their seniority at General Motors. By accepting a job with Ford and leaving General Motors, Gaddis and Starr would have forfeited all their rights at General Motors. Ford's offer did not include retroactive seniority to the time of the 1971 hirings. Ford presented Gaddis and Starr with an offer of mere beginning employment.

We have twice held under Title VII that victims of discrimination need not accept job offers which include a loss of seniority in order to preserve their back pay rights. In *UTU*, 532 F.2d at 340, we explained:

> A refusal to commit seniority suicide is not an acceptable reason to deny back pay. Victims of discrimination should not be required to forfeit wage and security benefits accruing because of their seniority

8. Of course, if a discrimination victim accepts permanent employment with substantially equivalent wages and remains at that job, the back pay period would end when she accepted the permanent job, because thereafter she would suffer no damages. Her actual earnings from that point on would be equal to or more than what she would have earned if she had not been a victim of discrimination. See Butta v. Anne Arundel County, 473 F.Supp. 83, 89 (D.Md.1979); Milton v. Bell Laboratories, Inc., 428 F.Supp. 502, 515 & n. 19 (D.N.J.1977). In this case, however, Gaddis and Starr were unable to remain at General Motors, because they were once again laid off after working for about a year. They thus suffered additional damages during the period following their layoff from General Motors, a period when they would probably have been employed if Ford had not discriminated against them in 1971.

> in order to remain eligible for purely speculative future back pay relief. A general rule requiring such action would frustrate the central purposes of Title VII.

Accord, Hairston v. McLean Trucking Co., 520 F.2d 226, 232 (4 Cir. 1975) (plaintiff's refusal of promotion or transfer because of a discriminatory loss of seniority is not a defense to plaintiff's back pay claim).

Ford would present Gaddis and Starr with a similarly intolerable choice. Under Ford's legal theory, if Gaddis and Starr rejected Ford's offer and stayed at General Motors, they would forego their rights to further back pay benefits. On the other hand, if they accepted the job offered by Ford, which they had not held for the previous two years because of Ford's discriminatory hiring policy, they would lose their seniority rights at General Motors. Thus, Ford's job offer was tainted by the effects of the discrimination it had practiced in 1971. Gaddis and Starr could accept the offer only by forfeiting the seniority they had accumulated at General Motors and without a compensating offer of seniority at Ford to alleviate the effects of the discrimination against them in 1971. As in *Hairston* and *UTU*, the result advocated by Ford would "frustrate the central purposes of Title VII."

Our decision is in accord with the decisions of three other circuits. In Comacho v. Colorado Electronic Technical College, Inc., 590 F.2d 887 (10 Cir. 1979) (per curiam), a woman sued a college under Title VII for discriminatorily firing her. She prevailed and was awarded back pay. The college argued that her right to back pay was terminated when the college made her an offer of reinstatement. The Tenth Circuit replied:

> 42 U.S.C. § 2000e–5(g) * * * gives the trial court discretion as to the remedies. The obvious purpose of the Act is to compensate persons for injuries suffered on account of unlawful discrimination. Congress clearly intended that the remedies employed would "make whole" as nearly as possible any person injured under the Act. * * * An offer of reinstatement without back pay does not "make whole" the person injured by an illegal firing. Such a holding would circumvent the objectives of Title VII. The college thus did not offer to fully compensate plaintiff, but merely offered to reemploy her. * * * Thus we must hold that a reinstatement offer without back pay does not relieve a guilty employer from further liability.

Id. at 889.

In Jurinko v. Edwin L. Wiegand Co., 477 F.2d 1038 (3 Cir.), vacated on other grounds, 414 U.S. 970, 94 S.Ct. 293, 38 L.Ed.2d 214 (1973), the district court held that discrimination against the plaintiffs ceased when they were offered jobs by the defendant. The Third Circuit rejected this portion of the district court's opinion, stating:

> The terms of the 1969 job offers were within Wiegand's control, and it did not offer the plaintiffs back seniority or back pay. The offer

> that was made did not rectify the effects of its past discrimination, and the plaintiffs were under no duty to accept such an offer.

Id. at 1047.

Similarly, in Claiborne v. Illinois Central Railroad, 583 F.2d 143, 153 (5 Cir. 1978), cert. denied, 442 U.S. 934, 99 S.Ct. 2869, 61 L.Ed.2d 303 (1979), the Fifth Circuit held that: "Failure to accept an offer of reinstatement in a Title VII case does not necessarily terminate the right to relief, so long as those amounts earned elsewhere or earnable with reasonable diligence are deducted from each plaintiff's award." Furthermore, the Fifth Circuit explained that "the disadvantages to an employee returning to the railroad without retroactive seniority" would "more than justify" an employee's decision to refuse an offer of reinstatement. Thus, the Fifth Circuit, like the Third and the Tenth, would find, as we do, that Ford's job offers to Gaddis and Starr did not end their back pay periods.[9]

Further, it should be noted that Ford was benefited by the employment of Gaddis and Starr at General Motors. Their earnings at General Motors were deducted in the calculation of their back pay awards. Gaddis and Starr reduced Ford's back pay liability by working at General Motors.

In sum, the district court reached an eminently reasonable result. It did not permit Ford to cut off the back pay period by making Gaddis and Starr an incomplete and unacceptable offer, and it denied Gaddis and Starr a double recovery by deducting their General Motors wages from their back pay awards. We affirm this aspect of the district court's decision.[10]

9. Ford points to several NLRA decisions in which the NLRB has held that an offer of reinstatement terminates an employer's back pay liability to a discriminatorily discharged employee. E.g., D'Armigene, Inc., 148 NLRB 2 (1964), enf'd as modified, 353 F.2d 406 (2 Cir. 1965). For several reasons we do not find these decisions persuasive.

The decisions cited by Ford discuss offers of reinstatement. In the instant case, Ford did not make the women offers of reinstatement, but only offers of beginning employment. An offer of reinstatement carries with it seniority rights, whereas an offer of beginning employment includes no seniority rights. This failure of Ford to offer retroactive seniority prevents Ford from relying on its offers to Gaddis and Starr.

In fact, our decision in this case is consistent with at least one decision of the NLRB. See note 11 infra. In NLRB v. Hilton Mobile Homes, 387 F.2d 7 (8 Cir. 1967), the employer offered a discharged employee reinstatement, but *without* seniority rights. The Board held that this offer did not terminate the company's back pay liability because the offer did not include seniority. The court agreed and enforced the Board's order. The offer in the instant case is almost identical to the offer in *Hilton Mobile Homes*, but significantly different from the offer of reinstatement addressed in *D'Armigene*.

Also, Gaddis and Starr mitigated damages. In some situations, refusal of an offer of employment or reinstatement might amount to a failure to mitigate damages, and, under 42 U.S.C. § 2000e–5(g), the discrimination victim's recovery might be reduced by the amount of wages she could have earned in the offered job, as "amounts earnable with reasonable diligence." In the case of Gaddis and Starr, they reduced Ford's liability by continuing to work at General Motors.

10. In addition to its finding that the women did not want to lose their General Motors seniority, the district court found that neither Gaddis nor Starr wanted to be the only woman employed at the warehouse. In fact, Ford's warehouse manager testified that he warned Gaddis and Starr

(c) *Nurses Training*

In September, 1975, Gaddis and Starr entered a nurses training program, a CETA program for the unemployed. Ford asked the district court to terminate the back pay period of Gaddis and Starr upon their entry into the program. The district court refused. Instead, the court accepted the special master's report which treated the training program as employment and reduced the back pay awards by forty hours of minimum wage earnings for each week the women spent in the program.

On appeal, Ford again presses the argument that its back pay liability should not extend beyond the date when Gaddis and Starr entered the nurses training program. We think that there are four reasons why Ford should not prevail.

First of all, Gaddis and Starr did not remove themselves from the labor market when they entered the CETA program. Both testified that they would have accepted work had it been offered to them. The special master's report credited their testimony. He found that the two women had not removed themselves from the labor market, and his finding was adopted by the district court. Because this determination was a reasonable credibility determination, we cannot treat it as clearly erroneous.

Two courts have decided similar cases in which Title VII claimants entered school after suffering discrimination at the hands of an employer. Those courts have decided that the critical determination is whether the claimant remained "ready, willing, and available" for employment. Taylor v. Safeway Stores, Inc., 524 F.2d 263, 267 (10 Cir. 1975); United States v. Wood, Wire & Metal Lathers Local 46, 328 F.Supp. 429, 439, 443–44 (S.D.N.Y.1971). If the claimant is ready, willing, and available for work, these courts have suggested, the back pay period does not come to a close when the claimant enters school.

The district court in this case followed the rationale of these cases by instructing the special master to ascertain whether Gaddis and Starr had removed themselves from the labor market. We conclude that the district court acted correctly in ordering the special master to examine the availability of these two particular women for work, rather than mechanically ending the back pay period upon their entry into the

that they might be subject to sexual harassment if they worked at the warehouse. He told them that "they may very well [be] subjected to passes, offensive remarks, off-color language" and that "there are not now nor, * * * have there ever been women working in the warehouse."

Incredibly, Ford tries to rely upon the discriminatory atmosphere of the warehouse to argue that Gaddis and Starr unreasonably rejected Ford's job offers. It would be ironic indeed if Ford could defeat the remedial purposes of Title VII by resting upon sexual harassment of women in its warehouse. Ford cannot escape the fact that its offer included no seniority rights to make Gaddis and Starr whole.

We note further that the warehouse manager told Gaddis and Starr that if Ford hired one of them it would hire the other to avoid subjecting a lone woman to sexual harassment. In 1973, Ford offered a single position to each of the women. It did not offer positions to both.

CETA training program. The "ready, willing, and able" test followed by the district court permits the relief in each case to be fitted to fit the circumstances of particular claimants.

Second, the CETA training program closely resembled employment. Both women received the minimum wage for the time they spent in the training program. Both testified that they regarded the program as employment. Indeed, the apparent intent of the CETA program is to provide the unemployed with work while at the same time preparing them for future employment.

The special master treated the training program as employment like the claimants' temporary employment at General Motors. As with the wages the women earned at General Motors, the special master subtracted the wages the women earned in the training program from Ford's back pay liability. 42 U.S.C. § 2000e–5(g). In addition, the district court took every precaution to insure that Ford was not unfairly burdened by back pay liability. Even though Gaddis and Starr sometimes attended the program for less than forty hours per week, the district court subtracted forty-hours of earnings for each week they spent in the program. In this fashion, the district court properly treated the nurses training program as the equivalent of employment and also guaranteed that Gaddis and Starr did not receive more than one full recovery.

Third, Gaddis and Starr were enrolled in the program as a result of their presence on the unemployment compensation rolls. Gaddis and Starr were receiving unemployment compensation when they began the training program. Both testified that they did not sign up for the CETA program on their own and that they enrolled at the urging of the state unemployment compensation office. In fact, a representative of the state agency testified that their unemployment benefits would have been cancelled if they had not enrolled in the CETA program. As the special master found, "[T]his course of action was recommended very strongly by the North Carolina Employment Security Commission."

Gaddis and Starr were unemployed as a direct result of the discrimination against them by Ford. As the employment histories of the men hired in 1971 demonstrate, if Ford had not discriminated against Gaddis and Starr in 1971, they probably would not have been receiving unemployment compensation. But for Ford's discriminatory hiring practices, they would have had no need of a CETA program. However, because they were unable to find work and because they were a burden on the state unemployment compensation fund, Gaddis and Starr were convinced by the state to enroll in the CETA training program. Ford cannot equitably be relieved of Title VII back pay liability because of an event which flowed directly from its discriminatory actions. The district court reached the proper result when it refused to terminate Ford's back pay liability upon the entry of Gaddis and Starr into the CETA training program.

Fourth, as has been detailed above, the district court did not abuse its discretion, see Franks v. Bowman Transportation Co., when it chose not to end these claimants' back pay period with their enrollment in the nurses training program. As the Tenth Circuit indicated in *Taylor*, 524 F.2d at 268, district courts have discretion to examine the particulars of a claimant's entry into school and to decide whether the employer's back pay liability should end or continue. In this case, the enrollment of Gaddis and Starr into nurses training is colored by several facts, including their availability for work, the similarity between the CETA program and employment, and the close connection between the state unemployment compensation agency and the CETA training program. When all these factors are considered, it is apparent that the district court did not abuse its discretion when it permitted Ford's back pay liability to continue during the training program, while giving Ford credit for the claimants' possible minimum wage earnings during the period.

(d) *Unemployment Compensation*

Ford argues that the awards of all three women should be reduced by the amount of unemployment compensation they received during the back pay period. The district court did not deduct unemployment compensation from the back pay awards. We conclude that the district court ruled correctly.

There is a division of authority over the deduction of unemployment compensation from Title VII back pay awards. Some district courts have subtracted unemployment compensation in computing back pay. See, e.g., Heelan v. Johns-Manville Corp., 451 F.Supp. 1382 (D.Colo. 1978).

On the other hand, one district court in this circuit has decided that monies received as "state unemployment compensation 'are made to carry out an independent social policy' and are not deductible from a back pay award under Title VII." Abron v. Black & Decker Manufacturing Co., 439 F.Supp. 1095, 1115 (D.Md.1977), quoting Inda v. United Air Line, Inc., 405 F.Supp. 426 (N.D.Calif.1975) aff'd in part and vacated in part, 565 F.2d 554 (9 Cir. 1977), cert. denied, 435 U.S. 1007, 98 S.Ct. 1877, 56 L.Ed.2d 388 (1978). See also Tidwell v. American Oil Co., 332 F.Supp. 424 (D.Utah 1971).

In an analogous context, the Supreme Court has decided that unemployment compensation need not be deducted from back pay awarded under the NLRA. NLRB v. Gullett Gin Co., 340 U.S. 361, 71 S.Ct. 337, 95 L.Ed. 337 (1951). The Supreme Court's analysis is particularly convincing:

> * * * To decline to deduct state unemployment compensation benefits in computing back pay is not to make the employees more than whole, as contended by respondent. Since no consideration has been given to collateral *losses* in framing an order to reimburse

employees for their lost earnings, manifestly no consideration need be given to collateral benefits which employees may have received. * * * Payments of unemployment compensation were not made to the employees by respondent but by the state out of state funds derived from taxation. True, these taxes were paid by employers, and thus to some extent respondent helped to create the fund. However, the payments to the employees were not made to discharge any liability or obligation of respondent, but to carry out a policy of social betterment for the benefit of the entire state. [citations omitted]. We think these facts plainly show the benefits to be collateral. It is thus apparent from what we have already said that failure to take them into account in ordering back pay does not make the employees more than "whole" as that phrase has been understood and applied.

Id. at 364, 71 S.Ct. at 339 (emphasis in original).[11]

Based on the *Abron* decision, the analysis of the Supreme Court, and the remedial policies of Title VII, we agree with the district court that "awards of back pay under Title VII should not be affected by a system of compensation which is designed to serve a wholly independent social policy." To decide otherwise would undercut to some degree the corrective force of a Title VII back pay award.

(3) *Conclusion*

Many of Ford's objections contest the factual findings and credibility determinations of the district court and the special master. Because we find none of them clearly erroneous, we do not overturn any of these resolutions of conflicting facts and testimony. Most of the rest of Ford's contentions challenge the district court's exercise of discretion in framing a remedy. As indicated above, we find that the district court did not abuse its discretion but, on the contrary, closely examined each issue to determine an equitable adjustment of Ford's back pay liability. Consequently, we affirm the district court's decision with respect to Gaddis, Starr, and Smith.

* * *

[The court affirmed the district court's finding that Ford had passed over eleven female job applicants in 1973 because of employment practices that had a disparate impact on women.]

(2) *Back Pay*

The district court awarded the 1973 women applicants back pay. Seven appeared before the special master to prove their damages. Under the instructions of the district court, the special master calculated each woman's back pay and awarded one-seventh of each sum,

11. This decision is particularly persuasive, because Congress turned to the "make whole" provisions of the NLRA when it framed the relief provisions of Title VII. *Albemarle Paper Co.*, 422 U.S. at 419–22, 95 S.Ct. at 2372–73.

because Ford only filled one vacancy in 1973. Ford does not contest this aspect of the district court's decision.

Ford does object to the length of the back pay period. After working several months, Simpson was laid off on February 6, 1974. Simpson's recall rights expired by the time Ford was ready to fill his vacant position. At that time, in September, 1975, Ford did not recall Simpson, but in his place hired Doris Baumgardner, who was Ford's first female permanent picker-packer.

The special master found that in the usual situation Ford recalled laid-off employees, even when their recall rights had expired. Because the hiring of Baumgardner was an unusual case, the special master did not terminate the back pay period with Simpson's layoff. Instead, the special master included Baumgardner's employment within the back pay period for the eleven women.

Ford argues that this extension of the back pay period was improper. According to Ford, "the court was required to track the actual work experience of the employee allegedly favored by Ford's alleged discrimination." Ford's proposed rule is unacceptable because it bears no relation to the purpose of a Title VII back pay award.

The purpose of a back pay award is to make the discrimination victim whole, to erase the effects of illegal discrimination. To accomplish that purpose, courts construct the hypothetical employment history of the discrimination victim to determine the appropriate back pay period. *UTU*, 532 F.2d at 341.

Frequently, the employment history of the applicant who was actually hired will provide the best guide to the hypothetical employment history of the discrimination victim. In fact, the district court in this case used the employment history of the men hired in 1971 to determine the back pay periods for Gaddis, Starr, and Smith. But the employment history of the employee is not controlling in and of itself. Actual employment histories are used only when they are the best available guide to the hypothetical employment history of the discrimination victim. The focus is on the probable job career of the victim, who is to be made whole, not on the career of the actual employee, who is of course not a party to the Title VII case.

In this instance, the special master tracked Simpson's work history, but only to a point. Simpson's employment history was used as the best indicator of the probable work history of the female applicants until Doris Baumgardner was hired to fill his job. At that point, the special master found that Simpson's employment history was abnormal. The testimony of Ford's warehouse manager revealed, as the special master found, that normally employees are recalled even after their recall rights had expired. In this case, Simpson was not recalled, and a woman was hired in his place. Ford's departure from its usual practice took place after EEOC filed this sex discrimination suit.

It was apparent, then, that Ford's decision not to recall Simpson was out of the ordinary, a product of unusual circumstances. As a result, Simpson's work history failed as an indicator of the probable work history that one of the seven women would have had. Since laid-off employees were usually recalled, the special master made the only reasonable decision when he abandoned Simpson's actual work history and concluded that one of the seven women would have probably been recalled if she had been hired. If the special master had instead followed Simpson's work history, the special master would have based the back pay period not on the hypothetical work history of the discrimination victim, but on the peculiarities of Simpson's situation. That approach would have been contrary to *UTU* and to the "make whole" doctrine of *Albemarle Paper Co.*

The special master adhered to the dictates of *UTU* and *Albemarle Paper Co.*, by constructing the hypothetical work histories of the women. In our view, the special master reasonably decided that if one of the women had been hired in 1973 she would have been recalled in 1975 even though Simpson was not.

III.

In its complaint, EEOC asked the district court to "make whole those persons adversely affected by [sex discrimination], by providing appropriate back pay, with interest, * * * and other affirmative relief necessary to eradicate the effects of unlawful employment practices." As described above, the district court meticulously formulated a back pay award to correct the effects of sex discrimination against the women applicants.

But the district court offered the women no further remedies. Under Title VII, district courts have discretion in the formulation of remedial orders. E.g., Franks v. Bowman Transportation Co. At the same time, district courts have a duty to grant the "fullest relief possible to the victims of discrimination," to insure that the effects of discrimination are totally removed from the lives of discrimination victims. *Albemarle Paper Co.*

In this case, the district court did not discuss possible remedies other than back pay. In its findings of fact and conclusions of law, in its referral order to the special master, and in its order adopting the special master's report, the district court did not address other remedial steps. Under *Albemarle Paper Co.*, then, the district court was obliged to consider other remedies and if it rejected them to articulate its reasons.

The district court may not have discussed other possible remedies because it concluded that Ford had made diligent efforts since 1975 to hire women. Although Ford's affirmative action program might justify the district court's decision not to order general affirmative relief against sex discrimination, Ford's anti-discrimination efforts do not alter the district court's responsibility to redress the discrimination suffered by these individual women. Ford's good faith since 1975 does not remove the burden placed upon the ten women by discrimination practices in 1971 and 1973. See *UTU*, 532 F.2d at 340.

In fact, these women are not aided in any fashion by Ford's program. They still do not possess the seniority they would have accumulated had they been hired in earlier years, and they do not yet have the jobs they might well have had if Ford had not discriminated against them. Ford's affirmative action program, then, does not excuse the district court's failure to consider additional relief for the individual women.

One seemingly desirable remedy in this instance would be to grant the women hiring preferences at the parts warehouse, with retroactive seniority.

This remedy may be particularly appropriate for the three women who were not hired in 1971. Gaddis and Starr have had difficulty finding jobs since 1971. After their final layoffs from General Motors, they were forced to enter a CETA training program, apparently unable to find work in the auto parts field. If Ford had not discriminated against them in 1971, they might well have avoided this checkered employment career. Smith had been employed during much of the time since 1971, but at relatively low wages. She also might be entitled to a hiring preference with retroactive seniority.

The seven women who were not hired in 1973 present a more difficult case. Ford filled only one opening in 1973, and thus all seven cannot reasonably claim that they would have been employed by Ford since 1973 if Ford had not discriminated against them. However, the district court may be able to fashion a remedy, such as hiring preferences without seniority, which would grant them more complete relief than a back pay award.

If the district court decides to order Ford to hire any or all of these discrimination victims as positions come open, it should also consider whether the women should receive an additional monetary award to compensate them for the estimated earnings lost between the date of the district court's decision and the date of employment at the warehouse. See White v. Carolina Paperboard Corp., 564 F.2d 1073, 1091 (4 Cir. 1977). Such an award, along with back pay, preferential hiring, and retroactive seniority, would constitute the "fullest relief possible."

We emphasize that the terms and conditions of relief for discrimination victims is determined by district courts, not by this court. We only instruct the district court to consider these possible remedies; not necessarily to provide them. On remand, the district court should articulate its reasons for rejecting or accepting the additional relief proposed by EEOC.

IV.

We affirm the district court's decision as a proper exercise of discretion founded on not clearly erroneous factual determinations.

We remand for consideration of further remedies, so that the district court can fully exercise its discretion to formulate the most complete relief possible for these discrimination victims.

Affirmed and remanded.

[The dissenting opinion of JUDGE HOFFMAN is omitted.]

FORD MOTOR CO. v. EQUAL EMPLOYMENT OPPORTUNITY COMMISSION

Supreme Court of the United States, 1982.
458 U.S. 219, 102 S.Ct. 3057, 73 L.Ed.2d 721.

JUSTICE O'CONNOR delivered the opinion of the Court.

This case presents the question whether an employer charged with discrimination in hiring can toll the continuing accrual of backpay liability under § 706(g) of Title VII, 42 U.S.C. § 2000e–5(g), simply by unconditionally offering the claimant the job previously denied, or whether the employer also must offer seniority retroactive to the date of the alleged discrimination.[1]

The question has considerable practical significance because of the lengthy delays that too often attend Title VII litigation.[2] The extended time it frequently takes to obtain satisfaction in the courts may force a discrimination claimant to suffer through years of underemployment or unemployment before being awarded the job the claimant deserves. Court delays, of course, affect all litigants. But for the victim of job discrimination, delay is especially unfortunate. The claimant cannot afford to stand aside while the wheels of justice grind slowly toward the ultimate resolution of the lawsuit. The claimant needs work that will feed a family and restore self-respect. A job is needed—now. In this case, therefore, we must determine how best to fashion the remedies available under Title VII to fulfill this basic need.

* * *

1. The dissent asserts that by so "fram[ing] the question presented" we have "simply and completely misstate[d] the issue." Apparently, neither party agrees with the dissent. The petitioner summarizes the question presented as "whether back pay due an employment discrimination claimant continues to accrue after the claimant has rejected an unconditional job offer that does not include retroactive seniority or back pay." Brief for Petitioner i. The respondent sums up the question presented as "[w]hether an employer who unlawfully refused to hire job applicants because they were women can terminate its liability for back pay by subsequently offering the applicants positions without seniority at a time when they had obtained, and accumulated seniority in, other jobs." Brief for Respondent i.

To buttress the assertion that the Court has addressed a question not presented, the dissent claims that we have "misrea[d]" the Court of Appeals' decision, "transform[ing] a narrow Court of Appeals ruling into a broad one, just so [we could] reverse and install a broad new rule of [our] own choosing," rather than attempt, as best we are able, to decide the particular case actually before us. Because we believe we have correctly and fairly framed the question, we decline the opportunity to address further this *ad hominem* argument.

2. The discriminatory refusals to hire involved in this case occurred 11 years ago.

[The Court's statement of the Facts and of the procedural history of the case is omitted.]

II

Section 706(g) of the Civil Rights Act of 1964, governs the award of backpay in Title VII cases. * * *

Under § 706(g), then, "backpay is not an automatic or mandatory remedy[,] * * * it is one which the courts 'may' invoke" in the exercise of their sound "discretion [which] is equitable in nature." Albemarle Paper Co. v. Moody. Nonetheless, while "the power to award backpay is a discretionary power," id., at 447 (BLACKMUN, J., concurring in the judgment), a "court must exercise this power 'in light of the large objectives of the Act,' " and, in doing so, must be guided by "meaningful standards" enforced by "thorough appellate review." (opinion of the Court) (citations omitted). Moreover, as we emphasized in *Albemarle Paper*, in Title VII cases

> "such discretionary choices are not left to a court's 'inclination, but to its judgment; and its judgment is to be guided by sound legal principles.' United States v. Burr, 25 F.Cas. 30, 35 (No. 14,692d) (CC Va. 1807) (Marshall, C. J.). * * *
>
> "It is true that '[e]quity eschews mechanical rules * * * [and] depends on flexibility.' Holmberg v. Armbrecht, 327 U.S. 392, 396 (1946). But when Congress invokes the Chancellor's conscience to further transcendent legislative purposes, what is required is the principled application of standards consistent with those purposes and not 'equity [which] varies like the Chancellor's foot.' Important national goals would be frustrated by a regime of discretion that 'produce[d] different results for breaches of duty in situations that cannot be differentiated in policy.' Moragne v. States Marine Lines, 398 U.S. 375, 405 (1970)." Id., at 416–417.

In this case, Ford and the EEOC offer competing standards to govern backpay liability. Ford argues that if an employer unconditionally offers a claimant the job for which he previously applied, the claimant's rejection of that offer should toll the continuing accrual of backpay liability.[9] The EEOC, on the other hand, defends the lower court's rule,[10] contending that backpay liability should be tolled only by

9. It should be clear that the contested backpay in this suit stems from the period following Ford's offer, and during which Gaddis and Starr were unemployed, i.e., after the GM warehouse closed. Our decision today does not affect their right to claim backpay for the period before they rejected Ford's offers.

10. For reasons of its own, the dissenting opinion reads the decision below narrowly and takes us to task for discerning the outlines of a "general rule" in the opinion of the Court of Appeals. In this regard, we note that already at least one district court evidently not only has read the opinion below as prescribing a general rule, but in addition has interpreted that rule more broadly than we do. See Saunders v. Hercules, Inc., 510 F.Supp. 1137, 1142 (WD Virginia 1981) ("in view of the recent Fourth Circuit Court of Appeals decision in Equal Employment Opportunity Commission v. Ford Motor Company, 645 F.2d 183 (4th Cir. 1981) * * * [i]t is clear * * * that a person who has been discriminated against does not have to ac-

the rejection of an offer that includes seniority retroactive to the date on which the alleged discrimination occurred. Our task is to determine which of these standards better coincides with the "large objectives" of Title VII.

III

The "primary objective" of Title VII is to bring employment discrimination to an end, *Albemarle Paper*, supra, by "achiev[ing] equality of employment opportunities and remov[ing] barriers that have operated in the past to favor an identifiable group * * * over other employees." Ibid. "[T]he preferred means for achieving" this goal is through "[c] ooperation and voluntary compliance." Alexander v. Gardner-Denver Co.

To accomplish this objective, the legal rules fashioned to implement Title VII should be designed, consistent with other Title VII policies, to encourage Title VII defendants promptly to make curative, unconditional job offers to Title VII claimants, thereby bringing defendants into "voluntary compliance" and ending discrimination far more quickly than could litigation proceeding at its often ponderous pace. Delays in litigation unfortunately are now commonplace, forcing the victims of discrimination to suffer years of underemployment or unemployment before they can obtain a court order awarding them the jobs unlawfully denied them. In a better world, perhaps, law suits brought under Title VII would speed to judgment so quickly that the effects of legal rules on the behavior of the parties during the pendency of litigation would not be as important a consideration. We do not now live in such a world, however, as this case illustrates.

The rule tolling the further accrual of backpay liability if the defendant offers the claimant the job originally sought well serves the objective of ending discrimination through voluntary compliance, for it gives an employer a strong incentive to hire the Title VII claimant. While the claimant may be no more attractive than the other job applicants, a job offer to the claimant will free the employer of the threat of liability for further backpay damages. Since paying backpay damages is like paying an extra worker who never came to work, Ford's proposed rule gives the Title VII claimant a decided edge over other competitors for the job he seeks.

The rule adopted by the court below, on the other hand, fails to provide the same incentive, because it makes hiring the Title VII claimant more costly than hiring one of the other applicants for the same job. To give the claimant retroactive seniority before an adjudication of liability, the employer must be willing to pay the additional costs of the fringe benefits that come with the seniority that newly hired workers usually do not receive. More important, the employer must also be prepared to cope with the deterioration in morale, labor

cept an offer of reemployment where back pay has not been offered").

unrest, and reduced productivity that may be engendered by inserting the claimant into the seniority ladder over the heads of the incumbents who have earned their places through their work on the job. In many cases, moreover, disruption of the existing seniority system will violate a collective bargaining agreement, with all that such a violation entails for the employer's labor relations.[11] Under the rule adopted by the court below, the employer must be willing to accept all these additional costs if he hopes to toll his backpay liability by offering the job to the claimant. As a result, the employer will be less, rather than more, likely to hire the claimant.

In sum, the Court of Appeals' rule provides no incentive to employers to hire Title VII claimants. The rule advocated by Ford, by contrast, powerfully motivates employers to put Title VII claimants to work, thus ending ongoing discrimination as promptly as possible.[12]

IV

Title VII's primary goal, of course, *is* to end discrimination; the victims of job discrimination want jobs, not lawsuits.[13] But when unlawful discrimination does occur, Title VII's secondary, fallback purpose is to compensate the victims for their injuries. To this end, § 706(g) aims "to make the victims of unlawful discrimination whole" by restoring them, "so far as possible * * * to a position where they would have been were it not for the unlawful discrimination." *Albemarle Paper*, supra, at 421. We now turn to consider whether the rule urged by Ford not only better serves the goal of ending discrimination, but also properly compensates injured Title VII claimants.

A

If Gaddis and Starr had rejected an unconditional offer from Ford before they were recalled to their jobs at GM, tolling Ford's backpay liability from the time of Ford's offer plainly would be consistent with providing Gaddis and Starr full compensation for their injuries. An unemployed or underemployed claimant, like all other Title VII claim-

11. See American Tobacco Co. v. Patterson, 456 U.S. 63, ___ (1982) ("Seniority provisions are of 'overriding importance' in collective bargaining, * * * and they 'are universally included in these contracts'") (quoting Humphrey v. Moore, 375 U.S. 335, 346 (1964), and Trans World Airlines, Inc. v. Hardison, 432 U.S. 63, 79 (1977)).

12. In his dissent, JUSTICE BLACKMUN suggests that it is we who speak from the "comfor[t]" of the "sidelines," somewhere outside "the real world" of sex discrimination. For all the dissent's rhetoric, however, nowhere does the dissent seriously challenge our conclusion that the rule we adopt will powerfully motivate employers to offer Title VII claimants the jobs they have been denied. But Rebecca Starr's trial testimony eloquently explains what claimants need: "I was just wanting that job so bad because you can't, a woman, when you've got three children, I needed the money, and I was wanting the job so bad." IV Tr. 356. Thus, it is the rule applied by the court below which manifests a "studied indifference to the real-life concerns" of the victims of sex discrimination.

13. See 118 Cong.Rec. 7569 (remarks of Rep. Dent during debate on 1972 amendments to Title VII) ("Most people just want to work. That is all. They want an opportunity to work. We are trying to see that all of us, no matter of what race, sex, or religious or ethnic background, will have an equal opportunity in employment").

ants, is subject to the statutory duty to minimize damages set out in § 706(g).[14] This duty, rooted in an ancient principle of law,[15] requires the claimant to use reasonable diligence in finding other suitable employment. Although the un- or underemployed claimant need not go into another line of work, accept a demotion, or take a demeaning position,[16] he forfeits his right to backpay if he refuses a job substantially equivalent to the one he was denied.[17] Consequently, an employer charged with unlawful discrimination often can toll the accrual of backpay liability by unconditionally offering the claimant the job he sought, and thereby providing him with an opportunity to minimize damages.[18]

14. The provision expressly states that "[i]nterim earnings or amounts earnable with reasonable diligence by the person or persons discriminated against shall operate to reduce the back pay otherwise allowable." 42 U.S.C. § 2000e–5(g).

Claimants often take other lesser or dissimilar work during the pendency of their claims, even though doing so is not mandated by the statutory requirement that a claimant minimize damages or forfeit his right to compensation. See, e.g., Merriweather v. Hercules, Inc., 631 F.2d 1161 (CA5 1980) (voluntary minimization of damages in dissimilar work); Thornton v. East Texas Motor Freight, 497 F.2d 416, 422 (CA6 1974) (voluntary minimization of damages by moonlighting).

15. See generally, e.g., C. McCormick, Handbook on the Law of Damages 127–158 (1935). McCormick summarizes "the general rule" as follows:

> "Where one person has committed a tort, breach of contract, or other legal wrong against another, it is incumbent upon the latter to use such means as are reasonable under the circumstances to avoid or minimize the damages. The person wronged cannot recover for any item of damage which could thus have been avoided." Id., at 127.

In connection with the remedial provisions of the NLRA, we said: "Making the workers whole for losses suffered on account of an unfair labor practice is part of the vindication of the public policy which the Board enforces. Since only actual losses should be made good, it seems fair that deductions should be made not only for actual earnings by the worker but also for losses which he willfully incurred." Phelps Dodge Corp. v. NLRB, 313 U.S. 177, 197–198 (1941).

16. See, e.g., NLRB v. The Madison Courier, Inc., 153 U.S.App.D.C. 232, 245–246, 472 F.2d 1307, 1320–21 (1972) (employee need not "seek employment which is not consonant with his particular skills, background, and experience" or "which involves conditions that are substantially more onerous than his previous position"); Wonder Markets, Inc., 236 N.L.R.B. 787, 787 (1978) (offer of reinstatement ineffective when discharged employee offered a different job, though former position still existed), enforced sub nom. NLRB v. Eastern Smelting & Refining Corp., 598 F.2d 666, 676 (CA1 1979), supplemental decision, 249 N.L.R.B. 294 (1980); Good Foods Manufacturing & Processing Corp., 195 N.L.R.B. 418, 419 (1972) (offer of reinstatement ineffective because job offered had different conditions of employment and benefits), supplemental decision, 200 N.L.R.B. 623 (1972), enforced, 492 F.2d 1302 (CA7 1974); Harvey Carlton, 143 N.L.R.B. 295, 304 (1963) (offer of reinstatement ineffective because employees would return on probation).

Some lower courts have indicated, however, that after an extended period of time searching for work without success, a claimant must consider taking a lower-paying position. See, e.g., NLRB v. The Madison Courier, Inc., supra, at 245–246, 472 F.2d, at 1320–1321; NLRB v. Southern Silk Mills, Inc., 242 F.2d 697, 700 (CA6), cert. denied, 355 U.S. 821 (1957). If the claimant decides to go into a dissimilar line of work, or to accept a demotion, his earnings must be deducted from any eventual backpay award. See § 706(g); Merriweather v. Hercules, Inc., 631 F.2d 1161, 1168 (CA5 1980); Taylor v. Philips Industries, Inc., 593 F.2d 783, 787 (CA7 1979) (per curiam).

17. NLRB v. Arduini Mfg. Corp., 394 F.2d 420 (CA1 1968).

18. The claimant's obligation to minimize damages in order to retain his right to compensation does not require him to settle his claim against the employer, in whole or in part. Thus, an applicant or discharged employee is not required to ac-

An employer's unconditional offer of the job originally sought to an un- or underemployed claimant, moreover, need not be supplemented by an offer of retroactive seniority to be effective, lest a defendant's offer be irrationally disfavored relative to other employers' offers of substantially similar jobs. The claimant, after all, plainly would be required to minimize his damages by accepting another employer's offer even though it failed to grant the benefits of seniority not yet earned.[19] Of course, if the claimant fulfills the requirement that he minimize damages by accepting the defendant's unconditional offer, he remains entitled to full compensation if he wins his case.[20] A court may grant him backpay accrued prior to the effective date of the offer,[21] retroactive seniority,[22] and compensation for any losses suffered as a result of his lesser seniority before the court's judgment.[23]

In short, the un- or underemployed claimant's statutory obligation to minimize damages requires him to accept an unconditional offer of the job originally sought, even without retroactive seniority. Acceptance of the offer preserves, rather than jeopardizes, the claimant's right to be made whole; in the case of an un- or underemployed claimant, Ford's suggested rule merely embodies the existing requirement of § 706(g) that the claimant minimize damages, without affecting his right to compensation.

cept a job offered by the employer on the condition that his claims against the employer be compromised. See, e.g., NLRB v. St. Marys Sewer Pipe Co., 146 F.2d 995, 996 (CA3 1945).

19. For the same reasons, a defendant's job offer is effective to force minimization of damages by an un- or underemployed claimant even without a supplemental offer of backpay, since the claimant would be required to accept another employer's offer of a substantially similar job without a large front-end, lump-sum bonus. See, e.g., NLRB v. Midwest Hanger Co., 550 F.2d 1101, 1103 (CA8) ("It is clear that had the Company's offer of reinstatement been conditioned solely on its refusal to give back pay, as the Company strenuously argues, then the offer of reinstatement would not have been invalidated"), cert. denied, 434 U.S. 830 (1977); Reliance Clay Products Co., 105 N.L.R.B. 135, 137 (1953) ("The Board has consistently held that a discriminatorily discharged employee may not refuse" an unconditioned offer of reinstatement even though unaccompanied by backpay; refusal of such an offer tolls the employer's liability for back pay).

20. In tailoring a Title VII remedy a court " 'has not merely the power but the duty to render a decree which will so far as possible eliminate the discriminatory effects of the past as well as bar like discrimination in the future.' " Albemarle Paper Co. v. Moody, 422 U.S. 405, 418 (1975) (quoting Louisiana v. United States, 380 U.S. 145, 154 (1965)).

21. See, e.g., NLRB v. Huntington Hospital, Inc., 550 F.2d 921, 924 (CA4 1977).

22. See, e.g., Zipes v. Trans World Airlines, Inc., 455 U.S. ___ (1982); Teamsters v. United States, 431 U.S. 324 (1977); Franks v. Bowman Transportation Co., 424 U.S. 747 (1976).

Decisions construing the remedial provision of the NLRA, § 10(c), 29 U.S.C. § 160(c), are in accord. See, e.g., In re Nevada Consolidated Copper Corp., 26 N.L.R.B. 1182, 1235 (1940) (persons unlawfully refused jobs must be offered jobs with "any seniority or other rights and privileges they would have acquired, had the respondent not unlawfully discriminated against them") (quoted in Franks v. Bowman Transportation Co., supra, at 770), enforcement denied, 122 F.2d 587 (CA10 1941), reversed, 316 U.S. 105 (1942).

23. Both Ford and the EEOC agree on this point. See Brief for Respondent 19; Reply Brief for Petitioner 9.

B

Ford's proposed rule also is consistent with the policy of full compensation when the claimant has had the good fortune to find a more attractive job than the defendant's, because the availability of the better job terminates the ongoing ill effects of the defendant's refusal to hire the claimant. For example, if Gaddis and Starr considered their jobs at GM to be so far superior to the jobs originally offered by Ford that, even if Ford had hired them at the outset, they would have left Ford's employ to take the new work, continuing to hold Ford responsible for backpay after Gaddis and Starr lost their GM jobs would be to require, in effect, that Ford insure them against the risks of unemployment in a new and independent undertaking. Such a rule would not merely restore Gaddis and Starr to the " 'position where they would have been were it not for the unlawful discrimination.' " Albemarle Paper Co. v. Moody; it would catapult them into a better position than they would have enjoyed in the absence of discrimination.

Likewise, even if Gaddis and Starr considered their GM jobs only somewhat better or even substantially equivalent to the positions they would have held at Ford had Ford hired them initially,[24] their rejection of Ford's unconditional offer could be taken to mean that they believed that the lingering ill effects of Ford's prior refusal to hire them had been extinguished by later developments. If, for example, they thought that the Ford and GM jobs were identical in every respect, offering identical pay, identical conditions of employment, and identical risks of layoff, Gaddis and Starr would have been utterly indifferent as to which job they had—Ford's or GM's. Assuming that they could work at only one job at a time, the ongoing economic ill effects caused by Ford's prior refusal to hire them would have ceased when they found the identical jobs at GM, and they would have had no reason to accept Ford's offers. As in the case of a claimant who lands a better job, therefore, requiring a defendant to provide what amounts to a form of unemployment insurance to claimants, after they have found identical jobs and refused the defendant's unconditional job offer, would be, absent special circumstances, to grant them something more than compensation for their injuries.

In both of these situations, the claimant has the power to accept the defendant's offer and abandon the superior or substantially equivalent replacement job. As in the case of an un- or underemployed claimant, under the rule advocated by Ford acceptance of the defendant's unconditional offer would preserve fully the ultimately victorious claimant's right to full redress for the effects of discrimination. The claimant who

24. It is possible that they did so value the GM jobs, since they applied at Ford only after being laid off at GM, and since after being recalled to the GM jobs they rejected Ford's offer. Therefore, contrary to the dissent's erroneous suggestion, the possibility that Gaddis and Starr considered their GM jobs superior to the positions they would have had at Ford had Ford hired them at the outset is not merely a "hypothetical case." We cannot infer that they so valued their GM jobs, however, solely from their rejection of Ford's offer.

chooses not to follow this path does so, then, not because it provides inadequate compensation, but because the value of the replacement job outweighs the value of the defendant's job supplemented by the prospect of full court-ordered compensation. In other words, the victim of discrimination who finds a better or substantially equivalent job no longer suffers ongoing injury stemming from the unlawful discrimination.

C

Thus, the rule advocated by Ford rests comfortably both on the statutory requirement that a Title VII claimant must minimize damages and on the fact that a claimant is no longer incurring additional injury if he has been able to find other suitable work that, all things considered, is at least as attractive as the defendant's. For this reason, in almost all circumstances the rule is fully consistent with Title VII's object of making injured claimants whole.

The sole question that can be raised regarding whether the rule adequately compensates claimants arises in that narrow category of cases in which the claimant believes his replacement job to be superior to the defendant's job without seniority, but inferior to the defendant's job with the benefits of seniority. In the present case, for example, it is possible that Gaddis and Starr considered their GM jobs more attractive than the jobs offered by Ford, but less satisfactory than the positions they would have held at Ford if Ford had hired them initially. If so, they were confronted with two options. They could have accepted Ford's unconditional offer, preserving their right to full compensation if they prevailed on their Title VII claims, but forfeiting their favorable positions at GM. Alternatively, they could have kept their jobs at GM, retaining the possibility of continued employment there, but, under the operation of the rule advocated here by Ford, losing the right to claim further backpay from Ford after the date of Ford's offer. The court below concluded that under these circumstances Ford's rule would present Gaddis and Starr with an "intolerable choice," 645 F.2d 183, 192 (CA4 1981), depriving them of the opportunity to receive full compensation.

We agree that Gaddis and Starr had to choose between two alternatives. We do not agree, however, that their opportunity to choose deprived them of compensation. After all, they had the option of accepting Ford's unconditional offer and retaining the right to seek full compensation at trial, which would comport fully with Title VII's goal of making discrimination victims whole. Under the rule advocated by Ford, if Gaddis and Starr chose the option of remaining at their GM jobs rather than accept Ford's offer, it was because they thought that the GM jobs, plus their claims to backpay accrued prior to Ford's offer, were *more* valuable to them than the jobs they originally sought from

Ford, plus the right to seek full compensation from the court.[26] It is hard to see how Gaddis and Starr could have been deprived of adequate compensation because they chose to venture upon a path that seemed to them more attractive than the Ford job plus the right to seek full compensation in court.

If the choice presented to Gaddis and Starr was difficult, it was only because it required them to assess their likelihood of prevailing at trial. But surely it cannot be contended for this reason alone that they were deprived of their right to adequate compensation. It is a fact of life that litigation is risky and that a plaintiff with a claim to compensation for his losses must consider the possibility that the claim might be lost at trial, either wrongly, because of litigation error, or rightly, because the defendant was innocent. Ford's rule merely requires the Title VII claimant to decide whether to take the job offered by the defendant, retaining his rights to an award by the court of backpay accrued prior to the effective date of the offer, and any court-ordered retroactive seniority plus compensation for any losses suffered as a result of his lesser seniority before the court's judgment, or, instead, whether to accept a more attractive job from another employer and the limitation of the claim for backpay to the damages that have already accrued. The rule urged by the EEOC and adopted by the court below, by contrast, would have the perverse result of requiring the employer in effect to insure the claimant against the risk that the employer might win at trial.

Therefore, we conclude that, when a claimant rejects the offer of the job he originally sought, as supplemented by a right to full court-ordered compensation, his choice can be taken as establishing that he considers the ongoing injury he has suffered at the hands of the defendant to have been ended by the availability of better opportunities elsewhere. For this reason, we find that, absent special circumstances,[27] the simple rule that the ongoing accrual of backpay liability

26. Employees value a job for many reasons besides the rate of pay, including, for example, the presence of other workers of the employee's own sex, the availability of recreational facilities at the worksite, staggered work hours, better health benefits, longer vacations, and so forth. What makes one job better than another varies from one employee to another.

Gaddis and Starr presumably rejected Ford's offer because they thought their jobs at GM were worth more to them than full compensation (Ford's offer plus a court award) discounted by the risks of litigation. In essence, the position adopted by the court below and advocated here by the EEOC turns on the fact that we cannot be sure that, had Gaddis and Starr known they were going to win their lawsuit, they still would have rejected Ford's offer. Had they known they were going to win, of course, they would have rejected the Ford job only if they valued the GM jobs more than they valued the combination of Ford's job plus the value of court-ordered compensation *un*discounted by the risks of litigation. To agree with the EEOC is, in effect, to contend that a claimant is not made whole for purposes of Title VII unless he decided to stay at a replacement job that was worth to him more than the sum of (1) the defendant's job, (2) the right to seek full court-ordered compensation, and, in addition, (3) a sum analogous to insurance against the risk of loss at trial. We discern, however, no reason for concluding that Title VII requires the defendant to insure the claimant against the possibility that the defendant might prevail in the lawsuit.

27. If, for example, the claimant has been forced to move a great distance to

is tolled when a Title VII claimant rejects the job he originally sought comports with Title VII's policy of making discrimination victims whole.

V

Although Title VII remedies depend primarily upon the objectives discussed above, the statute also permits us to consider the rights of "innocent third parties." City of Los Angeles Department of Water & Power v. Manhart, 435 U.S. 702, 723 (1978). See also Teamsters v. United States. The lower court's rule places a particularly onerous burden on the innocent employees of an employer charged with discrimination. Under the court's rule, an employer may cap backpay liability only by forcing his incumbent employees to yield seniority to a person who has not proven, and may never prove, unlawful discrimination. As we have acknowledged on numerous occasions, seniority plays a central role in allocating benefits and burdens among employees.[28] In light of the "overriding importance" of these rights, American Tobacco Co. v. Patterson, we should be wary of any rule that encourages job offers that compel innocent workers to sacrifice their seniority to a person who has only claimed, but not yet proven, unlawful discrimination.

The sacrifice demanded by the lower court's rule, moreover, leaves the displaced workers without any remedy against claimants who fail to establish their claims. If, for example, layoffs occur while the Title VII suit is pending, an employer may have to furlough an innocent worker indefinitely while retaining a claimant who was given retroactive seniority. If the claimant subsequently fails to prove unlawful discrimination, the worker unfairly relegated to the unemployment lines has no redress for the wrong done him. We do not believe that " 'the large objectives' " of Title VII, Albemarle Paper Co. v. Moody, 422 U.S. 405, 416 (1975) (citation omitted), require innocent employees to carry such a heavy burden.[29]

find a replacement job, a rejection of the employer's offer might reflect the costs of relocation more than a judgment that the replacement job was superior, all things considered, to the defendant's job. In exceptional circumstances, the trial court, in the exercise of its sound discretion, could give weight to such factors when deciding whether backpay damages accrued after the rejection of an employer's offer should be awarded to the claimant.

The dissent attempts to characterize "the loss of accumulated seniority at [a] replacement jo[b]" as such a cost of relocation. By so doing, the dissent simply confuses the costs of changing from one job to another—whatever the respective advantages and disadvantages of the two jobs might be—with the differences between the two jobs.

28. Seniority may govern, "not only promotion and layoff, but also transfer, demotion, rest days, shift assignments, prerogative in scheduling vacation, order of layoff, possibilities of lateral transfer to avoid layoff, 'bumping' possibilities in the face of layoff, order of recall, training opportunities, working conditions, length of layoff endured without reducing seniority, length of layoff recall rights will withstand, overtime opportunities, parking privileges, and [even] a preferred place in the punch-out line." Franks v. Bowman Transportation Co., 424 U.S. 747, 766–767 (1976) (quoting Stacy, Title VII Seniority Remedies in a Time of Economic Downturn, 28 Vand.L.Rev. 487, 490 (1975)).

29. In addition to the rights of innocent employees, the rule urged by the EEOC and adopted by the court below burdens

VI

In conclusion, we find that the rule adopted by the court below disserves Title VII's primary goal of getting the victims of employment discrimination into the jobs they deserve as quickly as possible. The rule, moreover, threatens the interests of other, innocent employees by disrupting the established seniority hierarchy, with the attendant risk that an innocent employee will be unfairly laid off or disadvantaged because a Title VII claimant unfairly has been granted seniority.

On the other hand, the rule that a Title VII claimant's rejection of a defendant's job offer normally ends the defendant's ongoing responsibility for backpay suffers neither of these disadvantages, while nevertheless adequately satisfying Title VII's compensation goals. Most important, it also serves as a potent force on behalf of Title VII's objective of bringing discrimination to an end more quickly than is often possible through litigation. For these reasons we hold that, absent special circumstances, the rejection of an employer's unconditional job offer ends the accrual of potential backpay liability. We reverse the judgment of the Court of Appeals and remand for proceedings consistent with this opinion.

So ordered.

JUSTICE BLACKMUN, with whom JUSTICE BRENNAN and JUSTICE MARSHALL join, dissenting.

After finding that petitioner Ford Motor Company had discriminated unlawfully against Judy Gaddis and Rebecca Starr because of their sex, the Court of Appeals affirmed the District Court's backpay award to the two women "as a proper exercise of discretion founded on not clearly erroneous factual determinations." The Court today reverses this unremarkable holding with a wide-ranging advisory ruling stretching far beyond the confines of this case. The Court's rule provides employers who have engaged in unlawful hiring practices with a unilateral device to cut off their backpay liability to the victims of their past discrimination.

innocent employers. An innocent employer—or one who believes himself innocent—has the right to challenge in court claims he considers weak or baseless. The approach endorsed by the lower court undermines this right by requiring the employer, if he wishes to offer some relief to the claimant and toll the mounting backpay bill, to surrender his defense to the charge that the claimant is entitled to retroactive seniority. If the employer offers the claimant retroactive seniority as well as a job, and then prevails at trial, he will have no recourse against the claimant for the costs of the retroactive seniority that the claimant erroneously received. The rule urged by Ford permits the parties to stem the ongoing effects of the alleged discrimination without compelling either claimant or employer to compromise his claims or surrender his defenses. Cf. Moro Motors Ltd., 216 N.L.R.B. 192, 193 (1975) ("were [an employer] required to offer to an employee, allegedly discharged for discriminatory reasons, reinstatement *with accrued back pay*, the [employer's] right to litigate the issue of whether the discharge was unlawful would for all practical purposes be nullified") (emphasis in original); National Screen Products Co., 147 N.L.R.B. 746, 747–748 (1964).

To justify its new rule, the Court mischaracterizes the holding of the Court of Appeals, undertakes an intricate economic analysis of hypothetical situations not presented here, and invokes the rights of " 'innocent third parties,' " who are not before the Court. By so doing, the Court not only supplants traditional district court discretion to mold equitable relief, but also ensures that Judy Gaddis and Rebecca Starr—the only Title VII claimants whose rights are at issue in this lawsuit—will not be made whole for injury they indisputably have suffered. I find the Court's ruling both unnecessary and unfair. I dissent.

I

A

The Court frames the question presented as "whether an employer charged with discrimination in hiring can toll the continuing accrual of backpay liability * * * simply by unconditionally offering the [Title VII] claimant the job previously denied, or whether the employer also must offer seniority retroactive to the date of the alleged discrimination."

In my view, the Court simply and completely misstates the issue. The question before us is not which of two inflexible standards should govern accrual of backpay liability in *all* Title VII cases, but whether the District Court's award of backpay relief to Gaddis and Starr *in this case* constituted an abuse of discretion.

The Court makes frequent and puzzling reference to the "onerous burden[s]" and "sacrifice demanded by the lower court's rule." * * * In fact, the Court of Appeals adopted no inflexible "rule" at all. Rather, it simply applied the well-settled and flexible principles of appellate review of Title VII remedies prescribed in Albemarle Paper Co. v. Moody and Franks v. Bowman Transportation Co.

In *Albemarle*, this Court directed that, in most Title VII matters, "the standard of [appellate] review will be the familiar one of whether the District Court was 'clearly erroneous' in its factual findings and whether it 'abused' its traditional discretion to locate 'a just result' in light of the circumstances peculiar to the case." With regard to Title VII backpay relief, however, the Court specified that " 'the [district] court has not merely the power but the duty to render a decree which will so far as possible eliminate the discriminatory effects of the past as well as bar like discrimination in the future.' " To achieve this purpose, "Congress took care to arm the courts with full equitable powers. For it is the historic purpose of equity to 'secur[e] complete justice.' " [1]

1. In passing the Equal Employment Opportunity Act of 1972, 86 Stat. 103, Congress specifically rejected several legislative efforts to limit the judicial power to award backpay. See Albemarle Paper Co. v. Moody, 422 U.S. 405, 420 (1975). The Section-by-Section Analysis accompanying the Conference Committee Report reaffirmed the "make whole" purpose of § 706(g), Title VII's backpay provision:

"The provisions of this subsection are intended to give the courts wide discretion exercising their equitable powers to fashion the most complete relief possible. In dealing with the present section 706(g) the courts have stressed that the

The Court in *Albemarle* and *Franks* made clear that, in Title VII cases, the equitable discretion of district courts should be guided by a heavy presumption in favor of full backpay awards. "Rather than limiting the power of district courts to do equity, the presumption insures that complete equity normally will be accomplished." Franks v. Bowman Transportation Co. By exercising their discretion to award full backpay relief, district courts further two broad purposes underlying Title VII. First, "the reasonably certain prospect of a backpay award * * * 'provide[s] the spur or catalyst which causes employers * * * to self-examine and to self-evaluate their employment practices and to endeavor to eliminate, so far as possible, the last vestiges'" of discrimination. Albemarle Paper Co. v. Moody. Second, backpay awards "make persons whole for injuries suffered on account of unlawful employment discrimination."

Thus, the goal of appellate review is to ensure that the district courts have exercised their remedial discretion in the way that "allow[s] the most complete achievement of the objectives of Title VII that is attainable under the facts and circumstances of the specific case." Franks v. Bowman Transportation Co. "The courts of appeals must maintain a consistent and principled application of the backpay provision, consistent with [Title VII's] twin statutory objectives, while at the same time recognizing that the trial court will often have the keener appreciation of those facts and circumstances peculiar to particular cases." Albemarle Paper Co. v. Moody.

B

In this case, the trial court's findings of fact were uncontroverted. In July 1971, Judy Gaddis and Rebecca Starr sought jobs at petitioner Ford's automotive parts warehouse in Charlotte, N. C. "Because of their experience, each was qualified to work at Ford as a 'picker-packer.'" Ford's stated hiring practice was to fill job vacancies at the warehouse by "taking the earliest filed applications first," and selecting employees by interviewing qualified candidates. At the time Gaddis and Starr applied, however, Ford had never hired any woman to work at the warehouse.[2] When Gaddis and Starr received their application forms, "a receptionist at Ford * * * told them in substance that Ford did not hire women to work in the warehouse."

Despite Gaddis' persistent requests for job interviews, petitioner interviewed neither woman immediately, supposedly because no job

scope of relief under that section of the Act is intended to make the victims of unlawful discrimination whole, and that the attainment of this objective * * * requires that persons aggrieved by the consequences and effects of the unlawful employment practice be, so far as possible, restored to a position where they would have been were it not for the unlawful discrimination." 118 Cong. Rec. 7168 (1972), quoted in Albemarle Paper Co. v. Moody, 422 U.S., at 421.

2. The District Court found, for example, that the job application of Zettie Smith, who sought employment at Ford about a month before Gaddis and Starr, and who was the first woman to apply for a warehouse job there, "was never seriously considered because she is a woman." App. to Pet. for Cert. A-157-A-158.

vacancy existed. The unit supervisor testified: "Ms. Gaddis called me on several occasions and asked if I was hiring, and I said no, * * * I just have too much work to do to sit down and interview people if I'm not hiring." Shortly thereafter, however, in August 1971, Ford hired male applicants to fill four job openings. "At least two of the men * * * were offered their jobs *after* Gaddis and Starr applied."

Gaddis filed a sex discrimination charge with respondent EEOC in September 1971. In January 1973, Gaddis and Starr were recalled to jobs at a nearby General Motors warehouse. In July 1973, petitioner made a vague job offer first to Gaddis, then to Starr.[3] The District Court found as a fact that "[t]he offer to the two women was made after Ford learned that a charge of sex discrimination had been filed with the Commission (and was prompted by a desire to bring some women into the warehouse in response to the charge)."[4]

Gaddis, and then Starr, turned down petitioner's job offer. The District Court found that the offer was "refused by both women since they were at that time back at work in the General Motors warehouse, having been recalled to work in January, 1973. Neither woman wished to lose accrued seniority at General Motors and neither wanted to be the only woman employed in the Ford warehouse."

Based on its factual findings, the District Court concluded as a matter of law that "Ford discriminated against * * * Gaddis and Starr on the basis of their sex by failing to employ them in its

3. At trial, Gaddis was asked:

"Q. Did [the clerk to the warehouse manager] say that the job was being offered to you, or did he discuss simply with you, in the form of an interview, the possibility of hiring you into some job?

A. It was so vague that I couldn't pinpoint anything down. They never did say what type of work it would be, whether it would be [parts] picking or whether it would be in sheet metal or whether it would be putting up stock or whether it would be on a day shift or night shift, whether it was a permanent or temporary job. At the time, I had a good seniority with General Motors and I had a secure job, and so on those grounds, I refused it." App. 43.

Similarly, Starr testified on cross-examination:

"I remember [the clerk to the warehouse manager] wasn't specific on the job about what it would be. I did have, at General Motors I had fifteen, I don't know if it was fourteen or fifteen people under me. I had seniority, and I also, this is the truth about [it,] I was scared. Whenever I had worked at Ford before, I had been badgered and I don't know, I was just, I wanted to look into the job. Yet, I had a fear to go back. I didn't know what I would be facing." Id., at 54.

4. The trial testimony of Ford's warehouse operations manager illuminates petitioner's motives:

"Q. Whose decision was it to call Ms. Gaddis and Ms. Starr?

A. It was my decision.

Q. Why?

A. Well, mainly because we had a suit, EEOC suit filed against us, and we wanted to give one of them an opportunity to go to work for us, and we only had one, maybe two openings at that time.

* * *

Q. Mr. Ely, you indicated in your testimony that you offered a job to one of the women, either Ms. Gaddis or Ms. Starr, in July, 1973. Is that correct?

A. Yes, that's correct.

Q. You also stated that you offered such job because of the EEOC charge which had been filed against Ford Motor Company. Is that correct?

A. That's correct." App. 17–18.

warehouse in the positions filled in August, 1971." In rulings not contested here, the District Court also found that 10 other women had established prima facie cases of unlawful sex discrimination by Ford.

To determine the backpay remedy to which Gaddis and Starr were entitled, the District Court attached no legal significance to the women's decision to decline beginning employment at Ford nearly two years after they unlawfully had been denied those same jobs and six months after they had begun accumulating seniority elsewhere.[5] In the ruling which the Court today implicitly deems an abuse of discretion, the District Court held that "[b]ack pay due to Gaddis and Starr shall not be affected by their refusal to accept the single position offered them in July, 1973, inasmuch as neither would have been confronted by that decision and its implications had both been hired in August, 1971."

Applying the standard of review specified in *Franks*, supra, and *Albemarle*, supra, the Court of Appeals affirmed "the district court's decision as a proper exercise of discretion founded on not clearly erroneous factual determinations." In particular, the Court of Appeals found no abuse of discretion in the District Court's failure to terminate the backpay awards in July 1973.[6]

The Court of Appeals rested its narrow ruling on two key facts: that "Gaddis and Starr could accept [Ford's] offer only by *forfeiting the seniority* they had accumulated at General Motors and *without a compensating offer of seniority at Ford* to alleviate the effects of the discrimination against them in 1971." The court expressed no view as to whether Ford's backpay liability would have been tolled if Gaddis and Starr could have accepted Ford's job offer without forfeiting seniority accumulated elsewhere. Nor did the Court of Appeals decide whether the women would have been obliged to accept Ford's offer had it encompassed *some* compensating offer of seniority, short of full retroactive seniority.

Contrary to this Court's suggestion today, the Court of Appeals announced no general *rule* that an employer's "backpay liability should be tolled *only* by the rejection of an offer that includes seniority retroactive to the date on which the alleged discrimination occurred." The Court of Appeals merely refused to announce a broad new rule, urged by Ford, requiring victims of Title VII discrimination to "accept

5. The District Court applied two equitable principles to shape relief in this case. It first concluded that an award of all backpay accruing after August 1971 would make Gaddis and Starr whole. The District Court therefore reconstructed a probable employment history at Ford for each woman, calculating what each would have received but for petitioner's unlawful discrimination. Second, the court obliged Gaddis and Starr to take all reasonable steps to mitigate damages. Accordingly, it subtracted from the backpay awards any amounts Gaddis and Starr actually earned or reasonably could have earned after August 1971. App. to Pet. for Cert. A–170.

6. "[T]he district court reached an eminently reasonable result. It did not permit Ford to cut off the back pay period by making Gaddis and Starr an incomplete and unacceptable offer, and it denied Gaddis and Starr a double recovery by deducting their General Motors wages from their back pay awards." 645 F.2d 183, 193 (CA4 1981).

job offers which include a loss of seniority in order to preserve their back pay rights." Such an inflexible approach, the court decided, would frustrate Title VII's central purposes by permitting employers to present discriminatees with an "intolerable choice." [7]

II

The Court today accepts Ford's invitation, wisely declined by the Court of Appeals, and adopts its broad new rule governing awards of backpay relief in Title VII cases: henceforth, "absent special circumstances, the rejection of an employer's unconditional job offer ends the accrual of potential backpay liability." [8] This ruling is disturbing in four respects.

First: The Court's new rule is flatly inconsistent with *Albemarle's* unambiguous directive "that, given a finding of unlawful discrimination, backpay should be denied only for reasons which, if applied generally, would not frustrate the central statutory purposes of eradicating discrimination throughout the economy and making persons whole for injuries suffered through past discrimination." Applied generally, the Court's rule interferes with both objectives.

The Court's approach authorizes employers to make "cheap offers" to the victims of their past discrimination. Employers may now terminate their backpay liability unilaterally by extending to their discrimination victims offers they cannot reasonably accept. Once an employer has refused to hire a job applicant, and that applicant has mitigated damages by obtaining and accumulating seniority in another job, the employer may offer the applicant the same job that she was denied unlawfully several years earlier. In this very case, for example, Ford offered Gaddis and Starr jobs only after they had obtained employment elsewhere and only because they had filed charges with the EEOC. If, as here, the applicant declines the offer to preserve existing job security, the employer has successfully cut off all future backpay liability to that applicant. By insulating a discriminating employer from proper liability for his discriminatory acts, the Court's rule reduces his "incentive to shun practices of dubious legality," and hinders the eradication of discrimination.

7. "[I]f Gaddis and Starr rejected Ford's offer and stayed at General Motors, they would forego their rights to further back pay benefits. On the other hand, if they accepted the job offered by Ford, which they had not held for the previous two years because of Ford's discriminatory hiring policy, they would lose their seniority rights at General Motors." 645 F.2d, at 192.

8. The Court's explanation for its misreading of the Court of Appeals' decision is that the United States District Court for the Western District of Virginia has interpreted that decision as stating a somewhat different proposition. But if one District Court in the Fourth Circuit has misconstrued the Fourth Circuit's opinion, surely that is a matter properly to be corrected by the United States Court of Appeals for the Fourth Circuit. This Court is not entitled to transform a narrow Court of Appeals ruling into a broad one, just so that it may reverse and install a broad new rule of its own choosing.

The Court's rule also violates Title VII's second objective—making victims of discrimination whole. Again, the rule's anomalies are well-illustrated by the facts of this case. Had petitioner not discriminated against Gaddis and Starr, both would have begun to work at Ford in August 1971. By July 1973, both would have accumulated nearly two years of seniority. Because of Ford's discrimination, however, each experienced long periods of unemployment and temporary employment before obtaining jobs elsewhere.[9] The District Court therefore determined that only full backpay awards, mitigated by wages earned or reasonably earnable elsewhere, would make Gaddis and Starr whole.

This Court now truncates those awards simply because Gaddis and Starr refused to accept Ford's offers of beginning employment in 1973. Yet even if Gaddis and Starr had accepted those offers, they would not have been made whole. Deprived of two years of seniority, Gaddis and Starr would have enjoyed lesser health, life, and unemployment insurance benefits, lower wages, less eligibility for promotion and transfer, and greater vulnerability to layoffs than persons hired after they were unlawfully refused employment. Even if Gaddis and Starr had continued to litigate the question of their retroactive seniority after accepting Ford's offer, they still would have spent many years at Ford "subordinate to persons who, but for the illegal discrimination, would have been[,] in respect to entitlement to [competitive seniority] benefits[,] [their] inferiors." Franks v. Bowman Transportation Co.

The Court claims that its new rule "powerfully motivates employers to put Title VII claimants to work, thus ending ongoing discrimination as promptly as possible." In fact, the discrimination is not ended, because a discrimination victim who accepts a "cheap offer" will be obliged to work at a seniority disadvantage, and therefore will suffer ongoing effects from the employer's discriminatory act. The Court also alleges that its rule promotes "cooperation and voluntary compliance" with Title VII by giving both employers and claimants incentives to make and accept "unconditional" job offers. If the Court's rule furthers this end, however, it does so only by weakening the bargaining position of a claimant vis-a-vis the employer. Discrimination victims will be forced to accept otherwise unacceptable offers, because they will know that rejection of those offers truncates their backpay recovery. A rule that shields discriminating employers from liability for their past discrimination and coerces bona fide Title VII claimants to accept incomplete job offers is fundamentally incompatible with the purposes of Title VII.

Second: The Court's rule unjustifiably limits a district court's discretion to make individual discrimination victims whole through awards of backpay. The Court suggests that, "absent special circum-

9. Gaddis, for example, sought employment in South Carolina, "at various parts places, independent part places, car dealers, such as Chrysler-Plymouth, the Ford place which was Lewis Ford at that time, all the car dealers, * * * some of the hosiery mills, * * * [and] Radiator Specialty Company," III Tr. 362, before obtaining her job at General Motors.

stances," a district court abuses its discretion *per se* if it fails to terminate an employer's backpay liability at the point where that employer has extended an unconditional job offer to a discrimination claimant. Yet "[i]n *Albemarle Paper* the Court read Title VII as creating a *presumption in favor* of backpay." Franks v. Bowman Transportation Co. (POWELL, J., concurring in part and dissenting in part) (emphasis added).[10] *Franks* supplied "emphatic confirmation that federal courts are empowered to fashion such relief as the *particular circumstances of a case may require* to effect restitution, making whole insofar as possible the victims of * * * discrimination in hiring."

The Court recognizes that its new rule interferes with district court discretion to make complete backpay awards in individual cases. Thus, the Court expressly preserves the principle of appellate deference to the "sound discretion" of the trial court in "exceptional circumstances." Yet, curiously, the Court offers no explanation why the facts of this very case fail to satisfy its own "exceptional circumstances" test.[11] Given the Court's concession that district courts must retain their discretion to make bona fide Title VII claimants whole in some cases, I see no advantage in prescribing a blanket rule that displaces that discretion in other cases where complete relief is equally justified.

Third: I am disturbed by the Court's efforts to justify its rule by relying on situations not presented by this case. For example, the Court partially rests its rule on an "un- or underemployed claimant's statutory obligation to minimize damages" by accepting an unconditional job offer without seniority. Because Gaddis and Starr were fully employed when Ford finally offered them jobs, however, neither the District Court nor the Court of Appeals exempted unemployed or underemployed victims of discrimination from accepting offers like Ford's.[12] Similarly, the Court analyzes the hypothetical case of a Title VII claimant who "has had the good fortune to find a more attractive

10. The Court cites language from *Albemarle* suggesting that a district court's discretion is not limitless. But the Court conspicuously omits *Albemarle*'s clear statement that if Congress intended to limit the equitable discretion of district courts in any way, it did so only by leaving " 'little room for the exercise of discretion *not* to order reimbursement.' " See Albemarle Paper Co. v. Moody, 422 U.S., at 417, citing Mitchell v. DeMario Jewelry, 361 U.S. 288, 296 (1960) (emphasis added).

11. The Court suggests, for example, that if a hypothetical Title VII "claimant has been forced to move a great distance to find a replacement job, a rejection of the employer's offer might reflect the costs of relocation more than a judgment that the replacement job was superior, all things considered, to the defendant's job." For Gaddis and Starr, however, the loss of their accumulated seniority at their replacement jobs certainly reflected "costs of relocation" at least as substantial as high moving expenses.

I expect that federal courts will find no meaningful distinction between a worker's refusal to accept a job offer because he believes that acceptance would force him to incur costs, and a similar refusal based on the worker's judgment that changing jobs would prove costly. In either case, for purposes of awarding Title VII relief, the reasonableness of the worker's refusal should be left to the trial court's discretion.

12. The purpose of § 706(g)'s "mitigation of damages" requirement is to encourage claimants to work while their Title VII claims are being adjudicated. The Court cannot deny that Gaddis and Starr fully mitigated damages by seeking and obtaining other employment while litigating their claims against Ford.

job than the defendant's." But, as the Court later recognizes, there is no assurance that the present case fits this category either. After speculating at length about how Gaddis and Starr may have valued the relative worth of their Ford and General Motors jobs, the Court finally acknowledges that on this paper record, "[w]e cannot infer" how much Gaddis and Starr "valued their GM jobs * * * solely from their rejection of Ford's offer."

Equally unconvincing is the Court's repeated invocation of, and preoccupation with, "the rights of 'innocent third parties,'" and the "disruption of the existing seniority system[s]," that would result from adoption of the Court of Appeals' "rule." The Court nowhere demonstrates how *petitioner's* labor relations would have suffered had Ford extended offers of retroactive seniority to Gaddis and Starr. The details of Ford's collective-bargaining agreement were not litigated in either the District Court or the Court of Appeals. Thus, those courts never passed on petitioner's obligation to offer retroactive seniority to Gaddis and Starr if such an offer would have disrupted its labor relations or existing seniority systems.[13] Nor did the Court of Appeals decide, as a general matter, whether or not offers of retroactive seniority to discrimination claimants adversely affect the rights of incumbent employees.[14] The Court cannot justify reversal in the case at hand by vague reference to classes of claimants and third parties who are not before the Court. To the extent that it seeks to do so. Its intricate argument is both irrelevant and advisory.

Fourth and finally: I am struck by the contrast between the Court's concern for parties who are not here and its studied indifference to the real-life concerns of the parties whose interests are directly affected. When the Court finally confronts the choice that actually faced Gaddis

13. The Court of Appeals did not foreclose the possibility that Ford could have terminated its backpay liability to Gaddis and Starr by offering them employment plus an award of *provisional* seniority, defeasible in the event that they lost their continuing lawsuit for backpay. Nor did the Court of Appeals deny that offering a job without seniority might terminate Ford's backpay liability, should any provision of Ford's collective-bargaining agreement preclude it from making offers of retroactive seniority. Had petitioner pointed to such a collective-bargaining agreement provision, or proved that its incumbent employees actually had objected to offers of retroactive seniority to Title VII claimants, the Court of Appeals would have considered those factors in determining whether the District Court abused its discretion in shaping Gaddis' and Starr's relief.

14. In any event, the Court's claim that offers of retroactive seniority would injure the rights of incumbent employees is vastly overstated. If any employer sued by a Title VII claimant could toll the accrual of backpay liability by making a unilateral offer that included some form of retroactive seniority, he still would have every incentive to make such an offer as soon as possible after the discriminatory act. The amount of retroactive seniority offered would necessarily be small, and the seniority rights of relatively few incumbent employees would be affected.

Under the Court's approach, in contrast, employers will no longer have any incentive to offer retroactive seniority. Any awards of retroactive seniority to bona fide Title VII claimants will thus be court-ordered, and will be entered only after "the lengthy delays that too often attend Title VII litigation." By delaying awards of retroactive seniority until final judgment in a significant number of cases, the Court's approach ensures that the seniority rights of comparatively greater numbers of incumbent employees will be affected adversely.

and Starr, it blithely suggests that "[a] fter all, they had the option of accepting Ford's unconditional offer and retaining the right to seek full compensation at trial" in the form of retroactive seniority. Yet the Court earlier acknowledges that "[d]elays in litigation unfortunately are now commonplace, forcing the victims of discrimination to suffer years of underemployment or unemployment before they can obtain a court order awarding them the jobs unlawfully denied them."

"If the choice presented to Gaddis and Starr was difficult," the Court continues, "it was only because it required them to assess their likelihood of prevailing at trial." Without consulting the record, the Court then states:

> "Gaddis and Starr presumably rejected Ford's offer because they thought their jobs at GM were worth more to them than full compensation (Ford's offer plus a court award) discounted by the risks of litigation. * * * Had they known they were going to win [their lawsuit], of course, they would have rejected the Ford job only if they valued the GM jobs more than they valued the combination of Ford's job plus the value of court-ordered compensation *un*discounted by the risks of litigation."

This is a comfortable rationale stated from the sidelines. Unfortunately, the abstract and technical concerns that govern the Court's calculations bear little resemblance to those that actually motivated Judy Gaddis and Rebecca Starr. When asked on cross-examination why she had turned down Ford's 1973 offer, Gaddis testified: "I had seniority [at General Motors] and I knew that I wasn't in danger of any layoff, where if I had accepted the job at Ford *I might have worked a week or two weeks and been laid off because I would have been low seniority.*" Similarly, Starr testified on cross-examination: "I had seniority at General Motors. I had about fifteen people working under me. *I could go to work at Ford and work a week and I knew that they could lay me off.*"

To a person living in the real world, the value of job security today far outstrips the value of full court-ordered compensation many years in the future. The Court's elaborate speculation about the concerns that "presumably" motivated Gaddis and Starr nowhere recognizes what a Ford job without seniority actually meant to Gaddis and Starr—a job from which they could be laid off at any moment. Unlike the Court, Gaddis and Starr recognized that if they traded their jobs with seniority for jobs without seniority, they could quickly become unemployed again, long before they had the chance to vindicate their rights at trial.

To people like Gaddis and Starr, the knowledge that they might someday establish their Title VII claims on the merits provides little solace for their immediate and pressing personal needs. Starr's trial testimony reveals just how much job security meant to her:

> "It was just a couple of days after I had [started working] there [at a temporary job] and this is, I was just wanting that job so bad

because you can't, a woman, when you've got three children, I needed the money, and I was wanting the job so bad. I worked so hard. I'll never forget one day when [the unit supervisor] came to me. I'll never forget that, and he said, I had just been there a few days, I'll have to let you go. * * * It broke my heart because I knew I had worked so hard."[15]

I agree with the Court that "the victims of job discrimination want jobs, not lawsuits." * * * When Ford made its 1973 offers to Gaddis and Starr, however, they *had* jobs, in which they had accumulated seniority despite Ford's discrimination. I therefore cannot accept the Court's conclusion that these women should have traded those jobs for uncertain employment in which back seniority could be won only by lawsuit. Nor can I justify penalizing Gaddis and Starr because they "discounted" the ultimate likelihood of obtaining court-ordered retroactive seniority at a different rate than the Court does today.

After hearing all the witnesses and appraising all the evidence, the District Court exercised its equitable discretion to shape complete backpay relief for Gaddis and Starr. In light of all the circumstances, the District Court refused to penalize Gaddis and Starr for declining Ford's 1973 job offer. Applying the correct standard of review over Title VII remedies, the Court of Appeals concluded that the District Court had exercised its remedial discretion properly. Sitting at this remove, I cannot say that Gaddis and Starr acted unreasonably. I would affirm the judgment of the Court of Appeals and thereby, for these two victims of discrimination, fulfill, and not defeat, the promise of Title VII.

NOTES AND PROBLEMS FOR DISCUSSION

1. Both the majority and the dissenting opinions of the Supreme Court in *Ford Motor Co.* rely on the Court's decision in Albemarle Paper Co. v. Moody. Which opinion is most consistent with the "make whole" philosophy of *Albemarle*? The majority opinion holds that an employer faced with a discrimination claim by an unsuccessful job applicant may choose not to gamble on the outcome of future litigation and may limit his potential liability for back pay by offering the claimant a position equivalent to that he originally applied for. The claimant, who has obtained other employment, on the other hand, must give up his current job (and any seniority rights which have accrued) in order to preserve his right to 'full" back pay and retroactive seniority if he prevails at trial. But the question of what constitutes full relief will only arise after the employer has been found guilty of discrimination. Why then should it be the innocent employee who is forced to gamble? Is the majority's opinion based on the assumption that the relief afforded to Gaddis and Starr by the courts below

15. Without embarrassment, the Court cites Rebecca Starr's testimony to support its argument that the Court of Appeals' "rule," and not its own new rule, is indifferent to the real-life concerns of victims of sex discrimination. Under the Court of Appeals' "rule," however, Rebecca Starr was awarded full backpay as compensation for Ford's sex discrimination. Under this Court's rule, a large portion of Starr's compensation will simply be cut off. By claiming that the Court of Appeals was somehow *more* indifferent to Starr's real-life concerns, the Court only confirms how far removed from the real world it is.

made them *more* than whole? Was there a middle ground which the Court could have adopted?

Under the Supreme Court's rule in *Ford Motor Co.*, can the employer terminate its backpay liability by offering the claimant a position different from the job originally sought? Compare, EEOC v. Exxon Shipping Co., 745 F.2d 967 (5th Cir. 1984) (offer of job not substantially equivalent to one sought by claimant does not terminate liability) with Cowen v. Standard Brands, Inc., 572 F.Supp. 1576 (N.D.Ala.1983) (offer of job in another city, while not as attractive to the plaintiff as one sought in local of his residence, was "comparable" in legal sense). Should the issue of "substantial equivalence" be one of fact or law?

Would the majority's reasoning also apply to a discriminatorily *discharged* employee offered reinstatement without accumulated back pay and seniority? See Comacho v. Colorado Electronic Technical College, Inc., 590 F.2d 887, 889 (10th Cir. 1979); Claiborne v. Illinois Central Railroad, 583 F.2d 143, 153 (5th Cir. 1978), cert. denied, 442 U.S. 934, 99 S.Ct. 2869, 61 L.Ed.2d 303 (1979). Can an employer who has discriminatorily denied promotions to employees limit his back pay liability by offering the promotions conditioned on a relinquishment of seniority accrued by the employees in their current jobs? In United Transportation Union v. Norfolk & Western Railway Co., 532 F.2d 336, 340 (4th Cir. 1975), cert. denied, 425 U.S. 934, 96 S.Ct. 1664, 48 L.Ed.2d 175 (1976), the court held that the refusal by black employees to accept promotions to predominantly white jobs, with a concomitant loss of seniority, did not cut off their back pay liability because "[a] refusal to commit seniority suicide is not an acceptable reason to deny back pay. Victims of discrimination should not be required to forfeit wage and seniority benefits *accruing* because of their seniority in order to remain eligible for purely speculative back pay relief." See also Hairston v. McLean Trucking Co., 520 F.2d 226, 232 (4th Cir. 1975). Are these cases distinguishable from *Ford Motor Co.*?

2. It is important to distinguish between the claimant's obligation to mitigate under § 706(g) and the kind of action the employer can take to terminate its back pay liability. The claimant's failure to look for alternative employment will generally bar recovery of back pay and this duty is not fulfilled by a readiness to accept only the job sought with the defendant. See, Miller v. Marsh, 766 F.2d 490 (11th Cir. 1985). There is however, no obligation to seek out work in another community, Hegler v. Board of Education, 447 F.2d 1078, 1081 (8th Cir. 1971), or to accept a position inferior in terms of pay, status or conditions to the position sought. See, EEOC v. Exxon Shipping Co., supra, 745 F.2d at 978; Spagnuolo v. Whirlpool Corp., 548 F.Supp. 104 (W.D.N.C.1982). In order to mitigate, must the claimant spend all her time looking for alternative employment? What if she enrolls in school in order to improve her prospects for employment by acquiring more marketable skills? Compare, Miller v. Marsh, supra, with Hanna v. American Motors Corp., 724 F.2d 1300 (7th Cir.), cert. denied, 467 U.S. 1241, 104 S.Ct. 3512, 82 L.Ed.2d 821 (1984).

The plaintiff in an ADEA case also has the duty to mitigate. The courts have held that the employer has the burden of proving failure to mitigate by establishing that comparable positions were available and discoverable by the claimant and that he failed to use reasonable care to find them. Jackson v. Shell Oil Co., 702 F.2d 197 (9th Cir. 1983); Coleman v. Omaha, 714 F.2d 804 (8th Cir. 1983).

How should the court determine back pay where the claimant has sought to mitigate, but, unable to find employment equivalent to that originally sought, has accepted on a permanent basis a job that pays less than that which he was illegally denied? Can the employer be required to pay back pay indefinitely? See, McIntosh v. Jones Truck Lines, Inc., 767 F.2d 433 (8th Cir. 1985).

3. If a back pay award must be reduced by "interim earnings," why should such an award not be reduced by a substitute for interim earnings, i.e., unemployment compensation? By awarding the claimants what they presumably would have earned had they been employed by Ford, in addition to unemployment compensation already received, did not the district court in EEOC v. Ford Motor Co. make them more than whole? There is a substantial division of authority over the application of the "collateral source" rule to unemployment compensation payments and pension benefits received by the claimant. Compare, Brown v. A. J. Gerrard Mfg. Co., 715 F.2d 1549 (11th Cir. 1983) (*en banc*); McDowell v. Avtex Fibers, Inc., 740 F.2d 214 (3d Cir. 1984), vacated and remanded on other grounds, ___ U.S. ___, 105 S.Ct. 1159, 84 L.Ed.2d 312 (1985); Maxfield v. Sinclair International, 766 F.2d 788 (3d Cir. 1985), cert. denied, ___ U.S. ___, 106 S.Ct. 796, 88 L.Ed.2d 773 (1986) (unemployment compensation, social security and pension benefits accruing between act of discrimination and award of relief not deducted from back pay) with Satty v. Nashville Gas Co., 522 F.2d 850 (6th Cir. 1975), vacated in part on other grounds, 434 U.S. 136, 98 S.Ct. 347, 54 L.Ed.2d 356 (1977) and EEOC v. Enterprise Association Steamfitters, Local 638, 542 F.2d 579 (2d Cir. 1976), cert. denied, 430 U.S. 911, 97 S.Ct. 1186, 51 L.Ed.2d 588 (1977) (back pay award should be reduced by unemployment benefits). The Third Circuit has held that unemployment compensation and public assistance payments must be deducted from back pay awards against the state where state law provided for the recoupment of such benefits in the event back pay is awarded. Dillon v. Coles, 746 F.2d 998 (3d Cir. 1984).

4. In order to "make whole" the economic loss suffered by the victim of discrimination, all fringe benefits which would have been obtained, but for the discrimination, should be included in the back pay award. See Crabtree v. Baptist Hospital of Gadsden, Inc., 749 F.2d 1501 (11th Cir. 1985) (executive retirement benefits); Patterson v. American Tobacco Co., 535 F.2d 257, 269 (4th Cir. 1976), cert. denied, 429 U.S. 920, 97 S.Ct. 314, 50 L.Ed.2d 286 (employer pension and profit sharing contributions); Pettway v. American Cast Iron Pipe Co., 494 F.2d 211, 263 (5th Cir. 1974), cert. denied, 439 U.S. 1115, 99 S.Ct. 1020, 59 L.Ed.2d 74 (1979) (overtime, shift differentials, sick pay and vacation pay); Love v. Pullman Co., 13 FEP Cases 423 (D.Colo.1976), affirmed, 569 F.2d 1074 (10th Cir. 1978) (insurance premiums, estimated tips, sick and vacation pay). In light of inflation and loss of use of the funds a victim of discrimination is hardly "made whole" by the award of the amount she should have earned years after she should have earned it. Courts have addressed this problem by awarding pre-judgment interest on the back pay award. See, EEOC v. County of Erie, 751 F.2d 79 (2d Cir. 1984); Parsons v. Kaiser Aluminum & Chemical Co., 727 F.2d 473 (5th Cir.), cert. denied, 467 U.S. 1243, 104 S.Ct. 3516, 82 L.Ed.2d 824 (1984); Washington v. Kroger Co., 671 F.2d 1072 (8th Cir. 1982). There is no consensus on the manner or rate of interest to be used in the calculation. See, Marshall v. Meyer Memorial Hospital, 35 EPD ¶ 34,681 (W.D.N.Y.1983) (adjusted prime interest rate, calculated from midpoint of back pay period); Pegues v. Mississippi State Employment Service, 35 EPD ¶ 34,645 (N.D.Miss.1984) (10% compounded annually); Association Against Discrimina-

tion in Employment, Inc. v. Bridgeport, 572 F.Supp. 494 (D.Conn.1983) (sliding scale interest rate tied to rates applicable to private money markets). The courts are divided, however, on the issue of whether prejudgment interest is available against the federal government. Compare, Cross v. United States Postal Service, 733 F.2d 1327 (8th Cir. 1984), cert. denied, ___ U.S. ___, 105 S.Ct. 1750, 84 L.Ed.2d 815 (1985) (holding that since federal government is immune from suit except to extent it consents to be sued, Congress must specifically authorize pre-judgment interest for it to be available) with Nagy v. United States Postal Service, 773 F.2d 1190 (11th Cir. 1985) (pre-judgment interest available against postal service because it has waived sovereign immunity).

The tax consequences of back pay awards continue to trouble the courts. Should, for example, federal and state income taxes that would otherwise be witheld from wages be deducted from back pay? Compare, Lewis v. J.P. Stevens & Co., 33 EPD ¶ 33,959 (D.S.C.1983) with Sweet v. General Tire & Rubber Co., 28 FEP Cases 804 (N.D.Ohio 1982). The payment of a lump-sum award representing years of lost wages may throw the plaintiff into a higher tax bracket than he otherwise would have in resulting in a larger share of the award going to the government than would have been the case absent the discrimination. The Tenth Circuit has upheld a "tax component" of the back pay award to compensate plaintiffs for their additional tax liability as a result of receiving over seventeen years of back pay in one lump sum. Sears v. Atchison, Topeka & Santa Fe Railway Co., 749 F.2d 1451 (10th Cir. 1984), cert. denied, ___ U.S. ___, 105 S.Ct. 2322, 85 L.Ed.2d 840 (1985).

5. Theoretically, in order to "make whole" an employee for lost wages, the back pay period would have to begin with the first act of discrimination that resulted in lost pay, regardless of how far in the past that incident occurred. A continuing pay violation, for example, may have begun decades before the employee initiated a Title VII claim by filing an EEOC charge. Section 706(g) of Title VII, however, provides in part that "[b]ack pay liability shall not accrue from a date more than two years prior to the filing of a charge with the [EEOC]." In an action filed under Section 1981 or 1983, courts will use the applicable state statute of limitations (see, supra, Chapter 8, Section D.) to determine the accrual date for back pay. See, EEOC v. Enterprise Assn. Steamfitters Local 638, supra, 542 F.2d at 590; Boudreaux v. Baton Rouge Marine Construction Co., 437 F.2d 1011, 1017 (5th Cir. 1971). In light of the wording of § 706(g), should a state statute of limitations of less than two years apply to the back pay claim in a Title VII case? See Stewart v. General Motors Corp., 542 F.2d 445 (7th Cir. 1976), cert. denied, 433 U.S. 919, 97 S.Ct. 2995, 53 L.Ed.2d 1105 (1977); EEOC v. Enterprise Association Steamfitters Local 638, supra; Draper v. United States Pipe & Foundry Co., 527 F.2d 515, 522 (6th Cir. 1976). Under both the Equal Pay Act and the ADEA, an employee may recover back pay for up to three years prior to the filing of his suit if the violation was "willful," but only for a two year period in the case of a "non willful" violation.

How should the cut-off date for the back pay period be determined? See, Gibson v. Mohawk Rubber Co., 695 F.2d 1093 (8th Cir. 1982).

6. In *Ford Motor Co.* back pay was calculated by creating a "hypothetical work history" for the plaintiffs based on the employment history of the men who were actually hired instead of the plaintiffs. The plaintiffs' interim earnings were subtracted from their hypothetical earnings to arrive at the amount of back pay. There is, of course, no way, particularly in a hiring case, to say with certainty that the plaintiffs' work histories, absent discrimination, would have resembled those of the male workers with whom they were

compared. At the stage where back pay is calculated, however, the burden of proof on the issue of quantum is significantly different than at the trial of the merits. The plaintiff's burden is to produce evidence sufficient to allow the court to reasonably estimate the wages lost as a result of the discrimination. The burden of proof then shifts to the defendant to rebut the evidence establishing the "hypothetical work history" or to show the plaintiff's failure to mitigate. Horn v. Duke Homes, Div. of Windsor Mobile Homes, Inc., 755 F.2d 599, 606–08 (7th Cir. 1985). Because of the speculative nature of the enterprise, the calculation cannot be precise, but unrealistic exactitude is not required in this context and "ambiguities in what an employee * * * would have earned but for the discrimination should be resolved against the discriminating employer." Stewart v. General Motors Corp., 542 F.2d 445, 452 (7th Cir. 1976), cert. denied, 433 U.S. 919, 97 S.Ct. 2995, 53 L.Ed.2d 1105 (1977).

It is not always possible to identify an employee who was not the victim of discrimination for purposes of creating a hypothetical work history for the plaintiff. In such cases courts exercise considerable discretion in the calculation of back pay. In Grimes v. Athens Newspaper, Inc., 604 F.Supp. 1166 (M.D. Ga.1985), for example, the court determined that female copy editors had been paid less than male sports reporters for equal work in violation of the Equal Pay Act. The court found it impossible to make individual comparisons between male and female employees because of significant differences in wage rates among the male employees which could not be justified by education, experience or seniority. Back pay was calculated for the plaintiffs by comparing their actual earnings "to the highest male salary being paid for the job at the time of performance." Was that calculation fair to the employer? Was it reasonable to assume that all the female workers would have been paid the same as the highest paid male absent discrimination? In Jepsen v. Florida Board of Regents, 754 F.2d 924 (11th Cir. 1985), the district court found that the plaintiff, a female university professor, had been denied promotions for a long period because of her sex. The plaintiff, who had retired prior to trial as an Associate Professor, urged that her back pay be determined by comparing her earnings to those of male professors who were hired near the time she was hired and who had advanced to full professor. The court found that the plaintiff, absent discrimination, would have been promoted at an earlier date to associate professor but could not conclude that she would have been promoted to full professor. Based on that conclusion, the plaintiff's back pay was determined by averaging the salaries of male faculty hired close to the time of plaintiff and who were promoted to associate professor close to the time she should have been promoted to arrive at an "adjusted salary." The Court of Appeals affirmed on the ground that the trial judge's finding that "Dr. Jepsen might well have remained an associate professor until her retirement" was not clearly erroneous. But if the employer has a history of discriminating against its employees, as did the university in *Jepsen,* why should it be entitled to the benefit of the doubt on the issue of whether the plaintiff would have been promoted?

The problems associated with back pay determinations are magnified in class actions. See discussion, infra, Chapter 14.

7. The Fourth Circuit in *Ford Motor Co.* remanded the case to the district court for reconsideration of the injunctive relief requested by the EEOC. Should the Supreme Court's decision that Gaddis' and Starr's right to back pay was terminated by their refusal to accept the job offers from Ford in 1973,

affect their entitlement to the injunctive relief (preferential hiring and retroactive seniority) suggested by the Circuit Court?

HARRIS v. RICHARDS MANUFACTURING COMPANY, INC.

United States Court of Appeals, Sixth Circuit, 1982.
675 F.2d 811.

REED, DISTRICT JUDGE.*

Richards Manufacturing Company appeals a District Court judgment in favor of Clara Harris for violation of her rights under Title VII of the Civil Rights Act of 1964, 42 U.S.C. Section 2000e–3(a), and Section 1 of the Civil Rights Act of 1866, 42 U.S.C. Section 1981, 511 F.Supp. 1193.

Richards, located in Memphis, Tennessee, is a manufacturer of medical supplies. Harris, a black woman, worked for Richards in various capacities from 1968 until her discharge on February 15, 1977. Her last position was that of "Final Inspector" in the otological products division. In 1976, and again in early 1977, Harris filed complaints with the Equal Employment Opportunity Commission (EEOC), alleging that Richards engaged in racially discriminatory employment practices. Two days after Harris lodged her second EEOC complaint, Richards informed her of its intention to transfer her to an inspection position in another department. Harris asserted her seniority rights and refused to accept the transfer. She was given overnight to reconsider, but again refused the following morning. Thereupon she was discharged, purportedly on the ground of "insubordination."

In November, 1977, Harris commenced this action in the United States District Court for the Western District of Tennessee, alleging racial discrimination by Richards in its hiring, promotion, compensation and termination of its employees. The Court narrowed Harris' allegations to the single issue of whether Harris was discharged in retaliation for her protests against Richards' discriminatory employment practices. In her complaint and amended complaint, Harris sought back pay, reinstatement, restored employment benefits, costs, including a reasonable attorneys' fee, and "such other and further relief as may be deemed necessary and proper." Not until the conclusion of the trial, when she submitted proposed Findings of Fact and Conclusions of Law, did she specifically ask for compensatory and punitive damages under 42 U.S.C. Section 1981.

After a bench trial, the District Judge issued findings of fact and conclusions of law which held: 1) that Harris had established a prima facie case of retaliatory discharge; 2) that Richards had rebutted this presumption by asserting a legitimate, nondiscriminatory reason for the discharge; and 3) that Harris proved by a preponderance of the evidence that Richards' explanation for her termination was pretextu-

* Honorable Scott Reed, United States District Judge for the Eastern District of Kentucky, sitting by designation.

al. In accordance with these findings, the court granted Harris Title VII relief in the form of reinstatement, back pay benefits, as well as attorney's fee and costs. It also awarded $10,000 in compensatory damages and $25,000 in punitive damages.

On appeal, Richards' arguments focus on two principal issues: first, whether the trial court's findings of fact are supported by substantial evidence; and second, whether a court may properly award compensatory and punitive damages in a joint Title VII and Section 1981 action. As a corollary to the second issue, Richards asserts that even if compensatory and punitive damages may, as a general rule, be awarded in a joint Title VII and Section 1981 case, Harris' failure to plead special damages at the outset deprived Richards of its right to demand a jury trial.

The district court's determination that Harris had established a prima facie case of retaliatory discharge, that Richards had rebutted the presumption by asserting a legitimate non-discriminatory reason for the discharge, and that Harris proved by a preponderance of the evidence that Richards' explanation for her termination was pretextual is supported by substantial evidence and is not clearly erroneous. Although there is conflicting testimony in the record, the District Judge had the benefit of hearing the witnesses and observing their demeanor. We note that the District Judge made very complete and detailed findings of fact. They cannot be disturbed by this Court. Fed.R.Civ.P. 52(a).

Although Richards emphasized the substantial evidence issue on appeal, this Court finds the damages issue more troublesome. In Equal Employment Opportunity Comm'n v. Detroit Edison Co., 515 F.2d 301 (6th Cir. 1975), vacated and remanded on other grounds, 431 U.S. 951, 97 S.Ct. 2668, 53 L.Ed.2d 267 (1976), this Court held "that a private plaintiff who sues under both Title VII and Section 1981 relief does not enlarge his right to relief beyond that authorized by Title VII." Id. at 309. Section 1981, it was noted, contains no provision for relief by way of damages or otherwise. When it is joined with a statutory right of action such as Title VII, which specifies broad equitable remedies, we concluded there is no justification for enlarging the Title VII remedies to include legal relief on the basis of Section 1981.

Shortly after this Court issued *Detroit Edison Co.,* supra, the United States Supreme Court rendered its opinion in Johnson v. Railway Express Agency, Inc., 421 U.S. 454, 95 S.Ct. 1716, 44 L.Ed.2d 295 (1975). The Supreme Court held therein that the timely filing of an employment discrimination charge with the EEOC pursuant to Title VII does not toll the running of the limitation period applicable to a Section 1981 action based on the same facts. In so holding, the Supreme Court discussed the characteristics of a Title VII action vis-a-vis the characteristics of a Section 1981 action.

Addressing the element of damages, the Court remarked that in Title VII actions, a court may award back pay for no more than the two-year period prior to the filing of the charge with the EEOC and order "such affirmative action as may be appropriate." 42 U.S.C. Section 2000e–5(g).[1] The court acknowledged that some district courts have ruled that neither compensatory nor punitive damages may be awarded in a Title VII suit. But the Court emphatically declared that an individual is not deprived of other remedies he possesses and is not limited to Title VII relief.

> "[T]he legislative history of Title VII manifests a congressional intent to allow an individual to pursue independently his rights under both Title VII and other applicable state and federal statutes." Alexander v. Gardner-Denver Co., 415 U.S. [36] at 48 [94 S.Ct. 1011 at 1019, 39 L.Ed.2d 260]. In particular, Congress noted "that the remedies available to the individual under Title VII are co-extensive with the indiv[i]dual's right to sue under the provisions of the Civil Rights Act of 1866, 42 U.S.C. Section 1981, and that the two procedures augment each other and are not mutually exclusive." H.R.Rep. No. 92–238, p. 19 (1971). See also S.Rep. No. 92–415, p. 24 (1971). Later, in considering the Equal Employment Opportunity Act of 1972, the Senate rejected an amendment that would have deprived a claimant of any right to sue under Section 1981. 118 Cong.Rec. 3371–3373 (1972).

Id. 421 U.S. at 459, 95 S.Ct. at 1719.

In examining Section 1981 actions, the Supreme Court joined the Federal Courts of Appeal in their holding that Section 1981 affords a federal remedy against discrimination in private employment on the basis of race. "An individual who establishes a cause of action under Section 1981 is entitled to both equitable and legal relief, including compensatory and, under certain circumstances, punitive damages." Id. at 460, 95 S.Ct. 1720. The Court generally concluded that Title VII remedies and Section 1981 remedies, although related and directed to most of the same results, are separate, distinct, and independent.

In light of the pronouncement in *Johnson,* supra, this Court feels constrained to reconsider that aspect of the *Detroit Edison* case which holds that a private plaintiff who sues under both Title VII and Section 1981 cannot obtain relief beyond that authorized by Title VII. Accordingly, we overrule that portion of *Detroit Edison Co.,* supra, and hold that a private plaintiff who sues under both Title VII and Section 1981

1. The full range of relief that a district court may award in Title VII actions is set forth in 42 U.S.C. Section 2000e–5(g). It states in relevant part:

> (g) If the court finds that the respondent has intentionally engaged in or is intentionally engaging in an unlawful employment practice charged in the complaint, the court may enjoin the respondent from engaging in such unlawful employment practice, and order such affirmative action as may be appropriate, which may include, but is not limited to, reinstatement or hiring of employees, with or without back pay (payable by the employer, employment agency, or labor organization, as the case may be, responsible for the unlawful employment practice), or any other equitable relief as the court deems appropriate. Back pay liability shall not accrue from a date more than two years prior to the filing of a charge with the Commission. * * *

may obtain the equitable relief provided by Title VII and such equitable relief as well as legal relief by way of compensatory and punitive damages afforded by Section 1981.

In both her complaint and amended complaint, Harris sought only equitable relief. She specifically sought a declaratory judgment that Richards violated her rights guaranteed by Title VII and Section 1981, injunctive relief, reinstatement, back pay, costs and "such other and further relief as may be deemed necessary and proper." In what was captioned a "Joint Pre-trial Order," it is stated: "Plaintiff is seeking reinstatement, back pay, restored employment benefits and her out-of-pocket litigation expenses including reasonable attorney fees." Finally, in the opening statement to the trial court, counsel for Harris asserted:

> If the plaintiff wins in her action in this matter, she seeks to have her job reinstated, to have her full employment benefits restored and back benefits to which she would have been entitled, and she seeks her full costs of litigation, including reasonable attorney's fees.

Not until her post-trial brief in the form of proposed findings of fact and conclusions of law did Harris seek compensatory and punitive damages. Richards contends that this belated demand for damages deprived it of its right to request a jury trial on that claim.

"[T]he Seventh Amendment guarantees a jury trial where a plaintiff is seeking legal relief, either compensatory or punitive damages, even though the right to such relief is created by a federal statute." Moore v. Sun Oil Co., 636 F.2d 154 (6th Cir. 1980), citing Curtis v. Loether, 415 U.S. 189, 94 S.Ct. 1005, 39 L.Ed.2d 260 (1974). To the extent that a plaintiff is seeking legal relief under Section 1981, the parties are entitled to a jury trial. *Moore,* supra. In an action brought under Title VII and Section 1981, both parties have a right to a jury trial on the legal claims stated under Section 1981. Bibbs v. Jim Lynch Cadillac, Inc., 653 F.2d 316 (8th Cir. 1981); Cf. Amburgey v. Cassady, 507 F.2d 728 (6th Cir. 1974). Plaintiff, alleging a violation of 42 U.S.C. Section 1983 and seeking both equitable and legal relief was entitled to a jury trial on the legal issues.[2]

This action originated as one seeking only equitable relief and remained in that posture throughout the pleading stage and the trial. Richards was in no position to assess the situation and demand a jury trial. Had Harris, at some point in the proceedings, amended her pleadings to include a prayer for legal relief, Richards could have then demanded a jury trial. But Harris failed to take such action until the end of trial and thereby deprived Richards of its right to demand a jury trial.

In United States v. Pelzer Realty Co., Inc., 377 F.Supp. 121 (M.D.Ala. 1974), aff'd 537 F.2d 841 (5th Cir. 1976), a case analogous to the one *sub judice,* the cause, brought under 42 U.S.C. Section 3604, was considered

2. Back pay is recoverable under either Title VII or Section 1981. Under the law of this circuit, back pay is equitable relief and the parties are therefore, not entitled to a jury trial on that issue. Moore v. Sun Oil Co., 636 F.2d 154, 156 (6th Cir. 1980).

on remand from the United States Court of Appeals for the Fifth Circuit. At that point, for the first time, the Government sought an award of damages. That court stated:

> While damages, even nominal damages, are proper relief for a violation of the Act, in the opinion of this Court, an award of damages, where none were prayed for or specifically proved and when the pleadings gave the Defendants no hint that damages were to be litigated so that the Defendants might litigate the issue or consider demanding a jury, would be a strange twist of the law in order to accommodate the Plaintiff.

377 F.Supp. at 123.

Harris' argument that the catchall phrase "and such other and further relief as may be deemed necessary and proper" is somehow magical and all encompassing and constitutes a prayer for legal relief in the form of damages is unpersuasive. First, of all, the phrase is limited, if the principle of *ejusdem generis* is applied, to relief of the same kind as that specifically enumerated, i.e., equitable relief. *Detroit Edison Co.*, supra at 309. Secondly, the joint pretrial order and the opening statement of Harris' counsel were limited to specifically enumerated equitable relief and accompanied by no allegedly saving catch-all phrase. Furthermore, both occurred after the pleading stage. We therefore hold that the District Judge erred in awarding compensatory and punitive damages where they were never sought, thereby depriving Richards of its right to consider the situation and to determine whether to demand a jury trial.

Accordingly, the judgment of the District Court is affirmed in part and reversed in part and remanded for proceedings not inconsistent with this opinion.

* * *

NOTES AND PROBLEMS FOR DISCUSSION

1. The principles of general tort law apply to damage actions under Sections 1981, 1983 and 1985. Carey v. Piphus, 435 U.S. 247, 98 S.Ct. 1042, 55 L.Ed.2d 252 (1978). Accordingly, in employment discrimination cases filed under one of the Reconstruction era civil rights statutes, recovery can be had for emotional distress, humiliation and other psychic injury, as well as for physical injury or economic loss. See, Stallworth v. Shuler, 777 F.2d 1431 (11th Cir. 1985) ($100,000 in compensatory damages to black employee denied promotions because of racial discrimination is within "acceptable universe" for injuries in light of plaintiff's testimony that he suffered stress, loss of sleep, marital strain and humiliation); Muldrew v. Anheuser-Busch, Inc., 728 F.2d 989 (8th Cir. 1984) ($125,000 award to employee discharged for racially discriminatory reasons where there was evidence that, as result of discharge, he lost his car and house, began experiencing marital problems and felt he had lost respect of his children). The Supreme Court has held, however, that compensatory damages must always be designed to compensate for injuries caused by unlawful actions, and not for the violation of a legal right in the abstract. In MEMPHIS COMMUNITY SCHOOL DISTRICT v. STACHURA, ___ U.S. ___,

106 S.Ct. 2537, 91 L.Ed.2d 249 (1986), the Court held that damages based on the abstract "value" or "importance" of constitutional rights are not a permissible element of compensatory damages in Section 1983 cases.

Punitive damages are available in a Section 1983 case where the violation is shown to be intentional or the result of reckless or callously indifferent conduct. Smith v. Wade, 461 U.S. 30, 103 S.Ct. 1625, 75 L.Ed.2d 632 (1983). A municipality which may be liable for an award of compensatory damages under Department of Social Services v. Monell, supra, has, however, a common law immunity from punitive damages. City of Newport v. Fact Concerts, Inc., 453 U.S. 247, 101 S.Ct. 2748, 69 L.Ed.2d 616 (1981). In Johnson v. Railway Express Agency, 421 U.S. 454, 95 S.Ct. 1716, 44 L.Ed.2d 295 (1975), the Court held that a plaintiff who proves a Section 1981 cause of action is entitled under certain circumstances to punitive damages. In light of the Court's subsequent ruling in General Building Contractors v. Pennsylvania, supra, that only purposeful discrimination will violate § 1981, what must the plaintiff prove to justify an award of punitive damages? See, Block v. R.H. Macy & Co., Inc., 712 F.2d 1241 (8th Cir. 1983).

As in other types of personal injury litigation, the difficulty of fixing dollar amounts for emotional injury and, in the case of punitive damages, for deterrence, has resulted in enormous variations in the amounts awarded. Compare, Rawson v. Sears, Roebuck & Co., 615 F.Supp. 1546 (D.Col.1985) (jury award of $5,000,000 for pain, suffering and humiliation, $10,000,000 in punitive damages and $849,910 in lost wages to victim of age discrimination allowed to stand); Rogers v. Fisher Body Div., General Motors Corp., 739 F.2d 1102 (6th Cir. 1984), cert. denied, ___ U.S. ___, 105 S.Ct. 1759, 84 L.Ed.2d 821 (1985) (awards of $300,000 compensatory and $500,000 punitive damages to black employee discharged for racially discriminatory reasons overturned as excessive); Phillips v. Smalley Maintenance Services, Inc., 711 F.2d 1524 (11th Cir. 1983) (award of $25,000 to victim of sexual harassment for mental suffering under state pendent cause of action upheld).

2. The Equal Pay Act, 29 U.S.C. § 206(d) and the Age Discrimination in Employment Act of 1967 (ADEA), 29 U.S.C. § 621 et seq., incorporate the remedial provisions of the Fair Labor Standards Act (FLSA), 29 U.S.C. § 201 et seq. The Equal Pay Act was enacted as an amendment to the FLSA and provides that "any amounts owing to any employee which have been withheld in violation of this subsection [of the FLSA] shall be deemed to be unpaid minimum wages or unpaid overtime compensation under this chapter." The applicable FLSA section provides, "[a]ny employer who violates the provisions of * * * this title shall be liable to the employee or employees affected in the amount of their unpaid minimum wages, or their unpaid overtime compensation, as the case may be, and in an additional equal amount as liquidated damages." 29 U.S.C. § 216(b). The ADEA also equates amounts owing to a person as a result of a violation of the Act to unpaid minimum wages or unpaid overtime compensation, 29 U.S.C. § 626(b), but incorporates a different remedial provision of § 216(b) of the FLSA which provides, "[a]ny employer who violates the provisions of * * * [this Act] shall be liable for such legal or equitable relief as may be appropriate to effectuate the purposes of * * * [the Act] including without limitation employment, reinstatement, promotion, and the payment of wages lost and an additional equal amount as liquidated damages." Liquidated damages are available under the ADEA where the violation has been willful. 29 U.S.C. § 626(b). In TRANS-WORLD AIRLINES, INC. v. THURSTON, 469 U.S. 111, 105 S.Ct. 613, 83 L.Ed.2d 523 (1985), the

Court held that the appropriate standard for determining a willful violation in connection with a claim for liquidated damages is whether the defendant knew its conduct violated the act or showed a reckless disregard as to whether its conduct was prohibited. The plaintiff's contention that a willful violation could be established by showing that the employer knew of the potential applicability of the ADEA to its conduct was rejected. The Tenth Circuit has held that under the Equal Pay Act willfulness is shown if the employer makes no effort to learn of the Act's requirements. Sinclair v. Automobile Club of Oklahoma, Inc., 733 F.2d 726 (10th Cir. 1984).

3. As noted by the Court of Appeals in *Harris,* where legal damages are claimed, as opposed to equitable relief, either party is entitled as a matter of right to a jury trial under the Seventh Amendment. Because Title VII expressly authorizes only equitable remedies, courts have generally agreed that neither party, in a pure Title VII case, is entitled to a jury trial. See e.g., Slack v. Havens, 522 F.2d 1091, 1094 (9th Cir. 1975); Johnson v. Georgia Highway Express, Inc., 417 F.2d 1122, 1125 (5th Cir. 1969). The Circuits are divided, however, on the question of whether a claim for back pay in a § 1981 case is a claim for equitable or legal relief. Compare, Moore v. Sun Oil Co., 636 F.2d 154 (6th Cir. 1980) (claim for back pay constitutes equitable rather than legal relief and plaintiff is entitled to jury trial in § 1981 case only if he asserts claim for compensatory or punitive damages) and Setser v. Novak Investment Co., 638 F.2d 1137 (8th Cir. 1981), cert. denied, 454 U.S. 1064, 102 S.Ct. 615, 70 L.Ed.2d 601 (1981) (back pay constitutes legal damages in § 1981 action).

Where a damage claim is joined with a Title VII claim and either party requests a jury trial, the jury will determine all the common factual issues of the claims as well as the amount of damages. The trial judge in such a case must decide the equitable (Title VII) claim but will be bound by the jury's findings of fact on common issues. Since the merits of the Title VII and the § 1981 claims will usually be the same, a jury verdict on the legal claim will, as a practical matter, determine the Title VII claim also. See, Cerminara v. Allegheny Housing Corp., 37 FEP Cases 998 (W.D.Pa.1985); Bolents v. City of Niagara Falls, 35 FEP Cases 597 (W.D.N.Y.1984). It has long been settled that the Seventh Amendment's right to trial by jury does not apply to actions against the federal government. See, Galloway v. United States, 319 U.S. 372, 388–89, 63 S.Ct. 1077, 1086, 87 L.Ed. 1458 (1943); Cuddy v. Carmen, 694 F.2d 853 (D.C.Cir. 1982).

In contrast to the treatment of back pay claims under Title VII as "equitable relief," private actions by employees for lost wages under the FLSA have consistently been held to include a right to trial by jury. See Lorillard v. Pons, 434 U.S. 575, 98 S.Ct. 866, 55 L.Ed.2d 40 (1978) (jury trial available in ADEA action for lost wages); Wirtz v. Jones, 340 F.2d 901, 904 (5th Cir. 1965); Olearchick v. American Steel Foundries, 73 F.Supp. 273, 279 (W.D.Pa.1947); see also Note, The Right to Jury Trial Under the Age Discrimination in Employment and Fair Labor Standards Acts, 44 U.Chi. L.Rev. 365, 376 (1977). But because of the element of discretion in awards of liquidated damages under the Portal-to-Portal Act, 29 U.S.C. § 260, such awards remain the province of the court, not the jury. See McClanahan v. Matthews, 440 F.2d 320, 322 (6th Cir. 1971); Hodgson v. Miller Brewing Co., 457 F.2d 221, 227 (7th Cir. 1972). In 1978, the ADEA was amended to specifically authorize trial by jury "of any issue of fact in any * * * action for recovery of amounts owing as a result of a violation of this chapter." 29 U.S.C. § 626(c)(2). Thus, under the ADEA all claims for monetary relief, whether back wages or liquidated damages, may be tried to a jury. See Criswell v. Western Air Lines, Inc., 514 F.Supp. 384, 393 (C.D.Cal.1981), affirmed, 709 F.2d 544 (9th Cir. 1983). A jury trial, however, is not available in an age claim against the federal government. Lehman v. Nakshian, 453 U.S. 156, 101 S.Ct. 2698, 69 L.Ed.2d 548 (1981). Under the Equal Pay Act, which has no explicit jury trial provision, jury trials, as in other FLSA cases, may be had on wage claims only with liquidated damages awarded by the court. See Altman v. Stevens Fashion Fabrics, 441 F.Supp. 1318, 1323 (N.D. Cal.1977).

4. The Eleventh Amendment to the Constitution bars an award of monetary relief against a state or state agency. Edelman v. Jordan, 415 U.S. 651, 94 S.Ct. 1347, 39 L.Ed.2d 662 (1974). Technically, the amendment also prohibits injunctive relief against a state, but the effect of the amendment is avoided by suing the appropriate state official. Ex Parte Young, 209 U.S. 123, 28 S.Ct. 441, 52 L.Ed. 714 (1908), held that illegal action of a state official is not action of the state for Eleventh Amendment purposes (even though it is simultaneously treated as "state action" for Fourteenth Amendment purposes). But see, Pennhurst State School and Hospital v. Halderman, 465 U.S. 89, 104 S.Ct. 900, 79 L.Ed.2d 67 (1984) (11th Amendment bars even injunctive relief against state officials if based on state pendent cause of action). The 1972 Amendments to Title VII expanded the Act's coverage to local and state employees as well as those of the federal government. In Fitzpatrick v. Bitzer, 427 U.S. 445, 96 S.Ct. 2666, 49 L.Ed.2d 614 (1976), a Title VII action against a state agency, the Court held that Congress had the power to abrogate Eleventh Amendment immunity by exercising its authority under section 5 of the Fourteenth Amendment to provide *expressly* for monetary relief against a state in federal court. Thus, an award of back pay against a state under Title VII is not barred by the Eleventh Amendment, but an award of back pay, or any other monetary relief, on a 42 U.S.C. § 1981 or 1983 cause of action will be precluded. Quern v. Jordan, 440 U.S. 332, 99 S.Ct. 1139, 59 L.Ed.2d 358 (1979); Sessions v. Rusk State Hospital, 648 F.2d 1066, 1069 (5th Cir. 1981). Note that the Eleventh Amendment does not apply to bar suits against political subdivisions of a state such as cities, counties, school districts, and like entities. Moor v. County of Alameda, 411 U.S. 693, 93 S.Ct. 1785, 36 L.Ed.2d 596 (1973); Goss v. San Jacinto Junior College, 588 F.2d 96 (5th Cir. 1979), modified on rehearing, 595 F.2d 1119. The Supreme Court has held, however, that municipalities enjoy a "common law" immunity from an award of punitive damages. City of Newport v. Fact Concerts, Inc., 453 U.S. 247, 101 S.Ct. 2748, 69 L.Ed.2d 616 (1981). While the Eleventh Amendment does not bar prospective injunctive relief against a state official, it does preclude an award of back pay or damages against him in his *official capacity*, because such a judgment would necessarily have to be paid with state funds. Edelman v. Jordan, supra. But the amendment does not immunize such officials from *personal* liability for their illegal acts, though they may benefit from other types of official immunity. See Scheuer v. Rhodes, 416 U.S. 232, 94 S.Ct. 1683, 40 L.Ed.2d 90 (1975) (executive immunity); Tenney v. Brandhove, 341 U.S. 367, 71 S.Ct. 783, 95 L.Ed. 1019 (1951). Public officials generally enjoy qualified immunity for "good faith" actions. See Wood v. Strickland, 420 U.S. 308, 95 S.Ct. 992, 43 L.Ed.2d 214 (1975).

Chapter 13

INJUNCTIVE RELIEF

FRANKS v. BOWMAN TRANSPORTATION CO., INC.

Supreme Court of the United States, 1976.
424 U.S. 747, 96 S.Ct. 1251, 47 L.Ed.2d 444.

MR. JUSTICE BRENNAN delivered the opinion of the Court.

This case presents the question whether identifiable applicants who were denied employment because of race after the effective date and in violation of Title VII of the Civil Rights Act of 1964, may be awarded seniority status retroactive to the dates of their employment applications.[1]

Petitioner Franks brought this class action in the United States District Court for the Northern District of Georgia against his former employer, respondent Bowman Transportation Co., and his unions, the International Union of District 50, Allied and Technical Workers of the United States and Canada, and its local, No. 13600,[2] alleging various racially discriminatory employment practices in violation of Title VII. Petitioner Lee intervened on behalf of himself and others similarly situated alleging racially discriminatory hiring and discharge policies limited to Bowman's employment of over-the-road (OTR) truck drivers. Following trial, the District Court found that Bowman had engaged in a pattern of racial discrimination in various company policies, including the hiring, transfer, and discharge of employees, and found further that the discriminatory practices were perpetrated in Bowman's collective-bargaining agreement with the unions. The District Court certified the action as a proper class action under Fed.Rule Civ.Proc. 23(b)(2), and of import to the issues before this Court, found that petitioner Lee represented all black applicants who sought to be hired or to transfer to OTR driving positions prior to January 1, 1972. In its final order and decree, the District Court subdivided the class represented by petitioner Lee into a class of black nonemployee applicants for OTR positions prior to January 1, 1972 (class 3), and a class of black employees who applied for transfer to OTR positions prior to the same date (class 4).

In its final judgment entered July 14, 1972, the District Court permanently enjoined the respondents from perpetuating the discriminatory practices found to exist, and, in regard to the black applicants for OTR positions, ordered Bowman to notify the members of both

1. Petitioners also alleged an alternative claim for relief for violations of 42 U.S.C. § 1981. In view of our decision we have no occasion to address that claim.

2. In 1972, the International Union of District 50 merged with the United Steelworkers of America, AFL–CIO, and hence the latter as the successor bargaining representative is the union respondent before this Court. Brief for Respondent United Steelworkers of America, AFL–CIO, and for American Federation of Labor and Congress of Industrial Organizations as *Amicus Curiae* 5.

subclasses within 30 days of their right to priority consideration for such jobs. The District Court declined, however, to grant to the unnamed members of classes 3 and 4 any other specific relief sought, which included an award of backpay and seniority status retroactive to the date of individual application for an OTR position.

On petitioners' appeal to the Court of Appeals for the Fifth Circuit, raising for the most part claimed inadequacy of the relief ordered respecting unnamed members of the various subclasses involved, the Court of Appeals affirmed in part, reversed in part, and vacated in part. 495 F.2d 398 (1974). The Court of Appeals held that the District Court had exercised its discretion under an erroneous view of law insofar as it failed to award backpay to the unnamed class members of both classes 3 and 4, and vacated the judgment in that respect. The judgment was reversed insofar as it failed to award any seniority remedy to the members of class 4 who after the judgment of the District Court sought and obtained priority consideration for transfer to OTR positions.[3] As respects unnamed members of class 3—nonemployee black applicants who applied for and were denied OTR positions prior to January 1, 1972—the Court of Appeals affirmed the District Court's denial of any form of seniority relief. Only this last aspect of the Court of Appeals' judgment is before us for review under our grant of the petition for certiorari. 420 U.S. 989, 95 S.Ct. 1421, 43 L.Ed.2d 699 (1975).

[The named plaintiffs included only one representative of class 3 (Lee). After being discriminatorily refused employment, Lee was hired by Bowman, but then was discharged before trial for cause. The district court awarded him back pay for the intervening period of discrimination. The defendant's argument that the class claim for seniority relief was moot, because the sole class representative's claim had become moot, was rejected by the Supreme Court. "The unnamed members of the class are entitled to the relief already afforded Lee, hiring and back pay, and thus to that extent have 'such a personal stake in the outcome of the controversy [whether they are also entitled to seniority relief] as to assure that concrete adverseness which sharpens the presentation of issues upon which the court so largely depends for illumination of difficult * * * questions.' [citation omitted] Given a properly certified class action, * * * mootness turns on whether, in the specific circumstances of the given case at the time it is before this Court, an adversary relationship sufficient to fulfill this function exists." 424 U.S. at 755–756, 96 S.Ct. 1259–1260. The Court also held that § 703(h) of Title VII, which recognizes the legality of bona fide seniority and merit systems, does not bar seniority relief to persons who were not seeking "modification or elimination of the existing seniority system, but only * * * an award of the seniority

3. In conjunction with its directions to the District Court regarding seniority relief for the members of other subclasses not involved in the issues presently confronting this Court, the Court of Appeals directed that class 4 members who transferred to OTR positions under the District Court's decree should be allowed to carry over all accumulated company seniority for all purposes in the OTR department. 495 F.2d, at 417.

status they would have individually enjoyed under the present system but for the illegal discriminatory refusal to hire." 424 U.S. at 758, 96 S.Ct. at 1261.]

* * *

II

In affirming the District Court's denial of seniority relief to the class 3 group of discriminatees, the Court of Appeals held that the relief was barred by § 703(h) of Title VII, 42 U.S.C. § 2000e–2(h). We disagree. Section 703(h) provides in pertinent part:

> "Notwithstanding any other provision of this title, it shall not be an unlawful employment practice for an employer to apply different standards of compensation, or different terms, conditions, or privileges of employment pursuant to a bona fide seniority or merit system * * * provided that such differences are not the result of an intention to discriminate because of race, color, religion, sex, or national origin * * *."

The Court of Appeals reasoned that a discriminatory refusal to hire "does not affect the bona fides of the seniority system. Thus, the differences in the benefits and conditions of employment which a seniority system accords to older and newer employees is protected [by § 703(h)] as 'not an unlawful employment practice.' " 495 F.2d, at 417. Significantly, neither Bowman nor the unions undertake to defend the Court of Appeals' judgment on that ground. It is clearly erroneous.

The black applicants for OTR positions composing class 3 are limited to those whose applications were put in evidence at the trial.[10] The underlying legal wrong affecting them is not the alleged operation of a racially discriminatory seniority system but of a racially discriminatory hiring system. Petitioners do not ask for modification or elimination of the existing seniority system, but only an award of the seniority status they would have individually enjoyed under the present system but for the illegal discriminatory refusal to hire. It is this context that must shape our determination as to the meaning and effect of § 703(h).

On its face, § 703(h) appears to be only a definitional provision; as with the other provisions of § 703, subsection (h) delineates which employment practices are illegal and thereby prohibited and which are not.[11] Section 703(h) certainly does not expressly purport to qualify or

10. By its terms, the judgment of the District Court runs to all black applicants for OTR positions prior to January 1, 1972, and is not qualified by a limitation that the discriminatory refusal to hire must have taken place after the effective date of the Act. However, only post-Act victims of racial discrimination are members of class 3. Title VII's prohibition on racial discrimination in hiring became effective on July 2, 1965, one year after the date of its enactment. Pub.L. 88–352, §§ 716(a)–(b), 78 Stat. 266. Petitioners sought relief in this case for identifiable applicants for OTR positions "whose applications were put in evidence at the trial." App. 20a. There were 206 unhired black applicants prior to January 1, 1972, whose written applications are summarized in the record and none of the applications relates to years prior to 1970. Id. at 52a, Table VA.

11. See Last Hired, First Fired Seniority, Layoffs, and Title VII: Questions of

proscribe relief otherwise appropriate under the remedial provisions of Title VII, § 706(g), 42 U.S.C. § 2000e–5(g), in circumstances where an illegal discriminatory act or practice is found. Further, the legislative history of § 703(h) plainly negates its reading as limiting or qualifying the relief authorized under § 706(g). The initial bill reported by the House Judiciary Committee as H.R. 7152 [12] and passed by the full House on February 10, 1964,[13] did not contain § 703(h). Neither the House bill nor the majority Judiciary Committee Report [14] even mentioned the problem of seniority. That subject thereafter surfaced during the debate of the bill in the Senate. This debate prompted Senators Clark and Case to respond to criticism that Title VII would destroy existing seniority systems by placing an interpretive memorandum in the Congressional Record. The memorandum stated: "Title VII would have no effect on established seniority rights. Its effect is prospective and not retrospective." 110 Cong.Rec. 7213 (1964).[15] Senator Clark also placed in the Congressional Record a Justice Department statement concerning Title VII which stated: "[I]t has been asserted that Title VII would undermine vested rights of seniority. This is not correct. Title VII would have no effect on seniority rights existing at the time it takes effect." Id., at 7207.[16] Several weeks thereafter,

Liability and Remedy, 11 Col.J.L. & Soc. Prob. 343, 376, 378 (1975).

12. See H.R.Rep.No.914, 88th Cong., 1st Sess., U.S.Code Cong. & Admin.News 1964, p. 2355 (1963).

13. 110 Cong.Rec. 2804 (1964).

14. H.R.Rep.No.914, supra.

15. The full text of the memorandum pertaining to seniority states:

"Title VII would have no effect on established seniority rights. Its effect is prospective and not retrospective. Thus, for example, if a business has been discriminating in the past and as a result has an all-white working force, when the title comes into effect the employer's obligation would be simply to fill future vacancies on a nondiscriminatory basis. He would not be obliged—or indeed, permitted—to fire whites in order to hire Negroes, or to prefer Negroes for future vacancies, or, once Negroes are hired, to give them special seniority rights at the expense of the white workers hired earlier. (However, where waiting lists for employment or training are, prior to the effective date of the title, maintained on a discriminatory basis, the use of such lists after the title takes effect may be held an unlawful subterfuge to accomplish discrimination.)"

16. The full text of the statement pertinent to seniority reads:

"First, it has been asserted that title VII would undermine vested rights of seniority. This is not correct. Title VII would have no effect on seniority rights existing at the time it takes effect. If, for example, a collective bargaining contract provides that in the event of layoffs, those who were hired last must be laid off first, such a provision would not be affected in the least by title VII. This would be true even in the case where owing to discrimination prior to the effective date of the title, white workers had more seniority than Negroes. Title VII is directed at discrimination based on race, color, religion, sex, or national origin. It is perfectly clear that when a worker is laid off or denied a chance for promotion because under established seniority rules he is 'low man on the totem pole' he is not being discriminated against because of his race. Of course, if the seniority rule itself is discriminatory, it would be unlawful under title VII. If a rule were to state that all Negroes must be laid off before any white man, such a rule could not serve as the basis for a discharge subsequent to the effective date of the title. I do not know how anyone could quarrel with such a result. But, in the ordinary case, assuming that seniority rights were built up over a period of time during which Negroes were not hired, these rights would not be set aside by the taking effect of title VII. Employers and labor organizations would simply be under a duty not to discriminate against Negroes because of their race. Any differences in treatment

following several informal conferences among the Senate leadership, the House leadership, the Attorney General and others, see Vaas, Title VII: Legislative History, 7 B.C.Ind. & Com.L.Rev. 431, 445 (1966), a compromise substitute bill prepared by Senators Mansfield and Dirksen, Senate majority and minority leaders respectively, containing § 703(h) was introduced on the Senate floor.[17] Although the Mansfield-Dirksen substitute bill, and hence § 703(h), was not the subject of a committee report, see generally Vaas, supra, Senator Humphrey, one of the informal conferees, later stated during debate on the substitute that § 703(h) was not designed to alter the meaning of Title VII generally but rather "merely clarifies its present intent and effect." 110 Cong. Rec. 12723 (1964). Accordingly, whatever the exact meaning and scope of § 703(h) in light of its unusual legislative history and the absence of the usual legislative materials, see Vaas, supra, at 457–458, it is apparent that the thrust of the section is directed toward defining what is and what is not an illegal discriminatory practice in instances in which the post-Act operation of a seniority system is challenged as perpetuating the effects of discrimination occurring prior to the effective date of the Act. There is no indication in the legislative materials that § 703(h) was intended to modify or restrict relief otherwise appropriate once an illegal discriminatory practice occurring after the effective date of the Act is proved—as in the instant case, a discriminatory refusal to hire. This accords with the apparently unanimous view of commentators, see Cooper & Sobol, Seniority and Testing Under Fair Employment Laws: A General Approach to Objective Criteria of Hiring and Promotion, 82 Harv.L.Rev. 1598, 1632 (1969); Stacy, Title VII Seniority Remedies in a Time of Economic Downturn, 28 Vand.L.Rev. 487, 506 (1975).[18] We therefore hold that the Court of Appeals erred in

based on established seniority rights would not be based on race and would not be forbidden by the title." 110 Cong. Rec. 7207 (1964).

Senator Clark also introduced into the Congressional Record a set of answers to a series of questions propounded by Senator Dirksen. Two of these questions and answers are pertinent to the issue of seniority:

"Question. Would the same situation prevail in respect to promotions, when that management function is governed by a labor contract calling for promotions on the basis of seniority? What of dismissals? Normally, labor contracts call for 'last hired, first fired.' If the last hired are Negroes, is the employer discriminating if his contract requires they be first fired and the remaining employees are white?

"Answer. Seniority rights are in no way affected by the bill. If under a 'last hired, first fired' agreement a Negroe happens to be the 'last hired,' he can still be 'first fired' as long as it is done because of his status as 'last hired' and not because of his race.

"Question. If an employer is directed to abolish his employment list because of discrimination what happens to seniority?

"Answer. The bill is not retroactive, and it will not require an employer to change existing seniority lists." Id., at 7217.

17. Id., at 11926, 11931.

18. Cf. Gould, Employment Security, Seniority and Race: The Role of Title VII of the Civil Rights Act of 1964, 13 How.L.J. 1, 8–9, and n. 32 (1967); see also Jurinko v. Edwin L. Wiegand Co., 477 F.2d 1038 (C.A.3), vacated and remanded on other grounds, 414 U.S. 970, 94 S.Ct. 293, 38 L.Ed.2d 214 (1973), wherein the court awarded back seniority in a case of discriminatory hiring after the effective date of Title VII without any discussion of the

concluding that, as a matter of law, § 703(h) barred the award of seniority relief to the unnamed class 3 members.

III

There remains the question whether an award of seniority relief is appropriate under the remedial provisions of Title VII, specifically, § 706(g).[19]

We begin by repeating the observation of earlier decisions that in enacting Title VII of the Civil Rights Act of 1964, Congress intended to prohibit all practices in whatever form which create inequality in employment opportunity due to discrimination on the basis of race, religion, sex, or national origin, Alexander v. Gardner-Denver Co., 415 U.S. 36, 44, 94 S.Ct. 1011, 1017, 39 L.Ed.2d 147, 155 (1974); McDonnell Douglas Corp. v. Green, 411 U.S. 792, 800, 93 S.Ct. 1817, 1823, 36 L.Ed. 2d 668, 676 (1973); Griggs v. Duke Power Co., 401 U.S. 424, 429–430, 91 S.Ct. 849, 852–853, 28 L.Ed.2d 158, 163–164 (1971), and ordained that its policy of outlawing such discrimination should have the "highest priority," Alexander, supra, 415 U.S., at 47, 94 S.Ct. at 1019, 39 L.Ed.2d at 158; Newman v. Piggie Park Enterprises, Inc., 390 U.S. 400, 402, 88 S.Ct. 964, 966, 19 L.Ed.2d 1263, 1265 (1968). Last Term's Albemarle Paper Co. v. Moody, 422 U.S. 405, 95 S.Ct. 2362, 45 L.Ed.2d 280 (1975), consistently with the congressional plan, held that one of the central purposes of Title VII is "to make persons whole for injuries suffered on account of unlawful employment discrimination." Id., at 418, 95 S.Ct., at 2372, 45 L.Ed.2d, at 297. To effectuate this "make whole" objective, Congress in § 706(g) vested broad equitable discretion in the federal courts to "order such affirmative action as may be appropriate, which may include, but is not limited to, reinstatement or hiring of employees, with or without back pay * * *, or any other equitable relief as the court deems appropriate." The legislative history supporting the 1972

impact of § 703(h) on the propriety of such a remedy.

19. Section 706(g) of Title VII, 42 U.S.C. § 2000e–5(g) (1970 ed., Supp. IV), provides:

> "If the court finds that the respondent has intentionally engaged in or is intentionally engaging in an unlawful employment practice charged in the complaint, the court may enjoin the respondent from engaging in such unlawful employment practice, and order such affirmative action as may be appropriate, which may include, but is not limited to, reinstatement or hiring of employees, with or without back pay (payable by the employer, employment agency, or labor organization, as the case may be, responsible for the unlawful employment practice), or any other equitable relief as the court deems appropriate. Back pay liability shall not accrue from a date more than two years prior to the filing of a charge with the Commission. Interim earnings or amounts earnable with reasonable diligence by the person or persons discriminated against shall operate to reduce the back pay otherwise allowable. No order of the court shall require the admission or reinstatement of an individual as a member of a union, or the hiring, reinstatement, or promotion of an individual as an employee, or the payment to him of any back pay, if such individual was refused admission, suspended, or expelled, or was refused employment or advancement or was suspended or discharged for any reason other than discrimination on account of race, color, religion, sex, or national origin or in violation of section 2000e–3(a) of this title."

amendments of § 706(g) of Title VII [20] affirms the breadth of this discretion. "The provisions of [§ 706(g)] are intended to give the courts wide discretion exercising their equitable powers to fashion the most complete relief possible. * * * [T]he Act is intended to make the victims of unlawful employment discrimination whole, and * * * the attainment of this objective * * * requires that persons aggrieved by the consequences and effects of the unlawful employment practice be, so far as possible, restored to a position where they would have been were it not for the unlawful discrimination." Section-by-Section Analysis of H.R. 1746, accompanying the Equal Employment Opportunity Act of 1972—Conference Report, 118 Cong.Rec. 7166, 7168 (1972). This is emphatic confirmation that federal courts are empowered to fashion such relief as the particular circumstances of a case may require to effect restitution, making whole insofar as possible the victims of racial discrimination in hiring.[21] Adequate relief may well

20. Equal Employment Opportunity Act of 1972, 86 Stat. 103, amending 42 U.S.C. § 2000e *et seq.*

21. It is true that backpay is the only remedy specifically mentioned in § 706(g). But to draw from this fact and other sections of the statute any implicit statement by Congress that seniority relief is a prohibited, or at least less available, form of remedy is not warranted. Indeed, any such contention necessarily disregards the extensive legislative history underlying the 1972 amendments to Title VII. The 1972 amendments added the phrase speaking to "other equitable relief" in § 706(g). The Senate Report manifested an explicit concern with the "earnings gap" presently existing between black and white employees in American society. S.Rep.No.92–415, p. 6 (1971). The Reports of both Houses of Congress indicated that "rightful place" was the intended objective of Title VII and the relief accorded thereunder. Ibid.; H.R. Rep.No.92–238, p. 4 (1971), U.S.Code Cong. & Admin.News 1972, p. 2137. * * * [R]ightful-place seniority, implicating an employee's *future* earnings, job security, and advancement prospects, is absolutely essential to obtaining this congressionally mandated goal.

The legislative history underlying the 1972 amendments completely answers the argument that Congress somehow intended seniority relief to be less available in pursuit of this goal. In explaining the need for the 1972 amendments, the Senate Report stated:

"Employment discrimination as viewed today is a * * * complex and pervasive phenomenon. Experts familiar with the subject now generally describe the problem in terms of 'systems' and 'effects' rather than simply intentional wrongs, and the literature on the subject is replete with discussions of, for example, the mechanics of seniority and lines of progression, perpetuation of the present effect of pre-act discriminatory practices through various institutional devices, and testing and validation requirements." S.Rep.No.92–415, supra, at 5. See also H.R.Rep.No.92–238, supra, at 8. In the context of this express reference to seniority, the Reports of both Houses cite with approval decisions of the lower federal courts which granted forms of retroactive "rightful place" seniority relief. S.Rep.No.92–415, supra, at 5 n. 1; H.R.Rep.No.92–238, supra, at 8 n.2. (The dissent would distinguish these lower federal court decisions as not involving instances of discriminatory *hiring*. Obviously, however, the concern of the entire thrust of the dissent—the impact of rightful-place seniority upon the expectations of other employees—is in no way a function of the specific type of illegal discriminatory practice upon which the judgment of liability is predicated.) Thereafter, in language that could hardly be more explicit, the analysis accompanying the Conference Report stated:

"In any area where the new law does not address itself, or in any areas where a specific contrary intention is not indicated, it was assumed *that the present case law as developed by the courts would continue to govern the applicability and construction of Title VII.*" Section-By-Section Analysis of H.R.1746, accompanying The Equal Employment Opportunity Act of 1972—Conference Report, 118 Cong.Rec. 7166 (1972) (emphasis added).

be denied in the absence of a seniority remedy slotting the victim in that position in the seniority system that would have been his had he been hired at the time of his application. It can hardly be questioned that ordinarily such relief will be necessary to achieve the "make-whole" purposes of the Act.

Seniority systems and the entitlements conferred by credits earned thereunder are of vast and increasing importance in the economic employment system of this Nation. S. Slichter, J. Healy, & E. Livernash, The Impact of Collective Bargaining on Management 104–115 (1960). Seniority principles are increasingly used to allocate entitlements to scarce benefits among competing employees ("competitive status" seniority) and to compute noncompetitive benefits earned under the contract of employment ("benefit" seniority). Ibid. We have already said about "competitive status" seniority that it "has become of overriding importance, and one of its major functions is to determine who gets or who keeps an available job." Humphrey v. Moore, 375 U.S. 335, 346–347, 84 S.Ct. 363, 370, 11 L.Ed.2d 370, 380 (1964). "More than any other provision of the collective[-bargaining] agreement * * * seniority affects the economic security of the individual employee covered by its terms." Aaron, Reflections on the Legal Nature and Enforceability of Seniority Rights, 75 Harv.L.Rev. 1532, 1535 (1962). "Competitive status" seniority also often plays a broader role in modern employment systems, particularly systems operated under collective-bargaining agreements:

> "Included among the benefits, options, and safeguards affected by competitive status seniority, are not only promotion and layoff, but also transfer, demotion, rest days, shift assignments, perogative in scheduling vacation, order of layoff, possibilities of lateral transfer to avoid layoff, 'bumping' possibilities in the face of layoff, order of recall, training opportunities, working conditions, length of layoff endured without reducing seniority, length of layoff recall rights will withstand, overtime opportunities, parking privileges, and, in one plant, a preferred place in the punch-out line." Stacy, 28 Vand. L.Rev., supra, at 490 (footnotes omitted).

Seniority standing in employment with respondent Bowman, computed from the departmental date of hire, determines the order of layoff and recall of employees.[22] Further, job assignments for OTR drivers are posted for competitive bidding and seniority is used to determine the highest bidder.[23] As OTR drivers are paid on a per-mile basis,[24] earnings are therefore to some extent a function of seniority. Additionally, seniority computed from the company date of hire determines the length of an employee's vacation [25] and pension benefits.[26] Obviously merely to require Bowman to hire the class 3 victim of

22. App. 46a–50a.

23. Ibid.

24. 2 Record 161.

25. App. 47a, 51a.

26. 2 Record 169.

discrimination falls far short of a "make whole" remedy.[27] A concomitant award of the seniority credit he presumptively would have earned but for the wrongful treatment would also seem necessary in the absence of justification for denying that relief. Without an award of seniority dating from the time when he was discriminatorily refused employment, an individual who applies for and obtains employment as an OTR driver pursuant to the District Court's order will never obtain his rightful place in the hierarchy of seniority according to which these various employment benefits are distributed. He will perpetually remain subordinate to persons who, but for the illegal discrimination, would have been in respect to entitlement to these benefits his inferiors.[28]

The Court of Appeals apparently followed this reasoning in holding that the District Court erred in not granting seniority relief to class 4 Bowman employees who were discriminatorily refused transfer to OTR positions. Yet the class 3 discriminatees in the absence of a comparable seniority award would also remain subordinated in the seniority system to the class 4 discriminatees. The distinction plainly finds no support anywhere in Title VII or its legislative history. Settled law dealing with the related "twin" areas of discriminatory hiring and discharges violative of the National Labor Relations Act, 49 Stat. 449, as amended, 29 U.S.C. § 151 et seq., provides a persuasive analogy. "[I]t would indeed be surprising if Congress gave a remedy for the one which it denied for the other." Phelps Dodge Corp. v. NLRB, 313 U.S. 177, 187, 61 S.Ct. 845, 849, 85 L.Ed. 1271, 1279 (1941). For courts to differentiate without justification between the classes of discriminatees "would be a differentiation not only without substance but in defiance of that against which the prohibition of discrimination is directed." Id., at 188, 61 S.Ct., at 850, 85 L.Ed., at 1280.

Similarly, decisions construing the remedial section of the National Labor Relations Act, § 10(c), 29 U.S.C. § 160(c)—the model for § 706(g), *Albemarle Paper*, 422 U.S., at 419, 95 S.Ct., at 2372, 45 L.Ed.2d, at 297 [29]—make clear that remedies constituting authorized "affirmative

27. Further, at least in regard to "benefit"-type seniority such as length of vacation leave and pension benefits in the instant case, any general bar to the award of retroactive seniority for victims of illegal hiring discrimination serves to undermine the mutually reinforcing effect of the dual purposes of Title VII; it reduces the restitution required of an employer at such time as he is called upon to account for his discriminatory actions perpetrated in violation of the law. See Albemarle Paper Co. v. Moody, 422 U.S. 405, 417–418, 95 S.Ct. 2362, 2371–2372, 45 L.Ed.2d 280, 296–297 (1975).

28. Accordingly, it is clear that the seniority remedy which petitioners seek does not concern only the "make-whole" purposes of Title VII. The dissent errs in treating the issue of seniority relief as implicating only the "make whole" objective of Title VII and in stating that "Title VII's 'primary objective' of eradicating discrimination is not served at all * * *." Nothing could be further from reality—the issue of seniority relief cuts to the very heart of Title VII's primary objective of eradicating present and future discrimination in a way that backpay, for example, can never do. "[S]eniority, after all, is a right which a worker exercises in each job movement in the future, rather than a simple one-time payment for the past." Poplin, Fair Employment in a Depressed Economy: The Layoff Problem, 23 U.C.L.A. L.Rev. 177, 225 (1975).

29. To the extent that there is a difference in the wording of the respective provi-

action" include an award of seniority status, for the thrust of "affirmative action" redressing the wrong incurred by an unfair labor practice is to make "the employees whole, and thus restor[e] the economic status quo that would have obtained but for the company's wrongful [act] ." NLRB v. Rutter-Rex Mfg. Co., 396 U.S. 258, 263, 90 S.Ct. 417, 420, 24 L.Ed.2d 405, 411 (1969). The task of the NLRB in applying § 10(c) is "to take measures designed to recreate the conditions and relationships that would have been had there been no unfair labor practice." Carpenters v. NLRB, 365 U.S. 651, 657, 81 S.Ct. 875, 879, 6 L.Ed.2d 1, 5 (1961) (Harlan, J., concurring). And the NLRB has often required that the hiring of employees who have been discriminatorily refused employment be accompanied by an award of seniority equivalent to that which they would have enjoyed but for the illegal conduct. See, e.g., In re Phelps Dodge Corp., 19 N.L.R.B. 547, 600, and n. 39, 603–604 (1940), modified on other grounds, 313 U.S. 177, 61 S.Ct. 845, 85 L.Ed. 1271 (1941) (ordering persons discriminatorily refused employment hired "without prejudice to their seniority or other rights and privileges"); In re Nevada Consolidated Copper Corp., 26 N.L.R.B. 1182, 1235 (1940), enforced, 316 U.S. 105, 62 S.Ct. 960, 86 L.Ed. 1305 (1942) (ordering persons discriminatorily refused employment hired with "any seniority or other rights and privileges they would have acquired, had the respondent not unlawfully discriminated against them"). Plainly the "affirmative action" injunction of § 706(g) has no lesser reach in the district courts. "Where racial discrimination is concerned, 'the [district] court has not merely the power but the duty to render a decree which will so far as possible eliminate the discriminatory effects of the past as well as bar like discrimination in the future.' " *Albemarle Paper*, supra, 422 U.S., at 418, 95 S.Ct., at 2372, 45 L.Ed.2d at 297.

IV

We are not to be understood as holding that an award of seniority status is requisite in all circumstances. The fashioning of appropriate remedies invokes the sound equitable discretion of the district courts. Respondent Bowman attempts to justify the District Court's denial of seniority relief for petitioners as an exercise of equitable discretion, but the record is its own refutation of the argument.

Albemarle Paper, supra, at 416, 95 S.Ct., at 2371, 45 L.Ed.2d, at 296, made clear that discretion imports not the court's " 'inclination, but * * * its judgment; and its judgment is to be guided by sound legal principles.' " Discretion is vested not for purposes of "limit[ing] appellate review of trial courts, or * * * invit[ing] inconsistency and

sions, § 706(g) grants, if anything, broader discretionary powers than those granted the National Labor Relations Board. Section 10(c) of the NLRA authorizes "such affirmative action including reinstatement of employees with or without back pay, as will effectuate the policies of this subchapter," 29 U.S.C. § 160(c), whereas § 706(g) as amended in 1972 authorizes "such affirmative action as may be appropriate, which may include, *but is not limited to*, reinstatement *or hiring* of employees, with or without back pay * * *, *or any other equitable relief as the court deems appropriate*." 42 U.S.C. § 2000e–5(g) (1970 ed., Supp. IV) (emphasis added).

caprice," but rather to allow the most complete achievement of the objectives of Title VII that is attainable under the facts and circumstances of the specific case. 422 U.S., at 421, 95 S.Ct., at 2373, 45 L.Ed. 2d, at 298. Accordingly, the District Court's denial of any form of seniority remedy must be reviewed in terms of its effect on the attainment of the Act's objectives under the circumstances presented by this record. No less than with the denial of the remedy of backpay, the denial of seniority relief to victims of illegal racial discrimination in hiring is permissible "only for reasons which, if applied generally, would not frustrate the central statutory purposes of eradicating discrimination throughout the economy and making persons whole for injuries suffered through past discrimination." Ibid.

The District Court stated two reasons for its denial of seniority relief for the unnamed class members.[30] The first was that those individuals had not filed administrative charges under the provisions of Title VII with the Equal Employment Opportunity Commission and therefore class relief of this sort was not appropriate. We rejected this justification for denial of class-based relief in the context of backpay awards in *Albemarle Paper*, and for the same reasons reject it here. This justification for denying class-based relief in Title VII suits has been unanimously rejected by the courts of appeals, and Congress ratified that construction by the 1972 amendments. *Albemarle Paper*, supra, at 414 n. 8, 95 S.Ct., at 2370, 45 L.Ed.2d, at 294.

The second reason stated by the District Court was that such claims "presuppose a vacancy, qualification, and performance by every member. There is no evidence on which to base these multiple conclusions." Pet. for Cert. A54. The Court of Appeals rejected this reason insofar as it was the basis of the District Court's denial of backpay, and of its denial of retroactive seniority relief to the unnamed members of class 4. We hold that it is also an improper reason for denying seniority relief to the unnamed members of class 3.

We read the District Court's reference to the lack of evidence regarding a "vacancy, qualification, and performance" for every individual member of the class as an expression of concern that some of the unnamed class members (unhired black applicants whose employment applications were summarized in the record) may not in fact have been actual victims of racial discrimination. That factor will become material however only when those persons reapply for OTR positions pursuant to the hiring relief ordered by the District Court. Generalizations concerning such individually applicable evidence cannot serve as a justification for the denial of relief to the entire class. Rather, at such time as individual class members seek positions as OTR drivers, posi-

30. Since the Court of Appeals concluded that an award of retroactive seniority to the unnamed members of class 3 was barred by § 703(h), a conclusion which we today reject, the court did not address specifically the District Court's stated reasons for refusing the relief. The Court of Appeals also stated, however, that the District Court did not "abuse its discretion" in refusing such relief, 495 F.2d 398, 418 (1974), and we may therefore appropriately review the validity of the District Court's reasons.

tions for which they are presumptively entitled to priority hiring consideration under the District Court's order,[31] evidence that particular individuals were not in fact victims of racial discrimination will be material. But petitioners here have carried their burden of demonstrating the existence of a discriminatory hiring pattern and practice by the respondents and, therefore, the burden will be upon respondents to prove that individuals who reapply were not in fact victims of previous hiring discrimination. Cf. McDonnell Douglas Corp. v. Green, 411 U.S. 792, 802, 93 S.Ct. 1817, 1824, 36 L.Ed.2d 668, 677 (1973); Baxter v. Savannah Sugar Rfg. Corp., 495 F.2d 437, 443–444 (C.A.5), cert. denied, 419 U.S. 1033, 95 S.Ct. 515, 42 L.Ed.2d 308 (1974).[32] Only if this burden is met may retroactive seniority—if otherwise determined to be an appropriate form of relief under the circumstances of the particular case—be denied individual class members.

Respondent Bowman raises an alternative theory of justification. Bowman argues that an award of retroactive seniority to the class of discriminatees will conflict with the economic interests of other Bowman employees. Accordingly, it is argued, the District Court acted within its discretion in denying this form of relief as an attempt to accommodate the competing interests of the various groups of employees.[33]

We reject this argument for two reasons. First, the District Court made no mention of such considerations in its order denying the seniority relief. As we noted in *Albemarle Paper*, 422 U.S., at 421 n. 14, 95 S.Ct., at 2373, 45 L.Ed.2d, at 299, if the district court declines, due to the peculiar circumstances of the particular case, to award relief generally appropriate under Title VII, "[i]t is necessary * * * that * * * it carefully articulate its reasons" for so doing. Second, and more fundamentally, it is apparent that denial of seniority relief to identifiable victims of racial discrimination on the sole ground that

31. The District Court order is silent as to whether applicants for OTR positions who were previously discriminatorily refused employment must be presently qualified for those positions in order to be eligible for priority hiring under that order. The Court of Appeals, however, made it plain that they must be. Id., at 417. We agree.

32. Thus Bowman may attempt to prove that a given individual member of class 3 was not in fact discriminatorily refused employment as an OTR driver in order to defeat the individual's claim to seniority relief as well as any other remedy ordered for the class generally. Evidence of a lack of vacancies in OTR positions at the time the individual application was filed, or evidence indicating the individual's lack of qualification for the OTR positions—under nondiscriminatory standards *actually applied* by Bowman to individuals who were in fact hired—would of course be relevant. It is true, of course, that obtaining the third category of evidence with which the District Court was concerned—what the individual discriminatee's job performance would have been but for the discrimination—presents great difficulty. No reason appears, however, why the victim rather than the perpetrator of the illegal act should bear the burden of proof on this issue.

33. Even by its terms, this argument could apply only to the award of retroactive seniority for purposes of "competitive status" benefits. It has no application to a retroactive award for purposes of "benefit" seniority—extent of vacation leave and pension benefits. Indeed, the decision concerning the propriety of this latter type of seniority relief is analogous, if not identical, to the decision concerning an award of backpay to an individual discriminatee hired pursuant to an order redressing previous employment discrimination.

such relief diminishes the expectations of other, arguably innocent, employees would if applied generally frustrate the central "make whole" objective of Title VII. These conflicting interests of other employees will, of course, always be present in instances where some scarce employment benefit is distributed among employees on the basis of their status in the seniority hierarchy. But, as we have said, there is nothing in the language of Title VII, or in its legislative history, to show that Congress intended generally to bar this form of relief to victims of illegal discrimination, and the experience under its remedial model in the National Labor Relations Act points to the contrary.[34] Accordingly, we find untenable the conclusion that this form of relief may be denied merely because the interests of other employees may thereby be affected. "If relief under Title VII can be denied merely because the majority group of employees, who have not suffered discrimination, will be unhappy about it, there will be little hope of correcting the wrongs to which the Act is directed." United States v. Bethlehem Steel Corp., 446 F.2d 652, 663 (C.A. 2 1971).[35]

34. With all respect, the dissent does not adequately treat with and fails to distinguish the standard practice of the National Labor Relations Board granting retroactive seniority relief under the National Labor Relations Act to persons discriminatorily discharged or refused employment in violation of the Act. The Court in Phelps Dodge Corp. v. NLRB, 313 U.S. 177, 196, 61 S.Ct. 845, 853, 85 L.Ed. 1271, 1284 (1941), of course, made reference to "restricted judicial review" as that case arose in the context of review of the policy determinations of an independent administrative agency, which are traditionally accorded a wide-ranging discretion under accepted principles of judicial review. "Because the relation of remedy to policy is peculiarly a matter for administrative competence, courts must not enter the allowable area of the Board's discretion." Id., at 194, 61 S.Ct., at 852, 85 L.Ed., at 1283. As we made clear in *Albemarle Paper*, however, the pertinent point is that in utilizing the NLRA as the remedial model for Title VII, reference must be made to actual operation and experience as it has evolved in administrating the Act. E.g., "We may assume that Congress was aware that the Board, since its inception, has awarded backpay as a matter of course." 422 U.S., at 419–420, 95 S.Ct., at 2372, 45 L.Ed.2d, at 298. "[T]he Board has from its inception pursued 'a practically uniform policy with respect to these orders requiring affirmative action.'" Id., at 2373 n. 12.

The dissent has cited no case, and our research discloses none, wherein the Board has ordered hiring relief and yet withheld the remedy of retroactive seniority status. Indeed, the Court of Appeals for the First Circuit has noted that a Board order requiring hiring relief "without prejudice to * * * seniority and other rights and privileges" is "language * * * in the standard form which has long been in use by the Board." NLRB v. Draper Corp., 159 F.2d 294, 296–297, and n. 1 (1947). The Board "routinely awards both back pay and retroactive seniority in hiring discrimination cases." Poplin, supra, n. 28, at 223. See also Edwards & Zaretsky, Preferential Remedies for Employment Discrimination, 74 Mich.L.Rev. 1, 45 n. 224 (1975) (a "common remedy"); Last Hired, First Fired Seniority, Layoffs and Title VII, supra, n. 11, at 377 ("traditionally and uniformly required"). This also is a "presumption" in favor of this form of seniority relief. If victims of racial discrimination are under Title VII to be treated differently and awarded less protection than victims of unfair labor practice discrimination under the NLRA, some persuasive justification for such disparate treatment should appear. That no justification exists doubtless explains the position of every union participant in the proceedings before the Court in the instant case arguing for the conclusion we have reached.

35. See also Vogler v. McCarty, Inc., 451 F.2d 1236, 1238–1239 (C.A. 5 1971):

> "Adequate protection of Negro rights under Title VII may necessitate, as in the instant case, some adjustment of the rights of white employees. The Court must be free to deal equitably with conflicting interests of white employees in order to shape remedies that will most effectively protect and redress the rights of the Negro victims of discrimination."

With reference to the problems of fairness or equity respecting the conflicting interests of the various groups of employees, the relief which petitioners seek is only seniority status retroactive to the date of individual application, rather than some form of arguably more complete relief.[36] No claim is asserted that nondiscriminatee employees holding OTR positions they would not have obtained but for the illegal discrimination should be deprived of the seniority status they have earned. It is therefore clear that even if the seniority relief petitioners seek is awarded, most if not all discriminatees who actually obtain OTR jobs under the court order will not truly be restored to the actual seniority that would have existed in the absence of the illegal discrimination. Rather, most discriminatees even under an award of retroactive seniority status will still remain subordinated in the hierarchy to a position inferior to that of a greater total number of employees than would have been the case in the absence of discrimination. Therefore, the relief which petitioners seek, while a more complete form of relief than that which the District Court accorded, in no sense constitutes "complete relief." [37] Rather, the burden of the past discrimination in hiring is with respect to competitive status benefits divided among discriminatee and nondiscriminatee employees under the form of relief sought. The dissent criticizes the Court's result as not sufficiently cognizant that it will "directly implicate the rights and expectations of perfectly innocent employees." We are of the view, however, that the result which we reach today—which, standing alone,[38] establishes that a sharing of the burden of the past discrimination is presumptively necessary—is entirely consistent with any fair characterization of equi-

36. Another countervailing factor in assessing the expected impact on the interests of other employees actually occasioned by an award of the seniority relief sought is that it is not probable in instances of class-based relief that all of the victims of the past racial discrimination in hiring will actually apply for and obtain the prerequisite hiring relief. Indeed, in the instant case, there appear in the record the rejected applications of 166 black applicants who claimed at the time of application to have had the necessary job qualifications. However, the Court was informed at oral argument that only a small number of those individuals have to this date actually been hired pursuant to the District Court's order ("five, six, seven, something in that order"), Tr. of Oral Arg. 23, although ongoing litigation may ultimately determine more who desire the hiring relief and are eligible for it. Id., at 15.

37. In no way can the remedy established as presumptively necessary be characterized as "total restitution," or as deriving from an "absolutist conception of 'make whole'" relief.

38. In arguing that an award of the seniority relief established as presumptively necessary does nothing to place the burden of the past discrimination on the wrongdoer in most cases—the employer—the dissent of necessity addresses issues not presently before the Court. Further remedial action by the district courts, having the effect of shifting to the employer the burden of the past discrimination in respect of competitive-status benefits, raises such issues as the possibility of an injunctive "hold harmless" remedy respecting all affected employees in a layoff situation, Brief for Local 862, United Automobile Workers, as *Amicus Curiae*; the possibility of an award of monetary damages (sometimes designated "front pay") in favor of each employee and discriminatee otherwise bearing some of the burden of the past discrimination, *ibid.*; and the propriety of such further remedial action in instances wherein the union has been adjudged a participant in the illegal conduct. Brief for United States et al. as *Amici Curiae*. Such issues are not presented by the record before us, and we intimate no view regarding them.

ty jurisdiction,[39] particularly when considered in light of our traditional view that "[a]ttainment of a great national policy * * * must not be confined within narrow canons for equitable relief deemed suitable by chancellors in ordinary private controversies." Phelps Dodge Corp. v. NLRB, 313 U.S., at 188, 61 S.Ct., at 850, 85 L.Ed., at 1280.

Certainly there is no argument that the award of retroactive seniority to the victims of hiring discrimination in any way deprives other employees of indefeasibly vested rights conferred by the employment contract. This Court has long held that employee expectations arising from a seniority system agreement may be modified by statutes furthering a strong public policy interest.[40] Tilton v. Missouri Pacific R. Co., 376 U.S. 169, 84 S.Ct. 595, 11 L.Ed.2d 590 (1964) (construing §§ 9(c)(1) and (c)(2) of the Universal Military Training and Service Act, 1948, 50 U.S.C. App. §§ 459(c)(1) and (2), which provided that a re-employed returning veteran should enjoy the seniority status he would have acquired but for his absence in military service); Fishgold v. Sullivan Drydock & Repair Corp., 328 U.S. 275, 66 S.Ct. 1105, 90 L.Ed. 1230 (1946) (construing the comparable provision of the Selective Training and Service Act of 1940). The Court has also held that a collective-bargaining agreement may go further, enhancing the seniority status of certain employees for purposes of furthering public policy interests beyond what is required by statute, even though this will to some extent be detrimental to the expectations acquired by other employees under the previous seniority agreement. Ford Motor Co. v. Huffman, 345 U.S. 330, 73 S.Ct. 681, 97 L.Ed. 1048 (1953). And the ability of the union and employer voluntarily to modify the seniority system to the end of ameliorating the effects of past racial discrimination, a national policy objective of the "highest priority," is certainly no less than in other areas of public policy interests. Pellicer v. Brotherhood of Ry. & S.S. Clerks, 217 F.2d 205 (C.A.5 1954), cert. denied, 349 U.S. 912, 75 S.Ct. 601, 99 L.Ed. 1246 (1955). See also Cooper & Sobol, 82 Harv.L. Rev. at 1605.

V

In holding that class-based seniority relief for identifiable victims of illegal hiring discrimination is a form of relief generally appropriate under § 706(g), we do not in any way modify our previously expressed view that the statutory scheme of Title VII "implicitly recognizes that

39. " 'The qualities of mercy and practicality have made equity the instrument for nice adjustment and reconciliation between the public interest and private needs as well as between competing private claims.' " " 'Moreover, * * * equitable remedies are a special blend of what is necessary, what is fair, and what is workable * * *.

" 'In equity, as nowhere else, courts eschew rigid absolutes and look to the practical realities and necessities inescapably involved in reconciling competing interests. * * * ' "

40. "[C]laims under Title VII involve the vindication of a major public interest * * *." Section-by-Section Analysis of H.R. 1746, accompanying the Equal Employment Opportunity Act of 1972—Conference Report, 118 Cong.Rec. 7166, 7168 (1972).

there may be cases calling for one remedy but not another, and—owing to the structure of the federal judiciary—these choices are, of course, left in the first instance to the district courts." *Albemarle Paper*, 422 U.S., at 416, 95 S.Ct., at 2370, 45 L.Ed.2d at 295. Circumstances peculiar to the individual case may, of course, justify the modification or withholding of seniority relief for reasons that would not if applied generally undermine the purposes of Title VII.[41] In the instant case it appears that all new hirees establish seniority only upon completion of a 45-day probationary period, although upon completion seniority is retroactive to the date of hire. Certainly any seniority relief ultimately awarded by the District Court could properly be cognizant of this fact. *Amici* and the respondent union point out that there may be circumstances where an award of full seniority should be deferred until completion of a training or apprenticeship program, or other preliminaries required of all new hirees.[42] We do not undertake to delineate all such possible circumstances here. Any enumeration must await particular cases and be determined in light of the trial courts' "keener appreciation" of peculiar facts and circumstances. *Albemarle Paper*, supra, at 421–422, 95 S.Ct., at 2373, 45 L.Ed.2d, at 299.

Accordingly, the judgment of the Court of Appeals affirming the District Court's denial of seniority relief to class 3 is reversed, and the case is remanded to the District Court for further proceedings consistent with this opinion.

It is so ordered.

Reversed and remanded.

MR. JUSTICE STEVENS took no part in the consideration or decision of this case.

MR. CHIEF JUSTICE BURGER, concurring in part and dissenting in part.

I agree generally with MR. JUSTICE POWELL, but I would stress that although retroactive benefit-type seniority relief may sometimes be appropriate and equitable, competitive-type seniority relief at the expense of wholly innocent employees can rarely, if ever, be equitable if that term retains traditional meaning. More equitable would be a monetary award to the person suffering the discrimination. An award such as "front pay" could replace the need for competitive-type seniori-

41. Accordingly, to no "significant extent" do we "[strip] the district courts of [their] equity powers." Rather our holding is that in exercising their equitable powers, district courts should take as their starting point the presumption in favor of rightful-place seniority relief, and proceed with further legal analysis from that point; and that such relief may not be denied on the abstract basis of adverse impact upon interests of other employees but rather only on the basis of unusual adverse impact arising from facts and circumstances that would not be generally found in Title VII cases. To hold otherwise would be to shield "inconsisten[t] and capri[cious]" denial of such relief from "thorough appellate review." *Albemarle Paper*, 422 U.S., at 421, 416, 95 S.Ct., at 2373, 2371, 45 L.Ed. 2d, at 299, 296.

42. Brief for United States et al. as *Amici Curiae* 26; Brief for Respondent United Steelworkers of America, AFL–CIO, and for American Federation of Labor and Congress of Industrial Organizations as *Amicus Curiae* 28 n. 32.

ty relief. Such monetary relief would serve the dual purpose of deterring wrongdoing by the employer or union—or both—as well as protecting the rights of innocent employees. In every respect an innocent employee is comparable to a "holder-in-due-course" of negotiable paper or a bona fide purchaser of property without notice of any defect in the seller's title. In this setting I cannot join in judicial approval of "robbing Peter to pay Paul."

I would stress that the Court today does not foreclose claims of employees who might be injured by this holding from securing equitable relief on their own behalf.

* * *

MR. JUSTICE POWELL, with whom MR. JUSTICE REHNQUIST joins, concurring and dissenting in part.

Although I am in accord with much of the Court's discussion in Parts III and IV, I cannot accept as correct its basic interpretation of § 706(g) as virtually requiring a district court, in determining appropriate equitable relief in a case of this kind, to ignore entirely the equities that may exist in favor of innocent employees. Its holding recognizes no meaningful distinction, in terms of the equitable relief to be granted, between "benefit"-type seniority and "competitive"-type seniority.[1] The Court reaches this result by taking an absolutist view of the "make whole" objective of Title VII, while rendering largely meaningless the discretionary authority vested in district courts by § 706(g) to weigh the equities of the situation. Accordingly, I dissent from Parts III and IV.

* * *

III

A

In *Albemarle Paper* the Court read Title VII as creating a presumption in favor of backpay. Rather than limiting the power of district courts to do equity, the presumption insures that complete equity normally will be accomplished. Backpay forces the employer[4] to account for economic benefits that he wrongfully has denied the victim of discrimination. The statutory purposes and equitable principles converge, for requiring payment of wrongfully withheld wages deters further wrongdoing at the same time that their restitution to the victim helps make him whole.

1. My terminology conforms to that of the Court. "Benefit"-type seniority refers to the use of a worker's earned seniority credits in computing his level of economic "fringe benefits." Examples of such benefits are pensions, paid vacation time, and unemployment insurance. "Competitive"-type seniority refers to the use of those same earned credits in determining his right, relative to other workers, to job-related "rights" that cannot be supplied equally to any two employees. Examples can range from the worker's right to keep his job while someone else is laid off, to his right to a place in the punch-out line ahead of another employee at the end of a work-day.

4. In an appropriate case, of course, Title VII remedies may be ordered against a wrongdoing union as well as the employer.

Similarly, to the extent that the Court today finds a like presumption in favor of granting *benefit*-type seniority, it is recognizing that normally this relief also will be equitable. As the Court notes, this type of seniority, which determines pension rights, length of vacations, size of insurance coverage and unemployment benefits, and the like, is analogous to backpay in that its retroactive grant serves "the mutually reinforcing effect of the dual purposes of Title VII." Benefit-type seniority, like backpay, serves to work complete equity by penalizing the wrongdoer economically at the same time that it tends to make whole the one who was wronged.

But the Court fails to recognize that a retroactive grant of *competitive*-type seniority invokes wholly different considerations. This is the type of seniority that determines an employee's preferential rights to various economic advantages at the expense of other employees. These normally include the order of layoff and recall of employees, job and trip assignments, and consideration for promotion.

It is true, of course, that the retroactive grant of competitive-type seniority does go a step further in "making whole" the discrimination victim, and therefore arguably furthers one of the objectives of Title VII. But apart from extending the make-whole concept to its outer limits, there is no similarity between this drastic relief and the granting of backpay and benefit-type seniority. First, a retroactive grant of competitive-type seniority usually does not directly affect the employer at all. It causes only a rearrangement of employees along the seniority ladder without any resulting increase in cost.[5] Thus, Title VII's "primary objective" of eradicating discrimination is not served at all,[6] for the employer is not deterred from the practice.

The second, and in my view controlling, distinction between these types of relief is the impact on other workers. As noted above, the

5. This certainly would be true in this case, as conceded by counsel for Bowman at oral argument. There the following exchange took place:

"QUESTION: How is Bowman injured by this action?

"MR. PATE [Counsel for Bowman]: By seniority? By the grant of this remedy?

"QUESTION: Either way.

"MR. PATE: It is not injured either way and the company, apart from the general interest of all of us in the importance of the question, has no specific tangible interest in it in this case as to whether seniority is granted to this group or not. That is correct." Tr. of Oral Arg. 42. In a supplemental memorandum filed after oral argument, petitioners referred to this statement by Bowman's counsel and suggested that he apparently was referring to the competitive aspects of seniority, such as which employees were to get the best job assignments, since Bowman certainly *would* be economically disadvantaged by the benefit-type seniority, such as seniority-related increases in backpay. I agree that in the context Bowman's counsel spoke, he was referring to the company's lack of a tangible interest, in whether or not competitive-type seniority was granted.

6. The Court in *Albemarle* noted that this primary objective had been recognized in Griggs v. Duke Power Co., 401 U.S. 424, 91 S.Ct. 849, 28 L.Ed.2d 158 (1971). See 422 U.S., at 417, 95 S.Ct., at 2371, 45 L.Ed. 2d, at 296; see also supra, at 1273. In *Griggs*, the Court found this objective to be "plain from the language of the statute." 401 U.S., at 429, 91 S.Ct., at 853, 28 L.Ed. 2d, at 163. In creating a presumption in favor of a retroactive grant of competitive-type seniority the Court thus exalts the make-whole purpose, not only above fundamental principles of equity, but also above the primary objective of the statute recently found to be plain on its face.

granting of backpay and of benefit-type seniority furthers the prophylactic and make-whole objectives of the statute without penalizing other workers. But competitive seniority benefits, as the term implies, directly implicate the rights and expectations of perfectly innocent employees.[7] The economic benefits awarded discrimination victims would be derived not at the expense of the employer but at the expense of other workers. Putting it differently, those disadvantaged—sometimes to the extent of losing their jobs entirely—are not the wrongdoers who have no claim to the Chancellor's conscience, but rather are innocent third parties.

As noted above in Part II, Congress in § 706(g) expressly referred to "appropriate" affirmative action and "other equitable relief as the court deems appropriate." And the 1972 Section-by-Section Analysis still recognized that the touchstone of any relief is equity. Congress could not have been more explicit in leaving the relief to the equitable discretion of the court, to be determined in light of all relevant facts and circumstances. Congress did underscore "backpay" by specific reference in § 706(g), but no mention is made of the granting of other benefits upon ordering reinstatement or hiring. The entire question of retroactive seniority was thus deliberately left to the discretion of the district court, a discretion to be exercised in accordance with equitable principles.

> "The essence of equity jurisdiction has been the power of the Chancellor to do equity and to mould each decree to the necessities of the particular case. Flexibility rather than rigidity has distinguished it. The qualities of mercy and practicality have made equity the instrument for nice adjustment and reconciliation between the public interest and private needs as well as between competing private claims." Hecht Co. v. Bowles, 321 U.S. 321, 329–330, 64 S.Ct. 587, 592, 88 L.Ed. 754 (1944). "Moreover, * * * equitable remedies are a special blend of what is necessary, what is fair, and what is workable. * * *" Lemon v. Kurtzman, 411 U.S. 192, 200, 93 S.Ct. 1463, 1469, 36 L.Ed.2d 151, 161 (1973) (opinion of Burger, C. J.)
>
> "In equity, as nowhere else, courts eschew rigid absolutes and look to the practical realities and necessities inescapably involved in reconciling competing interests * * *." Id., at 201, 93 S.Ct., at 1469, 36 L.Ed.2d 161.

The decision whether to grant competitive-type seniority relief therefore requires a district court to consider and weigh competing

7. Some commentators have suggested that the expectations of incumbents somehow may be illegitimate because they result from past discrimination against others. Cooper & Sobol, Seniority and Testing under Fair Employment Laws: A General Approach to Objective Criteria of Hiring and Promotion, 82 Harv.L.Rev. 1598, 1605–1606 (1969). Such reasoning is badly flawed. Absent some showing of collusion, the incumbent employee was not a party to the discrimination by the employer. Acceptance of the job when offered hardly makes one an accessory to a discriminatory failure to hire someone else. Moreover, the incumbent's expectancy does not result from discrimination against others, but is based on his own efforts and satisfactory performance.

equities. In any proper exercise of the balancing process, a court must consider both the claims of the discrimination victims and the claims of incumbent employees who, if competitive seniority rights are awarded retroactively to others, will lose economic advantages earned through satisfactory and often long service.[8] If, as the Court today holds, the district court may not weigh these equities much of the language of § 706(g) is rendered meaningless. We cannot assume that Congress intended either that the statutory language be ignored or that the earned benefits of incumbent employees be wiped out by a presumption created by this Court.[9]

IV

In expressing the foregoing views, I suggest neither that Congress intended to bar a retroactive grant of competitive-type seniority in all cases,[13] nor that district courts should indulge a presumption against

8. The Court argues that a retroactive grant of competitive-type seniority always is equitable because it "divides the burden" of past discrimination between incumbents and victims. Aside from its opacity, this argument is flawed by what seems to be a misperception of the nature of Title VII relief. Specific relief necessarily focuses upon the individual victim, not upon some "class" of victims. A grant of full retroactive seniority to an individual victim of Bowman's discriminatory hiring practices will place that person exactly where he would have been had he been hired when he first applied. The question for a district court should be whether it is equitable to place that individual in that position despite the impact upon all incumbents hired after the date of his unsuccessful application. Any additional effect upon the entire work force—incumbents and the newly enfranchised victims alike—of similar relief to still *earlier* victims of the discrimination, raises distinctly different issues from the equity, vis-à-vis incumbents, of granting retroactive seniority to each victim.

9. Indeed, the 1972 amendment process which produced the Section-by-Section Analysis containing the statement of the Act's "make whole" purpose, also resulted in an addition to § 706(g) itself clearly showing congressional recognition that total restitution to victims of discrimination is not a feasible goal. As originally enacted, § 706(g) contained simply an authorization to district courts to order reinstatement with or without backpay, with no limitation on how much backpay the courts could order. In 1972, however, the Congress added a limitation restricting the courts to an award to a date two years prior to the filing of a charge with EEOC. While it is true that Congress at the same time rejected an even more restrictive limitation, see Albemarle Paper Co. v. Moody, supra, 422 U.S., at 420 n. 13, 95 S.Ct., at 2373, 45 L.Ed.2d, at 298, its adoption of any limitation at all suggests an awareness that the desire to "make whole" must yield at some point to other considerations.

13. Nor is it suggested that incumbents have "indefeasibly vested rights" to their seniority status that invariably would foreclose retroactive seniority. But the cases cited by the Court for that proposition do not hold, or by analogy imply, that district courts operating under § 706(g) lack equitable discretion to take into account the rights of incumbents. In Tilton v. Missouri Pacific R. Co., 376 U.S. 169, 84 S.Ct. 595, 11 L.Ed.2d 590 (1964), and Fishgold v. Sullivan Corp., 328 U.S. 275, 66 S.Ct. 1105, 90 L.Ed. 1230 (1946), the Court only confirmed an express congressional determination, presumably made after weighing all relevant considerations, that for reasons of public policy veterans should receive seniority credit for their time in military service. See 376 U.S., at 174–175, 84 S.Ct., at 599–600, 11 L.Ed.2d, at 593–594. In Ford Motor Co. v. Huffman, 345 U.S. 330, 73 S.Ct. 681, 97 L.Ed. 1048 (1953), the Court affirmed the authority of a collective-bargaining agent, presumably after weighing the relative equities, see id., at 337–339, 73 S.Ct., at 685–687, 97 L.Ed., at 1057–1058, to advantage certain employees more than others. All I contend is that under § 706(g) a district court, like Congress in *Tilton* and *Fishgold*, and the bargaining agent in *Huffman*, also must be free to weigh the equities.

such relief.[14] My point instead is that we are dealing with a congressional mandate to district courts to determine and apply equitable remedies. Traditionally this is a balancing process left, within appropriate constitutional or statutory limits, to the sound discretion of the trial court. At this time it is necessary only to avoid imposing, from the level of this Court, arbitrary limitations on the exercise of this traditional discretion specifically explicated in § 706(g). There will be cases where, under all of the circumstances, the economic penalties that would be imposed on innocent incumbent employees will outweigh the claims of discrimination victims to be made entirely whole even at the expense of others. Similarly, there will be cases where the balance properly is struck the other way.

The Court virtually ignores the only previous judicial discussion directly in point. The Court of Appeals for the Sixth Circuit, recently faced with the issue of retroactive seniority for victims of hiring discrimination, showed a fine appreciation of the distinction discussed above. Meadows v. Ford Motor Co., 510 F.2d 939 (1975), cert. pending, No. 74–1349.[15] That court began with the recognition that retroactive competitive-type seniority presents "greater problems" than a grant of backpay because the burden falls upon innocent incumbents rather than the wrongdoing employer. Id., at 949.[16] The court further recognized that Title VII contains no prohibition against such relief. Then, noting that "the remedy for the wrong of discriminatory refusal to hire lies in the first instance *with the District Judge*," ibid. (emphasis added), the Court of Appeals for the Sixth Circuit stated:

> "For his guidance on this issue we observe * * * that a grant of retroactive seniority would not depend solely upon the existence of a record sufficient to justify back pay * * *. The court would, in dealing with job [i.e., competitive-type] seniority, need also to consider the interests of the workers who might be displaced * * *. We do not assume * * * that such reconciliation is impossible, but as is obvious, we certainly do foresee genuine difficulties. * * * " Ibid.

14. The Court suggests I am arguing that retroactive competitive-type seniority should be "less available" as relief than backpay. This is not my position. All relief not specifically prohibited by the Act is equally "available" to the district courts. My point is that equitable considerations can make competitive-type seniority relief less "appropriate" in a particular situation than backpay or other relief. Again, the plain language of § 706(g) compels careful determination of the "appropriateness" of each "available" remedy in a specific case, and does not permit the inflexible approach taken by the Court.

15. From the briefs of the parties it appears that *Meadows* is one of only three reported appellate decisions dealing with the question of retroactive seniority relief to victims of discriminatory hiring practices. In the instant case, of course, the Court of Appeals for the Fifth Circuit held such relief barred by § 703(h). In Jurinko v. Edwin L. Wiegand Co., 477 F.2d 1038, vacated and remanded on other grounds, 414 U.S. 970, 94 S.Ct. 293, 38 L.Ed.2d 214 (1973), the Court of Appeals for the Third Circuit ordered the relief without any discussion of equitable considerations.

16. The Sixth Circuit noted that no equitable considerations stand in the way of a district court's granting retroactive benefit-type seniority. 510 F.2d at 949.

The Sixth Circuit suggested that the District Court seek enlightenment on the questions involved in the particular fact situation, and that it should allow intervention by representatives of the incumbents who stood to be disadvantaged.[17]

In attempted justification of its disregard of the explicit equitable mandate of § 706(g) the Court today relies almost exclusively on the practice of the National Labor Relations Board under § 10(c) of the National Labor Relations Act, 29 U.S.C. § 160(c).[18] It is true that in the two instances cited by the Court, and in the few others cited in the briefs of the parties,[19] the Board has ordered reinstatement of victims of discrimination "without prejudice to their seniority or other rights and privileges." But the alleged precedents are doubly unconvincing. First, in none of the cases is there a discussion of equities either by the Board or the enforcing court. That the Board has granted seniority relief in several cases may indicate nothing more than the fact that in the usual case no one speaks for the individual incumbents. This is the point recognized by the court in *Meadows*, and the impetus for its

17. One of the commentators quoted by the Court today has endorsed the even-handed approach adopted by the Sixth Circuit: "In fashioning a remedy, * * * the courts should consciously assess the costs of relief to *all* the parties in the case, and then tailor the decree to minimize these costs while affording plaintiffs adequate relief. The best way to do this will no doubt vary from case to case depending on the facts: the number of plaintiffs, the number of [incumbents]affected and the alternatives available to them, the economic circumstances of the industry." Poplin, Fair Employment in a Depressed Economy: The Layoff Problem, 23 U.C.L.A. L.Rev. 177, 202 (1975) (emphasis in original); see id. at 224.

Another commentator has said that judges who fail to take account of equitable claims of incumbents are engaging in an "Alice in Wonderland" approach to the problem of Title VII remedies. See Rains, Title VII v. Seniority Based Layoffs: A Question of Who Goes First, 4 Hofstra L.Rev. 49, 53 (1975).

18. By gathering bits and pieces of the legislative history of the 1972 amendments, the Court attempts to patch together an argument that full retroactive seniority is a remedy equally "available" as backpay. There are two short responses. First, as emphasized elsewhere, supra, at 1278 n. 14, no one contends that such relief is less *available*, but only that it may be less *equitable* in some situations. Second, insofar as the Court intends the legislative history to suggest some presumption in favor of this relief, it is irrefutably blocked by the plain language of § 706(g) calling for the exercise of *equitable* discretion in the fashioning of *appropriate* relief. There are other responses. As to the committee citations of lower court decisions and the Conference Report Analysis reference to "present case law," it need only be noted that as of the 1972 amendments no appellate court had considered a case involving retroactive seniority relief to victims of discriminatory hiring practices. Moreover, the cases were cited only in the context of a general discussion of the complexities of employment discrimination, never for their adoption of a "rightful place" theory of relief. And by the terms of the Conference Report Analysis itself, the existing case law could not take precedence over the explicit language of § 706(g), added by the amendments, that told courts to exercise *equitable* discretion in granting *appropriate* relief.

Moreover, I find no basis for the Court's statement that the Committee Reports indicated "rightful place" to be the objective of Title VII relief. In fact, in both instances cited by the Court the term was used in the context of a general comment that minorities were still "far from reaching their rightful place in society." S.Rep. No.92–416, p. 6 (1971). There was no reference to the scope of relief under § 706(g), or indeed even to Title VII remedies at all.

19. The respondent Steelworkers cited seven Board decisions in addition to those mentioned in the Court's opinion. Brief for Respondent United Steelworkers of America AFL–CIO, and for American Federation of Labor and Congress of Industrial Organizations as *Amicus Curiae*, 27 n. 31.

suggestion that a representative of their interests be entertained by the district court before it determines "appropriate" § 706(g) relief.

I also suggest, with all respect, that the Court's appeal to Board practice wholly misconceives the lesson to be drawn from it. In the seminal case recognizing the Board's power to order reinstatement for discriminatory refusals to hire, this Court in a reasoned opinion by Mr. Justice Frankfurter was careful to emphasize that the decision on the type and extent of relief rested in the Board's discretion, subject to limited review only by the courts.

> "But in the nature of things Congress could not catalogue all the devices and stratagems for circumventing the policies of the Act. Nor could it define the whole gamut of remedies to effectuate these policies in an infinite variety of specific situations. Congress met these difficulties by leaving the adaptation of means to end to the empiric process of administration. The exercise of the process was committed to the Board, subject to limited judicial review. * * *
>
> * * *
>
> "* * * All these and other factors outside our domain of experience may come into play. Their relevance is for the Board, not for us. *In the exercise of its informed discretion the Board may find that effectuation of the Act's policies may or may not require reinstatement*. We have no warrant for speculating on matters of fact the determination of which Congress has entrusted to the Board. All we are entitled to ask is that the statute speak through the Board where the statute does not speak for itself." Phelps Dodge Corp. v. NLRB, 313 U.S. 177, 194–196, 61 S.Ct. 845, 852–853, 85 L.Ed. 1271, 1283–1284 (1941) (emphasis added).

The fallacy of the Court's reliance upon Board practice is apparent: the district courts under Title VII stand in the place of the Board under the NLRA. Congress entrusted to their discretion the appropriate remedies for violations of the Act, just as it previously had entrusted discretion to the Board. The Court today denies that discretion to the district courts, when 35 years ago it was quite careful to leave discretion where Congress had entrusted it. It may be that the district courts, after weighing the competing equities, would order full retroactive seniority in most cases. But they should do so only after determining in each instance that it *is* appropriate, and not because this Court has taken from them the power—granted by Congress—to weigh the equities.

In summary, the decision today denying district courts the power to balance equities cannot be reconciled with the explicit mandate of § 706(g) to determine "appropriate" relief through the exercise of "equitable powers." Accordingly, I would remand this case to the District Court with instructions to investigate and weigh competing equities before deciding upon the appropriateness of retroactive competitive-type seniority with respect to individual claimants.[20]

NOTES AND PROBLEMS FOR DISCUSSION

1. Following *Franks,* courts have treated retroactive seniority, like back pay, as a remedy to be denied the victim of discrimination only for the most compelling reasons. In EEOC v. M.D. Pneumatics, Inc., 779 F.2d 21 (8th Cir. 1985), the district court denied retroactive seniority to women who had been refused employment with the defendant because the employer "had gone the extra mile in remedying its past discrimination" and because there was "no evidence * * * from which a reasonable determination could be made as to a date on which a class member might have been hired absent the sex discrimination which was then practiced by the defendant." The Court of Appeals reversed. "Pneumatic's effort to remedy the effects of past discrimination, although commendable, are not the kind of compelling reasons which justify the denial of retroactive seniority." 779 F.2d at 23. With respect to computation of seniority dates, the court noted that all the district court needed was the womens' dates of application and the dates on which men were subsequently hired. That data was either in the record of the case or could be obtained from the parties. With retroactive seniority, as with back pay, "unrealistic exactitude" is not required. See also, Easley v. Anheuser-Busch, Inc., 758 F.2d 251, 263–64 (8th Cir. 1985).

In *Franks* the Court held that retroactive seniority may not be denied merely because of an adverse impact on the interests of other employees, but in a footnote qualified that rule by saying that, in exercising its equitable discretion, a court could deny such relief "on the basis of unusual adverse impact that would not be generally found in Title VII cases." In ROMASANTA v. UNITED AIR LINES, INC., 717 F.2d 1140 (7th Cir. 1983), cert. denied, 466 U.S. 944, 104 S.Ct. 1928, 80 L.Ed.2d 474 (1984), the Seventh Circuit relied on that footnote in denying immediate reinstatement, with full competitive seniority, to a class of 1400 former airline stewardesses who had been terminated pursuant to an unlawful no-marriage rule. The plaintiffs argued that, on reinstatement, each class member should receive the full seniority she would have enjoyed had she never been fired. The Court concluded that, though such an award of retroactive seniority would appear to be necessary to make the discriminatees whole, to award more competitive seniority than the time actually worked before termination would have an unusual adverse impact on incumbents, resulting in furloughs, possible discharges, involuntary transfers and curtailment of job opportunities for recently hired minorities. In balancing the interests of all affected parties, the Court ap-

20. This is not to suggest that district courts should be left to exercise a standardless, unreviewable discretion. But in the area of competitive-type seniority, unlike backpay and benefit-type seniority, the twin purposes of Title VII do not provide the standards. District courts must be guided in each instance by the mandate of § 706(g). They should, of course, record the considerations upon which they rely in granting or refusing relief, so that appellate review could be informed and precedents established in the area. In this case, for example, factors that could be considered on remand and that could weigh in favor of full retroactive seniority, include Bowman's high employee turnover rate and the asserted fact that few victims of Bowman's discrimination have indicated a desire to be hired. Other factors, not fully developed in the record, also could require consideration in determining the balance of the equities. I would imply no opinion on the merits and would remand for full consideration in light of the views herein expressed.

proved competitive seniority for time actually worked, but awarded noncompetitive seniority (used for pay and fringe benefit purposes) to cover the time from date of hire for each class member who was reinstated.

2. In *Franks*, as in *Albemarle*, the Court adopted as persuasive authority the National Labor Relations Act cases in which retroactive seniority was awarded to further the "make whole" purpose of the NLRA. Concentrating on the "make whole" purpose of Title VII, the *Franks* Court made only passing references to the statute's other, prophylactic, purpose. Justice Powell in his separate opinion argued that "Title VII's 'primary objective' of eradicating discrimination is not served at all [by an award of retroactive seniority] for the employer is not deterred from the practice." 424 U.S. at 788, 96 S.Ct. at 1275. Many structural seniority systems, however, are the products of collective bargaining between employers and unions. While an employer may be relatively unconcerned about the prospect of adjustments in seniority systems, unions have a great stake in protecting the seniority rights of their incumbent members. The unpleasant alternative of court-ordered changes in seniority should have the same "prophylactic" effect on a union's policies as the threat of back pay theoretically will have on an employer. In Wilson v. Southwest Airlines, 98 F.R.D. 725 (N.D.Tex.1983), a union was allowed to intervene in the action after judgment to contest provisions in a consent decree awarding retroactive seniority to men denied flight attendant positions. Wilson v. Southwest Airlines, supra, Chapter 3 at p. 255. The intervention was proper, according to the district court, because the employer had not taken a position on retroactive seniority and thus did not represent the interests of the union's members. Justice Powell's comments notwithstanding, some employers, for example educational institutions and law firms, have a strong institutional interest in the integrity of the "seniority rights" of their employees.

Courts have been reluctant to review tenure decisions of educational institutions in cases where discrimination is alleged to have infected the tenure process.

> Neither the district court nor this court is empowered to sit as a super tenure board. I believe that courts must be extremely wary of intruding into the world of university tenure decisions. These decisions necessarily hinge on subjective judgments regarding the applicant's academic excellence, teaching ability, creativity, contributions to the university community, rapport with students and colleagues, and other factors that are not susceptible of quantitative measurement. Absent discrimination, a university must be given a free hand in making such tenure decisions. Where, as here, the university's judgment is supportable and the evidence of discrimination negligible, a federal court should not substitute its judgment for that of the university.

Kumar v. Board of Trustees of the University of Massachusetts, 774 F.2d 1, 12 (1st Cir. 1985) (Campbell, J., concurring), cert. denied, ___ U.S. ___, 106 S.Ct. 1496, 89 L.Ed.2d 896 (1986). Even where illegal discrimination has been found to have influenced a tenure denial, courts have been reluctant to order an award of tenure. In Fields v. Clark University, 40 FEP Cases 670 (D.Mass.1986), for example, the court found that the plaintiff had been denied tenure because of a "pervasively sexist attitude" on the part of the male members of her department who had made the basic decision to deny her tenure and that male faculty members with similar qualifications to those of the plaintiff had been awarded tenure. But despite the finding that the decision to deny the plaintiff tenure was "impermissibly infected with sex discrimination," the court noted that there were questions as to her capacity as a teacher, and ordered the university to rehire her on a probationary basis for two years and then to renew the tenure process under circumstances free of discrimination. See also, Gurmankin v. Costanzo, 626 F.2d 1132 (3d Cir. 1980) (award of tenure not appropriate since school district entitled to further evaluation of plaintiff's performance as a teacher); Kunda v. Muhlenberg College, 621 F.2d 532 (3d Cir. 1980) (award of tenure conditioned on attainment of necessary degree). By contrast, in Ford v. Nicks, 741 F.2d 858 (6th Cir. 1984), cert. denied, ___ U.S. ___, 105 S.Ct. 1195, 84 L.Ed.2d 340 (1985), the Court held that an unlawfully discharged teacher was properly reinstated and awarded tenure where state law automatically granted tenure to any professor at a state university who successfully completed five years of employment and where the district court had found that, but for the discrimination the plaintiff would have completed five years of employment.

Could partnership interest in a law firm be awarded to an associate who proved she was denied partnership because of her sex or race? The full scope of relief to which the plaintiff in Hishon v. King & Spalding, supra, might have been entitled on remand was not addressed by the Supreme Court because she sought only declaratory relief, back pay and damages "in lieu of reinstatement and promotion to partnership." 467 U.S. at 72, 104 S.Ct. at 2232.

3. In International Brotherhood of Teamsters v. United States, 431 U.S. 324, 97 S.Ct. 1843, 52 L.Ed.2d 396 (1977) and American Tobacco Co. v. Patterson, 456 U.S. 63, 102 S.Ct. 1534, 71 L.Ed.2d 748 (1982), discussed supra, at p. 791, the Court held that under § 703(h) of Title VII a "bona fide" seniority system (one not designed or maintained for a discriminatory purpose) was not illegal because it perpetuated the effects of past discrimination. In both *Teamsters* and *American Tobacco* the discrimination which was perpetuated by the seniority systems either had occurred before the enactment of Title VII or had not been the subject of a timely EEOC charge. The Court's determination that such seniority systems did not themselves violate the Act in no way affected the holding in *Franks* that, where discrimination in hiring or job assignment *over which the court has jurisdiction* is established, retroactive seniority is a proper remedy to make the victim of the discrimination whole. The Court in *Teamsters* was careful to distinguish between pre-Act discrimination, which was not illegal and for which the courts could not provide a remedy, and post-Act discrimination. "Post-Act discriminatees * * * may obtain full 'make whole' relief, including retroactive seniority * * * without attacking the seniority system as applied to them." 431 U.S. at 347, 97 S.Ct. at 1860.

Assume that employee A, who is black, was hired in 1962 and assigned to an all-black maintenance job. Employees B and C, who are white, were hired the next day and were given machine operator positions to which only whites were assigned. A, B and C all started with identical qualifications. Under the employer's seniority system, competitive seniority is only acquired in the job and an employee who transfers from one job to another loses all seniority acquired in the old position. In 1968 and again in 1975 A attempted to transfer into a machine operator position but was denied the transfer because of his race. After his 1975 rejection, A filed an EEOC charge and subsequently a law suit under Title VII. If the court finds that he was discriminated against in 1962, 1968 and 1975, what seniority relief is A entitled to?

4. The seniority systems of many industrial employers are organized in "lines of progression." In such systems, employees can use their competitive seniority to bid on jobs in a line of progression only in the order in which the

jobs are ranked in the line: the employee must start at the bottom or "entry level" position and then can only use his seniority to bid on the next job up in the progression. The common rationale for such systems is that the employee needs to know the lower jobs in the progression before he can competently perform the "higher" positions. Sometimes progression line seniority is linked with the provision that an employee acquires competitive seniority only in a line of progression and relinquishes his seniority when he transfers to a new line of progression.

Line of progression seniority complicates the job of "making whole" the victim of discrimination. For example, an employee may have been excluded because of race or sex from a progression line. The court can, of course, order that the employee be placed in the seniority line from which he has been discriminatorily excluded, but if the progression line seniority system is not itself illegal (i.e. it is "bona fide" under *Teamsters*), how is he to be made whole for his earlier exclusion from the line? But for the discrimination the employee would be at a position in the line well above the entry level job which will typically be the lowest paying and most arduous job in the line. This kind of problem is addressed in Locke v. Kansas City Power & Light Co.

LOCKE v. KANSAS CITY POWER AND LIGHT CO.

United States Court of Appeals, Eighth Circuit, 1981.
660 F.2d 359.

McMillian, Circuit Judge.

Kansas City Power & Light Co. (KCP&L) appeals from a judgment entered in the District Court for the Western District of Missouri finding that KCP&L unlawfully discriminated against appellee Julius B. Locke on the basis of his race. The district court found that KCP&L had denied appellee employment in violation of Title VII of the Civil Rights Act of 1964, and awarded appellee backpay, reinstatement and attorney's fees.

For reversal appellant argues that the district court erred in (1) requiring appellant to show by a "preponderance of evidence" a legitimate, nondiscriminatory reason for refusing Locke's bid for employment; (2) finding the reason given by KCP&L for refusing Locke's bid to be a pretext; (3) ordering appellee reinstated to a higher position than that for which he had applied, with backpay computed, in part, at a rate commensurate with that higher position; and (4) eliminating the probationary period applied to all other employees.

For the reasons discussed below, we affirm in part and reverse in part and remand the case to the district court for further consideration of the remedy issue.

I. Background

On November 3, 1976, KCP&L hired Locke, a black male, as a "Temporary Plant Helper" at KCP&L's Hawthorn generating facility to work for a period of sixty days. Locke worked the full sixty-day term which ended on December 30, 1976. Shortly thereafter, on January 26, 1977, KCP&L rehired Locke, again as a "Temporary Plant Helper," this time for a period of ninety days. Locke completed this term of employment on April 27, 1977.

Temporary employees are hired by KCP&L for a specified period of time at the end of which the company automatically lays off the temporary employee unless he or she is transferred to a permanent position. (By contrast, in a permanent position at KCP&L after a probationary period the employee attains full permanent status, under which the employee automatically stays on unless appropriate steps are taken to end employment.)[2] While employed as a temporary plant helper at KCP&L Locke applied to fill openings in three permanent job positions—one in November, 1976, for a janitor, and two in March, 1977, for plant helpers. Each time KCP&L returned the application to Locke, indicating that it would not be considered because a company policy prohibited accepting applications from temporary employees until the end of their temporary stints. Concerning the November, 1976, application, the company explained it had been filed after the closing date on the job announcement for accepting applications and that Locke was not eligible to apply until his temporary job ended. Concerning the March, 1977, applications, KCP&L explained only that Locke was not eligible to apply until his temporary job ended.[3] The company personnel department returned each application to Locke with an explanatory note dated the same day the application was submitted.

KCP&L continued to seek applicants for the available positions and ultimately filled them. Acting contrary to company policy as it was represented to Locke, KCP&L hired three white male temporary employees for the permanent positions which Locke also had sought. The applications of these temporary employees were considered even before their projects had been substantially completed.

Locke's second period of temporary employment ended April 27, 1977, and he was not rehired by the company. On May 9, 1977, Locke filed a charge of discrimination with the Equal Employment Opportuni-

2. As KCP&L describes its policy, its plant supervisors may hire temporary employees only in an emergency or nonrecurring situation and must obtain authorization from the company which permits hiring of only a limited number of temporaries. The district court was not convinced, however, that this policy was actually followed, because the record suggested that at least in some instances KCP&L hired temporary plant helpers to do essentially the same job as permanent plant helpers on a regular basis. In addition to the groups of temporary plant helpers (including Locke) hired in late 1976 and 1977, a third group was hired later in 1977 in what appeared to be an ongoing process despite absence of any evidence in the record of a year-long emergency under the company's stated policy.

3. There is some indication that Locke made these latter two applications after the closing date listed on the job announcement. The district court, however, found specifically that KCP&L continued to accept applications after Locke was turned down. Locke v. Kansas City Power & Light Co., No. 78–0636–CV–W–1 (W.D.Mo. Apr. 19, 1980), slip op. at 3, and KCP&L does not challenge that finding on appeal. Indeed, KCP&L does not assign any error to the district court's finding that Locke established a *prima facie* case of racial discrimination under the analysis of McDonnell Douglas Corp. v. Green, 411 U.S. 792, 93 S.Ct. 1817, 36 L.Ed.2d 668 (1973) (McDonnell Douglas).

ty Commission, alleging generally that the company had discriminated against him on the basis of race and specifically that a "probationary period" was used as a pretext to discharge him. The EEOC processed this charge and found no reasonable cause to believe that Locke's allegations were true and on June 7, 1978, notified Locke of his right to sue. Locke commenced this proceeding on August 29, 1978, complaining that KCP&L had discriminatorily failed to hire him into a permanent position and discharged him from temporary employment on the basis of race, all in violation of Title VII of the Civil Rights Act of 1964 and of 42 U.S.C. § 1981.[4]

At trial it was stipulated that KCP&L had hired into the permanent plant helper positions in question three white males who had, like Locke, been temporary employees at the time of their applications and, like Locke, had not yet completed their temporary stints. KCP&L did not, however, attempt to justify its failure to hire Locke on the basis of the supposed policy against accepting applications from temporary workers before their jobs ended.[5] Instead, the company offered a new justification that it had actually given consideration to appellant's application and decided to reject him because of poor work performance. In particular KCP&L relied upon testimony by Glendon Paul Curry, the maintenance supervisor at the plant where Locke worked, that Curry had decided not to accept Locke's bid on the permanent plant helper jobs because of Locke's poor performance as a temporary employee. Curry testified that he had reports from foremen that Locke had been away from his work station, had argued with them, and had refused work assignments from more senior employees authorized by the foremen to direct him. The company also presented testimony of foremen and workers as direct evidence of Locke's poor performance.

The district court, however, determined this explanation was a pretext for a number of reasons which the court specified in an oral decision delivered from the bench.[6] The company had obtained written

4. KCP&L does not assert that the allegations in the complaint were not "like or related" to the substance of the EEOC charge. See Satz v. ITT Financial Corp., 619 F.2d 738, 741 (8th Cir. 1980). The EEOC determination of the charge is not in the record before us.

5. It was stipulated that

During the periods of [Locke's] employment, [KCP&L] maintained the following bidding procedure on permanent positions:

(a) Initially, regular bids will be considered.

(b) After regular employee bids are accepted or rejected, consideration may then be given to probationary employee bidders.

(c) Probationary employees are hired without time limitation and after six months of satisfactory service become employees.

(d) For the purposes of bidding, temporary employees are also probationary except that they are hired for a specific period of time only.

(e) The Company may elect to defer consideration of any bid submitted by a temporary employee until the project upon [which] they are working has been completed or nearly completed.

(f) The plant superintendent or his representative makes the decision regarding acceptance or rejection of bids.

6. Although the district court issued a document identified as written findings of fact and conclusions of law which had been approved as to form by counsel for both sides, the document does not fully reflect the substance of the factual findings and

reports from foremen on Locke's supposedly poor performance after Locke's employment ended; the timing, of course, casts some doubt on whether those reports were actually considered in deciding not to give a permanent position to Locke. Moreover, KCP&L witnesses could not name any other employee who had been the subject of such post-termination reports. Locke's supposedly poor performance had not been grounds for failing to rehire him for a second period of temporary employment or for dismissing him. In the district court's view Locke's supposed absence from his work station and failure to follow orders from senior nonsupervisory workers would not be unusual in a job like plant helper where new workers were shuffled between various tasks, some requiring movement around various areas of the plant. It was not clear from the record which KCP&L official was responsible for the decisions about Locke's future employment or what standards or considerations were normally applied in making the decision.[7] Finally, KCP&L's proffered justification for the failure to hire Locke was entirely different from what Locke was told when his application was returned to him.

The district court concluded that Locke had established a *prima facie* case of racial discrimination under the test of McDonnell Douglas v. Green, 411 U.S. 792, 93 S.Ct. 1817, 36 L.Ed.2d 668 (1973) (McDonnell Douglas), and that the reasons proffered by KCP&L for denying him a permanent position were pretextual. In its memorandum the court specified also that the "claim that [Locke] was less than a perfect employee fails to rebut [Locke's] prima facie case as it isn't necessary for [Locke] to 'show perfect performance or even average performance,' " Locke v. Kansas City Power & Light Co., No. 78–0636–CV–W–1 (W.D.Mo. Apr. 19, 1980), slip op. at 3, citing Flowers v. Crouch-Walker Corp., 552 F.2d 1277 (7th Cir. 1977), and that KCP&L's "claim that [Locke] was not entitled to further employment because of an alleged failure to get along with his co-workers fails to rebut [Locke's] prima facie case as [Locke] is not required to have a 'pleasing personality' in order to be entitled to further employment." Locke v. Kansas City Power & Light Co., supra, slip op. at 3, citing Kyriazi v. Western Electric Co., 461 F.Supp. 894 (D.N.J.1978). The district court also concluded that KCP&L had "failed to show by a 'preponderance of the evidence' that [the] failure to accept plaintiff's bid for regular employ-

legal reasoning relied on by the court in announcing from the bench its decision on liability. In evaluating the district court's decision we consider both the document and the transcript of Judge Oliver's remarks which do not contradict the document but supplement it.

7. For example, although KCP&L stipulated the decision would be made by the plant supervisor or his representative, KCP&L at trial took the position that the decision was delegated by the plant supervisor to the supervisor of maintenance in the plant. The district court remarked on the absence of any evidence that the plant manager made even a cursory review of a decision that was apparently his responsibility or that there were any standards at all to guide the decision. Although the court considered this as background evidence, it clearly did not hold the subjectiveness or vagueness of the decision making process *per se* improper, but rather went on to consider the ultimate question of whether race was a factor in this particular case.

ment was for a legitimate nondiscriminatory reason." Locke v. Kansas City Power & Light Co., supra, slip op. at 4, citing Vanguard Justice Society v. Hughes, 471 F.Supp. 670 (D.Md.1979).

Accordingly, the district court found that KCP&L had violated Title VII by denying Locke a permanent plant helper position as of April, 1977, because of his race. In fashioning a remedy the court sought to put Locke in the position he would have occupied but for the discrimination against him. As the white temporary employees hired in place of Locke had all been promoted from plant helper to relief man positions at KCP&L, the district court ruled that Locke also was entitled to a relief man position. The court also held that Locke would not be required to undergo the normal six-month probationary period for new permanent employees. Finally, the court awarded backpay from April 27, 1977, the date KCP&L filled the permanent plant helper position sought by Locke. Backpay was computed at the rate for a plant helper until January 18, 1978 (the date found by the court to be the "average date" for promotion to relief man of the three white plant helpers hired in April, 1977, ahead of Locke), and after January 18, 1978, at the rate for a relief man.[8]

* * *

[The court upheld the district court's finding that plaintiff was denied permanent employment because of his race and that the reasons put forward by the employer for its decisions were pretextual.]

III. Remedy

A. *Instatement as Permanent Plant Helper and Backpay at Plant Helper Rates*

As explained above, the district court found that absent discrimination Locke would have been hired as a plant helper on April 27, 1977 and continued in that position until January 20, 1978. The court awarded backpay at the plant helper rate until January 20, 1978; afterward it awarded backpay at the higher relief man rate. Including interest, a deduction for Locke's interim earnings, and probable overtime, the backpay award was $6,131.63 for 1977. During 1978 the award was zero because Locke's interim earnings fully offset his lost backpay even at the higher relief man rate. For 1979, the award was $7,359.14 and for 1980 up to the date of the district court's judgment the award was $2,060.80, all calculated at the relief man rate. In addition, the court ordered Locke instated as a relief man on a theory that Locke would have been promoted by that time in the absence of discrimination. The court further ordered that Locke should not have to undergo a six-month probationary period provided in KCP&L's contract with the union representing plant employees, because Locke

8. The award was increased by adding prejudgment interest and decreased by subtracting interim earnings of Locke.

would have served his probationary period long ago in the absence of discrimination.

On appeal KCP&L challenges certain aspects of this remedy, including the backpay award at the relief man rate, the instatement of Locke as a relief man, and the cancellation of the probationary period. KCP&L does not argue that backpay at the plant helper rate or instatement as a plant helper was improper as a remedy for the discrimination found by the district court and KCP&L did not appeal these matters. KCP&L's brief nevertheless seeks reversal of the entire judgment on grounds that, even if the district court was correct in finding discrimination, the remedy was an abuse of discretion. We take this to apply only to those parts of the remedy KCP&L objects to, and note that neither instatement of Locke as a plant helper nor backpay at the plant helper rate have been appealed. In view of our affirmance of the district court's finding of discrimination, no challenge remains to the portions of the judgment ordering Locke instated as a plant helper and $6,131.63 in backpay at the plant helper rate for 1977, and those parts of the judgment stand. However, as discussed below, the record before us is not adequate to support the other portions of the judgment. Therefore, we vacate and remand these questions for further consideration in light of this opinion.

B. *Standard of Review*

Preliminarily we note that we review the district court's remedial order only to correct abuse of discretion. Harper v. General Grocers Co., 590 F.2d 713, 717 (8th Cir. 1979). That discretion is not unbounded but must be exercised consistently with the strong remedial aims of Title VII.

> One of the central purposes of Title VII is "to make persons whole for injuries suffered on account of unlawful employment discrimination." Albemarle Paper Company v. Moody, supra, [422 U.S. 405] at 418, 95 S.Ct. [2362] at 2372, 45 L.Ed.2d 280. Accord, Franks v. Bowman Transportation Co., [424 U.S. 747,] 763, 96 S.Ct. 1251, [1264, 47 L.Ed.2d 444] [(1976)]. "To effectuate this 'make whole' objective, Congress [has] vested broad equitable discretion in the federal courts to 'order such affirmative action as may be appropriate, which may include, but is not limited to, reinstatement * * * with or without back pay * * *, or any other equitable relief as the court deems appropriate.'" Id. at 763, 96 S.Ct. at 1264.

Harper v. General Grocers Co., supra, 590 F.2d at 716. Under this standard none of the remedial measures ordered by the district court *per se* went beyond the broad equitable powers specifically granted in § 706(g) of Title VII, 42 U.S.C. § 2000e–5(g). The problem is that there are insufficient findings in the record for us to evaluate the soundness of the district court's exercise of discretion and we therefore vacate parts of the judgment and remand for further findings and reconsideration. See Rule v. International Ass'n of Bridge, Structural & Ornamental Ironworkers, Local Union No. 396, 568 F.2d 558, 568 (8th Cir. 1977).

C. *The Probationary Period*

The district court obviously had some basis for concern on this record that requiring Locke to go through a six-month probationary period, presumably giving him something less than the protection of a "just cause" clause in a typical collective bargaining agreement, would provide a ready pretext for further discrimination. There of course may well be valid nondiscriminatory reasons for requiring a probationary period. The probationary period has not been used to discriminate against Locke, however, and eliminating it may therefore be at odds with the equitable principle that the scope of the remedy should be tailored to the scope of the violation.

If the probationary period is a uniform requirement imposed by KCP&L on new employees for valid business purposes, we think Locke would be in the same position as other employees if he too was subject to it. If the probationary period in fact was not imposed uniformly, the district court may have been justified in exempting Locke from it in order to put him in the position he would have held but for the discrimination against him. Cf. Kansas City Power & Light Co. v. NLRB, 641 F.2d 553 (8th Cir. 1981) (another case involving same employer suggesting a possibility of erratic enforcement). We cannot tell what the outcome should be on this record, and the district court has not made adequate subsidiary findings to support this remedial measure.

Rather than make the substantial inquiry that may be required to resolve a matter of only peripheral importance in this case, we suggest that it may be more appropriate for the district court simply to require Locke to serve the six-month probationary period and retain jurisdiction over the case during that time. Such a resolution would provide opportunity for close scrutiny of any employment decision which Locke may claim to have a discriminatory taint, while allowing KCP&L to use the probationary period for valid business objectives. Of course any action disfavoring Locke would have to be viewed in the context of the finding of discrimination already made in this case.[11]

D. *Promotion to Relief Man*

The district court apparently considered Locke qualified for a relief man job and thought Locke would have been promoted to relief man

11. In this light, if the district court allows the probationary period and retains jurisdiction, further proceedings will not be on a clean slate and KCP&L should be required to carry the burden of persuasion that any dismissal of Locke is based entirely on legitimate, nondiscriminatory factors. Compare International Bhd. of Teamsters v. United States, 431 U.S. 324, 362, 97 S.Ct. 1843, 52 L.Ed.2d 396 (1977) (after finding of discrimination against class the burden may be on the employer to demonstrate legitimate reasons for denying employment opportunity to a member of the class) with Burdine, supra, 101 S.Ct. at 1095 (plaintiff's burden of persuasion as to existence of discriminatory disparate treatment).

but for the discrimination against him. We cannot tell whether the court was of the view that the relief man job required essentially the same qualifications as the plant helper job or that Locke had any additional qualifications required for the relief man job or for some other reason. In any event the findings concerning Locke's qualifications and KCP&L's promotion practices are inadequate for us to evaluate the promotion of Locke to relief man as a remedial measure.

A court can in appropriate circumstances order a promotion as make whole relief for a victim of discrimination, but cannot under Title VII properly order the promotion of an employee to a position for which he or she is not qualified. Our research has not, however, discovered any cases precisely similar to this one, where a court has ordered a Title VII plaintiff who has suffered discrimination in the hiring process instated to a higher position than entry level.

There is some support for the district court's action in a series of cases providing for "job-skipping" where an employer has discriminatorily excluded some employees from whole lines of progression within the employer's work force. E.g., Watkins v. Scott Paper Co., 530 F.2d 1159 (5th Cir.), cert. denied, 429 U.S. 861, 97 S.Ct. 163, 50 L.Ed.2d 139 (1976); Rogers v. International Paper Co., 510 F.2d 1340, 1354 (8th Cir.), vacated on other grounds, 423 U.S. 809, 96 S.Ct. 19, 46 L.Ed.2d 29 (1975); Long v. Georgia Kraft Co., 450 F.2d 557 (5th Cir. 1971); see also United States v. City of Philadelphia, 573 F.2d 802 (3d Cir.), cert. denied, 439 U.S. 830, 99 S.Ct. 105, 58 L.Ed.2d 123 (1978). Such "job-skipping" cases have involved lines of progression between lower and higher level jobs in a plant, where a certain amount of time in a lower level job is generally required before moving up to the next higher job. Victims of discriminatory exclusion from the whole line of progression, especially those who have worked in other jobs within a facility, may be left without any real remedy if, for example, they must take a reduction in pay to transfer into the line of progression at entry level. Courts have in this context carefully scrutinized the lower level jobs prerequisite for advancement within lines of progression and have allowed job-skipping to make whole victims of discrimination where it has specifically been found that the lower level jobs prerequisite is not justified by business necessity. But job-skipping is only appropriate where the beneficiary has demonstrated the skills or other qualifications legitimately required or the higher level job and the promotion is in a line of progression where a promotion is normally forthcoming after some interval of time in the lower level job. Young v. Edgcomb Steel Co., 499 F.2d 97 (4th Cir. 1974).

Under the job-skipping cases the district court has discretion to order Locke instated as a relief man only if it makes the following findings: (1) that Locke had the particular skills or other job-related qualifications required by KCP&L for a relief man, (2) that the relief man position was in a line of progression upward from the plant helper position, that is, a plant helper would normally be promoted to relief man after some interval of acceptable performance as a plant helper, and (3) that the prerequisite service as a plant helper is not itself justified by business necessity aside from the skills or other qualifications to perform the relief man job. Moreover, in exercising its discretion we think the court should consider the possibility for making Locke whole economically by other means such as retroactive seniority, see Franks v. Bowman Transportation Co., supra, 424 U.S. 747, 96 S.Ct. 1251, 47 L.Ed.2d 444, or front pay discussed below.

In any event, KCP&L does not appear to contend that Locke is not entitled to instatement as a plant helper on the basis of the district court's discrimination finding that we have affirmed above and to nondiscriminatory consideration for promotion in the future. Therefore, regardless of the decision on the relief man issue, Locke is in this posture of the case entitled to no less than instatement in a plant helper position.

E. *Backpay*

In view of our treatment of the promotion issue, the backpay award must be amended. If the district court finds that Locke is entitled under the above standards to a relief man position, Locke would be entitled to backpay at the relief man rate from the date his entitlement began, as under the present order. Otherwise, the backpay award must be recomputed at the lower plant helper rate for the year 1979 and any subsequent period of backpay award.

For the reasons stated above, the judgment of the district court is affirmed in part, vacated in part and remanded to the district court.

NOTES AND PROBLEMS FOR DISCUSSION

1. On remand, the district court was instructed by the Eighth Circuit to make certain findings with respect to Locke's qualifications for the relief man position and the functional relation of that job to the position of plant helper, in order to sustain that portion of the district court's judgment placing plaintiff in the relief man position. Who should have the burden of proof in these issues? Does Franks v. Bowman Transportation supply an answer? With the principal case compare, Curl v. Reavis, 740 F.2d 1323 (4th Cir. 1984) (discharged employee not entitled to reinstatement in position better than that for which her experience qualified her) and McClure v. Mexia Independent School District, 750 F.2d 396 (5th Cir. 1985) (district court did not abuse discretion in reinstating discharged employee in position she had never held where she had de facto exercised functions of the job and had been denied title because of her sex).

2. Assuming Locke is qualified for the relief man position and that service as plant helper is not a legitimate prerequisite to the relief man job, could the court displace a white employee from that position in order to put Locke in his "rightful place?" The extreme remedy of "bumping" the incumbent employee has been consistently rejected by the courts.

> The Act should be construed to prohibit the *future awarding* of vacant jobs on the basis of a seniority system that "locks in" prior racial classification. White incumbent workers should not be bumped out of their *present*

positions by Negroes with greater plant seniority; plant seniority should be asserted only with respect to new job openings. This solution accords with the purpose and history of the legislation.

Local 189, United Papermakers & Paperworkers v. United States, 416 F.2d 980, 988 (5th Cir. 1969), cert. denied, 397 U.S. 919, 90 S.Ct. 926, 25 L.Ed.2d 100 (1970). See also Patterson v. American Tobacco Co., 535 F.2d 257 (4th Cir. 1976), cert. denied, 429 U.S. 920, 97 S.Ct. 314, 50 L.Ed.2d 286 (1976); EEOC v. Detroit Edison Co., 515 F.2d 301 (6th Cir. 1975), vacated on other grounds 431 U.S. 951, 53 L.Ed.2d 267, 97 S.Ct. 2668 (1977). But the legislative history relied on by these Courts of Appeals shows only that the sponsors of Title VII did not intend that employees hired *before* the effective date of the Act be bumped by those claiming under the Act. 110 Cong.Rec. 6992 (1964) (interpretive memorandum of Senators Clark and Case). Title VII's operation was to be "prospective and not retrospective." Whites hired after the Act's passage are, however, unlike pre-Act employees, the beneficiaries of *illegal* discrimination, as was, presumably, the white temporary employed instead of Locke as plant helper.

In Franks v. Bowman Transportation Co., the employer argued that the denial of retroactive seniority was necessary to protect the seniority rights of incumbent employees. The Court rejected the argument because its acceptance would "frustrate the central 'make whole' objective of Title VII." 424 U.S. at 774, 96 S.Ct. at 1269. The Court also stressed that "make whole" relief cannot " 'be denied merely because the majority group of employees, who have not suffered discrimination, will be unhappy about it' " and that " 'adjustment of the rights of white employees' " may be necessary " 'to shape remedies that will most effectively protect and redress the rights of the Negro victims of discrimination.' " 424 U.S. at 775, n. 35, 96 S.Ct. at 1269, n. 35. (quoting United States v. Bethlehem Steel Corp., 446 F.2d 652, 663 (2d Cir. 1971); and Vogler v. McCarty, Inc., 451 F.2d 1236, 1238–1239 (5th Cir. 1971)). If this is so, why should the employee who has benefited from discrimination against minorities have any greater claim to his job than to seniority rights under a collective bargaining agreement? Are the equitable considerations surrounding the "bumping" of an employee from his job different from those surrounding deprivation to the employee of his "place" on a seniority roster?

The official position of the EEOC on bumping is that:

> Each identified victim of discrimination is entitled to an immediate and unconditional offer of placement in the employer's work force, to the position he or she would have occupied absent the discrimination, even if this results in displacement of another employee.

Equal Employment Opportunity Commission, Policy Statement, 2/5/85, 53 U.S. L.W. 2400–01. The Fourth Circuit has indicated that under certain circumstances, some kinds of incumbents can be bumped. In Spagnuolo v. Whirlpool Corp., 717 F.2d 114 (4th Cir. 1983) the district court in an ADEA case had entered an order requiring that plaintiff be offered a "comparable position" to the one from which he had been terminated when one became available and paid front pay in the interim. After sixteen months, the district judge concluded that the defendant was dragging its feet in complying with the order and entered a new order requiring that the plaintiff be immediately reinstated to his old job. This order necessitated the bumping of the plaintiff's successor from his position. The Court of Appeals reversed, holding that regardless of the lapse in time and the trial judge's well-founded suspicion regarding defendant's conduct, the district court's equitable discretion did not extend to ordering displacement of an "innocent" incumbent employee. The Court went on to explain, however, that on remand, the district judge could explore whether the defendant had in fact filled positions after the original order which should have been offered to the plaintiff and whether it could have offered jobs in other locations to the incumbent holding the plaintiff's old position.

> We think that should the response to the first inquiry reveal that Whirlpool has filled a vacancy in a job that the district court concludes is comparable to the original position, the district court is empowered to bump the "new" incumbent from that position and order that Spagnuolo be employed in that job. It is important to note that this is not bumping the original employee who was the unknowing beneficiary of discrimination, as that bumping is prohibited by Title VII. Rather, this is bumping an employee whose promotion or hiring was in violation of the court's rightful place order. This "authorized" bumping presumes that the employee who is promoted or hired after the judicial pronouncement of discrimination is no longer an innocent beneficiary. We conclude that such equitable action is authorized under both Title VII and under the district court's inherent powers to enforce its orders.

717 F.2d at 122. Why would the beneficiary of the company's effort to avoid compliance with the court order be any less "innocent" than the beneficiary of the original illegal employment decision?

3. Either because the claimant lacks the qualifications to move directly into a non-entry level job or because of the reluctance to displace incumbent employees, the victim of discrimination may be delayed in attaining his "rightful place" in the employment hierarchy. To financially compensate for this delay, monetary remedies have been developed.

Red Circling. In plants with functionally related lines of progression the minority employee, formerly excluded from bidding into a desirable department because of race or sex, may not be able to go directly into the job in that department to which he would have progressed absent discrimination (see the discussion of job-skipping in Locke v. Kansas City Power & Light Co.), but may be required to start at the entry level job for that line despite the award of retroactive seniority. But the employee may be dissuaded from seeking his rightful place, because the entry level job may pay less than the dead end position the employee now holds at the top of his formerly segregated line of progression. In such situations, the employer generally is required to "red circle" the employee's current wage rate, i.e., to allow the employee to carry it with him until he attains a job in the progression with a higher wage rate. See Grann v. City of Madison, 738 F.2d 786, 790 (7th Cir.), cert. denied, ___ U.S. ___, 105 S.Ct. 296, 83 L.Ed.2d 231 (1984); Rogers v. International Paper Co., 510 F.2d 1340, 1355–1356 (8th Cir. 1975), modified, 526 F.2d 722 (8th Cir. 1979); White v. Carolina Paperboard Corp., 564 F.2d 1073 (4th Cir. 1977). Red circling can be combined with the job-skipping remedy described in *Locke*.

Front Pay. The Eighth Circuit's opinion in *Locke* suggests that front pay (paying the employee the wage rate of the higher job even though he holds the lower position) might be an alternative to placing the plaintiff directly into the relief man job. (Compare Chief Justice Burger's separate opinion in *Franks*, suggesting front pay as an alternative to retroactive seniority). Front pay has become virtually mandatory in cases when the "rightful place" position pays a higher wage rate than the claimant's current salary and, for whatever reason, the employee cannot immediately attain his "rightful place."

> Some employees who have been victims of discrimination will be unable to move immediately into jobs to which their seniority and ability entitle them. The back pay award should be fashioned to compensate them until they can obtain a job commensurate with their status. * * * [B]ack pay * * * until the date of judgment * * * should be supplemented by an award equal to the estimated present value of lost earnings that are reasonably likely to occur between the date of judgment and the time when the employee can assume his new position. * * * Alternatively, the court may exercise continuing jurisdiction over the case and make periodic back pay awards until the workers are promoted to the jobs their seniority and qualifications merit.

Patterson v. American Tobacco Co., 535 F.2d 257, 269 (4th Cir.), cert. denied, 429 U.S. 920, 97 S.Ct. 314, 50 L.Ed.2d 286 (1976). Briseno v. Central Technical Community College Area, 739 F.2d 344, (8th Cir. 1984). Front pay is normally calculated, at specific post-judgment intervals, as the difference between the employee's actual earnings and those of a hypothetical employee in the claimant's "rightful place." See generally Note, Front Pay—Prophylactic Relief Under Title VII of the Civil Rights Act of 1964, 29 Vand. L.Rev. 211 (1976). Do front pay and red circling completely compensate an employee for the delay in reaching his "rightful place?" What if the "rightful place" position not only pays more, but is intellectually more challenging and physically less demanding than the claimant's current job?

4. Is there any circumstance, other than displacement of an incumbent, which might justify the denial of rightful place relief to a victim of discrimination? In Easley v. Anheuser-Busch, Inc., 758 F.2d 251, 264 (8th Cir. 1985), the Court of Appeals reversed a district court's order which had required the immediate hiring of two applicants who had been discriminatorily denied employment. Employees who had been hired at the time the two applicants would have been hired absent discrimination had been laid off in a reduction in force and not recalled. "In the circumstances of this case, we believe an award of back pay is sufficient to serve the 'make whole' purpose of Title VII." Could a change in the applicant's skills or abilities, occurring between the discriminatory act and the time of relief, make reinstatement inappropriate? The EEOC has stated that:

> An employer's contention that a discriminatee is no longer suitable for placement due to loss of skills or change in job content is not an acceptable excuse for failure to accomplish a placement. The employer has the burden to demonstrate that the discriminatee's inability to accept placement is unrelated to the discrimination.

Equal Employment Opportunity Commission: Policy Statement, 2/5/85, supra. See also, Whatley v. Skaggs Companies, Inc., 707 F.2d 1129 (10th Cir.), cert. denied, 464 U.S. 938, 104 S.Ct. 349, 78 L.Ed.2d 314 (1983) (discharged employee who had suffered partial physical disability after discharge entitled to reinstatement where disability would not have occurred had defendant not unlawfully terminated him).

Should animosity between the parties constitute a ground for denial of reinstatement or promotion? Compare, Taylor v. Teletype Corp., 648 F.2d 1129 (8th Cir.), cert. denied, 454 U.S. 969, 102 S.Ct. 515, 70 L.Ed.2d 386 (1981) (reinstatement of public relations representative proper despite employer's hostility) with EEOC v. Kallir, Philips, Ross, Inc., 420 F.Supp. 919 (S.D.N.Y. 1976), aff'd, 559 F.2d 1203 (2d Cir.) (*per curiam*), cert. denied, 434 U.S. 920, 98

S.Ct. 395, 54 L.Ed.2d 277 (1977) (unlawfully discharged advertising account executive not entitled to reinstatement in view of close working relationship required between plaintiff and employer). Most courts have agreed in principle that hostility generated by the litigation itself is not a sufficient reason to deny reinstatement. See, Dickerson v. Deluxe Check Printers, Inc., 703 F.2d 276, 281 (8th Cir. 1983); Armsey v. Nestle Co., 631 F.Supp. 717 (S.D.Ohio 1985). There has, however, been a growing trend among courts to deny reinstatement on the ground that animosity between the parties would make an effective working relationship impossible. See, McIntosh v. Jones Truck Lines, Inc., 767 F.2d 433, 435 (8th Cir. 1985) (reinstatement not proper remedy due to "animosity between the parties and likelihood that they could not work together in peace"); Cancellier v. Federated Department Stores, 672 F.2d 1312, 1319 (9th Cir.), cert. denied, 459 U.S. 859, 103 S.Ct. 131, 74 L.Ed.2d 113 (1982) (plaintiffs and employer could no longer co-exist in business relationship); Hoffman v. Nissan Motor Corp., 511 F.Supp. 352, 355 (D.N.H.1981) (reinstatement of plaintiff would be "harbinger of disaster"). In McIntosh v. Jones Truck Lines, Inc., supra, the dissent argued that animosity alone could not bar reinstatement because "an employer who has violated the law could always avoid reinstatement by making the job sufficiently uncomfortable for a successful plaintiff." 767 F.2d at 436. (Arnold, J., dissenting).

Courts that decide that reinstatement is not viable, normally award a fixed amount of "front pay" in lieu of reinstatement. See, EEOC v. Prudential Federal Savings and Loan Assn., 763 F.2d 1166 (10th Cir.), cert. denied, ___ U.S. ___, 106 S.Ct. 312, 88 L.Ed.2d 289 (1985) ($17,000 in pension benefits that would have vested absent discrimination, case remanded for articulation of why reinstatement not appropriate); Davis v. Combustion Engineering, Inc., 742 F.2d 916 (6th Cir. 1984) ($88,000 in lieu of reinstatement to discharged employee who was six years away from mandatory retirement). The calculation of this type of front pay, perhaps better characterized as future damages, is inherently more speculative than when back pay is determined. See, Shore v. Federal Express Corp., 777 F.2d 1155 (6th Cir. 1985) (award of $68,880 representing five years of "front pay" vacated and remanded for further findings: "Such an estimation must involve more than mere guesswork."); Foit v. Suburban Bancorp, 549 F.Supp. 264 (D.Md.1982) ("uncertain and speculative"). Should this type of "front pay" or future damages ever be appropriate if the employer is willing to reinstate the plaintiff? See, O'Donnell v. Georgia Osteopathic Hospital, 748 F.2d 1543 (11th Cir. 1984).

There remains substantial disagreement as to whether front pay of the type discussed above is available in ADEA cases. Because monetary relief under the Fair Labor Standards Act, which supplies the remedies for the ADEA, is arguably limited to unpaid wages and, in willful violation cases, liquidated damages, the First and Third Circuits have held that front pay is precluded by the statute. Kolb v. Goldring, Inc., 694 F.2d 869 (1st Cir. 1982); Wehr v. Burroughs Corp., 619 F.2d 276 (3d Cir. 1980). Other circuits, reasoning that the power to grant injunctive relief carries with it the power to award alternative monetary relief have approved the remedy. EEOC v. Prudential Federal Savings and Loan Assn., supra; Cancellier v. Federated Department Stores, supra; Blim v. Western Electric Co., 731 F.2d 1473 (10th Cir.), cert. denied, ___ U.S. ___, 105 S.Ct. 233, 83 L.Ed.2d 161 (1984).

5. As noted elsewhere in this book, employment discrimination cases can take a long time to litigate. A private Title VII action may not be filed until the EEOC issues a right-to-sue letter, and the Commission has no statutory

obligation to issue such a letter even if requested by the charging party, until six months after the charge was filed. Because of crowded court dockets and the voluminous discovery often required in such cases, delays of five to six years from filing suit to final judgment are not uncommon. Must a claimant who has been denied promotion or discharged wait for relief until final judgment on the merits? Issuance of a preliminary injunction under Rule 65 of the Federal Rules of Civil Procedure requires a showing of (1) likelihood of success on the merits, (2) irreparable injury, (3) a balance of hardships tipping in plaintiff's favor, and (4) the absence of harm to the public interest. See, 11 Wright & Miller, Federal Practice and Procedure § 2948 (1973).

Section 706(f)(2) of the Act, part of the 1972 amendments, provides in part that:

> Whenever a charge is filed with the Commission and the Commission concludes on the basis of a preliminary investigation that prompt judicial action is necessary to carry out the purposes of this Act, the Commission * * * may bring an action for appropriate temporary or preliminary relief pending final disposition of such charge. Any temporary restraining order or other order granting preliminary or temporary relief shall be issued in accordance with Rule 65 of the Federal Rules of Civil Procedures.

Courts have uniformly held that the failure of the Act to specify that private parties may seek preliminary relief during the EEOC's administrative process does not mean that Congress intended to preclude such a remedy, which existed under the general equitable powers of the courts prior to the 1972 amendments.

> [F]or the court to renounce its incidental equity jurisdiction to stay employer retaliation pending the EEOC's consideration would frustrate Congress's purposes. * * * Given the singular role in 1964 of the individual private action as the only method of enforcing Title VII, and the continued view in 1972 of that right of action as "paramount" we cannot conclude that Congress intended to preclude the courts' use of their incidental equity powers in these circumstances to prevent frustration of Congress's goals.

Sheehan v. Purolator Courier Corp., 676 F.2d 877, 885 (2d Cir. 1982). See also, Drew v. Liberty Mutual Insurance Co., 480 F.2d 69, 74 (5th Cir. 1973), cert. denied, 417 U.S. 935, 94 S.Ct. 2650, 41 L.Ed.2d 239 (1974).

Since a discharged employee who proves her termination or demotion was illegal will be entitled to back pay and reinstatement, how can such a person suffer "irreparable harm" if a preliminary injunction is not granted? Compare, Duke v. Langdon, 695 F.2d 1136 (9th Cir. 1983) (discharged IRS attorney not entitled to preliminary injunction because at trial merits would be entitled to reinstatement with back pay) and Stromfield v. Smith, 557 F.Supp. 995 (S.D.N.Y.1983) (any loss from allegedly retaliatory transfer is compensable and thus no showing of irreparable harm) with Aguilar v. Baine Service Systems, Inc., 538 F.Supp. 581 (S.D.N.Y.1982) (discharged employees who face eviction, cut-off utilities and inability to provide for their children have shown sufficient evidence of irreparable harm to support issuance of preliminary injunction; balance of equities favors reinstatement) and Morrow v. Inmont Corp., 30 EPD ¶ 33,142 (W.D.N.C.1982) (discharged sales person would suffer irreparable harm from loss of customers and sales contacts). The Second Circuit has held that a discharged employee does not establish irreparable harm by showing financial distress or inablility to find other employment absent "truly extraordinary circumstances," but where it is alleged that the discharge was in retaliation for filing an EEOC charge, the risk that other employees may be deterred from protecting their own rights or from providing testimony for the discharged employee may constitute irreparable injury. Holt v. The Continental Group, Inc., 708 F.2d 87 (2d Cir. 1983), cert. denied, 465 U.S. 1038, 104 S.Ct. 1316, 79 L.Ed.2d 712 (1984). See also, Segar v. Civiletti, 516 F.Supp. 314 (D.D.C.1981); Weintraub, Employment Discrimination Cases Under Title VII: The Presumption of Irreparable Harm in Preliminary Injunction Motions, 12 Mem. St. U.L.Rev. 197 (1982). There is a split in the Circuits as to whether the EEOC must demonstrate that irreparable injury would occur or that the balance of hardships is in its favor when it seeks preliminary relief under Section 706(f)(2). Compare, EEOC v. Anchor Hocking Corp., 666 F.2d 1037, 1041–43 (6th Cir. 1981) (irreparable injury must be shown) with EEOC v. Pacific Press Pub. Ass'n., 535 F.2d 1182, 1187 (9th Cir. 1976) and EEOC v. Pacific Southwest Airlines, 587 F.Supp. 686 (N.D.Cal.1984) (when EEOC seeks preliminary relief pursuant to statutory authority, injury to the public interest mandates injunction so long as procedural requirements are met).

6. In a hiring or promotion case the plaintiff who establishes that he was unlawfully denied the position will ordinarily be entitled to an injunction placing him in the position or, where an "innocent" incumbent would be affected, to a preference for the next vacancy (See supra, at p. 791). But what if discrimination is established, but there was more than one minority applicant for the position? Could *both* be entitled to injunctive relief? In Milton v. Weinberger, 696 F.2d 94 (D.C.Cir. 1982), the Court noted:

> [I]f two employees are denied the same promotion for concededly discriminatory reasons, the employer may nonetheless establish that one of the claimants is not entitled to a promotion * * * by offering clear and convincing evidence that there was only one job opening and that the other applicant was more qualified. Since only one of the two victims of discrimination would have been promoted 'but for' the discrimination, the other would not be entitled to an award of the job notwithstanding the unlawful reason for the denial.

696 F.2d at 99. The Court offered no explanation of what the outcome should be if the employer failed to meet its burden. Could the employer ever be ordered to hire both applicants if only one vacancy was originally available? If, as *Milton* assumes, both applicants are "victims of discrimination," would it be fair to at least award the less qualified of two applicants a hiring or promotion preference for a future vacancy? Is the winner-take-all approach to injunctive relief suggested in *Milton* consistent with the Fourth Circuit's method of dealing with the same problem, as it affected back pay, in EEOC v. Ford Motor Co., supra?

Chapter 14

THE PROBLEMS OF CLASS-WIDE RELIEF

Employment discrimination class actions are normally litigated in bifurcated proceedings. Class liability, the issue of whether the employer has engaged in a pattern and practice of discrimination, is tried in the first stage. Neither the class representatives nor individual class members are called upon to prove damages at this stage and remedy-oriented proof is usually not admitted. If classwide discrimination is found, a second proceeding, called "Stage II," is conducted for the purpose of determining the relief due the plaintiffs and individual class members. See generally, Craik v. Minnesota State University Board, 731 F.2d 465 (8th Cir. 1984); Sagers v. Yellow Freight System, Inc., 529 F.2d 721, 733–34 (5th Cir. 1976); Comment, Special Project: Back Pay in Employment Discrimination Cases, 35 Vand.L.Rev. 893, 978–92 (1982).

A finding that the employer has engaged in a pattern and practice of discrimination does not mean that every class member will be entitled to relief. For example, in a hiring case the employer may have discriminated against applicants generally on the basis of race, but some of the class members would not have been hired, absent discrimination, because they could not satisfy legitimate requirements of the position or because at the time of their applications there were no vacancies. Johnson v. Goodyear Tire & Rubber Co., 491 F.2d 1364, 1375 (5th Cir. 1974). Thus, in the Stage II proceeding the court must determine both which class members are entitled to relief and the kind and amount of relief to be awarded. Because discrimination against the class has been determined, however, the burden of proof on the issues before the court no longer rests solely with the plaintiffs as it does in the liability phase of the case. In Teamsters v. United States, 431 U.S. 324, 97 S.Ct. 1843, 52 L.Ed.2d 396 (1977), the defendants contended that at the remedial stage of class litigation individual class members should have to establish their entitlement to relief through the *McDonnell Douglas-Burdine* formula. The Supreme Court rejected the argument and held that when class-wide discrimination has been established, the burden "rests on the employer to demonstrate that the individual applicant was denied an employment opportunity for lawful reasons such as his lack of qualifications or the fact that a more qualified applicant would have been chosen for a vacancy." 431 U.S. at 362, 369 n. 53, 97 S.Ct. at 1868, 1872 n. 53. As the three cases in this chapter demonstrate, however, disagreement remains over the exact nature of the employers' burden in Stage II.

The accepted method for determining the amount of back pay and/or retroactive seniority, once entitlement is established, is by the construction of hypothetical work histories as was done in EEOC v.

Ford Motor Co., supra, for each class member. See, EEOC v. Korn Industries, 662 F.2d 256 (4th Cir. 1981); White v. Carolina Paperboard Corp., 564 F.2d 1073 (4th Cir. 1977). Under the best of conditions, this process can be a monumental task, but because of such factors as highly subjective decision-making, lack of records and fading memories, anything approaching an accurate reconstruction of what an individual employee's work history would have been absent discrimination is often impossible. In Pettway v. American Cast Iron Pipe Co., 494 F.2d 211, 260 (5th Cir. 1974) (*Pettway III*), the Court of Appeals described some of the problems facing courts in typical Stage II litigation.

> There is no way of determining which jobs the class members would have bid on and have obtained if discriminatory testing, seniority, posting and bidding system, and apprentice and on-the-job training programs not been in existence. Class members outnumber promotion vacancies; jobs have become available only over a period of time; the vacancies enjoy different pay rates; and a determination of who was entitled to the vacancy would have to be determined on a judgment of seniority and ability at that time. This process creates a quagmire of hypothetical judgments.

The efforts of courts to solve problems associated with class relief are illustrated by the following cases.

KYRIAZI v. WESTERN ELECTRIC CO.

United States District Court for New Jersey, 1979.
465 F.Supp. 1141.

OPINION

STERN, DISTRICT JUDGE.

At the conclusion of "Stage I" of this Title VII litigation—the liability phase—this Court found that Western Electric discriminated against its female employees, applicants and former employees in the areas of hiring, promotion, participation in job training programs, layoffs, wages and opportunities for testing.[1] We now enter "Stage II", the damage phase. Stage II requires adjudication of the claims of thousands of class members.[2]

To assist it in this formidable task, the Court has appointed three Special Masters pursuant to Rule 53(a) of the Federal Rules of Civil Procedure. The Court now addresses some of the procedural hurdles which confront it at this stage.

1. That opinion is reported at 461 F.Supp. 894 (D.N.J.1978). An earlier opinion of this Court on the discovery aspects of Stage I is reported at 74 F.R.D. 468 (D.C.1977).

2. Western reports that there are approximately 10,000 class members (Tr. 1/31/79 at 5), of which:

—1,131 are retired

—1,887 are active employees

—3,200 were laid off by Western

—3,500 were rejected by Western.

(Tr. 1/31/79 at 9–10).

1. Burden of Proof

The Supreme Court has made clear that once there has been a finding of classwide discrimination, the burden then shifts to the employer to prove that a class member was not discriminated against; that is, a finding of discrimination creates a rebuttable presumption in favor of recovery. The Court first addressed this in Franks v. Bowman, in which it held that:

> [P]etitioners here have carried their burden of demonstrating the existence of a discriminatory hiring pattern and practice by the respondents and, therefore, the burden will be upon respondents to prove that individuals who reapply were not in fact victims of previous hiring discrimination.

More recently, in International Brotherhood of Teamsters v. United States, the Court specifically rejected the contention that in the remedial stage of a pattern-or-practice case, the government must prove that the individual was actually the victim of discrimination:

> That basic contention was rejected in the *Franks* case. As was true of the particular facts in *Franks,* and as is typical of Title VII pattern-or-practice suits, the question of individual relief does not arise until it has been proved that the employer has followed an employment policy of unlawful discrimination. The force of that proof does not dissipate at the remedial stage of the trial. The employer cannot, therefore, claim that there is no reason to believe that its individual employment decisions were discriminatorily based; it has already been shown to have maintained a policy of discriminatory decisionmaking.
>
> The proof of the pattern or practice supports an inference that any particular employment decision, during the period in which the discriminatory policy was in force, was made in pursuit of that policy. The Government need only show that an alleged individual discriminatee unsuccessfully applied for a job and therefore was a potential victim of the proved discrimination. As in *Franks,* the burden then rests on the employer to demonstrate that the individual applicant was denied an employment opportunity for lawful reasons.

(Footnote omitted; citation omitted).

Accordingly, the sole burden upon class members will be to demonstrate that they are members of the class, that is, that now or at any time since June 9, 1971, they were either employed by Western, applied for employment at Western or were terminated by Western. In practical terms, this will be reflected in the Proof of Claim forms which class members will be required to fill out. Those forms require only that the putative class member state the dates of her employment and/or application, the positions she held and/or sought.[3] The Court will not require individual class members to specify the manner in which they

3. Copies of the notice to the class and the Proof of Claim forms to be distributed to class members are reproduced in the Appendix to this opinion.

were discriminated against. As was held in Stage I, employees remained for the most part ignorant of the fact that they were being passed over for promotion and training programs, and unsuccessful applicants may well be unaware that they were rejected on the basis of their sex. The fact is that employment decisions are rarely put in discriminatory terms, no matter how discriminatorily bottomed. Individual employees should not be put to the almost impossible task of delving into the corporate consciousness to demonstrate how an already proven policy of discrimination exactly impacted each one of them.[4] Thus, once an individual demonstrates that she is a class member, the burden will then shift to Western to demonstrate that the individual class member was not the victim of discrimination.

2. *Notice*

Pursuant to Rule 23(d)(2), Federal Rules of Civil Procedure, Western is required to give notice to class members in the following manner. All class members whose addresses are known to Western will be sent a notice and Proof of Claim form together with a prepaid envelope. The remaining class members will be notified by publication in six local newspapers for two consecutive weeks in the Sunday editions and three weekday editions.[5] All costs of notification are, of course, to be borne by Western.

The Court has scanned the early returns from the newspaper notices and the mailings and has determined that it would be advisable to supplement the notice to the nearly 1,900 class members who are presently employed by Western by providing an opportunity for class counsel to communicate with them directly at the plant.[6] Accordingly, Western will permit counsel for the class to enter the plant for the purpose of meeting with class members who are presently employed by Western. Western may accomplish this in any manner that will minimize loss of productivity and disruption of its normal activities, provided that the manner selected gives employees advance notice and a reasonable opportunity to meet with counsel. Undoubtedly, mass

4. Compare Pettway v. American Cast Iron Pipe Co., 494 F.2d 211, 259 (5th Cir. 1974), which held that each class member has the "initial burden * * * to bring himself within the class and to describe the harmful effect of the discrimination on his individual employment position." It is noteworthy, however, that *Pettway* was decided before the Supreme Court's decisions in *Franks* and *Teamsters.*

5. Those newspapers are *The* New York *Times, The* Daily *News, The* Newark *Star Ledger, The* Bergen *Record, The* New York *Post,* and *The* Jersey *Journal.*

A substantial number of class members, approximately 3,500 are women who applied for positions at Western and were rejected. Western reports that it does not have the addresses of these women, only their social security numbers. Counsel for the plaintiff has been directed to prepare a form of notice acceptable to the Social Security Administration to be forwarded to the last known business addresses of these women.

6. In this Circuit, counsel is permitted to confer with members of the class—indeed, a restriction upon counsel's ability to communicate with class members has been held violative of the First Amendment. Coles v. Marsh, 560 F.2d 186 (3rd Cir.), cert. denied, 434 U.S. 985, 98 S.Ct. 611, 54 L.Ed.2d 479 (1977); Rodgers v. United States Steel Corp., 508 F.2d 152 (3rd Cir.), cert. denied, 423 U.S. 832, 96 S.Ct. 54, 46 L.Ed.2d 50 (1975). See also, Developments in the Law—Class Actions, 89 Harv.L.Rev. 1317, 1592–1604 (1976).

meetings will be required in order to minimize the number of visits which counsel will have to make. These meetings may take place before or after working hours, if Western prefers, but sufficient time must be allocated and a suitable facility must be provided. With these guidelines in mind, counsel are directed to meet and work out a schedule which will commence not later than March 12, 1979 and terminate not later than March 31, 1979, nine days before the April 9, 1979 cutoff date for the filing of claims by class members.

3. Computation of Back Pay Awards

The courts have adopted a number of approaches in connection with the computation of back pay awards.[7] One approach, the "pro rata" formula referred to in Pettway v. American Cast Iron Pipe Co., 494 F.2d 211 (5th Cir. 1974), and United States v. United States Steel, 520 F.2d 1043 (5th Cir. 1975), looks to the difference between the salary of the class members computed collectively and that received by employees of comparable skills and seniority, not the victims of discrimination. The class member then receives his pro rata share of that collective difference, based upon his salary differential and the number of competitors for the position. Another approach is the "test period" approach, used in Bowe v. Colgate, Palmolive Co., 489 F.2d 896 (7th Cir. 1973), in which the court awards class members the difference between the pay they receive after implementation of the Title VII decree and the pay they received while the discriminatory policies were in force. A variation of the "test period" approach was used in Stewart v. General Motors, 542 F.2d 445 (7th Cir. 1976), cert. denied, 433 U.S. 919, 97 S.Ct. 2995, 53 L.Ed.2d 1105 (1977), in which the court awarded the class members the difference between the wages of salaried white workers during a test period and that actually received by the class. Yet another approach was used in Stamps v. Detroit Edison Co., 365 F.Supp. 87, 121 (E.D. Mich.1973), rev'd on other grounds sub nom. EEOC v. Detroit Edison Co., 515 F.2d 301 (6th Cir. 1975), in which the court awarded class members the difference between their own actual earnings and the earnings of the skilled trade opportunity jobs from the effective date of Title VII.

The Court finds none of these approaches appropriate here. As we found in connection with Stage I, we deal with discrimination which manifests itself in a number of ways. For example, a woman might initially be hired at the lowest grade—32—while a comparable male would have been hired at grade 33. During the course of a ten-year period, the woman—perhaps unbeknownst to her—would be passed over for promotion, denied entry into job training programs and,

7. The back pay period commences two years before the filing of the EEOC charge. 42 U.S.C. § 2000e–5(g). At Stage I, the Court concluded that the nature of the discrimination alleged and proved brought this case within the "continuing violation" theory of Title VII, therefore, allowing class members to secure relief for acts of discrimination occurring since the effective date of Title VII. While it is clear that the back pay award is statutorily limited, the Court is considering what other forms of relief may be awarded for discrimination which occurred before the two year back pay period.

finally, notwithstanding her seniority, would be the first to be laid off because she was in the lowest job category. She may in fact have been laid off and rehired a number of times.[8] By contrast, the male, during the same period and having started at a higher grade, would be promoted several grades—perhaps even trained for a supervisory position—and would thus remain unscathed in times of layoffs. It is, therefore, apparent that a back pay award must take into account the fact that a male and a female entering Western with comparable skills would, over a period of time, take dramatically divergent paths.

While this approach will not yield an exact measure of damages, neither could any other approach. However, the law is clear that where one has been damaged by the wrong of another, the victim is not to be denied any recompense merely because the exact measure of damages is uncertain. The approach we adopt at least gives individual consideration to each claimant and, if not precise, it is no more imprecise than lumping claimants into groups and extracting averages, or otherwise depersonalizing victims of discrimination by running them through a mathematical blender.

Moreover, Western itself objects to any formula type or averaging approach in awarding back pay—that is, to any but an individual approach under which the merits of each woman's claim is separately considered. In the face of Western's objections, it may be that due process considerations require that any award to an individual be on the merits of that individual's case. In any event, it does seem that an individual approach is more fair both to class members and to Western.

In its proposed Order of Reference, Western proposes that:

> 45. If there is more than one eligible claimant for a given designated vacancy, net back pay awards shall be computed for each claimant. One award shall be made in an amount equal to the highest individual net award. Each claimant shall share that award in the proportion that her individual net back pay award bears to her total of all claimants' net back pay awards pursuant to the formula set forth in United States v. United States Steel, 520 F.2d 1043 (5th Cir. 1975).

The Court rejects this approach. According to Western, if there were three women who should have been considered for one promotion and none were, and if we cannot now determine which of the three women should have received the promotion, then each one receives one-third of the benefits. As Western notes, this approach does shield Western from having to pay three increases when only one was actually possible, but it also unjustly penalizes the one woman who was entitled to *all*—not just one-third—of the benefits of that promotion. Under Western's approach, two of the claimants get a windfall while the actual victim receives only one-third of the back pay to which she is statutorily entitled. If we know that all three claimants were discriminated

8. The preliminary responses already received from class members indicate that this is no rare experience for women at Western.

against in that they were not considered for promotion but that only one—which, we do not know—would have actually received the promotion, then all three should get the full benefit of the promotional opportunity. Where it is proved that an employer unlawfully disregarded women for promotion, it is better that it pay a little more than to permit an innocent party to shoulder the burdens of the guilty. Western *will* be permitted to demonstrate that the promotion would have gone to one class member, rather than the others. However, if Western cannot demonstrate which claimant would have received the promotion, Western cannot divide the benefits of the one job. It is no more unreal to construe three promotions out of one, than to divide the salary increase of one promotion among three prospects. Either smacks of some artificiality but the latter protects the wrongdoer at the expense of the innocent.

The Order of Reference to the Special Masters is reproduced in the Appendix. Among other requirements, in an effort to assure back pay awards on as individualized basis as possible, where appropriate class members will be compared to the male employee with comparable skills upon initial hire and comparable seniority. The class member will then be awarded the difference between her salary and that received by the male counterpart, including bonuses and any other fringe benefits. See Pettway v. American Cast Iron Pipe Co., supra.

4. Compensation of Special Masters

The final problem which confronts us at the outset of Stage II is the compensation of the Special Masters.

All parties have recognized that the number of potential claimants virtually mandates the appointment of Special Masters. The parties agree that if any significant portion of the 10,000 potential claimants respond, the existing court mechanism of a district judge and a magistrate is totally inadequate to deal with the issues which will confront the Court. Even 3,000 claimants out of the 10,000 eligible, for example, would exceed the yearly civil filings for this entire district of nine active judges and five magistrates. Moreover, unlike a rough sampling of the typical civil case cross section, many of which will be voluntarily dismissed, others of which will be settled without any judicial supervision, and the overwhelming majority of which will be settled without any judicial factfinding,[9] it appears that each one of the claims of Western's present or former employees will have to be individually considered and adjudicated. Western has objected to any formula approach, and has requested that each claim be considered upon its own merits. The Court agrees that not only is Western entitled to this approach, but that each claimant is also entitled to individual consideration. In many instances this approach requires that efforts be made to project the actual benefits lost by each Western employee who has

9. In 1978, approximately 90% of the civil actions filed in this District were terminated sometime prior to trial. *Management Statistics for United States Courts* (1978).

been found to have been a victim of Western's discrimination. Whole work histories will have to be recast, based on evaluations of the background, education, potential and abilities of each claimant, as compared with the opportunities available to and realized by similarly situated males at Western. In a very real sense, Stage II proceedings under this approach resemble a host of individual cases, sharing many common questions of law and fact, as much as it does the pure class action of more common experience.

Faced with this task, the parties agree not merely to the appointment of a Special Master, but to the appointment of three Special Masters. The parties also agree that these Special Masters should not only be lawyers, but experienced trial lawyers. Western has demanded, and the Court has granted, an opportunity for it to conduct "discovery regarding the * * * claims pursuant to the Federal Rules of Civil Procedure." If the past is any gauge of the future, the Special Masters will be occupied with discovery matters concerning many hundreds of claimants even before they get down to dealing with the merits of each.

[The Court found that the Special Masters should be compensated "in a manner roughly comparable to that which they receive in the practices from which they are being diverted"—i.e. at hourly rates of $125 and $115. The defendant was ordered to pay all the Masters' fees.]

Appendix "A"

TO: Female Applicants, Employees or Former Employees of Western Electric's Kearny Plant (including the Clark Shops)

RE: Sex Discrimination Action Against Western

If you are a woman and now or any time since June 9, 1971 you either: (a) applied for employment at Western's Kearny plant and were rejected; *or* (b) were employed in any position at Western's Kearny plant; *or* (c) were laid off or discharged from any position at Western's Kearny plant, please read this notice carefully.

On October 30, 1978, in a lawsuit brought by Kyriaki Cleo Kyriazi, a former employee of Western, the United States District Court for the District of New Jersey found that Western has been discriminating against its women employees at its Kearny plant in violation of federal law. It was found that women, *as a group,* were discriminated against in the following ways:

1) *Hiring*—Women are hired into the lowest grades, while men with equal skills and experience were hired into the higher grades.

2) *Promotion*—Women employees were not given promotional opportunities equal to male employees.

3) *Layoffs*—Women were not treated fairly when employees had to be laid off.

4) *Transfer into Kearny*—Women who transferred into the Kearny plant were placed in lower grades than they were in before they transferred.

5) *Discharge*—More women were fired than men.

6) *Participation in Job Training Programs*—Women were not given the opportunities given to men to participate in job training programs.

7) *Opportunities for Testing*—Women were not given the opportunity to take tests for promotion to better positions.

The Court has completed the first stage of this lawsuit by finding that Western had discriminated against women in its Kearny plant. Copies of the Court's opinion are on file in the United States District Court of the District of New Jersey.

There will be soon be a second stage, "Stage II", at which time the Court will determine the damages and other relief which it will award to individual women. If you are or were at any time since June 9, 1971 an employee of Western, or if you ever applied for a position at Western, you may be entitled to certain benefits, including monetary payments. The "Stage II" proceedings will determine this question. At these "Stage II" proceedings, any eligible woman will be presumed to have been discriminated against. It will be Western's duty to show that it did not deny a woman employment opportunities because of her sex. If Western fails to demonstrate this, that women will be entitled to recovery, which may include back pay and reinstatement.

If you wish to be considered, you must fill out the enclosed form. Your claim will not be considered if you do not do so and return the form by April 2nd, 1979. If you do fill out the form, you may be required, with no cost to yourself, to participate in court proceedings. You will be furnished an attorney without cost to you. That attorney will be Judith Vladeck, Attorney for plaintiff Kyriazi. If you prefer, you may retain an attorney of your own choosing. If you wish further information, you may contact the attorney for the plaintiff, Judith Vladeck, at (212) 354–8330

AS PART OF THE COURT'S ORDER, YOUR EMPLOYER MAY NOT PENALIZE YOU IN ANY WAY IF YOU CHOOSE TO FILE A CLAIM AGAINST IT.

APPENDIX "B"

Kyriazi v. Western Electric 475–73

____
NAME

____
ADDRESS

____
TELEPHONE NUMBER

Answer each question to the best of your ability.

1) Did you use any other name while employed at Western's Kearny Plant? (Indicate yes or no) ______. If so, please set forth the names you used and the dates you used each name.

NAME	DATES
__________	______ - ______
__________	______ - ______

2) What is your social security number?__________

3) Were you rejected for a position at Western's Kearny Plant? (Indicate yes or no) _____. If so, please set forth the date of your application and the position for which you applied.__________

____

4) Are you presently employed at Western's Kearny Plant? _____ If so, when did your employment begin? _____. Please list all positions you have held at Western, (the grade, if the position was graded), and the dates you held each position.

POSITION	GRADE	DATES
__________	_____	_____ - _____
__________	_____	_____ - _____
__________	_____	_____ - _____

5) Were you laid off or otherwise terminated by Western?_____. If so, when did your employment end? _____. What was the reason given for your termination?__________.
Set forth each of the positions you held at Western's Kearny plant and the dates you held each position.

__________ ______ - ______
__________ ______ - ______
__________ ______ - ______

6) Have you been employed since you left Western? _____. If so, please set forth the positions you have held since you left Western and the dates you held each position.

__________ ______ - ______
__________ ______ - ______
__________ ______ - ______

Please send the completed form to:

Angelo Locascio, Clerk
United States District Court
U.S. Post Office and Courthouse
Newark, New Jersey 07101

[Appendix "C" to the opinion, containing detailed guidelines for the Special Masters to follow in resolving the various types of claims to be raised by class members, is omitted.]

INGRAM v. MADISON SQUARE GARDEN CENTER

United States Court of Appeals for the Second Circuit.
709 F.2d 807, cert. denied, 464 U.S. 937, 104 S.Ct. 346, 78 L.Ed.2d 313 (1983).

Before VAN GRAAFEILAND, MESKILL and PRATT, CIRCUIT JUDGES.

VAN GRAAFEILAND, CIRCUIT JUDGE:

Local 3 of the International Brotherhood of Electric Workers appeals from a judgment of the United States District Court for the

Southern District of New York (Sand, J.) which awarded plaintiffs in a class employment discrimination suit retroactive seniority rights with back pay, front pay, and attorneys' fees, the total monetary award, with interest, being substantially in excess of $1 million. Four opinions written by the district court are reported at 482 F.Supp. 414, 482 F.Supp. 426, 482 F.Supp. 918, and 535 F.Supp. 1082. Although we find the evidence of discrimination somewhat less persuasive than did the district court, we are not prepared to hold that the district court's findings on this issue were clearly erroneous. See Pullman-Standard v. Swint, 456 U.S. 273, 102 S.Ct. 1781, 72 L.Ed.2d 66 (1982). Accordingly, we affirm the district court's adjudication of liability. However, for reasons hereafter discussed, we find it necessary to modify the relief which the court below granted.

Since 1965, Local 3 of the International Brotherhood, which has more than 4,300 black and Hispanic members, has represented the "maintenance group of utility men" (hereafter "laborers") at Madison Square Garden. These laborers prepare the Garden for its various featured events. The several contracts between the Union and the Garden placed no restrictions on the employer's method of hiring, merely requiring that all laborers become members of the Union within 31 days of their employment. However, in practice, the hirelings, of which there was an average of about 5 per year, were referred to the Garden by the Union representative for the Garden laborers. About 1 in 6 of the hirelings was either black or Hispanic.

Until 1969, the Garden also employed other groups of people as cleaners or porters, bowling alley and lavatory attendants, and elevator operators. In 1969, the Garden subcontracted its cleaning work to Allied Maintenance Corporation, retaining only the elevator operators as its own employees. All of the cleaners are represented by Local 54 of Service Employees International Union, and most of them are either black or Hispanic.

On August 13, 1973, appellees Ingram, Britt, Moody, and Floyd, all of whom were porters working at the Garden, filed charges against the Garden and Allied with the Equal Employment Opportunity Commission, pursuant to Title VII of the Civil Rights Act of 1964, 42 U.S.C. § 2000e et seq., alleging that these employers had discriminated against them and other black porters by paying them less than the white laborers for doing similar work and by maintaining segregated job classifications. The EEOC concluded that the Garden and Allied were violating Title VII, and, on October 4, 1976, following unsuccessful conciliation efforts, issued right-to-sue letters to the four complainants. On December 30, 1976, the porters filed a proposed class action suit against the Garden and Allied, alleging violations of 42 U.S.C. §§ 1981 and 1985 as well as Title VII. On June 22, 1977, Local 3 was added to the litigation by means of an amended complaint, which charged that the Union was discouraging competent minority cleaners from seeking and obtaining jobs as laborers and was conspiring with the Garden and

Allied towards this end by advising cleaners that the Garden was solely responsible for hiring, that no jobs were available, and that cleaners must do apprenticeships before becoming members of Local 3.

On November 24, 1975, appellees Anderson and Perry, black porters who worked at the Garden, also filed discrimination charges with the EEOC, their charges being directed against the Garden, Allied, and Local 3. On January 16, 1978, a right-to-sue letter issued, and on March 31, 1978, a proposed class action complaint on behalf of the Anderson group was filed.

The district court certified a Title VII class and a §§ 1981 and 1985 class in both actions. In the *Ingram* action, the Title VII class, whose claims, of necessity, were limited to the Garden and Allied, consisted of all blacks who, after February 14, 1973, had been or would be employed as cleaners at the Garden. The §§ 1981 and 1985 class consisted of all blacks and Hispanics who, after December 30, 1973, had been or would be employed as cleaners at the Garden. The §§ 1981 and 1985 class consisted of all blacks and Hispanics who, after December 30, 1973, had been or would be employed as cleaners at the Garden. Certification of both classes in *Ingram* was conditioned on the intervention of lavatory and bowling alley attendants and elevator operators as named plaintiffs. Thereafter, Williams, a black lavatory attendant, Milon, a black bowling alley attendant, Mitchell, a black elevator operator, Bruton, a retired black cleaner, and Garcia, an Hispanic cleaner, intervened. The *Anderson* classes were defined in the same manner as those of *Ingram,* except that the Title VII *Anderson* class limitation was May 28, 1975, and the §§ 1981 and 1985 *Anderson* class limitation was March 31, 1975, and both classes claimed against the Garden, Allied, and Local 3.

On July 13, 1978, the *Ingram* and *Anderson* actions were consolidated. On July 16, 1979, the district court denied the Union's motion to decertify the classes. Subsequently, the plaintiffs entered into a proposed consent decree with the Garden and Allied, in which the defendants agreed, among other things, to pay $117,500 in settlement of plaintiffs' monetary claims plus $47,500 in attorneys' fees. On October 23, 1979, the settlement was approved by the district court, subject only to the submission of an affidavit in support of counsel fees. See 482 F.Supp. at 426. In the meantime, the case had proceeded to trial against Local 3, the issue being limited to that of liability.

On October 3, 1979, in an opinion reported at 482 F.Supp. 414, the district court dismissed plaintiffs' § 1985 claims, relying on Great American Federal Savings & Loan Assoc. v. Novotny, but held the Union liable under both Title VII and § 1981.

[The Court's discussion of the statistical evidence (which showed that blacks and Hispanics had been referred by the Union in numbers significantly below their percentage in the relevant labor market) and of antecdotal testimony by class members is omitted.]

The Back Pay Award

In fashioning a remedy for employment discrimination, "the court must, as nearly as possible, 'recreate the conditions and relationships that would have been had there been no' unlawful discrimination." Int'l Bhd. of Teamsters v. United States. We believe that the remedy in the instant case went beyond that.

The district court referred the factual remedial issues to a Magistrate and instructed the Magistrate to award seniority to every class member who desired a laborer's job as of the date of the next laborer hire that followed his application or "qualifying desire", subject to a maximum date of July 2, 1965. The court instructed the Magistrate to make back pay awards on the same basis, subject to the 2-year limitation period of Title VII and the 3-year limitation period applicable in New York to § 1981. The computations, made as directed, produced some interesting results. Two class members were awarded retroactive competitive seniority dates to 1970, a year in which 5 laborers were hired, one of whom was Hispanic. If the district court was recreating the conditions that would have existed had there been no discrimination, presumably he intended that three of the five 1970 hirelings should have been either black or Hispanic. In 1974, 6 laborers were hired, one of whom was black. Nevertheless, 4 class members were awarded retroactive competitive seniority to 1974. In recreating the conditions for that year, the district court must have intended that 5 out of the 6 hirelings should have been either black or Hispanic. Although only one laborer, a white man, was hired in 1976, seniority retroactive to 1976 was awarded 4 class members.

According to appellees' own computations, in 1969, the laborer work force at the Garden consisted of 48 whites, 2 blacks and 2 Hispanics. Between 1970 and 1978, the Garden hired 33 laborers referred to it by the Union, of whom 6 were either black or Hispanic. The minority hiring rate during these years was thus 18.2%. The district court held that, for purposes of retroactive competitive seniority, 17 class members should have been hired during this period, for purposes of non-competitive seniority, 10 class members should have been hired, and for purposes of back pay awards, 13 class members should have been hired. Had 17 class members been hired, the racial composition of labor hirings during this period would have been 69% black or Hispanic. Had 13 class members been hired, the composition would have 57% black or Hispanic. Had 10 been hired, 48% of the hirelings would have been black or Hispanic. This is hardly a recreation of the conditions that would have existed had there been no discrimination.

A court that finds unlawful discrimination is not required to grant retroactive relief. City of Los Angeles v. Manhart, 435 U.S. 702, 718, 98 S.Ct. 1370, 1380, 55 L.Ed.2d 657 (1978). "To the point of redundancy, the statute stresses that retroactive relief 'may' be awarded if it is 'appropriate.'" Id. at 719, 98 S.Ct. at 1380. Moreover, such remedy as is given should not constitute a windfall at the expense of the employer, its union, or its white employees. Title VII imposes no duty to maximize the hiring of minority employees. Furnco Construction Corp. v. Waters. Remedial relief should be granted only to those class members who would have filled vacancies had there been no discrimination. The district court's judgment, based on the concept that all class members with unexpressed employment desires should have been hired regardless of the number of vacancies and competing applicants, is based upon a hypothetical hiring practice which the law did not require and which, in actuality, never would have been followed absent any trace of discrimination.

James O'Hara, the Union representative for the Garden laborers and the person who made job referrals, received over 300 requests for jobs during the period at issue, not a single one of which came from a class member. There is nothing in the record to indicate that, discrimination aside, class members would have been given preference over other applicants. Indeed, since the Union counted 4,300 blacks and Hispanics among its own members, it is unlikely that preferred treatment would have been given to members of another union. In view of the limited number of vacancies that occurred, we conclude that, to the extent that back pay was awarded to more than 7 class members, it constituted an unwarranted windfall and did not recreate the conditions that would have existed in the absence of discrimination.

Because of the statistical limitations inherent in the small samples available to plaintiffs' expert witness, her testimony concerning disproportionate hiring did not focus on any particular year. Faced with the same limitations, neither this Court nor the district court can state accurately when the 7 class members should have been hired. Under such circumstances, we think it would be inequitable to award back pay to only the first 7 class members who indicated a "desire" to become laborers. The fairer procedure, we believe, would be to compute a gross award for all the injured class members and divide it among them on a pro rata basis. See Stewart v. General Motors Corp., 542 F.2d 445, 452–53 (7th Cir. 1976), cert. denied, 433 U.S. 919, 97 S.Ct. 2995, 53 L.Ed.2d 1105 (1977); Pettway v. American Cast Iron Pipe Co., 494 F.2d 211, 263 n. 154 (5th Cir. 1974). In determining the amount of the gross award, however, we think it fair to both the Union and the class members to assume that the Union would have referred the 7 class members who first desired employment, had they applied, and to base the class award on the loss attributable to these 7 men.

The first 7 "applicants", determined by their seniority dates, and the back pay awards made them by the district court, are:

1. Clarence Lamar .... $ 55,120
2. Wilfred Boudreaux 51,010
3. William Moody 53,298
4. Herbert Holmes 57,604
5. Henry Ingram 27,202

6.	Kenneth Williams	61,494
7.	James Britt	39,988
		$345,716

The total award to these men, $345,716, is equal to approximately 52.14% of the total award of $663,085 which the district court made to all 18 back pay recipients. Proration by 52.14% of the 18 individual awards produces the following figures:

1.	Shelly Anderson	$ 16,578.43
2.	Wilfred Boudreaux	26,596.61
3.	James Britt	20,849.74
4.	John Carroll	9,630.78
5.	Russell Footman	11,123.03
6.	Waverly Green	10,675.67
7.	Graydon Griffith	18,963.84
8.	Lawrence Hawkins	24,746.17
9.	Francisco Hernandez	23,836.84
10.	Herbert Holmes	30,034.73
11.	Henry Ingram	14,183.12
12.	Clarence Lamar	28,739.57
13.	William Moody	27,789.58
14.	James Parrott	19,611.94
15.	James Perry	8,775.16
16.	James Pettigrew	11,628.78
17.	George Sharpe, Sr.	9,905.56
18.	Kenneth Williams	32,062.97
		$345,732.52

The district court's award of back pay is modified in accordance with the foregoing figures.

Front Pay

Since this action was begun, at least 6 class members to whom the district court made back pay awards have been hired by the Garden, 5 of them on November 5, 1979, and one on December 20, 1980. The district court has indicated that it intends to make front pay awards for future losses to the twelve remaining back pay recipients. For the reasons already expressed, we believe it is completely unrealistic to assume that all 18 back pay beneficiaries would have been hired had there been no discrimination practiced against them. Accordingly, we deem it unfair to the members of the defendant Union, black, Hispanic, and white, to impose a continuing liability upon their association for the loss of future benefits. This unfairness is exacerbated by the fact that the Union has no control over future hirings, which are the sole prerogative of the Garden, and is therefore in no position to bring its liability for front pay to an end. Under these circumstances, we believe that it would be an abuse of discretion for the district court to make front pay awards against the Union to class members not already hired.

Retroactive Seniority

The same factors which dictate the limitation of back pay and front pay awards also militate against the grant of retroactive seniority to future hirelings. In addition, we view pendent grants of retroactive seniority as self-defeating, in that they militate against the likelihood that the beneficiaries of the grants will be employed. Under the consent decree which terminated plaintiffs' action against the Garden, the Garden agreed that every second job opening would be offered to minorities until their representation among the Garden's laborers reached 27%. Because at least 9 minority laborers have been hired since the execution of the consent decree, 6 of whom were class members, it is not at all unlikely that the 27% quota has been reached and the compulsory hiring of class members has come to an end. Relations between the Garden and its presently employed laborers will not be improved by the voluntary hiring of additional class members who will be granted automatic seniority under the terms of the district court's judgment. For all the foregoing reasons, we think that the proper exercise of discretion would limit the grant of retroactive seniority to the 6 or more class members already hired.

[The Court's discussion of the attorney fee issue is omitted.]

NOTES AND PROBLEMS FOR DISCUSSION

1. How does the district court's treatment of the "limited vacancy" problem in *Kyriazi* differ from that of the Second Circuit in *Ingram?* Has the Second Circuit in fact put the burden of proof on the employer? Compare, Easley v. Anheuser-Busch, Inc., 758 F.2d 251 (8th Cir. 1985) (at remedial stage employer has burden of showing that applicant would not have been hired absent discrimination). Which process is likely to produce the larger judgment per class member?

2. The employer defendants in *Ingram* settled before trial for an amount that was roughly a third of the back pay award subsequently made against the union. The district court credited the settlement amount against the union's liability, but the union still claimed it was entitled to indemnity and/or contribution from the employers. In NORTHWEST AIRLINES, INC. v. TRANSPORT WORKERS UNION OF AMERICA, 451 U.S. 77, 101 S.Ct. 1571, 67 L.Ed.2d 750 (1981), the Supreme Court held that an employer guilty of violating Title VII does not possess an explicit or implied right of contribution from a union which was responsible in part for the violation. Noting that the legislative history of the Act was silent on the issue of contribution, the Court reasoned that it would be improper to imply a right of action for contribution because Congress had created a comprehensive remedial scheme which evidenced an intent not to allow additional remedies and because employers as a group were not the intended beneficiaries of the Act. But *Northwest Airlines* was distinguishable from *Ingram* because no charge of discrimination was ever filed against the union in that case and the Supreme Court stated in its opinion that: "A court's broad power * * * to fashion relief against all respondents named in a properly filed charge is not, of course, at issue in this litigation since no charge was filed against either of the respondent unions." 451 U.S. at

93 n. 28. The district court in the *Ingram* litigation, nevertheless relied on *Northwest Airlines* in rejecting the union's claims and the Second Circuit affirmed. Anderson v. Local Union No. 3, IBEW, 751 F.2d 546 (2d Cir. 1984). The Court of Appeals based its affirmance in part on the fear that recognition of a right of indemnity would encourage suits between defendants which would in turn discourage voluntary settlements. Is the Second Circuit's concern realistic? Is an employer's knowledge that it will not be able to obtain contribution from a union more likely to encourage settlement or to encourage it to take its chances on the court's apportionment of liability at trial?

3. In a subsequent decision in *Kyriazi,* the district court created a hypothetical work history for the named plaintiff, in a manner similar to that employed in EEOC v. Ford Motor Co., supra, by modifying the actual work history of a male employee who held the same job as the plaintiff and had similar qualifications. Kyriazi v. Western Electric Co., 476 F.Supp. 335 (D.N.J.1979), aff'd, 647 F.2d 388 (3d Cir. 1981). Presumably, the court contemplated similar constructions for all class members who filed claims. But if even a fraction of the potential class of 10,000 filed claims, the Stage II proceedings could last years. Is such a marathon proceeding in fact "fair both to class members and [the employer]?" The economic problems posed by such extended proceedings on class counsel are addressed in the next chapter.

SEGAR v. SMITH

United States Court of Appeals for the District of Columbia Circuit, 1984.
738 F.2d 1249, cert. denied, ___ U.S. ___, 105 S.Ct. 2357, 86 L.Ed.2d 258 (1985).

Before WRIGHT, WALD, and EDWARDS, CIRCUIT JUDGES.

J. SKELLY WRIGHT, CIRCUIT JUDGE:

Title VII of the Civil Rights Act of 1964 proclaims one of this nation's most fundamental, if yet unrealized, principles: a person shall not be denied full equality of employment opportunity on account of race, color, religion, sex, or national origin. Title VII bars both intentional discrimination and artificial, arbitrary, or unnecessary barriers to equal opportunity. In this case we review a decision of the United States District Court for the District of Columbia, Segar v. Civiletti, 508 F.Supp. 690 (D.D.C.1981), holding that the federal Drug Enforcement Agency (DEA) had engaged in a pattern or practice of discrimination against its black agents in violation of Title VII. A class comprising black agents initiated this suit in 1977 and the case came to trial in 1979. Finding that DEA had discriminated against black agents in salary, promotions, initial (GS) grade assignments, work assignments, supervisory evaluations, and imposition of discipline, the District Court ordered a comprehensive remedial scheme consisting of a class-wide backpay award, promotion goals and timetables to ensure that qualified black agents received promotions to the upper levels of DEA, and a class-wide frontpay award to compensate such qualified agents while they awaited the promotions they deserved. In the course of the proceedings the court also denied plaintiffs' request for prejudgment interest and issued a preliminary injunction barring transfer or demotion of Carl Jackson (the Jackson injunction), a black agent who was the subject of adverse employment decisions immediately after his testimony for plaintiffs in this lawsuit.

On appeal DEA challenges the liability determination, the remedial scheme, and the Jackson injunction. Plaintiffs cross-appeal the denial of prejudgment interest. As to the liability determination, DEA urges that the trial court erred in finding that plaintiffs had presented sufficient probative evidence to support any inference of discrimination at DEA, and urges that DEA had in any event effectively rebutted plaintiffs' showing. As to the remedial scheme, DEA argues that class-wide relief was inappropriate and that imposition of promotion goals and timetables both exceeded the court's remedial authority under Title VII and violated the equal protection component of the Fifth Amendment Due Process Clause. DEA also argues that Carl Jackson did not make a showing of retaliation sufficient to justify the preliminary injunction.

To resolve this appeal we have had to plumb some of the deepest complexities of Title VII adjudication. After careful review, we affirm the District Court's liability determination in its entirety. We also affirm the trial court's decision to use a class-wide backpay remedy, but we vacate the backpay formula imposed and remand for reformulation of the particular backpay award. We also vacate the part of the District Court's remedy that mandates promotion goals and timetables. We do not hold that such remedies exceed a court's remedial authority under Title VII. Nor do we hold that such remedies violate the Constitution. Nonetheless, we find that the District Court's particular order of goals and timetables was not appropriate on the current factual record. Because the frontpay remedy was specifically linked to the promotion goals and timetables, we vacate that part of the remedial order as well, and remand to the District Court for further consideration of appropriate remedies.[3] We affirm the preliminary injunction against demotion or transfer of Carl Jackson and we expect the District Court to undertake resolution of the status of the Jackson injunction on remand. We affirm the trial court's denial of prejudgment interest.

* * *

This Lawsuit

In January 1977 two black special agents of DEA, and an association representing all black special agents, brought suit alleging that DEA had engaged in a pattern or practice of racial discrimination against black special agents in violation of Title VII of the Civil Rights Act of 1964. These agents alleged discrimination in recruitment, hiring, initial grade assignments, salary, work assignments, evaluations, discipline, and promotions.

On September 9, 1977 the trial court, pursuant to Federal Rule of Civil Procedure 23(b)(2), certified the class of all blacks who then served

3. We vacate the frontpay remedy only because the trial court specifically linked it to the promotion timetables, and without prejudice to reinstatement of a new frontpay remedy if the trial court finds such a course appropriate on remand.

or had had been discharged as special agents at DEA, and who had applied for positions or would in the future apply. Before trial the parties settled the claims involving discriminatory recruitment and hiring, but could not come to terms on the other issues. As is common in Title VII class actions, the District Court bifurcated the trial into separate liability and remedial phases. After lengthy discovery, the liability issues came to trial in April 1979. The trial was in large measure a duel of experts armed with sophisticated statistical means of proof.

1. *The plaintiffs' case.* The plaintiffs presented a range of statistical and anecdotal evidence of discrimination. The statistical evidence included several multiple linear regression analyses as well as a number of studies considering the effects of particular employment practices.

Multiple regression is a form of statistical analysis used increasingly in Title VII actions that measures the discrete influence independent variables have on a dependent variable such as salary levels. See Valentino v. U.S. Postal Service, 674 F.2d 56, 70 (D.C.Cir. 1982). Typically the independent variables in Title VII cases will be race, age, education level, and experience levels. The first step in a multiple regression analysis is specification of the independent (or explanatory) variables thought likely to affect significantly the dependent variable. The choice of proper explanatory variables determines the validity of the regression analysis. A coherent theory, devised prior to observation of the particular data, must be employed to select the relevant explanatory variables. See Vuyanich v. Republic Nat'l Bank of Dallas (Vuyanich I), 505 F.Supp. 224, 269 (N.D.Tex.1980), vacated on other grounds, 723 F.2d 1195 (5th Cir. 1984). When the proper variables have been selected, the multiple regression analysis is conducted, generally by a computer. In essence, the regression measures the impact of each potential explanatory variable upon the dependent variable by holding all other explanatory variables constant. The analysis yields figures demonstrating how much of an observed disparity in salaries can be traced to race, as opposed to any of the other potential explanatory variables.

The computer analysis will generally also yield two other measurements that assist in evaluation of the explanatory power of the regression. The first is "T-Ratio." The T-Ratio measures the probability that the result obtained could have occurred by chance.[7] The second is R^2. The R^2 figure measures, to a certain extent, the degree to which a multiple regression analysis taken as a whole explains observed disparities in a dependent variable.

Having observed an average disparity in salary of about $3,000 between white and black special agents at DEA, plaintiffs' experts,

7. The T-Ratio figure for a particular measure of race-related disparity corresponds to the number of standard deviations for that figure. D. Baldus & J. Cole, Statistical Proof of Discrimination 297 n. 14 (1980).

Professors Bergmann and Straszheim,[8] formulated a regression analysis to discover whether and to what extent race explained the observed salary disparity. The experts based their analysis on a "human capital model." A widely accepted approach, the model builds on labor economists' findings that the human capital an employee brings to a job—such as education and experience—in large measure determines the employee's success. See Note, Beyond the Prima Facie Case in Employment Discrimination Law: Statistical Proof and Rebuttal, 89 Harv.L. Rev. 387, 408 n. 90 (1975); *Vuyanich I,* supra, 505 F.Supp. at 265–267.

Plaintiffs' experts selected education, prior federal experience, prior nonfederal experience, and race as the four independent variables that might explain the salary differential. Information regarding these independent variables came from the computerized JUNIPER personnel information tapes of the Department of Justice. Professors Bergmann and Straszheim then ran the regressions. They first evaluated the causes of salary disparities among all agents as of five dates: the first of January in 1975, 1976, 1977, and 1978 and the first of October in 1978. This study generated the following results:

DATE	RACE COEFFICIENT	T–RATIO
1/1/75	–$1,628	4.65
1/1/76	–$1,744	5.37
1/1/77	–$1,119	5.15
1/1/78	–$1,934	5.15
10/1/78	–$1,877	4.50

The race coefficient measures the salary disparities between white and black agents when education and prior experience are held constant. The T-Ratio figures here correspond to standard deviations of four or five. See D. Baldus & J. Cole, Statistical Proof of Discrimination 297 n. 14 (1980) (hereinafter "D. Baldus & J. Cole"). Since a standard deviation level higher than three indicates that the odds are less than one in a thousand that an observed result could have occurred by chance, these figures indicate that the odds are far less than one in a thousand that the observed disparities for any year could have occurred by chance. A study is generally considered to be statistically significant when the odds that the result occurred by chance are at best one in 20. See D. Baldus & J. Cole, supra, at 297.

Professors Bergmann and Straszheim then ran a second regression to measure salary disparities over the same time frame for agents hired after 1972. They intended this study to generate some measure of the effects of race discrimination at DEA after 1972. Title VII applies to DEA in this action only as of that date.[9] Because the first regression

8. Professors Bergmann and Straszheim both hold Ph.D.'s and teach labor economics at the University of Maryland. Findings ¶ 6, 508 F.Supp. at 695.

9. Plaintiffs are subject to the statutory limit on the period of actionable discrimination; under Title VII liability may not accrue for a period of more than two years before the date of filing of an administrative complaint with the Equal Employment Opportunity Commission. In this case the actionable period began on July 15, 1972.

measured disparities in the salaries of all black agents, including those hired before 1972, the race coefficient in that study may have reflected disparities resulting from the continuing effects of discrimination that occurred prior to 1972, rather than actionable post-1972 discrimination. This second regression generated the following results:

DATE	RACE COEFFICIENT	T–RATIO
1/1/75	–$ 378	.84
1/1/76	–$1,864	2.54
1/1/77	–$1,119	3.18
1/1/78	–$ 866	2.07
10/1/78	–$1,026	2.30

Again a significant salary disparity between agents with comparable education and experience was revealed. The T-Ratios indicate that for every year, save 1975, the possibility that the result could have occurred by chance was at most one in 20. Though these figures are not at as high a level of significance as were those of the first regression, they still meet the generally accepted test for statistical significance. The second regression, moreover, tends to understate the amount of post-1972 discrimination at DEA. Because the post-1972 study measures discrimination among newer agents, the study focuses on the speed with which the new recruits make their way through the lower levels of DEA. Promotions at these levels are relatively automatic, and discrimination thus has less opportunity to work its effects. Discrimination will most adversely affect older agents contending for upper level positions; promotion decisions at these levels incorporate far more discretionary elements and leave more room for bias. The study does not measure any post-1972 discrimination against those hired before 1972. Since these agents would have been the ones contending for the upper level positions during the time frame studied, they would have been the ones on whom discrimination would have been most likely to operate. The problem is particularly severe with respect to the 1975 race coefficient. Almost half of those studied to obtain this figure were hired in 1974. Since they were in their first year at the time of the study, they would not yet have been eligible for a grade promotion.

Having uncovered evidence of significant discrimination in salary levels, plaintiffs' experts undertook a more exacting inquiry into DEA's employment practices to pinpoint where discrimination was taking place. They first examined DEA's initial grade assignment practices. Through regression analyses they determined at a sufficient level of statistical significance that blacks were 16 percent less likely than comparably qualified whites to have been hired at GS–9 rather than GS–7. For those hired after 1972, blacks were 12 percent less likely to be hired at GS–9. The experts then evaluated work assignments,

Although not formally created until 1973, DEA was at its creation a consolidation of other federal agencies engaged in drug enforcement efforts, and agents serving these agencies became DEA agents.

supervisory evaluations, and discipline. In all three categories statistical analysis revealed significant levels of discrimination against black agents. Finally, plaintiffs' experts studied promotions at DEA. Promotions up to the GS–11 level were found to be relatively automatic. The promotion rate from GS–11 to GS–12 was 70 percent for blacks and 82 percent for whites. This differential met generally accepted levels of statistical significance. Differentials in promotion rates for positions above GS–12 were also found, but—largely because of the small sample size—these differentials did not achieve statistical significance at generally accepted levels.

To buttress the statistical proof plaintiffs introduced anecdotal testimony of discrimination. This evidence consisted of accounts by several black agents of perceived discrimination against them in initial grade assignments, work assignments, supervisory evaluations, and discipline. These agents also testified about their general perceptions of racial hostility at DEA.

2. *Defendant DEA's case.* DEA responded to plaintiffs' case in several ways. The rebuttal consisted of expert testimony attacking the methodological integrity and explanatory value of plaintiffs' statistics, alternative statistical analyses tending to show an absence of discrimination, testimonial evidence concerning DEA's equal employment opportunity programs, and cross-examination of plaintiffs' anecdotal accounts of individual discrimination

* * *

Testimonial evidence buttressed DEA's statistical rebuttal. DEA presented extensive general testimony on its efforts to establish equal opportunity programs and implement equal opportunity goals at the agency. Through cross-examination of plaintiffs' witnesses, DEA also sought to rebut every particular anecdotal account of discrimination.

The District Court Decision

1. *The liability determination.* Judge Robinson held that DEA had discriminated against black special agents in violation of Title VII across a range of employment practices. The court found that the salary differentials between white and black agents were a result of race discrimination, and that DEA had discriminated against black agents in grade-at-entry, work assignments, supervisory evaluations, and promotions. The finding of discrimination in promotions extended to promotions above the GS–12 level, even though the court did not credit plaintiffs' statistical evidence of discrimination at that level because the statistics had not achieved acceptable levels of statistical significance. The court based its finding of discrimination at the upper levels on inferences from proven discrimination at the immediately preceding levels and discrimination in the factors that bear most directly on promotions (work assignments, evaluations, and discipline).

To make these determinations the District Court credited the bulk of plaintiffs' statistical evidence [10] and rejected both DEA's critique of this evidence and DEA's alternative statistics. * * *

2. *The remedies determination.* Having found pervasive discrimination at DEA, the District Court—in a separate remedial proceeding—set out to formulate an appropriate remedial plan.[11] The essential elements of the plan were class-wide backpay, promotion goals and timetables, and class-wide frontpay.

Class-wide Backpay. Rather than order individualized relief hearings, see Int'l Brhd. of Teamsters v. United States, the District Court ordered a class-wide award of backpay for members of the plaintiff class. For successive one-year periods beginning in July 1972, a class-wide backpay pool figure would be calculated. The calculations would derive from plaintiffs' first salary regression study (which measured disparities among all agents including those hired before 1972). For every year for which figures were available—1975 to 1979—the class-wide pool figure would be the race coefficient multiplied by the number of black special agents. For the years before 1975 and after 1979 the race coefficient would be derived by extrapolating backward and forward from the available figures, and this extrapolated coefficient would be multiplied by the number of black agents.

The annual backpay pool would be distributed evenly among eligible black agents. Only agents above the GS–9 level during the year in question were made eligible. The court excluded agents at GS–7 and GS–9 because most discrimination was found to occur at the higher levels of DEA. The court did, however, permit individual plaintiffs to come forward and seek backpay for discrimination suffered in initial grade assignment (viz. assignment to GS–7 instead of GS–9). Any such individual awards would be subtracted from the class-wide pool in order to prevent double liability.

Promotion Goals and Timetables. Finding discrimination at the upper levels of DEA, the District Court ordered remedial promotion goals and timetables. Since black agents made up at least 10 percent of agents at every level through GS–12 the court held that a 10 percent goal was appropriate for all levels above GS–12. To meet this goal the court ordered DEA to promote one black agent for every two white agents until 10 percent black representation had been met at GS–13 and above (or until five years had passed).

Class-wide Frontpay. To compensate black agents awaiting promotion under the goals and timetables plan the court established a class-wide frontpay formula. Frontpay pool calculations were also based on extrapolations from the salary regression, but the pool was to be

10. The court did, however, refuse to credit most of plaintiffs' anecdotal accounts of specific instances of discrimination. Findings ¶ 51d, 508 F.Supp. at 710.

11. DEA sought at the remedial hearing to introduce its own regression analyses. These regressions purportedly showed an absence of race-related disparity at DEA. The District Court rejected this proffered evidence of DEA's nonliability as untimely.

adjusted to reflect progress DEA had made under the promotions goals and timetables. The pool was to be distributed to all black agents at GS–12 for at least two years and all black agents above GS–12.

3. *Other issues.* In the course of the proceeding two other issues arose. Plaintiffs sought and were refused an award of prejudgment interest on the backpay awards. Also, during the time between the liability and remedial determinations the court issued a preliminary injunction barring demotion or transfer of black special agent Carl Jackson. Shortly after Jackson had testified at trial in this case he became the target of harassment and eventually of adverse employment actions including demotion and transfer. The District Court concluded that there was a high likelihood that these actions were in retaliation for Jackson's testimony, and therefore preliminarily enjoined Jackson's demotion or transfer.

[The Court's analysis of the district court's liability determination is omitted.]

II. The Remedies Determination

Section 706(g) of Title VII empowers a court that has found illegal discrimination to "order such affirmative action as may be appropriate, which may include, but is not limited to, reinstatement or hiring of employees, with or without back pay * * * or any other equitable relief as the court deems appropriate." * * *

Having found pervasive discrimination at DEA, the District Court fashioned a tripartite remedial scheme: class-wide backpay for those at GS–11 and above,[35] promotion goals and timetables at DEA's upper levels, and class-wide frontpay for those at GS–11 and above. DEA raises three challenges to these remedies. First, the class-wide backpay award impermissibly circumvents the individualized remedial hearings required by *Teamsters,* supra. Second, the backpay award compensates for nonactionable pre-1972 discrimination. Third, the promotion goals and timetables exceed the court's remedial authority under Section 706(g) and violate the equal protection component of the Fifth Amendment to the Constitution.

A. *Individualized Hearings*

DEA objects to the District Court's decision to forego in this case the individualized relief hearings prescribed in *Teamsters,* supra. The gravamen of DEA's objection is that class-wide relief may benefit some black agents who were not victims of illegal discrimination. The Court in *Teamsters* stated that when plaintiffs seek relief as "victims of the discriminatory practice, a district court must usually conduct additional proceedings after the liability phase of the trial to determine the scope

35. Finding most discrimination took place at GS–11 and above, the court did not order classwide relief for discrimination against black agents at GS–7 or GS–9 during any given backpay year. The court did, however, permit these agents to bring individual claims for relief. Any individual awards at these levels are to be deducted from the class-wide backpay pool distributed to agents at GS–11 and above.

of individual relief." In the wake of *Teamsters* individualized hearings have been common features of Title VII class actions. See, e.g., McKenzie v. Sawyer, 684 F.2d 62, 75 (D.C.Cir. 1982).

Though *Teamsters* certainly raises a presumption in favor of individualized hearings, the case should not be read as an unyielding limit on a court's equitable power to fashion effective relief for proven discrimination.[36] The language of *Teamsters* is not so inflexible; after stating that individual hearings are "usually" required, *Teamsters,* supra, the Court went on to note that "[i]n determining the specific remedies to be afforded, a district court is 'to fashion such relief as the particular circumstances of a case may require to effect restitution.'" Later courts have often faced situations in which the *Teamsters* hearing preference had to bend to accommodate Title VII's remedial purposes. Primarily, courts have not required hearings when discrimination has so percolated through an employment system that any attempt to reconstruct individual employment histories would drag the court into "a quagmire of hypothetical judgments."

Applying these principles to the present controversy, we note at the outset that the District Court did not rush willy-nilly to impose class-wide relief. The court specifically ordered individual relief hearings where feasible. All claims of backpay for discrimination at levels below GS–11 will be resolved in individualized hearings. At these levels individualized hearings are appropriate because a small number of discernible decisions as to initial grade assignment and promotions will be in issue for each agent. These determinations are akin to those in *Teamsters,* where the required hearings were to involve a single determination as to whether individual plaintiffs had applied and were qualified for particular line driver positions in the trucking industry.

After careful consideration, the District Court here ordered class-wide relief only for discrimination above GS–11. The court had found that discrimination impeded black agents at every turn; blacks faced extra hurdles in DEA's initial grade assignments, work assignments, supervisory evaluations, imposition of discipline, and promotions. At the higher levels the cumulative effect of these pervasive discriminatory practices became severe, and the increased subjectivity in evaluations gave discrimination more room to work its effects. In such a situation "exact reconstruction of each individual claimant's work history, as if discrimination had not occurred, is not only imprecise but impractical." *Pettway,* supra, 494 F.2d at 262. The District Court here specifically found that "[e]ach major criterion in the promotion process

36. McKenzie v. Sawyer, 684 F.2d 62 (D.C.Cir. 1982), does not mandate individual hearings in every case. The panel in *Sawyer* affirmed a District Court's decision to require individual relief hearings. When, in an exercise of its remedial discretion, a trial court orders hearings, an appellate court is properly reluctant to interfere with that judgment. But the appellate panel in *Sawyer* was not faced with a trial court's decision that individual hearings would effectively preclude relief for most members of the plaintiff class. Thus, *Sawyer's* reiteration of the *Teamsters* hearing preference should not be taken as implying that class-wide relief in the present context would be improper.

at DEA was tainted by discrimination, making discrimination in the promotion process cumulative. Any attempt to recreate the employment histories of individual employees absent discrimination would result in mere guesswork." Our role in reviewing this determination is limited. "The framing of a remedial decree is left largely in the hands of the district judge, whose assessment of the needs of the situation is a factual judgment reviewable only for clear error * * *." McKenzie v. Sawyer, supra, 684 F.2d at 75.

We perceive no error in the District Court's finding that it would be impossible to reconstruct the employment histories of DEA's senior black agents. Examination of discrete promotion decisions, as difficult as even that might be, will not suffice. The decisive criteria for promotions decisions—supervisory evaluations, breadth of experience, and disciplinary history—were themselves found to be tainted with illegal discrimination. The court found that discrimination had skewed evaluations of black agents, but the court could have had no way of knowing how much more favorable a particular agent's evaluation should have been, or how a fair evaluation might have affected the agent's chances for obtaining a particular promotion. Similarly, the court found that discrimination in work assignments—leaving black agents with a disproportionately large share of undercover assignments—had impeded black agents in promotions, but the court could have had no way to divine what other broadening experiences a particular agent might have had, and no way to gauge how this hypothetical additional experience would have affected particular promotion decisions. And though the court found that black agents have been disciplined more frequently and more severely than white agents committing similar infractions, the court could have had no way of knowing exactly what effect the disproportionate disciplinary sanctions had on a particular agent's chances for particular promotions. Finally, because promotions at DEA are cumulative, the effects of discrimination in promotions are also cumulative. Denial of promotion to one grade affects the agent's eligibility for later promotions to higher grades.

To require individualized hearings in these circumstances would be to deny relief to the bulk of DEA's black agents despite a finding of pervasive discrimination against them. In effect, DEA would have us preclude relief unless the remedial order is perfectly tailored to award relief only to those injured and only in the exact amount of their injury. Though Section 706(g) generally does not allow for backpay to those whom discrimination has not injured, this section should not be read as requiring effective denial of backpay to the large numbers of agents whom DEA's discrimination has injured in order to account for the risk that a small number of undeserving individuals might receive backpay. Such a result cannot be squared with what the Supreme Court has told us about the nature of a court's remedial authority under Title VII. "[T]he scope of a district court's remedial powers under Title VII is determined by the purposes of the Act." A core purpose of Title VII is "to make persons whole for injuries suffered on account of unlawful employment discrimination." *Albemarle Paper Co.,* supra. "[F]ederal courts are empowered to fashion such relief as the particular circumstances require to effect restitution, making whole insofar as possible the victims of racial discrimination * * *." *Franks,* supra; accord *Albemarle Paper Co.,* supra, (the District Courts have "not merely the power but the duty to render a decree which will so far as possible eliminate the discriminatory effects of the past as well as bar like discrimination in the future"); *Teamsters,* supra. The trial court found that the particular circumstances of this case required classwide relief for black agents at GS–11 and above to ensure that they were made whole for the pervasive discrimination they have suffered. If effective relief for the victims of discrimination necessarily entails the risk that a few nonvictims might also benefit from the relief, then the employer, as a proven discriminator, must bear that risk. See Stewart v. General Motors Corp., supra, 542 F.2d at 452–453.

B. *The Allegation of Class-wide Overcompensation*

In calculating the backpay pool the District Court used the race coefficient of the first of plaintiffs' two salary regressions as the measure of average discrimination per agent. The first regression measured discrimination against all black agents, including those hired before 1972. This study may therefore have reflected the continuing effects of some discrimination occurring prior to 1972. Since the actionable period in this case commenced on July 15, 1972, use of the first regression might, according to DEA's argument, amount to compensation for some nonactionable discrimination.[37] Though the remedial order specifically states that backpay begins to accrue only as of July 15, 1972, DEA argues that a portion of the disparities between black and white agents as of that time (and thereafter) was caused by discrimination before 1972, and that DEA is therefore not liable for that portion.

The District Court found in the Liability Determination that "while pre-1972 discrimination may have affected the statistics * * *, post 1972 discrimination largely contributed to those statistics." The court also noted in the Remedial Order that plaintiffs' regressions "provide an accurate measure of the extent to which blacks at DEA were paid less than comparably qualified whites [and] * * * provide an appropriate basis for classwide relief." We are reluctant to disturb the trial

37. DEA also makes an argument that use of the first salary regression overcompensates plaintiffs based on the R^2 values for this study. DEA argues that, because the R^2 value was roughly .50, only about half of the race coefficient for the years in question actually represents race-related disparity. This argument reveals a basic misunderstanding of the meaning of R^2 figures. An R^2 of .50 does not mean that only half of the race coefficient is attributable to race. Rather, it means that half of the total salary disparity between black and white agents is attributable to the totality of the factors examined in the regression. See generally Fisher, Multiple Regression in Legal Proceedings, 80 Colum. L.Rev. 702, 720 (1980). In any event, R^2 is far from a wholly reliable measure of a study's accuracy. For these reasons, we hold that DEA's objection based on R^2 values is without force.

court's finding on this factual issue. See McKenzie v. Sawyer, supra, 684 F.2d at 75. Nonetheless on the record as it now stands, we cannot affirm the District Court's decision to use the first regression as a basis for calculating the backpay pool.

Although the court properly found that the plaintiff's evidence sufficed to support an inference of actionable discrimination, the court's reliance on the first regression to determine backpay is problematic. The court never found that *all* of that regression's race coefficient reflected actionable post-1972 discrimination.[38] To do so the court would have had to find either that all discrimination reflected in the salary disparities occurred after 1972 or that the small portion of "continuing effects" of pre-1972 discrimination reflected in the disparities was the result of a "continuing violation." The court made neither finding, and having found in the Liability Determination that pre-1972 discrimination had been "neither admitted nor proven," the court cannot plausibly rely on a continuing violation theory in the Remedial Order as grounds for using the first salary regression as a benchmark for the backpay pool.

It may be that plaintiffs' first regression does reflect only post-1972 discrimination. DEA's complete failure to present evidence showing pre-1972 discrimination in the regression certainly supports this view. It may also be that the portion of the disparity that reflects continuing effects of pre-1972 discrimination might be actionable on a continuing violation theory. Or it may be that the small amount of continuing effects cannot plausibly be factored out of the study; if so, and if no more precise methods of ascertaining the amount of actionable discrimination are reasonably available to the court, the court would be faced with using either a mildly overcompensatory formula based on the first regression or a significantly undercompensatory formula based on the second regression. Use of the first regression under these circumstances might be permissible.

We cannot, however, resolve these matters on the present appeal. As the Supreme Court stressed in Lehman v. Trout, supra, ___ U.S. at ___, 104 S.Ct. at 1404, this court must scrupulously respect the factfinding prerogative of the District Court. In this case the District Court has not yet determined whether the first regression reflects only post-1972 discrimination, whether a continuing violation occurred that might permit compensation for whatever continuing effects the regression reflects, or whether the small portion of nonactionable continuing effects that might be reflected in the regression cannot be factored out. On remand, if the District Court is unable to find that any of these three factual circumstances exists, the court must devise a new backpay formula.

38. Of course, the court need not have found that all of the discrimination reflected in the regression occurred after 1972 in order to find the regression sufficient to make out a prima facie case of actionable discrimination. See Part II-B-1-b; Valentino v. U.S. Postal Service, 674 F.2d 56, 71 n. 26 (D.C.Cir. 1982).

C. *Promotion Goals and Timetables*

The District Court ordered that one black be promoted for every two whites to positions above GS–12 at DEA until blacks made up 10 percent of all agents at each grade above GS–12 or until five years after the order was entered. DEA objects to this aspect of the remedy for the same reason that it objects to class-wide backpay: some individual agents might receive promotions they do not deserve. DEA argues that promotion goals and timetables exceed a court's remedial power under Title VII unless every person who potentially benefits from the relief has been individually shown to have been discriminatorily denied a specific promotion. According to DEA, Section 706(g) mandates this result. ("No order of the court shall require the * * * promotion of an individual as an employee, * * * if such individual was refused * * * advancement * * * for any reason other than discrimination * * *."). DEA also argues that such goals and timetables violate the equal protection component of the Fifth Amendment to the Constitution.

Though DEA's claims are not without some superficial appeal, Section 706(g) must not be read as requiring an exact fit between those whom an employer's discrimination has victimized and those eligible under promotion goals and timetables. The language on which DEA relies was aimed at ensuring that Title VII was not read as giving courts authority to remedy racial imbalance as an evil in itself, i.e., absent any finding that illegal discrimination caused the imbalance. See EEOC v. AT & T, 556 F.2d 167, 175 (3d Cir. 1977), cert. denied, 438 U.S. 915, 98 S.Ct. 3145, 57 L.Ed.2d 1161 (1978). The language should not be stretched to support a requirement of absolute precision in fashioning promotion goals and timetables when such a requirement would frustrate effective relief for those who were victimized by discrimination.[39] Every federal Court of Appeals in this nation has approved remedial use of goals and timetables without requiring that each and every potentially eligible person be shown to have been a victim of discrimination. Nor can the imposition of quotas to remedy proven discrimination be said to violate the Constitution's guarantees of equal protection. Whatever the current status of affirmative action absent a finding of discrimination, the Supreme Court has made clear that such relief is not unconstitutional when used to remedy proven

39. DEA has amassed an array of quotes from Title VII's legislative history in support of its contention that promotion goals and timetables are invalid if they benefit any individuals who are not proven victims of discrimination. See reply brief for appellants at 20–22. Many in Congress spoke in 1964, and again in 1972 when Title VII was amended, to assure wavering supporters that Title VII could not be applied to grant preferences for those who were not victims of discrimination. These statements are, however, inapposite to the question before us in this case. Those in Congress who made such statements were not considering the issue whether in affording relief for proven discrimination against a broad class some individual nonvictims might benefit in order to ensure that all actual victims benefitted. Rather, these statements were made with reference to the question whether Title VII could be used as a mandate to correct overall racial imbalance in an employer's workforce when such an imbalance had not been shown to be the result of discrimination.

discrimination. See Swann v. Charlotte-Mecklenburg School District, 402 U.S. 1, 91 S.Ct. 1267, 28 L.Ed.2d 554 (1971); Bakke v. Board of Regents of the University of California, 438 U.S. 265, 302, 98 S.Ct. 2733, 2754, 57 L.Ed.2d 750 (1978) (Powell, J., concurring); id. at 363–386, 98 S.Ct. at 2785–2797 (Brennan, White, Marshall and Blackmun, JJ, concurring).

Nonetheless promotion goals and timetables—even if as admirably crafted as those at issue here—must be used cautiously. Such relief intrudes into the structure of employment relations and may at times upset the legitimate promotion expectations of individuals in the majority group. We must take a careful look at the District Court's decision to use goals and timetables in this case.

We are persuaded that the District Court's order that one black be promoted for every two whites to positions above GS–12 was not appropriate. Strict goals and timetables should not be imposed when "alternative, equally effective methods could * * * supplant resort to a quota." Thompson v. Sawyer, supra, 678 F.2d at 294. The District Court did not consider whether less severe remedies might prove equally efficacious in this case. We therefore vacate the District Court's imposition of goals and timetables, and remand for additional consideration of the propriety of such remedies in this case.

In determining whether less severe remedies might prove equally effective the court must evaluate the likelihood that the employer will implement the remedy in good faith. One important indicium is the employer's past behavior in implementing equal opportunity programs, either voluntarily or in response to court order. This court has some doubt that DEA's past record on equal employment opportunity warrants application of strict goals and timetables. DEA has not been before this court in the past on identical or related claims of discrimination, and thus has not shown any recalcitrance in remedying discrimination pursuant to court order. Nor does DEA's overall approach to equal employment matters lead us to conclude that DEA will be unlikely to remedy the proven discrimination in promotions once this court orders it to do so. The record contains significant uncontradicted evidence of DEA's institutional good faith in implementing equal employment opportunity programs. Of course, the determination of appropriate relief is for the District Court in the first instance. We also vacate the District Court's order of class-wide frontpay because the frontpay order was premised on the existence of promotion goals and timetables. The District Court is free to impose a new frontpay order on remand if it deems one appropriate.

On remand we encourage the District Court to consider other remedial options to ensure that black agents attain their rightful places at the upper levels of DEA. We note in particular that a promotion bottleneck appears to exist at the GS–12 level. While black agents manage to arrive at this level eventually, few progress beyond this point. In remedying promotion discrimination at this point and at all levels, the court is of course free to establish promotion guidelines and to monitor DEA's progress in meeting those guidelines, or to fashion any other appropriate relief.

* * *

[The Court affirmed the district court's grant of a preliminary injunction barring the demotion and transfer of Special Agent Jackson. The Court reasoned that irreparable harm would follow from a refusal to grant such relief because other class members would be deterred from coming forward with claims at the relief stage. The district court's denial of prejudment interest was also affirmed on the ground that sovereign immunity barred such an award against the federal government. See, supra, n. 4. The concurring opinion of Judge Edwards is omitted.]

NOTES AND PROBLEMS FOR DISCUSSION

1. Courts have consistently held that difficulty in calculating back pay is not a ground for denying such relief altogether. See, e.g., Pettway v. American Cast Iron Pipe Co., 494 F.2d 211 (5th Cir. 1974), cert. denied, 439 U.S. 1115, 99 S.Ct. 1020, 59 L.Ed.2d 74 (1979) (*Pettway III*); Salinas v. Roadway Express, Inc., 735 F.2d 1574, 1578 (5th Cir. 1984). In a much-quoted section of *Pettway III,* the Fifth Circuit stated, "in computing a back pay award two principles are lucid: (1) unrealistic exactitude is not required, (2) uncertainties in determining what an employee would have earned but for the discrimination, should be resolved against the discriminating employer." 494 F.2d at 260–61. But does this reasoning justify the decision in *Segar* not to individualize the relief determinations? Was not the DEA entitled to show that particular class members would not have been promoted by introduction of objective evidence of their poor job performance? With *Segar* compare, Domingo v. New England Fish Co., 727 F.2d 1429 (9th Cir. 1984).

2. The hiring "goals and timetables" ordered by the district court in *Segar* were apparently designed to cure one of the effects of the DEA's discrimination, the absence of black agents above the rank of GS–12. Some of the beneficiaries of this relief would have been agents who had not actually been hurt by discrimination just as some of the recipients of back pay would not be victims of discrimination. Is it clear why the Court of Appeals reversed the district court's grant of injunctive relief? The justification for and problems surrounding "affirmative action" plans are explored in Chapter 16, infra.

Chapter 15

ATTORNEY FEES

JOHNSON v. GEORGIA HIGHWAY EXPRESS, INC.

United States Court of Appeals, Fifth Circuit, 1974.
488 F.2d 714.

Before THORNBERRY, AINSWORTH and RONEY, CIRCUIT JUDGES.

RONEY, CIRCUIT JUDGE.

The question on this appeal concerns the adequacy of attorneys' fees awarded by the District Court in a Title VII class action. Plaintiffs challenge as inadequate the $13,500.00 awarded for their alleged 659.5 billable hours accrued during more than four years of litigation. We are called upon to review the award and set appropriate standards to better enable District Courts to arrive at just compensation.

[In an "across-board-action," see, Chapter 7, supra, at p. 459, the district court found a variety of discriminatory practices and granted class relief to the plaintiffs. Plaintiffs' attorneys then requested a fee award of $30,145.50. The district court calculated a "reasonable fee" for the case based on an estimated sixty man days of pretrial work at $200 per day and three trial days for two attorneys at $250 per day. From this ruling both sides appealed.]

Section 706(k) of Title VII of the Civil Rights Act of 1964, provides that:

> In any action or proceeding under this subchapter the Court, in its discretion, may allow the prevailing party * * * a reasonable attorney's fee as part of the cost of the litigation.

The purpose of this provision is to effectuate the congressional policy against racial discrimination. Clark v. American Marine Corp., 320 F.Supp. 709 (E.D.La.1970), aff'd, 437 F.2d 959 (5th Cir. 1971). In discussing a similar provision in Title II, the United States Supreme Court observed that

> If [the plaintiff] obtains an injunction, he does so not for himself alone but also as a "private attorney general," vindicating a policy that Congress considered of the highest priority. If successful plaintiffs were routinely forced to bear their own attorneys' fees, few aggrieved parties would be in a position to advance the public interest by invoking the injunctive powers of the federal courts. Congress therefore enacted the provision for counsel fees—not simply to penalize litigants who deliberately advance arguments they know to be untenable but, more broadly, to encourage individuals injured by racial discrimination to seek judicial relief * * *.

Newman v. Piggie Park Enterprises, Inc., 390 U.S. 400, 401–402, 88 S.Ct. 964, 966, 19 L.Ed.2d 1263 (1968). This Court, as part of its obligation "to make sure that Title VII works," has liberally applied the attorney's fees provision of Title VII, recognizing the importance of private enforcement of civil rights legislation.

We are mindful that it is within the discretion of the District Court whether to award attorney's fees against a party. This Court, however, may review the District Court's determination as to a reasonable fee. It is under this authority that we undertake to review the award in this case.

The reasonableness of the award is to be judged by the abuse of discretion standard of review. But in utilizing this standard we must carefully review the basis upon which the District Court made its award.

It is at this juncture that we have difficulty with the District Court order. The judgment does not elucidate the factors which contributed to the decision and upon which it was based. No correlation to the facts and figures submitted by the plaintiff is visible. Sixty work days were allotted by the Court with six to seven productive hours per day as the standard. Compensation was computed at $200 per day which averages out to between $28.57 and $33.33 per hour depending on which productivity scale is used. Neither of these figures match the minimum fee scale in Atlanta, Georgia.[3] Furthermore, no differentiation was made by the District Court between the experienced and the non-experienced attorneys representing plaintiff. Yet, the award was supposedly considered in light of the Atlanta community practices. The District Court order leaves unexplained the disallowance of between 239.5 to 299.5 of the 659.5 hours claimed. Whether they reflected duplicated effort among the attorneys, improperly charged hours, time deemed unessential, or were merely overlooked is not answered in the order.

It is for these reasons that we must remand to the District Court for reconsideration in light of the following guidelines:

(1) *The time and labor required.* Although hours claimed or spent on a case should not be the sole basis for determining a fee, Electronics

3. The American Bar Association has recently recommended that state and local associations abandon "minimum" or "suggested" fee schedules which are under attack from the Justice Department as violations of the antitrust laws. See 59 A.B.A.J. p. 1435 (1973), reporting the adoption of the following resolution by the Association's Board of Governors:

In order to avoid possible future dispute or litigation, and

(a) Without the expression of any opinion upon questions of existing legal right or obligation, and

(b) Notwithstanding the most recent opinion issued by this Association's Committee on Ethics and Professional Responsibility with regard to ethical propriety of the voluntary consideration by lawyers of fees customarily charged for particular legal services in given localities;

The American Bar Association recommends that state and local bar associations that have not already done so give serious consideration to withdrawal or cancellation of all schedules of fees, whether or not designated as "minimum" or "suggested" fee schedules.

Capital Corp. v. Sheperd, 439 F.2d 692 (5th Cir. 1971), they are a necessary ingredient to be considered. The trial judge should weigh the hours claimed against his own knowledge, experience, and expertise of the time required to complete similar activities. If more than one attorney is involved, the possibility of duplication of effort along with the proper utilization of time should be scrutinized. The time of two or three lawyers in a courtroom or conference when one would do, may obviously be discounted. It is appropriate to distinguish between legal work, in the strict sense, and investigation, clerical work, compilation of facts and statistics and other work which can often be accomplished by non-lawyers but which a lawyer may do because he has no other help available. Such non-legal work may command a lesser rate. Its dollar value is not enhanced just because a lawyer does it.

(2) *The novelty and difficulty of the questions.* Cases of first impression generally require more time and effort on the attorney's part. Although this greater expenditure of time in research and preparation is an investment by counsel in obtaining knowledge which can be used in similar later cases, he should not be penalized for undertaking a case which may "make new law." Instead, he should be appropriately compensated for accepting the challenge.

(3) *The skill requisite to perform the legal service properly.* The trial judge should closely observe the attorney's work product, his preparation, and general ability before the court. The trial judge's expertise gained from past experience as a lawyer and his observation from the bench of lawyers at work become highly important in this consideration.

(4) *The preclusion of other employment by the attorney due to acceptance of the case.* This guideline involves the dual consideration of otherwise available business which is foreclosed because of conflicts of interest which occur from the representation, and the fact that once the employment is undertaken the attorney is not free to use the time spent on the client's behalf for other purposes.

(5) *The customary fee.* The customary fee for similar work in the community should be considered. It is open knowledge that various types of legal work command differing scales of compensation. At no time, however, should the fee for strictly legal work fall below the $20 per hour prescribed by the Criminal Justice Act, 18 U.S.C.A. § 3006A(d)(1), and awarded to appointed counsel for criminal defendants. As long as minimum fee schedules are in existence and are customarily followed by the lawyers in a given community,[4] they should be taken into consideration.

(6) *Whether the fee is fixed or contingent.* The fee quoted to the client or the percentage of the recovery agreed to is helpful in demon-

4. See n. 3, supra.

strating the attorney's fee expectations when he accepted the case. But as pointed out in Clark v. American Marine, supra,

> [t]he statute does not prescribe the payment of fees to the lawyers. It allows the award to be made to the prevailing party. Whether or not he agreed to pay a fee and in what amount is not decisive. Conceivably, a litigant might agree to pay his counsel a fixed dollar fee. This might be even more than the fee eventually allowed by the court. Or he might agree to pay his lawyer a percentage contingent fee that would be greater than the fee the court might ultimately set. Such arrangements should not determine the court's decision. The criterion for the court is not what the parties agreed but what is reasonable.

320 F.Supp. at 711. In no event, however, should the litigant be awarded a fee greater than he is contractually bound to pay, if indeed the attorneys have contracted as to amount.

(7) *Time limitations imposed by the client or the circumstances.* Priority work that delays the lawyer's other legal work is entitled to some premium. This factor is particularly important when a new counsel is called in to prosecute the appeal or handle other matters at a late stage in the proceedings.

(8) *The amount involved and the results obtained.* Title VII, 42 U.S. C.A. § 2000e–5(g), permits the recovery of damages in addition to injunctive relief. Although the Court should consider the amount of damages, or back pay awarded, that consideration should not obviate court scrutiny of the decision's effect on the law. If the decision corrects across-the-board discrimination affecting a large class of an employer's employees, the attorney's fee award should reflect the relief granted.

(9) *The experience, reputation, and ability of the attorneys.* Most fee scales reflect an experience differential with the more experienced attorneys receiving larger compensation. An attorney specializing in civil rights cases may enjoy a higher rate for his expertise than others, providing his ability corresponds with his experience. Longevity *per se*, however, should not dictate the higher fee. If a young attorney demonstrates the skill and ability, he should not be penalized for only recently being admitted to the bar.

(10) *The "undesirability" of the case.* Civil rights attorneys face hardships in their communities because of their desire to help the civil rights litigant. See NAACP v. Button, 371 U.S. 415, 443, 83 S.Ct. 328, 9 L.Ed.2d 405 (1963); Sanders v. Russell, 401 F.2d 241 (5th Cir. 1968). Oftentimes his decision to help eradicate discrimination is not pleasantly received by the community or his contemporaries. This can have an economic impact on his practice which can be considered by the Court.

(11) *The nature and length of the professional relationship with the client.* A lawyer in private practice may vary his fee for similar work in the light of the professional relationship of the client with his office.

The Court may appropriately consider this factor in determining the amount that would be reasonable.

(12) *Awards in similar cases.* The reasonableness of a fee may also be considered in the light of awards made in similar litigation within and without the court's circuit. For such assistance as it may be, we note in the margin a list of Title VII cases in this and other Circuits reviewed in the consideration of this appeal. [Omitted.]

These guidelines are consistent with those recommended by the American Bar Association's Code of Professional Responsibility, Ethical Consideration 2–18, Disciplinary Rule 2–106. They also reflect the considerations approved by us in Clark v. American Marine Co., supra.

To put these guidelines into perspective and as a caveat to their application, courts must remember that they do not have a mandate under Section 706(k) to make the prevailing counsel rich. Concomitantly, the Section should not be implemented in a manner to make the private attorney general's position so lucrative as to ridicule the public attorney general. The statute was not passed for the benefit of attorneys but to enable litigants to obtain competent counsel worthy of a contest with the caliber of counsel available to their opposition and to fairly place the economical burden of Title VII litigation. Adequate compensation is necessary, however, to enable an attorney to serve his client effectively and to preserve the integrity and independence of the profession. The guidelines contained herein are merely an attempt to assist in this balancing process.

We are mindful of the difficult job of the trial judge in cases of this kind, and that in all probability his decision will be totally satisfactory to no one. The cross-appeals taken in this case are witness to the usual view of parties litigant to such an award. The trial judge is necessarily called upon to question the time, expertise, and professional work of a lawyer which is always difficult and sometimes distasteful. But that is the task, and it must be kept in mind that the plaintiff has the burden of proving his entitlement to an award for attorney's fees just as he would bear the burden of proving a claim for any other money judgment.

In cases of this kind, we encourage counsel on both sides to utilize their best efforts to understandingly, sympathetically, and professionally arrive at a settlement as to attorney's fees. Although a settlement generally leaves every litigant partially dissatisfied, so does a judicial award for attorney's fees.

By this discussion we do not attempt to reduce the calculation of a reasonable fee to mathematical precision. Nor do we indicate that we should enter the discretionary area which the law consigns to the trial judge.

By remand of this case, we voice no observation or intimation as to the correctness of the amount awarded. We merely vacate the award and remand for reconsideration in the light of this opinion, and for the entry of an order fixing a reasonable fee which reflects the considerations which led to it. In sum, we hold it to be an abuse of discretion not to consider the factors we approved in Clark v. American Marine Co., and which we amplify here, and that a meaningful review requires a record that reflects such consideration.

Vacated and remanded.

COPELAND v. MARSHALL

United States Court of Appeals for the District of Columbia Circuit, 1980.
641 F.2d 880 (*en banc*).

ON REHEARING EN BANC

MCGOWAN, CIRCUIT JUDGE:

The court *en banc* has before it for review an order of the District Court awarding an attorney's fee of $160,000 for the successful prosecution of a gender-discrimination class suit against the United States Department of Labor. A panel of this court earlier reversed the District Court's award and remanded for reconsideration under the novel standards described in its opinion (*Copeland I*).[2] The panel denied rehearing, but issued a second opinion (*Copeland II*) clarifying the first. We granted rehearing *en banc*.

At issue in this appeal are (1) the standards to be applied in awarding attorney's fees in Title VII suits against the government, and (2) the reasonableness of the District Court's fee award in this case. For the reasons set forth below, we affirm the District Court's award.

* * *

[The history of the litigation is omitted. The Court of Appeals stated, however, that "the very intricacy of the litigation—which was a product, in part, of the government's vigorous and long-continued resistance to the claim asserted against it—is highly relevant to the reasonableness of the fee award."]

II

Title VII of the Civil Rights Act of 1964 allows the prevailing party to receive from the loser a reasonable attorney's fee in addition to other relief. * * *

* * *

Confronted by the explicit language of the statute and its accompanying legislative history, the government in the instant case concedes that plaintiff is entitled to an attorney's fee. Indeed, the parties so stipulated during the course of the lawsuit. At issue in this appeal is whether the District Court's fee award was reasonable.

The Court of Appeals for the Fifth Circuit explained, in general terms, how the fee should be calculated under Title VII in Johnson v.

2. Copeland v. Marshall, 594 F.2d 244 (1978).

Georgia Highway Express, Inc. In *Johnson,* the court suggested that district courts base fee awards on the following criteria: (1) the time and labor required; (2) the novelty and difficulty of the questions; (3) the skill requisite to perform the legal services properly; (4) the preclusion of other employment; (5) the customary fee in the community for similar work; (6) the fixed or contingent nature of the fee; (7) time limitations imposed by the client or the circumstances; (8) the amount involved and the results obtained; (9) the experience, reputation, and ability of the attorneys; (10) the undesirability of the case; (11) the nature and length of the professional relationship with the client; and (12) awards in similar cases.

We recognized the importance of considering the twelve *Johnson* factors in awarding fees in Evans v. Sheraton Park Hotel, 503 F.2d 177, 187–88 (1974). Many other courts have applied the *Johnson* factors in subsequent cases, and those factors remain central to any fee award.

Simply to articulate those twelve factors, however, does not itself conjure up a reasonable dollar figure in the mind of a district court judge. A formula is necessary to translate the relevant factors into terms of dollars and cents. This is particularly true because the twelve factors overlap considerably. For example, largely subsumed under the factor "time and labor required" is an assessment of the "difficulty of the questions." That is so because the more difficult the problem, the longer it will take adequately to solve it. Similarly, the customary hourly fee (*Johnson* factor # 5) is likely to be influenced by (# 3) the level of skill necessary to perform the services, (# 6) whether the fee is fixed or contingent, (# 7) time limitations, (# 8) the amount to be obtained, (# 9) the reputation of the attorneys, and (# 10) the undesirability of the case.

For these reasons, scholars have noted that the twelve *Johnson* factors, without more, cannot guarantee a rational setting of fees. One commented:

> The fundamental problem with an approach that does no more than assure that the lower courts will consider a plethora of conflicting and at least partially redundant factors is that it provides no analytical framework for their application. It offers no guidance on the relative importance of each factor, whether they are to be applied differently in different contexts, or, indeed, how they are to be applied at all.

Berger, Court Awarded Attorneys' Fees: What is "Reasonable"?, 126 U.Pa.L.Rev. 281, 286–87 (1977) (footnotes omitted); accord, Dawson, Lawyers and Involuntary Clients in Public Interest Litigation, 88 Harv. L.Rev. 849, 927 & n. 327 (1975); Note, Promoting the Vindication of Civil Rights Through the Attorney's Fees Awards Act, 80 Colum.L.Rev. 346, 372–73 & nn. 164–69 (1980).

District court judges for this reason have had difficulty applying the *Johnson* factors. A common, yet understandable, fault is for the trial judge to make the conclusory statement, "After considering each of the twelve factors in *Johnson,* I find that a reasonable fee is *X* dollars." This very often leads to reversal and remand.

Appellate courts have recognized that the *Johnson* factors, despite their substantial conceptual value, also are imprecise. Some courts, therefore, have incorporated the twelve factors into an analytical framework that can be easily applied by trial courts and that will make possible meaningful appellate review.

Any fee-setting formula must produce an award sufficient to fulfill the primary purpose of awarding fees in Title VII cases, namely, "to encourage individuals injured by * * * discrimination to seek judicial relief." *Piggie Park,* 390 U.S. at 402, 88 S.Ct. at 966. An award of fees provides an incentive to competent lawyers to undertake Title VII work only if the award adequately compensates attorneys for the amount of work performed. The Court of Appeals for the Third Circuit was the first to develop a fee-setting formula that reflects this principle. In Lindy Bros. Builders, Inc. v. American Radiator & Standard Sanitary Corp., 487 F.2d 161 (1973) (*Lindy I*), and its successor case, *Lindy II,* 540 F.2d 102 (1976) (*en banc*), the Third Circuit articulated a formula that considered all the relevant factors but eliminated the redundancy and imprecision that many have identified in other fee-setting schemes.

Lindy recognized that the starting point in fee setting—what it characterized as the "lodestar" fee—should be computed by multiplying a reasonable hourly rate by the number of hours reasonably expended on the lawsuit. Adjustments in this figure are appropriate, the court recognized, but the "lodestar" provides "the only reasonably objective" starting point for awarding a fee.

* * *

A. *The "Lodestar"*

Any fee-setting inquiry begins with the "lodestar": the number of hours reasonably expended multiplied by a reasonable hourly rate. The figure generated by that computation is the basic fee from which a trial court judge should work. We examine below some of the problems that arise in calculating the "lodestar."

1. *Hours Reasonably Expended*

The fundamental purpose of the fee award is to compensate the attorney for his efforts. The first task for the trial court judge, therefore, is determining the amount of time reasonably expended.

When a law firm seeks a fee, it should document the amount of work performed. The District Court then will be able to do more than merely lump together all the hours spent by the various attorneys associated with the enterprise; the judge instead can segregate into categories the kinds of work performed by each participating attorney. This project need not be unduly burdensome:

> It is not necessary to know the exact number of minutes spent nor the precise activity to which each hour was devoted nor the specific

> attainments of each attorney. But without some fairly definite information as to the hours devoted to various general activities, e.g., pretrial discovery, settlement negotiations, and the hours spent by various classes of attorneys, e.g., senior partners, junior partners, associates, the court cannot know the nature of the services for which compensation is sought.

Lindy I, 487 F.2d at 167.

Compiling raw totals of hours spent, however, does not complete the inquiry. It does not follow that the amount of time *actually* expended is the amount of time *reasonably* expended. In the private sector, "billing judgment" is an important component in fee setting. It is no less important here. Hours that are not properly billed to one's *client* also are not properly billed to one's *adversary* pursuant to statutory authority. Thus, no compensation is due for nonproductive time. For example, where three attorneys are present at a hearing when one would suffice, compensation should be denied for the excess time. Similarly, no compensation should be paid for time spent litigating claims upon which the party seeking the fee did not ultimately prevail.[18]

At this point in the computation, the District Judge might usefully construct a table that looks something like this example.

Attorney & Type of Work	Hours
Senior Partner: Court Appearances	17.3
Senior Partner: Review of pleadings	39.2
Junior Associate: Research & drafting	87.6
Junior Associate: Depositions	35.5

2. *A Reasonable Hourly Rate*

The remaining element in fixing a "lodestar" fee is the reasonable hourly rate.

The reasonable hourly rate is that prevailing in the community for similar work. As we noted a reasonable hourly rate is the product of a multiplicity of factors. *Evans* itself listed several of the relevant considerations: the level of skill necessary, time limitations, the amount to be obtained in the litigation, the attorney's reputation, and the undesirability of the case. It follows that there may be more than one reasonable hourly rate for each of the attorneys, and for each of the kinds of work, involved in the litigation. After receiving documenta-

18. E.g., Oldham v. Ehrlich, 617 F.2d 163, at 168 n. 9 (8th Cir. 1980); Dillon v. AFBIC Devel. Corp., 597 F.2d 556, 564 (5th Cir. 1979); Nadeau v. Helgemoe, 581 F.2d 275, 278–79 (1st Cir. 1978). However, it sometimes will be the case that a lawsuit will seek recovery under a variety of legal theories complaining of essentially the same injury. A district judge must take care not to reduce a fee award arbitrarily simply because a plaintiff did not prevail under one or more of these legal theories. No reduction in fee is appropriate where the "issue was all part and parcel of one matter," Lamphere v. Brown Univ., 610 F.2d 46, 47 (1st Cir. 1979), but only when the claims asserted "are truly fractionable," id.

tion and other submissions, and perhaps holding a hearing, the trial judge might complete the fee table in the following manner.

Attorney & Type of Work	Hours	Rate	Total
Senior Partner: Court appearances	17.3	$95	$1,643.50
Senior Partner: Review of pleadings	39.2	$85	$3,332.00
Junior Associate: Research & drafting	87.6	$40	$3,504.00
Junior Associate: Depositions	35.5	$40	$1,420.00
			$9,899.50

Thus, the "lodestar" fee in this hypothetical is $9,899.50

B. *Adjustments to the "Lodestar"*

The "lodestar" fee may be adjusted to reflect other factors. We discuss herein those applicable in Title VII and similar fee-setting cases.[22] The burden of justifying any deviation from the "lodestar" rests on the party proposing the deviation. *Lindy II,* 540 F.2d at 118.

1. *The Contingent Nature of Success*

Under statutes like Title VII, only the prevailing party is eligible for a court-awarded fee. An attorney contemplating representation of a Title VII plaintiff must recognize that no fee will be forthcoming unless the litigation is successful. An adjustment in the lodestar, therefore, may be appropriate to compensate for the risk that the lawsuit would be unsuccessful and that no fee at all would be obtained.

It is important to recognize that the contingency adjustment is designed solely to compensate for the possibility at the outset that the litigation would be unsuccessful and that no fee would be obtained. Contingency adjustments of this sort are entirely unrelated to the "contingent fee" arrangements that are typical in plaintiffs' tort representation. In tort suits, an attorney might receive one-third of whatever amount the plaintiff recovers. In those cases, therefore, the fee is directly proportional to the recovery. Such is not the case in contingency adjustments of the kind we describe herein. The contingency adjustment is a percentage increase in the "lodestar" to reflect the risk that no fee will be obtained. The contingency adjustment is *not* a percentage increase based on the amount of recovery.

To the extent, of course, that an hourly rate underlying the "lodestar" fee itself comprehends an allowance for the contingent nature of the availability of fees in Title VII litigation against the Government, no further adjustment duplicating that allowance will be made. The district judge has ample powers of inquiry into the makeup of hourly

22. Factors other than those discussed here may be relevant to the setting of fees under other statutes. For example, it is well established that it may not be necessary to award fees representing the full market value of an attorney's time to provide an incentive to vindicate certain Freedom of Information Act rights, because obtaining the information may result in private pecuniary gain. See LaSalle Extension Univ. v. FTC, 627 F.2d 481, 483–484 (D.C.Cir. 1980); Nationwide Bldg. Maintenance, Inc. v. Sampson, 559 F.2d 704, 711–12 (D.C.Cir. 1977). Other factors may be relevant in setting fees in other contexts.

rates to assure that the Government will not suffer from any such duplication or, indeed, from any excessive allowance for this purpose.

The delay in receipt of payment for services rendered is an additional factor that may be incorporated into a contingency adjustment. The hourly rates used in the "lodestar" represent the prevailing rate for clients who typically pay their bills promptly. Court-awarded fees normally are received long after the legal services are rendered. That delay can present cash-flow problems for the attorneys. In any event, payment today for services rendered long in the past deprives the eventual recipient of the value of the use of the money in the meantime, which use, particularly in an inflationary era, is valuable. A percentage adjustment to reflect the delay in receipt of payment therefore may be appropriate. *Lindy II,* 540 F.2d at 117.[23]

To the district court judge falls the task of calculating as closely as possible a contingency adjustment with which fairly to compensate the successful attorney. We have not, however, lost sight of the fact that this adjustment is inherently imprecise and that certain estimations must be made. For example, it is difficult in hindsight to determine the risk of failure at the commencement of a lawsuit that ultimately proved to be successful. Thus, we ask only that the district court judges exercise their discretion as conscientiously as possible, and state their reasons as clearly as possible.[24]

2. *Quality of Representation*

Next, the "lodestar" may be adjusted up or down to reflect "the quality of representation." It is important to make clear precisely the analysis that must accompany such an adjustment. A quality adjustment is appropriate only when the representation is unusually good or bad, *taking into account the level of skill normally expected* of an attorney commanding the hourly rate used to compute the "lodestar." In other words,

> the court must recognize that a consideration of "quality" inheres in the "lodestar" award: counsel who possess or who are reputed to possess more experience, knowledge and legal talent generally command hourly rates superior to those who are less endowed. Thus, the quality of an attorney's work *in general* is a component of the reasonabl[e] hourly rate; this aspect of "quality" is reflected in the "lodestar" and should not be utilized to augment or diminish the basic award under the rubric of "the quality of an attorney's work."

23. On the other hand, if the "lodestar" itself is based on *present* hourly rates, rather than the lesser rates applicable to the time period in which the services were rendered, the harm resulting from delay in payment may be largely reduced or eliminated.

24. The setting of contingency adjustments is particularly within the expertise of the District Judge. As the Supreme Court said long ago, the District Court "has far better means of knowing what is just and reasonable than an appellate court can have." Trustees v. Greenough, 105 U.S. 527, 537, 26 L.Ed. 1157 (1882).

> *Lindy I,* then permits an adjustment to the "lodestar"—up or down—based on the all-around performance of counsel in the specific case: "Any increase or decrease in fees to adjust for the quality of work is designed to take account of an unusual degree of skill, be it unusually poor or unusually good." 487 F.2d at 168. By this is meant simply that the district court may determine that the lawyer discharged the professional burden undertaken with a degree of skill above or below that expected for lawyers of the caliber reflected in the hourly rates.

Lindy II, 540 F.2d at 117–18 (emphasis in original).

Until now the calculations have entirely ignored the results of the litigation. Success was a threshold inquiry relevant to the entitlement *vel non* to a fee, but the amount or nature of recovery was not considered in setting the "lodestar." These latter factors should be considered now, under the rubric of "quality of representation."

Where exceptional results are obtained—taking into account the hourly rate commanded and number of hours expended—an increase in fee is justifiable. However, it is important again to emphasize that a huge dollar recovery does not itself justify a huge fee award. The "lodestar" itself generally compensates lawyers adequately for their time. An upward adjustment for quality is appropriate only when the attorney performed exceptionally well, or obtained an exceptional result for the client. For example, if a substantial monetary judgment was to be *expected,* that expectation normally is reflected in the hourly rate used to compute the "lodestar," and no further adjustment would be necessary.

Quality adjustments may be upward or downward. Thus, if a high-priced attorney performs in a competent but undistinguished manner, a decrease in the "lodestar" may be necessary under the "quality of representation" rubric because the hourly rate used to calculate the "lodestar" proved to be overly generous.

III

Copeland I and *Copeland II,* however, took an entirely different view from that expressed in this opinion. The fee approach we have described rests on compensating attorneys for the market value of services rendered. The panel had the notion that, at least where the government is the losing defendant, the fee should be the amount representing the "actual cost to the law firm plus a reasonable and controllable profit" for the legal work done.

[The Court concluded that both the language and the policy underlying the fee-shifting provision of the Act required that the fee calculation should not vary with the identity of the losing defendant. The panel's "cost-plus" approach to calculation was rejected as difficult to administer and as fundamentally inconsistent with the Congressional purpose in providing court awarded fees. Because "cost-plus" fee calculation would result in lower fee awards, particularly for "public interest" lawyers, than could be earned in the "market," the Court reasoned that the panel's approach would not provide the incentive for private enforcement of Title VII that Congress intended. Finally, the Court reviewed and found reasonable the district court's application of the lodestar and calculation of the fee.]

MACKINNON, CIRCUIT JUDGE.

I join in the court's opinion. In my view both the market value and the cost-plus standard can at times lead to exorbitant fees; but I view the market value approach as being more time honored and hence easier of application nationwide where all lawyers do not keep detailed records of overhead costs and other relevant expenditures. The bench and the bar are accustomed to market value in the area as representing reasonable attorney's fees and I believe that standard, when properly applied, includes within it its own elements of reasonableness. The only admonition I would include would be the caveat that the attorney's fee in the ordinary case must bear some *reasonable* relationship to the amount of money and equitable benefits that are involved. Attorneys in such cases should be forced to be mindful of the monetary and equitable benefits that are being sought and should not be permitted to run up bills that are greatly disproportionate to the ultimate benefits that may be reasonably attainable.

[The dissenting opinion of JUDGES WILKEY and TAMM is omitted.]

NOTES AND PROBLEMS FOR DISCUSSION

1. All federal causes of action for employment discrimination are covered by attorney fee statutes. The Civil Rights Attorney's Fees Awards Act of 1976, 42 U.S.C. § 1988, contains language identical to that in § 706(k) of Title VII and provides for attorney fees to prevailing parties in suits filed under 42 U.S.C. §§ 1981, 1982, 1983, 1985, 1986, Title IX [of the Education Amendments of 1972] (prohibiting discrimination on the basis of sex by institutions receiving federal funds) and Title VI of the Civil Rights Act of 1964 (prohibiting discrimination on the basis of race by institutions receiving federal funds). The legislative history of Section 1988 makes it clear that Congress intended that "the standards for awarding fees under (the Act) be generally the same as under the fee provisions of the 1964 Civil Rights Act." S.Rep. No. 1011, 94th Cong., 2d Sess. 4 (1976); H.R. Rep. No. 1558, 94th Cong., 2d Sess. 5–8 (1976). Section 505 of the Rehabilitation Act of 1973, 29 U.S.C. § 794a, covering suits for disabled persons, provides for reasonable attorney fees in language identical to that of § 706(k) and § 1988.[a] By contrast, the remedies section of the Fair Labor Standards Act, 29 U.S.C. § 216, which is incorporated in the Equal Pay Act and the Age Discrimination in Employment Act, provides in part that "[t]he court in such action shall, in addition to any judgment awarded to the plaintiff or plaintiffs, allow a reasonable attorney's fee to be paid by the defendant, and costs of the action." The courts have developed a common set of

a. Section 505 of the Rehabilitation Act which generally defines remedies under the Act applies only to § 501 actions (suits against the Federal government) and those filed under § 504 (suits against programs or activities receiving federal financial assistance). Section 503 (federal contractors) has been construed as not creating a private right of action. See infra, at 685.

standards for application of these attorney fee statutes. See e.g., Hensley v. Eckerhart, 461 U.S. 424, 433 n.7, 103 S.Ct. 1933, 1939 n.7, 76 L.Ed.2d 40 (1983) ("The standards set forth in this opinion are generally applicable in all cases in which Congress has authorized an award of fees to a 'prevailing party.' ") Cf. Richardson v. Alaska Airlines, Inc., 750 F.2d 763 (9th Cir. 1984) (fact that ADEA provides for recovery of fees only from "employer" precludes award of fees against a union which unsuccessfully opposed entry of consent decree).

2. When has a party "prevailed" within the meaning of § 706(k) or § 1988 so as to be entitled to attorney fees? If a plaintiff proves that the employer denied her a promotion because of her sex, but fails to establish that her discharge was discriminatory, she will be entitled to some back pay, but not reinstatement. Has she "prevailed" under the Act? Courts have generally held that plaintiffs are "prevailing parties" for attorney fee purposes, "if they succeed on any significant issue in the litigation which achieves some of the benefit the parties sought in bringing the suit." Nadeau v. Helgemoe, 581 F.2d 275, 278–79 (1st Cir. 1978). This "typical formulation" was approved by the Supreme Court in Hensley v. Eckerhart, supra, 461 U.S. at 435, 103 S.Ct. at 1940. For example, in Jones v. Roswell, 40 FEP Cases 705 (N.D.Ga.1986) the plaintiff was successful on only one of several claims. A jury found she had been sexually harrassed and awarded $1 in nominal damages rather than the $100,000 requested. Noting the "potential future benefits of this determination and the salutary effects it will have on conditions in the work place for other women employed by the City of Roswell Police Department," the court awarded plaintiff's counsel more than $10,000 in fees.

Although a party can "prevail" under the fee shifting statute through partial success, that success must be on the merits of the claim and must ultimately result in some of the relief prayed for. Thus, appellate reversal of a district court's dismissal of a suit with a remand for a trial on the merits does not constitute "prevailing" in the litigation. Hanrahan v. Hampton, 446 U.S. 754, 100 S.Ct. 1987, 64 L.Ed.2d 670 (1980). See also, Doe v. Busbee, 684 F.2d 1375 (11th Cir. 1982) (plaintiffs whose preliminary injunction was vacated because of change in law were not prevailing parties because success was only temporary). But cf., Frazier v. Board of Trustees, 765 F.2d 1278 (5th Cir. 1985) (discharged employee who obtained preliminary injunction reinstating her but who eventually lost on the merits of her action because of change in law was entitled to fees where relief obtained was coextensive with relief requested in complaint); Thompson v. Sawyer, 586 F.Supp. 635 (D.D.C.1984) (plaintiffs awarded fees against union which unsuccessfully sought to intervene in Title VII case to oppose relief sought by plaintiffs).

A plaintiff may be considered to have prevailed if the litigation is successfully terminated by a consent decree, out-of-court settlement, or voluntary cessation of an unlawful practice by the defendant. "Nothing in the language of sec. 1988 conditions the District Court's power to award fees on full litigation of the issues or on a judicial determination that the plaintiff's rights have been violated." Maher v. Gagne, 448 U.S. 122, 129, 100 S.Ct. 2570, 2574, 65 L.Ed.2d 653 (1980). But should fees be awarded where settlement results not from recognition of the meritorious grounds of the plaintiff's suit, but from the simple desire of the defendant to put an end to the controversy? A number of circuits have adopted the "catalyst" formula for determining whether a party has prevailed. As explained by the Fourth Circuit in Bonnes v. Long, 599 F.2d 1316, 1319 (4th Cir. 1979), cert. denied, 455 U.S. 961, 102 S.Ct. 1476, 71 L.Ed.2d

681 (1982) (a Section 1983 suit which ended in a consent decree without a determination of constitutional rights), the trial court must determine,

> * * * the precise factual/legal condition that the fee claimant has sought to change or affect so as to gain a benefit or be relieved of a burden. With this condition taken as a benchmark, inquiry may then turn to whether as a quite practical matter the outcome * * * is one to which the plaintiff fee claimant's efforts contributed in a significant way, and which does involve an actual conferral benefit or relief from the burden when measured against the benchmark condition.

See also, Hennigan v. Ouachita Parish School Board, 749 F.2d 1148 (5th Cir. 1985) (plaintiff must show that, as practical matter, goal of suit was achieved and then must demonstrate causal relationship between lawsuit and defendant's actions); Miller v. Staats, 706 F.2d 336 (D.C.Cir. 1983) (prevailing party is one who can show that final result of case furthers his interest and that his suit contributed to obtaining relief); cf. Ekanem v. The Health and Hospital Corp., 778 F.2d 1254 (7th Cir. 1985) (plaintiff's unsuccessful lawsuit not shown to have acted as catalyst in changing employer's disputed practices where practices were in place before lawsuit filed). By contrast, the First Circuit seems to require that the benefit not only result from the suit but be one to which the plaintiff was legally entitled.

> Even if plaintiffs can establish that their suit was causally related to the defendant's actions which improved their condition, this is only half of their battle. The test they must pass is legal as well as factual. If it has been judicially determined that defendant's conduct, however beneficial it may be to plaintiffs' interests, is not required by law, then defendants must be held to have acted gratuitously and plaintiffs have not prevailed in a legal sense.

Nadeau v. Helgemoe, supra, 581 F.2d at 281. Justice Rehnquist, joined by Justice O'Connor, dissented from the Court's denial of certiorari in Bonnes v. Long, supra, and used the occassion to express approval of the First Circuit's test in *Nadeau.*

> It is clear beyond peradventure that unless an action brought by a private litigant contains some basis in law for the benefits ultimately received by that litigant, the litigant cannot be said to have "enforced" the civil rights laws or to have promoted their policies for the benefit of the public at large. The Bonnes standard . . . seems largely to disregard this central purpose of sec. 1988, awarding attorney's fees even if the discernible benefit was conferred gratuitously by the defendant or was undertaken simply to avoid further litigation expenses.

Long v. Bonnes, 455 U.S. 961, 967, 102 S.Ct. 1476, 1479, 71 L.Ed.2d 681 (1982). What exactly is the "central purpose" of the fee shifting statutes according to Justice Rehnquist? A standard part of most settlement agreements is the formalistic denial by the defendant that the compromise constitutes an admission of liability. Faced with such a settlement, how should a court attempting to apply Justice Rehnquist's test, determine whether there was a "basis in law" for the settlement? The Sixth Circuit has stated that "the second prong of the test is legal in nature, essentially requiring a determination of whether the plaintiff's claim is frivolous." Johnston v. Jago, 691 F.2d 283, 287 (6th Cir. 1982). But can the "basis in law" for the settlement or the non-frivolousness of the plaintiff's case be determined on the basis of the pleadings without some factual inquiry? Should fees be awarded to a plaintiff whose Title VII case is mooted by her success in arbitration under a collective bargaining agreement?

See, Sullivan v. Pennsylvania Dept. of Labor, 663 F.2d 443 (3d Cir. 1981), cert. denied, 455 U.S. 1020, 102 S.Ct. 1716, 72 L.Ed.2d 138 (1982).

3. The "lodestar" method of fee calculation used by the D.C. Circuit in Copeland v. Marshall has been universally adopted. See e.g., Graves v. Barnes, 700 F.2d 220 (5th Cir. 1983); Ramos v. Lamm, 713 F.2d 546 (10th Cir. 1983); Fitzpatrick v. Internal Revenue Service, 665 F.2d 327 (11th Cir. 1982). The Supreme Court has implicitly approved the basic formula.

> The most useful starting point for determining the amount of a reasonable fee is the number of hours reasonably expended on the litigation multiplied by a reasonable hourly rate. This calculation provides an objective basis on which to make an initial estimate of the value of a lawyer's services.

Hensley v. Eckerhart, supra, 461 U.S. at 433, 103 S.Ct. at 1939.

Reasonable Hours. The fact that a partially successful plaintiff can be a "prevailing party" does not mean, of course, that his counsel should be compensated for all time spent on the case. Stressing that "the result is what matters," the Supreme Court in HENSLEY v. ECKERHART, 461 U.S. 424, 103 S.Ct. 1933, 76 L.Ed.2d 40 (1983) (an institutional reform case filed under Section 1983), provided the following guidelines.

> [1] Where the plaintiff has failed to prevail on a claim that is distinct in all respects from his successful claims, the hours spent on the unsuccessful claim should be excluded in considering the amount of a reasonable fee. [2] Where a lawsuit consists of related claims, a plaintiff who has won substantial relief should not have his attorney's fee reduced simply because the district court did not adopt each contention raised. [3] But where the plaintiff achieved only limited success, the district court should award only that amount of fees that is reasonable in relation to the results obtained.

461 U.S. at 440, 103 S.Ct. at 1943. The practical difficulty in applying these guidelines results from the fact that lawyers' work in litigation can seldom be so compartmentalized that all hours can be attributed to either "winning" or "losing" claims. For example, in depositions of the employer's officials all the contentions of the plaintiff are likely to be explored. Is such time to be fully compensated so long as some of the discovery was relevant to the winning claim? Who should have the burden of proving that given hours are related to the winning claim? The courts have not approached these problems with much consistency. See, Eddins v. West Georgia Medical Center, Inc., 39 FEP Cases 1499 (N.D.Ga.1985) (plaintiff who prevailed on hiring claim and achieved only partial success allowed 50% of time claimed for such tasks as telephone calls, conferences, research and discovery which were impossible to apportion clearly to various claims); Bruno v. Western Electric Co., 618 F.Supp. 398 (D.Colo.1985) (former employees failure to prevail on demotion issue and claim for punitive damages does not affect recovery of attorney fees where demotion was only one of a myriad of actions characterized as discriminatory and claim for punitive damages turned on same core of common facts as other issues on which he was successful); Brown v. Bolger, 102 F.R.D. 849 (D.D.C.1984) (hours for which court is unable to discern compensable time from noncompensable time excluded from fee award); Turgeon v. Howard University, 571 F.Supp. 679 (D.D.C.1983) (inability of court to divide hours on claim-by-claim basis precludes separation out of fee request). The Ninth Circuit has set forth a procedure for determining whether hours should be attributed to successful claims for purposes of fee calculation: in a hearing at which the fee applicant has the burden of proof,

evidence should be presented on time spent on successful claims, time spent on unsuccessful claims that are allegedly related to the ultimate goal of the litigation and the total time spent on all claims. Pate v. Alameda-Contra Costa Transit District, 697 F.2d 870 (9th Cir. 1983).

Even in a case where the plaintiff has prevailed on all the issues, the district court exercises considerable discretion in deciding whether the claimed hours are "reasonable." In Copeland v. Marshall the district judge, while finding that the plaintiffs' counsel had been highly successful, reduced the lodestar by 22% because of his determination that the inexperienced lawyers handling the case had "lacked experienced trial direction" and not all of the work proved productive. The Court of Appeals affirmed the reduction as within the judge's discretion. 641 F.2d at 902. Should time spent by counsel for a class on unsuccessful claims of class members in Stage II proceedings be excluded from the fee computation? See, Turner v. Orr, 785 F.2d 1498 (11th Cir. 1986).

Reasonable Hourly Rates. In BLUM v. STENSON, 465 U.S. 886, 104 S.Ct. 1541, 79 L.Ed.2d 891 (1984), the successful plaintiffs were represented by a non-profit legal services organization. The district court calculated the lodestar on the basis of prevailing commercial rates in the community (New York City) and the Court of Appeals affirmed. In the Supreme Court petitioners argued, as did the government in *Copeland,* that the rate portion of the lodestar should be based on the cost of providing the legal services and that use of market rates in this case would result in a windfall for counsel employed by a non-profit organization who were not engaged in the commercial practice of law. The Court held, however, that the legislative history of the fee-shifting statutes showed that Congress intended that fees be calculated according to market rates in the relevant community, not according to a cost-plus formula, regardless of whether the prevailing party is represented by private counsel or by non-profit organizations. The fee claimant has the burden of establishing the prevailing rate for attorneys of comparable experience and expertise in the community. Blum v. Stenson, supra, 465 U.S. at 895–96 n. 11, 104 S.Ct. at 1547 n. 11.

To what extent should the successful attorney's own billing rates determine what is reasonable? A number of courts have held that prevailing counsel's own rate is some evidence of, but not determinative of the "prevailing rate" in the community. See, EEOC v. Strasburger, Price, Kelton, Martin and Unis, 626 F.2d 1272, 1275 (5th Cir. 1980). But in Laffey v. Northwest Airlines, Inc., 746 F.2d 4 (D.C.Cir. 1984), cert. denied, ___ U.S. ___, 105 S.Ct. 3488, 87 L.Ed.2d 622 (1985), the Court of Appeals held that a private firm's normal billing rates cannot be exceeded in establishing the lodestar for that firm's work. The successful plaintiffs in *Laffey* were represented by a firm whose principal work was representation of labor unions. As is common among labor lawyers, the firm charged its union clients substantially less than the market rate for commercial legal work in the community because of their non-profit status, but argued that the lodestar should be established based on the prevailing community rates for lawyers of comparable skill, experience and reputation. The Court of Appeals held, however, that since the purpose of the fee statutes is to encourage counsel to take on civil rights work, the firms own billing rates were the best evidence of the economic incentive necessary to cause that firm to take on such work. See also, Palmer v. Shultz, 598 F.Supp. 382 (D.D.C.1984), aff'd, 38 FEP Cases 672 (D.C.Cir. 1985). Is the result of *Laffey* consistent with Blum v. Stenson? What if the firm's normal billing rate is above the "prevailing rate" in the community?

A major difference between the collection of fees under the fee-shifting statutes and in normal commercial work is that counsel in civil rights cases are not paid as they go and must wait a substantial time to realize their fees for successful cases. The attorneys in *Laffey,* for example, had worked on the case for over fourteen years. In recognition of this delay in payment factor, most courts have awarded fees based on current rates rather than on rates prevailing at the time the legal work for which compensation is sought was performed. See, Murray v. Weinberger, 741 F.2d 1423 (D.C.Cir. 1984) (rather than adjust lodestar upward to account for delay in payment, courts should award current rates); Johnson v. University College, 706 F.2d 1205 (11th Cir.), cert. denied, 464 U.S. 994, 104 S.Ct. 489, 78 L.Ed.2d 684 (1983) (delay in payment should be reflected through use of current rates or contingency adjustment of lodestar).

Should a prevailing attorney from outside the community be awarded fees based on the customary rates where he normally practices or on the prevailing rate in the community where the litigation takes place? Compare, Chrapliwy v. Uniroyal, Inc., 670 F.2d 760 (7th Cir. 1982), cert. denied, 461 U.S. 956, 103 S.Ct. 2428, 77 L.Ed.2d 1315 (1983) with Ramos v. Lamm, 713 F.2d 546 (10th Cir. 1983). Where a prevailing plaintiff's requested fees are challenged, should he be entitled to discover from defense counsel the hours charged their client for defense of the case and rates charged by defense counsel? See, Mitroff v. Xomox Corp., 631 F.Supp. 25 (S.D.Ohio 1985).

Enhancement or Reduction of the Lodestar. As explained in Copeland v. Marshall, courts have frequently applied a "multiplier" or upward adjustment to compensate counsel for the risk of non-recovery, the quality of representation or the high degree of success. In BLUM v. STENSON, supra, however, the Supreme Court, without flatly prohibiting such upward adjustments, established what amounts to a presumption against them. The district court in *Blum* had increased the lodestar by 50% because of the quality of representation, the complexity of the issues, the contingent nature of recovery of fees and the great benefit to the class that plaintiff achieved. Stressing that the lodestar is "presumed to be the reasonable fee," the Supreme Court reversed the 50% enhancement as "a clear case of double counting." The Court reasoned that ordinarily the novelty and complexity of the issues are reflected in number of hours put into the case by counsel, the quality of representation should be accounted for in the hourly rate and that benefit to a class is not normally an adjustment factor. Finally, the Court noted that the record was silent as to the "risks associated with the claim" and thus that there was no basis for an upward adjustment for the contingent nature of the case. 465 U.S. at 898–901, 104 S.Ct. at 1548–1550. In a footnote the Court stated:

> We have no occasion in this case to consider whether the risk of not being the prevailing party in a [section] 1983 case, and therefore, not being entitled to an award of attorney's fees from one's adversary, may ever justify an upward fee adjustment.

465 U.S. at 901 n. 17, 104 S.Ct. at 1550 n. 17. The Court also allowed that "in some cases of exceptional success an enhanced award may be justified." 465 U.S. at 897, 104 S.Ct. at 1548. Justices Brennan and Marshall concurred only to reaffirm their view (previously stated in Hensley v. Eckerhart, supra) "that Congress has clearly indicated that the risk of not prevailing, and therefore the risk of not recovering any attorney fees, is a proper basis on which a district court may award an upward adjustment to an otherwise compensatory fee." 465 U.S. at 902, 104 S.Ct. at 1550.

Despite the cautionary language of *Blum*, courts have continued to grant upward adjustments of lodestar figures on the basis of contingency risks and "exceptional results." See e.g., Crumbaker v. Merit Systems Protection Board, 781 F.2d 191 (Fed.Cir. 1986) (multiplier for contingency risks and delay in payment); Clayton v. Thurman, 775 F.2d 1096 (10th Cir. 1985) (33% upward adjustment for excellent results); Shaw v. Library of Congress, 747 F.2d 1469 (D.C.Cir. 1984), cert. granted, ___ U.S. ___, 106 S.Ct. 58, 88 L.Ed.2d 47 (1985) (multiplier to compensate for delay in payment). Contra, Laffey v. Northwest Airlines, supra, (no upward adjustment of fees despite contingent nature of case and fact that attorneys went unpaid for 14 years); Ridenour v. Montgomery Ward & Co., 786 F.2d 867 (8th Cir. 1986) (enhancement of fee award denied in ADEA case notwithstanding contingent nature of case and fact that plaintiff's attorney spent long hours on case with no guarantee of payment). Quantifying the degree of risk of non-success in a case is a highly speculative venture. One court has estimated the plaintiffs' chances of success in its district to be approximately 19%. Thompson v. Barrett, 599 F.Supp. 806, 815–16 (D.D.C. 1984) (granting 50% multiplier because chances of success were much lower than in typical case). One commentator has proposed that there should be a 50% multiplier where the plaintiff had a somewhat better than even chance of success, an enhancement of 100% where the odds were 50–50, and a 200% multiplier where the case was a long shot. Berger, Court Awarded Attorneys' Fees: What is "Reasonable?", 126 U.Pa.L.Rev. 281, 326 (1977). Should it be the business of the courts to encourage attorneys to take cases that have little realistic chance of success?

The Supreme Court in *Blum* also indicated that in some circumstances the lodestar should be reduced. There are few examples of such a reverse multiplier, but one circumstance that has troubled some courts is a great disparity between the fee award and monetary relief to the plaintiff where the principal relief sought has been money damages. Compare the concurring opinion of Judge MacKinnon in Copeland v. Marshall and Copper Liquor, Inc. v. Adolph Coors Co., 684 F.2d 1087 (5th Cir. 1982) (25% downward adjustment of lodestar in light of low damage recovery).

In CITY OF RIVERSIDE v. RIVERA, ___ U.S. ___, 106 S.Ct. 2686, 91 L.Ed. 2d 466 (1986), the Supreme Court considered whether an award of $245,456.25 in attorney fees pursuant to 42 U.S.C. § 1988 could be "reasonable" in light of the fact that a jury had awarded plaintiffs a total of $33,350 in compensatory and punitive damages. The award was made in a police misconduct case filed under Section 1983. The district court made findings required by Hensley v. Eckerhart and determined that plaintiffs' counsel were entitled to the full lodestar fee requested. The Court of Appeals affirmed on the basis of the district court's findings. Arguing that in civil rights cases in which only monetary relief is requested a "reasonable" fee should necessarily be proportionate to the damage award recovered, petitioners asked the Court to abandon the use of the lodestar method of calculation in such cases and suggested that fee awards in civil rights damage cases should be modeled upon the contingent fee arrangements commonly used in personal injury litigation.

In a plurality opinion, the Court rejected the analogy between civil rights cases seeking monetary relief and garden-variety tort litigation because, "damage awards do not reflect fully the public benefit advanced by civil rights litigation." 106 S.Ct. at 2695. The Court also held that limiting attorney fees in civil rights cases to a proportion of the damages awarded would undermine the Congressional purpose behind Section 1988.

> A rule of proportionality would make it difficult, if not impossible, for individuals with meritorious civil rights claims but relatively small potential damages to obtain redress from the courts. This is totally inconsistent with the Congress' purpose in enacting § 1988. Congress recognized that private-sector fee arrangements were inadequate to ensure sufficiently vigorous enforcement of civil rights. In order to ensure that lawyers would be willing to represent persons with legitimate civil rights grievances, Congress determined that it would be necessary to compensate lawyers for all time reasonably expended on a case.

Ibid.

In a dissenting opinion, Justice Rehnquist argued that the fees awarded were necessarily unreasonable because "[t]he very 'reasonableness' of the hours expended on a case by a plaintiff's attorney necessarily will depend, to a large extent, on the amount that may reasonably be expected to be recovered if the plaintiff prevails." According to the dissent, a "reasonable" fee under Section 1988 "means a fee that would have been deemed reasonable if billed to affluent plaintiffs by their own attorneys." Should the overall "reasonableness" of a fee award under the civil rights laws be determined by the same standard applied to fees charged to "affluent" clients motivated solely by the economics of the situation? Which view of "reasonableness," that of Justice Rehnquist or that of the plurality opinion, most closely accords with the purpose of the fee-shifting statutes?

4. The fee shifting statutes do not explicitly limit compensation to legal services in the litigation. The question of whether attorneys' time spent in administrative matters related to the litigation is compensable under the fee statutes has been disputed. In NEW YORK GASLIGHT CLUB, INC. v. CAREY, 447 U.S. 54, 100 S.Ct. 2024, 64 L.Ed.2d 723 (1980), the Court held that fees were properly awarded to plaintiff for time spent by her attorney in state deferral agency proceedings in which she obtained relief. But in WEBB v. BOARD OF EDUCATION OF DYER COUNTY, 471 U.S. 234, 105 S.Ct. 1923, 85 L.Ed.2d 233 (1985), a Section 1983 case in which the plaintiff challenged his discharge by a public school board, the Court held that time spent prior to filing suit in a series of administrative hearings before the board was not spent enforcing a federal right and could not be compensated under Section 1988. *Carey* was distinguished on the ground that Title VII requires the claimant to pursue state administrative remedies before commencing suit. Section 1983 on the other hand has no exhaustion requirement. See Chapter 8, Section B, supra. "Because § 1983 stands as 'an independent avenue of relief' and petitioner 'could go straight to court to assert it,' the school board proceedings in this case simply do not have the integral function under § 1983 that state administrative proceedings have under Title VII." 471 U.S. at ___, 105 S.Ct. at 1927. The Court stopped short of holding that fees for time spent at optional administrative proceedings can never be recovered. "The petitioner made no suggestion below that any discrete portion of the work product from the administrative proceedings was work that was both useful and of a type ordinarily necessary to advance the civil rights litigation to the stage it reached before settlement." Id. at 1929. In Chrapliwy v. Uniroyal, Inc., 670 F.2d 760 (7th Cir. 1982), cert. denied, 461 U.S. 956, 103 S.Ct. 2428, 77 L.Ed.2d 1315 (1983), a Title VII class action, plaintiffs supplemented their litigation efforts by persuading the Office of Federal Contract Compliance to take action against the employer for violation of executive orders barring discrimination by federal contractors. The Title VII action was subsequently settled and the defendant

admitted that it would not have settled had it not been for the threat of disbarment by the OFCCP. The district court awarded substantial fees to plaintiffs but denied compensation for time spent prodding the agency to take action as "not contemplated under Title VII's attorney fee provisions." Reasoning that "pursuit of disbarment was a service that contributed to the ultimate termination of the Title VII action, and in that sense was within the Title VII action," the Seventh Circuit reversed. 670 F.2d at 767. Is *Chrapliwy* consistent with *Webb?*

5. Employment discrimination cases are frequently lengthy and drawn out. As explained in Chapter 14, this is particularly the case in class litigation. The plaintiffs and their attorneys in class actions, even after establishing the defendant's liability, may have to go through protracted remedial proceedings before final judgment can be obtained. Recognizing the severe financial burdens imposed on plaintiff's counsel in such cases, courts have occasionally awarded interim fees to cover the liability phase of the trial. In James v. Stockham Valves & Fittings Co., 559 F.2d 310 (5th Cir. 1977), cert. denied, 434 U.S. 1034, 98 S.Ct. 767, 54 L.Ed.2d 781 (1978), the Fifth Circuit explained the award of fees pendente lite.

> There is a danger that litigants will be discouraged from bringing such suits because of the risks of protracted litigation and the extended financial drain represented by such a risk. An award of interim attorneys' fees will prevent extreme cash-flow problems for plaintiffs and their attorneys. * * * Here, where the litigation has consumed more than eleven years such an award is appropriate. Otherwise, the danger exists that defendants in Title VII suits may be tempted to seek victory through an economic war of attrition against plaintiffs.

559 F.2d at 358–59. See also, Carpenter v. Stephen F. Austin State University, 706 F.2d 608 (5th Cir. 1983) (district court directed on remand to award interim fees for pre-trial, trial and appellate work should relief be afforded plaintiffs). The denial or granting of interim fees is not immediately appealable as a final order. See, Morgan v. Kopecky Charter Bus Co., 760 F.2d 919 (9th Cir. 1985). The problem of recoupment of interim fees in the event plaintiff's victory is reversed on appeal has not been addressed.

6. Attorney fees may be awarded under § 706(k) of Title VII and Section 1988 against state and local governments. Unlike monetary damages, awards of attorney fees which ultimately run against the state are not barred by the Eleventh Amendment. Hutto v. Finney, 437 U.S. 678, 98 S.Ct. 2565, 57 L.Ed.2d 522 (1978); Fitzpatrick v. Bitzer, 427 U.S. 445, 96 S.Ct. 2666, 49 L.Ed.2d 614 (1976). Where plaintiffs obtain injunctive relief against government officials in their official capacities (See Chapter 8, Section B, supra) the fee award will run against the government agency even though it is not a formal party to the litigation. Hutto v. Finney, supra, 437 U.S. at 693–94, 98 S.Ct. at 2574–2575. But where officials are sued for damages in their individual capacities and where the government entity could not be liable for damages on the merits, it can not be assessed fees under Section 1988. Kentucky v. Graham, 473 U.S. ___, 105 S.Ct. 3099, 87 L.Ed.2d 114 (1985). The qualified "good faith" immunity of the public official from damage liability is irrelevant to the award of attorney fees if injunctive or declaratory relief has been awarded. See Aware Woman Clinic Inc. v. Cocoa Beach, supra, 629 F.2d at 1149, Bond v. Stanton, supra, 630 F.2d at 1234; see also S.Rep. No. 1011, 94th Cong., 2d Sess. 5 (1976). Nor will the absolute immunity from damages which certain public officials (judges, prosecutors, legislators) enjoy for discretionary actions in the scope of their

official duties bar an award of attorney fees against them in their official capacities where injunctive relief has been granted. See Morrison v. Ayoob, 627 F.2d 669 (3d Cir. 1980), cert. denied, 449 U.S. 1102, 101 S.Ct. 898, 66 L.Ed.2d 828 (1981).

CHRISTIANSBURG GARMENT CO. v. EQUAL EMPLOYMENT OPPORTUNITY COMMISSION

Supreme Court of the United States, 1978.
434 U.S. 412, 98 S.Ct. 694, 54 L.Ed.2d 648.

MR. JUSTICE STEWART delivered the opinion of the Court.

The question in this case is under what circumstances an attorney's fee should be allowed when the defendant is the prevailing party in a Title VII action—a question about which the federal courts have expressed divergent views.

I

Two years after Rosa Helm had filed a Title VII charge of racial discrimination against the petitioner Christiansburg Garment Co. (company), the Equal Employment Opportunity Commission notified her that its conciliation efforts had failed and that she had the right to sue the company in federal court. She did not do so. Almost two years later, in 1972, Congress enacted amendments to Title VII. Section 14 of these amendments authorized the Commission to sue in its own name to prosecute "charges pending with the Commission" on the effective date of the amendments. Proceeding under this section, the Commission sued the company, alleging that it had engaged in unlawful employment practices in violation of the amended Act. The company moved for summary judgment on the ground, inter alia, that the Rosa Helm charge had not been "pending" before the Commission when the 1972 amendments took effect. The District Court agreed, and granted summary judgment in favor of the company. 376 F.Supp. 1067 (W.D.Va.).

The company then petitioned for the allowance of attorney's fees against the Commission pursuant to § 706(k) of Title VII. Finding that "the Commission's action in bringing the suit cannot be characterized as unreasonable or meritless," the District Court concluded that "an award of attorney's fees to petitioner is not justified in this case." A divided Court of Appeals affirmed, 550 F.2d 949 (CA4), and we granted certiorari to consider an important question of federal law.

II

It is the general rule in the United States that in the absence of legislation providing otherwise, litigants must pay their own attorney's fees. Alyeska Pipeline Co. v. Wilderness Society, 421 U.S. 240, 95 S.Ct. 1612, 44 L.Ed.2d 141. Congress has provided only limited exceptions to this rule "under selected statutes granting or protecting various federal rights." Some of these statutes make fee awards mandatory for prevailing plaintiffs; others make awards permissive but limit them to certain parties, usually prevailing plaintiffs. But many of the statutes are more flexible, authorizing the award of attorney's fees to either plaintiffs or defendants, and entrusting the effectuation of the statutory policy to the discretion of the district courts. Section 706(k) of Title VII of the Civil Rights Act of 1964 falls into this last category, providing as it does that a district court may in its discretion allow an attorney's fee to the prevailing party.

In Newman v. Piggie Park Enterprises, 390 U.S. 400, 88 S.Ct. 964, 19 L.Ed.2d 1263, the Court considered a substantially identical statute authorizing the award of attorney's fees under Title II of the Civil Rights Act of 1964.[8] In that case the plaintiffs had prevailed, and the Court of Appeals had held that they should be awarded their attorney's fees "only to the extent that the respondents' defenses had been advanced 'for purposes of delay and not in good faith.'" We ruled that this "subjective standard" did not properly effectuate the purposes of the counsel-fee provision of Title II. Relying primarily on the intent of Congress to cast a Title II plaintiff in the role of "a 'private attorney general,' vindicating a policy that Congress considered of the highest priority," we held that a prevailing plaintiff under Title II "should ordinarily recover an attorney's fee unless special circumstances would render such an award unjust." We noted in passing that if the objective of Congress had been to permit the award of attorney's fees only against defendants who had acted in bad faith, "no new statutory provision would have been necessary," since even the American common-law rule allows the award of attorney's fees in those exceptional circumstances.

In Albemarle Paper Co. v. Moody, the Court made clear that the Piggie Park standard of awarding attorney's fees to a successful plaintiff is equally applicable in an action under Title VII of the Civil Rights Act. It can thus be taken as established, as the parties in this case both acknowledge, that under § 706(k) of Title VII a prevailing *plaintiff* ordinarily is to be awarded attorney's fees in all but special circumstances.

III

The question in the case before us is what standard should inform a district court's discretion in deciding whether to award attorney's fees to a successful *defendant* in a Title VII action. Not surprisingly, the parties in addressing the question in their briefs and oral arguments have taken almost diametrically opposite positions.

The company contends that the *Piggie Park* criterion for a successful plaintiff should apply equally as a guide to the award of attorney's fees

8. "In any action commenced pursuant to this subchapter, the court, in its discretion, may allow the prevailing party, other than the United States, a reasonable attorney's fee as part of the costs, and the United States shall be liable for costs the same as a private person." 42 U.S.C. § 2000a–3(b).

to a successful defendant. Its submission, in short, is that every prevailing defendant in a Title VII action should receive an allowance of attorney's fees "unless special circumstances would render such an award unjust." The respondent Commission, by contrast, argues that the prevailing defendant should receive an award of attorney's fees only when it is found that the plaintiff's action was brought in bad faith. We have concluded that neither of these positions is correct.

A

Relying on what it terms "the plain meaning of the statute," the company argues that the language of § 706(k) admits of only one interpretation: "A prevailing defendant is entitled to an award of attorney's fees on the same basis as a prevailing plaintiff." But the permissive and discretionary language of the statute does not even invite, let alone require, such a mechanical construction. The terms of § 706(k) provide no indication whatever of the circumstances under which either a plaintiff *or* a defendant should be entitled to attorney's fees. And a moment's reflection reveals that there are at least two strong equitable considerations counseling an attorney's fee award to a prevailing Title VII plaintiff that are wholly absent in the case of a prevailing Title VII defendant.

First, as emphasized so forcefully in *Piggie Park*, the plaintiff is the chosen instrument of Congress to vindicate "a policy that Congress considered of the highest priority." Second, when a district court awards counsel fees to a prevailing plaintiff, it is awarding them against a violator of federal law. As the Court of Appeals clearly perceived, "these policy considerations which support the award of fees to a prevailing plaintiff are not present in the case of a prevailing defendant." A successful defendant seeking counsel fees under § 706(k) must rely on quite different equitable considerations.

But if the company's position is untenable, the Commission's argument also misses the mark. It seems clear, in short, that in enacting § 706(k) Congress did not intend to permit the award of attorney's fees to a prevailing defendant only in a situation where the plaintiff was motivated by bad faith in bringing the action. As pointed out in *Piggie Park*, if that had been the intent of Congress, no statutory provision would have been necessary, for it has long been established that even under the American common-law rule attorney's fees may be awarded against a party who has proceeded in bad faith.

Furthermore, while it was certainly the policy of Congress that Title VII plaintiffs should vindicate "a policy that Congress considered of the highest priority," *Piggie Park*, it is equally certain that Congress entrusted the ultimate effectuation of that policy to the adversary judicial process, Occidental Life Ins. Co. v. EEOC, 432 U.S. 355, 97 S.Ct. 2447, 53 L.Ed.2d 402. A fair adversary process presupposes both a vigorous prosecution and a vigorous defense. It cannot be lightly assumed that in enacting § 706(k), Congress intended to distort that process by giving the private plaintiff substantial incentives to sue, while foreclosing to the defendant the possibility of recovering his expenses in resisting even a groundless action unless he can show that it was brought in bad faith.

B

The sparse legislative history of § 706(k) reveals little more than the barest outlines of a proper accommodation of the competing considerations we have discussed. The only specific reference to § 706(k) in the legislative debates indicates that the fee provision was included to "make it easier for a plaintiff of limited means to bring a meritorious suit." During the Senate floor discussions of the almost identical attorney's fee provision of Title II, however, several Senators explained that its allowance of awards to defendants would serve "to deter the bringing of lawsuits without foundation," "to discourage frivolous suits," and "to diminish the likelihood of unjustified suits being brought." If anything can be gleaned from these fragments of legislative history, it is that while Congress wanted to clear the way for suits to be brought under the Act, it also wanted to protect defendants from burdensome litigation having no legal or factual basis. The Court of Appeals for the District of Columbia Circuit seems to have drawn the maximum significance from the Senate debates when it concluded:

> "[From these debates] two purposes for § 706(k) emerge. First, Congress desired to 'make it easier for a plaintiff of limited means to bring a meritorious suit' * * *. But second, and equally important, Congress intended to 'deter the bringing of lawsuits without foundation' by providing that the 'prevailing party'—be it plaintiff or defendant—could obtain legal fees." Grubbs v. Butz, 79 U.S.App. D.C. 18, 20, 548 F.2d 973, 975.

The first federal appellate court to consider what criteria should govern the award of attorney's fees to a prevailing Title VII defendant was the Court of Appeals for the Third Circuit in United States Steel Corp. v. United States, 519 F.2d 359. There a District Court had denied a fee award to a defendant that had successfully resisted a Commission demand for documents, the court finding that the Commission's action had not been "'unfounded, meritless, frivolous or vexatiously brought.'" Id., at 363. The Court of Appeals concluded that the District Court had not abused its discretion in denying the award. Id., at 365. A similar standard was adopted by the Court of Appeals for the Second Circuit in Carrion v. Yeshiva University, 535 F.2d 722. In upholding an attorney's fee award to a successful defendant, that court stated that such awards should be permitted "not routinely, not simply because he succeeds, but only where the action brought is found to be unreasonable, frivolous, meritless or vexatious." Id., at 727.

To the extent that abstract words can deal with concrete cases, we think that the concept embodied in the language adopted by these two Courts of Appeals is correct. We would qualify their words only by pointing out that the term "meritless" is to be understood as meaning groundless or without foundation, rather than simply that the plaintiff has ultimately lost his case, and that the term "vexatious" in no way implies that the plaintiff's subjective bad faith is a necessary prerequisite to a fee award against him. In sum, a district court may in its discretion award attorney's fees to a prevailing defendant in a Title VII case upon a finding that the plaintiff's action was frivolous, unreasonable, or without foundation, even though not brought in subjective bad faith.

In applying these criteria, it is important that a district court resist the understandable temptation to engage in post hoc reasoning by concluding that because a plaintiff did not ultimately prevail, his action must have been unreasonable or without foundation. This kind of hindsight logic could discourage all but the most airtight claims, for seldom can a prospective plaintiff be sure of ultimate success. No matter how honest one's belief that he has been the victim of discrimination, no matter how meritorious one's claim may appear at the outset, the course of litigation is rarely predictable. Decisive facts may not emerge until discovery or trial. The law may change or clarify in the midst of litigation. Even when the law or the facts appear questionable or unfavorable at the outset, a party may have an entirely reasonable ground for bringing suit.

That § 706(k) allows fee awards only to *prevailing* private plaintiffs should assure that this statutory provision will not in itself operate as an incentive to the bringing of claims that have little chance of success. To take the further step of assessing attorney's fees against plaintiffs simply because they do not finally prevail would substantially add to the risks inhering in most litigation and would undercut the efforts of Congress to promote the vigorous enforcement of the provisions of Title VII. Hence, a plaintiff should not be assessed his opponent's attorney's fees unless a court finds that his claim was frivolous, unreasonable, or groundless, or that the plaintiff continued to litigate after it clearly became so. And, needless to say, if a plaintiff is found to have brought or continued such a claim in *bad faith*, there will be an even stronger basis for charging him with the attorney's fees incurred by the defense.[20]

20. Initially, the Commission argued that the "costs" assessable against the Government under § 706(k) did not include attorney's fees. See, e.g., United States Steel Corp. v. United States, 519 F.2d 359, 362 (CA3); Van Hoomissen v. Xerox Corp., 503 F.2d 1131, 1132–1133 (CA9). But the Courts of Appeals rejected this position and, during the course of appealing this case, the Commission abandoned its contention that it was legally immune to adverse fee awards under § 706(k). 550 F.2d, at 951.

It has been urged that fee awards against the Commission should rest on a standard different from that governing fee awards against private plaintiffs. One amicus stresses that the Commission, unlike private litigants, needs no inducement to enforce Title VII since it is required by statute to do so. But this distinction between the Commission and private plaintiffs merely explains why Congress drafted § 706(k) to preclude the recovery of attorney's fees by the Commission; it does not support a difference in treatment among private and Government plaintiffs when a prevailing defendant seeks to recover his attorney's fees. Several courts and commentators have also deemed significant the

IV

In denying attorney's fees to the company in this case, the District Court focused on the standards we have discussed. The court found that "the Commission's action in bringing the suit cannot be characterized as unreasonable or meritless" because "the basis upon which petitioner prevailed was an issue of first impression requiring judicial resolution" and because the "Commission's statutory interpretation of § 14 of the 1972 amendments was not frivolous." The court thus exercised its discretion squarely within the permissible bounds of § 706(k). Accordingly, the judgment of the Court of Appeals upholding the decision of the District Court is affirmed.

It is so ordered.

MR. JUSTICE BLACKMUN took no part in the consideration or decision of this case.

NOTES AND PROBLEMS FOR DISCUSSION

1. Under *Christianburg Garment,* should an employer ever be entitled to fees if the plaintiff has been able to establish a prima facie case? See, Glymph v. Spartanburg General Hospital, 783 F.2d 476 (4th Cir. 1986); EEOC v. Tarrant Distributors, Inc., 750 F.2d 1249 (5th Cir. 1984). Can the plaintiff's good faith in initiation of the litigation preclude an award of fees to the prevailing employer? Compare, Lane v. Sotheby Parke Bernet, Inc., 758 F.2d 71 (2d Cir. 1985) (district court which denied fees to employer on ground that plaintiff had pled nonfrivolous cause of action erred in failing to determine whether plaintiff should have continued action once discovery was complete); Eichman v. Linden & Sons, Inc., 752 F.2d 1246 (7th Cir. 1985) (fact that employee filed suit in face of EEOC's determination of no probable cause does not necessarily compel conclusion that action was frivolous); Charves v. Western Union Telegraph Co., 711 F.2d 462 (1st Cir. 1983) (a favorable EEOC evaluation of charge does not insure that court will not later conclude that case was frivolous and without foundation).

Government's greater ability to pay adverse fee awards compared to a private litigant. See, e.g., United States Steel Corp. v. United States, supra, 519 F.2d, at 364 n. 24; Heinsz, Attorney's Fees for Prevailing Title VII Defendants: Toward a Workable Standard, 8 U.Toledo L.Rev. 259, 290 (1977); Comment, Title VII, Civil Rights Act of 1964; Standards for Award of Attorney's Fees to Prevailing Defendants, 1976 Wis.L.Rev. 207, 228. We are informed, however, that such awards must be paid from the Commission's litigation budget, so that every attorney's fee assessment against the Commission will inevitably divert resources from the agency's enforcement of Title VII. See 46 Comp.Gen. 98, 100 (1966); 38 Comp.Gen. 343, 344–345 (1958). The other side of this coin is the fact that many defendants in Title VII claims are small- and moderate-size employers for whom the expense of defending even a frivolous claim may become a strong disincentive to the exercise of their legal rights. In short, there are equitable considerations on both sides of this question. Yet § 706(k) explicitly provides that "the Commission and the United States shall be liable for costs the same as a private person." Hence, although a district court may consider distinctions between the Commission and private plaintiffs in determining the reasonableness of the Commission's litigation efforts, we find no grounds for applying a different general standard whenever the Commission is the losing plaintiff.

Without stating so explicitly, *Christianburg Garment* suggests that, as an initial hurdle for obtaining fees, the prevailing employer would have to have been completely successful. The Fifth Circuit has indicated, however, that a defendant that has agreed to provide monetary and injunctive relief to a class of employees in a settlement may still qualify for an award of fees. In Commonwealth Oil Refining Co. v. EEOC, 720 F.2d 1383 (5th Cir. 1983), after six years of litigation the case was settled in a consent decree under which the employer changed certain of its challenged practices, began affirmative recruitment of minorities and provided a fund of one million dollars to satisfy individual back pay claims to be made to a special master who was also empowered to order preferential hiring and retroactive seniority. After the consent decree was finalized, the company sued the EEOC to recover $525,000 in counsel fees on the theory that it, not the Commission, had prevailed in the litigation because the settlement provided no relief for many of the employment practices initially challenged and that the final result was less relief than had been offered the EEOC in earlier negotiations. The district court granted summary judgment against the company. The Court of Appeals reversed and remanded for a hearing at which the district court was to weigh the claims made by the EEOC against the relief obtained to determine if Commonwealth was the prevailing party.

> In many, if not most lawsuits, whether tried or settled, it is possible to compare the allegations made with the results obtained and pick a winner: a plaintiff who carried the day on his major claim, a defendant who defected the major thrust of the lawsuit.

720 F.2d at 1385–86. A dissent characterized the majority opinion as "[i]gnoring controlling precedent of the Supreme Court, as well as flouting common sense * * *" Can the decision be reconciled with *Christianburg Garment?*

2. Where a defendant has established entitlement to fees, should its award be calculated in the same manner as that of a prevailing plaintiff? Most courts that have addressed the issue have ruled that the financial condition of the plaintiff should be taken into account in fixing the fee. See e.g., Durrett v. Jenkins Brickyard Inc., 678 F.2d 911 (11th Cir. 1982) (in light of plaintiff's ability to pay, reduced fee will fulfill the deterrent purpose of the Act without subjecting plaintiff to financial ruin); Faraci v. Hickey-Freeman Co., 607 F.2d 1025 (2d Cir. 1979) (abuse of discretion for district court not to take into account financial resources of plaintiff: fee of $200 dollars assessed instead of $11,500 awarded in lower court); Colucci v. New York Times Co., 533 F.Supp. 1011 (S.D. N.Y.1982) (defendant awarded $1,500 where $10,000 fee claimed by employer would force plaintiff into bankruptcy). Compare, Arnold v. Burger King Corp., 719 F.2d 63 (4th Cir. 1983), cert. denied, 469 U.S. 826, 105 S.Ct. 108, 83 L.Ed.2d 51 (1984) (not an abuse of discretion for for court to award full lodestar fee to employer given plaintiff's financial ability to pay); Charves v. Western Union Telegraph Co., supra, ($25,000 award upheld on ground that it would not completely ruin plaintiff financially). By contrast, the weak financial condition of a defendant has not been considered a factor in assessing fees. See, Jones v. Local 4B, Graphic Arts International Union, 595 F.Supp. 792 (D.D.C.1984); McPherson v. School District # 186, 465 F.Supp. 749 (S.D.Ill.1978).

3. The uncertain financial condition of many employment discrimination plaintiffs may frustrate the collection of any kind of an award made to a defendant and awards against plaintiffs do not have the kind of *in terrorem* effect often sought by prevailing defendants. These factors have resulted in

efforts to assess fees and costs against unsuccessful plaintiffs' counsel. In ROADWAY EXPRESS INC. v. PIPER, 447 U.S. 752, 100 S.Ct. 2455, 65 L.Ed.2d 488 (1980), the defendant argued that an award of fees should be shifted to plaintiffs' lawyers under Title VII and 28 U.S.C. § 1927, which allows the assessment of excess "costs" against attorneys who vexatiously multiply court proceedings. The Supreme Court construed "costs" under § 1927 not to include attorney fees and held that only a party may be assessed attorney fees under § 706(k) or § 1988. The Court noted, however, that in "narrowly defined circumstances federal courts have inherent power to assess attorney's fees against counsel" for abusive litigation practices. 447 U.S. at 765, 100 S.Ct. at 2463. After *Piper,* Congress amended § 1927 to expressly provide that an attorney who multiplies court proceedings "unreasonably or vexatiously may be required to satisfy personally the excess costs, expenses, and attorney's fees reasonably incurred because of such conduct." Pub.L. No. 96–349, § 3, 94 Stat. 1154, 1156 (Sept. 12, 1980). Acting under § 1927 or Rule 11 of the Federal Rules of Civil Procedure (which provides for sanctions including the assessment of attorney fees against attorneys who file pleadings not "well grounded in fact" or "warranted by existing law"), courts have increasingly made awards against counsel deemed responsible for frivolous or bad faith law suits. See e.g., Lewis v. Brown & Root, Inc., 711 F.2d 1287 (5th Cir. 1983), cert. denied, 467 U.S. 1231, 104 S.Ct. 2690, 81 L.Ed.2d 884 (1984) (irresponsible manner in which litigation conducted further multiplied needless proceedings); Morris v. Adams-Millis Corp., 758 F.2d 1352 (10th Cir. 1985) (fees awarded against counsel who commenced action without sufficient legal basis, continued to prosecute action when it was clear no grounds for prosecution would develop and abandoned client's cause when if became clear that defendant would not respond with nuisance value settlement of sufficient magnitude to justify his further involvement); Steinberg v. St. Regis/Sheraton Hotel, 583 F.Supp. 421 (S.D.N.Y.1984) ($10,000 award against lawyer who would have discovered that no factual basis for Title VII claim existed had he conducted minimal investigation). Cf. Textor v. Board of Regents, 711 F.2d 1387 (7th Cir. 1983) (lawyer should not be assessed fees without prior hearing to show that he acted in bad faith or otherwise abused judicial process so as to justify sanction). See also, Cochran, *Sanctions Under Rule 11,* 3 Fifth Cir.Rptr. 209 (1986).

PROBLEMS INVOLVING THE SETTLEMENT OF ATTORNEY FEE CLAIMS

Plaintiff's counsel in an employment discrimination, or other action where a fee-shifting statute is applicable, is in a markedly different position during settlement negotiations than a plaintiff's lawyer who is either paid by his client or who has a standard contingent fee contract which guarantees him a percentage of the recovery. Where the attorney looks to the defendant for his fee and must negotiate for his client and himself at the same time, there is the potential for a conflict of interest.

> [I]t is axiomatic that the overwhelming concern of counsel for the defendant in considering a proposed compromise is the total dollar cost of settlement. The defendant is uninterested in what portion of the total payment will go to the class and what percentage will go [to] the attorney. * * * [T]he spectre persists, absent appropriate judicial inquiry, that plaintiff's attorney may accept an insufficient judgment for the class in trade for immediate and certain compensation for himself in the form of legal fees deducted from the

> total available funds proffered by defendant. The actual presence and the potential consequences of such conflict of interest cannot be ignored.

Foster v. Boise-Cascade, Inc., 420 F.Supp. 674, 686 (S.D.Tex.1976), aff'd, 577 F.2d 335 (5th Cir. 1978). In recognition of the potential conflict, a number of courts have expressed disapproval of the simultaneous negotiation of the merits of the case and fees. See, Obin v. District No. 9 International Association of Machinists and Aerospace Workers, 651 F.2d 574, 582 (8th Cir. 1981) (counsel should not be "placed in the position of negotiating a fee ultimately destined for his pocket at the same time that all thoughts ought to be singlemindedly focused on the client's interests"); Prandini v. National Tea Co., 557 F.2d 1015, 1021 (3d Cir. 1977) ("Only after court approval of the damage settlement should discussion and negotiation of appropriate compensation for the attorneys begin."). The Bar Associations of the City of New York and of the District of Columbia have declared it unethical for defense counsel to attempt simultaneous negotiation of fees with the merits or to propose settlements conditioned on the waiver of fees authorized by fee-shifting statutes. Bar Ass'n of the City of New York, Committee on Professional and Judicial Ethics, Opinion No. 80–94 (Sept. 18, 1980); District of Columbia Bar Legal Ethics Committee, Op.No. 147 (1985). See generally, Calhoun, Attorney-Client Conflicts of Interest and the Concept of Non-Negotiable Fee Awards Under 42 U.S.C. § 1988, 55 U.Colo.L.Rev. 341 (1984); Comment, Settlement Offers Conditioned Upon Waiver of Attorneys' Fees: Policy, Legal and Ethical Considerations, 131 U.Pa.L.Rev. 793 (1983).

The Supreme Court has now rejected the idea that courts can prevent simultaneous negotiations and set aside fee waivers which are coerced by defendants. In EVANS v. JEFF D., ___ U.S. ___, 106 S.Ct. 1531, 89 L.Ed.2d 747 (1986) defendants proposed a settlement of a class action attacking institutional conditions and health care of emotionally handicapped children by the State of Idaho, conditioned on a complete waiver of attorney fees by class counsel. Counsel agreed to the settlement because he felt no better relief could be obtained through litigation, but then moved the district court to award fees despite the settlement because the waiver had been coerced. The district court denied the motion but the Ninth Circuit reversed, holding that courts in class actions could not approve coerced waiver of fees. The Court of Appeals also stated that ordinarily simultaneous negotiations were improper. The Supreme Court reversed the Ninth Circuit.

The Supreme Court ruled that, in the first place, the simultaneous negotiation of the merits and fees is not legally improper. "We agree that when the parties find such negotiations conducive to settlement, the public interest, as well as that of the parties, is served by simultaneous negotiations." ___ U.S. at ___, 106 S.Ct. at 1543 n. 30. With regard to the waiver issue, the Court could find nothing in the language or history of Section 1988 that mandated payment to successful counsel. On the other hand a general prohibition against attorney fee waivers in exchange for settlement would, according to the Court, actually "impede vindication of civil rights, at least in some cases, by reducing the attractiveness of settlement." ___ U.S. at ___, 106 S.Ct. at 1540. The Court recognized the difficulty faced by plaintiff's counsel but could see no "ethical dilemma" because the lawyer "had no *ethical* obligation to seek a statutory fee award." ___ U.S. at ___, 106 S.Ct. at 1537. The Court indeed suggested that the attorney would have acted unethically had he turned down the favorable offer because of the demand that fees be waived. Ibid.

In a dissent Justice Brennan, joined by Justices Marshall and Blackmun, criticized the majority's opinion as undermining the effectiveness of the fee-shifting statutes in encouraging of attorneys to take on civil rights cases.

> The cumulative effect this practice (coerced waivers) will have on the civil rights bar is evident. It does not denigrate the high ideals that motivate many civil rights practitioners to recognize that lawyers are in the business of practicing law, and that, like other business people, they are and must be concerned with earning a living. The conclusion that permitting fee waivers will seriously impair the ability of civil rights plaintiffs to obtain legal assistance is embarrassingly obvious.

— U.S. at —, 106 S.Ct. at 1553. Can plaintiff's counsel solve the problem, or at least shift the burden of the problem, by entering into retainer agreements which make the client ultimately responsible for fees in the event of a successful resolution of the case where fees are for any reason not awarded? Could such a strategy be used in a class action?

Another problem increasingly faced by plaintiff's counsel results from offers of judgment under Rule 68 of the Federal Rules of Civil Procedure which allows the defendant to serve on the plaintiff an offer to "allow judgment to be taken against him for the money or property or to the effect specified in his offer, with costs then accrued." If the offer is rejected and "the judgment finally obtained by the offeree is not more favorable than the offer, the offeree must pay the costs incurred after the making of the offer." In MAREK v. CHESNY, 473 U.S. —, 105 S.Ct. 3012, 87 L.Ed.2d 1 (1985), the Court held that the word "costs" in Rule 68 encompasses fees awarded under the fee-shifting statutes. Thus, where the defendant makes an offer to plaintiff before trial inclusive of fees, and the plaintiff subsequently recovers less than the amount offered, the court may deny all counsel fees incurred after the date of the offer. A proposed revision of Rule 68 would allow the court to impose sanctions, including attorney's fees, on an offeree who unreasonably declines an offer of settlement. See, Advisory Committee on Civil Rules, Preliminary Draft, 102 F.R.D. 432, 437 (1984). How would such a rule impact on litigation under the fee-shifting statutes? Would the sanction have any practical meaning for a defendant who unreasonably rejected a plaintiff's offer?

Chapter 16

AFFIRMATIVE ACTION

Read §§ 703(j) and 706(g) of Title VII.

Section 706(g) of Title VII provides that if a defendant is found to have intentionally engaged in or be intentionally engaging in an unlawful employment practice, the court may "order such affirmative action as may be appropriate, which may include, but is not limited to, reinstatement or hiring of employees * * * or any other equitable relief as the court deems appropriate." This remedial provision has generated several of the most complex and controversial issues in the entire field of employment discrimination law. The questions raised by the use of affirmative action fall into two broad categories. First, to what extent, if any, will a court's exercise of this statutory remedial authority conflict with the antidiscrimination provisions of § 703, the anti-preferential treatment mandate of § 703(j), the protection afforded seniority systems by § 703(h), or the equal protection guarantees of the Fifth or Fourteenth Amendments? Second, will any of these statutory or constitutional provisions be violated if an employer or union undertakes an affirmative action program on a voluntary basis?

LOCAL 28 OF SHEET METAL WORKERS v. EEOC

Supreme Court of the United States, 1986.
___ U.S. ___, 106 S.Ct. 3019, 92 L.Ed.2d 344.

JUSTICE BRENNAN announced the judgment of the Court and delivered the opinion of the Court with respect to Parts I, II, III, and VI, and an opinion with respect to Parts IV, V, and VII in which JUSTICE MARSHALL, JUSTICE BLACKMUN, and JUSTICE STEVENS join.

In 1975, petitioners were found guilty of engaging in a pattern and practice of discrimination against black and Hispanic individuals (nonwhites) in violation of Title VII of the Civil Rights Act of 1964, and ordered to end their discriminatory practices, and to admit a certain percentage of nonwhites to union membership by July 1982. In 1982 and again in 1983, petitioners were found guilty of civil contempt for disobeying the District Court's earlier orders. They now challenge the District Court's contempt finding, and also the remedies the court ordered both for the Title VII violation and for contempt. Principally, the issue presented is whether the remedial provision of Title VII, see 42 U.S.C. 2000e–5(g), empowers a district court to order race-conscious relief that may benefit individuals who are not identified victims of unlawful discrimination.

I

Petitioner Local 28 of the Sheet Metal Workers' International Association (Local 28) represents sheet metal workers employed by contractors in the New York City metropolitan area. Petitioner Local 28 Joint Apprenticeship Committee (JAC) is a management-labor committee which operates a 4-year apprenticeship training program designed to teach sheet metal skills. Apprentices enrolled in the program receive training both from classes and from on the job work experience. Upon completing the program, apprentices become journeyman members of Local 28. Successful completion of the program is the principal means of attaining union membership.[1]

In 1964, the New York State Commission for Human Rights determined that petitioners had excluded blacks from the union and the apprenticeship program in violation of state law. The State Commission found, among other things, that Local 28 had never had any black members or apprentices, and that "admission to apprenticeship is conducted largely on a nepot[is]tic basis involving sponsorship by incumbent union members," creating an impenetrable barrier for nonwhite applicants.[2] Petitioners were ordered to "cease and desist" their racially discriminatory practices. The New York State Supreme Court affirmed the State Commission's findings, and directed petitioners to implement objective standards for selecting apprentices. State Comm'n for Human Rights v. Farrell, 43 Misc.2d 958, 252 N.Y.S.2d 649 (1964).

When the court's orders proved ineffective, the State commission commenced other state-court proceedings in an effort to end petitioners' discriminatory practices. Petitioners had originally agreed to indenture two successive classes of apprentices using nondiscriminatory selection procedures, but stopped processing applications for the second apprentice class, thus requiring that the State Commission seek a court order requiring petitioners to indenture the apprentices. The court subsequently denied the union's request to reduce the size of the second apprentice class, and chastized the union for refusing "except for token gestures, to further the integration process." Petitioners proceeded to disregard the results of the selection test for a third apprentice class on the ground that nonwhites had received "unfair tutoring" and had passed in unreasonably high numbers. The state court ordered petitioners to indenture the apprentices based on the examination results.

1. In addition to completing the apprenticeship program, an individual can gain membership in Local 28 by (1) transferring directly from a "sister" union; (2) passing a battery of journeyman level tests administered by the union; and (3) gaining admission at the time a nonunion sheet metal shop is organized by Local 28. In addition, during periods of full employment, Local 28 issues temporary work permits which allow nonmembers to work within its jurisdiction.

2. The Sheet Metal Workers' International Union was formed in 1888, under a Constitution which provided for the establishment of "white local unions" and relegated blacks to membership in subordinate locals. Local 28 was established in 1913 as a "white local union." Although racial restrictions were formally deleted from the International Constitution in 1946, Local 28 refused to admit blacks until 1969.

In 1971, the United States initiated this action under Title VII and Executive Order 11246, 3 CFR 339 (1964–1965 Comp.) to enjoin petitioners from engaging in a pattern and practice of discrimination against black and Hispanic individuals (nonwhites).[3] The New York City Commission on Human Rights (City) intervened as plaintiff to press claims that petitioners had violated municipal fair employment laws, and had frustrated the City's efforts to increase job opportunities for minorities in the construction industry. In 1970, the City had adopted a plan requiring contractors on its projects to employ one minority trainee for every four journeyman union members. Local 28 was the only construction local which refused to comply voluntarily with the plan. In early 1974, the City attempted to assign six minority trainees to sheet metal contractors working on municipal construction projects. After Local 28 members stopped work on the projects, the District Court directed the JAC to admit the six trainees into the apprenticeship program, and enjoined Local 28 from causing any work stoppage at the affected job sites. The parties subsequently agreed to a consent order that required the JAC to admit up to 40 minorities into the apprenticeship program by September 1974. The JAC stalled compliance with the consent order, and only completed the indenture process under threat of contempt.

Following a trial in 1975, the District Court concluded that petitioners had violated both Title VII and New York law by discriminating against nonwhite workers in recruitment, selection, training, and admission to the union. 401 F.Supp. 467 (1975). Noting that as of July 1, 1974, only 3.19% of the union's total membership, including apprentices and journeymen, was nonwhite, the court found that petitioners had denied qualified nonwhites access to union membership through a variety of discriminatory practices. First, the court found that petitioners had adopted discriminatory procedures and standards for admission into the apprenticeship program. The court examined some of the factors used to select apprentices, including the entrance examination and high-school diploma requirement, and determined that these criteria had an adverse discriminatory impact on nonwhites, and were not related to job performance. The court also observed that petitioners had used union funds to subsidize special training sessions for friends and relatives of union members taking the apprenticeship examination.[4]

Second, the court determined that Local 28 had restricted the size of its membership in order to deny access to nonwhites. The court found that Local 28 had refused to administer yearly journeymen's examina-

3. The Equal Employment Opportunity Commission was substituted as named plaintiff in this case. The Sheet Metal and Air Conditioning Contractors' Association of New York City (Contractor's Association) was also named as a defendant. The New York State Division of Human Rights (State), although joined as a third and fourth-party defendant in this action, realigned itself as a plaintiff.

4. The court also noted that petitioners' failure to comply with EEOC regulations requiring them to keep records of each applicant's race had made it difficult for the court to evaluate the discriminatory impact of petitioners' selection procedures.

tions despite a growing demand for members' services.[5] Rather, to meet this increase in demand, Local 28 recalled pensioners who obtained doctors' certificates that they were able to work, and issued hundreds of temporary work permits to nonmembers; only one of these permits was issued to a nonwhite. Moreover, the court found that "despite the fact that Local 28 saw fit to request [temporary workers] from sister locals all across the country, as well as from allied New York construction unions such as plumbers, carpenters, and iron workers, it never once sought them from Sheet Metal Local 400," a New York City union comprised almost entirely of nonwhites. The court concluded that by using the temporary permit system rather than continuing to administer journeymen's tests, Local 28 successfully restricted the size of its membership with the "illegal effect, if not the intention, of denying non-whites access to employment opportunities in the industry." Ibid.

Third, the District Court determined that Local 28 had selectively organized nonunion sheet metal shops with few, if any, minority employees, and admitted to membership only white employees from those shops. The court found that "[p]rior to 1973 no non-white ever became a member of Local 28 through the organization of a non-union shop." The court also found that, despite insistent pressure from both the International Union and local contractors, Local 28 had stubbornly refused to organize sheet metal workers in the local blowpipe industry because a large percentage of such workers were nonwhite.

Finally, the court found that Local 28 had discriminated in favor of white applicants seeking to transfer from sister locals. The court noted that from 1967 through 1972, Local 28 had accepted 57 transfers from sister locals, all of them white, and that it was only after this litigation had commenced that Local 28 accepted its first nonwhite transfers, two journeymen from Local 400. The court also found that on one occasion, the union's president had incorrectly told nonwhite Local 400 members that they were not eligible for transfer.

The District Court entered an order and judgment (O & J) enjoining petitioners from discriminating against nonwhites, and enjoining the specific practices the court had found to be discriminatory. Recognizing that "the record in both state and federal court against these defendants is replete with instances of * * * bad faith attempts to prevent or delay affirmative action,"[6] the court concluded that "the

5. The Court noted that Local 28 had offered journeymen's examinations in 1968 and 1969 as a result of arbitration proceedings initiated by the Contractors' Association to force Local 28 to increase its manpower. Only 24 of 330 individuals, all of them white, passed the first examination and were admitted to the union. The court found that this examination had an adverse impact on nonwhites and had not been validated in accordance with EEOC guidelines, and was therefore violative of Title VII. Some nonwhites did pass the second examination, and the court concluded that Local 28's failure to keep records of the number of white and nonwhites tested made it impossible to determine whether that test had also had an adverse impact on nonwhites.

6. The court remarked:

"After [state] Justice Markowitz [in the 1964 state-court proceeding] ordered implementation of [a plan intended to] cre-

imposition of a remedial racial goal in conjunction with an admission preference in favor of non-whites is essential to place the defendants in a position of compliance with [Title VII]." The court established a 29% nonwhite membership goal, based on the percentage of nonwhites in the relevant labor pool in New York City, for the union to achieve by July 1, 1981. The parties were ordered to devise and to implement recruitment and admission procedures designed to achieve this goal under the supervision of a court-appointed administrator.[7]

The administrator proposed, and the court adopted, an Affirmative Action Program which, among other things, required petitioners to offer annual, nondiscriminatory journeyman and apprentice examinations, select members according to a white-nonwhite ratio to be negotiated by the parties, conduct extensive recruitment and publicity campaigns aimed at minorities,[8] secure the administrator's consent before issuing temporary work permits, and maintain detailed membership records, including separate records for whites and nonwhites. Local 28 was permitted to extend any of the benefits of the program to whites and other minorities, provided that this did not interfere with the program's operation.

The Court of Appeals for the Second Circuit affirmed the District Court's determination of liability, finding that petitioners had "consistently and egregiously violated Title VII." 532 F.2d 821, 825 (1976). The court upheld the 29% nonwhite membership goal as a temporary remedy, justified by a "long and persistent pattern of discrimination," and concluded that the appointment of an administrator with broad powers was clearly appropriate, given petitioners' refusal to change their membership practices in the face of prior state and federal court orders. However, the court modified the District Court's order to permit the use of a white-nonwhite ratio for the apprenticeship program only pending implementation of valid, job-related entrance tests. Local 28 did not seek certiorari in this Court to review the Court of Appeals' judgment.

ate a 'truly nondiscriminatory union[,]' Local 28 flouted the court's mandate by expending union funds to subsidize special training sessions designed to give union members' friends and relatives a competitive edge in taking the [apprenticeship examination]. JAC obtained an exemption from state affirmative action regulations directed towards the administration of apprentice programs on the ground that its program was operating pursuant to court order; yet Justice Markowitz had specifically provided that all such subsequent regulations, to the extent not inconsistent with his order, were to be incorporated therein and applied to JAC's program. More recently, the defendants unilaterally suspended court-ordered time tables for admission of forty non-whites to the apprentice program pending trial of this action, only completing the admission process under threat of contempt citations." 401 F.Supp., at 488.

7. The O & J also awarded backpay to those nonwhites who could demonstrate that they were discriminatorily excluded from union membership.

8. The District Court had concluded that petitioners had earned a well-deserved reputation for discriminating against nonwhites, and that this reputation "operated and still operates to discourage non-whites seeking membership in the local union or its apprenticeship program." The publicity campaign was consequently designed to dispel this reputation, and to encourage nonwhites to take advantage of opportunities for union membership.

On remand, the District Court adopted a Revised Affirmative Action Program and Order (RAAPO) to incorporate the Court of Appeals' mandate. RAAPO also modified the original Affirmative Action Program to accommodate petitioners' claim that economic problems facing the construction industry had made it difficult for them to comply with the court's orders. Petitioners were given an additional year to meet the 29% membership goal. RAAPO also established interim membership goals designed to "afford the parties and the Administrator with some device to measure progress so that, if warranted, other provisions of the program could be modified to reflect change (sic) circumstances." The JAC was directed to indenture at least 36 apprentices by February 1977, and to determine the size of future apprenticeship classes subject to review by the administrator.[9] A divided panel of the Court of Appeals affirmed RAAPO in its entirety, including the 29% nonwhite membership goal. 565 F.2d 31 (1977). Petitioners again chose not to seek certiorari from this Court to review the Court of Appeals' judgment.

In April 1982, the City and State moved in the District Court for an order holding petitioners in contempt.[10] They alleged that petitioners had not achieved RAAPO's 29% nonwhite membership goal, and that this failure was due to petitioners' numerous violations of the O & J, RAAPO, and orders of the administrator. The District Court, after receiving detailed evidence of how the O & J and RAAPO had operated over the previous six years, held petitioners in civil contempt. The court did not rest its contempt finding on petitioners' failure to meet the 29% membership goal, although nonwhite membership in Local 28 was only 10.8% at the time of the hearing. Instead, the court found that petitioners had "failed to comply with RAAPO * * * almost from its date of entry," identifying six "separate actions or omissions on the part of the defendants [that] have impeded the entry of non-whites into Local 28 in contravention of the prior orders of this court." Specifically, the court determined that petitioners had (1) adopted a policy of underutilizing the apprenticeship program in order to limit nonwhite membership and employment opportunities; [11] (2) refused to conduct the general publicity campaign required by the O & J and RAAPO to inform nonwhites of

9. The Affirmative Action Program originally had required the JAC to indenture at least 300 apprentices by July 1, 1976, and at least 200 apprentices in each year thereafter, up to and including 1981. These figures were adjusted downward after petitioners complained that economic conditions made it impossible for them to indenture this number of apprentices. The District Court also permitted petitioners to defer administration of the journeyman's examination for the same reason.

10. The Contractor's Association and individual Local 28 contractors were also named as respondents to the contempt proceeding.

11. The court explained that the "journeymen benefiting from this policy of underutilizing the apprenticeship program comprise Local 28's white incumbent membership." The court rejected Local 28's contention that any underutilization of the apprenticeship program could be blamed on difficult economic circumstances, emphasizing that the court had "not overlooked the obstacles or problems with which [petitioners] have had to contend," and that it had "given much consideration to the economic condition of the sheet metal trade in particular and the construction industry in general over the past six years."

membership opportunities; (3) added a job protection provision to the union's collective-bargaining agreement that favored older workers and discriminated against nonwhites (older workers provision); (4) issued unauthorized work permits to white workers from sister locals; and (5) failed to maintain and submit records and reports required by RAAPO, the O & J, and the administrator, thus making it difficult to monitor petitioners' compliance with the court's orders.

To remedy petitioners' contempt, the court imposed a $150,000 fine to be placed in a fund designed to increase nonwhite membership in the apprenticeship program and the union. The administrator was directed to propose a plan for utilizing the fund. The court deferred imposition of further coercive fines pending receipt of the administrator's recommendations for modifications to RAAPO.[12]

In 1983, the City brought a second contempt proceeding before the administrator, charging petitioners with additional violations of the O & J, RAAPO, and various administrative orders. The administrator found that the JAC had violated RAAPO by failing to submit accurate reports of hours worked by apprentices, thus preventing the court from evaluating whether non-white apprentices had shared in available employment opportunities, and that Local 28 had: (1) failed, in a timely manner, to provide the racial and ethnic data required by the O & J and RAAPO with respect to new members entering the union as a result of its merger with five predominately white sheet metal locals, (2) failed to serve copies of the O & J and RAAPO on contractors employing Local 28 members, as ordered by the administrator, and (3) submitted inaccurate racial membership records.[13]

The District Court adopted the administrator's findings and once again adjudicated petitioners guilty of civil contempt. The court ordered petitioners to pay for a computerized recordkeeping system to be maintained by outside consultants, but deferred ruling on additional contempt fines pending submission of the administrator's fund proposal. The court subsequently adopted the administrator's proposed Employment, Training, Education, and Recruitment Fund (Fund) to "be used for the purpose of remedying discrimination." The Fund was used for a variety of purposes. In order to increase the pool of qualified

12. The District Court found it necessary to modify RAAPO in light of the fact that the 29% nonwhite membership goal was no longer viable on the present timetable, and also because five other locals with predominantly white memberships had recently merged with Local 28. The court denied petitioners cross-motion for an order terminating both the O & J and RAAPO, finding that these orders had not caused petitioners unexpected or undue hardship.

13. The administrator's comments revealed that he was more concerned with Local 28's "inability to provide accurate data" than with the specific errors he had discovered. He emphasized that Local 28 had "no formal system to verify the racial and ethnic composition of [its] membership," and that "[s]uch verification that was done, was done on a totally haphazard basis." He concluded that "[t]he lack of any proper verification controls confirms * * * that Local 28 has not acted in the affirmative manner contemplated by the court." More generally, he observed that "[t]he violations found herein cannot be viewed in isolation, rather they must be seen as part of a pattern of disregard for state and federal court orders and as a continuation of conduct which led the court to find defendants in contempt."

nonwhite applicants for the apprenticeship program, the Fund paid for nonwhite union members to serve as liaisons to vocational and technical schools with sheet metal programs, created part-time and summer sheet metal jobs for qualified nonwhite youths, and extended financial assistance to needy apprentices. The Fund also extended counseling and tutorial services to nonwhite apprentices, giving them the benefits that had traditionally been available to white apprentices from family and friends. Finally, in an effort to maximize employment opportunities for all apprentices, the Fund provided financial support to employers otherwise unable to hire a sufficient number of apprentices, as well as matching funds to attract additional funding for job training programs.[14]

The District Court also entered an Amended Affirmative Action Plan and Order (AAAPO) which modified RAAPO in several respects. AAAPO established a 29.23% minority membership goal to be met by August 31, 1987. The new goal was based on the labor pool in the area covered by the newly expanded union. The court abolished the apprenticeship examination, concluding that "the violations that have occurred in the past have been so egregious that a new approach must be taken to solve the apprentice selection problem." Apprentices were to be selected by a three-member Board, which would select one minority apprentice for each white apprentice indentured. Finally, to prevent petitioners from underutilizing the apprenticeship program, the JAC was required to assign to Local 28 contractors one apprentice for every four journeymen, unless the contractor obtained a written waiver from respondents.

Petitioners appealed the District Court's contempt orders, the Fund order, and the order adopting AAAPO.[15] A divided panel of the Court of Appeals affirmed the District Court's contempt findings,[16] except the finding based on adoption of the older workers' provision.[17] The court

14. The Fund was to be financed by the $150,000 fine from the first contempt proceeding, plus an additional payment of $.02 per hour for each hour worked by a journeyman or apprentice. The Fund would remain in existence until the union achieved its nonwhite membership goal, and the District Court determined that the Fund was no longer necessary.

15. Petitioners did not appeal the denial of their cross-motion to terminate the O & J and RAAPO. The city cross-appealed from that part of AAAPO establishing a temporary 29.23% nonwhite membership goal, claiming that the percentage should be higher. The Court of Appeals denied the cross-motion.

16. With respect to the finding of underutilization of the apprenticeship program, the court noted that the District Court had mistakenly compared the total number of apprentices enrolled during the period before the O & J was entered against the number of new enrollees admitted during the period after entry of the O & J. However, the court found this error inconsequential, since the statistical comparison was "only a small part of the overall evidence showing underutilization of the apprenticeship program." 753 F.2d 1172, 1180 (1985). The court determined that the District Court's finding of underutilization was supported by strong evidence that despite a need for more apprentices, petitioners refused to advertise the apprenticeship program and thereby help fill the need. See n. 22, infra. The court also noted that "[m]any of the uncertainties about underutilization that are urged by defendants are due in large part to the union's noncompliance with the reporting provisions of RAAPO."

17. The court held that plaintiffs had failed to prove that the older workers' pro-

concluded that "[p]articularly in light of the determined resistance by Local 28 to all efforts to integrate its membership, * * * the combination of violations found by [the District Court] amply demonstrates the union's foot-dragging egregious noncompliance * * * and adequately supports [its] findings of civil contempt against both Local 28 and the JAC." The court also affirmed the District Court's contempt remedies, including the Fund order, and affirmed AAAPO with two modifications: it set aside the requirement that one minority apprentice be indentured for every white apprentice,[18] and clarified the Disrict Court's orders to allow petitioners to implement objective, nondiscriminatory apprentice selection procedures.[19] The court found the 29.23% nonwhite membership goal to be proper in light of Local 28's "long continued and egregious racial discrimination," and because it "will not unnecessarily trammel the rights of any readily ascertainable group of nonminority individuals." The court rejected petitioners' argument that the goal violated Title VII or the Constitution. The court also distinguished AAAPO from the race-conscious order invalidated by this Court in Firefighters v. Stotts, 467 U.S. 561, 104 S.Ct. 2576, 81 L.Ed.2d 483 (1984), on three grounds: (1) unlike the order in *Stotts*, AAAPO did not conflict with a bona fide seniority plan; (2) the *Stotts* discussion of § 706(g) of Title VII, applied only to "make whole" relief and did not address the prospective relief contained in AAAPO and the Fund order; and (3) this case, unlike *Stotts*, involved intentional discrimination.

Local 28 and the JAC filed a petition for a writ of certiorari. They present several claims for review: (1) that the District Court relied on incorrect statistical data; (2) that the contempt remedies ordered by the District Court were criminal in nature and were imposed without due process; (3) that the appointment of an administrator to supervise membership practices interferes with their right to self-governance; and (4) that the membership goal and Fund are unconstitutional. Principally, however, petitioners, supported by the Solicitor General, maintain that the membership goal and Fund exceed the scope of remedies available under Title VII because they extend race-conscious preferences to individuals who are not the identified victims of petitioners' unlawful discrimination. We granted the petition, and now affirm the Court of Appeals.

vision had either a discriminatory purpose or effect, because although negotiated, it was never actually implemented. The court instructed the District Court on remand to determine the status and effect of the provision. Because adoption of this provision was the only contemptuous conduct that the Contractors' Association had been charged with, the Court of Appeals vacated all contempt relief against the Association.

18. The court recognized that "temporary hiring rations may be necessary in order to achieve integration of a work force from which minorities have been unlawfully barred," but cautioned that "such race-conscious ratios are extreme remedies that must be used sparingly and 'carefully tailored to fit the violations found.'" Noting that petitioners had voluntarily indentured 45% nonwhites since January of 1981, the court concluded that a strict one-to-one hiring requirement was not needed to insure that a sufficient number of nonwhites were selected for the apprenticeship program.

19. The EEOC had argued that AAAPO prohibited the use of any new selection procedures until the 29.23% membership goal was reached.

II

Petitioners argue that the District Court relied on incorrect statistical evidence in violation of Title VII and of petitioners' right to due process.

A

Under the O & J and RAAPO, petitioners were directed to attain a 29% nonwhite membership goal by July of 1981. This goal was based on the percentage of minorities in the relevant labor pool within New York City. Petitioners argue that because members and applicants for Local 28 membership have always been drawn from areas outside of New York City, the nonwhite membership goal should have accounted for the percentage of minorities in the relevant labor pool in these areas. Although they concede that there is no evidence in the record from which the correct percentage could be derived, they insist that the District Court's figure is erroneous, and that this error was "significant." [20]

The 29% nonwhite membership goal was established more than a decade ago and was twice affirmed by the Court of Appeals. Petitioners did not seek certiorari from this Court to review either of the Court of Appeals' judgments. Consequently, we do not have before us any issue as to the correctness of the 29% figure. See Pasadena City Board of Education v. Spangler, 427 U.S. 424, 432, 96 S.Ct. 2697, 2703, 49 L.Ed.2d 599 (1976). Under AAAPO, petitioners are now obligated to attain a 29.23% nonwhite-membership goal by August 1987. AAAPO adjusted the original 29% membership goal to account for the fact that Local 28's members were now drawn from areas outside of New York City. Thus, even assuming that the original 29% membership goal was erroneous, it would not affect petitioners' existing obligations under AAAPO, or any other issue now before us.[21]

20. In their brief, petitioners also suggest that the District Court's 29% membership goal was used to confirm its original finding of discrimination, and was therefore invalid under Hazelwood School District v. United States, 433 U.S. 299, 97 S.Ct. 2736, 53 L.Ed.2d 768 (1977) (proof of a pattern of discrimination by statistical evidence must be drawn from relevant geographical locations). However, the Court of Appeals recognized that the District Court's finding of liability "did not rely on inferences from racial ratios of population and employment in the area," but rather "was based on direct and overwhelming evidence of purposeful racial discrimination over a period of many years." In any event, petitioners conceded at oral argument that they do not "challeng[e] any finding that there was deliberate discrimination."

21. Petitioners contend that "[i]nasmuch as [they] have now been held in contempt for not achieving the [29% membership] quota, the propriety of the evidence upon which it was derived is relevant." In the first place, the District Court expressly stated that petitioners were not held in contempt for failing to attain the 29% membership goal. In any event, a "contempt proceeding does not open to reconsideration the legal or factual basis of the order alleged to have been disobeyed and thus become a retrial of the original controversy." Maggio v. Zeitz, 333 U.S. 56, 69, 68 S.Ct. 401, 408, 92 L.Ed. 476 (1948); see also Walker v. City of Birmingham, 388 U.S. 307, 313–314, 87 S.Ct. 1824, 1828, 18 L.Ed.2d 1210 (1967); United States v. Rylander, 460 U.S. 752, 756–757, 103 S.Ct. 1548, 1552–1553, 75 L.Ed.2d 521 (1983); C. Wright & A. Miller, Federal

B

Petitioners argue that the District Court also relied on incorrect data in finding that they had underutilized the apprenticeship program. The Court of Appeals recognized this error, see n. 20, supra, but affirmed the finding based on other evidence presented to the District Court.[22] Petitioners do not explain whether, and if so, why, the Court of Appeals' evaluation of the evidence was incorrect. Based on our own review of the record, we cannot say that the District Court's resolution of the evidence presented on this issue was clearly erroneous. Moreover, because petitioners do not challenge three of the findings on which the first contempt order was based, any alleged use of incorrect statistical evidence by the District Court provides no basis for disturbing the contempt citation. As the Court of Appeals observed, petitioners' "failure to have the apprentices employed is both an independent ground for contempt and a symptom of the effects of defendants' other kinds of contemptuous conduct."

III

The District Court imposed a variety of contempt sanctions in this case, including fines to finance the Fund, a computerized recordkeeping requirement, and attorney's fees and expenses. Petitioners claim that these sanctions, while ostensibly imposed for civil contempt, are in fact punitive, and were issued without the procedures required for criminal contempt proceedings, see Fed.Rule Crim.Proc. 42(b); 42 U.S.C. § 2000h. We reject this contention.

Criminal contempt sanctions are punitive in nature and are imposed to vindicate the authority of the court. United States v. Mine Workers, 330 U.S. 258, 302, 67 S.Ct. 677, 700, 91 L.Ed. 884 (1947). On the other hand, sanctions in civil-contempt proceedings may be employed "for either or both of two purposes: to coerce the defendant into compliance with the court's order, and to compensate the complainant for losses sustained." Id., at 303–304, 67 S.Ct., at 701; see also McComb v. Jacksonville Paper Co., 336 U.S. 187, 191, 69 S.Ct. 497, 499, 93 L.Ed. 599 (1949); Penfield Co. of California v. S.E.C., 330 U.S. 585, 590, 67 S.Ct. 918, 921, 91 L.Ed. 1117 (1947); Nye v. United States, 313 U.S. 33, 42, 61 S.Ct. 810, 813, 85 L.Ed. 1172 (1941); McCrone v. United States, 307 U.S. 61, 64, 59 S.Ct. 685, 686–687, 83 L.Ed. 1108 (1939); 42 U.S.C.

Practice and Procedure § 2960, pp. 597–598.

22. The court pointed to evidence before the District Court showing that after the O & J was entered: (1) there was a "sharp increase" in the ratio of journeymen to apprentices employed by contractors; (2) the average number of hours worked annually by journeymen "increased dramatically"; (3) the percentage of unemployed apprentices decreased; and (4) the union issued hundreds of temporary work permits, mostly to white journeymen. Based on this evidence, the Court of Appeals concluded that despite the need for more apprentices, Local 28 had deliberately shifted employment opportunities from apprentices to predominately white journeymen, and had refused to conduct the general publicity campaign required by RAAPO to attract nonwhites to the apprenticeship program.

§ 2000h. Under this standard, the sanctions issued by the District Court were clearly civil in nature.

The District Court determined that petitioners' had underutilized the apprenticeship program to the detriment of nonwhites, and that this was one of the factors that had prevented petitioners even from approaching the court-ordered 29% nonwhite membership goal. The Fund—and the fines used to finance it—sought to remedy petitioners' contemptuous conduct by increasing nonwhite membership in the apprenticeship program in a variety of ways. In an attempt to encourage nonwhite interest in the apprenticeship program, petitioners were required to finance recruiting efforts at vocational schools, and to create summer and part-time sheet metal jobs for qualified vocational students. Nonwhite apprentices were provided with tutorial, counseling, and financial support services. In an effort to stimulate employment opportunities for *all* apprentices, the Fund helped subsidize contractors who could not afford to hire one apprentice for every four journeymen, and helped the union secure matching training funds. The court carefully considered "the character and magnitude of the harm threatened by continued contumacy, and the probable effectiveness of any suggested sanction in bringing about the result desired," *Mine Workers*, supra, 330 U.S., at 304, 67 S.Ct., at 701, and concluded that the Fund was necessary to secure petitioners' compliance with its earlier orders. Under the terms of the Fund order, petitioners could purge themselves of the contempt by ending their discriminatory practices and by achieving the court-ordered membership goal; they would then be entitled, with the court's approval, to recover any moneys remaining in the Fund. Thus, the sanctions levied by the District Court were clearly designed to coerce compliance with the court's orders, rather than to punish petitioners for their contemptuous conduct.[23]

IV

Petitioners, joined by the Solicitor General, argue that the membership goal, the Fund order, and other orders which require petitioners to grant membership preferences to nonwhites are expressly prohibited by § 706(g), which defines the remedies available under Title VII. Petitioners and the Solicitor General maintain that § 706(g) authorizes a district court to award preferential relief only to the actual victims of unlawful discrimination.[24] They maintain that the membership goal

23. The District Court had also determined that petitioners had failed to comply with the detailed recordkeeping requirements of the O & J and RAAPO. The computerized recordkeeping system was clearly designed to foster petitioners' compliance with these provisions. Finally, the assessment of attorney fees and expenses compensated respondents for costs occasioned by petitioners' contemptuous conduct.

24. Both petitioners and the Solicitor General present this challenge from a rather curious position. Petitioners did not seek review in this Court of the 29% membership goal twice approved by the Court of Appeals, even though that goal was similar to the 29.23% goal they now challenge. However, we reject the State's contention that either res judicata or the law of the case prohibits us from now ad-

and the Fund violate this provision, since they require petitioners to admit to membership, and otherwise to extend benefits to black and Hispanic individuals who are not the identified victims of unlawful discrimination.[25] We reject this argument, and hold that § 706(g) does not prohibit a court from ordering, in appropriate circumstances, affirmative race-conscious relief as a remedy for past discrimination. Specifically, we hold that such relief may be appropriate where an employer or a labor union has engaged in persistent or egregious discrimination, or where necessary to dissipate the lingering effects of pervasive discrimination.

A

Section 706(g) states:

> "If the court finds that the respondent has intentionally engaged in or is intentionally engaging in an unlawful employment practice * * *, the court may enjoin the respondent from engaging in such unlawful employment practice, and order such affirmative action as may be appropriate, which may include, but is not limited to, reinstatement or hiring of employees, with or without back pay * * *, or any other equitable relief as the court deems appropriate. * * * No order of the court shall require the admission or reinstatement of an individual as a member of a union, or the hiring, reinstatement, or promotion of an individual as an employee, or the payment to him of any back pay, if such individual was refused admission, suspended, or expelled, or was refused employment or advancement or was suspended or discharged for any

dressing the legality of the membership goal.

The Solicitor General challenges the membership goal and Fund order even though the EEOC has, throughout this litigation, joined the other plaintiffs in asking the courts to order numerical goals, implementing ratios, and timetables. In the complaint, the Government sought the "selection of sufficient apprentices from among qualified non-white applicants to overcome the effects of past discrimination." In its post-trial memorandum, the Government urged the court to "establish a goal of no less than 30 per cent non white membership in Local 28." To achieve this goal, the Government asked the court to order petitioners to select apprentices based on a one-to-one white to nonwhite ratio, and argued that "a reasonable preference in favor of minority persons to remedy past discriminatory injustices is permissable [*sic*]." Ibid.

25. The last sentence of § 706(g) addresses only court orders requiring the "admission or reinstatement of an individual as a member of a union." 42 U.S.C. § 2000e–5(g). Thus, even under petitioners' reading of § 706(g), that provision would not apply to several of the benefits conferred by the Fund, to wit the tutorial, liaison, counseling, stipend, and loan programs extended to nonwhites. Moreover, the District Court established the Fund in the exercise of its contempt powers. Thus, even assuming that petitioners correctly read § 706(g) to limit the remedies a court may impose *for a violation of Title VII*, that provision would not necessarily limit the District Court's authority to order petitioners to implement the Fund. The Solicitor General, without citing any authority, maintains that "contempt sanctions imposed to enforce Title VII must not themselves violate the statute's policy of providing relief only to the actual victims of discrimination." We need not decide whether § 706(g) restricts a court's contempt powers, since we reject the proposition that § 706(g) always prohibits a court from ordering affirmative race-conscious relief which might incidentally benefit individuals who were not the actual victims of discrimination.

reason other than discrimination on account of race, color, religion, sex, or national origin in violation of * * * this title." 42 U.S.C. § 2000e–5(g).

The language of § 706(g) plainly expresses Congress's intent to vest district courts with broad discretion to award "appropriate" equitable relief to remedy unlawful discrimination. Teamsters v. United States, 431 U.S. 324, 364, 97 S.Ct. 1843, 1869, 52 L.Ed.2d 396 (1977); Franks v. Bowman Transportation Co., 424 U.S. 747, 771, 96 S.Ct. 1251, 1267, 47 L.Ed.2d 444 (1976); Albermarle Paper Co. v. Moody, 422 U.S. 405, 421, 95 S.Ct. 2362, 2373, 45 L.Ed.2d 280 (1975).[26] Nevertheless, petitioners and the Solicitor General argue that the last sentence of § 706(g) prohibits a court from ordering an employer or labor union to take affirmative steps to eliminate discrimination which might incidentally benefit individuals who are not the actual victims of discrimination. This reading twists the plain language of the statute.

The last sentence of § 706(g) prohibits a court from ordering a union to admit an individual who was "refused admission * * * for any reason other than discrimination." It does not, as petitioners and the Solicitor General suggest, say that a court may order relief only for the actual victims of past discrimination. The sentence on its face addresses only the situation where a plaintiff demonstrates that a union (or an employer) has engaged in unlawful discrimination, but the union can show that a particular individual would have been refused admission even in the absence of discrimination, for example because that individual was unqualified. In these circumstances § 706(g) confirms that a court could not order the union to admit the unqualified individual. In this case, neither the membership goal nor the Fund order required petitioners to admit to membership individuals who had been refused admission for reasons unrelated to discrimination. Thus, we do not read § 706(g) to prohibit a court from ordering the kind of affirmative relief the District Court awarded in this case.

26. Section 706(g) was modeled after § 10(c) of the National Labor Relations Act, 29 U.S.C. § 160(c). See Franks v. Bowman Transportation Co., 424 U.S., at 769, 96 S.Ct., at 1266; Albermarle Paper Co. v. Moody, 422 U.S., at 419, 95 S.Ct., at 2372. Principles developed under the National Labor Relations Act "guide, but do not bind, courts tailoring remedies under Title VII." Ford Motor Co. v. EEOC, 458 U.S. 219, 226, n. 8, 102 S.Ct. 3057, 3062–3063, n. 8, 73 L.Ed.2d 721 (1982). Section 10(c) as we have noted, was intended to give the National Labor Relations Board broad authority to formulate appropriate remedies:

"[I]n the nature of things Congress could not catalogue all the devices and strategems for circumventing the policies of the Act. Nor could it define the whole gamut of remedies to effectuate these policies in an infinite variety of specific situations. Congress met these difficulties by leaving the adaption of means to end to the empiric process of administration." Phelps Dodge Corp. v. NLRB, 313 U.S. 177, 194, 61 S.Ct. 845, 852, 85 L.Ed. 1271 (1941).

See also *Franks*, supra, 424 U.S., at 769, n. 29, 96 S.Ct., at 1266 ("§ 706(g) grants * * * broader discretionary powers than those granted the [NLRB under section 10(c)].")

B

The availability of race-conscious affirmative relief under § 706(g) as a remedy for a violation of Title VII also furthers the broad purposes underlying the statute. Congress enacted Title VII based on its determination that racial minorities were subject to pervasive and systematic discrimination in employment. "[I]t was clear to Congress that '[t]he crux of the problem [was] to open employment opportunities for Negroes in occupations which have been traditionally closed to them,' * * * and it was to this problem that Title VII's prohibition against racial discrimination in employment was primarily addressed." Steelworkers v. Weber, 443 U.S. 193, 203, 99 S.Ct. 2721, 2727, 61 L.Ed.2d 480 (1979) (quoting 110 Cong.Rec. 6548 (1964) (remarks of Sen. Humphrey)). Title VII was designed "to achieve equality of employment opportunities and remove barriers that have operated in the past to favor an identifiable group of white employees over other employees." Griggs v. Duke Power Co., 401 U.S. 424, 429–430, 91 S.Ct. 849, 853, 28 L.Ed.2d 158 (1971); see *Teamsters,* supra, 431 U.S., at 364–365, 97 S.Ct., at 1869–1870; *Franks,* supra, 424 U.S., at 763, 771, 96 S.Ct., at 1263–1264, 1267; *Albemarle Paper,* 422 U.S., at 417–18, 95 S.Ct., at 2371–2372. In order to foster equal employment opportunities, Congress gave the lower courts broad power under § 706(g) to fashion "the most complete relief possible" to remedy past discrimination. *Franks,* supra, 424 U.S., at 770, 96 S.Ct., at 1267; *Albemarle Paper,* supra, 422 U.S., at 418, 95 S.Ct., at 2372.

In most cases, the court need only order the employer or union to cease engaging in discriminatory practices, and award make-whole relief to the individuals victimized by those practices. In some instances, however, it may be necessary to require the employer or union to take affirmative steps to end discrimination effectively to enforce Title VII. Where an employer or union has engaged in particularly longstanding or egregious discrimination, an injunction simply reiterating Title VII's prohibition against discrimination will often prove useless and will only result in endless enforcement litigation. In such cases, requiring recalcitrant employers or unions to hire and to admit qualified minorities roughly in proportion to the number of qualified minorities in the work force may be the only effective way to ensure the full enjoyment of the rights protected by Title VII.

Further, even where the employer or union formally ceases to engage in discrimination, informal mechanisms may obstruct equal employment opportunities. An employer's reputation for discrimination may discourage minorities from seeking available employment. In these circumstances, affirmative race-conscious relief may be the only means available "to assure equality of employment opportunities and to eliminate those discriminatory practices and devices which have fostered racially stratified job environments to the disadvantage of minority citizens." McDonnell Douglas Corp. v. Green, 411 U.S. 792, 800, 93 S.Ct. 1817, 1823, 36 L.Ed. 2d 668 (1973); see *Teamsters,* 431 U.S., at 348, 97 S.Ct., at

1861.[27] Affirmative action "promptly operates to change the outward and visible signs of yesterday's racial distinctions and thus, to provide an impetus to the process of dismantling the barriers, psychological or otherwise, erected by past practices." NAACP v. Allen, 493 F.2d 614, 621 (CA5 1974).

Finally, a district court may find it necessary to order interim hiring or promotional goals pending the development of nondiscriminatory hiring or promotion procedures. In these cases, the use of numerical goals provides a compromise between two unacceptable alternatives: an outright ban on hiring or promotions, or continued use of a discriminatory selection procedure.

We have previously suggested that courts may utilize certain kinds of racial preferences to remedy past discrimination under Title VII. See Fullilove v. Klutznick, 448 U.S. 448, 483, 100 S.Ct. 2758, 2777, 65 L.Ed.2d 902 (1980) (opinion of Burger, C.J.) ("Where federal antidiscrimination laws have been violated, an equitable remedy may in the appropriate case include a racial or ethnic factor"); id., at 513, 100 S.Ct., at 2792–2793 (Powell, J., concurring) ("The Courts of Appeals have approved temporary hiring remedies insuring that the percentage of minority group workers in a business or governmental agency will be reasonably related to the percentage of minority group members in the relevant population"); University of California Regents v. Bakke, 438 U.S. 265, 353, 98 S.Ct. 2733, 2780, 57 L.Ed.2d 750 (1978) (opinion of Brennan, White, Marshall, and Blackmun, JJ.) ("the Court has required that preferences be given by employers to members of racial minorities as a remedy for past violations of Title VII"). The Courts of Appeals have unanimously agreed that racial preferences may be used, in appropriate cases, to remedy past discrimination under Title VII.

C

Despite the fact that the plain language of § 706(g) and the purposes of Title VII suggest the opposite, petitioners and the Solicitor General maintain that the legislative history indicates that Congress intended that affirmative relief under § 706(g) benefit only the identified victims of past discrimination. To support this contention, petitioners and the Solicitor General rely principally on statements made throughout the House and Senate debates to the effect that Title VII would not require employers or labor unions to adopt quotas or preferences that would benefit racial minorities.

27. We have steadfastly recognized that affirmative race-conscious relief may provide an effective means of remedying the effects of past discrimination. See Wygant v. Jackson Board of Education, 476 U.S. ___, 106 S.Ct. 1842, 90 L.Ed.2d 260 (1986) (opinion of Powell, J.) ("to eliminate every vestige of racial segregation and discrimination * * * race-conscious remedial action may be necessary"); *id.*, at ___, 106 S.Ct., at 1861 (Marshall, J., dissenting) ("racial distinctions * * * are highly relevant to the one legitimate state objective of eliminating the pernicious vestiges of past discrimination"); Fullilove v. Klutznick, 448 U.S. 448, 100 S.Ct. 2758, 65 L.Ed.2d 902 (1980) (upholding 10% set aside of federal contract funds for minority businesses).

Our examination of the legislative history of Title VII convinces us that, when examined in context, the statements relied upon by petitioners and the Solicitor General do not indicate that Congress intended to limit relief under § 706(g) to that which benefits only the actual victims of unlawful discrimination. Rather, these statements were intended largely to reassure opponents of the bill that it would not require employers or labor unions to use racial quotas or to grant preferential treatment to racial minorities in order to avoid being charged with unlawful discrimination. See United Steelworkers of America, AFL CIO CLC v. Weber, (1979), 443 U.S. 193, at 205, 99 S.Ct. 2721, 2728, 61 L.Ed.2d 480. The bill's supporters insisted that this would not be the intent and effect of the legislation, and eventually agreed to state this expressly in § 703(j). Contrary to the arguments made by petitioners and the Solicitor General, these statements do not suggest that a court may not order preferential relief under § 706(g) when appropriate to remedy past discrimination. Rather, it is clear that the bill's supporters only wished to emphasize that an employer would not violate the statute merely by having a racially imbalanced work force, and, consequently, that a court could not order an employer to adopt racial preferences merely to correct such an imbalance.

1

H.R. 7152, the bill that ultimately became the Civil Rights Act of 1964, was introduced in the House by Representatives on June 20, 1963, and referred to the Committee on the Judiciary. The bill contained no provisions addressed to discrimination in employment, but the Judiciary Committee amended it by adding Title VII. Title VII as reported by the Judiciary Committee included a version of § 706(g), which read, in relevant part: "No order of the court shall require the admission or reinstatement of an individual as a member of a union * * * if such individual was refused admission, suspended, or expelled * * * for *cause.*" The word "cause" was deleted from the bill on the House floor and replaced by the language "any reason other than discrimination on account of race, color, religion, or national origin." Representative Celler, the Chairman of the House Judiciary Committee and the sponsor of this amendment, explained:

> "[T]he purpose of the amendment is to specify cause. Here the court, for example, cannot find any violation of the act which is based on facts other—and I emphasize 'other'—than discrimination on the grounds of race, color, religion, or national origin. The discharge might be based, for example, on incompetence or a morals charge or theft, but the court can only consider charges based on race, color, religion, or national origin. That is the purpose of this amendment."

2

Even before the Judiciary Committee's bill reached the House floor, opponents charged that Title VII would require that an employer maintain a racially balanced work force. The Minority Report of the

Judiciary Committee observed that "the word discrimination is nowhere defined in the bill," and charged that "the administration intends to rely upon its own construction of 'discrimination' as including the lack of racial balance." To demonstrate how the bill would operate in practice, the Report posited a number of hypothetical employment situations, concluding each time that Title VII would compel employers "to 'racially balance' those who work for him *in every job classification* or be in violation of Federal law." [30] In response, Republican proponents of the bill issued a statement emphasizing that the EEOC could not enforce the statute merely to achieve racial balance:

> "[T]he Commission must confine its activities to correcting abuse, not promoting equality with mathematical certainty. In this regard, nothing in the title permits a person to demand employment. Of greater importance, the Commission will only jeopardize its continued existence if it seeks to impose forced racial balance upon employers or labor unions."

When H.R. 7152 actually reached the House floor, Representative Celler attempted to respond to charges that the existence of racial imbalance would constitute "discrimination" under Title VII, or that the EEOC would be authorized to "order the hiring and promotion only of employees of certain races or religious groups." [31] Nevertheless, accusations similar to those made in the Judiciary Committee's Minority Report were repeatedly raised on the House floor. For example, Representative Alger charged that Title VII would "demand by law, special privileges for Negroes":

> "The Negro represents about 10 percent of the population of the United States and it cannot be said he is being kept from opportunity if he is represented in 10 percent of the working force. Now we

30. For illustrative purposes, we include two of these "examples":

"Under the power granted in this bill, if a carpenters' hiring hall, say, had 20 men awaiting call, the first 10 in seniority being white carpenters, the union could be forced to pass them over in favor of carpenters beneath them in seniority, but of the stipulated race. And if the union roster did not contain the names of the carpenters of the race needed to 'racially balance' the job, the union agent must, then, go into the street and recruit members of the stipulated race in sufficient number * * * else his local could be held in violation of Federal law."

"Assume two women of separate races apply to [a] firm for the position of stenographer; further assume that the employer for some indefinable reason, prefers one above the other, whether because of personality, superior alertness, intelligence, work history, or general neatness. Assume the employer has learned good things about the character of one and derogatory things about the character of the other which are not subject to proof. If his firm is not 'racially balanced,' [the employer] has no choice, he must employ the person of that race which, by ratio, is next up, even though he is certain in his own mind that the woman he is not allowed to employ would be a superior employee."

31. Representative Celler explained that the Commission would have no power "to rectify existing 'racial or religious imbalance' in employment by requiring the hiring of certain people * * * simply because they are of a given race or religion." He emphasized that "[n]o order could be entered against an employer except by a court," and that "[e]ven then, the court could not order that any preference be given to any particular race, religion or other group, but would be limited to ordering an end to discrimination."

are asked to ignore population ratios and force the hiring of Negroes even when it will mean, as in Government, that they are given preferential hiring far beyond the 10 percent of the population they represent."

Representative Abernathy raised the scenario of a "union [having] to send out a 'racially' balanced staff of organizers to sign up a crew of 'racially balanced' carpenters, a crew of 'racially balanced' laborers, 'racially balanced' plumbers, electricians, plasterers, roofers, and so forth, before a construction job could begin. Supporters of the bill stridently denied any intent to require "racial balancing." [32] Thus, in response to charges that an employer or labor union would be guilty of "discrimination" under Title VII simply because of a racial imbalance in its work force or membership roster, supporters of the bill insisted repeatedly that Title VII would not require employers or unions to implement hiring or promotional quotas in order to achieve racial balance. The question whether there should be any comparable restrictions with respect to a court's use of racial preferences as an appropriate *remedy for past discrimination* under § 706(g) simly did not arise during the House debates.

3

After passing the House by a vote of 290–130, the bill ran into equally strong opposition in the Senate. Opponents initially sought to have it sent to the Senate Judiciary Committee, which was hostile to civil rights legislation. The debate on this motion focused on the merits of the bill; many Senators again raised the specter of "racial balancing." Senator Ervin charged that under the substantive provisions of Title VII, "the Commission could * * * tell an employer that he had too few employees * * * and enter an order * * * requiring him to hire more persons, not because the employer thought he needed more persons, but because the Commission wanted to compel him to employ persons of a particular race." Similarly, Senator Robertson stated:

> "This title suggests that hiring should be done on some percentage basis in order that racial imbalance will be overcome. It is contemplated by this title that the percentage of colored and white population in a community shall be in similar percentages in every business establishment that employs over 25 persons. Thus, if there

32. See 110 Cong.Rec. 1540 (1964) (remarks of Rep. Lindsay) (The bill "does not impose quotas or any special privileges of seniority or acceptance. There is nothing whatever in this bill about racial balance as appears so frequently in the minority report of the committee"); id., at 1600 (remarks of Rep. Minish) ("[U]nder title VII. * * * no quota system will be set up, no one will be forced to hire incompetent help because of race or religion, and no one will be given a vested right to demand employment for a certain job"); id., at 1994 (remarks of Rep. Healy) ("Opponents of the bill say that it sets up racial quotas for job[s] * * *. The bill does not do that"); id., at 2558 (remarks of Rep. Goodell) ("There is nothing here as a matter of legislative history that would require racial balancing * * *. We are not talking about a union having to balance its membership or an employer having to balance the number of employees. There is no quota involved").

were 10,000 colored persons in a city and 15,000 whites, an employer with 25 employees would, in order to overcome racial imbalance, be required to have 10 colored personnel and 15 white. And, if by chance that employer had 20 colored employees he would have to fire 10 of them in order to rectify the situation."

Senator Humphrey, one of the most vocal proponents of H.R. 7152, rose to the bill's defense. He introduced a newspaper article quoting the answers of a Justice Department expert to common objections to Title VII. In response to the "objection" that "[w]hite people would be fired, to make room for Negroes," the article stated that "[t]he bill would not authorize anyone to order hiring or firing to achieve racial or religious balance." Later, responding to a political advertisement suggesting that federal agencies would interpret "discrimination" under Title VII as synonymous with racial imbalance, Senator Humphrey stressed that Title VII "does [not] in any way authorize the Federal Government to prescribe, as the advertisement charges, a 'racial balance' of job classifications or office staffs or 'preferential treatment of minorities' " to achieve such a balance. After 17 days of debate, the Senate voted to take up the bill directly without referring it to a committee.

Senators Humphrey and Kuchel, who served as bipartisan floor managers for H.R. 7152, opened formal debate on the merits of the bill and addressed opponent's charges that Title VII would require employers to implement quotas to achieve a certain racial balance. Senator Humphrey stressed that "[c]ontrary to the allegations of some opponents of this title, there is nothing in it that will give any power to the Commission or to any court to require hiring, firing, or promotion of employees in order to meet a racial 'quota' or to achieve a certain racial balance." Senator Kuchel elaborated:

"[Title VII] is pictured by its opponents and detractors as an intrusion of numerous Federal inspectors into our economic life. These inspectors would presumably dictate to labor unions and their members with regard to * * * racial balance in job classifications, racial balance in membership, and preferential advancement for members of so called minority groups. Nothing could be further from the truth * * *. [T]he important point * * * is that the court cannot order preferential hiring or promotion consideration for any particular race, religion, or other group."

These sentiments were echoed by Senators Case and Clark, who spoke as bipartisan team "captains" in support of Title VII. The Senators submitted an interpretative memorandum which explained that "[t]here is no requirement in title VII that an employer maintain a racial balance in his work force." Senator Clark also introduced a Justice Department memorandum which repeated what supporters of the bill had tried to make clear:

"There is no provision, either in title VII or in any other part of this bill, that requires or authorizes any Federal agency or Federal court to require preferential treatment for any individual or any group for the purpose of achieving racial balance. No employer is required to hire an individual because that individual is a Negro. No employer is required to maintain any ratio of Negroes to whites, Jews to gentiles, Italians to English, or women to men."

Opponents of the bill invoked a 2-month filibuster, again raising the charge that "discrimination" would be defined to include racial imbalance. Senator Robertson remarked: "What does discrimination mean? If it means what I think it does, and which it could mean, it means that a man could be required to have a quota *or he would be discriminating.*" Senators Smathers and Sparkman conceded that Title VII did not in so many words require the use of quotas, but feared that employers would adopt racial quotas or preferences to avoid being charged with discrimination. Even outsiders joined in the debate, Senator Javits referred to charges raised by Governor Wallace of Alabama that the bill "vested power in a federal inspector who, under an allegation of racial imbalance * * * can establish a quota system whereby a certain percentage of a certain ethnic group must be employed." The bill's supporters insisted that employers would not be required to implement racial quotas to avoid being charged with liability.[33] Nonetheless, opponents remained skeptical.

Recognizing that their own verbal assurances would not end the dispute over "racial balancing," supporters of the bill eventually agreed to insert an explicit disclaimer into the language of the bill to assuage opponents' fears. Senator Dirksen introduced the comprehensive "Dirksen-Mansfield" amendment as a substitute for the entire bill, which added several provisions defining and clarifying the scope of Title VII's substantive provisions. One of those provisions, § 703(j), specifically addressed the charges of "racial balancing":

> "Nothing contained in this subchapter shall be interpreted to require any * * * labor organization, or joint labor-management committee * * * to grant preferential treatment to any individual or to any group because of the race * * * of such individual or group on account of an imbalance which may exist with respect to the total number or percentage of persons of any race [admitted to the labor organization, or to any apprenticeship program] in comparison with the total number or percentage of persons of such race * * * in any community, State, section, or other area, or in the

33. See id., at 7420 (remarks of Sen. Humphrey) ("if [Senator Robertson] can find in title VII * * * any language which provides that an employer will have to hire on the basis of percentage or quota related to color, race * * * I will start eating the pages"); id., at 8500–8501 (remarks of Sen. Allott) ("if anyone sees in the bill quotas or percentages, he must read that language into it. It is not in the bill"); id., at 8921 (remarks of Sen. Williams) ("there is nothing whatever in the bill which provides for racial balance or quotas in employment"); id., at 11471 (remarks of Sen. Javits) (the bill "in no respect imposes a quota system or racial imbalance standard"); id., at 11848 (remarks of Sen. Humphrey) (the title "does not provide that any quota systems may be established to maintain racial balance in employment").

available work force in any community, State, section, or other area."

As Senator Humphrey explained:

> "A new subsection 703(j) is added to deal with the problem of racial balance among employees. The proponents of this bill have carefully stated on numerous occasions that title VII does not require an employer to achieve any sort of racial balance in his work force by giving preferential treatment to any individual or group. Since doubts have persisted, subsection (j) is added to state this point expressly. This subsection does not represent any change in the substance of the title. It does state clearly and accurately what we have maintained all along about the bill's intent and meaning."

* * * Section 703(j) apparently calmed the fears of most opponents, for complaints of "racial balance" and "quotas" died down considerably after its adoption.

In contrast to the heated debate over the substantive provisions of § 703, the Senate paid scant attention to the remedial provisions of § 706(g). Several Senators did emphasize, in reference to the last sentence of section 706(g), that "[t]he title does not provide for the reinstatement or employment of a person * * * if he was fired or refused employment or promotion for any reason other than discrimination prohibited by the Title." 110 Cong.Rec., at 11848 (remarks of Sen. Humphrey).[35] While both petitioners and the Solicitor General liberally quote from these excerpts, we do not read these statements as supporting their argument that a district court may not order affirmative race-conscious relief which may incidentally benefit individuals who are not identified victims of unlawful discrimination. To the contrary, these statements confirm our reading of the last sentence of § 706(g): that a court has no power to award relief to an individual who was denied an employment opportunity for reasons other than discrimination.

After 83 days of debate, the Senate adopted Title VII by a vote of 73 to 27. Rather than setting up a Conference Committee, the House voted directly upon, and passed, the Senate version of the bill. The bill's sponsors repeated, for the last time, that Title VII "[did] not require quotas, racial balance, or any of the other things that the opponents have been saying about it."

To summarize, many opponents of Title VII argued that an employer could be found guilty of discrimination under the statute simply

35. See id., at 6549 (remarks of Sen. Humphrey) ("No court order can require hiring, reinstatement, admission to membership, or payment of back pay for anyone who was not fired, refused employment or advancement or admission to a union by an act of discrimination forbidden by this title. This is stated expressly in the last sentence of [§ 706(g)], which makes clear what is implicit throughout the whole title; namely, that employers may hire and fire, promote and refuse to promote for any reason, good or bad, provided only that individuals may not be discriminated against because of race, religion, sex, or national origin").

because of a racial imbalance in his work force, and would be compelled to implement racial "quotas" to avoid being charged with liability. At the same time, supporters of the bill insisted that employers would not violate Title VII simply because of racial imbalance, and emphasized that neither the Commission nor the courts could compel employers to adopt quotas solely to facilitate racial balancing. The debate concerning what Title VII did and did not require culminated in the adoption of § 703(j), which stated expressly that the statute did not require an employer or labor union to adopt quotas or preferences simply because of a racial imbalance. However, while Congress strongly opposed the use of quotas or preferences merely to maintain racial balance, it gave no intimation as to whether such measures would be acceptable as *remedies* for Title VII violations.[36]

Congress' failure to consider this issue is not surprising, since there was relatively little civil rights litigation prior to the adoption of the 1964 Civil Rights Act. More importantly, the cases that had been litigated had not resulted in the sort of affirmative-action remedies that, as later became apparent, would sometimes be necessary to eliminate effectively the effects of past discrimination. Thus, the use of racial preferences as a *remedy* for past discrimination simply was not an issue at the time Title VII was being considered. Our task then, is to determine whether Congress intended to preclude a district court from ordering affirmative action in appropriate circumstances as a remedy for past discrimination. Our examination of the legislative policy behind Title VII leads us to conclude that Congress did not intend to prohibit a court from exercising its remedial authority in that way.[37] Congress deliberately gave the district courts broad authority under Title VII to fashion the most complete relief possible to eliminate "the last vestiges of an unfortunate and ignominious page in this country's history," *Albemarle Paper,* 422 U.S., at 418, 95 S.Ct., at 2372. As we noted above, affirmative race-conscious relief may in some

36. Cf. *Bakke,* 438 U.S., at 342, n. 17, 98 S.Ct., at 2774–2775, n. 17 (opinion of Brennan, White, Marshall, and Blackmun, JJ.) ("Even assuming that Title VII prohibits employers from deliberately maintaining a particular racial composition in their work force as an end in itself, this does not imply, in the absence of any consideration of the question, that Congress intended to ban the use of racial preferences as a tool for achieving the objective of remedying past discrimination or other compelling ends").

37. We also reject petitioners' argument that the District Court's remedies contravened § 703(j), since they require petitioners to grant preferential treatment to blacks and Hispanics based on race. Our examination of the legislative history convinces us that § 703(j) was added to Title VII to make clear that an employer or labor union does not engage in "discrimination" simply because of a racial imbalance in its workforce or membership, and would not be required to institute preferential quotas to avoid Title VII liability. See *Weber,* 443 U.S., at 205, n. 5, 99 S.Ct., at 2728, n. 5 ("§ 703(j) speaks to substantive liability under Title VII"); *Teamsters,* 431 U.S., at 339–340, n. 20, 97 S.Ct., at 1856–1857, n. 20 ("§ 703(j) makes clear that Title VII imposes no requirement that a work force mirror the general population"); *Franks,* 424 U.S., at 758, 96 S.Ct., at 1261 ("the * * * provisions of § 703 * * * delineat[e] which employment practices are illegal and thereby prohibited and which are not"). We reject the notion that § 703(j) somehow qualifies or proscribes a court's authority to order relief otherwise appropriate under § 706(g) in circumstances where an illegal discriminatory act or practice is established.

instances be necessary to accomplish this task. In the absence of any indication that Congress intended to limit a district court's remedial authority in a way which would frustrate the court's ability to enforce Title VII's mandate, we decline to fashion such a limitation ourselves.

4

Our reading of the scope of the district court's remedial powers under § 706(g) is confirmed by the contemporaneous interpretations of the EEOC and the Justice Department.[38] Following the enactment of the Civil Rights Act of 1964, both the Justice Department and the EEOC, the two federal agencies charged with enforcing Title VII, steadfastly maintained that race-conscious remedies for unlawful discrimination are available under the statute. Both agencies have, in appropriate cases, sought court orders and consent decrees containing such provisions. See, e.g., United States v. City of Alexandria, 614 F.2d 1358 (CA5 1980); see also Affirmative Action Appropriate Under Title VII of the Civil Rights Act of 1964, 29 CFR § 1608 (1985); Uniform Guidelines on Employee Selection Procedures, id., § 1607.17; 42 Op.Atty.Gen. 405 (1969). The agencies' contemporaneous reading of the statute lends strong support for our interpretation.

5

Finally, our interpretation of § 706(g) is confirmed by the legislative history of the Equal Employment Opportunity Act of 1972, which amended Title VII in several respects. One such change modified the language of § 706(g) to empower a court to order "such affirmative action as may be appropriate, which may include, *but is not limited to* reinstatement or hiring of employees * * * *or any other equitable relief as the court deems appropriate.*" (emphasized language added in 1972). This language was intended "to give the courts wide discretion exercising their equitable powers to fashion the most complete relief possible." While the section-by-section analysis undertaken in the

38. Although the Solicitor General now makes a contrary argument, we note that the brief for the EEOC submitted by the Solicitor General in *Weber,* supra, described the 1964 legislative history as follows:

"To be sure, there was considerable concern that the Act would be construed to require the use of quota systems to establish and maintain racial balance in employers' work forces. [citations omitted]. The sponsors of the bill repeatedly assured its opponents that this was not the intent and would not be the effect of the statute. [citations omitted]. But these assurances did not suggest restrictions on remedies that could be ordered after a finding of discrimination. Instead, they made it clear that the statute would not impose a duty on employers to establish racially balanced work forces and that it would not require or even permit employers to establish racial quotas for employment in the absence of discrimination of the kind prohibited by the Act. [citations omitted]." Brief for the United States and the Equal Employment Opportunity Commission in United Steelworkers of America v. Weber, O.T. 1978. Nos. 432, 435 and 436, pp. 29–30.

The brief concludes that "the last sentence of Section 706(g) simply state[s] that a court could not order relief under the authority of the Act if employers took action against employees or applicants on grounds other than those prohibited by the Act."

Conference Committee Report stressed the need for "make-whole" relief for the "victims of unlawful discrimination," nowhere did Congress suggest that a court lacked the power to award preferential remedies that might benefit nonvictims. Indeed, the Senate's rejection of two other amendments supports a contrary conclusion.

During the 1972 debates, Senator Ervin introduced an amendment to counteract the effects of the Department of Labor's so-called Philadelphia Plan. The Philadelphia Plan was established pursuant to Executive Order No. 11246, 3 CFR 339 (1964–1965 comp.), and required prospective federal contractors to submit affirmative-action programs including "specific goals of minority manpower utilization." Attacking the Plan as "[t]he most notorious example of discrimination in reverse," Senator Ervin proposed an amendment to Title VII that read, in relevant part: "No department, agency, or officer of the United States shall require an employer to practice discrimination in reverse by employing persons of a particular race * * * in either fixed or variable numbers, proportions, percentages, quotas, goals, or ranges." Senator Ervin complained that the amendment was needed because both the Department of Labor and the EEOC were ignoring § 703(j)'s prohibition against requiring employers to engage in preferential hiring for racial minorities.

Senator Javits vigorously opposed Senator Ervin's proposal. First, he recognized that the amendment, while targeted at the Philadelphia Plan, would also jettison "the whole concept of 'affirmative action' as it has been developed under Executive Order 11246 *and as a remedial concept under Title VII.*" (emphasis added). He explained that the amendment would "deprive the courts of the opportunity to order affirmative action under title VII of the type which they have sustained in order to correct a history of unjust and illegal discrimination in employment." * * * The Ervin amendment was defeated by a margin of 2 to 1.

Senator Ervin proposed a second amendment that would have extended § 703(j)'s prohibition against racial preferences to "Executive Order Numbered 11246, or any other law or Executive Order," this amendment was also defeated resoundingly. Thus, the legislative history of the 1972 amendments to Title VII confirms the availability of race-conscious affirmative action as a remedy under the statute. Congress was aware that both the Executive and Judicial Branches had used such measures to remedy past discrimination,[41] and rejected amendments that would have barred such remedies. Instead, Congress reaffirmed the breadth of the court's remedial powers under § 706(g) by

41. In addition, * * * other federal courts had, prior to the passage of the 1972 amendments, approved of the use of racial preferences to remedy the effects of illegal employment discrimination. See e.g., Carter v. Gallagher, 452 F.2d 315, 330 (CA8 1971) (en banc), cert. denied, 406 U.S. 950, 92 S.Ct. 2045, 32 L.Ed.2d 338 (1972); Local 53, Heat & Frost Insulators v. Volger, 407 F.2d 1047, 1055 (CA5 1969); United States v. Central Motor Lines, Inc., 338 F.Supp. 532, 560–562 (WDNC 1971); United States v. Sheet Metal Workers International Association, Local 10, 3 Empl.Prac.Dec. ¶ 8068 (D NJ 1970).

adding language authorizing courts to order "any other equitable relief as the court deems appropriate." 42 U.S.C. § 2000e–5(g). The section-by-section analysis undertaken by the Conference Committee Report confirms Congress' resolve to accept prevailing judicial interpretations regarding the scope of Title VII: "[I]n any area where the new law does not address itself, or in any area where a specific contrary intention is not indicated, it was assumed that the present case law as developed by the courts would continue to govern the applicability and construction of Title VII." 118 Cong.Rec., at 7166, 7564. Thus, "[e]xecutive, judicial, and congressional action subsequent to the passage of Title VII conclusively established that the Title did not bar the remedial use of race." *Bakke,* 438 U.S., at 353, n. 28, 98 S.Ct., at 2780 (opinion of Brennan, White, Marshall, and Blackmun, JJ.) [42]

D

Finally, petitioners and the Solicitor General find support for their reading of § 706(g) in several of our decisions applying that provision. Petitioners refer to several cases for the proposition that court-ordered remedies under § 706(g) are limited to make-whole relief benefiting actual victims of past discrimination. See Ford Motor Co. v. EEOC, 458 U.S. 219, 102 S.Ct. 3057, 73 L.Ed.2d 721 (1982); Connecticut v. Teal, 457 U.S. 440, 102 S.Ct. 2525, 73 L.Ed.2d 130 (1982); Teamsters v. United States, 431 U.S. 324, 97 S.Ct. 1843, 52 L.Ed.2d 396 (1977); Franks v. Bowman Transportation Co., 424 U.S. 747, 96 S.Ct. 1251, 47 L.Ed.2d 444 (1976); Albemarle Paper Co. v. Moody, 422 U.S. 405, 95 S.Ct. 2362, 45 L.Ed.2d 280 (1975). This reliance is misguided. The cases cited hold only that a court may order relief designed to make individual victims of racial discrimination whole. See *Teamsters,* supra (competitive seniority); *Franks,* supra, 424 U.S., at 779, 96 S.Ct., at 1271 (competitive seniority); *Albemarle Paper,* supra, 422 U.S., at 422, 95 S.Ct., at 2373–2374 (backpay). None of these decisions suggested that individual "make-whole" relief was the *only* kind of remedy available under the statute, on the contrary, several cases emphasized that the district court's remedial powers should be exercised both to eradicate the effects of unlawful discrimination as well as to make the victims of past discrimination whole. Neither do these cases suggest that § 706(g) prohibits a court from ordering relief which might benefit nonvictims; indeed several cases acknowledged that the district court has broad authority to "devise prospective relief designed to assure that employers found to be in violation of [Title VII] eliminate their discriminatory

42. Again, we note that the brief submitted by the Solicitor General in *Weber* urged this reading of the 1972 legislative history. The Solicitor General argued that "[a]ny doubts that Title VII authorized the use of race-conscious remedies were put to rest with the enactment of the Equal Employment Opportunity Act of 1972." Referring specifically to the amendment to the language of § 706(g), the Government argued: "In light of Congress's keen awareness of the kinds of remedies courts had been granting in Title VII cases, and in light of the protests from Senator Ervin and others over the use of race-conscious remedies, this amendment to Section 706(g) provides substantial support for the proposition that Congress intended that numerical, race-conscious relief is available under Title VII to remedy employment discrimination."

practices and the effects therefrom." *Teamsters,* supra, 431 U.S., at 361, n. 47, 97 S.Ct., at 1868, n. 47; see also *Franks,* supra, 424 U.S., at 770, 96 S.Ct. at 1267; *Albemarle Paper,* supra, 422 U.S., at 418, 95 S.Ct., at 2372.

Petitioners claim to find their strongest support in Firefighters v. Stotts, 467 U.S. 561, 104 S.Ct. 2576, 81 L.Ed.2d 483 (1984). * * *

First, we rejected the claim that the District Court was merely enforcing the terms of the consent decree since the parties had expressed no intention to depart from the existing seniority system in the event of layoffs. Second, we concluded that the District Court's order conflicted with § 703(h) of Title VII, which "permits the routine application of a seniority system absent proof of an intention to discriminate." Since the District Court had found that the proposed layoffs were not motivated by a discriminatory purpose, we held that the court erred in enjoining the city from applying its seniority system in making the layoffs.

We also rejected the Court of Appeals' suggestion that the District Court's order was justified by the fact that, had plaintiffs prevailed at trial, the court could have entered an order overriding the city's seniority system. Relying on *Teamsters,* supra, we observed that a court may abridge a bona fide seniority system in fashioning a Title VII remedy only to make victims of intentional discrimination whole, that is, a court may award competitive seniority to individuals who show that they had been discriminated against. However, because none of the firefighters protected by the court's order was a proven victim of illegal discrimination, we reasoned that at trial the District Court would have been without authority to override the city's seniority system, and therefore the court could not enter such an order merely to effectuate the purposes of the consent decree.

While not strictly necessary to the result, we went on to comment that "[o]ur ruling in *Teamsters* that a court can award competitive seniority only when the beneficiary of the award has actually been a victim of illegal discrimination is consistent with the policy behind § 706(g)" which, we noted, "is to provide 'make-whole' relief only to those who have been actual victims of illegal discrimination." Relying on this language, petitioners, joined by the Solicitor General, argue that both the membership goal and the Fund order contravene the policy behind § 706(g) since they extend preferential relief to individuals who were not the actual victims of illegal discrimination. We think this argument both reads *Stotts* too broadly and ignores the important differences between *Stotts* and this case.

Stotts discussed the "policy" behind § 706(g) in order to supplement the holding that the District Court could not have interfered with the city's senority system in fashioning a Title VII remedy. This "policy" was read to prohibit a court from awarding make-whole relief, such as competitive seniority, backpay, or promotion, to individuals who were denied employment opportunities for reasons unrelated to discrimination. The District Court's injunction was considered to be inconsistent with this "policy" because it was tantamount to an award of make-whole relief (in the form of competitive seniority) to individual black firefighters who had not shown that the proposed layoffs were motivated by racial discrimination.[44] However, this limitation on *individual* make-whole relief does not affect a court's authority to order race-conscious affirmative action. The purpose of affirmative action is not to make identified victims whole, but rather to dismantle prior patterns of employment discrimination and to prevent discrimination in the future. Such relief is provided to the class as a whole rather than to individual members; no individual is entitled to relief, and beneficiaries need not show that they were themselves victims of, discrimination.[45] In this case, neither the membership goal nor the Fund order required the petitioners to indenture or train particular individuals, and neither required them to admit to membership individuals who were refused admission for reasons unrelated to discrimination. We decline petitioners' invitation to read *Stotts* to prohibit a court from ordering any kind of race-conscious affirmative relief that might benefit nonvictims.[46] This reading would distort the language of § 706(g), and would deprive the courts of an important means of enforcing Title VII's guarantee of equal employment opportunity.[47]

44. We note that, consistent with *Stotts,* the District Court in this case properly limited make-whole relief to the actual victims of discrimination. The court awarded back pay, for example, only to those class members who could establish that they were discriminated against.

45. Even where the district court orders such relief, we note that § 706(g) protects the right of the employer or the union to exclude a particular individual from its workforce or membership for reasons unrelated to discrimination.

46. The Government urged a different interpretation of *Stotts* earlier in this lawsuit. In July 1984, petitioners' counsel, in a letter to the Court of Appeals, argued that *Stotts* "affects the propriety [of the remedies ordered] by the district court." In response, counsel for the EEOC submitted that "the decision in *Stotts* does not affect the disposition of the issues in this appeal." Counsel explained that "the court's discussion [in *Stotts*] of § 706(g) is not relevant to the relief challenged by the appellants since it relates only to the award of retroactive or 'make whole' relief and not to the use of prospective remedies," like those ordered by the District Court. With respect to the last sentence of § 706(g), counsel stated:

> "The last sentence of § 706(g) * * * deals with 'make whole' relief and does not even address prospective relief, let alone state that all prospective remedial orders must be limited so that they only benefit the specific victims of the employer's or union's past discriminatory acts. Moreover, the language and the legislative history of § 706(g) support the Commission's position that carefully tailored prospective race-conscious measures are permissible Title VII remedies. * * * [T]he fact that this interpretation was consistently followed by the Commission and the Department of Justice, during the years immediately following enactment of Title VII entitles the interpretation to great deference."

47. The federal courts have declined to read *Stotts* broadly, and have instead limited the decision to its facts. See Pennsylvania v. International Union of Operating Engineers, 770 F.2d 1068 (CA3 1985), cert. denied 474 U.S. ___, 106 S.Ct. 803, 88 L.Ed.2d 779 (1986); Paradise v. Prescott, 767 F.2d, at 1527–1530; Turner v. Orr, 759 F.2d 817, 823–826 (CA11 1985); Vanguards of Cleveland v. City of Cleveland, 753 F.2d, at 485–489, aff'd ___ U.S. ___, 106 S.Ct. ___, 90 L.Ed.2d ___ (1986); Diaz v. American Telephone & Telegraph, 752 F.2d 1356, 1360 n. 5 (CA9 1985); Van Aken v. Young, 750 F.2d 43, 44–45 (CA6 1984); Wygant v. Jackson Bd. of Educ., 746 F.2d 1152, 1157–1159 (CA6 1984), rev'd on other grounds, 476 U.S. ___, 106 S.Ct. 1842, 90 L.Ed.2d 260 (1986); Kromnick v. School Dist. of Philadelphia, 739 F.2d 894, 911 (CA3 1984), cert. denied, 469 U.S. 1107, 105 S.Ct. 782, 83

E

Although we conclude that § 706(g) does not foreclose a district court from instituting some sorts of racial preferences where necessary to remedy past discrimination, we do not mean to suggest that such relief is always proper. While the fashioning of "appropriate" remedies for a particular Title VII violation invokes the "equitable discretion of the district courts," *Franks,* 424 U.S., at 770, 96 S.Ct., at 1267, we emphasize that a court's judgment should be guided by sound legal principles. In particular, the court should exercise its discretion with an eye towards Congress' concern that race-conscious affirmative measures not be invoked simply to create a racially balanced work force. In the majority of Title VII cases, the court will not have to impose affirmative action as a remedy for past discrimination, but need only order the employer or union to cease engaging in discriminatory practices and award make-whole relief to the individuals victimized by those practices. However, in some cases, affirmative action may be necessary in order effectively to enforce Title VII. As we noted before, a court may have to resort to race-conscious affirmative action when confronted with an employer or labor union that has engaged in persistent or egregious discrimination. Or, such relief may be necessary to dissipate the lingering effects of pervasive discrimination. Whether there might be other circumstances that justify the use of court-ordered affirmative action is a matter that we need not decide here. We note only that a court should consider whether affirmative action is necessary to remedy past discrimination in a particular case before imposing such measures, and that the court should also take care to tailor its orders to fit the nature of the violation it seeks to correct.[48] In this case, several factors lead us to conclude that the relief ordered by the District Court was proper.

First, both the District Court and the Court of Appeals agreed that the membership goal and Fund order were necessary to remedy petitioners' pervasive and egregious discrimination. The District Court set the original 29% membership goal upon observing that "[t]he record in both state and federal courts against [petitioners] is replete with instances of their bad faith attempts to prevent or delay affirmative action." The court extended the goal after finding petitioners in contempt for refusing to end their discriminatory practices and failing

L.Ed.2d 777 (1985); Grann v. City of Madison, 738 F.2d 786, 795, n. 5 (CA7), cert. denied, 469 U.S. 918, 105 S.Ct. 296, 83 L.Ed.2d 231 (1984); Deveraux v. Geary, 596 F.Supp. 1481, 1485–1487 (Mass.1984) aff'd, 765 F.2d 268 (CA1 1985); NAACP v. Detroit Police Officers Assn., 591 F.Supp. 1194, 1202–1203 (ED Mich.1984).

48. This cautious approach to the use of racial preferences has been followed by the Courts of Appeals. As one commentator has noted:

"While the circuit courts of appeals have indicated that they possess [the] power [to award race-conscious affirmative relief], they have been reluctant to exercise it. The federal appellate courts have preferred to issue less harsh orders such as recruiting and posting of notices of vacancies. They have tended to impose hiring orders only after employer recalcitrance has been demonstrated." Blumrosen, 34 Rutgers L.Rev., at 41.

to comply with various provisions of RAAPO. In affirming the revised membership goal, the Court of Appeals observed that "[t]his court has twice recognized Local 28's long continued and egregious racial discrimination * * * and Local 28 has presented no facts to indicate that our earlier observations are no longer apposite." In light of petitioners' long history of "foot-dragging resistance" to court orders, simply enjoining them from once again engaging in discriminatory practices would clearly have been futile. Rather, the District Court properly determined that affirmative race-conscious measures were necessary to put an end to petitioners' discriminatory ways.

Both the membership goal and Fund order were similarly necessary to combat the lingering effects of past discrimination. In light of the District Court's determination that the union's reputation for discrimination operated to discourage nonwhites from even applying for membership, it is unlikely that an injunction would have been sufficient to extend to nonwhites equal opportunities for employment. Rather, because access to admission, membership, training, and employment in the industry had traditionally been obtained through informal contacts with union members, it was necessary for a substantial number of nonwhite workers to become members of the union in order for the effects of discrimination to cease. The Fund, in particular, was designed to insure that nonwhites would receive the kind of assistance that white apprentices and applicants had traditionally received through informal sources. On the facts of this case, the District Court properly determined that affirmative, race-conscious measures were necessary to assure the equal employment opportunities guaranteed by Title VII.

Second, the District Court's flexible application of the membership goal gives strong indication that it is not being used simply to achieve and maintain racial balance, but rather as a benchmark against which the court could gauge petitioners' efforts to remedy past discrimination. The court has twice adjusted the deadline for achieving the goal, and has continually approved of changes in the size of the apprenticeship classes to account for the fact that economic conditions prevented petitioners from meeting their membership targets; there is every reason to believe that both the court and the administrator will continue to accommodate *legitimate* explanations for the petitioners' failure to comply with the court's orders. Moreover, the District Court expressly disavowed any reliance on petitioners' failure to meet the goal as a basis for the contempt finding, but instead viewed this failure as symptomatic of petitioners' refusal to comply with various subsidiary provisions of RAAPO. In sum, the District Court has implemented the membership goal as a means by which it can measure petitioners' compliance with its orders, rather than as a strict racial quota.[49]

49. Other factors support the finding that the membership goal has not been applied as a strict racial quota. For example, the Court of Appeals has twice struck down provisions requiring petitioners to indenture one nonwhite apprentice for each white apprentice indentured. Petitioners, however, characterize the following com-

Third, both the membership goal and the Fund order are temporary measures. Under AAAPO "[p]referential selection of union members [w]ill end as soon as the percentage of [minority union members] approximates the percentage of [minorities] in the local labor force." *Weber,* 443 U.S., at 208–209, 99 S.Ct., at 2730. Similarly, the Fund is scheduled to terminate when petitioners achieve the membership goal, and the court determines that it is no longer needed to remedy past discrimination. The District Court's orders thus operate "as a temporary tool for remedying past discrimination without attempting to 'maintain' a previously achieved balance." *Weber,* supra, at 216, 99 S.Ct., at 2734 (Blackmun, J., concurring).

Finally, we think it significant that neither the membership goal nor the Fund order "unnecessarily trammel the interests of white employees." Id., 443 U.S., at 208, 99 S.Ct., at 2730; *Teamsters,* 431 U.S., at 352–353, 97 S.Ct., at 1863–1864. Petitioners concede that the District Court's orders did not require any member of the union to be laid off, and did not discriminate against *existing* union members. See *Weber,* supra, 443 U.S., at 208, 99 S.Ct., at 2729–2730. While whites seeking admission into the union may be denied benefits extended to their nonwhite counterparts, the court's orders do not stand as an absolute bar to such individuals; indeed, a majority of new union members have been white. Many provisions of the court's orders are race-neutral (for example, the requirement that the JAC assign one apprentice for every four journeymen workers), and petitioners remain free to adopt the provisions of AAAPO and the Fund Order for the benefit of white members and applicants.

V

Petitioners also allege that the membership goal and Fund order contravene the equal protection component of the Due Process Clause of the Fifth Amendment because they deny benefits to white individuals based on race. We have consistently recognized that government bodies constitutionally may adopt racial classifications as a remedy for past discrimination. See Wygant v. Jackson Board of Education, 476

ments by the District Court as evidence that the 29.23% membership goal is in reality an inflexible quota:

> "Although defendants were given seven years to attain [the 29% membership] goal * * * they have not. Indeed, they have a long way to go. In addition, they consistently have violated numerous court orders that were designed to assist in the achievement of that goal. The court therefore sees no reason to be lenient with defendants, for whatever reason, and orders that the * * * merged locals must reach a nonwhite membership of 29.23% by August 31, 1987. If the goal is not attained by that date, defendants will face fines that will threaten their very existence."

The District Court's comments express the understandable frustration of a court faced with 15 years of petitioners' deliberate resistance to ending discrimination. We do not view these statements as evidence that the court intends to apply the nonwhite membership goal as an inflexible quota. The record shows that the District Court has been willing to accommodate *legitimate* reasons for petitioners' failure to comply with court orders, and we have no reason to expect that this will change in the future.

U.S. ___, 106 S.Ct. 1842, 90 L.Ed.2d 260 (1986); Fullilove v. Klutznick, 448 U.S. 448, 100 S.Ct. 2758, 65 L.Ed.2d 902 (1980); University of California Regents v. Bakke, 438 U.S. 265, 98 S.Ct. 2733, 57 L.Ed.2d 750 (1978); Swann v. Charlotte-Mecklenburg Board of Education, 402 U.S. 1, 91 S.Ct. 1267, 28 L.Ed.2d 554 (1971). We have not agreed however, on the proper test to be applied in analyzing the constitutionality of race-conscious remedial measures. See *Wygant,* supra, at ___, 106 S.Ct. at ___ (opinion of Powell, J.) (means chosen must be "narrowly tailored" to achieve "compelling government interest"); id., at ___, 106 S.Ct., at ___ (O'Connor, J., concurring); id., at ___, 106 S.Ct., at ___ (Marshall, J., dissenting); id., at ___, 106 S.Ct., at ___ (Stevens, J., dissenting) (public interest served by racial classification and means pursued must justify adverse effects on the disadvantaged group); *Fullilove,* supra, 448 U.S., at 491, 100 S.Ct., at 2781 (opinion of Burger, C.J.) (racial preferences subject to "a most searching examination"); id., at 519, 100 S.Ct., at 2795–2796 (Marshall, J., concurring in the judgment) (remedial use of race must be substantially related to achievement of important governmental objectives); *Bakke,* supra, 438 U.S., at 305, 98 S.Ct., at 2756 (opinion of Powell, J.) (racial classification must be necessary to accomplishment of substantial state interest); id., at 359, 98 S.Ct., at 2783 (opinion of Brennan, White, Marshall and Blackmun, JJ.) (remedial use of race must be substantially related to achievement of important governmental objectives). We need not resolve this dispute here, since we conclude that the relief ordered in this case passes even the most rigorous test—it is narrowly tailored to further the Government's compelling interest in remedying past discrimination.

In this case, there is no problem, as there was in *Wygant,* with a proper showing of prior discrimination that would justify the use of remedial racial classifications. Both the District Court and Court of Appeals have repeatedly found petitioners guilty of egregious violations of Title VII, and have determined that affirmative measures were necessary to remedy their racially discriminatory practices. More importantly, the District Court's orders were properly tailored to accomplish this objective. First, the District Court considered the efficacy of alternative remedies, and concluded that, in light of petitioners' long record of resistance to official efforts to end their discriminatory practices, stronger measures were necessary. The court devised the temporary membership goal and the Fund as tools for remedying past discrimination. More importantly, the District Court's orders will have only a marginal impact on the interests of white workers. Again, petitioners concede that the District Court's orders did not disadvantage *existing* union members. While white applicants for union membership may be denied certain benefits available to their nonwhite counterparts, the court's orders do not stand as an absolute bar to the admission of such individuals; again, a majority of those entering the union after entry of the court's orders have been white. We therefore conclude that the District Court's orders do not violate the equal protection safeguards of the Constitution.[50]

VI

Finally, Local 28 challenges the District Court's appointment of an administrator with broad powers to supervise its compliance with the court's orders as an unjustifiable interference with its statutory right to self-governance. See 29 U.S.C. § 401(a). Preliminarily, we note that while AAAPO gives the administrator broad powers to oversee petitioners' membership practices, Local 28 retains complete control over its other affairs. Even with respect to membership, the administrator's job is to insure that petitioners comply with the court's orders and admit sufficient numbers of nonwhites; the administrator does not select the particular individuals that will be admitted, that task is left to union officials. In any event, in light of the difficulties inherent in monitoring compliance with the court's orders, and especially petitioners' established record of resistance to prior state and federal court orders designed to end their discriminatory membership practices, appointment of an administrator was well within the District Court's discretion. See Fed.Rule Civ. Proc. 53. While the administrator may substantially interfere with petitioners' membership operations, such "interference" is necessary to put an end to petitioners' discriminatory ways.

VII

To summarize our holding today, six members of the Court agree that a district court may, in appropriate circumstances, order preferential relief benefitting individuals who are not the actual victims of discrimination as a remedy for violations of Title VII, see supra, Parts IV–A—IV–D (opinion of Brennan, J., joined by Marshall, J., Blackmun, J., and Stevens, J.); post, at ___ (Powell, J., concurring in part and concurring in the judgment); post, at ___ (White, J., dissenting), that the District Court did not use incorrect statistical evidence in establishing petitioners' nonwhite membership goal, see supra, Part II–A, that the contempt fines and Fund order were proper remedies for civil contempt, see supra, Part III, and that the District Court properly appointed an administrator to supervise petitioners' compliance with the court's orders, see supra Part VI. Five members of the Court agree that in this case, the District Court did not err in evaluating petitioners' utilization of the apprenticeship program, see supra, Part II–B, and that the membership goal and the Fund order are not violative of either Title VII or the Constitution, see supra, Parts IV–E, V (opinion of Brennan, J., joined by Marshall, J., Blackmun, J., and Stevens, J.);

50. Petitioners also argue that "the construction of Title VII adopted by the Court of Appeals has the effect of making the Civil Rights Act an unconstitutional bill of attainder, visiting upon white persons the sins of past discrimination by others." We reject this contention as without merit.

post, at ___ (Powell, J., concurring in part and concurring in the judgment). The judgment of the Court of Appeals is hereby

Affirmed.

JUSTICE POWELL, concurring in part and concurring in the judgment.

I join Parts I, II, III, and VI of JUSTICE BRENNAN's opinion. I further agree that § 706(g) does not limit a court in all cases to granting relief only to actual victims of discrimination. I write separately * * * to explain why I think the remedy ordered under the circumstances of this case [did not violate] the Constitution.

I

* * * I have recently reiterated what I believe to be the standard for assessing a constitutional challenge to a racial classification:

> " 'Any preference based on racial or ethnic criteria must necessarily receive a most searching examination to make sure that it does not conflict with constitutional guarantees.' Fullilove v. Klutznick, 448 U.S. 448, 491 [100 S.Ct. 2758, 2781, 65 L.Ed.2d 902] (1980) (opinion of Burger, C.J.). There are two prongs to this examination. First, any racial classification 'must be justified by a compelling governmental interest' Palmore v. Sidoti, 466 U.S. 429, 432 [104 S.Ct. 1879, ___, 80 L.Ed.2d 421] (1984); see Loving v. Virginia, 388 U.S. 1, 11 [87 S.Ct. 1817, 1823, 18 L.Ed.2d 1010] (1967); cf. Graham v. Richardson, 403 U.S. 365, 375 [91 S.Ct. 1848, 1853–1854, 29 L.Ed.2d 534] (1971) (alienage). Second, the means chosen by the State to effectuate its purpose must be 'narrowly tailored to the achievement of that goal.' *Fullilove*, supra, 448 U.S., at 480 [100 S.Ct., at 2776]." Wygant v. Jackson Board of Education, 476 U.S. ___, ___, 106 S.Ct. 1842, 1846, 90 L.Ed.2d 260 (1986).

The finding by the District Court and the Court of Appeals that petitioners have engaged in egregious violations of Title VII establishes, without doubt, a compelling governmental interest sufficient to justify the imposition of a racially classified remedy. It would be difficult to find defendants more determined to discriminate against minorities. My inquiry, therefore, focuses on whether the District Court's remedy is "narrowly tailored," to the goal of eradicating the discrimination engaged in by petitioners. I believe it is.

The Fund order is supported not only by the governmental interest in eradicating petitioners' discriminatory practices, it also is supported by the societal interest in compliance with the judgments of federal courts. The Fund order was not imposed until *after* petitioners were held in contempt. In requiring the Union to create the Fund, the District Court expressly considered " 'the consequent seriousness of the burden' to the defendants." Moreover, the focus of the Fund order was to give minorities opportunities that for years had been available informally only to nonminorities. The burden this imposes on nonminorities is slight. Under these circumstances, I have little difficulty concluding that the Fund order was carefully structured to vindicate the compelling governmental interests present in this case.

The percentage goal raises a different question. In Fullilove v. Klutznick, 448 U.S. 448, 100 S.Ct. 2758, 65 L.Ed.2d 902 (1980), this Court upheld the constitutionality of the "minority business enterprise" provision of the Public Works Employment Act of 1977, which required, absent administrative waiver, that at least 10% of federal funds granted for local public works projects be used by grantees to procure services or supplies from businesses owned by minority group members. In my concurring opinion, I relied on four factors that had been applied by courts of appeals when considering the proper scope of race-conscious hiring remedies. Those factors were: (i) the efficacy of alternative remedies; (ii) the planned duration of the remedy; (iii) the relationship between the percentage of minority workers to be employed and the percentage of minority group members in the relevant population or work force; and (iv) the availability of waiver provisions if the hiring plan could not be met. A final factor of primary importance that I considered in *Fullilove,* as well as in *Wygant,* was "the effect of the [remedy] upon innocent third-parties." Application of those factors demonstrates that the goal in this case comports with constitutional requirements.

First, it is doubtful, given petitioners' history in this litigation, that the District Court had available to it any other effective remedy. That court, having had the parties before it over a period of time, was in the best position to judge whether an alternative remedy, such as a simple injunction, would have been effective in ending petitioners' discriminatory practices. Here, the court imposed the 29% goal in 1975 only after declaring that "[i]n light of Local 28's and JAC's failure to 'clean house' this court concludes that the imposition of a remedial racial goal * * * is essential to place the defendants in a position of compliance with the 1964 Civil Rights Act." On these facts, it is fair to conclude that absent authority to set a goal as a benchmark against which it could measure progress in eliminating discriminatory practices, the District Court may have been powerless to provide an effective remedy. Second, the goal was not imposed as a permanent requirement, but is of limited duration. Third, the goal is directly related to the percentage of nonwhites in the relevant workforce.

As a fourth factor, my concurring opinion in *Fullilove* considered whether waiver provisions were available in the event that the hiring goal could not be met. The requirement of a waiver provision or, more generally, of flexibility with respect to the imposition of a numerical goal reflects a recognition that neither the Constitution or Title VII requires a particular racial balance in the workplace. Indeed, the Constitution forbids such a requirement if imposed for its own sake. *Fullilove,* supra, 448 U.S., at 507, 100 S.Ct., at 2789–2790. "We have recognized, however, that in order to remedy the effects of prior discrimination, it may be necessary to take race into account." *Wygant,* supra, at 106 S.Ct., at 1850. Thus, a court may not choose a remedy for the purpose of attaining a particular racial balance; rather, remedies properly are confined to the elimination of proven discrimination. A goal is a means, useful in limited circumstances, to assist a court in determining whether discrimination has been eradicated.

The flexible application of the goal requirement in this case demonstrates that it is not a means to achieve racial balance. The contempt order was not imposed for the Union's failure to achieve the goal, but for its failure to take the prescribed steps that would facilitate achieving the goal. Additional flexibility is evidenced by the fact that this goal, originally set to be achieved by 1981, has been twice delayed and is now set for 1987.

It is also important to emphasize that on the record before us, it does not appear that nonminorities will be burdened directly, if at all. Petitioners' counsel conceded at oral argument that imposition of the goal would not require the layoff of nonminority union workers, and that therefore the District Court's order did not disadvantage existing union members. This case is thus distinguishable from *Wygant* where the plurality opinion noted that "layoffs impose the entire burden of achieving racial equality on particular individuals, often resulting in serious disruption of their lives." In contrast to the layoff provision in *Wygant,* the goal at issue here is akin to a hiring goal. In *Wygant* the plurality observed:

> "In cases involving valid *hiring* goals, the burden to be borne by individuals is diffused to a considerable extent among society generally. Though hiring goals may burden some innocent individuals, they simply do not impose the same kind of injury that layoffs impose." Id., at 14.[3]

My view that the imposition of flexible goals as a remedy for past discrimination may be permissible under the Constitution is not an endorsement of their indiscriminate use. Nor do I imply that the adoption of such a goal will always pass constitutional muster.[4]

JUSTICE O'CONNOR, concurring in part and dissenting in part.

3. Of course, it is too simplistic to conclude from the combined holdings in *Wygant* and this case that hiring goals withstand constitutional muster whereas layoff goals and fixed quotas do not. There may be cases, for example, where a hiring goal in a particularly specialized area of employment would have the same pernicious effect as the layoff goal in *Wygant.* The proper constitutional inquity focuses on the effect, if any, and the diffuseness of the burden imposed on innocent nonminorities, not on the label applied to the particular employment plan at issue.

4. If the record now before us supported the position taken by Justice O'Connor, I might well view this case differently. Justice O'Connor apparently assumes that the goal can be achieved by August 31, 1987, only if the District Court requires "the replacement of journeymen by apprentices on a strictly racial basis." If and when that happens, petitioners will be free to argue that an impermissible quota has been imposed on the union and the JAC. An examination of what *has occurred* in this litigation over the years makes plain that the District Court has not enforced the goal in the rigid manner that concerns Justice O'Connor. Based on the record actually before us, I am satisfied that the goal imposed by the District Court is a flexible one.

I join Parts II–A, III, and VI of the Court's opinion. I would reverse the judgment of the Court of Appeals on statutory grounds insofar as the membership "goal" and the Fund order are concerned, and I would not reach petitioners' constitutional claims. I agree with Justice White, however, that the membership "goal" in this case operates as a rigid racial quota that cannot feasibly be met through good-faith efforts by Local 28. In my view, § 703(j), and § 706(g), read together, preclude courts from ordering racial quotas such as this. I therefore dissent from the Court's judgment insofar as it affirms the use of these mandatory quotas.

In Firefighters v. Stotts, 467 U.S. 561, 104 S.Ct. 2576, 81 L.Ed.2d 483 (1984), the Court interpreted § 706(g) as embodying a policy against court-ordered remedies under Title VII that award racial preferences in employment to individuals who have not been subjected to unlawful discrimination. The dissenting opinion in *Stotts* urged precisely the position advanced by Justice Brennan's plurality opinion today—that any such policy extends only to awarding make-whole relief to particular non-victims of discrimination, and does not bar class-wide racial preferences in certain cases. Id., at 612–614, 104 S.Ct., at 2605–2607 (Blackmun, J., dissenting). The Court unquestionably rejected that view in *Stotts*. Although technically dicta, the discussion of § 706(g) in *Stotts* was an important part of the Court's rationale for the result it reached, and accordingly is entitled to greater weight than the Court gives it today.

It is now clear, however, that a majority of the Court believes that the last sentence of § 706(g) does not in all circumstances prohibit a court in a Title VII employment discrimination case from ordering relief that may confer some racial preferences with regard to employment in favor of non-victims of discrimination. Even assuming that some forms of race-conscious affirmative relief, such as racial hiring goals, are permissible as remedies for egregious and pervasive violations of Title VII, in my view the membership "goal" and fund order in this case were impermissible because they operate not as goals but as racial quotas. Such quotas run counter to § 703(j) of Title VII, and are thus impermissible under § 706(g) when that section is read in light of § 703(j), as I believe it should be.

The plurality asserts that § 703(j) in no way "qualifies or proscribes a court's authority to order relief otherwise appropriate under § 706(g) in circumstances where an illegal discriminatory act or practice is established." According to the plurality, § 703(j) merely provides that an employer or union does not engage in unlawful discrimination simply on account of a racial imbalance in its workforce or membership, and thus is not required to institute preferential quotas to avoid Title VII liability. Thus, the plurality concedes that § 703(j) is aimed at racial quotas, but interprets it as limiting only the substantive liability of employers and unions, not the remedial powers of courts.

This interpretation of § 703(j) is unduly narrow. * * *

In Steelworkers v. Weber, 443 U.S. 193, 205 n. 5, 99 S.Ct. 2721, 2728, n. 5, 61 L.Ed.2d 480 (1979) the Court stated that "Section 703(j) speaks to substantive liability under Title VII." While this is *one* purpose of § 703(j), the Court in *Weber* had no occasion to consider whether it was the *exclusive* purpose. In my view, the words "Nothing contained in this title shall be interpreted to require" plainly make § 703(j) applicable to the interpretation of *any* provision of Title VII, including § 706(g). Therefore, when a court interprets § 706(g) as authorizing it to require an employer to adopt a racial quota, that court contravenes § 703(j) to the extent that the relief imposed as a purported remedy for a violation of Title VII's substantive provisions in fact operates to require racial preferences "on account of [a racial] imbalance." In addition, since § 703(j) by its terms limits the circumstances in which an employer or union may be required to extend "preferential treatment to any individual *or to any group* because of * * * race," the plurality's distinction between make-whole and class-wide relief is plainly ruled out insofar as § 703(j) is concerned.

The plurality's restrictive reading of § 703(j) rests largely on its view of the legislative history, which the plurality claims establishes that Congress simply did not consider the use of racial preferences to remedy past discrimination when it enacted Title VII. According to the plurality, the sole focus of concern over racial quotas involved the scope of substantive liability under Title VII: the fear was that employers or unions would be found liable for violating Title VII merely on account of a racial imbalance. This reading of the legislative history ignores authoritative statements—relied on by the Court in *Stotts,* supra, 467 U.S., at 580–582, 104 S.Ct., at 2589–2590—addressing the relief courts could order, and making plain that racial *quotas,* at least, were not among the permissible remedies for past discrimination. See, e.g., 110 Cong.Rec. 6549 (1964) ("Contrary to the allegations of some opponents of this title, there is nothing in it that will give any power to the Commission or to any court to require hiring, firing, or promotion of employees in order to meet a racial 'quota' or to achieve a certain racial balance") (Sen. Humphrey); id., at 6566 ("[T]itle VII does not permit the ordering of racial quotas in businesses or unions * * *.") (memorandum of Republican House sponsors); id., at 14665 ("under title VII, not even a court, much less the Commission, could order racial quotas or the hiring, reinstatement, admission to membership or payment of back pay for anyone who is not discriminated against in violation of this title") (statement of Senate sponsors in a bipartisan newsletter delivered to Senators supporting the bill during an attempted filibuster).

The plurality's reading of the legislative history also defies common sense. Legislators who objected to racial quotas obviously did so because of the harm that such quotas would impose on innocent nonminority workers as well as because of the restriction on employer freedom that would follow from an across-the-board requirement of racial balance in every workplace. Racial quotas would inflict such harms on nonminority workers whether such quotas were imposed directly by federal law in the form of a requirement that every workforce be racially balanced, or imposed as part of a court-ordered remedy for an employer's violations of Title VII. The legislative history, fairly read, indicates that such racial quotas are impermissible as a means of enforcing Title VII, and that even racial preferences short of quotas should be used only where clearly necessary if these preferences would benefit nonvictims at the expense of innocent nonminority workers.

At bottom, the plurality recognizes that this is so, although it prefers to cut the congressional rejection of racial quotas loose from any statutory moorings and make this policy simply another factor that should inform the remedial discretion of district courts. Indeed, notwithstanding its claim that § 703(j) is irrelevant to interpretation of § 706(g), the plurality tacitly concedes that racial quotas are improper, and that they are improper by virtue of § 703(j). The plurality says that in considering whether to grant race-conscious affirmative relief "the court should exercise its discretion with an eye towards Congress' concern that race-conscious affirmative measures not be invoked simply to create a racially balanced work force." Since this is precisely the congressional concern that the plurality locates in § 703(j), the plurality appears to recognize that § 703(j) *is* relevant, after all, to the choice of remedies under § 706(g). Moreover, the plurality indicates that a hiring or membership goal must be applied flexibly in order that the goal not be "used simply to achieve and maintain racial balance, but rather as a benchmark against which the court [can] gauge [an employer's or union's] efforts to remedy past discrimination." It is fair to infer that the plurality approves the use of the membership goal in this case only because, in its view, that goal can be characterized as "a means by which [the court] can measure petitioners' compliance with its orders, rather than as a strict racial quota."

The plurality correctly indicates that, as to any racial goal ordered by a court as a remedy for past discrimination, the employer *always* has a potential defense by virtue of § 706(g) against a claim that it was required to hire a particular employee, to wit, that the employee was not hired for "reasons unrelated to discrimination." Although the plurality gives no clues as to the scope of this defense, it is clear that an employer would remain free to refuse to hire unqualified minority applicants, even if as a result the employer failed to meet a racial hiring goal. Thus, an employer's undoubted freedom to refuse to hire unqualified minority applicants, even in the face of a court-ordered racial hiring goal, operates as one important limitation on the extent of any racially preferential treatment that can result from such a goal.

The plurality offers little guidance as to what separates an impermissible quota from a permissible goal. Reference to benchmarks such as the percentage of minority workers in the relevant labor pool will often be entirely proper in order to *estimate* how an employer's workforce would be composed absent past discrimination. But it is completely unrealistic to assume that individuals of each race will gravitate with mathematical exactitude to each employer or union absent unlawful discrimination. That, of course, is why there must be a substantial statistical disparity between the composition of an employer's workforce and the relevant labor pool, or the general population, before an intent to discriminate may be inferred from such a disparity. Teamsters v. United States, 431 U.S. 324, 339–340, and n. 20, 97 S.Ct. 1843, 1856–1857, and n. 20, 52 L.Ed.2d 396 (1977). Thus, the use of a rigid quota turns a sensible rule of thumb into an unjustified conclusion about the precise extent to which past discrimination has lingering effects, or into an unjustified prediction about what would happen in the future in the absence of continuing discrimination. The imposition of a quota is therefore not truly remedial, but rather amounts to a requirement of racial balance, in contravention of § 703(j)'s clear policy against such requirements.

To be consistent with § 703(j), a racial hiring or membership goal must be intended to serve merely as a benchmark for measuring compliance with Title VII and eliminating the lingering effects of past discrimination, rather than as a rigid numerical requirement that must unconditionally be met on pain of sanctions. To hold an employer or union to achievement of a particular percentage of minority employment or membership, and to do so regardless of circumstances such as economic conditions or the number of available qualified minority applicants, is to impose an impermissible quota. By contrast, a permissible goal should require only a good faith effort on the employer's or union's part to come within a range demarcated by the goal itself.

This understanding of the difference between goals and quotas essentially comports with the definitions jointly adopted by the EEOC and the Departments of Justice and Labor in a 1973 memorandum, and reaffirmed on several occasions since then by the EEOC and the Department of Labor. Memorandum—Permissible Goals and Timetables in State and Local Government Employment Practices (Mar. 23, 1973), reprinted in 2 CCH Employment Practices ¶ 3776 (1985) (hereinafter Memorandum); see 41 Fed.Reg. 38815 (1976) (EEOC Policy Statement on Affirmative Action Programs for State and Local Government Agencies); Office of Federal Contract Compliance Programs v. Priester Construction Co., No. 78–OFCCP–11 (Feb. 22, 1983), summarized in OFCCP Order No. 970a3, reprinted in 2 BNA AACM D:9121 (1983). In the view of these federal agencies, which are charged with responsibility for enforcing equal employment opportunity laws, a quota "would impose a fixed number or percentage which must be attained, or which cannot be exceeded," and would do so "regardless of the number of potential applicants who meet necessary qualifications." Memorandum, 2 CCH Employment Practices, at 3856. By contrast, a goal is "a numerical objective, fixed realistically in terms of the number of vacancies expected, and the number of qualified applicants available in the relevant job market." Ibid. An employer's failure to meet a goal despite good faith efforts "is not subject to sanction, because [the employer] is not expected to displace existing employees or to hire unneeded employees to meet [the] goal." Ibid. This understanding of the difference between goals and quotas seems to me workable and far more consistent with the policy underlying § 703(j) and § 706(g) than the plurality's forced distinction between make-whole relief and class-wide relief. If, then, some racial preferences may be ordered by a court as a remedy for past discrimination even though the beneficiaries may be nonvictims, I would employ a distinction such as this between quotas and goals in setting standards to inform use by district courts of their remedial powers under § 706(g) to fashion such relief.

If, as the Court holds, Title VII sometimes allows district courts to employ race-conscious remedies that may result in racially preferential treatment for non-victims, it does so only where such remedies are truly necessary. In fashioning any such remedy, including racial hiring goals, the court should exercise caution and "take care to tailor its orders to fit the nature of the violation it seeks to correct." As the plurality suggests, goals should generally be temporary measures rather than efforts to maintain a previously achieved racial balance, and should not unnecessarily trammel the interests of nonminority employees. Furthermore, the use of goals is least likely to be consistent with § 703(j) where the adverse effects of any racially preferential treatment attributable to the goals will be "concentrated upon a relatively small, ascertainable group of non-minority persons." In sum, the creation of racial preferences by courts, even in the more limited form of goals rather than quotas, must be done sparingly and only where manifestly necessary to remedy violations of Title VII if the policy underlying § 703(j) and § 706(g) is to be honored.

In this case, I agree with Justice White that the membership "goal" established by the District Court's successive orders in this case has been administered and will continue to operate "not just [as] a minority membership goal but also [as] a strict racial quota that the union was required to attain." It is important to realize that the membership "goal" ordered by the District Court goes well beyond a requirement, such as the ones the plurality discusses approvingly, that a union "admit qualified minorities roughly in proportion to the number of qualified minorities in the work force." The "goal" here requires that the racial composition of Local 28's entire membership mirror that of the relevant labor pool by August 31, 1987, without regard to variables such as the number of qualified minority applicants available or the number of new apprentices needed. The District Court plainly stated that "[i]f the goal is not attained by that date, defendants will face fines that will threaten their very existence."

I see no reason not to take the District Court's mandatory language at face value, and certainly none is supplied by the plurality's conclusory assertion that "the District Court has been willing to accommodate *legitimate* reasons for petitioners' failure to comply with court orders." As Judge Winter persuasively argued in dissent below, the District

Court was clearly *not* willing to take due account of the economic conditions that led to a sharp decline in the demand for the union skills involved in this case. Indeed, notwithstanding that petitioners have "voluntarily indentured 45% nonwhites in the apprenticeship classes since January 1981," the District Court ordered the JAC to indenture one nonwhite apprentice for every white apprentice. 753 F.2d, at 1189. The Court of Appeals set this portion of the District Court's order aside as an abuse of discretion, ibid., but the District Court's willingness to impose such a rigid hiring quota certainly suggests that the District Court intended the membership "goal" to be equally absolute.

It is no answer to these observations that the District Court on two previous occasions postponed the final date for full compliance with the membership goal. At the time of the Court of Appeals' decision, Local 28's membership was approximately 10.8% nonwhite, and at oral argument counsel for petitioners represented that Local 28's membership of about 3,100 workers is now approximately 15.5% nonwhite. Absent an enormous expansion in the size of the apprentice program—which would be feasible only if the demand for the services of Local 28's members were dramatically to increase—it is beyond cavil that neither the "voluntary" 45% minority ratio now employed for apprenticeship classes nor the District Court's one-to-one order could achieve the 29.23% membership goal by Aug. 31, 1987. Indeed, at oral argument counsel for respondent conceded as much.

I do not question that petitioners' past violations of Title VII were egregious, or that in some respects they exhibited inexcusable recalcitrance in the face of the District Court's earlier remedial orders. But the timetable with which petitioners were ordered to comply was quite unrealistic and clearly could not be met by good-faith efforts on petitioners' part. In sum, the membership goal operates as a rigid membership quota, which will in turn spawn a sharp curtailment in the opportunities of nonminorities to be admitted to the apprenticeship program. Indeed, in order for the District Court's timetable to be met, this fixed quota would appear to require "the replacement of journeymen by apprentices on a strictly racial basis." 753 F.2d, at 1195 (Winter, J., dissenting).

Whether the unequivocal rejection of racial quotas by the Congress that enacted Title VII is said to be expressed in § 706(g), in § 703(j), or in both, a "remedy" such as this membership quota cannot stand. For similar reasons, I believe that the Fund order, which created benefits for minority apprentices that nonminority apprentices were precluded from enjoying, operated as a form of racial quota. Accordingly, I would reverse the judgment of the Court of Appeals on statutory grounds insofar as the membership "goal" and Fund order are concerned, without reaching petitioners' constitutional claims.

JUSTICE WHITE, dissenting.

As the Court observes, the general policy under Title VII is to limit relief for racial discrimination in employment practices to actual victims of the discrimination. But I agree that § 706(g) does not bar relief for nonvictims in all circumstances. Hence, I generally agree with Parts I through IV–D of the Court's opinion. It may also be that this is one of those unusual cases where nonvictims of discrimination were entitled to a measure of the relief ordered by the District Court and affirmed by the Court of Appeals. But Judge Winter, in dissent below, was correct in concluding that critical parts of the remedy ordered in this case were excessive under § 706(g), absent findings that those benefiting from the relief had been victims of discriminatory practices by the union. As Judge Winter explained and contrary to the Court's views, the cumulative effect of the revised affirmative action plan and the contempt judgments against the union established not just a minority membership goal but also a strict racial quota that the union was required to attain. We have not heretofore approved this kind of racially discriminatory hiring practice, and I would not do so now. Beyond this, I am convinced, as Judge Winter was, that holding the union in contempt for failing to attain the membership quota during a time of economic doldrums in the construction industry and a declining demand for the union skills involved in this case was for all practical purposes equivalent to a judicial insistence that the union comply even if it required the displacement of nonminority workers by members of the plaintiff class. The remedy is inequitable in my view, and for this reason I dissent from the judgment affirming the Court of Appeals.

JUSTICE REHNQUIST, with whom THE CHIEF JUSTICE joins, dissenting.

Today, in Local Number 93 v. City of Cleveland, (REHNQUIST, J., dissenting), I express my belief that § 706(g) forbids a court from ordering racial preferences that effectively displace non-minorities except to minority individuals who have been the actual victims of a particular employer's racial discrimination. Although the pervasiveness of the racial discrimination practiced by a particular union or employer is likely to increase the number of victims who are entitled to a remedy under the Act, § 706(g) does not allow us to go further than that and sanction the granting of relief to those who were not victims at the expense of innocent non-minority workers injured by racial preferences. I explain that both the language and the legislative history of § 706(g) clearly support this reading of § 706(g), and that this Court stated as much just two Terms ago in Firefighters v. Stotts, 467 U.S. 561, 104 S.Ct. 2576, 81 L.Ed.2d 483 (1984). Because of this, I would not reach the equal protection question, but would rely solely on § 706(g) to reverse the Court of Appeals' judgment approving the order of class-based relief for petitioners' past discrimination.

NOTES AND PROBLEMS FOR DISCUSSION

1. The opinions written by Justices Brennan and Powell state that an employer cannot be found in violation of Title VII "simply" because of a racial imbalance in its workforce and, therefore, that racial preferences cannot be imposed solely for the purpose of attaining or maintaining racial balance. Nevertheless, the opinions continue, racial preferences can be imposed as

remedies for Title VII violations. But if racial imbalance is not *per se* violative of Title VII, i.e., if discrimination means something more than the mere fact of imbalance, should racial balance constitute the objective of a remedy for discrimination? Isn't that the effect of including a specific numerical hiring or promotion goal in a court ordered affirmative action plan? If discrimination is not to be measured by the level of racial representation, should the effectiveness of efforts to remedy discrimination be gauged by racial proportionality?

2. The Court interpreted the last sentence of § 706(g) as permitting the awarding of race-conscious affirmative relief that might benefit non-victims as long as that relief was designed to remedy prior discrimination. In footnote 45, however, the Court added that specific individuals could be precluded from such relief where they are proven non-victims, i.e., where action taken against them was proven to be unrelated to discrimination. Yet if, as the Court also indicated, affirmative action is designed "to dismantle prior patterns of employment discrimination and to prevent discrimination in the future" and "is provided to the class as a whole rather than to individual members", is there a justification for distinguishing between proven and unproven non-victims? Does Justice O'Connor's opinion shed light on this question?

3. Justice Powell upheld the trial court's order, at least in part, because he concluded that incumbent nonminority workers would not be burdened directly, if at all, by the race-based hiring goal. Justices O'Connor and White, on the other hand, maintained that the plan would result in a "sharp curtailment in the opportunities of nonminorities to be admitted to the apprenticeship program." Justice Brennan, writing for the Court, concluded that while incumbents would not suffer any disadvantage under the challenged plan, whites seeking admission into the union might be temporarily disadvantaged in favor of minority candidates. What is the significance of this difference of opinion?

4. Do the opinions in *Local 28* reflect a consensus on the issue of whether court ordered affirmative action can respond to societal discrimination? The plurality opinion states that race-conscious relief "may be appropriate where an employer or a labor union has engaged in persistent or egregious discrimination, *or where necessary to dissipate the lingering effects of pervasive discrimination.*" (emphasis added). Justice Powell, whose critical swing vote produced a majority in favor of upholding the judgments below, while concentrating on the constitutional question, said only that such relief was permitted under Title VII "in cases involving particularly egregious conduct". Justice O'Connor declared that "assuming that some forms of race-conscious affirmative relief, such as racial hiring goals, are permissible as remedies for egregious and pervasive violations", such relief must be intended to serve as a benchmark for "eliminating the lingering effects of past discrimination". Justice White "agreed generally" with the plurality's statement on the issue. Justice Rehnquist and the Chief Justice dissented on the ground that affirmative relief that effectively displaced nonminority individuals could be awarded only to "actual victims of a particular employer's racial discrimination". The Court did address the issue of the propriety of voluntarily adopted affirmative responses to societal discrimination in *Weber* and *Wygant,* infra.

5. Note that on the critical question of whether a court can order race-conscious relief that might benefit non-victims, six members (Brennan, Marshall, Blackmun, Stevens, Powell and White) agreed that "in appropriate circumstances", Title VII would not preclude such relief. Only Justices O'Connor, Rehnquist and the Chief Justice agreed with the Solicitor General's contention that Title VII relief must be limited to proven victims of discrimina-

tion. This issue had been the subject of much controversy following the Supreme Court's prior ruling in *Stotts,* infra.

WYGANT v. JACKSON BOARD OF EDUCATION

Supreme Court of the United States, 1986.
___ U.S. ___, 106 S.Ct. 1842, 90 L.Ed.2d 260.

JUSTICE POWELL announced the judgment of the Court and delivered an opinion in which THE CHIEF JUSTICE and JUSTICE REHNQUIST joined, and which JUSTICE O'CONNOR joined in parts I, II, III–A, III–B, and V.

This case presents the question whether a school board, consistent with the Equal Protection Clause, may extend preferential protection against layoffs to some of its employees because of their race or national origin.

I

In 1972 the Jackson Board of Education, because of racial tension in the community that extended to its schools, considered adding a layoff provision to the Collective Bargaining Agreement (CBA) between the Board and the Jackson Education Association (the Union) that would protect employees who were members of certain minority groups against layoffs.[1] The Board and the Union eventually approved a new provision, Article XII of the CBA, covering layoffs. It stated:

> "In the event that it becomes necessary to reduce the number of teachers through layoff from employment by the Board, teachers with the most seniority in the district shall be retained, except that at no time will there be a greater percentage of minority personnel laid off than the current percentage of minority personnel employed at the time of the layoff. In no event will the number given notice of possible layoff be greater than the number of positions to be eliminated. Each teacher so affected will be called back in reverse order for positions for which he is certificated maintaining the above minority balance." App. 13.[2]

When layoffs became necessary in 1974, it was evident that adherence to the CBA would result in the layoff of tenured non-minority teachers while minority teachers on probationary status were retained. Rather than complying with Article XII, the Board retained the tenured teachers and laid off probationary minority teachers, thus failing to maintain the percentage of minority personnel that existed at the time of the layoff. The Union, together with two minority teachers

1. Prior to bargaining on this subject, the Minority Affairs Office of the Jackson Public Schools sent a questionnaire to all teachers, soliciting their views as to a layoff policy. The questionnaire proposed two alternatives: continuation of the existing straight seniority system, or a freeze of minority layoffs to ensure retention of minority teachers in exact proportion to the minority student population. Ninety-six percent of the teachers who responded to the questionnaire expressed a preference for the straight seniority system.

2. Article VII of the CBA defined "minority group personnel" as "those employees who are Black, American Indian, Oriental, or of Spanish descendancy." App. 15.

who had been laid off, brought suit in federal court, id., at 30, (Jackson Education Assn. v. Board of Education, (Jackson I) (mem. op.)), claiming that the Board's failure to adhere to the layoff provision violated the Equal Protection Clause of the Fourteenth Amendment and Title VII of the Civil Rights Act of 1964. They also urged the District Court to take pendent jurisdiction over state law contract claims. In its answer the Board denied any prior employment discrimination and argued that the layoff provision conflicted with the Michigan Teacher Tenure Act. App. 33. Following trial, the District Court *sua sponte* concluded that it lacked jurisdiction over the case, in part because there was insufficient evidence to support the plaintiffs' claim that the Board had engaged in discriminatory hiring practices prior to 1972, id., at 35–37, and in part because the plaintiffs had not fulfilled the jurisdictional prerequisite to a Title VII claim by filing discrimination charges with the Equal Employment Opportunity Commission. After dismissing the federal claims, the District Court declined to exercise pendent jurisdiction over the state law contract claims.

Rather than taking an appeal, the plaintiffs instituted a suit in state court, Jackson Education Assn. v. Board of Education (Jackson County Circuit Court, 1979) (*Jackson II*), raising in essence the same claims that had been raised in *Jackson I.* In entering judgment for the plaintiffs, the state court found that the Board had breached its contract with the plaintiffs, and that Article XII did not violate the Michigan Teacher Tenure Act. In rejecting the Board's argument that the layoff provision violated the Civil Rights Act of 1964, the state court found that it "ha[d] not been established that the board had discriminated against minorities in its hiring practices. The minority representation on the faculty was the result of societal racial discrimination." The state court also found that "[t]here is no history of overt past discrimination by the parties to this contract." Nevertheless, the court held that Article XII was permissible, despite its discriminatory effect on nonminority teachers, as an attempt to remedy the effects of societal discrimination.

After *Jackson II,* the Board adhered to Article XII. As a result, during the 1976–1977 and 1981–1982 school years, nonminority teachers were laid off, while minority teachers with less seniority were retained. The displaced nonminority teachers, petitioners here, brought suit in Federal District Court, alleging violations of the Equal Protection Clause, Title VII, 42 U.S.C. § 1983, and other federal and state statutes. On cross motions for summary judgment, the District Court dismissed all of petitioners' claims. With respect to the equal protection claim,[3] the District Court held that the racial preferences granted by the Board need not be grounded on a finding of prior discrimination. Instead, the court decided that the racial preferences were permissible under the Equal Protection Clause as an attempt to

3. Petitioners have sought review in this Court only of their claim based on the Equal Protection Clause.

remedy societal discrimination by providing "role models" for minority schoolchildren, and upheld the constitutionality of the layoff provision.

The Court of Appeals for the Sixth Circuit affirmed, largely adopting the reasoning and language of the District Court. 746 F.2d 1152 (1984). We granted certiorari to resolve the important issue of the constitutionality of race-based layoffs by public employers. We now reverse.

II

Petitioners' central claim is that they were laid off because of their race in violation of the Equal Protection Clause of the Fourteenth Amendment. Decisions by faculties and administrators of public schools based on race or ethnic origin are reviewable under the Fourteenth Amendment.[4] This Court has "consistently repudiated '[d]istinctions between citizens solely because of their ancestry' as being 'odious to a free people whose institutions are founded upon the doctrine of equality,'" Loving v. Virginia, 388 U.S. 1, 11, 87 S.Ct. 1817, 1823, 18 L.Ed.2d 1010 (1967) quoting Hirabayashi v. United States, 320 U.S. 81, 100, 63 S.Ct. 1375, 1385, 87 L.Ed. 1774 (1943). "Racial and ethnic distinctions of any sort are inherently suspect and thus call for the most exacting judicial examination." Regents of University of California v. Bakke, 438 U.S. 265, 291, 98 S.Ct. 2733, 2748, 57 L.Ed.2d 750 (1978) (opinion of Powell, J., joined by White, J.)

The Court has recognized that the level of scrutiny does not change merely because the challenged classification operates against a group that historically has not been subject to governmental discrimination. Mississippi University for Women v. Hogan, 458 U.S. 718, 724 n. 9, 102 S.Ct. 3331, 3336 n. 9, 73 L.Ed.2d 1090 (1982); *Bakke*, 438 U.S., at 291–299, 98 S.Ct., at 2748–2752; see Shelley v. Kraemer, 334 U.S. 1, 22, 68 S.Ct. 836, 846, 92 L.Ed. 1161 (1948); see also A. Bickel, The Morality of Consent 133 (1975). In this case, Article XII of the CBA operates against whites and in favor of certain minorities, and therefore constitutes a classification based on race. "Any preference based on racial or ethnic criteria must necessarily receive a most searching examination to make sure that it does not conflict with constitutional guarantees." Fullilove v. Klutznick, 448 U.S. 448, 491, 100 S.Ct. 2758, 2781, 65 L.Ed. 2d 902 (1980) (opinion of Burger, C.J.). There are two prongs to this examination. First, any racial classification "must be justified by a compelling governmental interest." Palmore v. Sidoti, 466 U.S. 429, 432, 104 S.Ct. 1879, 1882, 80 L.Ed.2d 421 (1984); see Loving v. Virginia, 388 U.S. 1, 11, 87 S.Ct. 1817, 1823, 18 L.Ed.2d 1010 (1967); cf. Graham v. Richardson, 403 U.S. 365, 375, 91 S.Ct. 1848, 1853, 29 L.Ed.2d 534 (1971) (alienage). Second, the means chosen by the State to effectuate its purpose must be "narrowly tailored to the achievement of that

4. School district collective bargaining agreements constitute state action for purposes of the Fourteenth Amendment. Abood v. Detroit Board of Ed., 431 U.S. 209, 218, and n. 12, 97 S.Ct. 1782, 1790, and n. 12, 52 L.Ed.2d 261 (1977).

goal." *Fullilove,* 448 U.S., at 480, 100 S.Ct., at 2776. We must decide whether the layoff provision is supported by a compelling state purpose and whether the means chosen to accomplish that purpose are narrowly tailored.

III

A

The Court of Appeals, relying on the reasoning and language of the District Court's opinion, held that the Board's interest in providing minority role models for its minority students, as an attempt to alleviate the effects of societal discrimination, was sufficiently important to justify the racial classification embodied in the layoff provision. The court discerned a need for more minority faculty role models by finding that the percentage of minority teachers was less than the percentage of minority students.

This Court never has held that societal discrimination alone is sufficient to justify a racial classification. Rather, the Court has insisted upon some showing of prior discrimination by the governmental unit involved before allowing limited use of racial classifications in order to remedy such discrimination. This Court's reasoning in Hazelwood School District v. United States, 433 U.S. 299, 97 S.Ct. 2736, 53 L.Ed.2d 768 (1977), illustrates that the relevant analysis in cases involving proof of discrimination by statistical disparity focuses on those disparities that demonstrate such prior governmental discrimination. In *Hazelwood* the Court concluded that, absent employment discrimination by the school board, " 'nondiscriminatory hiring practices will in time result in a work force more or less representative of the racial and ethnic composition of the population in the community from which the employees are hired.' " Id., at 307, 97 S.Ct., at 2741, quoting Teamsters v. United States, 431 U.S. 324, 340, n. 20, 97 S.Ct. 1843, 1856, n. 20, 52 L.Ed.2d 396 (1977). See also *Wygant,* supra, 746 F.2d, at 1160 (Wellford, J., concurring) ("Had the plaintiffs in this case presented data as to the percentage of qualified minority teachers in the relevant labor market to show that defendant Board's hiring of black teachers over a number of years had equalled that figure, I believe this court may well have been required to reverse * * *."). Based on that reasoning, the Court in *Hazelwood* held that the proper comparison for determining the existence of actual discrimination by the school board was "between the racial composition of [the school's] teaching staff and the racial composition of the qualified public school teacher population in the relevant labor market." 433 U.S., at 308, 97 S.Ct., at 2742. *Hazelwood* demonstrates this Court's focus on prior discrimination as the justification for, and the limitation on, a State's adoption of race-based remedies. See also Swann v. Charlotte-Mecklenburg Board of Education, 402 U.S. 1, 91 S.Ct. 1267, 28 L.Ed.2d 554 (1971).

Unlike the analysis in *Hazelwood,* the role model theory employed by the District Court has no logical stopping point. The role model theory allows the Board to engage in discriminatory hiring and layoff practices long past the point required by any legitimate remedial purpose. Indeed, by tying the required percentage of minority teachers to the percentage of minority students, it requires just the sort of year-to-year calibration the Court stated was unnecessary in *Swann,* 402 U.S., at 31–32, 91 S.Ct., at 1283–1284:

> "At some point these school authorities and others like them should have achieved full compliance with this Court's decision in *Brown I.* * * * Neither school authorities nor district courts are constitutionally required to make year-by-year adjustments of the racial composition of student bodies once the affirmative duty to desegregate has been accomplished and racial discrimination through official action is eliminated from the system."

Moreover, because the role model theory does not necessarily bear a relationship to the harm caused by prior discriminatory hiring practices, it actually could be used to escape the obligation to remedy such practices by justifying the small percentage of black teachers by reference to the small percentage of black students. Carried to its logical extreme, the idea that black students are better off with black teachers could lead to the very system the Court rejected in Brown v. Board of Education, 347 U.S. 483, 74 S.Ct. 686, 98 L.Ed. 873 (1954) (*Brown I*).

Societal discrimination, without more, is too amorphous a basis for imposing a racially classified remedy. The role model theory announced by the District Court and the resultant holding typify this indefiniteness. There are numerous explanations for a disparity between the percentage of minority students and the percentage of minority faculty, many of them completely unrelated to discrimination of any kind. In fact, there is no apparent connection between the two groups. Nevertheless, the District Court combined irrelevant comparisons between these two groups with an indisputable statement that there has been societal discrimination, and upheld state action predicated upon racial classifications. No one doubts that there has been serious racial discrimination in this country. But as the basis for imposing discriminatory *legal* remedies that work against innocent people, societal discrimination is insufficient and over expansive. In the absence of particularized findings, a court could uphold remedies that are ageless in their reach into the past, and timeless in their ability to affect the future.

B

Respondents also now argue that their purpose in adopting the layoff provision was to remedy prior discrimination against minorities by the Jackson School District in hiring teachers. Public schools, like other public employers, operate under two interrelated constitutional duties. They are under a clear command from this Court, starting with

Brown v. Board of Education, 349 U.S. 294, 75 S.Ct. 753, 99 L.Ed. 1083 (1955), to eliminate every vestige of racial segregation and discrimination in the schools. Pursuant to that goal, race-conscious remedial action may be necessary. North Carolina State Board of Education v. Swann, 402 U.S. 43, 46, 91 S.Ct. 1284, 1286, 28 L.Ed.2d 586 (1971). On the other hand, public employers, including public schools, also must act in accordance with a "core purpose of the Fourteenth Amendment" which is to "do away with all governmentally imposed distinctions based on race." Palmore v. Sidoti, 466 U.S., at 432, 104 S.Ct., at 1881–1882. These related constitutional duties are not always harmonious; reconciling them requires public employers to act with extraordinary care. In particular, a public employer like the Board must ensure that, before it embarks on an affirmative action program, it has convincing evidence that remedial action is warranted. That is, it must have sufficient evidence to justify the conclusion that there has been prior discrimination.

Evidentiary support for the conclusion that remedial action is warranted becomes crucial when the remedial program is challenged in court by nonminority employees. In this case, for example, petitioners contended at trial that the remedial program—Article XII—had the purpose and effect of instituting a racial classification that was not justified by a remedial purpose. In such a case, the trial court must make a factual determination that the employer had a strong basis in evidence for its conclusion that remedial action was necessary. The ultimate burden remains with the employees to demonstrate the unconstitutionality of an affirmative action program. But unless such a determination is made, an appellate court reviewing a challenge to remedial action by nonminority employees cannot determine whether the race-based action is justified as a remedy for prior discrimination.

Despite the fact that Article XII has spawned years of litigation and three separate lawsuits, no such determination ever has been made. Although its litigation position was different, the Board in *Jackson I* and *Jackson II* denied the existence of prior discriminatory hiring practices. This precise issue was litigated in both those suits. Both courts concluded that any statistical disparities were the result of general societal discrimination, not of prior discrimination by the Board. The Board now contends that, given another opportunity, it could establish the existence of prior discrimination. Although this argument seems belated at this point in the proceedings, we need not consider the question since we conclude below that the layoff provision was not a legally appropriate means of achieving even a compelling purpose.[5]

5. Justice Marshall contends that "the majority has too quickly assumed the absence of a legitimate factual predicate for affirmative action in the Jackson schools." In support of that assertion, he engages in an unprecedented reliance on non-record documents that respondent has "lodged" with this Court. This selective citation to factual materials not considered by the District Court or the Court of Appeals below is unusual enough by itself. My disagreement with Justice Marshall, however, is more fundamental than any disagreement over the heretofore unquestioned

IV

The Court of Appeals examined the means chosen to accomplish the Board's race-conscious purposes under a test of "reasonableness." That standard has no support in the decisions of this Court. As demonstrated in Part II above, our decisions always have employed a more stringent standard—however articulated—to test the validity of the means chosen by a state to accomplish its race-conscious purposes. See, e.g., *Palmore,* 466 U.S., at 432, 104 S.Ct., at 1882 ("to pass constitutional muster, [racial classifications] must be necessary * * * to the accomplishment of their legitimate purpose") (quoting McLaughlin v. Florida, 379 U.S. 184, 196, 85 S.Ct. 283, 290, 13 L.Ed.2d 222 (1964)); *Fullilove,* 448 U.S., at 480, 100 S.Ct., at 2775 (opinion of Burger, C.J.) ("We recognize the need for careful judicial evaluation to assure that any * * * program that employs racial or ethnic criteria to accomplish the objective of remedying the present effects of past discrimination is narrowly tailored to the achievement of that goal").[6] Under strict scrutiny the means chosen to accomplish the State's asserted purpose

rule that this Court decides cases based on the record before it. Justice Marshall does not define what he means by "legitimate factual predicate," nor does he demonstrate the relationship of these non-record materials to his undefined predicate. If, for example, his dissent assumes that general societal discrimination is a sufficient factual predicate, then there is no need to refer to respondents' lodgings as to its own employment history. No one disputes that there has been race discrimination in this country. If that fact alone can justify race-conscious action by the State, despite the Equal Protection Clause, then the dissent need not rely on non-record materials to show a "legitimate factual predicate." If, on the other hand, Justice Marshall is assuming that the necessary factual predicate is prior discrimination by the Board, there is no escaping the need for a factual determination below—a determination that does not exist.

The real dispute, then, is not over the state of the record. It is disagreement as to what constitutes a "legitimate factual predicate." If the necessary factual predicate is *prior discrimination*—that is, that race-based state action is taken to remedy prior discrimination by the governmental unit involved—then the very nature of appellate review requires that a factfinder determine whether the employer was justified in instituting a remedial plan. Nor can the respondent unilaterally insulate itself from this key constitutional question by conceding that it has discriminated in the past, now that it is in its interest to make such a concession. Contrary to the dissent's assertion, the requirement of such a determination by the trial court is not some arbitrary barrier set up by today's opinion. Rather, it is a necessary result of the requirement that race-based state action be remedial.

At any rate, much of the material relied on by Justice Marshall has been the subject of the previous lawsuit in *Jackson II,* where the court concluded that it "had not been established that the Board had discriminated against minorities in its hiring practices." Moreover, as noted supra, at 1852, in *Jackson I* the Board expressly denied that it had engaged in employment discrimination.

6. The term "narrowly tailored," so frequently used in our cases, has acquired a secondary meaning. More specifically, as commentators have indicated, the term may be used to require consideration whether lawful alternative and less restrictive means could have been used. Or, as Professor Ely has noted, the classification at issue must "fit" with greater precision than any alternative means. Ely, The Constitutionality of Reverse Racial Discrimination, 41 U.Chi.L.Rev. 723, 727, n. 26 (1974) (hereinafter Ely). "[Courts] should give particularly intense scrutiny to whether a nonracial approach or a more narrowly tailored racial classification could promote the substantial interest about as well and at tolerable administrative expense." Greenawalt, Judicial Scrutiny of "Benign" Racial Preference in Law School Admissions, 75 Colum.L.Rev. 559, 578–579 (1975).

must be specifically and narrowly framed to accomplish that purpose. *Fullilove,* 448 U.S., at 480, 100 S.Ct., at 2775 (opinion of Burger, C.J.).[7] "Racial classifications are simply too pernicious to permit any but the most exact connection between justification and classification." Id., at 537, 100 S.Ct., at 2805 (Stevens, J., dissenting).

We have recognized, however, that in order to remedy the effects of prior discrimination, it may be necessary to take race into account. As part of this Nation's dedication to eradicating racial discrimination, innocent persons may be called upon to bear some of the burden of the remedy. "When effectuating a limited and properly tailored remedy to cure the effects of prior discrimination, such a 'sharing of the burden' by innocent parties is not impermissible." Id., at 484, 100 S.Ct., at 2778, quoting Franks v. Bowman Transportation Co., 424 U.S. 747, 96 S.Ct. 1251, 47 L.Ed.2d 444 (1976).[8] In *Fullilove,* the challenged statute

7. Several commentators have emphasized, no matter what the weight of the asserted governmental purpose, that the *means* chosen to accomplish the purpose should be narrowly tailored. In arguing for a form of intermediate scrutiny, Professor Greenawalt contends that, "while benign racial classifications call for some weighing of the importance of ends they call for even more intense scrutiny of means, especially of the administrability of less onerous alternative classifications." Greenawalt 565. Professor Ely has suggested that "special scrutiny in the suspect classification context has in fact consisted not in weighing ends but rather in insisting that the classification in issue fit a constitutional permissible state goal with greater precision than any available alternative." Ely 727, n. 26. Professor Gunther argues that judicial scrutiny of legislative means is more appropriate than judicial weighing of the importance of the legislative purpose. Gunther, Foreword: In Search of Evolving Doctrine on a Changing Court: A Model For a Newer Equal Protection, 86 Harv.L.Rev. 1, 20–21 (1972).

8. Of course, when a state implements a race-based plan that requires such a sharing of the burden, it cannot justify the discriminatory effect on some individuals because other individuals had approved the plan. Any "waiver" of the right not to be dealt with by the government on the basis of one's race must be made by those affected. Yet Justice Marshall repeatedly contends that the fact that Article XII was approved by a majority vote of the Union somehow validates this plan. He sees this case not in terms of individual constitutional rights, but as an allocation of burdens "between two racial groups." Thus, Article XII becomes a political compromise that "avoided placing the entire burden of layoffs on either the white teachers as a group or the minority teachers as a group." But the petitioners before us today are not "the white teachers as a group." They are Wendy Wygant and other individuals who claim that they were fired from their jobs because of their race. That claim cannot be waived by petitioners' more senior colleagues. In view of the way union seniority works, it is not surprising that while a straight freeze on minority layoffs was overwhelmingly rejected, a "compromise" eventually was reached that placed the entire burden of the compromise on the most junior union members. The more senior union members simply had nothing to lose from such a compromise. The fact that such a painless accommodation was approved by the more senior union members six times since 1972 is irrelevant. The Constitution does not allocate constitutional rights to be distributed like bloc grants within discrete racial groups; and until it does, petitioners' more senior union colleagues cannot vote away petitioners' rights.

Justice Marshall also attempts to portray the layoff plan as one that has no real invidious effect, stating that "within the confines of constant minority proportions, it preserves the hierarchy of seniority in the selection of individuals for layoff." That phrase merely expresses the tautology that layoffs are based on seniority except as to those nonminority teachers who are displaced by minority teachers with less seniority. This is really nothing more than group-based analysis: "each group would shoulder a portion of [the layoff] burden equal to its portion of the faculty." The constitutional problem remains: the decision that petitioners would be laid off was based on their race.

required at least 10 percent of federal public works funds to be used in contracts with minority-owned business enterprises. This requirement was found to be within the remedial powers of Congress in part because the "actual burden shouldered by nonminority firms is relatively light." 448 U.S., at 484, 100 S.Ct., at 2778.[9]

Significantly, none of the cases discussed above involved layoffs. Here, by contrast, the means chosen to achieve the Board's asserted purposes is that of laying off nonminority teachers with greater seniority in order to retain minority teachers with less seniority. We have previously expressed concern over the burden that a preferential layoffs scheme imposes on innocent parties. See Firefighters v. Stotts, 467 U.S. 561, 574–576, 578–579, 104 S.Ct. 2576, ___-___, ___-___, 81 L.Ed. 2d 483 (1984); see also *Weber,* 443 U.S., at 208, 99 S.Ct., at 2730 ("The plan does not require the discharge of white workers and their replacement with new black hirees"). In cases involving valid *hiring* goals, the burden to be borne by innocent individuals is diffused to a considerable extent among society generally. Though hiring goals may burden some innocent individuals, they simply do not impose the same kind of injury that layoffs impose. Denial of a future employment opportunity is not as intrusive as loss of an existing job.

Many of our cases involve union seniority plans with employees who are typically heavily dependent on wages for their day-to-day living. Even a temporary layoff may have adverse financial as well as psychological effects. A worker may invest many productive years in one job and one city with the expectation of earning the stability and security of seniority. "At that point, the rights and expectations surrounding seniority make up what is probably the most valuable capital asset that the worker 'owns,' worth even more than the current equity in his home." Fallon & Weiler, Conflicting Models of Racial Justice, 1984 S.Ct.Rev. 1, 58. Layoffs disrupt these settled expectations in a way that general hiring goals do not.

While hiring goals impose a diffuse burden, often foreclosing only one of several opportunities,[11] layoffs impose the entire burden of achieving racial equality on particular individuals, often resulting in serious disruption of their lives. That burden is too intrusive. We

9. Similarly, the Court approved the hiring program in Steelworkers v. Weber, 443 U.S. 193, 208, 99 S.Ct. 2721, 2729, 61 L.Ed.2d 480 (1979), in part because the plan did not "unnecessarily trammel the interests of the white employees." Since *Weber* involved a private company, its reasoning concerning the validity of the hiring plan at issue there is not directly relevant to this case, which involves a state-imposed plan. No equal protection claim was presented in *Weber.*

11. The "school admission" cases, which involve the same basic concepts as cases involving hiring goals, illustrate this principle. For example, in DeFunis v. Odegaard, 416 U.S. 312, 94 S.Ct. 1704, 40 L.Ed. 2d 164 (1974), while petitioner's complaint alleged that he had been denied admission to the University of Washington Law School because of his race, he also had been accepted at the Oregon, Idaho, Gonzaga, and Willamette Law Schools. DeFunis v. Odegaard, 82 Wash.2d 11, 30, n. 11, 507 P.2d 1169, 1181, n. 11 (1973). The injury to Defunis was not of the same kind or degree as the injury that he would have suffered had he been removed from law school in his third year. Even this analogy may not rise to the level of harm suffered by a union member who is laid off.

therefore hold that, as a means of accomplishing purposes that otherwise may be legitimate, the Board's layoff plan is not sufficiently narrowly tailored.[12] Other, less intrusive means of accomplishing similar purposes—such as the adoption of hiring goals—are available. For these reasons, the Board's selection of layoffs as the means to accomplish even a valid purpose cannot satisfy the demands of the Equal Protection Clause.[13]

V

We accordingly reverse the judgment of the Court of Appeals for the Sixth Circuit.

It is so ordered.

JUSTICE O'CONNOR, concurring in part and concurring in the judgment.

This case requires us to define and apply the standard required by the Equal Protection Clause when a governmental agency agrees to give preferences on the basis of race or national origin in making layoffs of employees. The specific question posed is, as Justice Marshall puts it, "whether the Constitution prohibits a union and a local school board from developing a collective-bargaining agreement that apportions layoffs between two racially determined groups as a means of preserving the effects of an affirmative hiring policy." Post, at 1860 (Marshall, J., dissenting). There is no issue here of the interpretation and application of Title VII of the Civil Rights Act; accordingly, we have only the constitutional issue to resolve.

The Equal Protection Clause standard applicable to racial classifications that work to the disadvantage of "nonminorities" has been articulated in various ways. Justice Powell now would require that: (1) the racial classification be justified by a " 'compelling governmental interest,' " and (2) the means chosen by the State to effectuate its purpose be "narrowly tailored." This standard reflects the belief, apparently held by all members of this Court, that racial classifications of any sort must be subjected to "strict scrutiny," however defined. See, e.g., Fullilove v. Klutznick, 448 U.S. 448, 491, 100 S.Ct. 2758, 2781, 65 L.Ed.2d 902 (1980) (opinion of Burger, C.J., joined by White, J.) ("Any preference based on racial or ethnic criteria must necessarily receive a most searching examination to make sure that it does not conflict with constitutional guarantees"); id., at 537, 100 S.Ct., at 2805 (Stevens, J., dissenting)

12. We have recognized, however, that in order to provide make-whole relief to the actual, identified victims of individual discrimination, a court may in an appropriate case award competitive seniority. See Franks v. Bowman Transportation Co., 424 U.S. 747, 96 S.Ct. 1251, 47 L.Ed.2d 444 (1976).

13. The Board's definition of minority to include blacks, Orientals, American Indians, and persons of Spanish descent, n. 2, supra, further illustrates the undifferentiated nature of the plan. There is no explanation of why the Board chose to favor these particular minorities or how in fact members of some of the categories can be identified. Moreover, respondents have never suggested—much less formally found—that they have engaged in prior, purposeful discrimination against members of each of these minority groups.

("Racial classifications are simply too pernicious to permit any but the most exact connection between justification and classification"); Regents of University of California v. Bakke, 438 U.S. 265, 291, 98 S.Ct. 2733, 2748, 57 L.Ed.2d 750 (1978) (opinion of Powell, J., joined by White, J.) ("Racial and ethnic distinctions of any sort are inherently suspect and thus call for the most exacting judicial examination"); id., at 361–362, 98 S.Ct., at 2784 ("[O]ur review under the Fourteenth Amendment should be strict—not ' "strict" in theory and fatal in fact,' because it is stigma that causes fatality—but strict and searching nonetheless") (opinion of Brennan, White, Marshall, and Blackmun, JJ). Justices Marshall, Brennan, and Blackmun, however, seem to adhere to the formulation of the "strict" standard that they authored, with Justice White, in *Bakke:* "remedial use of race is permissible if it serves 'important governmental objectives' and is 'substantially related to achievement of those objectives.' " Supra, at 359, 98 S.Ct., at 2783 (opinion of Brennan, White, Marshall, and Blackmun, JJ.).

I subscribe to Justice Powell's formulation because it mirrors the standard we have consistently applied in examining racial classifications in other contexts. In my view,

> "the analysis and level of scrutiny applied to determine the validity of [a racial] classification do not vary simply because the objective appears acceptable to individual Members of the Court. While the validity and importance of the objective may affect the outcome of the analysis, the analysis itself does not change." Mississippi University for Women v. Hogan, 458 U.S. 718, 724, n. 9, 102 S.Ct. 3331, 3336, n. 9, 73 L.Ed.2d 1090 (1982).

Although Justice Powell's formulation may be viewed as more stringent than that suggested by Justices Brennan, White, Marshall, and Blackmun, the disparities between the two tests do not preclude a fair measure of consensus. In particular, as regards certain state interests commonly relied upon in formulating affirmative action programs, the distinction between a "compelling" and an "important" governmental purpose may be a negligible one. The Court is in agreement that, whatever the formulation employed, remedying past or present racial discrimination by a state actor is a sufficiently weighty state interest to warrant the remedial use of a carefully constructed affirmative action program. This remedial purpose need not be accompanied by contemporaneous findings of actual discrimination to be accepted as legitimate as long as the public actor has a firm basis for believing that remedial action is required. Additionally, although its precise contours are uncertain, a state interest in the promotion of racial diversity has been found sufficiently "compelling," at least in the context of higher education, to support the use of racial considerations in furthering that interest. See, e.g., *Bakke,* 438 U.S., at 311–315, 98 S.Ct., at 2759–2761 (opinion of Powell, J.). And certainly nothing the Court has said today necessarily forecloses the possibility that the Court will find other governmental interests which have been relied upon in the lower courts but which have not been passed on here to be sufficiently "important" or "compelling" to sustain the use of affirmative action policies.

It appears, then, that the true source of disagreement on the Court lies not so much in defining the state interests which may support affirmative action efforts as in defining the degree to which the means employed must "fit" the ends pursued to meet constitutional standards. Yet even here the Court has forged a degree of unanimity; it is agreed that a plan need not be limited to the remedying of specific instances of identified discrimination for it to be deemed sufficiently "narrowly tailored," or "substantially related," to the correction of prior discrimination by the state actor.

In the final analysis, the diverse formulations and the number of separate writings put forth by various members of the Court in these difficult cases do not necessarily reflect an intractable fragmentation in opinion with respect to certain core principles. Ultimately, the Court is at least in accord in believing that a public employer, consistent with the Constitution, may undertake an affirmative action program which is designed to further a legitimate remedial purpose and which implements that purpose by means that do not impose disproportionate harm on the interests, or unnecessarily trammel the rights, of innocent individuals directly and adversely affected by a plan's racial preference.

Respondent School Board argues that the governmental purpose or goal advanced here was the School Board's desire to correct apparent prior employment discrimination against minorities while avoiding further litigation. The Michigan Civil Rights Commission determined that the evidence before it supported the allegations of discrimination on the part of the Jackson School Board, though that determination was never reduced to formal findings because the School Board, with the agreement of the Jackson Education Association (Union), voluntarily chose to remedy the perceived violation. Among the measures the School Board and the Union eventually agreed were necessary to remedy the apparent prior discrimination was the layoff provision challenged here; they reasoned that without the layoff provision, the remedial gains made under the ongoing hiring goals contained in the collective bargaining agreement could be eviscerated by layoffs.

The District Court and the Court of Appeals did not focus on the School Board's unquestionably compelling interest in remedying its apparent prior discrimination when evaluating the constitutionality of the challenged layoff provision. Instead, both courts reasoned that the goals of remedying "societal discrimination" and providing "role models" were sufficiently important to withstand equal protection scrutiny. I agree with the Court that a governmental agency's interest in remedying "societal" discrimination, that is, discrimination not traceable to its own actions, cannot be deemed sufficiently compelling to pass constitutional muster under strict scrutiny. I also concur in the Court's assessment that use by the courts below of a "role model" theory to justify the conclusion that this plan had a legitimate remedial purpose was in error.* Thus, in my view, the District Court and the Court of Appeals clearly erred in relying on these purposes and in failing to give greater attention to the School Board's asserted purpose of rectifying its own apparent discrimination.

The error of the District Court and the Court of Appeals can be explained by reference to the fact that the primary issue argued by the parties on the cross motions for summary judgment was whether the School Board, a court, or another competent body had to have made a finding of past discrimination before or at the time of the institution of the plan in order for the plan to be upheld as remedial in purpose. The courts below ruled that a particularized, contemporaneous finding of discrimination was not necessary and upheld the plan as a remedy for "societal" discrimination, apparently on the assumption that in the absence of a specific, contemporaneous finding, any discrimination addressed by an affirmative action plan could only be termed "societal." I believe that this assumption is false and therefore agree with the Court that a contemporaneous or antecedent finding of past discrimination by a court or other competent body is not a constitutional prerequisite to a public employer's voluntary agreement to an affirmative action plan.

A violation of federal statutory or constitutional requirements does not arise with the making of a finding; it arises when the wrong is committed. Contemporaneous findings serve solely as a means by which it can be made absolutely certain that the governmental actor truly is attempting to remedy its own unlawful conduct when it adopts an affirmative action plan, rather than attempting to alleviate the wrongs suffered through general societal discrimination. Such findings, when voluntarily made by a public employer, obviously are desirable in that they provide evidentiary safeguards of value both to nonminority employees and to the public employer itself, should its affirmative action program be challenged in court. If contemporaneous findings were *required* of public employers in every case as a precondition to the constitutional validity of their affirmative action efforts, however, the relative value of these evidentiary advantages would diminish, for they could be secured only by the sacrifice of other vitally important values.

The imposition of a requirement that public employers make findings that they have engaged in illegal discrimination before they engage in affirmative action programs would severely undermine public employers' incentive to meet voluntarily their civil rights obligations. This result would clearly be at odds with this Court's and Congress'

* The goal of providing "role-models" discussed by the courts below should not be confused with the very different goal of promoting racial diversity among the faculty. Because this latter goal was not urged as such in support of the layoff provision before the District Court and the Court of Appeals, however, I do not believe it necessary to discuss the magnitude of that interest or its applicability in this case. The only governmental interests at issue here are those of remedying "societal" discrimination, providing "role models," and remedying apparent prior employment discrimination by the School District.

consistent emphasis on "the value of voluntary efforts to further the objectives of the law." *Bakke,* supra, 438 U.S., at 364, 98 S.Ct., at 2785 (opinion of Brennan, White, Marshall, and Blackmun, JJ.); see also Albemarle Paper Co. v. Moody, 422 U.S. 405, 417–418, 95 S.Ct. 2362, 2371–2372, 45 L.Ed.2d 280 (1975); Alexander v. Gardner-Denver Co., 415 U.S. 36, 44, 94 S.Ct. 1011, 1017, 39 L.Ed.2d 147 (1974). The value of voluntary compliance is doubly important when it is a public employer that acts, both because of the example its voluntary assumption of responsibility sets and because the remediation of governmental discrimination is of unique importance. See S.Rep. No. 92–415, p. 10 (1971) (accompanying the amendments extending coverage of Title VII to the States) ("Discrimination by government * * * serves a doubly destructive purpose. The exclusion of minorities from effective participation in the bureaucracy not only promotes ignorance of minority problems in that particular community, but also creates mistrust, alienation, and all too often hostility toward the entire process of government"). Imposing a contemporaneous findings requirement would produce the anomalous result that what private employers may voluntarily do to correct apparent violations of Title VII, Steelworkers v. Weber, supra, public employers are constitutionally forbidden to do to correct their statutory and constitutional transgressions.

Such results cannot, in my view, be justified by reference to the incremental value a contemporaneous findings requirement would have as an evidentiary safeguard. As is illustrated by this case, public employers are trapped between the competing hazards of liability to minorities if affirmative action *is not* taken to remedy apparent employment discrimination and liability to nonminorities if affirmative action *is* taken. Where these employers, who are presumably fully aware both of their duty under federal law to respect the rights of *all* their employees and of their potential liability for failing to do so, act on the basis of information which gives them a sufficient basis for concluding that remedial action is necessary, a contemporaneous findings requirement should not be necessary.

This conclusion is consistent with our previous decisions recognizing the States' ability to take voluntary race-conscious action to achieve compliance with the law even in the absence of a specific finding of past discrimination. See, e.g., United Jewish Organizations of Williamsburgh, Inc. v. Carey, 430 U.S. 144, 165–166, 97 S.Ct. 996, 1009–1010, 51 L.Ed.2d 229 (1977) (reapportionment); McDaniel v. Barresi, 402 U.S. 39, 91 S.Ct. 1287, 28 L.Ed.2d 582 (1971) (school desegregation). Indeed, our recognition of the responsible state actor's competency to take these steps is assumed in our recognition of the States' constitutional *duty* to take affirmative steps to eliminate the continuing effects of past unconstitutional discrimination. See, e.g., Swann v. Charlotte-Mecklenburg Board of Education, 402 U.S. 1, 15, 91 S.Ct. 1267, 1275, 28 L.Ed.2d 554 (1971); Green v. New Kent County School Board, 391 U.S. 430, 437–438, 88 S.Ct. 1689, 1693–1694, 20 L.Ed.2d 716 (1968).

Of course, as the Court notes, the public employer must discharge this sensitive duty with great care; in order to provide some measure of protection to the interests of its nonminority employees and the employer itself in the event that its affirmative action plan is challenged, the public employer must have a firm basis for determining that affirmative action is warranted. Public employers are not without reliable benchmarks in making this determination. For example, demonstrable evidence of a disparity between the percentage of qualified blacks on a school's teaching staff and the percentage of qualified minorities in the relevant labor pool sufficient to support a prima facie Title VII pattern or practice claim by minority teachers would lend a compelling basis for a competent authority such as the School Board to conclude that implementation of a voluntary affirmative action plan is appropriate to remedy apparent prior employment discrimination.

To be sure, such a conclusion is not unassailable. If a voluntary affirmative action plan is subsequently challenged in court by nonminority employees, those employees must be given the opportunity to prove that the plan does not meet the constitutional standard this Court has articulated. However, as the Court suggests, the institution of such a challenge does not automatically impose upon the public employer the burden of convincing the court of its liability for prior unlawful discrimination; nor does it mean that the court must make an actual finding of prior discrimination based on the employer's proof before the employer's affirmative action plan will be upheld. In "reverse discrimination" suits, as in any other suit, it is the plaintiffs who must bear the burden of demonstrating that their rights have been violated. The findings a court must make before upholding an affirmative action plan reflect this allocation of proof and the nature of the challenge asserted. For instance, in the example posed above, the nonminority teachers could easily demonstrate that the purpose and effect of the plan is to impose a race-based classification. But when the Board introduces its statistical proof as evidence of its remedial purpose, thereby supplying the court with the means for determining that the Board had a firm basis for concluding that remedial action was appropriate, it is incumbent upon the nonminority teachers to prove their case; they continue to bear the ultimate burden of persuading the court that the Board's evidence did not support an inference of prior discrimination and thus a remedial purpose, or that the plan instituted on the basis of this evidence was not sufficiently "narrowly tailored." Only by meeting this burden could the plaintiffs establish a violation of their constitutional rights, and thereby defeat the presumption that the Board's assertedly remedial action based on the statistical evidence was justified.

In sum, I do not think that the layoff provision was constitutionally infirm simply because the School Board, the Commission or a court had not made particularized findings of discrimination at the time the provision was agreed upon. But when the plan was challenged, the District Court and the Court of Appeals did not make the proper inquiry into the legitimacy of the Board's asserted remedial purpose; instead, they relied upon governmental purposes that we have deemed insufficient to withstand strict scrutiny, and therefore failed to isolate a sufficiently important governmental purpose that could support the challenged provision.

There is, however, no need to inquire whether the provision actually had a legitimate remedial purpose based on the record, such as it is, because the judgment is vulnerable on yet another ground: the courts below applied a "reasonableness" test in evaluating the relationship between the ends pursued and the means employed to achieve them that is plainly incorrect under any of the standards articulated by this Court. Nor is it necessary, in my view, to resolve the troubling questions of whether any layoff provision could survive strict scrutiny or whether this particular layoff provision could, when considered without reference to the hiring goal it was intended to further, pass the onerous "narrowly tailored" requirement. Petitioners have met their burden of establishing that this layoff provision is not "narrowly tailored" to achieve its asserted remedial purpose by demonstrating that the provision is keyed to a hiring goal that itself has no relation to the remedying of employment discrimination.

Although the constitutionality of the hiring goal as such is not before us, it is impossible to evaluate the necessity of the layoff provision as a remedy for the apparent prior employment discrimination absent reference to that goal. See, e.g., post, at 1858, (Marshall, J., dissenting). In this case, the hiring goal that the layoff provision was designed to safeguard was tied to the percentage of minority students in the school district, not to the percentage of qualified minority teachers within the relevant labor pool. The disparity between the percentage of minorities on the teaching staff and the percentage of minorities in the student body is not probative of employment discrimination; it is only when it is established that the availability of minorities in the relevant labor pool substantially exceeded those hired that one may draw an inference of deliberate discrimination in employment. See Hazelwood School District v. United States, 433 U.S. 299, 308, 97 S.Ct. 2736, 2741, 53 L.Ed.2d 768 (1977) (Title VII context). Because the layoff provision here acts to maintain levels of minority hiring that have no relation to remedying employment discrimination, it cannot be adjudged "narrowly tailored" to effectuate its asserted remedial purpose.

I therefore join in parts I, II, III–A, III–B, and V of the Court's opinion, and concur in the judgment.

JUSTICE WHITE, concurring in the judgment.

The school board's policy when layoffs are necessary is to maintain a certain proportion of minority teachers. This policy requires laying off non-minority teachers solely on the basis of their race, including teachers with seniority, and retaining other teachers solely because they are black, even though some of them are in probationary status. None of the interests asserted by the board, singly or together, justify this racially discriminatory layoff policy and save it from the strictures of the Equal Protection Clause. Whatever the legitimacy of hiring goals or quotas may be, the discharge of white teachers to make room for blacks, none of whom has been shown to be a victim of any racial discrimination, is quite a different matter. I cannot believe that in order to integrate a work force, it would be permissible to discharge whites and hire blacks until the latter comprised a suitable percentage of the work force. None of our cases suggest that this would be permissible under the Equal Protection Clause. Indeed, our cases look quite the other way. The layoff policy in this case—laying off whites who would otherwise be retained in order to keep blacks on the job—has the same effect and is equally violative of the Equal Protection Clause. I agree with the plurality that this official policy is unconstitutional and hence concur in the judgment.

JUSTICE MARSHALL, with whom JUSTICE BRENNAN and JUSTICE BLACKMUN join, dissenting.

When this Court seeks to resolve far-ranging constitutional issues, it must be especially careful to ground its analysis firmly in the facts of the particular controversy before it. Yet in this significant case, we are hindered by a record that is informal and incomplete. Both parties now appear to realize that the record is inadequate to inform the Court's decision. Both have lodged with the Court voluminous "submissions" containing factual material that was not considered by the District Court or the Court of Appeals. Petitioners have submitted 21 separate items, predominantly statistical charts, which they assert are relevant to their claim of discrimination. Respondents have submitted public documents that tend to substantiate the facts alleged in the brief accompanying their motion for summary judgment in the District Court. These include transcripts and exhibits from two prior proceedings, in which certain questions of discrimination in the Jackson schools were litigated, Jackson Education Association v. Board of Education, No. 4–72340 (ED Mich.1976) (*Jackson I*), and Jackson Education Association v. Board of Education, (Jackson Cty.Cir.Ct.1979) (*Jackson II*).

We should not acquiesce in the parties' attempt to try their case before this Court. Yet it would be just as serious a mistake simply to ignore altogether, as the plurality has done, the compelling factual setting in which this case evidently has arisen. No race-conscious provision that purports to serve a remedial purpose can be fairly assessed in a vacuum.

The haste with which the District Court granted summary judgment to respondents, without seeking to develop the factual allegations contained in respondents' brief, prevented the full exploration of the facts that are now critical to resolution of the important issue before us. Respondents' acquiescence in a premature victory in the District Court should not now be used as an instrument of their defeat. Rather, the District Court should have the opportunity to develop a factual record adequate to resolve the serious issue raised by the case. I believe, therefore, that it is improper for this Court to resolve the constitutional issue in its current posture. But, because I feel that the plurality has also erred seriously in its legal analysis of the merits of this case, I write further to express my disagreement with the conclusions that it has reached.

I, too, believe that layoffs are unfair. But unfairness ought not be confused with constitutional injury. Paying no heed to the true circumstances of petitioners' plight, the plurality would nullify years of negotiation and compromise designed to solve serious educational problems in the public schools of Jackson, Michigan. Because I believe that a public employer, with the full agreement of its employees, should be permitted to preserve the benefits of a legitimate and constitutional affirmative-action hiring plan even while reducing its work force, I dissent.

I

The record and extra-record materials that we have before us persuasively suggest that the plurality has too quickly assumed the absence of a legitimate factual predicate, even under the plurality's own view, for affirmative action in the Jackson schools. The first black teacher in the Jackson Public Schools was hired in 1954.[1] In 1969, when minority representation on the faculty had risen only to 3.9%, the Jackson branch of the NAACP filed a complaint with the Michigan Civil Rights Commission, alleging that the Board had engaged in various discriminatory practices, including racial discrimination in the hiring of teachers. The Commission conducted an investigation and concluded that each of the allegations had merit.[2]

In settlement of the complaint, the Commission issued an order of adjustment, under which the Jackson Board of Education (Board) agreed to numerous measures designed to improve educational opportunities for black public-school students. Among them was a promise to "[t]ake affirmative steps to recruit, hire and promote minority group teachers and counselors as positions bec[a]me available * * *." As a result of the Board's efforts to comply with the order over the next two years, the percentage of minority teachers increased to 8.8%.

1. Unless otherwise indicated, the historical facts herein recited have been taken from the Defendants' Brief in Support of its Motion for Summary Judgment before the District Court, Record, Doc. No. 4, pp. 1–6.

2. The Commission concluded that "[r]acial tension continues to be a part of the entire Jackson School System from the elementary level through high school. It would appear, therefore, that each of the allegations as stated in the complaint can be substantiated based upon organizational records, court files, school records, special committee reports and the appraisal conducted by the Superintendent of Schools." This conclusion is supported by extra-record materials suggesting that the shortage of minority teachers was the result of past discrimination in teacher hiring. For example, the then-Superintendent of Schools testified that "an administrator * * * told me she had tried to get a position in Jackson in the early 1950's and was told that they didn't hire colored people." This was the "type of thing," he stated, that led to adoption of Article XII.

In 1971, however, faculty layoffs became necessary. The contract in effect at that time, between the Board and the Jackson Education Association (Union), provided that layoffs would be made in reverse order of seniority. Because of the recent vintage of the school system's efforts to hire minorities, the seniority scheme led to the layoff of a substantial number of minority teachers, "literally wip[ing] out all the gain" made toward achieving racial balance. Respondent's Lodging No. 3, p. 24 (deposition of Superintendent of Schools). Once again, minority teachers on the faculty were a rarity.

By early 1972, when racial tensions in the schools had escalated to violent levels, school officials determined that the best course was full integration of the school system, including integration of the faculty. But they recognized that, without some modification of the seniority layoff system, genuine faculty integration could not take place. The Minority Affairs Office of the Jackson Public Schools submitted a questionnaire to all teachers, asking them to consider the possibility of abandoning the "last hired, first fired" approach to layoffs in favor of an absolute freeze on layoffs of minority teachers. The teachers overwhelmingly voted in favor of retaining the straight seniority system. Negotiations ensued between the two camps—on the one hand, the Board, which favored a freeze of minority layoffs and, on the other, the Union, urging straight seniority—and the negotiators ultimately reached accord. One union leader characterized the development of the layoff compromise as the most difficult balancing of equities that he had ever encountered.

The compromise avoided placing the entire burden of layoffs on either the white teachers as a group or the minority teachers as a group. Instead, each group would shoulder a portion of that burden equal to its portion of the faculty. Thus, the overall percentage of minorities on the faculty would remain constant. Within each group, seniority would govern which individuals would be laid off. This compromise was the provision at issue here, subsequently known as Article XII: * * *

The Board and the Union leadership agreed to the adoption of Article XII. The compromise was then presented to the teachers, who ratified it by majority vote. Each of the six times that the contract has been renegotiated, Article XII has been presented for reconsideration to the members of the Union, at least 80% of whom are white, and each time it has been ratified.

To petitioners, at the bottom of the seniority scale among white teachers, fell the lot of bearing the white group's proportionate share of layoffs that became necessary in 1982. Claiming a right not to lose their jobs ahead of minority teachers with less seniority, petitioners brought this challenge to Article XII under the Equal Protection Clause of the Fourteenth Amendment.

II

From the outset, it is useful to bear in mind what this case is not. There has been no court order to achieve racial balance, which might require us to reflect upon the existence of judicial power to impose obligations on parties not proven to have committed a wrong. There is also no occasion here to resolve whether a white worker may be required to give up his or her job in order to be replaced by a black worker. See Steelworkers v. Weber, 443 U.S. 193, 208, 99 S.Ct. 2721, 2729, 61 L.Ed.2d 480 (1979). Nor are we asked to order parties to suffer the consequences of an agreement that they had no role in adopting. See Firefighters v. Stotts, 467 U.S. 561, 575, 104 S.Ct. 2576, ___, 81 L.Ed.2d 483 (1984). Moreover, this is not a case in which a party to a collective-bargaining agreement has attempted unilaterally to achieve racial balance by refusing to comply with a contractual, seniority-based layoff provision. Cf. Teamsters v. United States, 431 U.S. 324, 350, 352, 97 S.Ct. 1843, 1862, 1863, 52 L.Ed.2d 396 (1977).

The sole question posed by this case is whether the Constitution prohibits a union and a local school board from developing a collective-bargaining agreement that apportions layoffs between two racially determined groups as a means of preserving the effects of an affirmative hiring policy, the constitutionality of which is unchallenged.[3]

III

Agreement upon a means for applying the Equal Protection Clause to an affirmative-action program has eluded this Court every time the issue has come before us. In University of California Regents v. Bakke, 438 U.S. 265, 98 S.Ct. 2733, 57 L.Ed.2d 750 (1978), four Members of the Court concluded that, while racial distinctions are irrelevant to nearly

3. Justice O'Connor rests her disposition of this case on the propriety of the hiring plan, even though petitioners have not challenged it. She appears to rely on language in the preamble to the collective-bargaining agreement, which suggests that the "goal of such [affirmative-action] policy shall be to have at least the same percentage of minority racial representation on each individual staff as is represented by the student population of the Jackson Public Schools." Believing that the school system's hiring "goal" ought instead to be the percentage of qualified minorities in the labor pool, Justice O'Connor concludes that the challenged layoff provision itself is overly broad. Among the materials considered by the District Court and Court of Appeals, however, there is no evidence to show the actual proportion of minority teachers in the Jackson schools, either in relation to the qualified minority labor force or in relation to the number of minority students. If the distinction between the two goals is to be considered critical to the constitutionality of the affirmative-action plan, it is incumbent on petitioners—plaintiffs below—to demonstrate that, at the time they were laid off, the proportion of minority teachers had equaled or exceeded the appropriate percentage of the minority labor force, and that continued adherence to affirmative-action goals, therefore, unjustifiably caused their injuries. This petitioners have failed to do. Outside of the First Amendment context, I know of no justification for invalidating a provision because it might, in a hypothetical case, apply improperly to other potential plaintiffs. Petitioners have attempted to fill the gap in their case by supplying statistical charts to this Court. Clearly, however, we are not equipped for such factfinding, and if the hortatory ceiling of the affirmative-action plan is indeed to be considered a significant aspect of the case, then that would be an appropriate subject of inquiry on remand.

all legitimate state objectives and are properly subjected to the most rigorous judicial scrutiny in most instances, they are highly relevant to the one legitimate state objective of eliminating the pernicious vestiges of past discrimination; when that is the goal, a less exacting standard of review is appropriate. We explained at length our view that, because no fundamental right was involved and because whites have none of the immutable characteristics of a suspect class, the so-called "strict scrutiny" applied to cases involving either fundamental rights or suspect classifications was not applicable. Id., at 357, 98 S.Ct., at 2782 (opinion of Brennan, White, Marshall, and Blackmun, JJ.). Nevertheless, we eschewed the least rigorous, "rational basis" standard of review, recognizing that any racial classification is subject to misuse. We determined that remedial use of race is permissible if it serves "important governmental objectives" and is "substantially related to achievement of those objectives." Id., at 359, 98 S.Ct., at 2783; see also id., at 387, 98 S.Ct., at 2797 (opinion of Marshall, J.); id., at 402, 98 S.Ct., at 2802 (opinion of Blackmun, J.). This standard is genuinely a "strict and searching" judicial inquiry, but is "not ' "strict" in theory and fatal in fact.' " Id., at 362, 98 S.Ct. at 2784 (opinion of Brennan, White, Marshall, and Blackmun, JJ.) (quoting Gunther, The Supreme Court, 1971 Term—Foreward: In Search of Evolving Doctrine on a Changing Court: A Model for a Newer Equal Protection, 86 Harv.L. Rev. 1, 8 (1972)). The only other Justice to reach the constitutional issue in *Bakke* suggested that, remedial purpose or no, any racial distinctions "call for the most exacting judicial examination." Id., at 291, 98 S.Ct., at 2748 (opinion of Powell, J.).

In Fullilove v. Klutznick, 448 U.S. 448, 100 S.Ct. 2758, 65 L.Ed.2d 902 (1980), the Court again disagreed as to the proper standard of review. Three Justices, of whom I was one, concluded that a statute reserving 10% of federal funds for minority contractors served important governmental objectives and was substantially related to achievement of those objectives, surviving attack under our *Bakke* test. 448 U.S., at 519, 100 S.Ct., at 2748 (Marshall, J., joined by Brennan and Blackmun, JJ., concurring in judgment). Three other Justices expressly declined to adopt any standard of review, deciding that the provision survived judicial scrutiny under either of the formulae articulated in *Bakke.* 448 U.S., at 492, 100 S.Ct., at 2781 (opinion of Burger, C.J., joined by White and Powell, JJ.).

Despite the Court's inability to agree on a route, we have reached a common destination in sustaining affirmative action against constitutional attack. In *Bakke,* we determined that a state institution may take race into account as a factor in its decisions, 438 U.S., at 326, 98 S.Ct., at 2766, and in *Fullilove,* the Court upheld a congressional preference for minority contractors because the measure was legitimately designed to ameliorate the present effects of past discrimination, 448 U.S., at 520, 100 S.Ct., at 2796.

In this case, it should not matter which test the Court applies. What is most important, under any approach to the constitutional analysis, is that a reviewing court genuinely consider the circumstances of the provision at issue. The history and application of Article XII, assuming verification upon a proper record, demonstrate that this provision would pass constitutional muster, no matter which standard the Court should adopt.

IV

The principal state purpose supporting Article XII is the need to preserve the levels of faculty integration achieved through the affirmative hiring policy adopted in the early 1970's. Justification for the hiring policy itself is found in the turbulent history of the effort to integrate the Jackson Public Schools—not even mentioned in the majority opinion—which attests to the bona fides of the Board's current employment practices.

The record and lodgings indicate that the Commission, endowed by the State Constitution with the power to investigate complaints of discrimination and the duty to secure the equal protection of the laws, Mich.Const., Art. V, § 29, prompted and oversaw the remedial steps now under attack.[4] When the Board agreed to take specified remedial action, including the hiring and promotion of minority teachers, the Commission did not pursue its investigation of the apparent violations to the point of rendering formal findings of discrimination.

Instead of subjecting an already volatile school system to the further disruption of formal accusations and trials, it appears that the Board set about achieving the goals articulated in the settlement. According to the then-Superintendent of Schools, the Board was aware, at every step of the way, that "[t]he NAACP had its court suit ready if either the Board postponed the [integration] operation or abandoned the attempts. They were willing to—they were ready to go into Federal court and get a court order, as happened in Kalamazoo." Rather than provoke the looming lawsuit, the Board and the Union worked with the committees to reach a solution to the racial problems plaguing the school system. In 1972, the Board explained to parents why it had adopted a voluntary integration plan:

> "Waiting for what appears the inevitable only flames passions and contributes to the difficulties of an orderly transition from a segregated to a desegregated school system. Firmly established

4. The Commission currently describes its participation in the Jackson matter as follows: "[T]he Commission investigated the allegations and sought *to remedy the apparent violations* by negotiating an order of adjustment with the Jackson Board. * * * [T]he out-of-line seniority layoff provisions in the Jackson Board of Education's employment contracts with its teachers since 1972 are consistent with overall desegregation efforts undertaken *in compliance with* the Commission's order of adjustment." Brief for Michigan Civil Rights Commission, Michigan Dept. of Civil Rights as *Amicus Curiae* 14 (emphasis added).

legal precedents mandate a change. Many citizens know this to be true.

"Waiting for a court order emphasizes to many that we are quite willing to disobey the law. * * * Further, court orders cost money for both the school system and the litigants." Respondents' Lodging No. 1, pp. 1–2 (Exhibit No. 8, *Jackson I*).

An explicit Board admission or judicial determination of culpability, which the petitioners and even the Solicitor General urge us to hold was required before the Board could undertake a race-conscious remedial plan, would only have exposed the Board in this case to further litigation and liability, including individual liability under 42 U.S.C. § 1983, for past acts. It would have contributed nothing to the advancement of the community's urgent objective of integrating its schools.

The real irony of the argument urging mandatory, formal findings of discrimination lies in its complete disregard for a longstanding goal of civil rights reform, that of integrating schools without taking every school system to court. Our school desegregation cases imposed an affirmative duty on local school boards to see that "racial discrimination would be eliminated root and branch." Green v. County School Board, 391 U.S. 430, 437–438, 88 S.Ct. 1689, 1693–1694, 20 L.Ed.2d 716 (1968); see Brown v. Board of Education, 349 U.S. 294, 299, 75 S.Ct. 753, 755, 99 L.Ed. 1083 (1955). Petitioners would now have us inform the Board, having belatedly taken this Court's admonitions to heart, that it should have delayed further, disputing its obligations and forcing the aggrieved parties to seek judicial relief. This result would be wholly inconsistent with the national policies against overloading judicial dockets, maintaining groundless defenses, and impeding good-faith settlement of legal disputes. Only last Term, writing for the Court, The Chief Justice reaffirmed that civil rights litigation is no exception to the general policy in favor of settlements: "Indeed, Congress made clear its concern that civil rights plaintiffs not be penalized for 'helping to lessen docket congestion' by settling their cases out of court. * * * In short, settlements rather than litigation will serve the interests of plaintiffs as well as defendants." Marek v. Chesny, 473 U.S. ——, ——, 105 S.Ct. 3012, 3018, 87 L.Ed.2d 1 (1985). It would defy equity to penalize those who achieve harmony from discord, as it would defy wisdom to impose on society the needless cost of superfluous litigation. The Court is correct to recognize, as it does today, that formal findings of past discrimination are not a necessary predicate to the adoption of affirmative-action policies, and that the scope of such policies need not be limited to remedying specific instances of identifiable discrimination.

Moreover, under the apparent circumstances of this case, we need not rely on any general awareness of "societal discrimination" to conclude that the Board's purpose is of sufficient importance to justify its limited remedial efforts. There are allegations that the imperative to integrate the public schools was urgent. Racially motivated violence had erupted at the schools, interfering with all educational objectives. We are told that, having found apparent violations of the law and a substantial underrepresentation of minority teachers, the state agency responsible for ensuring equality of treatment for all citizens of Michigan had instituted a settlement that required the Board to adopt affirmative hiring practices in lieu of further enforcement proceedings. That agency, participating as *amicus curiae* through the Attorney General of Michigan, still stands fully behind the solution that the Board and the Union adopted in Article XII, viewing it as a measure necessary to attainment of stability and educational quality in the public schools. See n. 4, supra. Surely, if properly presented to the District Court, this would supply the "[e]videntiary support for the conclusion that remedial action is warranted" that the plurality purports to seek. Since the District Court did not permit submission of this evidentiary support, I am at a loss as to why Justice Powell so glibly rejects the obvious solution of remanding for the factfinding he appears to recognize is necessary. See ante, at 1848–1849, n. 5.

Were I satisfied with the record before us, I would hold that the state purpose of preserving the integrity of a valid hiring policy—which in turn sought to achieve diversity and stability for the benefit of *all* students—was sufficient, in this case, to satisfy the demands of the Constitution.

V

The second part of any constitutional assessment of the disputed plan requires us to examine the means chosen to achieve the state purpose. Again, the history of Article XII, insofar as we can determine it, is the best source of assistance.

A

Testimony of both Union and school officials illustrates that the Board's obligation to integrate its faculty could not have been fulfilled meaningfully as long as layoffs continued to eliminate the last hired. In addition, qualified minority teachers from other States were reluctant to uproot their lives and move to Michigan without any promise of protection from imminent layoff. The testimony suggests that the lack of some layoff protection would have crippled the efforts to recruit minority applicants. Adjustment of the layoff hierarchy under these circumstances was a necessary corollary of an affirmative hiring policy.

B

Under Justice Powell's approach, the community of Jackson, having painfully watched the hard-won benefits of its integration efforts vanish as a result of massive layoffs, would be informed today, simply, that preferential layoff protection is never permissible because hiring policies serve the same purpose at a lesser cost. As a matter of logic as well as fact, a hiring policy achieves no purpose at all if it is eviscerated by layoffs. Justice Powell's position is untenable.

Justice Powell has concluded, by focusing exclusively on the undisputed hardship of losing a job, that the Equal Protection Clause always bars race-conscious layoff plans. This analysis overlooks, however, the important fact that Article XII does not cause the loss of jobs; someone will lose a job under any layoff plan and, whoever it is, that person will not deserve it. Any *per se* prohibition against layoff protection, therefore, must rest upon a premise that the tradition of basing layoff decisions on seniority is so fundamental that its modification can never be permitted. Our cases belie that premise.

The general practice of basing employment decisions on relative seniority may be upset for the sake of other public policies. For example, a court may displace innocent workers by granting retroactive seniority to victims of employment discrimination. Franks v. Bowman Transportation Co., 424 U.S. 747, 775, 96 S.Ct. 1251, 1269, 47 L.Ed.2d 444 (1976). Further, this Court has long held that "employee expectations arising from a seniority system agreement may be modified by statutes furthering a strong public policy interest." Id., at 778, 96 S.Ct., at 1271. And we have recognized that collective-bargaining agreements may go further than statutes in enhancing the seniority of certain employees for the purpose of fostering legitimate interests. See Ford Motor Co. v. Huffman, 345 U.S. 330, 339–340, 73 S.Ct. 681, 686–687, 97 L.Ed. 1048 (1953). Accordingly, we have upheld one collectively bargained provision that bestowed enhanced seniority on those who had served in the military before employment, id., at 340, 73 S.Ct., at 687, and another that gave preferred seniority status to union chairmen, to the detriment of veterans. Aeronautical Industrial District Lodge 727 v. Campbell, 337 U.S. 521, 529, 69 S.Ct. 1287, 1291, 93 L.Ed. 1513 (1949).

In Steelworkers v. Weber, 443 U.S. 193, 99 S.Ct. 2721, 61 L.Ed.2d 480 (1979), we specifically addressed a departure from the seniority principle designed to alleviate racial disparity. In *Weber,* a private employer and a union negotiated a collective agreement that reserved for black employees one half of all openings in a plant training program, replacing the prior system of awarding all seats on the basis of seniority. This plan tampered with the expectations attendant to seniority, and redistributed opportunities to achieve an important qualification toward advancement in the company. We upheld the challenged plan under the Civil Rights Act of 1964 because it was designed to "eliminate traditional patterns of racial segregation" in the industry and did not "unnecessarily trammel the interests of the white employees." Id., at 201, 208, 99 S.Ct., at 2726, 2730. We required no judicial finding or employer admission of past discrimination to justify that interference with the seniority hierarchy for the sake of the legitimate purposes at stake.

These cases establish that protection from layoff is not altogether unavailable as a tool for achieving legitimate societal goals. It remains to be determined whether the particular form of layoff protection embodied in Article XII falls among the permissible means for preserving minority proportions on the teaching staff.

C

Article XII is a narrow provision because it allocates the impact of an unavoidable burden proportionately between two racial groups. It places no absolute burden or benefit on one race, and, within the confines of constant minority proportions, it preserves the hierarchy of seniority in the selection of individuals for layoff. Race is a factor, along with seniority, in determining which individuals the school system will lose; it is not alone dispositive of any individual's fate. Cf. *Bakke,* 438 U.S., at 318, 98 S.Ct., at 2762 (opinion of Powell, J.). Moreover, Article XII does not use layoff protection as a tool for *increasing* minority representation; achievement of that goal is entrusted to the less severe hiring policies.[5] And Article XII is narrow in the temporal sense as well. The very bilateral process that gave rise to Article XII when its adoption was necessary will also occasion its demise when remedial measures are no longer required. Finally, Article XII modifies contractual expectations that do not themselves carry any connotation of merit or achievement; it does not interfere with the "cherished American ethic" of "[f]airness in individual competition," *Bakke,* supra, at 319, n. 53, 98 S.Ct., at 2763, n. 53, depriving individuals of an opportunity that they could be said to deserve. In all of these important ways, Article XII metes out the hardship of layoffs in a manner that achieves its purpose with the smallest possible deviation from established norms.

The Board's goal of preserving minority proportions could have been achieved, perhaps, in a different way. For example, if layoffs had been determined by lottery, the ultimate effect would have been retention of current racial percentages. A random system, however, would place every teacher in equal jeopardy, working a much greater upheaval of the seniority hierarchy than that occasioned by Article XII; it is not at all a less restrictive means of achieving the Board's goal. Another possible approach would have been a freeze on layoffs of minority teachers. This measure, too, would have been substantially more burdensome than Article XII, not only by necessitating the layoff of a greater number of white teachers, but also by erecting an absolute distinction between the races, one to be benefited and one to be burdened, in a way that Article XII avoids. Indeed, neither petitioners nor any Justice of this Court has suggested an alternative to Article XII

5. Justice White assumes that respondents' plan is equivalent to one that deliberately seeks to change the racial composition of a staff by firing and hiring members of predetermined rates. Ante, at 1857. That assumtion utterly ignores the fact that the Jackson plan involves only the means for selecting the employees who will be chosen for layoffs already necessitated by external economic conditions. This plan does not seek to supplant whites with blacks, nor does it contribute in any way to the number of job losses.

that would have attained the stated goal in any narrower or more equitable a fashion. Nor can I conceive of one.

VI

It is no accident that this least burdensome of all conceivable options is the very provision that the parties adopted. For Article XII was forged in the crucible of clashing interests. All of the economic powers of the predominantly white teachers' union were brought to bear against those of the elected Board, and the process yielded consensus.

The concerns that have prompted some Members of this Court to call for narrowly tailored, perhaps court-ordered, means of achieving racial balance spring from a legitimate fear that racial distinctions will again be used as a means to persecute individuals, while couched in benign phraseology. That fear has given rise to mistrust of those who profess to take remedial action, and concern that any such action "work the least harm possible to other innocent persons competing for the benefit." *Bakke,* supra, at 308, 98 S.Ct., at 2757 (opinion of Powell, J.). One Justice has warned that "if innocent employees are to be made to make any sacrifices * * * they must be represented and have had full participation rights in the negotiation process," Firefighters v. Stotts, 467 U.S., at 588, n. 3, 104 S.Ct., at 2593 (O'Connor, J., concurring), and another has called for a "principle for deciding whether preferential classifications reflect a benign remedial purpose or a malevolent stigmatic classification * * *" *Bakke,* supra, 438 U.S., at 294–295, n. 34, 98 S.Ct., at 2750, n. 34 (opinion of Powell, J.). This case answers that call.

The collective-bargaining process is a legitimate and powerful vehicle for the resolution of thorny problems, and we have favored "minimal supervision by courts and other governmental agencies over the substantive terms of collective-bargaining agreements." American Tobacco Co. v. Patterson, 456 U.S. 63, 76–77, 102 S.Ct. 1534, 1541, 71 L.Ed. 2d 748 (1982). We have also noted that "[s]ignificant freedom must be afforded employers and unions to create differing seniority systems," California Brewers Assn. v. Bryant, 444 U.S. 598, 608, 100 S.Ct. 814, 820, 63 L.Ed.2d 55 (1980).[6] The perceived dangers of affirmative action misused, therefore, are naturally averted by the bilateral process of negotiation, agreement, and ratification. The best evidence that Article XII is a narrow means to serve important interests is that representatives of all affected persons, starting from diametrically opposed perspectives, have agreed to it—not once, but six times since 1972.

6. This deference is warranted only if the union represents the interests of the workers fairly; a union's breach of that duty in the form of racial discrimination gives rise to an action by the worker against the union. See Steele v. Louisville & Nashville R. Co., 323 U.S. 192, 207, 65 S.Ct. 226, 234, 89 L.Ed. 173 (1944).

VII

The narrow question presented by this case, if indeed we proceed to the merits, offers no occasion for the Court to issue broad proclamations of public policy concerning the controversial issue of affirmative action. Rather, this case calls for calm, dispassionate reflection upon exactly what has been done, to whom, and why. If one honestly confronts each of those questions against the factual background suggested by the materials submitted to us, I believe the conclusion is inescapable that Article XII meets, and indeed surpasses, any standard for ensuring that race-conscious programs are necessary to achieve remedial purposes. When an elected school board and a teachers' union collectively bargain a layoff provision designed to preserve the effects of a valid minority recruitment plan by apportioning layoffs between two racial groups, as a result of a settlement achieved under the auspices of a supervisory state agency charged with protecting the civil rights of all citizens, that provision should not be upset by this Court on constitutional grounds.

The alleged facts that I have set forth above evince, at the very least, a wealth of plausible evidence supporting the Board's position that Article XII was a legitimate and necessary response both to racial discrimination and to educational imperatives. To attempt to resolve the constitutional issue either with no historical context whatever, as the plurality has done, or on the basis of a record devoid of established facts, is to do a grave injustice not only to the Board and teachers of Jackson and to the State of Michigan, but also to individuals and governments committed to the goal of eliminating all traces of segregation throughout the country. Most of all, it does an injustice to the aspirations embodied in the Fourteenth Amendment itself. I would vacate the judgment of the Court of Appeals and remand with instructions that the case be remanded to the District Court for further proceedings consistent with the views I have expressed.[7]

JUSTICE STEVENS, dissenting.

In my opinion, it is not necessary to find that the Board of Education has been guilty of racial discrimination in the past to support the conclusion that it has a legitimate interest in employing more black teachers in the future. Rather than analyzing a case of this kind by asking whether minority teachers have some sort of special entitlement to jobs as a remedy for sins that were committed in the past, I believe that we should first ask whether the Board's action advances the public interest in educating children for the future. If so, I believe we should

7. I do not envy the District Court its task of sorting out what this Court has and has not held today. It is clear, at any rate, that from among the many views expressed today, two noteworthy results emerge: a majority of the Court has explicitly rejected the argument that an affirmative-action plan must be preceded by a formal finding that the entity seeking to institute the plan has committed discriminatory acts in the past; and the Court has left open whether layoffs may be used as an instrument of remedial action.

consider whether that public interest, and the manner in which it is pursued, justifies any adverse effects on the disadvantaged group.[1]

I

The Equal Protection Clause absolutely prohibits the use of race in many governmental contexts. To cite only a few: the government may not use race to decide who may serve on juries,[2] who may use public services,[3] who may marry,[4] and who may be fit parents.[5] The use of race in these situations is "utterly irrational" because it is completely unrelated to any valid public purpose;[6] moreover, it is particularly pernicious because it constitutes a badge of oppression that is unfaithful to the central promise of the Fourteenth Amendment.

Nevertheless, in our present society, race is not always irrelevant to sound governmental decisionmaking.[7] To take the most obvious example, in law enforcement, if an undercover agent is needed to infiltrate a group suspected of ongoing criminal behavior—and if the members of the group are all of the same race—it would seem perfectly rational to employ an agent of that race rather than a member of a different racial class. Similarly, in a city with a recent history of racial unrest, the superintendent of police might reasonably conclude that an integrated

1. In every equal protection case, we have to ask certain basic questions.

"What class is harmed by the legislation, and has it been subjected to a 'tradition of disfavor' by our laws? What is the public purpose that is being served by the law? What is the characteristic of the disadvantaged class that justifies the disparate treatment?" Cleburne v. Cleburne Living Center, 473 U.S. ___, ___, 105 S.Ct. 3249, 3261–3262, 87 L.Ed.2d 313 (1985) (Stevens, J., concurring).

2. Batson v. Kentucky, 476 U.S. ___, 106 S.Ct. 1712, 89 L.Ed.2d ___ (1986); Vasquez v. Hillery, 474 U.S. ___, 106 S.Ct. 617, 88 L.Ed.2d 598 (1985); Rose v. Mitchell, 443 U.S. 545, 99 S.Ct. 2993, 61 L.Ed.2d 739 (1979); Strauder v. West Virginia, 10 Otto 303, 100 U.S. 303, 25 L.Ed. 664 (1880).

3. Turner v. City of Memphis, 369 U.S. 350, 82 S.Ct. 805, 7 L.Ed.2d 762 (1962) (per curiam); Burton v. Wilmington Parking Authority, 365 U.S. 715, 81 S.Ct. 856, 6 L.Ed.2d 45 (1961).

4. Loving v. Virginia, 388 U.S. 1, 87 S.Ct. 1817, 18 L.Ed.2d 1010 (1967).

5. Palmore v. Sidoti, 466 U.S. 429, 104 S.Ct. 1879, 80 L.Ed.2d 421 (1984).

6. *Cleburne,* supra, 473 U.S., at ___, 105 S.Ct., at ___ (Stevens, J., concurring in judgment) ("It would be utterly irrational to limit the franchise on the basis of height or weight; it is equally invalid to limit it on the basis of skin color"). See also Palmore v. Sidoti, 466 U.S., at 432, 104 S.Ct., at 1882 (1984) ("Classifying persons according to their race is more likely to reflect racial prejudice than legitimate public concerns; the race, not the person, dictates the category").

7. As Justice Marshall explains, although the Court's path in University of California Regents v. Bakke, 438 U.S. 265, 98 S.Ct. 2733, 57 L.Ed.2d 750 (1978) and Fullilove v. Klutznick, 448 U.S. 448, 100 S.Ct. 2758, 65 L.Ed.2d 902 (1980) is tortuous, the path at least reveals that race consciousness does not automatically violate the Equal Protection Clause. In those opinions, only two Justices of the Court suggested that race conscious governmental efforts were inherently unconstitutional. See id., at 522, 100 S.Ct., at 2797 (Stewart, J., dissenting, joined by Rehnquist, J.). Cf. id., at 548, 100 S.Ct., at 2810 (Stevens, J., dissenting) ("Unlike Mr. Justice Stewart and Mr. Justice Rehnquist, * * * I am not convinced that the Clause contains an absolute prohibition against any statutory classification based on race"). Notably, in this Court, petitioners have presented solely a constitutional theory, and have not pursued any statutory claims. Cf. *Bakke,* 438 U.S. at 408, 98 S.Ct., at 2808 (Stevens, J., concurring in judgment in part and dissenting in part) (suggesting that constitutional issue need not be reached because statutory issue was dispositive).

police force could develop a better relationship with the community and thereby do a more effective job of maintaining law and order than a force composed only of white officers.

In the context of public education,[8] it is quite obvious that a school board may reasonably conclude that an integrated faculty will be able to provide benefits to the student body that could not be provided by an all white, or nearly all white, faculty. For one of the most important lessons that the American public schools teach is that the diverse ethnic, cultural, and national backgrounds that have been brought together in our famous "melting pot" do not identify essential differences among the human beings that inhabit our land. It is one thing for a white child to be taught by a white teacher that color, like beauty, is only "skin deep"; it is far more convincing to experience that truth on a day to day basis during the routine, ongoing learning process.

In this case, the collective-bargaining agreement between the Union and the Board of Education succinctly stated a valid public purpose—"recognition of the desirability of multi-ethnic representation on the teaching faculty," and thus "a policy of actively seeking minority group personnel." App. to Pet. for Cert. 22a. Nothing in the record—not a shred of evidence—contradicts the view that the Board's attempt to employ, and to retain, more minority teachers in the Jackson public school system served this completely sound educational purpose. Thus, there was a rational and unquestionably legitimate basis for the Board's decision to enter into the collective-bargaining agreement that petitioners have challenged, even though the agreement required special efforts to recruit and retain minority teachers.

II

It is argued, nonetheless, that the purpose should be deemed invalid because, even if the Board of Education's judgment in this case furthered a laudable goal, some other boards might claim that their experience demonstrates that segregated classes, or segregated faculties, lead to better academic achievement. There is, however, a critical difference between a decision to *exclude* a member of a minority race

8. The Court has frequently emphasized the role of public schools in our national life. See Board of Education v. Pico, 457 U.S. 853, 864, 102 S.Ct. 2799, 2806, 73 L.Ed.2d 435 (1982) (plurality opinion) ("[P]ublic schools are vitally important * * * as vehicles for 'inculcating fundamental values necessary to the maintenance of a democratic political system' "); Ambach v. Norwick, 441 U.S. 68, 76, 99 S.Ct. 1589, 1594, 60 L.Ed.2d 49 (1979) ("The importance of public schools in the preparation of individuals for participation as citizens, and in the preservation of the values on which our society rests, long has been recognized by our decisions"); San Antonio Independent School District v. Rodriguez, 411 U.S. 1, 30, 93 S.Ct. 1278, 1295, 36 L.Ed.2d 16 (1973) (" 'the grave significance of education both to the individual and to our society' cannot be doubted"); Brown v. Board of Education, 347 U.S. 483, 493, 74 S.Ct. 686, 691, 98 L.Ed. 873 (1954) ("[E]ducation * * * is the very foundation of good citizenship. Today it is a principal instrument in awakening the child to cultural values, in preparing him for later professional training, and in helping him to adjust normally to his environment").

because of his or her skin color and a decision to *include* more members of the minority in a school faculty for that reason.

The exclusionary decision rests on the false premise that differences in race, or in the color of a person's skin, reflect real differences that are relevant to a person's right to share in the blessings of a free society. As noted, that premise is "utterly irrational," *Cleburne,* supra, 473 U.S., at ___, 105 S.Ct., at 3261, and repugnant to the principles of a free and democratic society. Nevertheless, the fact that persons of different races do, indeed, have differently colored skin, may give rise to a belief that there is some significant difference between such persons. The inclusion of minority teachers in the educational process inevitably tends to dispel that illusion whereas their exclusion could only tend to foster it. The inclusionary decision is consistent with the principle that all men are created equal; the exclusionary decision is at war with that principle. One decision accords with the Equal Protection Clause of the Fourteenth Amendment; the other does not. Thus, consideration of whether the consciousness of race is exclusionary or inclusionary plainly distinguishes the Board's valid purpose in this case from a race-conscious decision that would reinforce assumptions of inequality.[9]

III

Even if there is a valid purpose to the race consciousness, however, the question that remains is whether that public purpose transcends the harm to the white teachers who are disadvantaged by the special preference the Board has given to its most recently hired minority teachers. In my view, there are two important inquiries in assessing the harm to the disadvantaged teacher. The first is an assessment of the procedures that were used to adopt, and implement, the race-conscious action.[10] The second is an evaluation of the nature of the harm itself.

9. Cf. Palmore v. Sidoti, 466 U.S., at 434, 104 S.Ct., at 1882 (1984) ("The effects of racial prejudice, however real, cannot justify a racial classification removing an infant child from the custody of its natural mother found to be an appropriate person to have such custody"); Buchanan v. Warley, 245 U.S. 60, 81, 38 S.Ct. 16, 20, 62 L.Ed. 149 (1917) (rejecting legitimacy of argument that the "proposed segregation will promote the public peace by preventing race conflicts").

10. Cf. *Fullilove,* 448 U.S., at 548–549, 100 S.Ct., at 2810–2811 (Stevens, J., dissenting) (a race-based classification "does impose a special obligation to scrutinize any governmental decision-making process that draws nationwide distinctions between citizens on the basis of their race and incidentally also discriminates against non-citizens in the preferred racial classes. For just as procedural safeguards are necessary to guarantee impartial decisionmaking in the judicial process, so can they play a vital part in preserving the impartial character of the legislative process"). That observation is, of course, equally applicable to a context in which the governmental decision is reached through a nonlegislative process. Significantly, a reason given for what this Court frequently calls "strict scrutiny" of certain classifications is the notion that the disadvantaged class is one that has been unable to enjoy full procedural participation. See United States v. Carolene Products, Co., 304 U.S. 144, 152–153, n. 4, 58 S.Ct. 778, 783–784, n. 4, 82 L.Ed. 1234 (1938) ("[P]rejudice against discrete and insular minorities may be a special condition, which tends seriously to curtail the operation of those political processes ordinarily to be relied upon to protect minorities, and which may call for a correspondingly more searching judicial

In this case, there can be no question about either the fairness of the procedures used to adopt the race-conscious provision, or the propriety of its breadth. As Justice Marshall has demonstrated, the procedures for adopting this provision were scrupulously fair. The Union that represents the petitioners negotiated the provision and agreed to it; the agreement was put to a vote of the membership, and overwhelmingly approved. Again, not a shred of evidence in the record suggests *any* procedural unfairness in the adoption of the agreement. Similarly, the provision is specifically designed to achieve its objective—retaining the minority teachers that have been specially recruited to give the Jackson schools, after a period of racial unrest, an integrated faculty. Thus, in striking contrast to the procedural inadequacy and unjustified breadth of the race-based classification in Fullilove v. Klutznick, 448 U.S. 448, 100 S.Ct. 2758, 65 L.Ed.2d 902 (1980), the race-conscious layoff policy here was adopted with full participation of the disadvantaged individuals and with a narrowly circumscribed berth for the policy's operation.

Finally, we must consider the harm to the petitioners. Every layoff, like every refusal to employ a qualified applicant, is a grave loss to the affected individual. However, the undisputed facts in this case demonstrate that this serious consequence to the petitioners is not based on any lack of respect for their race, or on blind habit and stereotype. Rather, petitioners have been laid off for a combination of two reasons: the economic conditions that have led Jackson to lay off some teachers, and the special contractual protections intended to preserve the newly integrated character of the faculty in the Jackson schools. Thus, the same harm might occur if a number of gifted young teachers had been given special contractual protection because their specialties were in short supply and if the Jackson Board of Education faced a fiscal need for layoffs. A Board decision to grant immediate tenure to a group of experts in computer technology, an athletic coach, and a language teacher, for example, might reduce the pool of teachers eligible for layoffs during a depression and therefore have precisely the same impact as the racial preference at issue here. In either case, the harm would be generated by the combination of economic conditions and the special contractual protection given a different group of teachers—a protection that, as discussed above, was justified by a valid and extremely strong public interest.[14]

inquiry"); J. Ely, Democracy and Distrust 75–77 (1980).

14. The fact that the issue arises in a layoff context, rather than a hiring context, has no bearing on the equal protection question. For if the Board's interest in employing more minority teachers is sufficient to justify providing them with an extra incentive to accept jobs in Jackson, Michigan, it is also sufficient to justify their retention when the number of available jobs is reduced. Justice Powell's suggestion, ante, at 1850–1852, that there is a distinction of constitutional significance under the Equal Protection Clause between a racial preference at the time of hiring and an identical preference at the time of discharge is thus wholly unpersuasive. He seems to assume that a teacher who has been working for a few years suffers a greater harm when he is laid off than the harm suffered by an unemployed teacher who is refused a job for which he is qualified. In either event, the adverse decision

IV

We should not lightly approve the government's use of a race-based distinction. History teaches the obvious dangers of such classifications. Our ultimate goal must, of course, be "to eliminate entirely from governmental decisionmaking such irrelevant factors as a human being's race." In this case, however, I am persuaded that the decision to include more minority teachers in the Jackson, Michigan, school system served a valid public purpose, that it was adopted with fair procedures and given a narrow breadth, that it transcends the harm to petitioners, and that it is a step toward that ultimate goal of eliminating entirely from governmental decisionmaking such irrelevant factors as a human being's race. I would therefore affirm the judgment of the Court of Appeals.

NOTES AND PROBLEMS FOR DISCUSSION

1. The decision in *Wygant,* the first Supreme Court opinion dealing with a constitutional challenge to race-based affirmative relief in the employment context, revealed the Justices' positions on two important issues and offered insight into their likely views on two other questions.

(a) Unlike the opinion announcing the Court's judgment in *Fullilove,* the four member plurality in *Wygant* clearly stated that racial classifications, whether predicated on so called "benign" or invidious considerations, are subject to traditional strict scrutiny analysis. Justices Marshall, Brennan and Blackmun, on the other hand, reiterated their view that benign classifications; i.e., those designed to remedy the effects of prior discrimination, should be subjected to a less rigorous level of scrutiny. Justice White again, as in *Fullilove,* did not announce his view on this question. Justice Stevens' opinion, in this regard, may be the most intriguing. While citing the opinion in which he applied traditional strict scrutiny to the statutory minority-owned business set-aside program in *Fullilove,* his use in *Wygant* of such phrases as "legitimate interest", "sound purpose" and "valid purpose" and his reliance on an inclusionary/exclusionary consciousness dichotomy, at least suggests that he is moving closer to the dissenters' position.

(b) There seemed to be no disagreement with the notion that while eliminating the effects of prior employer-specific discrimination is a permissible justification for the use of race-based affirmative relief in the public sector, ameliorating the vestiges of societal discrimination is not a constitutionally sufficient state interest. Equally significantly, all of the seven Justices who discussed the issue (i.e., all but White and Stevens) agreed that the requisite employer-specific discrimination did not have to be documented in a contemporaneous judicial determination of discrimination. While the Justices may have quibbled over the exact characterization of the requisite standard of employer belief in the necessity for affirmative action, these seven concurred in rejecting the contention that affirmative relief must be predicated upon a judicial finding of liability.

forecloses "only one of several opportunities" that may be available, ante, at 1851, to the disappointed teacher. Moreover, the distinction is artificial, for the layoff provision at issue in this case was included as part of the terms of the *hiring* of minority and other teachers under the collective-bargaining agreement.

(c) While the Justices differed on the level of scrutiny to be applied to this racial classification, they all adhered to the traditional two tiered formula. With respect to the second prong of this bifurcated approach—the degree to which the chosen means accomplished the legitimate state interest in remedying prior discrimination by the defendant employer—the opinions suggest that although a majority of five invalidated the layoff policy, all nine might uphold a race-based hiring plan. Three members of the plurality, Justices Powell, Burger and Rehnquist, reasoned that race-based layoffs are more injurious to the innocent, non-preferred employees and are thus less acceptable than race-based hiring decisions. This consideration was enough for them to conclude that the layoff policy was not sufficiently narrowly tailored to pass constitutional muster. Nevertheless, they contrasted the layoff policy to hiring goals, which they characterized as a "less intrusive means" of accomplishing the permissible purpose. Justice White's somewhat perplexing opinion suggests that he also might treat a race-based hiring policy differently than a layoff plan. Justice O'Connor broke with the plurality on this issue. While she agreed that the layoff policy was not narrowly tailored, she based this conclusion on the ground that by tying layoffs to a policy of maintaining a balance between the level of teacher and student integration, the policy was unrelated to the permissible goal of eradicating the effects of racial discrimination in hiring. Her opinion implies, therefore, that had the hiring, and thus the layoff, policy been keyed to the percentage of qualified black workers in the relevant labor pool, it would have survived constitutional challenge. The four dissenters, including Justice Stevens, not only upheld the validity of the layoff plan but rejected Justice Powell's view that there was a constitutional difference between race-based layoff and hiring policies.

(d) Finally, while none of the opinions directly addressed the controversial issue of whether affirmative relief should be limited to identifiable victims of discrimination or made available on a group basis to members of the victimized class, footnote 12 of the plurality opinion implies that a race-based hiring remedy, as opposed to layoff protection, might not have to be limited to specific victims. The Court directly addressed this issue, in the statutory context, in *Local 28,* supra.

2. When nonminority individuals bring a *Wygant*-like claim of "reverse discrimination", should the validity of the affirmative action plan be viewed as part of plaintiff's *prima facie* case, as an element of the defendant's general denial, or as an affirmative defense? In other words, who should bear the burden of persuasion? An overwhelming majority of the Court in *Wygant* (all but Justices White and Stevens) placed this burden on the plaintiff. Prior to this decision, however, several lower courts had ruled that the defendant carried the burden of proving that the plan was appropriately tailored to a permissible state interest. See e.g., Britton v. South Bend Community School Corp., 775 F.2d 794 (7th Cir.1985); Warsocki v. Omaha, 726 F.2d 1358 (8th Cir. 1984).

3. The City of Apex announced that it had 19 vacancies for the position of Detective Grade I. It solicited applications from all persons holding the rank of Detective Grade II. The selection committee submitted 19 names to the Chief of Police. The Chief concluded that accepting these names would not promote the goals of the affirmative action plan that the City had voluntarily adopted. Accordingly, he agreed to promote the 19 individuals recommended by the selection committee but also requested that the selection committee propose four additional names to improve the representation of blacks and women at

the Detective Grade I level. The committee proffered the names of three black officers and one woman officer and these four were also given promotions. Four white male officers whose names were on neither the original nor supplemental list filed suit against the City under § 1983, alleging that they had been discriminated against on the basis of their race and sex in violation of the equal protection clause. What result? See LeDoux v. District of Columbia, 40 FEP Cases 1258 (D.D.C.1986).

UNITED STEELWORKERS OF AMERICA v. WEBER

Supreme Court of the United States, 1979.
443 U.S. 193, 99 S.Ct. 2721, 61 L.Ed.2d 480.

MR. JUSTICE BRENNAN delivered the opinion of the Court.

Challenged here is the legality of an affirmative action plan—collectively bargained by an employer and a union—that reserves for black employees 50% of the openings in an in-plant craft-training program until the percentage of black craftworkers in the plant is commensurate with the percentage of blacks in the local labor force. The question for decision is whether Congress, in Title VII of the Civil Rights Act of 1964, left employers and unions in the private sector free to take such race-conscious steps to eliminate manifest racial imbalances in traditionally segregated job categories. We hold that Title VII does not prohibit such race-conscious affirmative action plans.

I

In 1974, petitioner United Steelworkers of America (USWA) and petitioner Kaiser Aluminum & Chemical Corp. (Kaiser) entered into a master collective-bargaining agreement covering terms and conditions of employment at 15 Kaiser plants. The agreement contained, *inter alia*, an affirmative action plan designed to eliminate conspicuous racial imbalances in Kaiser's then almost exclusively white craftwork forces. Black craft-hiring goals were set for each Kaiser plant equal to the percentage of blacks in the respective local labor forces. To enable plants to meet these goals, on-the-job training programs were established to teach unskilled production workers—black and white—the skills necessary to become craftworkers. The plan reserved for black employees 50% of the openings in these newly created in-plant training programs.

This case arose from the operation of the plan at Kaiser's plant in Gramercy, La. Until 1974, Kaiser hired as craftworkers for that plant only persons who had had prior craft experience. Because blacks had long been excluded from craft unions,[1] few were able to present such credentials. As a consequence, prior to 1974 only 1.83% (5 out of 273) of the skilled craftworkers at the Gramercy plant were black, even though the work force in the Gramercy area was approximately 39% black.

1. Judicial findings of exclusion from crafts on racial grounds are so numerous as to make such exclusion a proper subject for judicial notice.

Pursuant to the national agreement Kaiser altered its craft-hiring practice in the Gramercy plant. Rather than hiring already trained outsiders, Kaiser established a training program to train its production workers to fill craft openings. Selection of craft trainees was made on the basis of seniority, with the proviso that at least 50% of the new trainees were to be black until the percentage of black skilled craftworkers in the Gramercy plant approximated the percentage of blacks in the local labor force.

During 1974, the first year of the operation of the Kaiser-USWA affirmative action plan, 13 craft trainees were selected from Gramercy's production work force. Of these, seven were black and six white. The most senior black selected into the program had less seniority than several white production workers whose bids for admission were rejected. Thereafter one of those white production workers, respondent Brian Weber (hereafter respondent), instituted this class action in the United States District Court for the Eastern District of Louisiana.

The complaint alleged that the filling of craft trainee positions at the Gramercy plant pursuant to the affirmative action program had resulted in junior black employees' receiving training in preference to senior white employees, thus discriminating against respondent and other similarly situated white employees in violation of §§ 703(a) and (d) of Title VII. The District Court held that the plan violated Title VII, entered a judgment in favor of the plaintiff class, and granted a permanent injunction prohibiting Kaiser and the USWA "from denying plaintiffs, Brian F. Weber and all other members of the class, access to on-the-job training programs on the basis of race." A divided panel of the Court of Appeals for the Fifth Circuit affirmed, holding that all employment preferences based upon race, including those preferences incidental to bona fide affirmative action plans, violated Title VII's prohibition against racial discrimination in employment. * * * We reverse.

II

We emphasize at the outset the narrowness of our inquiry. Since the Kaiser-USWA plan does not involve state action, this case does not present an alleged violation of the Equal Protection Clause of the Fourteenth Amendment. Further, since the Kaiser-USWA plan was adopted voluntarily, we are not concerned with what Title VII requires or with what a court might order to remedy a past proved violation of the Act. The only question before us is the narrow statutory issue of whether Title VII *forbids* private employers and unions from voluntarily agreeing upon bona fide affirmative action plans that accord racial preferences in the manner and for the purpose provided in the Kaiser-USWA plan. That question was expressly left open in McDonald v. Santa Fe Trail Transp. Co., 427 U.S. 273, 281 n. 8, 96 S.Ct. 2574, 2579, 49 L.Ed.2d 493 (1976), which held, in a case not involving affirmative action, that Title VII protects whites as well as blacks from certain forms of racial discrimination.

Respondent argues that Congress intended in Title VII to prohibit all race-conscious affirmative action plans. Respondent's argument rests upon a literal interpretation of §§ 703(a) and (d) of the Act. Those sections make it unlawful to "discriminate * * * because of * * * race" in hiring and in the selection of apprentices for training programs. Since, the argument runs, McDonald v. Santa Fe Trail Transp. Co., supra, settled that Title VII forbids discrimination against whites as well as blacks, and since the Kaiser-USWA affirmative action plan operates to discriminate against white employees solely because they are white, it follows that the Kaiser-USWA plan violates Title VII.

Respondent's argument is not without force. But it overlooks the significance of the fact that the Kaiser-USWA plan is an affirmative action plan voluntarily adopted by private parties to eliminate traditional patterns of racial segregation. In this context respondent's reliance upon a literal construction of §§ 703(a) and (d) and upon *McDonald* is misplaced. See McDonald v. Santa Fe Trail Transp. Co., supra, at 281 n. 8, 96 S.Ct., at 2579. It is a "familiar rule, that a thing may be within the letter of the statute and yet not within the statute, because not within its spirit, nor within the intention of its makers." Holy Trinity Church v. United States, 143 U.S. 457, 459, 12 S.Ct. 511, 512, 36 L.Ed. 226 (1892). The prohibition against racial discrimination in §§ 703(a) and (d) of Title VII must therefore be read against the background of the legislative history of Title VII and the historical context from which the Act arose. Examination of those sources makes clear that an interpretation of the sections that forbade all race-conscious affirmative action would "bring about an end completely at variance with the purpose of the statute" and must be rejected.

Congress' primary concern in enacting the prohibition against racial discrimination in Title VII of the Civil Rights Act of 1964 was with "the plight of the Negro in our economy." Before 1964, blacks were largely relegated to "unskilled and semi-skilled jobs." Because of automation the number of such jobs was rapidly decreasing. As a consequence, "the relative position of the Negro worker [was] steadily worsening. * * * "

Congress feared that the goals of the Civil Rights Act—the integration of blacks into the mainstream of American society—could not be achieved unless this trend were reversed. And Congress recognized that that would not be possible unless blacks were able to secure jobs "which have a future." * * * Accordingly, it was clear to Congress that "[t]he crux of the problem [was] to open employment opportunities for Negroes in occupations which have been traditionally closed to them," and it was to this problem that Title VII's prohibition against racial discrimination in employment was primarily addressed.

It plainly appears from the House Report accompanying the Civil Rights Act that Congress did not intend wholly to prohibit private and voluntary affirmative action efforts as one method of solving this problem. The Report provides:

> "No bill can or should lay claim to eliminating all of the causes and consequences of racial and other types of discrimination against minorities. There is reason to believe, however, that national leadership provided by the enactment of Federal legislation dealing with the most troublesome problems *will create an atmosphere conducive to voluntary or local resolution of other forms of discrimination.*"

Given this legislative history, we cannot agree with respondent that Congress intended to prohibit the private sector from taking effective steps to accomplish the goal that Congress designed Title VII to achieve. The very statutory words intended as a spur or catalyst to cause "employers and unions to self-examine and to self-evaluate their employment practices and to endeavor to eliminate, so far as possible, the last vestiges of an unfortunate and ignominious page in this country's history," Albemarle Paper Co. v. Moody, 422 U.S. 405, 418, 95 S.Ct. 2362, 2372, 45 L.Ed.2d 280 (1975), cannot be interpreted as an absolute prohibition against all private, voluntary, race-conscious affirmative action efforts to hasten the elimination of such vestiges. It would be ironic indeed if a law triggered by a Nation's concern over centuries of racial injustice and intended to improve the lot of those who had "been excluded from the American dream for so long," constituted the first legislative prohibition of all voluntary, private, race-conscious efforts to abolish traditional patterns of racial segregation and hierarchy.

Our conclusion is further reinforced by examination of the language and legislative history of § 703(j) of Title VII. Opponents of Title VII raised two related arguments against the bill. First, they argued that the Act would be interpreted to *require* employers with racially imbalanced work forces to grant preferential treatment to racial minorities in order to integrate. Second, they argued that employers with racially imbalanced work forces would grant preferential treatment to racial minorities, even if not required to do so by the Act. Had Congress meant to prohibit all race-conscious affirmative action, as respondent urges, it easily could have answered both objections by providing that Title VII would not require or *permit* racially preferential integration efforts. But Congress did not choose such a course. Rather Congress added § 703(j) which addresses only the first objection. The section provides that nothing contained in Title VII "shall be interpreted to *require* any employer * * * to grant preferential treatment * * * to any group because of the race * * * of such * * * group on account of" a *de facto* racial imbalance in the employer's work force. The section does *not* state that "nothing in Title VII shall be interpreted to *permit*" voluntary affirmative efforts to correct racial imbalances. The natural inference is that Congress chose not to forbid all voluntary race-conscious affirmative action.

The reasons for this choice are evident from the legislative record. Title VII could not have been enacted into law without substantial support from legislators in both Houses who traditionally resisted federal regulation of private business. Those legislators demanded as a price for their support that "management prerogatives, and union freedoms * * * be left undisturbed to the greatest extent possible." H. R. Rep. No. 914, 88th Cong., 1st Sess., pt. 2, p. 29 (1963). Section 703(j) was proposed by Senator Dirksen to allay any fears that the Act might be interpreted in such a way as to upset this compromise. The section was designed to prevent § 703 of Title VII from being interpreted in such a way as to lead to undue "Federal Government interference with private businesses because of some Federal employee's ideas about racial balance or racial imbalance." Clearly, a prohibition against all voluntary, race-conscious, affirmative action efforts would disserve these ends. Such a prohibition would augment the powers of the Federal Government and diminish traditional management prerogatives while at the same time impeding attainment of the ultimate statutory goals. In view of this legislative history and in view of Congress' desire to avoid undue federal regulation of private businesses, use of the word "require" rather than the phrase "require or permit" in § 703(j) fortifies the conclusion that Congress did not intend to limit traditional business freedom to such a degree as to prohibit all voluntary, race-conscious affirmative action.

We therefore hold that Title VII's prohibition in §§ 703(a) and (d) against racial discrimination does not condemn all private, voluntary, race-conscious affirmative action plans.

III

We need not today define in detail the line of demarcation between permissible and impermissible affirmative action plans. It suffices to hold that the challenged Kaiser-USWA affirmative action plan falls on the permissible side of the line. The purposes of the plan mirror those of the statute. Both were designed to break down old patterns of racial segregation and hierarchy. Both were structured to "open employment opportunities for Negroes in occupations which have been traditionally closed to them." [8]

At the same time, the plan does not unnecessarily trammel the interests of the white employees. The plan does not require the discharge of white workers and their replacement with new black hirees. Nor does the plan create an absolute bar to the advancement of white employees; half of those trained in the program will be white. Moreover, the plan is a temporary measure; it is not intended to maintain racial balance, but simply to eliminate a manifest racial imbalance. Preferential selection of craft trainees at the Gramercy

8. See n. 1, supra. This is not to suggest that the freedom of an employer to undertake race-conscious affirmative action efforts depends on whether or not his effort is motivated by fear of liability under Title VII.

plant will end as soon as the percentage of black skilled craftworkers in the Gramercy plant approximates the percentage of blacks in the local labor force.

We conclude, therefore, that the adoption of the Kaiser-USWA plan for the Gramercy plant falls within the area of discretion left by Title VII to the private sector voluntarily to adopt affirmative action plans designed to eliminate conspicuous racial imbalance in traditionally segregated job categories.[9] Accordingly, the judgment of the Court of Appeals for the Fifth Circuit is

Reversed.

MR. JUSTICE POWELL and MR. JUSTICE STEVENS took no part in the consideration or decision of these cases.

MR. JUSTICE BLACKMUN, concurring.

* * *

In his dissent from the decision of the United States Court of Appeals for the Fifth Circuit, Judge Wisdom pointed out that this case arises from a practical problem in the administration of Title VII. The broad prohibition against discrimination places the employer and the union on what he accurately described as a "high tightrope without a net beneath them." If Title VII is read literally, on the one hand they face liability for past discrimination against blacks, and on the other they face liability to whites for any voluntary preferences adopted to mitigate the effects of prior discrimination against blacks.

In this litigation, Kaiser denies prior discrimination but concedes that its past hiring practices may be subject to question. Although the labor force in the Gramercy area was approximately 39% black, Kaiser's work force was less than 15% black, and its craftwork force was less than 2% black. Kaiser had made some effort to recruit black painters, carpenters, insulators, and other craftsmen, but it continued to insist that those hired have five years prior industrial experience, a requirement that arguably was not sufficiently job related to justify under Title VII any discriminatory impact it may have had. The parties dispute the extent to which black craftsmen were available in the local labor market. They agree, however, that after critical reviews from the Office of Federal Contract Compliance, Kaiser and the Steelworkers established the training program in question here and modeled it along the lines of a Title VII consent decree later entered for the steel industry. Yet when they did this, respondent Weber sued, alleging that Title VII prohibited the program because it discriminated against him as a white person and it was not supported by a prior judicial finding of discrimination against blacks.

9. Our disposition makes unnecessary consideration of petitioners' argument that their plan was justified because they feared that black employees would bring suit under Title VII if they did not adopt an affirmative action plan. Nor need we consider petitioners' contention that their affirmative action plan represented an attempt to comply with Exec. Order No. 11246, 3 CFR 339 (1964–1965 Comp.).

Respondent Weber's reading of Title VII, endorsed by the Court of Appeals, places voluntary compliance with Title VII in profound jeopardy. The only way for the employer and the union to keep their footing on the "tightrope" it creates would be to eschew all forms of voluntary affirmative action. Even a whisper of emphasis on minority recruiting would be forbidden. Because Congress intended to encourage private efforts to come into compliance with Title VII, Judge Wisdom concluded that employers and unions who had committed "arguable violations" of Title VII should be free to make reasonable responses without fear of liability to whites. Preferential hiring along the lines of the Kaiser program is a reasonable response for the employer, whether or not a court, on these facts, could order the same step as a remedy. The company is able to avoid identifying victims of past discrimination, and so avoids claims for backpay that would inevitably follow a response limited to such victims. If past victims should be benefited by the program, however, the company mitigates its liability to those persons. Also, to the extent that Title VII liability is predicated on the "disparate effect" of an employer's past hiring practices, the program makes it less likely that such an effect could be demonstrated. And the Court has recently held that work-force statistics resulting from private affirmative action were probative of benign intent in a "disparate treatment" case. Furnco Construction Corp. v. Waters, 438 U.S. 567, 579–580, 98 S.Ct. 2943, 2950–951, 57 L.Ed.2d 957 (1978).

The "arguable violation" theory has a number of advantages. It responds to a practical problem in the administration of Title VII not anticipated by Congress. It draws predictability from the outline of present law and closely effectuates the purpose of the Act. Both Kaiser and the United States urge its adoption here. Because I agree that it is the soundest way to approach this case, my preference would be to resolve this litigation by applying it and holding that Kaiser's craft training program meets the requirement that voluntary affirmative action be a reasonable response to an "arguable violation" of Title VII.

The Court, however, declines to consider the narrow "arguable violation" approach and adheres instead to an interpretation of Title VII that permits affirmative action by an employer whenever the job category in question is "traditionally segregated." The sources cited suggest that the Court considers a job category to be "traditionally segregated" when there has been a societal history of purposeful exclusion of blacks from the job category, resulting in a persistent disparity between the proportion of blacks in the labor force and the proportion of blacks among those who hold jobs within the category.

"Traditionally segregated job categories," where they exist, sweep far more broadly than the class of "arguable violations" of Title VII. The Court's expansive approach is somewhat disturbing for me because, as MR. JUSTICE REHNQUIST points out, the Congress that passed Title VII probably thought it was adopting a principle of nondiscrimination that would apply to blacks and whites alike. While setting aside that principle can be justified where necessary to advance statutory policy by encouraging reasonable responses as a form of voluntary compliance that mitigates "arguable violations," discarding the principle of nondiscrimination where no countervailing statutory policy exists appears to be at odds with the bargain struck when Title VII was enacted.

A closer look at the problem, however, reveals that in each of the principal ways in which the Court's "traditionally segregated job categories" approach expands on the "arguable violations" theory, still other considerations point in favor of the broad standard adopted by the Court, and make it possible for me to conclude that the Court's reading of the statute is an acceptable one.

A. The first point at which the Court departs from the "arguable violations" approach is that it measures an individual employer's capacity for affirmative action solely in terms of a statistical disparity. The individual employer need not have engaged in discriminatory practices in the past. While, under Title VII, a mere disparity may provide the basis for a prima facie case against an employer, Dothard v. Rawlinson, 433 U.S. 321, 329–331, 97 S.Ct. 2720, 2726–2727, 53 L.Ed.2d 786 (1977), it would not conclusively prove a violation of the Act. Teamsters v. United States, 431 U.S. 324, 339–340, n. 20, 97 S.Ct. 1843, 1856, 52 L.Ed.2d 396 (1977). As a practical matter, however, this difference may not be that great. While the "arguable violation" standard is conceptually satisfying, in practice the emphasis would be on "arguable" rather than on "violation." The great difficulty in the District Court was that no one had any incentive to prove that Kaiser had violated the Act. Neither Kaiser nor the Steelworkers wanted to establish a past violation, nor did Weber. The blacks harmed had never sued and so had no established representative. The Equal Employment Opportunity Commission declined to intervene, and cannot be expected to intervene in every case of this nature. To make the "arguable violation" standard work, it would have to be set low enough to permit the employer to prove it without obligating himself to pay a damages award. The inevitable tendency would be to avoid hair-splitting litigation by simply concluding that a mere disparity between the racial composition of the employer's work force and the composition of the qualified local labor force would be an "arguable violation," even though actual liability could not be established on that basis alone.

B. The Court also departs from the "arguable violation" approach by permitting an employer to redress discrimination that lies wholly outside the bounds of Title VII. For example, Title VII provides no remedy for pre-Act discrimination, yet the purposeful discrimination that creates a "traditionally segregated job category" may have entirely predated the Act. More subtly, in assessing a prima facie case of Title VII liability, the composition of the employer's work force is compared to the composition of the pool of workers who meet valid job qualifications. When a "job category" is traditionally segregated, however, that pool will reflect the effects of segregation, and the Court's approach goes further and permits a comparison with the composition of the labor force as a whole, in which minorities are more heavily represented.

Strong considerations of equity support an interpretation of Title VII that would permit private affirmative action to reach where Title VII itself does not. The bargain struck in 1964 with the passage of Title VII guaranteed equal opportunity for white and black alike, but where Title VII provides no remedy for blacks, it should not be construed to foreclose private affirmative action from supplying relief. It seems unfair for respondent Weber to argue, as he does, that the asserted scarcity of black craftsmen in Louisiana, the product of historic discrimination, makes Kaiser's training program illegal because it ostensibly absolves Kaiser of all Title VII liability. Absent compelling evidence of legislative intent, I would not interpret Title VII itself as a means of "locking in" the effects of segregation for which Title VII provides no remedy. Such a construction, as the Court points out, would be "ironic," given the broad remedial purposes of Title VII.

MR. JUSTICE REHNQUIST's dissent, while it focuses more on what Title VII does not require than on what Title VII forbids, cites several passages that appear to express an intent to "lock in" minorities. In mining the legislative history anew, however, the dissent, in my view, fails to take proper account of our prior cases that have given that history a much more limited reading than that adopted by the dissent. For example, in Griggs v. Duke Power Co., 401 U.S. 424, 434–436, and n. 11, 91 S.Ct. 849, 855–856, 28 L.Ed.2d 158 (1971), the Court refused to give controlling weight to the memorandum of Senators Clark and Case which the dissent now finds so persuasive. And in quoting a statement from that memorandum that an employer would not be "permitted * * * to prefer Negroes for future vacancies," the dissent does not point out that the Court's opinion in Teamsters v. United States, 431 U.S., at 349–351, 97 S.Ct., at 1861–1862, implies that that language is limited to the protection of established seniority systems. Here, seniority is not in issue because the craft training program is new and does not involve an abrogation of pre-existing seniority rights. In short, the passages marshaled by the dissent are not so compelling as to merit the whip hand over the obvious equity of permitting employers to ameliorate the effects of past discrimination for which Title VII provides no direct relief.

* * *

MR. CHIEF JUSTICE BURGER, dissenting.

The Court reaches a result I would be inclined to vote for were I a Member of Congress considering a proposed amendment of Title VII. I cannot join the Court's judgment, however, because it is contrary to the explicit language of the statute and arrived at by means wholly incompatible with long-established principles of separation of powers. Under the guise of statutory "construction," the Court effectively rewrites

Title VII to achieve what it regards as a desirable result. It "amends" the statute to do precisely what both its sponsors and its opponents agreed the statute was *not* intended to do.

When Congress enacted Title VII after long study and searching debate, it produced a statute of extraordinary clarity, which speaks directly to the issue we consider in this case. * * *

Often we have difficulty interpreting statutes either because of imprecise drafting or because legislative compromises have produced genuine ambiguities. But here there is no lack of clarity, no ambiguity. The quota embodied in the collective-bargaining agreement between Kaiser and the Steelworkers unquestionably discriminates on the basis of race against individual employees seeking admission to on-the-job training programs. And, under the plain language of § 703(d), that is "an *unlawful* employment practice."

Oddly, the Court seizes upon the very clarity of the statute almost as a justification for evading the unavoidable impact of its language. The Court blandly tells us that Congress could not really have meant what it said, for a "literal construction" would defeat the "purpose" of the statute—at least the congressional "purpose" as five Justices divine it today. But how are judges supposed to ascertain the *purpose* of a statute except through the words Congress used and the legislative history of the statute's evolution? One need not even resort to the legislative history to recognize what is apparent from the face of Title VII—that it is specious to suggest that § 703(j) contains a negative pregnant that permits employers to do what §§ 703(a) and (d) unambiguously and unequivocally *forbid* employers from doing. Moreover, as MR. JUSTICE REHNQUIST's opinion—which I join—conclusively demonstrates, the legislative history makes equally clear that the supporters and opponents of Title VII reached an agreement about the statute's intended effect. That agreement, expressed so clearly in the language of the statute that no one should doubt its meaning, forecloses the reading which the Court gives the statute today.

* * *

MR. JUSTICE REHNQUIST, with whom THE CHIEF JUSTICE joins, dissenting.

* * *

* * * It may be that one or more of the principal sponsors of Title VII would have preferred to see a provision allowing preferential treatment of minorities written into the bill. Such a provision, however, would have to have been expressly or impliedly excepted from Title VII's explicit prohibition on all racial discrimination in employment. There is no such exception in the Act. And a reading of the legislative debates concerning Title VII, in which proponents and opponents alike uniformly denounced discrimination in favor of, as well as discrimination against, Negroes, demonstrates clearly that any legislator harbor-

ing an unspoken desire for such a provision could not possibly have succeeded in enacting it into law.

* * * In February 1974, under pressure from the Office of Federal Contract Compliance to increase minority representation in craft positions at its various plants,[2] and hoping to deter the filing of employment discrimination claims by minorities, Kaiser entered into a collective-bargaining agreement with the United Steelworkers of America (Steelworkers) which * * * required that no less than one minority applicant be admitted to the training program for every nonminority applicant until the percentage of blacks in craft positions equaled the percentage of blacks in the local work force. * * *

* * *

* * * To be sure, the reality of employment discrimination against Negroes provided the primary impetus for passage of Title VII. But this fact by no means supports the proposition that Congress intended to leave employers free to discriminate against white persons.[11] In most cases, "[l]egislative history * * * is more vague

2. The Office of Federal Contract Compliance (OFCC), subsequently renamed the Office of Federal Contract Compliance Programs (OFCCP), is an arm of the Department of Labor responsible for ensuring compliance by Government contractors with the equal employment opportunity requirements established by Exec. Order No. 11246, 3 CFR 339 (1964–1965 Comp.), as amended by Exec. Order No. 11375, 3 CFR 684 (1966–1970 Comp.), and by Exec. Order No. 12086, 3 CFR 230 (1979).

Executive Order 11246, as amended, requires all applicants for federal contracts to refrain from employment discrimination and to "take affirmative action to ensure that applicants are employed, and that employees are treated during employment, without regard to their race, color, religion, sex or national origin." The Executive Order empowers the Secretary of Labor to issue rules and regulations necessary and appropriate to achieve its purpose. He, in turn, has delegated most enforcement duties to the OFCC. See 41 CFR 60–20.1 et seq., 60–2.24 (1978).

The affirmative action program mandated * * * for nonconstruction contractors requires a "utilization" study to determine minority representation in the work force. Goals for hiring and promotion must be set to overcome any "underutilization" found to exist.

The OFCC employs the "power of the purse" to coerce acceptance of its affirmative action plans. Indeed, in this case, "the district court found that the 1974 collective bargaining agreement reflected less of a desire on Kaiser's part to train black craft workers than a self-interest in satisfying the OFCC in order to retain lucrative government contracts." 563 F.2d 216, 226 (CA5 1977).

11. The only shred of legislative history cited by the Court in support of the proposition that "Congress did not intend wholly to prohibit private and voluntary affirmative action efforts," ante, at 203, is the following excerpt from the Judiciary Committee Report accompanying the civil rights bill reported to the House:

"No bill can or should lay claim to eliminating all of the causes and consequences of racial and other types of discrimination against minorities. There is reason to believe, however, that national leadership provided by the enactment of Federal legislation dealing with the most troublesome problems *will create an atmosphere conducive to voluntary or local resolution of other forms of discrimination.*" H.R.Rep.No. 914, 88th Cong., 1st Sess., pt. 1, p. 18 (1963) (hereinafter H.R.Rep.), quoted ante, at 203–204.

The Court seizes on the italicized language to support its conclusion that Congress did not intend to prohibit voluntary imposition of racially discriminatory employment quotas. The Court, however, stops too short in its reading of the House Report. The words immediately following the material excerpted by the Court are as follows:

"It is, however, possible and necessary for the Congress to enact legislation which prohibits and provides the means of terminating *the most serious types of*

than the statute we are called upon to interpret." Here, however, the legislative history of Title VII is as clear as the language of §§ 703(a) and (d), and it irrefutably demonstrates that Congress meant precisely what it said in §§ 703(a) and (d)—that *no* racial discrimination in employment is permissible under Title VII, not even preferential treatment of minorities to correct racial imbalance.

* * *

In the opening speech of the formal Senate debate on the bill, Senator Humphrey addressed the main concern of Title VII's opponents, advising that not only does Title VII not require use of racial quotas, *it does not permit* their use. "The truth," stated the floor leader of the bill, "is that this title forbids discriminating against anyone on account of race. This is the simple and complete truth about Title VII." * * *

At the close of his speech, Senator Humphrey returned briefly to the subject of employment quotas: "It is claimed that the bill would require racial quotas for all hiring, when in fact it provides that race shall not be a basis for making personnel decisions."

* * *

A few days later the Senate's attention focused exclusively on Title VII, as Senators Clark and Case rose to discuss the title of H.R. 7152 on which they shared floor "captain" responsibilities. In an interpretative memorandum submitted jointly to the Senate, Senators Clark and Case took pains to refute the opposition's charge that Title VII would result

discrimination. This H.R. 7152, as amended, would achieve in a number of related areas. It would reduce discriminatory obstacles to the exercise of the right to vote and provide means of expediting the vindication of that right. It would make it possible to remove the daily affront and humiliation involved in discriminatory denials of access to facilities ostensibly open to the general public. It would guarantee that there will be no discrimination upon recipients of Federal financial assistance. It would prohibit discrimination in employment, and provide means to expedite termination of discrimination in public education. It would open additional avenues to deal with redress of denials of equal protection of the laws on account of race, color, religion, or national origin by State or local authorities." H.R.Rep., pt. 1, p. 18 (emphasis added).

When thus read in context, the meaning of the italicized language in the Court's excerpt of the House Report becomes clear. By dealing with "the most serious types of discrimination," such as discrimination in voting, public accommodations, employment, etc., H.R. 7152 would hopefully inspire "voluntary or local resolution of other forms of discrimination," that is, forms other than discrimination in voting, public accommodations, employment, etc.

One can also infer from the House Report that the Judiciary Committee hoped that federal legislation would inspire voluntary elimination of discrimination against minority groups other than those protected under the bill, perhaps the aged and handicapped to name just two. In any event, the House Report does not support the Court's proposition that Congress, by banning racial discrimination in employment, intended to permit racial discrimination in employment.

Thus, examination of the House Judiciary Committee's report reveals that the Court's interpretation of Title VII, far from being compelled by the Act's legislative history, is utterly without support in that legislative history. Indeed, as demonstrated in Part III, infra, the Court's interpretation of Title VII is totally refuted by the Act's legislative history.

in preferential treatment of minorities. Their words were clear and unequivocal:

> "There is no requirement in Title VII that an employer maintain a racial balance in his work force. On the contrary, any deliberate attempt to maintain a racial balance, whatever such a balance may be, would involve a violation of Title VII because maintaining such a balance would require an employer to hire or to refuse to hire on the basis of race. It must be emphasized that discrimination is prohibited as to any individual." Id., at 7213.

Of particular relevance to the instant case were their observations regarding seniority rights. As if directing their comments at Brian Weber, the Senators said:

> "Title VII would have no effect on established seniority rights. Its effect is prospective and not retrospective. Thus, for example, if a business has been discriminating in the past and as a result has an all-white working force, when the title comes into effect the employer's obligation would be simply to fill future vacancies on a nondiscriminatory basis. He would not be obliged—*or indeed permitted*—to fire whites in order to hire Negroes, *or to prefer Negroes for future vacancies, or, once Negroes are hired, to give them special seniority rights at the expense of the white workers hired earlier.*" *Ibid.* (emphasis added).[19]

19. A Justice Department memorandum earlier introduced by Senator Clark, see n. 18, supra, expressed the same view regarding Title VII's impact on seniority rights of employees:

> "Title VII would have no effect on seniority rights existing at the time it takes effect. * * * This would be true even in the case where owing to discrimination prior to the effective date of the title, white workers had more seniority than Negroes. * * * [A]ssuming that seniority rights were built up over a period of time during which Negroes were not hired, these rights would not be set aside by the taking effect of Title VII. Employers and labor organizations would simply be under a duty not to discriminate against Negroes because of their race." 110 Cong.Rec. 7207 (1964).

The interpretation of Title VII contained in the memoranda introduced by Senator Clark totally refutes the Court's implied suggestion that Title VII would prohibit an employer from discriminating on the basis of race in order to *maintain* a racial balance in his work force, but would permit him to do so in order to *achieve* racial balance.

The maintain-achieve distinction is analytically indefensible in any event. Apparently, the Court is saying that an employer is free to *achieve* a racially balanced work force by discriminating against whites, but that once he has reached his goal, he is no longer free to discriminate in order to maintain that racial balance. In other words, once Kaiser reaches its goal of 39% minority representation in craft positions at the Gramercy plant, it can no longer consider race in admitting employees into its on-the-job training programs, even if the programs become as "all-white" as they were in April 1974.

Obviously, the Court is driven to this illogical position by the glaring statement, quoted in text, of Senators Clark and Case that "any deliberate attempt to *maintain* a racial balance * * * would involve a violation of Title VII because *maintaining* such a balance would require an employer to hire or to refuse to hire on the basis of race." Achieving a certain racial balance, however, no less than maintaining such a balance, would require an employer to hire or to refuse to hire on the basis of race. Further, the Court's own conclusion that Title VII's legislative history, coupled with the wording of § 703(j), evinces a congressional intent to leave employers free to employ "private, voluntary, race-conscious affirmative action plans," is inconsistent with its maintain-achieve distinction. If

Thus, with virtual clairvoyance the Senate's leading supporters of Title VII anticipated precisely the circumstances of this case and advised their colleagues that the type of minority preference employed by Kaiser would violate Title VII's ban on racial discrimination. To further accentuate the point, Senator Clark introduced another memorandum dealing with common criticisms of the bill, including the charge that racial quotas would be imposed under Title VII. The answer was simple and to the point: "Quotas are themselves discriminatory."

* * * Senators Smathers and Sparkman, while conceding that Title VII does not in so many words require the use of hiring quotas, repeated the opposition's view that employers would be coerced to grant preferential hiring treatment to minorities by agencies of the Federal Government. Senator Williams was quick to respond:

> "Those opposed to H.R. 7152 should realize that to hire a Negro solely because he is a Negro is racial discrimination, just as much as a 'white only' employment policy. Both forms of discrimination are prohibited by Title VII of this bill. The language of that title simply states that race is not a qualification for employment. * * * Some people charge that H. R. 7152 favors the Negro, at the expense of the white majority. But how can the language of equality favor one race or one religion over another? Equality can have only one meaning, and that meaning is self-evident to reasonable men. Those who say that equality means favoritism do violence to common sense." * * *

While the debate in the Senate raged, a bipartisan coalition under the leadership of Senators Dirksen, Mansfield, Humphrey, and Kuchel was working with House leaders and representatives of the Johnson administration on a number of amendments to H. R. 7152 designed to enhance its prospects of passage. The so-called "Dirksen-Mansfield" amendment was introduced on May 26 by Senator Dirksen as a substitute for the entire House-passed bill. The substitute bill, which ultimately became law, left unchanged the basic prohibitory language of §§ 703(a) and (d), as well as the remedial provisions in § 706(g). It added, however, several provisions defining and clarifying the scope of Title VII's substantive prohibitions. One of those clarifying amendments, § 703(j), was specifically directed at the opposition's concerns regarding racial balancing and preferential treatment of minorities * * *.

* * *

Congress' primary purpose in enacting Title VII was to open employment opportunities previously closed to Negroes, it would seem to make little difference whether the employer opening those opportunities was achieving or maintaining a certain racial balance in his work force. Likewise, if § 703(j) evinces Congress' intent to permit imposition of race-conscious affirmative action plans, it would seem to make little difference whether the plan was adopted to achieve or maintain the desired racial balance.

Contrary to the Court's analysis, the language of § 703(j) is precisely tailored to the objection voiced time and again by Title VII's opponents. Not once during the 83 days of debate in the Senate did a speaker, proponent or opponent, suggest that the bill would allow employers *voluntarily* to prefer racial minorities over white persons. In light of Title VII's flat prohibition on discrimination "against any individual * * * because of such individual's race," § 703(a), such a contention would have been, in any event, too preposterous to warrant response. Indeed, speakers on both sides of the issue, as the legislative history makes clear, recognized that Title VII would tolerate no *voluntary* racial preference, whether in favor of blacks or whites. The complaint consistently voiced by the opponents was that Title VII, particularly the word "discrimination," would be *interpreted* by federal agencies such as the EEOC to *require* the correction of racial imbalance through the granting of preferential treatment to minorities. Verbal assurances that Title VII would not require—indeed, would not permit—preferential treatment of blacks having failed, supporters of H. R. 7152 responded by proposing an amendment carefully worded to meet, and put to rest, the opposition's charge. Indeed, unlike §§ 703(a) and (d), which are by their terms directed at entities—e.g., employers, labor unions—whose actions are restricted by Title VII's prohibitions, the language of § 703(j) is specifically directed at entities—federal agencies and courts—charged with the responsibility of interpreting Title VII's provisions.

In light of the background and purpose of § 703(j), the irony of invoking the section to justify the result in this case is obvious. The Court's frequent references to the "voluntary" nature of Kaiser's racially discriminatory admission quota bear no relationship to the facts of this case. Kaiser and the Steelworkers acted under pressure from an agency of the Federal Government, the Office of Federal Contract Compliance, which found that minorities were being "underutilized" at Kaiser's plants. See n. 2, supra. That is, Kaiser's work force was racially imbalanced. Bowing to that pressure, Kaiser instituted an admissions quota preferring blacks over whites, thus confirming that the fears of Title VII's opponents were well founded. Today, § 703(j), adopted to allay those fears, is invoked by the Court to uphold imposition of a racial quota under the very circumstances that the section was intended to prevent.

* * *

Reading the language of Title VII, as the Court purports to do, "against the background of [its] legislative history * * * and the historical context from which the Act arose," ante, at 201, one is led inescapably to the conclusion that Congress fully understood what it was saying and meant precisely what it said. Opponents of the civil rights bill did not argue that employers would be permitted under Title VII voluntarily to grant preferential treatment to minorities to correct racial imbalance. The plain language of the statute too clearly prohibited such racial discrimination to admit of any doubt. They argued, tirelessly, that Title VII would be interpreted by federal agencies and their agents to require unwilling employers to racially balance their work forces by granting preferential treatment to minorities. Supporters of H.R. 7152 responded, equally tirelessly, that the Act would not be so interpreted because not only does it not require preferential treatment of minorities, it does not *permit* preferential treatment of any race for any reason. * * *

To put an end to the dispute, supporters of the civil rights bill drafted and introduced § 703(j). Specifically addressed to the opposition's charge, § 703(j) simply enjoins federal agencies and courts from interpreting Title VII to require an employer to prefer certain racial groups to correct imbalances in his work force. The section says nothing about voluntary preferential treatment of minorities because such racial discrimination is plainly proscribed by §§ 703(a) and (d). Indeed, had Congress intended to except voluntary, race-conscious preferential treatment from the blanket prohibition of racial discrimination in §§ 703(a) and (d), it surely could have drafted language better suited to the task than § 703(j). It knew how. Section 703(i) provides:

> "Nothing contained in [Title VII] shall apply to any business or enterprise on or near an Indian reservation with respect to any publicly announced employment practice of such business or enterprise under which a preferential treatment is given to any individual because he is an Indian living on or near a reservation." 78 Stat. 257, 42 U.S.C. § 2000e–2(i).

* * *

WEBER v. KAISER ALUM. & CHEM. CORP.

United States Court of Appeals, Fifth Circuit, 1980.
611 F.2d 132.

ON REMAND FROM THE SUPREME COURT OF THE UNITED STATES, 443 U.S. 193, 99 S.Ct. 2721, 61 L.Ed.2d 480

Before WISDOM, GEE, and FAY, CIRCUIT JUDGES.

GEE, CIRCUIT JUDGE.

* * *

For myself only, and with all respect and deference, I here note my personal conviction that the decision of the Supreme Court in this case is profoundly wrong.

That it is wrong as a matter of statutory construction seems to me sufficiently demonstrated by the dissenting opinions of the Chief Justice and of Mr. Justice Rehnquist. To these I can add nothing. They make plain beyond peradventure that the Civil Rights Act of 1964 passed the Congress on the express representation of its sponsors that it would not and could not be construed as the Court has now construed it. What could be plainer than the words of the late Senator Humphrey—defending the bill against the charge that it adumbrated quotas and preferential treatment—that "the title would *prohibit* preferential treatment for any particular group * * * "? The Court now tells us that this is not so. That it feels it may properly do so seems to me a grievous thing.

But sadder still—tragic, in my own view—is the Court's departure from the long road that we have travelled from Plessy v. Ferguson, 163 U.S. 537, 16 S.Ct. 1138, 41 L.Ed. 256 (1896), toward making good Mr. Justice Harlan's anguished cry in dissent that "[o]ur Constitution is color-blind, and neither knows nor tolerates classes among citizens." Id. at 559, 16 S.Ct. at 1146. I voice my profound belief that this present action, like *Plessy*, is a wrong and dangerous turning, and my confident hope that we will soon return to the high, bright road on which we disdain to classify a citizen, *any* citizen, to any degree or for any purpose by the color of his skin.

Though for the above reasons I think it gravely mistaken, I do not say that the Court's decision is immoral or unjust—indeed, in some basic sense it may well represent true justice. But there are many actions roughly just that our laws do not authorize and our Constitution forbids, actions such as preventing a Nazi Party march through a town where reside former inmates of concentration camps or inflicting summary punishment on one caught redhanded in a crime.

Subordinate magistrates such as I must either obey the orders of higher authority or yield up their posts to those who will. I obey, since in my view the action required of me by the Court's mandate is only to follow a mistaken course and not an evil one.

Vacated and Remanded.

WISDOM, CIRCUIT JUDGE, specially concurring:

With deference to the views expressed by the majority of this Court, I express the view that the decision of the Supreme Court in this case is profoundly right for the reasons stated in my dissenting opinion. Weber v. Kaiser Aluminum & Chemical Corporation and United Steelworkers of America, AFL–CIO, 5 Cir. 1977, 563 F.2d 216, 227.

NOTES AND PROBLEMS FOR DISCUSSION

1. Was the result in *Weber* a necessary consequence of the Court's prior rulings in *Griggs* and *Albemarle*? Can it be explained as a response to the dilemma (alluded to in Justice Blackmun's concurring opinion) that confronts employers who artificially increase their proportion of black employees in order to either avoid liability under a disproportionate impact discrimination claim predicated on a showing of racial imbalance in the employers' workforce, or to eschew the burden of validating the job relatedness of their employment criteria? If so, how does the Court's opinion in Connecticut v. Teal, supra, fit into this calculation? See Blumrosen, The "Bottom Line" After Connecticut v. Teal, 8 Emp.Rel.L.J. 572 (1983).

2. Is the "traditional pattern of segregation" standard more or less satisfactory than Judge Wisdom's "arguable violation" theory? Is an individual employer competent to make a determination as to the existence of either of these two criteria? What about Justice Blackmun's concern that the "traditional pattern" standard can, and likely will, include consideration of lawful pre-Act discrimination? On the other hand, is the majority saying that affirmative action is permissible where current employment practices perpetuate the discriminatory effects of a lawful pre-Act tradition of racial bias? Does the "traditional pattern" criterion permit the use of affirmative action in an historically segregated industry by a nondiscriminating employer that played no part in creating or maintaining that tradition? Would this issue arise under the "arguable violation" standard? See Cohen v. Community College of Philadelphia, 484 F.Supp. 411, 434 (E.D.Pa.1980) ("* * * I do not read *Weber* as requiring an employer to establish a history of actual discrimination on his own part before he is permitted to adopt an affirmative action plan designed to eliminate that discrimination. Rather, I hold that under *Weber*, an employer's affirmative action plan can be justified by the existence of a history of racial discrimination in the relevant occupation or profession at large.") Didn't the Supreme Court in *Fullilove* address this issue when it upheld a federal statute that imposed affirmative action requirements on all contractors in a traditionally segregated industry? In light of the pressure directed at Kaiser by the Office of Federal Contract Compliance, was Kaiser's affirmative action plan truly voluntary?

3. Are you convinced by either the majority's or Justice Rehnquist's opinion as to whether Congress seriously considered the issue of voluntary affirmative action during its deliberations over Title VII? If not, what impact should an inconclusive legislative history have on the construction of a statute?

4. The majority opinion notes that Kaiser's craft training program was established as part of an affirmative action plan designed specifically to increase the number of black craft workers. Prior to the creation of this training program, Kaiser hired only craftworkers with craft experience. The plaintiff sought admission to the training program because he couldn't satisfy the experience requirement for a craft job. Thus, he sought and was denied a benefit—training—that was created for the sole purpose of helping train black workers. Clearly, Weber would not have benefitted from the termination of the affirmative action plan since this would have eliminated any opportunity for him to obtain a craft job with Kaiser. Does this diminish the extent of the injury Weber suffered from being denied admission to the program to the preference of a less senior black employee?

5. Was Kaiser's plan limited to providing training to identifiable victims of discrimination? If not, what was the purpose of the plan? Does this suggest anything about Kaiser's, and perhaps the Court's, view of equality?

6. The majority in *Weber* concluded that Kaiser's plan constituted a permissible form of affirmative action because, in part, it was a temporary measure—lasting until the percentage of black craftworkers in the plant approximated the percentage of blacks in the local labor force. The significance attached to the temporary nature of the preference indicates that the Court believed that racial preferences could be used to attain, but not maintain racial balance in traditionally segregated job classifications. Is this distinction justifiable or is it merely an attempt to effect a compromise of an extremely sensitive issue? Is Justice Rehnquist right in suggesting that this distinction is at variance with other portions of the majority's opinion?

7. What if an employer adopted an affirmative action plan that granted benefits on the basis of sex? Did the *Weber* Court intend to restrict affirmative action to members of only one of the statutorily protected classifications? Does the legislative history of Title VII's sex discrimination provision, as recounted in the Kanowitz article, supra at 282, serve as a basis for distinguishing sex from race with respect to this issue? See La Riviere v. EEOC, 682 F.2d 1275 (9th Cir. 1982) (*Weber* analysis applied to sex-based affirmative action plan employed by a public employer).

Suppose a university determines that the salaries of its female faculty members are significantly less than those of its male faculty members. It then decides to implement an affirmative action plan to eliminate this differential by creating a compensation scheme that provides each woman faculty member with a $6000 increase in salary. As a result of this scheme, Prof. Amy Michel receives a higher salary than Prof. Richard Winfield, even though both teach in the same department, hold the same academic rank, have essentially identical credentials and have worked at the university for the same length of time. Does this plan violate Title VII? See Grann v. Madison, 738 F.2d 786 (7th Cir. 1984), cert. denied, ___ U.S. ___, 105 S.Ct. 296, 83 L.Ed.2d 231 (1984). What about the Equal Pay Act? See Ende v. Board of Regents, 565 F.Supp. 501 (N.D. Ill.1983).

8. In determining whether a "traditional pattern" of discrimination exists, must a court compare the minority composition of the defendant's or industry's workforce with that minority's representation in the local area population? Minnick v. California Department of Corrections, 95 Cal.App.3d 506, 157 Cal. Rptr. 260 (1979), cert. dismissed for want of finality, 452 U.S. 105, 101 S.Ct. 2211, 68 L.Ed.2d 706 (1981) (neither Title VII nor U.S. Constitution violated by voluntarily adopted affirmative action hiring plan designed to have the percentage of minority prison employees approximate the proportion of minority persons in the State prison inmate population).

9. In light of the extensive factual inquiry associated with judicial review of affirmative action plans, is the issue of the validity of such a plan a question of law or of fact? Where the defendant is a public entity, is the validity of the plan a question of law to be determined by a court or is the plaintiff entitled under the Seventh Amendment to a jury determination on this issue? See Bratton v. Detroit, 704 F.2d 878 (6th Cir.1983), modified, 712 F.2d 222 (6th Cir. 1983), cert. denied, 464 U.S. 1040, 104 S.Ct. 703, 79 L.Ed.2d 168 (1984). Additionally, is the determination of the validity of a plan or hiring order subject to the "clearly erroneous" standard of review on appeal?

10. Among the most helpful and insightful of the many articles discussing *Weber* and its impact on affirmative action are Cox, The Question of "Voluntary" Racial Employment Quotas and Some Thoughts on Judicial Role, 23 Ariz. L.Rev. 87 (1981); Boyd, Affirmative Action in Employment—The *Weber* Decision, 66 Iowa L.Rev. 1 (1980); Belton, Discrimination and Affirmative Action: An Analysis of Competing Theories of Equality and *Weber*, 59 No.Car.L.Rev. 531 (1981); Blumrosen, Affirmative Action in Employment After *Weber*, 34 Rutg.L.Rev. 1 (1981); Meltzer, The *Weber* Case: The Judicial Abrogation of the Antidiscrimination Standard in Employment, 47 U. Chi. L.Rev. 423 (1980); Schatzki, United Steelworkers of America v. Weber: An Exercise in Understandable Indecision, 56 Wash. L.Rev. 51 (1980).

11. The affirmative action obligations imposed on federal government contractors and subcontractors are discussed at Part. V, infra.

FIREFIGHTERS LOCAL UNION NO. 1784 v. STOTTS

Supreme Court of the United States, 1984.
467 U.S. 561, 104 S.Ct. 2576, 81 L.Ed.2d 483.

JUSTICE WHITE delivered the opinion of the Court.

Petitioners challenge the Court of Appeals' approval of an order enjoining the City of Memphis from following its seniority system in determining who must be laid off as a result of a budgetary shortfall. Respondents contend that the injunction was necessary to effectuate the terms of a Title VII consent decree in which the City agreed to undertake certain obligations in order to remedy past hiring and promotional practices. Because we conclude that the order cannot be justified, either as an effort to enforce the consent decree or as a valid modification, we reverse.

I

In 1977 respondent Carl Stotts, a black holding the position of fire-fighting captain in the Memphis, Tennessee, Fire Department, filed a class action complaint in the United States District Court for the Western District of Tennessee. The complaint charged that the Memphis Fire Department and other city officials were engaged in a pattern or practice of making hiring and promotions decisions on the basis of race in violation of Title VII of the Civil Rights Act of 1964, as well as 42 U.S.C. §§ 1981 and 1983. The District Court certified the case as a class action and consolidated it with an individual action subsequently filed by respondent Fred Jones, a black fire-fighting private in the Department, who claimed that he had been denied a promotion because of his race. Discovery proceeded, settlement negotiations ensued, and in due course, a consent decree was approved and entered by the District Court on April 25, 1980.

The stated purpose of the decree was to remedy the hiring and promotion practices "of the Department with respect to blacks." Accordingly, the City agreed to promote 13 named individuals and to provide backpay to 81 employees of the Fire Department. It also adopted the long-term goal of increasing the proportion of minority representation in each job classification in the Fire Department to approximately the proportion of blacks in the labor force in Shelby County, Tennessee. However, the City did not, by agreeing to the decree, admit "any violations of law, rule or regulation with respect to the allegations" in the complaint. The plaintiffs waived any further relief save to enforce the decree and the District Court retained jurisdiction "for such further orders as may be necessary or appropriate to effectuate the purposes of this decree."

The long-term hiring goal outlined in the decree paralleled the provisions of a 1974 consent decree, which settled a case brought against the City by the United States and which applied citywide. Like the 1974 decree, the 1980 decree also established an interim hiring goal of filling on an annual basis 50 percent of the job vacancies in the Department with qualified black applicants. The 1980 decree contained an additional goal with respect to promotions: the Department was to attempt to ensure that 20 percent of the promotions in each job classification be given to blacks. Neither decree contained provisions for layoffs or reductions in rank, and neither awarded any competitive seniority. The 1974 decree did require that for purposes of promotion, transfer, and assignment, seniority was to be computed "as the total seniority of that person with the City."

In early May, 1981, the City announced that projected budget deficits required a reduction of non-essential personnel throughout the City Government. Layoffs were to be based on the "last hired, first fired" rule under which city-wide seniority, determined by each employee's length of continuous service from the latest date of permanent employment, was the basis for deciding who would be laid off. If a senior employee's position were abolished or eliminated, the employee could "bump down" to a lower ranking position rather than be laid off. As the Court of Appeals later noted, this layoff policy was adopted pursuant to the seniority system "mentioned in the 1974 decree and * * * incorporated in the City's memorandum with the Union."

On May 4, at respondents' request, the District Court entered a temporary restraining order forbidding the layoff of any black employee. The Union, which previously had not been a party to either of these cases, was permitted to intervene. At the preliminary injunction hearing, it appeared that 55 then-filled positions in the Department were to be eliminated and that 39 of these positions were filled with employees having "bumping" rights. It was estimated that 40 least-senior employees in the fire-fighting bureau of the Department [1] would be laid off and that of these 25 were white and 15 black. It also appeared that 56 percent of the employees hired in the Department since 1974 had been black and that the percentage of black employees had increased from approximately 3 or 4 percent in 1974 to 11½ percent in 1980.

On May 18, the District Court entered an order granting an injunction. The Court found that the consent decree "did not contemplate the method to be used for reduction in rank or lay-off," and that the layoff policy was in accordance with the City's seniority system and was not adopted with any intent to discriminate. Nonetheless, concluding that the proposed layoffs would have a racially discriminatory effect and that the seniority system was not a bona fide one, the District Court ordered that the City "not apply the seniority policy insofar as it will decrease the percentage of black lieutenants, drivers, inspectors and privates that are presently employed." On June 23, the District Court broadened its order to include three additional classifications. A

1. The Memphis Fire Department is divided into several bureaus, including fire-fighting, alarm office, administration, apparatus, maintenance, and fire prevention. Of the positions covered by the original injunction, all but one were in the fire-fighting bureau.

modified layoff plan, aimed at protecting black employees in the seven classifications so as to comply with the court's order, was presented and approved. Layoffs pursuant to the modified plan were then carried out. In certain instances, to comply with the injunction, non-minority employees with more seniority than minority employees were laid off or demoted in rank.[2]

On appeal, the Court of Appeals for the Sixth Circuit affirmed despite its conclusion that the District Court was wrong in holding that the City's seniority system was not bona fide. Characterizing the principal issue as "whether the district court erred in modifying the 1980 Decree to prevent minority employment from being affected disproportionately by unanticipated layoffs," the Court of Appeals concluded that the District Court had acted properly. After determining that the decree was properly approved in the first instance, the court held that the modification was permissible under general contract principles because the City "contracted" to provide "a substantial increase in the number of minorities in supervisory positions" and the layoffs would breach that contract. Alternatively, the court held that the District Court was authorized to modify the decree because new and unforeseen circumstances had created a hardship for one of the parties to the decree. Finally, articulating three alternative rationales, the court rejected petitioners' argument that the modification was improper because it conflicted with the City's seniority system, which was immunized from Title VII attack under § 703(h) of that Act.

The City and the Union filed separate petitions for certiorari. The two petitions were granted and the cases were consolidated for oral argument.

II

We deal first with the claim that these cases are moot. Respondents submit that the injunction entered in this case was a preliminary injunction dealing only with the 1981 layoffs, that all white employees laid off as a result of the injunction were restored to duty only one month after their layoff, and that those who were demoted have now been offered back their old positions. Assertedly, the injunction no longer has force or effect, and the cases are therefore moot. For several reasons, we find the submission untenable.

First, the injunction on its face ordered "that the defendants not apply the seniority policy proposed insofar as it will decrease the percentage of black" employees in specified classifications in the Department. The seniority policy was the policy adopted by the City and contained in the collective bargaining contract with the Union. The injunction was affirmed by the Court of Appeals and has never been

2. The City ultimately laid off 24 privates, three of whom were black. Had the seniority system been followed, six blacks would have been among the 24 privates laid off. Thus, three white employees were laid off as a direct result of the District Court's order. The number of whites demoted as a result of the order is not clear from the record before us.

vacated. It would appear from its terms that the injunction is still in force and that unless set aside must be complied with in connection with any future layoffs.

Second, even if the injunction itself applied only to the 1981 layoffs, the predicate for the so-called preliminary injunction was the ruling that the consent decree must be construed to mean and, in any event, must be modified to provide that layoffs were not to reduce the percentage of blacks employed in the fire department. Furthermore, both the District Court and the Court of Appeals, for different reasons, held that the seniority provisions of the City's collective bargaining contract must be disregarded for the purpose of achieving the mandated result. These rulings remain undisturbed, and we see no indication that respondents concede in urging mootness that these rulings were in error and should be reversed. To the contrary, they continue to defend them. Unless overturned, these rulings would require the City to obey the modified consent decree and to disregard its seniority agreement in making future layoffs.

Accordingly, the inquiry is not merely whether the injunction is still in effect, but whether the mandated modification of the consent decree continues to have an impact on the parties such that the case remains alive.[3] We are quite unconvinced—and it is the respondents' burden to convince us,—that the modification of the decree and the *pro tanto* invalidation of the seniority system is of no real concern to the City because it will never again contemplate layoffs that if carried out in accordance with the seniority system would violate the modified decree.[4] For this reason alone, the case is not moot.

Third, the judgment below will have a continuing effect on the City's management of the Department in still another way. Although the City has resorted or offered to restore to their former positions all white employees who were laid off or demoted, those employees have not been

3. The Court of Appeals, recognizing that the District Court had done more than temporarily preclude the City from applying its seniority system, stated that the "principal issue" before it was "whether the district court erred in modifying the 1980 Decree to prevent minority employment from being affected disproportionately by unanticipated layoffs."

4. Of course if layoffs become necessary, both the City and respondents will be affected by the modified decree, the City because it will be unable to apply its seniority system, respondents because they will be given greater protection than they would otherwise receive under that system. Moreover, the City will be immediately affected by the modification even though no layoff is currently pending. If the lower courts' ruling is left intact, the City will no longer be able to promise current or future employees that layoffs will be conducted solely on the basis of seniority. Against its will, the City has been deprived of the power to offer its employees one of the benefits that make employment with the City attractive to many workers. Seniority has traditionally been, and continues to be, a matter of great concern to American workers. * * * It is not idle speculation to suppose that the City will be required to offer greater monetary compensation or fringe benefits in order to attract and retain the same caliber and number of workers as it could without offering such benefits were it completely free to implement its seniority system. The extent to which the City's employment efforts will be harmed by the loss of this "bargaining chip" may be difficult to measure, but in view of the importance that American workers have traditionally placed on such benefits, the harm cannot be said to be insignificant. * * *

made whole: those who were laid off have lost a month's pay, as well as seniority that has not been restored; and those employees who "bumped down" and accepted lesser positions will also have back-pay claims if their demotions were unjustified. Unless the judgment of the Court of Appeals is reversed, however, the layoffs and demotions were in accordance with the law, and it would be quite unreasonable to expect the City to pay out money to which the employees had no legal right. Nor would it feel free to respond to the seniority claims of the three white employees who, as the City points out, lost competitive seniority in relation to all other individuals who were not laid off, including those minority employees who would have been laid off but for the injunction.[5] On the other hand, if the Court of Appeals' judgment is reversed, the City would be free to take a wholly different position with respect to backpay and seniority.

Undoubtedly, not much money and seniority are involved, but the amount of money and seniority at stake does not determine mootness. As long as the parties have a concrete interest in the outcome of the litigation, the case is not moot notwithstanding the size of the dispute. Moreover, a month's pay is not a negligible item for those affected by the injunction, and the loss of a month's competitive seniority may later determine who gets a promotion, who is entitled to bid for transfers or who is first laid off if there is another reduction in force. These are matters of substance, it seems to us, and enough so to foreclose any claim of mootness.[6]

* * *

III

The issue at the heart of this case is whether the District Court exceeded its powers in entering an injunction requiring white employees to be laid off, when the otherwise applicable seniority system would have called for the layoff of black employees with less seniority.[8] We

5. Since the District Court's order precludes the City from reducing the percentage of black employees holding particular jobs in the event of a layoff or reduction in rank and since competitive seniority is the basis for determining who will be laid off or bumped down, there is some question whether, in light of the judgment below, the City could legally restore to the laid-off employees the competitive seniority they had before the layoffs without violating the order.

6. The present case is distinguishable from University of Texas v. Camenisch, 451 U.S. 390, 101 S.Ct. 1830, 68 L.Ed.2d 175 (1981), on which the dissent relies in that the defendant in *Camenisch* was not a party to a decree that had been modified by the lower court. When the injunction in that case expired, the defendant was in all respects restored to its pre-injunction status. Here, the City is faced with a modified consent decree that prevents it from applying its seniority system in the manner that it chooses.

8. The dissent's contention that the only issue before us is whether the District Court so misapplied the standards for issuing a preliminary injunction that it abused its discretion, overlooks what the District Court did in this case. The District Court did not purport to apply the standards for determining whether to issue a preliminary injunction. It did not even mention them. Instead, having found that the consent decree did "not contemplate what method would be used for a reduction in rank or layoff," the court considered "whether or not * * * it should exercise its authority to modify the consent decree * * *". As noted above, the Court of Appeals correctly recognized that more

are convinced that the Court of Appeals erred in resolving this issue and in affirming the District Court.

A

The Court of Appeals first held that the injunction did no more than enforce the terms of the agreed-upon consent decree. This specific-performance approach rests on the notion that because the City was under a general obligation to use its best efforts to increase the proportion of blacks on the force, it breached the decree by attempting to effectuate a layoff policy reducing the percentage of black employees in the Department even though such a policy was mandated by the seniority system adopted by the City and the Union. A variation of this argument is that since the decree permitted the District Court to enter any later orders that "may be necessary or appropriate to effectuate the purposes of this decree," the City had agreed in advance to an injunction against layoffs that would reduce the proportion of black employees. We are convinced, however, that both of these are improvident constructions of the consent decree.

It is to be recalled that the "scope of a consent degree must be discerned within its four corners, and not by reference to what might satisfy the purposes of one of the parties to it" or by what "might have been written had the plaintiff established his factual claims and legal theories in litigation." United States v. Armour & Co., 402 U.S. 673, 681–682, 91 S.Ct. 1752, 1757, 29 L.Ed.2d 256 (1971). Here, as the District Court recognized, there is no mention of layoffs or demotions within the four corners of the decree; nor is there any suggestion of an intention to depart from the existing seniority system or from the City's arrangements with the Union. We cannot believe that the parties to the decree thought that the City would simply disregard its arrangements with the Union and the seniority system it was then following. Had there been any intention to depart from the seniority plan in the event of layoffs or demotions, it is much more reasonable to believe that there would have been an express provision to that effect. This is particularly true since the decree stated that it was not "intended to conflict with any provisions" of the 1974 decree, and since the latter decree expressly anticipated that the City would recognize seniority. It is thus not surprising that when the City anticipated layoffs and demotions, it in the first instance faithfully followed its preexisting seniority system, plainly having no thought that it had already agreed to depart from it. It therefore cannot be said that the express terms of the decree contemplated that such an injunction would be entered.

was at stake than a mere preliminary injunction, stating that the "principal issue" was "whether the district court erred in modifying the 1980 Decree to prevent minority employment from being affected disproportionately by unanticipated layoffs." By deciding whether the District Court erred in interpreting or modifying the consent decree so as to preclude the City from applying its seniority system, we do not, as the dissent shrills, attempt to answer a question never faced by the lower courts.

The argument that the injunction was proper because it carried out the purposes of the decree is equally unconvincing. The decree announced that its purpose was "to remedy past hiring and promotion practices" of the Department and to settle the dispute as to the "appropriate and valid procedures for hiring and promotion". The decree went on to provide the agreed-upon remedy, but as we have indicated, that remedy did not include the displacement of white employees with seniority over blacks. Furthermore, it is reasonable to believe that the "remedy", which it was the purpose of the decree to provide, would not exceed the bounds of the remedies that are appropriate under Title VII, at least absent some express provision to that effect. As our cases have made clear, however, and as will be reemphasized below, Title VII protects bona fide seniority systems, and it is inappropriate to deny an innocent employee the benefits of his seniority in order to provide a remedy in a pattern or practice suit such as this. We thus have no doubt that the City considered its system to be valid and that it had no intention of departing from it when it agreed to the 1980 decree.

Finally, it must be remembered that neither the Union nor the non-minority employees were parties to the suit when the 1980 decree was entered. Hence the entry of that decree cannot be said to indicate any agreement by them to any of its terms. Absent the presence of the Union or the non-minority employees and an opportunity for them to agree or disagree with any provisions of the decree that might encroach on their rights, it seems highly unlikely that the City would purport to bargain away non-minority rights under the then-existing seniority system. We therefore conclude that the injunction does not merely enforce the agreement of the parties as reflected in the consent decree. If the injunction is to stand, it must be justified on some other basis.

B

The Court of Appeals held that even if the injunction is not viewed as compelling compliance with the terms of the decree, it was still properly entered because the District Court had inherent authority to modify the decree when an economic crisis unexpectedly required layoffs which, if carried out as the City proposed, would undermine the affirmative action outlined in the decree and impose an undue hardship on respondents. This was true, the court held, even though the modification conflicted with a bona fide seniority system adopted by the City. The Court of Appeals erred in reaching this conclusion.[9]

9. The dissent seems to suggest and Justice Stevens expressly states that Title VII is irrelevant in determining whether the District Court acted properly in modifying the consent decree. However, this was Title VII litigation, and in affirming modifications of the decree, the Court of Appeals relied extensively on what it considered to be its authority under Title VII. That is the posture in which the case comes to us. Furthermore, the District Court's authority to impose a modification of a decree is not wholly dependent on the decree. "[T]he District's Court's authority to adopt a consent decree comes only from the statute which the decree is intended to enforce," not from the parties' consent to the decree. System Federation No. 91 v.

Section 703(h) of Title VII provides that it is not an unlawful employment practice to apply different standards of compensation, or different terms, conditions, or privileges of employment pursuant to a bona fide seniority system, provided that such differences are not the result of an intention to discriminate because of race. It is clear that the City had a seniority system, that its proposed layoff plan conformed to that system, and that in making the settlement the City had not agreed to award competitive seniority to any minority employee whom the City proposed to lay off. The District Court held that the City could not follow its seniority system in making its proposed layoffs because its proposal was discriminatory in effect and hence not a bona fide plan. Section 703(h), however, permits the routine application of a seniority system absent proof of an intention to discriminate. Teamsters v. United States, 431 U.S. 324, 352, 97 S.Ct. 1843, 1863, 52 L.Ed.2d 396 (1977). Here, the District Court itself found that the layoff proposal was not adopted with the purpose or intent to discriminate on the basis of race. Nor had the City in agreeing to the decree admitted in any way that it had engaged in intentional discrimination. The Court of Appeals was therefore correct in disagreeing with the District Court's holding that the layoff plan was not a bona fide application of the seniority system, and it would appear that the City could not be faulted for following the seniority plan expressed in its agreement with the Union. The Court of Appeals nevertheless held that the injunction was proper even though it conflicted with the seniority system. This was error.

To support its position, the Court of Appeals first proposed a "settlement" theory, i.e., that the strong policy favoring voluntary settlement of Title VII actions permitted consent decrees that encroached on seniority systems. But at this stage in its opinion, the Court of Appeals was supporting the proposition that even if the injunction was not merely enforcing the agreed-upon terms of the decree, the District Court had the authority to modify the decree over the objection of one of the parties. The settlement theory, whatever its merits might otherwise be, has no application when there is no "settlement" with respect to the disputed issue. Here, the agreed-upon decree

Wright, 364 U.S. 642, 651, 81 S.Ct. 368, 373, 5 L.Ed.2d 349 (1961). In recognition of this principle, this Court in *Wright* held that when a change in the law brought the terms of a decree into conflict with the statute pursuant to which the decree was entered, the decree should be modified over the objections of one of the parties bound by the decree. By the same token, and for the same reason, a district court cannot enter a disputed modification of a consent decree in Title VII litigation if the resulting order is inconsistent with that statute.

Thus, Title VII necessarily acted as a limit on the District Court's authority to modify the decree over the objections of the City; the issue cannot be resolved solely by reference to the terms of the decree and notions of equity. Since, as we note infra, Title VII precludes a district court from displacing a non-minority employee with seniority under the contractually established seniority system absent either a finding that the seniority system was adopted with discriminatory intent or a determination that such a remedy was necessary to make whole a proven victim of discrimination, the District Court was precluded from granting such relief over the City's objection in this case.

neither awarded competitive seniority to the minority employees nor purported in any way to depart from the seniority system.

A second ground advanced by the Court of Appeals in support of the conclusion that the injunction could be entered notwithstanding its conflict with the seniority system was the assertion that "[i]t would be incongruous to hold that the use of the preferred means of resolving an employment discrimination action decreases the power of a court to order relief which vindicates the policies embodied within Title VII, and 42 U.S.C. §§ 1981 and 1983." The court concluded that if the allegations in the complaint had been proved, the District Court could have entered an order overriding the seniority provisions. Therefore, the court reasoned, "[t]he trial court had the authority to override the Firefighter's Union seniority provisions to effectuate the purpose of the 1980 Decree."

The difficulty with this approach is that it overstates the authority of the trial court to disregard a seniority system in fashioning a remedy after a plaintiff has successfully proved that an employer has followed a pattern or practice having a discriminatory effect on black applicants or employees. If individual members of a plaintiff class demonstrate that they have been actual victims of the discriminatory practice, they may be awarded competitive seniority and given their rightful place on the seniority roster. This much is clear from Franks v. Bowman Transportation Co., 424 U.S. 747, 96 S.Ct. 1251, 47 L.Ed.2d 444 (1976) and *Teamsters. Teamsters,* however, also made clear that mere membership in the disadvantaged class is insufficient to warrant a seniority award; each individual must prove that the discriminatory practice had an impact on him. Even when an individual shows that the discriminatory practice has had an impact on him, he is not automatically entitled to have a non-minority employee laid off to make room for him. He may have to wait until a vacancy occurs,[11] and if there are non-minority employees on layoff, the Court must balance the equities in determining who is entitled to the job. Here, there was no finding that any of the blacks protected from layoff had been a victim of discrimination and no award of competitive seniority to any of them. Nor had the parties in formulating the consent decree purported to identify any specific employee entitled to particular relief other than those listed in the exhibits attached to the decree. It therefore seems to us that in light of *Teamsters,* the Court of Appeals imposed on the parties as an adjunct of settlement something that could not have been ordered had the case gone to trial and the plaintiffs proved that a pattern or practice of discrimination existed.

11. Lower courts have uniformly held that relief for actual victims does not extend to bumping employees previously occupying jobs. See e.g., Patterson v. American Tobacco Co., 535 F.2d 257, 267 (CA4), cert. denied, 429 U.S. 920, 97 S.Ct. 314, 50 L.Ed.2d 286 (1976); Local 189, United Papermakers and Paperworkers v. United States, 416 F.2d 980, 988 (CA5 1969), cert. denied, 397 U.S. 919, 90 S.Ct. 926, 25 L.Ed. 2d 100 (1970).

Our ruling in *Teamsters* that a court can award competitive seniority only when the beneficiary of the award has actually been a victim of illegal discrimination is consistent with the policy behind § 706(g) of Title VII, which affects the remedies available in Title VII litigation. That policy, which is to provide make-whole relief only to those who have been actual victims of illegal discrimination, was repeatedly expressed by the sponsors of the Act during the congressional debates. Opponents of the legislation that became Title VII charged that if the bill were enacted, employers could be ordered to hire and promote persons in order to achieve a racially-balanced work force even though those persons had not been victims of illegal discrimination. Responding to these charges, Senator Humphrey explained the limits on a court's remedial powers as follows:

> "No court order can require hiring, reinstatement, admission to membership, or payment of back pay for anyone who was not fired, refused employment or advancement or admission to a union by an act of discrimination forbidden by this title. This is stated expressly in the last sentence of Section 707(e) [enacted without relevant change as § 706(g)] * * *. Contrary to the allegations of some opponents of this title, there is nothing in it that will give any power to the Commission or to any court to require * * * firing * * * of employees in order to meet a racial 'quota' or to achieve a certain racial balance. That bugaboo has been brought up a dozen times; but is non-existent."

An interpretative memorandum of the bill entered into the Congressional Record by Senators Clark and Case [14] likewise made clear that a court was not authorized to give preferential treatment to non-victims. "No court order can require hiring, reinstatement, admission to membership, or payment of back pay for anyone who was not discriminated against in violation of [Title VII]. This is stated expressly in the last sentence of section [706(g)] * * *."

Similar assurances concerning the limits on a court's authority to award make-whole relief were provided by supporters of the bill throughout the legislative process. For example, following passage of the bill in the House, its Republican House sponsors published a memorandum describing the bill. Referring to the remedial powers given the courts by the bill, the memorandum stated: "Upon conclusion of the trial, the federal court may enjoin an employer or labor organization from practicing further discrimination and may order the hiring or reinstatement of an employee or the acceptance or reinstatement of a union member. *But Title VII does not permit the ordering of racial quotas in business or unions* * * *." (emphasis added). In like manner, the principal Senate sponsors, in a bi-partisan news letter delivered during an attempted filibuster to each senator supporting the

14. Senators Clark and Case were the bipartisan "captains" of Title VII. We have previously recognized the authoritative nature of their interpretative memorandum. American Tobacco Co. v. Patterson, 456 U.S. 63, 73, 102 S.Ct. 1534, 1539, 71 L.Ed.2d 748 (1982); *Teamsters*, supra, 431 U.S., at 352, 97 S.Ct., at 1863.

bill, explained that "[u]nder title VII, not even a Court, much less the Commission, could order racial quotas or the hiring, reinstatement, admission to membership or payment of back pay for anyone who is not discriminated against in violation of this title." [15]

The Court of Appeals holding that the District Court's order was permissible as a valid Title VII remedial order ignores not only our ruling in *Teamsters* but the policy behind § 706(g) as well. Accordingly, that holding cannot serve as a basis for sustaining the District Court's order.[16]

Finally, the Court of Appeals was of the view that the District Court ordered no more than that which the City unilaterally could have done by way of adopting an affirmative action program. Whether the City, a public employer, could have taken this course without violating the law is an issue we need not decide. The fact is that in this case the City took no such action and that the modification of the decree was imposed over its objection.[17]

15. The dissent suggests that Congress abandoned this policy in 1972 when it amended § 706(g) to make clear that a court may award "any other equitable relief" that the court deems appropriate. As support for this proposition the dissent notes that prior to 1972, some federal courts had provided remedies to those who had not proven that they were victims. It then observes that in a section-by-section analysis of the bill, it sponsors stated that "in any areas where a specific contrary intention is not indicated, it was assumed that the present case law as developed by the courts would continue to govern the applicability and construction of Title VII."

We have already rejected, however, the contention that Congress intended to codify all existing Title VII decisions when it made this brief statement. See *Teamsters,* supra, at n. 39. Moreover, the statement on its face refers only to those sections not changed by the 1972 amendments. It cannot serve as a basis for discerning the effect of the changes that were made by the amendment. Finally, and of most importance, in a later portion of the same section-by-section analysis, the sponsors explained their view of existing law and the effect that the amendment would have on that law.

"The provisions of this subsection are intended to give the courts wide discretion exercising their equitable powers to fashion the most complete relief possible. In dealing with the present § 706(g) *the courts have stressed that the scope of relief under that section of the Act is intended to make victims of unlawful discrimination whole,* and that the attainment of this objective rests not only upon the elimination of the particular unlawful employment practice complained of, but also requires that *persons aggrieved by the consequences and effects of the unlawful employment practice* be, so far as possible, restored to a position where they would have been were it not for the unlawful discrimination." (emphasis added).

As we noted in *Franks,* the 1972 amendments evidence "emphatic confirmation that federal courts are empowered to fashion such relief as the particular circumstances of a case may require to effect restitution, making whole insofar as possible *the victims of racial discrimination.*" (emphasis added).

16. Neither does it suffice to rely on the District Court's remedial authority under §§ 1981 and 1983. Under those sections relief is authorized only when there is proof or admission of intentional discrimination. Washington v. Davis, 426 U.S. 229, 96 S.Ct. 2040, 48 L.Ed.2d 597 (1976); General Building Contractors Association v. Pennsylvania, 458 U.S. 375, 102 S.Ct. 3141, 73 L.Ed.2d 835 (1982). Neither precondition was satisfied here.

17. The Court of Appeals also suggested that under United States v. Swift & Co., 286 U.S. 106, 114–115, 52 S.Ct. 460, 462, 76 L.Ed. 999 (1932), the decree properly was modified pursuant to the District Court's equity jurisdiction. But *Swift* cannot be read as authorizing a court to impose a modification of a decree that runs counter to statutory policy, see n. 9, supra, here §§ 703(h) and 706(g) of Title VII.

We thus are unable to agree either that the order entered by the District Court was a justifiable effort to enforce the terms of the decree to which the City had agreed or that it was a legitimate modification of the decree that could be imposed on the City without its consent. Accordingly, the judgment of the Court of Appeals is reversed.

It is so ordered.

JUSTICE O'CONNOR, concurring.

The various views presented in the opinions in this case reflect the unusual procedural posture of the case * * *.

I

* * *

Respondents now claim that the case has become moot on certiorari to this Court. The recession is over, the employees who were laid off or demoted have been restored to their former jobs, and petitioners apparently have no current need to make seniority-based layoffs. The res judicata effects of the District Court's order can be eliminated by the Court's usual practice of vacating the decision below and remanding with instructions to dismiss. Thus, respondents conclude that the validity of the preliminary injunction is no longer an issue of practical significance and the case can be dismissed as moot.

I agree with the Court that petitioners and respondents continue to wage a controversy that would not be resolved by merely vacating the preliminary injunction. As a result of the District Court's order, several black employees have more seniority for purposes of future job decisions and entitlements than they otherwise would have under the city's seniority system. This added seniority gives them an increased expectation of future promotion, an increased priority in bidding on certain jobs and job transfers, and an increased protection from future layoffs. These individuals, who are members of the respondent class, have not waived their increased seniority benefits. Therefore, petitioners have a significant interest in determining those individuals' claims in the very litigation in which they were originally won. As the Court of Appeals noted, if petitioner-employer does not vigorously defend the implementation of its seniority system, it will have to cope with deterioration in employee morale, labor unrest, and reduced productivity. Likewise, if petitioner-union accedes to discriminatory employment actions, it will lose both the confidence of its members and bargaining leverage in the determination of who should ultimately bear the burden of the past (and future) fiscal shortages. Perhaps this explains why, in respondents' words, "the city and union have expended substantial time and effort * * * in [an] appeal which can win no possible relief for the individuals on whose behalf it has ostensibly been pursued."

* * *

II

* * *

[T]he preliminary injunction could only be justified as a reasonable interpretation of the consent decree or as a permissible exercise of the District Court's authority to modify that consent decree. Neither justification was present here. * * * [T]he consent decree itself cannot fairly be interpreted to bar use of the seniority policy or to require maintenance of racial balances previously achieved in the event layoffs became necessary. Nor can a district court unilaterally modify a consent decree to adjust racial imbalances or to provide retroactive relief that abrogates legitimate expectations of other employees and applicants. See Steelworkers v. Weber, 443 U.S. 193, 205–207, 99 S.Ct. 2721, 2728–2729, 61 L.Ed.2d 480 (1979). A court may not grant preferential treatment to any individual or group simply because the group to which they belong is adversely affected by a bona fide seniority system. Rather, a court may use its remedial powers, including its power to modify a consent decree, only to prevent future violations and to compensate identified victims of unlawful discrimination. See *Teamsters;* University of California Regents v. Bakke, 438 U.S. 265, 307–309, and n. 44, 98 S.Ct. 2733, 2757–2758, and n. 44, 57 L.Ed.2d 750 (1978) (Powell, J., announcing the judgment of the Court). Even when its remedial powers are properly invoked, a district court may award preferential treatment only after carefully balancing the competing interests of discriminatees, innocent employees, and the employer. In short, no matter how significant the change in circumstance, a district court cannot unilaterally modify a consent decree to adjust racial balances in the way the District Court did here.[2]

To be sure, in 1980, respondents could have gone to trial and established illegal discrimination in the Department's past hiring practices, identified its specific victims, and possibly obtained retroactive seniority for those individuals. Alternatively, in 1980, in negotiating the consent decree, respondents could have sought the participation of the union, negotiated the identities of the specific victims with the union and employer, and possibly obtained limited forms of retroactive relief. But respondents did none of these things. They chose to avoid the costs and hazards of litigating their claims. They negotiated with the employer without inviting the union's participation. They entered into a consent decree without establishing any specific victim's identity. And, most importantly, they waived their right to seek further relief. To allow respondents to obtain relief properly reserved for only identified victims or to prove their victim status now would undermine the certainty of obligation that is condition precedent to employers' acceptance of, and unions' consent to, employment discrimination settlements. * * * Modifications requiring maintenance of racial balance

2. Unlike the dissenters and Justice Stevens, I find persuasive the Court's reasons for holding Title VII relevant to analysis of the modification issue and the Court's application of Title VII's provisions to the facts of the present controversy.

would not encourage valid settlements of employment discrimination cases. They would impede them. Thus, when the Court states that this preferential relief could not have been awarded even had *this case* gone to trial, it is holding respondents to the bargain they struck during the consent decree negotiations in 1980 and thereby furthering the statutory policy of voluntary settlement.

In short, the Court effectively applies the criteria traditionally applicable to the review of preliminary injunctions. When the Court disapproves the preliminary injunction issued in this case, it does so because respondents had no chance of succeeding on the merits of their claim. The District Court had no authority to order the Department to maintain its current racial balance or to provide preferential treatment to blacks. It therefore abused its discretion. On this understanding, I join the opinion and judgment rendered by the Court today.

JUSTICE STEVENS, concurring in the judgment.

* * *

In my judgment, the Court's discussion of Title VII is wholly advisory. This case involves no issue under Title VII; it only involves the administration of a consent decree. The District Court entered the consent decree on April 25, 1980, after having given all parties, including all of the petitioners in this Court, notice and opportunity to object to its entry. The consent decree, like any other final judgment of a district court, was immediately appealable. No appeal was taken. Hence, the consent decree became a final judgment binding upon those who had had notice and opportunity to object; it was and is a legally enforceable obligation. If the consent decree justified the District Court's preliminary injunction, then that injunction should be upheld irrespective of whether Title VII would authorize a similar injunction.[3] Therefore, what governs this case is not Title VII, but the consent decree.[4]

There are two ways in which the District Court's injunction could be justified. The first is as a construction of the consent decree. If the District Court had indicated that it was merely enforcing the terms of the consent decree, and had given some indication of what portion of that decree it was interpreting, I might be hard pressed to consider the

3. The Court seems to suggest that a consent decree cannot authorize anything that would not constitute permissible relief under Title VII. I share Justice Blackmun's doubts as to whether this is the correct test. The provisions on which the Court relies, 42 U.S.C. §§ 2000e–2(h) and 2000e–5(g), merely state that certain seniority arrangements do not violate Title VII, and define the limits of appropriate relief for a Title VII violation, respectively. They do not place any limitations on what the parties can agree to in a consent decree. The Court does not suggest that any other statutory provision was violated by the District Court. The Court itself acknowledges that the administration of a consent decree must be tested by the four corners of the decree, and not by what might have been ordered had respondents prevailed on the merits, which makes it subsequent discussion of Title VII all the more puzzling.

4. If the decree had been predicated on a finding that the city had violated Title VII, the remedial policies underlying that Act might be relevant, at least as an aid to construction of the decree. But since the settlement expressly disavowed any such finding, the Court's exposition of Title VII law is unnecessary.

entry of the injunction an abuse of discretion. However, the District Court never stated that it was construing the decree, nor did it provide even a rough indication of the portion of the decree on which it relied. There is simply nothing in the record to justify the conclusion that the injunction was based on a reasoned construction of the consent decree.[5]

The second justification that could exist for the injunction is that the District Court entered it based on a likelihood that it would modify the decree, or as an actual modification of the decree.[6] As Justice Blackmun explains, modification would have been appropriate if respondents had demonstrated the presence of changed circumstances. However, the only "circumstance" found by the District Court was that the city's proposed layoffs would have an adverse effect on the level of black employment in the fire department. This was not a "changed" circumstance; the percentage of blacks employed by the Memphis Fire Department at the time the decree was entered meant that even then it was apparent that any future seniority-based layoffs would have an adverse effect on blacks. Thus the finding made by the District Court was clearly insufficient to support a modification of the consent decree, or a likelihood thereof.

Accordingly, because I conclude that the District Court abused its discretion in entering the preliminary injunction at issue here, I concur in the judgment.

JUSTICE BLACKMUN, with whom JUSTICE BRENNAN and JUSTICE MARSHALL join, dissenting.

Today's opinion is troubling less for the law it creates than for the law it ignores. * * * The Court * * * rejects respondents' claim that these cases are moot because the Court concludes that there are continuing effects from the preliminary injunction and that these create a continuing controversy. The Court appears, oblivious, however, to the fact that any continuing legal consequences of the preliminary injunction would be erased by simply vacating the Court of Appeals'

5. Justice Blackmun explains how the consent could be construed to justify the injunction. I find nothing in the record indicating that this is the theory the District Court actually employed. While I recognize that preliminary injunction proceedings are often harried affairs and that district courts need substantial leeway in resolving them, it nevertheless remains the case that there must be something in the record explaining the reasoning of the District Court before it may be affirmed. That is the purpose of Fed.Rule Civ.P. 65(d)'s requirement that "[e]very order granting an injunction and every restraining order shall set forth the reasons for its issuance. * * *"

6. It seems likely that this second justification was the actual basis for the entry of the injunction. The District Court's phrasing of the question it faced was whether "it should exercise its authority to modify a Consent Decree". The focus of the Court of Appeals' opinion reviewing the preliminary injunction was the "three grounds upon which a Consent Decree may later be modified". Most important, the practical effect of the District Court's action indicates that it should be treated as a modification. Until it is reviewed, it will effectively govern the procedure that the city must follow in any future layoffs, and that procedure is significantly different from the seniority system in effect when the consent decree was negotiated and signed.

judgment, which is this Court's longstanding practice with cases that become moot.

Having improperly asserted jurisdiction, the Court then ignores the proper standard of review. The District Court's action was a preliminary injunction reviewable only on an abuse of discretion standard; the Court treats the action as a permanent injunction and decides the merits, even though the District Court has not yet had an opportunity to do so. On the merits, the Court ignores the specific facts of these cases that make inapplicable the decisions on which it relies. Because, in my view, the Court's decision is demonstrably in error, I respectfully dissent.

I

Mootness. * * * Since the preliminary injunction was entered, * * * the layoffs all have terminated and the city has taken back every one of the workers laid off pursuant to the modified plan. Accordingly, the preliminary injunction no longer restrains the city's conduct, and the adverse relationship between the opposing parties concerning its propriety is gone. A ruling in this situation thus becomes wholly advisory * * *. The proper disposition, therefore, is to vacate the judgment and remand the cases with directions to dismiss them as moot.

* * *

II

Because there is now no justiciable controversy in these cases, today's decision by the Court is an improper exercise of judicial power. It is not my purpose in dissent to parallel the Court's error and speculate on the appropriate disposition of these nonjusticiable cases. In arriving at its result, however, the Court's analysis is misleading in many ways, and in other ways it is simply in error. Accordingly, it is important to note the Court's unexplained departures from precedent and from the record.

A

Assuming *arguendo* that these cases are justiciable, then the only question before the Court is the validity of a *preliminary* injunction that prevented the city from conducting layoffs that would have reduced the number of Negroes in certain job categories within the Memphis Fire Department. In granting such relief, the District Court was required to consider respondents' likelihood of success on the merits, the balance of irreparable harm to the parties, and whether the injunction would be in the public interest. The question before a reviewing court "is simply whether the issuance of the injunction, in light of the applicable standard, constituted an abuse of discretion."

The Court has chosen to answer a different question. The Court's opinion does not mention the standard of review for a preliminary injunction, and does not apply that standard to these cases. Instead, the Court treats the cases as if they involved a *permanent* injunction, and addresses the question whether the city's proposed layoffs violated the consent decree.[6] That issue was never resolved in the District Court because the city did not press for a final decision on the merits. The issue, therefore, is not properly before this Court. After taking jurisdiction over a controversy that no longer exists, the Court reviews a decision that was never made.

In so doing, the Court does precisely what in *Camenisch,* supra, it unanimously concluded was error. *Camenisch* involved a suit in which a deaf student obtained a preliminary injunction requiring that the University of Texas pay for an interpreter to assist him in his studies. While appeal of the preliminary injunction was pending before the Court of Appeals, the student graduated. The Court of Appeals affirmed the District Court. In so doing, the appellate court rejected Camenisch's suggestion that his graduation rendered the case moot because the District Court had required Camenisch to post a bond before granting the preliminary injunction, and there remained the issue whether the University or Camenisch should bear the cost of the interpreter. This Court granted certiorari and vacated and remanded the case to the District Court. The Court explained:

> "The Court of Appeals correctly held that the case as a whole is not moot, since, as that Court noted, it remains to be decided who should ultimately bear the cost of the interpreter. However, *the issue before the Court of Appeals was not who should pay for the interpreter, but rather whether the District Court had abused its discretion in issuing a preliminary injunction requiring the University to pay for him.* * * * *The two issues are significantly different, since whether the preliminary injunction should have issued depended on the balance of factors [for granting preliminary injunctions], while whether the University should ultimately bear the cost*

6. The Court's attempt to recharacterize the preliminary injunction as a permanent one is wholly unpersuasive. Respondents' request for injunctive relief specifically sought a preliminary injunction, and carefully laid out the standards for the issuance of such an injunction. Petitioners' response in opposition to the request for injunctive relief was devoted entirely to explaining that the standards for a preliminary injunction had not been met. The District Court's order granting injunctive relief was entitled an "Order Granting Preliminary Injunction," and a later order expanding the injunctive relief to include more positions was entitled an "Order Expanding Preliminary Injunction." The Court of Appeals expressly defined the nature of its inquiry by stating:

"We must weigh whether the plaintiffs have shown a possibility of success on the merits, whether the plaintiff or defendant would suffer irreparable harm and whether the public interest warrants the injunction * * *. The standard of appellate review is whether the district court abused its discretion in granting the preliminary injunction.

"[The District Judge] did not abuse his discretion in granting the preliminary injunction."

It is hard to imagine a clearer statement that the issue considered by the Court of Appeals was the propriety of a preliminary injunction. In any event, even if the Court of Appeals went beyond the scope of its appropriate review, it would be our duty to correct the error, not to follow it.

of the interpreter depends on a final resolution of the merits of Camenisch's case.

* * *

Until [a trial on the merits] has taken place, it would be inappropriate for this Court to intimate any view on the merits of the lawsuit." (emphasis added).

Camenisch makes clear that a determination of a party's entitlement to a preliminary injunction is a separate issue from the determination of the merits of the party's underlying legal claim, and that a reviewing court should not confuse the two. Even if the issues presented by the preliminary injunction in these cases were not moot, therefore, the only issue before this Court would be the propriety of preliminary injunctive relief.[7] It is true, of course, that the District Court and the Court of Appeals had to make a preliminary evaluation of respondents' likelihood of success on the merits, but that evaluation provides no basis for deciding the merits:

> "Since Camenisch's likelihood of success on the merits was one of the factors the District Court and the Court of Appeals considered in granting Camenisch a preliminary injunction, it might be suggested that their decisions were tantamount to decisions on the underlying merits and thus that the preliminary-injunction issue is not truly moot. * * * *This reasoning fails, however, because it improperly equates 'likelihood of success' with 'success,' and what is more important, because it ignores the significant procedural differences between preliminary and permanent injunctions."* (emphasis added).

B

After ignoring the appropriate standard of review, the Court then focuses on an issue that is not in these cases. It begins its analysis by stating that the "issue at the heart of this case" is the District Court's power to "ente[r] an injunction requiring white employees to be laid off." That statement, with all respect, is simply incorrect. On its face, the preliminary injunction prohibited the city from conducting layoffs in accordance with its seniority system "insofar as it will decrease the percentage of black[s] * * * presently employed" in certain job categories. The preliminary injunction did not require the city to lay off

7. The distinction between the preliminary and final injunction stages of a proceeding is more than mere formalism. The time pressures involved in a request for a preliminary injunction require courts to make determinations without the aid of full briefing or factual development, and make all such determinations necessarily provisional. Like the proceedings in *Camenisch,* those in this litigation "bear the marks of the haste characteristic of a request for a preliminary injunction." The hearing on the preliminary injunction was held four days after the layoffs had been announced. With the exception of a single deposition the day before the hearing, there was no discovery. * * * It is true that the District Court made a few of what generously could be described as findings and conclusions, but, as the Court in *Camenisch* pointed out, "findings of fact and conclusions of law made by a court granting a preliminary injunction are not binding at trial on the merits." Accordingly, there is simply no proper basis on which this Court legitimately can decide the question whether the city's proposed layoffs violated the consent decree.

any white employees at all. In fact, several parties interested in the suit, including the union, attempted to persuade the city to avoid layoffs entirely by reducing the working hours of all fire department employees. Thus, although the District Court order reduced the city's options in meeting its fiscal crisis, it did not require the dismissal of white employees. The choice of a modified layoff plan remained that of the city.

This factual detail is important because it makes clear that the preliminary injunction did not abrogate the contractual rights of white employees. If the modified layoff plan proposed by the city to comply with the District Court's order abrogated contractual rights of the union, those rights remained enforceable. This Court recognized this principle just last Term in W.R. Grace & Co. v. Local Union 759, — U.S. —, 103 S.Ct. 2177, 76 L.Ed.2d 298 (1983), which presented a situation remarkably similar to the one here. In that case, an employer sought to conduct layoffs and faced a conflict between a Title VII conciliation agreement protecting its female employees and the seniority rights of its male employees. The employer chose to lay off male employees, who filed grievances and obtained awards for the violation of their contractual rights. In upholding the awards, this Court explained that the dilemma faced by the employer did not render the male employees' contractual rights unenforceable:

> "Given the Company's desire to reduce its workforce, it is undeniable that the Company was faced with a dilemma: it could follow the conciliation agreement as mandated by the District Court and risk liability under the collective bargaining agrement, or it could follow the bargaining agreement and risk both a contempt citation and Title VII liability. The dilemma, however, was of the Company's own making. The Company committed itself voluntarily to two conflicting contractual obligations."

It is clear, therefore, that the correctness of the District Court's interpretation of the decree is irrelevant with respect to the enforceability of the union's contractual rights; those rights remained enforceable regardless of whether the city had an obligation not to lay off blacks. The question in these cases remains whether the District Court's authority pursuant to the consent decree enabled it to enjoin a layoff of more than a certain number of blacks. The issue is not whether the District Court could require the city to lay off whites, or whether the District Court could abrogate contractual rights of white firefighters.

III

Assuming, as the Court erroneously does, that the District Court entered a permanent injunction, the question on review then would be whether the District Court had authority to enter it. In affirming the District Court, the Court of Appeals suggested at least two grounds on which respondents might have prevailed on the merits.

The first of these derives from the contractual characteristics of a consent decree. Because a consent decree "is to be construed for enforcement purposes essentially as a contract," respondents had the right to specific performance of the terms of the decree. If the proposed layoffs violated those terms, the District Court could issue an injunction requiring compliance with them. Alternatively, the Court of Appeals noted that a court of equity has inherent power to modify a consent decree in light of changed circumstances. Thus, if respondents could show that changed circumstances justified modification of the decree, the District Court would have authority to make such a change.

Respondents based their request for injunctive relief primarily on the first of these grounds, and the Court's analysis of this issue is unpersuasive. The District Court's authority to enforce the terms and purposes of the consent decree was expressly reserved in ¶ 17 of the decree itself: "The Court retains jurisdiction of this action for such further orders as may be necessary or appropriate to effectuate the purposes of this decree." Respondents relied on that provision in seeking the preliminary injunction. The decree obligated the city to provide certain specific relief to particular individuals, and to pursue a long-term goal to "raise the black representation in each job classification on the fire department to levels approximating the black proportion of the civilian labor force in Shelby County." The decree set more specific goals for hiring and promotion opportunities as well. To meet these goals, the decree "require[d] reasonable, good faith efforts on the part of the City."

In support of their request for a preliminary injunction, respondents claimed that the proposed layoffs would adversely affect blacks significantly out of proportion to their representation. They argued that the proposed layoffs were "designed to thwart gains made by blacks" under the decree. Their argument emphasized that the Mayor had "absolute discretion to choose which job classifications" were to be affected by the layoffs and that the "ranks chosen by the Mayor for demotion are those where blacks are represented in the greatest number." Respondents claimed that such a layoff plan "violates the spirit of the 1980 Consent Decree." Had respondents been able to prove these charges at trial, they may well have constituted a violation of the city's obligation of good faith under the decree. On the basis of these claims, the limited evidence presented at the hearing prior to the issuance of the preliminary injunction, and the District Court's familiarity with the city's past behavior, the District Court enjoined the city from laying off blacks where the effect would have been to reduce the percentage of black representation in certain job categories. By treating the District Court's injunction as a permanent one, however, the Court first deprives respondents of the opportunity to substantiate these claims, and then faults them for having failed to do so. But without determining whether these allegations have any substance, there is simply no way to determine whether the proposed layoff plan violated the terms of the consent decree.

Even if respondents could not have shown that the proposed layoff plan conflicted with the city's obligation of good faith, ¶ 17 of the Decree also empowered the District Court to enter orders to "effectuate the purposes" of the decree. Thus, if the District Court concluded that the layoffs would frustrate those purposes, then the decree empowered the District Court to enter an appropriate order. Once again, however, on the limited factual record before the Court, it is improper to speculate about whether the layoffs would have frustrated the gains made under the consent decree sufficiently to justify a permanent injunction.

The Court rejects the argument that the injunctive relief was a proper exercise of the power to enforce the purposes of the decree principally on the ground that the remedy agreed upon in the consent decree did not specifically mention layoffs. This treatment of the issue is inadequate. The power of the District Court to enter further orders to effectuate the purposes of the decree was a part of the agreed remedy. The parties negotiated for this, and it is the obligation of the courts to give it meaning. In an ideal world, a well-drafted consent degree requiring structural change might succeed in providing explicit directions for all future contingencies. But particularly in civil rights litigation in which implementation of a consent decree often takes years, such foresight is unattainable. Accordingly, parties to a consent decree typically agree to confer upon supervising courts the authority to ensure that the purposes of a decree are not frustrated by unforeseen circumstances. The scope of such authority in an individual case depends principally upon the intent of the parties. Viewed in this light, recourse to such broad notions as the "purposes" of a decree is not a rewriting of the parties' agreement, but rather a part of the attempt to implement the written terms. The District Judge in these cases, who presided over the negotiation of the consent decree, is in a unique position to determine the nature of the parties' original intent, and he has a distinctive familiarity with the circumstances that shaped the decree and defined its purposes. Accordingly, he should be given special deference to interpret the general and any ambiguous terms in the decree. It simply is not a sufficient response to conclude, as the Court does, that the District Court could not enjoin the proposed layoff plan merely because layoffs were not specifically mentioned in the consent decree.

In this regard, it is useful to note the limited nature of the injunctive relief ordered by the District Court. The preliminary injunction did not embody a conclusion that the city could never conduct layoffs in accordance with its seniority policy. Rather, the District Court preliminarily enjoined a particular application of the seniority system as a basis for a particular set of layoffs. Whether the District Court would enjoin a future layoff presumably would depend on the factual circumstances of that situation. Such a future layoff presumably would affect a different proportion of blacks and whites; the black representation in the fire department presumably would be higher, the layoffs presumably would negate a smaller portion of the gains made under the decree; and the judge would have worked with the parties at implementing the decree for a longer period of time. There is no way of knowing whether the District Court would conclude that a future layoff conducted on the basis of seniority would frustrate the purposes of the decree sufficiently to justify an injunction. For this reason, the Court is wrong to attach such significance to the fact that the consent decree does not provide for a suspension of the seniority system during all layoffs, for that is not what the District Court ordered in these cases.

B

The Court of Appeals also suggested that respondents could have prevailed on the merits because the 1981 layoffs may have justified a modification of the consent decree. This Court frequently has recognized the inherent "power of a court of equity to modify an injunction in adaption to changed conditions though it was entered by consent." United States v. Swift & Co., 286 U.S. 106, 114, 52 S.Ct. 460, 462, 76 L.Ed. 999 (1932). * * * The test for ruling on a plaintiff's request for a modification of a consent decree is "whether the change serve[s] to effectuate * * * the basic purpose of the original consent decree." Chrysler Corp. v. United States, 316 U.S. at 562, 62 S.Ct. at 1149.

The Court rejects this ground for affirming the preliminary injunction, not by examining the purposes of the *consent decree* and whether the proposed layoffs justified a modification of the decree, but rather by reference to Title VII. The Court concludes that the preliminary injunction was improper because it "imposed on the parties as an adjunct of settlement something that could not have been ordered had the case gone to trial and the plaintiffs proved that a pattern or practice of discrimination existed." Thus, the Court has chosen to evaluate the propriety of the preliminary injunction by asking what type of relief the District Court could have awarded had respondents litigated their Title VII claim and prevailed on the merits. Although it is far from clear whether that is the right question,[9] it is clear that the Court has given the wrong answer.

Had respondents prevailed on their Title VII claims at trial, the remedies available would have been those provided by § 706(g). Under

9. The Court's analysis seems to be premised on the view that the consent decree cannot provide relief that could not be obtained at trial. In addressing the Court's analysis, I do not mean to imply that I accept its premise as correct. In Steelworkers v. Weber, 443 U.S. 193, 99 S.Ct. 2721, 61 L.Ed.2d 480 (1979), this Court considered whether an affirmative action plan adopted voluntarily by an employer violated Title VII because it discriminated against whites. In holding that the plan was lawful, the Court stressed that the voluntariness of the plan informed the nature of its inquiry. Because a consent decree is an agreement that is enforceable in court, it has qualities of both voluntariness and compulsion. The Court has explained that Congress intended to encourage voluntary settlement of Title VII suits and cooperative private efforts to eliminate the lingering effects of past discrimination. It is by no means clear, therefore, that the permissible scope of relief available under a consent decree is the same as could be ordered by a court after a finding of liability at trial.

that section, a court that determines that an employer has violated Title VII may "enjoin the respondent from engaging in such unlawful employment practice, and order such affirmative action as may be appropriate, which may include, *but is not limited to,* reinstatement or hiring of employees, with or without back pay * * *, *or any other equitable relief as the court deems appropriate*" (emphasis added). The scope of the relief that could have been entered on behalf of respondents had they prevailed at trial therefore depends on the nature of relief that is "appropriate" in remedying Title VII violations.

In determining the nature of "appropriate" relief under § 706(g), courts have distinguished between individual relief and race-conscious class relief. Although overlooked by the Court, this distinction is highly relevant here. In a Title VII class-action suit of the type brought by respondents, an individual plaintiff is entitled to an award of individual relief only if he can establish that he was the victim of discrimination. That requirement grows out of the general equitable principles of "make whole" relief; an individual who has suffered no injury is not entitled to an individual award. See *Teamsters.* If victimization is shown, however, an individual is entitled to whatever retroactive seniority, backpay, and promotions are consistent with the statute's goal of making the victim whole. Franks v. Bowman Transportation Co.

In Title VII class-action suits, the Courts of Appeals are unanimously of the view that race-conscious affirmative relief can also be "appropriate" under § 706(g). See University of California Regents v. Bakke, 438 U.S. 265, 301–302, 98 S.Ct. 2733, 2753–2754, 57 L.Ed.2d 750 (opinion of Powell, J.); id., at 353, n. 28, 98 S.Ct., at 2780, n. 28 (1978) (opinion of Brennan, White, Marshall and Blackmun, JJ.). The purpose of such relief is not to make whole any particular individual, but rather to remedy the present class-wide effects of past discrimination or to prevent similar discrimination in the future. Because the discrimination sought to be alleviated by race-conscious relief is the class-wide effects of past discrimination, rather than discrimination against identified members of the class, such relief is provided to the class as a whole rather than to its individual members. The relief may take many forms, but in class actions it frequently involves percentages—such as those contained in the 1980 consent decree between the city and respondents—that require race to be taken into account when an employer hires or promotes employees. The distinguishing feature of race-conscious relief is that no individual member of the disadvantaged class has a claim to it, and individual beneficiaries of the relief need not show that they were themselves victims of the discrimination for which the relief was granted.

In the instant case, respondents' request for a preliminary injunction did not include a request for individual awards of retroactive seniority—and, contrary to the implication of the Court's opinion, the District Court did not make any such awards. Rather, the District

Court order required the city to conduct its layoffs in a race-conscious manner; specifically, the preliminary injunction prohibited the city from conducting layoffs that would "decrease the percentage of black[s]" in certain job categories. The city remained free to lay off any individual black so long as the percentage of black representation was maintained.

Because these cases arise out of a consent decree, and a trial on the merits has never taken place, it is of course impossible for the Court to know the extent and nature of any past discrimination by the city. For this reason, to the extent that the scope of appropriate relief would depend upon the facts found at trial, it is impossible to determine whether the relief provided by the preliminary injunction would have been appropriate following a trial on the merits. Nevertheless, the Court says that the preliminary injunction was inappropriate because, it concludes, respondents could not have obtained similar relief had their cases been litigated instead of settled by a consent decree.

The Court's conclusion does not follow logically from its own analysis. As the Court points out, the consent decree arose out of a Title VII suit brought by respondents alleging, inter alia, that the city had engaged in a pattern and practice of discrimination against members of the plaintiff class. Mr. Stotts, the named plaintiff, claimed that he and the class members that he represented had been denied promotions solely because of race, and that because of that discrimination, he and other members of the class had been denied their rightful rank in the Memphis Fire Department. Had respondents' case actually proceeded to trial, therefore it would have involved the now familiar two-stage procedure established in *Teamsters* and *Franks*. The first stage would have been a trial to determine whether the city had engaged in unlawful discrimination; if so, the case would proceed to the second stage, during which the individual members of the class would have the opportunity to establish that they were victims of discrimination. * * * Were respondents to prevail at trial on their claims of discrimination, therefore, they would have been entitled to individual awards of relief, including appropriate retroactive seniority. Thus, even treating the District Court's preliminary injunction as if it granted individual awards of retroactive seniority to class members, it is relief that respondents might have obtained had they gone to trial instead of settling their claims of discrimination. Thus, the Court's conclusion is refuted by its own logic and by the very cases on which it relies to come to its result.[11]

11. The Court's opinion is sufficiently ambiguous to suggest another interpretation. The Court concludes that the preliminary injunction was improper because it gave respondents something they could not have obtained had they proved that "a pattern or practice of discrimination existed." It is possible, therefore, that the Court is suggesting that the limit on relief available under a consent decree is that which could be awarded if a plaintiff prevailed in "stage I" of a case but failed to proceed to "stage II" during which the plaintiff seeks to identify actual victims of discrimination. But the Court has failed to provide any support for this odd notion. The rationale underlying its opinion seems to be that the limit of the District Court's remedial power is that which could have been ordered following a trial on the al-

For reasons never explained, the Court's opinion has focused entirely on what respondents have actually shown, instead of what they might have shown had trial ensued. It is improper and unfair to fault respondents for failing to show "that any of the blacks protected from layoff had been a victim of discrimination," for the simple reason that the claims on which such a showing would have been made never went to trial. The whole point of the consent decree in these cases—and indeed the point of most Title VII consent decrees—is for both parties to avoid the time and expense of litigating the question of liability and identifying the victims of discrimination. In the instant consent decree, the city expressly denied having engaged in any discrimination at all. Nevertheless, the consent decree in this case provided several persons with both promotions and backpay. By definition, all such relief went to persons never determined to be victims of discrimination, and the Court does not indicate that it means to suggest that the original consent decree in these cases was invalid. Any suggestion that a consent decree can provide relief only if a defendant concedes liability would drastically reduce, of course, the incentives for entering into consent decrees. * * *

The Court's reliance on *Teamsters* is mistaken at a more general level as well, because *Teamsters* was concerned with individual relief, whereas these cases are concerned exclusively with classwide, race-conscious relief. *Teamsters* arose out of two pattern-or-practice suits filed by the Government alleging that a union and an employer had discriminated against minorities in hiring truck drivers. Prior to a finding of liability, the Government entered into a consent decree in partial resolution of the suit. In that decree, the defendants agreed to a variety of race-conscious remedial actions, including a requirement that the company hire "one Negro or Spanish-surnamed person for every white person" until a certain percentage of minority representation was achieved. The decree did not settle the claims of individual class members, however, and allowed the individuals whom the court found to be victims of discrimination to seek whatever retroactive seniority was appropriate under Title VII.

In *Teamsters,* therefore, all class-wide claims had been settled before the case reached this Court. The case concerned only the problems of determining victims and the nature of appropriate individual relief. *Teamsters* did not consider the nature of appropriate affirmative class relief that would have been available had such relief not been provided in the consent decree between the parties. The issue in the present cases, as posed by the Court, is just the reverse. Respondents have not requested individual awards of seniority, and the preliminary injunction made none. Thus, the issue in these cases is the appropriate scope of classwide relief—an issue not present in *Teamsters* when that case came here. *Teamsters* therefore has little relevance for these cases.

leged discrimination, not just the first stage of such a trial.

The Court seeks to buttress its reliance on *Teamsters* by stressing on the last sentence of § 706(g). That sentence states that a court cannot order the "hiring, reinstatement, or promotion of an individual as an employee * * * if such individual * * * was refused employment or advancement or was suspended or discharged for any reason other than discrimination" in violation of Title VII. The nature of the Court's reliance on that sentence is unclear, however, because the Court states merely that the District Court "ignores" the "policy behind § 706(g)." For several reasons, however, it appears that the Court relies on the policy of § 706(g) only in making a particularized conclusion concerning the relief granted in these cases, rather than a conclusion about the general availability of race-conscious remedies.

In discussing § 706(g), the Court relies on several passages from the legislative history of the Civil Rights Act of 1964 in which individual legislators stated their views that Title VII would not authorize the imposition of remedies based upon race. And while there are indications that many in Congress at the time opposed the use of race-conscious remedies, there is authority that supports a narrower interpretation of § 706(g). Under that interpretation, the last sentence of § 706(g) addresses only the situation in which a plaintiff demonstrates that an employer has engaged in unlawful discrimination, but the employer can show that a particular individual would not have received the job, promotion or reinstatement even in the absence of discrimination because there was also a lawful justification for the action. The provision, for example, prevents a court from granting relief where an employment decision is based in part upon race, but where the applicant is unqualified for the job for nondiscriminatory reasons. In that sense, the section merely prevents a court from ordering an employer to hire someone unqualified for the job, and has nothing to do with prospective class-wide relief.

Much of the legislative history supports this view. What is now § 706(g) had its origin in § 707(e) of H.R. 7152, 88th Cong., 1st Sess. (1963). That original version prevented a court from granting relief to someone that had been refused employment, denied promotion, or discharged "for cause." The "for cause" provision presumably referred to what an employer must show to establish that a particular individual should not be given relief. That language was amended by replacing "for cause" with "for any reason other than discrimination on account of race, color, religion or national origin," which was the version of the sentence as passed by the House. The author of the original version and the amendment explained that the amendment's only purpose was to specify cause, and to clarify that a court cannot find a violation of the act that is based upon facts other than unlawful discrimination. There is no indication whatever that the amendment was intended to broaden its prohibition to include all forms of prospective race-conscious relief.

In any event, § 706(g) was amended by the Equal Employment Opportunity Act of 1972. The legislative history of that amendment strongly supports the view that Congress endorsed the remedial use of race under Title VII. The amendment added language to the first sentence of § 706(g) to make clear the breadth of the remedial authority of the courts. As amended, the first sentence authorizes a court to order "such affirmative action as may be appropriate which may include, *but is not limited to,* reinstatement or hiring of employees, with or without backpay * * * *or any other equitable relief as the court deems appropriate.*" (emphasized language added in 1972).

In addition, during consideration of the amendment, Congress specifically rejected an attempt to amend Title VII to *prohibit* the use of prospective race-conscious employment goals to remedy discrimination. Senator Ervin proposed an amendment to Title VII intended to prohibit government agencies from requiring employers to adopt goals or quotas for the hiring of minorities. Senator Javits led the debate against the amendment. Significantly, Senator Javits stressed that the amendment would affect not only the activities of federal agencies, but also the scope of judicial remedies available under Title VII. He referred repeatedly to court decisions ordering race-conscious remedies, and asked that two such decisions be printed in the Congressional Record.[12] He stated explicitly his view that "[w]hat this amendment seeks to do is to undo * * * those court decisions." The amendment was rejected by a 2 to 1 margin.

With clear knowledge, therefore, of courts' use of race-conscious remedies to correct patterns of discrimination, the 1972 Congress rejected an attempt to amend Title VII to prohibit such remedies. In fact, the Conference Committee stated: "In any area where the new law does not address itself, or in any areas where a specific contrary intention is not indicated, it was assumed that the present case law as developed by the courts would continue to govern the applicability and construction of Title VII." Relying on this legislative history of the 1972 amendment and other actions by the Executive and the courts, four members of this Court, including the author of today's opinion, stated in University of California Regents v. Bakke: "Executive, judicial and congressional action subsequent to the passage of Title VII conclusively established that the Title did not bar the remedial use of race" (opinion of Brennan, White, Marshall, and Blackmun, JJ.). As has been observed, moreover, the Courts of Appeals are unanimously of the view that race-conscious remedies are not prohibited by Title VII. Because the Court's opinion does not even acknowledge this consensus, it seems clear that the Court's conclusion that the District Court "ignored the policy" of § 706(g) is a statement that the race-conscious relief ordered in these cases was broader than necessary, not that race-conscious relief is never appropriate under Title VII.

12. * * * Senator Javits also noted the Justice Department's practice of seeking consent decrees in Title VII cases containing percentage hiring goals.

IV

By dissenting, I do not mean glibly to suggest that the District Court's preliminary injunction necessarily was correct. Because it seems that the affected whites have no contractual rights that were breached by the city's modified layoff plan, the effect of the preliminary injunction was to shift the pain of the city's fiscal crisis onto innocent employees. This Court has recognized before the difficulty of reconciling competing claims of innocent employees who themselves are neither the perpetrators of discrimination nor the victims of it. * * * If the District Court's preliminary injunction was proper, it was because it correctly interpreted the original intent of the parties to the consent decree, and equitably enforced that intent in what admittedly was a zero-sum situation. If it was wrong, it was because it improperly interpreted the consent decree, or because a less painful way of reconciling the competing equities was within the court's power. In either case, the District Court's preliminary injunction terminated many months ago, and I regret the Court's insistence upon unnecessarily reviving a past controversy.

NOTES AND PROBLEMS FOR DISCUSSION

1. Does the majority's reference to *Teamsters* and the notion of limiting affirmative relief to identifiable victims of discrimination suggest that the Court may be backing away from the theories of discrimination and equality that underlie its prior decisions in *Griggs* and *Weber*?

2. Does this decision provide employers with the opportunity to retreat from their affirmative action commitments by claiming economic difficulty? Will the answer depend upon whether the affirmative action obligation was voluntarily adopted, judicially imposed, or the result of a consent decree?

3. To what extent can this decision be limited to the Court's treatment of the preliminary injunction modification issue? Isn't that distinction reflected in the decisions in *Wygant* and *Local #28*? The Court also addressed this point in the following case.

LOCAL NUMBER 93, INTERNATIONAL ASSOCIATION OF FIREFIGHTERS v. CLEVELAND

Supreme Court of the United States, 1986.
___ U.S. ___, 106 S.Ct. 3063, 92 L.Ed.2d 405.

JUSTICE BRENNAN delivered the opinion of the Court.

The question presented in this case is whether § 706(g) of Title VII of the Civil Rights Act of 1964, as amended, 42 U.S.C. § 2000e–5(g), precludes the entry of a consent decree which provides relief that may benefit individuals who were not the actual victims of the defendant's discriminatory practices.

I

On October 23, 1980, the Vanguards of Cleveland (the Vanguards), an organization of black and Hispanic firefighters employed by the City of Cleveland, filed a complaint charging the City and various municipal officials (hereinafter referred to collectively as the City) with discrimination on the basis of race and national origin "in the hiring, assignment and promotion of firefighters within the City of Cleveland Fire Department." The Vanguards sued on behalf of a class of blacks and Hispanics consisting of firefighters already employed by the City, applicants for employment, and "all blacks and Hispanics who in the future will apply for employment or will be employed as firemen by the Cleveland Fire Department."

The Vanguards claimed that the City had violated the rights of the plaintiff class under the Thirteenth and Fourteenth Amendments to the United States Constitution, Title VII of the Civil Rights Act of 1964, and 42 U.S.C. §§ 1981 and 1983. Although the complaint alleged facts to establish discrimination in hiring and work assignments, the primary allegations charged that black and Hispanic firefighters "have * * * been discriminated against by reason of their race and national origin in the awarding of promotions within the Fire Department." [1] The complaint averred that this discrimination was effectuated by a number of intentional practices by the City. The written examination used for making promotions was alleged to be discriminatory. The effects of this test were said to be reinforced by the use of seniority points and by the manipulation of retirement dates so that minorities would not be near the top of promotion lists when positions became available. In addition, the City assertedly limited minority advancement by deliberately refusing to administer a new promotional examination after 1975, thus cancelling out the effects of increased minority hiring that had resulted from certain litigation commenced in 1973.

As just noted, the Vanguards' lawsuit was not the first in which the City had to defend itself against charges of race discrimination in hiring and promotion in its civil services. In 1972, an organization of black police officers filed an action alleging that the Police Department discriminated against minorities in hiring and promotions. See Shield Club v. City of Cleveland, 370 F.Supp. 251 (ND Ohio 1972). The District Court found for the plaintiffs and issued an order enjoining

1. The Cleveland Fire Department has six ranks of officers. From the lowest to the highest rank, these are: Lieutenant, Captain, Battalion Chief, Assistant Chief and Chief. To obtain a promotion, a firefighter must satisfy minimum experience requirements and pass a written examination. The examination is apparently quite difficult; approximately 80% of the applicants failed the 1984 promotional examination. Firefighters who pass the written examination are assigned a place on a promotion eligibility list. Although rankings on the lists are based primarily on test scores, additional points are assigned on the basis of seniority. There is a separate list for each rank. These lists are to remain effective for one year, but may be extended for an additional year, and, as a practical matter, lists are ordinarily used for the full 2-year period. Promotions are made from the lists as positions become available.

certain hiring and promotion practices and establishing minority hiring goals. In 1977, these hiring goals were adjusted and promotion goals were established pursuant to a consent decree. Thereafter, litigation raising similar claims was commenced against the Fire Department and resulted in a judicial finding of unlawful discrimination and the entry of a consent decree imposing hiring quotas similar to those ordered in the *Shield Club* litigation. See Headen v. City of Cleveland, No. C73–330 (ND Ohio, Apr. 25, 1975). In 1977, after additional litigation, the *Headen* court approved a new plan governing hiring procedures in the Fire Department.

By the time the Vanguards filed their complaint, then, the City had already unsuccessfully contested many of the basic factual issues in other lawsuits. Naturally, this influenced the City's view of the Vanguards' case. As expressed by counsel for the City at oral argument in this Court:

> "[W]hen this case was filed in 1980, the City of Cleveland had eight years at that point of litigating these types of cases, and eight years of having judges rule against the City of Cleveland.
>
> "You don't have to beat us on the head. We finally learned what we had to do and what we had to try to do to comply with the law, and it was the intent of the city to comply with the law fully * * *."

Thus, rather than commence another round of futile litigation, the City entered into "serious settlement negotiations" with the Vanguards.

On April 27, 1981, Local Number 93 of the International Association of Firefighters, AFL–CIO, C.L.C. (Local 93 or Union), which represents a majority of Cleveland's firefighters, moved pursuant to Federal Rule of Civil Procedure 24(a)(2) to intervene as a party-plaintiff. The District Court granted the motion and ordered the Union to submit its complaint in intervention within 30 days.

Local 93 subsequently submitted a three-page document entitled "Complaint of Applicant for Intervention." Despite its title, this document did not allege any causes of action or assert any claims against either the Vanguards or the City. It expressed the view that "[p]romotions based upon any criterion other than competence, such as a racial quota system, would deny those most capable from their promotions and would deny the residents of the City of Cleveland from maintaining the best possible fire fighting force," and asserted that "Local #93's interest is to maintain a well trained and properly staffed fire fighting force and [Local 93] contends that promotions should be made on the basis of demonstrated competency, properly measured by competitive examinations administered in accordance with the applicable provisions of Federal, State, and Local laws." The "complaint" concluded with a prayer for relief in the form of an injunction requiring the City to award promotions on the basis of such examinations.

In the meantime, negotiations between the Vanguards and the City continued, and a proposed consent decree was submitted to the District Court in November, 1981. This proposal established "interim procedures" to be implemented "as a two-step temporary remedy" for past discrimination in promotions. The first step required that a fixed number of already planned promotions be reserved for minorities: specifically, 16 of 40 planned promotions to Lieutenant, 3 of 20 planned promotions to Captain, 2 of 10 planned promotions to Battalion Chief, and 1 of 3 planned promotions to Assistant Chief were to be made to minority firefighters. The second step involved the establishment of "appropriate minority promotion goal[s]," for the ranks of Lieutenant, Captain, and Battalion Chief. The proposal also required the City to forgo using seniority points as a factor in making promotions. The plan was to remain in effect for 9 years, and could be extended upon mutual application of the parties for an additional 6-year period.

The District Court held a 2-day hearing at the beginning of January to consider the fairness of this proposed consent decree. Local 93 objected to the use of minority promotional goals and to the 9-year life of the decree. In addition, the Union protested the fact that it had not been included in the negotiations. This latter objection particularly troubled the District Judge. Indeed, although hearing evidence presented by the Vanguards and the City in support of the decree, the Judge stated that he was "appalled that these negotiations leading to this consent decree did not include the intervenors * * *," and refused to pass on the decree under the circumstances. Instead, he concluded, "I am going to at this time to defer this proceeding until another day and I am mandating the City and the [Vanguards] to engage the Fire Fighters in discussions, in dialogue. Let them know what is going on, hear their particular problems." At the same time, Judge Lambros explained that the Union would have to make its objections more specific to accomplish anything: "I don't think the Fire Fighters are going to be able to win their position on the basis that, 'Well, Judge, you know, there's something inherently wrong about quotas. You know, it's not fair.' We need more than that."

A second hearing was held on April 27. Local 93 continued to oppose any form of affirmative action. Witnesses for all parties testified concerning the proposed consent decree. The testimony revealed that, while the consent decree dealt only with the 40 promotions to Lieutenant already planned by the City, the Fire Department was actually authorized to make up to 66 offers; similarly, the City was in a position to hire 32 rather than 20 Captains and 14 rather than 10 Battalion Chiefs. After hearing this testimony, Judge Lambros proposed as an alternative to have the City make a high number of promotions over a relatively short period of time. The Judge explained that if the City were to hire 66 Lieutenants rather than 40, it could "plug in a substantial number of black leadership that can start having some influence in the operation of this fire department" while still promoting the same nonminority officers who would have obtained promotions under the existing system. Additional testimony revealed that this approach had led to the amicable resolution of similar litigation in Atlanta, Georgia. Judge Lambros persuaded the parties to consider revamping the consent decree along the lines of the Atlanta plan. The proceedings were therefore adjourned and the matter was referred to a United States Magistrate.

Counsel for all three parties participated in 40 hours of intensive negotiations under the Magistrate's supervision and agreed to a revised consent decree that incorporated a modified version of the Atlanta plan. However, submission of this proposal to the court was made contingent upon approval by the membership of Local 93. Despite the fact that the revised consent decree actually increased the number of supervisory positions available to nonminority firefighters, the Union members overwhelmingly rejected the proposal.

On January 11, 1983, the Vanguards and the City lodged a second amended consent decree with the court and moved for its approval. This proposal was "patterned very closely upon the revised decree negotiated under the supervision of [the] Magistrate * * *," and thus its central feature was the creation of many more promotional opportunities for firefighters of all races. Specifically, the decree required that the City immediately make 66 promotions to Lieutenant, 32 promotions to Captain, 16 promotions to Battalion Chief and 4 promotions to Assistant Chief. These promotions were to be based on a promotional examination that had been administered during the litigation. The 66 initial promotions to Lieutenant were to be evenly split between minority and nonminority firefighters. However, since only 10 minorities had qualified for the 52 upper-level positions, the proposed decree provided that all 10 should be promoted. The decree further required promotional examinations to be administered in June 1984 and December 1985. Promotions from the lists produced by these examinations were to be made in accordance with specified promotional "goals" that were expressed in terms of percentages and were different for each rank. The list from the 1985 examination would remain in effect for two years, after which time the decree would expire. The life of the decree was thus shortened from nine years to four. In addition, except where necessary to implement specific requirements of the consent decree, the use of seniority points was restored as a factor in ranking candidates for promotion.

Local 93 was mentioned twice in the proposal. Paragraph 16 required the City to submit progress reports concerning compliance to both the Union and the Vanguards. In paragraph 24, the court reserved exclusive jurisdiction with respect to applications or claims made by "any party, including Intervenor." The decree imposed no legal duties or obligations on Local 93.

On January 19, the City was ordered to notify the members of the plaintiff class of the terms of the proposed decree. In addition, persons who wished to object to the proposal were ordered to submit their objections in writing. Local 93 filed the following formal objection to the proposed consent decree:

> "Local # 93 has consistently and steadfastly maintained that there must be a more equitable, more fair, more just way to correct the problems caused by the [City]. Many alternatives to the hopefully soon to be unnecessary 'remedial' methods embodied in the law have been explored and some have been utilized.
>
> "Local # 93 reiterates it's [*sic*] absolute and total objection to the use of racial quotas which must by their very nature cause serious racial polarization in the Fire Service. Since this problem is obviously the concern of the collective representative of all members of the fire service, Intervenors, Local # 93. [*sic*] We respectfully urge this court not to implement the 'remedial' provisions of this Decree."

Apart from thus expressing its opinion as to the wisdom and necessity of the proposed consent decree, the Union still failed to assert any legal claims against either the Vanguards or the City.[3]

The District Court approved the consent decree on January 31, 1983. Judge Lambros found that "[t]he documents, statistics, and testimony presented at the January and April 1982 hearings reveal a historical pattern of racial discrimination in the promotions in the City of Cleveland Fire Department." He then observed:

> "While the concerns articulated by Local 93 may be valid, the use of a quota system for the relatively short period of four years is not unreasonable in light of the demonstrated history of racial discrimination in promotions in the City of Cleveland Fire Department. It is neither unreasonable nor unfair to require nonminority firefighters who, although they committed no wrong, benefited from the effects of the discrimination to bear some of the burden of the remedy. Furthermore, the amended proposal is more reasonable and less burdensome than the nine-year plan that had been proposed originally."

The Judge therefore overruled the Union's objection and adopted the consent decree "as a fair, reasonable, and adequate resolution of the claims raised in this action." The District Court retained exclusive jurisdiction for "all purposes of enforcement, modification, or amendment of th[e] Decree upon the application of any party * * *."

The Union appealed the overruling of its objections. A panel for the Court of Appeals for the Sixth Circuit affirmed, one judge dissenting. Vanguards of Cleveland v. City of Cleveland, 753 F.2d 479 (1985). The court rejected the Union's claim that the use of race-conscious relief was "unreasonable," finding such relief justified by the statistical evidence presented to the District Court and the City's express admission that it had engaged in discrimination. The court also found that the consent decree was "fair and reasonable to non-minority firefighters," emphasizing the "relatively modest goals set forth in the plan,"

3. In addition to Local 93, three individual members of the Union voiced objections to the proposed consent decree in personal letters to the District Court. The basis of their objections was the same as the Union's.

the fact that "the plan does not require the hiring of unqualified minority firefighters or the discharge of any non-minority firefighters," the fact that the plan "does not create an absolute bar to the advancement of non-minority employees," and the short duration of the plan.

After oral argument before the Court of Appeals, this Court decided Firefighters v. Stotts, 467 U.S. 561, 104 S.Ct. 2576, 81 L.Ed.2d 483 (1984). "Concerned with the potential impact of *Stotts*," the Court of Appeals ordered the parties to submit supplemental briefs, but ultimately concluded that *Stotts* did not affect the outcome of the case. The court noted that the District Court in *Stotts* had issued an injunction requiring layoffs over the objection of the City, while in this case the City of Cleveland had agreed to the plan. The court reasoned that even if *Stotts* holds that Title VII limits relief to those who have been actual victims of discrimination, "[t]he fact that this case involves a consent decree and not an injunction makes the legal basis of the *Stotts* decision inapplicable." [4]

Local 93 petitioned this Court for a writ of certiorari. The sole issue raised by the petition is whether the consent decree is an impermissible remedy under § 706(g) of Title VII.[5] Local 93 argues that the consent decree disregards the express prohibition of the last sentence of § 706(g) that

> "*[n]o order of the court shall require* the admission or reinstatement of an individual as a member of a union, or *the hiring, reinstatement, or promotion of an individual as an employee,* or the payment to him of any back pay, *if such individual* was refused admission, suspended, or expelled, or *was refused employment or advancement* or was suspended or discharged *for any reason other than discrimination on account of race,* color, religion, sex, or national origin or in violation of section 2000e–3(a) of this title" (emphasis added).

4. The Court of Appeals also distinguished *Stotts* on the ground that the injunction imposed by the District Court in that case "had the direct effect of abrogating a valid seniority system to the detriment of non-minority workers," while "[i]n this case, the consent decree assured the integrity of the existing seniority system."

5. The petition for certiorari sets forth two questions:

"1. May a District Court adopt provisions in a consent decree purporting to remedy a Title VII violation that it would have had no authority to order as a remedy if the matter had gone to trial?

"2. May a municipal employer voluntarily adopt an affirmative action promotional scheme over the objections of an intervenor union duly elected to represent all employees when said promotional scheme adversely affects the rights and interests of the employees and awards relief to minority employees regardless of whether they were actual victims of past racial discrimination?"

The first of these questions plainly asks only whether Title VII precludes the entry of this consent decree. Although the second question can conceivably be read to embody a more general challenge respecting the effect of the consent decree on petitioner's legal rights, neither the petition for certiorari nor the brief on the merits discusses any issue other than whether this consent decree was prohibited by § 706(g) of Title VII. Moreover, petitioner limited its challenge below to whether the consent decree was "reasonable," and then, after *Stotts* was decided, to whether the consent decree was permissible under § 706(g). Finally, the District Court's retention of jurisdiction leaves it open for petitioner to press whatever other claims it might have before that court, see infra at ___. Therefore, we deem it necessary to decide only the question whether § 706(g) precluded the District Court from entering this consent decree.

According to Local 93, this sentence precludes a court from awarding relief under Title VII that may benefit individuals who were not the actual victims of the employer's discrimination. The Union argues further that the plain language of the provision that "[n]o order of the court" shall provide such relief extends this limitation to orders entered by consent in addition to orders issued after litigation. Consequently, the Union concludes that a consent decree entered in Title VII litigation is invalid if—like the consent decree approved in this case—it utilizes racial preferences that may benefit individuals who are not themselves actual victims of an employer's discrimination. The Union is supported by the United States as *amicus curiae.*[6]

We granted the petition in order to answer this important question of federal law. The Court holds today in Sheet Metal Workers v. EEOC, that courts may, in appropriate cases, provide relief under Title VII that benefits individuals who were not the actual victims of a defendant's discriminatory practices. We need not decide whether this is one of those cases, however. For we hold that whether or not § 706(g) precludes a court from imposing certain forms of race-conscious relief after trial, that provision does not apply to relief awarded in a consent decree.[7] We therefore affirm the judgment of the Court of Appeals.

II

We have on numerous occasions recognized that Congress intended for voluntary compliance to be the preferred means of achieving the objectives of Title VII. Alexander v. Gardner-Denver Co., 415 U.S. 36, 44, 94 S.Ct. 1011, 1017, 39 L.Ed.2d 147 (1974); Albermarle Paper Co. v. Moody, 422 U.S. 405, 417–418, 95 S.Ct. 2362, 2371–72, 45 L.Ed.2d 280 (1975). This view is shared by the Equal Employment Opportunity Commission (EEOC), which has promulgated guidelines setting forth its understanding that "Congress strongly encouraged employers * * * to act on a voluntary basis to modify employment practices and systems which constituted barriers to equal employment opportunity * * *." 29 CFR § 1608.1(b) (1985). According to the EEOC:

> "The principle of nondiscrimination in employment because of race, color, religion, sex, or national origin, and the principle that each person subject to Title VII should take voluntary action to correct the effects of past discrimination and to prevent present and future discrimination without awaiting litigation, are mutually consistent and interdependent methods of addressing social and economic conditions which precipitated the enactment of Title VII. Voluntary

6. The United States took exactly the opposite position in Steelworkers v. Weber, 443 U.S. 193, 99 S.Ct. 2721, 61 L.Ed.2d 480 (1979).

7. We emphasize that, in light of this holding, nothing we say here is intended to express a view as to the extent of a court's remedial power under § 706(g) in cases where that provision does apply. That question is addressed in Sheet Metal Workers v. EEOC.

affirmative action to improve opportunities for minorities and women must be encouraged and protected in order to carry out the Congressional intent embodied in Title VII." § 1608.1(c) (footnote omitted).

It is equally clear that the voluntary action available to employers and unions seeking to eradicate race discrimination may include reasonable race-conscious relief that benefits individuals who were not actual victims of discrimination. This was the holding of Steelworkers v. Weber, 443 U.S. 193, 99 S.Ct. 2721, 61 L.Ed.2d 480 (1979). In *Weber*, an employer and a union agreed in collective bargaining to reserve for black employees 50% of the openings in an in-plant craft-training program until the percentage of black craftworkers in the plant was commensurate with the percentage of blacks in the local labor force. After considering both the purposes of Title VII and its legislative history, we concluded that "[i]t would be ironic indeed if a law triggered by a Nation's concern over centuries of racial injustice and intended to improve the lot of those who had 'been excluded from the American dream for so long' constituted the first legislative prohibition of all voluntary, private, race-conscious efforts to abolish traditional patterns of racial segregation and hierarchy." Accordingly, we held that Title VII permits employers and unions voluntarily to make use of reasonable race-conscious affirmative action, although we left to another day the task of "defin[ing] in detail the line of demarcation between permissible and impermissible affirmative action plans."

Of course, *Weber* involved a purely private contractual agreement rather than a consent decree. But, at least at first blush, there does not seem to be any reason to distinguish between voluntary action taken in a consent decree and voluntary action taken entirely outside the context of litigation.[8] Indeed, in Carson v. American Brands, Inc., 450 U.S. 79, 88, n.14, 101 S.Ct. 993, 998, n.14, 67 L.Ed.2d 59 (1981), we

8. Unlike *Weber*, which involved a private employer, this case involves a public employer whose voluntary actions are subject to the strictures of the Fourteenth Amendment as well as to the limitations of § 703 of Title VII. In the posture in which this case comes to us, we have no occasion to address the circumstances, if any, in which voluntary action by a public employer that is permissible under § 703 would nonetheless be barred by the Fourteenth Amendment. Rather, as is explained below, we leave questions regarding the application of the Fourteenth Amendment to the underlying agreement to further proceedings before the District Court. Nor need we decide what limits § 703 places on an employer's ability to agree to race-conscious relief in a voluntary settlement that is not embodied in a consent decree, or what showing the employer would be required to make concerning possible prior discrimination on its part against minorities in order to defeat a challenge by nonminority employees based on § 703. Cf. Wygant v. Jackson Board of Education, 476 U.S. ___, 106 S.Ct. 1842, 90 L.Ed.2d 260 (1986). In any event, there may be instances in which a public employer, consistent with both the Fourteenth Amendment as interpreted in *Wygant* and § 703 as interpreted in *Weber*, could voluntarily agree to take race-conscious measures in pursuance of a legitimate remedial purpose. The only issue before us is whether, assuming *arguendo* that § 706(g) would bar a court from ordering such race-conscious relief after trial in some of these instances, § 706(g) also bars a court from approving a consent decree entered into by the employer and providing for such relief.

held that a District Court's order denying entry of a consent decree is appealable under 28 U.S.C. § 1292(a)(1) because such an order undermines Congress' "strong preference for encouraging voluntary settlement of employment discrimination claims" under Title VII. Moreover, the EEOC's guidelines concerning "Affirmative Action Appropriate Under Title VII of the Civil Rights Act of 1964," 29 CFR pt. 1608 (1985), plainly contemplate the use of consent decrees as an appropriate form of voluntary affirmative action. See, e.g., § 1608.8.[9] True, these guidelines do not have the force of law, General Electric Co. v. Gilbert, 429 U.S. 125, 141, 97 S.Ct. 401, 410, 50 L.Ed.2d 343 (1976), but still they " 'constitute a body of experience and informed judgment to which courts and litigants may properly resort for guidance.' " Id., at 142, 97 S.Ct., at 411 (quoting Skidmore v. Swift & Co., 323 U.S. 134, 140, 65 S.Ct. 161, 164, 89 L.Ed. 124 (1944)). Therefore, absent some contrary indication, there is no reason to think that voluntary, race-conscious affirmative action such as was held permissible in *Weber* is rendered impermissible by Title VII simply because it is incorporated into a consent decree.

Local 93 and the Solicitor General find a contrary indicator in § 706(g), which governs the courts' remedial power under Title VII. They contend that § 706(g) establishes an independent limitation on what *courts*—as opposed to employers or unions—can do, prohibiting any "order of the court" from providing relief that may benefit nonvictims. They argue that a consent decree should be treated as an "order" within the meaning of § 706(g) because it possesses the legal force and character of a judgment decreed after a trial. They rely for this conclusion on several characteristics of consent decrees: first, that a consent decree looks like and is entered as a judgment; second, that the court retains the power to modify a consent decree in certain circumstances over the objection of a signatory, see United States v. Swift & Co., 286 U.S. 106, 114, 52 S.Ct. 460, 462, 76 L.Ed. 999 (1932) (*Swift II*); third, that noncompliance with a consent decree is enforceable by citation for contempt of court, see United States v. City of Miami, 664 F.2d 435, 440, and n.8 (CA5 1981) (opinion of Rubin, J.).

To be sure, consent decrees bear some of the earmarks of judgments entered after litigation. At the same time, because their terms are arrived at through mutual agreement of the parties, consent decrees also closely resemble contracts. See United States v. ITT Continental Baking Co., 420 U.S. 223, 235–237, 95 S.Ct. 926, 933–35, 43 L.Ed.2d 148 (1975); United States v. Armour & Co., 402 U.S. 673, 91 S.Ct. 1752, 29 L.Ed.2d 256 (1971). More accurately, then, as we have previously recognized, consent decrees "have attributes both of contracts and of judicial decrees," a dual character that has resulted in different treatment for different purposes. United States v. ITT Continental Baking

9. The EEOC has not joined the Brief for United States in this case. The Solicitor General's brief has been filed only on behalf of the Attorney General, who has some limited enforcement responsibility under Title VII, see 42 U.S.C. § 2000e–5(f)(1), and the Federal Government in its capacity as an employer, § 2000e–16.

Co., supra, 420 U.S., at 235–237, and n.10, 95 S.Ct., at 934, and n.10. The question is not whether we can label a consent decree as a "contract" or a "judgment," for we can do both. The question is whether, given their hybrid nature, consent decrees implicate the concerns embodied in § 706(g) in such a way as to require treating them as "orders" within the meaning of that provision.

Because this Court's cases do not treat consent decrees as judicial decrees in all respects and for all purposes, we think that the language of § 706(g) does not so clearly include consent decrees as to preclude resort to the voluminous legislative history of Title VII. The issue is whether, when Congress used the phrase "[n]o order of the court shall require" in § 706(g), it unmistakably intended to refer to *consent* decrees. In addition to the fact that consent decrees have contractual as well as judicial features, the use of the verb "require" in § 706(g) suggests that it was the coercive aspect of a judicial decree that Congress had in mind. We turn therefore to the legislative history, since the language of § 706(g) does not clearly settle the matter.

The conclusion in *Weber* that "Congress chose not to forbid all voluntary race-conscious affirmative action" when it enacted Title VII was largely based upon the legislative history, which shows that Congress was particularly concerned to avoid undue federal interference with managerial discretion. As originally enacted, Title VII regulated only private enterprises; the liberal Republicans and Southern Democrats whose support was crucial to obtaining passage of the bill expressed misgivings about the potential for Government intrusion into the managerial decisions of employers and unions beyond what was necessary to eradicate unlawful discrimination. Their votes were obtained only after they were given assurances that "management prerogatives, and union freedoms are to be left undisturbed to the greatest extent possible." As one commentator points out, rather than seeking to outlaw voluntary affirmative action, the more conservative proponents of Title VII who held the balance of power in 1964 "were far more concerned to avoid the intrusion into business autonomy that a rigid color-blind standard would entail." Note, Preferential Relief Under Title VII, 65 Va.L.Rev. 729, 771, n. 224 (1979). See also, *Weber*, supra, at 207–208, n. 7, 99 S.Ct., at 2729, n. 7 (quoting 110 Cong.Rec. 15893 (1964) (remarks of Rep. MacGregor)) (Congress was not legislating about " 'preferential treatment or quotas in employment' " because it believed that " 'the problems raised by these controversial questions are more properly handled at a governmental level closer to the American people and by communities and individuals themselves' ").

The legislative history pertaining specifically to § 706(g) suggests that it was drafted with this concern in mind and, in fact, that a principal purpose of the last sentence of § 706(g) was to protect managerial prerogatives of employers and unions.[10] See H.R.Rep. No. 914,

10. Title VII was expanded to cover municipalities by the Equal Employment Opportunity Act of 1972, Pub.L. 92–261, 86 Stat. 103. Although the legislative history of the 1972 amendments does not reflect the same concern with preserving the man-

88th Cong., 2nd Sess., pt. 1, p. 11 (1963) (first version of § 706(g) preserving employer defense of "cause"); 110 Cong.Rec. 2567–2571 (1964) (amending this version to substitute "for any reason other than discrimination" in place of "cause"); id., at 2567 (remarks of Rep. Celler, the amendment's sponsor, that the amendment's purpose was "to specify cause"); id., at 6549 (remarks of Sen. Humphrey that § 706(g) makes clear "that employers may hire and fire, promote and refuse to promote for any reason, good or bad" except when such decisions violate the substantive provisions of Title VII). Thus, whatever the extent of the limits § 706(g) places on the power of the federal courts to compel employers and unions to take certain actions that the employers or unions oppose and would not otherwise take, § 706(g) by itself does not restrict the ability of employers or unions to enter into voluntary agreements providing for race-conscious remedial action. The limits on such agreements must be found outside § 706(g).[11]

From this, it is readily apparent that consent decrees are not included among the "orders" referred to in § 706(g), for the voluntary nature of a consent decree is its most fundamental characteristic. As we observed in United States v. Armour & Co.:

> "Consent decrees are entered into by parties to a case after careful negotiation has produced agreement on their precise terms. The parties waive their right to litigate the issues involved in the case and thus save themselves the time, expense, and inevitable risk of litigation. Naturally, the agreement reached normally embodies a compromise; in exchange for the saving of cost and elimination of risk, the parties each give up something they might have won had they proceeded with the litigation. Thus, the *decree* itself cannot be said to have a purpose; rather the *parties* have purposes, generally opposed to each other, and the resultant decree embodies as much of those opposing purposes as the respective parties have the bargaining power and skill to achieve." 402 U.S., at 681–682, 91 S.Ct., at 1757 (emphasis in original) (footnote omitted).

Indeed, it is the parties' agreement that serves as the source of the court's authority to enter any judgment at all. More importantly, it is

agerial discretion of governmental employers that was evident in 1964 with respect to the private sector, there is also no indication that Congress intended to leave governmental employers with less latitude under Title VII than had been left to employers in the private sector when Title VII was originally enacted. See generally, Subcommittee on Labor of the Senate Committee on Labor and Public Welfare, Legislative History of the Equal Employment Opportunity Act of 1972, 92d Cong., 2d Sess. (Comm.Print 1972).

11. Thus, we do not suggest that voluntary action by employers or unions is outside the ambit of Title VII regardless of its effect on non-minorities. We already rejected such arguments in McDonald v. Santa Fe Trail Transp. Co., 427 U.S. 273, 96 S.Ct. 2574, 49 L.Ed.2d 493 (1976), and Steelworkers v. Weber, 443 U.S. 193, 99 S.Ct. 2721, 61 L.Ed.2d 480 (1979). Section 706(g), by its own terms, limits courts, not employers or unions, and focuses on preserving certain management prerogatives from interference by the federal courts. The rights of non-minorities with respect to action by their employers are delineated in § 703 of Title VII, and, in cases involving governmental employees, by the Fourteenth Amendment. See *Weber*, supra; Wygant v. Jackson Board of Education, 476 U.S. ——, 106 S.Ct. 1842, 90 L.Ed.2d 260 (1986).

the agreement of the parties, rather than the force of the law upon which the complaint was originally based, that creates the obligations embodied in a consent decree. Consequently, whatever the limitations Congress placed in § 706(g) on the power of federal courts to impose obligations on employers or unions to remedy violations of Title VII, these simply do not apply when the obligations are created by a consent decree.

The features of consent decrees designated by the Union and the Solicitor General do not require a contrary result. The fact that a consent decree *looks* like a judgment entered after a trial obviously does not implicate Congress' concern with limiting the power of federal courts unilaterally to require employers or unions to make certain kinds of employment decisions. The same is true of the court's conditional power to modify a consent decree; the mere *existence* of an *unexercised* power to modify the obligations contained in a consent decree does not alter the fact that those obligations were created by agreement of the parties rather than imposed by the court.[12] Finally, we reject the argument that a consent decree should be treated as an "order" within the meaning of § 706(g) because it can be enforced by a citation for contempt. There is no indication in the legislative history that the availability of judicial enforcement of an obligation, rather than the creation of the obligation itself, was the focus of congressional concern. In fact, judicial enforcement is available whether race-conscious relief is provided in a collective-bargaining agreement (as in *Weber*) or in a consent decree; only the form of that enforcement is different. But the difference between contractual remedies and the contempt power is not significant in any relevant sense with respect to § 706(g). For the choice of an enforcement scheme—whether to rely on contractual remedies or to have an agreement entered as a consent decree—is itself made voluntarily by the parties.[13] Thus, it does not

12. However, as is discussed below, the court's *exercise* of the power to modify the decree over the objection of a party to the decree does implicate § 706(g).

13. Parties may choose to settle their disputes by consent decree rather than by private contract for a number of reasons. As one commentator points out, "[p]ublic law settlements are often complicated documents designed to be carried out over a period of years, * * * so any purely out-of-court settlement would suffer the decisive handicap of not being subject to continuing oversight and interpretation by the court." Schwarzschild, Public Law by Private Bargain: Title VII Consent Decrees and the Fairness of Negotiated Institutional Reform, 1984 Duke L.J. 887, 899. In addition to this advantage, the National League of Cities adds:

> "A consent decree has several other advantages as a means of settling litigation. It is easier to obtain enforcement of a consent decree because it will be unnecessary to prove many facts that would otherwise have to be shown in order to establish the validity of an ordinary contract. A court that maintains continuing jurisdiction over a consent decree will have a more flexible repertoire of enforcement measures. And it is likely to be easier to channel litigation concerning the validity and implications of a consent decree into a single forum—the court that entered the decree—thus avoiding the waste of resources and the risk of inconsistent or conflicting obligations." Brief for National League of Cities *et al.* as *Amicus Curiae* 25.

For all of these reasons, consent decrees have become widely used as devices to facilitate settlement. Indeed, we have little doubt that the interpretation of § 706(g) proposed by the Union and the Solicitor General would make it substantially more difficult to settle Title VII litigation, con-

implicate Congress' concern that federal courts not impose unwanted obligations on employers and unions any more than the decision to institute race-conscious affirmative action in the first place; in both cases the parties have themselves created obligations and surrendered claims in order to achieve a mutually satisfactory compromise.

III

Relying upon Firefighters v. Stotts, 467 U.S. 561, 104 S.Ct. 2576, 81 L.Ed.2d 483 (1984), and Railway Employees v. Wright, 364 U.S. 642, 81 S.Ct. 368, 5 L.Ed.2d 349 (1961), Local 93—again joined by the Solicitor General—contends that we have recognized as a general principle that a consent decree cannot provide greater relief than a court could have decreed after a trial. They urge that even if § 706(g) does not directly invalidate the consent decree, that decree is nonetheless void because the District Court "would have been powerless to order [such an injunction] under Title VII, had the matter actually gone to trial."

We concluded above that voluntary adoption in a consent decree of race-conscious relief that may benefit nonvictims does not violate the congressional objectives of § 706(g). It is therefore hard to understand the basis for an independent judicial canon or "common law" of consent decrees that would give § 706(g) the effect of prohibiting such decrees anyway. To be sure, a federal court is more than "a recorder of contracts" from whom parties can purchase injunctions; it is "an organ of government constituted to make judicial decisions. * * *" 1B J. Moore, J. Lucas & T. Currier, Moore's Federal Practice ¶ 0.409[5], p. 331 (1984) (hereinafter Moore). Accordingly, a consent decree must spring from and serve to resolve a dispute within the court's subject-matter jurisdiction. Furthermore, consistent with this requirement, the consent decree must "com[e] within the general scope of the case made by the pleadings," Pacific R. Co. v. Ketchum, 11 Otto 289, 297, 101 U.S. 289, 297, 25 L.Ed. 932 (1880), and must further the objectives of the law upon which the complaint was based. However, in addition to the law which forms the basis of the claim, the parties' consent animates the legal force of a consent decree. See Pacific R. Co. v. Ketchum, supra; Citizens for a Better Environment v. Gorsuch, supra, 231 U.S.App.D.C., at 89–90, 718 F.2d, at 1127–1128; Note, The Consent Judgment as an Instrument of Compromise and Settlement, 72 Harv.L.Rev. 1314, 1317 (1959). Therefore, a federal court is not necessarily barred from entering a consent decree merely because the decree provides broader relief than the court could have awarded after a trial. See, e.g. Pacific R. Co. v. Ketchum, supra, 101 U.S., at 295–297; Swift & Co. v. United States, 276 U.S. 311, 327–331, 48 S.Ct. 311, 315–16, 72 L.Ed. 587 (1928) (*Swift I*) (Brandeis, J.).

This is not to say that the parties may agree to take action that conflicts with or violates the statute upon which the complaint was

trary to the expressed congressional preference for voluntary remedial action.

based. As noted above, the fact that the parties have consented to the relief contained in a decree does not render their action immune from attack on the ground that it violates § 703 of Title VII or the Fourteenthe Amendment. However, inasmuch as the limits placed by § 706(g) on the remedial authority of a federal court—whatever these may be—are not implicated by voluntary agreements, there is no conflict with or violation of § 706(g) when a federal court enters a consent decree that provides such relief. Accordingly, to the extent that the consent decree is not otherwise shown to be unlawful, the court is not barred from entering a consent decree merely because it might lack authority under § 706(g) to do so after a trial.

This simply was not the case in either Railway Employees v. Wright or Firefighters v. Stotts, in both of which the Court found conflicts between a judicial decree and the underlying statute. In *Wright*, a railroad and the unions representing most of its employees were charged with discriminating against nonunion employees in violation of the Railway Labor Act, 45 U.S.C. § 151 et seq. The parties entered a consent decree that prohibited, among other things, the establishment of a union shop, a restriction that was also contained in the Railway Labor Act at the time. When the Act was amended several years later to permit union shops, the unions moved to modify the consent decree; their motion was opposed by the plaintiffs and by the railroad. This Court reversed the District Court's denial of this motion, holding that refusal to modify the consent decree constituted an abuse of discretion under the circumstances. The Court recognized that the District Court retained power to modify the consent decree and that "a sound judicial discretion" may call for such modification "if the circumstances, whether of law or fact, obtaining at the time of its issuance have changed, or new ones have arisen." Because it viewed the intervening amendment of the Railway Labor Act as rendering the consent decree incompatible with the terms of the Act, the Court regarded as "established" the conclusion that, had the decree represented relief awarded after trial, it would have been an abuse of discretion to deny modification. This left only the question whether "th[e] result [is] affected by the fact that we are dealing with a consent decree." Citing *Swift II* for the proposition that the power to modify a consent decree is the same as the power to modify a litigated decree, the Court held that District Court "must * * * be free to modify the terms of the consent decree when a change in law brings those terms in conflict with statutory objectives."

Firefighters v. Stotts, 467 U.S. 561, 104 S.Ct. 2576, 81 L.Ed.2d 483 (1984), also involved a consent decree that the Court concluded was in conflict with the underlying statute, in that case Title VII. The plaintiffs and the City of Memphis entered into a consent decree that included the use of racial preferences for hiring and promoting firefighters. After the decree had been in effect for just over a year, budget deficits forced Memphis to lay off a number of firemen. Because layoffs pursuant to Memphis' "last hired, first fired" rule would undo the gains made by minority firefighters under the decree, the plaintiffs sought and obtained an injunction requiring Memphis to modify its seniority rules to protect new black employees. We reversed. We held first that the injunction could not be upheld as merely enforcing the terms of the consent decree. The plaintiffs argued in the alternative that the injunction was justified by the change in circumstances brought about by the budget deficits and that it thus constituted a proper modification of the decree. We rejected this argument, reasoning that "the District Court's authority to impose a modification of a decree is not wholly dependent on the decree," but must also be consistent with the underlying statute. Noting that the Court in *Wright* "held that when a change in the law brought the terms of the decree into conflict with the statute pursuant to which the decree was entered, the decree should be modified over the objections of one of the parties bound by the decree," we reasoned: "By the same token, and for the same reason, a district court cannot enter a disputed modification of a consent decree in Title VII litigation if the resulting order is inconsistent with that statute". Because we concluded that the District Court would have been precluded by Title VII from issuing an injunction such as the one it had issued after a trial, we rejected the plaintiffs' argument and held that "the District Court was precluded from granting such relief over the City's objection" by modifying the consent decree.

Because § 706(g) is not concerned with voluntary agreements by employers or unions to provide race-conscious relief, there is no inconsistency between it and a consent decree providing such relief, although the court might be barred from ordering the same relief after a trial or, as in *Stotts*, in disputed proceedings to modify a decree entered upon consent.

IV

Local 93 and the Solicitor General also challenge the validity of the consent decree on the ground that it was entered without the consent of the Union. They take the position that because the Union was permitted to intervene as of right, its consent was required before the court could approve a consent decree. This argument misconceives the Union's rights in the litigation.

A consent decree is primarily a means by which parties settle their disputes without having to bear the financial and other costs of litigating. It has never been supposed that one party—whether an original party, a party that was joined later, or an intervenor—could preclude other parties from settling their own disputes and thereby withdrawing from litigation. Thus, while an intervenor is entitled to present evidence and have its objections heard at the hearings on whether to approve a consent decree, it does not have power to block the decree merely by withholding its consent. See Zipes v. Trans World Airlines, Inc., 455 U.S. 385, 392, 400, 102 S.Ct. 1127, 1131, 1136, 71 L.Ed.2d 234 (1982); Kirkland v. New York State Dept. of Correctional Services, 711

F.2d 1117, 1126 (CA2 1983), cert. denied, 465 U.S. 1005, 104 S.Ct. 997, 79 L.Ed.2d 230 (1984). Here, Local 93 took full advantage of its opportunity to participate in the District Court's hearings on the consent decree. It was permitted to air its objections to the reasonableness of the decree and to introduce relevant evidence; the District Court carefully considered these objections and explained why it was rejecting them. Accordingly, "the District Court gave the union all the process that [it] was due * * *." *Zipes*, supra, 455 U.S., at 400, 102 S.Ct., at 1136.

Of course, parties who choose to resolve litigation through settlement may not dispose of the claims of a third party, and *a fortiori* may not impose duties or obligations on a third party, without that party's agreement. A court's approval of a consent decree between some of the parties therefore cannot dispose of the valid claims of nonconsenting intervenors; if properly raised, these claims remain and may be litigated by the intervenor. And, of course, a court may not enter a consent decree that imposes obligations on a party that did not consent to the decree. However, the consent decree entered here does not bind Local 93 to do or not to do anything. It imposes no legal duties or obligations on the Union at all; only the parties to the decree can be held in contempt of court for failure to comply with its terms. Moreover, the consent decree does not purport to resolve any claims the Union might have under the Fourteenth Amendment, see Wygant v. Jackson Board of Education, 476 U.S. ___, 106 S.Ct. 1842, 90 L.Ed.2d 260 (1986), § 703 of Title VII, see McDonald v. Santa Fe Trail Transp. Co., 427 U.S. 273, 96 S.Ct. 2574, 49 L.Ed.2d 493 (1976); Steelworkers v. Weber, 443 U.S. 193, 99 S.Ct. 2721, 61 L.Ed.2d 480 (1979), or as a matter of contract, see W.R. Grace & Co. v. Rubber Workers, 461 U.S. 757, 103 S.Ct. 2177, 76 L.Ed.2d 298 (1983). Indeed, despite the efforts of the District Judge to persuade it to do so, the Union failed to raise any substantive claims. Whether it is now too late to raise such claims, or—if not—whether the Union's claims have merit are questions that must be presented in the first instance to the District Court, which has retained jurisdiction to hear such challenges. The only issue before us is whether § 706(g) barred the District Court from approving this consent decree. We hold that it did not. Therefore, the judgment of the Court of Appeals is

Affirmed.

JUSTICE O'CONNOR, concurring.

I join the Court's opinion. I write separately to emphasize that the Court's holding is a narrow one. The Court holds that the relief provided in a consent decree need not conform to the limits on court-ordered relief imposed by § 706(g), whatever those limits may be. Rather, the validity of race-conscious relief provided in a consent decree is to be assessed for consistency with the provisions of § 703, such as § 703(a) and § 703(d), which were at issue in Steelworkers v. Weber, 443 U.S. 193, 99 S.Ct. 2721, 61 L.Ed.2d 480 (1979), and, in the case of a public employer, for consistency with the Fourteenth Amendment. As the Court explains, nonminority employees therefore remain free to challenge the race-conscious measures contemplated by a proposed consent decree as violative of their rights under § 703 or the Fourteenth Amendment. Even if nonminority employees do not object to the consent decree, a court should not approve a consent decree that on its face provides for racially preferential treatment that would clearly violate § 703 or the Fourteenth Amendment. Finally, the Court refrains from deciding "what showing [an] employer would be required to make concerning prior discrimination on its part against minorities in order to defeat a challenge by nonminority employees based on § 703."

It is clear, then, that the Court's opinion does not hold or otherwise suggest that there is no "necessary predicate for race conscious practices * * * favoring one race over another," post, at ___ (White, J., dissenting), when those practices are embodied in a voluntary settlement or in a consent decree rather than ordered by the court over the objection of an employer or union. If *Weber* indicates that an employer's or union's "prior discriminatory conduct" is the necessary "predicate for a temporary remedy favoring black employees," id., at ___, the Court's opinion leaves that requirement wholly undisturbed. The Court leaves open the question whether the race-conscious measures provided for in the consent decree at issue here were permissible under § 703. I agree with the Court that it is not necessary to decide that question in the present posture of this case, and that any challenge petitioner may make to the consent decree on substantive grounds, whether based on § 703 or the Fourteenth Amendment, should be left for resolution on remand.

JUSTICE WHITE, dissenting.

For several reasons, I am unable to join either the Court's opinion or judgment.

Title VII forbids racially discriminatory employment practices. The general proscription of § 703 is that an employer may not discriminate against either blacks or whites in either hiring or promotion. An employer may not, without violating Title VII, simply decide for itself or in agreement with its employees to have a racially balanced work force and displace employees of any race to make room for employees of another race. Even without displacing any present employees, Title VII would forbid quota hiring or promotion such as reserving every third vacancy or promotion for a black, or for a white for that matter. And if this is the case, it must be wholly untenable to permit a court to enter a consent decree requiring conduct that would violate Title VII.

Under the present law, an employer may adopt or be ordered to adopt racially discriminatory hiring or promotion practices favoring actual or putative employees of a particular race only as a remedy for its own prior discriminatory practices disfavoring members of that race. The Court's opinion pays scant attention to this necessary predicate for race conscious practice, whether judicially imposed or voluntarily adopted, favoring one race over another. Instead, the Court seeks to avoid the issue whether the consent decree at issue violates the Title VII rights of nonminority employees by limiting itself to holding that § 706(g), which deals with remedies for violations of Title VII, has no application whatsoever to agreements and consent decrees such as are involved in this case. In so doing, the Court not only ignores the fact that the intervenors in this case have never restricted their claims to those based on § 706(g), see Pet. for Cert., at 7, but also adopts an unduly restricted view of the place of § 706(g) in the statute.

The Court purports to find support for its position in *Weber*, but this is not my understanding of that case. There, it was clear that the company had been hiring only those craft workers with prior experience and that the craft unions had excluded blacks. Hence, the company's craft workers were almost totally white. The company and the union negotiated a contract to break this discriminatory pattern, and we held that there was no violation of Title VII. But the company's prior discriminatory conduct provided the predicate for a temporary remedy favoring black employees. The *Weber* opinion stated that the agreement was a voluntary, private, race-conscious effort to abolish traditional patterns of segregation and hierarchy, and held that the agreement was not an undue attempt to overcome these racial barriers. The case did not hold that without such a predicate, an employer, alone or in agreement with the union, may adopt race conscious hiring practices without violating Title VII.

Under current law, an employer who litigates a Title VII case to judgment cannot lose unless it is proved that it has discriminated within the meaning of § 703. It is therefore untenable to conclude, as the Court does, that a district court may nevertheless enter a consent decree ordering an employer to hire or promote on a racial basis in a way that could not be ordered after a contested trial. Title VII was not enacted to protect employers against themselves, but to protect applicants and employees from racially discriminatory practices. There is no statutory authority for concluding that if an employer desires to discriminate against a white applicant or employee on racial grounds he may do so without violating Title VII but may not be ordered to do so if he objects. In either case, the harm to the discriminatee is the same, and there is no justification for such conduct other than as a permissible remedy for prior racial discrimination practiced by the employer involved. The Court should not deprecate that requirement and in effect make Title VII's proscription a one-way racial street, thus disserving the goal of ending racial discrimination in this country.

I agree with Justice Rehnquist that the consent decree in this case was not immune from examination under § 706(g). I also agree with Justice Brennan's opinion in *Local 28* that in Title VII cases enjoining discriminatory practices and granting relief only to victims of past discrimination is the general rule, with relief for non-victims being reserved for particularly egregious conduct that a District Court concludes cannot be cured by injunctive relief alone. I disagree, however, with the Court in this case that we need not decide whether the remedy conforms to the limitations of § 706(g); and for the reasons stated below, I am convinced that the remedy imposed in this case exceeds the limits of a permissible remedy for the discriminatory practices that were recited in the consent decree and that required a remedy consonant with the provisions of Title VII. Even if I agreed that § 706(g) is beside the point in the case, the Court itself concedes that there are limits to the racial discrimination that an employer and a union may voluntarily visit upon non-minorities, *ante*, at n. 10, and those limits, which in my view run parallel to those placed on judicial decrees by § 706(g), are exceeded in this case.

This case primarily concerns promotions in the Cleveland Fire Department. Reciting that there had been discrimination against minorities in promotions, but identifying no actual victims of such discrimination, the decree required that those proved eligible for promotion after examination be divided into two lists, one list comprising minority eligibles and one list made up of non-minority eligibles. Promotions were to proceed two at a time, one from the minority list and one from the non-minority roster. Of course, the names on each list were ranked in accordance with seniority and examination results. It is also evident, and it is conceded, that under the decree minority eligibles would be promoted who would not have been promoted had the lists been merged; that is, black and Hispanic firefighters who would have ranked below white firefighters eligible for promotion actually displaced and were preferred over the latter on a strictly racial basis. This kind of leapfrogging minorities over senior and better qualified whites is an impermissible remedy under Title VII, just as in *Stotts* laying off senior whites was an excessive remedy for an employer's prior discrimination, and just as in *Wygant*, the Equal Protection Clause did not require or permit the layoff of white teachers in order to maintain a particular racial balance in the work force. * * * None of the racially preferred blacks in the present case was shown to have been a victim of discriminatory promotion practices; and none of the whites denied promotion was shown to have been responsible or in any way implicated in the discriminatory practices recited in the decree. In view of the burdens placed on non-minority employees by the decree, the remedy imposed was inequitable, could not have been ordered after a trial, and is no more valid when agreed to by the employer but contested by those who claim their right not to be discriminated against on racial grounds.

JUSTICE REHNQUIST, with whom THE CHIEF JUSTICE joins, dissenting.

Petitioners challenge a District Court decree that ordered preferential treatment in promotions for minority firefighters at the expense of nonminority firefighters who would have been promoted under the City's existing seniority system. There was no requirement in the decree that the minority beneficiaries have been victims of the City's allegedly discriminatory policies. One would have thought that this question was governed by our opinion only two Terms ago in Firefighters v. Stotts, 467 U.S. 561, 578–579, 104 S.Ct. 2576, 2588, 81 L.Ed.2d 483 (1984), in which we said:

> "If individual members of a plaintiff class demonstrate that they have been actual victims of the discriminatory practice, they may be awarded competitive seniority and given their rightful place on the seniority roster. This much is clear from Franks v. Bowman Transportation Co., 424 U.S. 747 [96 S.Ct. 1251, 47 L.Ed.2d 444] (1976), and Teamsters v. United States, [431 U.S. 324 [97 S.Ct. 1843, 52 L.Ed.2d 396] (1977)]. *Teamsters,* however, also made clear that mere membership in the disadvantaged class is insufficient to warrant a seniority award; each individual must prove that the discriminatory practice had an impact on him * * *. Here, there was no finding that any of the blacks protected from layoff had been a victim of discrimination and no award of competitive seniority to any of them. Nor had the parties in formulating the consent decree purported to identify any specific employee entitled to particular relief other than those listed in the exhibits attached to the decree. It therefore seems to us that in light of *Teamsters,* the Court of Appeals imposed on the parties as an adjunct of settlement something that could not have been ordered had the case gone to trial and the plaintiffs proved that a pattern or practice of discrimination existed."

But a majority of the Court today holds that the District Court properly entered the decree in this case because it was a consent decree, whereas *Stotts* involved the *modification* of a consent decree. The Court apparently views a consent decree as one which may be structured almost entirely by the parties, even though the statute which the decree enforces may not authorize any such relief, and, indeed, may actually prohibit such relief.

To support its distinction of a "consent decree" from other types of decrees, the Court finds it necessary to implicitly repudiate language in the two of our cases most closely in point—*Stotts,* supra, and Railway Employees v. Wright, 364 U.S. 642, 81 S.Ct. 368, 5 L.Ed.2d 349 (1961), in favor of citations to cases that simply do not speak to the question presently before us, or to cases that deal only with the question of whether a party that has consented to a decree may nonetheless challenge it. For the decree entered by the District Court in this case was a consent decree only between Vanguards of Cleveland, an organization of black and Hispanic firefighters employed by the City of Cleveland, and the City; the petitioner union, representing the majority of firefighters, never consented to the decree at all. And the Court's suggestion in Part IV of its opinion that "the consent decree entered here does not bind Local 93 to do or not to do anything," verges on the pharisaical; the decree *does* bind the City of Cleveland to give preferential promotions to minority firemen who have not been shown to be the victims of discrimination in such a way that nonminority union members who would otherwise have received these promotions are obviously injured.

In Firefighters v. Stotts, supra, 467 U.S., at 576, n. 9, 104 S.Ct., at 2587, the Court said:

> " '[T]he District Court's authority to adopt a consent decree comes only from the statute which the decree is intended to enforce,' not from the parties' consent to the decree. Railway Employees v. Wright, 364 U.S. 642, 651 [81 S.Ct., at 373] (1961)."

The observations of Justice Harlan's opinion for the Court in Railway Employees v. Wright, supra, can best be understood when set forth more fully than it was in *Stotts:*

> "In a case like this the District Court's authority to adopt a consent decree comes only from the statute which the decree is intended to enforce. Frequently of course the terms arrived at by the parties are accepted without change by the adopting court. But just as the adopting court is free to reject agreed-upon terms as not in furtherance of statutory objectives, so must it be free to modify the terms of a consent decree when a change in law brings those terms in conflict with statutory objectives. In short, it was the Railway Labor Act, and only incidentally the parties, that the District Court served in entering the consent decree now before us." 364 U.S., at 651, 81 S.Ct., at 373.

The Court simply ignores the statements in *Stotts* and *Wright,* in favor of bare citations to various other cases and a commentator. But when we ask precisely what these "other cases" say about the issue presented in this case, the answer is virtually nothing. No one would dispute that a consent decree requires the consent of the parties, and that a consent decree may be an effective way to settle a law suit. But the Court's excerpt from Moore's Federal Practice, ante, at ___, does not aid its conclusions, and is in fact quite misleading in what it fails to include; the full sentence from Moore's reads thus:

> "But the fact remains that the judgment is not an *inter partes* contract; the Court is not properly a recorder of contracts, but is an organ of government constituted to make judicial decisions and when it has rendered a consent judgment it has made an adjudication." 1B J. Moore, J. Lucas, & T. Currier, Moore's Federal Practice ¶ 0.409[5], pp. 330–331 (1984).

The two prior cases principally relied upon by the Court are Pacific R. Co. v. Ketchum, 11 Otto 289, 101 U.S. 289, 25 L.Ed. 932 (1880), and Swift & Co. v. United States, 276 U.S. 311, 48 S.Ct. 311, 72 L.Ed. 587 (1928). No language from either of these cases is quoted to explain their citation for the proposition that "a federal court is not necessarily barred from entering a consent decree merely because the decree provides broader relief than the court could have awarded after a trial." *Ketchum* was an equity receivership case in federal court only by reason of diversity of citizenship, and there was no question of a federal statute or federal policy to be enforced other than the policy of hearing and deciding cases in which the parties could show diversity jurisdiction. The long and short of the Court's discussion of consent decrees in *Swift & Co.,* supra, is that while some of the paragraphs of a decree might be objectionable if they had been challenged on appeal, "the defendants by their consent lost the opportunity of raising the question on appeal." 276 U.S., at 328, 48 S.Ct., at 315. Here, of course, petitioner intervened in the District Court pursuant to Fed.Rule Civ.Proc. 24(a), and never in any way consented to the entry of the decree.*

Thus the Court abandons considered and repeated observations in *Stotts* and *Wright,* not because they are inconsistent with any cases recognizing that parties may agree in a consent decree to relief broader than a court would otherwise be authorized to impose, but because the statements in *Wright* and *Stotts* are inconsistent with the result which the Court is apparently determined to reach in this case. I would adhere to these well considered observations, which properly restrain the scope of a consent decree to that of implementation of the federal statute pursuant to which the decree is entered.

Even if I did not regard the above quoted language in *Stotts* as controlling, I would conclude—just as five Members of this Court did only two years ago in another passage from *Stotts*—that § 706(g) bars the relief which the District Court granted in this case. The critical language of § 706(g)—which is the only section of Title VII dealing with the Court's remedial authority—is:

> "No order of the Court shall require the * * * promotion of an individual * * * if such individual was refused * * * advancement * * * for any reason other than discrimination on account of race, color, religion, sex, or national origin * * *"

The Court today concludes that this language "simply is not concerned with obligations that are created by voluntary action of employers or unions." This conclusion rests on the premise that the overrid-

* The Court asserts that a three-party dispute may be ended by consent decree even if one of the parties refuses to tender his consent. It cites Zipes v. Trans World Airlines, Inc., 455 U.S. 385, 102 S.Ct. 1127, 71 L.Ed.2d 234 (1982), and Kirkland v. New York State Dept. of Correctional Services, 711 F.2d 1117 (CA2 1983), cert. denied, 465 U.S. 1005 (1984), for this novel proposition. But neither of these cases make statements anywhere as broad as the proposition for which they are cited. *Zipes* involved a union that was "permitted" to intervene nine years after the litigation had commenced, after a judgment on liability had been entered and affirmed, and just before a settlement on the remedy was reached. *Kirkland* involved permissive intervention under Fed.Rule Civ.Proc. 24(b), see 711 F.2d, at 1124, which of course raises significantly different equitable concerns from intervention as of right. An intervenor as of right becomes a party to the action because "the disposition of the action may as a practical matter impair or impede his ability to protect his interest," Fed.Rule Civ.Proc. 24(a), whereas a permissive intervenor typically becomes a party only to ward off the potential effects of *stare decisis.* The question whether a party or an intervenor as of right may block the entry of a consent decree is therefore left unresolved by these cases. Of course, *a judicial decree* to which the parties agree may be entered over the objections of an intervenor as of right; but the question is whether such a decree is properly called a "consent decree" or a coercive court order.

ing policy behind § 706(g) is to prevent courts from unduly interfering with the managerial discretion of employers or unions. Focusing on this single policy, the Court finds it natural to conclude that § 706(g) was intended *not* to apply to consent decrees to which an employer consents. But this construction flies in the face of the language just quoted, which by its terms deals with *any* "order" of the Court in a Title VII case. It also conflicts with the legislative history cited in *Stotts* which shows that § 706(g) serves the additional policy of protecting innocent nonminority employees from the evil of court-sanctioned racial quotas. * * *

The Court today repeats arguments made by the dissenters in *Stotts,* which did not command a majority two years ago, and also suggests that a restriction such as § 706(g) should apparently be narrowly construed because, if it were to limit the authority of the Court to enter a consent decree, it might hinder settlement of some cases. It would be just as sensible to say that the Norris-LaGuardia Act should be narrowly construed so as not to prevent a consent decree which would violate the Norris-LaGuardia Act since more consent decrees might be entered under that construction of the statute. Congress undoubtedly expressed a preference for conciliation in cases arising under Title VII, but not conciliation reached by violation of its express statutory commands.

Legislative history can obviously be mustered in support of the Court's interpretation of § 706(g), just as *Stotts* referred to the legislative history supporting the construction adopted in that case. But while the legislative history may be fairly apportioned among both sides, the language of the statutes is clear. *No order of the Court* shall require promotion of an individual whose failure to receive promotion was for a reason other than discrimination prohibited by the statute. Here the failure of the District Court to make any finding that the minority firemen who will receive preferential promotions were the victims of racial discrimination requires us to conclude on this record that the City's failure to advance them was *not* "on account of race, color, religion, sex, or national origin."

Section 706(g) is the one section in the entire text of Title VII which deals with the sort of relief which a court may order in a Title VII case; it is simply incredible that the Court today virtually reads it out of existence. Surely an order of the Court entered by the consent of the parties does not become any less an order of the Court; in the very words of the sentence quoted by the Court from 1B J. Moore, J. Lucas, & T. Currier, Moore's Federal Practice ¶ 0.409[5], pp. 330–331 (1984):

> "[T]he fact remains that the judgment is not an *inter partes* contract; the court is not properly a recorder of contracts, but is an organ of government constituted to make judicial decisions and when it has rendered a consent judgment it has made an adjudication."

Just as it has made an adjudication, it has also entered an order, and that order is by definition subject to the prohibitions of § 706(g).

NOTES AND PROBLEMS FOR DISCUSSION

1. It is important to keep in mind the very limited scope of the Court's holding in *Local 93.* Six members agreed with the conclusion that § 706(g) does not limit the ability of a court to approve a voluntarily adopted consent decree that contains race-conscious affirmative relief. But as footnote 8 makes clear, the Court did not rule on four other important issues, i.e., (1) the constitutional limits on race-conscious relief voluntarily adopted by a public employer; (2) the degree to which § 703 limits the authority of a public employer to voluntarily implement race-based relief in a form other than a consent decree; (3) whether the consent decree in the instant case violated the § 703 rights of nonminority individuals; or (4) the nature of the showing a public employer would have to make to defend its affirmative action from attack under § 703. Wasn't the first of these questions, however, answered in *Wygant?* Isn't *Weber* dispositive of the second issue? On remand, won't the trial court find *Weber* similarly instructive as to the union's § 703 claim? And don't the opinions in *Weber, Wygant* and *Local 128* suggest how the Court might resolve the fourth issue?

2. Do you agree with the way in which the Court distinguished the instant case from *Stotts?* When you consider that court approval was necessary to the enforcement of the consent decree in *Local 93,* do you remain convinced that the level of judicial involvement was less significant than where the trial court, as in *Stotts,* modified a consent decree over the objections of a party? Should, as the majority concluded, the validity of race-conscious consent decrees be governed by *Wygant* and *Weber* rather than by *Local 128?*

Part V

THE PRESIDENTIAL RESPONSE TO DISCRIMINATION: EXECUTIVE ORDERS

Over the past four decades, U.S. Presidents, beginning with Franklin D. Roosevelt in 1941, have issued Executive Orders designed to eliminate employment discrimination by the federal government and private employers who have contracts with the federal government, or their subcontractors. The most comprehensive current Order is Executive Order No. 11246,[a] as amended by Order No. 11375[b] and No. 12086,[c] which imposes nondiscrimination and affirmative action obligations on federal government contractors and their subcontractors with respect to race, color, religion, national origin and sex.[d] These dual obligations are contained within an equal opportunity clause that the Order requires all contracting federal agencies to include in their contracts with private employers. The Order also assigns to the Secretary of Labor the task of administering and enforcing its provisions and the authority to promulgate rules and regulations deemed necessary to achieve its purposes. The Secretary has delegated this responsibility to the Office of Federal Contract Compliance Programs (OFCCP),[e] which has issued an extensive body of regulations[f] to implement the requirements of the Order.

The OFCCP regulations provide that all contracts and subcontracts exceeding $10,000 must contain an equal opportunity clause that prohibits the contractors from discriminating and requires them to take affirmative action to ensure against discrimination on the basis of race, color, religion, sex and national origin. Contractors and subcontractors having 50 or more employees and a nonconstruction prime contract or subcontract worth $50,000 or more also must develop a written affirmative action plan for each of their establishments within 120 days of the

[a] 30 F.R. 12319, 3 CFR 339 (1965).

[b] 32 F.R. 14303, 3 CFR 684 (1967).

[c] 43 F.R. 46501 (1978).

[d] Executive Order No. 11478, 34 F.R. 12985, 3 CFR 841 (1969), declares that it is the policy of the federal government to prohibit employment discrimination in each executive department and agency based on race, color, religion, sex, national origin, handicap, or age. It requires all such departments and agencies to establish and maintain an "affirmative program of equal employment opportunity" and directs the EEOC to issue rules and regulations deemed necessary to implement the Order. The extension of Title VII to federal employees by the Equal Employment Opportunity Act of 1972, however, has significantly reduced the importance of this Order. Similarly, the impact of Executive Order No. 11141, 29 F.R. 2477, 3 CFR 179 (1964), which states that federal contractors and their subcontractors shall not discriminate on the basis of age, was sharply curtailed by the subsequent enactment of the Age Discrimination in Employment Act.

[e] 41 CFR 60–1.2 (1981).

[f] 41 CFR 60–1 et seq. (1981).

commencement of the contract. These plans must analyse the utilization of minority workers for each job category and include specific goals and timetables designed to increase minority participation in those categories in which minority workers are currently "underutilized". Underutilization is defined as "having fewer minorities or women in a particular job group than would reasonably be expected by their availability." These nonconstruction contractors also are required to submit annual reports of the results of such programs to the OFCCP.

Construction contractors and subcontractors holding federal or federally assisted contracts in excess of $10,000 also must engage in affirmative action. To obtain such a contract, the applicant's bid must include an affirmative action clause requiring the contractor to comply with goals and timetables for minority and female employment set periodically, according to the geographic location of the construction project, by the OFCCP.[g] Alternatively, if a construction contractor or subcontractor is participating in a "Hometown Plan" [h] approved by the Department of Labor, it must comply with the affirmative action requirements, including goals and timetables, set forth in that plan. And, if the Hometown Plan doesn't extend to women, the contractor must establish its own goals for female representation, at a level at least as high as the goals established by the OFCCP.[i]

Order No. 11246 provides that the Secretary of Labor can receive and investigate complaints by employees and job applicants of a contractor's failure to comply with its nondiscrimination or affirmative action obligations, or engage in such an investigation on its own initiative. The Secretary also is given the authority to impose a variety of penalties for noncompliance, including publishing the names of nonconforming contractors, recommending to the EEOC that proceedings be instituted under Title VII, requesting the Attorney General to bring suit to enforce the Order in cases of actual or threatened substantial violations of the contractual equal opportunity clause, directing the contracting agency to cancel, terminate or suspend the contract or any portion thereof, or debarring the noncomplying contractor from entering into further government contracts until the contractor has satisfied the Secretary that it will abide by the provisions of the Order. The Secretary must make reasonable efforts to secure compliance by conciliation, mediation and persuasion before requesting enforcement action by the Attorney General or cancelling or surrending a contract. A hearing is required before the Secretary can debar a contractor and may be granted before any other sanction is imposed. The OFCCP regulations, pursuant to a delegation of authority by the Secretary, set forth in detail the procedures used to administer and enforce the Order.

[g] 41 CFR 60–4.2, 4.3 (1981).

[h] A program voluntarily developed by unions and contractors, in consultation with minority group representatives, whereby these groups agree to commit themselves to goals and timetables for minority participation in all construction projects in a designated geographical area.

[i] 41 CFR 60–4.4(b) (1981).

As a consequence of the emphasis placed on administrative enforcement of Executive Order No. 11246, the courts have played a limited role in defining the equal employment obligations of government contractors. Most of the cases involving the Order have addressed two questions: (1) the availability of a private right of action to enforce the provisions of the Order; and (2) the relationship between the Order and the requirements of Title VII and the Due Process Clause of the Fifth Amendment.

CONTRACTORS ASSOCIATION OF EASTERN PENNSYLVANIA v. SECRETARY OF LABOR

United States Court of Appeals, Third Circuit, 1971.
442 F.2d 159, cert. denied, 404 U.S. 854, 92 S.Ct. 98, 30 L.Ed.2d 95.

* * *

The complaint challenges the validity of the Philadelphia Plan, promulgated by the federal defendants under the authority of Executive Order No. 11246. That Plan is embodied in two orders issued by officials of the United States Department of Labor, dated June 27, 1969 and September 23, 1969, respectively. * * * In summary, they require that bidders on any federal or federally assisted construction contracts for projects in a five-county area around Philadelphia, the estimated total cost of which exceeds $500,000, shall submit an acceptable affirmative action program which includes specific goals for the utilization of minority manpower in six skilled crafts: ironworkers, plumbers and pipefitters, steamfitters, sheetmetal workers, electrical workers, and elevator construction workers.

* * * The Executive Order empowers the Secretary of Labor to issue rules and regulations necessary and appropriate to achieve its purpose. On June 27, 1969 Assistant Secretary of Labor Fletcher issued an order implementing the Executive Order in the five-county Philadelphia area. The order required bidders, prior to the award of contracts, to submit "acceptable affirmative action" programs "which shall include specific goals of minority manpower utilization." The order contained a finding that enforcement of the "affirmative action" requirement of Executive Order No. 11246 had posed special problems in the construction trades. Contractors and subcontractors must hire a new employee complement for each job, and they rely on craft unions as their prime or sole source for labor. The craft unions operate hiring halls. "Because of the exclusionary practices of labor organizations," the order finds "there traditionally has been only a small number of Negroes employed in these * * * trades." The June 27, 1969 order provided that the Area Coordinator of the Office of Federal Contract Compliance, in conjunction with the federal contracting and administering agencies in the Philadelphia area, would determine definite standards for specific goals in a contractor's affirmative action program. After such standards were determined, each bidder would be required to commit itself to specific goals for minority manpower

utilization. The order set forth factors to be considered in determining definite standards, including:

"1) The current extent of minority group participation in the trade.

2) The availability of minority group persons for employment in such trade.

3) The need for training programs in the area and/or the need to assure demand for those in or from existing training programs.

4) The impact of the program upon the existing labor force."

Acting pursuant to the June 29, 1969 order, representatives of the Department of Labor held public hearings in Philadelphia on August 26, 27 and 28, 1969. On September 23, 1969, Assistant Secretary Fletcher made findings with respect to each of the listed factors and ordered that the following ranges be established as the standards for minority manpower utilization for each of the designated trades in the Philadelphia area for the following four years:

Identification of Trade	**Range of Minority Group Employment**			
	Until 12/31/70	**for 1971**	**for 1972**	**for 1973**
Ironworkers	5%–9%	11%–15%	16%–20%	22%–26%
Plumbers & Pipefitters	5%–8%	10%–14%	15%–19%	20%–24%
Steamfitters	5%–8%	11%–15%	15%–19%	20%–24%
Sheetmetal workers	4%–8%	9%–13%	14%–18%	19%–23%
Electrical workers	4%–8%	9%–13%	14%–18%	19%–23%
Elevator construction workers	4%–8%	9%–13%	14%–18%	19%–23%

The order of September 23, 1969 specified that on each invitation to bid each bidder would be required to submit an affirmative action program. The order further provided:

"4. No bidder will be awarded a contract unless his affirmative action program contains goals falling within the range set forth * * * above. * * *

* * *

6. The purpose of the contractor's commitment to specific goals as to minority manpower utilization is to meet his affirmative action obligations under the equal opportunity clause of the contract. This commitment is not intended and shall not be used to discriminate against any qualified applicant or employee. Whenever it comes to the bidder's attention that the goals are being used in a discriminatory manner, he must report it to the Area Coordinator of the Office of Federal Contract Compliance of the U. S. Department of Labor in order that appropriate sanction proceedings may be instituted.

* * *

8. The bidder agrees to keep such records and file such reports relating to the provisions of this order as shall be required by the contracting or administering agency."

In November, 1969, the General State Authority of the Commonwealth of Pennsylvania issued invitations to bid for the construction of an earth dam on Marsh Creek in Chester County, Pennsylvania. Although this dam is a Commonwealth project, part of the construction cost, estimated at over $3,000,000 is to be funded by federal monies under a program administered by the Department of Agriculture. The Secretary of Agriculture, one of the federal defendants, as a condition for payment of federal financial assistance for the project, required the inclusion in each bid of a Philadelphia Plan Commitment in compliance with the order of September 23, 1969. On November 14, 1969, the General State Authority issued an addendum to the original invitation for bids requiring all bidders to include such a commitment in their bids. It is alleged and not denied that except for the requirement by the Secretary of Agriculture that the Philadelphia Plan Commitment be included, the General State Authority would not have imposed such a requirement on bidders.

The Association consists of more than eighty contractors in the five-county Philadelphia area who regularly employ workers in the six specified crafts, and who collectively perform more than $150,000,000 of federal and federally assisted construction in that area annually. Each of the contractor plaintiffs is a regular bidder on federal and federally assisted construction projects. The complaint was filed prior to the opening of bids on the Marsh Creek dam. It sought injunctive relief against the inclusion of a Philadelphia Plan Commitment requirement in the invitation for bids. By virtue of a stipulation that the General State Authority would issue a new and superseding invitation for bids if the district court held the Plan to be unlawful, the parties agreed that bids could be received without affecting the justiciability of the controversy. Bids were received on January 7, 1970. One of the intervening contractor plaintiffs submitted a low bid and appeared at the time of the district court decision to be entitled to an award of the contract.

The complaints of the Association and the Contractors refer to the fact that the Comptroller General of the United States has opined that the Philadelphia Plan Commitment is illegal and that disbursement of federal funds for the performance of a contract containing such a promise will be treated as unlawful. The plaintiffs point out that the withholding of funds after a contractor has commenced performance would have catastrophic consequences, since contractors depend upon progress payments, and are in no position to complete their contracts without such payments. They allege that the Philadelphia Plan is illegal and void for the following reasons:

1. It is action by the Executive branch not authorized by the constitution or any statute and beyond Executive power.
2. It is inconsistent with Title VII of the Civil Rights Act of 1964.

3. It is inconsistent with Title VI of the Civil Rights Act of 1964.

* * *

5. It is substantively inconsistent with and was not adopted in procedural accordance with Executive Order No. 11246.
6. It violates due process because
   a) it requires contradictory conduct impossible of consistent attainment;
   b) it unreasonably requires contractors to undertake to remedy an evil for which the craft unions, not they, are responsible;
   c) it arbitrarily and without basis in fact singles out the five-county Philadelphia area for discriminatory treatment without adequate basis in fact or law; and
   d) it requires quota hiring in violation of the Fifth Amendment.

* * *

The plaintiffs contend that the Philadelphia Plan is social legislation of local application enacted by the Executive without the benefit of statutory or constitutional authority. They point out, probably correctly, that the Plan imposes on the successful bidder on a project of the Commonwealth of Pennsylvania record keeping and hiring practices which violate Pennsylvania law.[14] If the Plan was adopted pursuant to a valid exercise of presidential power its provisions would, of course, control over local law. But, say the plaintiffs, where there is neither statutory authorization nor constitutional authority for the Executive action, no substantive federal requirements may be imposed upon a contract between the Commonwealth and its contractor.

* * *

The limitations of Executive power have rarely been considered by the courts. One of those rare instances is Youngstown Sheet & Tube Co. v. Sawyer, 343 U.S. 579, 72 S.Ct. 863, 96 L.Ed. 1153 (1952). From the six concurring opinions and one dissenting opinion in that case, the most significant guidance for present purposes may be found in that of Justice Jackson:

"We may well begin by a somewhat oversimplified grouping of practical situations in which a President may doubt, or others may challenge, his powers, and by distinguishing roughly the legal consequences of this factor of relativity.

1. When the President acts pursuant to an express or implied authorization of Congress, his authority is at its maximum, for it

14. The Pennsylvania Human Relations Act, specifically prohibits an employer from keeping any record of or using any form of application with respect to the race, color, religion, ancestry, sex or national origin of an applicant for employment. The Act also prohibits the use of a quota system for employment based on the same criteria. The record keeping prohibition may be of limited force due to certain requirements of Title VII of the Civil Rights Act of 1964. Moreover, we do not know how the Pennsylvania courts or the Pennsylvania Human Relations Commission would react to a scheme of "benign" quota hiring.

includes all that he possesses in his own right plus all that Congress can delegate. In these circumstances, and in these only, may he be said (for what it may be worth) to personify the federal sovereignty. If his act is held unconstitutional under these circumstances, it usually means that the Federal Government as an undivided whole lacks power. A seizure executed by the President pursuant to an Act of Congress would be supported by the strongest of presumptions and the widest latitude of judicial interpretation, and the burden of persuasion would rest heavily on any who might attack it.

2. When the President acts in absence of either a congressional grant or denial of authority, he can only rely upon his own independent powers, but there is a zone of twilight in which he and Congress may have concurrent authority, or in which its distribution is uncertain. Therefore, congressional inertia, indifference or quiescence may sometimes, at least as a practical matter, enable, if not invite, measures on independent presidential responsibility. In this area, any actual test of power is likely to depend on the imperatives of events and contemporary imponderables rather than on abstract theories of law.

3. When the President takes measures incompatible with the expressed or implied will of Congress, his power is at its lowest ebb, for then he can rely only upon his own constitutional powers minus any constitutional powers of Congress over the matter. Courts can sustain exclusive presidential control in such a case only by disabling the Congress from acting upon the subject. Presidental claim to a power at once so conclusive and preclusive must be scrutinized with caution, for what is at stake is the equilibrium established by our constitutional system."

Plaintiffs contend that the Philadelphia Plan is inconsistent with the will of Congress expressed in several statutes. We deal with these statutory contentions hereinafter. Thus for the moment we may set to one side consideration of Justice Jackson's third category, and turn to category (1), action expressly or impliedly authorized, and category (2), action in which the President has implied power to act in the absence of congressional preemption. To determine into which category the Philadelphia Plan falls a review of Executive Orders in the field of fair employment practices is helpful.

The first such order, Executive Order No. 8802, was signed by President Roosevelt on June 25, 1941. It established in the Office of Production Management a Committee on Fair Employment Practice, and it required that all Government contracting agencies include in all defense contracts a covenant not to discriminate against any worker because of race, creed, color, or national origin. The order contained no specific statutory reference, and describes the action "as a prerequisite to the successful conduct of our national defense production effort." In December 1941 Congress enacted "An Act to expedite the prosecution of the war effort," and on December 27, 1941, pursuant to that Act the

President issued Executive Order No. 9001 which granted to the War and Navy Departments and the Maritime Commission broad contracting authority. This order among other provisions stated that a non-discrimination clause would be deemed incorporated by reference in all such contracts. On May 27, 1943, Executive Order No. 8802 was amended by Executive Order No. 9346 which established in the Office for Emergency Management of the Executive Office of the President a Committee on Fair Employment Practice. This order required the antidiscrimination clause in all government contracts rather than in defense contracts only. Still, the order was quite clearly bottomed on the President's war mobilization powers and was by its terms directed toward enhancing the pool of workers available for defense production.

On December 18, 1945, President Truman signed Executive Order No. 9664, which continued the Committee established by Executive Orders Nos. 8802 and 9346 "for the periods and subject to the conditions stated in the National War Agencies Appropriation Act, 1946. On February 2, 1951, the President signed Executive Order No. 10210, which transferred to the Department of Defense the contracting powers referred to in Executive Order No. 9001. The order continued the provision that a non-discrimination clause would be deemed incorporated by reference in all defense contracts. It referenced the First War Powers Act, 1941, as amended. By a subsequent series of Executive Orders, Executive Order No. 10210 was extended to other Government agencies engaged in defense related procurement. On December 3, 1951 the President signed Executive Order No. 10308, creating the Committee on Government Contract Compliance, which was charged with the duty of obtaining compliance with the non-discrimination contract provisions. The statutory authorities referenced in Executive Order No. 10308 are the Defense Production Act of 1950 and 31 U.S.C. § 691.[34] Reference to the Defense Production Act of 1950 shows that the President was still acting, pursuant to his national defense powers, to assure maximum utilization of available manpower.

President Eisenhower on August 13, 1953, by Executive Order No. 10479 revoked Executive Order No. 10308 and transferred the compliance functions of the Committee on Government Contract Compliance to the Government Contract Committee. In this order for the first time there is no mention of defense production. For the first time the Committee is authorized to receive complaints of violations, and to conduct activities not directly related to federal procurement. On September 3, 1954, by Executive Order No. 10557 the required form of Government contract provision was revised. The new provision was much more specific, required the imposition of the contractor's obligation on his subcontractors, and required the posting of appropriate notices. The Eisenhower orders, while they did not refer to defense production and did authorize the Compliance Committee to encourage

34. This latter reference is to the source of appropriations for salaries and expenses for committee members and staff. It appears in numerous subsequent Executive Orders, but has no significance other than fiscal.

nondiscrimination outside the field of Government contracts, were still restricted in direct application to federal government procurement. While the orders do not contain any specific statutory reference other than the appropriations statute, they would seem to be authorized by the broad grant of procurement authority with respect to Titles 40 and 41. No less than in the case of defense procurement it is in the interest of the United States in all procurement to see that its suppliers are not over the long run increasing its costs and delaying its programs by excluding from the labor pool available minority workmen. In the area of Government procurement Executive authority to impose non-discrimination contract provisions falls in Justice Jackson's first category: action pursuant to the express or implied authorization of Congress.

Executive Order No. 10925 signed by President Kennedy on March 6, 1961, among other things enlarged the notice requirements and specified that the President's Committee on Equal Employment Opportunity could by rule, regulation or order impose sanctions for violation. Coverage still extended only to federal government contracts. Significantly for purposes of this case, however, the required contract language was amended to add the provision:

> "The Contractor will take affirmative action to ensure that applicants are employed, and that employees are treated during employment, without regard to their race, creed, color, or national origin."

The Philadelphia Plan is simply a refined approach to this "affirmative action" mandate. Applied to federal procurement the affirmative action clause is supported by the same Presidential procurement authority that supports the non-discrimination clause generally.

The most significant change in the Executive Order program for present purposes occurred on June 22, 1963 when the President signed Executive Order No. 11114, which amended Executive Order No. 10925 by providing that the same non-discrimination contract provisions heretofore required in all federal procurement contracts must also be included in all federally assisted construction contracts. By way of Executive Order No. 11246 issued in 1965, President Johnson transferred to the Secretary of Labor the functions formerly specified in Executive Order Nos. 10925 and 11114, and he continued both the affirmative action requirement and the coverage of federally assisted construction contracts.

While all federal procurement contracts must include an affirmative action covenant, the coverage on federally assisted contracts has been extended to construction contracts only. This choice is significant, for it demonstrates that the Presidents were not attempting by the Executive Order program merely to impose their notions of desirable social legislation on the states wholesale. Rather, they acted in the one area in which discrimination in employment was most likely to affect the cost and the progress of projects in which the federal government had both financial and completion interests. In direct procurement the federal government has a vital interest in assuring that the largest possible pool of qualified manpower be available for the accomplishment of its projects. It has the identical interest with respect to federally assisted construction projects. When the Congress authorizes an appropriation for a program of federal assistance, and authorizes the Executive branch to implement the program by arranging for assistance to specific projects, in the absence of specific statutory regulations it must be deemed to have granted to the President a general authority to act for the protection of federal interests. In the case of Executive Order Nos. 11246 and 11114 three Presidents have acted by analogizing federally assisted construction to direct federal procurement. If such action has not been authorized by Congress (Justice Jackson's first category), at the least it falls within the second category. If no congressional enactments prohibit what has been done, the Executive action is valid. Particularly is this so when Congress, aware of Presidential action with respect to federally assisted construction projects since June of 1963, has continued to make appropriations for such projects. We conclude, therefore, that unless the Philadelphia Plan is prohibited by some other congressional enactment, its inclusion as a pre-condition for federal assistance was within the implied authority of the President and his designees. We turn, then to a consideration of the statutes on which plaintiffs rely.

Plaintiffs suggest that by enacting Title VII of the Civil Rights Act of 1964, * * * Congress occupied the field. The express reference in that statute to Executive Order No. 10925 or any other Executive Order prescribing fair employment practices for Government contractors, 42 U.S.C. § 2000e–8(d), indicates, however, that Congress contemplated continuance of the Executive Order program. Moreover we have held that the remedies established by Title VII are not exclusive.

But while Congress has not prohibited Presidential action in the area of fair employment on federal or federally assisted contracts, the Executive is bound by the express prohibitions of Title VII. The argument most strenuously advanced against the Philadelphia Plan is that it requires action by employers which violates the Act. Plaintiffs point to § 703(j). * * * The Plan requires that the contractor establish specific goals for utilization of available minority manpower in six trades in the five-county area. Possibly an employer could not be compelled, under the authority of Title VII, to embrace such a program, although § 703(j) refers to percentages of minorities in an area work force rather than percentages of minority tradesmen in an available trade work force. We do not meet that issue here, however, for the source of the required contract provision is Executive Order No. 11246. Section 703(j) is a limitation only upon Title VII not upon any other remedies, state or federal.

Plaintiffs, and more particularly the union amici, contend that the Plan violates Title VII because it interferes with a bona fide seniority system. * * * The unions, it is said, refer men from the hiring halls on the basis of seniority, and the Philadelphia Plan interferes with this arrangement since few minority tradesmen have high seniority. Just as with § 703(j), however, § 703(h) is a limitation only upon Title VII, not upon any other remedies.

Plaintiffs contend that the Plan, by imposing remedial quotas, requires them to violate the basic prohibitions of Section 703(a). * * * Because the Plan requires that the contractor agree to specific goals for minority employment in each of the six trades and requires a good faith effort to achieve those goals, they argue, it requires (1) that they refuse to hire some white tradesmen, and (2) that they classify their employees by race, in violation of § 703(a). This argument rests on an overly simple reading both of the Plan and of the findings which led to its adoption.

The order of September 23, 1969 contained findings that although overall minority group representation in the construction industry in the five-county Philadelphia area was thirty per cent, in the six trades representation was approximately one per cent. It found, moreover, that this obvious underrepresentation was due to the exclusionary practices of the unions representing the six trades. It is the practice of building contractors to rely on union hiring halls as the prime source for employees. The order made further findings as to the availability of qualified minority tradesmen for employment in each trade, and as to the impact of an affirmative action program with specific goals upon the existing labor force. The Department of Labor found that contractors could commit to the specific employment goals "without adverse impact on the existing labor force." Some minority tradesmen could be recruited, in other words, without eliminating job opportunities for white tradesmen.

To read § 703(a) in the manner suggested by the plaintiffs we would have to attribute to Congress the intention to freeze the status quo and to foreclose remedial action under other authority designed to overcome existing evils. We discern no such intention either from the language of the statute or from its legislative history. Clearly the Philadelphia Plan is color-conscious. Indeed the only meaning which can be attributed to the "affirmative action" language which since March of 1961 has been included in successive Executive Orders is that Government contractors must be color-conscious. Since 1941 the Executive Order program has recognized that discriminatory practices exclude available minority manpower from the labor pool. * * * It has been said respecting Title VII that "Congress did not intend to freeze an entire generation of Negro employees into discriminatory patters that existed before the Act." * * * We reject the contention that Title VII prevents the President acting through the Executive Order program from attempting to remedy the absence from the Philadelphia construction labor of minority tradesmen in key trades.

What we have said about Title VII applies with equal force to Title VI of the Civil Rights Act of 1964. That Title prohibits racial and other discrimination in any program or activity receiving federal financial assistance. This general prohibition against discrimination cannot be construed as limiting Executive authority in defining appropriate affirmative action on the part of a contractor.

We hold that the Philadelphia Plan does not violate the Civil Rights Act of 1964.

* * *

The absence of a judicial finding of past discrimination is also legally irrelevant. The Assistant Secretary acted not pursuant to Title VII but pursuant to the Executive Order. Regardless of the cause, exclusion from the available labor pool of minority tradesmen is likely to have an adverse effect upon the cost and completion of construction projects in which the federal government is interested. Even absent a finding that the situation found to exist in the five-county area was the result of deliberate past discrimination, the federal interest in improving the availability of key tradesmen in the labor pool would be the same. While a court must find intentional past discrimination before it can require affirmative action under 42 U.S.C. § 2000e–5(g), that section imposes no restraint upon the measures which the President may require of the beneficiaries of federal assistance. The decision of his designees as to the specific affirmative action which would satisfy the local situation * * * was not prohibited by 42 U.S.C. § 2000e–5(g).

The plaintiffs argue that the affirmative action mandate of § 202 of Executive Order No. 11246 is limited by the more general requirement in the same section, "The contractor will not discriminate against any employee or applicant for employment because of race, creed, color, or national origin." They contend that properly construed the affirmative action referred to means only policing against actual present discrimination, not action looking toward the employment of specific numbers of minority tradesmen.

Section 201 of the Executive Order provides:

> "The Secretary of Labor shall be responsible for the administration of Parts II [Government contracts] and III [federal assistance] of this Order and shall adopt such rules and regulations and issue such orders as he deems necessary and appropriate to achieve the purposes thereof."

Acting under this broad delegation of authority the Labor Department in a series of orders of local application made it clear that it interpreted "affirmative action" to require more than mere policing against actual present discrimination. Administrative action pursuant to an Executive Order is invalid and subject to judicial review if beyond the scope of the Executive Order. But the courts should give more than ordinary deference to an administrative agency's interpretation of an Executive Order or regulation which it is charged to administer. The Attorney General has issued an opinion that the Philadelphia Plan is valid, and the President has continued to acquiesce in the interpretation of the Executive Order made by his designee. The Labor Department interpretation of the affirmative action clause must, therefore, be deferred to by the courts.

* * *

Plaintiffs urge that the Plan violates the Due Process Clause of the Fifth Amendment in several ways.

First, they allege that it imposes on the contractors contradictory duties impossible of attainment. This impossibility arises, they say, because the Plan requires both an undertaking to seek achievement of specific goals of minority employment and an undertaking not to discriminate against any qualified applicant or employee, and because a decision to hire any black employee necessarily involves a decision not to hire a qualified white employee. This is pure sophistry. The findings in the September 23, 1969 order disclose that the specific goals may be met, considering normal employee attrition and anticipated growth in the industry, without adverse effects on the existing labor force. According to the order the construction industry has an essentially transitory labor force and is often in short supply in key trades. The complaint does not allege that these findings misstate the underlying facts.

Next the plaintiffs urge that the Plan is arbitrary and capricious administrative action, in that it singles out the contractors and makes them take action to remedy the situation created by acts of past discrimination by the craft unions. They point to the absence of any proceedings under Title VII against the offending unions, and urge that they are being discriminated against. This argument misconceives the source of the authority for the affirmative action program. Plaintiffs are not being discriminated against. They are merely being invited to bid on a contract with terms imposed by the source of the funds. The affirmative action covenant is no different in kind than other covenants specified in the invitation to bid. The Plan does not impose a punishment for past misconduct. It exacts a covenant for present performance.

Some amici urge that selection of the five-county Philadelphia area was arbitrary and capricious and without basis in fact. The complaint contains a conclusive allegation to this effect. No supporting facts are alleged. It is not alleged, for example, that the specific goals for minority manpower utilization would be different if more or fewer counties were to be included in the September 23, 1969 order. The union amici do question the findings made by the Assistant Secretary of Labor, but the complaint, fairly read, does not put these findings in issue. We read the allegation with respect to the five-county area as putting in issue the legal authority of the Secretary to impose a specific affirmative action requirement in any separate geographic area. The simple answer to this contention is that federally assisted construction contracts are performed at specific times and in specific places. What is appropriate affirmative action will vary according to the local manpower conditions prevailing at the time.

Finally, the plaintiffs urge that the specific goals specified by the Plan are racial quotas prohibited by the equal protection aspect of the Fifth Amendment. The Philadelphia Plan is valid Executive action designed to remedy the perceived evil that minority tradesmen have not been included in the labor pool available for the performance of construction projects in which the federal government has a cost and performance interest. The Fifth Amendment does not prohibit such action.

* * *

The judgment of the district court will be affirmed.

NOTES AND PROBLEMS FOR DISCUSSION

1. Does the court's discussion in *Contractors Association* of the equal protection challenge to the Philadelphia Plan survive the Supreme Court's ruling in Fullilove v. Klutznick, supra? Is a determination by a federal agency as to the existence of and appropriate response to discrimination in the construction industry entitled to the same deference accorded to a Congressional finding? See note 1 following Fullilove, supra.

2. What is the impact of the Supreme Court's opinion in United Steelworkers v. Weber, supra, on the relationship between the affirmative action component of Order No. 11246 and Title VII? Does the nonvolitional nature of this obligation, as exemplified by the Philadelphia Plan, distinguish it from the affirmative action plan that survived a Title VII attack in *Weber*? Is the Order's affirmative action requirement consistent with the *Weber* majority's desire to reduce governmental interference with private business? On the other hand, what about the connection, noted in Justice Rehnquist's dissenting opinion in *Weber*, between the implementation of the craft training program and the pressure directed at Kaiser, a federal contractor, by the OFCCP to increase minority representation in its craft positions? See Note, Doing Good the Wrong Way: The Case for Delimiting Presidential Power Under Executive Order No. 11,246, 33 Vand.L.Rev. 921 (1980).

3. Do you agree with the court in the principal case that § 703(j) only limits the remedies available under Title VII? If not, must you conclude that the affirmative action requirements of Order No. 11246 violate Title VII? Assuming *arguendo* that the *Weber* Court's interpretation of § 703(j) would not be controlling, do decisions such as Association Against Discrimination v. City of Bridgeport, supra, nevertheless suggest that involuntarily imposed affirmative action requirements may not be prohibited by § 703(j)?

4. Is the *Contractors Association* court's analysis of the applicability of § 703(h) consistent with International Brotherhood of Teamsters v. United States, supra? Suppose the Secretary of Labor claims that a contractor did not comply with the antidiscrimination clause in the federal contract. Could the contractor justify its action on the ground that it acted pursuant to a facially neutral, bona fide seniority plan? While the Third Circuit Court of Appeals in *Contractors Association* rejected the extension of the terms of § 703(h) to Order No. 11246, in UNITED STATES v. EAST TEXAS MOTOR FREIGHT SYSTEM, INC., 564 F.2d 179 (5th Cir. 1977), the court disagreed, reasoning that a President could not make unlawful—or penalize—that which Congress had declared to be lawful. How does this aspect of *Contractors Association* comport with cases such as Johnson v. Ryder Truck Lines, 575 F.2d 471 (4th Cir. 1978),

cert. denied, 440 U.S. 979, 99 S.Ct. 1785, 60 L.Ed.2d 239 (1979), that hold that the § 703(h) defense should be read into 42 U.S.C. § 1981? See United States v. Trucking Management, Inc., 662 F.2d 36 (D.C.Cir.1981). For a discussion of this and other issues relating to the relationship between Title VII and Executive Order No. 11246, see Brody, Congress, The President and Federal Equal Employment Policymaking: A Problem In Separation of Powers, 60 B.U.L.Rev. 239 (1980).

5. Executive Order No. 11246 does not explicitly provide for a private right of action against a government contractor for an alleged failure to satisfy its nondiscrimination or affirmative action obligations and most courts have refused to recognize such an implied right of action. See Weise v. Syracuse University, 522 F.2d 397 (2d Cir. 1975), Farkas v. Texas Instrument, Inc., 375 F.2d 629 (5th Cir. 1967), cert. denied 389 U.S. 977, 88 S.Ct. 480, 19 L.Ed.2d 471. On the other hand, the courts do permit private actions against the federal officials charged with enforcing the Order where the plaintiff seeks relief in the nature of *mandamus*—i.e., to compel performance of the non-discretionary aspects of administrative action required by the Order. See Legal Aid Society v. Brennan, 608 F.2d 1319 (9th Cir. 1979), cert. denied, 447 U.S. 921, 100 S.Ct. 3010, 65 L.Ed.2d 1112 (1980). Moreover, individual relief is available in an enforcement action brought by the Justice Department pursuant to § 209(a)(2) of Executive Order No. 11246. While the Order authorizes the Justice Department to bring an "appropriate proceeding * * * including the enjoining * * * of organizations, individuals, or groups who * * * prevent directly or indirectly, compliances with the provisions of this Order * * *", it has been held to support a suit for back pay for employee victims of discrimination by government contractors. See United States v. Duquesne Light Co., 423 F.Supp. 507 (W.D.Pa.1976).

For a comprehensive description and analysis of the history of administrative and judicial enforcement efforts under Executive Order # 11246 see Jones, Twenty-One Years of Affirmative Action: The Motivation of the Administrative Enforcement Process Under The Executive Order 11246 As Amended, 59 Chi.K.L.Rev. 67 (1982).

APPENDIX

TITLE VII OF CIVIL RIGHTS ACT OF 1964

42 U.S.C.A. § 2000e et seq.

§ 701. Definitions

For the purposes of this Title—

(a) The term "person" includes one or more individuals, governments, governmental agencies, political subdivisions, labor unions, partnerships, associations, corporations, legal representatives, mutual companies, joint-stock companies, trusts, unincorporated organizations, trustees, trustees in cases under Title 11, or receivers.

(b) The term "employer" means a person engaged in an industry affecting commerce who has fifteen or more employees for each working day in each of twenty or more calendar weeks in the current or preceding calendar year, and any agent of such a person, but such term does not include (1) the United States, a corporation wholly owned by the Government of the United States, an Indian tribe, or any department or agency of the District of Columbia subject by statute to procedures of the competitive service (as defined in section 2102 of Title 5), or (2) a bona fide private membership club (other than a labor organization) which is exempt from taxation under section 501(c) of Title 26, except that during the first year after March 24, 1972, persons having fewer than twenty-five employees (and their agents) shall not be considered employers.

(c) The term "employment agency" means any person regularly undertaking with or without compensation to procure employees for an employer or to procure for employees opportunities to work for an employer and includes an agent of such a person.

(d) The term "labor organization" means a labor organization engaged in an industry affecting commerce, and any agent of such an organization, and includes any organization of any kind, any agency, or employee representation committee, group, association, or plan so engaged in which employees participate and which exists for the purpose, in whole or in part, of dealing with employers concerning grievances, labor disputes, wages, rates of pay, hours, or other terms or conditions of employment, and any conference, general committee, joint or system board, or joint council so engaged which is subordinate to a national or international labor organization.

(e) A labor organization shall be deemed to be engaged in an industry affecting commerce if (1) it maintains or operates a hiring hall or hiring office which procures employees for an employer or procures for employees opportunities to work for an employer, or (2) the number of its members (or, where it is a labor organization composed of other labor organizations or their representatives, if the aggregate number of the members of such other labor organization) is (A) twenty-five or more during the first year after March 24, 1972, or (B) fifteen or more thereafter, and such labor organization—

(1) is the certified representative of employees under the provisions of the National Labor Relations Act, as amended, or the Railway Labor Act, as amended;

(2) although not certified, is a national or international labor organization or a local labor organization recognized or acting as the representative of employees of an employer or employers engaged in an industry affecting commerce; or

(3) has chartered a local labor organization or subsidiary body which is representing or actively seeking to represent employees of employers within the meaning of paragraph (1) or (2); or

(4) has been chartered by a labor organization representing or actively seeking to represent employees within the meaning of paragraph (1) or (2) as the local or subordinate body through which such employees may enjoy membership or become affiliated with such labor organization; or

(5) is a conference, general committee, joint or system board, or joint council subordinate to a national or international labor organization, which includes a labor organization engaged in an industry affecting commerce within the meaning of any of the preceding paragraphs of this subsection.

(f) The term "employee" means an individual employed by an employer, except that the term "employee" shall not include any person elected to public office in any State or political subdivision of any State by the qualified voters thereof, or any person chosen by such officer to be on such officer's personal staff, or an appointee on the policy making level or an immediate adviser with respect to the exercise of the constitutional or legal powers of the office. The exemption set forth in the preceding sentence shall not include employees subject to the civil service laws of a State government, governmental agency or political subdivision.

(g) The term "commerce" means trade, traffic, commerce, transportation, transmission, or communication among the several States; or between a State and any place outside thereof; or within the District of Columbia, or a possession of the United States; or between points in the same State but through a point outside thereof.

(h) The term "industry affecting commerce" means any activity, business, or industry in commerce or in which a labor dispute would hinder or obstruct commerce or the free flow of commerce and includes any activity or industry "affecting commerce" within the meaning of the Labor-Management Reporting and Disclosure Act of 1959, and further includes any governmental industry, business, or activity.

(i) The term "State" includes a State of the United States, the District of Columbia, Puerto Rico, the Virgin Islands, American Samoa, Guam, Wake Island, the Canal Zone, and Outer Continental Shelf lands defined in the Outer Continental Shelf Lands Act.

(j) The term "religion" includes all aspects of religious observance and practice, as well as belief, unless an employer demonstrates that he is unable to reasonably accommodate to an employee's or prospective employee's religious observance or practice without undue hardship on the conduct of the employer's business.

(k) The terms "because of sex" or "on the basis of sex" include, but are not limited to, because of or on the basis of pregnancy, childbirth, or related medical conditions; and women affected by pregnancy, childbirth, or related medical conditions shall be treated the same for all employment-related purposes, including receipt of benefits under fringe benefit programs, as other persons not so affected but similar in their ability or inability to work, and nothing in section 703(h) of this Act shall be interpreted to permit otherwise. This subsection shall not require an employer to pay for health insurance benefits for abortion, except where the life of the mother would be endangered if the fetus were carried to term, or except where medical complications have arisen from an abortion: *Provided*, That nothing herein shall preclude an employer from providing abortion benefits or otherwise affect bargaining agreements in regard to abortion.

§ 702. Exemptions

This Title shall not apply to an employer with respect to the employment of aliens outside any State, or to a religious corporation, association, educational institution, or society with respect to the employment of individuals of a particular religion to perform work connected with the carrying on by such corporation, association, educational institution, or society of its activities.

§ 703. Unlawful employment practices

(a) It shall be an unlawful employment practice for an employer—

(1) to fail or refuse to hire or to discharge any individual, or otherwise to discriminate against any individual with respect to his compensation, terms, conditions, or privileges of employment, because of such individual's race, color, religion, sex, or national origin; or

(2) to limit, segregate, or classify his employees or applicants for employment in any way which would deprive or tend to deprive any individual of employment opportunities or otherwise adversely af-

fect his status as an employee, because of such individual's race, color, religion, sex, or national origin.

(b) It shall be an unlawful employment practice for an employment agency to fail or refuse to refer for employment, or otherwise to discriminate against, any individual because of his race, color, religion, sex, or national origin, or to classify or refer for employment any individual on the basis of his race, color, religion, sex, or national origin.

(c) It shall be an unlawful employment practice for a labor organization—

(1) to exclude or to expel from its membership, or otherwise to discriminate against, any individual because of his race, color, religion, sex, or national origin;

(2) to limit, segregate, or classify its membership or applicants for membership, or to classify or fail or refuse to refer for employment any individual, in any way which would deprive or tend to deprive any individual of employment opportunities, or would limit such employment opportunities or otherwise adversely affect his status as an employee or as an applicant for employment, because of such individual's race, color, religion, sex, or national origin; or

(3) to cause or attempt to cause an employer to discriminate against an individual in violation of this section.

(d) It shall be an unlawful employment practice for any employer, labor organization, or joint labor-management committee controlling apprenticeship or other training or retraining, including on-the-job training programs to discriminate against any individual because of his race, color, religion, sex, or national origin in admission to, or employment in, any program established to provide apprenticeship or other training.

(e) Notwithstanding any other provision of this subchapter, (1) it shall not be an unlawful employment practice for an employer to hire and employ employees, for an employment agency to classify, or refer for employment any individual, for a labor organization to classify its membership or to classify or refer for employment any individual, or for an employer, labor organization, or joint labor-management committee controlling apprenticeship or other training or retraining programs to admit or employ any individual in any such program, on the basis of his religion, sex, or national origin in those certain instances where religion, sex, or national origin is a bona fide occupational qualification reasonably necessary to the normal operation of that particular business or enterprise, and (2) it shall not be an unlawful employment practice for a school, college, university, or other educational institution or institution of learning to hire and employ employees of a particular religion if such school, college, university, or other educational institution or institution of learning is, in whole or in substantial part, owned, supported, controlled, or managed by a particular religion or by a particular religious corporation, association, or society, or if the curriculum of such school, college, university, or other educational institution or institution of learning is directed toward the propagation of a particular religion.

(f) As used in this subchapter, the phrase "unlawful employment practice" shall not be deemed to include any action or measure taken by an employer, labor organization, joint labor-management committee, or employment agency with respect to an individual who is a member of the Communist Party of the United States or of any other organization required to register as a Communist-action or Communist-front organization by final order of the Subversive Activities Control Board pursuant to the Subversive Activities Control Act of 1950.

(g) Notwithstanding any other provision of this subchapter, it shall not be an unlawful employment practice for an employer to fail or refuse to hire and employ any individual for any position, for an employer to discharge any individual from any position, or for an employment agency to fail or refuse to refer any individual for employment in any position, or for a labor organization to fail or refuse to refer any individual for employment in any position, if—

(1) the occupancy of such position, or access to the premises in or upon which any part of the duties of such position is performed or is to be performed, is subject to any requirement imposed in the interest of the national security of the United States under any security program in effect pursuant to or administered under any statute of the United States or any Executive order of the President; and

(2) such individual has not fulfilled or has ceased to fulfill that requirement.

(h) Notwithstanding any other provision of this subchapter, it shall not be an unlawful employment practice for an employer to apply different standards of compensation, or different terms, conditions, or privileges of employment pursuant to a bona fide seniority or merit system, or a system which measures earnings by quantity or quality of production or to employees who work in different locations, provided that such differences are not the result of an intention to discriminate because of race, color, religion, sex, or national origin, nor shall it be an unlawful employment practice for an employer to give and to act upon the results of any professionally developed ability test provided that such test, its administration or action upon the results is not designed, intended or used to discriminate because of race, color, religion, sex or national origin. It shall not be an unlawful employment practice under this subchapter for any employer to differentiate upon the basis of sex in determining the amount of the wages or compensation paid or to be paid to employees of such employer if such differentiation is authorized by the provisions of the Equal Pay Act.

(i) Nothing contained in this subchapter shall apply to any business or enterprise on or near an Indian reservation with respect to any publicly announced employment practice of such business or enterprise under which a preferential treatment is given to any individual because he is an Indian living on or near a reservation.

(j) Nothing contained in this subchapter shall be interpreted to require any employer, employment agency, labor organization, or joint labor-management committee subject to this subchapter to grant preferential treatment to any individual or to any group because of the race, color, religion, sex, or national origin of such individual or group on account of an imbalance which may exist with respect to the total number or percentage of persons of any race, color, religion, sex, or national origin employed by any employer, referred or classified for employment by any employment agency or labor organization, admitted to membership or classified by any labor organization, or admitted to, or employed in, any apprenticeship or other training program, in comparison with the total number or percentage of persons of such race, color, religion, sex, or national origin in any community, State, section, or other area, or in the available work force in any community, State, section, or other area.

§ 704. Other unlawful employment practices

(a) It shall be an unlawful employment practice for an employer to discriminate against any of his employees or applicants for employment, for an employment agency, or joint labor-management committee controlling apprenticeship or other training or retraining, including on-the-job training programs, to discriminate against any individual, or for a labor organization to discriminate against any member thereof or applicant for membership, because he has opposed any practice made an unlawful employment practice by this Title, or because he has made a charge, testified, assisted, or participated in any manner in an investigation, proceeding, or hearing under this Title.

(b) It shall be an unlawful employment practice for an employer, labor organization, employment agency, or joint labor-management committee controlling apprenticeship or other training or retraining, including on-the-job training programs, to print or publish or cause to be printed or published any notice or advertisement relating to employment by such an employer or membership in or any classification or referral for employment by such a labor organization, or relating to any classification or referral for employment by such an employment agency, or relating to admission to, or employment in, any program established to provide apprenticeship or other training by such a joint labor-management committee, indicating any preference, limitation, specification, or discrimination, based on race, color, religion, sex, or national origin, except that such a notice or advertisement may indicate a preference, limitation, specification, or discrimination based on religion, sex, or national origin when religion, sex, or national origin is a bona fide occupational qualification for employment.

§ 705. Equal Employment Opportunity Commission

(a) There is hereby created a Commission to be known as the Equal Employment Opportunity Commission, which shall be composed of five members, not more than three of whom shall be members of the same political party. Members of the Commission shall be appointed by the President by and with the advice and consent of the Senate for a term of five years. Any individual chosen to fill a vacancy shall be appointed only for the unexpired term of the member whom he shall succeed, and all members of the Commission shall continue to serve until their successors are appointed and qualified, except that no such member of the Commission shall continue to serve (1) for more than sixty days when the Congress is in session unless a nomination to fill such vacancy shall have been submitted to the Senate, or (2) after the adjournment sine die of the session of the Senate in which such nomination was submitted. The President shall designate one member to serve as Chairman of the Commission, and one member to serve as Vice Chairman. The Chairman shall be responsible on behalf of the Commission for the administrative operations of the Commission, and, except as provided in subsection (b) of this section, shall appoint, in accordance with the provisions of Title 5 governing appointments in the competitive service, such officers, agents, attorneys, administrative law judges, and employees as he deems necessary to assist it in the performance of its functions and to fix their compensation in accordance with the provisions of chapter 51 and subchapter III of chapter 53 of Title 5, relating to classification and General Schedule pay rates: *Provided*, That assignment, removal, and compensation of administrative law judges shall be in accordance with sections 3105, 3344, 5372, and 7521 of Title 5.

(b)(1) There shall be a General Counsel of the Commission appointed by the President, by and with the advice and consent of the Senate, for a term of four years. The General Counsel shall have responsibility for the conduct of litigation as provided in sections 706 and 707 of this Act. The General Counsel shall have such other duties as the Commission may prescribe or as may be provided by law and shall concur with the Chairman of the Commission on the appointment and supervision of regional attorneys. The General Counsel of the Commission on the effective date of this Act shall continue in such position and perform the functions specified in this subsection until a successor is appointed and qualified.

(2) Attorneys appointed under this section may, at the direction of the Commission, appear for and represent the Commission in any case in court, provided that the Attorney General shall conduct all litigation to which the Commission is a party in the Supreme Court pursuant to this Title.

(c) A vacancy in the Commission shall not impair the right of the remaining members to exercise all the powers of the Commission and three members thereof shall constitute a quorum.

(d) The Commission shall have an official seal which shall be judicially noticed.

(e) The Commission shall at the close of each fiscal year report to the Congress and to the President concerning the action it has taken and the moneys it has disbursed. It shall make such further reports on the cause of and means of eliminating discrimination and such recommendations for further legislation as may appear desirable.

(f) The principal office of the Commission shall be in or near the District of Columbia, but it may meet or exercise any or all its powers at any other place. The Commission may establish such regional or State offices as it deems necessary to accomplish the purpose of this Title.

(g) The Commission shall have power—

(1) to cooperate with and, with their consent, utilize regional, State, local, and other agencies, both public and private, and individuals;

(2) to pay to witnesses whose depositions are taken or who are summoned before the Commission or any of its agents the same witness and mileage fees as are paid to witnesses in the courts of the United States;

(3) to furnish to persons subject to this subchapter such technical assistance as they may request to further their compliance with this Title or an order issued thereunder;

(4) upon the request of (i) any employer, whose employees or some of them, or (ii) any labor organization, whose members or some of them, refuse or threaten to refuse to cooperate in effectuating the provisions of this Title, to assist in such effectuation by conciliation or such other remedial action as is provided by this Title;

(5) to make such technical studies as are appropriate to effectuate the purposes and policies of this Title and to make the results of such studies available to the public;

(6) to intervene in a civil action brought under section 706 of this Act by an aggrieved party against a respondent other than a government, governmental agency or political subdivision.

(h) The Commission shall, in any of its educational or promotional activities, cooperate with other departments and agencies in the performance of such educational and promotional activities.

(i) All officers, agents, attorneys, and employees of the Commission shall be subject to the provisions of section 7324 of Title 5, notwithstanding any exemption contained in such section.

§ 706. Enforcement provisions

(a) The Commission is empowered, as hereinafter provided, to prevent any person from engaging in any unlawful employment practice as set forth in section 703 or 704 of this Act.

(b) Whenever a charge is filed by or on behalf of a person claiming to be aggrieved, or by a member of the Commission, alleging that an employer, employment agency, labor organization, or joint labor-management committee controlling apprenticeship or other training or retraining, including on-the-job training programs, has engaged in an unlawful employment practice, the Commission shall serve a notice of the charge (including the date, place and circumstances of the alleged unlawful employment practice) on such employer, employment agency, labor organization, or joint labor-management committee (hereinafter referred to as the "respondent") within ten days, and shall make an investigation thereof. Charges shall be in writing under oath or affirmation and shall contain such information and be in such form as the Commission requires. Charges shall not be made public by the Commission. If the Commission determines after such investigation that there is not reasonable cause to believe that the charge is true, it shall dismiss the charge and promptly notify the person claiming to be aggrieved and the respondent of its action. In determining whether reasonable cause exists, the Commission shall accord substantial weight to final findings and orders made by State or local authorities in proceedings commenced under State or local law pursuant to the requirements of subsections (c) and (d) of this section. If the Commission determines after such investigation that there is reasonable cause to believe that the charge is true, the Commission shall endeavor to eliminate any such alleged unlawful employment practice by informal methods of conference, conciliation, and persuasion. Nothing said or done during and as a part of such informal endeavors may be made public by the Commission, its officers or employees, or used as evidence in a subsequent proceeding without the written consent of the persons concerned. Any person who makes public information in violation of this subsection shall be fined not more than $1,000 or imprisoned for not more than one year, or both. The Commission shall make its determination on reasonable cause as promptly as possible and, so far as practicable, not later than one hundred and twenty days from the filing of the charge or, where applicable under subsection (c) or (d) of this section, from the date upon which the Commission is authorized to take action with respect to the charge.

(c) In the case of an alleged unlawful employment practice occurring in a State, or political subdivision of a State, which has a State or local law prohibiting the unlawful employment practice alleged and establishing or authorizing a State or local authority to grant or seek relief from such practice or to institute criminal proceedings with respect thereto upon receiving notice thereof, no charge may be filed under subsection (b) of this section by the person aggrieved before the expiration of sixty days after proceedings have been commenced under the State or local law, unless such proceedings have been earlier terminated, provided that such sixty-day period shall be extended to one hundred and twenty days during the first year after the effective date of such State or local law. If any requirement for the commencement of such proceedings is imposed by a State or local authority other than a requirement of the filing of a written and signed statement of the facts upon which the proceeding is based, the proceeding shall be deemed to have been commenced for the purposes of this subsection at the time such statement is sent by registered mail to the appropriate State or local authority.

(d) In the case of any charge filed by a member of the Commission alleging an unlawful employment practice occurring in a State or political subdivision of a State which has a State or local law prohibiting the practice alleged and establishing or authorizing a State or local authority to grant or seek relief from such practice or to institute criminal proceedings with respect thereto upon receiving notice thereof, the Commission shall, before taking any action with respect to such charge, notify the appropriate State or local officials and, upon request, afford them a reasonable time, but not less than sixty days (provided that such sixty-day period shall be extended to one hundred and twenty days during the first year after the effective day of such State or local law), unless a shorter period is requested, to act under such State or local law to remedy the practice alleged.

(e) A charge under this section shall be filed within one hundred and eighty days after the alleged unlawful employment practice occurred and notice of the charge (including the date, place and circumstances of the alleged unlawful employment practice) shall be served upon the person against whom such charge is made within ten days thereafter, except that in a case of an unlawful employment practice with respect to which the person aggrieved has initially instituted proceedings with a State or local agency with authority to grant or seek relief from such practice or to institute criminal proceedings with respect thereto upon receiving notice thereof, such charge shall be filed by or on behalf of the person aggrieved within three hundred days after the alleged unlawful employment practice occurred, or within thirty days after receiving notice that the State or local agency has terminated the proceedings under the State or local law, whichever is earlier, and a copy of such charge shall be filed by the Commission with the State or local agency.

(f)(1) If within thirty days after a charge is filed with the Commission or within thirty days after expiration of any period of reference under subsection (c) or (d) of this section, the Commission has been unable to secure from the respondent a conciliation agreement acceptable to the Commission, the Commission may bring a civil action against any respondent not a government, governmental agency, or political subdivision named in the charge. In the case of a respondent which is a government, governmental agency, or political subdivision, if the Commission has been unable to secure from the respondent a conciliation agreement acceptable to the Commission, the Commission shall take no further action and shall refer the case to the Attorney General who may bring a civil action against such respondent in the appropriate United States district court. The person or persons aggrieved shall have the right to intervene in a civil action brought by the Commission or the Attorney General in a case involving a government, governmental agency, or political subdivision. If a charge filed with the Commission pursuant to subsection (b) of this section is dismissed by the Commission, or if within one hundred and eighty days from the filing of such charge or the expiration of any period of reference under subsection (c) or (d) of this section, whichever is later, the Commission has not filed a civil action under this section or the Attorney General has not filed a civil action in a case involving a government, governmental agency, or political subdivision, or the Commission has not entered into a conciliation agreement to which the person aggrieved is a party, the Commission, or the Attorney General in a case involving a government, governmental agency, or political subdivision, shall so notify the person aggrieved and within ninety days after the giving of such notice a civil action may be brought against the respondent named in the charge (A) by the person claiming to be aggrieved or (B) if such charge was filed by a member of the Commission, by any person whom the charge alleges was aggrieved by the alleged unlawful employment practice. Upon application by the complainant and in such circumstances as the court may deem just, the court may appoint an attorney for such complainant and may authorize the commencement of the action without the payment of fees, costs, or security. Upon timely application, the court may, in its discretion, permit the Commission, or the Attorney General in a case involving a government, governmental agency, or political subdivision, to intervene in such civil action upon certification that the case is of general public importance. Upon request, the court may, in its discretion, stay further proceedings for not more than sixty days pending the termination of State or local proceedings described in subsection (c) or (d) of this section or further efforts of the Commission to obtain voluntary compliance.

(2) Whenever a charge is filed with the Commission and the Commission concludes on the basis of a preliminary investigation that prompt judicial action is necessary to carry out the purposes of this Act, the Commission, or the Attorney General in a case involving a government, governmental agency, or political subdivision, may bring an action for appropriate temporary or preliminary relief pending final disposition of such charge. Any temporary restraining order or other order granting preliminary or temporary relief shall be issued in accordance with rule 65 of the Federal Rules of Civil Procedure. It shall be the duty of a court having jurisdiction over proceedings under this section to assign cases for hearing at the earliest practicable date and to cause such cases to be in every way expedited.

(3) Each United States district court and each United States court of a place subject to the jurisdiction of the United States shall have jurisdiction of actions brought under this Title. Such an action may be brought in any judicial district in the State in which the unlawful employment practice is alleged to have been committed, in the judicial

district in which the employment records relevant to such practice are maintained and administered, or in the judicial district in which the aggrieved person would have worked but for the alleged unlawful employment practice, but if the respondent is not found within any such district, such an action may be brought within the judicial district in which the respondent has his principal office. For purposes of sections 1404 and 1406 of Title 28, the judicial district in which the respondent has his principal office shall in all cases be considered a district in which the action might have been brought.

(4) It shall be the duty of the chief judge of the district (or in his absence, the acting chief judge) in which the case is pending immediately to designate a judge in such district to hear and determine the case. In the event that no judge in the district is available to hear and determine the case, the chief judge of the district, or the acting chief judge, as the case may be, shall certify this fact to the chief judge of the circuit (or in his absence, the acting chief judge) who shall then designate a district or circuit judge of the circuit to hear and determine the case.

(5) It shall be the duty of the judge designated pursuant to this subsection to assign the case for hearing at the earliest practicable date and to cause the case to be in every way expedited. If such judge has not scheduled the case for trial within one hundred and twenty days after issue has been joined, that judge may appoint a master pursuant to rule 53 of the Federal Rules of Civil Procedure.

(g) If the court finds that the respondent has intentionally engaged in or is intentionally engaging in an unlawful employment practice charged in the complaint, the court may enjoin the respondent from engaging in such unlawful employment practice, and order such affirmative action as may be appropriate, which may include, but is not limited to, reinstatement or hiring of employees, with or without back pay (payable by the employer, employment agency, or labor organization, as the case may be, responsible for the unlawful employment practice), or any other equitable relief as the court deems appropriate. Back pay liability shall not accrue from a date more than two years prior to the filing of a charge with the Commission. Interim earnings or amounts earnable with reasonable diligence by the person or persons discriminated against shall operate to reduce the back pay otherwise allowable. No order of the court shall require the admission or reinstatement of an individual as a member of a union, or the hiring, reinstatement, or promotion of an individual as an employee, or the payment to him of any back pay, if such individual was refused admission, suspended, or expelled, or was refused employment or advancement or was suspended or discharged for any reason other than discrimination on account of race, color, religion, sex, or national origin or in violation of section 704 of this Act.

(h) The provisions of sections 101 to 115 of Title 29 shall not apply with respect to civil actions brought under this section.

(i) In any case in which an employer, employment agency, or labor organization fails to comply with an order of a court issued in a civil action brought under this section, the Commission may commence proceedings to compel compliance with such order.

(j) Any civil action brought under this section and any proceedings brought under subsection (i) of this section shall be subject to appeal as provided in sections 1291 and 1292, Title 28.

(k) In any action or proceeding under this Title the court, in its discretion, may allow the prevailing party, other than the Commission or the United States, a reasonable attorney's fee as part of the costs, and the Commission and the United States shall be liable for costs the same as a private person.

§ 707. Civil Actions by Attorney General

(a) Whenever the Attorney General has reasonable cause to believe that any person or group of persons is engaged in a pattern or practice of resistance to the full enjoyment of any of the rights secured by this Title, and that the pattern or practice is of such a nature and is intended to deny the full exercise of the rights herein described, the Attorney General may bring a civil action in the appropriate district court of the United States by filing with it a complaint (1) signed by him (or in his absence the Acting Attorney General), (2) setting forth facts pertaining to such pattern or practice, and (3) requesting such relief, including an application for a permanent or temporary injunction, restraining order or other order against the person or persons responsible for such pattern or practice, as he deems necessary to insure the full enjoyment of the rights herein described.

(b) The district courts of the United States shall have and shall exercise jurisdiction of proceedings instituted pursuant to this section, and in any such proceeding the Attorney General may file with the clerk of such court a request that a court of three judges be convened to hear and determine the case. Such request by the Attorney General shall be accompanied by a certificate that, in his opinion, the case is of general public importance. A copy of the certificate and request for a three-judge court shall be immediately furnished by such clerk to the chief judge of the circuit (or in his absence, the presiding circuit judge of the circuit) in which the case is pending. Upon receipt of such request it shall be the duty of the chief judge of the circuit or the presiding circuit judge, as the case may be, to designate immediately three judges in such circuit, of whom at least one shall be a circuit judge and another of whom shall be a district judge of the court in which the proceeding was instituted, to hear and determine such case, and it shall be the duty of the judges so designated to assign the case for hearing at the earliest practicable date, to participate in the hearing and determination thereof, and to cause the case to be in every way expedited. An appeal from the final judgment of such court will lie to the Supreme Court.

In the event the Attorney General fails to file such a request in any such proceeding, it shall be the duty of the chief judge of the district (or in his absence, the acting chief judge) in which the case is pending immediately to designate a judge in such district to hear and determine the case. In the event that no judge in the district is available to hear and determine the case, the chief judge of the district, or the acting chief judge, as the case may be, shall certify this fact to the chief judge of the circuit (or in his absence, the acting chief judge) who shall then designate a district or circuit judge of the circuit to hear and determine the case.

It shall be the duty of the judge designated pursuant to this section to assign the case for hearing at the earliest practicable date and to cause the case to be in every way expedited.

(c) Effective two years after March 24, 1972, the functions of the Attorney General under this section shall be transferred to the Commission, together with such personnel, property, records, and unexpended balances of appropriations, allocations, and other funds employed, used, held, available, or to be made available in connection with such functions unless the President submits, and neither House of Congress vetoes, a reorganization plan pursuant to chapter 9 of Title 5, inconsistent with the provisions of this subsection. The Commission shall carry out such functions in accordance with subsections (d) and (e) of this section.

(d) Upon the transfer of functions provided for in subsection (c) of this section, in all suits commenced pursuant to this section prior to the date of such transfer, proceedings shall continue without abatement, all court orders and decrees shall remain in effect, and the Commission shall be substituted as a party for the United States of America, the Attorney General, or the Acting Attorney General, as appropriate.

(e) Subsequent to March 24, 1972, the Commission shall have authority to investigate and act on a charge of a pattern or practice of discrimination, whether filed by or on behalf of a person claiming to be aggrieved or by a member of the Commission. All such actions shall be conducted in accordance with the procedures set forth in section 706 of this Act.

§ 708. Effect on State laws

Nothing in this Title shall be deemed to exempt or relieve any person from any liability, duty, penalty, or punishment provided by any present or future law of any State or political subdivision of a State, other than any such law which purports to require or permit the doing of any act which would be an unlawful employment practice under this Title.

§ 709. Investigations

(a) In connection with any investigation of a charge filed under section 706 of this Act, the Commission or its designated representative shall at all reasonable times have access to, for the purposes of examination, and the right to copy any evidence of any person being investigated or proceeded against that relates to unlawful employment practices covered by this Title and is relevant to the charge under investigation.

(b) The Commission may cooperate with State and local agencies charged with the administration of State fair employment practices laws and, with the consent of such agencies, may, for the purpose of carrying out its functions and duties under this Title and within the limitation of funds appropriated specifically for such purpose, engage in and contribute to the cost of research and other projects of mutual interest undertaken by such agencies, and utilize the services of such agencies and their employees, and, notwithstanding any other provision of law, pay by advance or reimbursement such agencies and their employees for services rendered to assist the Commission in carrying out this Title. In furtherance of such cooperative efforts, the Commission may enter into written agreements with such State or local agencies and such agreements may include provisions under which the Commission shall refrain from processing a charge in any cases or class of cases specified in such agreements or under which the Commission shall relieve any person or class of persons in such State or locality from requirements imposed under this section. The Commission shall rescind any such agreement whenever it determines that the agreement no longer serves the interest of effective enforcement of this Title.

(c) Every employer, employment agency, and labor organization subject to this Title shall (1) make and keep such records relevant to the determinations of whether unlawful employment practices have been or are being committed, (2) preserve such records for such periods, and (3) make such reports therefrom as the Commission shall prescribe by regulation or order, after public hearing, as reasonable, necessary, or appropriate for the enforcement of this Title or the regulations or orders thereunder. The Commission shall, by regulation, require each employer, labor organization, and joint labor-management committee subject to this Title which controls an apprenticeship or other training program to maintain such records as are reasonably necessary to carry out the purposes of this Title, including, but not limited to, a list of applicants who wish to participate in such program, including the chronological order in which applications were received, and to furnish to the Commission upon request, a detailed description of the manner in which persons are selected to participate in the apprenticeship or other training program. Any employer, employment agency, labor organization, or joint labor-management committee which believes that the application to it of any regulation or order issued under this section would result in undue hardship may apply to the Commission for an exemption from the application of such regulation or order, and, if such application for an exemption is denied, bring a civil action in the United States district court for the district where such records are kept. If the Commission or the court, as the case may be, finds that the application of the regulation or order to the employer, employment agency, or labor organization in question would impose an undue hardship, the Commission or the court, as the case may be, may grant appropriate relief. If any person required to comply with the provisions of this subsection fails or refuses to do so, the United States district court for the district in which such person is found, resides, or transacts business, shall, upon application of the Commission, or the Attorney General in a case involving a government, governmental agency or political subdivision, have jurisdiction to issue to such person an order requiring him to comply.

(d) In prescribing requirements pursuant to subsection (c) of this section, the Commission shall consult with other interested State and Federal agencies and shall endeavor to coordinate its requirements with those adopted by such agencies. The Commission shall furnish upon request and without cost to any State or local agency charged with the administration of a fair employment practice law information obtained pursuant to subsection (c) of this section from any employer, employment agency, labor organization, or joint labor-management committee subject to the jurisdiction of such agency. Such information shall be furnished on condition that it not be made public by the recipient agency prior to the institution of a proceeding under State or local law involving such information. If this condition is violated by a recipient agency, the Commission may decline to honor subsequent requests pursuant to this subsection.

(e) It shall be unlawful for any officer or employee of the Commission to make public in any manner whatever any information obtained by the Commission pursuant to its authority under this section prior to the institution of any proceeding under this Title involving such information. Any officer or employee of the Commission who shall make public in any manner whatever any information in violation of this subsection shall be guilty of a misdemeanor and upon conviction thereof, shall be fined not more than $1,000, or imprisoned not more than one year.

§ 710. Conduct of hearings and investigations

For the purpose of all hearings and investigations conducted by the Commission or its duly authorized agents or agencies, section 161 of Title 29 shall apply.

§ 711. Posting of notices; penalties

(a) Every employer, employment agency, and labor organization, as the case may be, shall post and keep posted in conspicuous places upon its premises where notices to employees, applicants for employment, and members are customarily posted a notice to be prepared or approved by the Commission setting forth excerpts from or, summaries of, the pertinent provisions of this Title and information pertinent to the filing of a complaint.

(b) A willful violation of this section shall be punishable by a fine of not more than $100 for each separate offense.

§ 712. Veterans' special rights or preference

Nothing contained in this Title shall be construed to repeal or modify any Federal, State, territorial, or local law creating special rights or preference for veterans.

§ 713. Regulations and reliance on interpretations and instructions of Commission

(a) The Commission shall have authority from time to time to issue, amend, or rescind suitable procedural regulations to carry out the provisions of this Title. Regulations issued under this section shall be in conformity with the standards and limitations of subchapter II of chapter 5 of Title 5.

(b) In any action or proceeding based on any alleged unlawful employment practice, no person shall be subject to any liability or punishment for or on account of (1) the commission by such person of an unlawful employment practice if he pleads and proves that the act or omission complained of was in good faith, in conformity with, and in reliance on any written interpretation or opinion of the Commission, or (2) the failure of such person to publish and file any information required by any provision of this Title if he pleads and proves that he failed to publish and file such information in good faith, in conformity with the instructions of the Commission issued under this Title regarding the filing of such information. Such a defense, if established, shall be a bar to the action or proceeding, notwithstanding that (A) after such act or omission, such interpretation or opinion is modified or rescinded or is determined by judicial authority to be invalid or of no legal effect, or (B) after publishing or filing the description and annual reports, such publication or filing is determined by judicial authority not to be in conformity with the requirements of this Title.

* * *

§ 715. Coordination of efforts and elimination of competition among Federal departments, agencies, etc. in implementation and enforcement of equal employment opportunity legislation, orders, and policies; report to President and Congress

The Equal Employment Opportunity Commission shall have the responsibility for developing and implementing agreements, policies and practices designed to maximize effort, promote efficiency, and eliminate conflict, competition, duplication and inconsistency among the operations, functions and jurisdictions of the various departments, agencies and branches of the Federal Government responsible for the implementation and enforcement of equal employment opportunity legislation, orders, and policies. On or before October 1 of each year, the Equal Employment Opportunity Commission shall transmit to the President and to the Congress a report of its activities, together with such recommendations for legislative or administrative changes as it concludes are desirable to further promote the purposes of this section.

* * *

§ 717. Employment by Federal Government

(a) All personnel actions affecting employees or applicants for employment (except with regard to aliens employed outside the limits of the United States) in military departments as defined in section 102 of Title 5, in executive agencies as defined in section 105 of Title 5 (including employees and applicants for employment who are paid from nonappropriated funds), in the United States Postal Service and the Postal Rate Commission, in those units of the Government of the District of Columbia having positions in the competitive service, and in those units of the legislative and judicial branches of the Federal Government having positions in the competitive service, and in the Library of Congress shall be made free from any discrimination based on race, color, religion, sex, or national origin.

(b) Except as otherwise provided in this subsection, the Equal Employment Opportunity Commission shall have authority to enforce the provisions of subsection (a) of this section through appropriate remedies, including reinstatement or hiring of employees with or without back pay, as will effectuate the policies of this section, and shall issue such rules, regulations, orders and instructions as it deems necessary and appropriate to carry out its responsibilities under this section. The Equal Employment Opportunity Commission shall—

(1) be responsible for the annual review and approval of a national and regional equal employment opportunity plan which each department and agency and each appropriate unit referred to in subsection (a) of this section shall submit in order to maintain an affirmative program of equal employment opportunity for all such employees and applicants for employment;

(2) be responsible for the review and evaluation of the operation of all agency equal employment opportunity programs, periodically obtaining and publishing (on at least a semiannual basis) progress reports from each such department, agency, or unit; and

(3) consult with and solicit the recommendations of interested individuals, groups, and organizations relating to equal employment opportunity.

The head of each such department, agency, or unit shall comply with such rules, regulations, orders, and instructions which shall include a provision that an employee or applicant for employment shall be notified of any final action taken on any complaint of discrimination filed by him thereunder. The plan submitted by each department, agency, and unit shall include, but not be limited to—

(1) provision for the establishment of training and education programs designed to provide a maximum opportunity for employees to advance so as to perform at their highest potential; and

(2) a description of the qualifications in terms of training and experience relating to equal employment opportunity for the principal and operating officials of each such department, agency, or unit responsible for carrying out the equal employment opportunity program and of the allocation of personnel and resources proposed by such department, agency, or unit to carry out its equal employment opportunity program.

With respect to employment in the Library of Congress, authorities granted in this subsection to the Equal Employment Opportunity Commission shall be exercised by the Librarian of Congress.

(c) Within thirty days of receipt of notice of final action taken by a department, agency, or unit referred to in subsection (a) of this section, or by the Equal Employment Opportunity Commission upon an appeal from a decision or order of such department, agency, or unit on a complaint of discrimination based on race, color, religion, sex or national origin, brought pursuant to subsection (a) of this section, Executive Order 11478 or any succeeding Executive orders, or after one hundred and eighty days from the filing of the initial charge with the department, agency, or unit or with the Equal Employment Opportunity Commission on appeal from a decision or order of such department, agency, or unit until such time as final action may be taken by a department, agency, or unit, an employee or applicant for employment, if aggrieved by the final disposition of his complaint, or by the failure to take final action on his complaint, may file a civil action as provided in section 706 of this Act, in which civil action the head of the department, agency, or unit, as appropriate, shall be the defendant.

(d) The provisions of section 706(f) through (k) of this Act, as applicable, shall govern civil actions brought hereunder.

(e) Nothing contained in this Act shall relieve any Government agency or official of its or his primary responsibility to assure nondiscrimination in employment as required by the Constitution and statutes or of its or his responsibilities under Executive Order 11478 relating to equal employment opportunity in the Federal Government.

§ 718. Procedure for denial, withholding, termination, or suspension of Government contract

No Government contract, or portion thereof, with any employer, shall be denied, withheld, terminated, or suspended, by any agency or officer of the United States under any equal employment opportunity law or order, where such employer has an affirmative action plan which has previously been accepted by the Government for the same facility within the past twelve months without first according such employer full hearing and adjudication under the provisions of section 554 of Title 5, and the following pertinent sections: *Provided*, That if such employer has deviated substantially from such previously agreed to affirmative action plan, this section shall not apply: *Provided further*, That for the purposes of this section an affirmative action plan shall be deemed to have been accepted by the Government at the time the appropriate compliance agency has accepted such plan unless within forty-five days thereafter the Office of Federal Contract Compliance has disapproved such plan.

SELECTED CONSTITUTIONAL AMENDMENTS

Amendment V

No person shall * * * be deprived of life, liberty, or property, without due process of law; nor shall private property be taken for public use, without just compensation.

Amendment XIII [1865]

Section 1. Neither slavery nor involuntary servitude, except as a punishment for crime whereof the party shall have been duly convicted, shall exist within the United States, or any place subject to their jurisdiction.

Section 2. Congress shall have power to enforce this article by appropriate legislation.

[Amendment XIV [1868]

Section 1. All persons born or naturalized in the United States, and subject to the jurisdiction thereof, are citizens of the United States and of the State wherein they reside. No State shall make or enforce any law which shall abridge the privileges or immunities of citizens of the United States; nor shall any State deprive any person of life, liberty, or property, without due process of law; nor deny to any person within its jurisdiction the equal protection of the laws.

* * *

Section 5. The Congress shall have power to enforce, by appropriate legislation, the provisions of this article.

RECONSTRUCTION CIVIL RIGHTS ACTS

42 U.S.C.A. § 1981. Equal rights under the law

All persons within the jurisdiction of the United States shall have the same right in every State and Territory to make and enforce contracts, to sue, be parties, give evidence, and to the full and equal benefit of all laws and proceedings for the security of persons and property as is enjoyed by white citizens, and shall be subject to like punishment, pains, penalties, taxes, licenses, and exactions of every kind, and to no other.

42 U.S.C.A. § 1983. Civil action for deprivation of rights

Every person who, under color of any statute, ordinance, regulation, custom, or usage, of any State or Territory or the District of Columbia, subjects, or causes to be subjected, any citizen of the United States or other person within the jurisdiction thereof to the deprivation of any rights, privileges, or immunities secured by the Constitution and laws, shall be liable to the party injured in an action at law, suit in equity, or other proper proceeding for redress. For the purposes of this section, any Act of Congress applicable exclusively to the District of Columbia shall be considered to be a statute of the District of Columbia.

42 U.S.C.A. § 1985(c). Conspiracy to interfere with civil rights

If two or more persons in any State or Territory conspire or go in disguise on the highway or on the premises of another, for the purpose of depriving, either directly or indirectly, any person or class of persons of the equal protection of the laws, or of equal privileges and immunities under the laws; or for the purpose of preventing or hindering the constituted authorities of any State or Territory from giving or securing to all persons within such State or Territory the equal protection of the laws; or if two or more persons conspire to prevent by force, intimidation, or threat, any citizen who is lawfully entitled to vote, from giving his support or advocacy in a legal manner, toward or in favor of the election of any lawfully qualified person as an elector for President or Vice President, or as a Member of Congress of the United States; or to injure any citizen in person or property on account of such support or advocacy; in any case of conspiracy set forth in this section, if one or more persons engaged therein do, or cause to be done, any act in furtherance of the object of such conspiracy, whereby another is injured in his person or property, or deprived of having and exercising any right or privilege of a citizen of the United States, the party so injured or deprived may have an action for the recovery of damages occasioned by such injury or deprivation, against anyone or more of the conspirators.

41 U.S.C.A. § 1988. Proceedings in vindication of civil rights, attorney's fees

* * * In any action or proceeding to enforce a provision of sections 1981, 1982, 1983, 1985, and 1986 of this title, title IX of Public Law 92–318, or title VI of the Civil Rights Act of 1964, the court, in its discretion, may allow the prevailing party, other than the United States, a reasonable attorney's fee as part of the costs.

EQUAL PAY ACT

29 U.S.C.A. § 206(d).

§ 206(d). Prohibition of sex discrimination

(1) No employer having employees subject to any provisions of this section shall discriminate, within any establishment in which such

employees are employed, between employees on the basis of sex by paying wages to employees in such establishment at a rate less than the rate at which he pays wages to employees of the opposite sex in such establishment for equal work on jobs the performance of which requires equal skill, effort, and responsibility, and which are performed under similar working conditions, except where such payment is made pursuant to (i) a seniority system; (ii) a merit system; (iii) a system which measures earnings by quantity or quality of production; or (iv) a differential based on any other factor other than sex: *Provided*, That an employer who is paying a wage rate differential in violation of this subsection shall not, in order to comply with the provisions of this subsection, reduce the wage rate of any employee.

(2) No labor organization, or its agents, representing employees of an employer having employees subject to any provisions of this section shall cause or attempt to cause such an employer to discriminate against an employee in violation of paragraph (1) of this subsection.

(3) For purposes of administration and enforcement, any amounts owing to any employee which have been withheld in violation of this subsection shall be deemed to be unpaid minimum wages or unpaid overtime compensation under this Act.

(4) As used in this subsection, the term "labor organization" means any organization of any kind, or any agency or employee representation committee or plan, in which employees participate and which exists for the purpose, in whole or in part, of dealing with employers concerning grievances, labor disputes, wages, rates of pay, hours of employment, or conditions of work.

29 U.S.C. § 216. Remedies [§ 16(b) of Fair Labor Standards Act of 1938, as amended]

(b) Any employer who violates the provisions of section 206 or section 207 of this title shall be liable to the employee or employees affected in the amount of their unpaid minimum wages, or their unpaid overtime compensation, as the case may be, and in an additional equal amount as liquidated damages. Any employer who violates the provisions of section 215(a)(3) of this title shall be liable for such legal or equitable relief as may be appropriate to effectuate the purposes of section 215(a)(3) of this title, including without limitation employment, reinstatement, promotion, and the payment of wages lost and an additional equal amount as liquidated damages. An action to recover the liability prescribed in either of the preceding sentences may be maintained against any employer (including a public agency) in any Federal or State court of competent jurisdiction by any one or more employees for and in behalf of himself or themselves and other employees similarly situated. No employee shall be a party plaintiff to any such action unless he gives his consent in writing to become such a party and such consent is filed in the court in which such action is brought. The court in such action shall, in addition to any judgment awarded to the plaintiff or plaintiffs, allow a reasonable attorney's fee to be paid by the defendant, and costs of the action. The right provided by this subsection to bring an action by or on behalf of any employee, and the right of any employee to become a party plaintiff to any such action, shall terminate upon the filing of a complaint by the Secretary of Labor in an action under section 217 of this title in which (1) restraint is sought of any further delay in the payment of unpaid minimum wages, or the amount of unpaid overtime compensation, as the case may be, owing to such employee under section 206 or section 207 of this title by an employer liable therefor under the provisions of this subsection or (2) legal or equitable relief is sought as a result of alleged violations of section 215(a)(3) of this title.

AGE DISCRIMINATION IN EMPLOYMENT ACT OF 1967

29 U.S.C.A. § 621 et seq.

§ 2. Congressional statement of findings and purpose

(a) The Congress hereby finds and declares that—

(1) in the face of rising productivity and affluence, older workers find themselves disadvantaged in their efforts to retain employment, and especially to regain employment when displaced from jobs;

(2) the setting of arbitrary age limits regardless of potential for job performance has become a common practice, and certain otherwise desirable practices may work to the disadvantage of older persons;

(3) the incidence of unemployment, especially long-term unemployment with resultant deterioration of skill, morale, and employer acceptability is, relative to the younger ages, high among older workers; their numbers are great and growing; and their employment problems grave;

(4) the existence in industries affecting commerce, of arbitrary discrimination in employment because of age, burdens commerce and the free flow of goods in commerce.

(b) It is therefore the purpose of this chapter to promote employment of older persons based on their ability rather than age; to prohibit arbitrary age discrimination in employment; to help employers and workers find ways of meeting problems arising from the impact of age on employment.

* * *

§ 4. Prohibition of age discrimination

(a) It shall be unlawful for an employer—

(1) to fail or refuse to hire or to discharge any individual or otherwise discriminate against any individual with respect to his compensation, terms, conditions, or privileges of employment, because of such individual's age;

(2) to limit, segregate, or classify his employees in any way which would deprive or tend to deprive any individual of employment opportunities or otherwise adversely affect his status as an employee, because of such individual's age; or

(3) to reduce the wage rate of any employee in order to comply with this chapter.

(b) It shall be unlawful for an employment agency to fail or refuse to refer for employment, or otherwise to discriminate against, any individual because of such individual's age, or to classify or refer for employment any individual on the basis of such individual's age.

(c) It shall be unlawful for a labor organization—

(1) to exclude or to expel from its membership, or otherwise to discriminate against, any individual because of his age;

(2) to limit, segregate, or classify its membership, or to classify or fail or refuse to refer for employment any individual, in any way which would deprive or tend to deprive any individual of employment opportunities, or would limit such employment opportunities or otherwise adversely affect his status as an employee or as an applicant for employment, because of such individual's age;

(3) to cause or attempt to cause an employer to discriminate against an individual in violation of this section.

(d) It shall be unlawful for an employer to discriminate against any of his employees or applicants for employment, for an employment agency to discriminate against any individual, or for a labor organization to discriminate against any member thereof or applicant for membership, because such individual, member or applicant for membership has opposed any practice made unlawful by this section, or because such individual, member or applicant for membership has made a charge, testified, assisted, or participated in any manner in an investigation, proceeding, or litigation under this chapter.

(e) It shall be unlawful for an employer, labor organization, or employment agency to print or publish, or cause to be printed or published, any notice or advertisement relating to employment by such an employer or membership in or any classification or referral for employment by such a labor organization, or relating to any classification or referral for employment by such an employment agency, indicating any preference, limitation, specification, or discrimination, based on age.

(f) It shall not be unlawful for an employer, employment agency, or labor organization—

(g)(1) For purposes of this section, any employer must provide that any employee aged 65 or older, and any employee's spouse aged 65 or older, shall be entitled to coverage under any group health plan offered to such employees under the same conditions as any employee, and the spouse of such employee, under age 65.

(2) For purposes of paragraph (1), the term "group health plan" has the meaning given to such term in section 162(i)(2) of the Internal Revenue Code of 1954.

(h)(1) If an employer controls a corporation whose place of incorporation is in a foreign country, any practice by such corporation prohibited under this section shall be presumed to be such practice by such employer.

(2) The prohibitions of this section shall not apply where the employer is a foreign person not controlled by an American employer.

(3) For the purpose of this subsection the determination of whether an employer controls a corporation shall be based upon the—

(A) interrelation of operations,

(B) common management,

(C) centralized control of labor relations, and

(D) common ownership or financial control, of the employer and the corporation.

(i) It shall not be unlawful for an employer which is a State, a political subdivision of a State, an agency or instrumentality of a State or a political subdivision of a State, or an interstate agency to fail or refuse to hire or to discharge any individual because of such individual's age if such action is taken—

(1) with respect to the employment of an individual as a firefighter or as a law enforcement officer and the individual has attained the age of hiring or retirement in effect under applicable State or local law on March 3, 1983, and

(2) pursuant to a bona fide hiring or retirement plan that is not a subterfuge to evade the purposes of this Act. [Automatically repealed December 31, 1993.]

(i)(1) Except as otherwise provided in this subsection, it shall be unlawful for an employer, an employment agency, a labor organization, or any combination thereof to establish or maintain an employee pension benefit plan which requires or permits—

(A) in the case of a defined benefit plan, the cessation of an employee's benefit accrual, or the reduction of the rate of an employee's benefit accrual, because of age, or

(B) in the case of a defined contribution plan, the cessation of allocations to an employee's account, or the reduction of the rate at which amounts are allocated to an employee's account, because of age.

(2) Nothing in this section shall be construed to prohibit an employer, employment agency, or labor organization from observing any provision of an employee pension benefit plan to the extent that such provision imposes (without regard to age) a limitation on the amount of benefits that the plan provides or a limitation on the number of years

of service or years of participation which are taken into account for purposes of determining benefit accrual under the plan.

(3) In the case of any employee who, as of the end of any plan year under a defined benefit plan, has attained normal retirement age under such plan—

(A) if distribution of benefits under such plan with respect to such employee has commenced as of the end of such plan year, then any requirement of this subsection for continued accrual of benefits under such plan with respect to such employee during such plan year shall be treated as satisfied to the extent of the actuarial equivalent of in-service distribution of benefits, and

(B) if distribution of benefits under such plan with respect to such employee has not commenced as of the end of such year in accordance with section 206(a)(3) of the Employee Retirement Income Security Act of 1974 and section 401(a)(14)(C) of the Internal Revenue Code of 1986, and the payment of benefits under such plan with respect to such employee is not suspended during such plan year pursuant to section 203(a)(3)(B) of the Employee Retirement Income Security Act of 1974 or section 411(a)(3)(B) of the Internal Revenue Code of 1986, then any requirement of this subsection for continued accrual of benefits under such plan with respect to such employee during such plan year shall be treated as satisfied to the extent of any adjustment in the benefit payable under the plan during such plan year attributable to the delay in the distribution of benefits after the attainment of normal retirement age.

The provisions of this paragraph shall apply in accordance with regulations of the Secretary of the Treasury. Such regulations shall provide for the application of the preceding provisions of this paragraph to all employee pension benefit plans subject to this subsection and may provide for the application of such provisions, in the case of any such employee, with respect to any period of time within a plan year.

(1) to take any action otherwise prohibited under subsections (a), (b), (c), or (e) of this section where age is a bona fide occupational qualification reasonably necessary to the normal operation of the particular business, or where the differentiation is based on reasonable factors other than age;

(2) to observe the terms of a bona fide seniority system or any bona fide employee benefit plan such as a retirement, pension, or insurance plan, which is not a subterfuge to evade the purposes of this chapter, except that no such employee benefit plan shall excuse the failure to hire any individual, and no such seniority system or employee benefit plan shall require or permit the involuntary retirement of any individual specified by section 12(a) of this Act because of the age of such individual; or

(3) to discharge or otherwise discipline an individual for good cause.

* * *

§ 7. Record keeping, investigation, and enforcement

(a) The Secretary shall have the power to make investigations and require the keeping of records necessary or appropriate for the administration of this chapter in accordance with the powers and procedures provided in sections 9 and 11 of the Fair Labor Standards Act of 1938, as amended.

(b) The provisions of this chapter shall be enforced in accordance with the powers, remedies, and procedures provided in sections 11(b), 16 (except for subsection (a) thereof), and 17 of the Fair Labor Standards Act of 1938, as amended, and subsection (c) of this section. Any act prohibited under section 4 of this Act shall be deemed to be a prohibited act under section 15 of the Fair Labor Standards Act of 1938, as amended. Amounts owing to a person as a result of a violation of this chapter shall be deemed to be unpaid minimum wages or unpaid overtime compensation for purposes of sections 16 and 17 of the Fair Labor Standards Act of 1938, as amended: *Provided*, That liquidated damages shall be payable only in cases of willful violations of this chapter. In any action brought to enforce this chapter the court shall have jurisdiction to grant such legal or equitable relief as may be appropriate to effectuate the purposes of this chapter, including without limitation judgments compelling employment, reinstatement or promotion, or enforcing the liability for amounts deemed to be unpaid minimum wages or unpaid overtime compensation under this section. Before instituting any action under this section, the Secretary shall attempt to eliminate the discriminatory practice or practices alleged, and to effect voluntary compliance with the requirements of this chapter through informal methods of conciliation, conference, and persuasion.

(c)(1) Any person aggrieved may bring a civil action in any court of competent jurisdiction for such legal or equitable relief as will effectuate the purposes of this chapter: *Provided*, That the right of any person to bring such action shall terminate upon the commencement of an action by the Secretary to enforce the right of such employee under this chapter.

(2) In an action brought under paragraph (1), a person shall be entitled to a trial by jury of any issue of fact in any such action for recovery of amounts owing as a result of a violation of this chapter, regardless of whether equitable relief is sought by any party in such action.

(d) No civil action may be commenced by an individual under this section until 60 days after a charge alleging unlawful discrimination has been filed with the Secretary. Such a charge shall be filed—

(1) within 180 days after the alleged unlawful practice occurred; or

(2) in a case to which section 14(b) of this Act applies, within 300 days after the alleged unlawful practice occurred, or within 30 days

after receipt by the individual of notice of termination of proceedings under State law, whichever is earlier.

Upon receiving such a charge, the Secretary shall promptly notify all persons named in such charge as prospective defendants in the action and shall promptly seek to eliminate any alleged unlawful practice by informal methods of conciliation, conference, and persuasion.

(e)(1) Sections 55 and 59 of the Fair Labor Standards Act of 1938, as amended, shall apply to actions under this Act.

(2) For the period during which the Secretary is attempting to effect voluntary compliance with requirements of this chapter through informal methods of conciliation, conference, and persuasion pursuant to subsection (b) of this section, the statute of limitations as provided in section 55 of the Fair Labor Standards Act of 1938, as amended, shall be tolled, but in no event for a period in excess of one year.

§ 8. Notices to be posted

Every employer, employment agency, and labor organization shall post and keep posted in conspicuous places upon its premises a notice to be prepared or approved by the Secretary setting forth information as the Secretary deems appropriate to effectuate the purposes of this Act.

§ 9. Rules and regulations; exemptions

In accordance with the provisions of subchapter II of chapter 5 of Title 5, the Secretary of Labor may issue such rules and regulations as he may consider necessary or appropriate for carrying out this chapter, and may establish such reasonable exemptions to and from any or all provisions of this chapter as he may find necessary and proper in the public interest.

§ 10. Criminal penalties

Whoever shall forcibly resist, oppose, impede, intimidate or interfere with a duly authorized representative of the Secretary while he is engaged in the performance of duties under this chapter shall be punished by a fine of not more than $500 or by imprisonment for not more than one year, or by both: *Provided, however,* That no person shall be imprisoned under this section except when there has been a prior conviction hereunder.

§ 11. Definitions

For the purposes of this chapter—

(a) The term "person" means one or more individuals, partnerships, associations, labor organizations, corporations, business trusts, legal representatives, or any organized groups of persons.

(b) The term "employer" means a person engaged in an industry affecting commerce who has twenty or more employees for each working day in each of twenty or more calendar weeks in the current or preceding calendar year: *Provided*, That prior to June 30, 1968, employers having fewer than fifty employees shall not be considered employers. The term also means (1) any agent of such a person, and (2) a State or political subdivision of a State and any agency or instrumentality of a State or a political subdivision of a State, and any interstate agency, but such term does not include the United States, or a corporation wholly owned by the Government of the United States.

(c) The term "employment agency" means any person regularly undertaking with or without compensation to procure employees for an employer and includes an agent of such a person; but shall not include an agency of the United States.

(d) The term "labor organization" means a labor organization engaged in an industry affecting commerce, and any agent of such an organization, and includes any organization of any kind, any agency, or employee representation committee, group, association, or plan so engaged in which employees participate and which exists for the purpose, in whole or in part, of dealing with employers concerning grievances, labor disputes, wages, rates of pay, hours, or other terms or conditions of employment, and any conference, general committee, joint or system board, or joint council so engaged which is subordinate to a national or international labor organization.

(e) A labor organization shall be deemed to be engaged in an industry affecting commerce if (1) it maintains or operates a hiring hall or hiring office which procures employees for an employer or procures for employees opportunities to work for an employer, or (2) the number of its members (or, where it is a labor organization composed of other labor organizations or their representatives, if the aggregate number of the members of such other labor organization) is fifty or more prior to July 1, 1968, or twenty-five or more on or after July 1, 1968, and such labor organization—

(1) is the certified representative of employees under the provisions of the National Labor Relations Act, as amended, or the Railway Labor Act, as amended; or

(2) although not certified, is a national or international labor organization or a local labor organization recognized or acting as the representative of employees of an employer or employers engaged in an industry affecting commerce; or

(3) has chartered a local labor organization or subsidiary body which is representing or actively seeking to represent employees of employers within the meaning of paragraph (1) or (2); or

(4) has been chartered by a labor organization representing or actively seeking to represent employees within the meaning of paragraph (1) or (2) as the local or subordinate body through which such employees may enjoy membership or become affiliated with such labor organization; or

(5) is a conference, general committee, joint or system board, or joint council subordinate to a national or international labor organi-

zation, which includes a labor organization engaged in an industry affecting commerce within the meaning of any of the preceding paragraphs of this subsection.

(f) The term "employee" means an individual employed by any employer except that the term "employee" shall not include any person elected to public office in any State or political subdivision of any State by the qualified voters thereof, or any person chosen by such officer to be on such officer's personal staff, or an appointee on the policymaking level or an immediate adviser with respect to the exercise of the constitutional or legal powers of the office. The exemption set forth in the preceding sentence shall not include employees subject to the civil service laws of a State government, governmental agency, or political subdivision.

(g) The term "commerce" means trade, traffic, commerce, transportation, transmission, or communication among the several States; or between a State and any place outside thereof; or within the District of Columbia, or a possession of the United States; or between points in the same State but through a point outside thereof.

(h) The term "industry affecting commerce" means any activity, business, or industry in commerce or in which a labor dispute would hinder or obstruct commerce or the free flow of commerce and includes any activity or industry "affecting commerce" within the meaning of the Labor-Management Reporting and Disclosure Act of 1959.

(i) The term "State" includes a State of the United States, the District of Columbia, Puerto Rico, the Virgin Islands, American Samoa, Guam, Wake Island, the Canal Zone, and Outer Continental Shelf lands defined in the Outer Continental Shelf Lands Act.

(j) The term "firefighter" means an employee, the duties of whose position are primarily to perform work directly connected with the control and extinguishment of fires or the maintenance and use of firefighting apparatus and equipment, including an employee engaged in this activity who is transferred to a supervisory or administrative position.

(k) The term "law enforcement officer" means an employee, the duties of whose position are primarily the investigation, apprehension, or detention of individuals suspected or convicted of offenses against the criminal laws of a State, including an employee engaged in this activity who is transferred to a supervisory or administrative position. For the purpose of this subsection, "detention" includes the duties of employees assigned to guard individuals incarcerated in any penal institution.

§ 12. Age limits

(a) The prohibitions in this Act (except the provisions of section 4(g)) shall be limited to individuals who are at least forty years of age.

(b) In the case of any personnel action affecting employees or applicants for employment which is subject to the provisions of section 15 of this Act, the prohibitions established in section 15 of this Act shall be limited to individuals who are at least 40 years of age.

(c)(1) Nothing in this Act shall be construed to prohibit compulsory retirement of any employee who has attained 65 years of age, and who, for the 2-year period immediately before retirement, is employed in a bona fide executive or a high policymaking position, if such employee is entitled to an immediate nonforfeitable annual retirement benefit from a pension, profit-sharing, savings, or deferred compensation plan, or any combination of such plans, of the employer of such employee, which equals, in the aggregate, at least $44,000.

(2) In applying the retirement benefit test of paragraph (1) of this subsection, if any such retirement benefit is in a form other than a straight life annuity (with no ancillary benefits), or if employees contribute to any such plan or make rollover contributions, such benefit shall be adjusted in accordance with regulations prescribed by the Secretary [EEOC], after consultation with the Secretary of the Treasury, so that the benefit is the equivalent of a straight life annuity (with no ancillary benefits) under a plan to which employees do not contribute and under which no rollover contributions are made.

(d) Nothing in this Act shall be construed to prohibit compulsory retirement of any employee who has attained 70 years of age, and who is serving under a contract of unlimited tenure (or similar arrangement providing for unlimited tenure) at an institution of higher education (as defined by section 1201(a) of the Higher Education Act of 1965).

§ 13. Annual report to Congress

The Secretary shall submit annually in January a report to the Congress covering his activities for the preceding year and including such information, data, and recommendations for further legislation in connection with the matters covered by this chapter as he may find advisable. Such report shall contain an evaluation and appraisal by the Secretary of the effect of the minimum and maximum ages established by this chapter, together with his recommendations to the Congress. In making such evaluation and appraisal, the Secretary shall take into consideration any changes which may have occurred in the general age level of the population, the effect of the chapter upon workers not covered by its provisions, and such other factors as he may deem pertinent.

§ 14. Federal-State relationship

(a) Nothing in this Act shall affect the jurisdiction of any agency of any State performing like functions with regard to discriminatory employment practices on account of age except that upon commencement of action under this Act such action shall supersede any State action.

(b) In the case of an alleged unlawful practice occurring in a State which has a law prohibiting discrimination in employment because of age and establishing or authorizing a State authority to grant or seek relief from such discriminatory practice, no suit may be brought under section 7 of this Act before the expiration of sixty days after proceedings have been commenced under the State law, unless such proceedings have been earlier terminated: *Provided*, That such sixty-day period shall be extended to one hundred and twenty days during the first year after the effective date of such State law. If any requirement for the commencement of such proceedings is imposed by a State authority other than a requirement of the filing of a written and signed statement of the facts upon which the proceeding is based, the proceeding shall be deemed to have been commenced for the purposes of this subsection at the time such statement is sent by registered mail to the appropriate State authority.

§ 15. Nondiscrimination on account of age in Federal Government employment

(a) All personnel actions affecting employees or applicants for employment who are at least 40 years of age (except personnel actions with regard to aliens employed outside the limits of the United States) in military departments as defined in section 102 of Title 5, in executive agencies as defined in section 105 of Title 5 (including employees and applicants for employment who are paid from nonappropriated funds), in the United States Postal Service and the Postal Rate Commission, in those units in the government of the District of Columbia having positions in the competitive service, and in those units of the legislative and judicial branches of the Federal Government having positions in the competitive service, and in the Library of Congress shall be made free from any discrimination based on age.

(b) Except as otherwise provided in this subsection, the Civil Service Commission is authorized to enforce the provisions of subsection (a) of this section through appropriate remedies, including reinstatement or hiring of employees with or without backpay, as will effectuate the policies of this section. The Civil Service Commission shall issue such rules, regulations, orders, and instructions as it deems necessary and appropriate to carry out its responsibilities under this section. The Civil Service Commission shall—

(1) be responsible for the review and evaluation of the operation of all agency programs designed to carry out the policy of this section, periodically obtaining and publishing (on at least a semiannual basis) progress reports from each department, agency, or unit referred to in subsection (a) of this section;

(2) consult with and solicit the recommendations of interested individuals, groups, and organizations relating to nondiscrimination in employment on account of age; and

(3) provide for the acceptance and processing of complaints of discrimination in Federal employment on account of age.

The head of each such department, agency, or unit shall comply with such rules, regulations, orders, and instructions of the Civil Service Commission which shall include a provision that an employee or applicant for employment shall be notified of any final action taken on any complaint of discrimination filed by him thereunder. Reasonable exemptions to the provisions of this section may be established by the Commission but only when the Commission has established a maximum age requirement on the basis of a determination that age is a bona fide occupational qualification necessary to the performance of the duties of the position. With respect to employment in the Library of Congress, authorities granted in this subsection to the Civil Service Commission shall be exercised by the Librarian of Congress.

(c) Any person aggrieved may bring a civil action in any Federal district court of competent jurisdiction for such legal or equitable relief as will effectuate the purposes of this Act.

(d) When the individual has not filed a complaint concerning age discrimination with the Commission, no civil action may be commenced by any individual under this section until the individual has given the Commission not less than thirty days' notice of an intent to file such action. Such notice shall be filed within one hundred and eighty days after the alleged unlawful practice occurred. Upon receiving a notice of intent to sue, the Commission shall promply notify all persons named therein as prospective defendants in the action and take any appropriate action to assure the elimination of any unlawful practice.

(e) Nothing contained in this section shall relieve any Government agency or official of the responsibility to assure nondiscrimination on account of age in employment as required under any provision of Federal law.

(f) Any personnel action of any department, agency, or other entity referred to in subsection (a) of this section shall not be subject to, or affected by, any provision of this Act, other than the provisions of section 12(b) of this Act and the provisions of this section.

(g)(1) The Civil Service Commission shall undertake a study relating to the effects of the amendments made to this section by the Age Discrimination in Employment Act Amendments of 1978, and the effects of section 12(b) of this Act.

(2) The Civil Service Commission shall transmit a report to the President and to the Congress containing the findings of the Commission resulting from the study of the Commission under paragraph (1) of this subsection. Such report shall be transmitted no later than January 1, 1980.

* * *

[See also § 16(b) of the Fair Labor Standards Act of 1938, as amended, reprinted in this Appendix as part of the Equal Pay Act]

REORGANIZATION PLAN NO. 1 OF 1978

43 F.R. 19,807.

§ 1. Transfer of equal pay enforcement functions

All functions related to enforcing or administering § 6(d) of the Fair Labor Standards Act, as amended, (29 U.S.C. § 206(d)) are hereby transferred to the Equal Employment Opportunity Commission. Such functions include, but shall not be limited to, the functions relating to equal pay administration and enforcement now vested in the Secretary of Labor, the Administrator of the Wage and Hour Division of the Department of Labor and the Civil Service Commission pursuant to Sections 4(d)(1); 9; 11(a), (b) and (c); 16(b) and (c) and 17 of the Fair Labor Standards Act, as amended, (29 U.S.C. §§ 204(d)(1), 204(f), 209, 211(a), (b) and (c); 216(b) and (c) and 217) and § 10(b)(1) of the Portal-to-Portal Act of 1947, as amended, (29 U.S.C. § 259).

§ 2. Transfer of age discrimination enforcement functions

All functions vested in the Secretary of Labor or in the Civil Service Commission pursuant to Sections 2, 4, 7, 8, 9, 10, 11, 12, 13, 14, and 15 of the Age Discrimination in Employment Act of 1967, as amended, (29 U.S.C. §§ 621, 623, 626, 627, 628, 629, 630, 631, 632, 633, and 633a) are hereby transferred to the Equal Employment Opportunity Commission. All functions related to age discrimination administration and enforcement pursuant to Sections 6 and 16 of the Age Discrimination in Employment Act of 1967, as amended, (29 U.S.C. §§ 625 and 634) are hereby transferred to the Equal Employment Opportunity Commission.

REHABILITATION ACT OF 1973

29 U.S.C.A. §§ 706(7), 791, 793, 794, 794a.

§ 7. Definitions

(7)(A) Except as otherwise provided in subparagraph (B), the term "handicapped individual" means any individual who (i) has a physical or mental disability which for such individual constitutes or results in a substantial handicap to employment and (ii) can reasonably be expected to benefit in terms of employability from vocational rehabilitation services provided pursuant to subchapters I and III of this chapter.

(B) Subject to the second sentence of this subparagraph, the term "handicapped individual" means, for purposes of subchapters IV and V of this chapter, any person who (i) has a physical or mental impairment which substantially limits one or more of such person's major life activities, (ii) has a record of such an impairment, or (iii) is regarded as having such an impairment. For purposes of sections 503 and 504 as such sections relate to employment, such term does not include any individual who is an alcoholic or drug abuser whose current use of alcohol or drugs prevents such individual from performing the duties of the job in question or whose employment, by reason of such current alcohol or drug abuse, would constitute a direct threat to property or the safety of others.

§ 501. Employment of handicapped individuals

(a) There is established within the Federal Government an Interagency Committee on Handicapped Employees (hereinafter in this section referred to as the "Committee"), comprised of such members as the President may select, including the following (or their designees whose positions are Executive Level IV or higher): the Chairman of the Civil Service Commission, the Administrator of Veterans' Affairs, and the Secretaries of Labor and Health, Education, and Welfare. The Secretary of Health, Education, and Welfare and the Chairman of the Civil Service Commission shall serve as co-chairmen of the Committee. The resources of the President's Committees on Employment of the Handicapped and on Mental Retardation shall be made fully available to the Committee. It shall be the purpose and function of the Committee (1) to provide a focus for Federal and other employment of handicapped individuals, and to review, on a periodic basis, in cooperation with the Civil Service Commission, the adequacy of hiring, placement, and advancement practices with respect to handicapped individuals, by each department, agency, and instrumentality in the executive branch of Government, and to insure that the special needs of such individuals are being met; and (2) to consult with the Civil Service Commission to assist the Commission to carry out its responsibilities under subsections (b), (c), and (d) of this section. On the basis of such review and consultation, the Committee shall periodically make to the Civil Service Commission such recommendations for legislative and administrative changes as it deems necessary or desirable. The Civil Service Commission shall timely transmit to the appropriate committees of Congress any such recommendations.

(b) Each department, agency, and instrumentality (including the United States Postal Service and the Postal Rate Commission) in the executive branch shall, within one hundred and eighty days after September 26, 1973, submit to the Civil Service Commission and to the Committee an affirmative action program plan for the hiring, placement, and advancement of handicapped individuals in such department, agency, or instrumentality. Such plan shall include a description of the extent to which and methods whereby the special needs of handicapped employees are being met. Such plan shall be updated annually, and shall be reviewed annually and approved by the Commission, if the Commission determines, after consultation with the Committee, that such plan provides sufficient assurances, procedures and commitments to provide adequate hiring, placement, and advancement opportunities for handicapped individuals.

(c) The Civil Service Commission, after consultation with the Committee, shall develop and recommend to the Secretary for referral to the appropriate State agencies, policies and procedures which will facilitate the hiring, placement, and advancement in employment of individuals who have received rehabilitation services under State vocational rehabilitation programs, veterans' programs, or any other program for handicapped individuals, including the promotion of job opportunities for such individuals. The Secretary shall encourage such State agencies to adopt and implement such policies and procedures.

(d) The Civil Service Commission, after consultation with the Committee, shall, on June 30, 1974, and at the end of each subsequent fiscal year, make a complete report to the appropriate committees of the Congress with respect to the practices of and achievements in hiring, placement, and advancement of handicapped individuals by each department, agency, and instrumentality and the effectiveness of the affirmative action programs required by subsection (b) of this section, together with recommendations as to legislation which have been submitted to the Civil Service Commission under subsection (a) of this section, or other appropriate action to insure the adequacy of such practices. Such report shall also include an evaluation by the Committee of the effectiveness of the Civil Service Commission's activities under subsections (b) and (c) of this section.

* * *

§ 503. Employment under Federal contracts

(a) Any contract in excess of $2,500 entered into by any Federal department or agency for the procurement of personal property and nonpersonal services (including construction) for the United States shall contain a provision requiring that, in employing persons to carry out such contract the party contracting with the United States shall take affirmative action to employ and advance in employment qualified handicapped individuals as defined in section 7(7). The provisions of this section shall apply to any subcontract in excess of $2,500 entered into by a prime contractor in carrying out any contract for the procurement of personal property and nonpersonal services (including construction) for the United States. The President shall implement the provisions of this section by promulgating regulations within ninety days after September 26, 1973.

(b) If any handicapped individual believes any contractor has failed or refuses to comply with the provisions of his contract with the United States, relating to employment of handicapped individuals, such individual may file a complaint with the Department of Labor. The Department shall promptly investigate such complaint and shall take such action thereon as the facts and circumstances warrant, consistent with the terms of such contract and the laws and regulations applicable thereto.

(c) The requirements of this section may be waived, in whole or in part, by the President with respect to a particular contract or subcontract, in accordance with guidelines set forth in regulations which he shall prescribe, when he determines that special circumstances in the national interest so require and states in writing his reasons for such determination.

§ 504. Nondiscrimination under Federal grants and programs

No otherwise qualified handicapped individual in the United States, as defined in section 7(7) shall, solely by reason of his handicap, be excluded from the participation in, be denied the benefits of, or be subjected to discrimination under any program or activity receiving Federal financial assistance or under any program or activity conducted by any Executive agency or by the United States Postal Service. The head of each such agency shall promulgate such regulations as may be necessary to carry out the amendments to this section made by the Rehabilitation, Comprehensive Services, and Developmental Disabilities Act of 1978. Copies of any proposed regulation shall be submitted to appropriate authorizing committees of the Congress, and such regulation may take effect no earlier than the thirtieth day after the date on which such regulation is so submitted to such committees.

§ 505. Remedies and attorney fees

(a)(1) The remedies, procedures, and rights set forth in section 717 of the Civil Rights Act of 1964, including the application of sections 706(f) through 706(k), shall be available, with respect to any complaint under section 501 of this Act, to any employee or applicant for employment aggrieved by the final disposition of such complaint, or by the failure to take final action on such complaint. In fashioning an equitable or affirmative action remedy under such section, a court may take into account the reasonableness of the cost of any necessary work place accommodation, and the availability of alternatives therefor or other appropriate relief in order to achieve an equitable and appropriate remedy.

(2) The remedies, procedures, and rights set forth in title VI of the Civil Rights Act of 1964 shall be available to any person aggrieved by any act or failure to act by any recipient of Federal assistance or Federal provider of such assistance under section 504 of this Act.

(b) In any action or proceeding to enforce or charge a violation of a provision of this Act, the court, in its discretion, may allow the prevailing party, other than the United States, a reasonable attorney's fee as part of the costs.

EXECUTIVE ORDER NO. 11246

Under and by virtue of the authority vested in me as President of the United States by the Constitution and statutes of the United States, it is ordered as follows:

PART I—NONDISCRIMINATION IN GOVERNMENT EMPLOYMENT

[Superseded by Ex.Ord.No.11478, Aug. 8, 1969, 34 F.R. 12985]

PART II—NONDISCRIMINATION IN EMPLOYMENT BY GOVERNMENT CONTRACTORS AND SUBCONTRACTORS

SUBPART A—DUTIES OF THE SECRETARY OF LABOR

Sec. 201. The Secretary of Labor shall be responsible for the administration and enforcement of Parts II and III of this Order. The Secretary shall adopt such rules and regulations and issue such orders as are deemed necessary and appropriate to achieve the purposes of Parts II and III of this Order.

SUBPART B—CONTRACTORS' AGREEMENTS

Sec. 202. Except in contracts exempted in accordance with Section 204 of this Order, all Government contracting agencies shall include in every Government contract hereafter entered into the following provisions:

"During the performance of this contract, the contractor agrees as follows:

"(1) The contractor will not discriminate against any employee or applicant for employment because of race, color, religion, sex, or national origin. The contractor will take affirmative action to ensure that applicants are employed, and that employees are treated during employment, without regard to their race, color, religion, sex or national origin. Such action shall include, but not be limited to the following: employment, upgrading, demotion, or transfer; recruitment or recruitment advertising; layoff or termination; rates of pay or other forms of compensation; and selection for training, including apprenticeship. The contractor agrees to post in conspicuous places, available to employees and applicants for employment, notices to be provided by the contracting officer setting forth the provisions of this nondiscrimination clause.

"(2) The contractor will, in all solicitations or advertisements for employees placed by or on behalf of the contractor, state that all qualified applicants will receive consideration for employment without regard to race, color, religion, sex or national origin.

"(3) The contractor will send to each labor union or representative of workers with which he has a collective bargaining agreement or other contract or understanding, a notice, to be provided by the agency contracting officer, advising the labor union or workers' representative of the contractor's commitments under Section 202 of Executive Order No. 11246 of September 24, 1965, and shall post copies of the notice in conspicuous places available to employees and applicants for employment.

"(4) The contractor will comply with all provisions of Executive Order No. 11246 of Sept. 24, 1965, and of the rules, regulations, and relevant orders of the Secretary of Labor.

"(5) The contractor will furnish all information and reports required by Executive Order No. 11246 of September 24, 1965, and by the rules, regulations, and orders of the Secretary of Labor, or pursuant thereto, and will permit access to his books, records, and accounts by the contracting agency and the Secretary of Labor for purposes of investigation to ascertain compliance with such rules, regulations, and orders.

"(6) In the event of the contractor's noncompliance with the nondiscrimination clauses of this contract or with any of such rules, regulations, or orders, this contract may be cancelled, terminated or suspended in whole or in part and the contractor may be declared ineligible for further Government contracts in accordance with procedures authorized in Executive Order No. 11246 of Sept. 24, 1965, and such other sanctions may be imposed and remedies invoked as provided in Executive Order No. 11246 of September 24, 1965, or by rule, regulation, or order of the Secretary of Labor, or as otherwise provided by law.

"(7) The contractor will include the provisions of paragraphs (1) through (7) in every subcontract or purchase order unless exempted by rules, regulations, or orders of the Secretary of Labor issued pursuant to Section 204 of Executive Order No. 11246 of September 24, 1965 [section 204 of this Order], so that such provisions will be binding upon each subcontractor or vendor. The contractor will take such action with respect to any subcontract or purchase order as may be directed by the Secretary of Labor as a means of enforcing such provisions including sanctions for noncompliance: *Provided, however*, That in the event the contractor becomes involved in, or is threatened with, litigation with a subcontractor or vendor as a result of such direction, the contractor may request the United States to enter into such litigation to protect the interests of the United States."

Sec. 203. (a) Each contractor having a contract containing the provisions prescribed in Section 202 shall file, and shall cause each of his subcontractors to file, Compliance Reports with the contracting agency or the Secretary of Labor as may be directed. Compliance Reports shall be filed within such times and shall contain such information as to the practices, policies, programs, and employment policies, programs, and employment statistics of the contractor and each subcontractor, and shall be in such form, as the Secretary of Labor may prescribe.

(b) Bidders or prospective contractors or subcontractors may be required to state whether they have participated in any previous contract subject to the provisions of this Order, or any preceding similar Executive order, and in that event to submit, on behalf of themselves and their proposed subcontractors, Compliance Reports prior to or as an initial part of their bid or negotiation of a contract.

(c) Whenever the contractor or subcontractor has a collective bargaining agreement or other contract or understanding with a labor union or an agency referring workers or providing or supervising apprenticeship or training for such workers, the Compliance Report shall include such information as to such labor union's or agency's practices and policies affecting compliance as the Secretary of Labor may prescribe: *Provided*, That to the extent such information is within the exclusive possession of a labor union or an agency referring workers or providing or supervising apprenticeship or training and such labor union or agency shall refuse to furnish such information to the contractor, the contractor shall so certify to the Secretary of Labor as part of its Compliance Report and shall set forth what efforts he has made to obtain such information.

(d) The Secretary of Labor may direct that any bidder or prospective contractor or subcontractor shall submit, as part of his Compliance Report, a statement in writing, signed by an authorized officer or agent on behalf of any labor union or any agency referring workers or providing or supervising apprenticeship or other training, with which the bidder or prospective contractor deals, with supporting information, to the effect that the signer's practices and policies do not discriminate on the grounds of race, color, religion, sex or national origin, and that the signer either will affirmatively cooperate in the implementation of the policy and provisions of this order or that it consents and agrees that recruitment, employment, and the terms and conditions of employment under the proposed contract shall be in accordance with the purposes and provisions of the order. In the event that the union, or the agency shall refuse to execute such a statement, the Compliance Report shall so certify and set forth what efforts have been made to secure such a statement and such additional factual material as the Secretary of Labor may require.

Sec. 204. The Secretary of Labor may, when he deems that special circumstances in the national interest so require, exempt a contracting agency from the requirement of including any or all of the provisions of Section 202 of this Order in any specific contract, subcontract, or purchase order. The Secretary of Labor may, by rule or regulation, also exempt certain classes of contracts, subcontracts, or purchase orders (1) whenever work is to be or has been performed outside the United States and no recruitment of workers within the limits of the United States is involved; (2) for standard commercial supplies or raw materials; (3) involving less than specified amounts of money or specified numbers of workers; or (4) to the extent that they involve subcontracts below a specified tier. The Secretary of Labor may also provide, by rule, regulation, or order, for the exemption of facilities of a contractor which are in all respects separate and distinct from activities of the contractor related to the performance of the contract: *Provided*, That such an exemption will not interfere with or impede the effectuation of the purposes of this Order: *And provided further*, That in the absence of such an exemption all facilities shall be covered by the provisions of this Order.

SUBPART C—POWERS AND DUTIES OF THE SECRETARY OF LABOR AND THE CONTRACTING AGENCIES

Sec. 205. The Secretary of Labor shall be responsible for securing compliance by all Government contractors and subcontractors with this Order and any implementing rules or regulations. All contracting agencies shall comply with the terms of this Order and any implementing rules, regulations, or orders of the Secretary of Labor. Contracting agencies shall cooperate with the Secretary of Labor and shall furnish such information and assistance as the Secretary may require.

Sec. 206. (a) The Secretary of Labor may investigate the employment practices of any Government contractor or subcontractor to determine whether or not the contractual provisions specified in Section 202 of this Order have been violated. Such investigation shall be conducted in accordance with the procedures established by the Secretary of Labor.

(b) The Secretary of Labor may receive and investigate complaints by employees or prospective employees of a Government contractor or subcontractor which allege discrimination contrary to the contractual provisions specified in Section 202 of this Order.

Sec. 207. The Secretary of Labor shall use his best efforts, directly and through interested Federal, State, and local agencies, contractors, and all other available instrumentalities to cause any labor union engaged in work under Government contracts or any agency referring workers or providing or supervising apprenticeship or training for or in the course of such work to cooperate in the implementation of the purposes of this Order. The Secretary of Labor shall, in appropriate cases, notify the Equal Employment Opportunity Commission, the Department of Justice, or other appropriate Federal agencies whenever it has reason to believe that the practices of any such labor organization or agency violate Title VI or Title VII of the Civil Rights Act of 1964 [sections 2000d to 2000d–4 of this title and this subchapter] or other provision of Federal law.

Sec. 208. (a) The Secretary of Labor, or any agency, officer, or employee in the executive branch of the Government designated by rule, regulation, or order of the Secretary, may hold such hearings, public or private, as the Secretary may deem advisable for compliance, enforcement, or educational purposes.

(b) The Secretary of Labor may hold, or cause to be held, hearings in accordance with Subsection (a) of this Section prior to imposing, ordering, or recommending the imposition of penalties and sanctions under this Order. No order for debarment of any contractor from further Government contracts under Section 209(a)(6) shall be made without affording the contractor an opportunity for a hearing.

SUBPART D—SANCTIONS AND PENALTIES

Sec. 209. (a) In accordance with such rules, regulations, or orders as the Secretary of Labor may issue or adopt, the Secretary may:

(1) Publish, or cause to be published, the names of contractors or unions which it has concluded have complied or have failed to comply with the provisions of this Order or of the rules, regulations, and orders of the Secretary of Labor.

(2) Recommend to the Department of Justice that, in cases in which there is substantial or material violation or the threat of substantial or material violation of the contractual provisions set forth in Section 202 of this Order, appropriate proceedings be brought to enforce those provisions, including the enjoining, within the limitations of applicable law, of organizations, individuals, or groups who prevent directly or indirectly, or seek to prevent directly or indirectly, compliance with the provisions of this Order.

(3) Recommend to the Equal Employment Opportunity Commission or the Department of Justice that appropriate proceedings be instituted under Title VII of the Civil Rights Act of 1964 [this subchapter].

(4) Recommend to the Department of Justice that criminal proceedings be brought for the furnishing of false information to any contracting agency or to the Secretary of Labor as the case may be.

(5) After consulting with the contracting agency, direct the contracting agency to cancel, terminate, suspend, or cause to be cancelled, terminated, or suspended, any contract, or any portion or portions thereof, for failure of the contractor or subcontractor to comply with equal employment opportunity provisions of the contract. Contracts may be cancelled, terminated, or suspended absolutely or continuance of contracts may be conditioned upon a program for future compliance approved by the Secretary of Labor.

(6) Provide that any contracting agency shall refrain from entering into further contracts, or extensions or other modifications of existing contracts, with any noncomplying contractor, until such contractor has satisfied the Secretary of Labor that such contractor has established and will carry out personnel and employment policies in compliance with the provisions of this Order.

(b) Pursuant to rules and regulations prescribed by the Secretary of Labor, the Secretary shall make reasonable efforts, within a reasonable time limitation, to secure compliance with the contract provisions of this Order by methods of conference, conciliation, mediation, and persuasion before proceedings shall be instituted under subsection (a)(2) of this Section, or before a contract shall be cancelled or terminated in whole or in part under subsection (a)(5) of this Section.

Sec. 210. Whenever the Secretary of Labor makes a determination under Section 209, the Secretary shall promptly notify the appropriate agency. The agency shall take the action directed by the Secretary and shall report the results of the action it has taken to the Secretary of Labor within such time as the Secretary shall specify. If the contracting agency fails to take the action directed within thirty days, the Secretary may take the action directly.

Sec. 211. If the Secretary of Labor shall so direct, contracting agencies shall not enter into contracts with any bidder or prospective contractor unless the bidder or prospective contractor has satisfactorily complied with the provisions of this Order or submits a program for compliance acceptable to the Secretary of Labor.

Sec. 212. When a contract has been cancelled or terminated under Section 209(a)(5) or a contractor has been debarred from further Government contracts under Section 209(a)(6) of this Order, because of noncompliance with the contract provisions specified in Section 202 of this Order, the Secretary of Labor shall promptly notify the Comptroller General of the United States.

* * *

PART III—NONDISCRIMINATION PROVISIONS IN FEDERALLY ASSISTED CONSTRUCTION CONTRACTS

Sec. 301. Each executive department and agency which administers a program involving Federal financial assistance shall require as a condition for the approval of any grant, contract, loan, insurance, or guarantee thereunder, which may involve a construction contract, that the applicant for Federal assistance undertake and agree to incorporate, or cause to be incorporated, into all construction contracts paid for in whole of in part with funds obtained from the Federal Government or borrowed on the credit of the Federal Government pursuant to such grant, contract, loan, insurance, or guarantee, or undertaken pursuant to any Federal program involving such grant, contract, loan, insurance, or guarantee, the provisions prescribed for Government contracts by Section 202 of this Order or such modification thereof, preserving in substance the contractor's obligations thereunder, as may be approved by the Secretary of Labor, together with such additional provisions as the Secretary deems appropriate to establish and protect the interest of the United States in the enforcement of those obligations. Each such applicant shall also undertake and agree (1) to assist and cooperate actively with the Secretary of Labor in obtaining the compliance of contractors and subcontractors with those contract provisions and with the rules, regulations and relevant orders of the Secretary, (2) to obtain and to furnish to the Secretary of Labor such information as the Secretary may require for the supervision of such compliance, (3) to carry out sanctions and penalties for violation of such obligations imposed upon contractors and subcontractors by the Secretary of Labor pursuant to Part II, Subpart D, of this Order, and (4) to refrain from entering into any contract subject to this Order, or extension or other modification of such a contract with a contractor debarred from Government contracts under Part II, Subpart D, of this Order.

Sec. 302. (a) "Construction contract" as used in this Order means any contract for the construction, rehabilitation, alteration, conversion, extension, or repair of buildings, highways, or other improvements to real property.

(b) The provisions of Part II of this Order shall apply to such construction contracts, and for purposes of such application the administering department or agency shall be considered the contracting agency referred to therein.

(c) The term "applicant" as used in this Order means an applicant for Federal assistance or, as determined by agency regulation, other program participant, with respect to whom an application for any grant, contract, loan, insurance, or guarantee is not finally acted upon prior to the effective date of this Part, and it includes such an applicant after he becomes a recipient of such Federal assistance.

Sec. 303(a). The Secretary of Labor shall be responsible for obtaining the compliance of such applicants with their undertakings under this Order. Each administering department and agency is directed to cooperate with the Secretary of Labor and to furnish the Secretary such information and assistance as the Secretary may require in the performance of the Secretary's functions under this Order.

(b) In the event an applicant fails and refuses to comply with the applicant's undertakings pursuant to this Order, the Secretary of Labor may, after consulting with the administering department or agency, take any or all of the following actions: (1) direct any administering department or agency to cancel, terminate, or suspend in whole or in part the agreement, contract or other arrangement with such applicant with respect to which the failure or refusal occurred; (2) direct any administering department or agency to refrain from extending any further assistance to the applicant under the program with respect to which the failure or refusal occurred until satisfactory assurance of future compliance has been received by the Secretary of Labor from such applicant; and (3) refer the case to the Department of Justice or the Equal Employment Opportunity Commission for appropriate law enforcement or other proceedings.

(c) In no case shall action be taken with respect to an applicant pursuant to clause (1) or (2) of subsection (b) without notice and opportunity for hearing.

Sec. 304. Any executive department or agency which imposes by rule, regulation, or order requirements of nondiscrimination in employment, other than requirements imposed pursuant to this Order, may delegate to the Secretary of Labor by agreement such responsibilities with respect to compliance standards, reports, and procedures as would tend to bring the administration of such requirements into conformity with the administration of requirements imposed under this Order: *Provided,* That actions to effect compliance by recipients of Federal financial assistance with requirements imposed pursuant to Title VI of the Civil Rights Act of 1964 shall be taken in conformity with the procedures and limitations prescribed in Section 602 thereof and the regulations of the administering department or agency issued thereunder.

PART IV—MISCELLANEOUS

Sec. 401. The Secretary of Labor may delegate to any officer, agency, or employee in the Executive branch of the Government, any function or duty of the Secretary under Parts II and III of this Order.

* * *

*

INDEX

References are to pages

†